THE GOLF GUIDE

PGA

WHERE TO PLAY
WHERE TO STAY

1995

Endorsed by
The Professional Golfers' Association

FHG Publications
Paisley

Golfing Around Britain

Where to Play – Where to Stay

by Jane Carter

THERE IS a lot to be said for those people who manage to combine something they love with making a living. Professional sportsmen and women are among that elite group for just that very reason and professional golfers are no exception. The enviable part of their job is the fact they are able to enjoy some of the finest fairways the world can offer – and earn a great deal of money while they are doing it.

The growth of golf at every level, professional and amateur, women's and men's, means that golf courses up and down the country are now playing host to tournament after tournament throughout the year. In every corner of the country Championship venues nestle alongside golfing delights which players of every level, for fun or competition, can enjoy.

The PGA European Tour with the likes of Faldo, Ballesteros, Olazabal, Woosnam, Lyle, playing for hundreds of thousands of pounds week in, week out, has been responsible for catapulting the best of the country's venues into the limelight and many are now on the list of courses every golfer should play.

The tournament flagship for the South-West is undoubtedly St Mellion, home of

Lanteglos

Lanteglos Country House Hotel
Camelford, Cornwall, PL32 9RF.

**Phone
(01840) 213551
or Fax
(01840) 212732**

Pedn-Olva
HOTEL & RESTAURANTS
Guests are assured of a warm, friendly welcome, personal attention, comfort and good food at Pedn-Olva, situated just two minutes' walk from the harbour and the quaint, narrow streets of St. Ives.
The hotel has direct access to safe Porthminster beach for bathing, and arrangements can be made for water ski-ing, paragliding, windsurfing, fishing, clay-pigeon shooting and golf. Close to 5 links courses. Reduced fees agreed with certain clubs. Break prices available October to mid-May.
35 bedrooms with private facilities, tea-makers, TV and radio, telephone and baby listening. Car parking available.
*Open all year *Fully licensed *Heated swimming pool *Sun terrace
AA ★★ RAC
Porthminster Beach, St. Ives, Cornwall TR26 2EA
Telephone (01736) 796222 Fax (01736) 797710
ST. IVES (CORNWALL) HOTEL & GUESTHOUSE ASSOCIATION
SERVICE HOSPITALITY

"THE CREAM OF GOLF AT CORNWALL'S FINEST ..."

"set in 250 spectacular acres"

THE CARLYON BAY HOTEL and Golf Course is set amidst some of Cornwall's most breathtaking coastal scenery, the course itself stretching out along the cliff tops, enjoys magnificent views across St. Austell Bay and miles of golden sands.

Built in 1925 as a private enterprise, the course has been owned by the hotel since 1929. In its early days the glorious setting attracted the Duke of Windsor, probably the keenest of the all golfing Royals while Winston Churchill too spent a few of his finest hours at Carlyon Bay.

Considerable changes have occurred during the past decade or so. In 1978, golf architect Hamilton Stutt was commissioned to make alterations to various parts of the course, prior to the hotel coming under ownership of the Brend Family, whose emphasis has been on improving the quality of golf offered. The extensive clubhouse complex included spacious, modern locker rooms, bar, restaurant and lounge and the club professional's shop, offering a selection of equipment in addition to buggy hire and expert tuition.

The Hotel's location complements the interior, being unique with superb views of the bay. Set in two hundred and fifty acre ground and gardens, The Carlyon Bay Hotel has the perfect combination of luxury, location and leisure facilities, the highest standard of cuisine and personal attentive service.

From the moment of arrival, an atmosphere of relaxation and luxury greets you. Each bedroom has private bathroom facilities, colour TV, tea and coffee making facilities, direct dial telephone and most have sea views. Deluxe bedrooms offer very spacious accommodation with added luxuries, chocolates, bathrobes etc.

An excellent choice at all times.

the European Tour's Benson & Hedges International. Designed by Jack Nicklaus, it is not a test for the faint-hearted but having tamed the monster there are a host of other Cornish delights all featuring some magnificent scenery.

The Carlyon Bay Hotel at St Austell has a golf course and a place to rest your head, while on the West coast of Cornwall there are the more familiar Lelant, Trevose and St Enodoc – courses for which the county is synonymous.

Not to be outdone, the neighbouring county of Devon has Saunton on the North coast as its regular choice for major championships while the Manor House at Moretonhampstead is another familiar watering and golfing hole. These, coupled with Royal North Devon at Bideford, founded in 1864 and one not to be missed, the comparatively new complex of Dartmouth Golf and Country Club near Totnes, and the parkland courses of Tiverton and Honiton, mean you are never stuck for choice.

Head along the tournament venue trail into Somerset and you will surely reach Burnham & Berrow, looking out over the Bristol Channel and having recently undergone some changes which have only heightened its appeal. Nearby Weston-Super-Mare can act as the perfect base for the golfing delights of Somerset and Avon with Worlebury, Mendip Spring, Puxton Park and Enmore Park all within easy travelling distance.

When it comes to Dorset hosting a major Championship then you need look no further than Ferndown, on the edge of Bournemouth. The close proximity of some excellent hotels including the De Vere-owned Dormy, has seen it host some major events including the Women's British and European Opens in recent years. Nearby Parkstone and Broadstone and two highly regarded

MORETONHAMPSTEAD:
a secret no longer!

"The ubiquitous motorways are not everyone's choice of road, but they have proved of benefit to holidaymakers and visitors seeking easier access to the more remote corners of the country, not least the West Country.

The M5 to Exeter has been a boon to that part of England, a green and tranquil corner where countryside on the edge of Dartmoor has remained unchanged for centuries, compelling in its beauty and serenity. Here are to be found dozens of lovely villages, all thatched roofs and flowerpots, and miles of golden beaches.

Golf here is a particular delight and nowhere is it better or more appealing than at Moretonhampstead, where the gracious old Manor House Hotel sits in regal splendour overlooking a golf course that is a sight for sore eyes at any time of year.

Only 17 miles from the ancient cathedral city of Exeter, near the village of North Bovey, the Manor House and its golf course was once the best-kept secret in British golf, the haunt for those to whom it represented all that was best in life.

Set on the edge of the Dartmoor National Park, the course provides a stunning combination of natural beauty and ideal golf terrain perhaps without peer. It is a rare mix of moor and parkland folded into the floor of a valley that winds around the 270 acre estate hidden from the eyes of the unknowing who pass the gatehouse lodge and the entrance to the mile-long driveway which splits the course and leads to the elegant hotel.

Currently owned by Principal Hotels, The Manor has recently completed an extensive refurbishment programme encompassing the Golf Course, House and Bedrooms, the aim being to retain the old-fashioned quality of luxury that the house is renowned for. With an emphasis towards comfort, the high standards of service and friendly, efficient staff, ensure that your stay will be an enjoyable experience.

Stand on the hotel's terrace and immediately below is the first tee. Down to the right, tucked into a bend of the River Bovey, lies the first green.

The river is a recurring feature of the first eight holes as it threads its way through the valley imposing its presence on virtually every shot played.

After your game, relax at the '19th' in the traditional setting of the Oak Bar; with its convivial atmosphere and comfortable Chesterfields, it is the ideal spot to sit and discuss the finer points of your game.

Another bonus, and part of the formerly well-kept secret, is the elegant former country home that is now the Manor House, a hotel in the grand tradition with oak panelled lounges, lots of open fireplaces, wide sweeping staircases, superb cuisine and impeccable service.

The hotel also offers the additional sports of game and fly fishing, squash, tennis, croquet and a challenging par 3 course.

Add walks through countryside of matchless beauty where hidden villages offer a treasure trove of lovely restaurants and shops in a setting of total tranquillity, and the prospect is one of idyllic holidays you will want to re-live again and again".

By Barry Ward of "Golf Monthly".

COME AND EXPERIENCE THE SECRET.

Queen's Park, one of Bournemouth's courses.

public courses, Queen's Park and Meyrick Park, provide a worthy selection. The relatively new Dudsbury course and also Crane Valley deserve a visit as potential Championship venues of the future.

Wiltshire has been somewhat starved of tournament golf in the past but the new Bowood Golf & Country Club – which bills itself as the longest course in Britain – looks set to change all that in future years. Having tackled such a testing course, the 6,505 yards Marlborough and 6,220 yard Swindon golf courses will seem positively short!

Along the coast into Hampshire and then Sussex and you are truly in golfing country, with Hampshire's gems including Liphook with its heather and trees which over the years has tested the country's best amateurs as well as the club golfer. Nearby Old Thorns is an ideal location whether you are planning to

Old Thorns Golf Course, Hotel and Restaurants complex is a unique combination of old and new creating a country estate appeal with the traditional beauty of the old tile hung farmhouse providing blazing log fires in winter and terraces which overlook the magnificent 200 acres of Hampshire downs. The regal oaks, beeches and Scotch pines have been painstakingly conserved and the superb course is enhanced by the creation of water features fed from natural water springs.

Our testing 18-hole championship course provides a fine challenge for the enthusiastic golfer. The fairways wind their way through parkland, over lakes and streams and some holes cut through the pines or over the heathered slopes. A fleet of 30 golf cars has a track carefully incorporated within the contours of the fairways. Mid-week enjoyment for societies and golfing weekends is ensured by a driving range and practice green on hand for the individual golfer and adds up to perfect golf for everyone.

Our resident teaching professional will assess, encourage and monitor golfing skills. Everything needed to play is available on hire from the Pro's shop which carries a very comprehensive selection of golfing accessories. A wide range of brand name items are stocked as well as a variety of prizes for societies.

The tranquillity and peace of Old Thorns is complemented by the elegant new Japanese Centre carefully developed to blend naturally into the background of the undulating countryside thus cleverly uniting Eastern and Western culture.

Within one hour's drive of London, Heathrow and Gatwick airports, Old Thorns can provide the perfect venue for any business or social function.

watch a little golf or play some yourself with the excellent 18-hole course. Old Thorns has 32 en suite guest rooms and a host of restaurants and facilities on site. The Bell Inn at Lyndhurst and the Watersplash at Brockenhurst allow you to sample golf in the New Forest as well as along Hampshire's impressive coast.

Golfing attention has been centred on Sussex in recent years because of the development of East Sussex National, tournament venue extraordinaire. It plays host to the European Open on the men's Tour and for spectator golf is without rival, with mounds constructed at strategic points for easy watching. In golfing terms it is a test along American lines with bunkers and water everywhere.

Dale Hill Golf & Country Club already has 18 holes with another 18 holes under construction (the first Ian Woosnam design), while Royal Ashdown is another favourite. Further west at Chichester is the Goodwood Park Golf & Country Club, opened in 1989, and the rather older Goodwood Golf Club itself, designed by no less than James Braid.

Think of Kent and think of Royal St George's, perhaps one of the most famous venues of them all. Any course on the Open Championship rota is worth a visit and this is the only one south of Lancashire. Right next door are Royal Cinque Ports and Princes to complete a links trio, while North Foreland is within easy reach. In the city of Canterbury you will discover Broome Park Country Club with a host of leisure facilities on offer as well as superb golf, while Tudor Park Golf Club near Maidstone is one of the popular Country Club Hotel venues dotted throughout the country. The London Club near Brands Hatch is the latest addition to the Kent golfing scene and it has quickly climbed its way onto our Tour of tournament circuits by being chosen to host the Women's European Tour Ford Golf Classic this season (1995).

Golf-watching country beckons with a vengeance south of the Thames with Wentworth, Sunningdale, Royal Mid Surrey, Coombe Hill, Kingswood, and Walton Heath all within a nine-iron of each other and nearly all having hosted either a Professional or Amateur Championship. There is no shortage of excellent accommodation. Selsdon Park, near Croydon, is just one of many excellent hotels with its own golf course and leisure complex.

Go north into Hertfordshire, one of the country's most densely populated

NIZELS GOLF CLUB

Nizels Lane, Hildenborough, near Tonbridge, Kent TN11 8NX
Telephone: Tonbridge (01732) 833138; Fax: (01732) 833764

Our splendid Georgian Clubhouse complements our superb 18 hole Golf Course which features many water hazards. In addition to golf we have facilities for wedding receptions and private parties, also rooms for business meetings. Golf Societies and Corporate days are most welcome. Our bar and restaurant offer quality service and we are open every day. Breakfast from 7 a.m. Bar snacks at reasonable prices, plus full A La Carte. Why not call round and see the beautifully landscaped gardens with panoramic views and meet our Director of Golf and Marketing, John Bellamy for full membership details.

- **6408 yards Par 72**
- **Green Fees from £35 per day** (including £3 food voucher)
- **Society/Corporate days**
- **Private Functions Room**
- **Well equipped Pro Shop**
- **Fantastic Club Atmosphere**

Nizels LTD

The Prince Regent Hotel ...
... gateway to Essex

Ideally situated on the cusp of Essex, London and the Home Counties. If you are looking for the ideal combination of comfort and atmosphere you normally associate with country houses the Prince Regent has it all.
From corporate promotions to golfing weekends, fairytale weddings to AGM's – the Prince Regent is the perfect choice.

For further enquiries and bookings call 0181-505 9966.

Test yourself on probably the most challenging courses in Essex!

- Upper Course (Classic) 5891 yards, par 70.
- Lower Course (Championship) 6600 yards, Par 72.
- Outdoor Practice Area
- Pro Shop.
- We welcome Golf Societies, Business parties or individual players.
- No Membership or Handicap required.
- Discounted rounds if booked through The Prince Regent Hotel.

Telephone 0181-500 2470 for further details.
Hainault Forest Golf Complex, for all golfing abilities.

THE PRINCE REGENT HOTEL AND HAINAULT FOREST GOLF COMPLEX.
A GREAT COMBINATION FOR THE WHOLE FAMILY.

counties when it comes to golf courses. The flagship for the tournament scene is undoubtedly Moor Park which has hosted both women's and men's European Tour events, most notably the Bob Hope Classic when star golfers and stars of stage and screen trod the fairways.

While in the area the connoisseur golfer should not miss a trip to Ashridge or Berkhamsted – famous for its absence of bunkers. The latest addition to the Hertfordshire golf scene is Hanbury Manor, re-designed by Jack Nicklaus and with the benefit of what is rapidly becoming one of the country's finest country house hotels on site.

The golfing triangle of Berkshire, Buckinghamshire and Oxfordshire – or Berks, Bucks & Oxon – has Woburn Golf & Country Club, near Milton Keynes, as its flagship on the golf circuit. Host to the Dunhill Masters and the Weetabix Women's British Open, the Duchess and the Dukes Course are two of the most sought after by visitors to the area. People have been quick to spot its success and a host of new courses have opened up nearby including Three Locks, the Wavendon Golf Centre, Abbey Hill and Aylesbury Vale.

In Berkshire the established names of The Berkshire, Newbury & Crookham, Stoke Poges – famous for the scene in the James Bond film 'Goldfinger' – Maidenhead, Sonning and Calcot are well worth a visit while in the area. The Berkshire, particularly, is a regular host to some of the country's finest amateur competitions.

Oxfordshire's best known names are Huntercombe and Frilford Heath – both again regular venues for leading amateur contests – but there are a number of new names including Brailes at Banbury and Lyneham at Chipping Norton. Top marks for business to the White Horse Inn at Duns Tew who have their own 6,000-yards-plus golf course only open to residents!

Northamptonshire can thank one of its newest developments for putting it on the golfing tournament map. Collingtree Park, designed by Johnny Miller, plays host to a seniors event every year and is already carving a name for itself as one of the finest teaching establishments in the country. Another new course is Northampton Golf Club on Lord Spencer's Estate at Althorp, with the nearby Northampton Moat House Hotel offering an ideal resting place.

Nearby is the Northamptonshire County Club, one of the area's most established courses, which stands alongside the newer venues of Staverton Park and Cold Ashby.

Over the border in Cambridgeshire awaits a feast of golf with Gog Magog probably the best known of all its venues – who, after all could forget that name! – with Ely City and Cambridgeshire Moat House Hotel offering even more variety. Another name fast-growing in prominence is Abbotsley Golf & Country Club with golf, hotel and leisure facilities on site alongside one of the finest teaching academies run by Vivien Saunders.

Not to be outdone, Leicestershire too offers some excellent golf. Rothley Park, Glen Corse, Leicestershire and Willesley Park are all worth a mention. A visit to Willesley can be combined with a stay at the nearby Health Hydro at Ashby-de-la-Zouch for a really relaxing break.

Suffolk and Norfolk may be considered to be too far off the beaten track when it comes to hosting major tournament golf, but for the holiday golfer there is nothing better, with a huge variety of inland and seaside courses and some spectacular scenery. Barnham Broom Hotel, Golf & Country Club is the area's Country Club Hotels flagship – and a popular one at that – while surrounding nearby Norwich there are a variety of courses, accessible and relatively inexpensive, including Bawburgh, Cotessy Park, and Sprowston Park – with nearby Sprowston Manor offering excellent accommodation.

Suffolk is equally well served with Felixstowe Ferry – famous as the course where Bernard Darwin learned to play – and Aldeburgh and Thorpeness further up the coast. Hintlesham Hall with its superb hotel and leisure facilities as well as its own 18-hole golf course is one of the new breed of complexes to arrive in Suffolk, along with Ufford Park Hotel near Woodbridge which offers its own weekend golfing breaks.

When it comes to tournament golf the highlight of any calendar is undoubtedly the Ryder Cup. Held biennially in Europe, it has been staged at The Belfry for the past three matches before moving to Spain in 1997. Consequently The Belfry is the jewel in the crown of De Vere Hotels and one of the most sought-after venues for company and society days and the keen amateur golfer for whom the Ryder Cup venue is a must.

But The Belfry is not the only reason to visit the Midlands. Just a few miles away there is another Country Clubs Hotel venue, Forest of Arden Golf & Country Club, which plays host to the English Open, while surrounding Birmingham there are some of the oldest established clubs such as Little Aston, Kings Norton, Edgbaston, Harborne, Copt Heath and Handsworth.

In Gloucestershire Tewkesbury Park Hotel and Country Club is a popular destination together with the new and luxurious Puckrup Hall, complete with its own country house hotel. Cotswold Edge provides some of the spectacular scenery for which the area is famous.

Worcestershire can boast a similar complex in the Abbey Park Golf & Country Club near Redditch. The Worcestershire Golf Club at Malvern Wells, Worcester Golf and Country Club and Blackwell is one of the most picturesque trios you will find, while many believe the county's jewel in the crown is Ross-on-Wye.

The tournament flagship for Wales is undoubtedly another Country Club Hotel: St Pierre Golf & Country Club at Chepstow. Until recently it was the home of the Murphy's Open but continues to host major regional professional and amateur events. Royal Porthcawl has been described as the most noble of Welsh Championship links and along with Tenby, Ashburnham and Pyle & Kenfig provides a stark contrast to the parkland of St Pierre. In the north of the Principality, Conway, Llandudno and Prestatyn are familiar names, while how can we forget Royal St David's at Harlech. One of the newest venues to open its fairways is Northop Country Park near Chester, designed by John Jacobs and with the excellent St David's Park Hotel on its doorstep.

Just over the border lies Shropshire where the newly revamped Hawkstone Park, home of the county's favourite son, Sandy Lyle, still attracts hundreds of visitors every year. Another famous complex is the Hill Valley Golf & Country Club with accommodation right on the doorstep, while Patshull Park Hotel and

There's more than Golf at Gloucester

Excellent golfing facilities are just one reason why the Gloucester Hotel and Country Club is well worth a visit – but there are many more attractions for the whole family.

Set in over 200 acres of beautiful Cotswold countryside, this modern hotel has 107 luxury bedrooms. An investment of over £3.5 million has ensured it offers a unique combination of sporting and leisure facilities including ski-ing, snooker, swimming, squash and tennis. With so much on offer, your golfing break could well turn into a family holiday.

For the keen golfer the 6,127 yard par 70, 18 hole course features a strategically laid out bunker formation. The natural hazards – trees, copses, small lakes and a variety of hillside undulations test all golfing skills.

The 9 hole par 3 course appeals to those who don't have time for a full round of golf, and the 12 bay floodlit driving range is always available for practising your swing.

Catering for all levels of golfing skills, tailored courses and special breaks are available, with tuition from the Club's three resident professionals.

For those learning the game, the residential beginners' golf instruction week covers basic techniques, discussion of rules and etiquette by the experts, and, for fun, concludes with a competition on the 9 hole course.

Away from the fairways, members of the whole family may wish to try out the premier dry ski slopes in England – and the excellent 'après ski' facilities at the Ski Lodge. Perhaps a game of tennis or squash for the more energetic, or chalk your cues for a game of snooker or pool.

Warm and welcoming water attractions include an exciting leisure pool, complete with rapids, spa pool, steam room, sauna and jacuzzi to provide that period of relaxation.

Not only catering for leisure breaks, the Hotel has extensive conference facilities ranging from rooms for select confidential business meetings to a full scale delegation of 150 people. The Club House Restaurant, a popular venue for business lunches, offers haute cuisine standards and an extensive wine cellar.

Should you wish to make the most of your stay in this most attractive area, Gloucester boasts an excellent shopping centre, many surrounding sites of historic interest and scenic walking routes in the Cotswolds. Reception staff are fully informed on all seasonal activities in the area.

The complex enjoys easy access from the M5 motorway, and is just 1½ miles from the City Centre.

The Gloucester Hotel and Country Club is a member of Jarvis Hotels.

Country Club is equally as welcoming and picturesque.

Shropshire's courses are relatively few in number but Cheshire is undoubtedly the county where it has all been happening in recent years with new developments mushrooming. Sandiway, Mere and Oaklands Golf & Country Club are all well known but standing alongside them is the splendid Portal which opened in 1991 and is now a regular stopover for golfing visitors to the area. That, coupled with the magnificent Carden Park at Malpas, the well established Mottram Hall – part of the De Vere stable – the Tytherington Club, home of the Women Professional Golfers' European Tour, and Shrigley Hall, again with accommodation right on site, makes Cheshire a real mecca for golfing visitors, whether tournament watching or playing.

Although Lincolnshire, Derbyshire and Nottinghamshire are not familiar tournament venues at a professional

If you quiver at the thought, fear not. The Belton Woods Hotel, Lincolnshire, has the answer.

As sister hotel to the world famous Belfry, it aims to please both the serious golfer and his non-golfing partner.

Belton Woods Hotel
Telephone 01476 593200

So as well as having two superb championship length golf courses, it offers luxurious Leisure Club facilities such as a sauna, spa pool, heated indoor pool, sunbeds, beauty salon, tennis, aerobics and, of course, archery.

Going anywhere else could be more than your life's worth.

DE VERE HOTELS

De Vere House, Chester Rd, Daresbury, Warrington, Cheshire WA4 4BN. **Tel: 01925 265050.**

level, for amateur golf they provide some of the best golfing challenges in Central England. Sherwood Forest in Nottingham is a past venue for the Forte Seniors PGA Championship, while nearby Lindrick has been the scene of many national triumphs and agonies.

Lincolnshire's two Championship jewels are undoubtedly Seacroft and Woodhall Spa, but for the players rather than the watchers, Belton Woods Hotel & Country Club near Grantham is an ideal spot for a golfing break. Derbyshire can boast the Breadsall Priory Hotel & Country Club, another Country Club Hotels venue, and which now has two 18-hole courses to test your skills.

In Lancashire one need look no further for tournament venues then these two very 'Royal' courses, Royal Lytham & St Annes and Royal Birkdale, scene of many Opens down the years. But it is easy to overlook the other gems which the county has to offer – St Annes Old Links, Southport, Formby, Hillside, and Southport & Ainsdale which many do not realise has hosted two Ryder Cup matches.

And while you are enjoying this prolific array of coastal courses, why not hop on a plane at Blackpool Airport and make the short journey to the Isle of Man where you will discover Castletown and their own excellent hotel.

Fulford in Yorkshire is probably best known as the original home of the Benson & Hedges International, now played at St Mellion, while Pannal near Harrogate has also welcomed its share of professional tournaments. Leeds, too, can boast its share of excellent venues including Moortown and Moor Allerton, and although Headingley may be better known for its cricket venue, its golf course should not be overlooked either.

Up in Northumberland the spectacular Slaley Hall near Hexham is a Championship venue of the future, having already hosted regional PGA and amateur events. Berwick-upon-Tweed is undoubtedly the county's best course, a true links designed by James Braid back in 1890. Another magnificent links can be found in Durham, namely Seaton Carew which has also played host to many national championships.

If you have followed our Tournament trail, by now you will be heading into the home of golf itself, Scotland, where there are so many wonderful courses you will think you have died and gone to golfing heaven. St Andrews is the most obvious place to start, as home of golf and host to the Open Championship this year (1995) but you can't forget Muirfield, Carnoustie, Gleneagles, Loch Lomond, Troon, Turnberry – the list goes on and on.

Hundreds of hotels, guest houses, bed and breakfasts or even the local pub offer famous Scottish hospitality while some venues have hotels on site, including Dalmahoy Hotel & Country Club, venue for the 1992 Solheim Cup and the Women's Scottish Open, and Westerhill,

SIX
SCOTTISH
CLASSICS

• SELECT •
GOLF CLASSICS

GLENEAGLES •
ST ANDREWS •
TURNBERRY • •
DALMAHOY • • •
MURRAYSHALL
WESTERWOOD •

Scotland

In association with Scotland's finest golfing hotels, we are proud to welcome you to SELECT GOLF CLASSICS. This most flexible of golf tour programmes is designed specifically to meet the requirements of the international executive golfer, his or her family, friends, guests and associates.

For further details see our advert at the start of the Scottish Section.

SELECT
Scotland

Rothes Golf Club in the Spey Valley near Elgin; recently opened.

North Berwick, with the famous Forte Marine Hotel just down the road.

For the discerning golfer Aberdeen presents the testing Cruden Bay and the delights of Aboyne, Banchory and Ballater. Further inland you can follow the whisky trail to Grantown-on-Spey, Boat of Garten, Newtonmore and Kingussie – all superb courses with local hotels to match.

On to Inverness, Nairn and Royal Dornoch, and even further north to the links of Wicks and Reay which should feature in any golfer's itinerary.

Across the water in Ireland, Belfast is not normally the first place you would think of as a golfing haven but on either side of the city can be found two of the finest examples of golf courses anywhere: Royal Portrush and Royal County Down. Both have hosted numerous Irish Amateur and Professional Championships and no one should visit Ulster and play one without the other.

Mahoney's Point, one of the two fine courses at Killarney (Killarney Golf Club).

Golf in Northern Ireland is not confined to those two either with Portstewart and Castlerock both fine examples of links golf, while Belfast itself can boast Royal Belfast and Malone. Clandeboye and Bangor are two towns on the edge of the Belfast district with their own courses, not forgetting Balmoral, home of the legendary Fred Daly, Holywood and Shandon Park.

Golf in Eire deserves a book on its own but when continuing the trail of tournament golf, you can not ignore Portmarnock, a few miles south of Baltray and a course which has seen more great events than any other. Dublin itself is the start of a coastal sweep which ends in Galway and takes in the glories of Ballybunion, Lahinch, Tralee and Waterville. In the southern tip nestles Killarney surrounded by some of the most spectacular scenery you will ever see and a former home of the Carrolls Irish Open. That superb event has now moved to Mount Juliet, Co Kilkenny, one of the newest courses in Eire and one which has quickly established itself as one to play.

Connemara, Donegal, Enniscrone and Carne (Belmullet) are among the main attractions on the west coast while the south-east boasts Rosslare, Waterford and Lismore.

Also away from mainland Britain, but south rather than west, are the pleasant courses of the Channel Islands including such championship challenges as St Pierre Park on Guernsey and La Moye on Jersey.

With such a choice, there is no doubt that golf is unique in allowing the ordinary mortal to follow in the footsteps of Faldo, Ballesteros, Nicklaus and Watson along some of the most spectacular fairways in the world. There is something for everyone and once having sampled the traditional golfing hospitality or witnessed the stars in action on some famous links, there is no doubt you will be back for more!

Golf in the Gulf

DUBAI The United Arab Emirates

On the southern shores of the Arabian Gulf, Dubai is a bustling and booming commercial centre. Strategically located for both business and leisure, Dubai in recent years has taken huge steps – or swings – in the world of golf and is now recognised as a serious player. Large and far-sighted investment has created three clubs whose environment and facilities rank among the best and well justify Dubai's claim to be the golfing capital of the Middle East.

With its stunning clubhouse, whose design echoes a group of traditional Arab tented pavilions, the *Emirates Golf Club* sets the standard, sitting as an oasis of green on the fringes of the city. The club hosts the PGA Desert Classic tournament and its 7,100-yard long, par-72 course is a real test of champions. Equally dramatic with its dhow-like outlines, is the clubhouse of the *Dubai Creek Golf and Yacht Club*, which features a golf academy in addition to all the usual facilities of a top-class club. There are restaurants and bars and, of course, the Yacht Club itself. Most recent arrival is the *Dubai Golf and Racing Club* with its fully floodlit 18 and 9-hole courses, all within Dubai's prestigious horse-racing track.

Always a 'hot-spot', Dubai is certainly now a 'high-spot' of any international golfing tour.

Golf in the French Alps, at Chamonix.

Holiday Golf in France

by Michael Gedye

JUST AS British history has been inextricably linked with France down the ages, so early development of golf in the country had a distinctly British flavour. The first course in France was founded by expatriate British at Pau in the south-west in 1856. Further golf, under British influence, followed at nearby Biarritz and St. Jean-de-Luz. The northern coastline, a mere pitch across the Channel, proved especially popular, since it offered true sand dunes and linksland, golfing conditions the British were used to. Courses were created at the fashionable seaside resorts – Le Touquet, Wimereux, Deauville and Dinard – as playgrounds for the rich and famous. Golf had arrived in France as an essentially elitist activity and was to remain so for the best part of a century.

It is only in the last fifteen years that there has been a total change of image and playing opportunity with something of a mini-boom. In the aftermath of an enthusiasm for tennis, developers saw potential in golf and players caught the bug. From less than a hundred courses catering basically to a limited group of the wealthy and well-connected, the game has expanded in France to the point where there are some 470 courses, many deliberately planned for the travelling visitor.

By a fortunate co-operation between the French Golf Federation and the National Tourist Office, there are a large number of specified clubs – grouped under the umbrella of France Golf International – where the facilities reach minimum criteria laid down to suit the travelling golfer such as bi-lingual reception, well-maintained course condition, a good restaurant, pro shop and practice areas. These courses are generally in attractive coastal locations and perfectly placed for the holiday player. France leads the golfing world in deliberately targeting and maintaining courses at a level that is attractive to visitors.

Because of the explosion of golf in France, most players are new to the game and more likely to be found on the practice ground than the course. As members, they will have insisted on a high quality clubhouse with a good restaurant and facilities. All these factors are to the holiday golfer's benefit. Green fees are relatively cheap, courses comparatively empty and maintained to a high standard with clubhouse to match. A big advantage for the British is being able to travel easily across the Channel to enjoy an excellent selection of vacation golfing opportunities, whether for a weekend or a longer break.

Traditionally we have found (and founded) our holiday golf along the northern coast from the Pas de Calais through Normandy to the West Country look-alike charm of Brittany. The ease with which two or four can jump in a car

La Nivelle, Aquitaine.

with their clubs and be playing the same day cross-Channel has given many of these coastal courses an Anglicised flavour. But, for the more adventurous, there is now golf of the highest quality further south through the Loire valley, Poitou-Charentes, around the vineyards of Bordeaux and down through Aquitaine to Biarritz and the Spanish border, probably the most golf-rich region in France. There is also plenty of accessible holiday golf all along the south coast round to the Côte d'Azur as well as many other parts of the country, waiting to welcome the visitor warmly with excellent facilities, plenty of space to play and manageable costs.

One of the great pleasures of golfing in France is that there is so much more to enjoy. Superb cuisine, fine wines, the whole panoply of history expressed by noble forts and grand châteaux plus the rural charm of a countryside made famous through its many artists. With much to captivate the visitor, it is easy to overlook the fact that there are more places to play golf than in any other European country but England. (Yes, even more than in Scotland, the home of golf!). Superb holiday golfing opportunities lie right on the British doorstep – attractive, available, challenging and affordable. No player worth his salt could ask for more.

Holiday Golf in Portugal

by Michael Gedye

IN THE HISTORY of exploration, the Portuguese have produced the great navigators, discovering distant lands around the globe. However, for the holiday golfer, there is much to discover

Val do Lobo, near Faro, in the Algarve.

in Portugal itself – a rich harvest of places to play, spread around the country and its islands. In a colourful country blessed with a happy combination of culture, civility and charm, the visiting player can choose from over thirty excellent courses which take full advantage of the dramatic landscape.

As a holiday golf destination, the country has much to offer. Bordering the Atlantic, just north of Africa, it enjoys the benefits of year-round sunshine, temperate sea breezes and a wide range of topography. From inland mountains and wooded valleys providing gently rolling slopes planted with fig, olive and pomegranate, hillsides scented with mimosa, eucalyptus and pine or the natural beauty of craggy cliffs and broad white sandy beaches – golf has been created in magnificent surroundings to captivate the visitor and test every aspect of his game.

There is a sense of history in the north, where the game was first played more than a century ago by expatriate British port wine shippers by the sea near Oporto. Two other seaside links followed in the same area plus a course at the mountain spa resort of Vidago.

Some of the best golf in the country, however, is to be found around the capital Lisbon. To the west lies Estoril, with its classic course and three others, the newest of which is the palatial complex of Penha Longa. Cross the Tagus river to the south of the city and you arrive in the Costa Azul, an attractive region where three more courses lie in wait, protected by pine forest, olive groves and sand dunes. Two of these, Aroeira and Troia, rank among the best in the country.

But Portugal's main claim to golfing fame lies in the rich necklace of green oases strung along the craggy coast of the Algarve in the south. Here, sleepy fishing villages and rolling orchards have been joined by no less than eighteen courses, with more to come. Well-maintained and

Golf de Palmares in the Western Algarve.

beautifully manicured, they offer a wide and varied choice between tough championship tests and interesting, strategic layouts, all with a warm welcome for the holiday player.

A picturesque coastal drive of some two hours separates the most westerly course, Parque da Floresta from the relatively new layout of Pinheiros Altos, not far from Faro airport. Even further east, one finds the brand new resort of Islantilla, close to the Spanish border town of Huelva. In between one can find some of the best-known and internationally acclaimed golfing tests – Penina, Vilamoura, Vale do Lobo, Quinta do Lago and San Lorenzo – true championship golf from the back tees but highly playable from the normal markers if one can resist the multitude of scenic distractions. Latest developments to command attention are the two courses at Carvoeiro, laid out by Ronald Fream through rolling ancient olive groves, and Vila Sol, a fine test by Donald Steel undulating through ranks of umbrella pine.

Further afield, there is golf at Terceira in the Azores while on the semi-tropical island of Madeira, two fine new courses at altitude add a further dimension to this holiday garden location.

Valderrama, near Gibraltar, a championship course worthy of the Ryder Cup.

Holiday Golf in Spain

by Michael Gedye

THE FIRST Mediterranean country to climb on the holiday golfing bandwagon in the early 1960's, Spain has led the way in sports resort development, fairway-bordering second homes and relatively inexpensive winter golfing packages – now common denominators in an increasingly global travel market. Its more than 200 golf clubs have a higher percentage of courses developed primarily to cater to a visiting clientele than any other European nation. Just as it was the prime mover in the burgeoning package holiday tour industry, so Spain is once again in the news through the 1994 US Masters victory of Jose Maria Olazabal, following the example of his compatriot Seve Ballesteros.

For the sheer scale of attractive, sun-drenched golfing locations, purpose-built to appeal to legions of northern Europeans and others suffering from winter chills, Spain leads every country in the world with the exception of the United States. From the western tip of the Costa del Sol, where Andalucia nudges Gibraltar, the golfing coast curves east and upwards past Almeria, Murcia, Alicante and Valencia into the northern charms of the Costa Brava.

The southern shores of the Costa del Sol offer a concentrated embarrassment of riches. Of the fifty-eight courses in Andalucia, the majority fall within its region, including a number of world-calibre by such leading international architects as Robert Trent Jones, Jack Nicklaus, Cabell Robinson, Ron Kirby and Gary Player plus the domestic skills of Javier Arana, Pepe Gancedo and Severiano Ballesteros. Numerous major championships have been played here, notably the Spanish Open, the Volvo Masters and two World Cups. Global attention will focus on the tough test of Valderrama, just inland from Gibraltar, in 1997 for the first staging of the Ryder Cup in Continental Europe.

South-eastern Spain includes Murcia, with the internationally famous 54-hole sporting complex of La Manga and the Valencia coast, where a number of attractive courses vie for attention, none more than the dramatic seaside links of El Saler, possibly the peak of Arana's achievements and universally reckoned one of Europe's best.

Golf continues up the coast in Catalonia, where a chain of twenty-two courses run right up to the border with France, blending the well-established with the new. Golf of quality, whether in a cluster around the urban delights of Barcelona or tucked among the sheltered bays and hills of Girona, the holiday haven that is the Costa Brava. We have included a worthy selection of very playable courses in adding this region to the guide.

Offshore in the Mediterranean, there are golfing opportunities on each of the main Balearic islands, but most particularly in Majorca where a choice of ten courses, set greenly between the rugged mountains and sparkling views of the sea, adds a touch of class to this popular holiday island.

Holiday Golf in the USA

by Michael Gedye

THE AMERICANS may not have invented golf but they have certainly refined and developed it, particularly in the area of holiday golf resorts. The United States is a vast country of immense contrasts with more golf courses than the rest of the world put together. The British visitor (and we are going there in ever-increasing numbers) is genuinely spoiled for choice. Florida, one of the two most popular destinations, has over 1,000 courses to choose from. If it was detached from the mainland, it would rank as the fourth-largest golfing country in the world. Along with the Carolinas, North and South, it has become a highly viable competitor to the well-known winter golf destinations in Europe. Convenient flights, a healthy exchange rate plus reliable weather and course conditions are the main factors.

Resort golf American-style is a whole new experience, quite unlike the game as we know it in Europe. Golf is created as

The West Course, Greenlefe, Florida.

an integral component of the resort, acting as a promotional magnet to encourage holiday players to visit and occupy hotel or condominium accommodation on site. It also provides a setting for the development of second or retirement homes fronting the fairways. Because of this, the visitor can be confident of finding manicured green ribbons winding their way to immaculate greens backed by colourful flora and waving palms. No expense is spared to create courses in superb, if a touch artificial, condition. The American market has come to expect the best golfing situations that money can buy and they get them.

With many courses designed to suit the market rather than provide a stiff challenge, since the average American tends to be a high handicapper, holes are often more of a delight to the eye than a severe test of one's game, despite vast stretches of sand and water. There are exceptions and we have included a few in a selection to tempt you across.

Holiday golf in the USA is an exercise in luxury and self-indulgence. Everything is organised to make life easier for the player. This is a cart culture and your bags will be pre-loaded on your obligatory cart, ready to ferry you to a pre-booked tee. In strong southern sunshine, your hosts provide welcome shade and relaxing transport, as well as accommodating the snacks and drinks that often appear, either at a bar every three holes or from a mobile service vehicle. The pace of the game may be slow but that is all part of the holiday. You may not be a millionaire but the American way of golf will make you feel like one.

For our initial choice of places to play, we have concentrated on two areas – Florida, the sunshine state bordering the warm waters of the Gulf of Mexico and the Carolinas, where the seaside vacation playgrounds of Hilton Head and Myrtle Beach contrast with classic locations such as Pinehurst. A mere taste of the rich treasure waiting to reward the holiday visitor.

Foreword

Playing golf gives us the excuse, if one is needed, to travel around the country to the loveliest parts of the land to play on the most beautiful courses which test everybody's ability and preferences.

The choice of your golfing experience, whether for a day or on an untried golf course or a more ambitious tour encompassing a number of new courses will be greatly enhanced by consulting *THE GOLF GUIDE* with accommodation entries, course descriptions and advice to be found in its pages.

There is a vast number of golf courses to choose from in the Brtish Isles – heathland, links, parkland, downland – and an even wider range of accommodation, but the one common denominator at most of these golf courses is that you will find a PGA professional, who will welcome you and offer any advice you require.

Remember that the PGA professional is there to help you enjoy your visit, so make the professionals shop your first point of contact on arrival at any golf club. There are four thousand PGA professionals throughout the country who spend their lives looking after your golfing needs.

You will without doubt enjoy playing many of the hundreds of golf courses, listed in the guide together with the interesting articles it contains. The PGA tournaments are fully covered, together with a great deal of relevant information on wide ranging activities of the PGA, that will be of interest to the golfing enthusiast.

On behalf of The Professional Golfers' Association may I wish you hours of pleasure delving into the pages of *THE GOLF GUIDE* to select where you will stay and play in the greatest game in the world.

Ross Whitehead
Captain
The Professional Golfers' Association

Acknowledgements

The Publishers wish to acknowledge the assistance of the Professional Golfers' Association, their staff at The Belfry and their golfing correspondents in the preparation of this, the 18th edition of *THE GOLF GUIDE*. Thanks are particularly due to Jane Carter and Joanne Taylor.

For colour illustrations we wish to acknowledge Puckrup Hall Hotel, near Tewkesbury, Glos. (title page), Bournemouth Tourism (p 10), the Dubai Creek Golf and Yacht Club (p 30), and Michael Gedye (pp 32, 35, 37, 38 and 40).

Our Front Cover features the Manor House Hotel and Golf Course, Moretonhampstead, Devon, of the Principal Hotel Group, which also includes Woodhall Spa Hotel shown on our outside back cover.

We wish to thank all our advertisers and, finally, the Club Secretaries, Professionals and others who have co-operated in the annual updating of the golf club directory entries which are the essential ingredient of *THE GOLF GUIDE: Where To Play/Where To Stay*.

Cover design: Ted Carden, Glasgow

ISBN 1 85055 195 2

Published by FHG Publications, a member of the U.N. Group, Abbey Mill Business Centre, Seedhill, Paisley PA1 1TJ (0141-887 0428)

Distribution: **Book Trade:** WLM, 117 The Hollow, Littleover, Derby DE3 7BS
(Tel: 01332 272020 Fax: 01332 774287)
News Trade: UMD, 16-28 Tabernacle Street, London EC2A 4BN
(Tel: 0170-638 4666 Fax: 0171-638 4665)

Typeset by RD Composition Ltd., Glasgow
Printed and bound by Benham's Ltd., Colchester

PRINTED AND PUBLISHED IN BRITAIN

How to Use The Golf Guide

THE GOLF GUIDE Where to Play • Where to Stay, contains up-to-date basic information on every course (as far as we know) in Britain. Details are provided by the clubs themselves. You will also find sections on Spain & Majorca, Portugal, France, the USA and Dubai.

The guide carries entries from hotels, guest-houses and other accommodation convenient to specific courses or areas. These are generally 'paid' entries and usually follow a recommendation from a club. *THE GOLF GUIDE* itself is endorsed by the Professional Golfers' Association and is usually available for sale in golf clubs through the Professional and/or the Secretary – as well as bookshops etc.

Golf Course Information

For virtually every course you will find the following details, updated annually:

1. Name, address and telephone number.
2. Location. 3. Brief description.
4. Number of holes, length and Standard Scratch Score. 5. Green fees.
6. Details of facilities for visitors – individuals, groups and societies.
7. Name and telephone number of the Professional and the Secretary.

The accuracy of details published depends on the response of the clubs and to our best knowledge is correct at the time of going to press (October 1994). Where entry details have not been confirmed an asterisk (*) is shown.

Choosing a Course

The golf clubs and courses are listed alphabetically by nearest town or village within the appropriate county section for England, Scotland, Wales, Ireland, the Isle of Man and the Channel Islands. Courses overseas are also listed by region. We have chosen to classify by place-name rather than club or course name since this seems more straightforward and recognisable to the majority.

If you want to find a club or course by its name, you should simply refer to the Index where you will see the page number of the listing. In each entry the name of the club or course is always shown in bold type after the place-name heading.

Accommodation

Accommodation entries are placed as near a particular club or course as possible and there are also hotel displays in the front colour section. Most of the accommodation advertised has been recommended by the local golf club. A full index is provided.

Maps

At the back of *THE GOLF GUIDE* you will find a set of maps showing cities, towns and villages in Britain with counties, motorways and main roads. Although many of the place-names under which the courses are classified are on the maps, please note that the maps are not golf course or club location maps.

The location details supplied with each entry should get you there and if you are in any doubt at all you should ask directions from the club itself.

Please mention *THE GOLF GUIDE Where to Play • Where to Stay* when you make a hotel booking or play at courses after using our guide.

Publisher's Note

WE WELCOME a number of new courses this year as well as entries for courses not previously covered, to join the hundreds of well-established favourites whose details have appeared ever since the first edition of *THE GOLF GUIDE* almost twenty years ago. With Driving Ranges, we now have over 2500 listings, over 2300 of which are in Britain and Ireland.

Golf is a wonderful game! It's a great leveller – from 'rabbits' to Club Captains, from lady associates to PGA professionals, indeed from Presidents to comedians, the challenge is the course and that tiny ball! It's a game for all ages: from the youngest junior to the oldest member, perhaps now non-playing but still a regular attender and a severe critic! It's a social activity and it's a great sport. Bending the rules may improve the score and lower the handicap, but it won't change the actual number of strokes taken in the round! And professional golfers stand almost apart from other professional games players in their honesty and strict observance of the spirit as well as the letter of the laws. A toast to golf, therefore . . . and to golfers!

While our main focus in *THE GOLF GUIDE* remains golfing facilities and accommodation for the visiting golfer around the British Isles, we have widened our golfing horizons further by introducing a taster of Golf in the USA – and most interesting, Golf in Dubai. Additional courses in Spain plus an update of France and Portugal complete the overseas scene for our 1995 edition. As usual we offer the following advice to readers:

Enquiries and Bookings. It is quite normal to confirm a booking in writing and also to receive written confirmation – and a receipt for any advance payment. You should check prices and also any special requirements.

Cancellations. Any booking is a form of contract for both parties. If you have to cancel, try to give maximum notice. With reasonable notice the hotel should normally refund any advance payment but on short notice a full refund is not necessarily a legal entitlement.

Complaints. Most owners/managers are anxious to sort out problems on the spot so that you are a satisfied customer. If a problem persists you can get advice from a Citizens' Advice Bureau, Consumers' Association, Trading Standards Office, Tourist Board or indeed your own solicitor.

Serious complaints are unlikely to arise with the kind of accommodation you'll find on our pages. FHG Publications Ltd. do not inspect accommodation and an entry does not imply a firm recommendation. However, most of the advertisers have been recommended or proposed by local golf clubs and have standards which satisfy and in many cases far exceed those expected by inspecting authorities. In addition we will be pleased to hear from you if you have a serious complaint and although we cannot act as intermediaries or accept responsibility for our advertisers, we will record the complaint and follow it up with the advertiser in question.

We are grateful to all Club Secretaries and Club Professionals who assist in the supply and revision of entries and to the PGA for editorial support. We are happy to hear from any Club which for some reason does not already have an entry. We also thank our advertisers for the wide range of accommodation choices for golfers, their families, friends and colleagues available in this edition and welcome suggestions for the future. We are particularly keen to receive accommodation recommendations from clubs and golfers themselves.

When you make enquiries and bookings for golf, accommodation or both, please mention this latest edition of *THE GOLF GUIDE: Where to Play/Where to Stay.*

Peter Clark
Publishing Director

Contents

THE GOLF FOUNDATION

57 London Road, Enfield, Middlesex EN2 6DU

Telephone: 081-367 4404

Established in 1952 The Golf Foundation has the specific aims of introducing more young people to the game of golf and of promoting and developing their skills and enjoyment of the game. The basis of the Foundation's work is the Coaching Scheme, whereby qualified members of the PGA give instruction to students at schools and universities. The Foundation also sponsors Open Coaching Centres during vacations, and implements a Coaching Award Scheme for teachers. A four-stage Merit Award Scheme operates successfully throughout the country, and Age Group Championships help raise the standard of junior golf by providing real competition at all levels of ability.

A newsletter "Tee to Green" is published, as well as other coaching material, visual aids and films.

The Golf Foundation is a non-profit-making organisation and a Registered Charity, relying on support from organisations within the game, commerce and industry, and individual Golf Clubs and club members. As the national body responsible for junior golf it plays a vital role in the future development of the game.

The PGA Year

THE PROFESSIONAL GOLFERS' ASSOCIATION was formed over 92 years ago with 50 members. Perhaps its potential membership and influence was reflected by the standing of its first president, the Rt Hon. James Balfour who was shortly afterwards to become the Prime Minister! The current president is the equally distinguished Lord Derby and the membership has grown to just under 4,000, including 800 working abroad and more than 1,000 trainees.

The working club professional continues to give lessons, repair clubs and run his shop and increasingly he has to play the "business" game as well as he plays golf! His time is very much taken up with pro-ams, company days and regional tournaments which have become vital to the economics and the image of professional golf. Other competitive demands on the professional have less to do with golf than with shopkeeping – in the shape of the trading competition he faces from retail sports shop chains and large supermarkets.

However, the club professional still has prestigious national tournaments where he can put his skills on more public show and compete against the best in his business in his own selected game – golf. It is with these annual and important events that our review of the PGA year deals.

THE TRUSTHOUSE FORTE PGA SENIORS' CHAMPIONSHIP

"Why do I want to retire when I already go fishing and play golf," were the words of Forte PGA Seniors Championship winner John Morgan when he collected

John Morgan, proud winner of the 1994 Trusthouse Forte PGA Seniors Championship at Sunningdale.

yet another cheque in a supremely successful year on the PGA European Tour Seniors' circuit. They may have been pinched from the mouth of Julius Boros but summed up exactly just how the 50-year-old Englishman is enjoying himself alongside the likes of Neil Coles, Tommy Horton, Brian Waites and Brian Huggett "all of whom I have always admired because of their magnificent careers."

Morgan is not only standing alongside them in his first year on the Seniors' Tour but is beating them hands down when it comes to golf. His victory in the Forte Seniors' at Sunningdale was his third of the season and his second in succession having arrived at the Ascot course as the winner of the Lawrence Batley Seniors the previous week. The cheque for £12,500 took his earnings to just under £50,000 and he looks well in sight of passing the £56,900 PGA European Seniors' Order of Merit winning total set by Tommy Horton in 1993.

But whereas his win a week earlier had been a comfortable jog – if not a romp – the Forte proved a different kettle of fish with a pack of players snapping at his heels for much of the final round. His best round of the tournament, a 67, was finally enough to earn him victory by two shots over German-based Englishman David Creamer who had had to pre-qualify for the 54-hole event.

Morgan, whose wife Christine caddied for him during the week as she had done at the Lawrence Batley, said: "Winning seems to get harder not easier. We were neck and neck out there for ages and there was no way David was letting go.

"It is a tough golf course – a classic golf course – and what with that and the quality of the players chasing me it has just been a magnificent week. It is even more special to win an event which is so established and join the names of O'Connor, Peter Thomson, Neil Coles and Tommy Horton."

It was North Berwick's David Huish who signalled some early form with victory in the Pro-am with a round of 65. Many rated the Scottish professional's chances, who admitted he was starting to find his feet again on Tour and was looking for a good finish on a course he knew well.

The course won the admiration of all the players but was certainly playing a lot longer than they were used to. The little known Italian Alberto Croce – uncle of women's Tour professional Stefania Croce – topped the leaderboard at the end of the first day with a round of 67. He was clearly delighted, as was Berkhamsted's Basil Proudfoot who shot a 68 to tie with Morgan and Tommy Horton. He had hit the headlines a year earlier when he had led after the first round. American Terry Fine, founder of the Tommy Armour Tour in America and a regular competitor on the Japanese Tour, was competing in his first event in England and did so to fine effect with an opening round of 69 to be in contention.

Former PGA Cup player David Creamer, now based out of Marhoerdt in Germany, shot a round of 66 to tie for the second round lead with Morgan who had a round of 68. Creamer was a former table tennis star, having been ranked number two in England before turning to golf. One shot further back was Fine with Coles, a four times winner of the title, another shot back and one in front of Huish and Horton. Golf is certainly a humbling game as Proudfoot discovered when he followed his 68 with an 82 to miss the cut which fell at eight over par.

Morgan began as many felt he would with a 'birdie' at the opening hole to move into a one-shot lead but it soon became obvious he was not going to have it all his own way. Creamer tied with a birdie at the fourth before dropping a shot at the sixth. Meanwhile the rest of the field was vainly trying to make an impression on the lead with Fine holding on to be four under at the turn while the Coles, Horton and Huish campaign never really materialised.

Only Italian Renato Campagnoli was making any real headway on his way to a 65 – the lowest round of the tournament – for a total of four under par 206.

Morgan and Creamer continued to slug it out with just the one shot separating them until Morgan played his ace card at the par five 14th. There he holed a 20-foot 'eagle' putt, while Creamer could only manage a par, to immediately move into a three shot lead with just four holes left to go. Not even a dropped shot by Morgan at the next opened the door wide enough for Creamer and a level par finish by the Scunthorpe based professional was enough to give him a two shot

Malcolm Boyd of Glenmuir presents Irishman David Jones with the PGA Club Professional Championship Trophy, played at North Berwick.

victory on seven under par 203, with Campagnoli third on 206, Fine in fourth place on 207.

The 'big names' failed to feature, with Coles and Horton tied for seventh, while David Huish who had high hopes after a second round 67 fell away to a 74 to finish tied in 12th place.

Both the sponsors and the players were delighted with crowds who had turned out to watch the names from the not so distant past. It was the 14th year of sponsorship by Forte and they can now be proud that on the Seniors' Tour, theirs is the one everyone wants to win!

THE GLENMUIR PGA CLUB PROFESSIONAL CHAMPIONSHIP

The 1994 Glenmuir Club Professional Championship at North Berwick painted a picture of contrasts. Conditions ranged from idyllic to unplayable; emotions stretched between elation and devastation.

At the end of the dramatic week, it was Knockbracken's David Jones who had most to celebrate. The 47-year-old Irishman produced an outstanding final day performance to snatch victory and enter the record books as the first three times winner. A back-to-back winner in 1978 and 1979, Jones finished on six under par 278 to clinch the £7,000 winner's cheque by two shots from the experienced trio of Nick Job (Richmond), Robin Mann (Fynn Valley) and Hogan Stott (Lalchan).

The win also secured pole position in the ten man European team for the Johnnie Walker PGA Cup matches against America at PGA National, Florida, in September.

While Jones snatched the title with a late surge – he covered the final nine in just 31 blows – it was the battle for PGA

Cup places that provided the ultimate in ecstasy and frustration.

The places were decided on points accumulated from performances at the 1993 and 1994 Glenmuir Club Professional Championships, and the top eight finishers at North Berwick – Jones, Stott, Mann, Job, Craig Maltman (Eyemouth), Andrew Baguley (Leigh), John Harrison (Barnard Castle) and Joe Higgins (Patshull Park) – secured their places alongside the 1993 Glenmuir victor at Coventry, Bulwell Forest's Chris Hall. But the final spot came down to a sudden-death play-off, and it was Scotland's Russell Weir who took the coveted prize with a par at the fifth extra hole. For the defeated Mark Parker (Riverside) it was the most disappointing day of his career.

The practice round was greeted with brilliant sunshine. But then the wind blew in and David Scott (Letham Grange), fresh from a recent victory in the Volvo Pro-Captain Challenge at Wentworth, claimed the opening day lead with a level par 71. A member of the 1990 PGA Cup side, the 6′5″ Scot led by two from Andrew Baguley. Day One may have been tough, but Day Two was impossible. With wild, south-easterly gales sweeping across the links, officials had little alternative but to abandon play. After a six-week drought – 200,000 gallons of water a week had been poured on the course since the beginning of May – the combination of 35 mph gusting winds and lightning fast greens made it impossible to keep the balls steady on the putting surfaces.

When the delayed second round did get under way a day late, Richmond's Nick Job set the tournament alight with a superb course record of seven-under-par 64 for the recently lengthened course. The 45-year-old former European Tour player made the score with a superb outward half of seven-under 29, five 'birdies' from the 4th being followed by a 20 yard chip-in for an 'eagle' at the 9th. The score put Job back on track after his disappointing opening 79, but it was Maltman with a fine 67 who claimed the halfway lead on two under par 140.

The loss of the day's play meant that 36 holes had to be squeezed into the final day, and that just added to the dramatic finale. Jones came into the event in impressive form having finished runner-up to Des Smyth in the inaugural Irish Masters in Dublin the previous week. And, after a 74 in the opening day's testing mix of gusting winds and slick greens, he continued the hot streak with sub par rounds of 69, 69 and 66. Three behind Eyemouth's Craig Maltman at the halfway stage, he packed eleven birdies into the final day 36 holes to emerge a winner from a tightly-packed field.

Eventually, the outcome hinged on the final run-in, and it was Jones who raced home in front thanks to a blistering final nine of four-under-par 31, 'birdies' coming at the 10th, 13th, 15th and 17th.

Mann, playing alongside Jones, was a shot ahead with three holes to play. But the Fynn Valley professional, who won the Club Professional title in 1985, faltered with a bogey, bogey, par finish in 67. Maltman, three ahead at halfway, still led by one going into the final 18 holes after a third round 69. But the 41-year-old, who has been troubled by shoulder problems for the past 18 months, slipped back into a share of fifth after a closing 72.

But it was not just the titles and cheques that added to the final day pressures. Chasing PGA Cup places was equally exciting. And deciding the tenth berth could not have produced a more nail-biting climax. Weir and Parker were joint runner-up in the 1993 Glenmuir Championship, but both failed to finish in the points at North Berwick. Adding to the tension late on the final evening was the fact that Weir had played 36 holes that day, while Parker, having missed the cut, had been hanging around waiting for fate to play its part.

Mark Plummer, winner of the Standard Life PGA Assistants' Trophy, with R. Dunlop Stuart (left) of Standard Life and Sandy Jones (right) Executive Director of the PGA.

The play-off was sudden-death. But it turned out to be a slow, lingering execution for the unfortunate Parker. The first four holes were halved, before Weir produced the killer blow with a winning par at North Berwick's tricky 16th, the fifth of the extra time decider.

One could only sympathise with Parker, who had come so close to victory in the 1993 Glenmuir event before being pipped by a final day course record-equalling 64 from Hall. It must have been a long drive home to Kent from North Berwick. For Weir, the play-off win secured his fifth successive appearance in the PGA Cup. The 42-year-old Scot has had his own successes, but he has yet to figure in the winning side.

STANDARD LIFE PGA ASSISTANTS' CHAMPIONSHIP

Mark Plummer, from Burnham and Berrow, produced four sub-par rounds to score an impressive victory in the Standard Life PGA Assistants' Championship at Foxhills in Surrey. The 22-year-old led from start to finish, although he had to hold off a late charge from Londoner Matt Deal (Bush Hill Park) before claiming the £3,750 top prize with a 14 under par 278 total.

Four behind with nine to play, Deal produced two eagles and four birdies to stand level on the 72nd tee. But his charge ended when he pulled his second shot at the 441-yard final hole behind the sponsor's banner and, after a free drop, failed to get up and down for par. A relieved Plummer was then left with a regulation two putts for a final round 70 and the one-shot victory.

For Deal, whose closing 67 was the best round of the tournament, there was the consolation of the £2,700 runners-up cheque. Cameron Smellie (North Manchester) finished third on six-under-par 286, with Carl Green (Bawburgh) and Scot, Colin Gillies, last year's runner-up, another shot further back. After a slow

Chris Tyson, winner of the 1994 Lord Derby Knowsley Safari Park Tournament – champagne much in evidence!

start in which he survived the cut on the final mark, Craig Everett (Caldwell) put up a brave defence of the title he won at Oaklands in Cheshire last year with two closing rounds of 70 that left him in joint sixth place.

In the first round, Plummer, who played for the England Boys' team and turned professional three years ago, shot a 70 to stand one shot clear of Green and Ross Robertson (Aylesbury Park), and he was still one clear at the halfway stage after a second round 70. Another 70 on the morning of the final day, which included a run of four birdies from the turn, placed him three clear of Deal going into the final 18 holes.

Winner of this season's Welsh Professional Championship, a delighted Plummer said: "This is a major victory and I'm absolutely thrilled. But I really thought Matt had me when he came back over the final nine. He certainly put the pressure on." Mark Plummer also wins an invitation to this year's Titleist and Foot-Joy PGA of America Assistant Professional Championship at PGA West, Palm Springs, California, with travel and accommodation provided by Titleist & Foot-Joy Worldwide for himself and a guest.

LORD DERBY'S KNOWSLEY SAFARI PARK TOURNAMENT

Chris Tyson has no illusions about his future as a professional golfer. Despite repelling the challenge from some of the country's leading assistants to win the Lord Derby's Knowsley Safari Park Tournament at Bolton, Tyson does not see himself as a high flyer. "I will have a go for my card at the Tour School but my main ambition is to become a club professional," he says with refreshing honesty. "This victory will not change my mind. I enjoy teaching and that's how I see my career shaping up".

Tyson, a 23-year-old assistant at North Yorkshire Club, Malton and Norton, went about his business almost unnoticed for most of the time. While much of the attention was focused on overnight leader Chris Tingey and John Mellor, who was defending his title, Tyson was quietly compiling a second round of 68 to add to his opening 69 – a score which had not seemed likely after he had marked down a double bogey six at the first hole where he overhit his wedge into the hedge.

Four birdies helped his recovery, the one at the seventh courtesy of a 25-yard putt to leave him in a group of six players two shots off the pace. It was the opening hole, which had caused him so much grief the previous day, that gave him the perfect start to his second round. He rapped in a four footer for the first of three birdies, the others coming at the seventh and eighth, in an outward half of three-under-par 32.

He three-putted on the 11th from 18 feet for his first bogey, birdied the 12th then three-stabbed the 13th. Tyson reached the downwind long 15th with a driver and seven iron, two putts for birdie hoisting him to the top of the leaderboard at four-under. Like so many other players, he then dropped a shot at the last hole where he pulled his tee-shot into the trees then bunkered his four iron.

Worksop's Mellor, who struck the ball beautifully on the first day, missing only one green and seeing seven realistic birdie chances go astray, could not maintain his momentum and closed with 72 for a share of eighth place.

Despite Stephen Raybould shooting a best-of-the-tournament 66, his three-under-par total of 137 left the Scarborough South Cliff man a stroke off the pace and tied second with Coventry's Craig Phillips, who added 68 to his earlier 70.

It was all down to Tingey to sustain the challenge. A birdie at the 15th, which he really should have converted into an eagle, put him one ahead – and the Wycombe Heights assistant had a one stroke lead and one hand on the trophy.

Arbroath professional David Scott and his Club Captain Brian Robertson, winners of the Volvo Pro-Captain Challenge.

But Tingey, who had hardly mishit a shot over the two days, suddenly lost his rhythm. He pulled his drive into the rough at the 16th, which cost him a stroke, three putted the next, then bogeyed the last to close with a 72. It was a sad end to his challenge and relegated him to a share of the fourth prize.

As for Tyson, he celebrated his victory with a magnum of Moet at Chandon champagne!

THE VOLVO PRO-CAPTAIN CHALLENGE
THE VOLVO PGA CHAMPIONSHIP

Arbroath Professional David Scott and his Club Captain Brian Robertson basked in a little Spanish glory when they won the Volvo Pro-Captain Challenge over the West Course at Wentworth. Only a day earlier, on that same course, Masters Champion Jose Maria Olazabal had shot a last round 65 to beat South African

U.S. Masters' Champion Jose Maria Olazabal with the 1994 Volvo PGA Championship trophy which he won at Wentworth.

Ernie Els to the coveted Volvo PGA Championship title in yet another memorable tournament.

The pair may not have been able to match Olazabal's last round of 65 but their betterball score of two under par 71 was good enough to win the title for their club Letham Grange and earn Scott a cheque for £2,500. And as if that were not enough Scott was delighted to hear Executive Director Sandy Jones announce that the duo's win had earned him a place in next year's Volvo PGA Championship.

He said: "I am completely shell shocked. I had played in a European Tour event before which was a great experience but did not think I would ever do it again. It was a big thrill for us both to win today and getting into the Volvo PGA Championship next year is just a marvellous bonus."

Sixteen pairings competed over exactly the same course as Olazabal and the rest of Europe's top professionals had played a day earlier, having qualified from an initial entry of 1050 pairings, making the Volvo Pro-Captain Challenge the biggest professional entry for any tournament in this country except The Open.

Although every couple found the going tough and the speed of the greens 'terrifying', it was a close-run thing with Letham Grange winning by just one shot from Professional Gary Emerson and Captain Mike Pugsley (Salisbury & South Wilts) and Professional Bill McColl and Captain Peter Creasy (Thorpe Hall).

Scott and factory manager Robertson, playing off six, had got off to a shaky start, dropping a shot at the first. Despite a superb four iron to 15 feet to set up an eagle for Scott at the fourth, the pairing still turned in two over par 38 compared with playing partners Emerson and Pugsley who were out in 34. But then it all started to come together with Robertson making a gross birdie at 11, Scott another at the 12th and finally finishing with a blitz of three birdies; Robertson's at the last being made out of the greenside bunker where he hit to five feet and then holed the putt.

Their back nine of 33 for a total of 71 was good enough to hold off all challengers and collect the second Volvo Pro-Captain title. Every competitor was a 'winner', having qualified regionally and then enjoyed two days of superb hospitality and golf at Wentworth courtesy of Volvo.

On the previous day they were guests of The Professional Golfers' Association and watched in admiration as Olazabal became the fourth European golfer to follow success in the US Masters with a victory in the Volvo PGA Championship in the same year. He compiled an outstanding 65 which included six birdies – five in the last eight holes – and one eagle for a 17 under par total of 271.

Congratulations were also in order for the Association's top man, Scotland's Kevin Stables, who shot a last round 68 to add to three rounds of 71 to finish in a tie for 10th place and collect a cheque for £14,340.

Charles Hunter-Pease, Managing Director of Volvo U.K., said: "We are delighted with the entry to this year's Volvo Pro-Captain Challenge and hope the event continues to grow. An entry of 1200 pairings next year would be fantastic and I hope every Club Professional encourages his Captain to enter."

THE PGA CUP

Played between club professionals from Britain and Europe against their counterparts from the USA every two years.

Europe failed in their bid to become the first team to win the PGA Cup on American soil when they lost to a strong US team by 15 points to 11 at the PGA National, Florida. A poor performance in the eight fourball matches played over the two days in this Ryder Cup style competition was their downfall, with Europe winning just one point from a possible eight.

Despite losing, the Europeans can take heart from the fact that the scoreline was the best performance by a European side on American soil since the teams tied at Turnberry Isle, Florida in 1981.

Intense heat and humidity and continual rain and lightning delays made life difficult for the 10-man team led by Captain Mike Ingham (Cleckheaton). They got off to a flying start, winning the first morning's foursomes by 3-1 but then that fourball jinx struck with the US winning all four of the first fourball series, three of the matches having to be completed the following morning. A two-point deficit saw the Europeans move up a gear in the second morning foursomes to win the series by 3-1 and take their foursome points won to six out of a possible eight. But the afternoon fourballs, which again had to be completed on the morning of the third day due to lightning delays, saw the US take a grip on the match, winning the series by 3-1 to lead by 9 points to 7 with 10 singles remaining.

Europe needed 6½ points from the 10 available to win the Llandudno Trophy and it was just too much to ask as one by one the Europeans toppled. Chris Hall (Bulwell Forest) lifted European hopes with the first singles victory of the day by 2&1 over Todd Smith but from that point it was an uphill struggle. Suffolk's Robin Mann (Fynn Valley) narrowly failed to win Europe's second point when J.L. Lewis, unbeaten during the week with four points out of four, holed a monster forty foot putt at the last for an eagle and victory by one hole. Europe's leading man David Jones (Knockbracken), making his seventh PGA Cup appearance, was close to tears as he went down by 3&2 to the powerful Rick Acton, also a four out of five points earner.

Warrington Professional Andrew Baguley (Leigh) claimed his first victory of the week with a 3&2 win over Jeff Roth, the reigning PGA Club Professional Champion. Durham's John Harrison (Barnard Castle) was feeling the strain after playing in all four series and went down in his singles by 6&5, a defeat compensated a few moments later by Midlands Professional Joe Higgins (Patshull Park) with a 5&4 victory.

Scotland's Craig Maltman kept European hopes alive with a 2&1 victory over former PGA Club Champion Ron McDougal but with America requiring just one point for the 13 needed to retain the trophy it came from a birdie by John Lee to win by 2&1 over Surrey's Hogan Stott (Laleham). Outright victory was provided by Walt Chapman's 4&3 win over Scotland's Russell Weir, who had also played in all four foursome and fourball series and was clearly tired. Nick Job

The European club professional's team, captained by Mike Ingham of Cleckheaton, which narrowly failed to win the PGA Cup in Florida in September 1994.

(Richmond) was pipped at the post for his singles win when Tom Cleaver birdied the last for a one-hole victory.

Captain Mike Ingham said: "Our record in the fourballs was disappointing and left a lot for us to do. When we came out here I thought we could win but these guys are so strong and on their home patch in these conditions it had to be in their favour. All of our team played their hearts out and it has been an honour for them and for me to be out here. It is a performance they can be proud of and remember in years to come."

The Johnnie Walker PGA Cup returns to Scotland in 1996 when it will be played at Gleneagles over the Monarchs course.

GOLF IN ENGLAND

Golf in England

WHERE TO PLAY • WHERE TO STAY

Golf in England covers all kinds of clubs and courses ranging geographically from the Lizard in the South-west to Berwick-on-Tweed in Northumberland, and from Broadstairs in east Kent to St. Bees in west Cumbria. The courses themselves may be modest and friendly or they may represent the hostile challenge of the Open Championship. Facilities may be simple and few, perhaps no more than a basic clubhouse, but may also be part of a larger leisure complex and so profuse as almost to overwhelm!

From city to country, however, from humble to grand, all these clubs and courses meet the great leveller in the game of golf and in the attitudes and abilities of golfers themselves. The serious golfer, subject to local circumstances and conditions, will normally be welcome on most courses but the pressure on playing-times and therefore availability in some areas remains intense. Our section on England offers a huge choice of golfing opportunities but prospective visitors should always check well in advance that they or their group can in fact make suitable bookings.

The same is true, though to a lesser extent, of overnight accommodation at hotels whose entries appear or any other accommodation perhaps recommended by a host club.

Our entries for England start with London but thereafter follow by county in alphabetical order.

Where an asterisk (*) follows an entry, details have not been confirmed by the club for 1995.

London

ASHFORD. **Ashford Manor Golf Club,** Fordbridge Road, Ashford, Middlesex TW15 3RT (01784 252049). 18 holes, 6343 yards. S.S.S. 70. *Green Fees:* information not provided. *Visitors:* welcome with introduction. Professional: M. Finney (01784 255940). Secretary: B.J. Duffy.

BARNET. **North Middlesex Golf Club,** The Manor House, Friern Barnet Lane, Whetstone N20 0NL (0181-445 1732). *Location:* five miles north of Finchley, five miles south of Junction 23 of M25. 18 holes, 5611 yards. S.S.S. 67. *Green Fees:* weekday round/day £22.00; weekends and Bank Holidays £30.00. *Eating facilities:* luncheons, snacks and dining facilities. *Visitors:* welcome (with Official Handicap), weekends playing with a member and in possession of Official Handicap. Advisable to telephone Professional to book time. *Society Meetings:* catered for. Professional: A.S.R. Roberts (0181-445 3060). General Manager/Secretary: M.C.N. Reding (0181-445 1604).

BARNET. **Old Fold Manor Golf Club,** Hadley Green, Barnet, Herts EN5 4QN (0181-440 9185). *Location:* Junction 23 M25 – A1000 one mile north of Barnet. Heathland course. 18 holes, 6471 yards. S.S.S. 71. Practice nets and putting green. *Green Fees:* weekdays £22.00 per round (with a member £10.00), £27.00 per day (with a member £15.00); weekends £12.50 with member only. *Eating facilities:* restaurant and bar except Mondays and Wednesdays when cafeteria/snack bar is available. *Visitors:* welcome weekdays, special visitors' concessions at weekends by arrangement. *Society Meetings:* catered for Thursdays and Fridays. Professional: Daniel Fitzsimmons (0181-440 7488). Manager: A.W. Dickens (0181-440 9185).

BEXLEY HEATH. **Barnehurst Golf Course,** Mayplace Road East, Bexley Heath, Kent DA7 6JU (01322 523746). *Location:* just north of Crayford town centre. Mature inland course in traditional woodland setting. 9 greens (18 tees), S.S.S. 66. Designed by five times Open Champion James Braid in 1904. *Green Fees:* weekdays £5.70, weekends and Bank Holidays £9.20. Reduced rates for Senior Citizens and Juniors. Membership available. *Eating facilities:* fully licensed bar and catering. *Visitors:* welcome. Society Meetings: catered for. Large function room. Professional Patrick "Teach" Tallack.

BROMLEY. **Bromley Golf Club,** Magpie Hall Lane, Bromley, Kent BR2 8JF. *Location:* off A21 Bromley to Farnborough road. Short, flat, open course with a few trees. 9 holes, 2745 yards. S.S.S. 35. Putting green and teaching facilities. *Green Fees:* information not available. *Eating facilities:* snacks available. *Visitors:* no booking required as this is public course. *Society Meetings:* by arrangement with Bromley District Council. Professional: Robert Lee (0181-462 7014).

CHINGFORD. **Chingford Golf Club,** 158 Station Road, Chingford E4 (0181-529 2107). 18 holes, 6342 yards. S.S.S. 70. *Green Fees:* on application. *Visitors:* welcome weekdays only, an article of red must be worn. Professional: John Francis. Secretary: Bryan Sinden. *

CHINGFORD. **Royal Epping Forest Golf Club,** Forest Approach, Chingford, London E4 7AZ (0181-529 6407). *Location:* 200 yards east of Chingford (BR) Station. A private club on a public course. Wooded. 18 holes, 6342 yards. S.S.S. 71. *Green Fees:* weekdays £9.00; weekends £12.50. *Eating facilities:* public snack bar. *Visitors:* may play course but may not use clubhouse. Must wear red garment (trousers or shirt/sweater). Professionals: Robin Gowers/John Francis (0181-529 5708). Secretary: Mrs P. Runciman (0181-529 2195).

CHINGFORD. **West Essex Golf Club,** Bury Road, Sewardstonebury, Chingford, London E4 7QL (0181-529 0928). *Location:* two miles north of Chingford BR Station. M25 (Junction 26) and Waltham Abbey follow directions to Chingford (Daws Lane on left). Parkland, wooded, hilly. 18 holes, 6289 yards. S.S.S. 70. Driving range (for members, members' guests and societies). *Green Fees:* weekdays £25.00 per round, £30.00 per day; weekends with member only. *Eating facilities:* restaurant and bar facilities: *Visitors:* welcome weekdays except Tuesday mornings and Thursday afternoons; after 3pm competition days. Phone first. *Society Meetings:* catered for by arrangement Mondays, Wednesdays and Fridays. Professional: Robert Joyce (0181-529 4367). Secretary: P.H. Galley MBE (0181-529 7558).

DULWICH. **Dulwich and Sydenham Hill Golf Club,** Grange Lane, College Road, London SE21 (0181-693 3961). *Location:* off South Circular, Dulwich Common. 18 holes, 6051 yards. S.S.S. 69. *Green Fees:* £25.00 per round. *Eating facilities:* lunch every day. *Visitors:* welcome, with reservation on weekdays. *Society Meetings:* catered for, maximum 30. Professional: David Baillie. Secretary: Mrs Susan Alexander.

EDMONTON. **Leaside Golf Club,** Pickett's Lock Sports Centre, Edmonton N9 0AS (0181-803 4756). *Location:* near North Circular Road. Flat parkland. 9 holes, 2496 yards. S.S.S. 32. Driving range, putting green. *Green Fees:* information not available. Reductions weekdays for Senior Citizens and Juniors. *Eating facilities:* cafe and bar. *Visitors:* booking required at weekends. *Society Meetings:* by arrangement with Sports Centre. Professional: R. Gerken. *

EDMONTON. **Lee Valley Leisure Golf Course,** Lee Valley Leisure, (Picketts Lock), Edmonton, London N9 0AS. *Location:* off Meridian Way near North Circular Road, Edmonton. Flat parkland course with lake and River Lea as water hazards. 18 holes, 4902 yards. S.S.S. 64. 20 bay floodlit driving range. *Green Fees:* weekdays £9.00; weekends £12.00. Senior Citizens and Junior weekday concessions. *Eating facilities:* snack bar and bar. *Visitors:* open to public every day, weekend booking advisable (contact Professional). *Society Meetings:* small societies welcome weekdays. Professional: Richard Gerken (0181-803 3611). Manager: (0181-345 6666).

ELTHAM. **Eltham Warren Golf Club,** Bexley Road, Eltham SE9 2PE (0181-850 1166). *Location:* A210 Eltham. Parkland. 9 holes, 5840 yards. S.S.S. 68. *Green Fees:* £25.00 per day; with member £10.00. *Eating facilities:* two bars, diningroom. *Visitors:* welcome weekdays only, weekends with member only. *Society Meetings:* by arrangement. Professional: R.V. Taylor (0181-859 7909). Secretary: D.J. Clare (0181-850 4477).

ELTHAM. **Royal Blackheath Golf Club,** The Clubhouse, Court Road, Eltham SE9 5AF. *Location:* M25, A20 exit London bound, second set of traffic lights turn right, 600 yards up hill on right. Parkland, wooded with water. 18 holes, 6219 yards. S.S.S. 70. Practice area. *Green Fees:* £40.00 per day (£15.00 with member). *Eating facilities:* excellent diningroom and two bars. *Visitors:* welcome weekdays, weekends only if introduced by and playing with member. Museum. *Society Meetings:* catered for midweek, prior booking essential. Professional: Ian McGregor (0181-850 1763). Secretary: R. Barriball (0181-850 1795; Fax: 0181-859 0150).

ENFIELD. **Crews Hill Golf Club,** Cattlegate Road, Crews Hill, Enfield EN2 8AZ (0181-363 0787). *Location:* off Junction 24 M25, follow directions to Enfield. Parkland. 18 holes, 6230 yards. S.S.S. 70. Practice area. *Green Fees:* on application. *Eating facilities:* full bar and snacks available, restaurant by arrangement. No catering Mondays. *Visitors:* welcome weekdays. Handicap Certificate required. Weekends by invitation of member. *Society Meetings:* by arrangement. Professional: J.R. Reynolds (0181-366 7422). General Manager: E.J. Hunt (0181-363 6674; Fax: 0181-364 5641).

ENFIELD. **Enfield Golf Club,** Old Park Road South, Enfield, Middlesex EN2 7DA. *Location:* off Junction 24, M25; follow directions to Enfield. Parkland; designed by James Braid. 18 holes, 6200 yards. S.S.S. 70. *Green Fees:* on request. *Eating facilities:* full bar and catering facilities. *Visitors:* welcome weekdays only, with current Handicap Certificate. *Society Meetings:* catered for Mondays, Wednesdays and Fridays by prior arrangement. Professional: Lee Fickling (0181-366 4492). Secretary: Nigel Challis (0181-363 3970; Fax: 0181-342 0381). *

ENFIELD. **Whitewebbs Golf Club,** Clay Hill, Beggars Hollow, Enfield EN2 9JN (0181-363 2951). *Location:* A10 off M25, north of Enfield. Parkland course. 18 holes, 5863 yards. S.S.S. 68. Practice area, separate 9 hole pitch and putt. *Green Fees:* £10.60 weekdays; £12.40 weekends. *Eating facilities:* public cafe on site. *Visitors:* welcome, public course, no restrictions. *Society Meetings:* contact the Secretary. Professional: D. Lewis (0181-363 4454). Secretary: Victor Van Graan (0181-363 2951). *

FINCHLEY. **Finchley Golf Club,** Nether Court, Frith Lane, Finchley, London NW7 1PU (0181-349 2314). *Location:* close A1/M1 Mill Hill East tube station. Parkland course. 18 holes, 6411 yards. S.S.S. 71. *Green Fees:* weekdays £28.00; weekends £37.00. *Eating facilities:* bar; diningroom open daily except Mondays. *Visitors:* welcome weekdays except Thursdays, weekends after mid-day. *Society Meetings:* catered for Mondays, Wednesdays and Fridays. Special rates for parties. Professional: David Brown (0181-346 5086). Secretary: Keith Monk (0181-346 2436; Fax: 0181-343 4205).

GREENFORD. **Ealing Golf Club,** Perivale Lane, Greenford, Middlesex UB6 8SS (0181-997 2595). *Location:* on Western Avenue A40 half a mile from Hanger Lane Gyratory System. Flat parkland. 18 holes, 6216 yards. S.S.S. 70. *Green Fees:* £30.00 weekdays; weekends with a member only. *Eating facilities:* men's bar, mixed lounge, restaurant – lunches and snacks. *Visitors:* welcome weekdays with reservation through Professional. *Society Meetings:* catered for on Monday, Wednesday and Thursday. Professional: A. Stickley (0181-997 3959). Secretary: M. Scargill (0181-997 0937).

GREENFORD. **Horsenden Hill Golf Club,** Whitton Avenue, Woodland Rise, Greenford UB6 0RD (0181-902 4555). *Location:* off Whitton Avenue East, next door to Sudbury Golf Course. Very tough though short course. 9 holes, 1632 yards, 1490 metres. S.S.S. 55.

Practice area, nets and putting green. *Green Fees:* weekdays £3.75 for 9 holes; weekends £5.60 for 9 holes. *Eating facilities:* restaurant and bar. *Visitors:* welcome at all times, unrestricted. Professional: Andrew Rogers and Anthony Ferrier. Secretary: Mr Jim Kelly. *

GREENFORD. **Perivale Park Golf Club,** Stockdove Way, Greenford, Middlesex (0181-575 7116). *Location:* A40, turn off at sign for Ealing and Perivale. Flat parkland. 9 holes, 2667 yards. S.S.S. 34. Excellent practice ground. *Green Fees:* weekdays £6.00 for 9 holes; weekends £6.00 for 9 holes, £11.00 for 18 holes. Reductions for Senior Citizens and Juniors. *Eating facilities:* cafeteria. *Visitors:* welcome – public course. Professional: Peter Bryant. Secretary: George Taylor (0181-845 7376).

HAMPSTEAD. **Hampstead Golf Club,** Winnington Road, London N2 0TU (0181-455 0203). *Location:* off Hampstead Lane adjacent to Spaniards Inn. Undulating parkland with trees. 9 holes, 5812 yards. S.S.S. 68. *Green Fees:* £23.00 (£28.00 per day) weekdays; weekends £30.00. *Eating facilities:* bar; snacks and afternoon teas. *Visitors:* welcome weekdays (not Tuesdays); limited at weekends. *Society Meetings:* small societies catered for weekdays by prior arrangement. Professional: Peter Brown (0181-455 7089). Secretary: K.F. Young (0181-455 0203).

HAMPTON HILL. **Fulwell Golf Club,** Wellington Road, Hampton Hill, Middlesex TW12 1JY (0181-977 3188). *Location:* opposite Fulwell Railway Station and bus garage. Flat parkland course. 18 holes, 6544 yards. S.S.S. 71. Practice ground. *Green Fees:* weekdays £30.00; weekends £35.00. £12.00 with member. *Eating facilities:* lunches and teas. *Visitors:* welcome weekdays. *Society Meetings:* welcome Monday, Wednesday, Thursday and Fridays. Professional: D. Haslam (Tel & Fax: 0181-977 3844). Secretary: P.F. Butcher (0181-977 2733).

HAMPTON WICK. **Home Park Golf Club,** Hampton Wick, Kingston-upon-Thames KT1 4AD (0181-977 2658). *Location:* between Hampton Court and Kingston Bridge, entrance at Kingston Bridge roundabout. Flat parkland. 18 holes, 6598 yards. S.S.S. 71. *Green Fees:* weekdays £15.00 (£24.00 all day), weekends and Bank Holidays £20.00 (£30.00 all day). *Eating facilities:* full bar and dining facilities. *Visitors:* welcome – no advance booking. *Society Meetings:* catered for by arrangement. Professional: D.L. Roberts (0181-977 2658). Secretary: Mr B.W. O'Farrell (0181-977 2423). *

HENDON. **Hendon Golf Club,** off Sanders Lane, Devonshire Road, Mill Hill, London NW7 1DG (0181-346 8083). *Location:* leave M1 southbound at Junction 2. Turn off A1 into Holders Hill Road. 10 miles north of London. Parkland, wooded, well bunkered. 18 holes, 6266 yards. S.S.S. 70. *Green Fees:* weekdays £25.00 per round, £30.00 per day; weekends £35.00. *Eating facilities:* full bar and catering facilities. *Visitors:* welcome weekdays (limited at weekends and Bank Holidays), book through Pro Shop. *Society Meetings:* catered for by arrangement Tuesdays to Fridays, book through Secretary's office. Professional: Stuart Murray (0181-346 8990). Secretary: David Cooper (0181-346 6023; Fax: 0181-343 1974).

HIGHGATE. **Highgate Golf Club,** Denewood Road, Highgate, London N6 4AH (0181-340 1906). *Location:* near A1, turn down Sheldon Avenue, opposite Kenwood House and first left. Parkland. 18 holes, 5985 yards. S.S.S. 69. *Green Fees:* weekdays £27.00/£35.00; weekends only with member. *Eating facilities:* bar, restaurant. *Visitors:* welcome weekdays except Wednesdays before 3pm. *Society Meetings:* catered for Thursdays/Fridays. Professional: Robin Turner (0181-340 5467). Secretary: Gordon Wilson (0181-340 3745).

HILLINGDON. **Hillingdon Golf Club,** 18 Dorset Way, Hillingdon, Uxbridge, Middlesex UB10 0JR (01895 239810). *Location:* near A40, adjacent to RAF Uxbridge. Very undulating – well wooded course, sloping down to river. 9 holes, 5490 yards. S.S.S. 67. *Green Fees:* weekdays £17.50 for 18 holes, £25.00 per day. *Eating facilities:* bar meals available Tuesday to Saturday. *Visitors:* welcome Mondays, Tuesdays and Fridays; Thursdays – Ladies' Day, weekends with members only. *Society Meetings:* catered for by special arrangement only with Committee through Club Secretary. Professional: Mr Neil Wichelow (01895 251980). Secretary: Mrs A.M. Cooper (01895 233956).

HOUNSLOW. **Airlinks Golf Club,** Southall Lane, Hounslow, Middlesex TW5 9PE (0181-561 1418; Fax: 0181-813 6284). *Location:* Junction 3 on M4, A312 to

Hayes. Same entrance as D. Lloyd Tennis Centre. Flat parkland course with water holes and doglegs. 18 holes, 5885 yards. S.S.S. 68. Floodlit driving range. *Green Fees:* weekdays £10.40 per round, £18.50 per day; weekends £13.00. *Eating facilities:* full catering and bar facilities/restaurant area. *Visitors:* weekdays no restrictions, some restrictions weekends, bookings advised seven days in advance. *Society Meetings:* catered for all week. Professionals: Bill Mylward/Ken Wickham (0181-813 6282). PR Manager: P.D. Watson. *

HOUNSLOW. **Hounslow Heath Municipal Golf Course,** Staines Road, Hounslow TW4 5DS (0181-570 5271). *Location:* Staines Road A315 between Hounslow and Bedfont. Heath course, some water hazards, tight fairways. 18 holes, 5820 yards, 5322 metres. S.S.S. 69. Practice area. *Green Fees:* weekdays £7.30 per round, £11.20 per day; weekends and Bank Holidays £10.20 per round, £14.50 per day. Reduced rates for Juniors and Senior Citizens weekdays except Bank Holidays (Council Leisure Card must be held). *Eating facilities:* snacks; tea, coffee, soft drinks. *Visitors:* welcome at all times, bookings required at weekends and Bank Holidays. *Society Meetings:* by arrangement. Secretary: Mr Bob Leslie. *

ISLEWORTH. **Wyke Green Golf Club,** Syon Lane, Isleworth TW7 5PT (0181-560 4874). *Location:* situated half a mile north of A4 near Gillettes Corner. Fairly flat parkland. 18 holes, 6242 yards. S.S.S. 70. *Green Fees:* weekdays £28 per day; weekends £42 per day (£12 with a member). *Eating facilities:* catering daily except Mondays. *Visitors:* welcome with reservation weekdays; weekends only with member until after 3pm. *Society Meetings:* catered for on Tuesdays, Wednesdays and Thursdays by arrangement, minimum 20. Professional: David Holmes (0181-847 0685). Secretary: D. Wentworth-Pollock (0181-560 8777).

LONDON. **London Scottish Golf Club,** Windmill Enclosure, Wimbledon Common SW19 5NQ (0181-788 0135). *Location:* just off A3 – Tibbetts Corner – just south of Putney SW15. Wooded commonland. 18 holes, 5438 yards. S.S.S. 66. *Green Fees:* information not provided. *Eating facilities:* bar and catering. *Visitors:* welcome weekdays only. Check with Professional recommended. Red top must be worn, no jeans or sweatshirts. *Society Meetings:* minimum 20 players. Professional: Stephen Barr (0181-789 1207). Secretary: Peter Dell (0181-789 7517).

LONDON. **Mill Hill Golf Club,** 100 Barnet Way, Mill Hill, London NW7 3AL (0181-959 2282). *Location:* A1, south half a mile before Apex Corner left into clubhouse car park – signposted. Flat wooded parkland. 18 holes, 6247 yards, 5697 metres. S.S.S. 70. Practice ground. *Green Fees:* weekdays £20.00 per round, £25.00 per day; weekends £30.00 per round. Special rates November to mid-March – Mondays/Wednesdays/Fridays minimum of eight players coffee, golf, high tea £25.00 per head. *Eating facilities:* restaurant and bar. *Visitors:* welcome Monday to Friday; weekends and Bank Holidays bookings only. Two snooker tables. *Society Meetings:* catered for Mondays, Wednesdays and Fridays with prior booking. Professional: G.R. Harvey (0181-959 7261). Secretary: Mr F.H. Scott (0181-959 2339; Fax: 0181-906 0731).

LONDON. **Trent Park Public Golf Course,** Bramley Road, Southgate, London N14 (0181-366 7432). *Location:* opposite Oakwood Tube Station. Undulating parkland. 18 holes, 6008 yards. S.S.S. 69. Floodlit golf range, golf superstore. *Green Fees:* weekdays £10.00; weekends £12.00. Membership available. *Eating facilities:* bar and snacks. *Visitors:* open to public at all times. Bookings advised on weekdays and necessary at weekends. *Society Meetings:* welcome Monday to Thursday. Professional: Tony Sheaff. Proprietor: Jeremy Sturgess.

NORTHOLT. **The London Golf Centre,** Lime Trees Park Golf Club, Ruislip Road, Northolt, Middlesex UB5 6QZ (0181-845 0442; Fax: 0181-842 2097). *Location:* just off A40 at the Polish War Memorial roundabout. Undulating parkland with interesting water hazards. 9 holes, 5906 yards. S.S.S. 70/71. Floodlit driving range. *Green Fees:* weekdays £5.00 9 holes, £9.00 18 holes; weekends from £6.75 9 holes. *Eating facilities:* two bars/bistro. *Visitors:* welcome at all times. Golf superstore. *Society Meetings:* catered for. Professional: Gary Newall (0181-845 3180). Secretary: Nigel Sturgess (0181-842 0442). General Manager: Jonathan Clifford.

NORTHWOOD. **Northwood Golf Club Ltd,** Rickmansworth Road, Northwood, Middlesex HA5 2QW (01923 825329). *Location:* on A404 between Pinner and Rickmansworth. Parkland/wooded course. 18 holes, 6493 yards. S.S.S. 71. *Green Fees:* weekdays £21.00. *Visitors:* welcome weekdays only. *Society Meetings:* by arrangement. Professional: C.J. Holdsworth (01923 820112). Secretary: R.A. Bond.

NORTHWOOD. **Sandy Lodge Golf Club,** Sandy Lodge Lane, Northwood, Middlesex HA6 2JD. *Location:* adjacent to Moor Park Underground Station. Inland links. 18 holes, 6081 yards. S.S.S. 70. *Green Fees:* weekdays £28.00 per round. *Eating facilities:* full catering and bar service available. *Visitors:* weekdays only, please telephone in advance. Handicap Certificate required. *Society Meetings:* catered for Mondays, Thursdays and Fridays. Professional: Jeff Pinsent (01923 825321). General Manager: J.N. Blair (01923 825429; Fax: 01923 824319).

ORPINGTON. **Lullingstone Park Golf Club,** Park Gate Road, Chelsfield, Near Orpington, Kent BR6 7JS (01959 32928). *Location:* two miles from Junction 4 off M25, fifth exit on left (signposted). Undulating parkland. 18 holes, 6779 yards. S.S.S. 72. 9 holes, 2432 yards. Par 33. 22 bay driving range, pitch and putt course, putting green. *Green Fees:* weekdays £5.80 per 9 holes, £9.10 per 18 holes; weekends £7.80 per 9 holes, £11.40 per 18 holes. *Eating facilities:* cafeteria and bar. *Visitors:* welcome at all times, course open from dawn to dusk. *Society Meetings:* very welcome, phone for Package details. Professional: Robert Lee (01959 533793; Fax: 01959 533795).

PINNER. **Grim's Dyke Golf Club,** Oxhey Lane, Hatch End, Pinner, Middlesex HA5 4AL (0181-421 1286). *Location:* on A4008 Watford to Harrow (2 miles west of Harrow). Undulating parkland, tree lined, testing greens. 18 holes, 5600 yards. S.S.S. 67. Practice area. *Green Fees:* weekdays £20.00 per round, £25.00 per day; weekends only with a member. *Eating facilities:* bar snacks, lunches available on request. No catering on Mondays. *Visitors:* must produce Certificate of Handicap. *Society Meetings:* catered for Tuesdays and Fridays. Professional: John Rule (0181-428 7484). Secretary: P. Payne (0181-428 4539).

PINNER. **Pinner Hill Golf Club,** Southview Road, Pinner Hill HA5 3YA (0181-866 0963). *Location:* one mile west Pinner Green. 18 holes, 6280 yards. S.S.S. 70. *Green Fees:* £25.00 weekdays, £32.00 weekends by prior arrangement only; Public Days (no access to clubhouse), Wednesdays and Thursdays £8.10 per round, £11.15 per day. *Eating facilities:* light refreshments served at all times (except Wednesdays and Thursdays). *Visitors:* welcome with Handicap Certificate or letter of introduction. *Society Meetings:* Mondays, Tuesdays and Fridays. Professional: Mark Grieve (0181-866 2109). Secretary: Jeremy Devitt (0181-868 4817). *

ROEHAMPTON. **Roehampton Club Ltd,** Roehampton Lane, London SW15 5LR (0181-876 1621; Fax: 0181-392 2386). *Location:* just off South Circular Road between Sheen and Putney. Parkland. 18 holes, 6011 yards. S.S.S. 69. *Green Fees:* weekdays £16.00; weekends £22.00. *Eating facilities:* restaurant, carvery, buttery and bar. *Visitors:* welcome if introduced by member, Handicap Certificate required at weekends. *Society Meetings:* catered for by arrangement, if introduced by member. Professional: Alan L. Scott (0181-876 3858). Chief Executive: Martin Yates (0181-876 5505).

RUISLIP. **Ruislip Golf Club,** King's End, Ickenham Road, Ruislip, Middlesex HA4 7OQ (01895 638081). *Location:* two and a half miles from Junction 1, M40, first left after M40/A40 merge, onto B467, then left at T-Junction onto B466. Parkland course. 18 holes, 5702 yards. S.S.S. 68. Driving range (40 bays). *Green Fees:* £10.00 weekdays, £12.50 weekends. Juniors and Senior Citizens on income support £6.25 weekdays. *Eating facilities:* full restaurant facilities. *Visitors:* welcome, booking system at all times. *Society Meetings:* welcome by arrangement. Professional: Shop (01895 638835). Secretary: B.J. Channing.

SHEPPERTON. **Sunbury Golf Club,** Charlton Lane, Shepperton, Middlesex TW17 8QA (01932 772898). *Location:* just off Junction 1 of the M3. Flat parkland course. 9 holes, 6502 yards. S.S.S. 72. 32 bay floodlit range, green 8am to 10pm. *Green Fees:* information not provided. *Eating facilities:* two bars, restaurant. *Visitors:* welcome, no restrictions. *Society Meetings:* welcome. Professional: Alistair Hardaway. Secretary: Sally Clark. *

SHOOTERS HILL. **Shooters Hill Golf Club Ltd,** "Lowood", Eaglesfield Road, Shooters Hill, London SE18 3DA (0181-854 1216; Fax: 0(1)81-854 0469). *Location:* off A207 between Blackheath and Welling. Hilly wooded course. 18 holes, 5736 yards. S.S.S. 68. *Green Fees:* weekdays £30.00. *Eating facilities:* bar and diningroom. *Visitors:* members of other clubs welcome weekdays on production of letter of introduction, or official Handicap Certificate. Jacket, collar and tie required in clubhouse. *Society Meetings:* catered for Tuesdays and Thursdays only. Professional: Michael Ridge (0181-854 0073). Secretary: Brian Adams (0181-854 6368).

SOUTHALL. **West Middlesex Golf Club,** Greenford Road, Southall, Middlesex UB1 3EE (0181-574 0166). *Location:* junction of Uxbridge Road (A4020) and Greenford Road. 18 holes, 6242 yards. S.S.S. 70. *Green Fees:* information not provided. *Visitors:* welcome without reservation. *Society Meetings:* catered for by prior arrangement. Professional: I.P. Harris. Secretary: P.J. Furness (0181-574 3450).

SOUTHWARK. **Aquarius Golf Club,** Beachcroft Reservoir, Marmora Road, Honor Oak, Southwark SE22 0RY (0181-693 1626). *Location:* nearest main road — Forest Hill Road. The course is situated on and around a reservoir, testing first and eighth holes. 9 holes, 5246 yards. S.S.S. 66. *Green Fees:* £10.00. *Eating facilities:* limited. *Visitors:* welcome with member only. Professional: F. Private. Secretary: Mrs Marilyn Moss.

STANMORE. **Stanmore Golf Club,** 29 Gordon Avenue, Stanmore, Middlesex HA7 2RL (0181-954 2599). *Location:* turn off A410 by church to Old Church Lane, Gordon Avenue is to the right. Wooded, parkland course. 18 holes, 5860 yards. S.S.S. 68. Practice and putting areas. *Green Fees:* Tuesday, Wednesday and Thursday £25.00; Public Days, Monday and Friday £8.10; weekends with a member only. *Eating facilities:* lunch and dinner available. *Visitors:* welcome Tuesdays, Wednesdays and Thursdays, Handicap Certificates required on Wednesday and Thursday. Jacket and tie after 7pm. *Society Meetings:* catered for Wednesday and Thursday by prior booking only. Professional: Vivian Law (0181-954 2646). Secretary: L.J. Pertwee. Caterer: (0181-954 4661).

THAMESMEAD. **Riverside Golf Club,** Summerton Way, Thamesmead, London SE28 8PP (0181-310 7995: Fax: 0181-312 3441). *Location:* Thamesmead town/Abbey Wood. Wooded course with many water features. 9 holes, 5462 yards. S.S.S. 70. 31-bay driving range. *Green Fees:* weekdays 9 holes £6.50, 18 holes £10.50; weekends 9 holes £7.50, 18 holes £12.00. Reductions for Juniors and Senior Citizens; reduced rate twilight fees. *Eating facilities:* restaurant and two bars. *Visitors:* open to members of public. *Society Meetings:* all welcome. Professional: Paul Joiner. Secretary: Eddie Springham.

TOTTERIDGE. **South Herts Golf Club,** Links Drive, Totteridge N20 (0181-445 0117). *Location:* off Totteridge Lane one mile from Whetstone, nearest station Totteridge. Parkland. 18 holes, 6432 yards. S.S.S. 71. *Green Fees:* on application. *Eating facilities:* lunch, high tea (Dinner served by arrangement). *Visitors:* welcome with reservation Wednesday, Thursday, Friday; lunch, high tea, dinner. Professional: R.V. Mitchell (0181-445 4633). Secretary: P.F. Wise (0181-445 2035).

TWICKENHAM. **Strawberry Hill Golf Club,** Wellesley Road, Twickenham TW2 (0181-894 1246). *Location:* near Strawberry Hill Station. Parkland. 9 holes, 2381 (x2) yards. S.S.S. 62. *Green Fees:* weekdays £18.00 per round, £25.00 per day; weekends with member only. *Eating facilities:* course bar/lounge bar, bar snacks, lunches. *Visitors:* welcome, restrictions weekends and competition days. *Society Meetings:* small numbers (maximum 24) catered for by arrangement. Professional: P. Buchan (0181-898 2082). Secretary: F.E. Ingoldby (0181-894 0165). *

TWICKENHAM. **Twickenham Golf Course,** Staines Road, Twickenham (0181-783 1698). *Location:* just off A316. Parkland. 9 holes, 3050 yards. S.S.S 35. 27 bay floodlit driving range. *Green Fees:* information not provided. *Eating facilities:* Pavilion Bar and cafe. *Visitors:* welcome, public course. Function room available. *Society Meetings:* welcome, full banqueting facilities. Professional: Steve Lloyd (0181-783 1698). Secretary: Norman Harnett (0181-783 1748).

UPMINSTER. **Upminster Golf Club,** 114 Hall Lane, Upminster (014022 20249). *Location:* one mile from Upminster Station. Parkland/wooded – river runs through the course. 18 holes, 5931 yards. S.S.S. 68. *Green Fees:* £25.00 per round, £30.00 per day weekdays. *Eating facilities:* full catering at club, bookable. *Visitors:* welcome weekdays except Tuesday mornings and must produce evidence of handicap. *Society Meetings:* catered for Wednesdays, Thursdays and Fridays (max 40). Professional: Neil Carr (01708 220000). Secretary: Keith Moyse (01708 222788).

UXBRIDGE. **Uxbridge Golf Course,** The Drive, Harefield Place, Uxbridge UB10 8PA (01895 272457). *Location:* off Swalkelys Junction – M40. Undulating parkland. 18 holes, 5753 yards. S.S.S. 68. *Green Fees:* weekdays £10.00; weekends £15.00/£12.50. *Eating facilities:* bars, restaurant. *Visitors:* welcome anytime, booking required at weekends. Function suite. *Society Meetings:* welcome Thursdays. Professional: Phil Howard (01895 237287; Fax: 01895 810262). Secretary: Brian Russell.

WANDSWORTH. **Springfield Park Golf Club,** Burntwood Lane, Wandsworth SW17 0AT (0181-871 2468; Fax: 0181-871 2221). *Location:* in former grounds of Springfield Hospital, off Garrett Lane and Trinity Road. Attractive tree-lined setting, popular and testing course. 9 holes, 4658 yards (for 18 tees). S.S.S 62. Large practice putting green. *Green Fees:* weekdays £6.50 for 18 holes; weekends £8.50 for 18 holes. Membership £250 joining fee (direct debit £47.50 per month). *Eating facilities:* function room with its own bar, lounge bar. *Visitors:* welcome except Saturday and Sunday mornings to 12 noon. Pro shop, club room. Special facilities for blind and disabled golfers. *Society Meetings:* welcome, special terms on request. Professional: Patrick "Teach" Tallack. Secretary: Bryan Davies.

WANSTEAD. **Wanstead Golf Club,** Overton Drive, Wanstead E11 2LW (0181-989 0604). *Location:* one mile from junction of A12 and A406. Parkland bordering Epping Forest with featured lake. 18 holes, 6109 yards. S.S.S. 69. *Green Fees:* £25.00 per day weekdays; weekends as member's guest only. *Eating facilities:* dining room and bars. *Visitors:* welcome Mondays, Tuesdays and Fridays by prior arrangement with the Secretary. Handicap Certificate required. Weekends with member only. *Society Meetings:* welcome, apply Secretary. Professional: Gary Jacom (0181-989 9876). Secretary: Keith Jones (0181-989 3938).

WEMBLEY. **Sudbury Golf Club Ltd,** Bridgewater Road, Wembley, Middlesex HA0 1AL (0181-902 3713). *Location:* junction of A4005 (Bridgewater Road) and A4090 (Whitton Ave East). Undulating parkland. 18 holes, 6282 yards. S.S.S. 70. Practice ground. *Green Fees:* weekdays £20.00 per round, £30.00 two rounds. *Eating facilities:* dining room and bars. *Visitors:* welcome weekdays with Handicap Certificate. *Society Meetings:* catered for. Professional: Neil Jordan (0181-902 7910). General Manager: A.J. Poole. *

WEST DRAYTON. **Holiday Golf Club,** Stockley Road, West Drayton, Middlesex UB7 9NA (01895 444232; Fax: 01895 444323). *Location:* in grounds of Holiday Inn Hotel, Junction 4 M40. Undulating parkland course. 18 holes, 3856 yards. S.S.S. 62. *Green Fees:* weekdays £5.50; weekends £6.50. *Eating facilities:* catering and bars in Hotel. *Visitors:* welcome, no restrictions. *Society Meetings:* welcome at all times. Secretary: R. Webb (0181-561 3471). Proprietor: J. O'Loughlin.

WIMBLEDON. **Royal Wimbledon Golf Club,** 29 Camp Road, Wimbledon SW19 4UW. *Location:* one mile west of War Memorial in Wimbledon Village. 18 holes, 6300 yards. S.S.S. 70. *Visitors:* not permitted. *Society Meetings:* Wednesdays and Thursdays only, by arrangement. Professional: Hugh Boyle (0181-946 4606). Secretary: Maj. G.E. Jones (0181-946 2125). Caddiemaster (0181-946 1118).

WIMBLEDON. **Wimbledon Common Golf Club,** 19 Camp Road, Wimbledon Common, Wimbledon SW19 4UW (0181-946 0294). Links type wooded course. 18 holes, 5438 yards. S.S.S. 66. *Green Fees:* weekdays £15.00 per round, £22.00 per day. *Eating facilities:* light lunches available every day; bar. *Visitors:* welcome weekdays, but only with a member at weekends. *Society Meetings:* groups of up to 24 catered for. Professional: J.S. Jukes (0181-946 0294). Secretary: B.K. Cox (0181-946 7571).

WIMBLEDON. **Wimbledon Park Golf Club,** Home Park Road, Wimbledon, London SW19 7HR (0181-946 1002; Fax: 0181-944 8688). *Location:* Church Road, Arthur Road and Home Park Road from Wimbledon High Street, or by District Line to Wimbledon Park Station where signposted. 18 holes, 5492 yards. S.S.S. 66. *Green Fees:* £25.00 per round, £30 per day weekdays; £25.00 per round weekends. *Eating facilities:* dining room and bar snacks each day except Monday. *Visitors:* welcome weekdays, occasional weekends after 3.30pm (check with Professional). *Society Meetings:* catered for. Professional: D. Wingrove (0181-946 4053). Secretary: M.K. Hale (0181-946 1250).

WINCHMORE HILL. **Bush Hill Park Golf Club,** Bush Hill, Winchmore Hill, London N21 2BU (0181-360 5738). *Location:* Enfield, nine miles north of City. Parkland. 18 holes, 5825 yards. S.S.S. 68. Practice ground and nets. *Green Fees:* weekdays £20.00; weekends only with member. *Eating facilities:* full catering and bar facilities. *Visitors:* welcome weekdays, Handicap Certificate required. *Society Meetings:* catered for weekdays except Wednesdays. Professional: G. Low (0181-360 4103). Secretary: Michael Burnand (0181-360 5738). *

WOOD GREEN. **Muswell Hill Golf Club,** Rhodes Avenue, Wood Green, London N22 4UT (0181-888 2044; Fax: 0181-889 9380). *Location:* North Circular/ Bounds Green tube station one mile. Parkland/ wooded. 18 holes, 6438 yards. S.S.S. 71. *Green Fees:* weekdays £23.00 per round, £33.00 per day; weekends £35.00 per round. Bookings through Secretary and Professional. *Eating facilities:* available in Clubhouse. *Visitors:* welcome weekdays, weekends pre-booked with Professional. *Society Meetings:* catered for Monday, Wednesday, Thursday and Friday, charges on request. Professional: I. Roberts (0181-888 8046). Secretary: D.E. Beer (0181-888 1764).

Avon

BATH. **Bath Golf Club,** Sham Castle, North Road, Bath BA2 6JG (01225 425182). *Location:* off A36, one mile south-east of Bath City Centre. 18 holes, 6369 yards, 5824 metres. S.S.S. 70. *Green Fees:* weekdays £25.00; weekends and Bank Holidays £30.00. *Eating facilities:* catering every day. *Vistors:* with bona fide handicap welcome. *Society Meetings:* catered for Wednesday and Friday. Professional: Peter Hancox (Tel & Fax: 01225 466953). Managing Secretary: P.E. Ware (01225 463834).

BATH. **Entry Hill Golf Club,** Entry Hill, Bath BA2 5AN (01225 834248). *Location:* one mile south of city centre, off A367 road to Wells. Hilly parkland course with many young trees. 9 holes, 2103 yards, 1922 metres. S.S.S. 61 (18 holes). Practice net. *Green Fees:* weekdays £7.45; weekends £8.45. Weekdays: rounds completed before 12 noon £5.10. *Visitors:* no restrictions but pre-booking up to one week in advance essential. Well equipped Pro Shop. *Society Meetings:* as per Visitors. Professional: T. Tapley (01225 834248). Secretary: J. Sercombe (01225 834248).

BATH. **Fosseway Country Club and Centurion Hotel,** Charlton Lane, Midsomer Norton, Bath BA3 4BD (01761 412214; Fax: 01761 418357). *Location:* off A367 10 miles south of Bath; midway between Bath and Wells. Flat parkland course. 9 holes, 4278 yards. S.S.S. 65. *Green Fees:* weekdays £10.00; weekends and Bank Holidays £15.00. *Eating facilities:* table d'hôte/à la carte restaurant, full bar meals. *Visitors:* welcome except Saturday and Sunday mornings and Wednesday evenings. Indoor bowls, squash, snooker, heated indoor pool. *Society Meetings:* welcome. Secretary: R.F. Jones (01761 417711).

BATH. **Lansdown Golf Club,** Lansdown, Bath BA1 9BT (01225 425007). *Location:* M4 junction 18 follow signs for Park and Ride. Flat, parkland, 800ft above sea-level, panoramic views. 18 holes, 6299 yards, 5759 metres. S.S.S. 70. Practice ground. *Green Fees:* weekdays £18.00 per round, £24.00 per day; weekends £30.00. *Eating facilities:* snacks at all times, lunch or dinner by arrangement with Steward. *Visitors:* welcome anytime, must have Handicap Certificate. *Society Meetings:* Mondays/Fridays only. Professional: T. Mercer (01225 420242). Secretary: Ron Smith (01225 422138; Fax: 01225 339252).

BRISTOL. **Bristol and Clifton Golf Club,** Beggar Bush Lane, Failand, Bristol BS8 3TH (01275 393117). *Location:* two miles west of the Suspension Bridge or three miles south of the M5-Junction 19 access. 18 holes, 6294 yards. S.S.S. 70. Parkland course. *Green Fees:* weekdays £30.00; weekends £38.00. *Eating facilities:* available. *Visitors:* welcome weekdays without reservation, must have current golf club Handicap Certificate. *Society Meetings:* welcome. Professional: Peter Mawson (01275 393031). Secretary: J. Lafford (01275 393474).

BRISTOL. **Chipping Sodbury Golf Club,** Chipping Sodbury, Bristol BS17 6PU (01454 312024). *Location:* 12 miles north of Bristol, nine miles from Junction No. 14 on M5 and three miles from Junction 18 on M4. Parkland. 18 hole course, 6912 yards; 9 hole course, 3076 yards. S.S.S. 73. *Green Fees:* 18-hole course weekdays £20.00; weekends £25.00. 9 hole course £2.50 any day. *Eating facilities:* full catering available. *Visitors:* welcome except Saturday/Sunday morning and Bank Holidays. Must have Handicap Certificate. *Society Meetings:* catered for by prior arrangement weekdays only. Professional: Mike Watts (01454 314087). Secretary: K.G. Starr (01454 319042).

BRISTOL. **Farrington Golf Club,** Marsh Lane, Farrington Gurney, Bristol BS18 5TS (01761 241274). *Location:* main A37/A39 Farrington Gurney. Wooded, Par 3's, 80 to 240 yards USGA spec greens, tees up to 800 square yards. 9 holes (18 hole course opening Autumn 1995), 1440 yards. S.S.S. 54. Floodlit, covered driving range, practice putting green and sand bunker. *Green Fees:* weekdays £4.50 per round, £8.50 per day; weekends £5.50 per round, £9.50 per day. *Eating facilities:* available, dress rules apply. *Visitors:* welcome, booking essential weekends. No jeans/

collarless t-shirts. Video teaching studio. *Society Meetings:* welcome. Professional: Peter Thompson. Secretary: Patricia Thompson.

BRISTOL. **Filton Golf Club,** Golf Course Lane, Filton, Bristol BS12 7QS (01272 692021). *Location:* Off A38 north of Bristol. Parkland, 18 holes, 6277 yards. S.S.S. 70. Two practice fields. *Green Fees:* weekdays £20.00 per round, £25.00 per day, £12.00 with member; weekends £12.00 with member only. *Eating facilities:* meals available. *Visitors:* accepted daily subject to programme. *Society Meetings:* all catered for, subject to programme – must book well in advance. Professional: J.C.N. Lumb (01272 694158). Secretary: Mr M. Burns (01272 694169).

BRISTOL. **Henbury Golf Club,** Henbury Hill, Westbury-on-Trym, Bristol BS10 7QB (01272 500660). *Location:* north M5 Junction 17 A4018 to Westbury-on-Trym; right to Blaise Castle. Wooded parkland, 18 holes, 6039 yards. S.S.S. 70. *Green Fees:* weekdays £21.00 for 18 holes, £28.00 more than 18 holes; weekends with member only. *Eating facilities:* dining room and bar snacks. *Visitors:* welcome, restricted at weekends and Bank Holidays. *Society Meetings:* Tuesdays and Fridays by prior arrangement. Professional: Nick Riley (01272 502121). Secretary: (01272 500044).

BRISTOL. **Knowle Golf Club,** Fairway, Bristol BS4 5DF (0117 977 6341). *Location:* three miles south of city centre, left off Wells Road. A4 – Bath. Parkland course. 18 holes, 6100 yards. S.S.S. 69. Practice field. *Green Fees:* weekdays £22.00 for 18 holes, £27.00 for 27 holes; weekends £27.00 for 18 holes, £32.00 for 27 holes. *Eating facilities:* bar and snacks, dinners by arrangement with Stewardess. *Visitors:* welcome with Handicap Certificate. *Society Meetings:* Thursdays only with Handicap Certificate. Professional: Mr Gordon M. Brand (0117 977 9193). Secretary: Mrs J.D. King (0117 977 0660).

BRISTOL. **Mangotsfield Golf Club,** Carsons Road, Mangotsfield, Bristol (0117 9565501). *Location:* four miles M32 via Downend, one mile Warmley A420. Parkland, hilly course. 18 holes, 5337 yards, 4877 metres. S.S.S. 66. Small practice area. *Green Fees:* information not provided. *Eating facilities:* no restriction on food and drink. *Visitors:* welcome, no restrictions. *Society Meetings:* catered for weekdays only. Professional: Craig Trewin. Secretary: Terry Bindon (0117 9755432 daytime, evenings 0117 9697032). *

BRISTOL. **Mendip Spring Golf Club,** Honeyhall Lane, Congresbury, Bristol BS19 5JT (01934 852322; Fax: 01934 853021). *Location:* between Congresbury and Churchill off B3133 (A370 and A38). Fairly flat courses with a lot of water hazards. Two courses: 18 holes, 6328 yards. S.S.S. 70 men, 77 ladies; 9 holes, 2260 yards, S.S.S 65 men and ladies. 15 bay floodlit driving range. *Green Fees:* 18 hole course £15.00 per round, £20.00 per day; 9 hole course £5.00 per round, £10.00 per day. *Eating facilities:* full restaurant and bar facilities. *Visitors:* welcome at any time. *Society Meetings:* welcome, corporate days available by arrangement. Professional: John Blackburn (01934 853337; Fax: 01934 853465). Acting Secretary: Lyn Lovell.

BRISTOL. **Shirehampton Park Golf Club,** Park Hill, Shirehampton, Bristol BS11 0UL (0117 982 3059). *Location:* one mile from Junction 18 on M5 on B4054 to Shirehampton. Parkland course. 18 holes, 5521 yards. S.S.S. 67. *Green Fees:* weekdays £18.00, weekends £25.00 (check with Secretary/Professional). *Eating facilities:* lunches, snacks, teas, etc available daily. *Visitors:* welcome weekdays, with reservation (check with Secretary), not weekends or Public Holidays. *Society Meetings:* catered for on Mondays, application to Secretary. Professional: Brent Ellis (0117 982 2488). Secretary: Piers Drew-Wilkinson (0117 982 2083).

BRISTOL. **Tall Pines Golf Club,** Cooks Bridle Path, Downside, Backwell, Bristol BS19 3DJ (01275 474889). *Location:* off A38 next to Bristol Airport. Parkland. 18 holes, 5827 yards. S.S.S. 68. Practice ground, putting green. *Green Fees:* weekdays £12.00; weekends £14.00. *Eating facilities:* fully licensed bar and restaurant. *Visitors:* welcome at all times, bookings at weekends. *Society Meetings:* welcome except weekends. Professional/Manager: Terry Murray (Tel & Fax: 01275 472076).

BRISTOL. **The Long Ashton Golf Club,** The Club House, Long Ashton, Bristol BS18 9DW (01275 392229). *Location:* three miles south-west of Bristol on the B3129 Clevedon/Bristol Road. Wooded parkland. 18 holes, 6077 yards. S.S.S. 70. Practice ground. *Green Fees:* weekdays £26.00 (18 holes), £30.00. (36 holes), weekends £35 (18 holes). *Eating facilities:* full catering daily, bar open Monday to Saturday (11am – 11pm). *Visitors:* welcome, must have current Handicap Certificate. *Society Meetings:* by arrangement with Secretary. Professional: Denis Scanlan (01275 392265). Secretary: B. Manning (01275 392316; Fax 01275 394395).

BRISTOL. **Tracy Park Golf and Country Club,** Bath Road, Wick, Bristol BS15 5RN (0117 937 2251; Fax: 0117 937 4288). *Location:* M4 Junction 18, A46 towards Bath, A420 towards Bristol. Turn left at bottom of steep hill for Lansdown/Bath. Wooded parkland with water hazards. 27 holes, 6800, 6800, 6200 yards. S.S.S. 73, 73, 70. Practice ground. *Green Fees:* weekdays £20.00 per round, £30.00 per day; weekends £30.00 per round, £40 per day. *Eating* *facilities:* full catering available. *Visitors:* welcome – telephone ahead. *Society Meetings:* welcome. Tennis, swimming, squash, croquet, snooker available. Professional: Richard Berry (0117 937 3521). General Manager: Stewart Taylor.

CLEVEDON. **Clevedon Golf Club,** Castle Road, Walton, Clevedon BS21 7AA (01275 873140). *Location:* two miles from M5 Junction 20; M5 Junction 19 (A369) four miles. Picturesque, beautiful parkland course, hilly. 18 holes, 5799 yards. S.S.S. 69. Practice green and net. *Green Fees:* weekdays £22.00, weekends and Bank Holidays £35.00. *Eating facilities:* available every day except Mondays (snacks only). *Visitors:* welcome except Wednesdays. Handicap Certificate must be produced; must phone in advance for availability. *Society Meetings:* catered for Mondays (not Bank Holidays) and Tuesdays only. Professional: Martin Heggie (01275 874704). Secretary: Matt Sullivan (01275 874057; Fax: 01275 341228).

SALTFORD. **Saltford Golf Club,** Golf Club Lane, Saltford, Bristol BS18 3AA (01225 873220). *Location:* A4 between Bristol and Bath. Wooded parkland course. 18 holes, 6081 yards. S.S.S. 69. Practice area, chipping green. *Green Fees:* weekdays £22.00 single round, £26.00 more than one round; weekends £30.00 single round summer only. *Eating facilities:* restaurant, bar service. *Visitors:* welcome, restricted to one round of golf weekends and per day during Summer. *Society Meetings:* accepted by arrangement Mondays and Thursdays. Professional: Dudley Millensted (01225 872043). Secretary: Valerie Radnedge (01225 873513).

WESTON-SUPER-MARE. **Weston-Super-Mare Golf Club,** The Clubhouse, Uphill Road North, Weston-Super-Mare BS23 4NQ (01934 621360). *Location:* M5 Junction 21 – on the sea front. Flat links course with excellent greens. 18 holes, 6251 yards. S.S.S. 70. Practice area plus nets. *Green Fees:* weekdays £20.00, weekends £28.00. Half price with a member. *Eating facilities:* full bar and catering facilities. *Visitors:* welcome weekdays and weekends. Handicap Certificate required. *Society Meetings:* catered for weekdays. Professional: Paul Barrington (Tel & Fax: 01934 633360). Secretary: John Keight (Tel & Fax: 01934 626968).

WESTON-SUPER-MARE. **Worlebury Golf Club,** Monks Hill, Worlebury, Weston-Super-Mare BS22 9SX (01934 623214; Fax: 01934 625789). *Location:* from the M5 (Junction 21) then A370 main road to the town for two miles, turn right into Baytree Road and continue to top of Milton Hill. Hill top with extensive views of the Severn Estuary and Wales. 18 holes, 5936 yards. S.S.S. 69. *Green Fees:* weekdays £20.00 per day, £12.00 with a member; weekends and Bank Holidays £30.00 per day, £17.00 with a member. *Eating facilities:* bar and restaurant. *Visitors:* welcome without reservation. *Society Meetings:* catered for by arrangement. Professional: Gary Marks (01934 418473). Secretary: Mike W. Penny (01934 625789).

Bedfordshire

AMPTHILL. **Millbrook Golf Course,** Millbrook, Ampthill MK45 2JB (01525 840252; Fax: 01525 406249). *Location:* in Millbrook village off the A507 Ampthill to Woburn. Rolling links situated on the Greensand Ridge overlooking Bedfordshire. 18 holes, 7051 yards. S.S.S. 74. Two practice grounds and practice bunkers. *Green Fees:* weekdays £15.00 9 holes, £25.00 18 holes, £35.00 36 holes; weekends £40.00 per day after 11am. *Eating facilities:* bar/restaurant, lunches/dinners from 11am. *Visitors:* welcome weekdays all day except Thursdays (course closed), weekends after 11am. *Society Meetings:* bookings welcomed all year. Professional: Terry Devine (01525 402269). Secretary: Gael Sutherland.

BEADLOW. **Beadlow Manor Hotel, Golf and Country Club,** Beadlow, Near Shefford SG17 5PH (01525 860800; Fax: 01525 861345). *Location:* from M1 (J12) take A5120 east to Ampthill, then A507 to Shefford. From A1 (J10) take A507 west to Ampthill. Challenging, rolling parkland with water hazards. Two courses, 36 holes, 6619 yards. S.S.S. 73. Covered 25 bay floodlit driving range, practice area. *Green Fees:* weekdays £14.00; weekends £27.00. Special rates from £7. *Eating facilities:* restaurant, three bars, snacks, refreshments, two function rooms. *Visitors:* welcome at all times. Integral Health Farm offers steam room, sauna, sunbeds, spa baths, beauty salon, gym. Residential Golf and Health Breaks available. Professional shop. Special mid-week and weekend Breaks for Society and Company Groups. All reservations through Sales and Marketing Office. *

BEDFORD. **Bedford and County Golf Club,** Green Lane, Clapham, Bedford (01234 354010). *Location:* off A6 north of Bedford before Clapham Village. Parkland. 18 holes, 6290 yards. S.S.S. 70. *Green Fees:* weekdays £27.50, with member £11.00; weekends and Bank Holidays £16.00 with a member only. *Eating facilities:* full catering facilities and bar. *Visitors:* welcome without reservation except weekends. *Society Meetings:* catered for Mondays, Tuesdays, Thursdays and Fridays. Professional/Manager: Eddie Bullock (01234 359189/352617; Fax: 01234 357195).

BEDFORD. **Bedfordshire Golf Club,** Biddenham, Bedford MK40 4AF (01234 353241). *Location:* one mile west of Bedford town centre on the A428. Wooded parkland, flat. 18 holes, 6185 yards. S.S.S. 69. *Green Fees:* weekdays £20.00; £24.00 per day. *Eating facilities:* bar and catering; evening meals by arrangement. *Visitors:* welcome on weekdays, must be with members at weekends. *Society Meetings:* catered for weekdays. Professional: G. Buckle (01234 353653). Manager: J.K. White (01234 261669).

BEDFORD. **Mowsbury Golf Club,** Cleat Hill, Kimbolton Road, Bedford MK41 8DQ (01234 771493). *Location:* on B660 at northern limit of city boundary. 18 holes, 6510 yards. S.S.S. 71. Driving range. *Green Fees:* on request. *Eating facilities:* meals and bar snacks until 2pm; evening meals if booked in advance. *Visitors:* welcome. Squash courts. *Society Meetings:* not on Friday afternoons or weekends. Professional: Malcolm Summers (01234 216374), for tee reservations and fees. Secretary: L.W. Allan (01234 771041).

COLMWORTH. **Colmworth Golf Club,** New Road, Colmworth (01234 378181). *Location:* north of Bedford just off B660 Kimbolton road. Flat, easy walking, inland course with links design; water features at three holes. 18 holes, 6459 yards. S.S.S. 71. 9-hole Par 3 course. Practice area. *Green Fees:* weekdays £7.00 per round, weekends £15.00. *Eating facilities:* licensed clubhouse with bar. *Visitors:* no restrictions. *Society Meetings:* packages available from £13.00 per person. Professional: J. MacFarlane (01234 378181). Secretary: P. Watmough (01234 266636).

DUNSTABLE. **Dunstable Downs Golf Club,** Whipsnade Road, Dunstable LU6 2NB (01582 604472). *Location:* on B4541; from the south, leave M1 at Markyate, A5 to centre of town, turn left at roundabout into West Street, turn left into Whipsnade Road at third roundabout, club half a mile on left. Downland course, 18 holes, 6255 yards. S.S.S. 70. *Green Fees:* on application. *Eating facilities:* catering Tuesday to Sunday. *Visitors:* weekdays if members of recognised Golf Club, weekends with member only. Handicap Certificate required. *Society Meetings:* Tuesdays and Thursdays. Professional: M. Weldon (01582 662806). Secretary: C.D. Alexander (01582 604472; Fax: 01582 478700).

DUNSTABLE. **Tilsworth Golf Centre,** Dunstable Road, Tilsworth, Leighton Buzzard LU7 9PU (01525 210722). *Location:* two miles north of Dunstable off A5, Tilsworth turn-off. Parkland. 18 holes, 5303 yards. Par 69. *Green Fees:* weekdays £8.00; weekends £10.00. *Eating facilities:* bar snacks and restaurant available. *Visitors:* welcome any time (except Sundays before 11.45am). Bookings taken up to seven days in advance. *Society Meetings:* welcome by prior arrangement. Professional: Nick Webb (01525 210721).

HENLOW. **Mount Pleasant Golf Course,** Station Road, Lower Stowdon, Henlow SG16 6JL (01462 850999). *Location:* three-quarters of a mile west of A600 (Hitchin to Bedford) at Henlow Camp roundabout. Undulating meadowland. 9 holes, 3070 yards. S.S.S. 69. Practice chipping, putting and nets. *Green Fees:* weekdays £5.00 for 9 holes, £9.00 for 18 holes; weekends £7.00 for 9 holes, £13.00 for 18 holes. Monday to Thursdays £1 deduction for Senior Citizens and Juniors. *Eating facilities:* licensed, sandwiches, snacks available. *Visitors:* welcome anytime, booking required for weekends and summer evenings. *Society Meetings:* welcome Mondays to Thursdays. Professional: Zac Thompson. Secretary: Ron Westcott.

LEIGHTON BUZZARD. **Aylesbury Vale Golf Club,** Stewkley Road, Wing, Leighton Buzzard LU7 0UJ (01525 240196). *Location:* four miles west of Leighton Buzzard, on Stewkley to Wing road. Gently undulating course with lakes. 18 holes, 6622 yards. S.S.S. 72. 10 bay driving range. *Green Fees:* weekdays £12.00, with a member £8.50; weekends £18.50 (£10.00 after 4pm), with a member £14.00. *Eating facilities:* downstairs bar and restaurant, upstairs bar with balcony, views over course. *Visitors:* welcome any time, no restrictions apart from correct dress. *Society Meetings:* all welcome – please telephone. Professional: Lee Scarbrow (01525 240197). Secretary: Chris Wright (01525 240196).

LEIGHTON BUZZARD. **Leighton Buzzard Golf Club,** Plantation Road, Leighton Buzzard LU7 7JF (01525 373812). *Location:* off A5 between Dunstable and Milton Keynes at village of Heath and Reach. Wooded parkland course. 18 holes, 6101 yards. S.S.S. 70. Practice ground. *Green Fees:* weekdays £18.00 per round, £25.00 per day; weekends with member only, £14.00. *Eating facilities:* available – dining room and two bars. *Visitors:* welcome weekdays with Handicap Certificate only. (Tuesday Ladies' Day). Weekends and Bank Holidays with member only. *Society Meetings:* catered for weekdays only, except Tuesdays. Professional: Lee Muncey (01525 372143). Secretary: J. Burchell (01525 373811).

LEIGHTON BUZZARD near. **Ivinghoe Golf Club,** The Wellcroft, Ivinghoe, Near Leighton Buzzard LU7 9EF (01296 668881). *Location:* four miles from Tring and Dunstable, seven miles from Aylesbury. Parkland. 9 holes, 4508 yards. S.S.S. 62. *Green Fees:* weekdays £6.00, £4.00 after 6pm; weekends £7.00. *Eating facilities:* bar meals (between 11am and 2pm). *Visitors:* no restrictions weekdays or weekends after 8am. *Society Meetings:* all welcome and catered for. Professional: Bill Garrad (01296 668696; Fax: 01296 662755). Secretary: Mrs S. Garrad (01296 668696; Fax: 01296 662755).

LEIGHTON BUZZARD near. **Mentmore Golf and Country Club,** Mentmore, Near Leighton Buzzard LU7 0UA (01296 662020; Fax: 01296 662592). *Location:* Leighton Buzzard three miles, in village of Mentmore. Parkland – some water features and woodland. Two courses – Rothschild and Rosebery. 36 holes, 6777 & 6763 yards. S.S.S. 72. Driving range. *Green Fees:* £30.00, £15.00 with a member. *Eating facilities:* restaurant, two bars; function suite. *Visitors:* welcome. *Society Meetings:* welcome. Professional/Golf Director: Pip Elson.

LUTON. **South Beds. Golf Club,** Warden Hill Road, Luton LU2 7AA (01582 591500). *Location:* on east side A6, two and a half miles north of Luton. Undulating downland course. 18 holes, 6342 yards. S.S.S. 71. Also 9 holes, 4914 yards. S.S.S. 64. Practice fairway, hut and chipping area. *Green Fees:* 18 holes weekdays £26.00 per day, £17.00 per round; weekends £34.50 per day, £24.00 per round (not on Competition Days). 9 holes (twice round) weekdays £8.00, weekends £11.00. *Eating facilities:* full course meals (must be booked), snacks at all times. *Visitors:* welcome weekdays with reservation. Handicap Certificate essential. Tuesday afternoon is Ladies Day. *Society Meetings:* catered for by arrangement. Professional: Eddie Cogle (01582 591209). Secretary: S. Beaton (01582 591500).

LUTON. **Stockwood Park Golf Club,** London Road, Luton LU1 4LX (01582 23241). *Location:* adjacent Exit 10 of M1 exit Luton Airport. Parkland. 18 holes, 6409 yards. S.S.S. 69. Driving range, mini golf course and pitch and putt. *Green Fees:* weekdays Luton residents £6.10, non residents £7.30; weekends Luton residents £8.30, non residents £9.60. Subject to review. *Eating facilities:* two bars and restaurant. *Visitors:* always welcome, municipal club. *Society Meetings:* catered for Mondays, Tuesdays and Thursdays by prior arrangement. Professional: G. McCarthy (01582 413704). Secretary: A.J. Bland.

MILTON KEYNES. **Aspley Guise and Woburn Sands Golf Club,** West Hill, Aspley Guise MK17 8DX (01908 582264). *Location:* two miles west of Junction 13 M1, between Aspley Guise and Woburn Sands. Undulating parkland, 18 holes, 6135 yards, 5610 metres. S.S.S. 70. *Green Fees:* weekdays £22.00 per round, £27.00 per day. *Eating facilities:* full catering except Mondays. *Visitors:* welcome weekdays with bona fide handicaps – check with Secretary; only with a member at weekends. *Society Meetings:* Wednesdays and Fridays. Professional: Trevor Hill (01908 582974). Secretary: M.A. Beadle (01908 583596).

SANDY. **John O'Gaunt Golf Club,** Sutton Park, Sandy SG19 2LY (01767 260252; Fax: 01767 261381). *Location:* on B1040 off A1 two miles north of Biggleswade. Parkland courses. Two 18 hole courses: John O'Gaunt Course 6513 yards, S.S.S. 71 and Carthagena Course 5869 yards, S.S.S. 69. Small practice area. *Green Fees:* weekdays £40.00, weekends £50.00. *Eating facilities:* restaurant and bar. *Visitors:* welcome. Handicap Certificate required. Phone Professional to ascertain tee availability. *Society Meetings:* welcome weekdays, with some limitations on Thursdays and Fridays. Professional: P. Round (01767 260094). Secretary: I.M. Simpson (01767 260360).

SHARNBROOK. **Colworth Golf Club,** Colworth House, Sharnbrook MK44 1LQ. *Location:* Sharnbrook, near Rushden. Parkland course, very narrow. 9 holes, 2650 yards. S.S.S. 64. *Green Fees:* £5.00. *Eating facilities:* none. *Visitors:* must play with a member. Secretary: Mr T.G. Jones (01234 222165).

TODDINGTON. **Chalgrave Manor Golf Club,** Dunstable Road, Toddingtom, Near Dunstable. *Location:* two minutes from Junction 12 M1 (Toddington Services), on main A5120 between Toddington and Houghton Regis. Rolling, open course with many natural undulations; two holes with water features. 18 holes, 6417 yards, 5892 metres. S.S.S. 71. Practice areas. *Green Fees:* weekdays £15.00 per round, weekends £30.00 per round. Day tickets available. *Eating facilities:* clubhouse. *Visitors:* booking not required, but visitors may be restricted at weekends at peak times (telephone in advance). *Society Meetings:* welcome weekdays by prior arrangement. Professional: Martin Brewer. Secretary: Lynn Rumball (01582 391741).

WYBOSTON. **Wyboston Lakes Golf Club,** Wyboston Lakes, Wyboston MK44 3AL (01480 218411). *Location:* one mile south of St. Neots, off A1 and A45. Parkland with play round five lakes. 18 holes, 5803 yards. S.S.S. 69. Driving range. *Green Fees:* weekdays £10.00 per 18 holes; weekends £14.00 per 18 holes. £20.00 per 36 holes weekdays only. Twilight Ticket (play till dark) £7.00 from 5pm. *Eating facilities:* clubhouse catering. *Visitors:* welcome weekdays, booking times required for weekends. Motel on site. *Society Meetings:* catered for weekdays only. Professional: P. Ashwell (01480 212501). Secretary: B. Chinn (01480 219200).

Berkshire

ASCOT. **Lavender Park Golf Centre,** Swinley Road, Ascot SL5 1BD (01344 890940). *Location:* one mile outside Bracknell on the A329. Flat, semi wooded course. 9 holes, 1104 yards. S.S.S. 28. 26 bay floodlit driving range. *Green Fees:* weekdays £3.25; weekends £4.25. *Eating facilities:* hot and cold food available. *Visitors:* welcome at all times. *Society Meetings:* welcome. Professional: Tony Bowers (01344 886096). *

ASCOT. **Royal Ascot Golf Club,** Winkfield Road, Ascot SL5 7LJ (01344 22923). *Location:* Winkfield Road is off Ascot High Street (A329). Heathland. 18 holes, 5709 yards. S.S.S. 68. *Green Fees:* weekdays £11.50 as member's guest; weekends £14.00 as member's guest. *Eating facilities:* full catering available except Mondays. *Visitors:* welcome only as guests of members. *Society Meetings:* catered for Wednesdays and Thursdays, maximum 40. Professional: Garry Malia (01344 24656). Secretary: Derek Simmonds (01344 25175).

ASCOT. **Swinley Forest Golf Club,** Coronation Road, Ascot SL5 9LE (01344 20197). *Location:* between Ascot and Bagshot. 18 holes, 6001 yards. *Green Fees:* £65.00 only on the introduction of a member. *Eating facilities:* lunches served. *Visitors:* welcome only with a member. *Society Meetings:* catered for. Professional: R.C. Parker (01344 874811). Secretary: I.L. Pearce.

ASCOT. **The Berkshire Golf Club,** Swinley Road, Ascot SL5 8AY (01344 21495). *Location:* on A332 between Bagshot and Ascot. Heathland (wooded) course. 36 holes. Blue Course: 6260 yards, S.S.S. 71,

Par 71. Red Course: 6369 yards, S.S.S. 71, Par 72. Practice facilities. *Green Fees:* £50.00 per round, £65.00 per day weekdays. *Eating facilities:* dining room open daily except Monday, snack bar open daily; bar open every day. *Visitors:* welcome weekdays only by application to the Secretary. *Society Meetings:* catered for by prior bookings. Professional: P. Anderson (01344 22351). Secretary: Major P.D. Clarke (01344 21496).

CROWTHORNE. **East Berkshire Golf Club,** Ravenswood Avenue, Crowthorne RG11 6BD (01344 772041). *Location:* M3 Junction 3 – Bracknell turn off, follow signs to Crowthorne, Ravenswood Avenue opposite Railway Station. Heathland course. 18 holes, 6344 yards. S.S.S. 70. *Green Fees:* weekdays £33.00. *Eating facilities:* bar snacks. *Visitors:* welcome weekdays by prior notification, Handicap Certificate essential. *Society Meetings:* Thursdays and Fridays only. Professional: Arthur Roe (01344 774112). Secretary: W.H. Short (01344 772041; Fax: 01344 777378).

MAIDENHEAD near. **Bird Hills Golf Centre,** Drift Road, Hawthorn Hill, Near Maidenhead SL6 3ST (01628 771030. Fax: 01628 31023). *Location:* M4 Junction 8/9 to Maidenhead, A330 to Ascot. Parkland course. 18 holes. 6176 yards. S.S.S. 69. 38 bay floodlit driving range. *Green Fees:* £11.00 weekdays; £13.50 weekends. Juniors/Senior Citizens concessionary rates. *Eating facilities:* large clubhouse, restaurant, barbecue, private function hall. *Visitors:* always welcome, open every day except Christmas Day. Large Pro shop, Conference facilities. *Society Meetings:* always welcome. Professional: Adam Bishop. Secretary: Matt Williams.

MAIDENHEAD. **Maidenhead Golf Club,** Shoppenhangers Road, Maidenhead SL6 2PZ (01628 20545). *Location:* adjacent to Maidenhead Station (south side), one mile from M4. Flat parkland course. 18 holes, 6364 yards. S.S.S. 70. *Green Fees:* weekdays £27.00. *Eating facilities:* bar meals Monday to Friday. *Visitors:* welcome weekdays, no visitors after 12 noon Fridays, Handicap Certificate required. *Society Meetings:* welcome, main days Wednesdays and Thursdays. Professional: Steve Geary (01628 24693). Secretary: Iain Lindsay (01628 24693).

MAIDENHEAD. **Temple Golf Club,** Henley Road, Hurley, Near Maidenhead SL6 5LH (01628 824248; Fax: 01628 828119). *Location:* exit M4 Junction 8/9 or M40 at Junction 4. Leave A404 signposted Henley A4130. Parkland – exceptional drainage. 18 holes, 6206 yards. S.S.S. 70. Excellent practice area, putting and chipping green. *Green Fees:* £40.00 all day weekdays; £45.00 all day weekends. Special rate for one round of £25.00 all year. *Eating facilities:* bar and restaurant seven days a week. *Visitors:* welcome at all times. Handicap Certificate required. Two squash courts. *Society Meetings:* welcome by prior arrangement; booking accepted one year in advance. Professional: Alan Dobbins (01628 824254). Secretary: John C.F. Hunt (01628 824795).

MAIDENHEAD. **Winter Hill Golf Club,** Grange Lane, Cookham SL6 9RP (01628 527613). *Location:* M4 Junction 8/9, four miles from Maidenhead. Parkland. 18 holes, 6408 yards. S.S.S. 71. Large practice ground. *Green Fees:* £24.00 weekdays. *Eating facilities:* lunches/snacks available daily. *Visitors:* welcome weekdays – confirmatory telephone enquiry advisable. Dress – strictly no jeans/trainers/shell suits on course or in clubhouse. *Society Meetings:* welcome, main day Wednesday. Professional: Mr David Hart (01628 527610). Secretary: Mr G.B. Charters-Rowe (01628 527613).

NEWBURY. **Newbury and Crookham Golf Club Ltd,** Bury's Bank Road, Greenham, Newbury RG15 8BZ (01635 40035; Fax: 01635 4005). *Location:* on north side of Newbury. Varied and interesting with woods or trees on almost every hole. 18 holes, 5880 yards, 5380 metres. S.S.S. 68. *Green Fees:* weekdays £25.00; weekends £15.00 with a member only. Reduced rates for groups over 25 in number. *Eating facilities:* restaurant/bar. *Visitors:* welcome, except weekends and Bank Holidays unless with a member. *Society Meetings:* welcome Wednesdays, Thursdays and Fridays. Professional: Mr David Harris (01635 31201). Secretary: Mrs J.R. Hearsey (01635 40045).

NEWBURY. **West Berkshire Golf Club,** Chaddleworth, Newbury RG16 0HS (01488 638574). *Location:* M4 Junction 14. A338 towards Wantage, then follow signposts to RAF Welford. Downland. 18 holes, 7059 yards. S.S.S. 74. *Green Fees:* £24.00 per day, £16.00 per round weekdays; weekends members' guests only. *Eating facilities:* full catering available. *Visitors:* welcome weekdays, members and guests only at weekends. *Society Meetings:* welcome by arrangement. Professional: Wraith Grant (01488 638851). Secretary: (01488 63574).

NORTH ASCOT. **Mill Ride Golf Club,** Mill Ride Estate, North Ascot SL5 8LT (01344 886777). *Location:* off Junction 3 of M3 or Junction 6 of M4, one mile from Ascot Racecourse. Parkland; designed by Donald Steel. 18 holes, 6750 yards. Par 72. Putting green, chipping green, driving range. *Green Fees:* information not provided. *Eating facilities:* lounge bar/restaurant/ private dining room. *Visitors:* welcome. Gym/saunas/ steam rooms. Accommodation. Pro Shop: (01344 886777).

READING. **Calcot Park Golf Club,** Bath Road, Calcot, Reading RG3 5RN (01734 427124; Fax: 01734 453373). *Location:* off Exit 12, M4 along A4 towards Reading, approximately one mile. Undulating wooded parkland. 18 holes, 6283 yards. S.S.S. 70. Limited practice areas. *Green Fees:* weekdays £30.00. *Eating facilities:* fully licensed restaurant, snacks available, two bars. *Visitors:* welcome on production of Handicap Certificate. Not weekends or Bank Holidays. Advisable to ring first to check availability. *Society Meetings:* catered for Tuesday, Wednesday and Thursday. Professional: Albert MacKenzie (01734 427797). Secretary: A.L. Bray.

READING. **Hurst Golf Club,** Sandford Lane, Hurst, Reading (01734 344355). *Location:* five miles Reading towards Wokingham. Parkland by the side of a large lake. 9 holes, 3154 yards. S.S.S. 70. *Green Fees:* information not provided. *Eating facilities:* bar and bar snacks. *Visitors:* unrestricted, bookings accepted. *Society Meetings:* welcome. Professional: Paul Watson (01734 344355). Secretary E. Brewer (Fax: 01344 301020). *

READING. **Reading Golf Club,** 17 Kidmore End Road, Emmer Green, Reading RG4 8SG (01734 472169). *Location:* two miles north of Reading off the Peppard Road (B481). Parkland. 18 holes, 6212 yards. S.S.S. 70. Practice facilities. *Green Fees:* £28.00 per day, £15.00 with member. *Eating facilities:* available. *Visitors:* welcome Monday to Thursday if member of recognised club, with Handicap of 24 or less. Friday to Sunday with member only. *Society Meetings:* catered for by arrangement Tuesdays, Wednesdays and Thursdays. Professional: Andrew Wild (01734 476115). Secretary: to be appointed (01734 472909).

READING. **Sonning Golf Club,** Duffield Road, Sonning RG4 0GJ (01734 693332; Fax: 01734 448409). *Location:* left off A4 at Sonning Roundabout, then left again. Parkland. 18 holes, 6366 yards. S.S.S. 70. *Green Fees:* on application. *Eating facilities:* new restaurant – phone for booking 01734 272055. *Visitors:* welcome, must be member of a recognised golf club with an official handicap; weekends with members only. *Society Meetings:* catered for Wednesdays. Professional: R. McDougall (01734 692910). Secretary: P.F. Williams.

SINDLESHAM. **Bearwood Golf Club,** Mole Road, Sindlesham RG11 5DB (01734 761330). *Location:* on B3030 from Winnersh to Arborfield. Flat wooded course. 9 holes, 2802 yards. S.S.S. 68 (18 holes). 9 hole Pitch and Putt. *Green Fees:* weekdays £8.00 for 9 holes, £15.00 for 18 holes. *Eating facilities:* food available all day. *Visitors:* welcome weekdays, Handicap Certificate required. Weekends as guests of members only. *Society Meetings:* maximum of 21 catered for, Thursdays only. Professional: Mark Griffiths (01734 760156). Manager: Barry Tustin (01734 760060).

SLOUGH. **Datchet Golf Club,** Buccleuch Road, Datchet (01753 543887). *Location:* within two miles of both Windsor and Slough. 9 holes, 5978 yards. S.S.S. 69. *Green Fees:* £16.00 per round, £22.00 per day. *Visitors:* welcome without reservation during week up to 3pm. Lessons and club repairs for non members. *Society Meetings:* small societies welcome. Professional: Bill Mainwaring (01753 542755). Secretary: Anne Perkins (01753 541872). *

STREATLEY ON THAMES. **Goring and Streatley Golf Club,** Rectory Road, Streatley on Thames RG8 9QA (01491 872688; Fax: 01491 875224). *Location:* 10 miles north west of Reading off A417 Wantage Road. Parkland course on Berkshire Downs. 18 holes, 6255 yards. S.S.S. 70. *Green Fees:* £28.00 per day; £19.00 per round after 4pm except weekends. Weekends only playing with a member. *Eating facilities:* full restaurant and bar meals. Restaurant (01491 875122). *Visitors:* welcome on weekdays by telephone booking. *Society Meetings:* catered for. Professional: Roy Mason (01491 873715). Secretary: J. Menzies (01491 873229).

SUNNINGDALE. **Sunningdale Ladies' Golf Club,** Cross Road, Sunningdale SL5 9RX (01344 20507). *Location:* second left going west on A30, past Sunningdale level crossing. Heathland, 18 holes, 3622 yards. (Designed for Ladies' Golf). S.S.S. 60. *Green Fees:* £17.00/£22.00 weekdays; £19.00/£27.00 weekends. *Eating facilities:* snack lunches available except Sundays. *Visitors:* welcome, telephone first. Must have Handicap Certificate. *Society Meetings:* catered for (Ladies only). Secretary: John Darroch. *

WOKINGHAM. **Downshire Golf Course,** Easthampstead Park, Wokingham RG11 3DH (01344 302030). *Location:* between Bracknell and Wokingham, off the Nine Mile Ride. Parkland. 18 holes, 6395 yards. S.S.S. 71. 9 hole pitch and putt, 30 bay floodlit driving range and indoor golf academy. *Green Fees:* weekdays £12.00; weekends £15.00. *Eating facilities:* bar meals, grills, free house bar and restaurant. *Visitors:* welcome. Membership available. *Society Meetings:* welcome weekdays. Professionals: Paul Watson/Warren Humphreys (01344 302030; Fax: 01344 301020). Secretary: Mary Humphreys (01344 422708).

WOKINGHAM. **Sand Martins Golf Club,** Finchampstead Road, Wokingham RG11 3RQ (01734 792711; Fax: 01734 770282). *Location:* off Nine Mile Ride, two miles from Wokingham town centre. Parkland, links/wooded course. 18 holes. Practice area including bunker/pitching area. *Green Fees:* weekdays £25.00. *Eating facilities:* bar, bar food and restaurant. *Visitors:* welcome weekdays. *Society Meetings:* welcomed. Professional: Willie Milne (01734 770265). Secretary: Peter Watkin.

Where an asterisk (*) follows an entry, details have not been confirmed by the club for 1995.

Buckinghamshire

AYLESBURY. **Chiltern Forest Golf Club,** Aston Hill, Halton, Aylesbury (Steward: 01296 630899). *Location:* five miles south-east of Aylesbury, signposted St. Leonards. Wooded, hilly course. 18 holes, 5765 yards. S.S.S. 70. *Green Fees:* £22.00 weekdays; £13.00 with a member weekends. Subject to review. *Visitors:* weekdays unrestricted, weekends with a member. *Society Meetings:* welcome, preferably Wednesdays. Professional: Christopher Skeet (01296 631817). Secretary: L.E.A. Clark (01296 631267).

AYLESBURY. **Ellesborough Golf Club,** Butlers Cross, Aylesbury HP17 0TZ (01296 622375). *Location:* on B4010 one and a half miles from Wendover. Chiltern Hills course. Undulating links. 18 holes, 6283 yards, 6064 metres. S.S.S. 71. Practice net/ground. *Green Fees:* £30.00 per day, £20.00 per round weekdays. *Eating facilities:* full catering available. *Visitors:* welcome except Tuesday mornings and competition days, weekends with a member only. Must provide Handicap Certificate. *Society Meetings:* catered for Wednesdays and Thursdays only by arrangement with Secretary. Professional: Paul Warner (Tel & Fax: 01296 623126). Secretary: K.M. Flint (01296 622114).

AYLESBURY. **Weston Turville Golf & Squash Club,** New Road, Weston Turville, Near Aylesbury HP22 5QT (01296 24084). *Location:* two miles south east of Aylesbury off A41. Easy walking course at the foot of the Chiltern Hills. 18 holes, 6002 yards. S.S.S. 69. *Green Fees:* weekdays £15; weekends £20. *Eating facilities:* meals, snacks and visitors' bar. *Visitors:* truly welcome, booking advisable Saturday and Sunday. Squash courts available. *Society Meetings:* especially catered for. Professional: Tom Jones (01296 25949). General Manager: Mr Barry Hill (01296 24084).

BEACONSFIELD. **Beaconsfield Golf Club Ltd,** Seer Green, Near Beaconsfield HP9 2UR (01494 681180; Fax: 01494 681148). *Location:* from A40 at Beaconsfield, A355 Amersham Road, one mile turn right to Jordans, one mile signposted. Parkland course. 18 holes, 6469 metres. S.S.S. 71. Large practice ground. *Green Fees:* £42.00 per day, £34.00 per round. *Eating facilities:* dining room or bar menu; two bars. *Visitors:* welcome weekdays with accredited introduction – check with Pro. Handicap Certificate required. *Society Meetings:* catered for Tuesdays and Wednesdays. Professional: Mike Brothers (01494 676616). Secretary: P.I. Anderson (01494 676545/6; Fax: 01494 681148).

BUCKINGHAM. **Buckingham Golf Club,** Tingewick Road, Buckingham MK18 4AG (01280 813282). *Location:* one and a half miles south west of Buckingham on A421. Undulating parkland – eight holes affected by river. 18 holes, 6082 yards. S.S.S. 69. Practice ground. *Green Fees:* weekdays £28.00; weekends as members' guests only. *Eating facilities:* seven day catering – bars, lunch and evening. *Visitors:* welcome weekdays only. *Society Meetings:* pre-booked on Tuesdays or Thursdays. Professional: Tom Gates (01280 815210). Secretary: David Rolph (01280 815566).

BURNHAM. **Burnham Beeches Golf Club,** Green Lane, Burnham, Slough SL1 8EG (01628 661150). *Location:* on M4 for Slough two miles, M40 seven miles. Wooded parkland course. 18 holes, 6449 yards. S.S.S. 71. *Green Fees:* weekdays £26.00. *Eating facilities:* bar and restaurant, full catering available. *Visitors:* welcome weekdays, weekends only with a member. *Society Meetings:* welcome by arrangement. Professional: R. Bolton (01628 661661). Secretary: A.J. Buckner (01628 661448).

BURNHAM. **Lambourne Golf Club,** Dropmore Road, Burnham SL1 8NF (01628 666755; Fax: 01628 663301). *Location:* take M4 to Exit 7; take M40 to Exit 2. Parkland. 18 holes, 6765 yards. S.S.S. 72. Practice facilities available. *Green Fees:* weekdays £30.00 per round, weekends £30.00 only with a member. *Eating facilities:* bars and restaurants, open for lunch and dinner. *Visitors:* welcome. Handicap Certificate required weekdays. Weekends only with a member. Golf Director: R.A. Newman (01628 662936). Secretary: C.J. Lumley.

CHALFONT ST GILES. **Chalfont Park Golf Club,** Threehouseholds, Chalfont St Giles HP8 4LW (01494 876293). *Location:* off main A413 towards Amersham. Parkland course. 9 holes, 2900 yards. S.S.S. 68. Practice range, green and bunkers. *Green Fees:* weekdays 9 holes £6.00, 18 holes £10.50; weekends 9 holes £8.00, 18 holes £12.50. *Eating facilities:* clubhouse. *Visitors:* welcome anytime. Pay and play course. *Society Meetings:* welcome. Professional: David Hawes. Director of Golf: Grant Harvey.

CHALFONT ST. GILES. **Harewood Downs Golf Club,** Cokes Lane, Chalfont St. Giles HP8 4TA (01494 762308). *Location:* off A413, two miles east of Amersham. Rolling, tree lined. 18 holes, 5958 yards, 5448 metres. S.S.S. 69. Practice ground. *Green Fees:* weekdays £20.00 per round, £27.00 per day; weekends £30.00. *Eating facilities:* lunches served at club. *Visitors:* welcome on weekdays with current Handicap, weekends by prior arrangement only. *Society Meetings:* catered for by arrangement. Professional: G. Morris (01494 764102). Secretary: M.R. Cannon (01494 762184).

CHESHAM. **Chartridge Park Golf Club,** Chartridge, Chesham HP5 2TF (01494 791772 extension 3; Fax: 01494 786462). *Location:* Junction 18 seven miles to A41 Chesham. Flat parkland course with wooded areas and views over Chilterns. 18 holes, 5510 yards, 5061 metres. S.S.S. 68. Practice ground, nets and bunkers. *Green Fees:* weekdays £18.00; weekends £25.00. *Eating facilities:* snacks and cooked food available seven days a week. *Visitors:* always welcome. Buggies available. *Society Meetings:* always welcome. Professional: Peter Gibbins (01494 791772 extension 2). Secretary: Anita Gibbins (01494 791772 extension 1).

CHESHAM. **Chesham and Ley Hill Golf Club,** Ley Hill, Chesham HP5 1UZ (01494 784541). *Location:* off A41 on B4504 and follow signs for Ley Hill, nearest town – Chesham. Wooded parkland. 9 holes, 5296 yards. S.S.S. 66. Putting green and practice net. *Green Fees:* weekdays £15.00 per round, £20.00 per day. *Eating facilities:* licensed bar, food available at certain times. *Visitors:* welcome Mondays and Thursdays all day; Wednesdays after 12 noon; Fridays till 1pm. *Society Meetings:* Thursdays only by prior arrangement. Secretary: J.R. Taylor (01494 784541). *

DENHAM. **Buckinghamshire Golf Club,** Denham Court Drive, Denham UB9 5BG (01895 835777; Fax: 01895 835210). *Location:* Junction 1 M40 off Denham roundabout, follow signs to Denham Country Park. Gently undulating parkland, River Colne and River Misbourne run through course. 18 holes, 6880 yards. S.S.S. 73. Practice range with ball dispenser and collection. *Green Fees:* weekdays £47.00. *Eating facilities:* Heron Restaurant, spike bar; lunches and menu. *Visitors:* welcome weekdays only and pre-booking required. *Society Meetings:* welcome, golf company days up to 80 – details on application. Professional: Mr John O'Leary. Operations Manager: Mr Kevin Hunt.

DENHAM. **Denham Golf Club,** Tilehouse Lane, Denham UB9 5DE (01895 832022; Fax: 01895 835340). *Location:* off A412 near Uxbridge. Parkland – undulating. 18 holes, 6451 yards, 6159 metres. S.S.S. 71. Practice ground. *Green Fees:* £32.00 per round, £48.00 per day weekdays; weekends with a member only. *Eating facilities:* diningroom, bar snacks. *Visitors:* welcome Monday to Thursday by prior arrangement only. Handicap Certificate. *Society Meetings:* catered for Tuesdays, Wednesdays and Thursdays. Professional: John Sheridan (01895 832801). Secretary: Wg Cdr D. Graham (01895 832022; Fax: 01895 835340).

GERRARDS CROSS. **Gerrards Cross Golf Club,** Chalfont Park, Gerrards Cross SL9 0QA (01753 883263; Fax: 01753 883593). *Location:* alongside A413 (to Amersham) about one mile from junction with A40 (London to Oxford road). Wooded parkland course. 18 holes, 6295 yards. S.S.S. 70. *Green Fees:* weekdays £29.00 per round, £36.00 per day. *Eating facilities:* lunch available to order, bar snacks at all times. *Visitors:* welcome except at weekends and Public Holidays but must produce a letter of introduction or current Handicap Certificate. *Society Meetings:* catered for Thursdays and Fridays, maximum number 50. Professional: M. Barr (01753 885300). Secretary/Manager: P.H. Fisher.

HIGH WYCOMBE. **Flackwell Heath Golf Club Limited,** Treadaway Road, Flackwell Heath, High Wycombe HP10 9PE (01628) 520027). *Location:* M4 Exit 3 from London, Exit 4 from Oxford. 2 miles High Wycombe. Heath and woodland, some hills. 18 holes, 6207 yards. S.S.S. 70. *Green Fees:* weekdays £27.00; weekends £10.00 with member only. *Eating facilities:* restaurant and bars daily (limited catering Mondays). *Visitors:* welcome weekdays only with Handicap Certificate. Weekends with member only. *Society Meetings:* catered for by arrangement Wednesdays and Thursdays. Professional: Stephen Bryan (01628 523017). Secretary: Peter Jeans (01628 520929).

HIGH WYCOMBE. **Hazlemere Golf and Country Club,** Penn Road, Hazlemere, Near High Wycombe (01494 714722). *Location:* on B474 about half a mile from junction with A404 High Wycombe/Amersham Road – three miles from High Wycombe centre. Undulating parkland course. 18 holes, 5873 yards. S.S.S. 68. *Green Fees:* weekdays £28.00; weekends £42.00. *Eating facilities:* restaurant and bar. *Visitors:* restricted at weekends. *Society Meetings:* by prior arrangement. Professional: Steve Morvell (01494 718298). Secretary: D. Hudson (01494 714722).

IVER. **Iver Golf Course,** Hollow Hill Lane, Off Langley Park Road, Iver SL0 0JJ (Slough (01753) 655615). *Location:* situated off Langley Park Road leaving the town of Langley heading towards Iver. Flat parkland, easy walking with natural ditches and ponds. 9 holes, 5988 yards (men), 5230 yards (ladies). S.S.S. 70 (men), 72 (ladies). Driving range and practice ground for short game. *Green Fees:* weekdays £5.00 for 9 holes, £8.50 for 18; weekends £6.80 for 9 holes, £12.00 for 18. Special rates available, please enquire. *Eating facilities:* lunch served 12 noon to 2.30pm seven days, snacks and rolls always available. *Visitors:* always welcome, best to phone on day of play for booking. *Society Meetings:* always welcome. Professional: Geraldine Isles (01753 655615). Secretary: James Rice. *

LITTLE CHALFONT. **Little Chalfont Golf Club,** Lodge Lane, Little Chalfont HP8 4AJ (01494 764877). *Location:* Junction 18 M25, two miles towards Amersham on A404, first left past garden centre. Undulating parkland. 9 holes, 5852 yards S.S.S. 68. *Green Fees:* information not provided. *Eating facilities:* full bar and eating facilities. *Visitors:* always welcome. *Society Meetings:* welcome mid-week. Professionals: B. Woodhouse and A. Philpott (01494 762942). Secretary: J.M. Dunne (01494 764877). *

MILTON KEYNES. **Abbey Hill Golf Club,** Monks Way, Two Mile Ash, Milton Keynes MK8 8AA (01908 562408; Fax: 01908 265771). *Location:* 2 miles south of Stony Stratford, adjacent A5. Wooded course with tight fairways. 18 holes, 5732 metres. S.S.S. 69. 6 hole par 3 course, practice area. *Green Fees:* weekdays £6.80; weekends £9.00. *Eating facilities:* full clubhouse facilities. *Visitors:* welcome; dress restrictions in clubhouse. *Society Meetings:* catered for, apply to clubhouse. Professional: Gary George (01908 563845). Secretary: Brendan McCormack.

MILTON KEYNES. **Three Locks Golf Club,** Great Brickhill, Milton Keynes MK17 9BH (01525 270470). *Location:* A4146 Bletchley to Leighton Buzzard. Parkland with water hazards on eight holes. 9 holes, 3327 yards. S.S.S. 70. Practice ground. *Green Fees:* weekdays £9.50; weekends £11.00. *Eating facilities:* restaurant and bar. *Visitors:* welcome every day. Accommodation available in Club's hotel, free golf for residents. Pro shop. *Society Meetings:* all welcome. Professional: (01525 270050). Secretary: Mrs Darby (01525 270470).

MILTON KEYNES. **Wavendon Golf Centre,** Lower End Road, Wavendon, Milton Keynes MK17 8DA (01908 281296; Fax: 01908 281257). *Location:* two minutes from Junction 13 M1, just off A421 link road. Parkland with six small lakes as hazards. Two courses: 18 holes, 5479 yards. S.S.S. 67. 9 holes, 1424 yards. S.S.S. 27. 36 bay driving range, practice green and bunker. *Green Fees:* weekdays £9.00; weekends £12.00. Senior Citizens and Juniors half price, twilight evening rates. *Eating facilities:* 65-seater carvery restaurant and downstairs bar serving lunches. *Visitors:* welcome. *Society Meetings:* welcome weekend afternoons only. Professional: Gregg Iron (01908 281811). Secretary: Cynthia Cheney (01908 281897).

MILTON KEYNES. **Windmill Hill Golf Course,** Tattenhoe Lane, Bletchley, Milton Keynes MK3 7RB (01908 378623). *Location:* M1 Junction 13/14 A421 to Buckingham, 10 minutes from motorway. Flat parkland course, Henry Cotton design. 18 holes, 6773 yards. S.S.S. 72. 23 bay floodlit driving range. *Green Fees:* weekdays £6.00; weekends and Bank Holidays £8.50. Reduced rates Juniors and Senior Citizens; twilight ticket. *Eating facilities:* public bar and restaurant. *Visitors:* welcome at any time, booking seven days in advance. *Society Meetings:* welcome at all times. All bookings through Professional. Professional: C. Clingan (01908 378623; Fax: 01908 271478). Secretary: Pat Long.

MILTON KEYNES. **Woburn Golf and Country Club,** Bow Brickhill, Milton Keynes MK17 9LJ (Milton Keynes (01908) 370756; Fax: 01908 378436). *Location:* four miles west of junction 13 M1. Two courses: 36 holes, Duke's Course 6940 yards, S.S.S. 74; Duchess' Course 6641 yards, S.S.S. 72. Two practice grounds. *Green Fees:* on application. *Eating facilities:* two restaurants; breakfasts, lunches and dinners. *Visitors:* welcome weekdays with prior arrangement. Members' guests only at weekends. *Society Meetings:* catered for, details on application. Professional: Alex Hay (01908 647987). Secretary: Mrs G. Beasley (01908 370756). *

PRINCES RISBOROUGH. **Whiteleaf Golf Club Ltd,** The Clubhouse, Whiteleaf, Princes Risborough HP27 0LY (01844 343097). *Location:* A4010 from Princes Risborough. Hilly course with spectacular views. 9 holes, 5359 yards. S.S.S. 66. *Green Fees:* weekdays £18.00 per round. *Visitors:* welcome on weekdays only. *Society Meetings:* on application, Thursdays only. Professional: K.S. Ward (01844 345472). Administrator: Mrs B.A. Parsley (01844 274058).

SLOUGH. **Farnham Park Municipal Golf Course,** Park Road, Stoke Poges SL2 4PJ (01753 643335). *Location:* centrally situated between Stoke Poges and Farnham Royal, off Park Road. Parkland. 18 holes, 6172 yards. S.S.S. 69, 70 Ladies. *Green Fees:* weekdays £8.00; weekends £11.00. Reduced rates for Senior Citizens and Juniors. *Eating facilities:* available. *Visitors:* welcome Tuesdays and Thursdays. Professional: P. Harrison (01753 643332). Hon. Secretary: Maureen Brooker (01753 647065).

STOKE POGES. **Stoke Poges Golf Club,** North Drive, Park Road, Stoke Poges SL2 4PG (01753 526385). *Location:* one mile north of Slough. 18 holes, 6654 yards. S.S.S. 72. *Green Fees:* weekdays £35.00 single round, £50.00 per day. *Eating facilities:* lunch and snack restaurant. *Visitors:* welcome weekdays only with Handicap Certificate or letter of introduction; weekends as members' guests only. *Society Meetings:* catered for. Professional: Tim Morrison. Secretary/Manager: R.C. Pickering (01753 526385; Fax: 01753 693805).

STOWE. **Silverstone Golf Club,** Silverstone Road, Stowe MK18 5LH (01280 850005; Fax: 01280 850037). *Location:* A43 Oxford – Northampton Road, opposite Grand Prix Circuit – Silverstone. Flat, new copses bordered by woodland. 18 holes, 6012 yards. S.S.S. 70. Floodlit, covered driving range; circuit golf; two putting areas. *Green Fees:* weekdays £8.00 (£7.00 member's guest); weekends £12.00 non members,

£10.00 guests of members. *Eating facilities:* licensed bar, meals at all times. *Visitors:* welcome, booking 24 hours in advance. *Society Meetings:* welcome weekdays only. Professional: Rodney Holt. Secretary: Margaret Mears.

STOWE. **Stowe Golf Club,** Stowe, Buckingham MK18 5EH (01280 816264). *Location:* situated at Stowe School, four miles north of Buckingham. Parkland course with follies and lakes. 9 holes, 2189 yards. S.S.S. 63. *Green Fees:* information not provided. *Visitors:* only as a guest of a member. *Society Meetings:* catered for by appointment. Secretary: Mrs S.A. Cross (01280 813650). *

WEXHAM. **Wexham Park Golf Course,** Wexham Street, Slough SL3 6NB (01753 663271). *Location:* M40 to Beaconsfield, A40 to Gerrards Cross, direction to Fulmer on right hand side, near Wexham Park Hospital. Parkland. 18 holes, 5390 yards. S.S.S. 66. Also 9/18 hole course, 2851/5702 yards. S.S.S. 34/68; and 9 hole course, 2283 yards. S.S.S. 32. Driving range. *Green Fees:* weekdays £8.50 for 18 holes, £5.00 for 9 holes; weekends £12.00 for 18 holes, £6.90 for 9 holes. *Eating facilities:* clubhouse bar and full kitchen facilities. *Visitors:* welcome – Pay and Play, open to all. Hotel and sports complex. *Society Meetings:* weekdays only (except Bank Holidays), minimum 12 people. Professional: David Morgan (01753 663425). Secretary: P.J. Gale. *

Cambridgeshire

CAMBRIDGE. **Cambridge Meridian Golf Club,** Comberton Road, Toft, Cambridge CB3 7RY (01223 264700; Fax: 01223 264701). *Location:* off Junction 12 of M11 onto B1046. Heavily landscaped parkland with six lakes and 100 bunkers. 18 holes, 6651 yards. S.S.S. 72. Practice ground and putting green. *Green Fees:* weekdays £15.00, weekends £18.00. *Eating facilities:* available all day. *Visitors:* welcome at all times (subject to availability). *Society Meetings:* weekdays only. Professional: Neil Harvey (01223 264702). Secretary: Phil Lloyd.

CAMBRIDGE. **Cambridgeshire Moat House Hotel Golf Club,** Bar Hill, Cambridge CB3 8EU (01954 780555). *Location:* five miles north from Cambridge on A604 Huntingdon Road. Undulating parkland with a lake, ditches and many trees. 18 holes, 6734 yards. S.S.S. 72. Practice grounds. *Green Fees:* weekdays £15.00 per round, £20.00 per day; weekends and Public Holidays £25.00 per round. Daily and weekend golf packages. *Eating facilities:* restaurant, bars, bar meals (Mon-Fri lunch). *Visitors:* welcome anytime by prior phone call. 100 Bedroom Hotel, Squash, Tennis, Residents' Health and Fitness Club and Indoor Heated Swimming Pool. *Society Meetings:* welcome weekdays. Resident Societies only at weekends. Professional: David Vernon (01954 780098). Secretary: (01954 780555; Fax: 01954 780010).

CAMBRIDGE. **Girton Golf Club,** Dodford Lane, Girton, Cambridge CB3 0QE (01223 276143). *Location:* two miles north of Cambridge. Flat parkland. 18 holes, 6085 yards. S.S.S. 69. Large practice area. *Green Fees:* £20.00 per day with Handicap Certificate, £25.00 without; weekends with a member only. *Eating facilities:* diningroom, lounge and bar. *Visitors:* weekdays only. *Society Meetings:* welcome Tuesdays to Fridays. Professional: S. Thomson (01223 276991). Secretary: Mrs M.A. Cornwell (01223 276169).

CAMBRIDGE. **Gog Magog Golf Club,** Shelford Bottom, Cambridge CB2 4AB (01223 247626; Fax: 01223 414990). *Location:* two miles from A11 – A604 roundabout. Colchester – Cambridge Road A604. Open, undulating. Two courses. 18 holes, 6386 yards. S.S.S. 70. 9 holes, 5805 yards. S.S.S. 68. *Green Fees:* Old Course £29.00 per round, £35.00 per day. 9-hole course £19.00 per day. *Eating facilities:* diningroom, bar meals, mixed and men's bar. *Visitors:* welcome, only with members at weekends and Bank Holidays, Handicap Certificates required, Handicap limit on Old Course 22 and below. *Society Meetings:* catered for Tuesdays and Thursdays. Professional: I. Bamborough (01223 246058). Secretary: Ian Skellern (01223 247626).

ELY. **Ely City Golf Course Ltd,** Cambridge Road, Ely CB7 4HX (01353 663810). *Location:* on southern outskirts of city on A10 going to Cambridge. Parkland course, slightly undulating, magnificent views of the 12th century cathedral. 18 holes, 6602 yards. S.S.S. 72. Practice area. *Green Fees:* weekdays £22.00, weekends and Bank Holidays £30.00. *Eating facilities:* full bar and restaurant facilities. *Visitors:* welcome anytime with a member or if in possession of a valid Handicap Certificate. Jeans, T-shirts and trainers not allowed. Well equipped Pro Shop. Snooker. *Society Meetings:* welcome Tuesday to Friday inclusive by arrangement. Professional: Andrew George (01353 663317). General Manager: Michael Hoare (01353 662751; Fax: 01353 668636).

HUNTINGDON. **Brampton Park Golf Club,** Buckden Road, Brampton, Huntingdon PE18 8NF. *Location:* three quarter of a mile off A1, travelling north take first Huntingdon turn, south take second sign for "RAF Brampton". Picturesque parkland/meadowland with many water hazards and wooded areas. 18 holes, 6403 yards. S.S.S. 73. *Green Fees:* weekdays £18 per round, £24 per day; weekends £36 per day only. *Eating facilities:* bar snacks, restaurant, two bars. *Visitors:* welcome at all times, no restrictions save telephone for tee reservations prior to arrival. Accommodation and business conference facilities and banqueting for up to 120 available. *Society Meetings:* welcome. Professional: Alisdair Currie (Tel & Fax: 01480 434705). Secretary: Matthew Staveley (01480 434700; Fax: 01480 434705).

HUNTINGDON. **Lakeside Lodge Golf Centre,** Fen Road, Pidley, Huntingdon PE17 3DD (01487 740968). *Location:* on the B1040 St. Ives to Warboys Road. Course has 8 lakes and considerable landscaping. 18 holes, 6437 yards. S.S.S. 73. 9 hole Par 3 course, driving range. *Green Fees:* weekdays £8.50 for 18 holes, £5.00 for 9 holes; weekends £14.00 for 18 holes, £8.00 for 9 holes. *Eating facilities:* full bar serving all day snacks and meals. *Visitors:* everyone welcome anytime, no restrictions. *Society Meetings:* all welcome. Professional: Mr Alistair Headley PGA (01487 741541). Secretary: Mrs Jane Hopkins (01487 740540; Fax. 01487 740852).

HUNTINGDON. **Ramsey Golf Club,** 4 Abbey Terrace, Ramsey, Huntingdon (01487 813573). *Location:* 20 minutes from A1, 12 miles south of Peterborough, 10 miles north of Huntingdon. Parkland, 18 holes, 6133 yards. S.S.S. 70. Two practice grounds. *Green Fees:* weekdays £20.00 per round or day with Handicap Certificate. Weekends, Bank Holidays with member only. *Eating facilities:* full catering available. *Visitors:* welcome without reservation. *Society Meetings:* catered for by arrangement, weekdays only. Professional: S.J. Scott (01487 813022). Secretary: Mr R. Muirhead (01487 812600).

MARCH. **March Golf Club,** Frogs Abbey, Grange Road, March PE15 0YH (01354 52364). *Location:* one mile south of town centre on west side of A141. Flat parkland. 9 holes, 6210 yards. S.S.S. 70 men, 72 ladies. Practice area. *Green Fees:* weekdays £15.00 (£7.50 with a member); weekends £7.50 with a member only. *Eating facilities:* food available at weekends only, bar daily. *Visitors:* welcome without reservation. *Society Meetings:* accepted with prior arrangement. Professional: Nigel Pickerell. Secretary: J.B. Clapham.

PETERBOROUGH. **Elton Furze Golf Club,** Bullock Road, Haddon, Peterborough. *Location:* four miles west of Peterborough on old A604 Oundle to Peterborough road. New course opened April 1993. Scenic parkland, wooded. 18 holes, 6289 yards, 5715 metres. S.S.S. 70. Driving range. *Green Fees:* weekdays £20.00 per round, £30.00 per day. *Eating facilities:* available. *Visitors:* welcome Tuesdays and Thursdays. *Society Meetings:* welcome Tuesdays and Thursdays – need to pre book. Professional: Frank Kiddie (01733 267701). Secretary: Peter Robinson (01733 232440). *

PETERBOROUGH. **Orton Meadows Golf Club,** Ham Lane, Orton Waterville, Peterborough PE2 0UU (01733 237478). *Location:* four miles west of Peterborough on A605. Parkland. 18 holes, 5800 yards. S.S.S. 68. Practice ground. *Green Fees:* weekdays £8.00; weekends £11.00. Weekday reductions for Juniors and Senior Citizens. *Eating facilities:* restaurant attached to course. *Visitors:* unrestricted – public course. *Society Meetings:* welcome. Professional: J. Mitchell (01733 237478). Secretary: K. Boyer.

PETERBOROUGH. **Peterborough Milton Golf Club,** Milton Ferry, Peterborough PE6 7AG (01733 380204). *Location:* on A47 west of Peterborough, 3 miles east of A1. Parkland. 18 holes, 6431 yards, 5856 metres. S.S.S. 72. *Green Fees:* weekdays £20.00 per round, weekends £25.00 per round. Societies £30.00 per day. *Eating facilities:* available daily. *Visitors:* welcome weekdays; as member's guest at weekends. *Society Meetings:* Tuesdays, Wednesdays and Thursdays by arrangement with Secretary. Professional: Michael Gallagher (01733 380793). Secretary: Mrs D.K. Adams (01733 380489).

PETERBOROUGH. **Thorney Golf Centre,** English Drove, Thorney, Peterborough PE6 0TJ (01733 270570). *Location:* left at traffic lights in Thorney off A47 Peterborough to Wisbech road out of village. Flat course. 18 holes, 6104 yards. S.S.S. 69. Driving range, Par 3 course. *Green Fees:* weekdays £5.00; weekends £7.00. *Eating facilities:* full bar and restaurant. *Visitors:* welcome anytime. *Society Meetings:* welcomed. Professional: Mark Templeman. Secretary: Jane Hind.

PETERBOROUGH. **Thorpe Wood Golf Course,** Thorpe Wood, Peterborough PE3 6SE (01733 267701). *Location:* three miles west of town on A47. Parkland. 18 holes, 7086 yards. S.S.S. 74. Practice ground. *Green Fees:* weekdays £7.50; weekends and Bank Holidays £10.00. Weekday reductions for Senior Citizens and Juniors. *Eating facilities:* Public House attached to course. *Visitors:* unrestricted, booking required. Public Course. *Society Meetings:* welcome – book early. Professionals: Dennis and Roger Fitton (01733 267701; Fax: 01733 332774). Secretary: R. Palmer. *

ST. IVES. **St. Ives (Hunts) Golf Club,** Westwood Road, St. Ives PE17 4RS (01480 464459). *Location:* B1040 off A45. 9 holes, 6052 yards. S.S.S. 69. *Green*

Fees: information not provided. *Eating facilities:* lunches at club, except Mondays. Order in advance. *Visitors:* no visitors weekends or Bank Holidays. *Society Meetings:* catered for. Professional: Darren Clasby (01480 466067). Secretary: B.E. Dunn (01480 468392).

ST. NEOTS. **Abbotsley Golf and Squash Club,** Eynesbury Hardwicke, St. Neots PE19 4XN (01480 215153; Fax: 01480 403280). *Location:* two miles off A1 (M) from St. Neots, 12 miles off Junction 13 M11. Pleasantly undulating parkland. Two courses, 36 holes – Abbotsley 6311 yards. S.S.S. 71; Cromwell – 6087 yards. S.S.S 69. Driving range. *Green Fees:* weekdays Abbotsley £16.00, Cromwell £9.00; weekends Abbotsley £18.00, Cromwell £11.00. *Eating facilities:* available all day. *Visitors:* always welcome. Six squash courts. Accommodation available in 16 bedroom hotel. Residential golf schools. *Society Meetings:* always welcome, weekends on Cromwell course. Professional: Miss Vivien Saunders (01480 406463). Secretary: Miss Jenny Wisson (01480 474000/403300). *

ST. NEOTS. **St. Neots Golf Club,** Crosshall Road, St. Neots PE19 4AE (01480 474311). *Location:* A45 off A1, eastwards, one mile east of Great North Road. Undulating parkland with water hazards. 18 holes, 6027 yards. S.S.S. 69. *Green Fees:* on application. *Eating facilities:* full catering facilities available. *Visitors:* at weekends/Bank Holidays with member only. *Society Meetings:* welcome. Professional: G. Bithrey (01480 476513). Secretary: R.J. Marsden (Tel & Fax: 01480 472363).

Cheshire

ALDERLEY EDGE.**Alderley Edge Golf Club,** Brook Lane, Alderley Edge SK9 7RU (01625 585583). *Location:* off A34. 9 holes, 5836 yards. S.S.S. 68. *Green Fees:* weekends £22.00, weekdays £18.00. *Eating facilities:* meals served in clubhouse. *Visitors:* subject to restrictions on Tuesdays, Wednesdays and weekends. *Society Meetings:* welcome on Thursdays. Professional: A. Sproston (01625 584493). Secretary: J.B. Page. *

ALSAGER. **Alsager Golf and Country Club,** Audley Road, Alsager, Stoke-on-Trent ST7 2UR (01270 875700; Fax: 01270 882207). *Location:* off M6 at Junction 16 onto A500, first left to Alsager, course is two and a half miles on right. Parkland. 18 holes, 6192 yards. S.S.S. 70. *Green Fees:* weekdays £21.00, weekends with member only. *Eating facilities:* restaurant and bar snacks. *Visitors:* welcome weekdays without reservation. Disco, conference and banqueting facilities. *Society Meetings:* welcome, package available on request. Professional: Paul Preston (01270 877432). General Manager: A. Clarke.

APPLETON. **The Warrington Golf Club,** Hill Warren, London Road, Appleton, Near Warrington WA4 5BT (01925 261620). *Location:* M56 exit 10, A49 Warrington one and a half miles. Parkland course. 18 holes, 6305 yards. S.S.S. 70. *Green Fees:* weekdays £23.00; weekends £35.00. *Eating facilities:* available lunchtimes and evenings. *Visitors:* welcome with booking through Professional. *Society Meetings:* Wednesdays only, booked through Secretary. Professional: R. MacKay (01925 265431). Secretary: N.F. Morrall (01925 261775).

CHEADLE. **Gatley Golf Club Ltd,** Waterfall Farm, Styal Road, Heald Green, Cheadle SK8 3TW (0161-437 2091). *Location:* from Gatley village to South down Styal Road and follow directions into Yew Tree Grove, then Motcombe Grove to Club entrance. Parkland course. 9 holes, 5934 yards. S.S.S. 68. *Green Fees:* weekdays £18.00, £6.00 with member, weekends only if playing with member. Special rates by arrangement. *Eating facilities:* available except Monday, bar. *Visitors:* welcome Mondays, Wednesdays and Thursdays. *Society Meetings:* welcome Thursdays. Professional: A.J. Ayre (0161-436 2830). Secretary: P. Hannam F.C.A.(0161-437 2091).

CHESTER. **Carden Park Golf Club,** Near Broxton, Chester CH3 9DQ (01829 731000; Fax: 01829 731032). *Location:* turn towards Wrexham off the A41 at Broxton roundabout. Parkland course with trees and superb views over the Cheshire countryside. 18 hole Championship Course, 6288 yards. S.S.S 72. 9 hole Par 3. Golf Academy. *Green Fees:* weekdays £25.00; weekends £30.00. Special winter-month offers. *Eating facilities:* available at Hotel. *Visitors:* individuals and groups always welcome. Accommodation in 84-suite Hotel. *Society Meetings:* welcome. Professionals: David Williams and Stephen Bradbury (01829 731176).

CHESTER. **Chester Golf Club,** Curzon Park, Chester CH4 8AR (01244 675130). *Location:* one mile south west of city centre. From Chester Castle take A483 (Wrexham) to first roundabout over Grovesnor Bridge. Turn right into Curzon Park North and follow signs. Parkland on two levels overlooking the River Dee. 18 holes, 6508 yards. S.S.S. 71. *Green Fees:* weekdays £21.00 per day; weekends £26.00. Reductions if playing with a member. *Eating facilities:* full restaurant and bar facilities except Mondays, when snacks only are served except by special arrangement. *Visitors:* welcome most days but advisable to telephone first. *Society Meetings:* catered for by prior arrangement. Professional: George Parton (01244 671185). Secretary: V.F.C. Wood (01244 677760).

CHESTER. **Eaton Golf Club,** Guy Lane, Waverton, Chester CH3 7PH (01244 336862). *Location:* three miles south east of Chester off A41. 18 holes, 6562 yards. S.S.S. 71. Substantial practice area. *Green Fees:* weekdays £21.00; weekends £27.00. *Eating facilities:* catering available seven days. *Visitors:* welcome at all times but with Handicap Certificate and prior checking with either Secretary or Professional. *Society Meetings:* welcome except Wednesdays and weekends. Professional: Alex Mitchell (01244 335826). Secretary: G.C. Parry (01244 335885; Fax: 01244 335782).

CHESTER. **Upton-by-Chester Golf Club,** Upton Lane, Chester CH2 1EE (01244 381183). *Location:* off A41, near Zoo turn-off traffic lights. Flat parkland course. 18 holes, 5808 yards. S.S.S. 69. *Green Fees:* £20.00 per day weekdays; £25.00 per round weekends. *Eating facilities:* large restaurant and four bars. *Visitors:* no restrictions except Competition Days. *Society Meetings:* welcome except Mondays, Tuesdays and weekends. Minimum number 16. All day package £32.00, half day £29.00. Professional: P.A. Gardner (01244 381333). Secretary: John B. Durban (01244 381183). *

CHESTER. **Vicars Cross Golf Club,** Tarvin Road, Great Barrow, Chester CH3 7HN (01244 335174). *Location:* four miles east of Chester on the A51. Wooded parkland course. 18 holes, 6243 yards. S.S.S. 70. Two practice grounds. *Green Fees:* weekdays £20.00 per day or round; weekends and Bank Holidays as member's guest only, £10.00. After 4pm £14.00 per round. *Eating facilities:* men's bar, mixed bar, restaurant. *Visitors:* welcome Monday to Thursday only for day ticket, after 4pm any day. *Society Meetings:* catered for Tuesdays and Thursdays only. Professional: John Forsythe (01244 335595). Secretary: Andrew Rogers.

CONGLETON. **Astbury Golf Club,** Peel Lane, Astbury, Near Congleton CW12 4RE (01260 272772 – Steward). *Location:* on A34 Congleton to Newcastle-under-Lyme road. Parkland. 18 holes, 6139 yards. S.S.S. 69. Large practice area. *Green Fees:* weekdays £25.00; £8.00 with member. *Eating facilities:* dining-room and bar. *Visitors:* welcome weekdays, weekends with a member only. Must be members of recognised golf club with bona fide Handicap. *Society Meetings:* Thursdays only. £20.00 per player. Professional: Ashley Salt (01260 298663). Secretary: Mike Bates (01260 279139). Caterer: (01260 299266).

CONGLETON. **Congleton Golf Club,** Biddulph Road, Congleton CW12 3LZ (01260 273540). *Location:* one mile south of Congleton Railway Station on Biddulph Road. Parkland. 9 holes, 5080 yards. S.S.S. 65. *Green Fees:* weekdays £14.00 (£7.00 with a member); weekends £20.00 (£10.00 with a member). *Eating facilities:* lunches and evening meals served if ordered in advance. Snacks available except Monday evenings. *Visitors:* welcome. *Society Meetings:* catered for, one year's notice if accepted. Professional: John Colclough (01260 271083). Secretary: R. Walsh (01260 273540).

CREWE. **Crewe Golf Club Ltd,** Fields Road, Haslington, Crewe CW1 1TB (01270 584227). *Location:* off A534 between Crewe and Sandbach. Parkland course. 18 holes, 6201 yards. S.S.S. 70. *Green Fees:* £22.00 after 1pm, £27.00 before 1pm. Subject to review. *Eating facilities:* bar, diningroom. *Visitors:* welcome weekdays only, not Bank Holidays. Snooker room. *Society Meetings:* Tuesdays only. Professional: R.E. Rimmer (01270 585032). Secretary: J.R. Stewart (Tel & Fax: 01270 584099).

CREWE. **Onneley Golf Club,** Barrhill Road, Onneley, Near Crewe (01782 750577). *Location:* one mile from Woore off A51, 12 miles from Stoke-on-Trent. Parkland on gentle slope. 9 holes, 5584 yards. S.S.S. 67. *Green Fees:* weekdays £15.00 (£6.00 with member); Saturdays and Bank Holidays with member only. Juniors half normal price. *Eating facilities:* light bar snacks when bar is open in summer. *Visitors:* welcome weekdays unrestricted. *Society Meetings:* welcome, except Tuesdays and Fridays (£18.00 per day including meal). Hon. Secretary: Don Whittick (01630 647022).

CREWE. **Queens Park Golf Course,** Queens Park Drive, Crewe CW2 7SB (01270 662378). *Location:* next to Queens Park, one mile from Crewe Station. Parkland. 9 holes x 2, 4920 yards. S.S.S. 64. *Green Fees:* weekdays £4.70 per round; weekends £6.10 per round. *Eating facilities:* bar with excellent bar snacks. *Visitors:* welcome, restrictions Sunday mornings to 11am. *Society Meetings:* welcome. Professional: (01270 666724). Secretary: K. Lear (01270 628352).

FRODSHAM. **Frodsham Golf Club,** Simons Lane, Frodsham WA6 6HE (01928 732159). *Location:* Frodsham 10 minutes M56 Junction 12, Cheshire. Parkland with views over Mersey estuary; undulating. 18 holes, 6289 yards. S.S.S. 70. Two practice areas with bunkers, putting green and nets. *Green Fees:* weekdays £18.00; weekends £25.00. *Eating facilities:* clubhouse, spike bar, lounge bar, dining areas. *Visitors:* welcome at all times, no parties at weekends. Self catering dormy house accommodation available. *Society Meetings:* welcome weekdays, groups 12 minimum. Professional: Graham Tonge (01928 739442). Secretary: Eric Roylance (01928 732159; Fax: 01928 739037).

HELSBY. **Helsby Golf Club,** Towers Lane, Helsby, Warrington WA6 0JB (01928 723407). *Location:* M56 Junction 14 take B5117 to Helsby. Through traffic lights one mile, first right into Primrose Lane, then first right into Towers Lane (400 yards). Flat parkland course. 18 holes, 6229 yards. S.S.S. 70. Practice area available. *Green Fees:* £20.00 weekdays. *Eating facilities:* full facilities, except Mondays. *Visitors:* welcome weekdays, weekends must play with a member. Snooker facilities. *Society Meetings:* welcome Tuesdays and Thursdays by arrangement. Professional: I. Wright (01928 725457). Secretary: G.A. Johnson (01928 722021).

KNUTSFORD. **Heyrose Golf Club,** Budworth Road, Tabley, Knutsford WA16 0HY (01545 733623). *Location:* Junction 19 M6 right at Windmill Pub to Pickmere, three-quarters of a mile right fork, half a mile further on right. Undulating parkland, wooded course. 18 holes, 6510 yards. S.S.S. 71. Large practice area, bunker, driving net, putting green. *Green Fees:* weekdays £18.00 per round; weekends £23.00 per round. Subject to review. *Eating facilities:* bar and restaurant. *Visitors:* no visitors on Saturdays before 2pm, Ladies priority Wednesdays, Seniors priority Thursdays 8am to 10.30am. *Society Meetings:* welcome. Professional: Martin Redrup (01565 734267). Hon. Secretary: (Tel and Fax: 01565 733664).

KNUTSFORD. **Knutsford Golf Club,** Mere Heath Lane, Knutsford (01565 633355). *Location:* one mile east of town centre. 9 holes, 6200 yards. S.S.S. 70. *Green Fees:* information not provided. *Eating facilities:* by prior arrangement with Steward. *Visitors:* welcome with reservation except Tuesdays and Wednesdays. To be introduced by member. *Society Meetings:* catered for by special arrangement with Hon. Secretary. Professional: A. Gillies. Secretary: D. Francis.

KNUTSFORD. **Mere Golf and Country Club,** Chester Road, Mere, Knutsford WA16 6LJ (01565 830155; Fax: 01565 830518). *Location:* two miles east of Junction 19 M6 and three miles west of Junction 7 M56. Parkland Championship course. 18 holes, 6817 yards. S.S.S. 73. Practice area, two 9-hole putting greens, driving range (April to October). *Green Fees:* £45.00 weekdays, £55.00 weekends. *Eating facilities:* bistro, restaurant, bar snacks. *Visitors:* welcome by prior arrangement only. *Society Meetings:* Mondays, Tuesdays and Thursdays only by arrangement. Professional: Peter Eyre (01565 830219). Secretary: Karen Bucksey.

KNUTSFORD. **Wilmslow Golf Club,** Great Warford, Mobberley, Knutsford WA16 7AY (01565 872148). *Location:* two miles from Wilmslow off the Knutsford road. Parkland course. 18 holes, 6611 yards. S.S.S. 72. Practice facility. *Green Fees:* weekdays £25.00 per round, £37.50 per day; weekends £40.00 per round, £50.00 per day. *Eating facilities:* full catering except Monday, two bars. *Visitors:* welcome, Ladies' Day Wednesday. *Society Meetings:* Tuesdays and Thursdays only. Professional: L.J. Nowicki (01565 873620). Secretary: A. Laurence (Tel & Fax: 01565 872148). *

LYMM. **Lymm Golf Club,** Whitbarrow Road, Lymm WA13 9AN (01925 752177). *Location:* five miles south east of Warrington, two and a half miles from Junction 20 on M6 and Junction 9 on M56. Parkland. 18 holes, 6304 yards. S.S.S. 70. Practice ground. *Green Fees:* information not provided. *Eating facilities:* coffee, bar snacks, lunches and dinner, bar. *Visitors:* welcome with Handicap Certificates, no visitors on Thursdays until 1.30pm, weekends or Bank Holidays. *Society Meetings:* catered for Wednesdays with reservations. Professional: Steve McCarthy (01925 755054). Secretary: J.M. Pearson (01925 755020).

MACCLESFIELD. **Macclesfield Golf Club,** Hollins Road, Macclesfield SK11 7EA (01625 423227). *Location:* turn off A523 Leek Road into Windmill Street, half a mile fork right. Hilly course with extensive views. 18 holes, 5625 yards, 5388 metres. S.S.S. 67. *Green Fees:* £17.00 weekdays; £20.00 weekends and Bank Holidays. *Eating facilities:* full catering and bar facilities. *Visitors:* welcome by arrangement. *Society Meetings:* welcome by arrangement (Tuesdays and Wednesdays preferred). Professional: Tony Taylor (01625 616952). Secretary: N.H. Edwards (01625 615845). *

MACCLESFIELD. **Prestbury Golf Club,** Macclesfield Road, Prestbury, Near Macclesfield (01625 829388). *Location:* on the Macclesfield road leaving Prestbury village. 18 holes, 6359 yards. S.S.S. 71. *Green Fees:* information not provided. *Eating facilities:* lunches, teas and dinners. *Visitors:* welcome on weekdays with official club handicap; Bank Holidays and weekends only with a member. *Society Meetings:* Thursdays only. Professional: Nick Summerfield (01625 828241). Secretary: J. Wright (01625 828241). *

MACCLESFIELD. **Shrigley Hall Golf and Country Club,** Shrigley Park, Pott Shrigley, Near Macclesfield SK10 5SB (01625 575757; Fax: 01625 573323). *Location:* easily accessible by M56, M62/63, M6, A523 and A6. Parkland with magnificent views, home of the Norman Wisdom Classic. 18 holes, 6305 yards. S.S.S. 71. Driving range. *Green Fees:* weekdays £22.00; weekends £28.00. Special rates for residents and guests of members. *Eating facilities:* golf clubhouse and restaurant. *Visitors:* on availability. Handicap Certificate required. 156 bedroomed, four star hotel. *Society Meetings:* all welcome. Professional: Granville A. Ogden (01625 575626). Secretary: Sandra Major. *

MACCLESFIELD. **The Tytherington Club,** Macclesfield SK10 2JP (01625 434562; Fax: 01625 611076). *Location:* one mile north of Macclesfield off A523. Championship course in beautiful parkland setting, Headquarters of WPGET. 18 holes, 6756 yards, 6136 metres. S.S.S. 72 (men) 74 (ladies). Practice area. *Green Fees:* £25.00 18 holes, £35.00 36 holes weekdays; £30.00 18 holes, £40.00 36 holes weekends. *Eating facilities:* bar snacks, bistro, à la carte restaurant, private diningrooms. *Visitors:* welcome, Handicap Certificates required, no other restrictions. Full Country Club facilities, pool, tennis. Accommodation arranged. *Society Meetings:* very welcome weekdays. Professional: Sandy Wilson. Managing Director: P. Dawson.

NANTWICH. **Reaseheath Golf Club,** Reaseheath College, Nantwich. *Location:* A500 north of Nantwich. Flat parkland. 9 holes, 1700 yards. S.S.S. 55. Reaseheath Golf Club is primarily a 9 hole college golf course principally for the training of greenkeepers throughout the UK. *Green Fees:* weekdays £3.00. Only playing with a member as small parties. *Visitors:* subject to approval. *Society Meetings:* subject to approval. Secretary: D. Mortram (01270 625131).

NORTHWICH. **Delamere Forest Golf Club,** Station Road, Delamere, Northwich CW8 2JE (01606 883264). *Location:* opposite Delamere Station on the B5152 Tarporley to Frodsham road. Undulating heathland course. 18 holes, 6305 yards. S.S.S. 70. Two practice grounds and one indoor net. *Green Fees:* weekdays £25.00 per round, £35.00 per day; weekends and Bank Holidays £30.00 per round. *Eating facilities:* bar snacks, diningroom for parties of 30 plus. *Visitors:* welcome any day except Competition Days – advisable to check in advance. *Society Meetings:* welcome if 24 or more in number with prior booking – Tuesdays and Thursdays only. Professional: E.B. Jones (01606 883307). Secretary: R.H. Allardice (Tel & Fax: 01606 883800).

See Colour Advertisement on page 20.

PUBLISHER'S NOTE

While every effort is made to ensure accuracy, we regret that FHG Publications cannot accept responsibility for errors, omissions or misrepresentation in our entries or any consequences thereof. Prices in particular should be checked because we go to press early. We will follow up complaints, but cannot act as arbiters or agents for either party.

NORTHWICH. **Sandiway Golf Club,** Chester Road, Sandiway, Northwich CW8 2DJ (01606 883247). *Location:* off A556, Northwich by-pass. Undulating heavily wooded parkland. 18 holes, 6435 yards. S.S.S. 72. *Green Fees:* weekdays £30.00 per round, £35.00 per day; weekends £35.00 per round, £40.00 per day. *Eating facilities:* lunches and teas served daily, full restaurant facilities. *Visitors:* welcome on weekdays with letter of introduction and Handicap Certificate from home club. *Society Meetings:* restricted to Tuesdays, parties up to 120. Professional: William Laird (01606 883180). Secretary: M.C. Gilyeat. Caterer: (01606 882606).

PRESTBURY. **Mottram Hall Golf Course,** Wilmslow Road, Mottram St. Andrew, Prestbury SK10 4QT (01625 820064). *Location:* M56 and M6. Flat parkland/woodland course. 18 holes, 6905 yards, 6250 metres. S.S.S. 72. Practice area. *Green Fees:* £30.00 weekdays; £35.00 weekends. Reduced green fees for Hotel residents. *Eating facilities:* golf centre bar and restaurant. *Visitors:* no restrictions. Accommodation in 133 bedrooms. *Society Meetings:* no restrictions. Professional: Tim Rastall.

RUNCORN. **Runcorn Golf Club,** Clifton Road, Runcorn WA7 4SU (01928 572093). *Location:* signposted The Heath, A557. High parkland course. 18 holes, 6035 yards, 5514 metres. S.S.S. 69. *Green Fees:* weekdays £18.00 per round or day, weekends and Bank Holidays £22.00 per round/day. *Eating facilities:* bar snacks; meals by arrangement. *Visitors:* welcome weekdays except Tuesday mornings. No visitors weekends or Bank Holidays except with a member. Handicap Certificate required. *Society Meetings:* by arrangement Mondays and Fridays. Professional: S. Dooley (01928 564791). Secretary: W.B. Reading (01928 574214). *

SANDBACH. **Malkins Bank Golf Club,** Betchton Road, Malkins Bank, Sandbach CW11 0XN (01270 767878). *Location:* M6, Junction 17 south, one mile via Sandbach. Countryside course. 18 holes, 6071 yards. S.S.S. 69. Practice area. *Green Fees:* information not provided. *Eating facilities:* bar and meals available. *Visitors:* welcome at all times, pre-booking advised weekends via club Professional. *Society Meetings:* welcome by prior arrangement. Professional: David Wheeler (01270 765931). Secretary: Ken Lea. *

SANDBACH. **Sandbach Golf Club,** 117 Middlewich Road, Sandbach CW11 9EA (01270 762117). *Location:* two miles from Junction 17 of M6 on Middlewich Road. Meadowland course. 9 holes, 5397 yards. S.S.S. 67. Practice field. *Green Fees:* weekdays £16.00 per day, £8.00 with member; weekends and Bank Holidays must be accompanied by a member. *Eating facilities:* available except Mondays and Thursdays. *Visitors:* welcome weekdays, weekends by invitation only. *Society Meetings:* catered for only by advance arrangement with Hon. Secretary. Secretary: A.F. Pearson.

SOUTH WIRRAL. **Ellesmere Port Golf Club,** Chester Road, Hooton, South Wirral L66 1QH (0151-339 7502). *Location:* approximately six miles north of Chester on main A41 trunk road. to Birkenhead. Wooded with a lot of ponds. 18 holes, 6432 yards. S.S.S. 71. *Green Fees:* weekdays £5.30; weekends £6.10. Special fees for Juniors and Senior Citizens, and concessions for unemployed during weekdays. *Eating facilities:* bar and catering facilities. *Visitors:* welcome weekdays, weekends must be booked; booking fee of £1. *Society Meetings:* by arrangement with Professional. Professional: Mr D. Yates (0151-339 7689). Secretary: Mr S. Hough (0151-339 7689).

STALYBRIDGE. **Stamford Golf Club,** Oakfield House, Heyheads, Huddersfield Road, Stalybridge SK15 3PY (01457 832126). *Location:* on B6175 off A6018. Hilly moorland course. 18 holes, 5701 yards. S.S.S. 68. *Green Fees:* weekdays £17.50; weekends after 3pm £23.00. *Eating facilities:* meals lunchtime and evening (except Monday). *Visitors:* welcome without restrictions. *Society Meetings:* catered for by appointment only. Golf Shop: Brian Badger (01457 834829). Secretary: W.E. Ricardo.

STOCKPORT. **Davenport Golf Club,** Middlewood Road, Poynton, Near Stockport SK12 1TS (01625 877321). *Location:* A6 from Stockport, Macclesfield Road at Hazel Grove, left at Poynton Church. Undulating parkland course. 18 holes, 6065 yards. S.S.S. 69. *Green Fees:* weekdays £24.00 (£8.00 with member), weekends £30.00 (£10.00 with a member). *Eating facilities:* bar snacks daily except Mondays, full meals by arrangement. *Visitors:* welcome, tee booking in operation after consultation with Club Professional. *Society Meetings:* catered for Tuesdays and Thursdays only. Professional: Wyn Harris (01625 877319). Secretary: D.W. Scott (01625 876951).

TARPORLEY. **Oaklands Golf Club,** Forest Road, Tarporley CW6 0JA (01829 733884 for general enquiries; Fax: 01829 733666). *Location:* half a mile from Tarporley on A49. Undulating parkland with scenic views of Cheshire Plain. 18 holes, 6508 yards. Par 71. Practice area and putting green. *Green Fees:* weekdays £18.00 per round; weekends £25.00 per round. Golf packages from £25. *Eating facilities:* spike bar and visitors' lounge bar. *Visitors:* welcome. *Society Meetings:* welcome except weekends. Professionals: Judy Stratham (01829 733703). Secretary/Manager: Paul Burroughes.

WARRINGTON. **Birchwood Golf Club,** Kelvin Close, Birchwood, Warrington WA3 7PB (01925 818819). *Location:* Junction 11, two miles Leigh – Warrington road M62. Parkland with water. 18 holes, 6810 yards. S.S.S. 73. *Green Fees:* information not provided. *Eating facilities:* full restaurant facilities and bar snacks. Must book in advance. *Visitors:* conference and banqueting facilities for 200. *Society Meetings:* catered for weekdays except Fridays. Package deals available. Professional: Derrick Cooper. Hon. Secretary: R. Denning (01925 818819).

WARRINGTON. **Leigh Golf Club,** Kenyon Hall, Broseley Lane, Culcheth, Warrington WA3 4BG (01925 763130). *Location:* off A580 East Lancs Road to Culcheth Village. Parkland – tree lined fairways. 18 holes, 5876 yards. S.S.S. 68. Three practice areas, practice nets. *Green Fees:* weekdays £25.00, £9.00 playing with member; weekends and Bank Holidays £32.00. Subject to review. *Eating facilities:* two bars and restaurant. *Visitors:* check with Professional. *Society Meetings:* catered for Mondays (except Bank Holidays) and Tuesdays. Professional: Andrew Baguley (01925 762013). Secretary: G.D. Riley (01925 762943).

WARRINGTON. **Poulton Park Golf Club Ltd,** Dig Lane, Cinnamon Brow, Warrington WA2 0SH (01925 812034). *Location:* M6 (Junction 21), off A574 (Warrington/Leigh) Crab Lane. 9 holes, 4937 metres. S.S.S. 66. *Green Fees:* weekdays £16.00 (Winter £12.00); weekends £18.00. *Eating facilities:* available except Mondays. *Visitors:* welcome. *Society Meetings:* catered for except weekends, maximum 24. Golf Society Packages available. Professional: Darren Newing (01925 825220). Secretary: D.J. Coleman.

WARRINGTON. **Walton Hall Golf Club,** Warrington Road, Higher Walton, Warrington WA4 5LU (01925 266775). *Location:* two miles south of Warrington off A56. Wooded parkland. 18 holes, 6801 yards. S.S.S. 73, Par 72. Practice ground. *Green Fees:* weekdays £6.00; weekends £7.50. Six day advance booking system. *Eating facilities:* licensed clubhouse, meals and bar snacks. *Visitors:* unrestricted. *Society Meetings:* welcome, weekends after 1pm. Professional: Peter Maton (01925 263061). Secretary: R. Davies (01925 266775).

WIDNES. **St. Michael's Jubilee Golf Club,** Dundalk Road, Widnes WA8 8BS (0151-424 6230). *Location:* five minutes from M56 and M62. Undulating parkland. 18 holes, 5612 yards. S.S.S. 67. Putting and practice areas. *Green Fees:* information not available. *Eating facilities:* bar, meals in restaurant. *Visitors:* unrestricted. *Society Meetings:* by arrangement with Professional. Professional: B. Bilton. Secretary: W. Hughes. *

WIDNES. **Widnes Golf Club,** Highfield Road, Widnes WA8 7DT (0151-424 2440; Fax: 0151-495 2849). *Location:* near town centre, five miles from M56 and M62. Parkland course. 18 holes, 5471 yards. S.S.S. 68 White, 67 Yellow, 69 Ladies. *Green Fees:* weekdays £20.00; weekends £30.00. *Eating facilities:* two bars and full catering service. *Visitors:* welcome, Wednesdays by prior arrangement. *Society Meetings:* catered for by arrangement. Professional: Mr S. Forster (0151-420 7467). Secretary: Margaret M. Cresswell (0151-424 2995).

WIDNES. **Widnes Municipal,** Dundalk Road, Widnes (0151-424 6230). 18 holes, 5638 yards. S.S.S. 67, Par 69. *Visitors:*unrestricted. Secretary: W. Hughes. Professional: Bob Bilton. *

WINSFORD. **Knights Grange Golf Course,** Sports Complex, Grange Lane, Winsford CW7 2PT. *Location:* signposted "Sports Complex" from traffic lights Winsford Town Centre. 6 miles from M6. Very flat but a challenging course. 9 holes, 2860 yards. S.S.S. 35/37. Practice area. *Green Fees:* £2.70 for 9 holes, £3.50 for 18 holes weekdays; £3.95 & £5.10 weekends. *Eating facilities:* snacks and hot drinks from golf shop, public house adjacent. *Visitors:* unrestricted, advance booking 01606 552780. Bowls, tennis, football, athletics and crazy golf. *Society Meetings:* welcomed – booking in writing. Manager: R. Wright (01606 552780).

Cleveland

BILLINGHAM. **Billingham Golf Club,** Sandy Lane, Billingham TS22 5NA (01642 554494). *Location:* off A19 trunk road, one mile west of Billingham town centre. Undulating parkland. 18 holes, 6460 yards. S.S.S. 71. Practice area including pitching green and putting greens. *Green Fees:* weekdays £20.00, £12.00 with member; weekends £33.00, £17.00 with member. *Eating facilities:* full catering Tuesdays to Saturdays. Snacks only on Mondays. *Visitors:* welcome weekdays, proof of membership of another club or Handicap Certificate required. Prior booking advised. *Society Meetings:* catered for with prior arrangement with Secretary. Professional: P.S. Bradley (01642 557060). Secretary: E.I. Douglas (01642 533816).

BROTTON. **Hunley Hall Golf Club,** Brotton, Saltburn TS12 2QQ (01287 76216). *Location:* situated off A174 at McLean Road, signposted. 18 holes, 6918 yards. S.S.S. 73. *Green Fees:* weekdays £18.00, with a member £9.00; weekends and Bank Holidays £25.00, with a member £12.50. *Eating facilities:* full catering and bar facilities. *Visitors:* welcome. *Society Meetings:* welcome by arrangement. Professional: Andrew Brook (01287 77444). *

EAGLESCLIFFE. **Eaglescliffe Golf Club Ltd,** Yarm Road, Eaglescliffe, Stockton-on-Tees TS16 0DQ (01642 780098). *Location:* on A135 one mile north of Yarm and three miles south of Stockton. Hilly parkland course, sloping to River Tees. 18 holes, 6275 yards. S.S.S. 70. Practice area and putting green. *Green Fees:* weekdays £22.00, weekends and Bank Holidays £28.00. *Eating facilities:* two bars, meals available except Mondays, separate diningroom. *Visitors:* welcome weekdays, restriction on Tuesdays and Fridays. *Society Meetings:* catered for except weekends. Professional: N. Gilks (01642 790122). Secretary: A.H. Painter (01642 780238).

HARTLEPOOL. **Castle Eden and Peterlee Golf Club,** Castle Eden, Hartlepool TS27 4SS (01429 836220). *Location:* two miles south of Peterlee, use exits from A19. Picturesque parkland course. 18 holes, 6262 yards. S.S.S. 70. Practice ground. *Green Fees:* weekdays £20.00; weekends and Bank Holidays £30.00. *Eating facilities:* restaurant, lounge and bar. *Visitors:* welcome weekdays. Hours 9.30am – 11.30am, 1.45pm – 3.30pm. Tuesday Ladies' day. No visiting parties weekends or Bank Holidays. *Society Meetings:* weekdays only with reservation. Professional: Graham J. Laidlaw (01429 836689). Secretary: Peter Robinson (01429 836510).

HARTLEPOOL. **Hartlepool Golf Club Ltd,** Hart Warren, Hartlepool (01429 274398). *Location:* off A1086 at Hart Station (north of town). Seaside links course, 18 holes, 6255 yards. S.S.S. 70. Practice ground. *Green Fees:* weekdays £17.00; weekends £24.00. Half green fees if playing with a member. *Eating facilities:* meals and snacks available. *Visitors:* welcome (excluding Sunday) without reservation. *Society Meetings:* catered for by prior arrangement. Professional: M. E. Cole (01492 267473). Hon. Secretary: W.E. Storrow (01492 870282).

HARTLEPOOL. **Seaton Carew Golf Club,** Tees Road, Seaton Carew, Hartlepool (01429 266249). *Location:* two miles south of Hartlepool on A178. Seaside links. 22 holes. Old Course: 6604 yards. S.S.S. 72. Brabazon Course: 6802 yards. S.S.S. 73. *Green Fees:* to be arranged. *Eating facilities:* available. *Visitors:* welcome, some weekend restrictions. *Society Meetings:* catered for by arrangement. Professional: W. Hector (01429 266249). Secretary: P.R. Wilson (01429 261473).

MIDDLESBROUGH. **Middlesbrough Golf Club,** Brass Castle Lane, Marton, Middlesbrough TS8 9EE (01642 311515; Fax: 01642 319607). *Location:* five miles south of Middlesbrough west of the A172. Parkland course. 18 holes, 6111 yards. S.S.S. 70. *Green Fees:* weekdays £26.00; weekends £32.00. *Eating facilities:* lunches, teas and dinners. *Visitors:* welcome when tee not booked. *Society Meetings:* welcome Wednesdays, Thursdays and Fridays. Professional: Don Jones (01642 311766). Secretary: J.M. Jackson (01642 315430).

MIDDLESBROUGH. **Middlesbrough Municipal Golf Centre,** Ladgate Lane, Middlesbrough TS5 7YZ (01642 315533; Fax: 01642 300726). *Location:* three miles south of Middlesbrough on A174. Parkland course with featured streams. 18 holes, 6333 yards. S.S.S. 71. Floodlit driving range, practice area and putting green. *Green Fees:* weekdays £7.50 adult, £4.50 Senior Citizen/Junior; weekends £9.50 adult, £8.50 Senior Citizen/Junior. *Eating facilities:* bar meals provided, lunches available seven days. *Visitors:* welcome anytime, but starting times must be booked in advance. *Society Meetings:* by prior arrangement, special golf packages available. Professionals: Alan Hope and Dave Symington (01642 300720). Manager: Mr M. Gormley (01642 315533). Secretary: John Dilworth (01642 319416).

REDCAR. **Cleveland Golf Club,** Queen Street, Redcar TS10 1BT (01642 483693). *Location:* south bank of River Teesmouth by A174 then A1042 into Redcar. 18 holes, 6707 yards. S.S.S. 72. *Green Fees:* weekdays £18.00; weekends £27.00. Visiting parties 16+ £28. *Eating facilities:* all week except Monday. *Visitors:* welcome but not on weekends or Bank Holidays. *Society Meetings:* catered for by prior arrangement weekdays only. Professional: M. Nutter (01642 483462). Secretary: L.R. Manley (Tel & Fax: 01642 471798).

REDCAR. **Wilton Golf Club**, Wilton Castle, Wilton, Redcar TS10 4QY (01642 454626). *Location:* eight miles east of Middlesbrough (A174), four miles west of Redcar. Wooded parkland course. 18 holes, 6145 yards. S.S.S. 69. Small practice area. *Green Fees:* weekdays £18.00, £9.00 with member; Sundays and Bank Holidays £24.00 (£11.00 with a member). Guests may only be introduced on a reduced green fee once per calendar month. *Eating facilities:* lunches, except Sundays; evening meals by arrangement. *Visitors:* welcome except Saturdays; Tuesdays Ladies have priority on first tee all day. Weekdays not before 10am unless playing with member. Snooker, squash by arrangement. *Society Meetings:* by arrangement, except Saturdays and Tuesdays. Please write to Secretary. Professional: Miss P.D. Smillie (01642 452730). Secretary: J.C.P. Elder (01642 465265).

SALTBURN BY THE SEA. **Saltburn by the Sea Golf Club Ltd,** Hob Hill, Saltburn by the Sea TS12 1NJ (01287 622812). *Location:* from Saltburn take Guisborough Road, one mile out of town on left. 18 holes, 5846 yards. S.S.S. 68. *Green Fees:* weekdays £19.00 per day, weekends and Bank Holidays £22.00 per day. *Eating facilities:* available except Mondays. *Visitors:* welcome, limited Sundays and Thursdays and no visitors Saturdays. *Society Meetings:* catered for by arrangement. Professional: David Forsythe (01287 24653). Secretary: David Becker (01287 622812).

STOCKTON-ON-TEES. **Harper's Golf and Leisure Norton Golf Course,** Junction Road, Norton, Stockton-on-Tees TS20 2SU (Golf Shop: 01642 676385). *Location:* turn into Junction Road to Norton from A177 at Horse and Jockey, two miles north of Stockton roundabout. Slightly hilly course with five lakes. 18 holes, 5393 yards. S.S.S. 70. *Green Fees:* weekdays £8.50 for 18 holes, weekends and Bank Holidays £9.00. *Eating facilities:* catering and bar available. *Visitors:* must have golf shoes and own clubs; no jeans. Parties welcome weekdays. *Society Meetings:* rates on application. Secretary: Mrs Dianne Harper (01642 674636; Fax: 01642 608467).

STOCKTON-ON-TEES. **Knotty Hill Golf Centre,** Sedgefield, Stockton-on-Tees TS21 2BB (Tel & Fax: 01740 620320). *Location:* A1 (M) Junction 60, one mile north of Sedgefield A177. Undulating parkland course. 18 holes, 6517 yards, 5957 metres. S.S.S 71. Floodlit driving range, practice greens, open grass tee area. *Green Fees:* 9 holes £7.00; 18 holes £12.00. *Eating facilities:* restaurant, bar. *Visitors:* welcome at all times. *Society Meetings:* welcome, information on request. Professional: Mr N. Todd. Secretary: Mrs J. Reynolds.

STOCKTON-ON-TEES. **Teesside Golf Club,** Acklam Road, Thornaby, Stockton-on-Tees TS17 7JS (01642 676249). *Location:* A19 – A1130 to Thornaby, 0.7 miles on right hand side. Flat parkland, partly tree lined. 18 holes, 6504 yards. S.S.S. 71. Practice ground. *Green Fees:* weekdays £18.00, £9.00 with a member; weekends £24.00, £13.00 with a member. Parties over 10 £14.00. *Eating facilities:* catering except Mondays, bars 11am to 11pm. *Visitors:* welcome mid-week up to 4.30pm, weekend after 11am subject to starting sheet. *Society Meetings:* catered for midweek only. Professional: K. Hall (01642 673822). Secretary: Mr W. Allen (01642 616516). *

Cornwall

BODMIN. **Lanhydrock Golf Club,** Lostwithiel Road, Bodmin PL30 5AQ (01208 73600; Fax: 01208 77325). *Location:* one-and-a-half miles outside Bodmin on B3269. Parkland, 8 bunkers only, with brooks and natural water hazards. 18 holes, 6185 yards, 5656 metres, S.S.S. 69. Practice range, club fitting. *Green Fees:* on application. 36 holes from £25.00; five-day/seven-day tickets unlimited golf. *Eating facilities:* full catering facilities available, two bars. *Visitors:* welcome, please book tee times. Lanhydrock Golf Club is part of St. Mellion International. *Society Meetings:* welcome by arrangement, private suite available. Professional: Jason Broadway. Manager: Graham Bond.

BUDE. **Bude and North Cornwall Golf Club,** Burn View, Bude EX23 8BY (01288 352006). *Location:* seaside links course situated in the centre of the town adjacent to beaches. 18 holes, 6202 yards. S.S.S. 77. Practice net and grounds. *Green Fees:* weekdays £20.00 per round or day; weekends £25.00 (subject to review). *Eating facilities:* catering and bar snacks. *Visitors:* welcome without reservation. Snooker, billiards and pool. *Society Meetings:* catered for by bookings. Professional: John Yeo (01288 353635). Secretary: Kevin Brown (01288 352006).

CAMBORNE. **Tehidy Park Golf Club,** Camborne TR14 0HH (01209 842208). *Location:* A30 via Blackwater and Camborne by-passes to sign for Portreath. Parkland, wooded, 3 new lakes. 18 holes, 6241 yards. S.S.S. 70. *Green Fees:* weekdays £21.00 per round, £27.00 per day; weekends £26.00 per round, £32.00 per day. *Eating facilities:* bar snacks, à la carte restaurant except Mondays. *Visitors:* welcome with Handicap Certificate. *Society Meetings:* by arrangement; early booking essential. Professional: J. Dumbreck (01209 842914). Secretary: John Prosser (01209 842208).

CAMELFORD. **Bowood Golf Club,** Valley Truckle, Camelford PL32 9RT (01840 213017). *Location:* M4, M5, A30, A39 through Camelford, half a mile out turn right for Tintagel/Boscastle. First left after garage. Parkland, set in an old deer park, once owned by the Black Prince. Plenty of wild life, trees and water and American style greens. Rating 10/10 Golf Monthly (October 1992). 18 holes, 6692 yards. S.S.S. 72. Teaching/practice areas, driving range. *Green Fees:* weekdays £23.00 per round, £30.00 per day; weekends £25.00 per round. *Eating facilities:* catering and bar all year round. *Visitors:* welcome, phone for tee reservations. *Society Meetings:* welcome by prior booking. Professional: Bryan Patterson. Secretary: Tony Japes. Proprietor: Ross Cobbledick. *

FALMOUTH. **Budock Vean Golf and Country House Hotel,** Near Mawnan Smith, Falmouth TR11 5LG (01326 250288). *Location:* between Helford and Falmouth, area of Helford River. 9 holes/18 tees, 5222 yards. Par 68. S.S.S. 65. *Green Fees:* weekdays and Saturdays £14.00; Sundays and Bank Holidays £18.00 for non-residents, Hotel Guests Free. *Eating facilities:* catering and bars available. *Visitors:* daily only for outside visitors who are most welcome, but must have Handicap Certificate. Hotel accommodation. Secretary: E. Duncan. Golf Manager: A. Ramsden.

FALMOUTH. **Falmouth Golf Club,** Swanpool Road, Falmouth TR11 5BQ (01326 311262).*Location:* quarter-of-a- mile west of Swanpool Beach, Falmouth, on the road to Maenporth. Wooded parkland course with magnificent views. 18 holes, 5680 yards, 5192 metres. S.S.S. 68. Five acres of practice ground. *Green Fees:* on application. Weekly or monthly tickets obtainable. *Eating facilities:* catering and bar all year round. *Visitors:* welcome at all times, except during major competitions. *Society Meetings:* are always welcome, four weeks' notice required. Professional: David Short (01326 316229). Secretary: D.J. de C. Sizer (01326 311262).

HELSTON. **Helston Golf and Leisure Pay and Play,** Wendron, Helston TR13 0LX (01326 572518). *Location:* one mile north of Helston on B3297 Redruth Road. Parkland, downland, open countryside – valley. Tee to green short course golf, 18 holes, distance 2100 yards. Par 60. Duration of play: two hours, 70 to 190 yards. *Green Fees:* £4.50 per round. *Eating facilities:* public bar, cafe, patio beer garden. The Ballpark Guest House offers accommodation and good food in the pub at £16.00 per person per night Bed and Breakfast. Free complimentary short golf for guests staying over 2 days in accommodation. Joint Owners/Proprietors: Carmen and David Robinson.

HELSTON. **Mullion Golf Club,** Cury, Helston TR12 7BP (01326 240276). *Location:* from Helston on the A3083 past Culdrose Air Station, take first right past roundabout; signposted three miles. Cliff top and links. 18 holes, 6022 yards. S.S.S. 69. *Green Fees:* £20.00 from 1st April to 30th September; £16.00 from 1st October to 31st March. *Eating facilities:* bar and catering available each day. Caterers: (01326 241231). *Visitors:* welcome, with Handicap only. *Society Meetings:* by prior arrangement. Professional: R. Goodway (01326 241176). Secretary/Treasurer: D. Watts, F.C.A. (01326 240685).

HELSTON. **RNAS Culdrose Golf Club,** Royal Naval Air Station, Helston TR12 7RH (01326 574121 ext. 2413). *Location:* at Helston on the Helston to Lizard road. Flat parkland course built around part of the airfield. 12 holes (18 tees), 6132 yards (men), 5293 (ladies). S.S.S. 70. Large practice area. *Green Fees:* weekdays £4.00, weekends £6.00. *Eating facilities:* large clubhouse with bar and hot and cold snacks. *Visitors:* must be accompanied by a club member. Professional: Custom Golf (01326 221242). Secretary: John C. Edwards (01326 562020).

LAUNCESTON. **Launceston Golf Club,** St. Stephens, Launceston PL15 8HF (01556 773442). *Location:* one mile north of town on Bude road (B3254). Parkland. 18 holes, 6407 yards. S.S.S. 71. *Green Fees:* weekdays £20.00 per day. *Eating facilities:* available. *Visitors:* welcome without reservation, no visitors weekends between 1st April and 30th September. *Society Meetings:* catered for. Professional: J. Tozer (01566 775359). Secretary: B.J. Grant (01566 773442).

LOOE. **Looe Golf Club,** Bin Down, Looe PL13 1PX (01503 240239). *Location:* three miles east of Looe on A387. Downland/parkland, fabulous views of S.E. Cornwall and beyond; designed by Harry Vardon. 18

holes, 5940 yards. S.S.S. 68. Large practice ground. *Green Fees:* on application. Five and seven day membership available. *Eating facilities:* full catering facilities available. *Visitors:* welcome, phone for tee reservations. Clubs for hire.Golf tuition available. *Society Meetings:* welcome by arrangement. Professional: Alistair MacDonald. Manager: Graham Bond.

LOSTWITHIEL. **Lostwithiel Golf and Country Club,** Lower Polscoe, Lostwithiel PL22 0HQ (01208 873550; Fax: 01208 873479). *Location:* in Lostwithiel. 9 holes hillside, 9 holes valley. 18 holes, 6101 yards. S.S.S. 71. Driving range. *Green Fees:* weekdays £15.00; weekends £19.00. *Eating facilities:* restaurant and bar snacks. *Visitors:* welcome anytime. 18 bedrooms; tennis court, indoor pool. *Society Meetings:* welcome anytime. Society rate of £25 including meals. Professional: Martin Hammond (01208 873822). Secretary: David Higman.

NEWQUAY. **Newquay Golf Club,** Tower Road, Newquay TR7 1LT (01637 872091). *Location:* 400 yards from Newquay Town Centre. Seaside links with 107 bunkers. 18 holes, 6140 yards, 5526 metres. S.S.S. 69. *Green Fees:* £20.00 per round; £75.00 per week. *Eating facilities:* lunches and bar snacks, evening meal by arrangement with the caterer on 0637 872091. *Visitors:* welcome at all times. *Society Meetings:* catered for except Sundays (£15.00). Professional: P. Muscroft (01637 874830). Secretary: G. Binney (01637 874354; Fax: 01637 874006).

NEWQUAY. **Merlin Golf Club,** Mawgan Porth, Newquay TR8 4AD (01841 540222). *Location:* on coast road between Newquay and Padstow (near Mawgan Porth). Fairly flat course. 9 holes (additional 9 holes in process of construction), 4706 yards. S.S.S. 64. Floodlit driving range. *Green Fees:* £9.00. Special rates on request. *Eating facilities:* snacks only. *Visitors:* very welcome. *Society Meetings:* very welcome. Secretary/ Proprietor: Ross Oliver (01841 540222; Fax: 01637 881057).

NEWQUAY near. **Carvynick Golf and Country Club,** Carvynick, Summercourt, Near Newquay (01872 510716). *Location:* turn off the A30 at Summercourt then take B3058 towards Newquay. Half a mile on left. Parkland and wooded course. 9 holes, 1246 yards. S.S.S. 27. *Green Fees:* information not provided. *Eating facilities:* at 16th century village inn and restaurant. *Visitors:* welcome all year. Sauna, gym, indoor swimming pool and badminton court. Holiday cottages available. Secretary: Peter Barton. *

NEWQUAY. **Treloy Golf Club,** Newquay TR7 4JN (01637 878554). *Location:* five minutes' drive from Newquay on the A3059 Newquay to St. Columb Major road. Parkland, seaside. 9 hole Executive golf course. First of its kind in Cornwall – sculptured greens, American Pencross grass, extensive mouldings and bunkers. 9 holes, 2143 yards, 1955 metres. S.S.S. 31. Practice green. *Green Fees:* 9 holes £7.50, 18 holes £11.50. *Eating facilities:* available, bar. *Visitors:* welcome. *Society Meetings:* welcome. Changing facilities, golf shop, club hire and professional tuition available on site. Secretary: Jim Reid.

PADSTOW. **Trevose Golf and Country Club,** Constantine Bay, Padstow PL28 8JB (01841 520208; Fax: 01841 521057). *Location:* off B3276, four miles west of Padstow at Constantine Bay. Seaside links course. Championship course 18 holes, 6461 yards. S.S.S. 71. 9 hole full length course (Par 35) and one 9 hole short course (Par 29). *Green Fees:* £15.00 to £30.00 depending on season. Weekly and fortnightly rates available. *Eating facilities:* restaurant 8am to 10pm, bars open 11am to 11pm. *Visitors:* welcome if checked by telephone beforehand; Handicap Certificate required. Tennis, summer outdoor swimming pool available, also self catering accommodation. *Society Meetings:* welcome if arrangements have been made. Professional: G. Alliss (01841 520261). Secretary: L. Grindley (01841 520208).

PENZANCE. **Cape Cornwall Golf and Country Club,** Cape Cornwall, St. Just, Penzance TR19 7NL (01736 788611). *Location:* signposted from St. Just-in-Penwith, seven miles west of Penzance. Cliff top course with spectacular coastal views. 18 holes, 5462 yards. S.S.S. 68. Practice putting green and golf area. *Green Fees:* weekdays £16.00; weekends £22.00. Special rates available for parties/societies over 15. *Eating facilities:* restaurant facilities lunchtime and evenings, bar all day. *Visitors:* welcome, telephone booking recommended. Heated indoor swimming pool, function room, games room. Accommodation available on site. *Society Meetings:* welcome. Professional: Mr B. Hamilton. Clubhouse Manager: Graham Addison.

PENZANCE. **Praa Sands Golf Club,** Germoe Crossroads, Near Penzance TR20 9TQ (01736 763445; Fax: 01736 763399). *Location:* midway between Helston and Penzance on A394. Seaside, parkland – beautiful sea views from all holes. 9 holes, 4104 yards. S.S.S. 60, Par 62. Putting green – net. *Green Fees:* £14.00 per round, £20.00 per day. *Eating facilities:* restaurant, bar snacks. *Visitors:* welcome every day except Sunday mornings and Friday evenings after 5pm. *Society Meetings:* catered for by arrangement. Professional: Mike Singleton. Secretary: Tony Chadwick. Proprietors: Kate and David Phillips.

PERRANPORTH. **Perranporth Golf Club,** Budnick Hill, Perranporth TR6 0AB (01872 572454). Seaside course overlooking Perranporth and beach. 18 holes, 6208 yards. S.S.S. 70. Par 72. *Green Fees:* information on request. *Eating facilities:* lunch and dinner. *Visitors:* welcome without reservation. Concessionary rates from selected holiday accommodation. *Society Meetings:* catered for with advance notice; concessionary rates. Professional: D. Michell (01872 572317). Secretary: P.D.R. Barnes (01872 573701).

REDRUTH. **Radnor Golf and Ski Centre,** Radnor Road, Treleigh, Redruth TR16 5EL (01209 211059). *Location:* two miles north east of Redruth, signposted from A3047 at Treleigh and North Country crossroads. Purpose-built Par 3 – interesting layout. 9 holes, 1312 yards. S.S.S. 52. Covered floodlit 18-bay driving range. *Green Fees:* £4.50 for 9 holes, £7.00 for 18 holes. *Eating facilities:* available. *Visitors:* welcome. Indoor ski training machine. Professional: Gordon Wallbank.

SALTASH. **St. Mellion Golf and Country Club,** Near Saltash PL12 6SD (01579 50101; Fax: 01579 50116). *Location:* A38 to Saltash, A388 from Saltash to Callington. Old Course: 18 holes, 5927 yards, par 70. S.S.S. 68. Nicklaus Course. 18 holes, 6626 yards, par 72, S.S.S. 72. *Green Fees:* on application. *Eating facilities:* many within club complex. *Visitors:* welcome, Handicap Certificate required. *Society Meetings:* welcome. Hotel accommodation: 24 rooms, full facilities (badminton, squash, swimming, tennis, sauna, solarium, multi-gym). Golf Director: D.M. Webb. Professional: Tony Moore (01579 50724).

ST. AUSTELL. **Carlyon Bay Hotel Golf Course,** Carlyon Bay, St. Austell. *Location:* St. Austell A390. Clifftop course running into parkland. 18 holes, 6505 yards. S.S.S. 71. Six acre practice ground. *Green Fees:* £20.00. Subject to review. *Eating facilities:* bar open 11.30am to 10.30pm, food available 11.30am to 9pm. *Visitors:* welcome, must phone Professional for starting times. Accommodation available in four star hotel. *Society Meetings:* catered for by arrangement. Professional: Nigel Sears (0172681 4228; Fax: 0172681 5604).

ST. AUSTELL. **St. Austell Golf Club,** Tregongeeves, Tregongeeves Lane, St. Austell PL26 7DS (01726 72649). *Location:* one mile west of St. Austell on A390 St. Austell to Truro road. Parkland course. 18 holes, 6089 yards, 5569 metres. S.S.S. 69. *Green Fees:* information on request. *Eating facilities:* full service; arrange for hot meals before play. *Visitors:* welcome with reservation, must be club members and hold

TREVOSE GOLF & COUNTRY CLUB

Constantine Bay, Padstow, North Cornwall PL28 8JJ
Telephone: (01841) 520208 Fax: (01841) 521057

Trevose offers not only Golf (Championship 18 hole Course, 9 hole Short Course plus a second 9 hole Course par 35, length 3100 yds) but also first class Club House and Restaurant, 3 hard all-weather Tennis Courts; Heated Outdoor Swimming Pool from mid May to mid September; a Pro-shop and a Boutique. Accommodation is in Bungalows, Chalets, Luxury Flats, and Double and Single Dormy Suites. Send for our detailed full colour brochure.

PRAA SANDS GOLF CLUB

PRAA SANDS,
GERMOE CROSS ROADS,
PENZANCE, CORNWALL.
Tel. PENZANCE (01736) 763445
Proprietors: David & Kate Phillips

This 9-hole golf course offers outstanding views and a deceptively challenging par 62. Situated on the main A394 Helston to Penzance Holiday Route (7 miles east of Penzance), David and Kate offer a warm welcome to one and all. After playing why not relax further in the licensed bar and enjoy a quiet meal or snack with your family? Clubs for hire. Green Fees from £14, weekly ticket £84.

Contact Kate and Dave Phillips for further details.

FAIRWAYS CARAVANS

Perranporth Golf Club

Luxury 6 berth caravans sited in Cornwall's finest links course. Families and Societies equally well catered for.
Free Golf Available. Contact: **Perranporth G.C., Budnic Hill, Perranporth, Cornwall TR6 0AB**

Telephone 01872 573701

"THE CREAM OF GOLF AT CORNWALL'S FINEST..."

"...set in 250 spectacular acres."

This spectacular clifftop 6,505 yard course stretches through the beautiful countryside of Cornwall. The Carlyon Bay Hotel Golf Course proves both interesting and challenging to golfers of all handicaps. Telephone for information and a full course layout.

- Spectacular Location
- One of Cornwall's Premier Courses
- 4 star luxury at Cornwall's finest Hotel
- Professionally managed

The Carlyon Bay Hotel

AND GOLF COURSE

AA ★★★★ RAC

St. Austell, South Cornwall PL25 8RD
Telephone St. Austell (01726) 812304

PRB
Brend Hotels
A Member of The Brend Group of Exclusive Hotels

See colour advertisement on page 6.

Pedn-Olva
HOTEL & RESTAURANTS
Porthminster Beach,
St. Ives, Cornwall TR26 2EA
Tel: 01736 796222
Fax: 01736 797710

Pedn-Olva sits on a rocky promontory overlooking St. Ives harbour. Close to 5 Links Courses. Reduced fees agreed with certain Clubs. The Hotel has 35 bedrooms, all with panoramic views of the sea. All rooms have private facilities and are very comfortably furnished. Guests can enjoy the sun on the sun soaked terrace with heated pool overlooking the beach. Break prices available October to mid-May. For further details see our colour advertisement on page 5.

DUNMAR HOTEL

Pednolver Terrace, St Ives, Cornwall TR26 2EL Tel. 01736 796117

On main road in St Ives, two minutes from town centre, one mile from seaside links.
** Wonderful coastal views ** Easy access to other courses
Family-run hotel with magnificent sea views. Most rooms ensuite.
So whether you love golf or just want a quiet break, call us on 01736 796117

THE OLD MILL COUNTRY HOUSE & Trevose Golf Club

Little Petherick, Near Padstow
Cornwall PL27 7QT
Tel: 01841 540388

This 16th century converted corn mill nestles next to a stream, retaining its character and charm whilst providing guests with modern amenities. Padstow is just two miles away and the hotel is situated close to the St. Enodoc Golf Club. Personal attention is assured from Proprietors, Michael and Pat Walker, and the dishes served in the Mill Room represent traditional cuisine at its best; residential licence.
Car parking. RAC Acclaimed, AA QQQ. ETB Commended.

The Cornish Arms

The 'CORNISH ARMS', a delightful 16th century coaching inn, must be the perfect place to stay to really enjoy your golfing holiday. ST ENODOC GOLF CLUB is just 10 minutes away with TREVOSE GOLF AND COUNTRY CLUB and ST MERRYN just a short drive, along with many other Cornish courses.

Whilst retaining the character of a traditional coaching inn, the 'CORNISH ARMS' offers all modern facilities in every bedroom; colour and satellite TV, telephone, trouser press, tea and coffee-making facilities and a complimentary copy of 'Country Life'.

The highly recommended restaurant, renowned for its food, specialises in locally caught sea food, roast duck with brandy, fillet steak stuffed with oysters and many other tempting dishes. Complement your meal with wine from our extensive cellars. 'Pendoggett Special Bitter', brewed for the Cornish Arms is famous for its strength, 'Bass' straight from the barrel, together with other real ales, makes you understand why both CAMRA and 'The Good Pub Guide', along with many others, recommend the 'CORNISH ARMS'.

A 5 MINUTE DRIVE FROM BOWOOD GOLF CLUB, CAMELFORD · SPECIAL RATES AVAILABLE

PENDOGGETT, PORT ISAAC, NORTH CORNWALL PL30 3HH
TELEPHONE 01208 880263 FACSIMILE 01208 880335

Handicap Certificate. *Society Meetings:* catered for weekdays by arrangement. Professional: M. Rowe (01726 68621). Secretary: S.H. Davey (01726 74756).

ST. IVES. **Tregenna Castle Hotel Golf Club,** Trelyon Avenue, St. Ives TR26 2DE (01736 795254; Fax: 01736 796066). *Location:* on the main road between Carbis Bay and St. Ives, half a mile from town centre. Seaside links course, wooded, with panoramic views overlooking St. Ives Harbour and Atlantic coast. 18 holes, 3549 yards. S.S.S. 59. *Green Fees:* £10.00 per round, £15.00 per day. *Eating facilities:* bar serving light snacks and refreshments. *Visitors:* welcome. 85 bedroom Hotel with restaurant, bar and wide range of leisure facilities. *Society Meetings:* prices on application; day packages available. Professional: Miss Ingrid Kemp. *

ST IVES. **West Cornwall Golf Club,** Church Lane, Lelant, St. Ives TR26 3DZ (01736 753319). *Location:* two miles from St. Ives. Seaside links – wonderful coastal views. 18 holes, 5884 yards. S.S.S. 69. Practice ground. *Green Fees:* weekdays £20.00; weekends £25.00. Five Day ticket £60.00, Seven Day ticket £80.00. *Eating facilities:* bar and restaurant. *Visitors:* must be golf club members with Handicap Certificate. Snooker table. *Society Meetings:* on written application. Professional: P. Atherton (01736 753177). Secretary: M. Lack (01736 753401).

TORPOINT. **Whitsand Bay Hotel Golf Club,** Portwrinkle, Torpoint PL11 3BU (01503 30276). *Location:* on coast six miles from Torpoint. Clifftop course. 18 holes, 5796 yards. S.S.S. 68. *Green Fees:* weekdays £12.50; weekends £15.00. *Eating facilities:* clubhouse and hotel. *Visitors:* welcome at all times with Handicap Certificate. Swimming/leisure complex. *Society Meetings:* catered for and hotel accommodation arranged on application to hotel. Professional: D.S. Poole (01503 30778). Secretary: G.G. Dyer (01503 30418). Hotel: (01503 30276).

TRURO. **Killiow Golf Club,** Killiow, Kea, Truro (01872 70246; Fax: 01872 40915). *Location:* three miles from Truro on A39 Truro/Falmouth road. Wooded parkland, picturesque setting with water features. 18 holes, 3542 yards. S.S.S. 57. All-weather floodlit driving range, practice bunker and putting green. *Green Fees:* £10.00 per round. *Eating facilities:* club bar and bar snacks. *Visitors:* course restricted to members until 10.30am at weekends, available at all other times. *Society Meetings:* welcome by arrangement through office – tel or fax. Professional: (visiting) David Short; D. Mitchell. Secretary: J. Penrose (01872 72768).

TRURO. **Truro Golf Club,** Treliske, Truro TR1 3LG (01872 72640). *Location:* two miles west of Truro on A390 to Redruth. Undulating parkland. 18 holes, 5357 yards. S.S.S. 66. *Green Fees:* weekdays £18.00 per day or round, weekends and Bank Holidays £22.00 per day or round. *Eating facilities:* available. *Visitors:* welcome with Handicap Certificates but restrictions on competition days, Tuesdays and weekends. *Society Meetings:* catered for on weekdays. Professional: N.K. Bicknell (01872 76595). Secretary: B.E. Heggie (01872 78684).

WADEBRIDGE. **St. Enodoc Golf Club,** Rock, Wadebridge PL27 6LB (01208 863216; Fax: 01208 862976). *Location:* take the B3314 from Wadebridge, signposted Rock (three miles). Seaside links. Two courses: Church Course 18 holes, 6243 yards. S.S.S. 69; Holywell Course 18 holes, 4134 yards. S.S.S. 61. Practice range, putting greens, etc. *Green Fees:* Church Course – weekdays £22.00 per round, £35.00 per day; weekends £27.00 per round, £40.00 per day. Holywell Course – £12.00 per round, £18.00 per day. *Eating facilities:* restaurant and bar snacks. *Visitors:* Handicap Certificates (24 and below) required for Church Course; no restrictions for Holywell Course. *Society Meetings:* all welcome by arrangement with the Secretary. Professional: Nick Williams (01208 862402). Secretary: Mr L. Guy.

Isles of Scilly

ST MARY'S. **Isles of Scilly Golf Club,** St. Mary's, Isles of Scilly (01720 22692). *Location:* one mile from Hugh Town, St. Mary's. Heathland by the sea with magnificent views. 9 holes, 3025 yards, 2791 metres. S.S.S. 69. Par 73. *Green Fees:* information not provided. *Eating facilities:* lunches and evening meals available. *Visitors:* welcome weekdays; Sunday play with member only. Secretary: Steve Watt (01720 22536).

Cumbria

ALSTON. **Alston Moor Golf Club,** The Hermitage, Middleton in Teesdale Road, Alston CA9 3DB (01434 381675). *Location:* one-and-three-quarter miles from Alston on B6277 to Barnard Castle. Penrith, Hexham, Carlisle all within 30 miles. Parkland with panoramic views (highest golf course in England). 10 holes, 5456 yards. S.S.S. 66. Practice ground. *Green Fees:* weekdays £8.00; Saturdays and Bank Holidays £10.00, Sundays £15.00. Reduction when playing with a member. *Eating facilities:* 19th Hole bar, catering available by prior notice. *Visitors:* welcome anytime, prior notice required for groups. Competitions most Sundays, tee reserved 9am to 10am and 1pm to 2.30pm. *Society Meetings:* welcome by arrangement. Secretary: Mr H. Robinson (01434 381354).

APPLEBY. **Appleby Golf Club,** Brackenber Moor, Appleby-in-Westmorland (Appleby (017683) 51432). *Location:* off A66 at Coupland Beck, two miles south of Appleby. Moorland course. 18 holes, 5914 yards. S.S.S. 68. *Green Fees:* weekdays £12.00; weekends £16.00. *Eating facilities:* available except Tuesdays. *Visitors:* welcome without reservation. *Society Meetings:* catered for by prior arrangement. Secretary: B.W. Rimmer.

ASKAM-IN-FURNESS. **Dunnerholme Golf Club,** Duddon Road, Askam-in-Furness LA16 7AW (01229 462675). *Location:* A595 Askam-in-Furness, over level crossing. Seaside links with stream on four holes. 10 holes (18 tees), 6154 yards. S.S.S. 69 white, 70 red. Practice area. *Green Fees:* weekdays £12.00 per day; weekends £15.00 per day. *Eating facilities:* catering for groups by arrangement. *Visitors:* welcome without reservation, excluding competition days. Handicap Certificate required. Competitions Saturday mornings and Sundays May to October. Pool. *Society Meetings:* catered for by prior arrangement. Secretary: M.E. Tyson (01229 581400 mornings, 01229 889326 pm).

BARROW-IN-FURNESS. **Barrow Golf Club,** Rakesmoor Lane, Hawcoat, Barrow-in-Furness LA14 4QB (01229 825444). *Location:* one mile from Barrow town centre, approach via Dalton By-pass, turn left at Dalton Lane opposite "Scotts" Paper Mill. Clubhouse 400 yards on the left. 18 holes, 6209 yards, 5679 metres. S.S.S. 70. *Green Fees:* weekdays £15.00, £10.00 if playing with a member; weekends and Bank Holidays £25.00. *Eating facilities:* available. *Visitors:* welcome without reservation, must be member of recognised golf club. Ladies' Day – Fridays. *Society Meetings:* up to 40 catered for by prior arrangement. Professional: N. Hyde (01229 831212). Secretary: J. Slater (01229 826968).

BARROW-IN-FURNESS. **Furness Golf Club,** Central Drive, Walney Island, Barrow-in-Furness LA14 3LN (01229 471232). *Location:* A590 into Barrow, follow sign to Walney Island, over bridge, straight on at lights. Clubhouse half a mile on right hand side. Seaside links. 18 holes, 6363 yards. S.S.S. 71. Practice area. *Green Fees:* weekdays £15.00, (£10.00 with member); Societies £8.00 per head for parties numbering over 12. *Eating facilities:* full bar meals, lunch and evening meals. *Visitors:* parties by prior arrangement, others without reservation; must hold current Handicap Certificate. Ladies' Day – Wednesdays; Competition Days – Saturdays or Sundays in summer. *Society Meetings:* welcome (tee reservation by prior arrangement). Secretary: W.T. French.

BRAMPTON. **Brampton Golf Club,** Talkin Tarn, Brampton CA8 1HN (016977 2255). *Location:* situated on the Brampton-Castle Carrock road (B6413), approximately one and a half miles from Brampton. Rolling fell countryside, excellent views. 18 holes, 6420 yards. S.S.S. 71. *Green Fees:* on application. Practice facilities available plus snooker and pool tables. *Eating facilities:* catering available every day during playing season and on most days during winter period. *Visitors:* welcome without reservation, but should avoid Sunday, Monday, Wednesday and Thursday mornings. *Society Meetings:* catered for, limited numbers at weekends. Contact for visiting Societies, J.F. Swift (01228 36699). Professional: S. Harrison (016977 2000). Secretary: Ian J. Meldrum (01228 23155). *

CARLISLE. **Carlisle Golf Club,** Aglionby, Carlisle CA4 8AG (01228 513303). *Location:* on A69 Newcastle Road, half a mile from Junction 43 of M6. Parkland. 18 holes, 6278 yards. S.S.S. 70. Practice area. *Green Fees:* weekdays £20.00 per round, £27.50 per day; £35.00 Sundays only. Package deals for parties of 12 or more on application. *Eating facilities:* snacks, lunches, dinners and high teas. *Visitors:* welcome Mondays to Fridays and Sundays. *Society Meetings:* catered for Mondays, Wednesdays and Fridays, parties of 12 of more. Professional: John S. Moore (01228 513241). Administrator/Secretary: J. Hook.

CARLISLE. **Dalston Hall Golf Club,** Dalston Hall, Dalston, Carlisle CA5 7JX (01228 710165). *Location:* leave M6 at Exit 42, take road to Dalston; at Dalston turn onto B5299, course on the right after one mile. Scenic parkland course. 9 holes, 5294 yards. S.S.S. 67. Practice area. *Green Fees:* weekdays £4.00 9 holes, £7.00 18 holes; weekends £6.00 9 holes, £11.00 18 holes. *Eating facilities:* full catering and bar facilities. *Visitors:* welcome, tee reservation is required at weekends and after 4pm during the week. *Society Meetings:* welcome by prior arrangement. Secretary: Jane Simpson (01228 710165).

CARLISLE. **Stoneyholme Municipal Golf Club,** St. Aidans Road, Carlisle (01228 33208). *Location:* off A69 between M6 Junction 42 and town. Parkland course, 18 holes, 6000 yards. S.S.S. 68. Large practice area, changing rooms. *Green Fees:* information not available. *Eating facilities:* bar and restaurant. *Visitors:* welcome without reservation, but booking advisable weekends and Bank Holidays. *Society Meetings:* welcome by prior arrangement. Professional: Stephen Ling (01228 34856). *

CARLISLE. **The Eden Golf Course,** Crosby-on-Eden, Carlisle CA6 4RA (01228 573003; Fax: 01228 818435). *Location:* M6 Junction 44, take A689 to Crosby-on-Eden village. Championship parkland course featuring six lakes and the River Eden adjacent. 18 holes, 6368 yards. S.S.S. 72. 16 bay floodlit driving range and practice area. *Green Fees:*weekdays £15.00; weekends £20.00. Discount for visiting parties of over 10 players. *Eating facilities:* new clubhouse offering full catering facilities. *Visitors:* welcome at all times. *Society Meetings:* welcome at all times. Professional: Phil Harrison. Secretary: Denis Willey.

EMBLETON. **Cockermouth Golf Club,** The Clubhouse, Embleton, Near Cockermouth CA13 9SG (017687 76223). *Location:* second exit A66 to Embleton across Old Road and up 1:5 hill. Scenic fell land course. 18 holes, 5457 yards. S.S.S. 67. *Green Fees:* weekdays £12.00; weekends and Bank Holidays £18.00. *Eating facilities:* meals by arrangement with Stewardess. *Visitors:* welcome; only with members at weekends. *Society Meetings:* catered for mid week only. Secretary: R.D. Pollard (01900 822650).

GRANGE-OVER-SANDS. **Grange Fell Golf Club,** Fell Road, Grange-over-Sands LA11 6HB (015395 32536). *Location:* Cartmel Road from Grange one mile. Hillside course with panoramic views. 9 holes, 4826 metres. S.S.S. 66. *Green Fees:* weekdays £10.00, weekends and Bank Holidays £15.00. *Visitors:* welcome without reservation. *Society Meetings:* not catered for. Secretary: J.B. Asplin (015395 32021).

GRANGE-OVER-SANDS. **Grange-over-Sands Golf Club,** Meathop Road, Grange-over-Sands LA11 6QX (015395 33180). *Location:* leave the A590 at roundabout signposted Grange, take the B5277 for approximately three miles. Flat parkland. 18 holes, 5958 yards, 5422 metres. S.S.S. 69. Practice area, bunker, green. *Green Fees:* weekdays £15.00 per round, £20.00 per day; weekends and Bank Holidays £20.00 per round, £25.00 per day. *Eating facilities:* diningroom, bar open every day except Tuesdays. *Visitors:* welcome without reservation weekdays and most weekends. *Society Meetings:* by arrangement with Secretary. Professional: Steve Sumner-Roberts (015395 35937). Secretary: J.R. Green (015395 33754).

KENDAL. **Kendal Golf Club,** The Heights, Kendal (01539 724079). *Location:* off A6 at Town Hall, signposted. 18 holes, 5515 yards. S.S.S. 67. *Green Fees:* £16.00 (£8.00 with member), weekends £20.00 (£10.00 with member). *Eating facilities:* meals available any day except Mondays. *Visitors:* welcome without reservation. Professional: D.J. Turner (01539 723499). Secretary: D. Leack (01539 733708). Manager: R.E. Maunder.

KESWICK. **Keswick Golf Club,** Threlkeld Hall, Threlkeld, Keswick CA12 4SX (017687 79013). *Location:* four miles from Keswick on A66 road to Penrith. Scenic fell and parkland course. 18 holes, 6175 yards. S.S.S. 72, Par 71. Extensive practice area. *Green Fees:* weekdays £15.00; weekends £20.00. Societies 12 or more £12.00 weekdays, £15.00 weekends and Public Holidays. *Eating facilities:* daily by arrangement (Caterer: (017687 79013); bar. *Visitors:* welcome, Ladies' Day Thursdays 12 noon to 1.30pm. *Society Meetings:* welcome by arrangement, unrestricted weekdays, 11.30am to 12.30pm weekends. Professional: Craig Hamilton (017687 79010). Secretary: Richard Bell (017687 79324).

KIRKBY LONSDALE. **Kirkby Lonsdale Golf Club,** Scalebar Lane, Barbon, Kirkby Lonsdale, Carnforth, Lancs LA6 2LJ (01468 36366). *Location:* three and a half miles from Kirkby Lonsdale on the A638 Sedbergh Road. Parkland, over Barbon Beck and sweeping down to the River Lune. 18 holes, 6280 yards. S.S.S. 70. Practice area. *Green Fees:* weekdays £16.00; weekends £20.00. Subject to review. *Eating facilities:* limited dining and bar facilities. *Visitors:* welcome, no restrictions except on competition days. Handicap Certificates required. *Society Meetings:* welcome by arrangement. Package deal available. Professional: Chris Barrett (015242 76366). Secretary: Mike Curtin (015242 76365).

MARYPORT. **Maryport Golf Club,** Bankend, Maryport (01900 812605). *Location:* approximately one mile northeast of Maryport on B5300 towards Silloth. 9 holes links extended to 18 with new holes parkland type, exposed, relatively flat. 18 holes, 6088 yards. S.S.S. 69. *Green Fees:* weekdays £15.00 per round/day; weekends £20.00. £10.00 per round/day if playing with a member. *Eating facilities:* available. *Visitors:* welcome, no restrictions. *Society Meetings:* catered for by prior arrangement. Secretary: F.L. Moss (01900 812140).

MILLOM. **Silecroft Golf Club,** Silecroft, Millom LA18 4NX (01229 774250). *Location:* on the coast near Junction A595 and A5093. Three miles north of Millom, eight miles west of Broughton-in-Furness. Flat/seaside links – good greens. 9 holes (18 tees), 5877 yards. S.S.S. 68 (67 off Yellow tees). Practice area. *Green Fees:* weekdays £10; weekends £15. *Eating facilities:* catering available at nearby public house (Silecroft Miners Arms), bar at club. *Visitors:* welcome, though generally not in the evenings, weekends, Bank Holidays or on competition days. Secretary: D. MacLardie (01229 774342).

PENRITH. **Penrith Golf Club,** Salkeld Road, Penrith CA11 8SG (01768 65429). *Location:* off M6 at Junction 41, course on north east of town. Parkland course with panoramic views to Lakeland hills. 18 holes, 6026 yards. S.S.S. 69. *Green Fees:* weekdays £20.00 first round, £25.00 second round; weekends and Bank Holidays £25.00 first round, £30.00 second round. *Eating facilities:* all day catering. *Visitors:* casual visitors in parties of less than 8, no booking except at weekends when tee time required. *Society Meetings:* by appointment. Professional: C.B. Thomson (01768 891919). Secretary: D. Noble (01768 891919).

SEASCALE. **Seascale Golf Club,** The Banks, Seascale CA20 1QL (Tel & Fax: 019467 28202). *Location:* B5344 off A595 to north of village. Links. 18 holes, 6416 yards. S.S.S. 71. 16-acre practice ground. *Green Fees:* weekdays £19.00; weekends £23.00. Three-day rate £45.00. 10% reduction for parties up to 12. *Eating facilities:* catering limited on Mondays and Tuesdays, bar available every day. *Visitors:* welcome when no tee reservations in force. *Society Meetings:* catered for by arrangement with Secretary. Secretary: C. Taylor.

SEDBERGH. **Sedbergh Golf Club,** Catholes – Abbot Holme, Sedbergh LA10 5SS (015396 21551). *Location:* one mile out of Sedbergh on road to Dent, well signposted. Superbly scenic course in Yorkshire Dales National Park – easy walking, not hilly. 9 holes, 5588 yards. S.S.S. 68. *Green Fees:* weekdays £12.00 per round, £18.00 per day; weekends £15.00 per round, £21.00 per day. *Eating facilities:* all day catering, normal bar hours. *Visitors:* welcome but prior booking advisable, weekends booking essential. Good local accommodation easily arranged via Secretary. *Society Meetings:* very welcome by prior arrangement. Secretary: David Lord (Tel & Fax: 015396 20993).

SILLOTH. **Silloth on Solway Golf Club,** The Clubhouse, Silloth, Carlisle (016973 31304). *Location:* M6 Junction 41 – B5305 to Wigton, B5302 Silloth. Seaside links, rated in the best five links courses in England. 18 holes, 6445 yards. S.S.S. 72. Practice facilities. *Green Fees:* weekdays £25 per day; weekends and Bank Holidays £30 per round. Subject to review. Restriction, only one round allowed per day at weekends. *Eating facilities:* full bar and catering. *Visitors:* welcome without reservation. *Society Meetings:* welcome midweek, maximum 40 catered for weekends, one round per day. Professional: John Burns. Secretary: John G. Proudlock (016973 31782).

ULVERSTON. **Ulverston Golf Club Ltd,** Bardsea Park, Ulverston LA12 9QJ (01229 52824). *Location:* Exit 36, M6. A590 to Barrow then A5087 to Bardsea village. Wooded parkland. 18 holes, 6142 yards. S.S.S. 70. *Green Fees:* weekdays £20.00, weekends and Bank Holidays £25.00. November to February £14.00 and £18.00; Juniors half price. *Eating facilities:* lunch and bar snacks (except Mondays and Fridays after 1.45pm). *Visitors:* welcome except Saturdays (competition day), and Tuesdays (Ladies' day). Must be members of accredited golf club and have a handicap. *Society Meetings:* welcome, write with reservation to the Match Secretary. Professional: M.R. Smith (01229 52806). Secretary: P. Wedgwood.

WHITEHAVEN. **St. Bees Golf Club,** Whitehaven (Whitehaven (01946) 822695). *Location:* four miles south of Whitehaven. 9 holes, 5079 yards. S.S.S. 65. *Green Fees:* information not provided. *Visitors:* unrestricted. Secretary: J.B. Campbell, Rhoda Grove, Rheda, Frizington CA26 3TE (01946 812105). *

WINDERMERE. **Windermere Golf Club,** Cleabarrow, Windermere LA23 3NB (015394 43123). *Location:* one mile from Bowness-on-Windermere on Crook road, B5284. Idyllic National Park setting. 18 holes, 5006 yards. S.S.S. 65. Practice ground. *Green Fees:* weekdays £23.00; weekends £28.00. *Eating facilities:* restaurant. *Visitors:* welcome with bona fide handicaps and if members of recognised golf clubs. *Society Meetings:* catered for by prior arrangement with Secretary, numbers from twelve to 50, corporate days by arrangement. Professional: W.S.M. Rooke (015394 43550). Secretary: K.R. Moffat (015394 43123).

WORKINGTON. **Workington Golf Club Ltd,** Branthwaite Road, Workington (01900 603460). *Location:* on A596, two miles east of town. Meadowland. 18 holes, 6252 yards. S.S.S. 70. *Green Fees:* weekdays £17.00, weekends and Bank Holidays £22.00. *Eating facilities:* lunches and dinners except Mondays and Thursdays. *Visitors:* welcome without reservation, must be members of recognised golf club. *Society Meetings:* welcome by prior arrangement. Professional: A. Drabble (01900 67828). Secretary: M.W. Addison (01900 603460).

NOTE

All the information in this book is given in good faith in the belief that it is correct. However, the publishers cannot guarantee the facts given in these pages, neither are they responsible for changes in policy, ownership or terms that may take place after the date of going to press. Readers should always satisfy themselves that the facilities they require are available and that the terms, if quoted, still apply.

Derbyshire

ALFRETON. **Alfreton Golf Club,** Wingfield Road, Alfreton (01773 832070). *Location:* B6024 (Matlock Road) one mile from Alfreton. 9 holes, 5012 yards. S.S.S. 65. *Green Fees:* £13.00 per round, £17.00 per day weekdays; weekends only with member. *Eating facilities:* lunches except Mondays. *Visitors:* welcome with reservation. *Society Meetings:* catered for. Professional: N. Hallam. Secretary: T. McKenzie.

ASHBOURNE. **Ashbourne Golf Club Ltd,** Clifton, Ashbourne (01335 42078). *Location:* on A515 Ashbourne to Lichfield, one and a half miles out of Ashbourne. Undulating parkland. 9 holes, 4960 yards. S.S.S. 66. *Green Fees:* weekdays £14.00. *Eating facilities:* catering available by prior arrangement with Steward; bar. *Visitors:* welcome most weekdays. *Society Meetings:* by arrangement. Secretary: N.P.A. James (01335 42077). *

BAKEWELL. **Bakewell Golf Club,** Station Road, Bakewell (01629 812307). *Location:* Sheffield Road out of Bakewell, turn right over River Bridge. Parkland, scenic hillside course. 9 holes, 5240 yards. S.S.S. 68. *Green Fees:* weekdays £12.00; weekends £16.00 by arrangement only. *Eating facilities:* available except Mondays. *Visitors:* welcome weekdays only unless accompanied by a member. *Society Meetings:* welcome, but available weekdays only. Professional: T.E. Jones. Secretary: T.P. Turner.

BURTON-ON-TRENT. **Burton-on-Trent Golf Club,** 43 Ashby Road East, Burton-on-Trent DE15 0PS (01283 68708). *Location:* three miles east of Burton-on-Trent on the left hand side of the A50. Undulating and mature parkland course. 18 holes, 6579 yards, 6017 metres. S.S.S. 71. Practice ground. *Green Fees:* weekdays £20.00 per round, £25.00 per day, weekends and Bank Holidays £25.00 per round, £30.00 per day. *Eating facilities:* bar open daily, diningroom/bar snacks except Mondays. *Visitors:* welcome during the week, not weekends. Ladies' day Tuesday, therefore some restrictions. *Society Meetings:* catered for, write to enquire. Professional: Gary Stafford (01283 62240). Secretary: D. Hartley (01283 44551).

BUXTON. **Buxton and High Peak Golf Club,** Town End, Buxton SK17 7EN (01298 23453). *Location:* A6 one mile north of Buxton. Gently undulating open Peak District countryside. 18 holes, 5980 yards. S.S.S. 69. *Green Fees:* weekdays £20.00; weekends £25.00. *Eating facilities:* full catering facilities except Thursdays. *Visitors:* welcome without reservation, ring at weekends. *Society Meetings:* up to 40 welcome. Contact Mrs S. Arnfield. Professional: A. Hoyles (01298 23112). Secretary: J.M. Williams (01298 26263).

BUXTON. **The Cavendish Golf Club Ltd,** Gadley Lane, Buxton SK17 6XD (01298 23494). *Location:* three quarters of a mile from town centre, on Leek Road A53, signposted. Parkland/moorland course, designed by Dr Alastair McKenzie who designed Augusta. 18 holes, 5833 yards. S.S.S. 68. Practice ground. *Green Fees:* £25.00 per round weekdays; £35.00 per round weekends. Juniors half price and visitors half price if playing with a member. Visiting parties £22.00. *Eating facilities:* usual bar hours, snacks, meals available at all times. *Visitors:* apply to Professional. Snooker. *Society Meetings:* catered for weekdays only except Thursdays, apply to the Professional for booking arrangements. Professional: Paul Hunstone (01298 25052). Secretary: J.A. Lockley (01298 23494).

CHAPEL-EN-LE-FRITH. **Chapel-en-le-Frith Golf Club,** The Cockyard, Manchester Road, Chapel-en-le-Frith SK12 6UH (01298 812118). *Location:* midway between Sheffield and Manchester, 25 miles from each on the B5470. Parkland, scenic. 18 holes, 6119 yards. S.S.S. 69. Practice ground. *Green Fees:* weekdays £20.00, weekends £30.00. *Eating facilities:* all meals daily except Mondays. *Visitors:* welcome, small numbers without reservation. *Society Meetings:* catered for by arrangement. Professional: D. Cullen (01298 812118). Secretary: J.W. Dranfield (01298 813943).

CHESTERFIELD. **Chesterfield Golf Club Ltd,** The Clubhouse, Walton, Chesterfield S42 7LA (01246 279256). *Location:* two miles from Chesterfield town centre on Matlock road (A632). Parkland. 18 holes, 6247 yards. S.S.S. 70. Practice ground. *Green Fees:* weekdays £22.00 per round, £27.00 per day; weekends as member's guest only. *Eating facilities:* full catering (dining room), two bars. *Visitors:* weekdays only. *Society Meetings:* catered for on application except weekends. Professional: Michael McLean (01246 276297). Secretary: K. Bradshaw (01246 279256).

CHESTERFIELD. **Chesterfield Municipal Golf Course,** Murray House, Crow Lane, Chesterfield S41 0EQ (01246 203960). *Location:* behind railway station. Wooded parkland course. 18 hole course and 9 hole pitch and putt course. 27 holes, 6025 yards. S.S.S. 69. *Green Fees:* weekdays £5.50, £3.00 9 holes; weekends £7.00, £4.00 9 holes. Concessions for unemployed and retired persons. *Eating facilities:* bar open to the public; restaurant. *Visitors:* welcome. Professional: Carl Weatherhead. Secretary: Mr J. Hearnshaw. *

CHESTERFIELD. **Grassmoor Golf Centre,** North Wingfield Road, Grassmoor, Chesterfield S42 5EA (01246 856044). *Location:* Grassmoor near Chesterfield, M1 Junction 29 or A61. Heathland course incorporating many water hazards. 18 holes, 5715 yards. S.S.S. 68. 26 bay floodlit driving range. *Green Fees:* non members £6.00, members £5.00 weekdays; non members £7.00, members £6.00 weekends. Driving range open daily till 10pm, £2.00 per 80 balls. *Eating facilities:* available 8am to 11pm seven days a week. *Visitors:* welcome. *Society Meetings:* all welcome including at weekends. Professional: Jim Gallagher. Secretary: Andrew Clark (01246 856044).

CHESTERFIELD. **Stanedge Golf Club,** Walton Hay Farm, Chesterfield S45 0LW (01246 566156). *Location:* five miles south-west of Chesterfield, off B5057 near "Red Lion" public house. 9 holes, 4867 yards. S.S.S. 64. *Green Fees:* weekdays £15.00, £7.50 with member; Saturdays and Bank Holidays £15.00, must be playing with member. *Visitors:* welcome by prior arrangement. Must book in by 2pm Monday to Fridays. No visitors on Sundays until 4pm and they must be with member. *Society Meetings:* catered for by prior arrangement. Secretary: W.C. Tyzack (01246 276568).

CHESTERFIELD. **Tapton Park Golf Club,** Murray House, Crow Lane, Chesterfield (01246 203960). *Location:* head for Chesterfield railway station, turn left onto Crow Lane, 250 yards on. Parkland course. 18 holes, 6025 yards. S.S.S. 69. Also 9 hole course, 2478 yards. *Green Fees:* information not provided. *Eating facilities:* meals and bar all day. *Visitors:* welcome without reservation. Coaching by qualified PGA staff. *Society Meetings:* welcome with reservations. Municipal course, open to general public. Professional: Carl Weatherhead. Secretary: G.C. Howard (01246 854588). *

CODNOR. **Ormonde Fields Golf Club,** Nottingham Road, Codnor, Ripley DE5 9RG (01773 744157). *Location:* five miles M1 Junction 26 towards Ripley on A610. Parkland. 18 holes, 6011 yards. S.S.S. 69. Practice area, putting green. *Green Fees:* £15.00 weekdays, £20.00 weekends. *Eating facilities:* full restaurant available. *Visitors:* unrestricted. *Society Meetings:* catered for; book through Secretary. Professional: P. Buttifant (01773 742987). Secretary: R.N. Walters (01773 570043).

DERBY. **Allestree Park Golf Club,** Allestree Hall, Allestree, Derby (Derby (01332) 552971). *Location:* 2 miles north of city centre on A6. Municipal course – hilly parkland. 18 holes, 5749 yards. S.S.S. 68. *Green Fees:* information not provided. *Eating facilities:* full bar, catering arranged with Steward. *Visitors:* booking sheet at weekends, weekday bookings available for parties through Professional. Professional: C. Henderson (01332 550616). Secretary: G. Rawson. *

DERBY. **Breadsall Priory Hotel, Golf and Country Club,** Moor Road, Morley DE7 6DL (Tel & Fax: 01332 832534 leisure club). *Location:* turn off the A61 towards Breadsall, proceed on Croft Lane, turn left into Rectory Lane, then bear right onto Moor Road, continue past the Church for approximately one mile. Two courses – Priory is a parkland course and Moorland is a contrast of open moorland. Priory – 18 holes, 5871 yards. S.S.S. 68 off yellow tees; Moorland – 18 holes, 5820 yards. S.S.S.S. 68 off yellow tees. Practice area and putting green. *Green Fees:* £27.50 weekdays; £29.50 weekends. Golf Packages available. *Eating facilities:* Hotel – Priory Restaurant and cocktail bar; leisure club – poolside bar and Mullarkeys Restaurant. *Visitors:* welcome any time subject to availability. *Society Meetings:* catered for by prior arrangement, rates on application. Hotel has 91 bedrooms, leisure club and conference facilities. Professional: Andrew Smith (01332 834425). Golf Manager: Patricia Straw (01332 832534).

DUFFIELD. **Chevin Golf Club,** Golf Lane, Duffield DE56 4EE (01332 840497). *Location:* five miles north of Derby on A6 at Duffield village. Hilly course. 18 holes, 6057 yards, 5451 metres. S.S.S. 69. Two practice areas. *Green Fees:* £27.00 per day. *Eating facilities:* bar snacks and diningroom. *Visitors:* welcome weekdays, Handicap Certificates required. Snooker. *Society Meetings:* welcome weekdays, but never weekends. Professional: W. Bird (01332 841112). Secretary: C.P. Elliott (01332 841864).

GLOSSOP. **Glossop and District Golf Club,** Sheffield Road, Glossop SK13 9PU (01457 865247). *Location:* off A57, one mile from town centre. Moorland course. 11 holes, 5800 yards. S.S.S. 68. *Green Fees:* weekdays £15.00 per round; weekends £20.00 per round. *Eating facilities:* full catering facilities available. *Visitors:* welcome with reservation through Professional, except Saturdays during playing season. *Society Meetings:* welcome, same restrictions as visitors. Professional: Gary S. Brown (01457 853117). Secretary: D.M. Pridham (0161-339 3959). *

HORSLEY. **Horsley Lodge Golf Club,** Smalley Mill Road, Horsley DE21 5BL (01332 780838; Fax: 01332 781118). *Location:* north of Derby on A61, past Little Eaton, right turn signposted. Parkland. 18 holes, 6432 yards, 5901 metres. S.S.S. 71. Driving range. *Green Fees:* £17.00; £12.00 societies. Free golf for residents. *Eating facilities:* two bars, bar meals, à la carte restaurant; function room seats 140. *Visitors:* welcome weekdays and some weekends but not on competition days. Four bedroom accommodation available. *Society Meetings:* by appointment. Professional: Simon Berry (01332 781400). Company Secretary: Richard Salt. Hon. Secretary (club): George Johnson (01332 880599).

ILKESTON. **Erewash Valley Golf Club Ltd,** Stanton-by-Dale, Near Ilkeston DE7 4QR (01602 323258). *Location:* Junction 25 of the M1, Stanton-by-Dale village. Parkland with two holes in an old quarry. 18 holes, 6487 yards. S.S.S. 71. *Green Fees:* weekdays £22.00 per round, £27.00 per day; weekends and Bank Holidays £27.00 per round. DUGC Card half price. *Eating facilities:* bar snacks available at all times, diningroom service on request. *Visitors:* welcome all week subject to club events and society bookings. *Society Meetings:* welcome weekdays only. Professional: Mike Ronan (01602 324667). Secretary: J.A. Beckett (01602 322984).

ILKESTON. **Ilkeston Borough Golf Club,** Peewit Municipal Golf Course, West End Drive, Ilkeston (01602 304550). *Location:* one mile west of Ilkeston market place. Slightly hilly meadowland. 9 holes, 4116 yards. S.S.S. 60. *Green Fees:* information not available. *Eating facilities:* not available. *Visitors:* welcome, no restrictions. Secretary: B. Smith (01602 302114).

MATLOCK. **Matlock Golf Club Ltd,** Chesterfield Road, Matlock DE4 5LF (01629 582191). *Location:* Matlock-Chesterfield road, A632, one mile out of Matlock, left hand side main road. Moorland with extensive views. 18 holes, yellow tees, 5801 yards. S.S.S. 68. *Green Fees:* weekdays £25.00; weekends and Bank Holidays £12.50 with a member only. *Eating facilities:* snacks available, luncheons and evening meals by arrangement (except on Mondays). *Visitors:* welcome weekdays. *Society Meetings:* catered for Tuesday to Friday. Professional: M.A. Whithorn (01629 584934). Secretary: A.J. Box.

MICKLEOVER. **Mickleover Golf Club,** Uttoxeter Road, Mickleover, Derby DE3 5AD (01332 513339). *Location:* three miles west of Derby on the A516/B5020 to Uttoxeter. Undulating. 18 holes, 5708 yards, 5222 metres. S.S.S. 68. *Green Fees:* weekdays £20.00, weekends and Bank Holidays £25.00. Society rates on request. *Eating facilities:* bar snacks available. *Visitors:* welcome, no restrictions – telephone Professional before arrival. *Society Meetings:* Tuesdays and Thursdays. Professional: Tim Coxon (01332 518662). Secretary: Doug Rodgers (01332 516011).

MICKLEOVER. **Pastures Golf Club,** Pastures Hospital, Mickleover (01332 521074 extension 419). *Location:* four miles west of Derby, A516. Undulating meadowland. 9 holes, 5005 yards, 4578 metres. S.S.S. 64. Practice area. *Green Fees:* £10.00 weekdays and Saturdays, no green fees Sundays. *Eating facilities:* bar facilities/snacks. *Visitors:* welcome every day except Sundays when must be with a member. *Society Meetings:* by arrangement. Secretary: S. McWilliams (01332 521074 extension 348).

QUARNDON. **Kedleston Park Golf Club,** Kedleston, Quarndon, Derby DE22 5JD. *Location:* four miles north of Derby on Kedleston Hall Estate – National Trust. Parkland with lakes. 18 holes, 6636 yards, 6068 metres. S.S.S. 72. *Green Fees:* weekdays £25.00 per round, £35.00 per day. *Eating facilities:* full catering, bars. *Visitors:* welcome Monday to Friday; weekends with member. *Society Meetings:* welcome Monday to Friday. Professional: J. Hetherington (01332 841685). Secretary: K. Wilson (01332 840035).

RISLEY. **Maywood Golf Club,** Off Rushy Lane, Risley, Draycott (0115 939 2306). *Location:* between Derby and Nottingham at Risley, two minutes from Junction 25 M1. Parkland course. 18 holes, 6424 yards. S.S.S. 71. Practice area. *Green Fees:* weekdays £15.00, weekends £20.00. *Eating facilities:* licensed bar and snacks. *Society Meetings:* rates on request. Proprietors: P. and B. Moon.

SHEFFIELD. **Renishaw Park Golf Club,** Golf House, Station Road, Renishaw, Sheffield S31 9UZ (01246 432044). *Location:* A616 Barlborough (Junction 30 M1) to Sheffield. Parkland/meadowland. 18 holes, 6523 yards. S.S.S. 70. Practice net. *Green Fees:* weekdays £20.00 per round, £28.00 per day; weekends £33.00 per round/day. *Eating facilities:* bar meals, full restaurant. *Visitors:* welcome without reservation (advisable to ring Pro prior to arrival). *Society Meetings:* by prior arrangement. Full day package available. Professional: S. Elliott (01246 435484). Secretary: L.T. Hughes (01246 432044).

SHEFFIELD. **Sickleholme Golf Club,** Bamford, Sheffield S30 2BH (01433 651306). *Location:* A625 west of Sheffield, right at Marquis of Granby, Bamford. 18 holes, 6064 yards. S.S.S. 69. *Green Fees:* information not available. *Eating facilities:* by arrangement. *Visitors:* must be members of a recognised Golf Club. *Society Meetings:* catered for by arrangement. Professional/Manager: P. H. Taylor (01433 651252). *

SHIRLAND. **Shirland Golf Club,** Lower Delves, Shirland DE5 6AU (01773 834969/834935). *Location:* one mile north of Alfreton off A61, three miles from M1 Junction 28 via A38. Tree-lined rolling parkland, 18 holes, 6072 yards. S.S.S. 69. Par 71. Two practice grounds. *Green Fees:* £15.00 per round, £25.00 per day weekdays; £20.00 per round, £30.00 per day weekends. *Eating facilities:* full restaurant, bar meals. Conference and banquet rooms. *Visitors:* unrestricted weekdays, but must book through Professional at weekends. County standard bowling green available. *Society Meetings:* welcome. Professional: Neville Hallam (01773 834935). Secretary: Mrs C.S. Fincham (01773 832515).

SINFIN. **Derby Golf Club,** Shakespeare Street, Sinfin, Derby DE24 9HD (01332 766323). *Location:* two miles town centre, access via Wilmore Road. Parkland. 18 holes, 6144 yards, 5618 metres. S.S.S. 69. Practice area. *Green Fees:* on request. *Eating facilities:* bar and catering available. *Visitors:* welcome weekdays. *Society Meetings:* welcome weekdays. Professional: Andrew Carnell (01332 766462). Secretary: P. Davidson.

STOCKPORT. **New Mills Golf Club,** Shaw Marsh, New Mills (01663 743485). *Location:* off A6015. 9 holes, 5633 yards. S.S.S. 67. *Green Fees:* £15.00 weekdays only. *Eating facilities:* catering except Thursdays. *Visitors:* welcome weekdays with reservation, weekends with members. No visitors competition days. *Society Meetings:* catered for by appointment (except Thursdays). Professional: Stephen James. Secretary: R. Tuson.

WIRKSWORTH near. **Carsington Water Golf Course,** Carsington, Near Wirksworth (0162985 650). *Location:* off B5035 (Ashbourne – Wirksworth Road) half a mile north of Reservoir Visitors Centre. Undulating meadowland overlooking Carsington Water Reservoir. 18 holes, 6200 yards. Driving range, practice area. *Green Fees:* on request. *Eating facilities:* bar and snack foods. *Visitors:* welcome, unrestricted. *Society Meetings:* welcome by prior arrangement. Manager: Guy R.W. Coleman (Tel & Fax: 01403 784864).

Devon

AXMOUTH. **Axe Cliff Golf Club,** Squires Lane, Axmouth, Seaton EX12 4AZ (01297 20499). *Location:* A35 from Lyme Regis, turn left on to B3172 at junction with A358 Seaton. Seaside wooded course. 18 holes, 5057 yards. S.S.S. 65. Practice area. *Green Fees:* on request. *Eating facilities:* bar and small restaurant. *Visitors:* welcome without reservation, course closed until 11am on Sundays and Wednesdays. *Society Meetings:* welcome. Secretary: Diane Rogers (01297 24371).

BIDEFORD near. **Clovelly Golf and Country Club,** Woolfardisworthy, Near Bideford EX39 5RA (01237 431442; Fax: 01237 431734). *Location:* between Bideford and Bude A39, signposted from main A39 road. Parkland with pond and lakes. 18 holes, 5641 yards. S.S.S. 67. *Green Fees:* £12.00. *Eating facilities:* restaurant and bar. *Visitors:* welcome at all times. Heated swimming pool, sauna, solarium, jacuzzi, fitness room. *Society Meetings:* welcome. Secretary: T. Woolnough. *

BIGBURY. **Bigbury Golf Club Ltd,** Bigbury, Kingsbridge TQ7 4BB (01548 810207). *Location:* off main Plymouth to Kingsbridge road, turn right at Harraton Cross. Two courses: No 1 – 18 holes, 5902 yards. S.S.S. 68. No. 2 (Comp) – 18 holes, 6076 yards. S.S.S. 69. *Green Fees:* weekdays £20.00; weekends £24.00. *Eating facilities:* buffet catering always available: medium to full catering order in advance. *Visitors:* welcome, Handicap Certificate required. *Society Meetings:* catered for by prior arrangement. Professional: Simon Lloyd. Secretary: B.J. Perry (01548 810557).

BRAUNTON. **Saunton Golf Club,** Saunton, Braunton (01271 812436; Fax: 01271 814241). *Location:* eight miles west of Barnstaple on Linksland at north side of Barnstaple Bay. East course 18 holes, 6708 yards. S.S.S. 73. West course 18 holes, 6356 yards. S.S.S. 71. *Green Fees:* weekdays £28.00, weekends £33.00. Subject to review. *Eating facilities:* full catering available. *Visitors:* welcome with reservation, must be members of other golf club and must be able to produce Handicap Certificate. *Society Meetings:* catered for by arrangement. Professional: J.A. McGhee (01271 812013). Secretary: P.R. Stevens (01271 812436).

BRIXHAM. **Churston Golf Club Ltd,** Churston, Near Brixham TQ5 0LA (01803 842218). *Location:* Torquay – follow road signs to Brixham. Seaside parkland course overlooking Torbay. 18 holes, 6243 yards. S.S.S. 70. *Green Fees:* weekdays £22.00, weekends £27.00. *Eating facilities:* available all day. *Visitors:* welcome, must be members of recognised club. Handicap Certificate required. *Society Meetings:* catered for by arrangement. Professional: Richard Penfold (01803 842218). Secretary: R.E. Freeman (0803 842751; Fax: 0803 845738).

BUDLEIGH SALTERTON. **East Devon Golf Club,** North View Road, Budleigh Salterton EX9 6DQ (01395 442018). *Location:* three miles from Exmouth. Heathland, 18 holes, 6214 yards. S.S.S. 70. *Green Fees:* weekdays £25.00 per round, £30.00 per day; weekends and Bank Holidays £30.00 per round, £35.00 per day. *Eating facilities:* full bar and catering facilities (no catering Mondays). *Visitors:* welcome with letter of introduction, Handicap Certificate or Devon County card. *Society Meetings:* catered for by arrangement. Professional: Trevor Underwood (01395 445195). Secretary: J.C. Tebbet (01395 443370).

CHULMLEIGH. **Chulmleigh Golf Course** Leigh Road, Chulmleigh EX18 7BL (01769 580519). *Location:* midway between Barnstaple and Crediton on A377. Undulating course. 18 holes, 1450 yards. S.S.S. 54. Mid December to end of March 9 holes x 2, 2352 yards. *Green Fees:* £6.00 per round, 2 rounds £9.00. Day ticket £12.00. Reductions for Juniors. *Eating facilities:* snacks, bar. *Visitors:* welcome. Large luxury apartment available. Giant TV screen for watching all major tournaments and own videos made on premises. *Society Meetings:* welcome by prior arrangement. Owner/Secretary: P.N. Callow.

CREDITON. **Downes Crediton Golf Club,** Hookway, Crediton (01363 773991). *Location:* off Crediton-Exeter road. Part flat, part hilly course featuring woods and water. 18 holes, 5920 yards. S.S.S. 68. *Green Fees:* £16.00 weekdays, £22.00 weekends. *Eating facilities:* available from 11.30am to one hour before bar closes. *Visitors:* welcome, advisable to phone first and must produce Handicap Certificate. *Society Meetings:* by arrangement. Professional: Howard Finch (01363 774464). Secretary: Mrs Paula Humphries (01363 773025).

CREDITON near. **Waterbridge Golf Course,** Down St. Mary, Near Crediton EX17 5LG (01363 85111). *Location:* on the A377 north of Crediton (one mile north of Copplestone). Attractive, gentle parkland course in a beautiful setting. 9 holes (18 tees), 1954 yards. S.S.S. 62. *Green Fees:* weekdays £5.00 9 holes, £9.00 18 holes; weekends £6.50 9 holes, £12.00 18 holes. 10% discount on parties of 10 and over. *Eating facilities:* tea, coffee, light snacks. *Visitors:* welcome. Club, shoe and trolley hire available. *Society Meetings:* welcome. Professional: Michael Blackwell. Secretary: Mrs C. Petherick.

CULLOMPTON. **Padbrook Park Golf Club,** Padbrook Park, Cullompton (01884 38286; Fax: 01884 34359). *Location:* Junction 28 of M5, one mile away. Parkland. 9 holes (18 tees), 6108 yards. S.S.S. 70. Nets. *Green Fees:* weekdays £7.00 9 holes, £10.00 18 holes; weekends £8.00 9 holes, £16.00 18 holes. Juniors half price. *Eating facilities:* two bars and restaurant. *Visitors:* always welcome. Indoor bowls, fishing. *Society Meetings:* welcome by prior arrangement. Professional: Stewart Adwick. General Manager: Richard Chard.

DAWLISH. **Warren Golf Club,** Dawlish EX7 0NF (01626 862738). *Location:* 12 miles south of Exeter off A379. Links golf course lying on a spit of land between the sea and Exe Estuary. 18 holes, 5973 yards. S.S.S. 69. *Green Fees:* weekdays £21.00, weekends and Bank Holidays £24.00 (half price with a member). *Eating facilities:* bar and full catering available. *Visitors:* welcome with Handicap Certificate. *Society Meetings:* welcome by arrangement, Special Packages available. Professional: A. Naldrett (01626 864002). Secretary: P.G. Tomlinson (01626 862255).

EXETER. **Exeter Golf and Country Club,** Countess Wear, Exeter EX2 7AE (Tel & Fax: 01392 874139). *Location:* near M5, exit Junction 30. Parkland course. 18 holes, 6000 yards. S.S.S. 69. Large practice ground. *Green Fees:* £22.00. *Eating facilities:* sports bar, lounge bar, diningroom. *Visitors:* welcome except Tuesdays (Ladies' Day) and weekends (very busy with members), booking number 01392 876303. *Society Meetings:* catered for Thursdays only. Professional: Mike Rowett (01392 875028). Secretary: C.H.M. Greetham (01392 874023).

EXETER near. **Fingle Glen Family Golf Centre,** Tedburn St. Mary, Near Exeter EX6 6AF (01647 61817; Fax: 01647 61135). *Location:* A30 five miles from Exeter on the Okehampton Road. Parkland with streams and lakes. 9 holes, 2475 yards. S.S.S. 63 (18 holes). Golf academy, 12 bay floodlit driving range. *Green Fees:* weekdays £7.50 9 holes, £11.00 18 holes; weekends £8.50 9 holes, £13.50 18 holes. *Eating facilities:* restaurant, bar snacks, families welcome, sun terrace. *Visitors:* welcome at all times. 3 crown en suite accommodation available. *Society Meetings:* welcome at all times. Professional: Stephen Gould. Golf Manager: Evan Pugh.

EXETER near. **Woodbury Park Golf and Country Club,** Woodbury Castle, Woodbury, Near Exeter EX5 1JJ (01395 233382; Fax: 01395 233384). *Location:* Junction 30 M5, A3052 towards Sidmouth, turn right B3052. Seven miles from motorway. Parkland through mature woodland with several water features. 18 hole championship course and 9 hole course. 18 holes, 6707 yards. S.S.S. 72. 12 bay driving range. *Green Fees:* weekdays £20.00 for 18 holes, £8.00 for 9 holes; weekends £25.00 for 18 holes, £9 for 9 holes. *Eating facilities:* bar snacks; meals available on request. *Visitors:* welcome at all times. *Society Meetings:* welcome, please ring; Golf Packages available. Professional: Alan Richards. Manager: Frances Carter.

HOLSWORTHY. **Holsworthy Golf Club,** Kilatree, Holsworthy (01409 253177). *Location:* leave Holsworthy on Bude road, A3072; one and a half miles on left. Parkland, 18 holes, 6062 yards. S.S.S. 69. Practice field. *Green Fees:* weekdays £15.00; weekends £20.00. *Eating facilities:* snacks at bar, diningroom. *Visitors:* welcome without reservation, Sundays afternoons only. *Society Meetings:* catered for by arrangement. Special reductions for parties of 12 or more. Professional: Tim McSherry (01409 254771). Secretary: Barry Megson (01409 253177).

HONITON. **Honiton Golf Club,** Middlehills, Honiton EX14 8TR (01404 47167). *Location:* one mile south of town proceed from New Street to Farway. Flat parkland. 18 holes, 5940 yards. S.S.S. 68. Small practice ground. *Green Fees:* weekdays £20.00 per day, weekends and Bank Holidays £25.00. *Eating facilities:* bar and restaurant. *Visitors:* bona fide members of other clubs welcome, with restrictions on Wednesdays (ladies' day) and weekends (club competitions). *Society Meetings:* bookable on Thursdays only. Professional: Adrian Cave (01404 42943). Secretary: J.L. Carter (01404 44422).

ILFRACOMBE. **Ilfracombe and Woolacombe Golf Range,** Woolacombe Road, Ilfracombe EX34 7HF (01271 866222). *Location:* on main road between Ilfracombe and Woolacombe. Flat course. 9 holes, 695 yards. 300 yard driving range with covered bays, 18 hole putting course, golf shop. *Green Fees:* weekdays £2.00 for 9 holes; weekends £3.00 for 9 holes. *Eating facilities:* pre-packed snacks and drinks available. *Visitors:* everyone is welcome. Bowling green. Lessons provided by David Hoare, Professional at Ilfracombe Golf Club. Secretary: Mr R.J. Howes.

ILFRACOMBE. **Ilfracombe Golf Club,** Hele Bay, Ilfracombe EX34 9RT (01271 862050). *Location:* on main coastal road between Ilfracombe and Combe Martin. Undulating parkland with spectacular views of sea and moors from every tee and green. 18 holes, 5893 yards. S.S.S. 69. Practice area and green. *Green Fees:* weekdays £17.00; weekends £20.00. *Eating facilities:* full catering available; normal club bar hours. *Visitors:* welcome (Handicap/membership Certificate preferred). Members only 12 noon to 2pm daily and before 10am weekends. *Society Meetings:* welcome, but book in advance. Professional: David Hoare (01271 863328). Secretary: Rodney C. Beer (0271 862176; Fax: 01271 867731).

MORETONHAMPSTEAD. **Manor House Hotel and Golf Course,** Moretonhampstead TR13 8RE (01647 40355). *Location:* Junction 31 from M5, B3212 for two miles. Parkland with rivers. 18 holes, 6016 yards.

S.S.S. 69. Extensive practice facilities. Practice ground, Par 3 course. *Green Fees:* weekdays £22.50; weekends £28.00. *Eating facilities:* brunch service, cream teas, two bars. *Visitors:* welcome. Please book in advance. Accommodation (Hotel), squash courts, tennis courts. *Society Meetings:* by prior arrangement. Professional/Golf Manager: Richard Lewis (01647 40355; Fax: 01647 40961).

NEWTON ABBOT. **Dainton Park Golf Club,** Ipplepen, Newton Abbot TQ12 5TN (01803 813812). *Location:* A381 midway between Newton Abbot and Totnes. Downland. 18 holes. 6200 yards. S.S.S. 70. Practice ground. *Green Fees:* weekdays £12.00; weekends £15.00. *Eating facilities:* full catering; bar. *Society meetings:* welcomed by arrangement. *Visitors:* unrestricted. Professional: Richard Jessop.

MORTEHOE. **Mortehoe and Woolacombe Golf Club,** Easewell Farm, Mortehoe (01271 870225). *Location:* just outside Mortehoe village. Parkland course. 9 holes (18 tees), 4690 yards, S.S.S. 63. *Green Fees:* £6.00 9 holes, £10.00 18 holes. *Eating facilities:* available. *Visitors:* welcome anytime. Holiday Park touring site accommodation available (special rates for golfing). *Society Meetings:* welcome anytime if booked. Secretary: M. Wilkinson.

NEWTON ABBOT. **Newton Abbot (Stover) Golf Club,** Bovey Road, Newton Abbot TQ12 6QQ (01626 52460). *Location:* A382 three miles north of Newton Abbot. Wooded parkland with river. 18 holes, 5899 yards. S.S.S. 68. *Green Fees:* £22.00 per day; half price with a member. *Eating facilities:* full catering daily from 11am. *Visitors:* welcome, but must telephone in advance and produce proof of membership of a county affiliated golf club. *Society Meetings:* catered for on Thursdays, parties of 24 and over. Professional: M. Craig (01626 62078). Secretary: R. Smith (01626 52460).

OKEHAMPTON near. **Ashbury Golf Hotel,** Higher Maddaford, Ashbury, Near Okehampton EX20 4NL (01837 55453; Fax: 01837 55468). *Location:* sign-posted "Ashbury" off the B3218, three miles west of Okehampton. Hilly, wooded courses. Two courses: Exmoor Course 18 holes, 5848 yards. S.S.S. 68; Bodmin Moor Course 18 holes, 2032 yards, Par 3. Practice nets and range. *Green Fees:* Exmoor – weekdays £12.00 per day; weekends £15.00 per day. Bodmin Moor – weekdays £6.00 per day; weekends £8.00 per day. *Eating facilities:* fully licensed bar, bar snacks 12 noon to 5pm, evenings by arrangement. *Visitors:* welcome, no restrictions. 40 bedroomed hotel. *Society Meetings:* welcome, no restrictions. Secretary: Mr David Fensom.

OKEHAMPTON. **Okehampton Golf Club,** Off Tors Road, Okehampton EX20 1EF (01837 52113) *Location:* from A30 take turning from centre of Okehampton then follow the signposts. Parkland. 18 holes, 5223 yards. S.S.S. 67. *Green Fees:* weekdays £15.00; Saturdays £20.00; Sundays £17.00, £12.00 after 1pm. *Eating facilities:* bar and dining room. *Visitors:* welcome; contact by telephone or letter. *Society Meetings:* welcome by prior arrangement. Professional: Philip J. Blundell (01837 53541). Secretary: Spencer Chave (01837 52113).

PLYMOUTH. **Elfordleigh Hotel, Golf and Country Club,** Near Colebrook, Plympton, Plymouth PL7 5EB (01752 336428). *Location:* one mile from Plympton. Woodland course in picturesque countryside. 9 holes, 5470 yards (twice round). S.S.S. 67. Practice area. *Green Fees:* £15.00 weekdays, £20.00 weekends. Special rates available on request. *Eating facilities:* bar meals available from Country Club bar. *Visitors:* welcome. Hotel accommodation available. *Society Meetings:* catered for by arrangement. Secretary: Mrs P. Parfitt (01752 348425; Fax: 01752 344581).

PLYMOUTH. **Sparkwell Golf Club,** Sparkwell, Plympton, Plymouth PL7 5DF (Tel & Fax: 01752 837219). *Location:* Sparkwell village centre. Parkland course. 9 holes, 5772 yards, S.S.S. 68. Practice area, pitch and putt. *Green Fees:* weekdays £5.00 9 holes, £9.00 18 holes; weekends £6.00 9 holes, £11.00 18 holes. Juniors/Senior Citizens weekdays £3.50 per 9 holes until 3pm. *Eating facilities:* restaurant and bar. *Visitors:* all welcome – pay as you play course. Hotel accommodation available. *Society Meetings:* all welcome. Secretary: Alan Price.

PLYMOUTH. **Staddon Heights Golf Club,** Staddon Heights, Plymstock, Plymouth PL9 9SP. *Location:* from Plymouth city follow signs to Plymstock. Seaside links. 18 holes, 5874 yards. S.S.S. 68. Practice area. *Green Fees:* weekdays £15.00; weekends £20.00. *Eating facilities:* diningroom open daily. *Visitors:* welcome except when tee booked for club competitions. *Society Meetings:* by arrangement with Secretary. Professional: John Cox (01752 492630). Secretary: Mike Holliday (01752 402475).

SIDMOUTH. **Sidmouth Golf Club,** Cotmaton Road, Peak Hill, Sidmouth EX10 8SX (01395 513023). *Location:* half a mile from town centre, 12 miles south east of M5 Junction 30. Parkland with breathtaking views over Sid Valley and Lyme Bay. 18 holes, 5109 yards. S.S.S. 65. *Green Fees:* £18.00 per day. *Eating facilities:* catering available except Mondays. All day bar Saturdays. *Visitors:* welcome anytime other than club competitions, tee reservations. *Society Meetings:* catered for, contact Secretary. Professional: Haydn Barrell (01395 516407). Secretary: I.M. Smith (01395 513451).

SOUTH BRENT. **Wrangaton Golf Club,** Golf Links Road, Wrangaton, South Brent TQ10 9HJ (01364 73001). *Location:* heading south take next exit off A38 after South Brent. Undulating parkland/moorland course. 18 holes, 6041 yards. S.S.S 69. Practice area and net. *Green Fees:* weekdays £16.00 per day, weekends and Bank Holidays £20.00. *Eating facilities:* full catering and bar facilities available. *Visitors:* welcome, restricted on club competition days; phoning beforehand advised during season. Special Offer days, period tickets and country membership available. *Society Meetings:* all welcome, written notice required. Professional: Adrian Whitehead (01364 72161). Secretary: Brian Cook (01364 73229).

TAVISTOCK. **Hurdwick Golf Club,** Tavistock Hamlets, Tavistock PL19 8PZ (01822 612746). *Location:* one mile north of Tavistock on the Brentor Road. Parkland. 18 holes, 4800 yards. S.S.S. 64. *Green Fees:* £10.00. *Eating facilities:* fresh sandwiches, licensed bar. *Visitors:* welcome anytime. *Society Meetings:* (10 or more) 36 holes and buffet for £15 a head. Professional: available. Secretary: Derek Bettany.

TAVISTOCK. **Tavistock Golf Club,** Down Road, Tavistock PL19 9AQ (01822 612049). *Location:* Whitchurch Down one mile from Tavistock. 18 holes, 6250 yards. S.S.S. 70. *Green Fees:* £18.00 weekdays, £23.00 weekends and Bank Holidays. *Eating facilities:* full catering facilities. *Visitors:* welcome with reservation. *Society Meetings:* catered for. Professional: R.M. Cade (01822 612316). Secretary: B. G. Steer (01822 612344).

TEIGNMOUTH. **Teignmouth Golf Club,** Haldon Moor, Teignmouth (01626 773614). *Location:* two miles north of Teignmouth on the Exeter Road – B3192. Level heathland course, designed by Dr MacKenzie, with panoramic views. 18 holes, 6227 yards. S.S.S. 71. *Green Fees:* £22.00. *Eating facilities:* full catering service midday to 6pm. *Visitors:* welcome with reservation if members of another club with Handicap Certificate. *Society Meetings:* catered for weekdays only. Professional: P. Ward (01626 772894). Secretary: D. Holloway (01626 774194).

THURLESTONE. **Thurlestone Golf Club,** Thurlestone, Kingsbridge TQ7 3NZ (01548 560221). *Location:* turn off A379 near Kingsbridge. Downland with superb views. 18 holes, 6303 yards, 5818 metres. S.S.S. 70. Practice area. *Green Fees:* £24.00 per day. *Eating facilities:* catering available from 10.00am until 5.30pm daily. *Visitors:* must produce Handicap Certificate, please telephone in advance. *Society Meetings:* not catered for. Professional: Neville Whitley (01548 560715). Secretary: R.W. Marston (01548 560405).

TIVERTON. **Tiverton Golf Club,** Post Hill, Tiverton EX16 4NE (01884 252114). *Location:* three miles east of Tiverton, Junction 27 of M5, proceed through Sampford Peverell and Halberton. Parkland, tree-lined fairways. 18 holes, 6263 yards. S.S.S. 71. *Green Fees:* on application. *Eating facilities:* snacks, lunches and teas; evening meals by arrangement. *Visitors:* welcome with reservation, Handicap Certificate or introduction required. *Society Meetings:* by arrangement with Secretary/Manager. Professional: D. Sheppard (01884 254836). Secretary: Martin Lowry (01884 252187).

TORQUAY. **Torquay Golf Club,** 30 Petitor Road, St Marychurch, Torquay TQ1 4QF (01803 327471). *Location:* north east of Torquay at St. Marychurch. Parkland. 18 holes, 6192 yards. S.S.S. 70. *Green Fees:* on application. *Eating facilities:* lunches, teas and evening meals available. *Visitors:* welcome if members of a golf club with Handicap Certificate. *Society Meetings:* catered for. Professional: M. Ruth (01803 329113). Secretary: B.G. Long (01803 314591).

TORRINGTON. **Torrington Golf Club,** Weare Trees, Torrington EX38 7EZ (01805 622229). *Location:* one mile north of Torrington on Weare Giffard road. Exposed common land with excellent views. 9 holes, 4373 yards. S.S.S. 61. Small practice area. *Green Fees:* weekdays £12.50; weekends £15.00. Reduced rates if playing with a member. *Eating facilities:* full meals and bar snacks available during bar hours. *Visitors:* welcome except on Saturday and Sunday mornings and during club and open competitions. 1995 is our Centenary year. *Society Meetings:* catered for by arrangement. Secretary: Geoffrey S.C. Green (01237 472792).

TOTNES. **Dartmouth Golf and Country Club,** Blackawton, Totnes TQ9 7DG (01803 712686; Fax: 01803 712628). *Location:* five miles from Dartmouth on the A3122. Undulating inland course with lakes, rock faces and multiple tees. Club Course: 9 holes, 2583 yards. S.S.S. 33; Championship Course: 18 holes, 7191 yards. S.S.S 74. 15 bay driving range. *Green Fees:* weekdays £32.00; weekends £35.00. *Eating facilities:* bar, bar snacks and restaurant. *Visitors:* welcome at all times except weekends when restrictions will apply. Cottage accommodation on site. Leisure Club (pool, sauna, etc). *Society Meetings:* welcome weekdays, details of golf packages available on request. Professional: Peter Laugher (01803 712650).

UMBERLEIGH. **Highbullen Hotel Golf Course,** Chittlehamholt, Umberleigh EX37 9HG (01769 540561; Fax: 01769 540492). *Location:* M5 Tiverton Exit (27) to South Molton, B3226 five miles. Right uphill to Chittlehamholt. Pleasant parkland setting amongst mature specimen trees and water hazards, spectacular views. *Green Fees:* non-residents only (free to hotel guests) £8.00 weekdays; £10.00 weekends. £2.00 reduction after 5pm. *Eating facilities:* in hotel – including snack lunches. *Visitors:* welcome anytime. *Society Meetings:* welcome, small numbers only. Professional: Paul Weston (01769 540530). Secretary: Martin Neil (Hotel).

UMBERLEIGH. **Libbaton Golf Club,** High Bickington, Umberleigh EX37 9BS (01769 60269; Fax: 01769 60342). *Location:* A377 Exeter to Barnstaple, turn off on B3227 to Torrington, at Atherington, turn of B3217 to High Bickington. Parkland, rolling countryside, NOT steep up and down slopes. 18 holes, 6428 yards. S.S.S. 72. Floodlit all-weather driving range. *Green Fees:* weekdays £12.00; weekends £14.00. *Eating facilities:* bar, bar meals and first class restaurant. *Visitors:* always welcome, seven days a week. Dress code must be observed. Luxury accommodation available. *Society Meetings:* welcome by prior arrangement. Special Society Packages. Professional: John Phillips (01769 60147). Secretary: Jack Brough.

WESTWARD HO!. **Royal North Devon Golf Club,** Golf Links Road, Westward Ho!, Bideford EX39 1HD (01237 473824). *Location:* A39 Tiverton. Links course. 18 holes, 6662 yards, 6089 metres. S.S.S. 72. Practice area. *Green Fees:* on application. *Eating facilities:* full catering available. *Visitors:* welcome with Handicap Certificate. Tee reservations should be made in advance. *Society Meetings:* catered for. Professional: G. Johnston (01237 477598). General Manager/ Secretary: J.E. Linaker (01237 473817).

YELVERTON. **Yelverton Golf Club,** Golf Links Road, Yelverton PL20 6BN (01822 853618). *Location:* eight miles north of Plymouth on A386 road. Moorland course. 18 holes, 6363 yards. S.S.S. 70. Practice ground. *Green Fees:* £20.00 per day or round. *Eating facilities:* full catering available, licensed. *Visitors:* welcome if member of a recognised golf club or golf society. Handicap Certificate required. *Society Meetings:* catered for, welcome by arrangement with Secretary. Professional: Mr R.J. Tibbs (01822 853593). Secretary: D.R. Bettany (01822 852824).

Dorset

BLANDFORD. **Ashley Wood Golf Club,** Wimborne Road, Blandford DT11 9HN (01258 452253). *Location:* half a mile south of Blandford on B3082. Downland with magnificent views. 18 holes, 6227 yards. S.S.S. 70. Practice ground, putting green. *Green Fees:* weekdays £17.00; weekends £25.00. *Eating facilities:* hot and cold snacks all day also restaurant. *Visitors:* welcome, Ladies only Tuesday mornings. *Society Meetings:* welcome by arrangement with Secretary. Professional: Spencer Taylor (01258 480379). Secretary: Peter Lillford (01258 452253).

BOURNEMOUTH. **Bournemouth & Meyrick Park Golf Club,** Meyrick Park, Bournemouth BH2 6LH (01202 314333). *Location:* one mile from town centre. Beautiful woodland. 18 holes, 5663 yards. S.S.S. 68. Practice area. *Green Fees:* weekdays £10 (Juniors £6); weekends £11 (Juniors £7). Dusk tickets available. Subject to review. *Eating facilities:* clubhouse restaurant and bar available if signed in by member; public cafe. *Visitors:* welcome at anytime (pay as you play) but must be signed in by members. *Society Meetings:* catered for. Tee Bookings (01202 290862/318661). Professional: Warren Butcher (01202 290862). Secretary: Major (Rtd) John Wood (01202 290307).

BOURNEMOUTH. **Knighton Heath Golf Club,** Francis Avenue, Bournemouth BH11 8NX (01202 577870). *Location:* A348 and A3049 roundabout exit Francis Avenue. Undulating heathland, 18 holes, 5987 yards. S.S.S. 69. *Green Fees:* on application. *Eating facilities:* meals and bar snacks available daily, except Monday. *Visitors:* welcome with reservation, after 9.30am weekdays. Restrictions on competition days. Not at weekends unless with a member. Handicap Certificate required. *Society Meetings:* catered for if arranged in advance. Professional: Jane Miles (01202 578275). Secretary: R.C. Bestwick (01202 572633).

BOURNEMOUTH. **Queens Park Golf Club,** Queens Park West Drive, Bournemouth BH8 9BY (01202 394466). *Location:* off Wessex Way. Parkland course in centre of Bournemouth. 18 holes, 6072 yards. S.S.S. 72. Small practice area. *Green Fees:* £11.40; day ticket £15.80. *Eating facilities:* restaurant and bar. *Visitors:* welcome anytime, last tee off times Sundays 12 noon. *Society Meetings:* by prior booking. Professional: R. Hill (01202 396817). Secretary: M.J. Poole (01202 302611).

BRIDPORT. **Bridport and West Dorset Golf Club,** East Cliff, West Bay, Bridport DT6 4EP (01308 422597). *Location:* one and a half miles south of Bridport, east of West Bay harbour. Clifftop links course. 18 holes, 5246 yards, 4795 metres. S.S.S. 66. 9 hole pitch and putt, 18 hole putting green. *Green Fees:* weekdays and weekends £18.00 (£12.00 after 2pm). *Eating facilities:* lounge and diningroom. *Visitors:* welcome. Members only 8am – 9.30am and 12.30pm to 2pm. *Society Meetings:* catered for by prior arrangement. Professional: John Parish (01308 421491). Secretary: P.J. Ridler (01308 421095).

BROADSTONE. **Broadstone (Dorset) Golf Club,** Wentworth Drive, Broadstone BH18 8DQ (01202 693363). *Location:* off A349 to B3072 to Broadstone. Heathland. 18 holes, 6315 yards. S.S.S. 70. Practice area. *Green Fees:* weekdays £27.00 per round, £33.00 per day; weekends £40.00. *Eating facilities:* full catering service. *Visitors:* welcome weekdays, weekends by prior arrangement, current Handicap Certificate required. *Society Meetings:* welcome by arrangement except weekends. Professional: Nigel Tokely (Tel & Fax: 01202 692835). Secretary: Colin Robinson (Tel & Fax: 01202 692595).

CHRISTCHURCH. **Dudmoor Farm Golf Course,** Dudmoor Farm Road, Christchurch BH23 6AQ (01202 483980). *Location:* off Fairmile road, near Christchurch Hospital. Wooded course. 9 holes. Longest hole 244 metres. *Green Fees:* £4.50 for 18 holes. *Eating facilities:* tea, coffee, crisps, chocolate. *Visitors:* welcome, no need to book. Bed and Breakfast accommodation available, livery yard.

CHRISTCHURCH. **Highcliffe Castle Golf Club,** 107 Lymington Road, Highcliffe on Sea, Christchurch BH23 4LA (01425 272953). *Location:* on the coastal road linking Lymington and Christchurch. Flat, wooded course. 18 holes, 4686 yards, 4284 metres. S.S.S. 63. *Green Fees:* weekdays £18.00, after 4pm £11.00; weekends before noon £27.00; afternoon £22.00, after 4pm £15.00. Must be in possession of Handicap Certificate. *Eating facilities:* full catering available. *Visitors:* welcome after 9.30am if member of recognised golf club, after 3.00pm on competition days. *Society Meetings:* catered for Tuesdays only by prior arrangement, all must be members of recognised golf clubs. Professional: R.E. Crockford (01425 276640). Secretary: Mrs E. Thompson (01425 272210).

CHRISTCHURCH. **Iford Bridge Golf Club,** Barrack Road, Christchurch BH23 2BA (01202 473817). *Location:* on the Christchurch/Bournemouth borders, on the bank of the River Stour. 9 greens (18 tees), S.S.S. 63. Driving range. *Green Fees:* weekdays £5.55; weekends and Bank Holidays £6.26. Juniors (under 16) £2.60. *Visitors:* welcome. Membership available. *Society Meetings:* welcome. Resident Golf Professional: Peter Troth.

DORCHESTER. **Came Down Golf Club,** Came Down, Dorchester DT2 8NR (01305 812531). *Location:* two miles south of Dorchester. Downland course on chalk downs with excellent drainage and magnificent views. 18 holes, 6224 yards, 5914 metres. S.S.S. 71. Practice area and nets. *Green Fees:* £20.00 weekdays; £25.00 weekends and Bank Holidays. *Eating facilities:* full catering facilities. *Visitors:* welcome without reservation except Sunday mornings – phone in advance. All visitors must have Handicap Certificate. *Society Meetings:* Wednesdays only. Package (around £30) includes golf (36 holes), morning coffee, lunch and evening meal. Professional: Robert Preston (01305 812670). Secretary: David E. Matthews (01305 813494).

DORCHESTER. **Lyons Gate Golf Club,** Lyons Gate, Dorchester DT2 7AZ (01300 345239). *Location:* on A352 going north from Dorchester about 11 miles, or south from Sherborne about seven miles. Parkland with spectacular views, probably England's most spectacular 9 hole course, famous for its wild flowers. 9 holes, 2000 yards. S.S.S. 30. Practice nets, greens. *Green Fees:* £4.50 for 9 holes, £7.50 for 18 holes. Children under 17 years half price. *Eating facilities:* snacks in shop, vending machine. *Visitors:* welcome, no restrictions, dogs on leads. *Society Meetings:* by arrangement. Secretary: Mr H. Wood.

FERNDOWN. **Dudsbury Golf Club,** Christchurch Road, Ferndown BH22 8ST (01202 593499; Fax: 01202 594555). *Location:* Ferndown town centre. Follow signs for Poole on A348, turn left at first mini roundabout, turn left to Hurn Airport, 200 yards. Club on right hand side. Parkland course designed by Donald Steel, featuring three lakes in beautiful Dorset countryside rolling gently down to the River Stour. 18 holes, 6620 yards. S.S.S 72. 5 hole teaching academy, practice range. *Green Fees:* weekdays £22.50 per round, £30.00 per day; weekends £45.00 per day. *Eating facilities:* two bars, spikes bar, snacks. *Visitors:* welcome. Handicap Certificate required. *Society Meetings:* welcome Monday to Friday, Handicap Certificates required. Professional: Kevin Spurgeon (01202 594488). Secretary/Manager: Kevin Legg.

FERNDOWN. **Ferndown Forest Golf Club,** Forest Links Road, Ferndown BH22 9QE (01202 876096). *Location:* off main A31 trunk road Ferndown bypass. Flat, wooded parkland. 18 holes, 3441 yards. S.S.S 56, Par 61. 19 bay covered driving range. *Green Fees:* weekdays £7.00 per round; weekends £8.00 per round. *Eating facilities:* tea, coffee/snacks; no bar, no meals. Club is still in early development stages; clubhouse/lounge available for members only or prior bookings. *Visitors:* welcome anytime. *Society Meetings:* welcome. Professional: Guy Hunt. Secretary: Ivor Williams.

FERNDOWN. **Ferndown Golf Club,** 119 Golf Links Road, Ferndown BH22 8BU (01202 872022). *Location:* off A31. Wooded heathland. 18 holes, 6452 yards. S.S.S. 71. 9 holes, 5604 yards. S.S.S. 68. Practice ground. *Green Fees:* Old Course: £35.00 weekdays, £40.00 weekends. President's Course: £15.00 weekdays, £20.00 weekends. Societies £50.00 for the day. *Eating facilities:* available. *Visitors:* welcome but prior permission recommended. Handicap Certificate required from a recognised golf club. Professional: D.N. Sewell (01202 873825). Secretary: E. Robertson (01202 874602).

LYME REGIS. **Lyme Regis Golf Club,** Timber Hill, Lyme Regis DT7 3HQ (01297 442043). *Location:* between Lyme Regis and Charmouth. Cliff top course (not hilly) with fine coastal views. 18 holes, 6220 yards. S.S.S. 70. *Green Fees:* £24.00 per day, £20.00 after 2pm. *Eating facilities:* restaurant and bar; newly extended and refurbished clubhouse. *Visitors:* welcome, but not before 9.30am and restrictions Thursdays and Sundays; best to check with Professional. Handicap Certificate or proof of membership of a golf club required. *Society Meetings:* minimum for Tee Booking 12. Professional: Mr A. Black (01297 443822). Secretary: Mr R.G. Fry (01297 442963).

OKEFORD FITZPAINE. **Mid-Dorset Golf Club,** Belchalwell, Okeford Fitzpaine, Near Blandford DT11 0EG (01258 861386). *Location:* A357 Sturminster Newton, Bulbarrow Hill. Parkland/wooded course. 18 holes, 6162 yards. S.S.S. 70. Large practice ground, putting green. *Green Fees:* weekdays £10.00 per round, £18.00 per day; weekends £15.00 per round, £25.00 per day. Reductions for groups of 20 or more. *Eating facilities:* bar and restuarant. *Visitors:* welcome all week. *Society Meetings:* welcome by appointment only. Professional: Spencer Taylor (01258 861184). Secretary: Jayne Burton (01258 861386; Fax: 01258 860656).

POOLE near. **Bulbury Woods Golf Club,** Halls Road, Lytchett Matravers, Near Poole BH16 6EP (01929 459574; Fax: 01929 459000). *Location:* Poole – Bere Regis Road A35. Wooded parkland. 18 holes, 6065 yards. S.S.S. 69. Practice ground. *Green Fees:* £15.00 per round, £25.00 per day. *Eating facilities:* bar and restaurant. *Visitors:* welcomed; dress requirements – recognised golf attire, no jeans, vests or training shoes. Accommodation from £30 per night including golf available. *Society Meetings:* welcome by prior arrangement; packages available. Professional: John Sharkey. Secretary: Peter Dickinson.

Where an asterisk (*) follows an entry, details have not been confirmed by the club for 1995.

POOLE. **Parkstone Golf Club,** Links Road, Parkstone, Poole BH14 9JU (01202 707138). *Location:* off A35 Bournemouth to Poole. Wooded heathland. 18 holes, 6250 yards. S.S.S. 70. *Green Fees:* £25.00 per round, £34.00 per day weekdays; £30.00 per round, £40.00 per day weekends and Bank Holidays (subject to review). *Eating facilities:* catering available daily. *Visitors:* welcome with reservation and Handicap Certificate. *Society Meetings:* catered for as above. Professional: Mark Thomas (01202 708092). Secretary: A.S. Kinnear (01202 707138).

SHAFTESBURY. **Port Regis Golf Club,** Motcombe Park, Shaftesbury SP7 9QA (01747 852566; Fax: 01747 854684). *Location:* one-and-a-half miles from Shaftesbury on Shaftesbury to Gillingham Road (B3081). Wooded parkland in lee of Shaftesbury Ridge. Mock-Tudor mansion overlooking course. 9 holes, 1291 yards. S.S.S.56 (18 holes). Practice net. *Green Fees:* £7 day, £5 Juniors (under 16). Group rate for schools. *Eating facilities:* none available. *Visitors:* welcome at any time. Course occasionally closed for competitions. Club Secretary: David Beaton. Members' Secretary: Ron Peet.

SHERBORNE. **Sherborne Golf Club,** Higher Clatcombe, Sherborne DT9 4RN (01935 812475). *Location:* one mile north of town on B3145 to Wincanton. Parkland. 18 holes, 5949 yards. S.S.S. 68. Practice facilities. *Green Fees:* £20.00 weekdays, £25.00 weekends and Bank Holidays. *Eating facilities:* snacks, lunches, suppers, teas; dinners to order. *Visitors:* as commitment allows, telephone in advance. Handicap Certificates required. Thursday is Ladies' Day. *Society Meetings:* catered for Tuesdays and Wednesdays. Professional: Stewart Wright (01935 812274). Secretary/Manager: Mrs J.M.C. Guy (01935 814431).

SOUTH PERROTT. **Chedington Court Golf Club,** Holt Farm, South Perrott DT8 3HU (01935 891413). *Location:* Crewkerne to Dorchester Road. Parkland course surrounded by woods, very picturesque. 9 holes, 6800 yards, S.S.S. 72. Being extended to 18 holes, designed by Donald Steel/Jim Arthur – Par 72, S.S.S. 71. 9 hole pitch and putt, 15 acre practice area. *Green Fees:* weekdays £6.50 9 holes, £10.00 18 holes; weekends £8.00 9 holes, £12.00 18 holes. *Eating facilities:* lounge bar with catering. *Visitors:* all welcome, bookings taken. Dress restrictions. *Society Meetings:* all welcome, special rates available. Secretary: Ray Gudge.

STUDLAND. **Isle of Purbeck Golf Club,** Studland, Swanage BH19 3AB (01929 44210). *Location:* A351 towards Swanage, at Corfe Castle turn onto B3351 to Studland. Heathland courses with wonderful views. Purbeck – 18 holes, 6248 yards, 5823 metres. S.S.S. 71. Dene – 9 holes, 2022 yards. S.S.S. 30. *Green Fees:* £22.50 per round, £30.00 per two rounds weekdays; £27.50 per round, £35.00 per two rounds weekends. *Eating facilities:* bar and restaurant. *Visitors:* welcome. *Society Meetings:* catered for by arrangement, minimum 8. Professional: Ian Brake (01929 44354). Secretary: Mrs J. Robinson (01929 44361).

VERWOOD. **Crane Valley Golf Club,** Verwood BH31 6LE (01202 814088; Fax: 01202 813407). *Location:* on B3081 Verwood to Cranborne Road. Parkland featuring lakes and River Crane. 18 holes, 6400 yards. S.S.S. 71. 9 hole course, 2100 yards. Covered driving range. *Green Fees:* weekdays £18.00; weekends £24.00. *Eating facilities:* restaurant and spikes bar. *Visitors:* welcome at all times except weekend mornings. Accommodation adjoining course at West Farm. *Society Meetings:* by appointment. Professional: Alan Egford. Secretary: Martin Wilson.

WAREHAM. **East Dorset Golf Club,** Hyde, Wareham BH20 7NT (01929 472244). *Location:* take A352 off Wareham by-pass, enter Puddletown Road, Worgret Heath. Proceed four miles, turn right immediately before ARC Blockworks (signposted), 200 yards to clubhouse. Two courses: Lakeland Course 18 holes, 6556 yards. S.S.S. 71. Woodland Course 18 holes, 4853 yards. S.S.S. 64. Driving range and Pro Shop. *Green Fees:* weekdays £25.00; weekends £35.00. *Eating facilities:* excellent bar and restaurant. *Visitors:* welcome anytime with prior tee reservation. New Dormy bungalow overlooking course for parties of four to eight people. *Society Meetings:* welcome by advance booking. Professional: Kim Thomas (01929 472272). Secretary: Brian R. Lee (01929 472244; Fax: 01929 471294). *

WAREHAM near. **Hyde House Country Club,** Hyde House, Near Wareham BH20 7NX (01929 471219 London Office). *Location:* from Wareham take road to Bere Regis for 2.9 miles, turn left up gravelled track, signposted Hyde House, for one and three-quarters miles in a straight line. Flat, wooded parkland. 24 holes (arranged in three 18 hole configurations), 6450 yards (Executive Course 4400 yards). S.S.S. 72. *Green Fees:* on application. *Eating facilities:* bar and snacks. *Visitors:* only groups possible by prior arrangement. Simple accommodation available by arrangement. *Society Meetings:* very welcome by prior arrangement. Secretary: C. Reynard (0181 940 7782; Fax: 0181 948 4999).

WAREHAM. **Wareham Golf Club,** Sandford Road, Wareham BH20 4DH (01929 554156). *Location:* adjoining A351 near railway station. Partly wooded course. 18 holes, 5603 yards. S.S.S. 67. *Green Fees:* weekdays £15.00 per round, £20.00 per day; weekends with a member only £10.00. *Eating facilities:* bar and restaurant. *Visitors:* welcome, after 9.30am weekdays only. *Society Meetings:* catered for by arrangement. Secretary: Major J.L. Hollaway (01929 554147).

WEYMOUTH. **Wessex Golf Centre,** Radipole Lane, Weymouth DT4 9HX (01305 784737). *Location:* north of Weymouth off Wetser roundabout on bypass road. Flat public course. 9 holes, 1432 yards. Par 27. Practice ground, putting green. *Green Fees:* £3.50. *Visitors:* welcome; public course. Professional: N. Statham.

WEYMOUTH. **Weymouth Golf Club Ltd,** Links Road, Weymouth DT4 0PF (01305 784994). *Location:* A354 from Dorchester, take last exit at Manor roundabout then second left at Chafeys roundabout. Undulating parkland. 18 holes, 6030 yards. S.S.S. 69 (Par 70). Practice area. *Green Fees:* weekdays £18.00, weekends and Bank Holidays £24.00. Half price playing with a member. Juniors half price. *Eating facilities:* full restaurant and bar. *Visitors:* welcome, but only with Handicap Certificate. *Society Meetings:* catered for Tuesdays and Thursdays, arrange with Secretary. Professional: Mr Des Lochrie (01305 773997). Secretary: Dennis Frost (01305 773981).

WIMBORNE. **Sturminster Marshall Golf Club,** Moor Lane, Sturminster Marshall, Wimborne BH21 4AH (01258 858444). *Location:* Wimborne to Bere Regis Road. Parkland. 9 holes, 2325 yards. S.S.S. 63. Practice net. *Green Fees:* £5.00 for 9 holes, £8.00 for 18 holes. *Eating facilities:* tea, coffee and soft drinks; snack meals. *Visitors:* welcome, no restrictions. *Society Meetings:* by arrangement. Professional: Mr J. Sharkey. Secretary: Mr K. Iball.

FOR THE MUTUAL GUIDANCE OF GUEST AND HOST

Every year literally thousands of holidays, short-breaks and overnight stops are arranged through our guides, the vast majority without any problems at all. In a handful of cases, however, difficulties do arise about bookings, which often could have been prevented from the outset.

It is important to remember that when accommodation has been booked, both parties — guests and hosts — have entered into a form of contract. We hope that the following points will provide helpful guidance.

GUESTS: When enquiring about accommodation, be as precise as possible. Give exact dates, numbers in your party and the ages of any children. State the number and type of rooms wanted and also what catering you require — bed and breakfast, full board, etc. Make sure that the position about evening meals is clear — and about pets, reductions for children or any other special points.

Read our reviews carefully to ensure that the proprietors you are going to contact can supply what you want. Ask for a letter confirming all arrangements, if possible.

If you have to cancel, do so as soon as possible. Proprietors do have the right to retain deposits and under certain circumstances to charge for cancelled holidays if adequate notice is not given and they cannot re-let the accommodation.

HOSTS: Give details about your facilities and about any special conditions. Explain your deposit system clearly and arrangements for cancellations, charges, etc, and whether or not your terms include VAT.

If for any reason you are unable to fulfil an agreed booking without adequate notice, you may be under an obligation to arrange alternative suitable accommodation or to make some form of compensation.

While every effort is made to ensure accuracy, we regret that FHG Publications cannot accept responsibility for errors, omissions or misrepresentation in our entries or any consequences thereof. Prices in particular should be checked because we go to press early. We will follow up complaints but cannot act as arbiters or agents for either party.

County Durham

BARNARD CASTLE. **Barnard Castle Golf Club,** Harmire Road, Barnard Castle DL12 8QN (01833 37237). *Location:* one mile north of Barnard Castle Town Centre on the B6278. Open parkland, 18 holes, 5838 yards. S.S.S. 68. *Green Fees:* weekdays £15.00 per round, £18.00 per day; weekends and Bank Holidays £24.00. Reduced rates playing with member. *Eating facilities:* full catering. *Visitors:* welcome, but booking system at weekends and Bank Holidays. *Society Meetings:* catered for by prior arrangement. Professional: D. Pearce (01833 31980). Secretary: J.C. Angel (01833 38355).

BISHOP AUCKLAND. **Bishop Auckland Golf Club,** High Plains, Durham Road, Bishop Auckland DL14 8DL (01388 602198). *Location:* leave Bishop Auckland Market Place on route to Spennymoor/Durham, half a mile on left. Parkland, 18 holes, 6420 yards, 6124 metres. S.S.S. 71 (Par 72). Practice fairways. *Green Fees:* weekdays £20.00 per round, £24.00 per day; weekends £26.00 per round. Visiting parties over 20 have day reduction to £18.00. *Eating facilities:* bar, full catering facilities except Mondays. *Visitors:* welcome mid-week only. Ladies' day Tuesday. Two snooker tables. *Society Meetings:* catered for on application, not weekends and Christmas period, and official Handicap desirable. Professional: Mr D. Skiffington (01388 661618). Secretary: Mr G. Thatcher (01388 663648).

BRANCEPETH. **Brancepeth Castle Golf Club,** Brancepeth DH7 8EA (0191-378 0075). *Location:* four miles west of Durham city on A690. Parkland. 18 holes, 6415 yards. S.S.S. 71. Practice ground. *Green Fees:* weekdays £24.00 per day, weekends by prior booking £30.00. *Eating facilities:* available every day. *Visitors:* welcome weekdays, weekends by prior arrangement. *Society Meetings:* catered for Monday to Friday only. Professional: D.C. Howdon (0191-378 0183). Secretary: J.T. Ross (0191-378 0075).

CHESTER-LE-STREET. **Chester-le-Street Golf Club,** Lumley Park, Chester-le-Street DH3 4NS (0191-388 3218). *Location:* Off A1 adjacent to Lumley Castle, half a mile east of Chester-le-Street. Parkland, 18 holes, 6054 yards, 5535 metres. S.S.S. 69. *Green Fees:* weekdays £20.00, weekends and Public Holidays £25.00. *Eating facilities:* lunches, snacks, dinners, bar. *Visitors:* welcome weekdays with letter of introduction or Handicap Certificate, but some restrictions weekends and Public Holidays. *Society Meetings:* catered for but not weekends and Public Holidays. Professional: A. Hartley (0191-389 0157). Secretary: W.B. Dodds (0191-388 3218).

CHESTER-LE-STREET. **Roseberry Grange Golf Club,** Grange Villa, Chester-le-Street DH2 3NF (0191-370 0670). *Location:* three miles west of Chester-le-Street on A693. Parkland course. 18 holes, 5809 yards. S.S.S. 68. Driving range. *Green Fees:* weekdays £8.00 per round, £12.00 per day; weekends £11.00 per round, £15.00 per day ticket. Half price weekdays for Juniors and Senior Citizens. *Eating facilities:* bar meals 12 noon to 2pm and 7pm to 9.30pm. *Visitors:* welcome, no restrictions. Professional: A. Hartley (0191-370 0660). Secretary: Raymond McDermott (0191-370 2047).

CONSETT. **Consett and District Golf Club,** Elmfield Road, Consett DH8 5NN (01207 502186). *Location:* A691 from Durham (12 miles), A692 from Gateshead (12 miles). 18 holes, 6013 yards. S.S.S. 69. *Green Fees:* weekdays £15.00; weekends £20.00. *Eating facilities:* full catering available. *Visitors:* most welcome without reservation. *Society Meetings:* catered for by arrangement, enquiries welcomed. Professional: S. Corbally (01207 580210). Secretary: Mr J. Horrill (01207 562261).

CROOK. **Crook Golf Club,** Low Jobs Hill, Crook DL15 9AA (01388 762429). *Location:* six miles west of Durham City on A690. Hilly, demanding parkland course. 18 holes, 6075 yards. S.S.S. 69. Practice nets and fairway. *Green Fees:* weekdays £12.00; weekends £20.00. *Eating facilities:* full catering facilities. *Visitors:* at any time other than when club competitions are held. Caravan Club Site (5 Vans) adjacent clubhouse. *Society Meetings:* catered for by arrangement with Secretary. Secretary: Peter N. Willis (01388 762429; Fax: 0191-378 9711).

DARLINGTON. **Blackwell Grange Golf Club,** Briar Close, Blackwell, Darlington DL3 8QX (01325 464464). *Location:* one mile south of Darlington on A66 turn into Blackwell. Signposts to Club. Parkland course. 18 holes, 5621 yards. S.S.S. 67. *Green Fees:* weekdays £15.00 per round, £18.00 per day; weekends and Bank Holidays £20 per round. *Eating facilities:* full menu except Sundays and Mondays. *Visitors:* welcome without reservation except weekends. *Society Meetings:* catered for except Wednesday and weekends. Professional: Ralph Givens (01325 462088). Secretary: F. Hewitson (01325 464458).

DARLINGTON. **Dinsdale Spa Golf Club,** Neasham Road, Middleton-St-George, Darlington DL2 1DW (01325 332222). *Location:* near Teesside Airport. Parkland. 18 holes, 6090 yards. S.S.S. 70. *Green Fees:* weekdays £16.00 per round, £20.00 per day; weekends with a member only (£8.00). *Eating facilities:* bar, catering except Mondays. *Visitors:* welcome weekdays except Tuesdays (Ladies Day). *Society Meetings:* catered for Wednesday, Thursday and Friday by advance booking. Professional: C. Imlah (Tel & Fax: 01325 332515). Secretary: Mr P.J. Wright (01325 332297).

DARLINGTON. **Stressholme Golf Club,** Snipe Lane, Darlington (01325 353073). *Location:* one mile south of Darlington town centre near junction of A66 and A167. 18 holes, 6511 yards, 5953 metres. S.S.S. 71. Practice ground. *Green Fees:* information not provided. *Eating facilities:* two bars, three course meals to snacks. *Visitors:* always welcome anytime. *Society Meetings:* all welcome any time – reserved tees available. Professional: Tim Jenkins (01325 461002). Secretary: Graham A. Patrick (01325 466587). *

DARLINGTON. **The Darlington Golf Club (Members) Ltd,** Haughton Grange, Darlington DL1 3JD (01325 355324). *Location:* northern outskirts of town, A1150 off A167, approximately 800 yards. Flat wooded parkland. 18 holes, 6271 yards. S.S.S. 70. Large practice ground. *Green Fees:* weekdays £22.00 per day; weekends with member only. *Eating facilities:* first class catering, Men's Bar, lounge bar available. *Visitors:* welcome weekdays with reservation, must be members of recognised golf club. *Society Meetings:* by arrangement weekdays, no more than 40 members. Professional: Mark Rogers (01325 484198). Secretary: Norman Adair (01325 355324).

DURHAM. **Durham City Golf Club,** Littleburn, Langley Moor, Durham DH7 8HL (0191 3780806). *Location:* from Durham City take A690 to Crook – course signposted in Langley Moor. Parkland with river. 18 holes, 6326 yards. S.S.S. 70. Large practice area. *Green Fees:* weekdays £18.00, weekends £24.00. Half fees if playing with a member. £14.00 per person for parties of 20 or more. *Eating facilities:* no catering Mondays or Thursday evenings. *Visitors:* welcome, only restrictions when club competitions are being held – ring Professional for details. *Society Meetings:* welcome, but restricted to weekdays. Professional: S. Corbally (0191 3780029). Secretary: I. Wilson (0191 3780069). *

DURHAM. **Mount Oswald Golf Club,** South Road, Durham DH1 3TQ (0191-386 7527; Fax: 0191-384 0975). *Location:* A1(M) Junction marked Bowburn. A177 Durham City A1050. Parkland, partially wooded. 18 holes, 6101 yards. S.S.S. 69. *Green Fees:* weekdays £10 per round, weekends and Bank Holidays £12 per round. *Eating facilities:* bar meals, Sunday lunches, set meals, etc. *Visitors:* welcome except Sunday mornings before 10am (members only). Bookings only at weekends and Bank Holidays. *Society Meetings:* welcome, same restrictions as visitors, must order food. General Manager: S.E. Reeve (0191-386 7527).

NEWTON AYCLIFFE. **Aycliffe Golf Club,** Oak Leaf Sports Complex, School Aycliffe Lane, Newton Aycliffe DL5 4EF (01325 300600). *Location:* three miles from A1M and A68. Rolling parkland. 18 holes, 5422 yards. S.S.S. 67. Driving range (floodlit). *Green Fees:* information not provided. Reduced rates for Senior Citizens and under 16's. *Eating facilities:* bar, limited eating facilities. Contact Stewardess (01325 300700). *Visitors:* welcome anytime (booking system), slight restrictions weekends. *Society Meetings:* all welcome by prior arrangement. Professional: Robert Lister (01325 310820). Secretary: W.J. Findley (01325 312994). *

NEWTON AYCLIFFE. **Woodham Golf and Country Club,** Burnhill Way, Newton Aycliffe DL5 4PN (01325 320574; Fax: 01325 315254). *Location:* A167, one mile north of Newton Aycliffe on the Shildon road. Parkland, wooded with lakes. 18 holes, 6727 yards. S.S.S. 72. Practice grounds, putting green. *Green Fees:* weekdays £15.00 per round, £20.00 per day; weekends £20.00 per round, £25.00 per day. *Eating facilities:* bar snacks, meals and restaurant available. *Visitors:* unlimited weekdays; tee restrictions weekends and Bank Holidays. *Society Meetings:* welcome by arrangement. Professional: Ernie Wilson (01325 315257). Secretary: John D. Jenkinson. Steward: (01325 301551). *

SEAHAM. **Seaham Golf Club,** Shrewsbury Street, Seaham SR7 7RD (0191-581 2354). *Location:* Dawdon, two miles north east of A19 leave for Seaham. Heathland. 18 holes, 6017 yards. S.S.S. 69. Practice area. *Green Fees:* weekdays £15.00 (£9.00 playing with a member); weekends and Bank Holidays £18.00 (£11.00 playing with a member). *Eating facilities:* snacks available, meals on request. *Visitors:* welcome, unrestricted weekdays, booking for weekends. *Society Meetings:* welcome on application. Professional: D. Patterson (0191-513 0837). Secretary: Vincent Smith (0191-581 5413).

STANLEY. **Beamish Park Golf Club,** Beamish, Stanley DH9 0RH (0191-370 1382). *Location:* follow directions to Beamish Museum. Parkland, 18 holes, 6205 yards. S.S.S. 70. Two practice areas. *Green Fees:* weekdays £16.00 per round, £20.00 per day; weekends £24.00 per round, £30.00 per day. *Eating facilities:* bar and à la carte menu. *Visitors:* welcome, Monday to Friday. Professional: C. Cole (0191-370 1984). Secretary: L. Gilbert (0191-370 1382).

STANLEY. **South Moor Golf Club,** The Middles, Craghead, Stanley DH9 6AG (01207 232848). *Location:* eight miles north-west of Durham, seven miles west of A1 (M) from Chester-le-Street. Parkland and moorland. 18 holes, 6445 yards. S.S.S. 71. *Green Fees:* weekdays £14.00 per round, £21.00 per day; with a member £10 per round, £15.00 per day; weekends and Bank Holidays £25.00 per day; with a member £12.00 per round, £18.00 per day. *Eating facilities:* available. *Visitors:* members only before 9.30am and 12 – 2pm. No casual visitors weekends or Bank Holidays unless with member. *Society Meetings:* catered for except Sundays. Professional: S. Cowell (01207 283525). Secretary: B. Davison (01207 232848).

Essex

BASILDON. **Basildon Golf Club,** Clay Hill Lane, Basildon (01268 533297). *Location:* off A13 or A127 on A176 – Kingswood Roundabout. Undulating woodland. 18 holes, 6153 yards. S.S.S. 69. Practice area. *Green Fees:* £8.70 weekdays; £14.50 weekends. *Eating facilities:* snack meals/bar. *Visitors:* welcome anytime, booking system at weekends and Bank Holidays. *Society Meetings:* catered for – apply to Basildon Council. Professional: (01268 533352). Secretary: A. M. Burch (01268 533849).

BASILDON. **Pipps Hill Country Club,** Cranes Farm Road, Basildon SS14 3DG (01268 523456). *Location:* A127 – Basildon. Flat course. 9 hole course, 5658 yards. *Green Fees:* on request. *Eating facilities:* Golfer Arms Public House nearby. *Visitors:* unrestricted at all times. Golf days catered for. *

BILLERICAY. **Stock Brook Manor Golf Club,** Queens Park Avenue, Stock, Near Billericay CM11 0SP (01277 633063). *Location:* nearest main road A12, Billericay. Parkland – gently undulating with featured lakes. 18 holes, 6728 yards. S.S.S. 72. Manor – 9 holes, 2997 yards. Driving range, putting green and three par 3 practice holes. *Green Fees:* weekdays £25.00; weekends £30.00. *Eating facilities:* available. *Visitors:* welcome. Handicap Certificate required. *Society Meetings:* welcome. Professional: Kevin Merry (01277 653616). Secretary: Kevin Roe. *

BRAINTREE. **Braintree Golf Club,** Kings Lane, Stisted, Braintree CM7 8DA (01376 24117). *Location:* A120 to Colchester, 300 yards east of Braintree by-pass, signposted Stisted and Golf Club. Parkland, with slopes down to the river. 18 holes, 6153 yards, S.S.S. 69. Practice ground, pitching area. *Green Fees:* weekdays £25.00, £18.00 after 2pm; £45.00 Saturdays only. *Eating facilities:* available. *Visitors:* welcome Monday to Friday (Fridays must have Handicap Certificate). *Society Meetings:* catered for Mondays, Wednesdays and Thursdays. Professional: A.K. Parcell (01376 343465). Secretary: G.J. Bardsley (01376 346079).

BRAINTREE. **Towerlands Golf Club,** Panfield Road, Braintree CM7 5BJ (01376 326802; Fax: 01376 552487). *Location:* off A120 into Braintree, then B1053. Undulating course. 9 holes, 2703 yards. S.S.S. 66. Golf range. *Green Fees:* weekdays £8.50 for 9 holes, £10.50 for 18 holes; weekends and Bank Holidays £12.50 for 18 holes only after 12 noon. *Eating facilities:* full bar and restaurant. *Visitors:* welcome. Wide range of other sports facilities. *Society Meetings:* by arrangement. Professional: (01376 347951). Secretary: Mr K. Cooper (01376 347951).

BRENTWOOD. **Hartswood Golf Club,** (Play on Brentwood Municipal), King George's Playing Fields, Ingrave Road, Brentwood (01277 217128). *Location:* one mile south of Brentwood on A128. Parkland, 18 holes, 6238 yards. S.S.S. 70. *Green Fees:* information not provided. *Eating facilities:* full catering available. *Visitors:* welcome without reservation. *Society Meetings:* limited number of society bookings. Professional: Mr Martin Siggins (01277 230474). Secretary: (01277 218850).

BRENTWOOD. **The Warley Park Golf Club,** Magpie Lane, Little Warley, Brentwood CM13 3DX (01277 224891). *Location:* leave M25 at Intersection 29. A127 towards Southend. Turn left three-quarters-of-a-mile Little Warley, Hall Lane. Turn left into Magpie Lane. Parkland, 3 Courses, (27 holes). S.S.S. 70-70-69. Large practice area, putting greens. *Green Fees:* weekdays £24.00 per round, £36.00 per day. *Eating facilities:* lounge bar and restaurant/spike bar. *Visitors:* welcome Monday to Friday, must produce club Handicap Certificate. *Society Meetings:* catered for. Professional: P. O'Connor (01277 212552). Secretary: K. Regan (01277 224891).

BRENTWOOD. **Thorndon Park Golf Club Ltd,** Thorndon Park, Ingrave, Brentwood CM13 3RH (01277 811666). *Location:* three miles south of Brentwood on A128. 18 holes, 6481 yards. S.S.S. 71. *Green Fees:* £40.00 per day, £25.00 per round weekdays, weekends with members only. *Eating facilities:* lunches served at club. *Visitors:* welcome with reservation, weekdays subject to prior permission. *Society Meetings:* catered for. Professional: Brian White (01277 810736). Secretary: J.E. Leggitt (01277 810345).

BRENTWOOD.**Bentley Golf Club,** Ongar Road, Brentwood CM15 9SS (01277 373179). *Location:* situated on A128 approximately five miles from Junction 28 of M25. Flat parkland course. 18 holes, 6709 yards, 6136 metres. S.S.S. 72. Practice field. *Green Fees:* weekdays £21.00 per round, £27.00 day ticket; weekends with a member only. Reductions for Senior Citizens and under 18s. *Eating facilities:* food and bar available all day. *Visitors:* welcome weekdays; Bank Holidays after 11am. *Society Meetings:* welcome by prior arrangement. Professional: Nick Garrett (01277 372933). Secretary: J.A. Vivers (01277 373179).

BULPHAN. **The Langdon Hills Golf Club,** Lower Dunton Road, Bulphan RM14 3TY (01268 548444; Fax: 01268 548065). *Location:* 8 miles from M25, Dartford River crossing, Basildon three miles between A127 and A13. Gently undulating parkland. 18 holes, 6485 yards. S.S.S. 71. 9 hole course, 22 bay floodlit driving range, large shortgame practice area. *Green Fees:* weekdays £18.50 per round, £26.50 per day; weekends £25.00 per round. *Eating facilities:* restaurant, two bars and private function room. *Visitors:* welcome most times, ring for details. 25 bedroomed hotel. *Society Meetings:* welcomed. Professional: John Slinger (Golf Director). Secretary: Mrs C. Hammond. *

BURNHAM-ON-CROUCH. **Burnham-on-Crouch Golf Club Ltd,** Ferry Road, Creaksea CM0 8PQ (01621 782282). *Location:* one mile west of Burnham-on-Crouch, turn right off B1010. Undulating meadowland. 18 holes, 6056 yards. S.S.S. 70. Practice ground. *Green Fees:* £20.00 weekdays. *Eating facilities:* full bar, lunch and evening meals. *Visitors:* no visitors weekends and Bank Holidays. Must commence play Mondays to Fridays (except Thursdays) 9.30am to 2pm. Thursdays 12 noon to 2pm. *Society Meetings:* catered for Tuesdays and Fridays only. Secretary: W.F. Miller.

CANVEY ISLAND. **Castle Point Golf Club,** Somnes Avenue, Canvey Island SS8 9FG (01268 511149). *Location:* A13 to Southend, A130 to Canvey Island, opposite sports centre. Links course, flat; views of Hadleigh Downs and Castle. 18 holes, 6176 yards. S.S.S. 69. Driving range. *Green Fees:* weekdays £8.75; weekends £13.00. Juniors and Senior Citizens £4.50 weekdays. *Eating facilities:* restaurant and bar available. *Visitors:* welcome anytime, booking required at weekends. Changing facilities, showers. *Society Meetings:* welcome, catered for weekdays only. Professional: John Hudson (01268 510830). Secretary: Vic Russell (01268 698909). *

CHELMSFORD. **Channels Golf Club,** Belsteads Farm Lane, Little Waltham, Chelmsford CM3 3PT (01245 440005). *Location:* three miles north east of Chelmsford on A130. Reclaimed gravel workings, many lakes, hazards and an abundance of wild life. Two courses – Channels 6271 yards, S.S.S. 71; Belsteads 4779 yards, S.S.S. 63. 14 bay floodlit driving range, 9 hole public pay and play course. *Green Fees:* £28.00 per day weekdays; weekends only with a member. Juniors and Senior Citizens £15.00 per round, £22.00 per day weekdays. *Eating facilities:* excellent restaurant in 13th century clubhouse. *Visitors:* welcome weekdays only. *Society Meetings:* catered for weekdays. Professional: I.B. Sinclair (01245 441056). Secretary: Mr A.M. Squire (01245 440005; Fax: 01245 442032).

CHELMSFORD. **Chelmsford Golf Club,** Widford Road, Chelmsford (01245 250555). *Location:* close to Widford roundabout on A1016. 18 holes, 5944 yards. S.S.S. 68. *Green Fees:* information not provided. *Eating facilities:* dining room and bar. *Visitors:* welcome Monday to Friday with reservation. Professional: D. Bailey. Manager: Wg. Cdr. B.A. Templeman-Rooke DSO, DFC, AFC, RAF (Retd.) (01245 256483).

CHIGWELL. **Chigwell Golf Club,** The Clubhouse, High Road, Chigwell IG7 5BH (0181-500 2059). *Location:* on A113, 14 miles from London, seven miles Waltham Abbey exit M25. Testing undulating parkland course. 18 holes, 6279 yards. S.S.S. 70. Practice shed and ground. *Green Fees:* weekdays £28.00 per round, £35.00 per day; weekends with introduction by member only. *Eating facilities:* restaurant and bars available. *Visitors:* weekdays by prior arrangement, Handicap Certificate required and membership of authorised Golf Club. *Society Meetings:* weekdays by arrangement. Professional: R. Beard (0181-500 2384). Secretary: Mr M. McL. Farnsworth (0181-500 2059).

CHIGWELL. **Hainault Forest Golf Club,** Romford Road, Chigwell IG7 4QW (0181-500 2097). *Location:*

off A12 towards Chigwell-Hainault. Flat wooded course with several lakes. 18 holes, 6600 yards. S.S.S. 71. 18 holes, 5754 yards. S.S.S. 67. Practice field and putting green. *Green Fees:* weekdays £9.20; weekends £11.50. *Eating facilities:* course restaurant; bars in private club. *Visitors:* public course. *Society Meetings:* weekdays by arrangement with Secretary. Professional: T. Dungate (0181-500 2131). *

CLACTON. **Clacton Golf Club,** West Road, Clacton (01255 421919). Seaside course. 18 holes, 6244 yards. S.S.S. 71. *Green Fees:* £20.00 weekdays, £30.00 weekends and Bank Holidays. *Eating facilities:* full catering by prior arrangement. *Visitors:* welcome with reservation and current Handicap Certificate. Weekends and Bank Holidays not before 11am. *Society Meetings:* Monday to Friday catered for by arrangement. Professional: S.J. Levermore. Secretary: H.F. Lucas.

COLCHESTER. **Birch Grove Golf Club,** Layer Road, Colchester CO2 0HS (01206 734276). *Location:* on B1026, two miles south of town. Parkland – small but challenging. 9 holes, 4038 yards. S.S.S. 60. *Green Fees:* £10.00 weekdays, £12.00 weekends and Bank Holidays for 18 holes. *Eating facilities:* hot meals and snacks are available during opening hours. *Visitors:* welcome without reservation Monday to Saturday and after 1pm Sundays. *Society Meetings:* catered for weekdays. Secretary: Mrs M. Marston.

COLCHESTER. **Colchester Golf Club,** Braiswick, Colchester CO4 5AU (01206 853396). *Location:* one mile north-west of Colchester North Station, on A133. Parkland. 18 holes, 6319 yards. S.S.S. 70. *Green Fees:* £22.00 per day weekdays; £30.00 weekends. *Eating facilities:* catering available all day. *Visitors:* welcome except Saturday and Sunday mornings. *Society Meetings:* catered for by prior arrangement. Professional: Mark Angel (01206 853920). Secretary: Mrs J. Boorman (01206 853396; Fax: 01206 852698).

COLCHESTER. **Earls Colne Golf and Leisure Centre,** Earls Colne, Colchester CO6 2NS (01787 224466; Fax: 01787 224410). *Location:* situated on the B1024 off the A120 opposite Coggeshall. Flat parkland courses (3). 4 hole teaching course; The Honeywood Course – 9 holes, 3100 yards. Par 34; 18 hole course 6715 yards. Par 73. 20 bay floodlit, covered driving range. *Green Fees:* weekdays £15.00; weekends £18.00. *Eating facilities:* à la carte restaurant, poolside grill and spike bar meals. *Visitors:* pay and play course – visitors welcome anytime. Full leisure centre including gym, swimming pool, whirlpool spa; conference facilities. *Society Meetings:* welcome weekdays. Professional: Owen McKenna. Secretary: Malcolm Hobbs.

COLD NORTON. **Three Rivers Golf and Country Club,** Stow Road, Cold Norton, Purleigh, Near Chelmsford CM3 6ET (01621 828631; Fax: 01621 828060). *Location:* 10 minutes from South Woodham Ferrers. Parkland with lakes and wooded areas. 18 holes, 6536 yards. S.S.S. 71. 9 hole Par 3 course. *Green Fees:* weekdays £19.00 per round; weekends £25.00 per round. *Eating facilities:* à la carte, carvery three times a week, bar meals all day. *Visitors:* welcome. Computer club fitting service/swing analysis centre; six bedroomed hotel, tennis courts, squash courts, snooker. *Society Meetings:* catered for mainly Tuesdays to Fridays. Professional/Golf Director: Graham Packer.

EPPING. **Theydon Bois Golf Club,** Theydon Road, Epping CM16 4EH. *Location:* M25 Waltham Abbey/ Epping A121 London to Cambridge, turn right at Bell Hotel. Wooded course. 18 holes, 5472 yards. S.S.S. 68. Practice area. *Green Fees:* (1994 rates) £23.00 per day, £20.00 after 2pm. Subject to review. *Eating facilities:* restaurant and bar. *Visitors:* welcome except Wednesday and Thursday morning. Not available November to March. *Society Meetings:* Monday and Tuesday £32 per person plus catering per day. Professional: R. Hall (01992 812460). Secretary: D. Jones (01992 813054).

FRINTON-ON-SEA. **Frinton Golf Club,** 1 The Esplanade, Frinton-on-Sea CO13 9EP. *Location:* 17 miles east of Colchester, A12 – A133, B1033. Flat seaside links course, strength of wind always a feature. 18 holes, 6265 yards. S.S.S. 70. Short Course 2508 yards, no Handicap Certificate required. Practice facilities. *Green Fees:* £22.00. *Eating facilities:* snack and restaurant facilities. *Visitors:* welcome, check with Secretary. Handicap Certificate required. *Society Meetings:* catered for Wednesday and Thursday by arrangement. Professional: Peter Taggart (Tel & Fax: 01255 671618). Secretary: Lt Col R.W. Attrill (01255 674618).

HARLOW. **Canons Brook Golf Club,** Elizabeth Way, Harlow CM19 5BE (01279 25142). *Location:* A414. 18 holes, 6745 yards. S.S.S. 73. *Green Fees:* £25.00 per weekday. *Eating facilities:* full catering except Mondays. *Visitors:* welcome weekdays. *Society Meetings:* catered for except Mondays. Professional: Alan McGinn (01279 418357). Secretary: G.E. Chambers (01279 421482). *

HARWICH. **Harwich and Dovercourt Golf Club,** Station Road, Parkeston, Harwich CO12 4NZ (01255 3616). *Location:* A604 thence to sign Parkeston Quay. Course marked on left hand side of Parkeston Road. 9 holes, 5862 yards. S.S.S. 68. *Green Fees:* information not provided. No visitors Saturdays, Sundays and Bank Holidays unless playing with a member. *Eating facilities:* order before playing. *Visitors:* welcome with Handicap Certificates. *Society Meetings:* catered for. Secretary: Mr B.Q. Dunham.

ILFORD. **Fairlop Waters,** Forest Road, Barkingside, Ilford IG6 3JA (0181-500 9911). *Location:* two miles north of Ilford, half a mile from A12, one and a half miles from southern end of M11. Parkland course. 18 holes, 6281 yards. S.S.S. 70. *Green Fees:* £7.50 weekdays; £11.00 weekends. Pay as you play, no membership required. *Eating facilities:* Daltons American Diner open from breakfast till late 7 days a week, lunchtime bar food. *Visitors:* welcome all week. Banqueting for 250 and conferences. Professional: Tony Bowers (0181-501 1881). Manager: Keith Robson. *

ILFORD. **Ilford Golf Club,** 291 Wanstead Park Road, Ilford RG1 3TR (0181-554 5174). *Location:* at end of M11. Parkland with winding river. 18 holes, 5787 yards. S.S.S. 68. *Green Fees:* weekdays £13.50, weekends £16.00. *Eating facilities:* restaurant and bar. *Visitors:* welcome weekdays, restricted times at weekends. *Society Meetings:* welcome. Professional: S. Dowsett (0181-554 0094). Secretary: P.H. Newson (0181-554 2930). *

LEIGH-ON-SEA. **Belfairs Golf Club,** Eastwood Road North, Leigh-on-Sea SS9 4LR (01702 526911). Park front 9, heavy woodland back 9; easy walking but challenging golf. Play over Belfairs Municipal course, 18 holes, 5857 yards. S.S.S. 68. *Green Fees:* weekdays £13.20, weekends and Bank Holidays £16.80 (approximately). *Visitors:* unrestricted on the course but no clubhouse facilities available. Bookings required at weekends, Bank Holidays and during school holidays. Professional: Roger Foreman (01702 520202). Secretary: J.W. Pacey (01702 520322).

LOUGHTON. **Loughton Golf Club,** Clay's Lane, Debden Green, Loughton IG10 2RZ (0181-502 2923). *Location:* just north of Loughton, on edge of Epping Forest. Hilly parkland, wooded. 9 holes, 4700 yards. S.S.S. 63. Practice range. *Green Fees:* weekdays £5.00 9 holes, £8.00 18 holes; weekends £6.00 for 9 holes, £10.00 for 18 holes. *Eating facilities:* bar, snacks available. *Visitors:* welcome, telephone to book. *Society Meetings:* welcome. Manager: Alan Day.

MALDON. **Bunsay Downs Golf Club,** Little Baddow Road, Woodham Walter, Maldon CM9 6RW (01245 222648; Fax: 01245 223989). *Location:* 7 miles east of Chelmsford off A414 at Woodham Walter, left onto Little Baddow Road. Undulating landscaped partly wooded course. 9 holes, 2932 yards. S.S.S. 68. Par 3 course, indoor range. *Green Fees:* weekdays 9 holes £8.00, 18 holes £10.00; weekends 9 holes £9.00, 18 holes £11.00. *Eating facilities:* bar/grill restaurant. *Visitors:* welcome at all times. Gift shop. *Society Meetings:* small societies welcome. Professional: Mickey Walker. Secretary: Mr M. Durham (01245 223258).

MALDON. **Forrester Park Golf and Tennis Club,** Beckingham Road, Great Totham, Near Maldon CM9 8EA (01621 891406). *Location:* three miles off A12 Rivenhall turn-off, on B1022 in Great Totham, near Maldon between Compasses and Bull. Parkland course. 18 holes, 6073 yards. S.S.S. 69. *Green Fees:* weekdays £17.00; weekends £22.00. *Eating facilities:* full catering and bar facilities. *Visitors:* welcome subject to prior booking, but not before 9.30am Tuesdays and Wednesdays and not before 12.30pm Saturdays and Sundays. *Society Meetings:* welcome subject to prior booking. Professional: Gary Pike (01621 893456). Manager: Tim Forrester-Muir (01621 891406).

MALDON. **Maldon Golf Club,** Beeleigh, Langford, Maldon CM9 6LL (01621 853212). *Location:* B1019 two miles northwest of Maldon, turn off at the Essex Waterworks. Flat parkland. 9 holes, 6197 yards, 5667 metres. S.S.S. 69. *Green Fees:* 18 holes £15.00, all day £20.00 weekdays; weekends 18 holes £12.00, all day £17.00 with a member only. *Eating facilities:* light meals, snacks; bar. *Visitors:* welcome weekdays, Handicap Certificates required. *Society Meetings:* catered for by arrangement. Secretary: G.R. Bezant.

MALDON. **Quietwaters Hotel, Golf and Country Club,** Colchester Road, Tolleshunt Knights, Maldon CM9 8HX (01621 868888; Fax: 01621 869696). *Location:* eight miles from Colchester on B1026. Links type courses. (Two courses). Links Course – 18 holes, 6222 yards, 5690 metres. S.S.S. 70. Lakes Course – 18 holes, 6767 yards, 6186 metres. S.S.S. 72. *Green Fees:* Links – weekdays £18.00, weekends £22.50; Lakes – weekdays and weekends £30.00. *Eating facilities:* full catering and bar snacks. *Visitors:* welcome at most times except Sunday mornings. *Society Meetings:* catered for. Director of Golf: P.D. Keeble (01621 868888).

MALDON. **Warren Golf Club,** Woodham Walter, Maldon CM9 6RW (01245 223198/223258; Fax: 01245 223989). *Location:* close to Chelmsford. A414 turn off to Maldon. Undulating wooded course. 18 holes, 6211 yards. S.S.S. 70. Large practice area. *Green Fees:* weekdays £28.00 18 holes, £35.00 36 holes. *Eating facilities:* restaurant, bar, bar snack menu. *Visitors:* welcome with reservation weekdays except Wednesday mornings. Handicap Certificate required. Golf Academy. *Society Meetings:* catered for weekdays – up to 40 players. Professional: Mickey Walker (01245 224662). Manager: M.F.L. Durham.

OCKENDON. **Belhus Park Golf Club,** Belhus Park, Aveley By-Pass, South Ockendon RM15 4QR (01708 852248 complex, 01708 854748 office). *Location:* on A13 London – Southend Road, approximately one mile from Dartford Tunnel. Parkland. 18 holes, 5188 yards. S.S.S. 68. Driving range. *Green Fees:* information not provided. *Eating facilities:* cafe and bar. *Visitors:* welcome anytime (municipal course), but booking essential weekends and Bank Holidays. Swimming pool. *Society Meetings:* by arrangement, telephone complex. Professional: Gary Lunn (01708 854260). Secretary: D.A. Faust (01708 446224).

ONGAR. **Toot Hill Golf Club,** School Road, Toot Hill, Ongar CM5 9PU (01277 365523). *Location:* between Epping and Ongar. Rolling Essex countryside. 18 holes, 6053 yards. S.S.S. 69. Practice ground. *Green Fees:* £25.00. Society Days (Tuesdays and Thursdays): 18 holes £31.00, 27 holes £42.00. *Eating facilities:* available. *Visitors:* welcome during week. *Society Meetings:* welcome. Professional: Geoff Bacon (01277 365747). Secretary: Mrs C. Cameron.

ORSETT. **Orsett Golf Club,** Brentwood Road, Orsett RM16 3DS (01375 891352). *Location:* A13 Junction roundabout with A128. South towards Chadwell St. Mary on A128. Heathland course. 18 holes, 6614 yards. S.S.S. 72. *Green Fees:* weekdays £30.00 per day, £20 per round after 1pm. *Eating facilities:* full catering available. *Visitors:* welcome on weekdays only by arrangement. Must be members of a club and have handicap. Proof must be produced. *Society Meetings:* welcome on Mondays, Tuesdays and Wednesdays. Professional: Robert Newberry (01375 891797). Secretary: P.M. Pritchard (01375 891226).

RAYLEIGH. **Hanover Golf and Country Club,** Hullbridge Road, Rayleigh SS6 9QS (01702 232377; Fax: 01702 231811). *Location:* A130, A127 Rayleigh. Parkland course, seven lakes. 18 holes, 6523 yards. S.S.S. 71. Putting green. *Green Fees:* weekdays £25.00 per round, £35.00 per day. Members' guests £15.00 per round, £20.00 per day. *Eating facilities:* two bars, restaurant, bar meals, function rooms. *Visitors:* welcome weekdays, Club Handicap required. *Society Meetings:* welcome weekdays. Professional: A. Blackburn (01702 230033). Secretary: G. Harrold.

ROCHFORD near. **Ballards Gore Golf Club,** Gore Road, Canewdon, Near Rochford SS4 2DA (01702 258917). *Location:* Southend Airport three miles, London via A127, club two miles from Rochford. Parkland with lakes. 18 holes, 7062 yards. S.S.S. 74. Practice area. *Green Fees:* weekdays £16.00 per round, £22.00 per day. *Eating facilities:* diningroom (100 covers). *Visitors:* welcome weekdays only. *Society Meetings:* catered for by arrangement. Professional: Ian Marshall (01702 258924). Secretary: N.G. Patient (01702 258917).

ROCHFORD. **Rochford Hundred Golf Club,** Hall Lane, Rochford SS4 1NW (01702 544302). *Location:* B1013 four miles north of Southend. Parkland course. 18 holes, 6132 yards. S.S.S. 69. *Green Fees:* information not provided. *Eating facilities:* full restaurant and snack facilities and bars. *Society Meetings:* catered for. Professional: Gary Shipley (01702 548968). Secretary: A.H. Bondfield. *

ROMFORD. **Maylands Golf and Country Club,** Harold Park, Romford RM3 0AZ (01708 342055). *Location:* directly on A12 between Romford and Brentwood. 18 holes, 6182 yards. S.S.S. 70. Practice field and putting green. *Green Fees:* £20.00 per round, £30.00 per day. *Eating facilities:* bar, spike bar, restaurant and bar snacks. *Visitors:* welcome midweek if members of recognised clubs with Handicap Certificates. *Society Meetings:* catered for Mondays, Wednesdays and Fridays. Professional: John Hopkin (01708 346466). Secretary/Proprietor: P. S. Taylor (Tel & Fax: 01708 373080).

ROMFORD. **Risebridge Golf Centre,** Risebridge Chase, Romford RM1 4DG (01708 727376). *Location:* Gallows Corner, Strait Road, left turn into Lower Bedfords Road, first left Risebridge Chase. Parkland. 18 holes, 6342 yards. S.S.S. 70. Par 3 course. *Green Fees:* weekdays £8.65; weekends £10.65. *Eating facilities:* cafe. *Visitors:* welcome without reservation. Professional: Paul Jennings. Secretary: Jean Pettite.

SAFFRON WALDEN. **Saffron Walden Golf Club,** Windmill Hill, Saffron Walden CB10 1BX (01799 22786). *Location:* end of town on A130 to Cambridge. 18 holes, 6609 yards. S.S.S. 72. *Green Fees:* £28.00 per day or round (weekdays only). *Eating facilities:* lunches and snacks available. *Visitors:* welcome with current Handicap Certificate. *Society Meetings:* catered for Mondays, Wednesdays and Thursdays. Professional: Philip Davis. General Manager: David Smith.

SOUTH BENFLEET. **Boyce Hill Golf Club Ltd,** Vicarage Hill, South Benfleet SS7 1PD (01268 793625). *Location:* one-and-a-half-miles from A13 or A127. Hilly course, 18 holes. S.S.S. 68. *Green Fees:* weekdays £20.00 per round, £25.00 per day. *Eating facilities:* full dining facilities. *Visitors:* welcome, except Tuesday mornings. *Society Meetings:* catered for Thursdays only. Professional: G. Burroughs (01268 752565). Secretary: J.E. Atkins (01268 793625). *

SOUTHEND-ON-SEA. **Southend-on-Sea Golf Club,** Belfairs Lodge, Belfairs Park, Leigh-on-Sea SS9 4LR (01702 524836). *Location:* A127 London to Southend Road. Parkland/wooded course (Belfairs Municipal course). 18 holes, 5877 yards. S.S.S. 68. *Green Fees:* weekdays £11.20; weekends £16.80. *Eating facilities:* restaurant in the park. *Visitors:* welcome, unrestricted, but bookings required for weekends and Bank Holidays. Booking by phone to Starters Hut (01702 525345). Professional: Martin Foreman (01702 520202). Secretary: Peter Metcalfe (01702 344300).

SOUTHEND-ON-SEA. **Thorpe Hall Golf Club,** Thorpe Hall Avenue, Thorpe Bay, Southend-on-Sea. *Location:* one mile east of Southend-on-Sea. Parkland. 18 holes, 6286 yards. S.S.S. 71. *Green Fees:* on application. *Eating facilities:* restaurant open every day except Mondays. *Visitors:* welcome weekdays with Handicap Certificate, weekends with members only. *Society Meetings:* catered for. Professional: Bill McColl (01702 588195). Secretary: G.R.G. Winckless (01702 582205).

STANFORD LE HOPE. **St. Cleres Golf Club,** St. Cleres Hall, Stanford le Hope (01375 361565). Downland course. 18 holes, 6500 yards. S.S.S. 71. Practice ground. *Green Fees:* weekdays £15.00; weekends £20.00. *Visitors:* unrestricted. *Society Meetings:* welcome.

STAPLEFORD ABBOTTS. **Stapleford Abbotts Golf Club,** Horsemans Side, Tysea Hill, Stapleford Abbotts RM4 1JU. *Location:* three miles from Junction 28 M25. Off main Romford – Ongar Road B175 at Stapleford Abbotts, Essex. Parkland with many water hazards. Abbotts – 18 holes, 6684 yards. S.S.S. 71. Priors – 18 holes, 6005 yards. S.S.S. 70. Friars – 9 holes, 1140 yards. S.S.S. 27. Two practice areas. *Green Fees:* Abbotts – £20.00 per round; Priors £15.00 per round; Friars £5.00 per round. *Eating facilities:* stud bar and restaurant. *Visitors:* midweek no restrictions. *Society Meetings:* ring for booking brochure. Professional: Dominic Eagle (01708 381278). Secretary: Keith Fletcher (01708 381108). Tee Reservations: Abbotts (01708 370040); Priors (01277 373344).

STAPLEFORD TAWNEY. **Abridge Golf and Country Club,** Epping Lane, Stapleford Tawney RM4 1ST (01708 688388). *Location:* A113 from London through Chigwell to Abridge, left at White Hart, right after 300 yards. Two miles on. Parkland. 18 holes, 6690 yards. S.S.S. 72. *Green Fees:* on application. *Eating facilities:* restaurant Saturdays to Thursdays, lunch; bar Saturday to Thursday, drinks and snacks; no service Fridays. *Visitors:* welcome but must be a member of a recognised golf club and produce evidence of current Handicap, weekdays only. Tennis courts and heated swimming pool. *Society Meetings:* catered for on Mondays and Wednesdays only by arrangement. Professional: Mike Herbert (01708 688333). Secretary: P.G. Pelling (01708 688396). *

STOCK. **Crondon Park Golf Club**, Stock Road, Stock CM4 9DP (01277 841115). *Location:* on B1007, off the A12 in the direction of Billericay. Set in parkland valley with trees, lakes and magnificent greens. 18 holes, 6270 yards (Club). S.S.S. 70. 9-hole Par 3 course. Changing rooms, driving range and putting green. *Green Fees:* weekdays £15.00. *Eating facilities:* bar, buffet food. *Visitors:* welcome weekdays; weekends as members' guests only. *Society Meetings:* welcome weekdays. Professional: P. Wernham. Secretary: J.W.T. Lewes.

WITHAM. **Braxted Park Golf Club**, Braxted Park, Witham CM8 3EN (01621 891393). *Location:* A12 south of Witham; from Chelmsford take Rivenhall turn-off, if travelling towards Colchester take Silver End turn-off. Mature parkland with specimen trees and lake. 9 holes, 3000 yards. S.S.S. 34. Practice ground. *Green Fees:* weekdays 9 holes £9.00, 18 holes £12.00. *Eating facilities:* catering available. *Visitors:* welcome weekdays 7.30am to 7.30pm; limited weekend play in August and September. *Society Meetings:* welcome, restrictions as for Visitors. The course and Braxted House may be hired for the day. Professional: Roger Smith (01702 558955). Secretary: Michael Clark (01621 891393; Fax: 01621 892840).

WOODFORD GREEN. **Woodford Golf Club**, Sunset Avenue, Woodford Green (0181-504 4254). *Location:* near Castle Public House, Woodford High Road. Public forest land. 9 holes, 5806 yards. S.S.S. 68. *Green Fees:* £15.00 per round. *Eating facilities:* bar. *Visitors:* no green fees Tuesday or Thursday mornings and Sundays after 12.30pm. Red (scarlet) clothing must be worn – trousers or top. *Society Meetings:* welcome. Professional: A. Johns (0181-504 4254). Secretary: G.J. Cousins (0181-504 3330).

Gloucestershire

BROADWAY. **Broadway Golf Club**, Willersey Hill, Broadway WR12 7LG (01386 853683). *Location:* one-and-a-half-miles east Broadway (A44). 18 holes, 6211 yards. S.S.S. 70 *Green Fees:* on application. *Eating facilities:* available daily (except Monday). *Visitors:* welcome; reservation advised. Handicap Certificates required. Saturdays (April/September) with member only before 3pm. October/March no restrictions. *Society Meetings:* by arrangement (Wednesday, Thursday and Friday). Professional: Martyn Freeman (01386 853275). Managing Secretary: B. Carnie (01386 853683).

CHELTENHAM. **Cleeve Cloud Golf Club**, Cleeve Hill, Near Cheltenham (01242 672025). *Location:* three miles north of Cheltenham on B4632. Inland links with gorse. 18 holes, 6411 yards. S.S.S. 71. *Green Fees:* information not provided. *Eating facilities:* full restaurant and bar snack every day. *Visitors:* welcome. *Society Meetings:* welcome with reservation. *

CHELTENHAM. **Lilley Brook Golf Club**, Cirencester Road, Charlton Kings, Cheltenham GL53 8EG (01242 526785). *Location:* two miles south-east of Cheltenham on main Cirencester road (A435). Parkland, 18 holes, 6226 yards, 5979 metres. S.S.S. 70. Practice field. *Green Fees:* weekdays £20.00. *Eating facilities:* full catering available. *Visitors:* welcome weekdays, weekends as a guest of a member only. Handicap Certificates required. *Society Meetings:* by arrangement. Professional: Forbes E. Hadden (01242 525201). Secretary: K.A. Skeen (01242 526785).

CHELTENHAM. **Naunton Downs Golf Club Ltd**, Naunton, Cheltenham GL54 3AE (01451 850093; Fax: 01451 850091). Rolling Cotswold countryside with a valley running through course. 18 holes, 6174 yards. S.S.S. 69. Practice ground. *Green Fees:* £19.95. *Eating facilities:* available. *Visitors:* welcome anytime, must book at weekends. *Society Meetings:* welcome. Director of Golf: Nigel Powell (01451 850092). Secretary: Charlotte Eager (01451 850090).

CHELTENHAM near. **Cotswold Hills Golf Club Ltd,** Ullenwood, Near Cheltenham GL53 9QT (01242 522421). *Location:* at Ullenwood, off the A436 south of Cheltenham (two miles from town). Undulating Cotswold country course, excellent drainage. 18 holes, 6750 yards. S.S.S. 72. Large practice ground. *Green Fees:* weekdays £21.00 per round; weekends £26.00 per round. *Eating facilities:* full restaurant and bars. *Visitors:* no restrictions as a rule, but it is wise to telephone. *Society Meetings:* catered for by arrangement with Secretary. Professional: Noel Boland (01242 515263). Secretary: Andrew O'Reilly (01242 515264).

CIRENCESTER. **Cirencester Golf Club,** Cheltenham Road, Cirencester (01285 653939; Fax: 01285 650665). *Location:* one mile north of Cirencester on A435 Cheltenham road. 18 holes, 6008 yards. S.S.S. 69. *Green Fees:* weekdays £20.00, weekends and Bank Holidays £25.00. *Eating facilities:* lunches and suppers by arrangement. Hot and cold snacks always available. *Visitors:* welcome, Handicap Certificate required. *Society Meetings:* catered for Tuesday, Wednesday and Friday only. Professional: Geoff Robbins (01285 656124). Secretary: N.D. Jones (01285 652465).

COLEFORD. **Forest Hills Golf Club Ltd.,** Mile End Road, Coleford (01594 810620). *Location:* 10 miles from Severn Bridge, six miles from Monmouth M5, M50. Coleford town centre on Gloucester Road. Parkland with panoramic views to Welsh hills. 18 holes, 6000 yards. S.S.S. 68. Practice ground. *Green Fees:* weekdays £13.00; weekends £15.00. All-inclusive packages available. *Eating facilities:* bar, restaurant. *Visitors:* welcome, no restrictions. *Society Meetings:* very welcome. Professional: T. Morgan. Secretary: Mr G. Kear.

COLEFORD. **Royal Forest of Dean Golf Club,** Lords Hill, Coleford GL16 8BD (01594 832583; Fax: 01594 832584). *Location:* quarter of a mile from Coleford town centre on B4431 Coleford to Parkend Road, 10 miles from Severn Bridge, M4, M5 and M50. Parkland course in Forest of Dean. 18 holes, 5535 yards. S.S.S. 67. Practice area. *Green Fees:* weekdays £11.00, weekends £13.00. Society Days – 36 holes golf, snack lunch, dinner only £25.00 available Mondays to Thursdays. *Eating facilities:* food available all day – breakfast, coffee, lunches, teas and dinner. Table d'hôte restaurant, bar open all day. *Visitors:* always welcome, please book teeing-off times with Professional. Own 32 bedroom Hotel (all en-suite), outdoor swimming pool, tennis court, bowling green, golf cars available. *Society Meetings:* welcome. Professional: John Nicol (01594 833689). Secretary: Mrs J. Sandalls (01594 832583).

DURSLEY. **Stinchcombe Hill Golf Club,** Stinchcombe Hill, Dursley GL11 6AQ (01453 542015). *Location:* M5 between Junctions 13 and 14, A38 to Dursley. At traffic lights in centre of Dursley enter May Lane, continue to top of Hill and turn right onto Golf Course. A gently undulating course situated on a hilltop at the southern edge of the Cotswolds, extensive views. 18 holes, 5734 yards. S.S.S. 68. Practice and teaching areas. *Green Fees:* £12.50 per round, £20.00 per day weekdays (£10.00 with member); £25.00 weekends and Bank Holidays (£12.50 with member). *Eating facilities:* full catering and bar service available. *Visitors:* welcome with recognised Handicaps, time restrictions at weekends and Bank Holidays. *Society Meetings:* catered for by arrangement. Professional: Brendan Wynne (01453 543878). Secretary: John R. Clarke (01453 542015).

GLOUCESTER. **Gloucester Hotel, Golf and Country Club,** Matson Lane, Gloucester GL4 9EA (01452 525653 Ext. 316). *Location:* situated on Robinwood Hill, turn off Gloucester to Painswick Road and head for Ski slopes. Parkland-type. Back 9 holes on top of hill. 18 holes, 6137 yards, 5613 metres. S.S.S. 69. 9 hole Par 3 course, driving range. *Green Fees:* information not provided. *Eating facilities:* full catering available. *Visitors:* welcome any time but booking recommended by telephoning Secretary. *Society Meetings:* welcome weekdays, weekends by special arrangement. Professional/Manager: P. Darnell (01452 411331). *

LYDNEY. **Lydney Golf Club,** The Links, off Lakeside Avenue, Lydney GL15 5QA (01594 842614). *Location:* on front left-hand side of town when entering on A48 Chepstow Road from Gloucester. Flat meadowland with views over the River Severn. 9 holes, 5382 yards. S.S.S. 66. Small practice area. *Green Fees:* £12.00 per day weekdays; weekends with a member only. Reduction of £3.00 when playing with a member. *Eating facilities:* snack meals only. *Visitors:* welcome weekdays, only with a member at weekends/Bank Holidays. *Society Meetings:* welcome by prior arrangement (maximum 36). Hon. Secretary: D.A. Barnard (01594 843940).

MINCHINHAMPTON. **Minchinhampton Golf Club (New Courses),** Minchinhampton, Stroud GL6 9BE (01453 833866). *Location:* between Minchinhampton and Avening. Two courses: both 18 holes, Cherington 6360 yards, Avening 6303 yards. S.S.S. 71. Practice area. *Green Fees:* on request. *Eating facilities:* available. *Visitors:* welcome, advance booking essential. Handicap Certificate required. *Society Meetings:* by arrangement, must have Handicaps. Professional: Chris Steele (Tel & Fax: 01453 833860). Secretary: David Vickers (01453 833866).

MINCHINHAMPTON. **Minchinhampton Golf Club (Old Course),** Minchinhampton, Stroud GL6 9AW (01453 832642). *Location:* between Minchinhampton and Stroud. 18 holes, 6295 yards. S.S.S. 70. Practice site. *Green Fees:* on request. *Eating facilities:* available. *Visitors:* welcome. *Society Meetings:* by arrangement. Professional: C. Steele (01453 836382). Administrator: R.W. Clarke (01453 832642). Secretary: D.R. Vickers (01453 833866).

PAINSWICK. **Painswick Golf Club,** Painswick, Near Stroud (01452 812180). *Location:* one mile north of Painswick village on A46 turn left. Hilltop, wooded course. 18 holes, 4900 yards. S.S.S. 64. *Green Fees:* weekdays £10.00; Saturdays £15.00. *Eating facilities:* lunches at clubhouse bar by arrangement. *Visitors:* welcome weekdays and Saturday mornings. Saturday afternoons, Sunday mornings and Public Holidays only with member. *Society Meetings:* welcome weekdays. Secretary: A.R. Green.

TETBURY. **Westonbirt Golf Course,** c/o Bursar, Westonbirt School Ltd, Westonbirt, Near Tetbury GL8 8QP (01666 880 242). *Location:* three miles south from Tetbury on A433, A439 to Bath on Bath road. Parkland. 9 holes, 4504 yards. S.S.S. 61. Practice area and green. *Green Fees:* weekdays £7.00 per day adults, £4.50 per day Juniors; weekends £7.00 per round adults, £4.50 per round Juniors. Eating facilities: tea and refreshments, outdoor table and chairs. *Visitors:* welcome without reservation. *Society Meetings:* catered for. Professional: C. Steele (visiting from Minchinhampton Golf Club). Secretary: Mr J. Nolan.

TEWKESBURY. **Puckrup Hall Hotel & Golf Club,** Puckrup, Tewkesbury GL20 6EL (01684 296200; Fax: 01684 850788). *Location:* three miles north of Tewkesbury on A38, half a mile from Junction 1 M50. Undulating parkland with water hazards, spectacular views of the Malverns. 18 holes, 6431 yards. S.S.S. 71. *Green Fees:* weekdays £19.50; weekends £25.00. Day ticket £27.50 weekdays, £30.00 weekends. *Eating facilities:* three bars, à la carte restaurant, brasserie, snack bar. *Visitors:* welcome, subject to golfing ability and course availability. 84 bedroomed hotel with full leisure facilities. *Society Meetings:* welcome. Golf Breaks available. Professional/Secretary: Kevin Pickett.

TEWKESBURY. **Tewkesbury Park Hotel, Golf and Country Club,** Lincoln Green Lane, Tewkesbury GL20 7DN (01684 295405; Fax: 01684 292386). *Location:* leave Junction 9 of M5, continue into Tewkesbury onto Gloucester Road. Parkland. 18 holes, 6533 yards. S.S.S. 72. 9 holes, Par 3 course. *Green Fees:* weekdays £25.00; weekends £30.00. Special rates available by arrangement. *Eating facilities:* full facilities available. *Visitors:* welcome, reservation required weekends. Valid Handicap Certificate required. Leisure complex. 78 bedroomed hotel. *Society Meetings:* all welcome by prior arrangement. Professional: Mr Robert Taylor (01684 294892). Secretary: Mr Bob Nichol (01684 299452).

WOTTON-UNDER-EDGE. **Cotswold Edge Golf Club,** Upper Rushmire, Wotton-under-Edge GL12 7PT (01453 844167). *Location:* eight miles from Junction 14 M5, on B4058 Tetbury road. Fairly flat course with magnificent views. 18 holes, White Tees – 6170 yards. S.S.S. 70; Yellow Tees – 5816 yards. S.S.S. 69. *Green Fees:* weekdays £15.00. Subject to review. *Eating facilities:* good catering service, usual bar facilities. *Visitors:* welcome weekdays. Telephone call in advance advisable. *Society Meetings:* by arrangement with Secretary. Professional: David Gosling (01453 844398). Secretary: N.J. Newman (01453 844167).

Hampshire

ALDERSHOT. **Army Golf Club,** Laffan's Road, Aldershot GU11 2HF (01252 540638; Fax: 01252 376562). Clubhouse (01252 541104). Pro's Shop (01252 547232). *Location:* access from Eelmoor Bridge off A323 Aldershot Fleet Road. 18 holes, 6533 yards. S.S.S. 71. *Green Fees:* special rates for servicemen. *Eating facilities:* a range of catering is available by arrangement with the Secretary. *Visitors:* weekdays only, members' guests anytime. *Society Meetings:* catered for. Professional: Mr Nigel Turner. Secretary/Manager: R.T. Crabb.

ALRESFORD. **Alresford Golf Club,** Cheriton Road, Tichborne Down, Alresford S024 0PN. *Location:* one mile south of A31 (Winchester/Alton). Two miles north A272 (Winchester/Petersfield). Rolling downland, wooded. 18 holes, 5905 yards. S.S.S. 68. Practice area. *Green Fees:* weekdays £16.50; weekends and Bank Holidays £32.00 per round (not before 12 noon). *Eating facilities:* full catering except Mondays. *Visitors:* welcome but not before 12 noon weekends/Bank Holidays. *Society Meetings:* catered for by prior arrangement. Professional: Malcolm Scott (01962 733998). Secretary: Peter Kingston (01962 733746).

ALTON. **Alton Golf Club,** Old Odiham Road, Alton GU34 4BU (01420 82042). *Location:* off A32, two miles north of Alton. Odiham six miles. Undulating wooded course. 9 holes, alternate tees. 5744 yards. S.S.S. 68. Practice area. *Green Fees:* weekdays £10.00 per round, £14.00 per day; weekends £20.00 per round, £30.00 per day. Half green fees if with a member. *Eating facilities:* bar. *Visitors:* weekdays welcome without reservation, except on competition days. Weekends and Bank Holidays with member or 18 Handicap maximum. *Society Meetings:* welcome weekdays only, catering provided. Professional: Mr A. Lamb (01420 86518). Secretary: W.J. Cleveland (Home: 01420 84774; Office: 01420 82042).

AMPFIELD. **Ampfield Par Three Golf and Country Club,** Winchester Road, Ampfield, Near Romsey SO51 9BQ (01794 368480). *Location:* A31 Winchester to Romsey road, next door to White Horse Public House. Parkland course designed by Henry Cotton. All holes par 3. 18 holes, 2478 yards. S.S.S. 53. *Green Fees:* on application. *Eating facilities:* light meals and snacks, bar facilities. *Visitors:* welcome, but best to phone first. Handicap Certificate required at weekends and Bank Holidays. Recognised golf shoes must be worn. *Society Meetings:* catered for by prior arrangement. Professional: Richard Benfield (01794 368750). Secretary: Mrs Stella Baker.

ANDOVER. **Andover Golf Club,** 51 Winchester Road, Andover SP10 2EF (01264 323980). *Location:* half-mile south of town centre on the A3057 Winchester/Stockbridge road. Parkland. 9 holes, 5933 yards. S.S.S. 68. *Green Fees:* weekdays £10.00 per round, £15.00 per day; £22.00 weekends. *Eating facilities:* full catering available. *Visitors:* welcome but not before 12 noon weekends and Bank Holidays. *Society Meetings:* welcome Mondays to Wednesdays by arrangement. Professional: A. Timms (01264 324151). Secretary: D.A. Fairweather (01264 358040). Clubhouse Manager: (01264 323980).

ANDOVER. **The Hampshire Golf Club,** Winchester Road, Goodworth Clatford, Andover SP11 7TB (01264 357555). *Location:* one mile south of Andover on A3057 Stockbridge Road. Downland with new trees and lakes. 18 holes, 6318 yards. S.S.S. 70. Driving range. *Green Fees:* weekdays £11.00; weekends £15.00. Discount for Juniors. *Eating facilities:* bar. *Visitors:* always welcome. *Society Meetings:* all welcome. Professional: Tony Ashton. Secretary: T.C. Fiducia (01264 357555; Fax: 01264 352965).

BARTON-ON-SEA. **Barton-on-Sea Golf Club,** Milford Road, New Milton BH25 5PP (01425 615308; Fax: 01425 621457). *Location:* one mile from centre of New Milton on B3058 towards Milford-on-Sea. Flat landscaped course on cliff edge – superb views of Isle of Wight and Christchurch Bay to Swanage. 27 holes. S.S.S. 72 any 18 holes. *Green Fees:* £25.00 per day weekdays; £30.00 weekends. *Eating facilities:* lunch, snacks and teas daily, full bar service. *Visitors:* welcome after 8.30am weekdays; weekends and Bank Holidays after 11.15am. Handicap Certificate required. *Society Meetings:* welcome by arrangement Mondays, Wednesdays and Fridays. Professional: P. Coombs (01425 611210). General Manager: A. Ross. *

BASINGSTOKE. **Basingstoke Golf Club,** Kempshott Park, Basingstoke RG23 7LL (01256 465990). *Location:* on A30, three miles west of town on road to Winchester; from Winchester leave M3 at Exit 7. Parkland course. 18 holes, 6350 yards. S.S.S. 70. *Green Fees:* information not provided. *Eating facilities:* full catering available seven days. *Visitors:* welcome on weekdays if member of a golf club, visitors at weekends and Bank Holidays only if playing with a member. *Society Meetings:* by arrangement through the Secretary. Professional: I. Hayes (01256 51332). Secretary: Gordon Hogg (01256 465990).

BASINGSTOKE. **Bishopswood Golf Club,** Bishopswood Lane, Tadley, Basingstoke RG26 6AT (01734 812200). *Location:* six miles north of Basingstoke off the A340. Parkland/wooded course. 9 holes, 6474 yards. S.S.S. 71. 12 bay floodlit driving range open seven days a week. *Green Fees:* weekdays £8.00 for 9 holes, £13.00 for 18 holes. *Eating facilities:* lounge and spike bars – snacks, bar meals and 50 seater restaurant facility. *Visitors:* welcome weekdays only by prior booking. *Society Meetings:* welcome by arrangement. Professional: S. Ward (Tel & Fax: 01734 815213). Manager: M.W. Phillips (01734 812200).

BASINGSTOKE. **Sandford Springs Golf Club,** Sandford Springs, Wolverton, Basingstoke RG26 5RT (01635 297881; Fax: 01635 298065). *Location:* north of A339 Basingstoke to Newbury road at Kingsclere. Wooded parkland course with lakes, undulating, with excellent views of surrounding area. Three loops of 9 holes. 27 holes. S.S.S. 69/70/69. Practice ground and putting green. *Green Fees:* weekdays £23.00. *Eating facilities:* available all day; also conference and banqueting facilities. *Visitors:* welcome weekdays. *Society Meetings:* always welcome weekdays. Golf Manager: G. Edmunds. Secretary/Director: G. Tipple. Managing Director: K. Brake.

BASINGSTOKE. **Test Valley Golf Club,** Micheldever Road, Overton, Basingstoke RG25 3DS (01256 771737). *Location:* on the C79, one mile north of M3/A303 signposted Overton. Downland in the style of the traditional Scottish/Irish links with hidden pot bunkers, etc. 18 holes, 6811 yards. S.S.S. 73. Full practice facilities. *Green Fees:* weekdays £14.00; weekends £20.00. *Eating facilities:* snacks in spike bar; breakfast, full meals, etc in diningroom. *Visitors:* welcome but may be restricted weekend mornings. *Society Meetings:* welcome (from £18.00 per person). Professional: Terry Notley. Secretary: Mrs J. McDonagh.

BASINGSTOKE. **Tylney Park Golf Club,** Rotherwick, near Basingstoke (01256 762079). *Location:* one mile Hook A30. Parkland. 18 holes, 6135 yards. S.S.S. 69, Par 70. *Green Fees:* weekdays £20.00; weekends £28.00. *Eating facilities:* catering available. *Visitors:* weekdays unrestricted, weekends with Handicap Certificate or as guest of a member. Professional: C. DeBruin. Secretary: A.D. Bewley. *

BASINGSTOKE. **Weybrook Park Golf Club,** Aldermaston Road, Sherborne St. John, Basingstoke RG24 9ND (01256 64074). *Location:* two miles north west of Basingstoke town centre, signposted off A339, leave at Newbury Road roundabout. Parkland. 18 holes, 6093 yards, 5571 metres. S.S.S. 69. Practice area. *Green Fees:* weekdays £12.00, with a member £7.00, Juniors £6.00, Senior Citizens £7.00; weekends and Bank Holidays £14.00, with a member £8.00. *Eating facilities:* clubhouse with bar and snacks. *Visitors:* welcome – advisable to telephone for availability. All players must have their own clubs, suitable casual/smart attire must be worn. *Society Meetings:* welcome, telephone for booking and costs. Secretary: Mr G.E. Carpenter (01256 20347).

BORDON. **Blackmoor Golf Club,** Bordon GU35 9EH (01420 472775). *Location:* lies midway between Petersfield and Farnham on A325. 18 holes, 6213 yards. S.S.S. 70. *Green Fees:* £35.00 per day, after 1pm £26.00. *Eating facilities:* dining room. *Visitors:* welcome with reservation, Handicaps necessary. *Society Meetings:* catered for all day. Morning coffee, lunch, evening meal. Professional: Stephen Clay (01420 472345; Fax: 01420 476110). Secretary: Major (Retd) H.R.G. Spiller (01420 472775; Fax: 01420 487666).

BORDON near. **Dean Farm Golf Club,** Kingsley, Near Bordon GU35 9NG (01420 489478). *Location:* B3004 off A325 (Farnham to Petersfield Road). Parkland public course, a challenging short course. 9 holes, 1797 yards. S.S.S. Men 53, Ladies 60. *Green Fees:* £4.00 9 holes. *Eating facilities:* bar and cafeteria. *Visitors:* welcome seven days. *Society Meetings:* welcome. Secretary: G. Doggrell.

BROCKENHURST. **Brokenhurst Manor Golf Club,** Sway Road, Brockenhurst SO42 7SG (01590 22383). *Location:* from M27 take A337 to Brockenhurst then B3055 (to Sway). Approximately one mile to golf club. Beautiful New Forest parkland course – wet in winter. 18 holes, 6222 yards. S.S.S. 70. Practice ground. *Green Fees:* weekdays £25.00 per round, £30.00 per day; weekends and Bank Holidays £35.00. *Eating facilities:* full catering and bar facilities. *Visitors:* welcome by arrangement except Tuesday mornings. Handicap Certificate required. *Society Meetings:* Thursdays by arrangement. Professional: J. Lovell (01590 23092). Secretary: A.S. Craven (01590 23332; Fax: 01590 24140).

CRONDALL. **Oak Park Golfing Complex,** Heath Lane, Crondall, Near Farnham, Surrey GU10 5PB (01252 850880; Fax: 01252 850851). *Location:* one and a half miles off A287 Farnham-Odiham road, five miles from Junctions 4 and 5 of M3 motorway. Gently undulating parkland course. 18 holes, 6437 yards. S.S.S. 71. Putting green and 16 bay covered driving range. *Green Fees:* weekdays £16.00 per round, £25.00 per day (reductions for Juniors); weekends £22.50 per round, £40 per day. *Eating facilities:* à la carte restaurant: Mon to Fri lunchtime and Sunday lunch. Tues to Sat evenings. Bar snacks available. *Visitors:* welcome; must book through Professional; reserved tee system weekends and Public Holidays. *Society Meetings:* by arrangement with Secretary, welcome every day subject to availability. Professional: Simon Coaker (01252 850066). Secretary: Mrs R. Smythe (01252 850850).

DIBDEN. **Dibden Golf Centre,** Main Road, Dibden, Southampton (01703 207508). *Location:* half-mile off A326 Totton to Fawley road at Dibden very close to New Forest. 18 holes, 6206 yards. S.S.S. 70. 9 hole course and 19 bay driving range. *Green Fees:* summer rate: weekdays £6.90, weekends £10.00. *Eating facilities:* available. *Visitors:* welcome without reservation. *Society Meetings:* catered for. Professional: Alan Bridge (01703 845596). Course administration by Professional.

EASTLEIGH. **Fleming Park Golf Club,** Magpie Lane, Eastleigh (01703 643671). *Location:* two miles off M27 Eastleigh Airport turning. Parkland. 18 holes, 4376 yards. S.S.S. 61. *Green Fees:* weekdays 9 holes £3.85, 18 holes £5.95, per day £10.65; weekends 9 holes £5.90, 18 holes £8.65, per day £15.10. *Eating facilities:* bar. *Visitors:* welcome, book on day or one week in advance. *Society Meetings:* all welcome. Professional: C. Strickett (01703 612797). Secretary: D. Ainsworth-Lay (01703 612797).

FAREHAM. **Cams Hall Estate Golf Club,** Cams Hill, Fareham PO16 8UP (01329 827222; Fax: 01329 827111). *Location:* Junction 9 M27 following signs to Portchester. Parkland, wooded course. Creek course 18 holes, Park Course 9 holes. Practice range. *Green Fees:* Creek Course: weekdays £18.00, weekends as member's guest only. Park Course: weekdays £7.00, weekends £12.00. *Eating facilities:* à la carte restaurant and two bars. *Visitors:* welcome. *Society Meetings:* welcome. Professional: Jason Neve (01329 827732). General Manager: Nigel Brunner.

FAREHAM. **Southwick Park Golf Club,** Pinsley Drive, Southwick, Fareham PO17 6EL (01705 370683). *Location:* near Southwick village, within HMS Dryad. Parkland. 18 holes, 5972 yards. S.S.S. 69. Practice area, pitch and putt. *Green Fees:* information not provided. *Eating facilities:* bar and snacks available. *Visitors:* weekdays only. *Society Meetings:* Tuesdays only, book through Manager. Professional: J. Green (01705 380442). Manager: N.W. Price (Tel & Fax: 01705 380131).

FARNBOROUGH. **Southwood Golf Course,** Ively Road, Cove, Farnborough GU14 0LJ (01252 515139). *Location:* approximately half a mile west of A325. Flat parkland. 18 holes, 5553 yards. S.S.S. 67. Putting green. *Green Fees:* weekdays £11.00; weekends £14.00. *Eating facilities:* bar and diningroom available. *Visitors:* welcome, bookable at all times. *Society Meetings:* catered for by arrangement. Professional: Bob Hammond (01252 548700).

FLEET. **Hartley Wintney Golf Club,** London Road, Hartley Wintney, Basingstoke RG27 8PT (01252 842214). *Location:* on A30 between Camberley and Basingstoke. Parkland, wooded. 9 holes, 6096 yards. S.S.S. 69. Practice area. *Green Fees:* under review. *Eating facilities:* full catering facilities available except Mondays. *Visitors:* restricted Wednesdays (Ladies' Day); weekends and Bank Holidays with member only. *Society Meetings:* catered for Tuesdays and Thursdays on application. Professional: Martin Smith (01252 843379). Secretary: B.D. Powell (01252 844211).

FLEET. **North Hants Golf Club,** Minley Road, Fleet GU13 8RE (01252 616443). *Location:* B3013 off A30, M3 Junction 4a. 400 yards from railway station. Heathland. 18 holes, 6257 yards. S.S.S. 70. Practice ground. *Green Fees:* weekdays £24.00 per round, £30.00 per two rounds. *Eating facilities:* lunch daily, evening meals by prior arrangement. *Visitors:* welcome weekdays only by prior arrangement, Handicap Certificates required, Thursdays ladies' day. *Society Meetings:* Tuesdays and Wednesdays only, maximum 42. Professional: Steve Porter (01252 616655). Secretary: I.R. Goodliffe (01252 616443; Fax: 01252 811627).

GOSPORT. **Fleetlands Golf Club,** RNAY Fleetlands, Fareham Road, Gosport PO13 0AW. *Location:* two miles south of Fareham on Fareham/Gosport Road. Flat/wooded course. 9 holes, 4852 yards. S.S.S. 64. *Green Fees:* £4.00 weekdays; £6.00 weekends. *Eating facilities:* bar/clubhouse. *Visitors:* by appointment with member only. *Society Meetings:* by appointment with member only. Secretary: Mr A. Eade (01705 822351 extension 44384).

GOSPORT. **Gosport and Stokes Golf Club,** off Fort Road, Haslar, Gosport (01705 581625). *Location:* A32 to Gosport, course is one mile east of Stokes Bay, near Gilkicker Point. Water course, natural hazards. 9 holes, 5800 yards. S.S.S. 68. Nets and putting green. *Green Fees:* weekdays £12.00; weekends £15.00. *Eating facilities:* bar snacks, meals by arrangement. *Visitors:* welcome all week, restricted Sundays and Thursdays. *Society Meetings:* by arrangement. Secretary: A.P. Chubb (01705 527941).

HAVANT. **Rowlands Castle Golf Club,** 31 Links Lane, Rowlands Castle PO9 6AE (01705 412216). *Location:* four miles north of Havant or Horndean/Rowlands Castle Junction from A3M. Flat parkland, wooded course. 18 holes, 6627 yards White Tees, 6381 yards Yellow Tees. S.S.S. 72 (White), 70 (Yellow). *Green Fees:* weekdays £23.00 per round/day; weekends £28.00. Subject to review. *Eating facilities:* full catering available except Mondays. *Visitors:* welcome, except Saturdays unless playing with a member, maximum 12 visitors on a Sunday and Bank Holidays. *Society Meetings:* catered for Tuesdays and Thursdays, bookings through Secretary. Professional: Peter Klepacz (01705 412785). Secretary: Mr K.D. Fisher (01705 412784).

HAYLING ISLAND. **Hayling Golf Club,** Links Lane, Hayling Island PO11 0BX (01705 463777). *Location:* A3023 five miles south of Havant. Seaside links. 18 holes, 6521 yards, 5965 metres. S.S.S. 71. *Green Fees:* weekdays £30.00 per day, weekends £35.00. *Eating facilities:* lunches and afternoon teas available. *Visitors:* welcome with current Handicap Certificate and must be members of recognised clubs. *Society Meetings:* Tuesdays and Wednesdays only by arrangement with the Secretary. Professional: Ray Gadd (01705 464491). Secretary: M.D. Harrison (01705 464446).

LEE-ON-THE-SOLENT. **Lee-On-The-Solent Golf Club,** Brune Lane, Lee-on-the-Solent PO13 9PB (01750 550207). *Location:* M27 Exit 9 eastbound, Exit 11 westbound, three miles south of Fareham. Flat parkland course. 18 holes, 5959 yards. S.S.S. 69. Practice range. *Green Fees:* weekdays £25.00; weekends £30.00. *Eating facilities:* full catering, extensive bar snack menu, lounge bar. *Visitors:* welcome weekdays, Handicap Certificate required. *Society Meetings:* welcome Thursdays, other days by special arrangement. Professional: Mr. John Richardson (01705 551181). Secretary: Michael Topper (01705 551170; Fax: 01705 554233).

LIPHOOK. **Liphook Golf Club,** Wheatsheaf Enclosure, Liphook GU30 7EH (01428 723271). *Location:* one mile south of Liphook off the old A3 Portsmouth road. Heathland. 18 holes, 6250 yards. S.S.S. 70. *Green Fees:* on application. *Eating facilities:* bar and restaurant. *Visitors:* welcome, Handicap Certificate required, check with Secretary. *Society Meetings:* catered for. Professional: Ian Large (01428 723271). Secretary: Major J.B. Morgan MBE (01428 723785).

LIPHOOK. **Old Thorns Golf Course and Hotel,** Longmoor Road, Liphook GU30 7PE (01428 724555). *Location:* A3 to Griggs Green exit then 500 yards. Parkland, wooded, with natural streams and lakes. 18 holes, 6529 yards. S.S.S. 72. Practice ground and putting green. *Green Fees:* £25.00 per round, £40.00 per weekday. £35.00 per round weekends. Telephone to arrange a starting time. *Eating facilities:* full catering available. Choice of European or Japanese cuisine. *Visitors:* welcome at all times. *Society Meetings:* welcome all week. Society Days £57.00. Company Days: Prices on request. Facilities: 33 en suite bedrooms, indoor heated swimming pool, sauna, solarium, massage, two tennis courts, conference and banqueting rooms. Professional: Philip Loxley. General Manager: G.M. Jones.

LYNDHURST. **Bramshaw Golf Club,** Brook, Lyndhurst (01703 813433). *Location:* M27 (Interchange 1) one mile from M27 (north) at Brook. Two courses: one parkland, one woodland. Both 18 holes. Forest Course 5774 yards. S.S.S. 68. Manor Course 6233 yards. S.S.S. 70. Practice facilities. *Green Fees:* £30.00 weekdays, weekends with member only or Bell Inn Hotel guest. *Eating facilities:* clubhouse and restaurant, also Bell Inn close by. *Visitors:* welcome Monday to Friday. No visitors at weekends unless playing with a member or Bell Inn resident. Accommodation in 22 bedroomed hotel. *Society Meetings:* catered for by arrangement. Professional: Clive Bonner (01703 813434). General Manager: Bob Tingey (01703 813433).

LYNDHURST. **New Forest Golf Club,** Southampton Road, Lyndhurst SO43 7BU (01703 282752). *Location:* on the A35 between Ashurst and Lyndhurst. Forest heathland course. 18 holes, 5742 yards. S.S.S. 68. Practice area and net. *Green Fees:* weekdays £12.00; weekends and Bank Holidays £14.00. *Eating facilities:* bar and lounge, dining room, garden. *Visitors:* welcome, weekdays after 9am, Saturdays after 10am and Sundays after 2.30pm. *Society Meetings:* advance booking only; maximum number of 24. Professional: (01703 282752). Secretary: Mr M.J. Wilson (01703 282752).

PETERSFIELD. **Petersfield Golf Club,** Heath Road, Petersfield GU31 4EJ (01730 263725; Fax: 01730 262386). *Location:* turn off A3 in town centre, clubhouse one mile east. Flat heathland and parkland. 18 holes, 5649 yards. S.S.S. 67. Practice ground. *Green Fees:* £15.00 per round weekdays; £21.00 per round weekends. *Eating facilities:* full catering and bar facilities. *Visitors:* welcome all day weekdays, Saturday and Sunday afternoons only. *Society Meetings:* welcome, must book in advance. Professional: Greg Hughes (01730 267732). General Manager: Richard Hine (01730 262386).

PORTSMOUTH. **Great Salterns Municipal Golf Course,** Burrfields Road, Portsmouth PO3 5HH. *Location:* south on A2030 off M27 signposted "Southsea". Flat links course. 18 holes, 5894 yards. S.S.S. 68. Floodlit driving range. *Green Fees:* summer £9.40, winter £6.90. Senior Citizens/Under 18's summer £5.70, winter £4.20. *Eating facilities:* full bar and catering service at Farmhouse Pub next door. *Visitors:* always welcome, tee time booking required one week ahead. *Society Meetings:* welcome. Professional: Terry Healy (01705 664549; Fax: 01705 650525).

PORTSMOUTH. **Portsmouth Golf Club (1926),** Crookhorn Lane, Widley, Portsmouth PO7 5QL (01705 375999). *Location:* two thirds of a mile from junction of B2177 and A3. Hilly course with views of harbour; outstanding 6th hole. 18 holes, 6139 yards. S.S.S. 69. Practice area, putting green. *Green Fees:* £9.70 Summer; £7.10 Winter. *Eating facilities:* full restaurant and bar. *Visitors:* welcome, tee bookings required. *Society Meetings:* welcome by prior arrangement with Pro Shop. Professional: Ian Roper (01705 372210; Fax: 01705 200766). Secretary: D. Houlihan (01705 201827).

PORTSMOUTH. **Southsea Golf Club,** Eastern Road, Portsmouth. *Location:* half a mile from M27 exit A2030 Southsea. Plays over Great Salterns Golf Course. Flat parkland. 18 holes, 6050 yards. S.S.S. 68. Floodlit golf driving range. *Green Fees:* information not provided. *Eating facilities:* at adjacent farmhouse bar/restaurant. *Visitors:* welcome – public course. Professional: Terry Healy (01705 690816). Secretary: K. Parker (01705 812435).

PORTSMOUTH. **Waterlooville Golf Club,** Cherry Tree Avenue, Cowplain, Waterlooville PO8 8AP. *Location:* off A3 or A3 (M), 10 miles north of Portsmouth. Parkland course. 18 holes, 6647 yards. S.S.S. 72. *Green Fees:* £20.00 per round, £30.00 per day, weekdays only. *Eating facilities:* full catering service available, bar facilities. *Visitors:* welcome weekdays, weekends as members' guests only. *Society Meetings:* catered for by prior arrangement. Professional: John Hay (01705 256911). Secretary: Mr C. Chamberlain (Tel & Fax: 01705 263388).

RINGWOOD. **Burley Golf Club,** Cott Lane, Burley, Ringwood BH24 4BB (01425 403737). *Location:* A31 from Ringwood and turn right at Picket Post and on through Burley Street. Heathland course, 9 holes, 6149 yards. S.S.S. 69. *Green Fees:* weekdays £14.00, weekends £16.00. Under 18's £8.00 weekdays, £9 weekends. *Eating facilities:* bar open, food available lunchtimes most days. *Visitors:* welcome, but not before 4pm Saturdays and 1.45pm Wednesdays. *Society Meetings:* not catered for. Secretary: Major G.R. Kendall (01425 402431).

RINGWOOD. **Moors Valley Golf Centre,** Horton Road, Ashley Heath, Ringwood BH24 2ET. *Location:* signposted from A338/A31 roundabout. Public heathland course. 18 holes, 6270 yards. S.S.S. 72. 14 bay floodlit driving range. *Green Fees:* weekdays £5.00 9 holes, £8.50 18 holes; weekends £6.00 9 holes, £11.00 18 holes. Youth rates available. *Eating facilities:* snack bar and bar. *Visitors:* welcome. *Society Meetings:* welcome by arrangement. Professional: Michael Torrens (Tel & Fax: 01425 479776). *

ROMSEY. **Dunwood Manor Golf Club,** Shootash Hill, Near Romsey SO51 0GF (01794 340549; Fax: 01794 341215). *Location:* four miles from Romsey off A27. Undulating parkland. 18 holes, 6004 yards. S.S.S. 69. Practice area. *Green Fees:* £20.00 per round, £28.00 per day weekdays; £30.00 per round weekends. Society rates from £23.00. *Eating facilities:* full catering, all day bar. *Visitors:* welcome, by arrangement. Self catering accommodation for up to eight people available. *Society Meetings:* welcome, by arrangement. Professional: Jonathan Simpson (01794 340663). Secretary: Hazel Johnson (01794 340549; Fax: 01794 341215).

ROMSEY. **Paultons Golf Centre,** Old Salisbury Road, Ower, near Romsey SO51 6AN (01703 813345; Fax: 01703 813993). *Location:* off M3 at Junction 2 towards Salisbury on A36; at first roundabout take first exit, then first right at Vine Public House. Parkland/ woodland laid out within the original grounds of Paulton House, landscaped by Capability Brown. 18 holes, 6200 yards, 5670 metres. S.S.S. 71. 9-hole academy course. 24-bay floodlit driving range. *Green Fees:* weekdays £17.50, weekends £18.50; 9-hole course £6.50. Reductions for Senior Citizens on Mondays and for Ladies on Tuesdays. *Eating facilities:* full bar and restaurant. *Visitors:* welcome anytime. *Society Meetings:* welcome anytime with prior booking. Professionals: John Cave and Heather Teschner (01703 814626). Secretary: J.R. Smith (01703 813992).

ROMSEY. **Wellow Golf Club,** Ryedown Lane, East Wellow, Romsey SO51 6BD (01794 322872). *Location:* M27 Junction 2 – A36 Salisbury, one mile right to East Wellow, one mile right Ryedown Lane. Parkland. 18 holes (further 9 under construction), 5966 yards. S.S.S. 69. Excellent practice facilities. *Green Fees:* weekdays £15.00; weekends £20.00. *Eating facilities:* food available all day. *Visitors:* welcome – advise ringing before playing. Correct dress code must be observed. *Society Meetings:* all welcome. Professional: Mr Neil Bratley (01994 323833). Secretary: Mrs C. Gurd.

SHEDFIELD. **Meon Valley Hotel, Golf and Country Club,** Sandy Lane, Shedfield SO32 2HQ (01329 833455; Fax: 01329 834411). *Location:* leave M27 at exit 7, take A334 to Botley then towards Wickham. Sandy Lane is 2 miles on the left. Wooded course. 18 holes, 6519 yards. S.S.S. 71. 9 holes, 2714 yards. S.S.S. 34. *Green Fees:* weekdays £25.00 per round; weekends £30.00. *Eating facilities:* Treetops Restaurant, poolside grillroom and three bars. *Visitors:* welcome, no restrictions. Handicap Certificates required to play. *Society Meetings:* catered for. Professional: Mr John Stirling (01329 832184). Secretary: Mr George McMenemy.

SOUTHAMPTON. **Botley Park Golf Club,** Winchester Road, Botley, Southampton SO3 2UA (01489 780888; Fax: 01489 789242). *Location:* approximately two miles from Junction 7 on M27. Parkland. 18 holes, 6200 yards. S.S.S. 70. Driving range. *Green Fees:* £23.00. *Eating facilities:* two bars, main restaurant and club lounge. *Visitors:* welcome by prior booking by phone. Handicap Certificate required. 100 bedroomed hotel on site; tennis, squash, swimming, sauna, solarium, steam room, fitness suite, snooker. *Society Meetings:* Wednesdays and Thursdays only. Professional: Tim Barter (01489 789771; Fax: 01489 789242). Secretary: David Taylor.

SOUTHAMPTON. **Corhampton Golf Club,** Corhampton, Southampton SO32 3LP (01489 877279). *Location:* one mile from Corhampton on the Bishops Waltham – Corhampton road (B3135). 18 holes, 6088 yards. S.S.S. 69. *Green Fees:* weekdays £20.00 per round, £30.00 per day; weekends £10.00 with a member only. *Eating facilities:* full catering, except Tuesdays. *Visitors:* welcome Monday to Friday; weekends and Bank Holidays with a member. *Society Meetings:* Mondays and Thursdays. Professional: Garry Stubbington (01489 877638). Secretary: P. Taylor (01489 877279). Steward: E. Easson (01489 878749).

SOUTHAMPTON. **Romsey Golf Club,** Nursling, Southampton SO16 0XW (01703 734637; Fax: 01703 741036). *Location:* two miles south east of Romsey on A3057, M27/M271 Junction 3. Well wooded, undulating course with extremely good views. 18 holes, 5856 yards. S.S.S. 68. *Green Fees:* weekdays £19.50 per round, £24.00 per day; weekends with a member only. *Eating facilities:* bar and restaurant. *Visitors:* welcome weekdays only. *Society Meetings:* welcome. Professional: Mark Desmond (01703 736673). Secretary: Phil Hargraves.

SOUTHAMPTON. **Southampton Golf Club** (Play over the Municipal Golf Course), Course Road, Southampton. 18 holes, 6218 yards, S.S.S. 70. Also 9 hole separate course, S.S.S. 33. *Green Fees:* 18 holes weekdays £7.40, weekends and Bank Holidays £10.80; 9 holes weekdays £3.70, weekends and Bank Holidays £5.40. *Eating facilities:* bar and full catering. *Visitors:* welcome but must book at weekends. *Society Meetings:* by arrangement with Sports Centre Manager's Office (01703 790732). Professional: John Cave (01703 768407). Hon. Secretary: K.G. Kennard (01703 760472). *

SOUTHAMPTON. **Stoneham Golf Club,** Monks Wood Close, Southampton SO16 3TT (01703 768151; Fax: 01703 769272). *Location:* A33/M27 north of Southampton find Chilworth roundabout, take road to Airport (A27), half mile on left. Hilly, heathery course. 18 holes, 6310 yards. S.S.S. 70. *Green Fees:* £27.00 per round or day; weekends £30.00. Telephone re availability. *Eating facilities:* full catering, bar open all day. *Visitors:* welcome, except competition days. *Society Meetings:* catered for. Professional: Ian Young (01703 768397). Secretary: R.G.M. Bennett (01703 769272).

WINCHESTER. **Hockley Golf Club,** Twyford, Near Winchester SO21 1PL (01962 713461). *Location:* on A333 (Twyford road), two miles south east of Winchester off M3. Parkland course. 18 holes, 6296 yards. S.S.S. 70. Practice areas. *Green Fees:* £25.00 per day or round. *Eating facilities:* restaurant and bar available. *Visitors:* welcome weekdays, weekends with members only. Check first with Professional. *Society Meetings:* welcome, catered for Wednesdays only. Professional: Terry Lane (01962 713678). Secretary: J.R. Digby (01962 713165).

WINCHESTER. **Royal Winchester Golf Club,** Sarum Road, Winchester SO22 5QE (01962 852462). *Location:* exit Winchester on Romsey Road, Hospital on left, right at roundabout, first left into Sarum Road. Downland. 18 holes, 6212 yards. S.S.S. 70. *Green Fees:* weekdays £26.00. Weekends with member only. *Eating facilities:* full catering available. *Visitors:* welcome weekdays, Handicap Certificate required. *Society Meetings:* by prior arrangement. Professional: Steven A. Hunter (01962 862473). Secretary: A.D. Bluck (01962 852462).

WINCHESTER. **South Winchester Golf Club,** Pitt, Winchester SO22 5QW (01962 877800; Fax: 01962 877900). *Location:* situated between Winchester and Hursley in the village of Pitt. Championship links-style course. 18 holes, 7086 yards. S.S.S. 74. Driving range. *Green Fees:* no casual green fees. *Eating facilities:* two bars, one dining room – food available all day. *Visitors:* as guests of members only. Golf days for non members by arrangement with the Secretary. Professional: Richard Adams (01962 840469). Secretary: Stephen Wright.

Hereford & Worcester

BELMONT. **Belmont Lodge and Golf Course,** Belmont, Hereford HR2 9SA (01432 352666; Fax: 01432 358090). *Location:* one and a half miles south of Hereford. Parkland running alongside the River Wye. 18 holes, 6490 yards. S.S.S. 71. *Green Fees:* weekdays £16.00 per round, £24.00 per day, £8.00 twilight ticket; weekends £20.00 per round, £28.00 per day, £10.00 twilight ticket. Special rates Mondays and Tuesdays. *Eating facilities:* restaurant and bar (snacks). *Visitors:* welcome at all times. 30 bedroomed hotel – bowls, snooker, tennis, fishing, meeting rooms. *Society Meetings:* catered for, special packages available. Professional: Mike Welsh (01432 352717).

BEWDLEY. **Little Lakes Golf Club,** Lye Head, Bewdley, Worcester DY12 2UZ (01299 266385). *Location:* three miles west of Bewdley on A456, turn left into Lye Head Lane opposite Alton Tea Rooms. Parkland course with superb views. 18 holes, 6100 yards. S.S.S. 69. Practice ground. *Green Fees:* weekdays £12.00; weekends £15.00. *Eating facilities:* restaurant and cafe facilities. *Visitors:* welcome, telephone bookings accepted.Tennis and swimming facilities. *Societies:* welcome by prior arrangement with Professional. Professional: M. Laing (01299 266385; Fax: 01299 266178). Secretary: D. Reinman (01299 266385).

BEWDLEY. **Wharton Park Golf Club,** Longbank, Bewdley DY12 2QW (01299 405222; Fax: 01299 405121). *Location:* A456 from Kidderminster, top of Bewdley by-pass. Championship course with woods and parkland. 18 holes, 6617 yards. S.S.S. 72. Par 73. Practice range. *Green Fees:* weekdays £20-£25 per day; weekends £25-£35 per day. *Eating facilities:* full facilities available. *Visitors:* welcome by arrangement (please telephone). Some restrictions at weekends. Snooker room. Functions/Conferences catered for. *Society Meetings:* welcome anytime including weekends. Professional: Angus Hoare (01299 405163). Secretary: C.J. Price.

BLACKWELL. **Blackwell Golf Club,** Blackwell, Near Bromsgrove B60 1PY (0121-445 1994). *Location:* approximately 10 miles south of Birmingham and three miles east of Bromsgrove. Parkland. 18 holes, 6202 yards. S.S.S. 71. *Green Fees:* weekdays £36.00 per day; weekends with a member only. *Eating facilities:* bar snacks at all times, meals by arrangement. *Visitors:* welcome by arrangement. *Society Meetings:* catered for by arrangement through Secretary. Professional: Nigel Blake (0121-445 3113). Secretary: R.W.A. Burns (0121-445 1994).

BLAKEDOWN. **Churchill and Blakedown Golf Club,** Churchill Lane, Blakedown, Near Kidderminster DY10 3NB (01562 700200). *Location:* off A456 Birmingham/Kidderminster road at Blakedown. Undulating parkland, partially wooded course. 9 holes, 6472 yards. S.S.S. 71. *Green Fees:* weekdays £17.50, with a member £7.50; weekends £10.00 with a member only. *Eating facilities:* snacks and full meals except Monday. *Visitors:* welcome weekdays, weekends and Bank Holidays with member only. Handicap Certificate required. *Society Meetings:* weekdays only by arrangement through the Secretary. Professional: Mr Keith Wheeler (01562 700454). Secretary: B.G. Pendry (01562 700018).

BRANSFORD. **Bransford Golf Club,** Bank House Hotel, Golf and Country Club, Bransford, Worcester WR6 5JD (01886 833551; Fax: 01886 832461). *Location:* on A4103 Hereford Road, four miles southwest of Worcester, at Bank House Hotel. Flat, undulating course incorporating 14 lakes – "Florida" style course – island greens, etc. 18 holes, 6101 yards. S.S.S. 70. 20 bay driving range. *Green Fees:* weekdays £20.00 18 holes; weekends £25.00. *Eating facilities:* available in Bank House Hotel. *Visitors:* welcome but not before 9.30am. Handicap Certificates required. Smart golf attire. Accommodation in hotel. *Society Meetings:* welcome after 10am – accommodation and meals available. Professional: Graham Hawkings (01886 833621). Secretary: Patrick A.D. Holmes (01886 833551; Fax: 01886 832461).

BROMYARD near. **Sapey Golf Club,** Upper Sapey, Worcester WR6 6XT (01886 853567). *Location:* situated six miles north of Bromyard on B4203. Parkland course with trees, ditches and water; outstanding views over Malvern Hills. 18 holes, 5885 yards. S.S.S. 69. Driving range. *Green Fees:* weekdays £15.00; weekends £20.00. *Eating facilities:* bar and restaurant meals available Wednesday to Sunday. *Visitors:* welcome always. *Society Meetings:* catered for Wednesdays to Sundays. Professional: Chris Knowles (01886 853288). Secretary: Shirley Dykes (01886 853506).

CLEOBURY MORTIMER. **Cleobury Mortimer Golf Club,** Wyre Common, Cleobury Mortimer, Near Kidderminster (01299 271320). *Location:* two miles out of Cleobury on B4201. Wooded parkland course. 18 holes, 6424 yards. S.S.S. 71. Covered driving range, putting green and pitching area. *Green Fees:* weekdays £15.00 per day (£7.50 with member), weekends £18.00 per day (£10.00 with member). *Eating facilities:* restaurant and Spike Bar. *Visitors:* welcome midweek; weekends by arrangement. Snooker room. *Society Meetings:* welcome by prior arrangement, ring for details. Professional: G. Farr (Tel and Fax: 01299 271112). Secretary: Graham Pain (01299 271112).

DROITWICH. **Droitwich Golf and Country Club Ltd,** Westford House, Ford Lane, Droitwich WR9 0BQ (01905 770129). *Location:* between Junction 5 of M5 and Droitwich just off A38. Parkland – undulating – wooded. 18 holes, 6040 yards. S.S.S. 69. Practice area. *Green Fees:* £24.00 weekdays, with a member £8.00; £10.00 weekends playing with a member only. *Eating facilities:* full catering available. *Visitors:* welcome without reservation Mondays to Fridays, weekends with member only. *Society Meetings:* catered for Wednesdays or Fridays. Professional: C.S. Thompson (01905 770207). Secretary: M.J. Taylor (01905 774344).

DROITWICH near. **Ombersley Golf Club,** Bishops Wood Road, Lineholt, Ombersley, Near Droitwich WR9 0LE (01905 620747; Fax: 01905 621016). *Location:* A449. High undulating course above the Severn

Valley. 18 holes, 6289 yards. S.S.S. 68. Practice range £1.40 per 45 balls. *Green Fees:* £9.60 weekdays (£7.00 veterans and juniors); £12.80 weekends. *Eating facilities:* bar facilities, snacks and meals available. *Visitors:* all visitors welcome. *Society Meetings:* welcome by arrangement. Professional/Secretary: Mr Graham Glenister.

EVESHAM. **Evesham Golf Club,** Craycombe Links, Fladbury Cross, Pershore WR10 2QS (01386 860395). *Location:* M5 at Junction 6, A4538 and B4084 to Evesham approximately 10 miles. Evesham take B4084 towards Worcester about three miles. Meadowland, heavily bunkered, tree-lined fairways. 9 holes (18 tees), 6415 yards, 5866 metres. S.S.S. 71. Practice area. *Green Fees:* £15.00 or £7.00 per round if playing with member. *Eating facilities:* diningroom and bar, except Mondays. *Visitors:* must be members of recognised club and have a certified handicap. On Tuesdays, Ladies' Day, play is not possible in Summer until after 3.15pm approx. *Society Meetings:* catered for by prior arrangement. Professional: Charles Haynes (01386 861144). Hon. Secretary: Frank G. Vincent (home 01386 552373). Steward: J.A. Webber.

HAGLEY. **Hagley Country Club Golf Club,** Wassell Grove, Hagley (01562 883701). *Location:* Wassell Grove is off A456 Birmingham to Kidderminster Road. 18 holes, 6353 yards. S.S.S. 72. *Green Fees:* £20.00 per round, £25.00 per day weekdays. *Eating facilities:* à la carte restaurant and bar snacks, Tuesday to Saturday. *Visitors:* welcome. *Society Meetings:* welcome by prior arrangement. Professional: Iain Clark (01562 883852). Secretary: Graham F. Yardley.

HEREFORD. **Burghill Valley Golf Club,** Tillington Road, Burghill, Hereford HR4 7RW (01432 760456; Fax: 01432 760315). *Location:* three miles north-west of Hereford. Take A4110, turn left at traffic lights after Three Elms Inn and then first right. Follow signs to club. Pleasantly undulating parkland including two lakes, and easy walking with some interesting holes through mature cider orchards. 18 holes, 6239 yards. S.S.S. 70. Large practice area. *Green Fees:* weekdays £14.00; weekends £16.00. *Eating facilities:* bar and new dining room with full catering available every day. *Visitors:* welcome at any time, must book tee time at weekends. *Society Meetings:* by prior arrangement with the Professional. Special rates available, please enquire. Professional: Peter Cane PGA. Secretary: Mrs P. Barnett.

HEREFORD. **Hereford Municipal Golf Course,** Holmer Road, Hereford HR4 9UD (01432 278178; Fax: 01432 266281). *Location:* on A49 approaching town centre from Leominster, next to race course and leisure centre. Flat parkland course with excellent greens all year round. 9 holes, 3060 yards. S.S.S. 69 for 18 holes. Large practice area, bunker and practice green. *Green Fees:* weekdays £3.20 per 9 holes, £5.20 per 18 holes, Juniors and Senior Citizens £2.00; weekends £4.40 per 9 holes, £7.00 per 18 holes. *Eating facilities:* full catering in Leisure Centre. *Visitors:* welcome at all times. *Society Meetings:* welcome. Professional/Secretary: Philip Brookes.

HEREFORD. **The Herefordshire Golf Club,** Ravens Causeway, Wormsley, Hereford HR4 8LY (01432 830219). *Location:* six miles north-west of Hereford on a B road to Weobley. Undulating parkland course. 18 holes, 6036 yards. S.S.S. 69. *Green Fees:* £14.00 per round, £20.00 per day weekdays; £18.00 per round, £26.00 per day weekends and Bank Holidays. Half price as members' guests. *Eating facilities:* catering available at all times. *Visitors:* welcome. *Society Meetings:* welcome, packages arranged through Secretary. Professional: David Hemming (01432 830465). Secretary: W.J. Bullock (01432 830219).

KIDDERMINSTER. **Habberley Golf Club,** Habberley, Kidderminster DY11 5LG (01562 822381). *Location:* north west side of Kidderminster. Hilly parkland course. 9 holes, 5481 yards. S.S.S. 68. *Green Fees:* information not provided. *Eating facilities:* food and bar available. *Visitors:* welcome weekdays, without reservation; weekends with member only. *Society Meetings:* by negotiation. Secretary: Mr D.B. Lloyd (01562 745756).

KIDDERMINSTER. **Kidderminster Golf club,** Russell Road, Kidderminster DY16 3HT (01562 822303). *Location:* signposted off A449 Worcester-Wolverhampton Road. Wooded parkland course. 18 holes, 6405 yards. S.S.S. 71. Practice ground. *Green Fees:* £22.00 weekdays. *Eating facilities:* bar and restaurant available. *Visitors:* welcome weekdays only if bona fide member of another club, weekends if guest of member. Snooker room with bar. *Society Meetings:* catered for Thursdays only. Professional: N.P. Underwood (01562 740090). Secretary: Alan Biggs (01562 822303; Fax: 01562 862041).

KINGTON. **Kington Golf Club,** Bradnor Hill, Kington (01544 230340). *Location:* one mile out of Kington, on B4355 to Presteigne. Hill course, with views of seven counties. Highest 18 hole course in England and Wales. 18 holes, 5820 yards. S.S.S. 68. *Green Fees:* £13.00 per round, £16.00 per day weekdays; weekends and Bank Holidays £18.00 per round, £22.00 per day. *Eating facilities:* meals at club. *Visitors:* welcome. Please contact Professional to ensure course is available. *Society Meetings:* catered for by arrangement. Professional: Dean Oliver (01544 231320). Hon. Secretary: G.E. Long (01497 820542).

LEOMINSTER. **Leominster Golf Club,** Ford Bridge, Leominster HR6 0LE (01568 612863). *Location:* three miles south of Leominster on A49 bypass, clearly signed. Undulating parkland with some holes alongside River Lugg. 18 holes, 6104 yards. S.S.S. 69. Small practice area and putting green, driving range adjacent to course. *Green Fees:* weekdays £12.50 per round, £17.00 per day; weekends £21.00. *Eating facilities:* bar open daily, full catering daily except Mondays. *Visitors:* welcome weekdays, weekends by prior arrangement. *Society Meetings:* most welcome Tuesdays to Fridays inclusive, some weekends available by prior booking. Golf and catering £25 weekdays, £32 weekends. Professional: Gareth Bebb (01568 611402). Secretary: J.A. Ashcroft (01432 880493).

MALVERN WELLS. **The Worcestershire Golf Club,** Wood Farm, Malvern Wells WR14 4PP (01684 575992). *Location:* two miles south of Great Malvern, near junction of A449 and B4209. Exceptionally scenic – Malvern Hills and Vale of Evesham. 18 holes, 6449 yards. S.S.S. 71. *Green Fees:* £25.00 weekdays; £30.00 weekends. With member £10. Seven Day ticket £80. Subject to review. *Eating facilities:* available. *Visitors:* visitors unaccompanied by a member must provide evidence of Golf Club membership. Weekends after 10am. *Society Meetings:* catered for Thursdays and Fridays only on application. Professional: G.M. Harris (01684 564428). Secretary: G.R. Scott (01684 575992).

PERSHORE. **The Vale Golf and Country Club,** Hill Furze Road, Bishampton, Near Pershore WR10 2LZ (01386 82781; Fax: 01386 82597). *Location:* off the B4084 Evesham to Worcester road, Fladbury crossroads. Feature lakes and wooded surrounds. Two courses: 1: The Lenches, 9 holes, 2628 to 2918 yards. S.S.S 66 to 68. 2: The International Championship Course, 18 holes, 7114 yards. S.S.S. 74. Driving range. *Green Fees:* weekdays £20.00 International, £7.00 Lenches; weekends £24.00 International, £9.00 Lenches. *Eating facilities:* Vale restaurant, spike bar, Sir William Lyons Suite. *Visitors:* welcome anytime on the Lenches, not before 10.30am weekends on International. *Society Meetings:* welcome any time, possible restriction at weekends. Professional: Caroline Griffiths (01386 82520; Fax: 01386 82660). General Manager: Robin Fischer.

REDDITCH. **Abbey Park Golf and Country Club,** Abbey Park, Dagnell End Road, Redditch B98 7BD (01527 63918; Fax: 01527 65872). *Location:* leave M42 at Junction 2 onto A441 towards Redditch, at garage turn onto A4101. Parkland. 18 holes, 6411 yards, 5827 metres. S.S.S. 71. Driving range. *Green Fees:* weekdays £10.00; weekends £12.50. *Eating facilities:* restaurant and bars. *Visitors:* welcome, no restrictions. Booking advisable. 31 bedroomed hotel, leisure facilities including swimming pool. *Society Meetings:* welcome, including weekends by arrangement. Professional: R.K. Cameron (01527 68006). Secretary: M.E. Bradley.

REDDITCH. **Pitcheroak Golf Course,** Plymouth Road, Redditch B97 4PB (01527 541043). *Location:* Plymouth Road, Redditch bus station. Parkland, wooded. 9 holes, 2206 yards. S.S.S. 62. Practice nets. *Green Fees:* weekdays £4.00 9 holes, £5.50 18 holes; weekends £4.50 9 holes, £6.50 18 holes. Senior Citizens and Juniors half price weekdays. *Eating facilities:* available, cafe and bar. *Society Meetings:* welcome. Professional: Mr David Steuart (01527 541054). Secretary: Mr Kent Hill (01527 585163).

REDDITCH. **Redditch Golf Club,** Green Lane, Lower Grinsty, Callow Hill, Redditch B97 5PJ (01527 543309). *Location:* three miles west of Redditch town centre, off Redditch to Bromsgrove road (A448), or Astwood Bank to Redditch (A441), take Windmill Drive, look for Callow Hill signs. First 9 holes parkland, second 9 holes wooded. White – 18 holes, 6671 yards. S.S.S. 72; Yellow – 18 holes, 6285 yards. S.S.S. 70. Two practice areas. *Green Fees:* £27.50 weekdays; weekends £8.00 with member only. *Eating facilities:*

restaurant and bar with bar snacks except Mondays. *Visitors:* welcome, weekends with member. *Society Meetings:* catered for by arrangement. Professional: Mr F. Powell (01527 546372). Secretary: Mr C. Holman.

REDDITCH. **Redditch Kingfisher Golf Club,** Plymouth Road, Redditch (01527 541054). *Location:* bus station, traffic lights. Parkland, wooded course. 9 holes, 4527 yards. S.S.S. 62. Practice nets. *Green Fees:* weekdays £4.00 9 holes, £5.50 18 holes; weekends £4.50 9 holes, £6.50 18 holes. Senior Citizens £3.50 18 holes, £2.50 9 holes weekdays. *Eating facilities:* full catering and bar facilities. *Visitors:* welcome at all times. Showers/changing rooms. *Society Meetings:* welcome at all times. Professional: Mr David Stewart (01527 541054). Secretary: J.A. Pullen (01527 541043). *

ROSS-ON-WYE. **Ross-on-Wye Golf Club,** Two Park, Gorsley, Ross-on-Wye HR9 7UT (01989 720457). *Location:* adjacent Junction 3 M50, five miles north of Ross-on-Wye. Parkland course. 18 holes, 6500 yards. S.S.S. 73. Large and small practice areas. *Green Fees:* weekdays £25.00; weekends £30.00. Societies of 16 and over £24 for 27 holes. *Eating facilities:* full catering, restaurant. *Visitors:* welcome any day if prior arrangement made with Professional or Secretary. Snooker tables (2). *Society Meetings:* welcome Wednesdays to Fridays. Professional: Nick Catchpole (01989 720439). Secretary: G.H. Cason (01989 720267).

TENBURY WELLS. **Cadmore Lodge Golf and Country Club,** Berrington Green, Tenbury Wells WR15 8TQ (01584 810044). *Location:* two miles south of Tenbury Wells, just off A4112 to Leominster. Parkland with lake and streams in constant play. *Green Fees:* weekdays £7.00; weekends £10.00. *Eating facilities:* hotel bar and restaurant. *Visitors:* welcome, no restrictions. 10 bedroomed (eight en suite) Hotel. *Society Meetings:* welcome. Secretary: R. Farr (01584 810306).

WORCESTER. **Tolladine Golf Club,** The Fairway, Tolladine Road, Worcester WR4 9BA (01905 21074). *Location:* M5, exit 6. Warndon turn off, one mile. Tolladine Road, opposite Virgin Tavern. Hilly course. 9 holes, 5630 yards (for 18 holes). S.S.S. 67. *Green Fees:* £15.00. *Eating facilities:* bar (limited opening). *Visitors:* welcome, phone Professional. *Society Meetings:* welcome, phone Professional for details. Professional: Miss Clare George (01905 726180). Secretary: K.T. Reveley (01905 27416).

WORCESTER. **Worcester Golf and Country Club,** Boughton Park, Worcester WR2 4EZ (01905 421132). *Location:* one-and-a-quarter miles west of city on A4103 (to Hereford). Parkland. 18 holes, 6313 yards. S.S.S. 70. Practice ground(s). *Green Fees:* £23.00 per weekday. Weekends only with a member. *Eating facilities:* full catering available. *Visitors:* welcome weekdays, telephone Professional. Handicap Certificate required. *Society Meetings:* welcome, telephone Secretary. Professional: Colin Colenso (01905 422044). Secretary: J.M. Kennedy (01905 422555). Caterer: Mrs M. Frutos (01905 421132).

WYTHALL. **Fulford Heath Golf Club Ltd,** Tanners Green Lane, Wythall (01564 822806). *Location:* one mile from Alcester Road, via Tanners Green Lane. 18 holes, 6216 yards. S.S.S. 70. *Green Fees:* weekdays £25.00 (Societies £20). *Eating facilities:* available. *Visitors:* welcome weekdays with reservation, not at weekends and Bank Holidays. *Society Meetings:* catered for on application. Professional: Mr D. Down (01564 822930). Secretary: R. Bowen (01564 824758).

Hertfordshire

BARNET. **Arkley Golf Club,** Rowley Green Road, Barnet EN5 3HL (0181-449 0394). *Location:* A1 from London, turn by Elstree Moat House, two miles from Barnet. Parkland. 9 holes, 6045 yards. S.S.S. 69. *Green Fees:* weekdays £15.00 per round, £20.00 per day; weekends with a member only. *Eating facilities:* available, no catering Mondays. *Visitors:* welcome weekdays, please phone, weekends with member only. *Society Meetings:* catered for Wednesdays, Thursdays and Fridays; special rates available. Professional: M. Squire (0181-440 8473). Secretary: G.D. Taylor (0181-499 0394).

BARNET. **Hadley Wood Golf Club,** Beech Hill, Near Barnet (0181-449 4328). *Location:* off the exit from M25 at Junction 24 on to A111 Cockfosters. Down hill, third turning on the right. Very attractive undulating parkland with lakes. 18 holes, 6473 yards. S.S.S. 71. Two practice areas and putting area. *Green Fees:* on application. *Eating facilities:* available weekdays. *Visitors:* welcome weekdays, (not Tuesday a.m.), with club Handicap Certificate or letter of introduction. *Society Meetings:* catered for weekdays except Tuesday mornings. Professional: Peter Jones (0181-449 3285). Secretary/General Manager: P.S. Bryan (Fax: 0181-364 8633).

BERKHAMSTED. **Ashridge Golf Club,** Little Gaddesden, Berkhamsted HP4 1LY (01442 842379). *Location:* on B450, five miles north west of Berkhamsted. Parkland. 18 holes, 6547 yards. S.S.S. 72. Practice area, putting green. *Green Fees:* weekdays £35.00 per round, £50.00 per day. Juniors (under 18) £7.00 per round. *Eating facilities:* dining room and spike bar, mixed lounge. *Visitors:* welcome with reservation weekdays only. *Society Meetings:* catered for. Professional: Geoff Pook (01442 842307). Secretary: Mrs Maggie West (01442 842244; Fax: 01442 843770).

BERKHAMSTED. **Berkhamsted Golf Club,** The Common, Berkhamsted HP4 2QB (01442 863730). *Location:* A41 to Berkhamsted, up past the castle to the common. Heathland, wooded, grass bunkers. 18 holes, 6605 yards. S.S.S. 72. Two practice grounds. *Green Fees:* weekdays £20.00 per round, £35.00 per day; weekends £35.00 per day. *Eating facilities:* daily although limited on Mondays. *Visitors:* welcome most days by arrangement. Handicap Certificate required. *Society Meetings:* catered for Wednesdays and Fridays. Professional: B.J. Proudfoot (01442 865851). Secretary: Colin Nextall (01442 865832).

BISHOP'S STORTFORD. **The Bishop's Stortford Golf Club,** Dunmow Road, Bishop's Stortford CM23 5HP (01279 654027). *Location:* M11 Junction 8, follow signs for Bishop's Stortford, after third (mini) roundabout entrance about half a mile on left hand side of road. Parkland. 18 holes, 6440 yards. S.S.S. 71. *Green Fees:* weekdays £21.00, with a member £10.50; weekends £16.00 (with full member only). *Eating facilities:* restaurant and bar meals. *Visitors:* welcome weekdays; weekends and Public Holidays with member only. *Society Meetings:* catered for weekdays except Tuesdays (minimum 15, maximum 40). Professional: Vince Duncan (01279 651324). Secretary: Mr Brian Hunt (01279 654715).

BUNTINGFORD. **East Herts Golf Club Ltd,** Hamels Park, Buntingford SG9 9NA (01920 821978). *Location:* one mile north of Puckeridge on A10. 18 holes, 6416 yards. S.S.S. 71. *Green Fees:* details on application. *Eating facilities:* separate restaurant. *Visitors:* welcome, with members only at weekends. *Society Meetings:* catered for weekdays. Professional: J. Hamilton (01920 821922). Secretary: G.N. Taylor (Tel & Fax: 01920 821978).

BUSHEY. **Bushey Hall Golf Club,** Bushey Hall Drive, Bushey WD2 2EP (01923 222253; Fax: 01923 229759). *Location:* one mile from M1 Junction 5, off Aldenham Road roundabout. Undulating parkland. 18 holes, 6099 yards, 6670 metres. S.S.S. 69. Practice nets, putting green. *Green Fees:* weekdays £12.00; weekends £15.00. *Eating facilities:* full catering available, two bars. *Visitors:* welcome, no restrictions. *Society Meetings:* catered for weekdays. Professional: Ken Wickham (01923 225802). Secretary/Manager: Julian Smith (01923 222253).

BUSHEY HEATH. **Hartsbourne Golf and Country Club,** Hartsbourne Avenue, Bushey Heath WD2 1JW. *Location:* five miles south east of Watford. Parkland. 18 holes, 6305 yards. S.S.S. 70. 9 holes, 5342 yards. S.S.S. 66. *Green Fees:* information not supplied. *Eating facilities:* restaurant and snack bar available. *Visitors:* guests of members only. *Society Meetings:*

catered for Mondays and Fridays. Professionals: Geoff Hunt and Martin Hattam (0181-950 2836). Secretary: David J. Woodman (0181-950 1133 or 4346).

CHORLEYWOOD. **Chorleywood Golf Club Ltd.,** Common Road, Chorleywood WD3 5LN (01923 282009). *Location:* half a mile off A404, three miles from Rickmansworth. Flat common land with woods. 9 holes, 5676 yards. S.S.S. 67. *Green Fees:* £14.00 weekdays, £17.50 weekends. *Eating facilities:* meals served if ordered by phone. *Visitors:* welcome weekdays except Tuesday and Thursday mornings, restricted at weekends. Secretary: R.M. Lennard.

DAGNALL. **Whipsnade Park Golf Club,** Studham Lane, Dagnall HP4 1RH (0144-284 2330/2331; Fax: 0144-284 2090). *Location:* between Dagnall and Studham. Junction 11 M1 (from north), Junction 9 (from south). Parkland. 18 holes, 6800 yards. S.S.S. 72. Large practice area. *Green Fees:* £20.00 per round, £30.00 per day weekdays, weekends with member only. *Eating facilities:* restaurant open daily, two bars. *Visitors:* welcome weekdays with reservation. *Society Meetings:* welcome with reservation. Professional: Mike Lewendon (0144-284 2310). Secretary: Andrea King (0144-284 2330).

ELSTREE. **Elstree Golf Club,** Watling Street, Elstree WD6 3AA (0181-953 6115; Fax: 0181 207 6390). *Location:* between Radlett and Elstree. Watling Street is also known as A5 (A5183) road. Close to M1, M25, A41, A1 (map available on request). Parkland course – undulating with ponds and ditches. 18 holes, 6830 yards. S.S.S. 72. 60 bay driving range. *Green Fees:* weekdays £20.00 per round, £30.00 per day; £25.00 weekends. Members' guests £10 per round, £15 per day. *Eating facilities:* bar, restaurant, conservatory available all day. *Visitors:* welcome weekdays anytime, weekends after 2pm unless earlier tee available. Ingolf Simulator, trolley hire, lockers/showers; large car park. *Society Meetings:* welcome, information pack sent on request. Professionals: Marc Warwick, Mark Wood (0181-207 5680). Director/Manager: Ken Ellis.

GRAVELEY. **Chesfield Downs Family Golf Centre,** Jack's Hill, Graveley, Near Hitchin SG4 7EQ (01462 482929). *Location:* just off Junction 8 of the A1 (M), approximately two miles along the B197. Inland links/downland. Two Courses: Chesfield Downs – 18 holes, 6709 yards. S.S.S. 72. Par 71. Lannock Links – 9 holes, 975 yards. S.S.S. 27. 25 bay floodlit driving range, putting green. *Green Fees:* weekdays £13.75 (£2.50 for 9 hole course); weekends £19.75 (£3.50). Special rates for over 50's every Monday and Tuesday 10am to 1pm. *Eating facilities:* "Chesfields Restaurant and Bar". *Visitors:* welcome, advance booking system available to reserve tee-off times. Golf Superstore, Golf Academy, changing facilities, creche/playground. *Society Meetings:* catered for by arrangement. Professional: Beverly Huke. Secretary: David C.M. Carter.

HARPENDEN. **Harpenden Common Golf Club,** East Common, Harpenden AL5 1BL (01582 712856). *Location:* on A1081 between Harpenden and St. Albans. Flat heathland. 18 holes, 5664 yards. S.S.S. 67. *Green Fees:* weekdays £20.00 per round, £25.00 per day; weekends £25.00 per day. *Eating facilities:* bar and restaurant daily. *Visitors:* welcome weekdays only with reservation (not Tuesdays). Weekends with member only. *Society Meetings:* Thursday and Friday only. Professional: B. Puttick (01582 460655). Secretary: R.D. Parry (Tel & Fax: 01582 715959).

HARPENDEN. **Harpenden Golf Club,** Hammonds End, Redbourn Lane, Harpenden (01582 712580). *Location:* turn off A1081, four miles after St. Albans on B487. Parkland course. 18 holes, 6363 yards. S.S.S. 70. *Green Fees:* £30 per day. *Eating facilities:* lunches at club, order in advance. *Visitors:* welcome by arrangement. *Society Meetings:* by arrangement only. Professional: Doug Smith. Secretary: J.R. Newton.

HATFIELD. **Brookmans Park Golf Club,** Golf Club Road, Brookmans Park, Hatfield AL9 7AT (01707 652459). *Location:* between A1 and A1000, also just off M25, exit for Potters Bar. Parkland. 18 holes, 6459 yards. S.S.S. 71. Practice ground and putting green. *Green Fees:* weekdays £27.00 per round, £32.00 per day. Handicap Certificate required. *Eating facilities:* bar snacks and lunches weekdays. *Visitors:* welcome weekdays; weekends with member only. *Society Meetings:* catered for Wednesdays and Thursdays. Professional: I. Jelley (01707 652468). Secretary: P.A. Gill (01707 652487; Fax: 01707 661851).

HATFIELD. **Hatfield London Country Club,** Bedwell Park, Essendon, Hatfield AL9 6JA (01707 642624 or 642626). *Location:* four miles south of Junction 4 A1(M), five miles north east of Junction 24 M25 Potters Bar. 9 holes Pitch and Putt. 18 holes, 6385 yards, Par 72. *Green Fees:* from £14.00. *Eating facilities:* lunch except Mondays. *Visitors:* welcome, advance bookings only. Tennis courts. *Society Meetings:* catered for. Professional: Norman Greer. *

HEMEL HEMPSTEAD. **Boxmoor Golf Club,** 18 Box Lane, Boxmoor, Hemel Hempstead HP1 1DZ (01442 242434). *Location:* two miles from Hemel Hempstead, three-quarters of a mile from Hemel Hempstead Station on A41. Hilly/moorland course, 9 holes, 4112 yards. S.S.S. 62. *Green Fees:* £10.00 weekdays; £15.00 weekends. Half fee if playing with member. *Eating facilities:* ring Steward. *Visitors:* welcome without reservation, except on Sundays. *Society Meetings:* catered for on application. Secretary: E. Duell.

HEMEL HEMPSTEAD. **Little Hay Golf Complex,** Box Lane, Bovingdon, Hemel Hempstead HP3 0DQ (01442 833798). *Location:* just off A41, along Chesham Road from Hemel Hempstead. Parkland. 18 holes, 6678 yards. S.S.S. 72. 9 hole pitch & putt course, 18 hole putting green, floodlit driving range. *Green Fees:* weekdays £7.50 per round; weekends £11.25 per round. *Eating facilities:* available, open all day. *Visitors:* welcome. *Society Meetings:* welcome by arrangement; special rates. Professional: David Johnson and Stephen Proudfoot (01442 833798). Director of Golf: David Johnson (01442 833798).

HERTFORD. **Brickendon Grange Golf and Country Club,** Brickendon, Near Hertford SG13 8PD (01992 511411). *Location:* three miles south of Hertford, one mile from Bayford Railway Station. Undulating parkland with specimen trees. 18 holes, 6315 yards.

S.S.S. 70. Excellent practice area. *Green Fees:* weekdays £30.00 day ticket, £24.00 per round. *Eating facilities:* bar and restaurant, snack meals available lunchtimes. *Visitors:* welcome weekdays only, Handicap Certificate required. *Society Meetings:* catered for by arrangement. Professional: J. Hamilton (01992 511218). Secretary: C.T. MacDonald (01992 511258).

KNEBWORTH. **Knebworth Golf Club,** Deards End Lane, Knebworth SG3 6NL (01438 814681). *Location:* one mile south of Stevenage. Parkland. 18 holes, 6492 yards. S.S.S. 71. *Green Fees:* details on application. *Eating facilities:* available. *Visitors:* welcome (with members only at weekends). *Society Meetings:* welcome Mondays, Tuesdays and Thursdays only. Professional: R.Y. Mitchell (01438 812757). Secretary: J.C. Wright (01438 812752).

LETCHWORTH. **Letchworth Golf Club,** Letchworth Lane, Letchworth SG6 3NQ. *Location:* two miles from A1 (M) near village of Willian, adjacent to Letchworth Hall Hotel. Parkland course. 18 holes, 6181 yards. S.S.S. 69. Practice ground. *Green Fees:* weekdays £23.50 per round, £32.50 per day; weekend accompanied only. Special rates Mondays – £12.00 per round, £20.00 per day. *Eating facilities:* bars and restaurant except Mondays. *Visitors:* weekdays Handicap Certificate required, weekends accompanied only. *Society Meetings:* catered for Wednesdays, Thursdays and Fridays. Professional: John Mutimer (01462 682713). Secretary: A.R. Bailey (01462 683203).

POTTERS BAR. **Potters Bar Golf Club,** Darkes Lane, Potters Bar EN6 1DF (01707 652020; Fax: 01707 655051). *Location:* one mile north of M25 exit 24 signposted Potters Bar, turn right at second traffic lights, club on left at end of shopping centre. Parkland course, well wooded, undulating, with streams. 18 holes, 6279 yards. S.S.S. 70. Small practice ground. *Green Fees:* weekdays £18.00 per round, £27.50 per day; weekends with member only. *Eating facilities:* luncheons and bar available from 11.30am. *Visitors:* weekdays only, must produce valid Handicap Certificate. *Society Meetings:* Mondays/Tuesdays/Fridays only. Professional: Kevin Hughes (01707 652987). Secretary: Arthur Williams (01707 652020).

RADLETT. **Porters Park Golf Club,** Shenley Hill, Radlett WD7 7AZ (01923 856262). *Location:* approximately 3 miles south west of Junction 22 (M25), three miles north-east Junction 5 (M1), half a mile north of Radlett Station on Shenley Hill. Park-type course with fine trees and a brook. 18 holes, 6313 yards. S.S.S. 70. Two practice areas, putting. *Green Fees:* £28.00 per round, £42.00 per day. Societies £65 inclusive. *Eating facilities:* full diningroom and bar snack menus. *Visitors:* welcome weekdays if pre-booked, with members only at weekends and Bank Holidays. Handicap Certificate required. *Society Meetings:* catered for Wednesday and Thursday March to October only. Professional: David Gleeson (01923 854366). Manager: J.H. Roberts (01923 854127). *

RICKMANSWORTH. **Moor Park Golf Club,** Moor Park, Rickmansworth WD3 1QN (01923 773146; Fax: 01923 777109). *Location:* A404 to Northwood Hills, Batchworth Heath. Course no. 1: 18 holes, 6695 yards. S.S.S. 72. Course no. 2: 18 holes, 5823 yards. S.S.S. 68. *Green Fees:* weekdays High Course – £30.00, West Course – £25.00; £50.00 per day for either. *Eating facilities:* full catering always available at club. *Visitors:* welcome on weekdays by prior arrangement, and on weekends with a member. Professional: L. Farmer (01923 774113). Secretary: J.A. Davies.

RICKMANSWORTH. **Rickmansworth Public Golf Course,** Moor Lane, Rickmansworth WD3 1QL (01923 773163). *Location:* from town centre along A404 to Waterworks, left along B4504, then first right. Testing, undulating parkland course. 18 holes, 4500 yards, 4115 metres. S.S.S. 62. *Green Fees:* weekdays £8.50, Juniors and Senior Citizens £4.25; weekends £12.00 (subject to review). *Eating facilities:* bars, restaurant. *Visitors:* welcome. *Society Meetings:* catered for, contact Professional. Professional: Iain Duncan (01923 775278). Secretary: Jim Devan (01923 238734).

ROYSTON. **Heydon Grange Golf and Country Club,** Heydon, Royston SG8 7NS (01763 208988; Fax: 01763 208926). *Location:* on A505 between Royston and Duxford; Junction 10 on M11. Undulating downland course. 18 holes. S.S.S. 71, Par 72. 9 holes, Par 36. *Green Fees:* weekdays £15.00, weekends £20.00. After 5pm £10.00. *Eating facilities:* two restaurants and large bar. *Visitors:* welcome anytime. *Society Meetings:* welcome. Professional: Stephen Bonham. Secretary: John Riches.

ROYSTON. **Royston Golf Club,** Baldock Road, Royston SG8 5BG (01763 242177). *Location:* alongside the A505 on right hand side when approaching from Baldock, clubhouse at top of hill before entering town. Links – undulating heathland. 18 holes, 6032 yards. S.S.S. 69 yellow, 67 white. Practice fairway. *Green Fees:* £20.00 weekdays; weekends with a member only £12.50. *Eating facilities:* lounge bar – 19th bar, diningroom and bar meals. *Visitors:* welcome weekdays; weekends only with member. *Society Meetings:* weekdays only, book through Secretary. Professional: M. Hatcher (01763 243476). Secretary: Mr D. Mear (01763 242696).

If you are writing, a stamped, addressed envelope is always appreciated.

SAWBRIDGEWORTH. **The Manor of Groves Golf and Country Club,** High Wych, Sawbridgeworth CM21 0LA (01279 722333; Fax: 01279 726972). *Location:* Junction 7 off M11 follow A414 to High Wych. Parkland/woodland course with water features. 18 holes, 6309 yards. S.S.S. 70. Large practice ground. *Green Fees:* £18.00/£25.00 weekdays; weekends £23.00. *Eating facilities:* restaurant, bar, grill room. *Visitors:* welcome anytime weekdays, advise preliminary phone call. Must have Handicap Certificate or proficiency certificate. Accommodation available in our 35 bedroomed Hotel. Snooker, tennis court, swimming pool. *Society Meetings:* welcome weekdays. Fourball Special £19.00 per person including lunch. Professional: Lee Jones. Secretary: Kevin Moss.

ST. ALBANS. **Batchwood Hall Golf Club,** Batchwood Drive, St. Albans AL3 5XA (01727 833349). *Location:* north west corner of town. Flat, parkland, wooded course with a monster Par 4 first hole. 18 holes, 6463 yards. S.S.S. 71. *Green Fees:* on application from Pro's shop. *Eating facilities:* bar meals. *Visitors:* welcome with reservation (01727 844250) except 0630 to 1000 hours weekends. *Society Meetings:* with reservations as above. Professional: Jimmy Thompson (01727 852101). Secretary: John Collantine (01727 853561).

ST. ALBANS. **Mid-Herts Golf Club,** Gustard Wood, Wheathampstead, St. Albans (01582 833385). *Location:* B651, six miles north of St. Albans. Heathland, short and tight course. 18 holes, 6094 yards. S.S.S. 69. Course record 63. *Green Fees:* weekdays £21.00 per round; weekends and Bank Holidays with member only. *Eating facilities:* by arrangement. *Visitors:* welcome weekdays with reservation; Handicap Certificate required. *Society Meetings:* catered for by arrangement. Professional: N. Brown (01582 832788). Secretary: R.J.H. Jourdan (01582 832242).

ST. ALBANS. **Redbourn Golf Club,** Kinsbourne, Green Lane, Redbourn, Near St. Albans AL3 7QA (01582 793363). *Location:* four miles north of St. Albans, four miles south of Luton, one mile south of M1 Junction 9. Parkland. 18 holes, 6407 yards. S.S.S. 71. 9 holes, 1361 yards. S.S.S. 27. Driving range. *Green Fees:* £14.00 weekdays, £18.00 weekends and Bank Holidays. *Eating facilities:* licensed bar, snacks and hot meals readily available. *Visitors:* welcome weekdays except between 4.15pm – 6pm, weekends and Bank Holidays after 3.00pm. *Society Meetings:* catered for by arrangement Mondays to Thursdays. Professional: Dale Brightman (01582 793493). Secretary: Chris Gyford (01582 792150). *

ST. ALBANS. **Verulam Golf Club,** 226 London Road, St. Albans AL1 1JG (01727 839016; Fax: 01727 812201). *Location:* M25 Junction 22a or 22 to A1081 to St. Albans, course is off London Road (A1081) near railway bridge. Easy walking parkland course. 18 holes, 6457 yards. S.S.S. 71. Practice nets/ground, putting green. *Green Fees:* Mondays £13.00 per round, £20.00 per day, rest of weekdays £25.00 per round, £30.00 per day; weekends with member only (£15.00). *Eating facilities:* bar snacks from 7.30am to close, other dining by prior arrangement. *Visitors:* welcome all day Mondays, rest of weekdays unintroduced with Handicap Certificate. *Society Meetings:* welcome by advance booking with deposit. Professional: Nick Burch (01727 861401). Secretary: A.R. Crichton-Smith (01727 853327).

STEVENAGE. **Stevenage Golf Centre,** Aston Lane, Stevenage SG2 7EL (01438 880424). *Location:* turn off A1(M) at Stevenage South Junction onto A602 to Hertford. 18 holes, 6451 yards. S.S.S. 71. Par 72. 20-bay driving range. *Green Fees:* telephone the Professional for details. *Eating facilities:* restaurant and bar. *Visitors:* welcome, Municipal course, advance booking system available to reserve tee-off times. Shower facilities. *Society Meetings:* catered for by arrangement. Professional: K. Bond. Hon. Secretary: J.M. Ryder.

TRING near. **Stocks Hotel and Country Club,** Stocks Road, Aldbury, Near Tring HP23 5RX (01442 851341; Fax: 01442 851253). *Location:* M1 and M25 easily accessible via A41(T) dual carriageway. Parkland. 18 holes, 7016 yards. S.S.S. 73. Teaching academy, practice range and putting green. *Green Fees:* weekdays £30.00; weekends £40.00. *Eating facilities:* conservatory – snack food menu, Tapestry Restaurant offering à la carte and table d'hôte, cocktail bar. *Visitors:* welcome weekdays, by prior arrangement weekends. Leisure facilities include heated outdoor swimming pool (May to September), jacuzzi, sauna, steam room, solarium, gymnasium, snooker, horse riding, croquet. Hotel accommodation on site. *Society Meetings:* welcome by prior arrangement with Sales Office. Professional: Derwynne Honan (01442 851491; Fax: 01442 851253).

WALTHAM CROSS. **Cheshunt Golf Club,** The Clubhouse, Park Lane, Cheshunt EN7 6QD (01992 629777). *Location:* M25 Junction 25, then A10 towards Hertford, second set of traffic lights turn left, right at mini roundabout. Flat parkland course. 18 holes, 6608 Yards. S.S.S. 71. Practice ground. *Green Fees:* on request. *Eating facilities:* public cafe. *Visitors:* welcome any time. For tee-off times phone Pro's shop (01992 624009). *Society Meetings:* catered for by arrangement through Pro Shop. Professional: Mr A.C. Newton (01992 624009). Secretary: Mr J.G. Duncan (01992 629777).

WARE. **Chadwell Springs Golf Club,** Hertford Road, Ware SG12 9LE (01920 461447). *Location:* A10 Hertford or Ware. Heathland. 9 holes, 6418 yards. S.S.S. 71. *Green Fees:* £14.00 weekdays; weekends £10.00 with a member only. *Eating facilities:* bar meals. *Visitors:* welcome weekdays; weekends with member only. *Society Meetings:* by arrangement. Professional: Adrian Shearn (01920 462075). Secretary: D. Evans (01920 461447). *

WARE. **Hanbury Manor Golf and Country Club,** Ware SG12 0SD (01920 487722; Fax: 01920 487692). *Location:* turn right off the A10, 25 miles north of London, near Ware. Parkland and Championship course designed by Jack Nicklaus II. 18 holes, 7016 yards. S.S.S. 74 (from blue tees). *Green Fees:* for hotel guests – £35.00 weekdays, £40.00 weekends. *Eating facilities:* three "acclaimed" restaurants under the guidance of Albert Roux in five star 96 room hotel. *Visitors:* golf available only to Club members or hotel guests. *Society Meetings:* Corporate Golf Days are available. Director of Golf: Mr David MacLaren.

WARE. **Whitehill Golf Club,** Whitehill Golf Centre, Dane End, Ware SG12 0JS (01920 438495; Fax: 01920 438891). *Location:* turn off A10 at Happy Eater, High Cross. Undulating course. 18 holes, 6636 yards. S.S.S. 72. 25 bay floodlit driving range. *Green Fees:* weekdays £15.00 per round, £20.00 per day; weekends £18.00. *Eating facilities:* bar, restaurant, function room. *Visitors:* welcome, must have Handicap Certificate. Snooker room. *Society Meetings:* catered for, groups of 12 or more. Professional: David Ling (01920 438326). Secretary: Andrew Smith.

WATFORD. **Aldenham Golf and Country Club,** Church Lane, Aldenham, Near Watford WD2 8AL (01923 853929; Fax: 01923 858472). *Location:* Junction 5 on M1, take A41 to South Watford, turn left at first roundabout to Church Lane. Flat parkland. 18 holes, 6500 yards. S.S.S. 71. New 9 hole course, 2500 yards. Practice area. *Green Fees:* weekdays £20.00; weekends £25.00. 9 hole course £10.00. *Eating facilities:* three bars, snack bar, restaurant. *Visitors:* welcome weekdays, weekends not before 12 noon. Teaching. *Society Meetings:* by arrangement. Golf Shop: (01923 857889). Secretary: Mrs J.I. Phillips (01923 853929).

WATFORD. **West Herts Golf Club,** Cassiobury Park, Watford WD1 7SL (01923 224264). *Location:* off Rousebarn Lane from Links Way, A412 at Croxley Green. Parkland. 18 holes, 6488 yards. S.S.S. 71. *Green Fees:* weekdays £20.00 per round; weekends £30.00. *Eating facilities:* catering (including breakfast) available seven days a week. *Visitors:* welcome weekdays only. Handicap Certificate required. *Society Meetings:* catered for Wednesdays and Fridays. Professional: C.S. Gough (01923 220352). Secretary: C.M. Brown (01923 236484).

WELWYN GARDEN CITY. **Panshanger Golf Complex,** Old Herns Lane, Panshanger, Welwyn Garden City AL7 2ED (01707 333312). *Location:* Junction 6 A1(M), 10 minutes from M25. Parkland set in the Mimram Valley. 18 holes, 6347 yards. S.S.S. 70. Practice ground, 9 hole pitch and putt. *Green Fees:* information not provided. *Eating facilities:* Fairway Tavern pub and servery. *Visitors:* municipal course, pay as you play, all welcome, dress conditions. *Society Meetings:* welcome. Professionals: Bryan Lewis and Mick Corlass (01707 333350). Secretary: Sheila (01707 332837). *

WELWYN GARDEN CITY. **Welwyn Garden City Golf Club Ltd.,** Mannicotts, High Oaks Road, Welwyn Garden City AL8 7BP (01707 336986). *Location:* from north Junction 5 on A1M and take B197 to Valley Road. From south Junction 4 on A1M to Lemsford Lane and Valley Road. Undulating parkland. 18 holes, 6200 yards. S.S.S. 69. Practice ground. *Green Fees:* £25.00 weekdays. *Eating facilities:* by order for lunches; sandwiches available. *Visitors:* welcome weekdays with Handicap Certificate; weekends with member only. *Society Meetings:* Wednesdays and Thursdays only (£48.00 per person per day). Professional: Simon Bishop (01707 325525). General Manager: M. Flint (01707 325243; Fax: 01707 393213).

Humberside

BEVERLEY. **Beverley and East Riding Golf Club,** Westwood, Beverley HU17 8RG (01482 867190). *Location:* one mile from Beverley town centre. Common pastureland. 18 holes, 6127 yards. S.S.S. 68. *Green Fees:* £11.00 weekdays, £15.00 weekends and Bank Holidays. *Eating facilities:* lunch and evening meals by prior ordering. *Visitors:* welcome except weekends. *Society Meetings:* catered for, prior notice for approval of committee. Professional: Ian Mackie (01482 869519). Secretary: A. Walker (01482 868757).

BEVERLEY. **Hainsworth Park Golf Club,** Brandesburton, Near Driffield YO25 8RT (Tel & Fax: 01964 542362). *Location:* eight miles northeast of Beverley on A165 road to Bridlington. Well drained parkland course with mature trees. 18 holes, 6003 yards. S.S.S. 69. Practice area. *Green Fees:* weekdays £10.00 per round, £15.00 per day; weekends £15.00. *Eating facilities:* bar and full catering. *Visitors:* welcome anytime. Hotel accommodation. *Society Meetings:* welcome. General Manager: Major R. Kilpatrick (01964 542362).

BRIDLINGTON. **Bridlington Golf Club,** Belvedere Road, Bridlington YO15 3NA (01262 672092). *Location:* south side of the town alongside the A165, Bridlington to Hull. Flat parkland. 18 holes, 6491 yards. S.S.S. 71. Practice area. *Green Fees:* weekdays £10.00 per round, £15.00 per day; weekends and Bank Holidays £20.00. Subject to review. Reductions for parties over 25 in number. *Eating facilities:* full catering, bar meals, etc. *Visitors:* welcome most days but limited on Wednesdays/Sundays. Advisable to book in advance. *Society Meetings:* catered for. Professional: Anthony Howarth (01262 674721). Hon. Secretary: Clive Wilson (01262 606367).

BRIDLINGTON. **Flamborough Head Golf Club,** Flamborough, Bridlington (01262 850333). *Location:* five miles north-east of Bridlington on B1255. 18 holes, 5438 yards. S.S.S. 66. *Green Fees:* weekdays £12.00 per day; weekends and Bank Holidays £16.00 per day. *Visitors:* welcome, limited Sunday and Wednesday mornings. *Society Meetings:* catered for, apply to Secretary. Secretary: W.R. Scarle (01262 676494).

BRIDLINGTON. **The Links at Bridlington Bay,** Flamborough Road, Marton, Bridlington (01262 401584; Fax: 01262 401702). *Location:* at Bridlington on Flamborough Road. Links course with spectacular views. 18 holes, 6719 yards. S.S.S. 72. 9-hole course. Driving range and Golf Academy. Golf schools weekly during Summer. *Green Fees:* weekdays £12.50 per round, £15.00 per day; weekends £15.00 per round, £20.00 per day (subject to review). *Eating facilities:* bar snacks and carvery. *Visitors:* welcome at all times, no restrictions. *Society Meetings:* very welcome. Director of Golf and Head Professional: David Edwards.

BRIGG. **Elsham Golf Club,** Barton Road, Elsham, Brigg, South Humberside DN20 0LS (01652 688382). *Location:* off M180 at Barnetby Top or A15 through Brigg to Barton. Flat parkland. 18 holes, 6411 yards. S.S.S. 71. Indoor and outdoor practice ground. *Green Fees:* weekdays £22.00, with a member £12; weekends only with a member £18.00. *Eating facilities:* full catering. *Visitors:* welcome weekdays except Thursdays. *Society Meetings:* catered for on weekdays except Thursdays. Steward (01652 688382). Professional: Stuart Brewer (01652 680432). Secretary: B.P. Nazer (01652 680291).

BROUGH. **Brough Golf Club,** Cave Road, Brough HU15 1HB (01482 667374). *Location:* 10 miles west of Hull off A63. Parkland. 18 holes, 6153 yards. S.S.S. 69 (white tees). Practice facilities. *Green Fees:* on application. *Eating facilities:* full restaurant and bar snack menu available on request. *Visitors:* welcome Mondays, Tuesdays, Thursdays and Fridays after 9.30am. *Society Meetings:* on application. Professional: G. Townhill (01482 667483). Secretary/Manager: W.G. Burleigh (01482 667291).

BROUGH. **Cave Castle Hotel Golf Club,** South Cave, Brough HU15 2EU (01430 422245; Fax: 01430 421118). *Location:* end of M62 east, 10 miles from Hull. Parkland at the foot of the wolds with views of the River Humber. 18 holes, 6400 yards. S.S.S. 71. *Green Fees:* £12.50 per round, £18.00 per day weekdays; £18.00 per round, £25.00 per day weekends. *Eating facilities:* golf bar plus hotel à la carte, banqueting and conference facilities for 300. *Visitors:* welcome, no restrictions. Hotel has 30 bedrooms; swimming pool and extra rooms planned for 1995 season. *Society Meetings:* welcome. Professional: Karl Worby (01430 421286). Secretary: Max Freling (01430 421286).

CLEETHORPES. **Cleethorpes Golf Club Ltd.,** Golf House, Kings Road, Cleethorpes DN35 0PN (01472 812059). *Location:* approximately one mile south of Cleethorpes Leisure Centre. Flat meadowland crossed by large dykes. 18 holes, 6349 yards. S.S.S. 70. Large and small practice areas. *Green Fees:* weekdays £18.00; weekends £25.00. Reductions when playing with member. *Eating facilities:* bar lunches, evening meals by arrangement. *Visitors:* welcome anytime except Wednesdays, but must be member of another golf club. *Society Meetings:* Tuesdays, Thursdays and Fridays only by arrangement with the Secretary. Professional: P. Davies (01472 814060). Secretary: G.B. Standaloft (01472 814060).

CONISTON. **Ganstead Park Golf Club,** Longdales Lane, Coniston, Near Hull HU11 4LB (01482 811280). *Location:* A165 to Bridlington. Flat course with lakes. 18 holes, 6495 yards. S.S.S. 71. Practice area. *Green Fees:* weekdays £15.00; weekends £24.00. *Eating facilities:* full catering facilities. *Visitors:* welcome without reservation except Wednesday 9am – 11am and Sunday 8am – 1pm. *Society Meetings:* catered for subject to availability. Professional: Mike Smee (01482 811121).

COTTINGHAM. **Hessle Golf Club,** Westfield Road, Raywell, Cottingham (01482 659187). *Location:* three miles south west of Cottingham. Parkland. 18 holes, 6290 yards, S.S.S. 70. Two practice areas. *Green Fees:* £20.00 per round, £25.00 per day weekdays; weekends and Bank Holidays £25.00 per round. *Eating facilities:* snack lunches Tuesday to Sunday, set lunches by arrangement. *Visitors:* mid-week unrestricted except Tuesdays 9am – 1pm. Weekends visitors may play after 11am at Professional's discretion. *Society Meetings:* catered for weekdays only by arrangement. Professional: G. Fieldsend (01482 650190). Secretary: R. L. Dorsey (01482 650171). *

DRIFFIELD. **Driffield Golf Club,** Sunderlandwick, Driffield YO25 9AD (01377 43116). *Location:* one mile south of Driffield off the A161. Parkland, wooded. 18 holes, 6199 yards. S.S.S. 70. Practice area. *Green Fees:* weekdays £15.00; weekends £20.00. *Eating facilities:* bar, dining facilities. *Visitors:* welcome weekdays except Ladies' Day (Tuesdays), restrictions weekends and Bank Holidays. *Society Meetings:* welcome weekdays. Professional: (01377 240448). Secretary: M. Winn (Tel & Fax: 01377 240599).

GRIMSBY. **Grimsby Golf Club Ltd,** Littlecoats Road, Grimsby DN34 4LU (01472 342823). *Location:* one mile west of Grimsby town centre off A18. 18 holes, 6058 yards. S.S.S. 69. Practice area. *Green Fees:* weekdays £17.00, £12 with member; weekends £22.00, £12.00 with member. *Eating facilities:*snack lunches most days, set lunches by arrangement, afternoon teas most days, evening meals by arrangement with Steward. *Visitors:* welcome weekdays, must be members of golf clubs. Ladies do not play Saturday between 1.00pm – 5.00pm and Sunday mornings. *Society Meetings:* catered for Mondays and Fridays by arrangement with Secretary (Club ladies' day Tuesday, club ladies have priority). Professional: Mike Grantham (01472 356981). Secretary: A.D. Houlihan (01472 342630). *

GRIMSBY. **The Manor Golf Course,** Laceby, Grimsby DN37 7EA (01472 873468; Fax: 01472 276706). *Location:* A18 to Louth – half a mile on left hand side from Oaklands Hotel, situated at roundabout (Laceby). Flat parkland course. 9 holes, 3127 yards. S.S.S. 70 for 18 holes. Practice driving net, chipping area, putting green. *Green Fees:* weekdays £6.00 9 holes, £9.00 18 holes; weekends £7.00 9 holes, £11.00 18 holes. *Eating facilities:* bar, bar snacks available most lunchtimes. *Visitors:* welcome on those days when competitions are not being held; tees booked 8-10.30am every Tuesday for Ladies and Seniors; telephone for details of competitions. *Society Meetings:* welcome by prior arrangement with the Secretary. Professional: Mr Tony Hallam. Secretary: Mrs Judith MacKay.

HORNSEA. **Hornsea Golf Club,** Rolston Road, Hornsea HU18 1XG (01964 535488). *Location:* follow signs for Hornsea Pottery – Golf Course 200 yards past Pottery. Parkland. 18 holes, 6440 yards. S.S.S. 72. Practice area. *Green Fees:* weekdays £18.50; weekends after 3pm £30.00. *Eating facilities:* available every day. *Visitors:* welcome, please ring Professional for a time. Ladies' Day Tuesdays. Snooker room. *Society Meetings:* catered for by arrangement with the Secretary. Professional: B. Thompson (01964 534989). Secretary: B.W. Kirton (01964 532020).

HOWDEN. **Boothferry Golf Club,** Spaldington Lane, Howden, Near Goole DN14 7NG (01430 430371). *Location:* two and a half miles from Junction 37 of the M62 on the B1228 road between Howden and Bubwith. Flat meadowland, with ditches and ponds. 18 holes, 6651 yards. S.S.S. 72. Large practice area and driving range. *Green Fees:* weekdays £7.90 per round, weekends £11.50 per round. *Eating facilities:* restaurant and bar facilities available. *Visitors:* welcome at all times. Certain dress restrictions for play on golf course. *Society Meetings:* all Golf Societies and individual parties welcome with prior booking through the Professional. Professional: Stewart Wilkinson (01430 430364; Fax: 01430 430567).

HULL. **Hull Golf Club (1921) Ltd.,** The Hall, 27 Packman Lane, Kirk Ella, Hull HU10 7TJ (01482 653026). *Location:* five miles west of Hull. Parkland and wooded. 18 holes, 6242 yards. S.S.S. 70. *Green Fees:* on application. *Eating facilities:* available. *Visitors:* welcome weekdays except Wednesday. *Society Meetings:* by prior arrangement. Professional: D. Jagger (01482 653074). General Manager: R. Toothill (01482 658919).

HULL. **Springhead Park Golf Club,** Willerby Road, Hull HU5 5JE (01482 656309). *Location:* west boundary. Parkland (municipal). 18 holes, 6402 yards. S.S.S. 71. *Green Fees:* weekdays adults £5.20 per round, Senior Citizens £3.10; weekends adults £6.75 per round. *Visitors:* welcome, restricted Sundays from dawn to 3pm. Professional: B. Herrington (01482 594969). Secretary: A. Farr (01482 501126).

HULL. **Sutton Park Municipal Golf Club,** Saltshouse Road, Hull HU8 9HF (01482 74242). *Location:* three miles east of city centre, half a mile north of inner ring road. Flat parkland course. 18 holes, 6251 yards, 5719 metres. S.S.S. 70. Practice area and nearby golf range. *Green Fees:* weekdays £5.00; weekends £6.50. Reductions for Juniors and Senior Citizens. *Eating facilities:* available, parties by pre-booking. *Visitors:* Municipal course, pay as you play. *Society Meetings:* by application to Hull City Leisure Services Dept. Professional: Paul Rushworth (01482 711450). Secretary: J.R. Allen.

IMMINGHAM. **Immingham Golf Club,** St. Andrew's Lane, off Church Lane, Immingham DN40 2EU (01469 575298). *Location:* two miles off A180, behind St. Andrew's Church, Immingham. Flat-ridge and furrow, wide and deep dykes. 18 holes, 6161 yards, 5633 metres. S.S.S. 72. Small practice area. *Green Fees:* weekdays £14.00 per round; weekends £20.00. *Eating facilities:* full catering facilities, normal bar. *Visitors:* welcome anytime except Thursday pm, Saturday pm and Sunday am. *Society Meetings:* catered for if booked in advance. £14.00 per player (minimum 12). Professional: Geoffrey Norton (01469 575493). Secretary: (01469 575298).

SCUNTHORPE. **Grange Park Golf Club,** Butterwick Road, Messingham, Scunthorpe DN17 3PP (01724 762945). *Location:* five miles south of Scunthorpe between Messingham and East Butterwick, four miles south of Junction 3 of M180. New parkland course. 9 holes, 2970 yards. S.S.S. 69. Par 35. Additional 9 hole course now open – Flat parkland course, 1300 yards. S.S.S. 27. Floodlit driving range. *Green Fees:* £4.00 weekdays; £6.00 weekends. Juniors half price. Additional course – £2 per round weekdays, £3.00 per round weekends. *Eating facilities:* coffee bar. *Visitors:* welcome at all times. Pro shop. Manager: Ian Cannon.

SCUNTHORPE. **Holme Hall Golf Club,** Holme Lane, Bottesford, Scunthorpe DN16 3RF (01724 849185). *Location:* M180 Exit 4 (Scunthorpe East). Heathland with sandy subsoil. 18 holes, 6475 yards. S.S.S. 71. *Green Fees:* £20 per day weekdays, weekends as members' guests only. *Eating facilities:* bar meals and restaurant daily except Mondays. *Visitors:* welcome weekdays only. *Society Meetings:* catered for by arrangement with Secretary. Professional: Richard McKiernan (01724 851816). Secretary: Mr G.D. Smith (01724 862078).

SCUNTHORPE. **Normanby Hall Golf Club,** Normanby Park, Near Scunthorpe DN15 9HU (01724 720252). *Location:* five miles north of Scunthorpe on B1130. Follow signs for Normanby Country Park. Parkland. 18 holes, 6500 yards. S.S.S. 71. Practice area. *Green Fees:* weekdays £10.00 per round, £16.00 per day; weekends £12.00 per round. Twilight Ticket £5.00 weekdays, £6.00 weekends. *Eating facilities:* fully licensed Clubhouse, restaurant; meals most times.

Visitors: welcome on most occasions, check times in advance with Professional. *Society Meetings:* bookings taken for weekdays, except Bank Holidays. Professional: Mr Chris Mann (01724 720226). Bookings Secretary: I.D. Reekie (01724 280444). Secretary: Mr Graham Kirk (01724 280280).

SCUNTHORPE. **Scunthorpe Golf Club,** Burringham Road, Scunthorpe DN17 2AB (01724 842913). *Location:* leave M181 Scunthorpe South, opposite Asda Superstore. Flat wooded course. 18 holes, 6281 yards. S.S.S. 71. *Green Fees:* weekdays £20.00 per round, £24.00 per day. *Eating facilities:* full catering and bar available. *Visitors:* welcome weekdays only, not Sundays, Saturdays with members. *Society Meetings:* catered for weekdays. Professional: A. Lawson (01724 868972). Secretary: K.R. Ford (01724 866561).

WITHERNSEA. **Withernsea Golf Club,** Chestnut Avenue, Withernsea HU19 2PG (01964 612078 or 612258). *Location:* 25 miles north-east of Hull on main road into Withernsea (signposted). Flat course. 9 holes, 5112 yards. S.S.S. 64. *Green Fees:* weekdays £8.00 per day, £5.00 if with a member; weekends £8.00 with a member only. *Eating facilities:* bar and meals available (prior notice for meals if possible). *Visitors:* welcome weekdays, weekends must be playing with a member. *Society Meetings:* by arrangement. Special rates available. Professional: G. Harrison. Secretary: B. Williams (01964 612078).

Isle of Wight

COWES. **Cowes Golf Club,** Crossfield Avenue, Cowes, Isle of Wight PO31 8HN (01983 292303). *Location:* entrance adjacent Cowes High School. Parkland with sea views. 9 holes, 5934 yards. S.S.S. 68. *Green Fees:* weekdays £15.00; weekends £18.00. *Eating facilities:* snack meals available in bar in summer. Bar open 11am to 2pm summer months. *Visitors:* welcome except Sunday before 1pm and Thursday, Ladies' Day (11.30am to 3pm). *Society Meetings:* by arrangement with Secretary. Society rates by arrangement. Secretary: D.C. Weaver.

EAST COWES. **Osborne Golf Club,** Osborne House, East Cowes PO32 6JX (01983 295421). *Location:* off A3027 north of East Cowes, in Osborne Estate. Parkland. 9 holes, 6286 yards. S.S.S. 70. Practice area. *Green Fees:* weekdays £18.00; weekends and Bank Holidays £20.00. *Eating facilities:* catering available each day. *Visitors:* welcome except on Saturdays and Sundays before 12.00 noon and Tuesdays before 1.00pm. *Society Meetings:* catered for (24 maximum). Professional: Andrew Scullion (01983 295649). Secretary: Roy Jones.

FRESHWATER. **Freshwater Bay Golf Club,** Afton Down, Freshwater (01983 752955). *Location:* western end of Island, approximately half-a-mile east of Freshwater Bay on coast road to Ventnor. 18 holes, 5725 yards. S.S.S. 68. *Green Fees:* £18.00 per day, £22.00 weekends and Bank Holidays. *Eating facilities:* licensed bar, catering. *Visitors:* welcome. *Society Meetings:* by arrangement. Secretary: G. Smith.

NEWPORT. **Newport (Isle of Wight) Golf Club,** St. Georges Down, Near Shide, Newport, Isle of Wight (01983 525076). *Location:* one mile south east of Newport. Testing downland course. 9 holes, 5704 yards. S.S.S. 68. *Green Fees:* £15.00 per day weekdays; £17.50 weekends. *Eating facilities:* hot snacks available. *Visitors:* welcome, except Saturday after 3.30pm and Sunday afternoons. *Society Meetings:* groups of 12 plus welcome by arrangement weekdays except Wednesday afternoons. Secretary: Mr P.J. Mills (01983 525076).

RYDE. **Ryde Golf Club,** Binstead Road, Ryde, Isleof Wight PO33 3NF (01983 614809). *Location:* on A3054 very close to town. Parkland course. 9 holes, 5287 yards. S.S.S. 66. Practice area. *Green Fees:* weekdays £15.00 per day; weekends and Bank Holidays £20.00. *Eating facilities:* available during bar hours. *Visitors:* welcome, restrictions Wednesdays and Sundays. *Society Meetings:* catered for. Professional: Mark Wright. Secretary: A.R.J. Goodall (01983 614809).

SANDOWN. **Shanklin and Sandown Golf Club,** The Fairway, Lake, Sandown PO36 9PR (01983 403170). *Location:* one mile from Sandown. Heathland. 18 holes, 6068 yards. S.S.S. 69. Practice ground. *Green Fees:* £22/£27 weekdays; £27/£30 weekends. Three day ticket weekdays £50. *Eating facilities:* available all day. *Visitors:* welcome, weekends after 12 noon/1pm; bona fide golfers only. Handicap Certificate preferred. *Society Meetings:* by arrangement. Professional: Peter Hammond (01983 404424). Secretary: G.A. Wormald (01983 403217).

UPPER VENTNOR. **Ventnor Golf Club,** Steephill Down Road, Upper Ventnor (01983 853326). *Location:* northwest boundary of Ventnor. Downland undulating with side slopes windy. 12 holes, 5767 yards. S.S.S. 68. *Green Fees:* weekdays £12.00; weekends £14.00. Ladies £2.00 less; Juniors under 16 half price. *Eating facilities:* bar snacks only. *Visitors:* welcome, Sundays after 1pm, Ladies' Day Fridays 12 noon to 3pm. Secretary: K.M. Tomes (01983 566456).

Kent

ASHFORD. **Ashford (Kent) Golf Club,** Sandyhurst Lane, Ashford TN25 4NT (01233 620180). *Location:* just off A20, one and a half miles west of Ashford. Parkland – stream cutting through course. 18 holes, 6246 yards. S.S.S. 70. *Green Fees:* weekdays £27.00, weekends and Bank Holidays £42.00 (November to February reduced green fees). *Eating facilities:* available every day. *Visitors:* welcome. Handicap Certificate required. *Society Meetings:* catered for Tuesdays and Thursdays by arrangement. Professional: Hugh Sherman (01233 629644). Secretary: A.H. Story (01233 622655).

ASHFORD. **Chart Hills Golf Club,** Biddenden, Ashford TN27 8JX (01580 292222; Fax: 01580 292233). *Location:* M25, M20 Leeds Castle turn off (B2163), A274 to Tenterden. Wooded course designed by Nick Faldo. 18 holes, 7086 yards. S.S.S. 74. Short game area, golf academy. *Green Fees:* £45 per round, £60 per day weekdays, £48 per round, £65 per day weekends. *Eating facilities:* restaurant, bar snacks, bar, conference facilities. *Visitors:* restricted play – please contact the Pro Shop. Gymnasium, fitness centre. *Society Meetings:* mid-week only, contact Pro Shop. Professional: Roger Hyder (01580 292148). General Manager: Jeff Levine.

BECKENHAM. **Beckenham Place Park Golf Club,** Beckenham Hill Road, Beckenham. *Location:* on A222 north of Bromley. Parkland. 18 holes, 5672 yards. S.S.S. 68. Practice ground, nets, putting green. *Green Fees:* information not available. *Eating facilities:* bar and cafeteria. *Visitors:* welcome without reservation on weekdays, but must book for weekends. *Society Meetings:* not catered for. Other facilities include tennis courts and putting green. Professional: B. Woodman (0181-658 5374). Secretary: K. Tregunno (0181-778 4116). *

BECKENHAM. **Braeside Golf Club,** Beckenham Place Park, Beckenham Hill, Beckenham (0181-650 2292). Parkland course. 18 holes, 5722 yards, 5230 metres. S.S.S. 68. Practice area and nets. *Green Fees:* information not provided. *Eating facilities:* cafe and bar. *Visitors:* welcome any time. Professional: Bill Woodman (0181-658 5374). Secretary: R. Oliver (0181-304 3818). *

BECKENHAM. **Langley Park Golf Club,** Barnfield Wood Road, Beckenham BR3 2SZ (0181-650 2090). *Location:* one mile from Bromley South station. Flat wooded parkland. 18 holes, 6488 yards, 5931 metres, S.S.S. 71. Practice areas and nets. *Green Fees:* weekdays £35.00; weekends with member only. *Eating facilities:* bar snacks, restaurant/dining room. *Visitors:* welcome weekdays by arrangement with Pro Shop. Handicap Certificate required. *Society Meetings:* Wednesdays and Thursdays only by arrangement with Secretary. Professional: Colin Staff (0181-650 1663). Secretary: J.L. Smart (0181-658 6849).

BEXLEY HEATH. **Bexley Heath Golf Club,** Mount Road, Bexley Heath DA6 8JS (0181-303 6951). *Location:* adjacent to A2. Hilly parkland. 9 holes, 5239 yards, 4788 metres. S.S.S. 66. *Green Fees:* £20 (approximately). Weekends with member only. *Eating facilities:* catering available. *Visitors:* weekdays only. Professional: To be appointed. Secretary: S.E. Squires.

BIGGIN HILL. **Cherry Lodge Golf Club,** Jail Lane, Biggin Hill, Near Westerham TN16 3AX (01959 572250). *Location:* A233 to M25 Junction 5, nearest town Bromley, eight miles. Parkland. 18 holes, 6652 yards, 6084 metres. S.S.S. 73. Extensive practice ground. *Green Fees:* weekdays £18.00 per round, £23.00 per day; weekends with member only. *Eating facilities:* restaurant, lounge snacks, full bar. *Visitors:* welcome weekdays except Bank Holidays. *Society Meetings:* welcome weekdays only by arrangement. Professional: Nigel Child (01959 572989). Secretary: Alex Kemsley (01959 572250; Fax: 01959 540672).

BROADSTAIRS. **North Foreland Golf Club,** The Clubhouse, Convent Road, Broadstairs CT10 3PU (01843 862140). *Location:* outside Broadstairs, near North Foreland Lighthouse. Seaside downland. 18 holes, 6382 yards. S.S.S. 71. Short Course: 18 holes, 1752 yards. Par 3. *Green Fees:* £25.00 per round; £35.00 per day weekdays. Short Course: £5.50 weekdays, £6.50 weekends and Public Holidays. *Eating facilities:* bar and dining room. *Visitors:* welcome weekdays and weekend afternoons with current Handicap Certificate. Tennis. *Society Meetings:* Wednesdays and Fridays by prior arrangement with Secretary. Professional: Mike Lee (01843 869628). Secretary: B.J. Preston (01843 862140).

BROMLEY. **Magpie Hall Lane Municipal Golf Club,** Magpie Hall Lane, Bromley. *Location:* off Bromley Common on A21. 9 holes, 5490 yards, 5014 metres. S.S.S. 67. *Green Fees:* weekdays £4.70 per 9 holes; weekends £6.00 per 9 holes. *Eating facilities:* bar/bar food. *Visitors:* welcome anytime without reservation. *Society Meetings:* phone the Professional for details. Professional: Bob Lee (0181-462 7014). Secretary: Michael Arnold (0181-695 1296 or 0181-460 8581).

BROMLEY. **Shortlands Golf Club,** Postal Meadow Road, Shortlands, Bromley BR2 0PB (0181-460 2471). *Location:* car park and entrance in Ravensbourne Avenue, off the main Beckenham to Bromley Road, adjacent Shortlands B.R. Station. 9 holes, 5261 yards. S.S.S. 66. *Green Fees:* no green fees allowed except when introduced and playing with a member: £10.00. *Eating facilities:* available. *Visitors:* restricted to playing with a member. *Society Meetings:* only when member involved. Professional: J. Bates (0181-464 6182). Hon. Secretary: Mrs Leah Burrows (0181-460 8828 or 2471). *

BROMLEY. **Sundridge Park Golf Club,** Garden Road, off Plaistow Lane, Bromley BR1 3NE (0181-460 1822). *Location:* five minutes' walk from Sundridge Park station. Wooded parkland. 36 holes. East 6467 yards. West 6007 yards. S.S.S. 71 and 69. Two practice grounds. *Green Fees:* £36.00 per day weekdays. *Eating facilities:* restaurant, spike bar, lounge bar, members' bar. *Visitors:* welcome weekdays only, with Handicap Certificate. *Society Meetings:* catered for by arrangement. Professional: Bob Cameron (0181-460 5540). Secretary: Derek Lowton (0181-460 0278).

CANTERBURY. **Broome Park Golf and Country Club,** Broome Park Estate, Barham, Near Canterbury CT4 6QX (01227 831701; Fax: 01227 831973). *Location:* off the A2 at the A260 in the direction of Folkestone, half a mile on right. Undulating parkland, lake in front of 18th green. 18 holes, 6610 yards, S.S.S. 72. Driving range and practice ground. *Green Fees:* £26.00 weekdays; £30.00 weekends (after midday only). *Eating facilities:* available all week. *Visitors:* welcome. Handicap Certificate required. *Society Meetings:* weekdays only. Professional: Tienie Britz (01227 831701 extension 264). Hon. Secretary: John Cowling (01227 831701 extension 298).

CANTERBURY. **Canterbury Golf Club,** Scotland Hills, Littlebourne Road, Canterbury CT1 1TW (01227 781871). *Location:* one mile from town centre on the A257 road to Sandwich. 18 holes, 6209 yards. S.S.S. 70. *Green Fees:* weekdays £27.00 per round, £36.00 per day; weekends £36.00 per round. Saturday/Sunday after 3pm only. *Eating facilities:* snacks, sandwiches, lunches, dinners each day. *Visitors:* welcome without reservation. *Society Meetings:* catered for Tuesday and Thursday. Professional: Paul Everard (01227 462865). Secretary: E.L. Ruckert (01227 453532). *

CHISLEHURST. **Chislehurst Golf Club,** Camden Park Road, Chislehurst BR7 5HJ (0181-467 3055). *Location:* between Bromley and junction of A222 and Sidcup bypass. Parkland. 18 holes, 5128 yards. S.S.S. 65. *Green Fees:* £25.00 weekdays; £10.00 weekends with member only. *Eating facilities:* catering available. Large parties by prior arrangement. *Visitors:* welcome but restricted to weekdays (except Wednesday mornings) and only with a member at weekends. *Society Meetings:* catered for by arrangement, 36 hole Societies only on Thursdays. Professional: Mark Lawrence (0181-467 6798). Secretary: N.E. Pearson (0181-467 2782; Fax: 0181-295 0874).

CRANBROOK. **Cranbrook Golf Club Ltd.,** Benenden Road, Cranbrook TN17 4AL (01580 712833; Fax: 01580 714274). *Location:* situated between Sissinghurst and Benenden. Parkland – tree lined. 18 holes, 6351 yards. S.S.S. 70. Practice area. *Green Fees:* weekdays £19.00, £11.00 with a member; weekends £27.50, £16.00 with a member. *Eating facilities:* clubhouse facilities open all day. *Visitors:* welcome anytime weekdays except before 9.30am Tuesdays and before 10.30am Thursdays; weekends welcome 12 noon to 12.30pm and after 3.30pm. *Society Meetings:* company days available. Secretary: (01580 712833).

DARTFORD. **Corinthian Golf Club,** Valley Road, Fawkham, Dartford DA3 8LZ (01474 707559). *Location:* off the A2 east of Dartford/off A20 north of Brands Hatch. Wooded course (tree lined), special feature being lake in front of the 9th green. 9 holes, 6303 yards. S.S.S. 70. Practice area. *Green Fees:* weekdays £12.00, with a member £7.00; weekends £16.00, with a member £7.00 after 1pm. *Eating facilities:* members bar, sports bar. *Visitors:* welcome except weekends and Bank Holiday mornings. *Society Meetings:* welcome Mondays, Wednesdays and Fridays. Professional: D. Private. Secretary: R. Fletton.

DARTFORD. **Dartford Golf Club Ltd.,** The Clubhouse, Dartford Heath, Dartford DA1 2TN (01322 223616). *Location:* backing on to A2, one mile from Dartford Tunnel and M25. Flat parkland. 18 holes, 5914 yards. S.S.S. 69. *Green Fees:* weekdays £28.00. *Eating facilities:* catering available. *Visitors:* welcome on weekdays with reservation, must be member of another golf club. *Society Meetings:* welcome on Mondays and Fridays by prior arrangement with Secretary. Professional: G. Cooke (01322 226409). Secretary: Margaret Gronow (01322 226455).

DEAL. **Royal Cinque Ports Golf Club,** Golf Road, Deal CT14 6RF (01304 374007; Fax: 01304 379530). *Location:* A258 from Sandwich. In Upper Deal leave for Middle Deal Road, left turn into Albert Road, Western Road, on to Golf Road (or from Dover, A258 via Sea front and Godwin Road). Links course. 18 holes, Championship 6785 yards, Medal 6406 yards. S.S.S. 71. *Green Fees:* weekdays £45.00 per day/round, £35.00 after 1pm. No fees accepted at weekends. *Eating facilities:* bar snacks. *Visitors:* welcome. Maximum handicap 18. Handicap Certificate must be produced. *Society Meetings:* catered for weekdays only on application. Professional: Andrew Reynolds (01304 374170). Secretary: Colin Hammond (01304 367856).

DEAL. **Walmer and Kingsdown Golf Club,** The Leas, Kingsdown, Deal CT14 8EP (01304 373256). *Location:* on A258 from Dover (A2) to Deal, club signposted at village of Ringwood. Seaside links on clifftop near Dover. 18 holes, 6451 yards. S.S.S. 71. *Green Fees:* weekdays £22.00 per round, £28.00 per day; weekends £24.00 per round, £30.00 per day. *Eating facilities:* full catering and bar service. *Visitors:* welcome without reservation if members of another club. *Society Meetings:* catered for except Saturdays and Sundays. Professional: Ian Coleman (01304 363017). Secretary: B.W. Cockerill.

EDENBRIDGE. **Edenbridge Golf and Country Club,** Crouch House Road, Edenbridge TN8 5LQ (01732 865097). *Location:* from M25 take A25, at Limpsfield take B2026 to Edenbridge. Parkland. First course 18 holes, 6643 yards. S.S.S. 73. Second course 18 holes, 5671 yards. S.S.S. 67. 16 bay floodlit driving range. *Green Fees:* weekdays £15.00 per round, weekends and Bank Holidays £18.00 per round; Skeynes Course £12.00 weekdays, £15.00 weekends. *Eating facilities:* bar and restaurant. *Visitors:* welcome, call for start time. *Society Meetings:* welcome by arrangement. Professional: Keith Burkin (01732 865202). Secretary: Judith Scully (01732 867381; Fax: 01732 867029).

EYNSFORD. **Austin Lodge Golf Club,** Upper Austin Lodge Road, Eynsford DA4 0HU (01322 863000; Fax: 01322 862406). *Location:* Enysford – 10 minutes' drive from Junction 3 of M25, M20, A20. Secluded rolling countryside with lakes. 18 holes, 6575 yards Yellow Tees, 7118 yards White Tees. S.S.S. 73. Practice ground. *Green Fees:* weekdays £15.00; weekends £23.00. *Eating facilities:* bar, restaurant with light meals all day. *Visitors:* welcome weekdays, possibly after 2pm weekends, telephone booking only. *Society Meetings:* welcome, telephone booking only. Professional: Nigel Willis (01322 868944). Secretary: S. Bevan.

FARNBOROUGH. **High Elms Golf Club,** High Elms Road, Downe (01689 858175). *Location:* two miles from Farnborough Hospital on A21, turn right at Shire Lane, second on left. Beautiful parkland. 18 holes, 5626 metres. S.S.S. 70. *Green Fees:* weekdays £9.45; weekends £12.00. *Eating facilities:* food by arrangement with publican, ring (01689 50177). *Society Meetings:* apply to Bromley Council. Professional: Bob Lee. Secretary: Mrs P. O'Keeffe.

FAVERSHAM. **Faversham Golf Club Ltd.,** Belmont Park, Faversham ME13 0HB (01795 890251). *Location:* M2 Faversham Exit (A251) to A2 junction, left to Brogdale Road, left to Belmont. 18 holes, 6021 yards. S.S.S. 69. *Green Fees:* weekdays £23.00 per round, £30.00 all day; weekends with members only £24.00 per round, £32.00 per day. Societies £25.00 per round, £32.00 per day. Fees subject to review. *Eating facilities:* by arrangement with Steward. *Visitors:* welcome with member. *Society Meetings:* Wednesdays and Fridays catered for, Tuesdays limited numbers. Professional: (01795 890275). Secretary: D.B. Christie (01795 890561).

FOLKESTONE. **Sene Valley Golf Club Ltd.,** Blackhouse Hill, Sene, Folkestone CT18 8BZ (01303 266726). *Location:* A20 then B2065 towards Hythe. Downland course overlooking sea. 18 holes, 6287 yards. S.S.S. 70. Practice ground. *Green Fees:* weekdays £20.00 per round, £30.00 per day; weekends £30.00 per round, £32.00 per day. *Eating facilities:* bar and restaurant (no catering Mondays). *Visitors:* welcome with Handicap Certificate (preferably not weekends or Bank Holidays). *Society Meetings:* welcome Wednesdays to Fridays. Professional: P. Moger (01303 268514). Secretary: R.W. Leaver (01303 268513).

GILLINGHAM. **Gillingham Golf Club Ltd.,** Woodlands Road, Gillingham ME7 2AP (01634 850999; Fax: 01634 574749). *Location:* A2 Gillingham. Flat parkland. 18 holes, 5879 yards. S.S.S. 68. Practice nets. *Green Fees:* weekdays £15.00; weekends £11.00 with a member only. Special rates on application. *Eating facilities:* available. *Visitors:* welcome at all times except weekends. Must have proof of Handicap or membership of another club. *Society Meetings:* welcome, maximum 30/36 players. Professional: Brian Impett (01634 855862). Secretary: L.P. O'Grady (01634 853017).

GRAVESEND. **Mid-Kent Golf Club,** Singlewell Road, Gravesend DA11 7RB (01474 352387). *Location:* A227 off A2. Parkland. 18 holes, 6199 yards. S.S.S. 69. *Green Fees:* weekdays £20.00 per round, £30.00 per day; weekends with member only. *Eating facilities:* breakfast, dinner by arrangement, lunch every day, bar 11am to 11pm. *Visitors:* welcome weekdays except competition days with Handicap Certificate. *Society Meetings:* catered for Tuesdays only. Professional: Neil Hansen (01474 332810). Secretary: T. Potter (01474 568035; Fax: 01474 564218).

HALSTEAD. **Broke Hill Golf Club,** Sevenoaks Road, Halstead TN14 7HR (01959 533225). *Location:* two minutes from M25 Junction 4, A21 four miles from Bromley and two miles from Orpington. Parkland course, exposed on high ground. 18 holes, 6454 yards. Two practice grounds. *Green Fees:* weekdays £25.00 per round, £40.00 per day. Reductions for members' guests. *Eating facilities:* full bar and restaurant facilities. *Visitors:* welcome. *Society Meetings:* accepted weekdays only. Professional: (01959 533810). Secretary: Trevor Collingwood (01959 533225; Fax: 01959 532880).

HAWKHURST. **Hawkhurst Golf Club,** High Street, Hawkhurst TN18 4JS (01580 752396). *Location:* on A268 from Hawkhurst to Flimwell. Parkland. 9 holes, 5709 yards. S.S.S. 68. *Green Fees:* £18.00 weekdays; weekends £10.00 only with member. Can play without a member after 4pm (Summer only). *Eating facilities:* all facilities, prior notice for Societies. *Visitors:* welcome weekdays, weekends with member only. Handicap Certificate recommended. Squash courts. *Society Meetings:* weekdays, catered for with prior notice. Professional: Tony Collins (01580 753600). Secretary: Richard C. Fowles (01580 830287).

HEADCORN. **Weald of Kent Golf Course,** Maidstone Road, Headcorn TN27 9PT (01622 891671; Fax: 01622 891793). *Location:* Junction 8 M20, five miles south of Maidstone on A274. Scenic undulating parkland course with many ditches, ponds and lakes. 18 holes, 6169 yards. S.S.S. 69. *Green Fees:* weekdays £14.50; weekends £18.50. *Eating facilities:* 65 cover silver service restaurant and an extensive bar menu available from 7.30am to 10pm. Banqueting and conference facilities also available (30 to 200 delegates). *Visitors:* welcome at anytime, bookings available three days in advance (01622 890866). *Society Meetings:* welcome weekdays, minimum 12. Professional: Nick McNally. Manager: John Millen.

HERNE BAY. **Herne Bay Golf Club,** Canterbury Road, Herne Bay (01227 373964). 18 holes, 5466 yards. S.S.S. 67. *Green Fees:* weekdays £18.00 per round, £25.00 per day; weekends £25.00. *Eating facilities:* available except Monday. *Visitors:* welcome;

weekdays unrestricted, weekends and Bank Holidays after 12 noon only. Handicap Certificate required. *Society Meetings:* catered for weekdays. Professional: D. Lambert. Secretary: B. Warren.

HEVER. **Hever Golf Club,** Hever TN8 7NP (01732 700771; Fax: 01732 700775). *Location:* at Junction 6 take A22 turning to Godstone, then turn left onto the A25 to Sevenoaks, after three and a half miles take the Edenbridge road. Follow signs for Hever Castle. Go past the entrance to castle and the club is one mile further on the right. Parkland, wooded. 18 holes, 6951 yards, 6319 metres. S.S.S. 73. Large practice area. *Green Fees:* on application. *Eating facilities:* available in the clubhouse. *Society Meetings:* on application. Professional/Secretary: John Powell (01732 700785 or 700771; Fax: 01732 700775).

HYTHE. **Hythe Imperial Golf Club,** Princes Parade, Hythe CT21 6AE (01303 267441). *Location:* come off M20 Junction 11, directions for Hythe A261. Flat seaside course. 9 holes, 5533 yards. S.S.S. 67. Practice ground. *Green Fees:* £15.00 weekdays. Reductions if playing with a member. *Eating facilities:* available at the hotel. *Visitors:* welcome weekdays, no fees weekends up to 1pm. *Society Meetings:* welcome weekdays only. Professional: Gordon Ritchie (01303 267441). Secretary: Mr R. Barrett (01303 267554).

LYDD. **Lydd Golf Club,** Romney Road, Lydd, Romney Marsh TN29 9LS (01797 320808). *Location:* B2075 Lydd. Seaside links course with many lakes. 9 holes, 3234 yards. S.S.S. 71. (Additional 9 holes open May 1995). 20-bay floodlit driving range. *Green Fees:* weekdays 9 holes £9.00, 18 holes £15.00; weekends 9 holes £12.00, 18 holes £20.00. *Eating facilities:* bar and restaurant. *Visitors:* no restrictions. *Society Meetings:* welcome, discount rates available. Professional: Mark Chilcott (01797 321921). Secretary: David Astill (01797 320808; Fax: 01797 321482).

MAIDSTONE. **Bearsted Golf Club,** Ware Street, Bearsted, Maidstone ME14 4PQ (01622 738389). *Location:* Junction 7 off M20. Secluded parkland course with view of North Downs. 18 holes, 6253 yards, 5715 metres. S.S.S. 70. Practice area/net. *Green Fees:* £24/£32 weekdays; weekends with members only. *Eating facilities:* bar/restaurant. *Visitors:* welcome on proof of membership of bona fide golf club. Handicap Certificate required. Weekends with member only. *Society Meetings:* catered for Tuesdays and Thursdays, limited numbers Wednesdays/Fridays. Professional: T. Simpson (01622 738024). Secretary: Mrs L.M. Siems (01622 738198).

MAIDSTONE. **Cobtree Manor Park Golf Club,** Chatham Road, Sandling, Maidstone ME14 3AZ (01622 681560). *Location:* M20, A229 Chatham (not Maidstone). Undulating course with trees, and interesting 6th hole over lake. 18 holes, 5716 yards. S.S.S. 68. Tuition, practice, putting. *Green Fees:* information on request. *Eating facilities:* restaurant and bar. *Visitors:* welcome, book one week in advance through Professional. *Society Meetings:* weekdays by arrangement only. Professional: Martin Drew (01622 753276).

MAIDSTONE. **Leeds Castle Golf Course,** Leeds Castle, Leeds, Maidstone ME17 1PL (Tel & Fax: 01622 880467). *Location:* M20-A20 near Maidstone. Situated in the grounds of Leeds Castle, parkland. 9 holes, 2790 yards. S.S.S. 34. Practice putting green and nets. *Green Fees:* weekdays £8.50; weekends £9.50. Reduced second 9 holes weekdays £6.50; Senior Citizens and Juniors £6.50 9 holes. *Eating facilities:* Park Gate Inn (situated in golf course car park). *Visitors:* welcome anytime, bookings taken from six days in advance. Correct dress must be worn – no denim jeans allowed, golf shoes preferred. *Society Meetings:* welcome midweek. Professional: Chris Miller PGA. Secretary: Jill Skinner.

MAIDSTONE. **The Ridge Golf Club,** Chartway Street, East Sutton, Maidstone ME17 3DL (01622 844382; Fax: 01622 844168). *Location:* Junction 8 M20, past Leeds Castle on Sutton Valence Road to A274 turn left and first turning on left. Wooded parkland. 18 holes, 6254 yards. S.S.S. 71. Driving range. *Green Fees:* weekdays £25.00; weekends £30.00. *Eating facilities:* spikes bar, three bars, 80-seater restaurant, function room. *Visitors:* welcome. Handicap Certificate required. *Society Meetings:* welcome. Professional: Allen Robertson (01622 844243). Secretary: Graham Sones.

MAIDSTONE. **Tudor Park Golf and Country Club,** Ashford Road, Bearsted ME14 4NQ (01622 735891). *Location:* east of Maidstone, on A20 at Bearsted. Off Junction 8 of M20. Parkland. 18 holes, 6041 yards. S.S.S. 69. Practice area. *Green Fees:* information not provided. *Eating facilities:* restaurants and bars. *Visitors:* current Handicap Certificate required. Hotel, leisure and conference facilities. *Society Meetings:* Societies and Company Days catered for. Professional: Marc Boggia (01622 39412). Secretary: Christopher May (01622 34334). *

MAIDSTONE. **West Malling Golf Club,** London Road, Addington, West Malling ME19 5AR (01732 844785). *Location:* A228 turn off M20. Parkland, 18 holes, 6142 yards. S.S.S. 70 (Spitfire Course). 18 holes, 6300 yards. S.S.S. 70 (Hurricane Course). *Green Fees:* weekdays £20.00 per round, £28.00 per day; weekends £30.00 per round after 12 noon. *Eating facilities:* restaurant available. *Visitors:* welcome except Bank Holidays or before 12 noon weekends. Conference/function facilities available. *Society Meetings:* catered for. Professional: Paul Foston (01732 844022). Secretary: Mike Ellis (01732 844785).

NEW ROMNEY. **Littlestone Golf Club,** St. Andrews Road, Littlestone, New Romney TN28 8RB (01797 362231). *Location:* A20 to Ashford, B2070 to New Romney, one mile from New Romney. Seaside links course. 18 holes, 6460 yards. S.S.S. 72. Driving range. *Green Fees:* £26.00 per round, £36.00 per day weekdays; £32.00 per round, £40.00 per day weekends. *Eating facilities:* available. *Visitors:* Handicap Certificate required, visitors not allowed at weekends in Winter, in Summer only after 3pm. Weekdays by prior arrangement with the Secretary. Professional: Stephen Watkins (01797 362231). Secretary: J.D. Lewis (01797 363355).

NEW ROMNEY. **Romney Warren Golf Club,** St. Andrews Road, Littlestone New Romney TN28 8RB (01797 362231). *Location:* A20 to Ashford, B2070 to New Romney. Undulating seaside links crisscrossed with dykes. 18 holes, 5126 yards. S.S.S. 67. Practice area. *Green Fees:* weekdays £10.00 per round, £20.00 per day; weekends £13.00 per round. Seven days £65, 14 days £110. *Eating facilities:* full facilities daily. *Visitors:* welcome. *Society Meetings:* welcome by arrangement. Professional: Steve Watkins (01797 362231). Secretary: J.D. Lewis (01797 363355).

ORPINGTON. **Cray Valley Golf Club,** Sandy Lane, St. Paul's Cray, Orpington BR5 3HY (01689 831927). *Location:* Ruxley roundabout A20; turn off into Sandy Lane, half-a-mile on left. Parkland. 18 holes, 5624 yards. S.S.S. 67. *Green Fees:* weekdays £11.00, weekends £16.80. Also 9 hole course: weekdays £4.00, weekends £5.50. *Eating facilities:* hot meals available lunchtimes, also bar. *Visitors:* welcome all week. *Society Meetings:* welcome weekdays. Professional: Mr John Gregory (01689 837909). Secretary: Ron Hill (01689 839677).

ORPINGTON. **Hewitts Golf Centre,** Court Road, Orpington BR6 9BX (01689 896266; Fax: 01689 824577). *Location:* M25 Junction 4, take A224 Orpington (Court Road), quarter of a mile on left. Parkland with orchards throughout, two lakes. 18 holes, 6077 yards, 5556 metres. S.S.S. 69. 9 hole par 3 course, 40 bay floodlit driving range. *Green Fees:* weekdays £13.00; weekends £16.00. *Eating facilities:* bar snacks and restaurant. *Visitors:* welcome anytime except during members' tee-off times at weekends (please ring for times). *Society Meetings:* all welcome, contact Centre Manager. Professional: Head Teaching Professional Nigel Lee. Centre Manager: Ken Weatherley.

ORPINGTON. **Ruxley Park Golf Centre,** Sandy Lane, St. Paul's Cray, Orpington BR5 3HY (01689 871490). *Location:* off Ruxley roundabout on the old A20. Parkland course. 18 holes, 6031 yards, 5388 metres. S.S.S. 69. Floodlit driving range. *Green Fees:* weekdays £10.30; weekends £15.50. Weekend afternoon rate £11.00. *Eating facilities:* bar snacks and bar facilities. *Visitors:* welcome. *Society Meetings:* welcome. Professional: Mark Woodman. Secretary: Paul Davis.

ORPINGTON. **West Kent Golf Club,** West Hill, Downe, Near Orpington BR6 7JJ (01689 853737). *Location:* from Downe village south along Luxted Lane, 600 yards turn right into West Hill. 18 holes, 6399 yards. S.S.S. 70. *Green Fees:* £25.00 per round, £40.00 per day. *Eating facilities:* meals by arrangement. *Visitors:* welcome with letter of introduction and recognised handicap. Casual golfers must phone at least 24 hours in advance. *Society Meetings:* catered for. Professionals: R.S. Fidler and G. Ryan (01689 856863). Secretary: A.J. Messing (01689 851323).

RAMSGATE. **St. Augustine's Golf Club,** Cottington Road, Cliffsend, Ramsgate CT12 5JN (01843 590333). *Location:* two miles south-west of Ramsgate – approaching from A253 or A256 follow signs to St. Augustine's Cross. Entrance 75 yards beyond Cross by railway bridge. Mainly parkland, flat – tight and challenging course. 18 holes, 4999 yards, 4572 metres. S.S.S. 64. *Green Fees:* £20.00 weekdays; £22.00 weekends and Bank Holidays. Weekly £65.00, monthly £195. *Eating facilities:* full catering except Mondays when sandwiches and beverages only, usual bar facilities. *Visitors:* welcome, proof of Handicap required, advisable to ring Professional the day before to check periods booked for competitions, societies, etc. *Society Meetings:* catered for, book through Secretary. Professional: D. Scott (01843 590222). Secretary: R.G. Worthington (01843 590333).

ROCHESTER. **Deangate Ridge Golf Club,** Hoo, Rochester (Medway (01634) 250374). *Location:* three miles from Rochester off A228 towards Isle of Grain. Wooded. 18 holes, 6300 yards. S.S.S. 70. 9 hole Pitch and Putt. *Green Fees:* £8.60 weekdays, £11.30 weekends. *Eating facilities:* available. *Visitors:* welcome without reservation, bookings required for weekends. *Society Meetings:* catered for. Professional: Barry Aram (01634 251180). Secretary: R. Worthington (01634 271749). *

ROCHESTER. **Rochester and Cobham Park Golf Club,** Park Pale, by Rochester ME2 3UL (0147 482 3411). *Location:* on A2, two miles east of Gravesend turn-off. 18 holes, 6467 yards. S.S.S. 71. *Green Fees:* weekdays £26 per round, £35 per day. *Eating facilities:* lunch, tea, dinner and snacks available, lunches should be ordered in advance. *Visitors:* with Handicap Certificates – welcome without reservation on weekdays. *Society Meetings:* catered for on Tuesdays and Thursdays. Professional: Matt Henderson (0147 482 3658). Manager: J.W. Irvine (0147 482 3411; Fax: 01474 824446).

SANDWICH. **Royal St. Georges Golf Club,** Sandwich CT13 9PB (01304 617308; Fax: 01304 611245). *Location:* one mile from Sandwich on the road to Sandwich Bay. From Canterbury A257, from Dover A258. Links. 18 holes, Championship 6903 yards, Medal 6534 yards. S.S.S. Championship 74, Medal 72. Large practice ground. *Green Fees:* £50.00 per round, £70.00 per day weekdays. *Eating facilities:* snack bar and dining room. *Visitors:* welcome weekdays only. Must have Handicap Certificate and be member of club with membership of E.G.U. *Society Meetings:* catered for by arrangement. All players must meet requirements for visitors. Professional: Niall Cameron (01304 615236). Secretary: Gerald E. Watts (01304 613090).

SANDWICH BAY. **Prince's Golf Club,** Sandwich Bay. (01304 611118). *Location:* four miles from Sandwich through the Sandwich Bay Estate. Seaside links. 27 holes arranged as 3 loops of 9 holes named "Dunes", "Himalayas", "Shore". D & H 6262 – 6776 yds, Par 71, S.S.S. 70-73. H & S 6238 – 6813 yds, Par 71, S.S.S. 70-73. S & D 6466-6947 yds, Par 72, S.S.S. 71-73. Driving range, full practice facilities. *Green Fees:* weekdays £31.00 per round, £36.00 day; Saturdays £35.50 round, £41.00 day; Sundays £35.50 round, £46.50 day. Special winter offer rates October to May, check by telephone. *Eating facilities:* breakfast, lunch, dinner available every day (pre-booking advisable); bar buffet/Ploughman's lunchtime & evenings; light snacks throughout the day. *Visitors & Societies:* welcome without restriction, Company days and private parties our speciality. Brochure available on request. *Starting Times:* Philip Sparks. Professional: Chris Evans (01304 613797). Information & Bookings: Bob Duncan (01304 611118). Secretary/General Manager: W.M. Howie.

SEVENOAKS. **Darenth Valley Golf Course,** Station Road, Shoreham, Near Sevenoaks TN14 7SA (01959 522944; Fax: 01959 525089). *Location:* A225 between Otford and Eynsford, approximately four miles north of Sevenoaks. Parkland course. 18 holes, 6327 yards. S.S.S. 72. Practice area, putting greens. *Green Fees:* weekdays £11.00; weekends and Bank Holidays £15.00. *Eating facilities:* bar snacks, dining-room, functions up to 130 covers. *Visitors:* welcome with reservation through Pro's shop. *Society Meetings:* catered for by arrangement. Professional: Scott Fotheringham (01959 522922). Clubhouse Manager/ Steward: Neil Morgan (Fax: 01959 525089).

SEVENOAKS. **Knole Park Golf Club,** Seal Hollow Road, Sevenoaks TN15 0HJ (01732 452709). *Location:* one mile south-east of Sevenoaks town. Parkland. 18 holes, 6249 yards, 5711 metres. S.S.S. 70. *Green Fees:* weekdays only, £26 per round, £37 for two rounds. *Eating facilities:* full catering and bar. *Visitors:* by appointment only, must have a club handicap. *Society Meetings:* catered for by arrangement only. Professional: P.E. Gill (01732 451740). Secretary: D.J.L. Hoppe (01732 452150).

SEVENOAKS. **Wildernesse Golf Club,** Park Lane, Seal, Sevenoaks TN15 0JE (01732 761526). *Location:* A25 between Sevenoaks and Borough Green. Park and woodland. 18 holes, 6438 yards. S.S.S. 72. Large practice ground. *Green Fees:* £26.00/£37.00 weekdays. *Eating facilities:* by arrangement. *Visitors:* welcome weekdays only by prior arrangement; letter of introduction. *Society Meetings:* catered for Mondays, Thursdays and Fridays. Professional: Bill Dawson (01732 761527). Secretary: R.A. Foster (01732 761199).

SEVENOAKS. **Woodlands Manor Golf Club,** Tinkerpot Lane, Woodlands, Near Otford, Sevenoaks TN15 6AB (01959 523805). *Location:* Junction 3, M25 take "Brands Hatch" sign on A20, seven miles. Parkland. 18 holes, 6000 yards. S.S.S. 68. Six acre practice ground. *Green Fees:* on application. *Eating facilities:* bar daily. *Visitors:* welcome weekdays, Handicap Certificate required at weekends after 1pm. *Society Meetings:* welcome by arrangement Monday to Friday. Professional: Andrew Brooks (01959 524161). Secretary: E.F. Newman (01959 523806).

SEVENOAKS. **Wrotham Heath Golf Club,** Seven Mile Lane, Comp, Sevenoaks TN15 8QZ (01732 884800). *Location:* on B2016 half-a-mile south of junction with A20. Woods and heather. 9 holes with alternate tees for 18. 6000 yards. S.S.S. 69. *Green Fees:* weekdays £22.00; weekends only with a member. *Eating facilities:* bar and snacks, meals by arrangement, except Mondays. *Visitors:* welcome on weekdays with Handicap Certificate, but not Bank Holidays. *Society Meetings:* catered for Fridays only, no more than 30 people. Professional: H. Dearden (01732 883854). Secretary: L.J. Byrne (01732 884800).

SHEERNESS. **Sheerness Golf Club,** Power Station Road, Sheerness ME12 3AE (01795 662585). *Location:* follow A249 then A250 towards Sheerness. Flat marshland/meadowland – numerous water hazards. 18 holes, 6460 yards. S.S.S. 71. Practice area. *Green Fees:* weekdays £15.00 (£8.00) per round, £20.00 (£12.00) per day; weekends £12.00 only if playing with a member. *Eating facilities:* available. *Visitors:* weekdays only except with member. *Society Meetings:* catered for Tuesdays, Wednesdays and Thursdays by previous arrangement (16-40). Secretary: Lt Col R. Pearce.

SIDCUP. **Sidcup Golf Club (1926) Ltd,** 7 Hurst Road, Sidcup DA15 9AE (0181-300 2150). *Location:* three minutes' walk from Sidcup Station. Parkland. 9 holes, 5722 yards. S.S.S. 68. Practice area. *Green Fees:* weekdays £18.00. *Eating facilities:* restaurant and bar. *Visitors:* welcome weekdays except Bank Holidays. *Society Meetings:* (up to 30 members) catered for by arrangement. Professional: Nick Terry (0181-309 0679). Secretary: Sandy Watt (0181-300 2150).

SITTINGBOURNE near. **Upchurch River Valley Golf Courses,** Oak Lane, Upchurch, near Sittingbourne ME9 7AY (01634 360626; Fax: 01634 387784). *Location:* M2, Junction 4 (A278) A2 Rainham 2.5 miles L, Upchurch (opposite Little Chef). Undulating parkland with ponds and panoramic views. 18 holes, 6160 yards. S.S.S. 69. Driving range. *Green Fees:* weekdays £9.95 18 holes, £5.95 9 holes; weekends £12.95 18 holes, £6.95 9 holes. Reductions for Senior Citizens. *Eating facilities:* 120 seater à la carte restaurant, all day food and drinks lounge. *Visitors:* unrestricted. Swimming pool. *Society Meetings:* welcome weekdays. Professional: Martin Daniels (01634 379592). Secretary: (Members only) A.J. New ACIB (01634 260594). Course Controller: URVGC Ltd.

SITTINGBOURNE. **Sittingbourne and Milton Regis,** Wormdale, Newington, Sittingbourne ME9 7PX (01795 842261). *Location:* Junction 5 M2, A249 to Sheerness three quarters of a mile. Undulating course with trees. 18 holes, 6272 yards, 5754 metres. S.S.S. 70. *Green Fees:* £20.00 (18 holes), £32.00 (36 holes) weekdays. No green fees weekends. *Eating facilities:* available. *Visitors:* welcome weekdays, Handicap Certificate or letter of introduction required. *Society Meetings:* catered for Tuesdays and Thursdays by arrangement. Professional: J. Hearn (01795 842775). Manager: H.D.G. Wylie.

SNODLAND. **Oastpark Golf Club,** Malling Road, Snodland ME6 5LG (01634 242661). *Location:* quarter of a mile off Junction 4 of M20 (Snodland A228). Easy walking, good test of golf, lots of water/sand/trees. 18 holes, 6173 yards. S.S.S. 69. Extensive practice facilities. *Green Fees:* weekdays £10.00; weekends £13.00. Twilight ticket (two and a half hours before dusk) weekdays £7.00 per round, weekends £8.00. *Eating facilities:* full bar and catering service. *Visitors:* welcome, no restrictions. No jeans, tracksuits; golf shoes must be worn. *Society Meetings:* all welcome weekdays. Professional: Terry Cullen (01634 242661). Secretary: Valerie Hagger (01634 242818).

TENTERDEN. **Tenterden Golf Club,** Woodchurch Road, Tenterden TN30 7DR. *Location:* one mile south east of Tenterden on B2067. Parkland course. 18 holes, 6030 yards. S.S.S. 69. *Green Fees:* weekdays £20.00. *Eating facilities:* catering available. *Visitors:* welcome except weekends and Bank Holidays. *Society Meetings:* by prior arrangement. Professional: Darren Lewis (01580 762409). Secretary: J.B. Shaw (01580 763987).

TONBRIDGE. **Nizels Golf Club,** Nizels Lane, Hildenborough, Near Tonbridge TN11 8NX (01732 833138; Fax: 01732 833764). *Location:* five minutes from M25 between Sevenoaks and Tonbridge. Lakes and woodland. 18 holes, 6408 yards. S.S.S. 71. Par 72. *Green Fees:* weekdays £35.00 per round. *Eating facilities:* open all day, high class catering. *Visitors:* welcome weekdays, bookings taken. *Society Meetings:* weekdays. Professional: N. Way (01732 838926). Secretary: L.P. Dyke (01732 833138).

TONBRIDGE. **Poult Wood Public Golf Course,** Higham Lane, Tonbridge (01732 364039 – Golf Shop). *Location:* A227, two miles north of town centre. Wooded, 18 holes, 5569 yards. S.S.S. 67. 9 hole course, practice ground. *Green Fees:* £8.40 per round (£4.90 Juniors/Senior Citizens) weekdays; £12.60 per round weekends. Day ticket (Society) £23.00, £11.50 for 18 holes. *Eating facilities:* full catering available. *Visitors:* all welcome. *Society Meetings:* by arrangement with Clubhouse Manager. Other facilities include squash courts, meeting room, showers, toilets, changing rooms, lockers. Club House Manager: (01732 366180).

TUNBRIDGE WELLS. **Lamberhurst Golf Club,** Church Road, Lamberhurst TN3 8DT (01892 890241). *Location:* A21 from Tunbridge Wells to Hastings, turn left prior to descending hill to Lamberhurst then first right. Attractive parkland course. 18 holes, 6232 yards. S.S.S. 70. Small practice ground. *Green Fees:* weekdays £20.00 per round, £30.00 per day; £36.00 weekends and Bank Holidays. *Eating facilities:* full catering by arrangement. *Visitors:* welcome after 8am weekdays, 12 noon weekends and Bank Holidays. Handicap Certificate required. *Society Meetings:* catered for Tuesdays, Wednesdays and Thursdays by arrangement. Professional: M. Travers (01892 890552). Secretary: Mr P. Gleeson (Tel & Fax: 01892 890591).

TUNBRIDGE WELLS. **Nevill Golf Club,** Benhall Mill Road, Tunbridge Wells TN2 5JW (01892 527820). *Location:* off Forest Road, follow signs. 18 holes, 6336 yards. S.S.S. 70. *Green Fees:* £33.00 weekdays; £46.00 weekends and Bank Holidays. *Eating facilities:* lunches at club by prior arrangement. *Visitors:* welcome with reservation. Handicap Certificate required. *Society Meetings:* catered for. Professional: Paul Huggett (01892 532941). Secretary: Miss K.N.R. Pudner (01892 525818).

TUNBRIDGE WELLS. **Tunbridge Wells Golf Club,** Langton Road, Tunbridge Wells (01892 523034). *Location:* behind Marchants Garages. Parkland. 9 holes, 4525 yards. S.S.S. 62. *Green Fees:* weekdays £22.00. *Eating facilities:* snacks at bar or by arrangement. *Visitors:* welcome weekdays except Tuesdays. Weekends with member only. *Society Meet-*

ings: only by previous arrangement. Professional: K. Smithson (01892 541386). Secretary: P.F. Janes (01892 536918).

WESTGATE ON SEA. **Westgate and Birchington Golf Club,** 176 Canterbury Road, Westgate on Sea CT8 8LT (01843 833905). Seaside course between Westgate on Sea and Birchington (A28). Seaside links course. 18 holes, 4926 yards, 4547 metres. S.S.S. 64. *Green Fees:* weekdays £15.00 per day (after 10am), weekends and Bank Holidays £18.00 (after 11am, Sun after 12 noon). *Eating facilities:* full service available except Mondays and Fridays. *Visitors:* welcome if members of a recognised golf club. *Society Meetings:* by arrangement with Secretary. Professional: R. Game (01843 831115). Secretary: J.M. Wood (01843 831115).

WHITSTABLE. **Chestfield (Whitstable) Golf Club,** 103 Chestfield Road, Chestfield, Whitstable CT5 3LU (01227 792243). *Location:* half a mile south of Thanet Way (A299). Parkland with sea views. 18 holes, 6181 yards. S.S.S. 70. *Green Fees:* £18 weekdays, weekends with a member only. *Eating facilities:* full catering facilities 12 noon to 3pm, bar 11am to 11pm. *Visitors:* welcome weekdays with Handicap Certificate, weekends with member only. *Society Meetings:* catered for weekdays (except Thursdays). Professional: John Brotherton (01227 793563). Secretary: M.A. Sutcliffe (01227 794411).

WHITSTABLE. **Whitstable and Seasalter Golf Club,** Collingwood Road, Whitstable CT5 1EB (01227 272020). *Location:* course adjoins town centre, take Nelson Road turning off main street. Flat seaside links. 9 holes, 5276 yards. S.S.S. 63. Practice net. *Green Fees:* £15.00, green fees are accepted at weekends only if accompanied by a member. *Eating facilities:* bar snacks. *Society Meetings:* welcome (limited in size). Secretary: Mr G.A. Hodson.

Lancashire

ACCRINGTON. **Accrington and District Golf Club,** New Barn Farm, West End, Oswaldtwistle, Accrington (01254 232734). *Location:* on A679, 2 miles from Blackburn. 18 holes, 5954 yards. S.S.S. 69. *Green Fees:* weekdays £15.00, weekends £18.00. *Eating facilities:* lunches and evening meals. *Visitors:* welcome without reservation. *Society Meetings:* prior bookings catered for. Professional: Bill Harling (01254 231091). Hon Secretary: J. Pilkington (01254 232734).

ACCRINGTON. **Green Haworth Golf Club,** Green Haworth, Accrington (01254 237580). *Location:* off A679, one mile Town Centre, via Willows Lane, turn left 300 yards beyond Red Lion Inn. Moorland. 9 holes, 5513 yards. S.S.S. 67. *Green Fees:* weekdays £10.00; weekends and Bank Holidays £14.00. *Eating facilities:* full catering and bar facilities. *Visitors:* welcome, no visitors on Sundays March to October. *Society Meetings:* catered for weekdays only. Secretary: Mr Kevin Lynch (01282 35900).

BACUP. **Bacup Golf Club,** Bankside Lane, Bacup (01706 3170). *Location:* one mile from Bacup centre. 9 holes, 6008 yards. S.S.S. 69. *Green Fees:* weekdays £12.00; weekends £15.00. *Eating facilities:* by arrangement except Mondays. *Visitors:* welcome without reservation except Mondays. Secretary: J. Garvey (01706 874485).

BLACKBURN. **Blackburn Golf Club,** Beardwood Brow, Blackburn BB2 7AX. *Location:* off A677 within easy reach of M6 (Junction 31), M61 and M65; west end of Blackburn. Parkland with superb views of Lancashire coast and Pennine Hills. 18 holes, 6140 yards, 5614 metres. S.S.S. 70. Par 71. Practice area. *Green Fees:* weekdays £19.00 (£7.00 with a member); weekends and Bank Holidays £22.00 (£8.00 with a member). Special rates for parties of 20 or more. *Eating facilities:* full catering and bar facilities (restricted Mondays). *Visitors:* welcome without reservation except on competition days. *Society Meetings:* catered for by arrangement (not Tuesdays or weekends). Professional: Alan Rodwell (01254 55942). Secretary: Peter D. Haydock (01254 51122).

BLACKBURN. **Great Harwood Golf Club,** Harwood Bar, Great Harwood, Blackburn BB6 7TE (01254 884391). Flat wooded course. 9 holes, 6411 yards, 5862 metres. S.S.S. 71. Practice area. *Green Fees:* weekdays £13.00; weekends £16.00. *Eating facilities:* all meals catered for, bar hours 12-2pm, 4-11pm. *Visitors:* welcome Tuesday – Friday. *Society Meetings:* catered for by advance bookings. Secretary: A. Garraway (01254 886802).

BLACKBURN. **Pleasington Golf Club,** Pleasington, Near Blackburn (01254 202177). *Location:* M6 north to Junction 31. Blackburn eight miles. Undulating woodland. 18 holes, 6445 yards. S.S.S. 71. *Green Fees:* weekdays £26.00, weekends and Bank Holidays £30.00. *Eating facilities:* full catering available. *Visitors:* welcome by prior arrangement. *Society Meetings:* Mondays, Wednesdays, Fridays by arrangement. Professional: G.J. Furey (01254 201630). Secretary: A.A. Cook (01254 202177).

BLACKBURN. **Rishton Golf Club,** Eachill Links, Rishton (01254 884442). *Location:* three miles east of Blackburn. 9 holes, 6098 yards. S.S.S. 69. *Green Fees:* weekdays £13.00, £8.00 with a member; weekends £9.00 with a member only. *Eating facilities:* full catering by prior arrangement. *Visitors:* welcome on weekdays and with a member at weekends and on Bank Holidays. *Society Meetings:* visiting parties welcome by prior arrangement, special rates can be obtained. Secretary: I. Baron.

BLACKBURN. **Whalley Golf Club,** Portfield Lane, Whalley, Blackburn BB6 9DR (01254 822236). *Location:* seven miles east of Blackburn on A59. Parkland. 9 holes, 6258 yards, 5727 metres. S.S.S. 72. *Green Fees:* weekdays £15.00 (with a member £8.00); weekends £20.00 (with a member £12.00). *Eating facilities:* full catering and bar facilities. *Visitors:* welcome except Thursday afternoons and Saturdays April to September. *Society Meetings:* welcome by appointment. Professional: H. Smith (01254 824766). Secretary: R. Bolsover (01254 824259).

BLACKBURN. **Wilpshire Golf Club Ltd,** Whalley Road, Wilpshire, Blackburn (01254 248260 or 249691). *Location:* A666 three miles north of Blackburn on Blackburn to Whalley road. 18 holes, 5911 yards. S.S.S. 68. *Green Fees:* £25.00 weekdays; £30.00 weekends. *Eating facilities:* lunch, high tea, dinner except Mondays. *Visitors:* welcome without reservation except competition days. *Society Meetings:* catered for by prior booking through the Secretary. Professional: W. Slaven. Secretary: B. Grimshaw.

BLACKPOOL. **Blackpool North Shore Golf Club,** Devonshire Road, Blackpool FY2 0RD (01253 351017). *Location:* north Blackpool on A587 behind North Prom. Undulating parkland. 18 holes, 6431 yards. S.S.S. 71. *Green Fees:* £25.00 weekdays; £30.00 weekends. Special Package – day's golf with meals £35.00. *Eating facilities:* full catering and bar facilities. *Visitors:* welcome except Thursdays and Saturdays. *Society Meetings:* welcome except Thursdays and weekends. Professional: Brendan Ward (01253 354640). Secretary: Mr R. Yates (01253 352054).

BLACKPOOL. **Blackpool Park Golf Club,** North Park Drive, Blackpool FY3 8LS (01253 393960). *Location:* one mile east of Tower. Parkland course. 18 holes, 6060 yards. S.S.S. 69. *Green Fees:* £7.50 weekdays; £9.50 weekends. Bookings for tee reservation must be made to Blackpool Borough Council. *Eating facilities:* full catering services except Tuesday, bar. *Visitors:* welcome. *Society Meetings:* welcome (booking to be made through Blackpool Borough Council). Professional: B. Purdie (01253 391004). Secretary: Diane Woodman (01253 397916).

BLACKPOOL. **Knott End Golf Club Ltd,** Wyre Side, Knott End, Poulton-le-Fylde FY6 0AA (01253 810254). *Location:* M55 Exit 3, A585 Fleetwood Road then A588 to Knott End, or by passenger ferry from Fleetwood. Scenic riverside course, slight undulations. 18 holes, 5852 yards. S.S.S. 68. Practice ground. *Green Fees:* £20.00 per day weekdays, weekends £24.00. *Eating facilities:* full catering and bar. *Visitors:* welcome, time sheet in use, contact Professional with 24 hours notice. *Society Meetings:* by arrangement weekdays only. Professional: Paul Walker (01253 811365). Secretary: Keith E. Butcher (01253 810576).

BLACKPOOL. **Poulton-le-Fylde Golf Club,** Myrtle Farm, Breck Road, Poulton-le-Fylde, Blackpool FY6 7HJ (01253 893150). *Location:* three miles east of Blackpool. 9 holes, 2972 yards. *Green Fees:* £5.50 weekdays, £7.50 weekends per round. *Eating facilities:* meals at lunch time and light snacks available all day. *Visitors:* welcome without reservation. *Society Meetings:* catered for by prior booking. Professional: D. Spencer (01253 892444). Secretary: K. Audis. *

BLACKPOOL. **The Village Golf Club,** Herons Reach Golf Course, East Park Drive, Blackpool FY3 8LL (01253 838866). *Location:* from Junction 4 off M55 follow signs for Blackpool Zoo, complex is opposite Stanley Park and near to the Zoo. Championship standard parkland course incorporating links features and 10 lakes. 6416 yards. S.S.S. 71. 18 bay floodlit driving range. *Green Fees:* weekdays £20.00 per round; weekends and Bank Holidays £30.00 per round. *Eating facilities:* Spikes Bar, leisure bar, grill restaurant. *Visitors:* welcome. Must hold current Handicap Certificate. 166 bedroomed hotel, leisure facilities, conference and banqueting facilities; Hotel Reservations (01253 838866; Fax: 01253 798800). *Society Meetings:* welcome. Golf Packages available. Professional: Richard Hudson. Golf Manager: David Hughes.

BOLTON. **Bolton Municipal Golf Course,** Links Road, Chorley New Road, Bolton BL2 9XX (01204 844170). *Location:* midway between Horwich and Bolton, A673. Fairly flat parkland. 18 holes, 6336 yards, 5570 metres. S.S.S. 70. Practice ground. *Green Fees:* weekdays £5.00; weekends £6.50. *Eating facilities:* snack and meal facilities available and bar. *Visitors:* welcome at any time. *Society Meetings:* advance booking. Mid-week Society package available. Professional: Bob Longworth (01204 42336). Secretary: K. Taylor (01204 652882). *

BOLTON. **Bolton Open Golf Course,** Longsight Park, Longsight Lane, Harwood, Bolton (01204 597779). *Location:* one and a half miles north east of Bolton town centre. Parkland, mature wooded, superb layout. 9 holes, 2962 yards. S.S.S. 35. *Green Fees:* weekdays £5.00 18 holes (£3.50 9 holes); weekends £6.50 18 holes (£4.00 9 holes). *Eating facilities:* under construction. *Visitors:* welcome, pay as you play course. *Society Meetings:* welcome. Professional: TBA. Secretary: Peter Openshaw (01625 872652).

BURNLEY. **Burnley Golf Club,** Glen View, Burnley BB11 3RW (01282 421045). *Location:* 300 yards from junction of A56 and A646. Moorland. 18 holes, 5899 yards, 5391 metres. S.S.S. 69. *Green Fees:* weekdays £18.00; weekends and Bank Holidays £24.00. *Eating facilities:* available except Wednesdays from lunchtime and Mondays. *Visitors:* welcome except Saturdays. *Society Meetings:* catered for. Professional: W.P. Tye (Tel & Fax: 01282 455266). Secretary: G.J. Butterfield (01282 451281).

BURNLEY. **Towneley Golf Club,** Todmorden Road, Burnley (01282 451636). *Location:* A617 Burnley to Halifax, approximately one mile east of Burnley town centre. Parkland course, mostly flat. 18 holes, 5862 yards, 5357 metres. S.S.S. 68, Par 70. 9 hole course. Small practice area. *Green Fees:* £6.00 weekdays, £7.00 weekends. *Eating facilities:* clubhouse with diningroom, lounge bar and games room. *Visitors:* welcome but make tee reservations in advance. *Society Meetings:* contact Steward at clubhouse for catering requirements (01282 451636). Secretary: I. Kippax (01282 33972).

CARNFORTH. **Silverdale Golf Club,** Redbridge Lane, Silverdale, Carnforth LA5 0SP (01524 701300). *Location:* M6 to Carnforth, then two miles west, adjacent to railway station. Testing heathland course with rock outcrops and excellent views. 12 holes, 5417 yards. S.S.S. 67. *Green Fees:* weekdays £12.00, weekends and Bank Holidays £17.00. *Eating facilities:* not available. *Visitors:* welcome except Sundays in the Summer unless with a member. *Society Meetings:* welcome by arrangement with Secretary. Professional: S. Sumner Roberts. Secretary: P.J. Watts (01524 701307).

CHORLEY. **Chorley Golf Club,** Hall o' the Hill, Heath Charnock, Chorley PR6 9HX (01257 480263; Fax: 01257 480722). *Location:* south of Chorley, just off the A673 at the junction with the A6. Scenic course. 18 holes, 6317 yards. S.S.S. 70. *Green Fees:* weekdays £25.00. *Eating facilities:* restaurant and lounge bar. *Visitors:* welcome by prior arrangement except Mondays, Bank Holidays or weekends. *Society Meetings:* catered for by arrangement. Professional: Mark Tomlinson (01257 481245). Secretary: A.K. Tyrer. Catering: (01257 474664).

CHORLEY. **Duxbury Park Golf Club (Municipal),** Duxbury Hall Road, Duxbury Park, Chorley PR7 4AS (01257 241634). *Location:* one mile south of town centre off A6. Wooded parkland with water hazards on several holes. 18 holes, 6390 yards, 5843 metres. S.S.S. 70. Practice area. *Green Fees:* weekdays £6.50; weekends £8.50. *Eating facilities:* can be arranged. *Visitors:* welcome, book seven days in advance. *Society Meetings:* book in advance. Professional: David Clarke (01257 265380). Secretary: Reg Blease (01257 268665).

CHORLEY. **Euxton Park Golf Centre,** Euxton Lane, Chorley PR7 6DL (01257 261601; Fax: 01772 611603). *Location:* Euxton Lane, Euxton Road between A6 and A49, next to Royal Ordnance factory. 9 holes, Par 3. 40 bay driving range, practice bunkers. *Green Fees:* £2.50. *Eating facilities:* coffee lounge. *Visitors:* welcome, pay and play course. *Society Meetings:* welcome. Professional: Mark Tomlinson (01257 233500). Secretary: T.R. Evans.

CHORLEY. **Shaw Hill Hotel Golf and Country Club,** Preston Road, Whittle-le-Woods, Chorley PR6 7PP (01257 269221; Fax: 01257 261223). *Location:* one mile north of Junction 8 on M61 and two miles M6 Junction 28. Championship course in superb parkland with the clubhouse in a beautiful Georgian mansion. 18 holes, 6405 yards. S.S.S. 71. Practice area. *Green Fees:* weekdays £30.00 per round; weekends £40.00 per round. *Eating facilities:* spike bar and formal bar, à la carte restaurant. *Visitors:* welcome all week, must hold current Handicap Certificate. Accommodation available. Golf trolleys and buggies also available. *Society Meetings:* catered for midweek only. Professional: David Clarke (01257 279222). General Manager: Mr G. Tyrer. Secretary: Mr F. Wharton. *

CLITHEROE. **Clitheroe Golf Club,** Whalley Road, Pendleton, Clitheroe BB7 1PP (01200 22618). *Location:* A59, junction A671 (south of Clitheroe); 300m turn left (signposted Barrow) clubhouse 100m on right. Parkland with extensive countryside views. 18 holes, 6326 yards, 5785 metres. S.S.S. 71. Practice ground and range. *Green Fees:* (1994 Rates) weekdays £25.00; weekends and Bank Holidays £30.00. With a member £10.00. All rates subject to increase for 1995. *Eating facilities:* full service available. *Visitors:* welcome but restricted to times available. No jeans, trainers, track/shell suits. *Society Meetings:* catered for, maximum 48 on Mondays, Tuesdays and Wednesdays, maximum 24 on Thursdays, Fridays and Sundays. No parties Saturdays. Professional: John E. Twissell (01200 24242). Secretary: G. Roberts JP (01200 22292).

COLNE. **Colne Golf Club,** Law Farm, Skipton Old Road, Colne BB8 7EB (01282 863391). *Location:* come off eastern end of M65. Carry on one mile to next roundabout and take first exit on left, Goup Hill. Flat scenic moorland course with trees. 9 holes, 5961 yards, 5451 metres. S.S.S. 69. Full practice facilities. *Green Fees:* £14.00 weekdays, £18.00 weekends and Bank Holidays (subject to review). Parties of 12 or more £13.00 per person (not weekends, Thursdays or competition days). *Eating facilities:* available daily except Mondays. *Visitors:* welcome except on competition days; two-balls only on Thursdays. *Society Meetings:* welcome except weekends, Thursdays and competition days. Secretary: J.T. Duerden.

DARWEN. **Darwen Golf Club,** Winter Hill, Darwen BB3 0LB (01254 701287). *Location:* one and a half miles from Darwen centre. Moorland. 18 holes, 5752 yards. S.S.S. 68. Large practice area. *Green Fees:* weekdays £15.00; weekends and Bank Holidays £20.00. *Eating facilities:* full catering. *Visitors:* welcome, except Saturdays. *Society Meetings:* welcome, except Saturdays. Professional: Wayne Lennon (01254 776370). Secretary: J. Kenyon (01254 704367). *

FLEETWOOD. **Fleetwood Golf Club Ltd.,** The Golf House, Princes Way, Fleetwood FY7 8AF (01253 873114). *Location:* on Fylde Coast, eight miles from Blackpool, Coast Road Blackpool to Fleetwood, two miles west of Fleetwood Centre. Seaside, true links. White course 18 holes, 6723 yards, S.S.S. 72; Yellow course 18 holes, 6433 yards, S.S.S. 71. *Green Fees:* weekdays £20.00; weekends £25.00. *Eating facilities:* full catering and bar service. *Visitors:* welcome with Handicap Certificate. *Society Meetings:* catered for by arrangement. Professional: C.T. Burgess (01253 873661). Secretary: H. Fielding (01253 773573).

HEYSHAM. **Heysham Golf Club,** Trumacar Park, Middleton Road, Heysham LA3 3JH (01524 851240). *Location:* five miles from M6 via Lancaster and Morecambe. Parkland, flat, part-wooded. 18 holes, 6338 yards. S.S.S. 70. Two practice grounds. *Green Fees:* weekdays £18.00 per round, £23.00 per day; weekends and Bank Holidays £28.00. Special rates for parties on application. *Eating facilities:* full catering seven days. *Visitors:* welcome with Handicap Certificates. Tee reserved for members 1pm to 1.45pm. *Society Meetings:* catered for by arrangement with Secretary. Professional: S. Fletcher (01524 852000). Secretary: F.A. Bland (01524 851011).

LANCASTER. **Lancaster Golf and Country Club Ltd,** Ashton Hall, Ashton-with-Stodday, Lancaster LA2 0AJ (01524 752090). *Location:* three miles south of Lancaster on A588. Parkland. 18 holes, 6282 yards. S.S.S. 71. *Green Fees:* weekdays £26.00. *Eating facilities:* available (Caterer: 01524 751105). *Visitors:* welcome weekdays only unless staying in the Dormy House. Club has a Dormy House (part of Ashton Hall) which accommodates 18 persons, 2 nights minimum stay. *Society Meetings:* catered for weekdays only. Professional: David Sutcliffe (01524 751802). Secretary: Mr D.D.J. Palmer (01524 751247). *

LANCASTER. **Lansil Golf Club,** Caton Road, Lancaster LA1 3PE (01524 39269). *Location:* A683, towards Lancaster from Junction 34 M6. Parkland. 9 holes, 5608 yards. S.S.S. 67. *Green Fees:* £15.00 (£8.00 with a member). *Eating facilities:* full meals available all day. *Visitors:* welcome weekdays, not before 1pm Saturday and Sunday. Handicap Certificate required. *Society Meetings:* groups of 12 plus welcome weekdays by prior arrangement. Secretary: John McIntyre (01524 823732).

LEYLAND. **Leyland Golf Club Ltd.,** Wigan Road, Leyland, Preston PR5 2UD (01772 421359). *Location:* leave M6 at Exit 28, turn right to traffic lights, (200 yards) turn right onto the A49, course located one mile on left. Flat parkland. 18 holes, 6123 yards. S.S.S. 69. *Green Fees:* £24.00 weekdays. *Eating facilities:* full catering except Mondays. *Visitors:* welcome weekdays; weekends only with a member. *Society Meetings:* welcome by arrangement with Secretary. Professional: C. Burgess (01772 423425). Secretary/Manager: J. Ross (01772 436457).

LYTHAM ST. ANNES. **Fairhaven Golf Club Ltd.,** Lytham Hall Park, Ansdell, Lytham St. Annes FY8 4JU (01253 736741). *Location:* on B5261, two miles from Lytham, eight miles from Blackpool. 18 holes, 6880 yards. S.S.S. 73. Practice ground and net. *Green Fees:* weekdays £25.00 per round, £35.00 per day; weekends £30.00 per round. *Eating facilities:* full catering except Mondays. *Visitors:* welcome with reservation. *Society Meetings:* catered for by arrangement Mondays, Tuesdays, Wednesdays and Fridays. Professional: B. Plucknett (01253 736976). Secretary: Brian Hartley.

LYTHAM ST. ANNES. **Lytham Green Drive Golf Club,** Ballam Road, Lytham St. Annes FY8 4LE (01253) 734782. Fax: 01253 731350). *Location:* one mile from Lytham Square. 18 holes, 6159 yards. S.S.S. 69. *Green Fees:* £21.00 per round, £26.00 per day weekdays; £33.00 per round weekends. *Eating facilities:* catering available daily. *Visitors:* welcome without reservation. *Society Meetings:* weekdays except Wednesdays. Professional: A. Lancaster (01253 737379). Secretary: R. Kershaw (01253 737390).

LYTHAM ST. ANNES. **Royal Lytham and St. Annes Golf Club,** Links Gate, Lytham St. Annes FY8 3LQ (01253 724206; Fax: 01253 780946). *Location:* within one mile of the centre of St. Annes on Sea. Seaside links course. 18 holes, 6673 yards. S.S.S. 73. Practice ground. *Green Fees:* information not provided. *Eating facilities:* restaurant and bar. *Visitors:* welcome weekdays, limited Sundays, times by arrangement. Dormy House accommodation available. *Society Meetings:* by arrangement. Professional: Eddie Birchenough (01253 720094). Secretary: Major A.S. Craven. *

LYTHAM ST. ANNES. **St. Annes Old Links Golf Club,** Highbury Road, Lytham St. Annes FY8 2LD (01253 723597). *Location:* M55 via Blackpool South Shore, following airport signs. Past airport down to coast road, turn left and first left at next real traffic lights. The only true links course in Lancashire. 18 holes, 6616 yards. S.S.S. 72. Practice ground, putting and chipping greens. *Green Fees:* £28.00 weekdays; £35.00 weekends. *Eating facilities:* restaurant and snack facilities, bar. *Visitors:* welcome, not Saturdays, restricted Sundays. Tuesday is ladies' day. *Society Meetings:* restricted to those with Handicaps and membership of other clubs. Professional: G.G. Hardiman (01253 722432). Secretary: P.W. Ray (01253 723597; Fax: 01253 781506).

MORECAMBE. **Morecambe Golf Club Ltd.,** The Club House, Bare, Morecambe LA4 6AJ (01524 418050). *Location:* on A589 leaving Morecambe towards Carnforth. Parkland course affected by sea breezes and offering superb views. 18 holes, 5766 yards. S.S.S. 68. *Green Fees:* weekdays £16.00 per round, £21.00 per day; weekends and Bank Holidays £21.00 per round, £26.00 per day. *Eating facilities:* diningroom and bar snacks, except Mondays. *Visitors:* welcome at all times, tee reserved for members up to 9.30am and from 12 noon to 1.30pm. *Society Meetings:* welcome at all times. Professional: P. De Valle (01524 415596). Secretary: T.H. Glover (01524 412841).

NELSON. **Marsden Park Golf Club,** Nelson Municipal Golf Course, Townhouse Road, Nelson BB9 8DG (01282 67525). *Location:* just off M65, heading towards Colne. Hilly parkland. 18 holes, 5806 yards. S.S.S. 68. *Green Fees:* information not available. *Eating facilities:* bar, meals to order. *Visitors:* welcome without restriction. Shop (01282 617525). *Society Meetings:* by arrangement. Secretary: J.L. Beck (01282 699181). *

NELSON. **Nelson Golf Club,** King's Causeway, Brierfield, Nelson BB9 0EU (01282 614583). *Location:* leave M65 at Junction 12, take A682 for Brierfield, turn left at Brierfield centre traffic lights, course on the right at top of the hill. Wooded moorland, good views on clear days, No's 5 and 8 holes hilly. 18 holes, 5967 yards, 5457 metres. S.S.S. 69. Large practice area. *Green Fees:* weekdays £20.00; weekends £24.00. *Eating facilities:* lunches, dinners by arrangement except Mondays. *Visitors:* weekdays except Thursdays (Ladies Day), or Saturdays during Competition season. Formal dress (jacket, collar and tie) weekend evenings. *Society Meetings:* weekdays except Thursdays. Professional: Mr Nigel Sumner (01282 617000). Secretary: Mr D.T. Ingham (01282 611834).

ORMSKIRK. **Ormskirk Golf Club,** Cranes Lane, Lathom L40 5UJ (01695 572112). *Location:* two miles east of Ormskirk. 18 holes, 6358 yards. S.S.S. 70. *Green Fees:* information not provided. *Eating facilities:* available except Monday. *Visitors:* welcome, Handicap Certificates required, notice advised with reservation. *Society Meetings:* catered for, book in advance. Professional: J. Hammond. Secretary: P.D. Dromgoole. *

PRESTON. **Ashton and Lea Golf Club Ltd,** Tudor Avenue, off Blackpool Road, Lea, Preston PR4 0XA (01772 726480). *Location:* on A583, three miles west of Preston, turn right opposite Pig and Whistle Hotel. Parkland with water features. 18 holes, 6346 yards. S.S.S. 70. Small practice ground. *Green Fees:* weekdays £20.00; weekends and Bank Holidays £24.00. Reduced rates if playing with member. *Eating facilities:* full catering every day. *Visitors:* welcome but please telephone the Professional to reserve tee time. Conference facilities available. *Society Meetings:* catered for weekdays only, contact the Secretary. Professional: Mr M.R. Greenough (01772 720374). Secretary: Mr M.G. Gibbs (01772 735282).

PRESTON. **Fishwick Hall Golf Club,** Glenluce Drive, Farringdon Park, Preston PR1 5TD (01772 798300). *Location:* two minutes from Exit 31 M6, off A59 Blackburn to Preston Road. Parkland, part wooded, bounded by river. 18 holes, 6028 yards. S.S.S. 69. Practice ground and net. *Green Fees:* weekdays £20.00; weekends and Public Holidays £25.00. Reductions if playing with members. *Eating facilities:* bar, full catering available. *Visitors:* welcome by arrangement. *Society Meetings:* catered for by arrangement. Professional: S. Bence (01772 795870). Secretary: R.R. Gearing (01772 798300).

PRESTON. **Ingol Golf and Squash Club,** Tanterton Hall Road, Ingol, Preston PR7 1BY (01772 734556). *Location:* two miles from Junction 32 M6 (joins M55). Parkland. 18 holes, 5868 yards. S.S.S. 68. *Green Fees:* weekdays £20.00 (reduction with member), weekends and Bank Holidays £25.00 (reduction with member). Reductions for parties. *Eating facilities:* bar/restaurant. *Visitors:* welcome anytime, please telephone to check tee reservations. Snooker, pool and squash. *Society Meetings:* welcome by arrangement. Professional: S. Laycock. Secretary: Amanda Parker. *

PRESTON. **Longridge Golf Club,** Fell Barn, Jeffrey Hill, Longridge, Preston PR3 2TU (01772 783291). *Location:* eight miles north-east of Preston off B6243. Moorland with extensive spectacular views. 18 holes, 5726 yards. S.S.S. 68. *Green Fees:* £18.00 Mondays to Thursdays, £21.00 Fridays, Saturdays, Sundays and Bank Holidays. *Eating facilities:* full catering except Mondays. *Visitors:* welcome at all times. *Society Meetings:* welcome by arrangement. Professional: Neil James. Secretary: J. Greenwood (01772 782765 evenings).

PRESTON. **Penwortham Golf Club Ltd.,** Blundell Lane, Penwortham, Preston PR1 0AX (01772 743207). *Location:* one mile west of Preston on main Southport to Liverpool road. Parkland. 18 holes, 5667 yards. S.S.S. 68. *Green Fees:* £22.00 weekdays; £28.00 weekends. *Eating facilities:* lunches and dinners served at Club. *Visitors:* weekdays only. *Society Meetings:* catered for by arrangement. Professional: J. Wright (01772 742345; Fax: 01772 741677). Secretary: J. Parkinson (01772 744630).

PRESTON. **Preston Golf Club,** Fulwood Hall Lane, Fulwood, Preston PR2 4DD (01772 700011). *Location:* exit 32 on M6 marked Preston & Garstang, partway to Preston turning at Watling Street Road. Parkland course. 18 holes, 6267 yards. S.S.S. 70. *Green Fees:* weekdays £22.00 per round, £27.00 per day. *Eating facilities:* first class diningroom, bars. *Visitors:* welcome weekdays, weekends or Bank Holidays must be accompanied by a member. *Society Meetings:* catered for, Handicap Certificate required. Professonal: P. Wells (01772 700022). Secretary: J.R. Spedding (01772 700011).

ROSSENDALE. **Rossendale Golf Club Ltd.,** Ewood Lane Head, Haslingden, Rossendale BB4 6LH (01706 213056). *Location:* 14 miles north of Manchester, easy access from M66 and A56. 18 holes, 6260 yards. S.S.S. 70. *Green Fees:* weekdays £22.50; weekends and Bank Holidays £27.50. *Eating facilities:* full catering except Mondays; bar. *Visitors:* welcome except Saturdays during season. *Society Meetings:* special terms including full catering available. Professional: S.J. Nicholls (01706 213616). Secretary: J.R. Swain (01706 831339).

SCARISBRICK. **Hurlston Hall Golf Club,** Hurlston Lane, Scarisbrick L40 8JD (01704 840400; Fax: 01704 841404). *Location:* six miles from Southport and two miles from Ormskirk along A570 trunk road; eight miles from M58. Parkland with several lakes and streams. 18

holes, 6746 yards. S.S.S. 72. Golf centre with 18-bay driving range, putting green, large shop with nets. *Green Fees:* weekdays £25.00, weekends £30.00. Winter (tee mats) £20.00. *Eating facilities:* three bars; à la carte restaurant (food served 8.30am to 10pm). *Visitors:* welcome, must book in advance. Handicap Certificate or letter of introduction required. *Society Meetings:* by arrangement, registered Golf Societies only. Professional: Gerry Bond (01704 841120; Fax: 01704 841404). Club Administrator: Hilary Griffiths.

SKELMERSDALE. **Beacon Park Golf Club,** Beacon Lane, Dalton, Upholland WN8 7RU (01695 622700). *Location:* M6 Junction 26, follow signs for Upholland. Parkland, tree lined – undulating. 18 holes, 5995 yards. S.S.S. 72. Large practice ground, 24 bay floodlit driving range. *Green Fees:* information not provided. *Eating facilities:* bar/restaurant. *Visitors:* welcome anytime. Public course, open seven days. *Society Meetings:* Society and Group bookings available on request. Professional: Ray Peters (01695 622700; Fax: 01695 633066). *

UPHOLLAND. **Dean Wood Golf Club,** Lafford Lane, Upholland, Skelmersdale WN8 0QZ (01695 622980). *Location:* Exit 26 from M6 signposted for Southport. Follow A577 to Upholland, first right after church. Wooded parkland course. 18 holes, 6137 yards. S.S.S. 70. *Green Fees:* weekdays £26.00; weekends £30.00. *Eating facilities:* daily catering available, bar. *Visitors:* welcome with reservation, not before 10.30am weekends and Bank Holidays. *Society Meetings:* catered for by prior arrangement. Professional: Tony Coop. Secretary: T.F. Hehir (01695 622219).

Leicestershire

ASHBY DE LA ZOUCH. **Willesley Park Golf Club,** Tamworth Road, Ashby de la Zouch LE65 5PF (01530 411532). *Location:* on B5006 towards Tamworth, one mile from centre of Ashby. Wooded park, semi-heathland. 18 holes, 6304 yards. S.S.S. 70. *Green Fees:* weekdays £27.50 per round/day, weekends and Bank Holidays £32.50. *Eating facilities:* dining room and bar, no catering Mondays. *Visitors:* welcome with reservation. *Society Meetings:* catered for Wednesday, Thursday and Friday. Professional: C.J. Hancock (01530 414820). Secretary: N.H. Jones (01530 414596).

BIRSTALL. **Birstall Golf Club,** Station Road, Birstall LE4 3BB (0116 267 4450). *Location:* 3 miles north of Leicester just off the A6 Leicester to Derby. Parkland. 18 holes, 6222 yards. S.S.S. 70. Practice ground and net. *Green Fees:* weekdays £25.00 per day. *Eating facilities:* bar, diningroom. No catering Mondays. *Visitors:* welcome Mondays, Wednesdays and Fridays. *Society Meetings:* minimum 20, catered for by prior arrangement £20.00 per person. Professional: D. Clark (0116 267 5245). Secretary: Mrs S.E. Chilton (0116 267 4322).

COSBY. **Cosby Golf Club,** Chapel Lane, off Broughton Road, Cosby, Leicester (01533 864759). *Location:* eight miles south of Leicester, four miles from Junction 21 M1. Undulating parkland. 18 holes, 6418 yards. S.S.S. 71. *Green Fees:* weekdays £22.00 per round, £24.00 per day; weekends £8.00 but only with a member. Special rates for societies over 20 in number. *Eating facilities:* bar and food available by arrangement with the Steward. *Visitors:* no visitors after 4pm weekdays. Handicap Certificates may be required for all visitors. 1995 – Centenary Celebrations. *Society Meetings:* welcome, prior booking essential. Professional: Martin Wing (01533 848275). Secretary: M.D. Riddle (01533 864759; Fax: 01533 864484).

EAST GOSCOTE. **Beedles Lake Golf Club,** 170 Broome Lane, East Goscote (0116 260 6759). *Location:* off A46 just north of Leicester, near Syston/East Goscote. Fairly flat course in river valley, adjoining lake with fishing. 18 holes, 6573 yards, 6008 metres. S.S.S. 71. *Green Fees:* weekdays £6.00, weekends £8.00. Twilight fees £4.00. *Eating facilities:* catering available; bar. Steward: Roy Jones. *Visitors:* welcome, no restrictions. Changing rooms and Pro shop. *Society Meetings:* please ring in advance for details. Golf Manager: Gary Meardon.

ENDERBY. **Enderby Golf Club,** Enderby Golf Course, Enderby Leisure Centre, Mill Lane, Enderby (01162 849388). *Location:* two miles from M1/M69 junction 21 roundabout. Flat parkland course. 9 holes, 2178 yards. S.S.S. 61. *Green Fees:* information not provided. *Eating facilities:* bar open normal bar hours, light snacks available at lunchtime. *Visitors:* welcome at all times. Full range of recreational facilities available – swimming, squash, indoor bowls, sauna, solarium, badminton, snooker, etc. Professional: Chris d'Araujo.

HINCKLEY. **Hinckley Golf Club,** Leicester Road, Hinckley LE10 3DR (01455 615124). *Location:* situated one mile from Hinckley on A47 Leicester-Hinckley road. Parkland with lakeside features. 18 holes, 6517 yards, 5959 metres. S.S.S. 71. Practice area for members. *Green Fees:* weekdays £20.00 per round, £25.00 per day. *Eating facilities:* bar meals daily except Sundays. *Visitors:* welcome except Tuesdays and weekends. *Society Meetings:* Mondays and Wednesdays by appointment. Professional: R. Jones (Tel & Fax: 01455 615014). Secretary: J. Toon (01455 615124).

KIRBY MUXLOE. **Kirby Muxloe Golf Club,** Station Road, Kirby Muxloe LE9 9EP (01533 393107). *Location:* four miles west of Leicester on A47. M1 Exit 21. Undulating parkland with lake. 18 holes, 6303 yards, 5766 metres. S.S.S. 70. Driving range, practice area and tuition from Professional. *Green Fees:* weekdays £20.00 per round, £25.00 per day; weekends with member only. *Eating facilities:* bars, dining room. *Visitors:* welcome weekdays except after 4pm. Advisable to phone in advance. Snooker room. *Society Meetings:* Monday afternoons, Wednesdays, Thursdays, Friday afternoons only. Full tariff only. Professional: R.T. Stephenson (Tel & Fax: 01533 392813). Secretary: S.F. Aldwinckle (01533 393457).

LEICESTER. **Humberstone Heights Golf Club,** Gipsy Lane, Leicester LE5 0TB (0116 276 1905). *Location:* A563 ring road, Uppingham side of Leicester. Parkland. 18 holes, 6343 yards. S.S.S. 70. Practice area, pitch and putt course. *Green Fees:* weekdays £6.50 per round; weekends £8.50 (reduced rates for Juniors). *Eating facilities:* bar, snacks; clubhouse closed Mondays. *Visitors:* welcome (Municipal Golf Course). Green Fee ticket gains entry to Clubhouse. *Society Meetings:* welcome. Professional: Philip Highfield (0116 276 4674). Secretary: F. Lock (0116 276 1905).

LEICESTER. **Kibworth Golf Club,** Weir Road, Kibworth Beauchamp, Leicester LE8 0LP (01533 796172). *Location:* A6, four miles Market Harborough, 12 miles Leicester. Flat wooded course. 18 holes, 6333 yards. S.S.S. 70. 8 bay golf range. *Green Fees:* £21.00. *Eating facilities:* available, advance booking through Mrs Pritchard would be appreciated. *Visitors:* welcome, Handicap Certificate required or introduction from club member. *Society Meetings:* welcome, prior booking essential. Professional: Alan Strange (01533 792283). Secretary: Mrs Ann Towers (01533 792301).

LEICESTER. **Leicestershire Golf Club,** Evington Lane, Leicester LE5 6DJ (01533 736035). *Location:* two miles from city centre off A6 road. Parkland. 18 holes, 6312 yards. S.S.S. 70. *Green Fees:* weekdays £25.00, weekends £30.00. *Eating facilities:* bar snacks, full catering available by order. *Visitors:* welcome, Handicap Certificate required. *Society Meetings:* by arrangement. Professional: John R. Turnbull (01533 736730). Secretary: J.L. Adams (01533 738825).

LEICESTER. **Scraptoft Golf Club,** Beeby Road, Scraptoft, Leicester LE7 9SJ (01533 419000). *Location:* off A47 Peterborough. Undulating. 18 holes, 6166 yards. S.S.S. 69. *Green Fees:* £20.50 weekdays, £25.50 weekends. Sunday mornings with club member only. *Eating facilities:* full restaurant service except Mondays. *Visitors:* welcome, proof of Handicap required. *Society Meetings:* catered for on application weekdays only. Professional: Simon Sherratt (01533 419138). Secretary: A.M. Robertson (01533 418863).

LEICESTER. **Western Park Golf Club,** Scudamore Road, Braunstone Frith, Leicester (01533 876158). *Location:* four miles west of Junction 21 on M1 motorway. Flat, wooded course. 18 holes, 6532 yards. S.S.S. 71. Practice area. *Green Fees:* information not available. *Eating facilities:* full catering facilities. *Visitors:* contact Professional. *Society Meetings:* contact Professional. Professional: Bruce Whipham (01533 872339). Secretary: Brian Wells (01533 773543).

LEICESTER. **Whetstone Golf Club and Driving Range,** Cambridge Road, Cosby (0116 286 1424). *Location:* south of Leicester between Cosby and Whetstone. Parkland. 18 holes, 5795 yards. S.S.S. 68. Driving range, putting green. *Green Fees:* weekdays £12.00; weekends £13.00. *Eating facilities:* bar/lounge serving full range of meals. *Visitors:* welcome midweek and after 1pm Saturday and Sunday. *Society Meetings:* welcome by prior arrangement. Professionals: N. Leatherland and D. Raitt.

LOUGHBOROUGH. **Charnwood Forest Golf Club,** Breakback Road, Woodhouse Eaves, Near Loughborough LE12 8TA (01509 890259). *Location:* Beacon Hill, Charnwood Forest. A6 to B591 two miles; M1 Junction 22 two miles east. Rocks, bracken, heather, woods – in the heart of Charnwood Forest. No bunkers. 9 holes, 5960 yards. S.S.S. 69. *Green Fees:* weekdays £20.00 (£8.00 with member); weekends £25.00 (£12.50 with member). *Eating facilities:* full catering except Mondays, snacks available. *Visitors:* welcome, but not Tuesdays (Ladies' Day). *Society Meetings:* welcome by prior arrangement on Wednesdays and Thursdays, no more than 40 in party. Hon. Secretary: A.G. Stanley (01509 890259).

LOUGHBOROUGH. **Longcliffe Golf Club,** Snell's Nook Lane, Nanpantan, Loughborough (01509 216321). *Location:* two miles west of Loughborough Town Centre, 13 miles north of Leicester. Approximately one mile from Exit 23, M1. 18 holes, 6551 yards. S.S.S. 71. *Green Fees:* £22.00 per round, £27.00 per day. *Eating facilities:* full catering facilities, except Tuesdays. *Visitors:* restricted, must be introduced and playing with member at weekends and Bank Holidays. *Society Meetings:* welcome by arrangement only on Mondays, Wednesdays, Thursdays and Fridays. Professional: I. Bailey (01509 231450). Secretary: G. Harle (01509 239129).

LOUGHBOROUGH. **Park Hill Golf Club,** Park Hill, Seagrave, Loughborough LE12 7NG. *Location:* six miles north of Leicester on A46 at Seagrove turn. Parkland, rolling fairways, excellent views. 18 holes, 7230 yards. S.S.S. 74. Practice ground. *Green Fees:* weekdays £15.00, with a member £8.00; weekends and Bank Holidays £20.00, with a member £10.00. *Eating facilities:* lunch/dinner/bar snacks, fully licensed bar. *Visitors:* welcome at all times, by prior arrangement if no Handicap or non bona fide club member. *Society Meetings:* all welcome. Professional: D.C. Mee. Secretary: S.G. Winterton (01509 815454; Fax: 01509 816062).

LUTTERWORTH. **Lutterworth Golf Club,** Rugby Road, Lutterworth, Leicester LE17 4HN (01455 557141). *Location:* on A4114. Hilly parkland-type course – open fairways. 18 holes, 5570 yards. S.S.S. 67. *Green Fees:* £16.00 per round, £22.00 per day. *Eating facilities:* lunches and evening meals available every day. *Visitors:* welcome on weekdays and with a member at weekends. Professional: N. Melvin (01455 557199). Secretary: John Jaynes (01455 552532). Steward: C.D. Sholl (01455 557141).

LUTTERWORTH near. **Ullesthorpe Court Golf Club,** Frolesworth Road, Ullesthorpe, Near Lutterworth LE17 5BZ (01455 209023; Fax: 01455 202537). *Location:* 10/15 minutes M1, M69, M6, between Leicester and Coventry. 18 holes, 6650 yards. S.S.S. 72. *Green Fees:* £19.00 weekdays. Golf Day Specials from £22.00. *Eating facilities:* restaurant, bar snacks and functions. *Visitors:* welcome weekdays except Bank Holidays. 40 bedroomed hotel and leisure centre. *Society Meetings:* catered for weekdays except Bank Holidays. Professional: David Bowrins. Secretary: Mrs P. Woolley. *

MARKET HARBOROUGH. **Market Harborough Golf Club,** Great Oxendon Road, Market Harborough (01858 463684). *Location:* one mile south of Market Harborough on A508. Parkland. An excellent testing new 9 holes were opened in May 1993. 18 holes, 6022 yards. S.S.S. 69. Practice ground. *Green Fees:* weekdays £16.00 per round, £22.00 per day; weekends £14.00 with a member. *Eating facilities:* bar snacks and full meals available. *Visitors:* welcome weekdays; weekends only with a member. *Society Meetings:* welcome on application. Professional: F. Baxter. Secretary: J. Lord (01536 771771). *

MELTON MOWBRAY. **Melton Mowbray Golf Club,** Thorpe Arnold, Melton Mowbray LE14 4SD (01664 62118). *Location:* A607 road two miles north-east of Melton Mowbray. Undulating parkland. 18 holes, 6222 yards, S.S.S. 70. Practice ground. *Green Fees:* weekdays £18.00; weekends £25.00. *Eating facilities:* full catering and bar facilities. *Visitors:* welcome before 3pm. *Society Meetings:* by prior arrangement weekdays only. Professional: Tony Westwood (01664 69629). Secretary: E.A. Sallis.

NORTH KILWORTH. **Kilworth Springs Golf Club,** South Kilworth Road, North Kilworth (01858 575082; Fax: 01858 575078). *Location:* M1 Junction 20, A427 Lutterworth to Market Harborough. Links type, parkland course. 18 holes, 6718 yards. S.S.S. 72. Driving range. *Green Fees:* weekdays £16.00; weekends £20.00. *Eating facilities:* restaurant, bar food, bar. *Visitors:* welcome at all times subject to tee times being available. *Society Meetings:* welcome. Secretary: Ken Mattock.

OADBY. **Glen Gorse Golf Club,** Glen Road, Oadby LE2 4RF (01533 712226). *Location:* on A6, four and a half miles south of Leicester between Oadby and Great Glen. Fairly flat parkland course. 18 holes, 6603 yards, 6038 metres. S.S.S. 72. Par 72. *Green Fees:* weekdays £22.00 per round, £25.00 per day (£7.50 with member); weekends £7.50 with member only. *Eating facilities:* bar and meals/snacks (not Mondays). *Visitors:* welcome weekdays, weekends with members only. Snooker room. *Society Meetings:* welcome Tuesday to Friday by prior arrangement. Professional: Bob Larratt (01533 713748). Secretary: M. Goodson (01533 714159).

OADBY. **Oadby Golf Club,** Leicester Road, Oadby, Leicester LE2 4AB (0116) 270 0215. *Location:* on A6 south of Leicester, one mile from City boundary, at Leicester Racecourse. Parkland. 18 holes, 6376 yards, 5827 metres. S.S.S. 70. Practice ground, coaching. *Green Fees:* information not provided. *Eating facilities:* snacks always available, bar with meals on prior notice. *Visitors:* welcome on application to the Professional or booked through Oadby and Wigston Borough Council. *Society Meetings:* booking as for Visitors (weekdays only). Professional: Simon Ward (0116 270 9052). Hon. Secretary: C. Chamberlain (0116 288 9862 home). *

ROTHLEY. **Rothley Park Golf Club,** Westfield Lane, Rothley, Leicester LE7 7LH (01533 302019). *Location:* off A6, north of Leicester. Parkland. 18 holes, 6481 yards. S.S.S. 71. *Green Fees:* £25.00 per round, £30.00 per day (midweek). *Eating facilities:* available except Mondays. *Visitors:* welcome except Tuesdays, weekends and Bank Holidays, must be members of recognised golf club with Handicap. *Society Meetings:* catered for Wednesdays and Thursdays. Professional: Andrew Gerald Collins (01533 303023). Secretary: Bernard Durham (01533 302809).

RUTLAND. **Greetham Valley Golf Club,** Wood Lane, Greetham, Near Oakham, Rutland LE15 7RG (01780 460444; Fax: 01780 460623). *Location:* one mile off A1, B668. Parkland, flat. 18 holes, 6550 yards, S.S.S. 72; 9 holes course 1472 yards, S.S.S. 27. 21 bay floodlit driving range. *Green Fees:* weekdays 18 holes £15.00, £25.00 per day; weekends £25.00 18 holes, £35.00 per day. *Visitors:* welcome any time. Bowls green, meeting room, conference facilities. *Society Meetings:* welcome except weekends and Bank Holidays. Professional: Mark Cunningham (01780 460666). Secretary: Mr Chris Evans.

WOODHOUSE EAVES. **Lingdale Golf Club,** Joe Moore's Lane, Woodhouse Eaves, Near Loughborough LE12 8TF (01509 890035). *Location:* on B5300, Anstey-Shepshed road, three miles from Exit 23 on M1. Woodland and parkland – set in Charnwood Forest. 18 holes, 6545 yards. S.S.S. 71. Practice ground. *Green Fees:* weekdays £18.00 per day; weekends £20.00. Societies £15.00 per round, £18.00 per day. *Eating facilities:* full catering available. *Visitors:* welcome, but please telephone first. *Society Meetings:* catered for Mondays, Wednesdays, Thursdays and Fridays (one month's notice required). Professional: P. Sellears (01509 890684). Secretary: M. Green (01509 890703).

Where an asterisk (*) follows an entry, details have not been confirmed by the club for 1995.

Lincolnshire

ALFORD. **Woodthorpe Hall Golf Club,** Woodthorpe, Alford LN13 0DD (01507 450294). *Location:* three and a half miles from Alford off B1371. Undulating parkland. 18 holes, 4659 yards. S.S.S. 63. *Green Fees:* £9.00. *Eating facilities:* at Woodthorpe Country Inn on site. *Visitors:* welcome, unrestricted. *Society Meetings:* by prior arrangement with the Secretary. Secretary: P.C. Bell (Tel and Fax: 01507 463664). See also Display Advertisement on this page.

BOSTON. **Boston Golf Club Ltd,** Cowbridge, Horncastle Road, Boston PE22 7EL (01205 362306). *Location:* two miles north of Boston on B1183. Look for sign to right if travelling north. Parkland with featured water. 18 holes, 6566 yards, 6060 metres. S.S.S. 71. *Green Fees:* weekdays £16.00 per round, £22.00 per day; weekends and Bank Holidays £22.00 per round, £30.00 per day. *Eating facilities:* daily by arrangement with resident Steward (01205 352533). *Visitors:* welcome without reservation. *Society Meetings:* small groups catered for midweek. Professional: T.R. Squires (01205 362306). Secretary: D.E. Smith (Tel & Fax: 01205 350589).

BOSTON. **Kirton Holme Golf Club,** Holme Road, Kirton Holme, Boston PE20 1SY (01205 290669). *Location:* half a mile off A52 Boston to Swineshead road. Flat parkland. 9 holes, 2884 yards. S.S.S. 34. Small practice area includes net. *Green Fees:* weekdays £4.40 per 9 holes, £7.70 per day; weekends £5.50 per 9 holes, £8.80 per day. *Eating facilities:* bar open 11am to dusk, snack meals available. *Visitors:* always welcome – smart dress required. *Society Meetings:* by arrangement. Professional: Alison Johns (01205 369948). Secretary: Mrs T. Welberry (01205 290560).

BOURNE. **The Toft Hotel Golf Club,** Toft, Near Bourne PE10 0JT (01778 590616; Fax: 01778 590264). *Location:* in Toft village on A6121 Stamford to Bourne road. Undulating course with lake. 18 holes, 6486 yards. S.S.S. 71. Practice area. *Green Fees:* weekdays £18.00 per day, weekends £25.00 per day. *Eating facilities:* bar open all day; bar snacks and restaurant. *Visitors:* welcome at all times, prior booking essential. Hotel has 22 bedrooms. *Society Meetings:* welcome, prior booking essential. Professional: Mark Jackson. Secretary: Roger Atkin.

GAINSBOROUGH. **Gainsborough Golf Club,** Thonock, Gainsborough DN21 1PZ (01427 613088). *Location:* one mile north east of Gainsborough, between A159 and A631 signposted. Parkland. 18 holes, 6620 yards. S.S.S. 72. 20 bay floodlit driving range. Second 18 hole course under construction. *Green Fees:* weekdays £20.00 per round, £25.00 per day. *Eating facilities:* restaurant and coffee shop. *Visitors:* welcome weekdays without reservation; weekends with member only. *Society Meetings:* welcome if booked in advance. Professional: S. Cooper (01427 612278). Secretary: J.D. Bowers.

GRANTHAM near. **De Vere Belton Woods Hotel and Country Club,** Belton, Near Grantham NG32 2LN (01476 593200; Fax: 01476 74547). *Location:* two miles north of Grantham on A607 to Lincoln. Five minutes off A1 at Gonerby Moor. Parkland course. Three courses – Lancaster Course: 18 holes, 7021 yards. S.S.S. 74; Wellington Course: 18 holes, 6875 yards. S.S.S. 73; Spitfire Course: 9 holes, 1184 yards. 24 bay floodlit driving range. *Green Fees:* on application. Special rates for Societies and groups. *Eating facilities:* three bars, three restaurants. *Visitors:* welcome at all times, check in advance for availability. Accommodation in Hotel, 96 luxurious bedrooms and suites, with extensive leisure and conference facilities. Golfing Breaks and society meetings a speciality. *Society Meetings:* welcome. Golf and Leisure Manager: Lorna Bainbridge. Golf Professional: Tony Roberts (01476 593200; Fax: 01476 74547).

GRANTHAM. **Stoke Rochford Golf Club,** Stoke Rochford, Near Grantham NG33 5EW (01476 83275). *Location:* five miles south of Grantham on A1. Entrance at "A.J.S." service area. Parkland. 18 holes, 6232 yards. S.S.S. 70. Small practice ground. *Green Fees:* £17.00 per round, £24.00 per day weekdays (estimated); weekends and Bank Holidays £26.00 per round, £35.00 per day (estimated). If playing with a member £8.00 weekdays, £10.00 weekends. *Eating facilities:* meals available daily, to be booked before playing. *Visitors:* cannot commence play before 10.30am at weekends or on Public Holidays. No visitors at weekends November, December and January. *Society Meetings:* by prior arrangement. Professional: A.E. Dow (01476 83218). Secretary: J.M. Butler (01476 67030).

GRANTHAM. **Belton Park Golf Club,** Belton Lane, Londonthorpe Road, Grantham NG31 9SH (01476 63355; Fax: 01476 592078). *Location:* two miles from Grantham. 250 acre Deer Park adjacent to the historical Belton House. Three courses as follows: Brownlow Course 6420 yards (Championship). S.S.S. 71. Ancaster Course 6252 yards. S.S.S. 70. Belmont Course 6016 yards. S.S.S. 69. Two large practice areas. *Green Fees:* weekdays £18.00 per round, £23.00 per day; weekends and Bank Holidays £26.00 per round, £31.00 per day. All including VAT. *Eating facilities:* full restaurant facilities every day; three bars. *Visitors:* welcome without reservation. *Society Meetings:* catered for by arrangement weekdays only (except Tuesday). Special day package. Professional: B. McKee (01476 63911). Secretary and General Manager: T. Measures (01476 67399 – all enquiries; Fax: 01476 592078).

GRANTHAM. **Sudbrook Moor Golf Club,** Charity Street, Carlton Scroop, Grantham (01400 50876). *Location:* A607 Lincoln to Grantham, six miles north-east of Grantham. Private course in picturesque valley; easy walking, flat parkland/meadowland. 9 holes, 4566 yards. S.S.S. 61/62/63. Practice ground and net. *Green Fees:* weekdays £5.00 per day, weekends £7.00 per day. *Eating facilities:* Spike Bar and dining room (alcohol-free). *Visitors:* welcome by appointment. Professionals: Tim Hutton and Alison Johns. Secretary: Judith M. Hutton (Tel and Fax: 01400 50796).

HORNCASTLE near. **Horncastle Golf Club,** West Ashby, Near Horncastle LN9 5PP (01507 526800). *Location:* just off A158 between Horncastle and Baumber. Parkland course – water features on 14 holes. 18 holes, 5800 yards. S.S.S. 70. Floodlit golf range. New 9 hole Par 3 course £2.50 per round. *Green Fees:* £10.00 per round, £15.00 per day. *Eating facilities:* bar, restaurant. *Visitors:* welcome anytime but helpful to phone. Special package available golf range, golf course, food and drink. Ballroom and conference facilities. Accommodation available in 24 bedrooms. Fishing lake. *Society Meetings:* please phone in advance. Professional: E.C. Wright. Secretary: R. Chantry.

LINCOLN. **Blankney Golf Club,** Blankney, near Metheringham, Lincoln LN4 3AZ (01526 320263). *Location:* on B1188, 10 miles south of Lincoln. Parkland, slightly undulating. 18 holes, 6500 yards. S.S.S. 71. Practice area. *Green Fees:* weekdays £15.00 per round, £20.00 per day; weekends £20.00 per round, £30.00 per day. *Eating facilities:* dining room, bar meals or snacks. *Visitors:* welcome, limited number weekends. Accommodation for six persons. *Society Meetings:* by advance booking only. Professional: Graham Bradley (01526 320202). General Manager: D.A. Priest (01526 320263; Fax: 01526 322521).

LINCOLN. **Canwick Park Golf Club,** Canwick Park, Washingborough Road, Lincoln LN4 1EF (01522 522166). *Location:* one and a half miles approximately east of Lincoln, first left (turning) off Canwick Road from Lincoln is Washingborough Road. Wooded parkland course. 18 holes, 6257 yards, 5726 metres, S.S.S. 70. Practice ground. *Green Fees:* £15.00 weekdays; £19.00 weekends. *Eating facilities:* bar snacks and meals to order. *Visitors:* welcome weekdays; weekends after 3pm. Locker rooms. *Society Meetings:* welcome. Professional: Steve Williamson (01522 536870). Secretary: Mr John Arnold (01522 690810; Fax: 01522 690810).

LINCOLN. **Carholme Golf Club,** Carholme Road, Lincoln LN1 1SE (01522 523725). *Location:* one mile from city centre on A57 to Worksop. Flat parkland. 18 holes, 6150 yards. S.S.S. 69. *Green Fees:* on application. *Eating facilities:* full service except Mondays. *Visitors:* welcome (not Sundays). *Society Meetings:* by prior arrangement only. Professional: G. Leslie (01522 536811). Secretary: R.D. Motts (01522 523725).

LINCOLN. **Lincoln Golf Club,** Torksey, Lincoln (0142 771 210). *Location:* West Lincolnshire, between Lincoln, Gainsborough and Newark. Flat testing inland course with quick drying sandy subsoil. 18 holes, 6438 yards. S.S.S. 71. *Green Fees:* £18.00 per round, £23.00 per day. *Eating facilities:* full facilities except Tuesday (ladies' day). *Visitors:* welcome by arrangement, weekends with members only. *Society Meetings:* catered for. Professional: Ashley Carter (0142 771 273). Secretary: M.A. Colls (0142 771 721).

LOUTH. **Louth Golf Club,** 59 Crowtree Lane, Louth LN11 9LJ (01507 602554). *Location:* western outskirts of Louth. Undulating parkland. 18 holes, 6477 yards. S.S.S. 71. Practice ground. *Green Fees:* £16.00 per round, £20.00 per day weekdays; £25.00 per round, £30.00 per day weekends and Bank Holidays. *Eating facilities:* full catering 10am to 10pm (to order). *Visitors:* welcome without reservation. Squash courts. *Society Meetings:* catered for. Professional: A.J. Blundell (01507 604648). Secretary/Manager: M. Covey (Tel & Fax: 01507 603681). Assistant Secretary: T. Curtis (01507 604864).

MABLETHORPE. **Sandilands Golf Club,** Roman Bank, Sandilands, Sutton-on-Sea LN12 2RJ (01507 441432). *Location:* A52 one mile south of Sutton-on-Sea. Seaside links adjacent to sea and sand. 18 holes, 5995 yards. S.S.S. 69. 40 acre practice area. *Green Fees:* weekdays £12.00 round; weekends and Bank Holidays £18.00 per round. *Eating facilities:* bar and restaurant. *Visitors:* welcome. *Society Meetings:* catered for weekdays. Secretary: Dennis Mumby (01507 441617).

MARKET RASEN. **Market Rasen and District Golf Club,** Legsby Road, Market Rasen LN8 3DZ (01673 842319). *Location:* A46 to Market Rasen – one mile east of town. Wooded course. 18 holes, 6043 yards, 5527 metres. S.S.S. 69. Practice ground. *Green Fees:* weekdays £20.00 per day, £15.00 per round; weekends only with member. *Eating facilities:* by arrangement with the Steward, but not Mondays. *Visitors:* welcome with reservation, must be member of bona fide golf club. Not Wednesdays after 10.30am. Weekends with members only. *Society Meetings:* catered for Tuesdays and Fridays. Professional: A.M. Chester (01673 842416). Secretary: J.A. Brown (01673 842319).

MARKET RASEN. **Market Rasen Racecourse 9-Hole Pay and Play Course,** Legsby Road, Market Rasen LN8 3EA. *Location:*on A631 Market Rasen to Louth road, midway between Lincoln and Grimsby. Course is in centre of picturesque National Hunt racecourse. 9 holes, 2532 yards. S.S.S. 33. *Green Fees:* weekdays 9 holes £4.00, 18 holes £6.00; weekends 9 holes £5.00, 18 holes £8.00. Reductions for Juniors and reduced rates for groups. *Eating facilities:* hot and cold drinks available. *Visitors:* no restrictions. Golf course is closed on race days. *Society Meetings:* welcome on application to Secretary. Secretary: Gaynor Haxby (01673 843434; Fax: 01673 844532).

NOTE

All the information in this book is given in good faith in the belief that it is correct. However, the publishers cannot guarantee the facts given in these pages, neither are they responsible for changes in policy, ownership or terms that may take place after the date of going to press. Readers should always satisfy themselves that the facilities they require are available and that the terms, if quoted, still apply.

SKEGNESS. **North Shore Hotel and Golf Club,** North Shore Road, Skegness PE25 1DN (01754 763298). *Location:* north of town one mile. Half seaside links, half parkland overlooking the sea. 18 holes, 6134 yards. S.S.S. 71. *Green Fees:* information not provided. *Eating facilities:* hotel on the course. *Visitors:* welcome, prior notice essential. *Society Meetings:* welcome. Professional: Golf instruction given by John Cornelius (01754 764822). *

SKEGNESS. **Seacroft Golf Club,** Seacroft, Skegness PE25 3AU (01754 763020). *Location:* towards Gibraltar Nature Reserve. Seaside links course. 18 holes, 6490 yards. S.S.S. 71. *Green Fees:* weekdays £20.00 per round, £28.00 per day; weekends and Bank Holidays £25.00 round, £35.00 per day. *Eating facilities:* available on prior booking. *Visitors:* welcome after 9.30am if members of recognised club, Handicap Certificate required; not between 12noon and 2pm. *Society Meetings:* catered for, limited to 24 at weekends. Professional: R. Lawie (01754 769624). Secretary: H.K. Brader (01754 763020).

SLEAFORD. **Sleaford Golf Club,** Willoughby Road, South Rauceby, Sleaford NG34 8PL (01529 488273). *Location:* off A153, two miles west of Sleaford. Inland links-type course, fairly flat and lightly wooded. 18 holes, 6443 yards, 5947 metres. S.S.S. 71. Practice field, 6 hole pitch and putt. *Green Fees:* weekdays £20.00 per round/day; weekends £28.00. *Eating facilities:* full catering except Mondays. Bar open seven days. *Visitors:* welcome without reservation, except winter weekends. Handicap Certificate required and must be members of a recognised club. *Society Meetings:* catered for weekdays only by prior arrangement. Professional: J.N. Wilson (01529 488644). Secretary: T.G.E. Churms (01529 488326/488207 – home).

SOUTH KYME. **South Kyme Golf Club,** Skinners Lane, South Kyme LN4 4AE (01526 861113). *Location:* approximately four miles off A153 road from Sleaford to Horncastle, turn right before North Kyme. Six miles off A17 from Sleaford to Boston, turn left before East Heckington. A long and testing fenland course. 18 holes, 6597 yards. S.S.S. Men 71, Ladies 70. 6 hole pitch and putt. *Green Fees:* weekdays £10.00; weekends £12.00. £2.00 reduction when playing with a member. *Eating facilities:* bar and restaurant. Snacks available all day. Lunch menu available. *Visitors:* no restrictions at present but advisable to check at weekends in case of competitions. *Society Meetings:* welcome with prior booking. Secretary: Anne Maplethorpe.

SPALDING near. **Gedney Hill Golf Course,** West Drove, Gedney Hill, Near Spalding PE12 0NT (01406 330183). *Location:* six miles from Radar Tower near Crowland, off B1073 follow signs or follow B1066 off A47. Flat, testing conditions; playing characteristics of a links course with fen winds. 18 holes, 5429 yards. S.S.S. 66. 10 bay driving range. *Green Fees:* weekdays £5.75; weekends £9.75. *Eating facilities:* two bars (one casual spike bar), restaurant (80 seater). *Visitors:* welcome by arrangement, no restrictions. Full snooker room/snookerette table. *Society Meetings:* by arrangement. Professional: David Creek (01406 330922). Secretary: Steve McGregor (01406 330922).

SPALDING. **Sutton Bridge Golf Club,** New Road, Sutton Bridge, Spalding (01406 350323). *Location:* off A17, 18 miles east of Spalding. 9 holes, 5804 yards. S.S.S. 68. *Green Fees:* weekdays £15.00. *Eating facilities:* available. *Visitors:* welcome, except weekends, Bank Holidays and match or competition days. *Society Meetings:* not catered for. Professional: R. Wood (01406 351080). Secretary: K.C. Buckle (01945 870455).

SPALDING. **The Spalding Golf Club,** Surfleet, Spalding PE11 4EA (01775 680234). *Location:* four miles from Spalding on A16 to Boston. Parkland. 18 holes, 6432 yards. S.S.S. 71. Practice area. *Green Fees:* £20.00 weekdays; £25.00 weekends. *Eating facilities:* full bar facilities and dining facilities (no meals Tuesdays). *Visitors:* welcome, Handicap Certificates required. *Society Meetings:* catered for on Thursdays and Tuesday afternoons only April to October. Professional: John W. Spencer (01775 680386). Secretary: B.W. Walker (01775 680386).

STAMFORD. **Burghley Park (Stamford) Golf Club,** St. Martins Without, Stamford PE9 3JX (01780 53789). *Location:* leave A1 at roundabout south of Stamford, club one mile on right. Flat parkland. 18 holes, 6236 yards. S.S.S. 70. *Green Fees:* weekdays £20.00, weekends as members' guests only. Half price after 5pm May to September. *Eating facilities:* restaurant (closed Mondays) and bar. *Visitors:* welcome weekdays. Handicap Certificates required. Visit Stamford, now made more famous as the background for "Middlemarch". *Society Meetings:* Wednesdays and Thursdays only. Professional: Glenn Davies (01780 62100). Secretary: Howard Mulligan (01780 53789).

STAMFORD. **Luffenham Heath Golf Club,** Ketton, Stamford PE9 3UU (01780 721095). *Location:* one-and-a-half miles south-west of Ketton on A6121. Undulating heathland, in conservation area for flora and fauna. 18 holes, 6254 yards. S.S.S. 70. Practice ground. *Green Fees:* weekdays £30.00 per day/per round; weekends £35.00 per day/per round. *Eating facilities:* snacks available daily, full meals by arrangement. *Visitors:* welcome, advisable to contact Professional first. Handicap Certificate required. Changing room/showers. *Society Meetings:* by arrangement through the Secretary. Professional: J.A. Lawrence (Tel & Fax: 01780 720298). Secretary: Ian F. Davenport (01780 720205).

STAMFORD. **Rutland County Golf Club,** Great Casterton, Stamford PE9 4AQ (01780 460330). *Location:* five miles north of Stamford on A1 Great North Road. Open rolling fairways, heavily bunkered, some water, inland links style. 27 holes, 6189 yards. S.S.S. 70. 20 bay driving range, grass practice area, putting green, practice bunker. *Green Fees:* weekdays £15.00; weekends £18.00. £25.00 day ticket, £30.00 weekend. *Eating facilities:* coffee bar, dining lounge, players bar, new clubhouse bars and lounge. *Visitors:* welcome. Must have Handicap Certificate or be signed in by Pro. *Society Meetings:* welcome except weekends. Professional: James Darroch. Secretary: Steve Cowe (01780 86330).

WOODHALL SPA. **Woodhall Spa Golf Club,** Woodhall Spa LN10 6PU (01526 352511; Fax: 01526 352778). *Location:* 19 miles from Lincoln, Boston, Sleaford; 33 miles from Skegness; 50 miles from Nottingham. Flat, wooded heathland. 18 holes, 6907 yards. S.S.S. 73. Practice ground and driving net. *Green Fees:* weekdays £26.00 per round, £40.00 per day; weekends and Bank Holidays £30.00 per round, £45.00 per day (all fees are estimates). *Eating facilities:* full catering available. *Visitors:* welcome with reservation. Handicap Certificates required (maximum handicap permitted Gents 20, Ladies 30). *Society Meetings:* catered for if booked in advance. Professional: C.C. Elliot (01526 353229). Secretary: B.H. Fawcett.

Greater Manchester

ALTRINCHAM. **Altrincham Golf Course,** Stockport Road, Timperley, Altrinchram, Cheshire (0161-928 0761). *Location:* one mile east of Altrincham on A560. Parkland. 18 holes, 6190 yards, 5659 metres. S.S.S. 69. Driving range. *Green Fees:* £6.00 weekdays; £8.00 weekends. *Eating facilities:* Old Hall Hotel attached to course. *Visitors:* welcome any time, book one week in advance. Public course. Professional: John Jackson. Secretary: David G. Barton.

ALTRINCHAM. **Dunham Forest Golf and Country Club,** Oldfield Lane, Altrincham WA14 4TY (0161-928 2605; Fax: 0161-929 8975). *Location:* approximately 9 miles south of Manchester off A56. Wooded parkland. 18 holes, 6772 yards. S.S.S. 72. *Green Fees:* weekdays £25.00, weekends and Bank Holidays £30.00. *Eating facilities:* clubhouse restaurant and bar open daily. *Visitors:* welcome, but should telephone to check availability. *Society Meetings:* welcome by prior arrangement. Professional: I. Wrigley (0161-928 2727). Secretary: Mrs S. Klaus (0161-928 2605).

ALTRINCHAM. **Hale Golf Club,** Rappax Road, Hale, Altrincham WA15 0NU (0161-980 4225). Pleasant undulating parkland. 9 holes (2 rounds), 5780 yards, S.S.S. 68. *Green Fees:* weekdays £20.00 per round, £25.00 per day; weekends only with member. *Eating facilities:* by arrangement with Steward. *Visitors:* welcome weekdays (except Thursday) with reservation. *Society Meetings:* by arrangement with Hon. Secretary. Professional: J. Jackson (0161-904 0835). Secretary: J.W. Hughes (0161-980 4320).

ALTRINCHAM. **The Ringway Golf Club Ltd,** Hale Mount, Hale Barns, Altrincham WA15 8SW (0161-904 9609). *Location:* Junction 6, M56 then A538 towards Altrincham for one mile. Parkland. 18 holes, 6494 yards. S.S.S. 71. *Green Fees:* weekdays £28.00, weekends and Bank Holidays £34.00. *Eating facilities:* full diningroom facilities available. *Visitors:* generally not on Tuesdays or Saturdays which are Ladies' and Gentlemen's Competition Days, or Fridays (members only). *Society Meetings:* catered for by arrangement. Professional: Nick Ryan (0161-980 8432). Secretary: D. Wright (0161-980 2630).

ASHTON-IN-MAKERFIELD. **Ashton-in-Makerfield Golf Club Ltd,** Garswood Park, Liverpool Road, Ashton-in-Makerfield (01942 727269). *Location:* M6, Junction 23 from south, M6 Junction 24 from north. Wooded course. 18 holes, 6205 yards. S.S.S. 70. *Green Fees:* £21.00. *Eating facilities:* available, except Mondays. *Visitors:* welcome mid-week (except Wednesday) with reservation but not before 9.45am. *Society Meetings:* catered for Tuesdays and Thursdays by prior appointment. Professional: P. Allan (01942 724229). Secretary: J.R. Hay (01942 719330).

ASHTON-UNDER-LYNE. **Ashton-under-Lyne Golf Club,** Gorsey Way, Ashton-under-Lyne OL6 9HT (0161-330 1537). *Location:* Hurst Cross – three miles from town centre, Mossley Road, left at Queens Road, right at Nook Lane, Clubhouse top of St. Christopher's Road. Wooded course. 18 holes, 6209 yards. S.S.S. 70. *Green Fees:* weekdays £22.00 per day, weekends with member only. *Eating facilities:* full catering except Mondays. *Visitors:* welcome weekdays except Wednesdays; members of recognised golf clubs welcome without reservation. *Society Meetings:* catered for on application: special daily rates. Professional: Mr Colin Boyle (0161-308 2095). Secretary: Mr K.J. Clayton.

BOLTON. **Bolton Golf Club Ltd,** Lostock Park, Chorley New Road, Bolton BL6 4AJ (01204 843278). *Location:* off main road half-way between Bolton and Horwich. 18 holes, 6215 yards. S.S.S. 70. *Green Fees:* weekdays £26.00 per round, £32.00 per day (except Wednesdays); weekends and Wednesdays £30.00 per round, £36 per day. *Eating facilities:* luncheons (evening meals except Monday and Sunday). *Visitors:* welcome with reservation. *Society Meetings:* catered for on Thursdays and Fridays. Professional: R. Longworth (01204 843073). Secretary: H. Cook (01204 843067).

BOLTON. **Breightmet Golf Club,** Red Bridge, Ainsworth, Bolton (01204 27381). *Location:* leave Bolton on main road to Bury, turn left two miles on Milnthorpe road for the bridge. 9 holes, 6418 yards. S.S.S. 71. *Green Fees:* weekdays £15.00, weekends and Bank Holidays £18.00 (half-price with a member). *Eating facilities:* lunches and light refreshments. *Visitors:* welcome, preliminary phone call advisable. *Society Meetings:* catered for on application. Secretary: R. Weir.

BOLTON. **Deane Golf Club,** Broadford Road, Deane, Bolton (01204 61944). *Location:* one mile east of Junction 5 of M61 towards Bolton Centre. Rolling parkland with number of small ravines to cross. 18 holes, 5583 yards, 5105 metres. S.S.S. 67. *Green Fees:* weekdays £18.00; weekends £22.50. *Eating facilities:* lunches and evening meals by arrangement. *Visitors:* welcome. *Society Meetings:* Tuesdays, Thursdays and Fridays only. Secretary: P. Flaxman (01204 651808).

BOLTON. **Dunscar Golf Club Ltd,** Longworth Lane, Bromley Cross, Bolton BL7 9QY (01204 303321). *Location:* one and a half miles north of Bolton on A666. Parkland, moorland course. 18 holes, 6085 yards. S.S.S. 69. Practice facilities available. *Green Fees:* prices on application. *Eating facilities:* available. *Visitors:* welcome except weekends. *Society Meetings:* catered for by arrangement. Professional: Gary Treadgold (01204 592992). Secretary: Thomas Michael Yates (01204 301090).

BOLTON. **Great Lever and Farnworth Golf Club Ltd,** Lever Edge Lane, Bolton BL3 3EN (01204 62582). *Location:* A666 or M61 (Junction 4), one and a half miles from Bolton town centre. Flat parkland. 18 holes, 5859 yards. S.S.S. 69. Practice ground. *Green Fees:* weekdays £15.00; weekends £25.00. *Eating facilities:* restaurant and bar every day except Mondays. *Visitors:* welcome, preferably by appointment. *Society Meetings:* catered for by arrangement weekdays. Professional: Donald Stirling (01204 656650). Secretary: Mrs J. Ivill (01204 656137).

BOLTON. **Harwood Golf Club,** Roading Brook Road, Harwood, Bolton BL2 4JD (01204 22878). *Location:* three miles east of Bolton – A58 to Bury, turn left through Ainsworth village. Flat meadowland. 9 holes, 5958 yards. S.S.S. 69. Small practice area. *Green Fees:* weekdays £15.00; weekends £6.00 with a member only. *Eating facilities:* bar open every day, lunchtime, tea time and evenings, catering on request. *Visitors:* welcome weekdays only, weekends only with a member. Should be members of recognised golf club or society. *Society Meetings:* on application to Secretary. Secretary: D. Bamber (01204 22878 or 0161-761 6022).

BOLTON. **Old Links (Bolton) Ltd,** Chorley Old Road, Montserrat, Bolton BL1 5SU (01204 840050). *Location:* on B6226, 400 yards north of roundabout on ring road. Championship course, moorland. 18 holes, 6410 yards. S.S.S. 72. Practice facilities. *Green Fees:* weekdays £26.00, weekends £30.00. Special rates for groups over 20. *Eating facilities:* available. *Visitors:* welcome, not Wednesdays or weekends. *Society Meetings:* catered for weekdays. Professional: P. Horridge (01204 843089). Secretary: K.G. Jennions (01204 842307).

BOLTON. **Regent Park Golf Club Ltd,** Links Road, Lostock, Bolton BL6 4AF (01204 844170). *Location:* midway between Bolton and Horwich off Chorley New Road. Parkland. 18 holes, 6217 yards. S.S.S. 70/71. Practice area. *Green Fees:* weekdays £5.50; weekends £7.00. *Eating facilities:* meals/bar available. *Visitors:* welcome seven days, telephone Professional to book time slot. *Society Meeetings:* welcome midweek, book in advance – booking through Bolton Metro Leisure Services, The Wellsprings Civic Centre, Bolton. Professional: Bob Longworth (01204 842336/495421). Secretary: K.J. Taylor (01204 652882).

BOLTON. **Turton Golf Club,** Wood End Farm, Chapeltown Road, Bromley Cross, Bolton (01204 852235). *Location:* three miles north of Bolton on the A666. Moorland course with extensive views. 18 holes, 5805 yards. S.S.S. 68. Practice area. *Green Fees:* £15.00 per day. *Eating facilities:* to order except Mondays. *Visitors:* welcome, restrictions Wednesdays (Ladies' Day). *Society Meetings:* welcome on Tuesdays and Thursdays by arrangement. Secretary: B.E. Stanley.

BURY. **Bury Golf Club,** Unsworth Hall, Blackford Bridge, Bury (0161-766 4897). *Location:* A56 eight miles north of Manchester. Undulating parkland. 18 holes, 5961 yards. S.S.S. 69. *Green Fees:* weekdays £20.00; weekends £26.00. *Eating facilities:* grill room service except Mondays. *Visitors:* welcome without reservation but Handicap Certificate will be required. *Society Meetings:* catered for. Professional: S. Crake (0161-766 2213). Secretary: J. Meikle.

BURY. **Greenmount Golf Club,** Greenhaigh Fold Farm, Greenmount, Bury (01204 883712). *Location:* three miles north of Bury. Undulating parkland. 9 holes, 4920 yards. S.S.S. 64. *Green Fees:* £12.00, £5.00 with member. *Eating facilities:* lunches at club except on Thursdays. *Visitors:* welcome, weekends with members only, Tuesday – ladies' day. *Society Meetings:* catered for by arrangement with Secretary. Professional: G. Pearson. Secretary: G.J. Lowe.

BURY. **Lowes Park Golf Club Ltd.,** Hill Top, Walmersley, Bury BL9 6SU (0161-764 1231). *Location:* take A56 north from Bury, turn right at Bury General Hospital into Lowes Road. Moorland course, exposed, easy walking. 9 holes, 6009 yards. S.S.S. 69. Small practice area. *Green Fees:* weekdays £13.50; weekends £20.00. *Eating facilities:* full catering except Mondays. *Visitors:* welcome weekdays except Wednesdays (Ladies' Day), not Saturday, Sunday by appointment. *Society Meetings:* catered for by appointment with Secretary. Secretary: John Entwistle (01204 76657).

BURY. **Walmersley Golf Club,** Garretts Close, Walmersley, Bury (0161-764 1429). *Location:* leave A56 approximately two miles north of Bury at Walmersley Post Office into Old Road, right at Masons Arms Inn. Moorland course. 9 holes (course being extended to 18 holes), 6114 yards, 5588 metres. S.S.S. 70. *Green Fees:* weekdays £15.00 per day, £6.00 with member; weekends £6.00 with a member only. *Eating facilities:* lunches and evening meals served except Mondays. *Visitors:* welcome weekdays except Tuesdays 12.30pm to 5.30pm. *Society Meetings:* catered for weekdays. Secretary: C. Stock (0161-764 5057).

CHEADLE. **Cheadle Golf Club,** Shiers Drive, Cheadle SK8 1HW (0161-428 2160). *Location:* one-and-a-half miles Junction 11 M63. Parkland. 9 holes, 5006 yards. S.S.S. 65. *Green Fees:* information not provided. *Eating facilities:* by arrangement with the Steward. *Visitors:* welcome, must be members of a bona fide golf club; current Handicap Certificate to be produced; no visitors on Tuesdays or Saturdays. *Society Meetings:* catered for by arrangement with the Secretary. Professional: G.J. Norcott (0161-428 9878). Secretary: P.P. Webster (0161-491 4452).

DAVYHULME. **Davyhulme Park Golf Club,** Gleneagles Road, Davyhulme, Urmston M41 8SA (0161-748 2856). *Location:* one mile from M63/M62. Wooded parkland course. 18 holes, 6237 yards. S.S.S. 70. *Green Fees:* information not provided. *Eating facilities:* lunches and dinners. *Visitors:* welcome except Competition days. *Society Meetings:* catered for by prior arrangement. Professional: Dean Butler (0161-748 3931). Secretary: H.A. Langworthy (0161-748 2260).

DENTON. **Denton Golf Club,** Manchester Road, Denton M34 2NU (0161-336 3218). *Location:* A57, five miles from Piccadilly, Manchester. 18 holes, 6290 yards. S.S.S. 70. *Green Fees:* information not provided. *Eating facilities:* meals catered for except all day Monday and Thursday afternoon. *Visitors:* welcome with club members and Handicap, without reservation weekdays only. *Society Meetings:* catered for on weekdays except Tuesday by application. Professional: Roger Vere. Secretary: R. Wickham. *

DUKINFIELD. **Dukinfield Golf Club,** Lyne Edge, Dukinfield (0161-338 2340). *Location:* six miles east of Manchester via Ashton-under-Lyne. Hillside with wooded areas. 18 holes, 5556 yards. S.S.S. 67. *Green Fees:* weekdays £16.50. *Eating facilities:* bar open from mid day, snacks and meals available. *Visitors:* welcome except Wednesdays noon to 2pm and 4-6pm (Ladies' Day) and weekends. Times may be booked in advance by phoning Pro's Shop. *Society Meetings:* catered for by prior arrangement; full and half day packages available. Professional: Mr Jason Peel. Secretary: K.P. Parker (0161-338 2669).

ECCLES. **Worsley Golf Club,** Stableford Avenue, Monton, Eccles M30 8AP (0161-789 4202). *Location:* one mile from Junction 13 M62. Parkland. 18 holes, 6200 yards. S.S.S. 70. *Green Fees:* weekdays £20.00; weekends and Bank Holidays £25.00 (£12.00 with member). *Eating facilities:* snacks, lunches and evening meals. *Visitors:* welcome, if past or present members of recognised golf clubs. *Society Meetings:* catered for Mondays, Wednesdays and Thursdays. Professional: Ceri Cousins. Secretary: R. Pizzey MBE.

FLIXTON. **Acre Gate Golf Club,** Pennybridge Lane, Flixton, Manchester M31 (0161-748 1226). *Location:* off Flixton Road. Flat parkland course. 18 holes, 4395 yards. S.S.S. 61. *Green Fees:* weekdays £6.00; weekends £8.00. *Eating facilities:* not available to visitors unless with member. *Visitors:* course is Municipal (William Wroe Municipal Course) therefore no restrictions, book 24 hours in advance. *Society Meetings:* small groups welcome on application to the Club Secretary. Secretary: D.J. Bostock.

HORWICH. **Horwich Golf Club,** Victoria Road, Horwich, Bolton BL6 5PH (01204 696980). *Location:* Junction 6 M61 – Chorley New Road – Victoria Road, Horwich. Parkland course. 9 holes. S.S.S. 65. *Green Fees:* £12.00 per day. *Eating facilities:* available. *Visitors:* Wednesday Ladies' Day but tee times still available. Snooker room. *Society Meetings:* weekdays only. Society rate £20.00 per day incl. soup/sandwich and evening meal. Professional: Ken Howarth. Secretary: C. Sherborne.

HYDE. **Werneth Low Golf Club Ltd,** Werneth Low Road, Hyde, Cheshire SK14 3AF (0161-368 2503). *Location:* A560 from Junction 4 of M67. Scenic, hilly course with excellent greens. 11 holes, 6550 yards. S.S.S. 69. *Green Fees:* weekdays £18.00; weekends £23.00 (Saturdays only). *Eating facilities:* light refreshments normally available except Wednesdays. *Visitors:* welcome any time except Sunday before 4pm and Tuesday mornings and evenings. *Society Meetings:* catered for by prior arrangement. Professional: T. Bacchus (0161-336 6908). Secretary: R. Clapham (0161-366 0837). *

LEIGH. **Pennington Golf Club (Municipal),** Pennington Golf Course, Pennington Country Park, off St. Helens Road, Leigh. *Location:* Junction 17 on M6 to Leigh. Flat parkland with water coursing through. 9 holes, 2919 yards. S.S.S. 34. *Green Fees:* on request. *Eating facilities:* snack bar facilities. *Visitors:* welcome without reservation. Professional: Mr T. Kershaw (01942 607278). Secretary: Mr P.A. Cartwright (0161-794 5316).

LITTLEBOROUGH. **Whittaker Golf Club,** Whittaker Lane, Littleborough OL15 0LH (01706 378310). *Location:* one mile from town centre along Blackstone Edge Old Road. Moorland course. 9 holes, 5632 yards. S.S.S. 67. *Green Fees:* weekdays £10.00; weekends £12.00. *Eating facilities:* bar only. *Visitors:* welcome without reservation, except Tuesday afternoons and Sundays. *Society Meetings:* weekdays and Saturdays only by prior arrangement with Secretary. Secretary: Mr G.A. Smith (01484 428546).

MANCHESTER. **Blackley Golf Club,** Victoria Avenue East, Blackley, Manchester M9 2HW (0161-643 2980). *Location:* five miles north from City Centre. Parkland. 18 holes, 6237 yards, 5708 metres. S.S.S. 70. *Green Fees:* £18.00 weekdays. *Eating facilities:* diningroom/bar. *Visitors:* welcome, Thursdays and weekends with member only. *Society Meetings:* catered for. Professional: Martin Barton (0161-643 3912). Secretary: C.B. Leggott (0161-654 7770).

MANCHESTER. **Brookdale Golf Club Ltd,** Ash Bridge, Woodhouses, Failsworth, Manchester (0161-681 4534). *Location:* five miles north of Manchester. 18 holes, 6040 yards. S.S.S. 68. *Green Fees:* weekdays £18.00; weekends and Bank Holidays £21.00. *Eating facilities:* available with ample notice. *Visitors:* welcome, only with a member weekends. *Society Meetings:* welcome except Tuesdays (Ladies Day). Package Deal £29.00 by arrangement. Professional: Mr Jason Spibey (0161-681 2655). Hon. Secretary: T. Warren.

MANCHESTER. **Chorlton-cum-Hardy Golf Club,** Barlow Hall Road, Chorlton-cum-Hardy M21 7JJ (0161-881 3139). *Location:* near junction of A5145 and A5103 (M63 Junction 9). Meadowland. 18 holes, 6003 yards. S.S.S. 69. *Green Fees:* weekdays £20.00; weekends and Bank Holidays £25.00. *Eating facilities:* catering provided – seasonal limited hours, sandwiches only Mondays. *Visitors:* welcome without reservation, except on Competition days, must provide proof of recognised handicap. *Society Meetings:* catered for Thursdays only by arrangement with Secretary. Professional: David Screeton (0161-881 9911). Secretary: Mrs H.M. Stuart (Tel & Fax: 0161-881-5830).

MANCHESTER. **Didsbury Golf Club Ltd,** Ford Lane, Northenden, Manchester M22 4NQ (0161-998 2743). *Location:* Junction 3 on M56 to Palatine Road, to Church Road, to Ford Lane. Parkland. 18 holes, 6276 yards. S.S.S. 70. Good practice facilities. *Green Fees:* weekdays £22.00; weekends £25.00. *Eating facilities:* fully-equipped bar and restaurant. *Visitors:* Thursday/Friday – Tuesday small societies. *Society Meetings:* catered for. Professional: P. Barber (0161-998 2811). Secretary/Manager: C.B. Turnbull (0161-998 9278).

MANCHESTER. **Ellesmere Golf Club,** Old Clough Lane, Worsley, Manchester M28 7HZ (0161-790 2122). *Location:* off A580 East Lancs Road, adjacent to M62 northbound, (eastbound) access. Wooded parkland. 18 holes, 5954 yards. S.S.S. 69. *Green Fees:* weekdays £18.00 per round, £24.00 per day; weekends £25.00. *Eating facilities:* bar; catering available, with or without reservation. *Visitors:* members of recognised golf clubs welcome, but not during club competitions or Bank Holidays, contact Professional for restrictions. *Society Meetings:* catered for by appointment. Professional: Terry Morley (0161-790 8591). Hon. Secretary: A.C. Kay (0161-799 0554).

MANCHESTER. **Fairfield Golf and Sailing Club,** "Boothdale", Booth Road, Audenshaw, Manchester M34 5GA (0161-370 1641). *Location:* off A635, five miles east of Manchester. Parkland bounded in part by reservoir. 18 holes, 4956 yards. S.S.S. 68. *Green Fees:* weekdays £16.00; weekends £22.00. *Eating facilities:* available. *Visitors:* welcome, restrictions Wednesdays, Thursdays and weekends. *Society Meetings:* catered for by prior arrangement mid-week. Professional: N. Harding (0161-370 2292). Hon. Secretary: J. Humphries (0161-336 3950).

MANCHESTER. **Flixton Golf Club,** Church Road, Flixton, Urmston (0161-748 2116). *Location:* five miles from Manchester on B5213. Parkland. 9 holes, 6410 yards. S.S.S. 71. *Green Fees:* £17.50 weekdays; £12.00 weekends, Bank Holidays and Christmas and New Year holiday period (playing with a member only). *Eating facilities:* daily except Tuesdays. *Visitors:* welcome with reservation. *Society Meetings:* catered for by arrangement. Professional: B. Ling (0161-746 7160). Hon. Secretary: J.G. Frankland (0161-747 0296). Catering: (0161-748 7545).

MANCHESTER. **Heaton Park Golf Club,** Heaton Park, Prestwich, Manchester (0161-798 0295). *Location:* north Manchester, M62 to exit 19 M66 to A576, right to park entrance (200 yards). Undulating parkland. 18 holes, 5840 yards. S.S.S. 68. *Green Fees:* weekdays £5.50, weekends and Bank Holidays £6.60 per round. *Visitors:* welcome, book week in advance. Secretary: F. Lewis (0161-773 1113). *

MANCHESTER. **Houldsworth Golf Club Ltd,** Houldsworth Street, Reddish, Stockport SK5 6HY (0161-442 1815). *Location:* off A6 between Manchester and Stockport, adjacent to M63 and M6. Flat parkland with water hazards. 18 holes, 6234 yards. S.S.S. 70. Practice area. *Green Fees:* weekdays £13.00 per round, £14.00 per day; weekends £16.00 per round. Reduced rates for parties. *Eating facilities:* bar snacks, or full restaurant service. *Visitors:* must be pre-arranged with Professional or Hon. Secretary. *Society Meetings:* catered for on application. Professional: David Naylor (0161-224 4571). Secretary: S.W. Zielinski (0161-224 5055). *

MANCHESTER. **Manchester Golf Club,** Hopwood Cottage, Middleton, Manchester M24 2QP (0161-643 2718). *Location:* Exit 20 from M62, three minutes from motorway. Moorland/parkland. 18 holes, 6454 yards, 5895 metres. S.S.S. 72. Large practice ground. Driving range. *Green Fees:* weekdays £26.00 per day, weekends £32.00 per day. *Eating facilities:* two bars and first class restaurant. *Visitors:* welcome weekdays. *Society Meetings:* parties up to 120 catered for by arrangement. Professional: B. Connor (0161-643 2638). Secretary: K.G. Flett (0161-643 3202).

MANCHESTER. **New North Manchester Golf Club Ltd,** Rhodes House, Manchester Old Road, Middleton, Manchester (0161-643 2941). *Location:* A576, less than one mile from Junction 18 on M62/M66. Undulating and sometimes hilly terrain. 18 holes, 6527 yards, 5987 metres. S.S.S. 72. Large practice ground. *Green Fees:* £22.00 per round, £25.00 per day. *Eating facilities:* catering every day. *Society Meetings:* welcome. Professional: P.J. Lunt (0161-643 7094). Secretary: (0161-643 9033).

MANCHESTER. **Northenden Golf Club,** Palatine Road, Northenden, Manchester M22 4FR (0161-998 4079). *Location:* half a mile off Junction 9 M56. Parkland with plenty of trees. 18 holes, 6622 yards. S.S.S. 72. Practice net. *Green Fees:* £25.00 weekdays, £27.50 weekends. *Eating facilities:* available (0161-998 4079). *Visitors:* welcome most days, preferably with reservation. Restrictions 8.30am to 9.15am Tuesdays and 12 noon to 1.15pm Fridays. *Society Meetings:* catered for Tuesdays and Fridays only. Professional: P. Wesselingh (0161-945 3386). Manager: R.N. Kemp (0161-998 4738; Fax: 0161-945 5592). Steward: Mr P. Massey.

MANCHESTER. **Pikefold Golf Club,** Cooper Lane, Blackley, Manchester M9 2QQ (0161-740 1136). *Location:* four miles north of city centre off Rochdale Road A664, then A6104 Victoria Avenue, located rear of St. Clare's RC church. Undulating wooded parkland course. 9 holes, 5789 yards. S.S.S. 68. *Green Fees:* weekdays £12.00 per day (£5.00 with member); Saturdays and Bank Holidays £7.00, must play with member. No visitors Sundays. *Eating facilities:* available by arrangement. *Visitors:* welcome weekdays without reservation. *Society Meetings:* catered for weekdays and Saturday mornings. Secretary: F.J. Ashworth. *

MANCHESTER. **Prestwich Golf Club,** Hilton Lane, Prestwich, Manchester M25 9XB (0161-773 2544). *Location:* on A6044, one mile from junction with A56. 18 holes, 4757 yards. S.S.S. 63. *Green Fees:* information not provided. *Eating facilities:* by arrangement. *Visitors:* welcome weekdays. *Society Meetings:* catered for weekdays, special rates for parties of 16 and over. Professional: A. Sproston. Secretary: V. Trees.

MANCHESTER. **Stand Golf Club,** The Dales, Ashbourne Grove, Whitefield, Bury, Manchester M25 7NL (0161-766 2388). *Location:* M62 Exit 17, A56/A665 one mile. Undulating parkland with sandy subsoil, playable all year round. 18 holes, 6426 yards. S.S.S. 71. *Green Fees:* weekdays £25.00; weekends £30.00. Reduced rates for societies over 20. *Eating facilities:* meals served daily and bar except Mondays, order in advance. *Visitors:* welcome Monday to Friday; weekends by prior arrangement. *Society Meetings:* welcome Wednesday/Friday by prior arrangement. Professional: Mark Dance (0161-766 2214). Hon. Secretary: Eric B. Taylor (0161-766 3197).

MANCHESTER. **Swinton Park Golf Club,** East Lancashire Road, Swinton, Manchester M27 5LX (0161-794 1785). *Location:* on the A580 Manchester to Liverpool road, five miles from Manchester centre. Parkland course. Three courses. Practice area. *Green Fees:* on application. *Eating facilities:* available. *Visitors:* welcome Tuesdays, Wednesdays and Fridays, tee reservations 10am-noon, 2pm-4pm. *Society Meetings:* catered for by prior arrangement. Professional: J. Wilson (0161-793 8077). General Secretary: F. Slater (0161-794 0861).

MANCHESTER. **Withington Golf Club,** 243 Palatine Road, West Didsbury, Manchester M20 8UD (0161-445 3912). *Location:* three miles from Manchester city centre, adjacent M56 and M63. Flat parkland. 18 holes, 6410 yards. S.S.S. 71. *Green Fees:* weekdays only (except Thursdays) £25.00 per round, £30.00 per day. *Eating facilities:* lunches and evening meals to order. Snacks available at all times except Mondays. *Visitors:* ring Professional for times. *Society Meetings:* catered for by arrangement with the Secretary. Professional: R.J. Ling (0161-445 4861). Secretary/ Manager: A. Larsen (0161-445 9544).

MARPLE. **Marple Golf Club,** Barnsfold Road, Marple, Stockport SK6 7EL (0161-427 2311). *Location:* off A6 at Hawk Green sign. Parkland. 18 holes, 5565 yards. S.S.S. 67. Practice area. *Green Fees:* weekdays £20.00 per day, £8.50 with member; weekends £30.00 per day (when no competitions), £11.00 with member. Subject to review. *Eating facilities:* full meals available except Mondays when bar snacks only. *Visitors:* welcome, not competition days or Thursday between 11am and 3.30pm. *Society Meetings:* all welcome by arrangement with Professional. Professional: Nick Hamilton (0161-449 0690). Secretary: F.W. Ogden (0161-427 1125).

OLDHAM. **Crompton and Royton Golf Club Ltd,** High Barn, Royton, Oldham OL2 6RW (0161-624 2154). *Location:* A671 Oldham to Rochdale, turn off in Royton. Heathland. 18 holes, 6215 yards. S.S.S. 70. Practice ground and nets. *Green Fees:* weekdays £24.00; weekends £30.00. *Eating facilities:* lunches and meals served, except Mondays. *Visitors:* welcome without reservation, not at weekends. *Society Meetings:* catered for by arrangement with Secretary. Professional: D.A. Melling (0161-624 2154). Secretary: Mr T.R. Jones (0161-624 0986).

OLDHAM. **Oldham Golf Club,** Lees New Road, Oldham (0161-624 4986). *Location:* B6194 between Ashton-under-Lyne and Oldham. Moorland course. 18 holes, 5045 yards. S.S.S. 65. *Green Fees:* weekdays £14.00; weekends £20.00. *Eating facilities:* full catering. *Visitors:* welcome, telephone to check for competitions, especially weekends. *Society Meetings:* catered for by prior arrangement with Secretary. Professional's shop (0161-626 8346). Secretary: J. Brooks (0161-624 1955).

OLDHAM. **Saddleworth Golf Club,** Mountain Ash, Ladcastle Road, Uppermill, Near Oldham OL3 6LT (01457 872059). *Location:* five miles from Oldham – M62. A moorland course with superb views of the Pennines. 18 holes, 5976 yards. S.S.S. 69. Practice area. *Green Fees:* weekdays £23.00 (£7.50 per day with member), weekends and Bank Holidays £26.00 (£10.50 per day with member). *Eating facilities:* snacks and meals available. *Visitors:* welcome weekdays. *Society Meetings:* groups of 12 or more catered for except weekends. Professional: T. Shard (01457 873653). Secretary: H.A. Morgan (Tel & Fax: 01457 873653).

OLDHAM. **Werneth Golf Club,** 124 Green Lane, Garden Suburb, Oldham (0161-624 1190). Semi moorland. 18 holes, 5363 yards. S.S.S. 66. Practice ground. *Green Fees:* £18.50 weekdays only. *Eating facilities:* full catering service available. *Visitors:* welcome Mondays and Wednesdays, ring for details. *Society Meetings:* catered for, ring for details. Professional: Roy Penny. Secretary: J.H. Barlow.

ROCHDALE. **Lobden Golf Club,** Whitworth, Near Rochdale (01706 343228). *Location:* take A671 from Rochdale, turn right at Dog and Partridge Pub in Whitworth. Moorland. 9 holes, 2885 yards. S.S.S. 68. *Green Fees:* weekdays £10.00; weekends £15.00. *Eating facilities:* by prior arrangement. *Visitors:* welcome all week except Saturday. *Society Meetings:* catered for by arrangement. Secretary: N.B. Danby (01706 43241).

ROCHDALE. **Rochdale Golf Club,** The Clubhouse, Edenfield Road, Bagslate, Rochdale OL11 5YR (01706 46024). *Location:* M62 at Exit 20, three miles on A680. Parkland. 18 holes, 6034 yards. S.S.S. 69. *Green Fees:* on request. *Eating facilities:* meals available on request except Mondays. *Visitors:* welcome, please check for tee closures. *Society Meetings:* catered for by prior arrangement Mondays, Wednesdays and Fridays. Professional: A. Laverty (01706 522104). Secretary: R. Cutteridge (01706 43818).

ROCHDALE. **Springfield Park Golf Club,** Springfield Park, Marland, Rochdale (01706 56401). *Location:* A58 out of Rochdale, along Bolton Road on right. Parkland. 18 holes, 5237 yards. S.S.S. 66. *Green Fees:* on request. *Eating facilities:* none available. *Visitors:* welcome, no restrictions. Professional: D. Wills (01706 49801). Secretary: B. Wynn (01706 526064).

SALE. **Ashton-on-Mersey Golf Club,** Church Lane, Ashton-on-Mersey, Sale M33 5QQ (0161-973 3220). *Location:* M63, two miles from Sale Station. Parkland course. 9 holes, 6242 yards. S.S.S. 69. *Green Fees:* £20.00 weekdays, £8.00 with a member. *Eating facilities:* available weekdays except Mondays. *Visitors:* welcome on weekdays. Saturdays, Sundays and Bank Holidays only with member. *Society Meetings:* Thursdays. Professional: M.J. Williams (0161-962 3727). Secretary: D. Singleton (0161-976 4390).

SALE. **Sale Golf Club,** Sale Lodge, Golf Road, Sale M33 2LU (0161-973 3404). *Location:* Junction 8 M63, A6144. Parkland. 18 holes, 6352 yards. S.S.S. 70. *Green Fees:* £22.00 weekdays, £30.00 weekends. *Eating facilities:* dining room and bar daily. *Visitors:* welcome weekdays except Thursdays, weekends and Bank Holidays with a member. *Society Meetings:* by arrangement with Manager. Professional: M. Stewart (0161-973 1730). Secretary/Manager: Harry Prow (0161-973 1638).

SALFORD. **Brackley Golf Club,** Bullows Road (off Captain Fold Road), Little Hulton, Worsley M38 9TR (0161-790 6076). *Location:* M61 to Junction 4 onto A6, left at roundabout onto A6 (Walkden), half a mile turn left at White Lion pub. Flat parkland course. 9 holes, 3003 yards, 2747 metres. S.S.S. 70. *Green Fees:* weekdays £3.50; £6.00 weekends. Senior Citizens £2.50, Juniors £3.00. *Visitors:* welcome anytime. *Society Meetings:* welcome. Secretary: R. Heyes.

STOCKPORT. **Bramall Park Golf Club,** 20 Manor Road, Bramhall, Stockport (0161-485 3119). *Location:* 10 miles south of Manchester, 3 miles south of Stockport, half a mile from Cheadle Hulme. Parkland. 18 holes, 6214 yards. S.S.S. 70. *Green Fees:* weekdays £25.00; weekends and Bank Holidays £35.00. *Eating facilities:* full eating facilities except Fridays. *Visitors:* welcome, apply to Professional. *Society Meetings:* catered for. Professional: M. Proffitt (0161-485 2205). Secretary: J.C. O'Shea (0161-485 3119).

STOCKPORT. **Bramhall Golf Club,** The Clubhouse, Ladythorn Road, Bramhall, Stockport SK7 2EY (0161-439 4057). *Location:* three quarters of a mile from Bramhall Railway Station, half a mile from Bramhall Moat House Hotel. Parkland. 18 holes, 6361 yards, 5816 metres. S.S.S. 70. *Green Fees:* weekdays £25.00; weekends £35.00. *Eating facilities:* Steward will provide meals on request, subject to club and visiting party occasions. *Visitors:* welcome except Thursdays and Competition Days. *Society Meetings:* catered for Wednesdays, minimum 24. Professional: R. Green (0161-439 1171). Secretary: J.G. Lee (0161-439 6092).

STOCKPORT. **Disley Golf Club Ltd,** Stanley Hall Lane, Disley, Stockport SK12 2JX (01663 762071). *Location:* off A6 at Disley Village. Open hillside/parkland course. 18 holes, 6015 yards, 5832 metres. S.S.S. 69. *Green Fees:* weekdays £25.00; weekends £30.00. *Eating facilities:* available except Mondays. *Visitors:* welcome weekdays. *Society Meetings:* catered for by arrangement. Professional: A.G. Esplin (01663 762884). Secretary: David English (01663 764001).

STOCKPORT. **Hazel Grove Golf Club,** Buxton Road, Hazel Grove, Stockport SK7 6LU (0161-483 3217). *Location:* A6 to Buxton out of Hazel Grove, three miles south of Stockport. Flat parkland with tree-lined fairways. 18 holes, 6310 yards. S.S.S. 71. *Green Fees:* weekdays £22.50; Friday, Saturday, Sunday and Bank Holidays £27.50. *Eating facilities:* available daily. *Visitors:* welcome, ring Professional for booking of tee times. *Society Meetings:* catered for on Thursdays and Fridays. Professional: M.E. Hill (0161-483 7272). Secretary: H.A.G. Carlisle (0161-483 3978).

STOCKPORT. **Heaton Moor Golf Club,** Mauldeth Road, Heaton Mersey, Stockport SK4 3NX (0161-432 2134). *Location:* A34 off M56. Flat parkland course, tree lined fairways. 18 holes, 5909 yards. S.S.S. 68. Practice area. *Green Fees:* weekdays £22.00; weekends £30.00. *Eating facilities:* lunches and evening meals by arrangement; bar. *Visitors:* welcome weekdays. *Society Meetings:* catered for. Professional: Clive Loydall (0161-432 0846). Secretary: A.D. Townsend. *

STOCKPORT. **Mellor and Townscliffe Golf Club Ltd,** Gibb Lane, Tarden, Mellor, Stockport SK6 5NA (0161-427 2208). *Location:* seven miles south east of Stockport off A626. Parkland with trees/moorland. 18 holes, 5925 yards. S.S.S. 69. *Green Fees:* weekdays £20.00 per day, £8.00 with a member; weekends and Bank Holidays £27.50, with a member £10.00. *Eating facilities:* available daily except Tuesdays. *Visitors:* welcome weekdays, no casual visitors weekends. *Society Meetings:* catered for by prior arrangement. Professional: Gary R. Broadley (0161-427 5759). Secretary: D.A. Ogden.

STOCKPORT. **Reddish Vale Golf Club,** Southcliffe Road, Reddish, Stockport SK5 7EE (0161-480 2359). *Location:* one mile north east of Stockport. Varied undulating heathland course, designed by Dr A. MacKenzie. 18 holes, 6086 yards. S.S.S. 69. *Green Fees:* weekdays £22.00. *Eating facilities:* bar and catering. *Visitors:* welcome on weekdays (not 12.30 – 1.30pm). *Society Meetings:* catered for by arrangement. Professional: Richard Brown (0161-480 3824). Secretary: J.L. Blakey.

STOCKPORT. **Romiley Golf Club Ltd,** Goosehouse Green, Romiley, Stockport SK6 4LJ (0161-430 2392). *Location:* B6104 off A560, signposted from Romiley village. Parkland. 18 holes, 6421 yards. S.S.S. 71. *Green Fees:* weekdays £22.00 per round, £28.00 per day; weekends and Bank Holidays £33.00 per round, £44.00 per day. Reduced rates for visitors by arrangement. *Eating facilities:* full catering by arrangement except Mondays. *Visitors:* welcome any day. *Society Meetings:* catered for by prior arrangement with Secretary. Professional: Gary Butler (0161-430 7122). Secretary: Paul Trafford (0161-430 7257).

STOCKPORT. **Stockport Golf Club Ltd,** Offerton Road, Offerton, Stockport, Cheshire SK2 5HL (0161-427 2001). *Location:* one mile from lights at Hazel Grove, along Torkington Road. Parkland. 18 holes, 6326 yards. S.S.S. 71. *Green Fees:* weekdays £30.00 per round, weekends £40.00 per round. *Eating facilities:* available, excellent. *Visitors:* welcome weekdays, contact Professional at weekends. *Society Meetings:* catered for. Professional: M. Peel (0161-427 2421). Secretary: P. Moorhead (Tel & Fax: 0161-427 8369).

TRAFFORD. **William Wroe Municipal Golf Course,** Pennybridge Lane, off Flixton Road, Flixton, Trafford M31 3DL (0161-748 8680). Course and shop managed by Trafford Borough Council, Acre Gate Golf Club play over the course. *Location:* M63 Exit 4, B5124 to Davyhulme Circle then one mile on B5158, left at Bird-in-Hand Pub. Flat course. 18 holes, 4395 yards. S.S.S. 61. *Green Fees:* weekdays £5.00 adults, £2.50 juniors; weekends £7.00 everyone. *Visitors:* welcome anytime, but advisable to book the day before. Teaching Professional: Roland West. Secretary: Mrs P. Rowan. Golf Course Manager: Mr B. Davies. *

WESTHOUGHTON. **Westhoughton Golf Club,** Long Island, School Street, Westhoughton, Bolton BL5 2BR (01942 811085). *Location:* four miles south west of Bolton on A58. Parkland. 9 holes, 5702 yards. S.S.S. 68. *Green Fees:* weekdays £15.00 per day; weekends with a member only £5.00. *Eating facilities:* bar meals and home cooking. *Visitors:* welcome, Tuesday Ladies' Day. Snooker room. *Society Meetings:* welcomed on Thursdays, maximum 32. Professional: A. Franklin. Secretary: D.J. Kinsella.

WHITEFIELD. **Whitefield Golf Club,** Higher Lane, Whitefield, Manchester (0161-766 2728). *Location:* Exit 17, off M62 then take road to Radcliffe for half a mile. 18 holes, 6045 yards. S.S.S. 69. *Green Fees:* on application. *Eating facilities:* restaurant facilities every day. *Visitors:* welcome. *Society Meetings:* catered for. Professional: P. Reeves. Secretary: Miss S. Addleman (0161-766 2904).

WIGAN. **Gathurst Golf Club,** 62 Miles Lane, Shevington, Wigan WN6 8EW (01257 254861). *Location:* one mile south of Junction 27 M6. Parkland. 12 holes, 3765 yards. S.S.S. 46. *Green Fees:* weekdays £20.00. *Eating facilities:* available bar hours, daily except Monday. *Visitors:* welcome Monday, Tuesday, Thursday and Friday with reservation. *Society Meetings:* catered for by appointment. Professional: D. Clarke (01257 254909). Secretary: J. Clarke (01257 255235).

WIGAN. **Haigh Hall Golf Club,** Haigh Country Park, Aspull, Near Wigan WN2 1PE (01942 833337). *Location:* Junction 27 M6, at Standish. Parkland. 18 holes, 6400 yards. S.S.S. 71. Practice area. *Green Fees:* weekdays £5.95; weekends £8.50. *Eating facilities:* cafeteria. *Visitors:* welcome, book by telephone. *Society Meetings:* welcome. Professional: Ian Lee (01942 831107). Secretary: W. Fleetwood.

WIGAN. **Hindley Hall Golf Club,** Hall Lane, Hindley, Wigan WN2 2SQ (01942 525020). *Location:* two miles east of Wigan, Junction 6 M61, or A58 to Ladies Lane/Hall Lane. 18 holes, 5841 yards. S.S.S. 68. *Green Fees:* £20.00 weekdays; £27.00 weekends and Bank Holidays. *Eating facilities:* book before playing. *Visitors:* welcome without reservation if members of a recognised golf club. *Society Meetings:* catered for by arrangement with the Secretary. Professional: N. Brazell (01942 55991). Secretary: R. Bell (01942 55131).

WIGAN. **Wigan Golf Club,** Arley Hall, Haigh, Near Wigan WN1 2UH (01257 421360). *Location:* M6 Exit 27, two miles on B5329, east of Standish. Parkland. 9 holes, 6058 yards. S.S.S. 69. *Green Fees:* weekdays £25.00; weekedns £30.00. *Eating facilities:* meals and bar available. *Visitors:* welcome anytime except Tuesdays and Saturdays. *Society Meetings:* catered for on Thursdays and Fridays. Secretary: E. Walmsley (01942 43455).

FOR THE MUTUAL GUIDANCE OF GUEST AND HOST

Every year literally thousands of holidays, short-breaks and overnight stops are arranged through our guides, the vast majority without any problems at all. In a handful of cases, however, difficulties do arise about bookings, which often could have been prevented from the outset.

It is important to remember that when accommodation has been booked, both parties — guests and hosts — have entered into a form of contract. We hope that the following points will provide helpful guidance.

GUESTS: When enquiring about accommodation, be as precise as possible. Give exact dates, numbers in your party and the ages of any children. State the number and type of rooms wanted and also what catering you require — bed and breakfast, full board, etc. Make sure that the position about evening meals is clear — and about pets, reductions for children or any other special points.

Read our reviews carefully to ensure that the proprietors you are going to contact can supply what you want. Ask for a letter confirming all arrangements, if possible.

If you have to cancel, do so as soon as possible. Proprietors do have the right to retain deposits and under certain circumstances to charge for cancelled holidays if adequate notice is not given and they cannot re-let the accommodation.

HOSTS: Give details about your facilities and about any special conditions. Explain your deposit system clearly and arrangements for cancellations, charges, etc, and whether or not your terms include VAT.

If for any reason you are unable to fulfil an agreed booking without adequate notice, you may be under an obligation to arrange alternative suitable accommodation or to make some form of compensation.

While every effort is made to ensure accuracy, we regret that FHG Publications cannot accept responsibility for errors, omissions or misrepresentation in our entries or any consequences thereof. Prices in particular should be checked because we go to press early. We will follow up complaints but cannot act as arbiters or agents for either party.

Merseyside

BIRKENHEAD. **Arrowe Park Golf Course,** Arrowe Park, Birkenhead L49 5LW. *Location:* Mersey Tunnel into Brough Road, then Woodchurch Road, head for Arrowe Park roundabout, bear left approximately 400 yards, turn right into Arrowe Park. Flat tree-lined parkland. 18 holes, 6435 yards, 5885 metres. S.S.S. 71. 9 hole pitch and putt, putting green. *Green Fees:* £6.00 per round. *Eating facilities:* restaurant/cafe – bar. *Visitors:* EVERYBODY WELCOME! *Society Meetings:* by arrangement through Professional. Professional: Clive Scanlon (0151-677 1527). Secretary: Ken Finlay.

BIRKENHEAD. **Prenton Golf Club,** Golf Links Road, Prenton, Birkenhead L42 8LW (0151-608 1053). *Location:* M53 Junction 3, off A552 towards Birkenhead. Parkland course. 18 holes, 6411 yards. S.S.S. 71. *Green Fees:* £23.00 weekdays; £25.00 weekends. *Eating facilities:* full catering facilities available. *Visitors:* welcome, reservation advisable. *Society Meetings:* catered for Wednesdays and Fridays. Professional: Robin Thompson (0151-608 1636). Secretary: W.F.W. Disley.

BIRKENHEAD. **The Wirral Ladies' Golf Club Ltd,** 93 Bidston Road, Oxton, Birkenhead (0151-652 5797). *Location:* on boundary of town, Bidston Hill area. Acid heath/gorse and heather course. 18 holes, 4966 yards (Ladies), 5170 yards (Men). S.S.S. 70 (Ladies), S.S.S. 66 (Men). *Green Fees:* £20.00 per round. *Eating facilities:* dining room, meals during day to order. *Visitors:* welcome with reservation. *Society Meetings:* welcome weekdays only. Professional: Philip Chandler (0151-652 2468). Secretary: Christine Piper (0151-652 1255; Fax: 0151-653 4323).

BLUNDELLSANDS. **West Lancashire Golf Club,** Hall Road West, Blundellsands, Liverpool L23 8SZ (0151-924 4115). *Location:* A565 Liverpool – Southport to Crosby, follow signposts for club or Waterloo Rugby Club. Links course. 6756 yards. S.S.S. 73. *Green Fees:* £33.00 per day, £22.00 per round; £40.00 per round weekends. *Eating facilities:* lunch, tea and dinner every day. *Visitors:* welcome on weekdays. Electric trolleys by prior agreement only. *Society Meetings:* catered for by advance application. Professional: D.G. Lloyd (0151-924 5662). Secretary: D.E. Bell (0151-924 1076; Fax: 0151-931 4448).

BOOTLE. **Bootle Golf Club,** 3 Dunnings Bridge Road, Bootle L30 2PP (0151-928 6196). *Location:* five miles north of Liverpool, one mile from M57 and M58. Links course. 18 holes, 6362 yards. S.S.S. 70. *Green Fees:* £3.60 weekdays; £5.05 weekends. *Eating facilities:* full catering as required by arrangement. *Visitors:* welcome weekdays and afternoons at weekends. *Society Meetings:* by appointment. Professional: Gary Brown (0151-928 1371). Secretary: John F. Morgan (0151-922 4792). *

BROMBOROUGH. **Bromborough Golf Club,** Raby Hall Road, Bromborough, Wirral, Merseyside L63 0NN (0151-334 2155). *Location:* Exit 4 Wirral Motorway M53. Parkland. 18 holes, 6650 yards, 6080 metres. S.S.S. 73. *Green Fees:* weekdays £26.00, weekends £30.00, reduced rates for Societies over 24. *Eating facilities:* bar and full catering facilities. *Visitors:* welcome weekdays, but essential to ring in advance for weekends and Bank Holidays. *Society Meetings:* catered for by prior arrangement. Professional: G. Berry (0151-334 4499). Secretary: J.T. Barraclough (0151-334 2978).

EASTHAM. **Eastham Lodge Golf Club,** 117 Ferry Road, Eastham, Wirral, Merseyside L62 0AP (0151-327 1483). *Location:* exit Junction 5 M53 into Eastham village from A41, follow signs for Eastham Country Park. Flat pleasant parkland course with many trees. 15 holes, 5876 yards (for 18). S.S.S. 68. *Green Fees:* weekdays £22.00; weekends with a member only £10.00. *Eating facilities:* bar snacks, full restaurant (book in advance). *Visitors:* welcome weekdays, with member weekends. *Society Meetings:* welcome mainly Tuesdays, some Mondays/Fridays by special arrangement; £22.00 per day, £18.00 per round. Professional: Bob Boobyer (0151-327 3008). Secretary: C.S. Camden (0151-327 3003).

FORMBY. **Formby Golf Centre,** Moss Side, Formby L37 0AF (01704 875952). *Location:* off Formby bypass (Liverpool to Southport road). Parkland. 9 holes. Driving Range, Par 3 putting green. *Green Fees:* £3.00 per 18 holes. *Visitors:* welcome anytime. Professional: Malcolm Welsh (01704 875952). Secretary: Mrs D. Robinson.

FORMBY. **Formby Golf Club,** Golf Road, Formby, Liverpool L37 1LQ (01704 872164). *Location:* one mile west of A565 by Freshfield Station. Seaside links, wooded. 18 holes, 6781 yards. S.S.S. 73. *Green Fees:* £45.00 per round or day. *Eating facilities:* available except Mondays. *Visitors:* welcome by arrangement with the Secretary (not before 9.30am weekends or before 10.30am Wednesdays). Accommodation available. *Society Meetings:* catered for Tuesdays, Thursdays and Fridays. Professional: C. Harrison (01704 873090). Secretary: R. Dixon (01704 872164; Fax: 01704 833028).

FORMBY. **Formby Ladies' Golf Club,** Golf Road, Formby, Liverpool L37 1YH (01704 874127). Seaside links. 18 holes, 5374 yards, 4914 metres. S.S.S. 71. Practice area. *Green Fees:* weekdays £27.00; weekends £32.00. *Eating facilities:* light lunches, afternoon teas. *Visitors:* welcome with prior reservation, contact the Secretary. *Society Meetings:* catered for with prior reservation. Professional: C. Harrison (01704 873090). Secretary: Mrs V. Bailey (01704 873493).

HESWALL. **Heswall Golf Club,** Cottage Lane, Gayton, Wirral L60 8PB (0151-342 2193). *Location:* off A540, eight miles north-west of Chester. Parkland on the banks of River Dee estuary overlooking Welsh coast and hills. 18 holes, 6472 yards, 5909 metres. S.S.S. 72. Large practice area. *Green Fees:* weekdays £30.00, weekends and Bank Holidays £35.00. *Eating facilities:* bar snacks, full meals by arrangement. *Visitors:* welcome anytime subject to availability. Must have accredited Handicaps. *Society Meetings:* catered for fully on Wednesdays and Fridays only, minimum 24 players. Professional: Alan Thompson (0151-342 7431). Secretary: (0151-342 1237). Catering (0151-342 2193).

HOYLAKE. **Royal Liverpool Golf Club,** Meols Drive, Hoylake, Wirral, Merseyside L47 4AL (0151-632 3101). *Location:* 10 miles southwest of Liverpool on Wirral Peninsula. Approach from M6, M56 and M53 Junction 2.Championship links. 18 holes, 6804 yards. S.S.S. 74. Large practice area. *Green Fees:* weekdays £40.00 per round, £55.00 per day; weekends £55.00 per round, £80.00 per day. Subject to review. *Eating facilities:* full dining room (jacket and tie), snacks or soup in locker room bar. *Visitors:* welcome weekdays except Thursday mornings (Ladies Day) and very limited at weekends. Proof of Handicap required. Caddies available. *Society Meetings:* catered for Tuesdays to Fridays. Professional: John Heggarty (0151-632 5868). Secretary: Group Captain C.T. Moore CBE (0151-632 3101).

HUYTON. **Bowring Golf Club,** Bowring Park, Roby Road, Huyton (0151-489 1901). 9 holes, 5580 yards. S.S.S. 66. *Green Fees:* on application. *Visitors:* unrestricted. Secretary: E. Hatton. Professional: Michael Sarsfield. *

HUYTON. **Huyton and Prescot Golf Club Ltd,** Hurst Park, Huyton Lane, Huyton, Liverpool L36 1UA (0151-489 1138). *Location:* Liverpool Road to Prescot town centre. Parkland. 18 holes, 5779 yards. S.S.S. 68 white, 67 yellow. *Green Fees:* weekdays £22.00; weekends £8.00 (one visitor with member only). *Eating facilities:* catering 11am to 5pm; normal bar hours. *Visitors:* welcome, midweek days 9.30am to 12.30pm, 2pm to 4pm. *Society Meetings:* catered for Mondays, Wednesdays, Thursdays and Friday afternoons. Professional: Mr M.J. Harrison (0151-489 2022). Secretary: Mrs E. Holmes (0151-489 3948).

LIVERPOOL. **Allerton Park Golf Club,** Allerton Road, Liverpool L18 3JT (0151-428 4074). *Location:* Menlove Avenue. Parkland. 18 holes, 5800 yards. S.S.S. 67. *Green Fees:* £6.50. *Eating facilities:* lunches at clubhouse. *Visitors:* welcome at all times. Professional: Barry Large. Secretary: H. O'Neill.

LIVERPOOL. **Dudley Golf Club,** Allerton Municipal Golf Course, Menlove Avenue, Allerton, Liverpool 18 (0151-428 8510). *Location:* end of M62, then two miles on Allerton road, five miles from city centre. Wooded parkland. Two courses. (1) 18 holes, 5459 metres. S.S.S. 67. (2) 9 holes, 1685 metres. S.S.S. 34. *Green Fees:* on application. *Eating facilities:* licensed bar, bar snacks. *Visitors:* welcome at any time, please book in advance. *Society Meetings:* welcome by advance booking. Professional: Barry Large (0151-428 1046). Secretary: Clive R. Mullins (0151-733 4731).

LIVERPOOL. **Lee Park Golf Club,** Childwall Valley Road, Liverpool L27 3YA (0151-487 9861). *Location:* Queens Drive, Childwall Valley Road. Parkland. 18 holes, 6074 yards. Medal tees: 5569 yards. Front tees: S.S.S. 68. Ladies' tee: 5650 yards. S.S.S. 72. *Green Fees:* information not provided. *Eating facilities:* restaurant and bar snacks daily. *Visitors:* welcome anytime except between 12.15pm and 2.15pm daily (reserved for members). *Society Meetings:* catered for. Secretary: Mrs Doris Barr (0151-487 3882).

LIVERPOOL. **The Childwall Golf Club Ltd.,** Naylors Road, Gateacre, Liverpool L27 2YB (0151-487 9982). *Location:* Exit 6 M62 to Liverpool follow Huyton A5080 to second set of traffic lights, turn left into Wheathill Road. Parkland, flat, designed by James Braid. 18 holes, 6425 yards. S.S.S. 72. Practice area. *Green Fees:* £19.50 weekdays; £28.00 weekends. *Eating facilities:* bar, snacks and restaurant. *Visitors:* no visitors weekends and Tuesdays. *Society Meetings:* catered for on weekdays, contact the Secretary. Groups over 20, £17.50. Professional: Mr N.M. Parr (0151-487 9871). Secretary: Mr L. Upton (0151-487 0654).

LIVERPOOL. **West Derby Golf Club,** Yew Tree Lane, West Derby, Liverpool L12 9HQ (0151-228 1540). Flat parkland course. 18 holes, 6346 yards. S.S.S. 70. *Green Fees:* weekdays £22.00 per round, £25.00 per day; weekends £30.00. *Eating facilities:* soup and sandwiches, light meals available at lunch. Evening meals by prior arrangement. *Visitors:* welcome if members of a recognised golf club. *Society Meetings:* catered for only by arrangement with Secretary. Professional: Nick Brace (0151-220 5478). Secretary/ Manager: S. Young (0151-254 1034).

LIVERPOOL. **Woolton Golf Club,** Doe Park, Speke Road, Woolton, Liverpool L25 7TZ (0151-486 1601). *Location:* south Liverpool, one mile from Woolton Village. Parkland, rolling terrain, excellent springy fairways affording inviting lies. 18 holes, 5717 yards. S.S.S. 68. *Green Fees:* weekdays £20.00; weekends £28.00. *Eating facilities:* bar snacks daily, evening dining by arrangement. *Visitors:* welcome, enquiries via Pro Shop. *Society Meetings:* catered for by arrangement with the Secretary. Professional Shop: (0151-486 1298). Secretary: C. Brereton (0151-486 2298).

MORETON. **Bidston Golf Club,** Scoresby Road, Leasowe, Moreton L46 1QQ (0151-638 3412). *Location:* M53 Junction 1 (from Chester direction) turn right at roundabout, course entrance 200 yards on dual carriageway. Mixture of links and parkland. 18 holes, 6140 yards. S.S.S. 69. Practice ground and nets. *Green Fees:* weekdays £23.00. *Eating facilities:* restaurant, snacks, lounge bar. *Visitors:* welcome weekdays with prior notification. *Society Meetings:* catered for by arrangement. Professional: J. Law (0151-630 6650). Secretary: John J. Gleeson.

MORETON. **Leasowe Golf Club,** Leasowe Road, Moreton, Wirral, Merseyside L46 3RD (0151-677 5852). *Location:* Exit 1 from M53, one mile towards Hoylake. Flat seaside links. 18 holes, 6227 yards. S.S.S. 71. Practice area. *Green Fees:* £18.00 weekdays; £22.00 weekends. *Eating facilities:* dining room or snacks. *Visitors:* welcome anytime, phone first. *Society Meetings:* catered for except Mondays and Saturdays. Professional: Neil Sweeney (0151-678 5460). Secretary: C. Peter R. Calvert.

NEWTON-LE-WILLOWS. **Haydock Park Golf Club,** Newton Lane, Newton-le-Willows WA12 0HX (01925 224389). *Location:* off East Lancs Road (A580) and M6, three quarters of a mile from Newton-le-Willows High Street. Flat, wooded parkland course in beautiful setting. 18 holes, 6043 yards. S.S.S. 69. Large practice ground. *Green Fees:* weekdays £25.00; weekends £8.00 with a member only. *Eating facilities:* restaurant and two bars. *Visitors:* welcome weekdays except Tuesdays, identification (club membership card) or letter of introduction required. *Society Meetings:* catered for by arrangement. Professional: P. Kenwright (01925 226944). Secretary: G. Tait (01925 228525).

SOUTHPORT. **Hesketh Golf Club,** Cockle Dicks Lane, Cambridge Road, Southport PR9 9QQ (01704 530226). *Location:* one mile north of town centre. Seaside links Championship course. 18 holes, 6407 yards. S.S.S. 72. Practice ground. *Green Fees:* weekdays £25.00 per round, £35.00 per day; weekends and Bank Holidays £40.00 per day. *Eating facilities:* bar snacks and dining room; three bars. *Visitors:* welcome by prior arrangement with Secretary. *Society Meetings:* catered for by arrangement with Secretary. Professional: John Donoghue (01704 530050). Secretary: Peter B. Seal (01704 536897; Fax: 0704 539250).

SOUTHPORT. **Hillside Golf Club,** Hastings Road, Hillside, Southport PR8 2LU (01704 569902). *Location:* three miles south of town centre, Hillside station one mile. Links. Championship course used for R&A, EGU and PGA events. 18 holes, 6850 yards. S.S.S. 74. Practice ground. *Green Fees:* weekdays £45.00 per day, £35.00 per round; weekends £45.00 per round. *Eating facilities:* diningroom, bars and lounges. *Visitors:* welcome Mondays, Wednesdays, Thursdays and Fridays, Tuesday pm only, limited times available Sundays. *Society Meetings:* welcome with prior reservations. Professional: Brian Seddon (01704 568360). Secretary: John G. Graham (01704 567169; Fax: 01704 563192).

SOUTHPORT. **Park Golf Club,** Park Road West, Southport (01704 530133). Play over Southport Municipal Links. S.S.S. 69. Secretary: J.A.V. Turner. Professional: (01704 535286). *

SOUTHPORT. **Royal Birkdale Golf Club,** Waterloo Road, Birkdale, Southport PR8 2LX (01704 567920; Fax: 01704 562327). *Location:* one mile south of Southport town centre. Classic Links on the Open Championship rota. 18 holes, 6703 yards. S.S.S. 73. *Green Fees:* contact the Secretary. *Visitors:* welcome by arrangement with Secretary, official golf Handicap required. *Society Meetings:* catered for, package prices for 20 plus, diningroom facilities. Professional: Richard Bradbeer (01704 568857). Secretary: Norman Crewe (01704 567920).

SOUTHPORT. **Southport and Ainsdale Golf Club,** Bradshaw's Lane, Off Liverpool Road, Ainsdale, Southport PR8 3LG (01704 570892). *Location:* south of Southport on A565. Links course. 18 holes, 6615 yards. S.S.S. 73. *Green Fees:* weekdays £30.00 per round, £40.00 per day; weekends £45.00 per day. *Eating facilities:* full catering available. *Visitors:* advance booking recommended. *Society Meetings:* catered for by arrangement. Professional: M. Houghton (01704 577316). Secretary: I.F. Sproule (01704 578000; Fax: 01704 570896).

If you are writing, a stamped, addressed envelope is always appreciated.

SOUTHPORT. **Southport Municipal Golf Club,** Park Road West, Southport (01704 55130). *Location:* Park Road West, north end of Promenade, near Marine Lake, Southport. Flat seaside links. 18 holes, 6139 yards. S.S.S. 70. *Green Fees:* information not available. *Eating facilities:* licensed cafe. *Visitors:* booking system operates up to seven days in advance (visitors unrestricted). *Society Meetings:* welcome, book in advance. Professional: William Fletcher (01704 35286). *

SOUTHPORT. **Southport Old Links Golf Club,** Moss Lane, Churchtown, Southport PR9 7QS (01704 28207). *Location:* end of Roe Lane, Churchtown, at the rear of Meols Hall. Tree lined links course. 9 holes, 6378 yards (x2). S.S.S. 71. *Green Fees:* weekdays £18.00 per round, £25.00 per day; weekends and Bank Holidays £25.00 per round only. Weekly ticket £75.00 to play any five out of seven days. For minimum number of 12 £30.00 per day including coffee on arrival, soup and sandwiches, three-course evening meal and two rounds of golf – £10 deposit. *Eating facilities:* available daily. *Visitors:* welcome except Wednesdays, Sundays and Bank Holidays. *Society Meetings:* catered for by arrangement, letter of application required. Professional: Mr P. Atkiss (01704 28207). Secretary: Mr B.E. Kenyon (01704 28207).

ST. HELENS. **Grange Park Golf Club,** Prescot Road, St. Helens WA10 3AD (01744 22980). *Location:* one and a half miles south west of St. Helens on A58. Wooded parkland. 18 holes, 6429 yards. S.S.S. 71. Practice area. *Green Fees:* weekdays £21.00; weekends £26.00. *Eating facilities:* full catering and bar facilities. *Visitors:* welcome anytime but times are often not available at weekends/Bank Holidays; reservation through Professional recommended. *Society Meetings:* catered for Mondays, Wednesdays, Thursdays or Fridays by advance reservation through Secretary. Professional: Paul Evans (01744 28785). Secretary: David A. Wood (01744 26318).

ST HELENS. **Sherdley Park Golf Club,** Sherdley Park, St. Helens (01744 815518). *Location:* Marshalls Cross Road A570. Undulating parkland course. 18 holes, 5974 yards. S.S.S. 71. Driving range. *Green Fees:* weekdays £5.50; weekends £6.60. 50% reductions for Senior Citizens and Juniors. *Eating facilities:* by arrangement with Secretary. *Visitors:* unrestricted. *Society Meetings:* by prior arrangement. Professional: P.R. Parkinson (01744 813149). Secretary: S. Nicholson (01744 812017).

ST. HELENS. **Sherdley Park Municipal Golf Course,** St. Helens (01744 813149; clubhouse 01744 815518). *Location:* two miles east of town on A570. 18 holes, 5974 yards. S.S.S. 69. *Green Fees:* information not provided. *Visitors:* welcome. Professional: P.R. Parkinson. Secretary: B.M. Healiss.

WALLASEY. **Wallasey Golf Club,** Bayswater Road, Wallasey L45 8LA (0151-639 3630). *Location:* via M53 through Wirral or 15 minutes from Liverpool centre via Wallasey Tunnel. Seaside links. 18 holes, 6607 yards, 6038 metres. S.S.S. 73. *Green Fees:* weekdays £26.50 per round, £31.50 per day; weekends and Bank Holidays £31.50 per round, £37.00 per day. *Eating facilities:* snacks and full catering facilities. *Visitors:* welcome with reservation. *Society Meetings:* catered for by arrangement. Professional: Mike Adams (0151-638 3888). Secretary: Mrs L.M. Dolman (0151-691 1024).

WALLASEY. **Warren Golf Club,** The Grange, Grove Road, Wallasey (0151-639 8323). *Location:* 300 yards Grove Road Station. Seaside links course. 9 holes, 5914 yards. S.S.S. 68. *Green Fees:* £5.40. Special rates for Senior Citizens and Juniors. *Visitors:* welcome Mondays to Saturdays. Showers. *Society Meetings:* welcome. Professional: Kenneth Lamb (0151-639 5730). Secretary: Paul Warrington.

WIRRAL. **Brackenwood Golf Club,** Bracken Lane, Bebington, Wirral (0151-608 5394). *Location:* M53 Junction 7 Clatterbridge turnoff. Parkland. 18 holes, 6285 yards, 5747 metres. S.S.S. 70. *Green Fees:* £6.00. There is a charge of £1.00 per person individual booking. *Eating facilities:* snacks available. *Visitors:* welcome anytime weekdays through the Professional, bookings at weekends. *Society Meetings:* welcome. Professional: Colin Disbury (0151-608 3093). Secretary: N.D. Taylor. *

WIRRAL. **Hoylake Golf Club,** Carr Lane, Hoylake, Wirral (0151-632 4883). *Location:* turn at roundabout Hoylake town centre, over railway. Part flat semi links. 18 holes, 6313 yards, 5780 metres. S.S.S. 70. *Green Fees:* £6.00. *Eating facilities:* cafe and bar. Phone Steward (M. Down) in advance (0151-632 4883). *Visitors:* welcome, booking fee required in advance. *Society Meetings:* weekdays only. Professional: S.N. Hooton (0151-632 2956). Secretary: Alan Peacock (0151-632 3164).

WIRRAL. **The Caldy Golf Club Ltd,** Links Hey Road, Caldy, Wirral L48 1NB (0151-625 5515). *Location:* one mile south of West Kirby on the River Dee, 10 miles from Chester. Undulating parkland, links, open aspect with views across the Dee to the North Wales hills. 18 holes, 6675 yards, 6105 metres. S.S.S. 73. Practice ground and putting green. *Green Fees:* weekdays £30.00 per round, £35.00 per day; weekends with member only. *Eating facilities:* bars and restaurant throughout the day. *Visitors:* welcome weekdays with advance booking and Handicap Certificate. Restrictions Tuesdays and Wednesdays. Jeans not allowed on course or in Clubhouse. *Society Meetings:* Thursdays by prior arrangement. Professional: Kevin Jones (0151-625 1818). Secretary: T.D.M. Bacon (0151-625 5660; Fax: 0151-625 7394).

Where an asterisk (*) follows an entry, details have not been confirmed by the club for 1995.

Norfolk

CROMER. **Links Country Park Hotel and Golf Club,** Sandy Lane, West Runton, Cromer NR27 9QH (01263 838383). *Location:* midway between Cromer and Sheringham on the A149, turn left opposite the village inn. Undulating parkland with narrow fairways and tricky greens. 9 holes, 4814 yards, S.S.S. 64. *Green Fees:* £19.00 per day weekdays, £23.00 weekends. *Eating facilities:* grill room, snacks, hotel restaurant table d'hôte and à la carte. *Visitors:* welcome weekdays, restrictions weekends. Adjoining Hotel offers free golf to residents; sauna, solarium, swimming pool etc. *Society Meetings:* welcome. Professional: Mike Jubb (01263 838215). Hon. Secretary: Charles Savage (01263 838383).

CROMER. **Royal Cromer Golf Club,** 145 Overstrand Road, Cromer NR27 0JH (01263 512219). *Location:* one mile east of town centre on coast road. Undulating seaside course. 18 holes, 6508 yards. S.S.S. 71. Large practice ground. *Green Fees:* £25.00 weekdays, £30.00 weekends. *Eating facilities:* full catering and bar snacks. *Visitors:* welcome, booking essential from 1st April to 31st October, Handicap Certificates required. *Society Meetings:* welcome except weekends. Professional: Robin J. Page (01263 512267). Secretary: B.A. Howson (01263 512884).

DEREHAM. **Dereham Golf Club,** Quebec Road, Dereham NR19 2DS (01362 695900). *Location:* three-quarters of a mile from town centre on B1110. Wooded parkland. 9 holes (double tees), 6225 yards. S.S.S. 70. Practice nets, practice ground. *Green Fees:* weekdays £16.00; weekends with member only £10. *Eating facilities:* full restaurant (limited Mondays). *Visitors:* welcome weekdays with prior notice, not weekends. Handicap Certificates required. *Society Meetings:* catered for with advance booking. Professional: Gary Kitley (01362 695631). Secretary: J. Holland (01362 695900).

DISS. **Diss Golf Club,** Stuston Common, Diss (01379 642847). The course is in Suffolk but Postal Address is Diss, Norfolk. *Location:* B1077 off A140, half-a-mile from Diss railway station, one mile from town centre. Flat common land. 18 holes, 6238 yards. S.S.S. 70. *Green Fees:* £20.00, £10.00 if playing with a member. *Eating facilities:* excellent facilities – newly refurbished. *Visitors:* welcome without reservation. *Society Meetings:* all welcome and catered for. Professional: N. Taylor (01379 644399). Secretary: J.A. Bell (01379 641025).

DOWNHAM MARKET. **Ryston Park Golf Club,** Ely Road, Denver, Downham Market PE38 0HH (01366 382133).*Location:* one mile south Downham Market on A10. 36 miles north Cambridge. Parkland. 9 holes, 6292 yards. S.S.S. 70. Practice ground. *Green Fees:* weekdays £20.00, £8.00 with a member. *Eating facilities:* meals served to order. *Visitors:* welcome weekdays, one guest per member weekends. *Society Meetings:* restricted, catered for by arrangement. Secretary: A.J. Wilson (01366 383834).

FAKENHAM. **Fakenham Golf Club,** Gallow Sports Centre, Hempton Road, Fakenham (01328 862867). *Location:* half-a-mile town centre on Swaffham Road. Parkland. 9 holes, 5992 yards. S.S.S. 69. Large practice area. *Green Fees:* weekdays £14.00, weekends and Bank Holidays £18.00 after 3pm. 10% reduction for Societies. *Eating facilities:* available in Sports Centre. *Visitors:* welcome by appointment. *Society Meetings:* welcome, reduced rates. Professional: J. Westwood (01328 863534). Secretary: G.G. Cocker (01328 855665).

GREAT YARMOUTH. **Caldecott Hall Golf Club,** Beccles Road, Fritton, Great Yarmouth NR31 9EY (01493 488488; Fax: 01493 488561). *Location:* on A143 just north of the village of Fritton. Parkland. 9 holes (double tees), 6711 yards. S.S.S. 72. Floodlit driving range. *Green Fees:* weekdays £15.00 per round, £20.00 per day; weekends £20.00 per round, £25 per day. Fees reduced winter months. *Eating facilities:* bar, restaurant. *Visitors:* welcome at all times, starting sheets weekends and Bank Holidays. *Society Meetings:* welcome by arrangement. Professional: Frank Hill. General Manager: D. Brooks.

GREAT YARMOUTH. **Gorleston Golf Club,** Warren Road, Gorleston, Great Yarmouth NR31 6JT (01493 661082). *Location:* A12 Lowestoft to Great Yarmouth. Seaside links. 18 holes, 6400 yards. S.S.S. 71. *Green Fees:* weekdays £20.00; weekends and Public Holidays £25.00 (weekly £60.00). Reductions if playing with member. *Eating facilities:* restaurant/bars open seven days. *Visitors:* welcome, advisable to check in advance for details of restrictions. *Society Meetings:* catered for by prior arrangement (membership of recognised club required). Professional: Nick Brown (01493 662103). Secretary: C.B. Court (01493 661911).

GREAT YARMOUTH. **Great Yarmouth and Caister Golf Club,** Beach House, Caister-on-Sea, Great Yarmouth NR30 5TD (01493 720214). *Location:* A149 coast road, two miles north of Great Yarmouth. Links. 18 holes, 6235 yards. S.S.S. 70. Practice ground. *Green Fees:* £23.50, £15.00 after 3.30pm weekdays; £28.00, £18.00 after 3.30pm weekends. Members' guests 50 per cent. *Eating facilities:* full range of catering; bar. *Visitors:* welcome, not before 10.30am Saturdays and not before 11.30am Sundays. *Society Meetings:* catered for. Professional: R. Foster (01493 720421). Secretary: H.J. Harvey (01493 728699).

HELLESDON. **Royal Norwich Golf Club,** Drayton High Road, Hellesdon, Norwich NR6 5AH (01603 429928). *Location:* centre of city and thence by A1067 Fakenham or via Ring Road, then 500 yards along A1067. Mature parkland. 18 holes, 6603 yards. S.S.S. 72. Large practice ground. *Green Fees:* on request. *Eating facilities:* lunches and teas served at club. *Visitors:* welcome during week only, but must have membership card of a recognised golf club and a bona fide Handicap. *Society Meetings:* welcome on application. Professional: Gary Potter (01603 408459). General Manager: John Meggy.

HUNSTANTON. **Hunstanton Golf Club,** Golf Course Road, Old Hunstanton PE36 6JQ (01485 532811; Fax: 01485 532319). *Location:* off A149. Adjoins Old Hunstanton village, approximately half a mile north east of Hunstanton. Championship links course with excellent fast greens. 18 holes, 6670 yards. S.S.S. 72. Practice ground. *Green Fees:* weekdays £32.00; weekends £38.00. Special rates in winter, also after 4pm all year. Subject to review. *Eating facilities:* catering and bar facilities. *Visitors:* welcome but limited times available at weekends. Prior booking advisable. Visitors must be member of recognised golf club and hold a current Handicap. *Society Meetings:* welcome. Professional: J. Carter (01485 532751). Secretary: Malcolm Whybrow (01485 532811).

KING'S LYNN. **Eagles Golf Club,** 39 School Road, Tilney All Saints, King's Lynn PE34 4RS (01553 827147). *Location:* off A47 between King's Lynn and Wisbech. Parkland. 9 holes, 4284 yards. S.S.S. 61. Par 3 course, driving range, practice bunkers and putting green. *Green Fees:* weekdays £5.50 9 holes; weekends £6.50 9 holes. *Eating facilities:* bar/restaurant. *Visitors:* welcome, no restrictions. *Society Meetings:* apply to Secretary. Professional: Nigel Pickerall. Secretary: S.D. Faires (Tel & Fax: 01553 829777).

KING'S LYNN. **King's Lynn Golf Club,** Castle Rising, King's Lynn PE31 6BD (01553 631227). *Location:* four miles north-east of King's Lynn. Undulating wooded course. 18 holes, 6646 yards. S.S.S. 72. Practice areas. *Green Fees:* weekdays £30.00, weekends £38.00. *Eating facilities:* snacks, lunches, teas available; dinners by arrangement; two bars. *Visitors:* welcome on production of Handicap Certificate. *Society Meetings:* catered for by prior arrangement. Professional: C. Hanlon (01553 631655). Secretary: G.J. Higgins (01553 631654; Fax: 01553 631036).

KING'S LYNN. **Royal West Norfolk Golf Club,** Brancaster, Near King's Lynn PE31 8AX (01485 210223). *Location:* one mile off A149, Beach Road junction, seven miles east of Hunstanton. Seaside links. 18 holes, 6428 yards. S.S.S. 71. *Green Fees:* weekdays £32.00 per day; weekends £42.50 per day. *Eating facilities:* available. *Visitors:* all visitors must be members of a recognised Golf Club, hold an official Handicap and must make prior arrangements with the Secretary to play. No visitors prior to 10am Sundays and no visitors during last week in July and until first week in September. Professional: R.E. Kimber (01485 210616). Secretary: Major N.A. Carrington Smith (01485 210087).

NORWICH. **Barnham Broom Hotel, Golf and Country Club,** Honingham Road, Norwich NR9 4DD (01603 759393; Fax: 01603 358224). *Location:* A11 to Norwich follow brown tourist signs marked "Barnham Broom" from Wymondham; A47 to Norwich follow brown tourist signs, 10 miles from Norwich. River valley parkland and hill courses. Two courses: Valley – 18 holes, 6470 yards, S.S.S. 71; Hill – 18 holes, 6628 yards, S.S.S. 72. Practice facilities. *Green Fees:* weekdays £25 per round, £30 per day; weekends on application. *Eating facilities:* all day buffet/bar and full restaurant. *Visitors:* welcome anytime, on application at weekends. 52 bedroomed hotel (en suites). Golfing "Getaway Breaks", residential Peter Ballingall Golf Schools, overnight stay tuition breaks. *Society Meetings:* welcome on application. Professional: Steven Beckenham (01603 759393 ext. 279). Director of Golf: Peter Ballingall (01603 759393; Fax: 01603 758224).

NORWICH. **Bawburgh Golf Club,** Long Lane, Bawburgh, Norwich NR9 3LX (01603 746390; Fax: 01603 811110). *Location:* directly off the new Norwich Southern Bypass/rear Royal Norfolk Showground. Undulating heathland and parkland. 18 holes, 6066 yards. S.S.S. 69. Driving range – covered and floodlit, group tuition. *Green Fees:* weekdays £14.00, weekends £17.00 on application. *Eating facilities:* bar snacks and licensed bar. *Visitors:* restricted on weekend mornings and Bank Holidays, advisable to ring in advance. Ladies have preference Monday mornings. Membership of "The Buggy Club" for disabled golfers. *Society Meetings:* welcome on application. Professional: C. Potter (01603 742323). Secretary: R.J. Mapes (01953 606776). *

NORWICH. **Costessey Park Golf Course,** Old Costessey, Norwich NR8 5AL (01603 746333). *Location:* off the A47 Norwich to King's Lynn road, in the village of Old Costessey (adjacent to Norwich). Set in river valley with some parkland. 18 holes, 5964 yards. S.S.S. 69. Par 72. Practice area. *Green Fees:* information not provided. *Eating facilities:* bar and bar snacks; carvery and set meals available. *Visitors:* welcome anytime except weekends when visitors allowed only after 11.30am. Golf cart available for hire by physically handicapped golfers. *Society Meetings:* catered for by arrangement. Professional: Simon Cook (01603 747085). Secretary: Colin House. *

NORWICH. **Dunston Hall Golf Club,** Ipswich Road, Norwich NR14 8PQ (01508 470444; Fax: 01508 471499). *Location:* on Ipswich road A140. Parkland with many water features; USGA spec. greens. 10 holes, 6054 yards. S.S.S. 69. *Green Fees:* weekdays £15.00, weekends £18.00. 9 holes £7.50. *Eating facilities:* four eating places, two bars. *Visitors:* pay and play course, all welcome at any time. Accommodation available in 72-bedroom Hotel. *Society Meetings:* all welcome. Professional: Peter Briggs. Secretary: George Robertson-Burnett.

NORWICH. **Eaton (Norwich) Golf Club,** Newmarket Road, Norwich NR4 6SF (01603 452881). *Location:* half a mile from A11, approximately one and a half miles from Norwich city centre. Parkland course. 18 holes, 6135 yards. S.S.S. 69. Practice areas available. *Green Fees:* £28.00 weekdays, £35.00 weekends and Bank Holidays. *Eating facilities:* snacks, lunches; dinners by arrangement. *Visitors:* welcome; only after 11.30am weekends. Handicap Certificate required. *Society Meetings:* welcome, fees by arrangement. Professional: Mr Nigel Bundy (01603 452478). Secretary: Mr David Sochon (Tel & Fax: 01603 451686).

NORWICH. **Sprowston Park Golf Club,** Wroxham Road, Norwich NR7 8RP (01603 409188). *Location:* A1151 Norwich to Wroxham. Parkland with plenty of trees. 18 holes, 5982 yards. S.S.S. 70. Huge practice putting area, new bunkers, 27 bay driving range. *Green Fees:* weekdays £12.00 per round; weekends £15.00 per round. *Eating facilities:* Fairways Bar and Restaurant. *Visitors:* always welcome. *Society Meetings:*

catered for anytime with notice. Packages available. Professional: P.G. Grice PGA (01603 417264). Secretary: J.A. Butterfield (Mrs) (01603 410657; Fax: 01603 788884).

NORWICH. **Mundesley Golf Club,** Links Road, Mundesley, Norwich NR11 8ES (01263 720297). *Location:* one mile from village centre. Undulating fairly exposed parkland course with fine panoramic views. 9 holes, 5410 yards, 4949 metres. S.S.S. 66. Small practice area. *Green Fees:* on application. *Eating facilities:* full catering facilities. *Visitors:* welcome, but course reserved for members until 11.30am at weekends and 12 noon to 3.30pm Wednesday. *Society Meetings:* catered for, restriction as for visitors. Professional: T.G. Symmons (01831 455461). Secretary: Peter Hampel (01263 720095).

NORWICH. **Wensum Valley Golf Club,** Beech Avenue, Taverham, Norwich NR8 6HP (01603 261012). *Location:* 5 miles north of Norwich on the A1067 to Taverham. Two courses. Parkland and very picturesque set in the valley. Wensum Course – 4862 yards, 4447 metres. S.S.S. 66. Valley Course – 18 holes, 6000 yards, 5486 metres. S.S.S. 69. Driving range. *Green Fees:* weekdays £12.00; weekends £15.00. *Eating facilities:* full catering and bar facilities. *Visitors:* always welcome, restrictions at weekends and Bank Holidays. Accommodation for 14 people available. *Society Meetings:* all welcome; package available. Professional: Peter Briggs (01603 261012 extension 5). Secretary: Bridgette Todd (01603 261012 extension 2).

SHERINGHAM. **Sheringham Golf Club,** Weybourne Road, Sheringham NR26 8HG (01263 822038). *Location:* one mile west of town on Weybourne Road (A149). Clifftop course. 18 holes, 6464 yards. S.S.S. 71. Large practice area. *Green Fees:* weekdays £29.00; weekends and Bank Holidays £34.00. *Eating facilities:* full catering to order. *Visitors:* welcome, telephone first, with reservation for members of other clubs, Handicap Certificate required. Accommodation in Dormy House, details from Secretary. *Society Meetings:* catered for by prior arrangement with Secretary except weekends from 1st April to 31st October. Professional: R.H. Emery (01263 822980). Secretary: M.J. Garrett (01263 823488; Fax: 01263 825189).

SWAFFHAM. **Swaffham Golf Club,** Cley Road, Swaffham PE37 8AE (01760 721611). *Location:* two miles south-west of Swaffham Market Place (signposted) on Cley Road. Heathland course. 9 holes, 6252 yards. S.S.S. 70. Practice ground. *Green Fees:* £18.00 weekdays. *Eating facilities:* full catering except Mondays and Tuesdays, bar snacks all week. *Visitors:* welcome without reservation weekdays, weekends only if playing with member. *Society Meetings:* catered for subject to prior notice being given. Professional: Peter Field. Secretary: R. Joslin.

THETFORD. **Feltwell Golf Club,** Thor Avenue, Feltwell, Thetford. *Location:* off the A10, beside RAF Feltwell. Inland links – can be windy! 9 holes, 6175 yards. S.S.S. 69. Practice ground. *Green Fees:* weekdays £12.00; weekends £20.00. *Eating facilities:* cafeteria and bar. *Visitors:* welcome at all times but check with Secretary. *Society Meetings:* welcome by prior arrangement. Secretary: B. Munday (01842 827644).

THETFORD. **Richmond Park Golf Club,** Saham Road, Watton, Thetford IP25 6EA (01953 881803; Fax: 01953 881817). *Location:* half a mile north west of Watton town centre. Parkland. 18 holes, 6289 yards. S.S.S. 70. Driving range. *Green Fees:* weekdays £15.00 per round, £20.00 per day; weekends £20.00. £10.00 with a member. *Eating facilities:* bar, bar food, restaurant. *Visitors:* always welcome. Mini gym. *Society Meetings:* welcome, excellent facilities available. Professional: Alan Hemsley. Secretary: Group Capt E. Durham.

THETFORD. **Thetford Golf Club,** Brandon Road, Thetford IP24 3NE (01842 752258). *Location:* half a mile from A11. Wooded heathland course. 18 holes, 6879 yards. S.S.S. 73. *Green Fees:* £26.00 weekdays. *Eating facilities:* bar snacks, teas, meals available. *Visitors:* welcome weekdays. *Society Meetings:* catered for Wednesdays, Thursdays and Fridays if members of a golf club. Professional: N. Arthur (01842 752662). Secretary: R.J. Ferguson (01842 752169).

Northamptonshire

CORBY. **Corby Public Golf Course,** Priors Hall Complex, Corby (01536 400497). *Location:* off A43 Kettering to Stamford Road one mile east of village of Weldon. 18 holes, 6677 yards. S.S.S. 72. *Green Fees:* information not provided. *Eating facilities:* available, and licensed bar. *Society Meetings:* by arrangement with Professional. Professional: M. Summers (01536 60756). Secretary: Jack Marr. *

CORBY near. **Priors Hall Golf Club,** Stamford Road, Weldon, Near Corby NN17 3JH (01536 400497). *Location:* on the A43, four miles from Corby on the Stamford Road. 18 holes, 6700 yards. S.S.S. 72. Practice nets and ground. *Green Fees:* weekdays £7.35; weekends £8.75. *Eating facilities:* bar meals. *Visitors:* no restrictions midweek, booking system. *Society Meetings:* no restrictions midweek. Professional: Garry Brown (01536 60756). Secretary: J. Marr.

DAVENTRY. **Daventry and District Golf Club,** Norton Road, Daventry (01327 702829). 9 holes, 5812 yards. S.S.S. 67. *Green Fees:* weekdays £9.00; weekends £12.00. *Visitors:* welcome weekdays and weekends. Summer all welcome except Sunday before 11am. Professional: Mike Higgins. Secretary: F. Higham.

DAVENTRY. **Staverton Park Golf Club,** Daventry Road, Staverton, Near Daventry NN11 6JT (01327 705911; Fax: 01327 311428). *Location:* one mile from Daventry on A425 to Leamington Spa. Easy access from M1 Junctions 16 or 18. Undulating parkland. 18 holes, 6661 yards. S.S.S. 71. Driving range, practice range, two putting greens. Trimnasium trim track. *Green Fees:* on application. *Eating facilities:* full catering available at all times. *Visitors:* welcome, no restrictions. 100 bedroomed hotel with leisure facilities. Residential golf packages available. *Society Meetings:* welcome, please enquire about our Society Package. Professional: Richard Mudge (01327 705506). General Manager: N.J. Lucas.

HELLIDON. **Hellidon Lakes Golf Club,** Hellidon NN11 6LN (01327 62550; Fax: 01327 62559). *Location:* one and a half miles from A361, six miles from Daventry, 12 miles from Banbury. Parkland. 18 holes, 6700 yards. S.S.S. 72. Driving range, putting green. *Green Fees:* on application. *Eating facilities:* bar and restaurant. *Visitors:* always welcome, Handicap Certificates required at weekends. Hotel, leisure centre, tennis. *Society Meetings:* all welcome. Professional: Gary Wills (01327 62551). Secretary: Mrs J.A. Nicoll.

KETTERING. **Kettering Golf Club,** Headlands, Kettering NN15 6XA (01536 512074). *Location:* course is at south end of Headlands which is continuation from High Street. Flat parkland. 18 holes, 6035 yards, 5515 metres. S.S.S. 69. *Green Fees:* weekdays £22.00 day/round; weekends £10.00 with member only. *Eating facilities:* by prior arrangement. *Visitors:* welcome weekdays only. *Society Meetings:* catered for Wednesdays and Fridays only by arrangement. Professional: K. Theobald (01536 81014). Secretary: D.G. Buckby (01536 511104).

NORTHAMPTON. **Cold Ashby Golf Club,** Cold Ashby, Northampton NN6 7EP (Tel & Fax: 01604 740548). *Location:* midway between Rugby, Leicester and Northampton, with easy access M1 Junction 18. Undulating parkland. 18 holes, 6004 yards. S.S.S. 69. *Green Fees:* midweek £14.00 per round, £20.00 per day; weekends £16.00 per round. *Eating facilities:* meals and bar snacks available daily. *Visitors:* welcome midweek anytime, weekends after 2pm. *Society Meetings:* catered for weekdays. Professional: Shane Rose (01604 740099). Secretary: David Croxton.

NORTHAMPTON. **Collingtree Park Golf Course,** Windingbrook Lane, Northampton NN4 0XN (01604 700000; Fax: 01604 702600). *Location:* take Junction 15 off M1-A508 Northampton. 18 holes, 6692 yards. S.S.S. 72. 18th hole is an island green, set in parkland. Driving range. *Green Fees:* weekdays: £20.00 18 holes, £30.00 36 holes; weekends: £30.00 18 holes, £40.00 36 holes. *Eating facilities:* Conservatory Restaurant, à la carte and table d'hôte, and bar snacks at all times. *Visitors:* welcome – advised to book in advance, members only before 12.30pm at weekends. Handicap Certificates required. *Society Meetings:* welcome, corporate golf packages available. Golf Academy which includes two par 4 and one par 3 practice holes, as well as 16 driving range bays. Hi-tech indoor teaching rooms also. The finest teaching facility for golf, 5 special programmes available. Professional: John Cook. Secretary: Janice Byrne.

NORTHAMPTON. **Delapre Park Golf Club,** Eagle Drive, Nene Valley Way, Northampton NN4 0DU (01604 764036; Fax: 01604 763957). *Location:* two and a half miles from Junction 15 (M1), A45 to Wellingborough (exit at Swallow Hotel). Parkland. 18 holes, 6943 yards. S.S.S. 70. Additional 9 holes, 2146 yards. S.S.S. 32. Floodlit covered driving range, 40 bays; Par 3 courses, pitch and putt course. *Green Fees:* weekdays £7.30; weekends and Bank Holidays £9.50; 9 hole courses £5.00 weekdays; £6.00 weekends and Bank Holidays. Pitch and putt £1.20 weekdays; £1.40 weekends. Par 3 Courses £3.15 weekdays; £3.50 weekends. *Eating facilities:* meals available all day 9am to 9.30pm, bar – regular hours. *Visitors:* welcome without reservation, except 18 hole and 9 hole course. Start times bookable and must be paid and booked in advance unless vacancies occur on the day. *Society Meetings:* catered for by appointment and advance payment. Professional/Secretary: John Corby (Tel & Fax: 01604 763957).

NORTHAMPTON. **Kingsthorpe Golf Club,** Kingsley Road, Northampton NN2 7BU (01604 711173). *Location:* off M1 and A43. Undulating parkland. 18 holes, 6006 yards. S.S.S. 69. *Green Fees:* (provisional) weekdays £22.00 per round/day; weekends £10.00 per round/day (must play with member). *Eating facilities:* full catering. *Visitors:* welcome weekdays, but must have a Certificate of Handicap. Weekends must be guest of member. *Society Meetings:* catered for by arrangement Thursdays and Fridays only. Professional: Paul Armstrong (01604 719602). Secretary: P.L. Voke (01604 710610).

NORTHAMPTON. **Northampton Golf Club,** Harlestone, Northampton NN7 4EF (01604 845102). *Location:* on A428 north-west of the village of Harlestone. Parkland with a lake coming into play 16th and 18th holes. 18 holes, 6534 yards. S.S.S. 71. Practice ground. *Green Fees:* £25.00 weekdays, weekends must play with a member. *Eating facilities:* restaurant and bar snacks. *Visitors:* welcome weekdays but must have a Certificate of Handicap. *Society Meetings:* weekdays except Wednesdays. Inclusive packages available. Professional: Mark Chamberlain (01604 845167). Secretary: I.M. Kirkwood (01604 845155; Fax: 01604 820262).

NORTHAMPTON. **Northamptonshire County Golf Club,** Sandy Lane, Church Brampton, Northampton NN6 8AZ (01604 842170). *Location:* four miles north of Northampton between A50 and A428. Heathland with woods, gorse and stream. 18 holes, 6503 yards, 5946 metres. S.S.S. 71. Practice ground, indoor net. *Green Fees:* £35.00 (£10.00 with a member). *Eating facilities:* restaurant and bar. *Visitors:* by prior arrangement, must have Club Handicap. *Society Meetings:* catered for Wednesdays, small groups on Mondays and Thursdays. Professional: T. Rouse (01604 842226). Secretary: M.E. Wadley (01604 843025).

NORTHAMPTON. **Overstone Park Golf and Country Club,** The Watermark Club, Billing Lane, Northampton NN6 0AP (01604 671471; Fax: 01604 671109). *Location:* seven miles from Junction 15 M1 A508 merges with A45. Follow signs for Overstone from Billing Aerodrome turn-off. Undulating parkland with some water features. 18 holes, 6602 yards. S.S.S. 72. Practice ground. *Green Fees:* members' guests only except by prior appointment. *Eating facilities:* bar, brasserie/restaurant. *Visitors:* members' guests only except by prior appointment. Leisure Club. Professional: Brian Mudge. General Manager: Allan McLundie.

OUNDLE. **Oundle Golf Club,** Benfield Road, Oundle, Peterborough PE8 4EZ (01832 273267). *Location:* one mile from Oundle on Corby Road A447. Undulating course. 18 holes. *Green Fees:* weekdays £20.00 per day; weekends £30.00. *Eating facilities:* bar meals/restaurant. *Visitors:* welcome, after 10.30am weekends; check with Professional regarding tee availability. *Society Meetings:* welcome by arrangement. Professional: R. Keys (01832 272273). General Manager: A.J. Dobson.

RUSHDEN. **Rushden Golf Club,** Kimbolton Road, Chelveston, Wellingborough NN9 6AN (01933 312581). *Location:* on A45 two miles east of Higham Ferrers. Undulating parkland. 10 holes, 6335 yards. S.S.S. 70. Small practice area. *Green Fees:* £15.00 per round/day, £10.00 with member. *Eating facilities:* bar and dining area – no catering Mondays. *Visitors:* welcome except Wednesday afternoons, weekends must play with member. *Society Meetings:* small societies catered for weekdays. Secretary: E.W. Richardson (01933 314910).

TOWCESTER near. **Farthingstone Golf Club,** Farthingstone, Near Towcester NN12 8NA (01327 361291; Fax: 01327 361645). *Location:* just a few minutes from Junction 16 of the M1, close to A5 and A45. Picturesque rolling countryside enfolded between mature woods. 18 holes, 6298 yards. S.S.S. 71. *Green Fees:* weekdays £7.50; weekends £12.50. *Eating facilities:* real ale bar, carvery restaurant. *Visitors:* welcome at all times. Golf cars for hire. 16 bedroomed hotel, pool, snooker, squash. *Society Meetings:* welcome weekdays.

TOWCESTER near. **West Park Golf and Country Club,** Whittlebury, Near Towcester NN12 8XW (01327 858092; Fax: 01327 858009). *Location:* 15 minutes from M1 and M40, from A43, via Whittlebury. 36-hole championship quality course, comprising three standard 9-holes and a dedicated 9-hole Academy Course. Mature oak parkland with freshwater lakes and ancient copses. Large range practice ground plus unique 9-hole Indoor Golf Course. *Green Fees:* weekdays £20.00 per round; weekends/Bank Holidays £25.00. *Eating facilities:* bar/bistro within clubhouse plus special function suites. *Visitors:* 'pay and play' or corporate guests welcome seven days. Other sports and activities offered. Accommodation planned. *Society Meetings:* welcome seven days, by arrangement. Secretary: Robert L. Jones. *Bookings:* please contact Events Management team on (01327 858092). *

WELLINGBOROUGH. **Wellingborough Golf Club,** Great Harrowden Hall, Wellingborough NN9 5AD (01933 673022). *Location:* one mile out of Wellingborough on A509, turn right at crossroads by Great Harrowden Church. Undulating parkland. 18 holes, 6617 yards, 6039 metres. S.S.S. 72. Practice ground. *Green Fees:* £22.00 per round, £27.00 per day weekdays; weekends as member's guest only. *Eating facilities:* bar with casual lunch or dinner menu, restaurant. *Visitors:* weekdays only by appointment and with Handicap Certificate. *Society Meetings:* welcome by appointment. Conference facilities available. Professional: David Clifford (01933 678752). Secretary: Roy Tomlin (01933 677234).

Northumberland

ALNMOUTH. **Alnmouth Golf Club Ltd,** Foxton Hall, Lesbury, Alnwick NE66 3BE (01665 830687). *Location:* four miles east of Alnwick. 18 holes, 6414 yards, 5855 metres. S.S.S. 71. *Green Fees:* weekdays £25.00. *Eating facilities:* diningroom and bars. *Visitors:* welcome Mondays, Tuesdays, Thursdays by prior arrangement, Handicap Certificate required. Dormy House accommodation available. *Society Meetings:* maximum numbers 30 catered for on Mondays, Tuesdays and Thursdays only. Secretary: Charles Jobson (01665 830231).

ALNMOUTH. **Alnmouth Village Golf Club,** Marine Road, Alnmouth (01665 830370; Fax: 01665 603395). *Location:* leave A1 from Alnwick to Alnmouth. Seaside links course. 9 holes, 6090 yards, 5572 metres. S.S.S. 70. *Green Fees:* weekdays £15.00 per 18 holes; weekends £20.00 per 18 holes. *Eating facilities:* available. *Visitors:* welcome, restrictions on club competition days. *Society Meetings:* book in advance and only with official Golf Club Handicaps. Secretary: W. MacLean (01665 602096).

ALNWICK. **Alnwick Golf Club,** Swansfield Park, Alnwick (01665 602632). *Location:* south-west of town, top of Swansfield Park Road, off A1. Mature wooded parkland. 9 holes (extending to 18 holes for 1994), 5387 yards. S.S.S. 66. *Green Fees:* weekdays £10.00 per round, £15.00 per day; weekends and Bank Holidays £15.00 per round, £20.00 per day. Half price with member at any time. *Eating facilities:* available on request; bar. *Visitors:* welcome without reservation, some restrictions on competition days. *Society Meetings:* welcome by prior arrangement. Secretary: L.E. Stewart (01665 602499). *

ALNWICK. **Dunstanburgh Castle Golf Club,** Embleton, Alnwick NE66 3XQ (01665 576562). *Location:* seven miles off A1, to the north-east of Alnwick. Seaside links course in area of outstanding natural beauty. Designed by James Braid. 18 holes, 6298 yards. S.S.S. 70. *Green Fees:* weekdays £12.50 per day; weekends £16.00 per round, £18.50 per day. *Eating facilities:* snacks, lunches, high teas; bar. *Visitors:* welcome without reservation. Clubs for hire. *Society Meetings:* catered for. Secretary: P.F.C. Gilbert.

BAMBURGH. **Bamburgh Castle Golf Club,** Bamburgh NE69 7DE (01668 214378). *Location:* midway between Alnwick and Berwick upon Tweed on A1, take B1341 or B1342 to Bamburgh village. Seaside links course with outstanding views of Farne Islands, Holy Island and magnificent coastal area. 18 holes, 5621 yards, 5132 metres. S.S.S. 67. Practice area. *Green Fees:* weekdays £25.00 per round, £30.00 per day; weekends and Bank Holidays £30.00 per round, £35.00 per day. Five-day weekday ticket £60.00. Reductions if playing with member. All rates reduced for Juniors. *Eating facilities:* bar snacks, lunch, tea/coffee, etc. *Visitors:* welcome, with members only conpetitions days and Bank Holidays. *Society Meetings:* welcome, by written application. Secretary: T.C. Osborne (01668 214321).

BEDLINGTON. **Bedlingtonshire Golf Club,** Acorn Bank, Bedlington NE22 6AA (01670 822457). *Location:* one mile south west of Bedlington on A1068. Parkland. 18 holes, 6546 metres. S.S.S. 73. Practice ground and putting green. *Green Fees:* weekdays £13.00 per round, £17.00 per day; weekends £16.00 per round, £19.00 per day (estimated). *Eating facilities:* catering available seven days a week. *Visitors:* welcome, but not before 10.30am weekends. *Society Meetings:* welcome, contact the Professional. Professional: Marcus Webb (01670 822087). Secretary: A.J. Gray (01670 826235).

BELFORD. **Belford Golf Club,** South Road, Belford NE70 7DP (01668 213433). *Location:* turn off A1 at sign for Belford, first turning on right. Parkland. 9 holes, 6304 yards, 5768 metres. S.S.S. 70. Floodlit driving range. *Green Fees:* weekdays £13.00 per round, £16.00 per day; weekends £15.00 per round, £20.00 per day. *Eating facilities:* meals and bar seven days a week. *Visitors:* welcome after 10am. *Society Meetings:* welcome. Secretary: A.M. Gilhome (01668 213587).

BERWICK-UPON-TWEED. **Berwick-upon-Tweed (Goswick) Golf Club,** Beal, Berwick-upon-Tweed TD15 2RW (01289 387256). *Location:* signposted off A1, seven miles south of Berwick-upon-Tweed. Seaside links. 18 holes, 6500 yards, 4070 metres. S.S.S. 71. Practice ground. *Green Fees:* weekdays £18.00 per round, £24.00 per day; weekends £32.00 per day, £24.00 per round. Special rate for parties of 20 plus. *Eating facilities:* full restaurant, bar – Mondays soup and sandwiches only. *Visitors:* welcome, must book at weekends. *Society Meetings:* welcome weekdays only. Professional: P. Terras (01289 387380). Secretary: A.E. French (01289 387256).

BERWICK-UPON-TWEED. **Magdalene Fields Golf Club,** Magdalene Fields, Berwick-upon-Tweed TD15 1NE (01289 306384). *Location:* approximately 700 yards from town centre. Seaside, parkland course in clifftop setting. 18 holes, 6300 yards. S.S.S. 71. Practice area. *Green Fees:* weekdays £18.00; weekends £20.00. Discount for party bookings. Fees subject to review. *Eating facilities:* bar and eating facilities. *Visitors:* welcome Monday to Saturday, restrictions on Sundays. *Society Meetings:* all welcome. Club Manager: M. Lynch (01289 330700). Secretary: P.J. Rae (01289 304452).

BLYTH. **Blyth Golf Club Ltd,** New Delaval, Blyth NE24 9DB (01670 367728). *Location:* 12 miles north of Newcastle near the coast. Flat parkland, water hazards. 18 holes, 6533 yards, 6300 metres. S.S.S. 71.

Large practice area. *Green Fees:* £16.00 per round, £18.00 per day (with a member £6.00) weekdays; weekends only with a member £6.00. *Eating facilities:* bar and full catering. *Visitors:* welcome weekdays before 3pm, weekends with member only. *Society Meetings:* welcome weekdays only by prior arrangement. Professional: Mr P. Chapman (01670 356514). Secretary: Miss J. Tate (01670 540110).

CARLISLE. **Haltwhistle Golf Course,** Banktop, Greenhead, Via Carlisle (016977 47367). *Location:* off the A69 at the village of Greenhead, two and a half miles west of Haltwhistle. Undulating parkland course with wooded areas. 12 holes, 6154 yards over 18 holes. S.S.S. 69. Practice area. *Green Fees:* £10.00 per day. £30.00 weekly ticket for bona fide holidaymakers. *Eating facilties:* clubhouse bar, catering by prior arrangement. *Visitors:* welcome, no restrictions except on club competition days when course is closed until 4pm. *Society Meetings:* welcome by arrangement. Professional: Joe Metcalfe. Secretary: Bill Barnes (01434 320337).

HEXHAM. **Allendale Golf Club,** High Studdon, Allenheads Road, Allendale, Hexham. *Location:* 10 miles south of Hexham on B6295. Parkland course, hilly but not too severe. 9 holes, 5044 yards. S.S.S. 65. Driving net and putting green. *Green Fees:* weekdays £5.00; weekends and Bank Holidays £7.00. Special rates for visiting parties. *Eating facilities:* no catering apart from tea-making facilities, but several good hotels and pubs in Allendale. *Visitors:* welcome anytime except Sunday mornings and August Bank Holiday Monday. *Society Meetings:* catered for by arrangement. Secretary: Jim Hall (0191-267 5875).

HEXHAM. **Bellingham Golf Club,** Boggle Hole, Bellingham, Hexham NE48 2DT (01434 220152). *Location:* four miles west of A68. Parkland with panoramic views of North Tyne Valley. 9 holes (18 tees), 5245 yards. S.S.S. 66. Large practice ground. *Green Fees:* weekdays £10.00; weekends and Bank Holidays £15.00. *Eating facilities:* meals available. *Visitors:* welcome, no visitors till 5pm Sundays and all visitors must adhere to starting sheet when in operation. *Society Meetings:* welcome midweek and Saturdays by prior booking. Secretary: Mr R. Calladine (01434 220530).

HEXHAM. **Hexham Golf Club,** Spital Park, Hexham NE46 3RZ (01434 602057). *Location:* 20 miles west of Newcastle upon Tyne, one mile west of Hexham town centre. 18 holes, 6272 yards. S.S.S. 70. *Green Fees:* weekdays £20.00; weekends and Bank Holidays £26.00. *Eating facilities:* lunch, high tea and dinner. *Visitors:* welcome without reservation. Preliminary booking advisable. *Society Meetings:* catered for Monday to Friday by arrangement. Professional: M.W. Forster (01434 604904). Secretary: J.C. Oates (01434 603072; Fax: 01434 601865).

HEXHAM. **Tynedale Golf Club,** Tynegreen, Hexham (01434 608154). *Location:* off A69 towards Hexham over Tyne Bridge; immediate right along riverside. Flat, private course owned by Tynedale Council. 9 holes, 5640 yards. S.S.S. 67. *Green Fees:* weekdays £10.00; weekends £12.00. Reductions for Juniors and Senior Citizens. *Eating facilities:* full catering available. *Visitors:* welcome, restricted Sunday mornings 7.30am to 11am. *Society Meetings:* welcome. Professional: C. Brown. Secretary: J. McDiarmid.

MATFEN. **Matfen Hall Golf Club,** Matfen (01661 886500). *Location:* 15 miles west of Newcastle, five miles north of Corbridge, off B6318 (Military Road). Lovely parkland setting directly in front of Matfen Hall, with natural and added water hazards. 18 holes, 6711 yards. Range and practice ground. *Green Fees:* on application. *Eating facilities:* bar, dining room. *Visitors:* very welcome any day, no restrictions. Ladies' and Gents' locker rooms, Pro's shop. *Society Meetings:* very welcome, no restrictions. Director of Golf: John Harrison.

MORPETH. **Burgham Park Golf and Country Club,** Near Felton, Morpeth NE65 8QP (01670 787898). *Location:* seven miles north of Morpeth, one mile west of A1 on Longhorsley Road. 18 holes, 6751 yards. S.S.S. 72. *Green Fees:* on application. *Eating facilities:* catering and bar available daily. *Visitors:* welcome; special rates for parties by arrangement. Professional: Steve McNally. Secretary: Jim Carr (Fax: 01670 787164).

MORPETH. **Swarland Hall Golf Club,** Coast View, Swarland, Morpeth NE65 9JG (01670 787940). *Location:* approximately one mile west of A1 trunk road, eight miles south of Alnwick. Undulating parkland course beside mature woodland. 18 holes, 6628 yards, 6060 metres. S.S.S. 72. *Green Fees:* Mondays to Saturdays £15.00 per round, Sundays £20.00. *Eating facilities:* full dining facilities, bar meals, licensed bar. *Visitors:* welcome Mondays to Saturdays, Sundays restricted to playing with members. *Society Meetings:* welcome. Secretary: K.S. Rutter.

MORPETH. **The Morpeth Golf Club (1992) Ltd.,** The Common, Morpeth NE61 2BT (01670 519980). *Location:* turn off A1 for Morpeth, A167 south side of town. Easy walking parkland. 18 holes, 6206 yards. S.S.S. 69. Practice area. *Green Fees:* weekdays £20.00 per round, £25.00 per day; weekends £25.00 per round, £33.00 per day. Weekly ticket £80, fortnightly ticket £150. *Eating facilities:* restaurant/bar meals/ snacks etc. *Visitors:* welcome, weekdays after 9.30am, Handicap Certificates may be asked for. *Society Meetings:* catered for weekdays by prior arrangement. discounts available for large parties. Professional: M.R. Jackson (01670 515675; Fax: 01670 512065). Secretary: K.D. Cazaly (01670 504942; Fax: 01670 504918).

MORPETH. **Warkworth Golf Club,** The Links, Warkworth, Morpeth NE65 0SW (01665 711596). *Location:* off A1 to B6345 at Felton, on to A1068 to Warkworth. Links course. 9 holes, 5817 yards. S.S.S. 66 (Medal 68). Practice area. *Green Fees:* weekdays £12.00 per day; weekends £20.00 per day. Half price with member. *Eating facilities:* by arrangement with Stewardess. *Visitors:* welcome except Tuesdays and Saturdays. *Society Meetings:* welcome by arrangement. Secretary: J.W. Anderson (01665 575608).

NEWBIGGIN-BY-THE-SEA. **Newbiggin-by-the-Sea Golf Club,** Clubhouse, Prospect Place, Newbiggin-by-the-Sea NE64 6DW (01670 817344). *Location:* take signpost for Newbiggin off A189 (spine road from Tyne Tunnel). Clubhouse at most easterly point of village, adjacent to Church Point Caravan Park. Seaside links. 18 holes, 6452 yards. S.S.S. 71. Practice area. *Green Fees:* weekdays £12.00, £8.00 with a member; weekends £17.00, £12.00 with a member. *Eating facilities:* bar, lounge bar, dining room. *Visitors:* welcome, not before 10am or on competition days, check by telephone with Professional. *Society Meetings:* catered for by prior arrangement with Secretary. Professional: D. Fletcher (01670 817833). Secretary: G.B. Walker (01670 811972).

NEWCASTLE. **Arcot Hall Golf Club Ltd,** Arcot Hall, Dudley, Cramlington NE23 7QP (0191-236 2794). *Location:* seven miles north of Newcastle. Turn off A1 for Ashington and then signposted. Flat, parkland – mostly tree lined. 18 holes, 6389 yards, 5840 metres. S.S.S. 70. Practice ground, chipping area, putting green. *Green Fees:* weekdays £25.00; weekends £28.00 by invitation only. *Eating facilities:* good restaurant, bar. *Visitors:* welcome, small parties only Fridays (Ladies' Day) and with a member only weekends. *Society Meetings:* catered for on application to Secretary. Professional: Graham Cant (0191-236 2147). Secretary: J.M. Forteath QGM (0191-236 2794).

NEWCASTLE-UPON-TYNE. **Ponteland Golf Club,** Bell Villas, Ponteland, Newcastle-upon-Tyne NE20 9BD (01661 822689). *Location:* A696, one and a half miles north of Newcastle Airport. Parkland. 18 holes, 6524 yards. S.S.S. 71. Large practice area. *Green Fees:* £22.50 per day or round (inclusive VAT). *Eating facilities:* full menu in restaurant and bar. *Visitors:* welcome Monday to Thursday, must be member's guest Friday, weekends and Bank Holidays. Handicap Certificate required. *Society Meetings:* Tuesdays or Thursdays, catered for with pre-booking agreed by Secretary/Manager. Professional: Alan Crosby (01661 822689). Secretary: Mr John Hillyer (01661 822689).

PRUDHOE. **Prudhoe Golf Club,** Eastwood Park, Prudhoe NE42 5DX (01661 832466). *Location:* 10 miles west of Newcastle upon Tyne, A695 to Hexham. Undulating parkland, highly rated course. 18 holes, 5856 yards, 5319 metres. S.S.S. 68. Large practice area. *Green Fees:* £20.00 weekdays; £25.00 weekends after 4.30pm only. Special rates for parties over 20. *Eating facilities:* bar snacks, dining room and evening meals. *Visitors:* welcome midweek with reservation (contact Professional); weekends after 4.30pm. *Society Meetings:* catered for weekdays with prior booking. Professional: John Crawford (01661 836188). Secretary: G.B. Garratt. Bookings Secretary: W. Wray.

ROTHBURY. **Rothbury Golf Club,** Old Race Course, Thorpton Road, Rothbury, Morpeth NE65 7TR (01669 21271). *Location:* 15 miles north of Morpeth, take A697 turn off at Weldon Bridge for Rothbury. Flat course on Haugh alongside river. 9 holes, 5560 yards. S.S.S. 67. *Green Fees:* £11.00 weekdays, £16.00 weekends. *Eating facilities:* bar open 11am to 2.30pm and 7.30pm to 11pm, bar meals and snacks available at lunchtimes only. *Visitors:* welcome during weekdays, but limited at weekends due to club competitions. *Society Meetings:* catered for weekdays by arrangement only. Hon. Secretary: W.T. Bathgate (01669 20718).

SEAHOUSES. **Seahouses Golf Club,** Beadnell Road, Seahouses NE68 7XT (01665 720794). *Location:* 15 miles north of Alnwick, turn off A1 for B1340. Flat seaside links with water hazards. 18 holes, 5462 yards. S.S.S. 67. Practice ground. *Green Fees:* weekdays £15.00 per day; weekends £20.00 per day. Juniors under 16 half rates. *Eating facilities:* full catering and bar. *Visitors:* welcome with no restrictions, please telephone clubhouse. *Society Meetings:* by arrangement. Secretary: J.A. Stevens (01665 720809).

PUBLISHER'S NOTE

While every effort is made to ensure accuracy, we regret that FHG Publications cannot accept responsibility for errors, omissions or misrepresentation in our entries or any consequences thereof. Prices in particular should be checked because we go to press early. We will follow up complaints, but cannot act as arbiters or agents for either party.

STOCKSFIELD. **Stocksfield Golf Club,** New Ridley, Stocksfield NE43 7RE (01661 843041). *Location:* 15 miles west of Newcastle on A69, and three miles east of A68. Wooded parkland. 18 holes, 5978 yards. S.S.S. 70. Practice area. *Green Fees:* weekdays £15.00 per round, £20.00 per day; weekends and Bank Holidays £20.00 per round. *Eating facilities:* available, also bar. *Visitors:* welcome except Wednesday mornings and not until 4.30pm Saturdays. *Society Meetings:* catered for by prior arrangement. Professional: Stephen McKenna. Secretary: W. Martin.

TYNEMOUTH. **Tynemouth Golf Club Ltd,** Spital Dene, Tynemouth (0191 257 4578). *Location:* on A695. 18 holes, 6403 yards. S.S.S. 71. *Green Fees:* weekdays £20.00; weekends and Bank Holidays must be signed in and play with a member. *Eating facilities:* lunches and high teas served at club. *Visitors:* welcome with reservation. *Society Meetings:* catered for. Professional: John McKenna. Secretary: W. Storey.

WOOLER. **Wooler Golf Club,** Dod Law, Doddington, Wooler. *Location:* situated on the high ground named Dod Law to the east of the B6525 Wooler – Berwick road. The route is signposted from Doddington village. 9 holes (18 tees), 6358 yards. S.S.S. 70. Limited practice area. *Green Fees:* weekdays £10.00 per day; weekends and Bank Holidays £15.00 per day. Juniors £2.00 per round. Sunday parties (10 plus) £12.50 per day. *Eating facilities:* bar open evenings (operated voluntarily). *Visitors:* always welcome except during all day competitions, check with Secretary. *Society Meetings:* welcome by arrangement with Secretary. Secretary: (01668 281956).

Nottinghamshire

BRAMCOTE. **Bramcote Hills Golf Course,** Thoresby Road, off Derby Road, Bramcote NG9 3EP (0115 928 1880). *Location:* A52 Nottingham to Derby road, close to Bramcote Leisure Centre. Parkland. 18 holes, 1500 yards. *Green Fees:* weekdays £4.90; weekends £5.40. *Eating facilities:* refreshments available. *Visitors:* always welcome anytime, pay and play course. *Society Meetings:* welcome.

BULWELL. **Bulwell Forest Golf Club,** Hucknall Road, Bulwell (0115 977 0576) *Location:* A610 north of Nottingham, M1 Junction 26, three miles from course. Parkland, very tight course. 18 holes, 5572 yards. S.S.S. 67. *Green Fees:* weekdays £6.50; weekends £8.10. *Eating facilities:* meals served at all times. *Visitors:* welcome except Tuesdays and weekends, time sheets in operation every day. *Society Meetings:* catered for, but book well in advance. Professional: C. D. Hall (0115 976 3172). Secretary: D. Stubbs. *

CALVERTON. **Ramsdale Park Golf Centre,** The Clubhouse, Oxton Road, Calverton NG14 6NU (01602 655600; Fax: 01602 654105). *Location:* course alongside B6386 between Calverton and Oxton north east of Nottingham. Flat first 9 holes then undulating back 9. Two courses: High Course – 18 holes, 6546 yards, 5985 metres. S.S.S. 71. Low Course – 18 holes, 2844 yards. S.S.S. 54. 25 bay floodlit driving range. *Green Fees:* High Course £12.00; Low Course £6.50. *Eating facilities:* bar food always available, also large dining room. *Visitors:* welcome, pay as you play; small membership. No Handicap required. Advance booking required for High Course. *Society Meetings:* welcome. Professional: Robert Macey. Secretary: Brian Jenkinson.

EAST LEAKE. **Rushcliffe Golf Club,** Stocking Lane, East Leake, Near Loughborough LE12 5RL (01509 852209). *Location:* on A60 signposted eight miles south of Nottingham. Wooded hills on edge of the Wolds. 18 holes, 6057 yards, 5539 metres. S.S.S. 70. Practice ground. *Green Fees:* weekdays £22.00; weekends £25.00. *Eating facilities:* full catering except Mondays when bar snacks only. *Visitors:* welcome with reservation, weekends without a member between 9.30am to 11am and 3pm to 4.30pm. *Society Meetings:* catered for Mondays, Wednesdays, Thursdays and Fridays strictly by prior booking. Professional: Tim Smart (01509 852701). Secretary: D.J. Barnes (01509 852959).

EDWALTON. **Edwalton Municipal Golf and Social Club,** Wellin Lane, Edwalton (0115 923 4713). *Location:* follow Nottingham ring road, course signposted from island on ring road. Gently sloping parkland. 9 holes, 3342 yards. S.S.S. 72. Also 9 hole par 3 course. Large practice ground. *Green Fees:* £4.30 for 9 holes. Senior Citizens, disabled and UB40's £2.60 before 5pm, weekdays only. Par 3 course £2.40, special rate £1.50. *Eating facilities:* first class catering, bar open all day. *Visitors:* welcome anytime except club competitions (contact Professional for dates). Professional: J.A. Staples (0115 923 4775). Secretary: K. Platkin (0115 952 4634).

KIRKBY-IN-ASHFIELD. **Notts. Golf Club Ltd,** Hollinwell, Kirkby-in-Ashfield, Nottingham NG17 7QR (01623 753225). *Location:* three miles from Exit 27 on M1, turn off M1 then left on A611. Testing heathland championship course. 18 holes, 7020 yards. S.S.S. 74. *Green Fees:* on application. *Visitors:* welcome on production of Handicap Certificate (weekends and Bank Holidays with member only). Advisable to book beforehand. *Society Meetings:* catered for Mondays and Tuesdays. Professional: Brian Waites. Secretary: S.F.C. Goldie.

LONG EATON. **Trent Lock Golf Centre,** Lock Lane, Sawley, Long Eaton NG10 3DD (0115 9464398; Fax: 0115 9461183). *Location:* Sawley/Long Eaton. Set in rural countryside, with six lakes and River Trent. 18 holes, 6300 yards. S.S.S. 72. 24-bay floodlit driving range. *Green Fees:* £8.50. *Eating facilities:* à la carte restaurant (0115 9461184), bar food, 200-seater function room. *Visitors:* welcome anytime. *Society Meetings:* all welcome. Professional: Mark Taylor. Director of Golf: E.W. McCausland.

MANSFIELD. **Coxmoor Golf Club,** Coxmoor Road, Sutton in Ashfield, Mansfield NG17 5LF (01623 559878). *Location:* exit Junction 27 M1, A611 for three miles. Heathland, undulating. 18 holes, 6251 yards, 5944 metres. S.S.S. 72. Practice area and nets. *Green Fees:* weekdays 27/36 holes £30.00, 18 holes £22.00. *Eating facilities:* restaurant and bars. *Visitors:* welcome except weekends and Bank Holidays, pre-book through Professional. (Tuesday Ladies' Day). *Society Meetings:* catered for by prior application to Secretary. Professional: David Ridley (01623 559906). Secretary: Ian McDonald (01623 557359).

MANSFIELD. **Mansfield Woodhouse Golf Club,** Leeming Lane North, Mansfield Woodhouse NG19 9EU (01623 23521). *Location:* Junction 27 of M1, A60 Mansfield-Warsop. Flat parkland. 9 holes, 2446 yards. S.S.S. 64. *Green Fees:* £2.95 9 holes, £4.30 18 holes. *Eating facilities:* bar snacks. *Visitors:* welcome, unrestricted – pay and play. Professional: L. Highfield Jnr. (01623 23521). Secretary: T. Mason.

MANSFIELD. **Sherwood Forest Golf Club,** Eakring Road, Mansfield NG18 3EW (01623 23327). *Location:* leave M1 at Exit 27, take signs for Mansfield, proceed via Southwell Road and Oak Tree Lane. Traditional heathland course designed by James Braid (Championship standard). 18 holes, 6710 yards. S.S.S. 73. Two practice grounds. *Green Fees:* weekdays £30.00 per round, £35.00 per day; weekends and Bank Holidays £35.00 per round. *Eating facilities:* two dining rooms, gents' bar and mixed lounge. *Visitors:* welcome Mondays, Thursdays and Fridays, must be member of a golf club with a handicap. *Society Meetings:* catered for Mondays, Thursdays and Fridays. Professional: K. Hall (Tel & Fax: 01623 27403). Secretary: K. Hall (01623 26689; Fax: 01623 27403).

MAPPERLEY. **Mapperley Golf Club,** Central Avenue, Plains Road, Mapperley NG3 5RH (01602 265611). *Location:* B684, four miles north east of centre of Nottingham. Hilly picturesque course. 18 holes, 6283 yards. S.S.S. 70. Practice ground. *Green Fees:* weekdays £17.00 per round (with a member £11.00), £20.00 per day; weekends £19.00 per round (with a member £14.00), £22.00 per day. *Eating facilities:* bar open all day. *Visitors:* welcome except on match and competition days; Ladies' Day Tuesdays. *Society Meetings:* catered for. Professional: Paul Richmond (01602 202227). Secretary: A. Newton.

NEWARK. **Newark Golf Club,** Coddington, Newark NG24 2QX (01636 626241). *Location:* off the A17 Sleaford road four miles east of Newark. Parkland, wooded course. 18 holes, 6486 yards. S.S.S. 71. Practice ground. *Green Fees:* £22.50 weekdays; weekends £28.00. *Eating facilities:* full catering, bar all day. *Visitors:* welcome with reservation. Handicap Certificates will be required. Restriction at peak times Saturday and Sunday, Ladies' Day Tuesday. Snooker. Professional tuition and computer/video analysis. *Society Meetings:* welcome except Tuesdays, weekends. Booking fee payable. Professional: H.A. Bennett (01636 626492). Secretary: A.W. Morgans (01636 626282).

NOTTINGHAM. **Beeston Fields Golf Club,** Old Drive, Wollaton Road, Beeston NG9 3DD (0115 925 7062). *Location:* Wollaton road off A52 Derby road, M1, Exit 25. Parkland. 18 holes, 6414 yards. S.S.S. 71. Practice ground and net available. *Green Fees:* weekdays £20.00; weekends £30.00. *Eating facilities:* available daily. *Visitors:* welcome with reservation, Tuesday not until 2.30pm. *Society Meetings:* catered for Mondays and Wednesdays. Professional: Alun Wardle (0115 922 0872). Secretary: J. Lewis (0115 925 7062).

NOTTINGHAM. **Chilwell Manor Golf Club,** Meadow Lane, Chilwell, Nottingham NG9 5AE (0115 925 8958). *Location:* four miles from Nottingham on main Nottingham to Birmingham road. 18 holes, 6379 yards. S.S.S. 70. *Green Fees:* £18.00. *Eating facilities:* available. *Visitors:* welcome weekdays with reservation, restricted at certain busy times. *Society Meetings:* societies catered for by appointment (minimum 30). Professional: P. Wilson. Hon. Secretary: G.A. Spindley.

NOTTINGHAM. **Nottingham City Golf Club,** Lawton Drive, Bulwell, Nottingham NG6 8BL (0115 927 8021). *Location:* exit 26 M1, at first roundabout follow signs for Bulwell. Parkland. 18 holes, 6218 yards. S.S.S. 70. Practice area. *Green Fees:* weekdays £8.00 per round; weekends £10.00. *Eating facilities:* available. *Visitors:* welcome, Saturdays to 2pm – telephone for times. *Society Meetings:* welcome by prior arrangement. Professional: C.R. Jepson (0115 927 2767). Secretary: Laurie Whyte (0115 927 6916 mornings). *

NOTTINGHAM. **Ruddington Grange Golf Club,** Wilford Road, Ruddington, Nottingham NG11 6NB (01602 214139). *Location:* M1 Junction 24 Nottingham road, A52 to Nottingham Knight island, right to Ruddington, half a mile outside Ruddington. Parkland. 18 holes, 6543 yards, 5984 metres. S.S.S. 72. *Green Fees:* weekdays £15.00; weekends £20.00. *Eating facilities:* full restaurant. *Visitors:* welcome all the time but at weekends members have priority. *Society Meetings:* welcome. Professional: Richard Daibell (01602 211951). Secretary: A.R. Dessaur (01602 846141).

NOTTINGHAM. **Wollaton Park Golf Club,** Wollaton Park, Nottingham (01602 787574). *Location:* turning off Ring Road Middleton Boulevard. 18 holes, 6545 yards. S.S.S. 71. *Green Fees:* weekdays £19.00 per round, weekends £22.00 per round. *Eating facilities:* meals and bar snacks available. *Visitors:* welcome, contact Professional for availability. *Society Meetings:* catered for Tuesdays and Fridays. Professional: J. Lower (01602 784834). Secretary: O.B. Kirk.

RADCLIFFE-ON-TRENT. **Radcliffe-on-Trent Golf Club,** Dewberry Lane, Cropwell Road, Radcliffe-on-Trent NG12 2JH (01602 333000). *Location:* A52 from Nottingham turn right at traffic lights on Cropwell Road. Flat, wooded parkland. 18 holes, 6423 yards. S.S.S. 71. Two large practice areas. *Green Fees:* weekdays £21.00 per day, weekends £26.00 per day (reductions for members' guests). *Eating facilities:* snacks, meals and bar. *Visitors:* welcome, confirm course availability with Professional or Secretary. *Society Meetings:* catered for on Wednesdays. Professional: Robert Ellis (01602 332396). Secretary: Les Wake (01602 333000).

RETFORD. **Retford Golf Club Ltd,** Brecks Road, Ordsall, Retford DN22 7UA (01777 703733). *Location:* south off A620 midway between Worksop and Gainsborough. Wooded parkland. 18 holes, 6301 yards. S.S.S. 70. Practice ground. *Green Fees:* weekdays £16.00 per round (£8.00 with a member), £20.00 per day; weekends and Bank Holidays £10.00 (must be accompanied by a member). *Eating facilities:* bar, meals available at the club. *Visitors:* welcome but advisable to telephone beforehand; weekends with member only. *Society Meetings:* welcome by prior arrangement weekdays only. Professional: S. Betteridge (01777 703733). Secretary: A. Harrison (01777 860682).

SOUTHWELL. **Oakmere Park Golf Club,** Oaks Lane, Oxton, Near Southwell NG25 0RH (01602 653545; Fax: 01602 655628). *Location:* eight miles north east of Nottingham on A614. Parkland course with longest Par 5 in Nottinghamshire. North Course – 18 holes, 6041 yards, S.S.S. 72. South Course – 9 holes, 3193 metres. S.S.S. 37. 30 bay floodlit driving range. *Green Fees:* North – weekdays £16.00; weekends £20.00. South – weekdays £6.00; weekends £8.00. Reductions for Senior Citizens and Juniors. *Eating facilities:* clubhouse bar, spike bar, restaurant and resident chef. *Visitors:* welcome at all times but need to book at weekends. *Society Meetings:* welcome, weekends require maximum notice possible. Professional: Stephen Meade (01602 655553). Operations Director: Malcolm Gibson (01602 653545; Fax: 01602 655628).

STANTON-ON-THE-WOLDS. **Stanton-on-the-Wolds Golf Club,** Stanton-on-the-Wolds NG12 5BH (0115 937 2044). *Location:* seven miles south of Nottingham, one mile west of main Nottingham – Melton road. Agricultural land. 18 holes, 6437 yards, 5886 metres. S.S.S. 71. Practice ground. *Green Fees:* weekdays £20.00; weekends with member only. *Eating facilities:* restaurant and bar. *Visitors:* welcome with prior arrangement with Secretary, weekends with member only. *Society Meetings:* catered for by arrangement with Secretary. Professional: Nick Hernon (0115 937 2390). Secretary: H.G. Gray, F.C.A. (0115 937 2006).

STRAGGLETHORPE. **Cotgrave Place Golf and Country Club,** Stragglethorpe, Nottingham NG12 3HB (01602 333344). *Location:* on the A52 towards Grantham, turn right to Cotgrave village. Lakeside and parkland course. 27 holes, 6154 yards. S.S.S. 69 – par 71. Driving range, putting green. *Green Fees:* weekdays £15; weekends £25. Midweek day ticket £22. *Eating facilities:* clubhouse, spike bar, conference suite. *Society Meetings:* catered for. Professional: Greg Towne. Secretary: David Roberts (01602 334686).

WORKSOP. **College Pines Golf Club,** College Lane, Worksop (01909 501431). Heathland course surrounded by woodland; very well drained, with Winter play a speciality. 18 holes, 6700 metres. S.S.S. 72. Driving range and short game practice area. *Green Fees:* weekdays £12.00, weekends £18.00. *Eating facilities:* light refreshments available all day. *Visitors:* welcome by appointment; starting times may be booked. *Society Meetings:* groups allowed occasionally. Professional: Charles Snell (01909 501431). Professional: R. Smith (01909 771924).

WORKSOP. **Kilton Forest Golf Club,** Blyth Road, Worksop S81 0TL (01909 472488). *Location:* main Worksop to Blyth road, right hand side. Undulating parkland. 18 holes, 6424 yards. S.S.S. 71, Par 72.

Practice area. *Green Fees:* weekdays £6.30; weekends £7.60. Reduction with Bassetlaw District Council leisure pass. *Eating facilities:* bar meals. *Visitors:* welcome, club competitions some Sundays – check with Professional. *Society Meetings:* by arrangement with Professional. Professional: Mr Peter Foster (01909 486563). Secretary: Mr Granville Lawman (01909 485994; Mobile 0850 199144).

WORKSOP. **Lindrick Golf Club,** Lindrick Common, Worksop S81 8BH (01909 485802). *Location:* on A57 four miles west of Worksop. M1 junction 31 on to A57 Worksop. Heathland. 18 holes, 6612 yards, 6046 metres. S.S.S. 72. Two practice areas. *Green Fees:* weekdays £40.00 per day; weekends £45.00 per round. *Eating facilities:* diningroom. *Visitors:* welcome weekdays, except Tuesday mornings. Prior booking required. *Society Meetings:* catered for weekdays. Professional: P. Cowen (01909 475820). Secretary: Lt Cdr R.J.M. Jack (01909 475282; Fax: 01909 488685).

WORKSOP. **Worksop Golf Club,** Windmill Lane, Worksop S80 2SQ (01909 472696). *Location:* just off Worksop bypass (A57), one mile south east of town centre. Heathland with gorse, broom, birch and oak; easy walking. 18 holes, 6651 yards. S.S.S. 73. Practice ground. *Green Fees:* £18.50 per round, £25.00 per day weekdays; £26.00 per round weekends and Bank Holidays. *Eating facilities:* dining room and bar. *Visitors:* welcome, except weekends November to March without member. Advise preliminary phone call to Professional. Snooker table. *Society Meetings:* weekdays only by arrangement with Professional. Not Bank Holidays. Professional: J.R. King (01909 477732). Secretary: P.G. Jordan (01909 477731).

Oxfordshire

ABINGDON. **Frilford Heath Golf Club,** Abingdon OX13 5NW (01865 390864). *Location:* on A338 Oxford/Wantage Road seven miles south-west of Oxford, four miles west of Abingdon. Flat, wooded heathland. Red course: 18 holes, 6768 yards. S.S.S. 73; Green course: 18 holes, 5763 yards. S.S.S. 69. Two practice areas. *Green Fees:* weekdays £45.00; weekends and Bank Holidays £55.00; after 5pm £25.00 all week. *Eating facilities:* first class restaurant and bars. *Visitors:* welcome weekdays with Handicap Certificate, phone ahead for weekends and Bank Holidays. *Society Meetings:* welcomed Mondays, Wednesdays and Fridays. Professional: D.C. Craik (01865 390887). Secretary: J. Kleynhans (01865 390864).

BANBURY. **Cherwell Edge Golf Club,** C/o Cherwell Edge Course, Chacombe, Banbury (01295 711591). *Location:* half a mile off M40 at Banbury. Parkland. 18 holes, 5840 yards. S.S.S. 68 men, 69 ladies. Practice area. *Green Fees:* weekdays £9.50; weekends £12.50. *Eating facilities:* restaurant and bar. *Visitors:* welcome, some time restrictions. *Society Meetings:* welcome, some time restrictions. Professional: Mr R. Jefferies (01295 711591). Secretary: Mr R.A. Beare (0295 275679 home).

BANBURY. **Tadmarton Heath Golf Club,** Wiggington, Banbury OX15 5HL (01608 737278). *Location:* off M40, off A41, off B4035, five miles west of Banbury. Heathland. 18 holes, 5917 yards. S.S.S. 69. Practice area. *Green Fees:* by application. *Eating facilities:* full catering. *Visitors:* welcome weekdays (restrictions Thursdays); weekends with member only. Must be member of another golf club with Handicap Certificate. *Society Meetings:* welcome weekdays except Thursdays. Professional: Les Bond (01608 730047). Secretary: R.E. Wackrill (01608 737278).

BICESTER. **Chesterton Golf Club,** Chesterton, Near Bicester OX6 8TE (01869 241204). *Location:* one mile off A421, Bicester/Oxford. Two miles south-west of Bicester. 18 holes, 6224 yards. S.S.S. 70. Practice ground and putting green. *Green Fees:* weekdays £12.00 per round, £15.00 per day; weekends and Bank Holidays £18.00 per round, £24.00 per day. *Eating facilities:* bars and lunchtime bar food, diningroom by arrangement. *Visitors:* welcome weekdays without reservation, weekends may book through Pro shop. Snooker room. *Society Meetings:* catered for. Professional: Jack Wilkshire (01869 242023). Secretary: Brian Carter (01869 241204).

BURFORD. **Burford Golf Club,** Burford OX18 4JG (01993 822149). *Location:* A40 – Burford roundabout. Flat parkland. 18 holes, 6405 yards, 6083 metres. S.S.S. 71. *Green Fees:* £25.00 per day weekdays. *Eating facilities:* full catering. *Visitors:* welcome weekdays by arrangement with the Secretary. *Society Meetings:* catered for on application. Professional: Norman Allen (01993 822344). Secretary: Richard Cane (01993 822583).

CHIPPING NORTON. **Chipping Norton Golf Club,** Southcombe, Chipping Norton OX7 5QH (01608 641150). *Location:* Junction of A3400 and A34, 18 miles from Oxford, 20 miles from Stratford-on-Avon. Downland, with many planted trees and lake. 18 holes, 6280 yards, 5743 metres. S.S.S. 70. Practice ground and putting green. *Green Fees:* weekdays £22.00; weekends only with a member £10.00. £40 per day for societies, including catering. *Eating facilities:* dining-room and bar. *Visitors:* welcome Monday to Friday but not Bank Holidays. *Society Meetings:* Mondays, Tuesdays, Wednesdays and some Fridays. Professional: Robert Gould (01608 643356). Secretary: John Norman (01608 642383).

CHIPPING NORTON. **Lyneham Golf Club,** Lyneham, Chipping Norton OX7 6QQ (01993 831841; Fax: 01993 831775). *Location:* six miles from Burford off the A361 Burford to Chipping Norton Road. Parkland. 18 holes, 6669 yards, 6099 metres. S.S.S. 72. Practice range. *Green Fees:* weekdays £13.00; weekends £16. *Eating facilities:* bar, function room. *Visitors:* welcome, can book start time three days in advance. *Society Meetings:* welcome, special rates available. Professional: Mark Stancer. Secretary: Cyril Howkins.

DIDCOT. **Hadden Hill Golf Club,** Wallingford Road, Didcot OX11 9BJ. *Location:* on A4130, half a mile east of Didcot on the Wallingford road. Well drained parkland with superb greens – never closed for rain! 18 holes, 6523 yards. S.S.S. 71. 20-bay driving range. *Green Fees:* weekdays £11.50, weekends £15.00. *Eating facilities:* good food all day, every day. *Visitors:* telephone bookings for tee times. *Society Meetings:* very welcome weekdays only. Professionals: Adrian Water and Dean Halford (01235 510410). Secretary: Michael Morley (01235 510410).

FARINGDON. **Carswell Golf and Country Club,** Carswell Home Farm, Carswell, Faringdon SN7 8PU. *Location:* just off A420 between Oxford and Swindon, near Faringdon. Undulating parkland course with many trees. 18 holes, 6200 yards. S.S.S. 70. Practice bunker and pitching green; golf range. *Green Fees:* visitors £12.00 weekdays, £15.00 weekends. Discounts if playing with members. *Eating facilities:* clubhouse serving varied menu. *Visitors:* no restrictions. *Society Meetings:* all welcome. Professional: Jon Nicholas. Secretary: (0136787 422).

HENLEY-ON-THAMES. **Badgemore Park Golf Club,** Badgemore, Henley-on-Thames RG9 4NR (01491 573667). *Location:* one mile from Henley town centre on Peppard Road. Flat parkland, wooded course. 18 holes, 6112 yards. S.S.S. 69. Chipping green. *Green Fees:* weekdays £27.00 per day; weekends £30.00. *Eating facilities:* full catering and bar facilities. *Visitors:* welcome though must play with a member weekends and Bank Holiday mornings. Handicap Certificate required. Telephone bookings required. *Society Meetings:* complete Company and Society Golf Days available except Tuesdays. Professional: J. Dunn (01491 574175). Manager: R. Park (01491 572206; Fax: 01491 567899).

HENLEY-ON-THAMES. **Henley Golf Club,** Harpsden, Henley-on-Thames RG9 4HG (01491 573304). *Location:* from centre of Henley-Reading, one mile from Harpsden Way to clubhouse. Parkland with many trees. 18 holes, 6329 yards. S.S.S. 70. *Green Fees:* £30.00; weekends with member only £10. *Eating facilities:* bar snacks at all times, meals by arrangement. *Visitors:* welcome with reservation weekdays, not at weekends or Bank Holidays (Handicap Certificate holders only). *Society Meetings:* catered for Wednesdays and Thursdays only. Professional: Mark Howell (01491 575710). Secretary: Andrew Chaundy (01491 575742).

HENLEY-ON-THAMES. **Huntercombe Golf Club,** Nuffield, Henley-on-Thames RG9 5SL (01491 641207). *Location:* A432, six miles west of Henley-on-Thames. Downland wooded course. 18 holes, 6301 yards. S.S.S. 70. Practice ground. *Green Fees:* £31.50 per day weekdays, £31.50 per round weekends. *Eating facilities:* catering and bar facilities. *Visitors:* welcome by prior arrangement only. *Society Meetings:* Tuesdays and Thursdays by arrangement. Professional: J.B. Draycott (01491 641241). Secretary: Lt Col T.J. Hutchinson.

MAPLEDURHAM. **Mapledurham Golf Club,** Chazey Heath, Mapledurham, Reading RG4 7UD (01734 463353; Fax: 01734 463363). *Location:* leave Reading on A4074 towards Mapledurham, Woodcote and Wallingford, club is on the right immediately after leaving built up area. Parkland. 18 holes, 5621 yards. S.S.S. 66. Practice ground. *Green Fees:* weekdays £13.00; weekends £16.00. *Eating facilities:* bar/

lounge, food available. *Visitors:* welcome, no restrictions. *Society Meetings:* welcome. Professional: Douglas Burton. Manager: Kevin Bailey.

OXFORD. **North Oxford Golf Club,** Banbury Road, Oxford OX2 8ED (01865 54415). *Location:* just north of Oxford on the Banbury Road to Kidlington. 18 holes, 5805 yards, S.S.S. 67. *Green Fees:* on request. *Eating facilities:* limited on Mondays. *Visitors and Societies:* welcome. Professional: Bob Harris (01865 53977). Secretary: G.W. Pullin (01865 54924).

OXFORD. **Southfield Golf Club,** Hill Top Road, Oxford OX4 1PF. *Location:* one mile from Rover Works, along Cowley Road, turn right into Southfield Road, then right at end of road. Hilly parkland. 18 holes, 6328 yards. S.S.S. 70. *Green Fees:* £24.00 per day weekdays. *Eating facilities:* full catering except Mondays, bar open seven days. *Visitors:* welcome except weekends and Public Holidays. Handicap Certificates required. *Society Meetings:* welcome by arrangement (not weekends or Bank Holidays). Professional: Tony Rees (01865 244258). Secretary: A.G. Hopcraft (01865 242158).

OXFORD. **Waterstock Golf Club,** Thame Road, Waterstock, Oxford OX33 1HT (01844 338093; Fax: 01844 338036). *Location:* on Junction 8 M40 next to Wheatley. Rolling parkland with 14500 young trees. 18 holes, 6535 yards. S.S.S. 73. Practice bunkers and putting facilities; 22-bay driving range. *Green Fees:* weekdays £6.50 for 9 holes, £12.00 for 18 holes, £18.00 per day; weekends £8.50 for 9 holes, £16.00 for 18 holes, £24.00 per day. *Eating facilities:* full bar and restaurant. *Visitors:* no restrictions, welcome at all times. Changing rooms. *Society Meetings:* fully catered for, packages available on request. Professional: Andy Wyatt. Secretary: Andrew Wyatt.

WALLINGFORD near. **RAF Benson,** Near Wallingford OX10 6AA. *Location:* three and a half miles north-east of Wallingford, follow signposts to RAF Benson. Airfield course, through airfield installations. 9 holes, 4395 yards. S.S.S. 61. *Green Fees:* £5.00. *Visitors:* casual visitors not permitted, must be accompanied by members. Secretary: Flt Lt G. Clark (01491 837766).

WITNEY. **Witney Golf Club Ltd,** Witney Golf Centre, Downs Road, Witney OX8 5SY (01993 779000; Fax: 01993 778866). *Location:* one mile off B4047 west out of Witney; turn into Downs Road by West Oxfordshire Motor Auctions. Parkland with four large lakes. 18 holes, 6675 yards, 6102 metres. S.S.S. 71, Par 71. 24-bay floodlit driving range. *Green Fees:* weekdays £12.00, weekends £15.00. *Eating facilities:* bar and full catering. *Visitors:* no restrictions. Function/conference room, two large shops, sauna. *Society Meetings:* all welcome. Professional: Paul Sowerby. Manager: Mike Bennett.

Shropshire

BRIDGNORTH. **Bridgnorth Golf Club,** Stanley Lane, Bridgnorth WV16 4SF (01746 763315). *Location:* one mile from town centre on Broseley road. Parkland, alongside River Severn. 18 holes, 6627 yards. S.S.S. 72. Practice ground. *Green Fees:* £18.00 – £22.00 weekdays; £25.00 – £30.00 weekends and Bank Holidays. *Eating facilities:* full catering available except Mondays. *Visitors:* welcome weekdays except Wednesday with Handicap Certificate or if bona fide club member. *Society Meetings:* catered for Tuesday, Thursday, Friday only. Professional: Paul Hinton (01746 762045). Secretary: K.D. Cole (01746 764179).

CHURCH STRETTON. **Church Stretton Golf Club,** "Hunters Moon", Trevor Hill, Church Stretton SY6 6JH (01694 722281). *Location:* one mile west of A49, adjacent to Carding Mill Valley. Hillside, heathland course. 18 holes, 5008 yards. S.S.S. 65. *Green Fees:* £12.00 weekdays, £18.00 weekends and Bank Holidays. *Eating facilities:* snacks and meals by arrangement; bar. *Visitors:* welcome, Saturdays not 9am to 10.30am or 1pm to 3pm, Sundays not before 10.30am or between 12.30pm and 3pm. *Society Meetings:* catered for by arrangement with Secretary. Hon. Secretary: R. Broughton (01694 722633).

NOTE

All the information in this book is given in good faith in the belief that it is correct. However, the publishers cannot guarantee the facts given in these pages, neither are they responsible for changes in policy, ownership or terms that may take place after the date of going to press. Readers should always satisfy themselves that the facilities they require are available and that the terms, if quoted, still apply.

LUDLOW. **Ludlow Golf Club,** Bromfield, Ludlow SY8 2BT (01584 77285). *Location:* A49 one mile north of Ludlow bypass, turn right onto the Bridgnorth road. Well signposted. Parkland with hills to north east; two quarry holes. 18 holes, 6239 yards. S.S.S. 70. Practice ground. *Green Fees:* weekdays £18.00; weekends £24.00 (£8.00 with member). *Eating facilities:* full catering and bar service. *Visitors:* welcome weekdays with prior booking, weekends with member only. *Society Meetings:* catered for Wednesdays and Thursdays April to October. Professional: Russell Price (01584 77366). Administrator: C.R. Vane Percy.

MARKET DRAYTON. **Market Drayton Golf Club,** Sutton, Market Drayton (01630 652266). *Location:* south of town leaving by Walkmill Road one mile past the swimming baths. Parkland with exceptional views. 18 holes, 6214 yards, 5702 metres. S.S.S. 70. *Green Fees:* weekdays £20.00; weekends only with a member. Reduced fees if playing with member. *Eating facilities:* bar with high class catering open all day. *Visitors:* welcome weekdays only. Tuesday Ladies' Day, first tee closed 9am to 11am. Bungalow (sleeps 6) available for letting. *Society Meetings:* catered for weekdays by prior arrangement. Professional: R. Clewes. Secretary: C. Price (01630 657496).

NEWPORT. **Lilleshall Hall Golf Club,** Lilleshall, Near Newport TF10 9AS (01952 603840). *Location:* at Lillyhurst turn north off Abbey Road, which joins Wellington Road near Lilleshall and the B4379 near Sheriffhales. Wooded parkland. 18 holes, 5906 yards. S.S.S. 68. Practice ground. *Green Fees:* weekdays £18.00 (half price with member), weekends £15.00 only with member. Bank Holidays and following day plus Christmas holiday week £30.00 (half price with a member). *Eating facilities:* meals served 9am to 5pm, order in advance. *Visitors:* welcome on weekdays, check with Professional for tee restrictions. *Society Meetings:* catered for by prior arrangement with Secretary. Professional: N.W. Bramall (01952 604104). Secretary: B.G. Weaver (01952 604776).

OSWESTRY. **Llanymynech Golf Club,** Pant, Near Oswestry SY10 8LB (01691 830542). *Location:* one mile west of A483 Welshpool to Oswestry, six miles south of Oswestry. Turn by Cross Guns Inn, Pant. Upland course with extensive views part in England, part in Wales! 18 holes, 6114 yards, 5899 metres. S.S.S. 69. Practice area. *Green Fees:* weekdays £19.00 per day, £14.00 per round; weekends £24.00 per day, £20.00 per round. Half price with member. Reductions for Juniors. *Eating facilities:* restaurant and bar (not Mondays). *Visitors:* welcome weekdays; some weekends by prior arrangement. *Society Meetings:* by arrangement with the Secretary. Professional: A.P. Griffiths (01691 830879). Secretary: D.R. Thomas (01691 830983).

OSWESTRY. **Mile End Golf Club,** Mile End, Oswestry SY11 4JE. *Location:* signposted off A5, one mile south-east of Oswestry. Gently undulating course. 9 holes, 6130 yards (for 18 holes). S.S.S. 69. Further 9 holes under construction. Driving range. *Green Fees:* weekdays £10.00 for 18 holes, £14.00 per day; weekends £14.00 for 18 holes, £18.00 per day. *Eating facilities:* catering available lunchtimes, telephone for details. *Visitors:* welcome at all times. *Society Meetings:* available midweek. Professional: Scott Carpenter (01691 671246). Secretary: Richard Thompson (01691 670580).

OSWESTRY. **Oswestry Golf Club,** Aston Park, Oswestry SY11 4JJ (01691 610221). *Location:* four miles south-east of Oswestry on A5. Parkland course. 18 holes, 6038 yards. S.S.S. 69. Practice ground. *Green Fees:* weekdays £18.00; weekends £25.00. *Eating facilities:* diningroom and bar. *Visitors:* welcome; must be members of another club or playing with a member. *Society Meetings:* catered for Wednesdays and Fridays only by arrangement, application necessary. Professional: D. Skelton (01691 610448). Secretary: Mrs P.M. Lindner (01691 610535).

SHIFNAL. **Shifnal Golf Club,** Decker Hill, Shifnal TF11 8QL (01952 460330). *Location:* one mile north east of Shifnal, one mile from A5, Junction 4 M54. Parkland course. 18 holes, 6504 yards. S.S.S. 71. *Green Fees:* £22.00 per round, £30.00 per day; weekends with member only. *Eating facilities:* full catering service except Mondays. *Visitors:* welcome, phone first, not weekends or Bank Holidays. *Society Meetings:* catered for by arrangement with Secretary. Professional: J. Flanagan (01952 460457). Secretary: P.W. Holden (01952 460330).

SHREWSBURY. **Arscott Golf Club,** Arscott, Pontesbury, Shrewsbury SY5 0XP (01743 860114). *Location:* 10 minutes from Shrewsbury off the A488 Bishops Castle road. Set in mature parkland with stunning views of South Shropshire and Welsh Borders. 18 holes, 6025 yards. S.S.S. 69. Practice area, putting green and driving net. *Green Fees:* weekdays £15.00 before 12 noon, £10.00 after 12 noon; weekends £20.00 at all times. *Eating facilities:* bar and full restaurant open from 11am daily. *Visitors:* welcome at all times on production of Handicap Certificate. Please telephone Pro Shop to book tees. *Society Meetings:* weekdays only by arrangement, please telephone Secretary. Professional: Gary Sawyer (01743 860881). Secretary: B.K. Harper.

SHREWSBURY. **Hawkstone Park Leisure Ltd,** Weston-under-Redcastle, Shrewsbury SY4 5UY (01939 200611; Fax: 01939 200311). Where Sandy Lyle, '85 Open Champion, learned his game. *Location:*

14 miles north of Shrewsbury off A49. Parkland/woodland courses (three). Hawkstone Course – 18 holes, 6465 yards. S.S.S. 71; Windmill Course (designed by Brian Huggett) – 18 holes, 6734 yards. S.S.S. 72; Academy Par 3 Course – 6 holes, 741 yards. Par 18, S.S.S. 18. Practice range, teaching academy. *Green Fees:* £25.00 per round Summer; weekends £31.00 Summer, from £15.00 Winter. *Eating facilities:* Terrace bar, restaurant. *Visitors:* welcome at all times. Handicap Certificate required for main courses. Hotel accommodation. *Society Meetings:* welcome, special terms for 12 players or more. Professional: Keith Williams (01939 200209). Secretary: Mrs Dilys Airey.

SHREWSBURY. **Shrewsbury Golf Club,** Condover, Shrewsbury SY5 7BL (01743 872776). *Location:* A49 two miles south west of Shrewsbury. Parkland. 18 holes, 6212 yards. S.S.S. 70. Large practice ground. *Green Fees:* £15.00 per round, £20.00 per day weekdays; £25.00 per day or round weekends and Bank Holidays. *Eating facilities:* full restaurant facilities available seven days. *Visitors:* welcome at all times. *Society Meetings:* by arrangement if over 16 players, not Wednesdays, preferably Mondays and Fridays, some Sundays. Professional: Peter Seal (01743 873751). Secretary: Mrs S.M. Kenny (01743 872977).

TELFORD. **Telford Hotel, Golf and Country Club,** Great Hay, Sutton Hill, Telford TF7 4DT (01952 585642; Fax: 01952 586602). *Location:* turn off A442 between Bridgnorth and Telford, two miles to M54 Junction 4. Rolling wooded parkland with lake features, full irrigation. 18 holes, 6766 yards, 6187 metres. S.S.S. 72. 9 hole par 3 course. All-weather driving range. *Green Fees:* £25.00 weekdays; £30.00 weekends. *Eating facilities:* clubroom, coffee bar and restaurant, also private rooms for Societies. *Visitors:* welcome anytime but advance booking essential. Handicap Certificates or membership of bona fide golf club essential. Leisure Centre with swimming pool, gym, etc. *Society Meetings:* by arrangement with Golf Co-ordinator, extension 297. Professional: Graham Farr (01952 586052). Secretary: Dave Paterson (01952 585642 extension 274).

TELFORD. **The Shropshire Grange Golf Club,** The Shropshire Limited, Muxton Grange, Muxton, Telford TF2 8PQ (01952 677866; Fax: 01952 677622). *Location:* M54 from M6 Junction 4 turn right follow signs. Undulating parkland. 27 holes, 3286 yards, 3303 yards, 3334 yards. S.S.S. 71, 72, 72. 31 bay floodlit driving range, 12 hole short course, 18 hole putting green. *Green Fees:* weekdays £10.00; weekends £17.00. *Eating facilities:* restaurant, private rooms, four bars. *Visitors:* welcome, no restrictions. Trout fishing, equestrian centre. *Society Meetings:* very welcome. Professional: Mr K. Craggs (Fax: 01952 677644). Secretary: Mrs G.V. Bell.

TELFORD. **Wrekin Golf Club,** Ercall Woods, Wellington, Telford (01952 244032). *Location:* end of M54, turn back along Holyhead road to golf club sign. Undulating parkland. 18 holes, 5699 yards. S.S.S. 67. Small practice ground. *Green Fees:* weekdays £20.00; weekends £25.00 (numbers limited). *Eating facilities:* by arrangement with Stewardess. *Visitors:* welcome except weekends and Bank Holidays. *Society Meetings:* by arrangement. Professional: K. Houseden (01952 223101). Secretary: S. Leys (01952 255586 after 7pm). *

WHITCHURCH. **Hill Valley Golf and Country Club,** Terrick Road, Whitchurch SY13 4JZ (01948 663584; Fax: 01948 665927). *Location:* fully signposted off A49/A41 trunk road in Whitchurch. Undulating parkland courses. No 1 Course – 18 holes, 6050 yards. S.S.S. 69, Par 72. No 2 Course – 18 holes, 5283 yards. S.S.S. 65, Par 66. *Green Fees:* No 1 Course – weekdays £18.00, weekends and Bank Holidays £24.00; No 2 Course – weekdays £9.00, weekends and

Bank Holidays £12.00. *Eating facilities:* full restaurant and bar facilities 8am – 9pm. *Visitors:* welcome without reservation. Motel accommodation, squash, tennis, snooker room. *Society Meetings:* fully catered for every day. Professional: A.R. Minshall (01948 663032). Secretary: R.B. Walker (01948 663584). *

WOLVERHAMPTON. **Patshull Park Hotel, Golf and Country Club,** Patshull Park, Pattingham, Near Wolverhampton WV6 7HR (Tel/Fax: 01902 700100/ 700874). *Location:* take Junction 3 off M54, turn left on A41 back towards Wolverhampton and fork right into Albrighton. From main crossroads turn right along Cross Road, taking T-junction with A464 Wolverhampton/Shifnal Road and turning right towards Shifnal. Signposted Patshull Park Golf Course. Set in glorious parkland landscaped by Capability Brown; John Jacobs designed course. 18 holes, 6412 yards. S.S.S. 72. Excellent practice area. *Green Fees:* weekdays £20.00 per 18 holes, £35.00 per 36 holes; weekends £25.00 per 18 holes, £40.00 per 36 holes. *Eating facilities:* Lakeside Restaurant and three bars, Bunkers coffee shop. *Visitors:* welcome on application. 48 bedroomed hotel, leisure club and swimming pool, fishing lakes (80 acres). Residential Breaks. *Society Meetings:* corporate and society meetings welcome; special group rates and facilities. Professional: Joe Higgins. Golf Manager: David Thorp.

WORFIELD. **Worfield Golf Club,** Bridgnorth Road, Worfield, Near Bridgnorth WV15 5HE (017464 541). *Location:* A454 Wolverhampton to Bridgnorth Road, three miles from Bridgnorth. Parkland course set on rolling countryside.18 holes, 6801 yards. S.S.S. 73. Large practice ground, bunker and putting green. *Green Fees:* weekdays £15.00 per round, £20.00 per day; weekends £20.00 per round, £25 per day. *Eating facilities:* lounge, spike bar and restaurant. *Visitors:* welcome, no visitors before 10am weekends. *Society Meetings:* all welcome. Professional: Steve Russell (017464 372). Secretary: William Weaver (017464 541).

Somerset

BRIDGWATER. **Cannington Golf Course,** Cannington College, Cannington, Bridgwater TA5 2LS (01278 652226; Fax: 01278 652479). *Location:* M5 Junction 24, off A39 Bridgwater to Minehead road. Flat, with slight undulations, on parkland turf; exposed to sea breezes. 9 holes, 2929 yards. S.S.S. 34. Small practice area. *Green Fees:* weekdays £10.00, weekends £12.00. Economy 9 £6.50 (after 2.30pm Winter, 5.30pm Summer). *Eating facilities:* College restaurant. *Visitors:* pay and play course. *Society Meetings:* by arrangement with Professional/Course Manager. Professional: Ron Macrow (01278 652394).

BRIDGWATER. **Enmore Park Golf Club,** Enmore, Bridgwater TA5 2AN (01278 671244). *Location:* M5 Exit 23, left at lights in town for one mile, course signposted two miles on right. Wooded parkland course on Quantock foothills. 18 holes, 6406 yards, 5910 metres. S.S.S. 71. Large practice area. *Green Fees:* £18.00 per round, £25.00 per day weekdays; £25.00 per round, £30.00 per day weekends. *Eating facilities:* lunch and evening meal available. *Visitors:* welcome weekdays, weekends if no competitions. *Society Meetings:* welcome by arrangement. Professional: Nigel Wixon (01278 671519). Secretary: David Weston (01278 671481).

BURNHAM-ON-SEA. **Brean Golf Club,** Coast Road, Brean Sands, Burnham-on-Sea TA8 2RF (Tel & Fax: 01278 751595). *Location:* leave M5 at Junction 22, follow Brean signs to Brean Leisure Park (five miles). Flat moorland. 18 holes, 5714 yards. S.S.S. 68 (Par 69). Practice green and area. *Green Fees:* weekdays £12.00 per round; weekends £15.00 per round. Reduced rates with a member. *Eating facilities:* snacks at Clubhouse; meals at adjoining Leisure Centre on request. *Visitors:* welcome weekdays, Saturdays and Sundays after 1pm. *Society Meetings:* welcome by arrangement. Professional: Sue Spencer (01278 751570). Secretary: W.S. Martin (01278 751409). Manager: Mr A. Clarke.

See our display advertisement in the Colour Section on page 7.

BURNHAM-ON-SEA. **Burnham and Berrow Golf Club,** St. Christopher's Way, Burnham-on-Sea TA8 2PE (01278 783137). *Location:* one mile north of Burnham-on-Sea. Leave M5 at Exit 22. Seaside links. 18 holes, 6447 yards. S.S.S. 72; 9 holes, 6332 yards. S.S.S. 70. *Green Fees:* £30.00 weekdays, £40.00 weekends and Bank Holidays; 9 hole course £8.00. *Eating facilities:* catering available daily 11am to 6pm (other meals by arrangement). *Visitors:* welcome with reservation if members of a recognised golf club and with Handicap Certificate. *Society Meetings:* catered for. Professional: M. Crowther-Smith (01278 784545). Secretary: Mrs E.L. Sloman (01278 785760).

CHARD. **Windwhistle Golf, Squash and Country Club Ltd,** Cricket St. Thomas, Near Chard TA20 4DG (01460 30231; Fax: 01460 30055). *Location:* on A30 between Chard and Crewkerne, opposite Cricket St. Thomas Wildlife Park, follow signs. Unique elevated course with unsurpassed panoramic scenery, flora and fauna. 18 holes, 6500 yards. S.S.S. 71, Par 73. Practice areas. *Green Fees:* on application. *Eating facilities:* comprehensive and extensive clubhouse facilities. *Visitors:* welcome weekdays, weekends and holidays, booking preferred. Senior PGA tuition available. Trolley hire. *Society Meetings:* catered for – comprehensive arrangements available. Professional: visiting. Secretary/Manager: Ian Neville Dodd. *

LANGPORT near. **Long Sutton Golf Club,** Near Langport TA10 9JU (01458 241017). *Location:* from Podimore roundabout on A303 towards Langport turn left for Long Sutton. Gently undulating course. 18 holes, 6368 yards. S.S.S. 70. Floodlit driving range. *Green Fees:* weekdays £12.00; weekends £16.00. *Eating facilities:* bar and bar food. *Visitors:* welcome at all times, phone for tee reservations at weekends. *Society Meetings:* welcome. Professional: Stewart Adwick. Secretary: G.C. Bennett.

MINEHEAD. **Minehead and West Somerset Golf Club,** The Warren, Minehead TA24 5SJ (01643 702057). *Location:* beside the beach at eastern end of the town, three-quarters of a mile from town centre. Flat seaside links. 18 holes, 6137 yards. S.S.S. 70. *Green Fees:* weekdays £19.50; weekends and Bank Holidays £23.00. *Eating facilities:* available at clubhouse, bar open every day. *Visitors:* welcome with tee reservation at Pro's shop. *Society Meetings:* catered for, subject to prior arrangement with the Secretary. Society groups numbering 15 or more qualify for 10 per cent discount. Wide wheel trolleys only. Professional: Ian Read (01643 704378). Secretary: Laurie Harper (01643 702057).

SHEPTON MALLET. **Mendip Golf Club Ltd.,** Gurney Slade, Shepton Mallet, Near Bath BA3 4UT (01749 840570). *Location:* three miles north of Shepton Mallet (A37). Downland, undulating course. 18 holes, 6330 yards. S.S.S. 70. Practice ground. *Green Fees:* weekdays £20.00 per round, £25.00 per day (with a member £8.00); weekends and Bank Holidays £30.00 per day (with a member £10.00). *Eating facilities:* bar and restaurant open seven days a week. *Visitors:* welcome every day, telephone Professional to check availability. *Society Meetings:* catered for Mondays to

Fridays by arrangement. Professional: R.F. Lee (01749 840793). Secretary: Mrs J.P. Howe (01749 840570).

STREET. **Kingweston Golf Club,** (Millfield School), Street (01458 43921). *Location:* one mile south of Butleigh Village, near Street, Somerset. Flat course – trees. 9 holes, 2378 yards. S.S.S. 62. Practice area. *Green Fees:* £4.00. *Eating facilities:* pub half a mile. *Visitors:* welcome only with a member. Secretary: D.J. Thomas (01458 833689).

TAUNTON. **Oake Manor Golf Club,** Oake, Milverton, Taunton (01823 400214; Fax: 01823 461993). *Location:* off B3227, village of Oake between Taunton and Wellington or Wiveliscombe. Parkland course with lakes. 18 holes, 6109 yards. S.S.S. 69. *Green Fees:* weekdays £12.00; weekends £15.00. *Eating facilities:* bar, restaurant, lounge. *Visitors:* always welcome. No dogs allowed. *Society Meetings:* by arrangement. Professional: R. Gardner. *

TAUNTON. **Taunton and Pickeridge Golf Club,** Corfe, Taunton TA3 7BY (01823 421240). *Location:* four miles south of Taunton on the B3170. Undulating parkland. 18 holes, 5926 yards. S.S.S. 68. Practice ground, indoor shed. *Green Fees:* weekdays £20.00; weekends £25.00. *Eating facilities:* restaurant and bar. *Visitors:* welcome by arrangement with the Secretary. *Society Meetings:* by arrangement with the Secretary. Professional: G. Glen (01823 421790). Secretary: G.W. Sayers (01823 421537; Fax: 01823 421742).

TAUNTON. **Taunton Golf Club,** Vivary Park, Taunton (01823 81946). 18 holes, 4280 yards. S.S.S. 62. *Green Fees:* information not provided. *

TAUNTON. **Taunton Vale Golf Club,** Creech, Heathfield, Taunton TA3 5EY (01823 412220; Fax: 01823 413583). *Location:* just off A361 at Junction with A38 between Junctions 24 and 25 of M5; easily accessible. Parkland. Two courses. 18 holes, 6072 yards. S.S.S. 69. 9 holes, 1943 yards. S.S.S. 31. 10 bay floodlit driving range. *Green Fees:* weekdays £14.00 for 18 holes, £7.00 for 9 holes; weekends £17.50 for 18 holes, £8.75 for 9 holes. Special daily rates and Society rates available, please enquire. *Eating facilities:* two bars with dining facilities. *Visitors:* welcome at all times, telephone for bookings. *Society Meetings:* welcome except Saturdays, telephone Professional for bookings. Professional: Martin Keitch (01823 412880). Secretary: Mrs Janice Thomas.

TAUNTON. **Vivary Park Public Golf Course,** Vivary Park, Fons George, Taunton TA1 3JW. *Location:* one mile from town centre off main Wellington road. Access to course is through Vivary Park in central Taunton. Pleasant parkland course with spectacular water hazards. 18 holes, 4620 yards. S.S.S. 63. Practice ground. *Green Fees:* information not available. *Eating facilities:* restaurant and bar available. *Visitors:* always welcome but will need to book on the day of play. *Society Meetings:* catered for by prior arrangement. Professional: Jeremy Wright (01823 33875). *

WEDMORE. **Isle of Wedmore Golf Club,** Lineage, Lascot Hill, Wedmore BS28 4QT (01934 713649). *Location:* from A38 Bristol/Bridgwater Road, take Wedmore Road from Lower Weare. Gently undulating fairways with magnificent views. 18 holes, 5900 yards. S.S.S. 68. Small practice area. *Green Fees:* weekdays £12.00 per round, £15.00 per day, with a member £8.00 per round; weekends £15.00 per round, £18.00 per day, with a member £12.00 per round. *Eating facilities:* large bar and restaurant. *Visitors:* always welcome. *Society Meetings:* all welcome, various packages available. Professional: Graham Coombe (01934 712452). Secretary: Andrew Edwards.

WELLS. **Wells (Somerset) Golf Club Ltd,** East Horrington Road, Wells BA5 3DS (01749 672868). *Location:* one mile east of city centre off B3139. Parkland, wooded. 18 holes, 6015 yards. S.S.S. 69. Practice area. *Green Fees:* weekdays £16.00 per round, £19.00 per day; weekends and Bank Holidays £20.00 per round, £22.00 per day. *Eating facilities:* restaurant and bars. *Visitors:* welcome, Handicaps required weekends and no play before 9.30am weekends and Public Holidays. Caravan park adjacent. *Society Meetings:* catered for weekdays. Professional: Adrian Bishop (01749 679059). Secretary: George Ellis (01749 675005).

WINCANTON. **Wincanton Golf Club,** The Racecourse, Wincanton BA9 8BJ (01963 34606; Fax: 01963 34668). *Location:* in the middle of the racecourse, half a mile from the town centre. Very flat course, testing layout; large bunkers protecting very well maintained greens. 9 holes, 3333 yards. S.S.S. 36. Good practice facilities. Teaching/coaching on individual or group basis; hire of clubs/trolley/buggy. *Green Fees:* weekdays 9 holes £5.00, 18 holes £8.00; weekends 9 holes £6.00, 18 holes £9.00. *Eating facilities:* not available. *Visitors:* welcome at all times. *Society Meetings:* can be catered for if booked in advance. Professional: Andrew England.

YEOVIL. **Yeovil Golf Club,** Sherborne Road, Yeovil BA21 5BW (01935 75949). *Location:* on A30, one mile from town centre towards Sherborne on right before Babylon Hill. Parkland. 18 holes, 6144 yards. S.S.S. 70. 9 holes, 5016 yards. S.S.S. 66. Practice ground and putting green. *Green Fees:* 18 hole course weekdays £20.00 per round or day, 9 hole course £12.00 per round or day; weekends and Bank Holidays 18 holes £25.00, 9 holes £15.00. *Eating facilities:* bars and dining room. Tuesdays 11.45am to 4.45pm only. *Visitors:* welcome, Handicap Certificates required for 18 hole course, telephone Pro shop to check times. *Society Meetings:* welcome Mondays, Wednesdays and Thursdays. Professional: G. Kite (01935 73763; Fax: 01935 78605). Secretary/Manager: J. Riley (01935 22965; Fax: 01935 411283).

Staffordshire

BARLASTON. **Barlaston Golf Club,** Meaford Road, Stone ST15 8UX (01782 372795). *Location:* one mile south of Barlaston off A34. 18 holes, 5800 yards. S.S.S. 68. *Green Fees:* weekdays £18.00; £22.50 weekends. *Eating facilities:* available on request in advance. *Visitors:* welcome anytime except before 10am at weekends and Bank Holidays. Professional: Ian Rogers. Secretary: M.J. Degg (01782 372867).

BURTON UPON TRENT. **Craythorne Golf Centre,** Craythorne Road, Stretton, Burton upon Trent DE13 0AZ (01283 564329; Fax: 01283 511908). *Location:* A38 (Burton North) A5121 signposted Stretton. Parkland. 18 holes, 5350 yards. S.S.S. 67. Floodlit driving range. *Green Fees:* £17.00 weekdays; £21.00 weekends and Bank Holidays. Evening rate available during summer. *Eating facilities:* bars and restaurant open daily. *Visitors:* welcome every day, booking necessary at weekends. Tennis courts. *Society Meetings:* welcome, special rates for parties over 16. Professional: Steve Hadfield (01283 533745). Managing Director: Tony Wright.

BURTON-ON-TRENT. **Branston Golf and Country Club,** Burton Road, Branston, Burton-on-Trent DE14 3DP (01283 43207). *Location:* A38 Junction A5121. Flat parkland. 18 holes, 6632 yards, 6064 metres. S.S.S. 71. Driving range. *Green Fees:* weekdays £19.00, weekends £23.00. *Eating facilities:* restaurant. *Visitors:* welcome, weekend restrictions only. *Society Meetings:* welcome, special rates. Professional: S.D. Warner (01283 43207). General Manager: K. Heathcote (01283 512211; Fax: 01283 66984).

CANNOCK. **Beau Desert Golf Club,** Hazel Slade, Cannock WS12 5PJ (01543 422773). *Location:* A460 Hednesford, signposted. Heathland course. 18 holes, 6300 yards. S.S.S. 71. Practice ground. *Green Fees:* £30.00 weekdays; £45.00 weekends. *Eating facilities:* full catering and bar. *Visitors:* welcome weekdays. *Society Meetings:* catered for weekdays. Professional: Barrie Stevens (01543 422492). Secretary: A.J.R. Fairfield (01543 422626).

CANNOCK. **Cannock Park Golf Club,** Stafford Road, Cannock WS11 2AL. *Location:* on the A34 Stafford Road, quarter of a mile from Cannock town centre. Parkland course, playing alongside Cannock Chase. 18 holes, 5048 yards. S.S.S. 65. *Green Fees:* £6.00 weekdays, £7.50 weekends. Phone bookings same day midweek for after 12 noon, weekends personal bookings before 12 noon. Reductions for Juniors. *Eating facilities:* available. *Visitors:* welcome every day. Golf shop, inside leisure centre. *Society Meetings:* welcome weekdays. Professional: David Dunk (Tel & Fax: 01543 578850). Secretary: E.G. Jones.

CHEADLE near. **Whiston Hall Golf Club,** Whiston, Near Cheadle ST10 2HZ (01538 266260; Fax: 01538 383600). *Location:* A52 Stoke to Ashbourne road, three miles from Alton Towers. Scenic course set in beautiful countryside. 18 holes, 5742 yards. S.S.S. 69. *Green Fees:* weekdays £10.00 per round, £15.00 per day; weekends £14.00 per round, £21.00 per day. *Eating facilities:* full bar and catering at weekends and by prior arrangement. *Visitors:* welcome at any time except 7am to 10am Sundays and 10.30am to 1.30pm Saturdays. Snooker, fly fishing. *Society Meetings:* all welcome. Manager: Howard L. Wainscott (01850 903815).

LEEK. **Leek Golf Club,** Birchall, Cheddleton Road, Leek (01538 385889). *Location:* one mile south of Leek on A520. Undulating semi-moorland. 18 holes, 6240 yards. S.S.S. 70. *Green Fees:* weekdays £24.00; weekends £30.00. *Eating facilities:* full bar facilities 11.30am-2pm and 4-11.30pm. Light refreshments from 9am. *Visitors:* welcome most times by prior arrangement. *Society Meetings:* catered for by arrangement Wednesdays only. Professional: P.A. Stubbs (01538 384767). Secretary: Frank Cutts B.E.M. (01538 384779).

LEEK. **Westwood Golf Club,** Newcastle Road, Leek ST13 7AA (01538 398385). *Location:* A53 south of Leek. Moorland/parkland. 18 holes, 6156 yards. S.S.S. 69. *Green Fees:* weekdays £18.00. *Eating facilities:* full facilities. *Visitors:* welcome weekdays, Saturdays with member, no visitors Sundays. *Society Meetings:* weekdays by arrangement with Secretary. Professional: Colin Smith (01538 398897). Secretary: Joe Clarke (01538 398385).

LICHFIELD near. **The Seedy Mill Golf Club,** Elmhurst, Near Lichfield WS13 8HE (01543 417333; Fax: 01543 418098). *Location:* A51 three miles north of Lichfield. Parkland with lakes, ponds and streams. The Mill – 18 holes, 6247 yards. S.S.S. 70; The Spires – 9 holes, Par 3. 26 bay floodlit driving range. *Green Fees:* weekdays £12.00; weekends £18.00. *Eating facilities:* full clubhouse facilities open 7.30am to 11pm. *Visitors:* welcome at all times. *Society Meetings:* welcome weekdays and weekends. Professional: Andrew Bolton. Director of Golf: Simon Lloyd. *

LICHFIELD. **Whittington Barracks Golf Club,** Tamworth Road, Lichfield WS14 9PW (01543 432212). *Location:* on A51 Tamworth-Lichfield Road. Wooded heathland. 18 holes, 6457 yards. S.S.S. 71. *Green Fees:* weekdays £32.00. *Eating facilities:* lunches served at club. *Visitors:* welcome with prior notification and Handicap Certificate or letter of introduction. *Society Meetings:* catered for Wednesdays and Thursdays by arrangement. Professional: Adrian Sadler (01543 432261). Secretary: D.W.J. Macalester (01543 432317). Golf Administrator: N.A. Spence (01543 432317).

NEWCASTLE. **Newcastle-under-Lyme Golf Club,** Whitmore Road, Newcastle (01782 616583). *Location:* M6 Junction 15, one mile from Newcastle-under-Lyme. Parkland. 18 holes, 6404 yards. S.S.S. 71 white, 70 yellow. *Green Fees:* weekdays £25.00; weekends with a member only (£7.50). *Eating facilities:* restaurant and bar meals. *Visitors:* welcome. Restrictions at weekends. *Society Meetings:* Wednesdays 10am to 12 noon then 2pm to 4pm; Thursdays 2pm to 4pm. Professional: P. Symonds (01782 618526). Secretary: (01782 617006).

NEWCASTLE-UNDER-LYME. **Newcastle-under-Lyme Municipal Golf Club,** Keele Road, Newcastle-under-Lyme (01782 627596). *Location:* A525 Newcastle to Whitchurch, opposite University of Keele. Undulating parkland. 18 hoies, 6300 yards, 5822 metres. S.S.S. 70. Driving range. *Green Fees:* weekdays £6.95, Juniors £3.10; weekends £8.40, Juniors £6.95. *Eating facilities:* available. *Visitors:* welcome, no restrictions but start times must be prebooked. Professional: Mr M. Shryane. Secretary: Mr G.A. Bytheway (01782 619317).

RUGELEY. **Lakeside Golf Club,** Rugeley Power Station, Armitage Road, Rugeley WS15 1PR (01889 575667). *Location:* nearest town Rugeley (between Lichfield and Stafford), course over power station grounds. Flat parkland adjacent River Trent. 18 holes, 5508 yards, 5037 metres. S.S.S. 67. Limited practice area. *Green Fees:* £6.00 with member. *Eating facilities:* evening snacks and bar facilities. *Visitors:* must be accompanied by member. *Society Meetings:* by arrangement. Secretary: Mr E.G. Jones (Tel & Fax: 01889 584472).

STAFFORD. **Brocton Hall Golf Club,** Brocton, Stafford ST17 0TH (01785 662627). *Location:* off A34 Stafford to Cannock four miles south east of Stafford. Undulating parkland. 18 holes, 6095 yards. S.S.S. 69. *Green Fees:* weekdays £25.00; weekends and Bank Holidays £30.00. *Visitors:* by arrangement. *Society Meetings:* by arrangement Tuesdays and Thursdays. Professional: Bob Johnson (01785 661485).Secretary: W.R. Lanyon (01785 661901).

STAFFORD. **Ingestre Park Golf Club,** Ingestre, Near Stafford (01889 270061). *Location:* six miles east of Stafford, between Tixall and Great Haywood. Parkland. 18 holes, 6334 yards. S.S.S. 70. *Green Fees:* 18 holes £20.00, £25.00 per day weekdays. *Eating facilities:* lunch and dinner menu. *Visitors:* welcome weekdays. Handicap Certificate required if playing before 3.30pm. *Society Meetings:* welcome with reservation except Wednesday. £30 all inclusive 27 holes package for Societies. Professional: Danny Scullion (01889 270304). Manager: D.D. Humphries (01889 270845).

STAFFORD. **Stafford Castle Golf Club,** Newport Road, Stafford ST16 1BP (01785 223821). *Location:* M6 Junction 13 or 14, two miles from club. Parkland course. 9 holes, 6071 yards. S.S.S. 69, Par 71. *Green Fees:* £14.00 weekdays; £18.00 weekends. *Eating facilities:* snacks and full catering available except Mondays. *Visitors:* welcome except Sunday mornings. Handicap Certificate required. *Society Meetings:* catered for by arrangement. Secretary: D.H. Fellowes. *

STOKE-ON-TRENT. **Burslem Golf Club Ltd,** Wood Farm, High Lane, Tunstall, Stoke-on-Trent ST6 7ST (01782 837006). *Location:* leave Burslem centre by Hamil Road, turn left at High Lane junction, 2 miles on right. 9 holes, 5800 yards. S.S.S. 68. *Green Fees:* information not provided. *Eating facilities:* meals and refreshments by arrangement except Wednesday and Sunday. *Visitors:* welcome weekdays with reservation. Bona fide golf club members only. *Society Meetings:* catered for. Secretary: F. Askey.

STOKE-ON-TRENT. **Greenway Hall Golf Club,** Greenway Hall, Stockton Brook, Stoke-on-Trent (01782 50318). 18 holes, 5803 yards. *Green Fees:* information not provided. *Visitors:* only with member during week, not weekends. *

STOKE-ON-TRENT. **Parkhall Golf Course,** Hulme Road, Weston Coyney, Stoke on Trent ST3 5BH (01782 599584). *Location:* one mile outside Longton. Parkland. 18 holes, 2335 yards, 2136 metres. S.S.S. 54. *Green Fees:* information not provided. *Visitors:* welcome. Seven days advance booking required for weekends and Bank Holidays. *Society Meetings:* welcome. Professional: T. Clingan. *

STOKE-ON-TRENT. **Trentham Golf Club,** 14 Barlaston Old Road, Trentham, Stoke-on-Trent ST3 8HB (01782 642347). *Location:* off A34 travelling south of Newcastle (Staffs.). Turn left at Trentham Gardens on Longton Road. Turn right at National Westminster Bank. Parkland with a sprinkling of trees. 18 holes, 6644 yards. S.S.S. 72. Practice ground. *Green Fees:* £30.00 weekdays; Sundays 12 noon onwards £35.00. Playing with member £8.00. *Eating facilities:* lunches and dinners available. *Visitors:* welcome except weekends, can play only from 12 noon onwards. Handicap Certificate required. *Society Meetings:* limited numbers catered for. Professional: Mark Budz (01782 657309). Secretary: R.B. Irving (01782 658109).

STOKE-ON-TRENT. **Trentham Park Golf Club,** Trentham Park, Trentham, Stoke-on-Trent ST4 8AE (01782 642245). *Location:* off A34 adjoining Trentham Gardens near Junction 15 on M6. 18 holes, 6403 yards. S.S.S. 71. *Green Fees:* £20.00 weekdays, £25.00 weekends. *Eating facilities:* available at clubhouse except Mondays. *Visitors:* welcome weekdays with reservation. *Society Meetings:* catered for Wednesdays and Fridays only. Professional: Jim McLeod (01782 642125). Secretary: R.N. Portas (01782 658800).

STONE. **Stone Golf Club,** Filleybrooks, Stone ST15 0NB (01785 813103). *Location:* one mile north of Stone on the A34 adjacent to the Wayfarer Hotel. Parkland. 9 holes, 6299 yards. S.S.S. 70. *Green Fees:* weekdays £15.00. *Eating facilities:* full meals to order, snacks always available, bar. *Visitors:* welcome weekdays only, not Bank Holidays. Snooker table. *Society Meetings:* catered for by arrangement. Secretary: M.G. Pharaoh (01889 508224).

STOURBRIDGE. **Enville Golf Club Ltd,** Highgate Common, Enville, Stourbridge DY7 5BN (01384 872551). *Location:* leave A449 at Stewpony Hotel taking Bridgnorth Road A458, fork right after Fox Inn following signs for Halfpenny Green Airport. Two flat wooded heathland courses. Highgate Course – 18 holes, 6556 yards. S.S.S 72; Lodge Course – 18 holes, 6217 yards. S.S.S. 70. *Green Fees:* weekdays £22.00 18 holes, £26.50 27 holes, £32.00 36 holes. *Eating facilities:* meals available except Mondays. *Visitors:* welcome weekdays with Handicap Certificate, advisable to phone prior to visit. Ladies' day Thursday; weekends with members only. *Society Meetings:* welcome except Thursdays and weekends. Professional: S. Power (01384 872585). Secretary/Manager: R.J. Bannister (01384 872074).

STREETLY. **Little Aston Golf Club,** Streetly, Sutton Coldfield B74 3AN (0121-353 2066). *Location:* off A454. Parkland course. 18 holes, 6670 yards. S.S.S. 73. *Green Fees:* on application. *Eating facilities:* lunches and dinner except Mondays. *Visitors:* welcome on weekdays by prior arrangement, weekends with a member. *Society Meetings:* catered for on weekdays only. Professional: John Anderson (0121-353 2942). Secretary: N.H. Russell (0121-353 2942).

TAMWORTH. **Drayton Park Golf Club,** Drayton Park, Tamworth B78 3TN (01827 251139). *Location:* two miles south of Tamworth on A4091, next to Drayton Manor Leisure Park. Parkland with wooded areas. 18 holes, 6214 yards. S.S.S. 70. Practice area. *Green Fees:* weekdays £27.00 per round/day. Special rates for Societies over 12. *Eating facilities:* full catering facilities. *Visitors:* welcome weekdays, weekends with member only. *Society Meetings:* catered for Tuesdays and Thursdays, booked through Secretary. Professional: M.W. Passmore (01827 251478). Secretary: A.O. Rammell (01827 251139).

TAMWORTH. **Tamworth Municipal Golf Club,** Eagle Drive, Amington, Tamworth B77 4EG (01827 53858). *Location:* M42 off B5000 Amington, Tamworth, signposted. Parkland course used by NAPGC for Juniors and Ladies Championships. 18 holes, 6083 metres. S.S.S. 72. Practice area. *Green Fees:* £7.80. Reduced rates during the week for unemployed. *Eating facilities:* bar, snacks. *Visitors:* welcome every day, no restrictions. *Society Meetings:* welcome weekdays. Professional: Barry Jones (01827 53850). Secretary: Mrs Brenda Read-Jones (01827 373333).

UTTOXETER. **Uttoxeter Golf Club,** Woodgate Farm, Wood Lane, Uttoxeter ST14 7LZ (01889 565108). *Location:* quarter of a mile past racecourse, about half a mile from town centre. Undulating parkland, very picturesque scenery. 18 holes, 5468 yards. S.S.S. 68. Par 68. Practice net and putting area. *Green Fees:* £13.00 per round, £20.00 per day weekdays; £17.00 per round weekends and Bank Holidays. *Eating facilities:* by arrangement with Steward. *Visitors:* always welcome, but not on major competition days. *Society Meetings:* welcome (groups of four and over). Rates for visiting parties £27.50 per day including refreshments. Professional: Mr John Pearsall (01889 564884). Secretary: Mrs G. Davies (01889 566552).

WOLSTANTON. **Wolstanton Golf Club,** Dimsdale Old Hall, Hassam Parade, Wolstanton, Newcastle (01782 616995). *Location:* one mile north of Newcastle, turn right off A34 (Dimsdale Parade), first right (Hassam Parade) then right again 75 yards. Flat parkland. 18 holes, 5807 yards. S.S.S. 68. *Green Fees:* weekdays £18.00, £7.00 as member's guest; weekends as member's guest only £18.00. *Eating facilities:* full catering service and bar. *Visitors:* welcome weekdays; weekends only as member's guest. *Society Meetings:* catered for by arrangement. Professional: (01782 622718). Secretary: M.A. Staniforth (01782 622413).

Suffolk

ALDEBURGH. **Aldeburgh Golf Club,** Aldeburgh IP15 5PE (01728 452408). *Location:* one mile from town centre on A1094. Heathland course. 18 holes, 6366 yards. S.S.S. 71; also 9 holes, 2114 yards. S.S.S. 32. *Green Fees:* weekdays £30.00 per day, £20.00 after 12 noon; weekends £36.00 per day, £25.00 after 12 noon. *Eating facilities:* available, no evening meals. *Visitors:* welcome, to play on 18 hole course must have club Handicap Certificate. No three or four balls allowed. *Society Meetings:* by arrangement. Professional: K.R. Preston (01728 453309). Secretary: R.C. Van de Velde (01728 452890).

BECCLES. **Wood Valley (Beccles) Golf Club,** The Common, Beccles NR34 9BX (01502 712244). *Location:* A146 Norwich, Lowestoft, River Waveney, Church Tower, Safeway. Flat heathland. 9 holes, 5558 yards, 5084 metres. S.S.S. 67. *Green Fees:* weekdays £10.00 (with member £8.00); weekends and Bank Holidays £12.00 (with member £10.00). *Eating facilities:* two bars, snacks available. Meals to order. *Visitors:* welcome, must play with member on Sundays and Bank Holidays, course closed Sunday 1.30pm-5.30pm April to September. *Society Meetings:* catered for (not weekends or Bank Holidays). Secretary: Mrs L.W. Allen (01502 712479).

BUNGAY. **Bungay and Waveney Valley Golf Club,** Outney Common, Bungay NR35 1DS (01986 892337). *Location:* a quarter mile from town centre and alongside A143. Flat, links-type course. 18 holes, 6063 yards. S.S.S. 69. *Green Fees:* £18.00 per day. *Eating facilities:* available except Mondays. *Visitors:* welcome weekdays, weekends with member only. *Society Meetings:* by arrangement with Secretary. Professional: N. Whyte (01986 892337). Secretary: W.J. Stevens (01986 892337).

BURY ST. EDMUNDS. **Bury St. Edmunds Golf Club,** Tut Hill, Bury St. Edmunds IP28 6LG (01284 755977). *Location:* B1106 just off A45. Flat parkland. 18 holes, 6615 yards. S.S.S. 72; 9 holes, 4664 yards. S.S.S. 63. Practice facilities. *Green Fees:* weekdays £24.00 on 18 hole course, £11.00 on 9 hole course; weekends 9 hole course Saturdays only £12.00. *Eating facilities:* available. *Visitors:* welcome Monday to Friday on both courses; Saturday on 9 hole course. *Society Meetings:* catered for. Professional: Mark Jillings (01284 755978). Secretary: John C. Sayer (01284 755979).

BURY ST. EDMUNDS. **Flempton Golf Club,** Flempton, Bury St. Edmunds IP28 6EQ (01284 728291). *Location:* follow A1101 from Bury St. Edmunds towards Mildenhall for about four miles, course on right. 9 holes, 6240 yards. S.S.S. 70. *Green Fees:* weekdays £18.50 per round of 18 holes, £24.00 per day, weekends only with member. *Eating facilities:* by arrangement. *Visitors:* not weekends or Bank Holidays. Must produce Handicap Certificate. Professional: Jamie Perks (01284 728817). Secretary: P.H. Nunn.

BURY ST. EDMUNDS. **Fornham Park Golf and Country Club,** The Street, Fornham All Saints, Bury St. Edmunds IP28 6JQ (01284 706777; Fax: 01284 706721). *Location:* two miles from Bury St. Edmunds (A45), off A1101 to Mildenhall, village of Fornham All Saints. Flat parkland, interesting water hazards. 18 holes, 6209 yards. S.S.S. 70. Practice ground and putting green. *Green Fees:* weekdays £8.00 per round; weekends £10.00 per round. *Eating facilities:* bar and food available all week. Some concessions, details on application. *Visitors:* welcome anytime (public course). Advance bookings accepted. *Society Meetings:* welcome by arrangement. Professional: Sean Clark (01284 706777; Fax: 01284 706721). Operations Manager: Amanda Nunn.

COLCHESTER. **Stoke by Nayland Golf Club,** Keepers Lane, Leavenheath, Colchester CO6 4PZ (01206 262836; Fax: 01206 263356). *Location:* just off A134 Colchester to Sudbury on B1068 towards Stoke by Nayland. Undulating parkland with water hazards. Two courses (1) Gainsborough – 18 holes, 6516 yards. S.S.S. 71. (2) Constable – 18 holes, 6544 yards. S.S.S. 71. 20 bay covered range, practice area. *Green Fees:* on request. Handicap golfers only. *Eating facilities:* full catering and bars. *Visitors:* welcome weekdays, phone call advisable; weekends after 10.30am, must produce Handicap Certificate. Accommodation, squash courts, sauna and fishing also available. *Society Meetings:* welcome weekdays, book well in advance. Professional: Kevin Lovelock (01206 262769). Secretary/ Manager: Jonathan Loshak (01206 262836).

FELIXSTOWE. **Felixstowe Ferry Golf Club,** Ferry Road, Felixstowe IP11 9RY (01394 283060). *Location:* follow signs to Yacht Centre. Seaside links course. 18 holes, 6308 yards. S.S.S. 70. Practice area. *Green Fees:* £21.00 per day, weekends and Bank Holidays £25.00. *Eating facilities:* diningroom and bar. *Visitors:* welcome, but advisable to check first. Two self catering flats available, free golf included in charges. *Society Meetings:* catered for Tuesdays, Wednesdays and Fridays. Professional: Ian MacPherson (01394 283975). Secretary: Ian H. Kimber (01394 286834).

FRAMLINGHAM. **Cretingham Golf Club,** Cretingham, Woodbridge IP13 7BA (01728 685275). *Location:* A1120 to Earl Soham, Cretingham Golf Club signposted. Wooded inland course, undulating terrain. 9 holes, 4024 yards (for 18 holes). S.S.S. 62. Practice area. *Green Fees:* weekdays £7.00, £6.00 with a member; weekends and Bank Holidays £10.00, £9.00

with a member. *Eating facilities:* full bar and catering available. *Visitors:* always welcome, no handicap required, smart casual dress. Caravan park. *Society Meetings:* welcome. Professional: Colin Jenkins. Secretary: Marion Jenkins.

HALESWORTH. **St. Helena Golf Club,** Bramfield Road, Halesworth IP19 9XA (01986 875567; Fax: 01986 874565). *Location:* A12, A144 through Bramfield; over crossroad, then first right. Undulating parkland course just inland from the Heritage Coast. St. Helena Course: 18 holes, 6580 yards. S.S.S. 72. Halesworth Course: 9 holes, 3059 yards. S.S.S. 36. Practice ground. *Green Fees:* 9 hole course £7.50; 18 hole course £15.00 weekdays, £18.00 weekends. *Eating facilities:* available. *Visitors:* no restrictions. *Society Meetings:* welcome. Professional: P.M. Heil. Secretary: Mrs R.K. Ward.

HAVERHILL. **Haverhill Golf Club Ltd,** Coupals Road, Haverhill CB9 7UW (01440 61951; Fax: 01440 714883). *Location:* A604 Sturmer road turn into Chalkestone Way, near railway viaduct, right into Coupals Road. Club is one mile on right. Undulating parkland with river features. 9 holes, 5707 yards. S.S.S. 68. Practice ground. *Green Fees:* weekdays £10.00 per 18 holes, £15.00 per day; weekends and Bank Holidays £15.00 per 18 holes, £20.00 per day. Half price if playing with a member. Practice ground fee of £1.00 for non-members. *Eating facilities:* bar (rolls available). *Visitors:* welcome at all times except when first tee booked for matches and societies. *Society Meetings:* by arrangement with Secretary. Professional: Simon Mayfield (01440 712628). Secretary: Jill Edwards (01440 61951).

IPSWICH. **Fynn Valley Golf Club,** Witnesham, Ipswich IP6 9JA (01473 785202). *Location:* two miles due north of Ipswich on B1077. Rolling, undulating parkland along the Fynn Valley. 18 holes, 5850 yards, 5400 metres. S.S.S. 68. Floodlit covered golf range. *Green Fees:* £15.00 weekdays; £20.00 weekends. *Eating facilities:* bar terrace, gourmet restaurant. *Visitors:* welcome, members only Sunday mornings, Ladies priority Wednesday mornings. Weekly residential courses available at all levels. *Society Meetings:* welcome weekdays, 25% discounts. Professional: Robin Mann (Tel & Fax: 01473 785463). Secretary: Merryn Tyrrell (01473 785267; Fax: 01473 785632).

IPSWICH. **Hintlesham Hall Golf Club,** Hintlesham, Ipswich IP8 3NS (01473 652761; Fax: 01473 652750). *Location:* four miles west of Ipswich on the A1071 to Sudbury. Parkland, championship standard – Architect: Martin Hawtree. 18 holes, 6638 yards. S.S.S. 72. Full practice facilities. *Green Fees:* weekdays £26.00; weekends £45.00. *Eating facilities:* full catering facilities. *Visitors:* please telephone for tee off times. Accommodation available at Hintlesham Hall Hotel. *Society Meetings:* telephone enquiries welcome. We have a growing national reputation for the organisation of golf days. Professional: Alastair Spink.

IPSWICH. **Ipswich Golf Club,** Purdis Heath, Bucklesham Road, Ipswich IP3 8UQ (01473 727474). *Location:* three miles east of Ipswich on Bucklesham Road, A12 and A45. Heathland. 18 holes, 6405 yards. S.S.S. 71. 9 holes, 1930 yards. S.S.S. 59. *Green Fees:* 18 hole course £30.00 weekdays, £36.00 weekends per day. 9 hole course £8.00 per day, £10.00 weekends and Bank Holidays. *Eating facilities:* full catering facilities available for visitors to 18 hole course only. *Visitors:* by prior arrangement for 18 hole course, and must produce Handicap Certificate or letter of introduction. No restriction for 9 hole course. *Society Meetings:* by special reservation only and on Society terms. Professional: S.J. Whymark (01473 724017). Secretary: Brig A.P. Wright MBE (01473 728941).

IPSWICH. **Rushmere Golf Club,** Rushmere Heath, Woodbridge Road, Ipswich IP4 5QQ (01473 727109). *Location:* off A1214 north from Ipswich, 300 yards signposted. Heathland course. 18 holes, 6287 yards. S.S.S. 70. Practice facilities. *Green Fees:* £18.00. *Eating facilities:* full catering available. *Visitors:* welcome except 4.30 – 5.30pm, weekends after 2.30pm. Handicap Certificate required. *Society Meetings:* welcome. Professional: N.T.J. McNeill (01473 728076). Secretary: P.L. Coles (01473 725648).

LOWESTOFT. **Rookery Park Golf Club,** Beccles Road, Carlton Colville, Lowestoft (01502 574009). *Location:* west of Lowestoft on A146. Flat parkland. 18 holes, 6898 yards, S.S.S. 72. 9 hole Par 3 course. Practice ground. *Green Fees:* weekdays £20.00; weekends £25.00. Half price when playing with a member. *Eating facilities:* full catering and two bars. *Visitors:* welcome if members of recognised golf club, please telephone before coming. *Society Meetings:* welcome. Professional: M. Elsworthy (01502 515103). Secretary: S.R. Cooper (01502 560380).

MILDENHALL. **Royal Worlington and Newmarket Golf Club,** Golf Links Road, Worlington, Mildenhall IP28 8SD (01638 712216). *Location:* six miles north east of Newmarket, signposted off A11 just south of Barton Mills roundabout. Inland links type course. 9 holes, 3105 yards, 2840 metres. S.S.S. 70 (18 holes). Practice ground. *Green Fees:* weekdays £32.00 per day, £21 per half day. *Eating facilities:* lunch and tea available with prior notice; no evening meals. *Visitors:* welcome weekdays, Handicap Certificate or letter of introduction from home club required. *Society Meetings:* catered for Tuesdays or Thursdays – booking well in advance essential. Charge £42.00, foursomes only. Professional: M. Hawkins (01638 715224). Secretary: Major G. Hipkin (01638 712216; Fax: 01638 717787).

NEWMARKET. **Links Golf Club,** Cambridge Road, Newmarket CB8 0TG (01638 662708). *Location:* one and a half miles south of Newmarket High Street, opposite racecourse. Relatively flat parkland. 18 holes, 6424 yards. S.S.S. 71. Two practice grounds. *Green Fees:* £24.00 weekdays; £28.00 weekends and Bank Holidays. *Eating facilities:* diningroom daily, normal bar hours. *Visitors:* current Handicap Certificate required weekdays/weekends except for members of organised golf societies. Not before 11.30am Sunday unless member's guest. *Society Meetings:* mid-week only by prior arrangement. Professional: Mr John Sharkey (Tel & Fax: 01638 662395). Secretary: Mrs T. MacGregor (01638 663000).

RAYDON. **Brett Vale Golf Club,** Noakes Road, Raydon, Ipswich IP7 5LR (01473 310718). *Location:* midway between Colchester and Ipswich, just off A12 on B1070 to Hadleigh – head for Raydon Water Tower. Within Dedham Vale, the course is designed to complement its natural valley setting. 18 holes, 5808 yards. S.S.S. 68. 5-bay indoor Golf Academy, practice ground, Pro's shop; electric buggy and power trolley hire. *Green Fees:* weekdays £15.00, day ticket £25.00; weekends £17.50, day ticket £27.50. Reductions for Juniors. *Eating facilities:* clubroom bar and restaurant; society/function room and bar. *Visitors:* welcome anytime. *Society Meetings:* welcome anytime, various packages available. Professional: Andrew Boulter. Secretary: Mrs Lesley Morrison (01473 310718; Fax: 01473 824482).

SOUTHWOLD. **Southwold Golf Club,** The Common, Southwold (01502 723234). *Location:* from A12 Blythburgh turn off on A1095 to Southwold. Flat common land with sea views. 9 holes, 6050 yards. S.S.S. 69. *Green Fees:* £14.00 per round weekdays; £18.00 weekends. *Visitors:* welcome, phone for availability. *Society Meetings:* welcome, subject to availability. Professional: B.G. Allen (01502 723790). Secretary: Mr D.F. Randall (01502 723248).

STOWMARKET. **Stowmarket Golf Club Ltd,** Lower Road, Onehouse, Stowmarket IP14 3DA (01449 736473). *Location:* on B1508 from Stowmarket to Onehouse. Parkland. 18 holes, 6101 yards. S.S.S. 69. Driving range. *Green Fees:* weekdays £20.00 per round, £25.00 per day; weekends £25.00 per round, £33.00 per day. *Eating facilities:* lunches except Mondays, snacks all week. *Visitors:* welcome, avoid Wednesdays. Handicap Certificate required at weekends. *Society Meetings:* catered for Thursdays and Fridays only. Professional: C. S. Aldred (01449 736392). Secretary: J. Edwards-Hayes (01449 736473).

SUDBURY. **Newton Green Golf Club,** Newton Green, Sudbury (01787 377501). *Location:* on A134 east of Sudbury. Flat course. 9 holes, 5488 yards, 5022 metres. S.S.S. 67. *Green Fees:* £15.00, weekends only with member. *Eating facilities:* available. *Visitors:* welcome Monday to Friday (except Tuesday). *Society Meetings:* catered for, not more than 20 persons. Professional: K. Lovelock (01787 210910). Secretary: G. Bright (01787 377217). *

THORPENESS. **Thorpeness Golf Club and Hotel,** Thorpeness, Leiston IP16 4NH (01728 452176; Fax: 01728 453868). *Location:* leave A12 at Aldeburgh turnoff. Gorse and heather inland course. 18 holes, 6241 yards. S.S.S. 71. *Green Fees:* weekdays £25.00 per round, £35.00 per day; weekends £30.00 per round, £45.00 per day. *Visitors:* welcome without reservation. Accommodation available – 22 bedrooms. *Society Meetings:* catered for. Professional: Mr M. Grantham (01728 454926). General Manager: N. Griffin.

WOODBRIDGE. **Seckford Golf Club,** Seckford Hall Road, Great Bealings, Woodbridge (01394 388000; Fax: 01394 382818). *Location:* between Martlesham and Woodbridge just off A12. Undulating parkland course. 18 holes, 5088 yards. S.S.S. 64. Golf range next to Hotel. *Green Fees:* weekdays £12.00 per day, weekends £12.00 per round. *Eating facilities:* catering available. *Visitors:* no restrictions. *Society Meetings:* welcome. Professional/Secretary: T. Pennock.

PUBLISHER'S NOTE

While every effort is made to ensure accuracy, we regret that FHG Publications cannot accept responsibility for errors, omissions or misrepresentation in our entries or any consequences thereof. Prices in particular should be checked because we go to press early. We will follow up complaints, but cannot act as arbiters or agents for either party.

WOODBRIDGE. **Ufford Park Hotel, Golf and Leisure Centre,** Yarmouth Road, Ufford, Woodbridge IP12 1QW (01394 383555). *Location:* A12 northwards to A1152 to Melton. In Melton turn left at traffic lights one mile on the right hand side. Parkland course with 10 water hazards. 18 holes, 6078 yards (6335 Medal). S.S.S. 70. *Green Fees:* weekdays £14.00; weekends £18.00. *Eating facilities:* spikes bar, restaurant, bar and patio. *Visitors:* welcome anytime. Hotel, conference and banqueting. Large leisure centre and indoor swimming pool. *Society Meetings:* welcome. Golf Director: Jon Marks (01394 382836). Golf Co-ordinator: David Cotton.

WOODBRIDGE. **Waldringfield Heath Golf Club,** Newbourne Road, Waldringfield, Woodbridge IP12 4PT (01473 736426). *Location:* three miles north of Ipswich off old A12. Flat, easy walking, heathland course. 18 holes, 6153 yards. S.S.S. 69. Limited practice area. *Green Fees:* weekdays £10.00 per round, £15.00 per day; weekends £13.00 per round. Special rates available by arrangement. *Eating facilities:* full service. *Visitors:* welcome weekdays, weekends after 12 noon. *Society Meetings:* welcome weekdays by arrangement. Professional: A. Dobson (01473 736417). Secretary: L.J. McWade (01473 736768).

WOODBRIDGE. **Woodbridge Golf Club,** Bromeswell Heath, Woodbridge IP12 2PF (01394 383212). *Location:* leave A12 at Melton Roundabout. After traffic lights, follow A1152 over level crossing, fork left at roundabout. Club is 400 yards on right. Heathland. 18 holes, 6314 yards. S.S.S. 70. 9 holes, 2243 yards. S.S.S. 62. Large practice ground. *Green Fees:* £28.00 weekdays. Societies £32.00 per round or day. *Eating facilities:* main bar, casual bar and restaurant. *Visitors:* not before 9.30am, not at weekends. Handicap Certificates mandatory on 18 hole course, no restriction on 9 hole course. Telephone call advisable. *Society Meetings:* by prior arrangement, maximum number 36. Professional: L.A. Jones (01394 383213). Secretary: Capt. L.A. Harpum RN (01394 382038; 01394 382392).

Surrey

BAGSHOT. **Pennyhill Park Hotel and Country Club,** London Road, Bagshot GU19 5ET (01276 471774; Fax: 01276 475570). *Location:* just off A30 at Bagshot. Wooded, hilly course. 9 holes, 2000 yards. S.S.S. 64. *Green Fees:* weekdays £10.00; weekends £15.00. *Eating facilities:* on site bar and light snacks – in Hotel full à la carte restaurant. *Visitors:* welcome anytime, booking for Sunday advisable. Hotel with 76 de luxe rooms; tennis, horse riding, clay pigeon shooting, etc. *Society Meetings:* welcome anytime. Professional: lessons on request. Manager: Sharon Millen. *

BANSTEAD. **Cuddington (Banstead) Golf Club Ltd,** Banstead Road, Banstead SM7 1RD (0181-393 0952; Fax: 0181-786 7025). *Location:* 200 yards from Banstead Railway Station. 18 holes, 6394 yards. S.S.S. 70. *Green Fees:* on application. *Visitors:* welcome with reservation. *Society Meetings:* catered for on Thursdays. Professional: J. Morgan. Secretary: D. M. Scott.

BLETCHINGLEY. **Bletchingley Golf Club,** Church Lane, Bletchingley (01883 744666). *Location:* off A25, three miles Junction 6 M25. Parkland course. 18 holes, 6504 yards. S.S.S. 71. Practice area. *Green Fees:* weekdays £20.00 per round. *Eating facilities:* lounge/ dining room, bar. *Visitors:* welcome weekdays only. Handicap Certificate or competence check. *Society Meetings:* welcome. Professional: Paul Webster (01883 744848). Manager: Colin Manktelow (01883 744666; Fax: 01883 744284).

BROOKWOOD. **West Hill Golf Club,** Bagshot Road, Brookwood GU24 0BH (01483 472110). *Location:* M3, Junction 3, A322 entrance adjacent railway bridge Brookwood. Heather, heathland, wooded course. 18 holes, 6368 yards. S.S.S. 70. Practice range and net. *Green Fees:* weekdays £42.00 per day. *Eating facilities:* bar snacks available, meals including dinner by prior arrangement. *Visitors:* by arrangement through the Professional. *Society Meetings:* catered for by arrangement through the Secretary. Professional: J.C. Clements (01483 473172). Secretary: M.C. Swatton (01483 474365).

CAMBERLEY. **Camberley Heath Golf Club,** Golf Drive, Portsmouth Road, Camberley GU15 1JG (01276 23258; Fax: 01276 692505). *Location:* adjacent to Ravenswood roundabout on the A325. Heathland and pine, designed by Harry Colt – his best. 18 holes, 6337 yards. S.S.S. 70. Practice ground. *Green Fees:* weekdays £30.00 per round, Saturdays accompanied by a member, £40.00 per round. *Eating facilities:* restaurants and Teppan Yaki (Japanese cuisine). *Visitors:* welcome weekdays only. *Society Meetings:* welcome by prior arrangement weekdays only. Professional: Gary Smith (01276 27905). Secretary/General Manager: J. Greenwood (01276 23258). *

CARSHALTON. **Oaks Sports Centre Ltd,** Woodmansterne Lane, Carshalton SM5 4AN (0181-643 8363; Fax: 0181-770 7303). *Location:* on the B2032 past Carshalton Beeches Station, Oaks Sports Centre signposted north of A2022, half way between A217 and A237. Meadowland course. 18 holes, 5975 yards. S.S.S 69. 9 holes, 1590 yards. S.S.S 28. 18 bay golf range. *Green Fees:* £10.00 per 18 holes, £4.50 per 9 holes weekdays; £12.00 per 18 holes, £5.50 per 9 holes weekends. *Eating facilities:* bar lounge, restaurant (no smoking). *Visitors:* public course, everyone welcome. Five squash courts, changing rooms. *Society Meetings:* by arrangement. Professional: Mr G.D. Horley. Secretary: Mr J. Greenaway.

CHERTSEY. **Barrow Hill Golf Club,** Longcross, Chertsey KT16 0DS. *Location:* four miles west of Chertsey. 18 holes, 3090 yards. S.S.S. 53. *Green Fees:* information not provided. *Visitors:* only with a member. *Society Meetings:* not accommodated. Secretary: R.W. Routley (01932 848117).

CHERTSEY. **Laleham Golf Club,** Laleham Reach, Mixnams Lane, Chertsey KT16 8RP (01932 562188; Fax: 01932 564448). *Location:* M25 to Junction 10, follow directions to Thorpe Park, entrance opposite roundabout. Flat but interesting parkland course with water features. 18 holes, 6211 yards. S.S.S. 70. Practice ground and nets. *Green Fees:* weekdays £25.00 per day, £16.50 per round; weekends with member only. Special 50% discount of full day rate for bona fide members of recognised golf club with CONGU or USGA Handicaps. *Eating facilities:* full restaurant and bar facilities. *Visitors:* welcome weekdays only, please phone to ensure no tee reservations and to take advantage of discount scheme. *Society Meetings:* catered for weekdays at competitive rates. Professional: Hogan Stott (01932 562877). Secretary: Rob Fry (01932 564211).

CHESSINGTON. **Chessington Golf Club,** Garrison Lane, Chessington KT9 2LW (0181-391 0948). *Location:* off A243, 500 yards from Chessington World of Adventure. Opposite Chessington South Station, Junction 9 M25. Flat course. 9 holes, 1530 yards, 1401 metres. S.S.S. 28. Covered floodlit driving range. Green Fees: weekdays £3.85; weekends and Bank Holidays £4.75 (for 9 holes). Reductions for Juniors and Senior Citizens. *Eating facilities:* bar, coffee, catering available. *Visitors:* welcome, must book for weekend mornings. Facilities open to public 8am until 10pm seven days a week. *Society Meetings:* welcome. Professional: (0181-391 0948). Secretary: Tony Maxted (0181-974 1705).

CHESSINGTON. **Surbiton Golf Club,** Woodstock Lane, Chessington KT9 1UG (0181-398 2056; Fax: 0181-339 0992). *Location:* two miles east of Esher, off A3 at Ace of Spades roundabout. Undulating parkland.

18 holes, 6055 yards. S.S.S. 69, Par 70. Limited practice area. *Green Fees:* £27.00 per round, £40.50 per day. *Eating facilities:* snacks and lunches to order by reservation weekdays. *Society Meetings:* catered for Monday and Friday only. Professional: Paul Milton (0181-398 6619). Secretary: G.A. Keith MBE (0181-398 3101).

CHIDDINGFOLD. **Shillinglee Park Golf Club,** Chiddingfold, Godalming GU8 4TA (01428 653237; Fax: 01428 644391). *Location:* off A283 near Chiddingfold. Parkland. 9 holes, 5300 yards. S.S.S. 64. 6 hole pitch and putt course, ideal for learners. Well equipped Pro Shop. *Green Fees:* weekdays £7.50 for 9 holes, £11.00 for 18; weekends £8.50 for 9 holes, £13.00 for 18 holes. Daily rate, plus Senior Citizens' and Junior rates. Season tickets and club membership available. Gradually reducing twilight green fees – the later you play the less you pay. Special rates for unemployed and students. *Eating facilities:* excellent menu from snacks to à la carte. *Visitors:* welcome at all times, advisable to book. Instruction available. *Society Meetings:* always welcome. Professional/Secretary: Roger Mace.

CHIPSTEAD. **Chipstead Golf Club Ltd,** How Lane, Coulsdon CR5 3PR (01737 551053). *Location:* by Chipstead Station (Tattenham Corner Line). Parkland. 18 holes, 5454 yards, 4351 metres. S.S.S. 67. *Green Fees:* £25.00 before 2.00pm, £20.00 after 2.00pm. *Eating facilities:* available. *Visitors:* welcome weekdays only. *Society Meetings:* catered for Thursdays. Professional: Gary Torbett (01737 554939). Secretary: S. Spencer-Skeen (01737 555781).

COBHAM. **Silvermere Golf and Leisure Complex,** Redhill Road, Cobham (01932 866007). Individual bookings (01932 867275). Open for the public seven days a week. Administration enquiries for Society bookings and Company Days (01932 866007). *Location:* from Junction 10, M25 take A3 then A245, B366 to Byfleet, half a mile on right. From London take Cobham turn-off then A245 to Byfleet, half a mile on left into Redhill Road. London 25 minutes, Heathrow 15 minutes, Gatwick 25 minutes. Seven holes tight heathland, 10 holes open parkland, one hole (17th) completely over water. 18 holes, 6333 yards. S.S.S. 71. 34 bay floodlit (till 10.00pm) driving range. *Green Fees:* weekdays £16.50; weekends £22.00 bookable by telephone. Professional's Golf Superstore open seven days till 10.00pm. All top named brands stocked. Clubs may be tried on range prior to purchase. *Eating facilities:* full service from 7.00am – breakfast, lunch, snacks and dinner; bar facilities seven days a week. *Society Meetings:* welcome, £49.50 for full day including dinner. All enquiries to Secretary. Professional: Doug McClelland PGA (01932 867275). Secretary: Mrs Pauline Devereux (01932 866007).

COULSDON. **Coulsdon Manor Golf Centre,** Coulsdon Road, Coulsdon CR5 2LL (0181-668 0414). *Location:* off M23/M25 A23 London to Brighton road. Parkland. 18 holes, 6030 yards. S.S.S. 68. *Green Fees:* weekdays £12.00; weekends £15.00. *Eating facilities:* elegant restaurant offering table d'hôte and à la carte menus. Two relaxing bars with top quality bar food. *Visitors:* welcome. *Society Meetings:* welcome. Extensive banquet and conference facilities, 35 luxurious bedrooms, all en-suite. Professional: Mike Homewood (0181-660 6083). General Manager: Mr Rhodes.

COULSDON. **Woodcote Park Golf Club Ltd,** Meadow Hill, Bridle Way, Coulsdon CR5 2QQ (0181-660 2577). *Location:* south of Croydon, on B2030. 18 holes, 6669 yards. S.S.S. 72. *Green Fees:* information not available. *Eating facilities:* meals by arrangement, bar snacks. *Visitors:* welcome with reservation. *Society Meetings:* up to 60 catered for, by arrangement. Professional: Mr David Hudspith (0181-668 1843). Secretary: T.J. Fenson (Tel & Fax: 0181-668 2788).

CRANLEIGH. **Fernfell Golf and Country Club,** Barhatch Lane, Cranleigh GU6 7NG (01483 268855). *Location:* Guildford A281 Horsham take Cranleigh turn-off. Interesting parkland course. 18 holes, 5599 yards. S.S.S. 67. Par 68. *Green Fees:* £20.00 per round, £30.00 per two rounds weekdays. *Eating facilities:* bar, bar snacks, banqueting facilities available. *Visitors:* welcome weekdays only. Tennis. *Society Meetings:* welcome weekdays (£45.00). Professional: Trevor Longmuir (01483 277188). Secretary: Catherine Kimberley (01483 268855; Fax: 01483 267251). *

CROYDON. **Addington Court Golf Courses,** Featherbed Lane, Addington, Croydon CR0 9AA (0181-657 0281/3). *Location:* two miles east of Croydon. Leave B281 at Addington Village. Undulating. Four courses – Old Championship 5577 yards, S.S.S. 67. New Falconwood 5513 yards, S.S.S. 66. Lower 9 hole course 1812 yards, S.S.S 62. 18 hole, Par 3 course. *Green Fees:* £2.50 – £12.00. *Eating facilities:* full range available. *Visitors:* golfers and non-golfers welcome. *Society Meetings:* catered for weekdays only. Professional/Managing Director: G.A. Cotton. *

CROYDON. **Addington Palace Golf Club,** Gravel Hill, Addington, Croydon CR0 5BB (0181-654 2650). *Location:* two miles East Croydon Station. 18 holes, 6262 yards. S.S.S. 71. *Green Fees:* weekdays £25.00. *Visitors:* welcome weekdays, weekends and Bank Holidays must be accompanied by a member. Professional: Roger Williams (0181-654 1786). Secretary: Martin Moore (0181-654 3061).

CROYDON. **Croham Hurst Golf Club,** Croham Road, South Croydon CR2 7HJ (0181-657 2075). *Location:* midway between Croydon and Selsdon. Parkland. 18 holes, 6286 yards. S.S.S. 70. *Green Fees:* weekdays £32.00; weekends £42. *Eating facilities:* lunches, teas, snacks. *Visitors:* welcome with reservation on weekdays. *Society Meetings:* catered for booked one year ahead. Professional: E. Stillwell (0181-657 7705). Secretary: Ray Passingham (0181-657 5581).

CROYDON. **Shirley Park Golf Club Ltd,** 194 Addiscombe Road, Croydon CR0 7LB (0181-654 1143). *Location:* on A232 one and a half miles from East Croydon Station. Parkland. 18 holes, 6210 yards. S.S.S. 70. Practice area. *Green Fees:* £28.00 weekdays. *Eating facilities:* breakfast/snack lunch/ dinner, two bars. *Visitors:* welcome weekdays 9.30am/

12 noon and 1pm/4pm; weekends only with a member. *Society Meetings:* catered for Tuesdays and half day Mondays, Thursdays and Fridays (afternoon). Professional: Nick Allen (0181-654 8767). Secretary: Andrew Baird (0181-654 1143).

CROYDON. **Selsdon Park Hotel Golf Course,** Sanderstead, South Croydon, Surrey CR2 8YA (0181-657 8811; Fax: 0181-651 6171). *Location:* three miles south of Croydon on A2022 Purley-West Wickham road. Parkland course, designed by J.H. Taylor. 18 holes, 6407 yards, 5854 metres. S.S.S. 71. Practice ground. *Green Fees:* weekdays from £20.00 (18), £30.00 (36); Saturdays £35.00, Sundays and Bank Holidays £35.00. Reduced rates if starting after twilight. Reduced fees for resident guests. *Eating facilities:* hotel bars, restaurant and grill. *Visitors:* welcome all week with pre-bookable tee-off times, some times reserved for hotel guests. *Society Meetings:* welcome by prior arrangement. P.G.A. Professionals: Tom O'Keefe; Sam Torrance Touring Golf Professional (0181-657 4129). Golf Reservations: (0181-657 8811). *

DORKING. **Betchworth Park Golf Club (Dorking) Ltd,** Reigate Road, Dorking (01306 885929). *Location:* on A25 half a mile east of Dorking on Reigate Road. Parkland course. 18 holes, 6266 yards. S.S.S. 70. *Green Fees:* weekdays £31.00; weekends (when permitted) £43.00. *Eating facilities:* lunches to order, bar snacks and bar facilities daily. *Visitors:* welcome all day Mondays and Thursdays, pm Tuesdays and Wednesdays, restricted on Fridays. Handicap Certificate required. *Society Meetings:* welcome Mondays and Thursdays. Professional: Rick Blackie (01306 884334). Secretary: D.A.S. Bradney (01306 882052).

DORKING. **Dorking Golf Club,** Chart Park, Dorking RH5 4BX (01306 886917). *Location:* on A24 half-a-mile south of junction with A25. Parkland/downland. 9 holes, alternative tees second 9, 5106 yards. S.S.S. 65. *Green Fees:* £16.00 per round. *Eating facilities:* full catering except Mondays. *Visitors:* weekdays only without reservation. *Society Meetings:* catered for up to 24, over this number by arrangement. Professional: P. Napier. Secretary: J.B. Hawkins.

DORKING. **Gatton Manor Hotel, Golf and Country Club,** Standon Lane, Ockley, Near Dorking RH5 5PQ (01306 627555; Fax: 01306 627713). *Location:* one and a half miles off A29 at Ockley, nine miles south of Dorking on A24, midway between London and South Coast. Undulating course, wooded and scenic water holes. 18 holes, 6903 yards. S.S.S. 72. *Green Fees:* weekdays £26.00 per day, £15.00 per round, £10.00 after 4pm; weekends £40.00 per day, £20.00 per round, £15.00 after 4pm. *Eating facilities:* bar meals and à la carte restaurant. *Visitors:* welcome every day except Sunday mornings. Hotel, conference suites. Fishing, tennis, bowls available. *Society Meetings:* welcome weekdays. Professional: Rae Sargent (01306 627557). Secretary: David G. Heath. *

EAST HORSLEY. **Drift Golf Club,** The Drift, East Horsley, Leatherhead KT24 5HD (01483 284641). *Location:* the club is located just off the Drift Road which runs between Ockham Road and Forest Road, East Horsley. 18 holes, 6425 yards. S.S.S. 72. *Green Fees:* weekdays £30.00 before 1pm, £20.00 after 1pm; weekends with a member only. *Eating facilities:* restaurant/buffet service. *Visitors:* welcome Monday to Friday. *Society Meetings:* catered for. Professional: Joe Hagan (01483 284772). Secretary: Charles Rose (01483 284641).

EFFINGHAM. **Effingham Golf Club,** Guildford Road, Effingham KT24 5PZ (01372 452203; Fax: 01372 459959). *Location:* A246 between Guildford and Leatherhead. Downland course with magnificent views towards London. 18 holes, 6542 yards. S.S.S. 71. Large practice ground. *Green Fees:* weekdays £35.00, weekends with a member only. *Eating facilities:* full bar and catering facilities. *Visitors:* welcome Monday-Friday. Handicap Certificate required. *Society Meetings:* welcome Wednesdays, Thursdays, Fridays. Professional: Steve Hoatson (01372 452606). Secretary: Lt Col (Rtd) Steve Manning OBE (01372 452203).

EPSOM. **Epsom Golf Club,** Longdown Lane South, Epsom KT17 4JR (01372 723363). *Location:* off A240 into B288, 200 yards south of Epsom Downs Station. Downland, links-type course with very fast, undulating greens. 18 holes, 6800 yards. S.S.S. 68. Practice nets and putting green. *Green Fees:* weekdays £16.00 per round, £24.00 per day; weekends £18.00 after 12 noon. *Eating facilities:* lounge and 19th hole bar with bar snack menu, two diningrooms with full catering facilities. *Visitors:* always welcome except Tuesday am (Ladies' Day), Saturday and Sunday before 12 noon (members and their guests only). *Society Meetings:* very welcome. Professional: R. Goudie (01372 721666). Secretary: J.H. Carter (01372 741867).

EPSOM. **Horton Park Country Club,** Hook Road, Epsom KT19 8QG (0181-393 8400; Fax: 0181-394 1369). *Location:* A3, M25 (Junction 9). Parkland with lake. 18 holes, 5197 yards. S.S.S. 65. Driving range, putting green. *Green Fees:* weekdays £11.00; weekends £13.00. *Eating facilities:* bars, restaurant and function suite. *Visitors:* welcome. *Society Meetings:* welcome except weekends. Professional: Gary Clements (0181-394 2626). General Manager: Mr P.R. Hart.

ESHER. **Moore Place Golf Club,** Portsmouth Road, Esher KT10 9LN (01372 463533). *Location:* half a mile from Esher town centre on Portsmouth Road. Undulating parkland course with featured trees. 9 holes, 2093 yards. S.S.S. 32. Large practice ground. *Green Fees:* weekdays £5.40; weekends £7.25. *Eating facilities:* two bars, snack bar and restaurant. *Visitors:* welcome, unrestricted. *Society Meetings:* welcome anytime. Professional: David Allen (01372 463533). Hon. Secretary: K.J. Sargeant (0181-941 1168).

ESHER. **Sandown Golf Centre,** More Lane, Esher KT10 8AN (01372 463340). *Location:* centre of Sandown Park racecourse. Parkland. 9 holes, 2829 yards. S.S.S. 67 (18 holes). 9-hole par 3; 9-hole Pitch and Putt. Floodlit 33-bay driving range, open until 10.30pm. *Green Fees:* £5.00 weekdays; £6.50 weekends. Subject to review. *Eating facilities:* bar and coffee shop. *Visitors:* welcome. *Society Meetings:* welcome. Professional: Neal Bedward. General Manager: Peter Barriball.

ESHER. **Thames Ditton and Esher Golf Club,** Marquis of Granby, Portsmouth Road, Esher (0181-398 1551). 9 holes played twice from different tees. 5190 yards. S.S.S. 65. *Green Fees:* £10.00 weekdays, £12.00 weekends. *Eating facilities:* breakfast-lunches, evening meals served on advance bookings by arrangement. *Society Meetings:* welcome except Sundays. Professional: R. Hutton. Secretary: D.I. Kaye.

FARNHAM. **Farnham Golf Club Ltd,** The Sands, Farnham GU10 1PX (01252 783163). *Location:* off A31 Crooksbury Road, Near "Jolly Farmer", signposted. Mixture of wooded parkland and heathland. 18 holes, 6313 yards. S.S.S. 70. Large practice ground. *Green Fees:* weekdays £25.00 round, £30.00 day; weekends with a member £10.00 per round, £12.00 per day. *Eating facilities:* two bars and diningroom, full high standard catering. *Visitors:* welcome weekdays with Handicap Certificate. *Society Meetings:* welcome Wednesday to Friday by prior booking. Professional: Grahame Cowlishaw (01252 782198). Secretary: James Pevalin (01252 782109).

FARNHAM. **Hankley Common Golf Club,** Tilford Road, Tilford, Farnham GU10 2DD (01252 792493). *Location:* off A3, right at lights at Hindhead. Off A31 (Farnham by-pass) left at lights, three miles beyond level crossing on A287. Heathland, dry and sandy links-type course. 18 holes, 6465 yards. S.S.S. 71. Practice ground. *Green Fees:* weekdays £28.00 per round; weekends £35.00 per round. *Eating facilities:* full range available, restaurant and two bars. *Visitors:* welcome weekdays, weekends after 2pm only. Handicap Certificate required. *Society Meetings:* catered for on Tuesdays and Wednesdays. Professional: Peter Stow (01252 793761). Secretary: J.K.A. O'Brien (01252 792493).

GODALMING near. **Hurtmore Golf Club,** Hurtmore Road, Near Godalming GU8 6AY (01483 426492; Fax: 01483 426121). *Location:* London to Portsmouth, four miles south of Guildford. M25 (15 minutes) A3 Exit Portsmouth. Undulating parkland with seven large lakes. 18 holes, 5500 yards. S.S.S. 66. Practice net. *Green Fees:* weekdays £12.00; weekends £15.00. Discounts for Senior Citizens and Juniors. *Eating facilities:* bar, restaurant. *Visitors:* welcome at all times, pay and play course with 200 members. Bookings taken per telephone. *Society Meetings:* welcome by prior booking. Professional: Tony White. Secretary: Maureen Searle (01483 424440).

GODALMING. **West Surrey Golf Club,** Enton Green, Godalming GU8 5AF (01483 421275). *Location:* off the A3 south of Guildford, half mile past Milford Station/crossing. Wooded parkland. 18 holes, 6259 yards, 5722 metres. S.S.S. 70. Practice ground. *Green Fees:* weekdays £24.50 and £35.00; weekends £43.00. *Eating facilities:* bar, diningroom. *Visitors:* welcome, must be member of recognised golf club and have current Handicap Certificate. *Society Meetings:* catered for by prior arrangement. Professional: J. Hoskison (01483 417278). Secretary: R.S. Fanshawe (01483 421275).

GUILDFORD. **Bramley Golf Club,** Bramley, Near Guildford GU5 0AL (01483 893042). *Location:* three miles south of Guildford on the Horsham road, A281. Parkland. 18 holes, 5990 yards. S.S.S. 69. Practice area, driving range. *Green Fees:* weekdays £25.00 per round, £30.00 per day; weekends with member only. *Eating facilities:* catering from 8am to 8pm, bar from 11am to 10pm. *Visitors:* welcome Monday to Friday. *Society Meetings:* by prior arrangement with Secretary. Professional: Gary Peddie (01483 893685). Secretary: Ms M. Lambert (01483 892696).

GUILDFORD. **Guildford Golf Club,** High Path Road, Merrow, Guildford (01483 63941). Steward: (01483 31842). *Location:* from Guildford take Epsom Road (A246) turn right at the third set of traffic lights. Downland course. 18 holes, 6090 yards. S.S.S. 70. Practice area. *Green Fees:* £25.00 per round, £35.00 per day weekdays; weekends with a member only. Subject to review. *Eating facilities:* snacks and restaurant service. *Visitors:* welcome weekdays, with member weekends. *Society Meetings:* catered for Monday to Friday. Professional: P. G. Hollington (01483 66765). Secretary: R.E. Thomas (01483 63941; Fax: 01483 453228).

GUILDFORD. **Puttenham Golf Club,** Guildford GU3 1AL (01483 810498). *Location:* Farnham and Guildford, 600 yards south of Hog's Back (A31). Wooded/heathland course. 18 holes, 6220 yards. S.S.S. 70. *Green Fees:* on application. *Visitors:* welcome weekdays only by prior arrangement. (Weekends playing with a member). *Society Meetings:* catered for Wednesdays and Thursdays. Secretary and Professional: Gary Simmons.

HINDHEAD. **Hindhead Golf Club,** Churt Road, Hindhead GU26 6HX (01428 604614). *Location:* one and a half miles north of Hindhead on A287 to Farnham. The course is played over heathland and wooded valleys. 18 holes, 6373 yards. S.S.S. 70. *Green Fees:* £35.00 per day weekdays; £42.00 weekends. *Eating facilities:* restaurant, snack bar, summer bar and members' bar. *Visitors:* welcome with Handicap Certificate, weekends by appointment.

Society Meetings: Wednesdays and Thursdays only. Professional: Neil Ogilvy (01428 604458). Secretary: Miss A. McMenemy.

KINGSTON-UPON-THAMES. **Coombe Hill Golf Club,** Golf Club Drive, off Coombe Lane West, Kingston KT2 7DG (0181-942 2284). *Location:* from A3 take A238 to Kingston. Hilly and tree lined. 18 holes, 6040 yards. S.S.S. 71. *Green Fees:* weekdays £45.00. *Eating facilities:* diningroom 11.30am to 5pm, bar (varying hours). *Visitors:* weekdays only. *Society Meetings:* please contact Secretary. Professional: Craig De Foy (0181-949 3713). Secretary: D.G. Seward. *

KINGSTON-UPON-THAMES. **Coombe Wood Golf Club,** George Road, Kingston Hill KT2 7NS (0181-942 3828). *Location:* on A307. Wooded course. 18 holes, 5296 yards, 4842 metres. S.S.S. 66. *Green Fees:* weekdays £26.00; weekends with member only. *Eating facilities:* catering all week. *Visitors:* welcome weekdays. *Society Meetings:* by arrangement Wednesday to Friday. Professional: D. Butler (0181-942 6764). Secretary: P.M. Urwin (0181-942 0388).

KINGSWOOD. **Kingswood Golf and Country Club Ltd,** Sandy Lane, Kingswood, Tadworth KT20 6NE (01737 833316: Fax: 01737 833920). *Location:* five miles south of Sutton just off A217/Junction 8 M25. 18 holes, 6855 yards. S.S.S. 73. Large practice area. *Green Fees:* weekdays £30.00 per round; weekends £42.00 per round. *Eating facilities:* full range available. *Visitors:* welcome anytime, restricted times at weekends. Squash courts, snooker tables. *Society Meetings:* catered for. Professional: Mr Martin Platts (01737 832334). Administrator: Miss Lynn Thompson (01737 832188). *

LEATHERHEAD. **Leatherhead Golf Club,** Kingston Road, Leatherhead KT22 0EE (01372 843966; Fax: 01372 842241). *Location:* off Junction 9 of M25, onto A243 to Kingston. Parkland, many mature trees. 18 holes, 6157 yards. S.S.S. 71. Practice ground, putting green. *Green Fees:* weekdays £25.00 one round, £35.00 two rounds; weekends £35.00 one round afternoons only. *Eating facilities:* à la carte restaurant, cafe/brasserie and lounge bar. *Visitors:* welcome, no visitors Saturday or Sunday mornings. *Society Meetings:* welcome, from 16 to 100 by reservation. Professional: Richard Hurst (01372 843956). Secretary: L. Laithwaite (01372 843966).

LEATHERHEAD. **Pachesham Golf Centre,** Oaklawn Road, Leatherhead KT22 0BT (01372 843453; Fax: 01372 844076). *Location:* half a mile outside Leatherhead on A244, quarter of a mile off Junction 9 M25. Flat parkland. 9 holes, 1756 yards. S.S.S. 56. 33 bay driving range, putting green, chipping area. *Green Fees:* weekdays £6.50 9 holes; weekends £7.50 9 holes. *Eating facilities:* fully licensed bar, restaurant. *Visitors:* welcome, bookings taken two days in advance. Must wear golf shoes. *Society Meetings:* welcome. Professional/Secretary: Phil Taylor.

LEATHERHEAD. **Tyrrells Wood Golf Club Ltd,** Leatherhead KT22 8QP (01372 376025). *Location:* south-east on A24 Leatherhead by-pass after A.A. caravan, one mile left to Headley, then 200 yards right. Hillside, wooded course with glorious views. 18 holes, 6234 yards. S.S.S. 70. Small practice ground. *Green Fees:* weekdays £32.00 per round, £48.00 per day; Sunday afternoons only, £42.00. *Eating facilities:* catering by arrangement with Manager. *Visitors:* no visitors Saturday or Sunday mornings. *Society Meetings:* catered for by arrangement with Manager. Professional: Max Taylor (01372 375200). Secretary: C.G.R. Kydd (01372 376025).

LINGFIELD. **Lingfield Park Golf Club,** Racecourse Road, Lingfield Park, Lingfield RH7 6PQ (01342 834602). *Location:* A22 turn off at Blindley Heath, six miles from M25 Junction 6. Parkland/wooded. 18 holes, 6500 yards. S.S.S. 72. Driving range and practice ground. *Green Fees:* weekdays £20.00 per round, £30.00 per day; weekends no casual green fees. *Eating facilities:* snacks available all day, other catering by arrangement. *Visitors:* welcome weekdays only. Horse racing. *Society Meetings:* catered for weekdays only. Professional: C.K. Morley (01342 832659). Manager: Greer Milne.

MITCHAM. **Mitcham Golf Club,** Carshalton Road, Mitcham Junction, Mitcham CR4 4HN (0181-648 1508). *Location:* Carshalton Road, aim for Mitcham Junction Station. Flat course. 18 holes, 5517 yards. S.S.S. 67. *Green Fees:* £10.00; Senior Citizens £5.50. *Eating facilities:* meals and snacks daily. *Visitors:* welcome, book via Professional. *Society Meetings:* catered for, book through Secretary. Professional: J.A. Godfrey (0181-640 4280). Secretary: C.A. McGahan (0181-648 4197). *

NEW MALDEN. **Malden Golf Club,** Traps Lane, New Malden KT3 4RS (0181-942 0654). *Location:* half a mile from Malden Station – near A3, between Wimbledon and Kingston. Parkland. 18 holes, 6295 yards. S.S.S. 70. *Green Fees:* weekdays £20.00 per round, £30.00 per day; weekends £45.00. *Eating facilities:* restaurant and bar. *Visitors:* welcome weekdays, weekends restricted. Advisable to telephone Professional. *Society Meetings:* catered for Wednesday, Thursday and Friday. Professional: Robert Hunter (0181-942 6009). Secretary: Peter G. Fletcher (0181-942 6433). *

NEWDIGATE. **Rusper Golf Club,** Rusper Road, Newdigate RH5 5BX (01293 871456; Fax: 01293 871987). *Location:* Dorking – Horsham A24, Beare Green roundabout left to Newdigate, through Newdigate, right to Rusper – course on right hand side. Parkland course with mature trees. 9 holes, 6065 yards. S.S.S. 69. Driving range. *Green Fees:* weekdays £7.00 per 9 holes, £11.50 per 18 holes; weekends £8.50 per 9 holes, £15.50 per 18 holes. *Eating facilities:* snack bar and full bar. *Visitors:* welcome every day, times bookable 48 hours in advance. No Handicaps required. *Society Meetings:* welcome, groups up to 50, various packages. Professional: Karl Spurrier (01293 871871). Secretary: G. Hems.

OTTERSHAW. **Foxhills Country Club,** Stonehill Road, Ottershaw KT16 0EL (01932 872050; Fax: 01932 874762). *Location:* Exit 11 M25, follow signs to Woking, right at roundabout, left at next roundabout, left at junction into Stonehill Road. Parkland course (Chertsey) 18 holes, 6734 yards, S.S.S. 72. Wooded course (Longcross) 18 holes, 6417 yards, S.S.S. 71. Par 3 course (9 holes). *Green Fees:* weekdays £45.00 per round, £65 per day; weekends £55.00 per round. *Eating facilities:* clubhouse restaurant (lunch only except Saturdays), Manor Restaurant (lunch and dinner, closed Sunday and Monday nights, Monday and Tuesday lunch). *Visitors:* welcome from 7.30am weekdays and after 12 noon at weekends. 16 rooms; tennis, squash, gym, swimming pools. *Society Meetings:* bookings for weekdays only. Professional: Bernard Hunt MBE (01932 873961).

OXTED. **Limpsfield Chart Golf Club,** Westerham Road, Limpsfield, Oxted RH8 0SL (01883 722106). *Location:* on A25 between Westerham and Oxted. Heathland, now well wooded, easy walking. 9 holes – alternate tees for 18 holes, 5718 yards. S.S.S. 68. Very small practice area. *Green Fees:* weekdays £18.00, weekends £20.00 with a member only. Evenings £8.00 *Eating facilities:* by prior arrangement, snacks always available, bar open 11.30am to 2.30pm then 6pm to 9.30pm. *Visitors:* welcome weekdays except Thursday (Ladies' Day) when only after 3.30pm, weekends by appointment. *Society Meetings:* catered for by prior arrangement. Secretary: Mr D.S. Adams (01883 723405).

OXTED. **Tandridge Golf Club,** Oxted (01883 712274). *Location:* A25 between Godstone and Sevenoaks. 18 holes, 6260 yards. S.S.S. 70. *Green Fees:* information not provided. *Eating facilities:* full catering facilities. *Visitors:* welcome Monday, Wednesday and Thursday only. *Society Meetings:* catered for Mondays, Wednesdays and Thursdays. Professional: A. Farquhar (01883 713701). Secretary: A.S. Furnival.

PIRBRIGHT. **Goal Farm Golf Course,** Golf Road, Pirbright, Woking GU24 0PZ (01483 433183). *Location:* between Woking and Guildford, off A322. Challenging, picturesque course. 9 holes, 1273 yards. S.S.S. 48. Practice net, putting green, bunker. *Green Fees:* information not provided. *Eating facilities:* bar, light refreshments. *Visitors:* welcome, restrictions Saturday and Thursday mornings (Club Competitions) Professional: Kevin Warn. Secretary: Bruce Tapsfield. *

PURLEY. **Purley Downs Golf Club,** 106 Purley Downs Road, Purley, South Croydon CR2 0RB (0181-657 1231). *Location:* three miles south of Croydon, one mile east of A235. Downland (hilly). 18 holes, 6212 yards. S.S.S. 70. Practice area, nets. *Green Fees:* weekdays £30.00. Visitors are not allowed to play at weekends unless with a Full Member of the club. *Eating facilities:* diningroom, bar snacks, two bars. *Visitors:* welcome weekdays, Handicap Certificate required. *Society Meetings:* catered for Mondays and Thursdays. Professional: G. Wilson (0181-651 0819). Secretary: P.C. Gallienne (0181-657 8347; Fax: 0181-651 5044).

REDHILL. **Redhill and Reigate Golf Club,** Clarence Lodge, Pendleton Road, Redhill (01737 244626). *Location:* one mile south of Reigate between A23 and A25. Well wooded course. 18 holes, 5261 yards. S.S.S. 66. Small practice area. *Green Fees:* weekdays £10.00 per round; weekends £15.00 per round. No green fees before 11.00am at weekends. No play after 2.00pm Sundays June to September. *Eating facilities:* available but very limited on Mondays. *Visitors:* welcome without reservation most days. Telephone enquiry advised weekends. *Society Meetings:* catered for by arrangement with Secretary. Professional: Barry Davies (01737 244433). Secretary: Frank R. Cole (01737 240777).

REIGATE. **Reigate Heath Golf Club,** The Clubhouse, Reigate Heath, Reigate RH2 8QR (01737 242610). *Location:* south of A25 on western boundary of Reigate. Heathland. 9 holes, 5658 yards. S.S.S. 67. *Green Fees:* on application. *Eating facilities:* meals by arrangement with Steward. Light lunches and snacks available except Mondays. *Visitors:* welcome weekdays, advisable to telephone before coming. *Society Meetings:* catered for Wednesdays or Thursdays. Professional: G. Gow (01737 243077). Secretary: R.J. Perkins (01737 226793).

RICHMOND. **Richmond Golf Club,** Sudbrook Park, Petersham, Richmond TW10 7AS (0181-940 1463). *Location:* off A307 two miles south of Richmond, end of Sudbrook Lane. Parkland. 18 holes, 6007 yards, 6566 metres. S.S.S. 69. Practice driving range. *Green Fees:* weekdays £38.00. *Eating facilities:* lunches available Monday to Friday; teas daily. *Visitors:* welcome weekdays without reservation. *Society Meetings:* welcome Tuesdays, Thursdays and Fridays by arrangement with Secretary. Professional: Nicholas Job (0181-940 7792). Secretary: R.L. Wilkins (0181-940 4351).

RICHMOND. **Royal Mid-Surrey Golf Club,** Old Deer Park, Richmond TW9 2SB (0181-940 1894). *Location:* in Old Deer Park off A316 at Richmond. Parkland course. Two 18 hole courses, Inner – 5544 yards, S.S.S. 67 men, 5446 yards, S.S.S. 71 ladies; Outer – 6337 yards, S.S.S. 70 men, 5755 yards, S.S.S. 73 ladies. *Green Fees:* weekdays £45.00 Summer, £32.00 Winter. *Eating facilities:* The Buttery daily, the diningroom daily except Mondays, the bar daily. *Visitors:* welcome weekdays only, with introduction from own club. *Society Meetings:* welcome by prior arrangement. Professional: D. Talbot (0181-940 0459). Secretary: M.S.R. Lunt.

SUNNINGDALE. **Sunningdale Golf Club,** Ridgemount Road, Sunningdale, Ascot SL5 9RR (01344 21681; Fax: 01344 24154). *Location:* 350 yards west of station, off A30, 25 miles from London. Heathland, 36 holes, 2 courses. *Green Fees:* weekdays £84.00 day ticket. Subject to review. *Eating facilities:* diningroom and three bars. *Visitors:* require introduction from Secretary of own club on weekdays. At weekends with member only. *Society Meetings:* accepted Tuesday, Wednesday, Thursday only, by arrangement. Professional: Keith Maxwell (01344 20128). Secretary: Stewart Zuill. Caddiemaster for bookings (01344 26064).

SUTTON. **Banstead Downs Golf Club,** Burdon Lane, Belmont, Sutton SM2 7DD (0181-642 2284; Fax: 0181-642 5252). *Location:* A217 (10 minutes from Belmont Station). 18 holes, 6190 yards. S.S.S. 69. *Green Fees:* weekdays £30.00 mornings, £20.00 afternoons. *Eating facilities:* lunches served at Club every day. *Visitors:* welcome on weekdays with letter of introduction, at weekends with member. *Society Meetings:* catered for all day Thursdays. Professional: Robert Dickman (0181-642 6884). Secretary: Roger Steele.

TADWORTH. **Walton Heath Golf Club,** Deans Lane, Walton-on-the-Hill, Tadworth KT20 7TP (01737 812060). *Location:* Junction 8 M25, A217 towards London, B2032 towards Dorking, turning right hand side Deans Lane. Two 18 hole heathland courses. Old – 6883 yards, S.S.S. 73. New – 6659 yards, S.S.S. 72. Large putting green; indoor and outdoor practice facilities. *Green Fees:* £57.00 weekdays, after 11.30am £47.00. Special rates November – mid March. *Eating facilities:* restaurant and two bars. *Visitors:* welcome by previous arrangement, Handicap Certificate or letter of introduction required. *Society Meetings:* catered for by arrangement. A variety of packages available for both summer and winter. Professional: Ken MacPherson (01737 812152). Secretary: G.R. James (01737 812380).

VIRGINIA WATER. **Wentworth Club Ltd,** Wentworth Drive, Virginia Water GU25 4LS (01344 842201; Fax: 01344 842804). *Location:* 21 miles south-west of London, just off the A30 at junction with A329 to Ascot. M25 and M3 three miles. Wooded heathland. West course – 18 holes, 6945 yards, S.S.S. 74; East course – 18 holes, 6176 yards, S.S.S. 70; Edinburgh course – 18 holes, 6979 yards, S.S.S. 73; Executive course – 9 holes. Driving range. *Green Fees:* weekdays from £70 – £90 including VAT. *Eating facilities:* dining room, private rooms, bar. *Visitors:* welcome weekdays only by appointment. Handicap Certificates required – Ladies 30, Men 20. Accommodation available. *Society Meetings:* welcome by prior arrangement. Professional: Bernard Gallacher (01344 843353). General Manager: Keith Williams (01344 842201). Golf Administrator: Niall Flanagan.

WALTON-ON-THAMES. **Burhill Golf Club,** Walton-on-Thames KT12 4BL (01932 227345). *Location:* off A3 to A245, right into Seven Hills Road and again into Burwood Road or from Walton Railway Bridge through Burwood Park. 18 holes, 6224 yards. S.S.S. 70. *Green Fees:* information not provided. Professional: Lee Johnson. Secretary: M.B. Richards.

WEST BYFLEET. **West Byfleet Golf Club,** Sheerwater Road, West Byfleet KT14 6AA (01932 343433). *Location:* Junction 10 M25 onto A245 – half a mile west of West Byfleet. Flat, wooded course. 18 holes, 6211 yards. S.S.S. 70. *Green Fees:* weekdays £27.00 per round, £33.00 per day. *Eating facilities:* lunches, bar snacks, teas and evening meals available. Catering: 01932 353525. Bar: 01932 352501. *Visitors:* welcome weekdays with reservation, weekends with member only. *Society Meetings:* catered for, advance bookings, minimum group size 25. Professional: David Regan (01932 346584). Secretary: D. Lee (01932 343433).

WEST CLANDON. **Clandon Regis Golf Club,** Epsom Road, West Clandon (01483 211781). Parkland, undulating, with feature lakes. Course designed by David Williams. 18 holes, 6500 yards. S.S.S. 71/72. Excellent practice facilities. *Green Fees:* on application. *Eating facilities:* bar, diningroom. *Visitors:* welcome weekdays, weekend afternoons. Handicap Certificate or competence test. *Society Meetings:* welcome. Professional: S. Brady. Secretary: M. Thomas. *

WEYBRIDGE. **New Zealand Golf Club,** Woodham Lane, Woodham, Addlestone KT15 3QD (01932 345049). *Location:* junction Woodham Lane and Sheerwater Road on A245. 18 holes, 6012 yards. S.S.S. 69. *Green Fees:* information on request. *Eating facilities:* lunch available Tuesdays to Fridays. *Visitors:* welcome Monday to Friday with reservation. *Society Meetings:* catered for Tuesday, Wednesday, Thursday and Friday. Professional: V.R. Elvidge. Secretary: Cdr J. Manley OBE RN.

WEYBRIDGE. **St. George's Hill Golf Club,** St. George's Hill, Weybridge KT13 0NL (01932 842406). *Location:* M25, Junction 10 take A3 off towards London, turn left at Byfleet, outer estate at S.P's St. George's Hill. Hilly, Surrey heathland – well wooded with plentiful heather and rhododendron. 27 holes, 6569 yards. S.S.S. 71. *Green Fees:* information not provided. *Eating facilities:* diningroom, two bars. *Visitors:* by prior arrangement. *Society Meetings:* catered for on Wednesdays, Thursdays and Fridays by prior arrangement. Professional: A.C. Rattue (01932 843523). Secretary: M.R. Tapsell (01932 847758). *

WOKING. **Chobham Golf Club,** Chobham Road, Knaphill, Woking GU21 2TU (01276 855584; Fax: 01276 855663). *Location:* on A3046 one mile outside Chobham village, three minutes from M3 Junction 3. Wooded parkland course. 18 holes, 5821 yards. S.S.S. 68. Practice area. *Green Fees:* weekdays £12.00 with a member; weekends £18.00 with a member. Non-member guests' green fee rates subject to Club Manager approval. *Eating facilities:* restaurant/dining area/ spikes bar/upstairs function room. *Visitors:* welcome subject to approval of Club Manager, must be member of a golf club and have an official Handicap. *Society Meetings:* bookings available from Spring 1996. Professional: Paul Young. Club Manager: Stuart Allen.

WOKING. **Hoebridge Golf Centre,** Old Woking Road, Old Woking GU22 8JH (01483 722611). Parkland with some trees on sand. 18 holes, 6536 yards. S.S.S. 71. Par 3 course. (9 hole intermediate course). Covered driving range. *Green Fees:* Main Course £13.00; Intermediate £7.00; 18-hole Par 3 £6.50. *Eating facilities:* large dining room and bar, open all day. *Visitors:* welcome. Snooker centre. *Society Meetings:* welcome midweek. Professional: Tim Powell. Secretary: Valerie Statham.

WOKING near. **Pyrford Golf Club 1993,** Warren Lane, Pyrford, Near Woking GU22 8XR (01483 723555; Fax: 01483 729777). *Location:* A3 – Ripley turn off, turn next to Suzuki garage, continue for approximately two miles, on left hand bend turn right into Warren Lane. Inland water links, 23 acres of lakes. 18 holes, 6230 yards. S.S.S. 72. Practice range. *Green Fees:* weekdays £35.00; weekends £50.00. Members' guests half price. *Eating facilities:* à la carte restaurant, bar meals, spikes bar open 7am-11pm every day. *Visitors:* welcome, no restrictions on visitors, tee times MUST be booked. Weekday play preferred. *Society Meetings:* welcome during week. Professional: Jeremy Bennett (01483 751070). Secretary: David Renton.

WOKING. **Windlemere Golf Club,** Windlesham Road, West End, Near Woking (01276 858727). *Location:* off A322. Well designed parkland course. 9 holes, 2673 yards. S.S.S. 33. Floodlit 12-bay driving range. *Green Fees:* weekdays £7.00, £5.50 Senior Citizens and Juniors; weekends £9.00, £7.00 Senior Citizens and Juniors. *Eating facilities:* bar with light menu, normal clubhouse facilities. *Visitors:* always welcome, may book up to one week in advance. Snooker, pool facilities. *Society Meetings:* welcome to book. Professional: Dave Thomas. Secretary: Simon Hodsdon (01276 857405).

WOKING. **Woking Golf Club,** Pond Road, Hook Heath, Woking GU22 0JZ (01483 760053). *Location:* via Hollybank Road, just south of first road bridge over Woking/Brookwood railway. 18 holes, 6365 yards. S.S.S. 70. *Green Fees:* on application. *Eating facilities:* lunches and snacks available. *Visitors:* welcome with reservation, please telephone. *Society Meetings:* catered for. Professional: J. Thorne (01483 769582). Secretary: I.J. Holmes.

WOKING. **Worplesdon Golf Club,** Heath House Road, Woking. *Location:* off A322 Guildford, Bagshot Road, Heath House Road, first left south of West Hill G.C. Wooded heathland course. 18 holes, 6440 yards. S.S.S. 71. *Green Fees:* £50.00 per day. *Eating facilities:* lunches served at club. *Visitors:* weekdays only. *Society Meetings:* by arrangement. Professional: Jim Christine (01483 473287). Secretary: Major R.E.E. Jones (01483 472277; Fax: 01483 473303).

WOLDINGHAM. **North Downs Golf Club,** Northdown Road, Woldingham, Caterham CR3 7AA (01883 653298). *Location:* Eastbourne Road roundabout at Caterham. 2 miles Woldingham road. 18 holes, 5843 yards, S.S.S. 68. *Green Fees:* enquire from Professional. *Eating facilities:* full restaurant facilities. *Visitors:* welcome with Handicap Certificate. *Society Meetings:* catered for. Professional: P. Ellis (01883 653004). Secretary: J.A.L. Smith (01883 652057).

East Sussex

BEXHILL-ON-SEA. **Cooden Beach Golf Club,** Cooden Sea Road, Bexhill-on-Sea TN39 4TR (01424 842040). *Location:* A259 Eastbourne to Hastings road, follow 'Cooden Beach' sign at Little Common roundabout (one mile). Seaside course, slightly undulating. 18 holes, 6450 yards. S.S.S. 71. Practice facilities. *Green Fees:* £26.00 weekdays, weekends and Bank Holidays £33.00. *Eating facilities:* catering and bar every day. *Visitors:* welcome, preferably by prior arrangement. Accommodation for five in Club's own guest house alongside 18th green. *Society Meetings:* prior booking necessary. Professional: Jeffrey Sim (01424 843938). Secretary: T.E. Hawes (01424 842040). Caterers: (01424 843936).

BEXHILL-ON-SEA. **Highwoods Golf Club,** Ellerslie Lane, Bexhill-on-Sea TN39 4LJ (01424 212625). *Location:* off A259 north west of town. Parkland, wooded course. 18 holes, 6218 yards. S.S.S. 70. *Green Fees:* on application. *Eating facilities:* snacks always available, lunch by prior arrangement. *Visitors:* Handicap Certificate required. Sunday mornings with member only. *Society Meetings:* welcome Thursdays by arrangement. Professional: M. Andrews (01424 212770). Secretary: Ian Osborough (01424 212625).

BRIGHTON. **Brighton and Hove Golf Club,** Dyke Road, Brighton BN1 8YJ (01273 507861). *Location:* south from A23, at Patcham traffic lights turn right and right again at mini roundabout to Devil's Dyke. Downland course. 9 holes, 5722 yards. S.S.S. 68. *Green Fees:* (18 holes) weekdays £12.50; weekends and Bank Holidays £21.00. *Eating facilities:* available every day except Mondays and Tuesdays. *Visitors:* welcome without reservation. *Society Meetings:* catered for. Professional: (01273 540560). Secretary: C. S. Cawkwell (01273 556482).

BRIGHTON. **Dyke Golf Club,** Dyke Road, Brighton BN1 8YJ (01273 857230). *Location:* off A23 on to A2038 on entering Brighton; follow signs to Devil's Dyke. Downland course. 18 holes, 6611 yards. S.S.S. 72. Practice fairway and putting green. *Green Fees:* weekdays £21.00 per round, £31.00 per day, after 4.30pm £10.50; weekends and Bank Holidays £31.00 per round. *Eating facilities:* full restaurant and bar available. *Visitors:* welcome with reservation, not before 12 noon Sundays. *Society Meetings:* catered for by appointment, £45.00 for full day inclusive of lunch and dinner. Professional: Mr P. Longmore (01273 857260). Secretary: Mr T.R. White (01273 857296; Fax: 01273 857078).

BRIGHTON. **East Brighton Golf Club,** Roedean Road, Brighton BN2 5RA (01273 603989). *Location:* east end of Brighton just off A259, overlooking the Marina. Undulating downland course. 18 holes, 6346 yards, 5802 metres. S.S.S. 70. *Green Fees:* weekdays £21.00, weekends and Bank Holidays £30.00. *Eating facilities:* diningroom and bars, lunches and teas served. *Visitors:* welcome from 9am weekdays, after 11am weekends. *Society Meetings:* catered for weekdays (not Wednesdays) on application. Professional: W. Street (01273 603989). Secretary/Manager: Colin P. Simpson (01273 604838).

BRIGHTON. **Hollingbury Park Golf Club,** Ditchling Road, Brighton (01273 552010). *Location:* between A23 and A27. 18 holes, 6502 yards. S.S.S. 71. *Green Fees:* weekdays £10.00 per round, £18.00 per day; weekends £14.00 per round. *Eating facilities:* full catering service seven days. *Visitors:* welcome without reservation. *Society Meetings:* catered for weekdays only. Professional: Peter Brown (01273 500086). Secretary: J. Walling.

BRIGHTON. **Pyecombe Golf Club,** Clayton Hill, Pyecombe BN4 7FF (01273 844176). *Location:* four miles north of Brighton on A273 Burgess Hill Road. Downland with magnificent views. 18 holes, 6278 yards. S.S.S. 70. Two practice areas. *Green Fees:* weekdays £15.00 per round, £18.00 per day; weekends and Bank Holidays £25.00. *Eating facilities:* catering 10.30am to 6pm every day or as booked. *Visitors:* welcome, after 9.15am weekdays, after 2pm weekends. *Society Meetings:* catered for on Mondays, Wednesdays and Thursdays. Professional: C.R. White (01273 845398). Secretary: W.M. Wise (01273 845372).

BRIGHTON. **Waterhall Golf Club,** Seddlescombe Road, off Devils Dyke Road, Brighton BN1 8YN (01273 508658). *Location:* three miles north of Brighton. Downland course. 18 holes, 5773 yards, 5328 metres. S.S.S. 68. Practice area. *Green Fees:* weekdays £10.00; weekends £14.00. *Eating facilities:* catering available every day except Tuesdays. *Visitors:* welcome except weekends. *Society Meetings:* catered for except Tuesdays, weekends or Bank Holidays by prior arrangement with Secretary. Professional: Paul Charman-Mitchell. Secretary: Peter Verner.

CROWBOROUGH. **Crowborough Beacon Golf Club,** Beacon Road, Crowborough (01892 661511). *Location:* nine miles south of Tunbridge Wells on the A26. Heathland. 18 holes, 6279 yards. S.S.S. 70. Practice ground. *Green Fees:* £24.00 per round, £36.00 per day weekdays. *Eating facilities:* available. *Visitors:* welcome after 9.30am weekdays, not allowed at weekends. *Society Meetings:* catered for. Professional: D. Newnham (01892 653877). Secretary: Mrs V. Harwood (01892 661511; Fax: 01892 667339).

EASTBOURNE. **Eastbourne Downs Golf Club,** East Dean Road, Eastbourne BN20 8ES (01323 21844). *Location:* five minutes from town centre via Old Town on A259. Downland. 18 holes, 6635 yards. S.S.S. 72. Practice area. *Green Fees:* weekdays £14.00; weekends £18.00. *Eating facilities:* food available except Monday and Tuesday, two bars. *Visitors:* welcome after 9am weekdays, after 11am weekends. *Society Meetings:* catered for by arrangement. Professional: Terry Marshall (01323 32264). Secretary: D.J. Eldrett (01323 20827).

EASTBOURNE. **Eastbourne Golfing Park,** Lottbridge Drove, Eastbourne BN23 6QJ (01323 520400; Fax: 01323 504134). *Location:* half a mile south of Hampden Park and one mile north of the sea. Parkland course with water on seven holes. 9 holes, 5046 yards. S.S.S. 65. 24 bay floodlit driving range. *Green Fees:* weekdays £7.00 9 holes, £12.00 18 holes; weekends £8.00 9 holes, £13.00 for 18 holes. Special rates for Senior Citizens. *Eating facilities:* all day snack bar and order by intercom from the course. *Visitors:* welcome at all times. *Society Meetings:* all welcome, please ring to book. Professional: Barrie Finch. Secretary: Clive Packham (01323 520400).

EASTBOURNE. **Royal Eastbourne Golf Club,** Paradise Drive, Eastbourne BN20 8BP (01323 730412). *Location:* one mile from town centre via Meads Road and Compton Place Road. (a) 18 holes, 6109 yards. S.S.S. 69. (b) 9 holes, 2147 yards 2. S.S.S. 61. *Green Fees:* weekdays £20.00; weekends and Bank Holidays £25.00. *Eating facilities:* full catering. *Visitors:* welcome. Handicap Certificate required Long Course only. Cottage accommodation for four people. *Society Meetings:* catered for. Professional: Richard Wooller (Tel & Fax: 01323 736986). Secretary: P. Robins (01323 729738).

EASTBOURNE. **Willingdon Golf Club,** Southdown Road, Eastbourne BN20 9AA (01323 410983). *Location:* north of Eastbourne, one mile from station, just off A22 at traffic lights (signposted). Downland course of particular beauty. 18 holes, 6113 yards, 5589 metres. S.S.S. 69. Practice ground and nets. *Green Fees:* weekdays £24.00; Saturdays and Bank Holidays £27.00. Winter rates on application. *Eating facilities:* diningroom, lounge and casual bar. *Visitors:* welcome after 9am weekdays, Saturdays check for tee bookings, not Sunday mornings, check for tee bookings. *Society Meetings:* welcome – book well in advance. Professional: J. Debenham (01323 410984). Secretary: Brian Kirby (01323 410981).

EAST GRINSTEAD near. **Royal Ashdown Forest Golf Club (Old Course),** Forest Row, Near East Grinstead RH18 5LR (01342 822018/823014). *Location:* four miles south of East Grinstead; take B2110 (off A22) in Forest Row and then turn right into Chapel Lane, bear left at top of Chapel Lane. Undulating heathland. 18 holes, 6477 yards. S.S.S. 71. *Green Fees:* weekdays £28.00 per round, £36.00 per day; weekends £34.00 per round, £40.00 per day. *Eating facilities:* lunch and tea (prior arrangement), bar snacks. *Visitors:* welcome but always phone beforehand. *Society Meetings:* catered for – prior reservation essential. Professional: M. Landsborough (01342 822247). Secretary: D.J. Scrivens (Fax: 01342 825211).

FOREST ROW. **Ashdown Forest Hotel and Royal Ashdown Forest New Course,** Chapel Lane, Forest Row RH18 5BB (01342 824866; Fax: 01342 824869). *Location:* three miles south of East Grinstead on A22 in village of Forest Row. Take Tunbridge Wells road. Chapel Lane is fourth turning on right. Undulating forest and heathland course – no sand bunkers! Adjoins Royal Ashdown Forest Old Course. 18 holes, 5586 yards. S.S.S. 67. *Green Fees:* on application. *Eating facilities:* bar snacks, restaurant, banqueting up to 100. *Visitors:* welcome, no 4 ball prior to mid-day weekends. Tees can be reserved six days in advance. 15 bedroom hotel. *Society Meetings:* welcome. Professional: Martyn Landsborough (01342 822047). Secretary: Robin Pratt.

HAILSHAM near. **Wellshurst Golf and Country Club,** North Street, Hellingly, Near Hailsham BN27 4EE (01435 813636; Fax: 01435 812444). *Location:* two miles north of the A22 roundabout at Hailsham on the A267. Parkland course. 18 holes, 5717 yards. S.S.S. 68. 16 bay driving range with two bunker bays. *Green Fees:* weekdays £12.00 per 18 holes; weekends £16.00 per 18 holes, £26.00 per day. *Eating facilities:* bar and restaurant open seven days a week. *Visitors:* no restrictions, pay as you play course; advisable to book at weekends. *Society Meetings:* all welcome at any time, good rates. Professional: Mr M. Barton (01435 813456). Secretary: Mr M. Adams.

HASTINGS. **Beauport Park Golf Club** (Associated to Hastings Golf Course), Battle Road, St. Leonards on Sea TN38 0TA (01424 851165). *Location:* A2100 Battle to Hastings Road. Parkland, wooded, hilly course. 18 holes, 6248 yards, 5767 metres. S.S.S. 70. Driving range. *Green Fees:* weekdays £10.00; weekends £12.50. *Eating facilities:* dining room. *Visitors:* welcome at all times. *Society Meetings:* catered for weekdays. Professional: M. Barton (01424 852981). Secretary: P.S. Irwin (01424 852977). *

HEATHFIELD. **Horam Park Golf Course,** Chiddingly Road, Horam, Near Heathfield TN21 0JJ (01435 813477; Fax: 01435 813677). *Location:* 13 miles north of Eastbourne, seven miles east of Uckfield. Follow signs to Heathfield and turn right onto the Eastbourne Road A267, go through Horam village, club on right hand side. A delightful parkland course with wooded areas and several lakes and ponds. 9 holes (18 tees), 5864 yards. S.S.S. 69. Floodlit driving range, practice ground, par 3 9-hole course. *Green Fees:* weekdays £7.50 for 9 holes, £10.50 for 18 holes, £12.50 all day; weekends £8.00 9 holes, £11.00 for 18 holes, £13.00 all day. *Eating facilities:* restaurant and bar facilities open all day seven days a week, also spike bar. *Visitors:* all facilities at Horam Park are open to the general public with no restrictions, everybody welcome. *Society Meetings:* welcome seven days per week, special cheap rates from January/March every year. Golf and food £23.00 per person April onwards. Professional: Mark Jarvis. Secretary: Gail Lloyd.

HOVE. **West Hove Golf Club,** Church Farm, Hangleton Valley, Hove BN3 8AN (01273 413411). *Location:* A27 Brighton bypass, second exit going west to Worthing from London Road A23. Downland course overlooking the sea. 18 holes, 6201 yards. S.S.S. 70. Practice range. *Green Fees:* £15.00 weekdays; £20.00 weekends. After 4.30pm in summer £8.00. *Eating facilities:* catering and bar. *Visitors:* welcome at all times. *Society Meetings:* welcome; 36 holes, lunch and evening meal £40.00. Professional: D. Mills (01273 413494). Secretary: Nicholas G. Hill (01273 419738; Fax: 01273 439988).

LEWES. **Lewes Golf Club,** Chapel Hill, Lewes BN7 2BB (01273 483245). *Location:* A27 – A22, east of Lewes town centre. Undulating downland with panoramic views. 18 holes, 6204 yards. S.S.S. 70. Practice area. *Green Fees:* £16.50 weekdays; £27.00 weekends. Twilight (after 4pm) £10.00 weekdays, £15.00 weekends. *Eating facilities:* full catering and bar facilities. *Visitors:* welcome without reservation. *Society Meetings:* catered for by prior arrangement. Professional: Paul Dobson (01273 483823). Secretary: Peter White (01273 483474).

NEWHAVEN. **Peacehaven Golf Club,** The Clubhouse, Brighton Road, Newhaven BN9 9UH (01273 514049). *Location:* one mile from Newhaven on the right hand side of A259 towards Brighton. Downland course, short but challenging. 9 holes, 5305 yards. S.S.S. 66. *Green Fees:* weekdays £12.00; weekends £16.00. *Eating facilities:* snacks (other catering by prior booking). *Visitors:* welcome except Saturday and Sunday mornings. *Society Meetings:* catered for up to 20. Professional: G. Williams. Secretary: A.A. Kemsley (01273 512571). *

ROTHERFIELD. **Dewlands Manor Golf Course,** Rotherfield TN6 3JN. *Location:* three quarters of a mile south of village of Rotherfield, just off B2101. Challenging undulating course on second highest point of Sussex. Fine bent and fescue greens. 9 holes, 3186 yards (18 – 6372 yards). Par 72. *Green Fees:* information not provided. *Eating facilities:* bar lunches/snacks on request. *Visitors:* welcome at all times by appointment. Handicap not required. Dress and etiquette a prerequisite. *Society Meetings:* Company Days a speciality. Professional: Nick Godin ETPD. Course Directors: Russell and Anna Page (01892 852266).

RYE. **Rye Golf Course,** Camber, Rye (01797 225241). *Location:* A259 from Rye, take Camber road to coast. Seaside links. 18 holes, 6310 yards. S.S.S. 71. 9 holes, 6141 yards. S.S.S. 71. *Green Fees:* information not provided. *Eating facilities:* lunch and tea only, but not Tuesdays. Bars. *Visitors:* welcome, only playing with a member or on introduction by a member. *Society Meetings:* very limited. Professional: Peter Marsh (01797 225218). Secretary: Lt Col C.J.W. Gilbert (01797 225241).

SEAFORD. **Seaford Golf Club,** East Blatchington, Seaford BN25 2JD (01323 892442). *Location:* turn inland at War Memorial in Seaford, follow the road for one and a quarter miles. Downland course. 18 holes, 6233 yards, 5700 metres. S.S.S. 70. Practice ground. *Green Fees:* weekdays from £15.00. *Eating facilities:* bar and restaurant open all day. *Visitors:* welcome weekdays other than Tuesdays. Telephone first. *Society Meetings:* catered for Wednesdays and Thursdays if club members with Handicap Certificates. Residential accommodation for 18 guests. Professional: P. Stevens (01323 894160). Secretary: M.B. Hichisson (01323 892442).

SEAFORD. **Seaford Head Golf Club,** Southdown Road, Seaford BN25 4JS (01323 894843). *Location:* midway between Eastbourne and Brighton on A259, signposted on entering Seaford. Downland course on cliff edge. 18 holes, 5812 yards. S.S.S. 68. *Green Fees:* information not provided. *Eating facilities:* available for Societies. *Visitors:* welcome without reservation. *Society Meetings:* catered for by written appointment. Professional: A. J. Lowles. Secretary: D. Strickland.

SEDLESCOMBE. **Sedlescombe Golf Course,** Kent Street, Sedlescombe TN33 0SD (01424 870898; Fax: 01424 870855). *Location:* five miles north of Hastings on the A21. Gently undulating parkland. 9 holes (18 tee positions), 3142 yards. S.S.S. 71. Driving range. Four courses available for play, ring for information. *Green Fees:* weekdays £7.50 9 holes, £10.50 18 holes; weekends £8.00 9 holes, £11.00 for 18 holes. Twilight rates and reduced rates for Senior Citizens and Juniors. *Eating facilities:* bar and restaurant facilities available all day seven days a week. *Visitors:* welcome, no restrictions. Course open to public. *Society Meetings:* welcome. Special rates golf and food all day £21.00 per person. Reduced rates January/March. Professional: Mr Ian Pearson. Secretary: Mrs Carole Johnson.

UCKFIELD. **East Sussex National Golf Club,** Little Horsted, Uckfield TN22 5ES (01825 880088; Fax: 01825 880066). *Location:* off the A22 Eastbourne road following the Uckfield by-pass, 30 minutes from Gatwick. American style, wooded, bent grasses. Two courses; 1: 18 holes, 7138 yards. S.S.S. 74 Championship; 2: 18 holes, 7154 yards. S.S.S. 74 Championship. 3 hole teaching academy, driving range. *Green Fees:* April to November: £55/£60 per round, £65/£80 27/36 holes weekdays. November to March: £45.00. Special rates on request. *Eating facilities:* full restaurant facilities. *Visitors:* welcome anytime booking six months in advance. Luxury country house hotel accommodation. *Society Meetings:* booking allowed one year in advance. Director of Golf: Mr Greg Dukart. C E O: Hon. John Sinclair.

UCKFIELD. **Piltdown Golf Club,** Piltdown, Uckfield TN22 3XB (01825 722033). *Location:* one mile west of Maresfield off A272, signposted Isfield. Undulating gorse and heather. 18 holes, 6070 yards. S.S.S. 69. Practice ground, putting green. *Green Fees:* any day round or day £27.50. Reductions after 3pm. County cards £18.00 per round. *Eating facilities:* bar, full catering – please telephone to book. *Visitors:* welcome but must bring Handicap Certificate or letter of introduction from own club Secretary. Some time restrictions. No visitors before 9.30am. Jacket and tie obligatory in lounge and diningroom. Smart dress on course. *Society Meetings:* catered for by prior arrangement. Professional: John Amos (01825 722389). Secretary: J.C. Duncan (01825 722033).

WADHURST. **Dale Hill Golf Club,** Ticehurst, Wadhurst TN5 7DQ (01580 200113). *Location:* on B2087, one mile off A21, 50 miles south of London. 16 miles north of Hastings. Wood/parkland course. 18 holes, men 6063 yards (ladies 5221). S.S.S. 69 (ladies 70). Practice area and green, indoor practice area. *Green Fees:* midweek £20.00; weekends £25.00. *Eating facilities:* breakfast and dinner to order, lunches and snacks always available. *Visitors:* welcome with reservation, handicap players only at weekends. 27 room luxury hotel with leisure centre. Buggy hire £10. *Society Meetings:* catered for by prior arrangement. Professional: Liam Greasley. Director of Golf: (01580 201090). Secretary: Mr P. Gaynor (01580 200112).

West Sussex

ALBOURNE. **Singing Hills Golf Course Ltd.,** Albourne BN6 9AJ (01273 835353; Fax: 01273 835444). *Location:* on the B2117 between Hurstpierpoint and Shaves Thatch. 36 holes (three courses). S.S.S. 70. 15 bay practice range. *Green Fees:* weekdays £20.00; weekends £25.00. £2 voucher to use in bar/restaurant included in above prices. *Eating facilities:* The Pavilion Restaurant offering catering all day, large bar. *Visitors:* welcome, not before 9am weekends. *Society Meetings:* welcome. Professional: Bob Wynn. Club Director: Derek T. Howe.

ANGMERING. **Ham Manor Golf Club Ltd,** Angmering BN16 4JE (01903 783288). *Location:* on A259 between Worthing and Littlehampton. 18 holes, 6216 yards. S.S.S. 70. *Green Fees:* on application. *Eating facilities:* lunches served at club except on Mondays. *Visitors:* welcome with reservation. Handicap Certificate required. *Society Meetings:* catered for weekdays only. Professional: Simon Buckley. Secretary: P.H. Saubergue.

BOGNOR REGIS. **Bognor Regis Golf Club,** Downview Road, Felpham, Bognor Regis PO22 8JD (01243 865867). *Location:* turn north at traffic lights on A259 at Felpham village. Flat parkland. 18 holes, 6238 yards. S.S.S. 70. Practice area. *Green Fees:* £25.00 weekdays, £30.00 weekends and Bank Holidays. *Eating facilities:* bar snacks available most days. *Visitors:* welcome weekdays, weekends only with a member. Handicap Certificate required. *Society Meetings:* catered for, minimum 20. Professional: A.P. Barr (01243 865209). Secretary: B.D. Poston (01243 821929).

BURGESS HILL. **Burgess Hill Golf Club,** Cuckfield Road, Burgess Hill RH15 8RE (01444 870615). *Location:* on A2306 from M23 Burgess Hill Junction on Cuckfield Road into Burgess Hill. Very attractive undulating course with River Adur on southern perimeter with many established trees. 9 holes, 4433 yards (for 18 holes), S.S.S. 62. 24 bay floodlit covered driving range. *Green Fees:* weekdays £5.00 per 18 holes; weekends £7.00 per 18 holes. Membership details on application. *Eating facilities:* converted Sussex barn clubhouse with bar and restaurant. *Visitors:* welcome except Saturday and Sunday mornings up to 12 noon. Pro shop. Special facilities for blind and disabled golfers. *Society Meetings:* welcome. Professional: Patrick "Teach" Tallack. Secretary: Bryan Davies.

CHICHESTER. **Goodwood Golf Club,** Goodwood, Chichester PO18 0PN (01243 785012; Fax: 01243 536650). *Location:* one mile north of roundabout at east end of Chichester Bypass (A27). Parkland, wooded. 18 holes, 6401 yards. S.S.S. 71. Practice ground, nets, putting greens. *Green Fees:* weekdays £28.00, weekends and Bank Holidays £38.00. Sussex County Cards 50% off normal charges. *Eating facilities:* full catering and bar. *Visitors:* welcome, must show Handicap Certificate. *Society Meetings:* all welcome on Wednesdays and Thursdays only. Professional: Keith MacDonald (01243 774944). Secretary: Colin Pickup (01243 774968). Steward: (01243 774105).

CHICHESTER. **Selsey Golf Club,** Golf Links Lane, Selsey, Chichester (01243 602203/602165). *Location:* B2145, seven miles south of Chichester. Flat course. 9 holes playing 18, 5932 yards. S.S.S. 68. *Green Fees:* information not available. *Eating facilities:* lunches served at club. *Visitors:* welcome weekends and Bank Holidays only if holding a bona fide Handicap Certificate or playing with a member. *Society Meetings:* small societies catered for weekdays only. Professional: P. Grindley. Secretary: B.G. Keen (01243 606442).

CRAWLEY. **Copthorne Golf Club,** Borers Arms Road, Copthorne, Crawley RH10 3LL (01342 712033). *Location:* off Exit 10 M23, one mile on A264 towards East Grinstead. Flat wooded course. 18 holes, 6505 yards. S.S.S. 71. Practice area. *Green Fees:* weekdays £25.00 per round, £33.00 per day; weekends £30.00 after 2pm. Half fees if playing with member. *Eating facilities:* catering all day, bar. *Visitors:* welcome weekdays without reservation, after 1pm weekends. *Society Meetings:* welcome with advance bookings. Professional: Joe Burrell (01342 712405). Secretary: I.J. Evans (01342 712508; Fax: 01342 717682).

CRAWLEY. **Cottesmore Country Club,** Buchan Hill, Pease Pottage, Crawley RH1 9AT (01293 528256; Fax: 01293 522819). *Location:* Junction 11 off M23 to Pease Pottage and Horsham. Undulating Sussex countryside lined by rhododendrons and birch, four holes over lakes. Old Course 18 holes, 6280 yards. S.S.S. 70; New Course 18 holes, 5489 yards. S.S.S. 68. *Green Fees:* Old Course – weekdays £30.00; weekends £38.00. New Course – weekdays £20.00; weekends £25.00. *Eating facilities:* three bars, two diningrooms, licensed Spike Bar with snacks. *Visitors:* welcome; only members' guests and residents may use the course at weekends before 11am. Indoor heated pool, health club, tennis, squash club; en-suite accommodation available. *Society Meetings:* catered for. Professional: Steve Laycock (01293 535399). Secretary: M.F. Rogerson (01293 529196). *

CRAWLEY. **Ifield Golf and Country Club,** Rusper Road, Ifield, Crawley RH11 0LN (01293 520590; Fax: 01293 612973). *Location:* outskirts of Crawley near A23 to Gossops Green. Undulating parkland. 18 holes, 6314 yards. S.S.S. 70. Practice fairway. *Green Fees:* £20.00 per round, £27.00 per day weekdays. *Eating facilities:* all day bar and catering. *Visitors:* welcome Monday, Tuesday and Wednesday afternoons, Thursday, Friday till 3.30pm. *Society Meetings:* welcome by arrangement. Professional: Jon Earl (01293 523088). Secretary: Brian Gazzard (01293 520222; Fax: 01293 612973).

CRAWLEY. **Tilgate Forest Golf Centre,** Titmus Drive, Tilgate, Crawley RH10 5EU (01293 530103). *Location:* Crawley, five minutes from Junction 11 M23. Wooded parkland. 18 holes, 6167 yards, 5643 metres. Par 72. 35 bay floodlit driving range. Par 3 course. *Green Fees:* weekdays £11.85; weekends £16.25. *Eating facilities:* restaurant and bar. *Visitors:* welcome at all times but there is a booking system in operation weekends. *Society Meetings:* welcome Mondays to Thursdays. Professional: Sean Trussell (01293 545411; Fax: 01293 523478).

EAST GRINSTEAD. **Chartham Park,** Lingfield Road, Felcourt, East Grinstead RH19 2JT (01342 870340; Fax: 01342 870719). *Location:* Lingfield Road off A22 on north side of East Grinstead. Parkland. 18 holes, 6680 yards. S.S.S. 72. Practice area, putting green. *Green Fees:* information not provided. *Eating facilities:* light snacks and refreshments available all day. *Visitors:* pre-booking required. Golf carts and trolleys can be hired. *Society Meetings:* by prior arrangement. Secretary: Lindsey Irvine. *

EAST GRINSTEAD. **Holtye Golf Club,** Holtye Common, Cowden, Near Edenbridge TN8 7ED (01342 850635). *Location:* four miles east of East Grinstead on A264, seven miles west of Tunbridge Wells. Undulating forest course; alternate tees. 9 holes, 5325 yards. S.S.S. 66. Large practice ground. *Green Fees:* information not available. *Eating facilities:* available every lunchtime, some evenings in summer season. *Visitors:* welcome, restrictions Thursday and weekend mornings. *Society Meetings:* catered for. Professional: Kevin Hinton (01342 850635). Secretary: J.P. Holmes (01342 850576).

EFFINGHAM. **Effingham Park Golf Club,** Copthorne Effingham Park Hotel, Copthorne (01342 716528). *Location:* Junction 10 M23, two miles east on A264. Wooded parkland around lake. 9 holes, 1750 yards. S.S.S. 57. *Green Fees:* information not provided. *Eating facilities:* Wellingtonia Restaurant, McLaren Restaurant and Charlie's Bar. *Visitors:* welcome but not before 1pm at weekends or on a Tuesday evening. Four star Hotel on site and leisure club. *Society Meetings:* catered for on request. Professional: I. Dryden. Secretary: Mr J.O'Donovan. *

HAYWARDS HEATH. **Haywards Heath Golf Club,** High Beech Lane, Haywards Heath RH16 1SL (01444 414310). *Location:* two miles north of Haywards Heath. Parkland. 18 holes, 6204 yards. S.S.S. 70. Practice area. *Green Fees:* weekdays £22.00 per round £27.00 for more than 18 holes; weekends and Bank Holidays £30.00 per round, £35.00 for more than 18 holes. *Eating facilities:* bar and catering both available. *Visitors:* welcome, by arrangement, phone Professional; members of another golf club only. *Society Meetings:* catered for Wednesdays and Thursdays only, numbers over 20. Professional: M. Henning (01444 414866). Secretary: John Duncan (01444 414457).

HORSHAM. **Horsham Golf Park,** Worthing Road, Horsham RH13 7AX (01403 271525; Fax: 01403 274528). *Location:* A24 Horsham bypass (southwest roundabout), 200 yards towards Horsham. Parkland. 9 holes, 4122 yards. S.S.S. 60. Practice area (£2.00 per bucket of balls). *Green Fees:* weekdays £6.00 9 holes; weekends £7.00 9 holes. *Eating facilities:* restaurant/bar open all day. *Visitors:* welcome at all times. *Society Meetings:* welcome with booking. Professional: N.J. Burke. Secretary: J. Ellwood.

HORSHAM. **Mannings Heath Golf Club,** Goldings Lane, Mannings Heath, Near Horsham RH13 6JU (01403 210228; Fax: 01403 270974). *Location:* off Junction 11 M23, three miles south-east of Horsham off A281. Undulating wooded course with featured streams. 18 holes, 6404 yards. S.S.S. 71. Second course under construction, due for completion Spring 1996. Practice net and practice ground with putting green. *Green Fees:* weekdays £27.00 per 18 holes, £36 per 36 holes; weekends £35.00 per 18 holes, £52.00 per 36 holes. *Eating facilities:* full restaurant and bar facilities. *Visitors:* welcome, must give seven days notice at most. Handicap Certificates essential. *Society Meetings:* welcome during week, full or half day. Professional: Peter Harrison. Director of Golf: Danny Pecorelli. Secretary: Jackie Brew/Danny Pecorelli.

HORSHAM near. **Slinfold Park Golf and Country Club,** Stane Street, Slinfold, Near Horsham RG13 7RE (01403 791154). *Location:* A29 Slinfold, near Horsham. Wooded parkland with lakes and streams. 18

holes. S.S.S. 72. 9 hole course, driving range, practice course. *Green Fees:* weekdays £18.00 18 hole course, £6.00 9 hole course; weekends £25.00 18 hole course, £8.00 9 hole course. *Eating facilities:* full restaurant and bar facilities. *Visitors:* welcome at all times. Pro shop. *Society Meetings:* all welcome. Professional: George McKay (01403 791555). Manager: Nigel Caplin. *

LITTLEHAMPTON. **Littlehampton Golf Club,** 170 Rope Walk, Riverside West, Littlehampton BN17 5DL (01903 717170). *Location:* leave A259 one mile west of Littlehampton at sign. Seaside links. 18 holes, 6244 yards. S.S.S. 70. *Green Fees:* £24.00 weekdays, £30.00 weekends. *Eating facilities:* restaurant and two bars. *Visitors:* welcome weekdays, weekends after midday, but phone prior to arrival. *Society Meetings:* recognised societies only. Professional: Guy McQuitty (01903 716369). Secretary: Keith Palmer.

MIDHURST. **Cowdray Park Golf Club,** Midhurst GU29 0BB (01730 812088). *Location:* one mile east of Midhurst on A272. Undulating parkland. 18 holes, 6212 yards. S.S.S. 70. Two practice grounds. *Green Fees:* £20.00 weekdays, £25.00 weekends. Reduction when playing with member. *Eating facilities:* restaurant and bar snacks. *Visitors:* welcome, weekends only after 11.00am. *Society Meetings:* catered for except Tuesdays, Fridays, weekends and Bank Holidays. Professional: Charles Giddins. Secretary: Mr J.K. McIver (01730 813599).

PULBOROUGH. **West Sussex Golf Club,** Golf Club Lane, Wiggonholt, Pulborough RH20 2EN (01798 872563). *Location:* between Storrington and Pulborough on the A283. Heathland. 18 holes, 6221 yards. S.S.S. 70. Large practice ground. *Green Fees:* on application. *Eating facilities:* lunch and tea daily, bars. *Visitors:* welcome by prior arrangement (not Fridays and weekends). No three or four balls. *Society Meetings:* catered for Wednesdays and Thursdays. Professional: T. Packham (01798 872426). Secretary: G.R. Martindale (01798 872563).

WEST CHILTINGTON. **West Chiltington Golf Club,** Broadford Bridge Road, West Chiltington RH10 2YA (01798 813574; Fax: 01798 812631). *Location:* A29 Bognor from London Road, left at Adversane village B2132 then signposted. Gently undulating parkland with spectacular views of South Downs. 18 holes, 6389 yards. S.S.S. 69. 9 holes, 1360 yard short pitch and putt course ideal for beginners. 13 bay driving range. *Green Fees:* weekdays £12.50, £5.00 after 5pm; weekends £15.00, £7.50 after 5pm. *Eating facilities:* bar and restaurant open all day every day. *Visitors:* always welcome, smart dress. Tee times may be booked through Pro Shop. *Society Meetings:* welcome, apply to Secretary. Professionals: Brian Barnes/ Roland Tisdall (01798 812115). Secretary: S.E. Coulson.

WORTHING. **Hill Barn Golf Course,** Hill Barn Lane, Worthing BN14 9AX (01903 233918). *Location:* signposted on the roundabout at the top of Broadwater, Worthing on the A27. Downland course with a few trees but generally fairly open. 18 holes, 6224 yards. S.S.S. 70. Small practice area (balls not provided) and putting green. *Green Fees:* weekdays £10.50, weekends £12.50. Juniors £4.50 weekdays only. *Eating facilities:* clubhouse and bar. *Visitors:* welcome at all times. *Society Meetings:* catered for by pre-booking, 25 people minimum. Professional/Secretary: A.P. Higgins (01903 237301). *

WORTHING. **Worthing Golf Club,** Links Road, Worthing BN14 9QZ (01903 260717; Fax: 01903 694664). *Location:* on A27 near junction with A24 (Offington Roundabout). Two downland courses. Lower course: 18 holes, 6519 yards. S.S.S. 72. Upper course: 5243 yards. S.S.S. 66. *Green Fees:* weekdays £30.00 per day, weekends and Bank Holidays £40.00 per day. *Eating facilities:* first class restaurant facilities. *Visitors:* welcome, check in advance with Secretary. No visitors at weekends during December, January and February. *Society Meetings:* catered for by arrangement. Professional: Stephen Rolley (01903 260718). Secretary: David Browse (01903 260801).

Tyne & Wear

BIRTLEY. **Birtley Golf Club,** Portobello Lane, Birtley (0191-410 2207). *Location:* just off old Durham road and main A1. Parkland. 9 holes, 5660 yards. S.S.S. 67. *Green Fees:* weekdays £12.00; weekends £12.00 with member only. *Eating facilities:* bar only after 7.30pm. *Visitors:* welcome weekdays, weekends with a member only. *Society Meetings:* welcome, limited. Secretary: T. Stobbart (0191-410 4021).

CHOPWELL. **Garesfield Golf Club,** Chopwell NE17 7AP (01207 561278). *Location:* leave A694 at Rowlands Gill, follow signposts for Chopwell, approximately three miles. Parkland, wooded. 18 holes, 6203 yards. S.S.S. 70. Practice nets and area. *Green Fees:* weekdays £14.00 per round, £16.00 per day; weekends and Bank Holidays after 4.30pm, £17.00. *Eating facilities:* full catering and bar service. *Visitors:* welcome weekdays, weekends and Bank Holidays after 4.30pm. *Society Meetings:* by arrangement with Secretary. Professional: D. Race (01207 563082). Secretary: J.R. Peart (01207 561309).

EASINGTON LANE. **Elemore Golf Course (Municipal),** Elemore View, Easington Lane (0191-526 9020). *Location:* follow signs to Easington Lane, located off A1068, following signs to Elemore/Pittington. Flat meadowland course. 9 holes, 5986 yards. S.S.S. 69. (Additional 9 holes under construction). Practice area. *Green Fees:* weekdays adults £5.00, concessions £2.50. Weekends adults £7.50 before noon, £6.50 after noon; concessions £5.00 before noon, £4.00 after noon. *Eating facilities:* clubhouse with bar/lounge serving snacks and meals. *Visitors:* welcome, no restrictions. *Society Meetings:* welcome throughout the year. Contact Course Manager for advance bookings (14 days' notice required). Course Manager: J. Burnikell.

EAST BOLDON. **Boldon Golf Club Ltd,** Dipe Lane, East Boldon NE36 0PQ (0191-536 4182). *Location:* near Sunderland, approximately one mile from roundabout at junction of A19 and A184 highways. Fairly flat parkland. 18 holes, 6348 yards. S.S.S. 70. *Green Fees:* weekdays £16.00, with a member £10.00; weekends £20.00, with a member £12.00. *Eating facilities:* bar snacks and restaurant. *Visitors:* welcome, not between 9am and 10am, 12.30pm and 1.30pm or 4.30pm and 6pm. Not before 3.30pm at weekends. *Society Meetings:* catered for. Professional: Phipps Golf (0191-536 5835). Hon. Secretary: R.E. Jobes (0191-536 5360).

GATESHEAD. **Heworth Golf Club,** Gingling Gate, Heworth, Gateshead (0191-469 2137). *Location:* A1 (M) south east boundary of Gateshead. Flat wooded course. 18 holes, 6437 yards. S.S.S. 71. Practice area. *Green Fees:* £15.00 weekdays; £18.00 weekends. Special rates for parties over 20. *Eating facilities:* diningroom, two bars. *Visitors:* weekdays up to 4pm, no visitors Saturdays; but after 10am on Sundays. *Society Meetings:* welcome mid-week only up to 4pm. Secretary: G. Holbrow (0191-469 9832). *

GATESHEAD. **Ravensworth Golf Club Ltd,** Moss Heaps, Wrekenton, Gateshead NE9 7UU (0191-4876014). *Location:* two miles south of Gateshead town centre. 18 holes, 5872 yards, 5374 metres. S.S.S. 68. *Green Fees:* £17.00 per round weekdays; £25.00 weekends and Bank Holidays. *Eating facilities:* meals served with reasonable notice (not Mondays). *Visitors:* welcome without reservation. *Society Meetings:* catered for. Professional: David Race. Secretary: L. Winter.

HEDDON-ON-THE-WALL. **Close House Golf Club,** Heddon-on-the-Wall, Newcastle-upon-Tyne NE15 0HT (01661 852953). *Location:* nine miles west of city on A69. Parkland/part wooded. 18 holes, 5587 yards. S.S.S. 67. Private golf club. *Eating facilities:* by arrangement with Close House Mansion (01661 852427). *Visitors:* with member only. *Society Meetings:* weekdays only by arrangement with Secretary. Secretary: J. Pearson (01661 852953).

HOUGHTON-LE-SPRING. **Houghton-le-Spring Golf Club,** Copt Hill, Houghton-le-Spring (0191 5841198). *Location:* off A690 Durham Road, take Houghton to Seaham road, course is situated at the top of Copt Hill bank. Testing hillside course. 18 holes, 6416 yards, 5867 metres. S.S.S. 71. *Green Fees:* information not provided. *Eating facilities:* available most days, bar open every day. *Visitors:* welcome most days but not on competition days (Sundays). *Society Meetings:* catered for by arrangement. Professional: K. Gow (0191 5847421). Secretary: N. Wales (0191 5285481).

NEWCASTLE UPON TYNE. **City of Newcastle Golf Club,** Three Mile Bridge, Gosforth, Newcastle upon Tyne NE3 2DR (0191-285 1775). *Location:* B1318 three miles north of city. Flat parkland. 18 holes, 6510 yards. S.S.S. 71. *Green Fees:* weekdays £19.00; weekends and Bank Holidays £21.00. *Eating facilities:* bar, meals. *Visitors:* welcome without reservation, restricted times Fridays. *Society Meetings:* very welcome. Professional/Secretary: A.J. Matthew (0191-285 5481).

NEWCASTLE UPON TYNE. **Gosforth Golf Club,** Broadway East, Gosforth, Newcastle upon Tyne NE3 5ER (0191-285 6710). *Location:* one mile from Gosforth Park Hotel, three miles north of Newcastle. Parkland with stream. 18 holes, 6024 yards. S.S.S. 69. *Green Fees:* £18.00. *Eating facilities:* by arrangement. *Visitors:* welcome weekdays. *Society Meetings:* catered for by arrangement with the Secretary. Not weekends or Bank Holidays. Professional: G. Garland (0191-285 0553). Secretary: P. Keady (0191-285 3495).

NEWCASTLE UPON TYNE. **Newcastle United Golf Club,** 60 Ponteland Road, Cowgate, Newcastle upon Tyne NE5 3JW (0191 2864693). *Location:* two miles west of city centre in direction of airport. Moorland. 18 holes, 6573 yards, 6010 metres. S.S.S. 71. Practice area. *Green Fees:* information not provided. *Eating facilities:* bar meals available. *Visitors:* no restrictions midweek, welcome weekends if no competitions. *Society Meetings:* welcome, book through Secretary. Professional: Brian Hall. Golf Shop: (0191 2869998). Secretary: J. Simpson. *

NEWCASTLE UPON TYNE. **Parklands Golf Club,** High Gosforth Park, Newcastle upon Tyne NE3 5HQ (0191-236 4867). *Location:* three miles north of centre of Newcastle, off the A1 follow signs for Gosforth Park. Parkland. 18 holes, 6060 yards, 5530 metres. S.S.S. 69. 9 holes pitch and putt, 45 bay floodlit driving range. *Green Fees:* weekdays £13.00; weekends £15.00. *Eating facilities:* restaurant and bar. *Visitors:* welcome, no restrictions. *Society Meetings:* catered for. Professional: Brian Rumney (0191-236 4480). Secretary: Brian Woof (0191-236 4480).

NEWCASTLE UPON TYNE. **The Northumberland Golf Club Ltd,** High Gosforth Park, Newcastle upon Tyne NE3 5HT (0191-236 2498). *Location:* off A1. 18 holes, 6629 yards. S.S.S. 72. *Green Fees:* information not provided. *Visitors:* welcome with prior reservation or introduction. *Society Meetings:* catered for except on Mondays, Wednesdays and weekends. Secretary: S.C. Owram (0191-236 2498).

NEWCASTLE UPON TYNE. **Westerhope Golf Club,** Whorlton Grange, Westerhope, Newcastle-upon-Tyne NE5 1PP (0191-286 9125). *Location:* A69, Jingling Gate Public House. Parkland/wooded. 18 holes, 6468 yards, 5912 metres. S.S.S. 71. Two practice areas. *Green Fees:* weekdays £16.00 per round, £8.00 with a member; £22.00 per day, £12.00 with a member; weekends £10.00 per round with a member only. *Eating facilities:* lunches and high teas. *Visitors:* welcome weekdays, weekends and Bank Holidays with a member only. *Society Meetings:* by appointment. Professional: N. Brown (0191-286 0594). Secretary: J.W. Hedley (0191-286 7636).

NEWCASTLE-UPON-TYNE. **Hobson Municipal Golf Club,** Hobson, Burnopfield, Newcastle-upon-Tyne (01207 271605). *Location:* on main Newcastle to Consett road. Fairly flat, well designed course. 18 holes, 6582 yards, 6018 metres. S.S.S. 71. Practice area. *Green Fees:* weekdays £8.50 per round; weekends £11.00 per round. *Eating facilities:* bar, lounge and restaurant. *Visitors:* no restrictions; booking system at weekends. *Society Meetings:* by prior arrangement with Professional (all bookings). Professional: J.W. Ord (01207 271605). Secretary: R.J. Handrick (01207 570189).

NEWCASTLE-UPON-TYNE. **Tyneside Golf Club Ltd,** Westfield Lane, Ryton NE40 3QE (0191-413 2177). *Location:* seven miles west of Newcastle-upon-Tyne, off A695 in Ryton Village. Parkland, hilly with water hazards. 18 holes, 6042 yards, 5522 metres. S.S.S. 69. Practice field. *Green Fees:* weekdays £18.00, weekends £28.00. *Eating facilities:* full catering. *Visitors:* bona fide golfers welcome. *Society Meetings:* by arrangement with Secretary, weekdays only. Professional: M. Gunn (0191-413 1600). Secretary: J.R. Watkin (0191-413 2742).

NEWCASTLE-UPON-TYNE. **Whickham Golf Club,** Hollinside Park, Whickham, Newcastle-upon-Tyne NE16 5BA (0191-488 7309). *Location:* five miles south west of Newcastle. Parkland. 18 holes, 6179 yards. S.S.S. 69. *Green Fees:* weekdays £20.00; weekends £25.00. *Eating facilities:* lunches, teas, evening meals available by prior order. *Visitors:* welcome without reservation. *Society Meetings:* catered for by arrangement. Professional: Brian Ridley (0191-488 8591). Secretary/Manager: M.J. Musto (0191-488 1576).

RYHOPE. **Ryhope Golf Course (Municipal),** Leechmere Way, Ryhope, Sunderland (0191-523 7333; Fax: 0191-521 3811). *Location:* off A1018 in the village of Ryhope. Undulating parkland course. 18 holes, 4601 yards. S.S.S. 63. *Green Fees:* weekdays adults £6.00, concessions £3.00. Weekends adults £9.00 before noon, £7.00 after noon; concessions £6.00 before noon, £4.00 after noon. *Visitors:* welcome, no restrictions. *Society Meetings:* welcome throughout the year. Please contact Course Manager for advance bookings (14 days' notice required). Course Manager: J. Burnikell.

RYTON. **Ryton Golf Club,** Dr. Stanners, Clara Vale, Ryton NE40 3TD (0191-413 3737). *Location:* off A695 eight miles west of Newcastle at Crawcrook to Clara Vale. Flat parkland, wooded, running alongside River Tyne. 18 holes, 6042 yards, 5524 metres. S.S.S. 69. *Green Fees:* weekdays £12.00 per round, £18.00 per day; weekends £16.00 per round. *Eating facilities:* available by arrangement with Steward. *Visitors:* welcome weekdays, weekends with member or by prior arrangement. *Society Meetings:* catered for by arrangement with Secretary. Secretary: Mr F.R. Creed (0191-413 3253).

SHIREMOOR. **Backworth Golf Club,** The Hall, Backworth, Shiremoor (0191 2681048). *Location:* from Newcastle to Shiremoor Crossroads then left for one mile. Parkland, flat. 9 holes, 5930 yards. S.S.S. 69. *Green Fees:* on request. *Eating facilities:* meals booked in advance, bar facilities, snacks, etc. *Visitors:* welcome by arrangement but not Tuesday pm (Ladies' day), not Saturday until 5pm (Summer), not Sunday mornings. *Society Meetings:* welcome booked in advance through Welfare Management Secretary. Secretary: D. Carruthers (0191 2581291 after 6.30pm).

SOUTH SHIELDS. **South Shields Golf Club Ltd,** Cleadon Hills, South Shields NE34 8EG (0191-456 0475). *Location:* near A19 and A1 M, Cleadon Chimney prominent landmark. 18 holes, 6264 yards, 5729 metres. S.S.S. 70. *Green Fees:* weekdays £20.00; weekends and Bank Holidays £25.00. *Eating facilities:* meals available at all times, bar. *Visitors:* welcome at all times without reservation. *Society Meetings:* catered for. Professional: Gary Parsons (0191-456 0110). Secretary: W.H. Loades (0191-456 8942).

SOUTH SHIELDS. **Whitburn Golf Club,** Lizard Lane, South Shields NE34 7AF (0191-529 2144). *Location:* between Sunderland and South Shields adjoining Coast Road. Parkland. 18 holes, 5773 yards, 5275 metres. S.S.S. 68. *Green Fees:* weekdays £15.00, introduced by and playing with member £10.00. Saturdays, Sundays and Bank Holidays £20.00, introduced by and playing with a member £12.00. *Eating facilities:* available. *Visitors:* welcome except on Saturday or Sunday when competitions being held and restricted Tuesdays (Ladies' Day). *Society Meetings:* catered for on weekdays by prior reservations. Professional: D. Stephenson (0191-529 4210). Secretary: Mrs V. Atkinson (0191-529 4944).

SUNDERLAND. **Wearside Golf Club,** Cox Green, Sunderland SR4 9JT (0191-534 2518). *Location:* on south bank of River Wear, one mile west of A19. From A19 exit for A183, direction Chester-le-Street, at 200 yards turn right, signposted Offerton/Cox Green, then left at T junction, down hill over humped bridge. Parkland, bordered on north by River Wear, deep wooded gully traverses course. 18 holes, 6323 yards. S.S.S. 70. 4 holes Par 3 field and separate practice tees. *Green Fees:* weekdays £24.00 per day; weekends and Bank Holidays £30.00. *Eating facilities:* full catering and bar service. *Visitors:* welcome most times, telephone Professional for information. *Society Meetings:* by advance application. Professional: Mr Doug Brolls (0191-534 4269). Secretary: N. Hildrew (0191-534 2518).

WALLSEND. **Wallsend Golf Club,** Bigges Main, Wallsend. *Location:* western boundary. Parkland. 18 holes, 6608 yards, 6043 metres. S.S.S. 72. *Green Fees:* weekdays £10.50; weekends £12.50. *Eating facilities:* meals available on request. *Visitors:* restricted weekends – not before 12.30pm April to October. *Society Meetings:* weekdays only. Professional: K. Phillips (0191-262 2431). Secretary: D. Souter (0191-262 1973).

WASHINGTON. **Washington Moat House Golf Club,** Stonecellar Road, Washington NE33 1PH (0191-417 2626). *Location:* half a mile from A1 M junction A94. Parkland. 18 holes, 6604 yards, 6038 metres. S.S.S. 72. 21 bay floodlit driving range, 9 hole pitch and putt. *Green Fees:* weekdays £16.00; weekends £23.00. *Eating facilities:* fully licensed hotel on site. *Visitors:* by arrangement. Special rates for visiting parties of over 15 mid-week. Hotel with 105 plus bedrooms. *Society Meetings:* by arrangement. Professional: Warren Marshall (0191-417 8346). Secretary: Stephen Purdy (0191-416 8341). Leisure Manager: B. Wardle (0191-417 2626).

WHITLEY BAY. **Whitley Bay Golf Club,** Claremont Road, Whitley Bay NE26 3UF (0191-252 0180). *Location:* north side of town. Undulating parkland. 18 holes, 6617 yards. S.S.S. 72. *Green Fees:* weekdays £18.00 per round, £26.00 per day. *Eating facilities:* available except Mondays. *Visitors:* welcome with reservation weekdays, weekends only with member. *Society Meetings:* catered for by arrangement with Secretary. Professional: G. Shipley (0191-252 5688). Secretary: B. Dockar (0191-252 0180).

Warwickshire

ATHERSTONE. **Atherstone Golf Club,** The Outwoods, Coleshill Road, Atherstone CV9 2RL (01827 713110). *Location:* five miles north of Nuneaton and seven miles south of Tamworth. Undulating parkland. 18 holes, 6239 yards. Practice ground. *Green Fees:* £17.00 per day/round weekdays, £8.00 with a member; Saturdays with member only. *Eating facilities:* bar and dining room. *Visitors:* welcome weekdays without reservation, Saturdays with member only, not Sundays. Ladies' Day Wednesday. *Society Meetings:* on application to Secretary. Professional: (01827 713110). Secretary: V.A. Walton (01827 892568).

BRAILES. **Brailes Golf Club Ltd,** Sutton Lane, Brailes, Banbury OX15 5BB (01608 685722). *Location:* between Banbury and Shipston-on-Stour, just off the B4035. Parkland/meadowland course. 18 holes, 6270 yards. S.S.S. 70. *Green Fees:* weekdays £11.00 per round, £16.00 per day, twilight (after 5pm) £7.00; weekends £15.00 per round, £22.00 per day, twilight (after 5pm) £9.00. *Eating facilities:* modern clubhouse; bar and restaurant facilities. *Visitors:* welcome subject to availability. Large car park. *Society Meetings:* welcome subject to availability. Professional: M. Bendall (01608 685633). Manager: R.A.S. Malir (01608 685336).

HENLEY-IN-ARDEN. **Crocketts Manor Golf and Country Club,** Birmingham Road, Henley-in-Arden (01564 793715; Fax: 01564 795754). *Location:* two miles from M40 Junction 16; 20 minutes from Birmingham, Solihull, Stratford-upon-Avon and Warwick. Parkland, with lovely countryside views. 18 holes, 6760 yards. S.S.S. 73. 9-hole Par 3 course. Practice range. *Green Fees:* weekdays £20.00 per round, £25.00 per day, £10.00 twilight fee; weekends £25.00 per round, £30.00 per day, £15.00 twilight fee. *Eating facilities:* bar lounge menu, "Greens Restaurant". *Visitors:* no restrictions, but must book in advance. Smart casual dress required, no denim. Tennis courts and Leisure Club with saunas and steam baths. *Society Meetings:* very welcome. Professional: Simon Edwin. Secretary; Neil Selwyn-Smith.

KENILWORTH. **Kenilworth Golf Club Ltd,** Crew Lane, Kenilworth (01926 54038). *Location:* A429 Coventry to Kenilworth adjacent to A46 Coventry to Warwick Road. Parkland and wooded course. 18 holes, 6413 yards. S.S.S. 71. Practice ground and 9 hole Par 3 course. *Green Fees:* £26.00 weekdays; £37.00 weekends and Bank Holidays. *Eating facilities:* diningroom, bar snacks, two bars. *Visitors:* must be members of another club with official Handicap Certificate. *Society Meetings:* groups (under 20 in number) weekdays, Societies (over 20) Wednesday only. Professional: S. Yates (01926 512732). Secretary: J.H. McTavish (Tel & Fax: 01926 58517).

LEAMINGTON SPA. **Leamington and County Golf Club,** Golf Lane, Whitnash, Leamington Spa (01926 420298). *Location:* two miles south of town centre of Royal Leamington Spa. 18 holes, 6430 yards, 5878 metres. S.S.S. 71. *Green Fees:* weekdays £25.00 per round, £30.00 per day; weekends £40.00 per round. *Eating facilities:* luncheons, teas, evening meals and snacks. *Visitors:* welcome without reservation. *Society Meetings:* catered for. Professional: I. Grant (01926 428014). Secretary: S.M. Cooknell (01926 425961).

LEAMINGTON SPA. **Newbold Comyn Golf Club,** Newbold Terrace East, Leamington Spa (01926 421157). *Location:* signposted off Willes Road. Parkland, front 9 hilly, back 9 flat. 18 holes, 6315 yards. S.S.S. 70. Practice area. *Green Fees:* weekdays £7.00; weekends £9.00. *Eating facilities:* bar, restaurant. *Visitors:* welcome, unrestricted. *Society Meetings:* catered for, book through Professional. Professional: D.R. Knight (01926 421157). Secretary: A.A. Pierce (01926 422660).

NORTH WARWICKSHIRE. **Purley Chase Golf and Country Club "1990",** Ridge Lane, Near Nuneaton CV10 0RB (01203 397468). *Location:* three miles off A5 between Atherstone and Nuneaton. Slightly undulating. 18 holes, 6650 yards, 6040 metres. S.S.S. 71. Driving range. *Green Fees:* information not provided. *Eating facilities:* restaurant. *Visitors:* welcome at all times. *Society Meetings:* all welcome, special rates. Professional/Secretary: David Llewellyn (01203 395348 or 393118). *

NUNEATON. **Bramcote Water Golf Club,** Bazzard Road, Bramcote, Nuneaton CV11. 9-hole course opening 1995 – full details not available.

NUNEATON. **Nuneaton Golf Club,** Golf Drive, Whitestone, Nuneaton CV11 6QF (01203 383281). *Location:* Junction 3 off M6. Wooded course. 18 holes, 6429 yards. S.S.S. 71. Practice ground. *Green Fees:* weekdays £22.00, with a member £6.00; weekends £22.00 playing with a member only. *Eating facilities:* catering available except Mondays; bar open usual hours. *Visitors:* welcome weekdays. *Society Meetings:* Wednesdays and Fridays only, must clear tee by 2pm on Fridays. Professional: (01203 340201). Secretary/ Manager: G. Pinder (01203 347810). *

NUNEATON. **Oakridge Golf Club,** Arley Lane, Ansley Village, Nuneaton CV10 9PH (01676 541389). *Location:* on outskirts of Nuneaton, approximately 15 minutes from town centre, 20 minutes from Coventry and 25 minutes from Tamworth. Immature woodland; undulating fairways with many water hazards. 18 holes, 6242 yards. S.S.S. 70. Practice area, Pro shop. *Green Fees:* weekdays £15.00 for 18 holes, £25.00 for 36 holes. *Eating facilities:* à la carte restaurant, bar meals, lounge bar. *Visitors:* welcome weekdays, weekends as members' guests only. Snooker room. *Society Meetings:* welcome weekdays (Friday mornings only). Professional: Ian Sadler (01676 540542). Secretary (Admin. and Society Bookings): Mrs S. Lovric; Golf Section Secretary: Les Grant.

RUGBY. **Rugby Golf Club,** Clifton Road, Rugby CV21 3RD (01788 542306). *Location:* one mile from Rugby town centre on the Clifton road. Parkland course. 18 holes, 5457 yards. S.S.S. 67. Practice ground. *Green Fees:* weekdays £20.00 per day; weekends with a member only. *Eating facilities:* bar and dining facilities daily except Tuesdays. *Visitors:* welcome weekdays; weekends and Bank Holidays only with a member. Ladies' Day Wednesday. Snooker room. *Society Meetings:* welcome if pre-booked. Professional: A. Peach (01788 575134). Secretary: R. Scott.

STRATFORD-UPON-AVON. **Stratford Oaks Golf Club,** Bearley Road, Snitterfield, Stratford-upon-Avon CV37 0JH (01789 731892). *Location:* from Junction 15 off M40 head south to Stratford-upon-Avon, take signpost to Snitterfield and club is between Snitterfield and Bearley. Flat parkland with lakes. 18 holes, 6100 yards. S.S.S. 69. 26 bay floodlit driving range. *Green Fees:* weekdays £12.00; weekends £15.00. Juniors half price. *Eating facilities:* available. *Visitors:* welcome, no restrictions. *Society Meetings:* catered for, no restrictions. Professional: Fraser Leek (01789 731571). Secretary: Simon Millington (01789 731571). *

STRATFORD-UPON-AVON. **Stratford-on-Avon Golf Club,** Tiddington Road, Stratford-upon-Avon CV37 7BA (01789 297296). *Location:* half a mile from town on B4086. Flat parkland. 18 holes, 6309 yards. S.S.S. 70. *Green Fees:* weekdays £25.00; weekends £35.00. *Eating facilities:* full catering/bar service. *Visitors:* welcome any time subject to domestic commitments. *Society Meetings:* catered for Tuesdays and Thursdays. Professional: D. Sutherland (01789 205677). Secretary: M.L. Wilson (01789 205749).

STRATFORD-UPON-AVON. **Welcombe Hotel Golf Course,** Warwick Road, Stratford-upon-Avon CV37 0NR (01789 299012). *Location:* exit M40 at Junction 15, follow signs to Stratford. Club is on A439 after five miles. Or take A439 out of town and club is on left after one mile. Undulating parkland with lakes and waterfall. 18 holes, 6217 yards. S.S.S. 70. Practice area and putting green. *Green Fees:* weekdays £35.00; weekends and Bank Holidays £40.00. *Eating facilities:* bar serving pub style food. *Visitors:* welcome subject to availability. Hotel on site, four star facilities. *Society Meetings:* weekdays by prior arrangement, rates on request. Golf Manager: (01789 295252).

WARWICK. **The Warwickshire Golf Club,** Leek Wootton, Near Warwick CV35 7QT (01926 409409; Fax: 01926 408409). *Location:* on B4115, just off A46, five minutes from M40 Junction 15. Parkland and woodland courses with many attractive holes over water. North/West Course: 18 holes, 7407 yards. S.S.S. 74. South/East Course: 18 holes, 7157 yards. S.S.S. 74. 9-hole Par 3 course. Driving range. *Green Fees:* £35.00 per round. *Eating facilities:* hot food available from 7.30am; bars open all day. *Visitors:* welcome at all times. Handicap Certificate required. *Society Meetings:* Golf Days arranged for groups from 12 to 300. Professional: S. Hutchinson. Secretary: A.J. Sledger. General Manager: P.A. Chubb.

WARWICK. **Warwick Golf Club,** Warwick Golf Centre, Racecourse, Warwick (01926 494316). *Location:* off M40, from A41/A46 junction, travel half a mile towards Warwick, turn right into racecourse. Flat parkland. 9 holes, 2682 yards. S.S.S. 66. Driving range (floodlit). *Green Fees:* weekdays £3.80 per 9 holes, weekends £5.50 per 9 holes. *Eating facilities:* bar open 7-10.30pm weekdays, no catering. *Visitors:* welcome any time except Sunday mornings. Professional: (01926 491284). Secretary: R. Dunkley.

West Midlands

BIRMINGHAM. **Brandhall Golf Club,** Heron Road, Oldbury, Warley B68 8AQ (0121-552 7475). *Location:* Junction 2 M5, A4123, right at traffic lights, signposted from there. Wooded course. 18 holes, 5734 yards, 5243 metres. S.S.S. 68. Practice area. *Green Fees:* weekdays £6.00, Juniors and Senior Citizens £4.00; weekends £8.00. *Eating facilities:* cafe (except Tuesdays) and bar (lunchtime only on Wednesdays). *Visitors:* welcome, no restriction except weekends. Tee reserved for club members only Saturdays 8-10am and Sundays 8-10.30am. *Society Meetings:* phone Pro Shop (0121-552 2195) to book times. Secretary: M. Butler (01676 42482).

BIRMINGHAM. **Cocks Moors Woods Golf Club,** Alcester Road, Kings Heath, Birmingham B14 4ER (0121-444 3584). *Location:* A435 Kings Heath, nearest motorway M42. Parkland/wooded course. 18 holes, 5820 yards. S.S.S. 68. *Green Fees:* £6.60 weekdays and weekends. *Eating facilities:* full catering and bars. *Visitors:* welcome at all times. Full range of leisure facilities within complex. *Society Meetings:* not catered for. Professional: Steve Ellis. Secretary: Glyn Williams. *

BIRMINGHAM. **Edgbaston Golf Club Ltd,** Church Road, Edgbaston, Birmingham B15 3TB (0121-454 1736). *Location:* from centre of city take A38 (Bristol Road). After one mile and at second traffic lights turn right into Priory Road, at end turn left into Church Road, club entrance 100 yards on left. Undulating parkland course designed by H.S. Colt. Clubhouse in historic Edgbaston Hall. 18 holes, 6118 yards, 5594 metres. S.S.S. 69. *Green Fees:* weekdays Summer £35.00, Winter £27.50; weekends Summer £45.00, Winter £37.50. Playing with a member £8.50. *Eating facilities:* fully licensed, lunches, teas daily and bar meals; other meals by prior arrangement. *Visitors:* welcome. Must have Handicap Certificate. Facilities for business meetings/seminars. *Society Meetings:* welcome by arrangement with Secretary. Societies of 20 players of more £32.00.Professional: A.H. Bownes (0121-454 3226; Fax: 0121-454 8295). Secretary: Andrew D. Mollett.

BIRMINGHAM. **Gay Hill Golf Club,** Hollywood Lane, Hollywood, Birmingham B47 5PP (0121-430 6523). *Location:* M42 Junction 3, three miles. Flat course. 18 holes, 6532 yards. S.S.S. 71. Practice area. *Green Fees:* £28.50 weekdays. *Eating facilities:* available. *Visitors:* welcome all week; weekends by invitation only. *Society Meetings:* catered for by arrangement Thursdays. Professional: Andrew Hill (0121-474 6001). Secretary: Mrs E.K. Devitt (0121-430 8544).

BIRMINGHAM. **Great Barr Golf Club,** Chapel Lane, Great Barr, Birmingham B43 7BA (0121-357 1232). *Location:* six miles north-west of Birmingham M6 Junction 7. Parkland. 18 holes, 6523 yards. S.S.S. 71. *Green Fees:* £25.00 weekdays and weekends. *Eating facilities:* meals served, order in advance. *Visitors:* welcome weekdays, restricted at weekends. Weekends maximum handicap 18. Handicap Certificate required. *Society Meetings:* small groups catered for. Professional: R. Spragg (0121-357 5270). Secretary: Mrs J.S.Pembridge (0121-358 4376).

BIRMINGHAM. **Handsworth Golf Club,** 11 Sunningdale Close, Handsworth Wood, Birmingham B20 1NP (0121-554 0599). *Location:* M5 Junction 1. A41 left at first lights, left at next set of lights, second left, second left/M6 Junction 7. A34 Birmingham Road, Old Walsall Road, Vernon Avenue, Westover Road, Craythorne Avenue. Parkland course. 18 holes, 6272 yards, 5733 metres. S.S.S. 70. Large practice area and putting green. *Green Fees:* £30.00 per day, £8.00 with a member; weekends with member only, £10.00. *Eating facilities:* bar snacks to à la carte menu in restaurant. *Visitors:* welcome weekdays with Handicap Certificate. *Society Meetings:* catered for by arrangement with Secretary. Special packages available. Professional: Mr L. Bashford (0121-523 3594). Secretary: P.S. Hodnett (0121-554 3387).

BIRMINGHAM. **Harborne (Church Farm) Golf Club,** Vicarage Road, Harborne, Birmingham B17 0SN (0121-427 1204). *Location:* signposted from Harborne Centre. Parkland. 9 holes, 4914 yards. S.S.S. 64. *Green Fees:* 9 holes £4.20, 18 holes £7.20. Reductions for Senior Citizens and students. *Eating facilities:* canteen serves hot and cold snacks. *Visitors:* welcome anytime – phone call required as a booking system is in operation. *Society Meetings:* by arrangement with the Professional. Professional: Mr Mark Hampton (0121-427 1204). Secretary: Mr William Flanagan.

BIRMINGHAM. **Harborne Golf Club,** 40 Tennal Road, Harborne, Birmingham B32 2JE (0121-427 1728). *Location:* A4123, A456, B4124 three miles west Birmingham city centre. Undulating parkland/moorland. 18 holes, 6235 yards. S.S.S. 70. *Green Fees:* weekdays £30.00 per round, £35.00 per day. *Eating facilities:* bar and dining area daily. *Visitors:* welcome except weekends and Bank Holidays. *Society Meetings:* welcome weekdays except Tuesdays. Special rates for parties comprising over 20 players. Professional: A. Quarterman (0121-427 3512). Secretary: E.J. Humphreys (0121-427 3058).

BIRMINGHAM. **Harborne Municipal Golf Club,** Vicarage Road, Harborne, Birmingham B17 0SN (0121-427 1204). *Location:* A456 to Harborne Village then course is signposted. Parkland course, beware of brooks! 9 holes, 2457 yards. S.S.S. 64. *Green Fees:* 9 holes £3.30, 18 holes £6.00. *Eating facilities:* restaurant. *Visitors:* welcome anytime, must pre book. Free car parking. *Society Meetings:* welcome anytime. Professional: M.J. Hampton (0121-427 1204; Fax: 0121-428 3126). Secretary: W. Flanagan (0121-427 1204).

BIRMINGHAM. **Hatchford Brook Golf Club,** Coventry Road, Sheldon, Birmingham B26 3PY (0121-743 9821). *Location:* A45 next to Birmingham Airport, M6 Exit 4. North of M42 Junction 6. Flat parkland. 18 holes, 6202 yards. S.S.S. 70. Practice ground. *Green Fees:* weekdays £6.60; weekends £7.00. *Eating facilities:* cafe. *Visitors:* welcome at all times. *Society Meetings:* contact Professional. Professional: Paul Smith (0121 743 9821). Secretary: D. Williams (01676 23383).

BIRMINGHAM. **Hilltop Public Golf Course,** Park Lane, Handsworth, Birmingham B21 8LJ (0121-554 4463). *Location:* M5 exit West Bromwich, take Birmingham road first left past W.B.A. football ground. Parkland, gently sloping fairways, large greens. 18 holes, 6114 yards. S.S.S. 69. *Green Fees:* information not provided. *Eating facilities:* cafe serving drinks and hot meals. *Visitors:* welcome anytime, Municipal course. *Society Meetings:* bookings available through Professional. Professional: Kevin Highfield. Secretary: M. Adams. *

BIRMINGHAM. **Kings Norton Golf Club Ltd,** Brockhill Lane, Weatheroak, Alvechurch, Birmingham B48 7ED (01564 822821). *Location:* M42 Junction 3, towards Birmingham. Sign on left to Weatheroak, follow for two miles, over first crossroads. Club on left hand side. Parkland. 27 holes, 7000 yards. S.S.S. 72. 12 hole short course. *Green Fees:* £27.00 per round; £29.50 per day. *Eating facilities:* available. *Visitors:* welcome weekdays only, weekends with member. *Society Meetings:* catered for weekdays only. Professional: Kevin Hayward (01564 822822). Secretary: L.N.W. Prince (01564 826789).

BIRMINGHAM. **Maxstoke Park Golf Club,** Castle Lane, Coleshill, Birmingham B46 2RD (01675 462158). *Location:* three miles north east of Coleshill on B4114, turn right for Maxstoke. Parkland with trees and lake. Water filled moat surrounding Maxstoke Castle. 18 holes, 6442 yards, S.S.S. 71. Two practice areas. *Green Fees:* £25.00 per round, £35.00 per day. *Eating facilities:* restaurant and bar. *Visitors:* welcome weekdays only, weekends with member. *Society Meetings:* catered for Tuesdays/Thursdays. Professional: N. McEwan (01675 464915). Secretary: D. Haywood (01675 466743).

BIRMINGHAM. **North Worcestershire Golf Club,** Frankley Beeches Road, Northfield, Birmingham B31 5LP (0121-475 1026). *Location:* A38 from Birmingham City Centre. Parkland, established inland course. 18 holes, 5959 yards. S.S.S. 69. *Green Fees:* £18.50 weekdays; weekends with a member only. *Eating facilities:* catering facilities on request, normal bar opening hours. *Visitors:* welcome weekdays. *Society Meetings:* catered for Tuesdays and Thursdays. Professional: K.E. Jones (0121-475 5721). Secretary: B.C. Lediard (0121-475 1047).

BIRMINGHAM near. **Rose Hill Golf Club,** Rose Hill, Rednal, Near Birmingham (0121-453 7600). *Location:* M5 Exit 4 to Birmingham South. Parkland, wooded. 18 holes, 6010 yards. S.S.S. 69. *Green Fees:* £7.80 per round. *Eating facilities:* cafe in clubhouse. *Visitors:* welcome without reservation. Professional: M. March (0121-453 3159). Secretary: M. Billingham (01374 409732).

BIRMINGHAM. **The Moseley Golf Club,** Springfield Road, Kings Heath, Birmingham B14 7DX (0121-444 2115). *Location:* close by A435 (south Birmingham). Parkland. 18 holes, 6227 yards. S.S.S. 70. *Green Fees:* £34.00. *Eating facilities:* in clubhouse. *Visitors:* welcome only by prior arrangement with Secretary. *Society Meetings:* catered for by prior arrangement with the Secretary Wednesdays or Thursdays. Professional: G. Edge (0121-444 2063). Secretary: R.A. Jowle (0121-444 4957; Fax: 0121-441 4662).

COVENTRY. **Ansty Golf Centre,** Brinklow Road, Ansty, Coventry CV7 9JH (01203 621347; Fax: 01203 602671). *Location:* half a mile from Junction 2 M6 from Rugby, half a mile from Junction 2 M69 from Hinckley. Parkland. 18 holes, 5814 yards. S.S.S. 67. Driving range. *Green Fees:* weekdays £9.00; weekends £11.00. Reductions for Juniors and Senior Citizens. *Eating facilities:* full restaurant/bar. *Visitors:* always welcome. John Reay Golf Shop. *Society Meetings:* welcome. Corporate Golf Days available. Professional: John Reay (01203 621305/621341). Secretary: R. Challis (01203 602671).

COVENTRY. **Brandon Wood Golf Course,** Brandon Lane, Wolston, Near Coventry CV8 3GQ (01203 543133). *Location:* six miles south of Coventry off southbound carriageway A45. Parkland on banks of River Avon. 18 holes, 6610 yards, 6043 metres. S.S.S. 72. Floodlit driving range. *Green Fees:* weekdays £8.25; weekends £10.85. *Eating facilities:* bar and restaurant. *Visitors:* welcome anytime, unrestricted. *Society Meetings:* phone Professional for details. Professional/Secretary: Chris Gledhill (01203 543141; Fax: 01203 545108).

COVENTRY. **City of Coventry Golf Club,** Brandon Wood, Brandon Lane, Wolston, Near Coventry CV8 3GQ (01203 543133). *Location:* six miles south-east from City centre off A45. Parkland on banks of River Avon. 18 holes, 6610 yards. S.S.S. 72. Floodlit driving range. *Green Fees:* weekdays £8.25; weekends £10.85. 10% discount for members, concession for locals. *Eating facilities:* "Brandons" Club House on site, licensed bar and restaurant. *Visitors:* anytime – advance bookings available any day up to seven days in advance on payment of one green fee – telephone bookings available 24 hours in advance. *Society Meetings:* telephone Professional for details. Professional/ Secretary: C. Gledhill (01203 543141).

COVENTRY. **Coventry Golf Club,** Finham Park, Coventry CV3 6PJ (01203 411123). *Location:* on A444 south of A45, one mile on left. Parkland, wooded. 18 holes, 6613 yards. S.S.S. 72. Practice ground. *Green Fees:* on application. *Eating facilities:* available. *Visitors:* welcome weekdays only, without reservation. *Society Meetings:* catered for on Wednesdays and Thursdays by arrangement. Rates dependent on numbers. Professional: P. Weaver (01203 411298). Secretary: J.E. Jarman (01203 414152).

COVENTRY. **Coventry Hearsall Golf Club,** Beechwood Avenue, Coventry CV5 6DF (01203 675809). *Location:* off A46 south of Coventry, one mile south of city centre. 18 holes, 5983 yards. S.S.S. 69. *Green Fees:* Mondays to Fridays £23.00, weekends only as guest of a member. *Eating facilities:* full restaurant facilities. *Visitors:* welcome weekdays. *Society Meetings:* limited. Professional: (01203 713156). Secretary: W.G. Doughty (01203 713470).

COVENTRY. **Forest of Arden Country Club Resort,** Maxstoke Lane, Meriden, Coventry CV7 7HR (01676 22335; Fax: 01676 23711). *Location:* three miles from Junction 6 M42, three miles from Junction 4 M6; very close to N.E.C. on A45 towards Coventry. Two 18 hole parkland courses. The Arden – 6915 yards. S.S.S. 73; The Aylesford – 6525 yards. S.S.S. 71. *Green Fees:* Arden £50.00, Aylesford £24.00 (subject to review). Discounts for residents. *Eating facilities:* bars and restaurant available. *Visitors:* welcome, residential visitors only at weekends. Groups less than 12 may only book 48 hours in advance. 152 bedroom four star hotel with extensive conference and luxurious leisure facilities. *Society Meetings:* enquiries welcome. Professional: Mike Tarn (01676 22118). Golf Operations Manager: Heid Fennan (01676 22335 extension 421; Fax: 01676 23711).

COVENTRY. **G.P.T. Golf Club,** Copeswood, Coventry (01203 563339). *Location:* three miles from centre of Coventry on A427/A428 road to Rugby, Lutterworth. 9 holes, 6002 yards. S.S.S. 69. *Green Fees:* weekdays £10.00 per round, Sundays £15.00 per round. *Visitors:* welcome except Saturdays, weekday evenings or Sunday mornings. Secretary: E. Soutar (01203 563127 office, 01203 456183 home).

COVENTRY. **North Warwickshire Golf Club Ltd,** Hampton Lane, Meriden, Coventry CV7 7LL (01676 22259). *Location:* on B4102, one mile from Stonebridge on A45, approximately midway between Birmingham and Coventry. 9 holes, 6352 yards. S.S.S. 70. *Green Fees:* £18.00 weekdays; weekends £18.00 with member only. *Eating facilities:* full catering and bar. *Visitors:* welcome without reservation except Thursdays and weekends. *Society Meetings:* catered for by prior arrangement, limited numbers. Professional: David Engram (01676 22259). Secretary: E.G. Barnes (01676 22915).

COVENTRY. **Windmill Village Hotel and Golf Club,** Birmingham Road, Allesley, Coventry CV5 9AL (01203 407241). *Location:* six miles from NEC Birmingham Airport on the A45 westbound. Parkland. 18 holes, 5131 yards. S.S.S. 67. Par 70. *Green Fees:* weekdays £9.40; weekends £10.50. *Eating facilities:* 180 seater restaurant, cellar bar, varied menus. *Visitors:* welcome, no restrictions. Leisure Club; 100 rooms, all en-suite, available at hotel; sauna, jaccuzi, etc. *Society Meetings:* welcome. Professional: Mr Rob Hunter. Secretary: Marc Harrhy. *

DUDLEY. **Dudley Golf Club Ltd,** Turners Hill, Rowley Regis, Warley (01384 253719). *Location:* one mile south of Dudley town centre on Blackheath Road. 18 holes, 6000 yards. S.S.S. 68. *Green Fees:* £18.00 weekdays. *Eating facilities:* full catering facilities available. *Visitors:* welcome but only with a member at weekends. *Society Meetings:* by prior arrangement. Professional: Paul Taylor (01384 254020). Secretary: R.P. Fortune (01384 233877).

DUDLEY. **Himley Hall Golf Centre,** Log Cabin, Himley Park, Himley Road, Dudley DY3 4DF (01902 895207). *Location:* just off A449 at Himley near Dudley. Parkland. 9 holes, 3145 yards. S.S.S. 35 for 9 holes. Practice ground, pitch and putt. *Green Fees:* weekdays £4.30 for 9 holes, £6.00 for 18 holes; weekends £4.50 for 9 holes, £6.50 for 18 holes. Juniors and Senior Citizens reduced rate. *Eating facilities:* snacks – hot and cold. *Visitors:* welcome weekdays, weekends with booking. *Society Meetings:* mid-week only. Secretary: Mr M. Harris (01384 239929).

DUDLEY. **Sedgley Golf Centre,** Sandyfields Road, Sedgley, Dudley DY3 3DL (01902 880503). *Location:* half a mile from Sedgley town centre near Cotwall End Valley Nature Reserve, just off the A463. Undulating contours and mature trees with extensive views over surrounding countryside. 9 holes, 3147 yards. S.S.S. 71 (18 holes). Covered and floodlit golf range. *Green Fees:* £4.00 9 holes, £6.00 18 holes weekdays; £4.50 9 holes, £6.50 18 holes weekends. Reductions weekdays for Juniors and Senior Citizens. *Eating facilities:* hot and cold snacks available on request. *Visitors:* pay and play course throughout the week, booking advisable at weekends. *Society Meetings:* weekdays preferred by prior arrangement. Professional: David Fereday (01384 287996). Secretary: J.A. Cox (01902 672452).

DUDLEY near. **Swindon Golf Club,** Bridgnorth Road, Swindon, Near Dudley DY3 4PU (01902 897031). *Location:* B4176 Dudley/Bridgnorth Road, three miles from A449 at Himley. Woodland and parkland course with exceptional views. 27 holes; 9 holes – 1135 yards, 18 holes – 6042 yards. S.S.S. (18) 69, 9 Par 3. *Fees:* £15.00 per round, £25.00 per day weekdays; £25.00 per round, £40.00 per day weekends and Bank Holidays. *Eating facilities:* fully licensed bar and restaurant. *Visitors:* always welcome, booking not required. Buggies available. Fishing. *Society Meetings:* by arrangement weekdays only. Secretary: Rosemary Pope (01902 897031).

DUDLEY. **Swindon Ridge Driving Range and Golf Club,** Bridgnorth Road, Swindon, Dudley DY3 4PU (01902 896765). *Location:* B4176 Bridgnorth/Dudley Road, three miles from Himley A449. Wooded. 18 holes, 6026 yards. S.S.S. 69. *Green Fees:* £15.00 per round weekdays; £25.00 per round weekends. *Eating facilities:* restaurant/bar. *Visitors:* welcome at all times. *Society Meetings:* welcome. Professionals: Phil Lester and Simon Price (01902 896191). Secretary: Rosemary Pope (01902 897031).

HALESOWEN. **Halesowen Golf Club,** The Leasowes, Leasowes Lane, Halesowen B62 8QF (0121-550 1041). *Location:* exit Junction 3 M5, A456 (Kidderminster) two miles, Halesowen town centre one mile. Parkland course. 18 holes, 5754 yards. S.S.S. 68. *Green Fees:* weekdays £16.00 per round, £23.00 per day; weekends must play with a member. *Eating facilities:* no catering Mondays. *Visitors:* welcome weekdays. *Society Meetings:* by arrangement with Secretary. Professional: Steve Fanning (0121-503 0593). Secretary: Mrs M. Bateman (0121-501 3606).

REDNAL. **Lickey Hills (Municipal) Golf Club,** Old Birmingham Road, Rednal, Near Birmingham (0121-453 3159). *Location:* M5 Exit 4 on city boundary. 18 holes, 5721 yards. S.S.S. 67. *Green Fees:* information not provided. *Eating facilities:* restaurant at club. *Visitors:* welcome.

SOLIHULL. **Copt Heath Golf Club,** 1220 Warwick Road, Knowle, Solihull B93 9LN (01564 772650). *Location:* on A4141 half a mile south of Junction 5 with M42. Flat parkland. 18 holes, 6500 yards. S.S.S. 71. Full practice facilities available. *Green Fees:* weekdays £35.00 per round, £40.00 per day. Weekends and Public Holidays must be introduced by a member. *Eating facilities:* lunch and evening meal available except Mondays. *Visitors:* no restrictions weekdays. *Society Meetings:* by arrangement with Secretary. Professional: Brian Barton. Secretary: W. Lenton.

SOLIHULL. **Ladbrook Park Golf Club Ltd,** Poolhead Lane, Tanworth-in-Arden, Solihull B94 5ED (0156474 2220). *Location:* south from Junction 3 M42. Parkland, gently undulating. 18 holes, 6427 yards. S.S.S. 71. *Green Fees:* weekdays £25.00 18 holes, £35.00 36 holes; weekends with a member only. *Eating facilities:* excellent dining. *Visitors:* welcome weekdays, prior telephone call suggested. Weekends with member only. *Society Meetings:* catered for by prior arrangement with Secretary. Professional: Steve Harrison (015644 2581). Secretary: J.R. Basford (015644 2264).

SOLIHULL. **Olton Golf Club Ltd,** Mirfield Road, Solihull B91 1JH (0121-705 1083; Fax: 0121-711 2010). *Location:* approximately two miles off Junction 5 (M42), A41 – Birmingham. Parkland. 18 holes, 6229 yards, 5694 metres. S.S.S. 71. *Green Fees:* £30.00 weekdays. *Eating facilities:* by arrangement. *Visitors:* welcome weekdays only except Wednesdays. *Society Meetings:* catered for by arrangement. Professional: David Playdon (0121-705 7296). Secretary: M.A. Perry (0121-704 1936 am).

SOLIHULL. **Robin Hood Golf Club,** St. Bernards Road, Solihull B92 7DJ (0121-706 0159). *Location:* eight miles south of Birmingham, off A41 Birmingham to Warwick road. Flat parkland. 18 holes, 6635 yards, 6067 metres. S.S.S. 72. *Green Fees:* £29.00 per round, £35.00 per day weekdays. *Eating facilities:* by prior arrangement with Steward (0121-706 0159). *Visitors:* welcome weekdays only subject to limitations. Arrange with Professional. *Society Meetings:* catered for by prior booking. Professional: A.R. Harvey (0121-706 0806). Secretary: A.J. Hanson (0121-706 0061).

SOLIHULL. **Shirley Golf Club,** Stratford Road, Monkspath, Shirley, Solihull B90 4EW (0121-744 7024). *Location:* Junction 4 M42, 500 yards on left of A34 to Birmingham. Parkland. 18 holes, 6411 yards. S.S.S. 71. *Green Fees:* £25.00 per round, £35.00 per day. *Eating facilities:* bar and catering. *Visitors:* welcome weekdays without reservation. *Society Meetings:* catered for weekdays by arrangement. Professional: Chris Wicketts (0121-745 4979). Secretary: A.J. Phillips (Tel & Fax: 0121-744 6001).

SOLIHULL. **Whitelakes Golf Club,** Tilehouse Lane, Tidbury Green, Solihull B90 1PT (01564 824414). *Location:* two miles from Shirley and three miles off the M42. To play over numerous ponds, lakes and the River Coal. 9 holes, 987 yards. S.S.S. 27. 15-bay golf range. *Green Fees:* information not available. *Eating facilities:* excellent bar and restaurant facilities. *Visitors:* welcome, no restrictions. Facilities for fishing, clay pigeon shooting, archery, swimming pool available. *Society Meetings:* catered for. *

SOLIHULL. **Widney Manor Golf Club,** Saintbury Drive, Widney Manor, Solihull B91 3SZ (0121-711 3646; Fax: 0121-711 3691). *Location:* entrance next to Widney Manor railway station, three miles off Junction 4 M42. Small but interesting pay and play parkland course. 18 holes, 5000 yards. *Green Fees:* weekdays £7.00; weekends £10.00. *Eating facilities:* normal bar hours, catering available all day. *Visitors:* welcome, bookings accepted. *Society Meetings:* welcome at all times. Professional/Manager: Tim Atkinson.

STOURBRIDGE. **Stourbridge Golf Club,** Worcester Lane, Pedmore, Stourbridge DY8 2RB (01384 393062). *Location:* situated between Hagley and Stourbridge on Worcester road. Parkland. 18 holes, 6231 yards. S.S.S. 70. Small practice ground. *Green Fees:* weekdays £25.00; weekends with a member only £11.00. *Eating facilities:* bar meals available, lunch, dinner if booked. *Visitors:* welcome weekdays, weekends with member. *Society Meetings:* catered for mainly Tuesdays. Professional: W.H. Firkins (01384 393129). Secretary: Ms M.A. Cooper (01384 395566).

SUTTON COLDFIELD. **Aston Wood Golf Club,** Blake Street, Little Aston, Sutton Coldfield (0121-353 0363; Fax: 0121-353 0354). *Location:* off A5127 Lichfield Road. Gently rolling course with trees and four lakes. 18 holes, 6480 yards. S.S.S. 71. Practice area, bunker and green. *Green Fees:* £35.00 per round; as member's guest £10.00. *Eating facilities:* large restaurant, bar lounge, Spike Bar. *Visitors:* weekdays only. *Society Meetings:* corporate facilities and function room available. Golf Operations Manager: Dave Whomsley.

SUTTON COLDFIELD. **Boldmere Municipal Golf Club,** Monmouth Drive, Sutton Coldfield (0121-354 3379). *Location:* A34, seven miles from centre of Birmingham. Flat parkland, wooded. 18 holes, 4482 yards. S.S.S. 62. *Green Fees:* £6.60 Subject to review. *Eating facilities:* meals daily. *Visitors:* welcome without reservation but "LinkCard" system in operation. *Society Meetings:* at least one month's notice required. Professional: Trevor Short. Secretary: I. Furlong.

SUTTON COLDFIELD. **Moor Hall Golf Club Ltd,** Moor Hall Drive, Sutton Coldfield B75 6LN (0121-308 0103). *Location:* one mile east of Sutton Coldfield, A446. Parkland. 18 holes, 6249 yards. S.S.S. 70. Practice area. *Green Fees:* £25.00 per round, £36.00 day ticket. *Eating facilities:* available weekdays except for Mondays. *Visitors:* welcome weekdays only (not Thursday mornings). *Society Meetings:* catered for Tuesdays and Wednesdays only. Professional: Alan Partridge (0121-308 5106). Secretary: R.V. Wood (0121-308 6130).

SUTTON COLDFIELD. **Pype Hayes Golf Club,** Eachelhurst Road, Walmley, Sutton Coldfield B76 8EP (0121-351 1014). *Location:* off the A38 Kingsbury Road by M6 Junction 5, one and a half miles from Junction 9 M42. Wooded course. Smallish demanding greens as well as four demanding Par 3 holes. 18 holes, 5972 yards. S.S.S. 69. *Green Fees:* £6.90. *Eating facilities:* available. *Visitors:* welcome, booking by Link Card is now required and can be used on eight courses in Birmingham area. Professional: J. Bayliss. Secretary: K. Haden (0121-779 2357). *

SUTTON COLDFIELD. **Sutton Coldfield Golf Club,** Thornhill Road, Streetly, Sutton Coldfield B74 3ER (0121-353 2014; Fax: 0121-353 5503). *Location:* situated in Sutton Park, one mile off A452, seven miles from centre of Birmingham. Natural heathland. 18 holes, 6541 yards. S.S.S. 71. *Green Fees:* weekdays £30.00. *Eating facilities:* by arrangement with Steward. *Visitors:* welcome without reservation. Handicap Certificate required. *Society Meetings:* catered for by arrangement with Secretary. Professional: J.K. Hayes (0121-353 9633). Administrator: Mrs T. Thomas.

SUTTON COLDFIELD. **Walmley Golf Club,** Brooks Road, Wylde Green, Sutton Coldfield B72 1HR (0121-373 0029). *Location:* Birmingham/Sutton Coldfield main road, turn right at Green Hill Road. Flat parkland. 18 holes, 6537 yards. S.S.S. 72. Practice area. *Green Fees:* weekdays £25.00 18 holes, £30.00 18+ holes; weekends playing with member only. *Eating facilities:* lunch and evening meals available except Mondays by arrangement with Steward. *Visitors:* welcome weekdays but should check with Professional prior to attending, weekends with a member only. *Society Meetings:* catered for weekdays except Mondays. 10% reductions on green fees if numbers are 30 or more. Professional: Mike Skerritt (0121-373 7103). Secretary: J.P.G. Windsor (0121-377 7272).

WALSALL. **Bloxwich Golf Club (1988) Ltd,** 136 Stafford Road, Bloxwich, Walsall WS3 3PQ (01922 405724). *Location:* off main Walsall-Cannock road (A34). Semi parkland. 18 holes, 6286 yards. S.S.S. 70. *Green Fees:* weekdays £20.00 per round, £25.00 per day. *Eating facilities:* available. *Visitors:* welcome with or without reservation except weekends and Bank Holidays. *Society Meetings:* catered for preferably midweek, reduced rates for 20 or more. Professional: Mr G. Broadbent (01922 476889). Secretary: Mrs J.N. Loveridge (01922 476593).

WALSALL. **Calderfields Golf Club Ltd,** Aldridge Road, Walsall WS4 2JS (01922 32243). *Location:* A454. Parkland, lake. 18 holes, 6700 yards, 6100 metres. S.S.S. 73. Practice holes and putting green. *Green Fees:* weekdays £12.00; weekends £16.00. *Eating facilities:* restaurant and bar. *Visitors:* always welcome. *Society Meetings:* very welcome, package deals available. Professional: Roger Griffin (01922 32243). Secretary: Mr Colin Andrews (01922 640540; Fax: 01922 38787).

WALSALL. **Druids Heath Golf Club,** Stonnall Road, Aldridge, Walsall WS9 8JZ (01922 55595). *Location:* between Sutton Coldfield and Walsall, near A452. 18 holes, 6914 yards. S.S.S. 73. *Green Fees:* £25.00 weekdays; £33.00 weekends. *Eating facilities:* dining-room and bar snacks. *Visitors:* welcome without reservation weekdays, with member at weekends. Ladies' Day Thursdays. *Society Meetings:* catered for on weekdays. Professional: M.P. Daubney (01922 59523). Secretary: P.J. Bradford.

WALSALL. **Walsall Golf Club,** The Broadway, Walsall WS1 3EY (01922 20014 or 22710). *Location:* one and a half miles from M6/M5 junction. Wooded course. 18 holes, 6243 yards. S.S.S. 70. *Green Fees:* £33.00 per round, £40.00 per day. Reduced rates for organised societies, minimum 16. *Eating facilities:* all facilities available. *Visitors:* welcome weekdays only. *Society Meetings:* catered for. Professional: R. Lambert (01922 26766). Secretary: E. Murray (01922 613512).

WARLEY. **Warley Golf Club,** Lightwood Hill, Warley (0121-429 2440). *Location:* five miles west of Birmingham centre, just off main Hagley Road West. 9 holes, 2606 yards. S.S.S. 64. *Green Fees:* £6.00. *Eating facilities:* cafe. *Visitors:* welcome without reservation. *Society Meetings:* catered for, but not advised (Municipal Golf Course). Professional: David Owen. Secretary: C. Lowndes.

WEST BROMWICH. **Dartmouth Golf Club,** Vale Street, West Bromwich B71 4DW (0121-588 2131). *Location:* one mile from West Bromwich town centre, rear of Churchfields High School, All Saints Way. Part flat, part undulating course. 9 holes, 6060 yards. S.S.S. 70. Practice area, putting green. *Green Fees:*weekdays £16.50 per day; weekends only with a member £14.00. *Eating facilities:* bar snacks always available, meals by prior arrangement. *Visitors:* welcome weekdays, weekends with a member only. *Society Meetings:* welcome by prior arrangement. Professional: Carl R. Yates (0121-588 2131). Secretary: Mike Morton (0121-588 2131).

WEST BROMWICH. **Sandwell Park Golf Club Ltd.,** Birmingham Road, West Bromwich (0121-553 0260). *Location:* on A41 to Birmingham close to Junction 1 M5. 18 holes, 6470 yards. S.S.S. 72. Two practice areas. *Green Fees:* weekdays £32.50. *Eating facilities:* full restaurant facilities and two bars. *Visitors:* welcome except weekends and Bank Holidays. Handicap Certificate required. *Society Meetings:* by prior arrangement, rates on request. Professional: N. Wylie (0121-553 4384). Secretary: J.B. Mawby (0121-553 4637).

WISHAW. **The Belfry,** Lichfield Road, Wishaw, Near Sutton Coldfield B76 9PR (01675 470301; Fax: 01675 470178). *Location:* M42 Junction 9 just off the Lichfield Road (A446). Two parkland courses. Championship Brabazon: 18 holes, 6905 yards. Par 72, S.S.S. 72. Derby: 18 holes, 6103 yards. Par 70, S.S.S. 70. Driving range and putting green. *Green Fees:* Brabazon: £50.00; Derby: £25.00. Reduced winter rates on request. *Eating facilities:* eight bars, four restaurants. *Visitors:* welcome, non residential golf can be booked 24 hours in advance during summer months. Residential Golf Packages from £72.50 per person in the Summer and £55 per person in the Winter to include two rounds of golf. 4 Star Hotel, 18 conference rooms, magnificent leisure complex and the Bel Air Night Club in the Hotel grounds. *Society Meetings:* welcome at all times. Professional: Peter McGovern.

WOLVERHAMPTON. **Oxley Park Golf Club Ltd,** Stafford Road, Bushbury, Wolverhampton WV10 6DE (01902 20506). *Location:* one and a half miles M54/A449 junction. One and a half miles Wolverhampton town centre. Undulating parkland. 18 holes, 6168 yards, 5639 metres. S.S.S. 69. *Green Fees:* weekdays £18.00 per round, £22.00 per day; weekends £20.00 per round, £24.00 per day. *Eating facilities:* each day except Monday. *Visitors:* welcome weekdays, weekends by arrangement with Professional. *Society Meetings:* catered for Wednesdays only. Professional: Leslie Burlison (01902 25445). Secretary: Mrs Kathryn Mann (01902 25892).

WOLVERHAMPTON. **Penn Golf Club,** Penn Common, Penn, Wolverhampton (01902 341142). *Location:* two miles south west of Wolverhampton, off A449. Heathland. 18 holes, 6462 yards. S.S.S. 71. *Green Fees:* £20.00 per round, £25.00 per day. *Eating facilities:* available, excluding Sunday and Monday. *Visitors:* welcome weekdays, without advance booking. *Society Meetings:* catered for. Professional: A. Briscoe (01902 330472). Secretary: P.W. Thorrington (01384 256220).

WOLVERHAMPTON. **Perton Park Golf Club,** Wrottesley Park Road, Perton, Wolverhampton WV6 7HL (01902 380103). *Location:* just off the A454 Bridgnorth Road or A41 Wolverhampton to Newport road. Flat meadowland. 18 holes, 7007 yards. S.S.S. 71. Driving range, putting green. *Green Fees:* Mondays to Thursdays £5.00, Fridays £7.00; weekends and Bank Holidays £12.00. *Eating facilities:* available, also bar. *Visitors:* pay as you play course. *Society Meetings:* catered for. Secretary: E.G.J. Greenway (01902 380073).

WOLVERHAMPTON. **The South Staffordshire Golf Club,** Danescourt Road, Tettenhall, Wolverhampton WV6 9BQ (01902 756401). *Location:* A41 out of Wolverhampton (approximately three miles). Parkland. 18 holes, 6513 yards. S.S.S. 71. Practice area (approximately 10 acres). *Green Fees:* weekdays £27.50 per round, £30.00 per day; weekends £35.00 by prior arrangement. *Eating facilities:* excellent catering facilities – Steward: Hugh Campbell (01902 756401). *Visitors:* welcome weekdays except Tuesdays. *Society Meetings:* by arrangement with the Secretary weekdays except Tuesdays before 2pm. Professional: J. Rhodes (01902 754816). Secretary: J.A. Macklin (01902 751065).

WOLVERHAMPTON. **Wergs Golf Club,** Keepers Lane, Tettenhall, Wolverhampton WV6 8UA (01902 742225; Fax: 01902 744748). *Location:* from centre of Wolverhampton, take A41 (to Newport), after two and a half miles turn right, half a mile on right. Open parkland. 18 holes, 6949 yards. S.S.S. 73. 20 acre practice area. *Green Fees:* weekdays £12.50; weekends and Bank Holidays £15.00. Senior Citizens and Juniors £10.00 weekdays, £12.50 weekends and Bank Holidays. *Eating facilities:* full catering and bar facilities. *Visitors:* always welcome. Membership available. *Society Meetings:* welcome anytime during week, after 10am at weekends. Professional: Martin Payne. Secretary: Mrs G. Parsons.

Wiltshire

CALNE. **Bowood Golf and Country Club,** Derry Hill, Calne SN11 9PQ (01249 822228; Fax: 01249 822218). *Location:* A4 between Marlborough and Chippenham, signposted off M4. Grade I listed, Capability Brown landscaped, parkland. 18 holes, 7317, 6890, 6566: 6229 yards. S.S.S. 74, 73, 71: 77. Three academy holes, driving range. *Green Fees:* weekdays £27.00 per round, £40.00 per day; weekends £32.00 per round. *Eating facilities:* private diningrooms, public restaurant. *Visitors:* welcome at all times except before 12 noon at weekends. Four (double/twin) bedroomed house in centre of course. *Society Meetings:* welcome. Director of Golf: Nigel Blenkarne. Professional: Gary Manham. Chief Executive: Sally-Jane Coode.

CASTLE COMBE. **Castle Combe Golf Club,** Castle Combe SN14 7PL. *Location:* five miles south M4 between Junctions 17 and 18. Parkland course in an area of outstanding natural beauty. 18 holes, 6340 yards. S.S.S. 71. *Green Fees:* information not provided. *Eating facilities:* bar and catering available all day. *Visitors:* welcome, book in advance. Snooker and sauna facilities. *Society Meetings:* welcome, book in advance. Professional: Christine Langford (01249 783101). Secretary: Stephen Wright (01249 782982; Fax: 01249 782992). *

CHIPPENHAM. **Chippenham Golf Club,** Malmesbury Road, Chippenham SN15 5LT (01249 652040). *Location:* A429 one mile from Chippenham, two miles from M4 (Junction 17). Parkland. 18 holes, 5540 yards. S.S.S. 67. *Green Fees:* weekdays £20.00, weekends £25.00. *Eating facilities:* snacks and evening à la carte (not Mondays). *Visitors:* welcome; current Handicap Certificate required. Prior arrangement necessary. *Society Meetings:* catered for weekdays only. Professional: Bill Creamer (01249 655519). Secretary: D. Maddison (01249 652040). *

CHIPPENHAM. **Monkton Park Golf Club,** Monkton Park, Chippenham SN15 3PE (Tel & Fax: 01249 653928). *Location:* centre of Chippenham, two miles from M4 Junction 17. Parkland Par 3 course. Probably the best Par 3 course in the south west of England. 9 holes, 1000 yards. S.S.S. 27. Crazy golf. *Green Fees:* weekdays £2.75; weekends £3.00; £7.00 per day. Senior Citizen rates available. *Eating facilities:* snack bar. *Visitors:* always welcome 364 days of the year! Golf clubs available. *Society Meetings:* welcome. Professional: M.R. Dawson. Secretary: Mrs B.J. Dawson.

CORSHAM. **Kingsdown Golf Club,** Corsham SN14 9BS (01225 742530). *Location:* five miles east of Bath. Heathland. 18 holes, 6445 yards, 5891 metres. S.S.S. 71. *Green Fees:* weekdays £22.00. *Eating facilities:* lounge bar and diningroom. *Visitors:* welcome except at weekends and Bank Holidays and must have current Handicap Certificate. *Society Meetings:* catered for by arrangement. Professional: Andrew Butler (01225 742634). Secretary: S.H. Phipps (01225 743472).

DEVIZES. **Erlestoke Sands Golf Club,** Erlestoke, Devizes SN10 5UA (01380 830507). *Location:* six miles east of Westbury on B3098. Downland course, on two levels with green 100ft below, spectacular 7th hole, 170 yards Par 3, one of the finest short holes in the West Country. 18 holes, 6619 yards. S.S.S. 72, Par 71. Large practice ground. *Green Fees:* weekdays £12.00; weekends £16.00. *Eating facilities:* full catering service, lounge, bar and diningroom. *Visitors:* welcome, booking advisable. *Society Meetings:* catered for by prior arrangement. Stewards: Pauline and Trevor Head (01380 830507). Professional: Tony Valentine (01380 831027). Office: R. Hampton (01380 831069).

DEVIZES. **North Wilts Golf Club,** Bishop's Cannings, Devizes SN10 2LP (01380 860257). *Location:* one and a half miles from A4 east of Calne. Four miles from Devizes. Downland, undulating course with spectacular views. 18 holes, 6332 yards, 5790 metres. S.S.S. 71. Practice ground. *Green Fees:* weekdays £18.00 per round, £25.00 per day; weekends £30.00 when accepted. *Eating facilities:* full catering service. *Visitors:* welcome all weekdays, some weekends but not December to March. *Society Meetings:* catered for by prior arrangement. Professional: Graham Laing (01380 860330; Fax: 01380 860061). Secretary: Stuart Musgrove (01380 860627).

HIGHWORTH. **Highworth Community Golf Centre,** Swindon Road, Highworth SN6 7SJ. *Location:* on A361 just south of the town. Undulating parkland. 9 holes, 3120 yards, 2851 metres. Par 35. 9 hole pitch and putt, practice ground. *Green Fees:* information not provided. *Eating facilities:* vending machines. *Visitors:* municipal course, no restrictions. *Society Meetings:* welcome any day. Professional: Kevin Pickett (01793 766014). *

HIGHWORTH. **Wrag Barn Golf Club,** Shrivenham Road, Highworth SN6 7QQ (01793 861327). *Location:* Junction 15 M4, take A419 Cirencester Road to Highworth roundabout fourth exit B1400. Undulating, set in beautiful Wiltshire countryside, three lakes and moat around 17th green. 18 holes, 6548 yards. S.S.S. 71. Excellent practice facilities. *Green Fees:* weekdays £15.00; weekends £22.00 after 11.30am. *Eating facilities:* good bar snacks available all day and bar – à la carte Friday, Saturday, Sunday and Sunday lunch. *Visitors:* welcome but members have priority, no green fee players at weekends before 11.30am. *Society Meetings:* welcome any weekday. Two rounds, coffee, lunch, dinner £35.00 per head, minimum of 20 players.

Professional: Barry Loughrey (01793 766027). Secretary: Mrs Suzanne Manners (01793 861327; Fax: 01793 861325).

MARLBOROUGH. **Marlborough Golf Club,** The Common, Marlborough SN8 1DU (01672 512147). *Location:* about one mile from town centre on A345 travelling towards Swindon. Downland. 18 holes, 6241 yards. S.S.S. 70. Practice ground and putting green. *Green Fees:* weekdays only £19.50 per round, £29.00 per day; weekends £40.00 per round. *Eating facilities:* restaurant serving snacks and full meals open most of day. *Visitors:* welcome generally, but it is best to telephone in advance as course may be too busy to allow green fees; some weekends course is closed to green fees. *Society Meetings:* catered for with advance notice. Professional: L. Ross (01672 512493). General Manager: Laurence Ross (01672 512147). *

SALISBURY. **Hamptworth Golf and Country Club,** Hamptworth Road, Hamptworth, Near Landford SP5 2DU (01794 390155; Fax: 01794 390022). *Location:* off A36Salisbury to Southampton Road, turning off B3079. Parkland, wooded course with river running through. 18 holes, 6512 yards, 5954 metres. S.S.S. 72. Practice area. *Green Fees:* weekdays £17.50; weekends £25.00. *Eating facilities:* bar snacks, bar. *Visitors:* welcome, must have Handicaps. *Society Meetings:* welcome, but limited catering. Secretary: Mark Pierson.

SALISBURY. **High Post Golf Club Ltd,** Great Durnford, Salisbury SP4 6AT (01722 73231). *Location:* midway between Salisbury and Amesbury on A345. Downland and blackthorn. 18 holes, 6267 yards, 5730 metres. S.S.S. 70. Large practice ground. *Green Fees:* weekdays £20.00 per round, £28.00 per day; weekends £25.00 per round, £33.00 per day. *Eating facilities:* full catering and bars available. *Visitors:* welcome with valid Handicap Certificate. *Society Meetings:* catered for mid-week by arrangement. Professional: A.J. Harman (01722 73219). Secretary: W. Goodwin (01722 73356).

SALISBURY. **Salisbury and South Wilts Golf Club,** Netherhampton, Salisbury SP2 8PR (01722 742131). *Location:* on A3094, two miles Salisbury, Wilton, opposite Netherhampton village. Parkland. 27 holes, 6528 yards. S.S.S. 71. Practice ground. *Green Fees:* weekdays £25.00 per day, weekends and Bank Holidays £40.00 per day. *Eating facilities:* full catering service and bar. *Visitors:* welcome without reservation at all times, but preliminary phone call advised. *Society Meetings:* catered for by prior arrangement. Professional: G. Emerson (01722 742929). Secretary: John Newcomb (01722 742645).

SHRIVENHAM. **Shrivenham Park Golf Course,** Penny Hooks, Near Swindon SN6 8EX (01793 783853; Fax: 01793 782999). *Location:* M4 Exit 15. Follow signs to Shrivenham, go through village, golf club on right. A delightful parkland course in excellent condition. 18 holes, 5553 yards. S.S.S 69 (men), 71 (ladies). Practice area. *Green Fees:* £10.00 per round weekdays; £13.00 per round weekends. Discounts for Senior Citizens and Juniors. *Eating facilities:* restaurant and bar facilities open all day seven days a week. *Visitors:* all facilities at Shrivenham Park are open to the general public with no restrictions, everybody welcome. *Society Meetings:* welcome seven days a week. Special cheap rates January/March every year. Golf and food all day £19.00 April onwards. Professional: Mr Simon Jefferies. Secretary: Mrs Trudy Mace (01428 653237) and Mrs Carole Johnson (014353 3477). Manager: Mr V. Sedgwick. *

SWINDON. **Broome Manor Golf Complex,** Pipers Way, Swindon SN3 1RG (01793 495761). *Location:* two miles from Junction 15, M4 (follow signs for "Golf Complex"). Wooded parkland. 18 holes, 6359 yards, 5815 metres. S.S.S. 71. 9 holes, 5610 yards, 5130 metres. S.S.S. 67. Floodlit covered driving range. *Green Fees:* weekdays £4.60 for 9 holes, £7.70 for 18 holes; weekends £5.70 for 9 holes, £9.40 for 18 holes. *Eating facilities:* full facilities. *Visitors:* welcome, no restrictions, booking essential for 18 hole course. *Society Meetings:* catered for Monday to Thursday. Full package available. Professional: Barry Sandry (01793 532403). Manager: Tom Watt (01793 495761). Catering: (01793 490939).

SWINDON. **Swindon Golf Club (changing name of club to Ogbourne Downs Golf Club),** Ogbourne St. George, Marlborough SN8 1TB (01672 841217). *Location:* A345, four miles south of Junction 15 (M4), three miles north of Marlborough. Downland course. 18 holes, 6226 yards. S.S.S. 70. Practice area, baskets of practice balls for hire. *Green Fees:* weekdays £17.00 per round, £23.00 per day; with a member only at weekends. *Eating facilities:* full catering and bar service. *Visitors:* welcome weekdays. Handicap Certificates required. *Society Meetings:* catered for weekdays only. Professional: Colin Harraway (01672 841287). Secretary: D.J. Knight (01672 841327).

TIDWORTH. **Tidworth Garrison Golf Club,** Bulford Road, Tidworth SP9 7AF (01980 42321). *Location:* A338 Salisbury to Marlborough Road, golf course off Bulford Road. Undulating downland course. 18 holes, 6075 yards. S.S.S. 69. Practice driving area, chipping and putting greens. *Green Fees:* £18.00. *Eating facilities:* full bar and catering facilities except for Mondays (sandwiches only). *Visitors:* welcome at all times, but normally after 2pm at weekends and Bank Holidays. *Society Meetings:* catered for Tuesdays, Thursdays and Fridays. Professional: T. Gosden (01980 42393). Secretary: Lt. Col. (retd) D.F.T. Tucker RE (01980 42301). *

UPAVON. **Upavon (RAF) Golf Club,** Douglas Avenue, Upavon SN9 6BQ (01980 630281). *Location:* off A342 south and east of Upavon one and a half miles. Parkland/downland course with two testing Par 3s across a ravine. 9 holes, 5589 yards, 5116 metres. S.S.S. 67. Practice area. *Green Fees:* weekdays £12.00 per round, £16.00 per day; weekends £24.00, reductions when playing with a member. *Eating facilities:* available by prior arrangement. *Visitors:* welcome at all times subject to club competitions, etc. Handicap Certificate required weekends. *Society Meetings:* welcome midweek by prior arrangement. Professional: Richard Blake (01980 630281). Secretary: Les Mitchell (01980 630787).

WARMINSTER. **West Wilts Golf Club,** Elm Hill, Warminster BA12 0AU (01985 212702). *Location:* on A350 half-a-mile out of Warminster on Westbury Road. Downland. 18 holes, 5709 yards. S.S.S. 68. *Green Fees:* weekdays £24.00; weekends £35.00. *Eating facilities:* full meals (must be ordered in advance) and snacks available at all times (restricted Winter evenings). *Visitors:* welcome, but must produce a Handicap Certificate. Afternoons only at weekends. *Society Meetings:* catered for Wednesday to Friday. Professional: John Jacobs (01985 212110). Secretary: I.D. Wheater (01985 213133).

WESTBURY near. **Thoulstone Park Golf Club,** Chapmanslade, Near Westbury BA13 4AQ (01373 832825; Fax: 01373 832821). *Location:* on A36, three miles north west of Warminster. Parkland course with trees and two lakes. 18 holes, 6312 yards. S.S.S. 70. Driving range, practice putting green. *Green Fees:* weekdays £12.00; weekends £18.00. *Eating facilities:* Spikes Bar (with bar snacks), coffee shop, function rooms. *Visitors:* welcome anytime except Saturday, Sunday and Bank Holiday mornings – suggest phone beforehand. *Society Meetings:* welcome weekdays, very attractive packages available. Professional: Derek Thomson (01373 832808). General Manager: Martin Sagar.

North Yorkshire

ALDWARK. **Aldwark Manor Golf Club,** Aldwark, Alne, York YO6 2NF (01347 838146; Fax: 01347 838867). *Location:* in village of Aldwark, five miles from A1 and five miles from A19. Flat parkland. 18 holes, 6171 yards. S.S.S. 69. Practice ground. *Green Fees:* weekdays £16.00 per round, £20.00 per day; weekends and Bank Holidays £20.00 per round, £24.00 per day. *Eating facilities:* two restaurants and two bars. *Visitors:* always welcome weekdays, restricted weekends. 20 bedroomed hotel. *Society Meetings:* always welcome, restricted weekends. Professional: Gary M. Platt (01347 838353). Golf Director: Geoff Platt (01347 838353; Fax: 01347 838867).

BARNOLDSWICK. **Ghyll Golf Club,** Ghyll Brow, Barnoldswick, Colne, Lancs BB8 6JQ (01282 842466). *Location:* M65 to Colne. Parkland, hilly course. 9 holes, 5706 yards, 5213 metres. S.S.S. 68. *Green Fees:* weekdays £14.00 (£7.00 with member), weekends and Bank Holidays £18.00 restricted (£12.00 with member). *Eating facilities:* bar, evening only. *Visitors:* welcome except Sundays and some Saturdays. *Society Meetings:* catered for by arrangement. Secretary: John L. Gill (01756 842511 (business) 01756 798592 (home)).

BEDALE. **Bedale Golf Club,** Leyburn Road, Bedale (01677 422568). *Location:* close to northern boundary of town. Parkland. 18 holes, 6565 yards. S.S.S. 71. *Green Fees:* £18.00 weekdays; £28.00 weekends. *Eating facilities:* caterer employed. *Visitors:* welcome without reservation. *Society Meetings:* catered for on application. Professional: A.D. Johnson (01677 422443). Secretary: G.A. Shepherdson (01677 422451).

BENTHAM. **Bentham Golf Club,** Robin Lane, Bentham, Near Lancaster LA2 7AG (015242 61018). *Location:* B6480 north-west of Lancaster towards Settle. Parkland with magnificent views. 9 holes, 5760 yards. S.S.S. 69. *Green Fees:* weekdays £14.00, Juniors £7.00; weekends and Bank Holidays £20.00, Juniors £9.00. Weekly tickets £40.00, Juniors £20.00. *Eating facilities:* hot and cold snacks and meals available. *Visitors:* welcome all week without reservation. *Society Meetings:* welcome – contact Secretary. Secretary: J.M. Philipson (015242 62455).

CATTERICK. **Catterick Garrison Golf Club,** Leyburn Road, Catterick Garrison, Catterick DL9 3QE (01748 833401). *Location:* six miles south-west Scotch Corner, A1 turn off to Catterick Garrison. Undulating parkland/moorland with spectacular views. 18 holes, 6331 yards, 5789 metres. S.S.S. 70. Practice ground. *Green Fees:* weekdays £18.00; weekends and Bank Holidays £25.00. *Eating facilities:* bar and restaurant. *Visitors:* welcome without reservation. *Society Meetings:* catered for by appointment only. Professional: Andy Marshall (01748 833671). Secretary: J.K. Mayberry (01748 833268; Fax: 01748 833263).

EASINGWOLD. **Easingwold Golf Club,** Stillington Road, Easingwold, York YO6 3ET (01347 21486). *Location:* 12 miles north of York, course one mile along Stillington Road. Flat, wooded parkland. 18 holes, 5679 metres. S.S.S. 70. *Green Fees:* weekdays £23.00 per day; weekends and Bank Holidays £28.00. £10.00 playing with a member at any time. *Eating facilities:* catering except Mondays, order in advance. *Visitors:* welcome without reservation. *Society Meetings:* weekdays only, prior booking essential. Contact G.C. Young. Professional: John Hughes (01347 21964). Secretary: K.C. Hudson (01347 22474).

FILEY. **Filey Golf Club,** The Clubhouse, West Avenue, Filey YO14 9BQ (01723 513116). *Location:* one mile from town centre. Seaside links. 18 holes, 5907 yards. S.S.S. 67. Practice area. *Green Fees:* weekdays £20.00, weekends £25.00. Subject to review. *Eating facilities:* full dining and bar facilities. *Visitors:* welcome most days if members of a golf club and hold current Handicap Certificate. *Society Meetings:* welcome, must be pre-arranged. Professional: D. England (01723 513134). Secretary: T.M. Thompson (01723 513293).

HARROGATE. **Crimple Valley Golf Club,** Hookstone Wood Road, Harrogate HG2 8PN (01423 883485; Fax: 01423 881018). *Location:* one mile south from town centre. Turn off A61 at Appleyards Garage on to Hookstone Road, signposted to right. Gently sloping fairways in rural setting. 9 holes, 2500 yards. S.S.S. 33. *Green Fees:* information not provided. *Eating facilities:* licensed bar, lunches available weekdays, breakfasts weekends. *Visitors:* welcome at all times. Professional: R.A. Lumb. Secretary: A.M. Grange.

HARROGATE. **Harrogate Golf Club Ltd,** Forest Lane Head, Harrogate HG2 7TF (01423 863158). *Location:* two miles from Harrogate on the A59 Harrogate/Knaresborough road. Parkland, wooded. 18 holes, 6241 yards, 5706 metres. S.S.S. 70. Large practice ground, covered net. *Green Fees:* weekdays £26.00 per round £30.00 per day; weekends £40.00. *Eating facilities:* chef catering and bar menu, lounge and casual spike bars. *Visitors:* welcome subject to club events. *Society Meetings:* catered for weekdays except Tuesdays. Parties of 12 or more welcome. Professional: P. Johnson (01423 862547). Secretary: Mr Peter H. Ince (01423 862999). Caterer: (01423 860278).

HARROGATE. **Oakdale Golf Club,** Oakdale Glen, Harrogate HG1 2LN (01423 502806). *Location:* off Ripon road into Kent Road follow signs. Parkland, with featured stream. 18 holes, 6456 yards. S.S.S. 71. Practice ground and nets. *Green Fees:* weekdays £25.00 per round, £30.00 per day; weekends £30.00 per round. *Eating facilities:* first class restaurant, bar. *Visitors:* welcome at all times, Tuesday Ladies' Day. *Society Meetings:* welcome weekdays by arrangement. Professional: Clive Dell (01423 560510). Secretary: Frank Hindmarsh (01423 567162).

HARROGATE. **Pannal Golf Club,** Follifoot Road, Pannal, Harrogate HG3 1ES (01423 871641; Fax: 01423 870043). *Location:* two miles south of Harrogate A61 (Leeds Road). 18 holes, 6659 yards. S.S.S. 72. Large practice ground. *Green Fees:* weekdays £29.00 per round, £36.00 per day; weekends and Bank Holidays £36.00 per round. *Eating facilities:* lunch available daily, dinner by arrangement. *Visitors:* welcome Monday to Friday without reservation, enquiry advised. *Society Meetings:* catered for Monday, Tuesday (pm only), Wednesday and Thursday, Friday (limited to 16 only). Professional: Murray Burgess (01423 872620). Secretary: T.B. Davey MBE (01423 872628).

HARROGATE. **Rudding Park Golf Course,** Rudding Park, Harrogate HG3 1DJ (01423 872100; Fax: 01423 873011). *Location:* off Harrogate south bypass, brown tourist signs indicate Rudding Park. Parkland. 18 holes, 6826 yards. S.S.S. 72. Driving range, academy holes. *Green Fees:* phone for details. *Eating facilities:* bar and restaurant. *Visitors:* welcome at all times. *Society Meetings:* welcome. Professional: S. Footman.

KIRKBYMOORSIDE. **Kirkbymoorside Golf Club,** Manor Vale, Kirkbymoorside, York YO6 6EG (01751 431525). *Location:* on A170 through Kirkbymoorside. Undulating parkland. 18 holes, 6000 yards, 4932 metres. S.S.S. 69. *Green Fees:* £17.00 weekdays, £25.00 weekends and Public Holidays. Reduced fees in winter when temporary greens and shortened course in use. *Eating facilities:* available except Mondays, bar food available every day. *Visitors:* welcome at all times except weekend medal competitions. Handicap Certificates required. *Society Meetings:* catered for by arrangement with Secretary. Secretary: D.G. Saunders.

KNARESBOROUGH. **Knaresborough Golf Club,** Boroughbridge Road, Knaresborough HG5 0QQ (01423 863219). *Location:* one-and-a-half miles from town centre, direction A1 Boroughbridge. Wooded parkland. 18 holes, 6481 yards, 5925 metres. S.S.S.71. Large practice area. *Green Fees:* weekdays £18.00 per round, £24.00 per day; weekends £24.00 per round, £29.00 per day. *Eating facilities:* resident Steward provides full catering. *Visitors:* welcome but not before

9.30am weekdays and 10am weekends. *Society Meetings:* welcome by prior arrangement. Professional: Gary J. Vickers (01423 864865). Manager: J.I. Barrow (01423 862690).

MALTON. **Malton and Norton Golf Club,** Welham Park, Malton YO17 9QE (01653 692959). *Location:* off A64 to Malton between York and Scarborough. One mile south on Welham road turn right at Norton level crossing. 27 holes – Longest 18: 6456 yards. S.S.S. 71. Medal Course: 6141 yards. S.S.S. 69 (Club). Practice ground. *Green Fees:* weekdays £20.00; weekends and Public Holidays £25.00. *Eating facilities:* full bar and catering available. *Visitors:* welcome without reservation except club match days, and weekends from 1st November to 31st March unless with member. *Society Meetings:* catered for by arrangement with Secretary. Professional: S. Robinson (01653 693882). Secretary: W.G. Wade (01653 697912).

NORTHALLERTON. **Romanby Golf Course,** Yafforth Road, Northallerton DL7 0PE. *Location:* west of Northallerton on the B6271 Richmond Road. Parkland course with formidable "Great Lake Complex" on the 2nd, 11th and 12th. 18 holes, 6666 yards. 12 bay floodlit driving range. *Green Fees:* on application. *Visitors:* always welcome, best to telephone for tee off times. Professional: Fred Thorpe (01609 779988; Fax: 01609 779084).

RICHMOND. **Richmond (Yorkshire) Golf Club,** Bend Hagg, Richmond DL10 5EX (01748 825319). *Location:* Scotch Corner (A1). Wooded, parkland, some hills. 18 holes, 5704 yards. S.S.S. 68. *Green Fees:* weekdays £16.00; weekends £25.00. *Eating facilities:* bar and catering. *Visitors:* welcome but not before 12 noon Sundays. *Society Meetings:* catered for, book with Professional. Professional: Paul Jackson (01748 822457). Secretary: B.D. Aston (01748 823231).

RIPON. **Masham Golf Club,** Masham, Ripon (01765 689379). *Location:* nine miles north of Ripon. 9 holes, 5308 yards. S.S.S. 66. *Green Fees:* £15.00 U/A. *Visitors:* welcome weekdays but must be accompanied by a member weekends and Bank Holidays. Party visits by arrangement. Secretary: Mrs M.A. Willis (01765 689491).

RIPON. **Ripon City Golf Club,** Palace Road, Ripon HG4 1UW (01765 603640). *Location:* one mile north of Ripon on A6108 (Masham). Undulating parkland with magnificent views. 18 holes, 6120 yards. S.S.S. White 69, Yellow 68. *Green Fees:* weekdays £18.00; weekends £25.00. Half price if playing with a member. *Eating facilities:* available every day except Mondays. *Visitors:* welcome, weekend start sheet in operation. *Society Meetings:* welcome, package deals available. Professional: S.T. Davis (01765 600411). Secretary: B. Denbigh-White (01765 603640).

SCARBOROUGH. **Ganton Golf Club Ltd,** Ganton, Near Scarborough YO12 4PA. *Location:* on A64, nine miles west of Scarborough. 18 holes, 6693 yards. *Green Fees:* on request. *Eating facilities:* available. *Visitors:* welcome by prior arrangement. *Society Meetings:* catered for with reservation. Professional: Gary Brown. Secretary: Air Vice-Marshal R.G. Price, CB.

SCARBOROUGH. **Raven Hall Country House Hotel Golf Course,** Ravenscar, Near Scarborough YO13 0ET (01723 870353; Fax: 01723 870072). *Location:* off main A171 (Whitby Road), 10 miles north of Scarborough. Open links, clifftop with a fair gradient. 9 holes, 3762 yards. S.S.S. 64. 18 hole putting green. *Green Fees:* £12.00 per day, every day. *Eating facilities:* Hotel bar and restaurant, Coach House bar facility. *Visitors:* welcome. 53 en-suite bedrooms plus a host of additional leisure facilities. *Society Meetings:* it is advisable for large societies to book in advance through Nick Davies or Caroline Connelly. Secretary: Mr Nicholas Davies. *

SCARBOROUGH. **Scarborough North Cliff Golf Club,** North Cliff Avenue, Scarborough YO12 6PP (01723 360786). *Location:* two miles north of Scarborough on coastal road to Whitby. Parkland. 18 holes, 6425 yards. S.S.S. 71. Practice area. *Green Fees:* weekdays £23.00 per day, weekends and Bank Holidays £28.00. *Eating facilities:* available. *Visitors:* welcome (restrictions on competition days, not allowed Sundays before 10am.). *Society Meetings:* catered for, parties from 8 to 40. Prior booking through Secretary. Professional: S.N. Deller (01723 365920). Secretary: J.R. Freeman (01723 360786).

SCARBOROUGH. **Scarborough South Cliff Golf Club Ltd,** Deepdale Avenue, Scarborough YO11 2UE (01723 360522). *Location:* one mile south of Scarborough off Filey road. Parkland and clifftop with panoramic sea views. 18 holes, 6039 yards. S.S.S. 69. Practice ground. *Green Fees:* weekdays £20.00 per round, £30.00 per day; £27.50 per round, £30.00 per day weekends and Bank Holidays. *Eating facilities:* full catering facilities. *Visitors:* welcome when course available. *Society Meetings:* catered for by prior arrangement. Professional: T. Skingle (01723 365150). Secretary: C.E. Lee (01723 374737).

SELBY. **Selby Golf Club,** Mill Lane, Brayton Barff, Selby YO8 9LD (01757 228622). *Location:* three miles south of Selby off A19 Selby-Doncaster road. Links type course, very well drained. 18 holes, 6246 yards. S.S.S. 70. Large practice ground. *Green Fees:* weekdays £22.00 per round, £24.00 per day; weekends members and guests only. *Eating facilities:* pleasant restaurant and bar. *Visitors:* welcome Wednesdays, Thursdays and Fridays. Handicap Certificate necessary. Snooker. *Society Meetings:* as visitors; special rate £25.00 per day including £2 evening meal voucher for parties. Professional: Andrew Smith (01757 228785). Secretary: Barrie Moore.

SETTLE. **Settle Golf Club,** Buck Haw Brow, Giggleswick, Settle (01729 825288). *Location:* one mile north of Settle on main A65. Moorland. 9 holes, 4600 yards. S.S.S. 62. *Green Fees:* £10.00. *Eating facilities:* bar facilities open Sundays only. *Visitors:* welcome, restrictions Sundays. *Society Meetings:* welcome, must book in advance through Secretary. Secretary: R.G. Bannier (01729 823596).

SKIPTON. **Skipton Golf Club,** off North West Bypass, Skipton BD23 1LL (01756 793922). *Location:* one and a half miles northwest of Skipton town centre on A65. Undulating, with panoramic views, some water hazards. 18 holes, 6049 yards. S.S.S. 69. Practice ground. *Green Fees:* weekdays £20.00; weekends and Bank Holidays £26.00. Half-price for Juniors (under 18). *Eating facilities:* full bar and catering daily (except Mondays during winter). *Visitors:* welcome at all times, some restrictions weekends and Thursdays. *Society Meetings:* welcome by prior arrangement. Special package rates. Professional: P. Robinson (01756 793257). Secretary/Manager: D. Farnsworth (01756 795657).

STUTTON. **Cocksford Golf Club,** Stutton, Tadcaster LS24 9NG (Tel and Fax: 01937 834253). *Location:* from A64 at Tadcaster to Stutton. Parkland course in picturesque valley with Cock Beck running through. 18 holes, 5570 yards. S.S.S. 68. (Additional 9 holes due for completion 1995). Practice facilities. *Green Fees:* on application. *Eating facilities:* Sparrows Restaurant and bar snacks daily except Mondays. *Visitors:* no restrictions apart from competitions – telephone prior to visit. Accommodation available at Cocksford Cottages, reduced green fees for guests. *Society Meetings:* welcome by prior arrangement. Professional: Graham Thompson. Secretary: Mrs Gill Coxon.

THIRSK. **Thirsk and Northallerton Golf Club,** Thornton-le-Street, Thirsk YO7 4AB (01845 522170). *Location:* off the A168 Northallerton Road, two miles north of Thirsk. Flat parkland with excellent views. 9 holes, 6342 yards. S.S.S. 70. Small practice area. *Green Fees:* weekdays £15.00 per round, £20.00 per day; Saturdays and Public Holidays £25.00; Sundays only with a member. *Eating facilities:* bars open normal times, food available except Tuesdays. *Visitors:* must be members of a recognised golf club and have a Handicap. Not at weekends. Dress regulations must be strictly followed. *Society Meetings:* application must be made in writing to, and confirmed by, the Secretary well in advance of a society visit. Not at weekends. Professional: Andrew Wright (01845 526216). Secretary: S. Weatherall (01845 525115).

WHITBY. **Whitby Golf Club,** Sandsend Road, Low Straggleton, Whitby YO21 3SR (01947 602768). *Location:* Sandsend Road (A174) out of Whitby. Coastal course. 18 holes, 6134 yards. S.S.S. 70. *Green Fees:* weekdays £17.50, weekends and Bank Holidays £25.00. Half price when playing with member. *Eating facilities:* meals available daily except Mondays, full bar facilities daily. *Visitors:* welcome, parties over 12 by prior reservation, all must be bona fide golfers. *Society Meetings:* catered for by prior arrangement. Professional: Brian English (Tel & Fax: 01947 602719). Secretary: Alan Dyson (01947 600660).

YORK. **Forest Park Golf Club,** Stockton on Forest, York YO3 9UX (01904 400425). *Location:* one and a half miles from east end of York bypass, follow signs for Stockton on Forest. Flat parkland type course with trees and stream running through. 18 holes, 6600 yards. S.S.S. 71; 9 holes, 3150 yards. S.S.S. 70 (twice round). Open air driving range and practice area. *Green Fees:* weekdays £14.50 per round, £20.00 per day; weekends £20.00 per round, £25.00 per day. Special party and package rates; quotation on request. *Eating facilities:* full bar and golf club catering facilities. *Visitors:* welcome mid week, limited availability weekends. *Society Meetings:* welcome by prior arrangement. Secretary: David Crossley (01904 400688).

YORK. **Fulford (York) Golf Club Ltd,** Heslington Lane, York YO1 5DY (01904 413579). *Location:* A19 (Selby) from city, turn left to Heslington (signposted to University). Heathland. 18 holes, 6775 yards. S.S.S. 72. Practice ground. *Green Fees:* weekdays £20.00 per round, £30.00 per day, £35.00 corporate fee. *Eating facilities:* lounge, diningroom and bar. *Visitors:* welcome Monday to Friday, prior reservation recommended. *Society Meetings:* Monday to Friday by arrangement with Secretary. Professional: B. Hessay (01904 412882). Secretary: R. Bramley (01904 413579; Fax: 01904 416918).

YORK. **Heworth Golf Club,** Muncaster House, Muncastergate, York YO3 9JX (01904 424618). *Location:* one and a half miles from City Centre on A1036 Malton/Scarborough road. Parkland, easy walking. 11 holes, 6141 yards. S.S.S. 69. *Green Fees:* weekdays £10.00 per round, £14.00 per day; weekends and Bank Holidays £14.00 per round, £17.00 per day. All-in rates for parties (coffee, 9 holes, soup and sandwiches, 18 holes, evening meal) £20.00. *Eating facilities:* bar (snacks), dining room. *Visitors:* generally welcome, advisable to telephone Professional in advance. *Society Meetings:* by arrangement with Secretary. Professional: Gregg Roberts (01904 422389). Secretary: J.R. Richards (01904 426156).

YORK. **Pike Hills Golf Club,** Tadcaster Road, Askham Bryan, York YO2 3UW (01904 706566). *Location:* four miles from York on Tadcaster Road, right hand side going west. Flat parkland surrounding wildlife reserve. 18 holes, 6120 yards. S.S.S. 69. *Green Fees:* £22.00 per day/round. *Eating facilities:* newly opened restaurant and bar facilities. *Visitors:* welcome except weekends or Bank Holidays. *Society Meetings:* welcome by arrangement. Professional: Ian Gradwell (01904 708756). Secretary: G. Rawlings (01904 706566).

YORK. **York Golf Club,** Lordsmoor Lane, Strensall, York YO3 5XF (01904 490304). *Location:* two miles north of York ring road (A1237). Wooded heathland. 18 holes, 6285 yards. S.S.S. 70. Practice ground; Professional shop. *Green Fees:* weekdays £20.00 per round, £26.00 per day; parties Sundays £32.00. *Eating facilities:* full catering except Fridays. *Visitors:* welcome weekdays, but advisable to ring before visiting. *Society Meetings:* catered for weekdays and Sundays. Professional: A.B. Mason (01904 490304). Secretary: Group Captain F. Appleyard (01904 491840; Fax: 01904 491852).

South Yorkshire

BARNSLEY. **Barnsley Golf Club,** Wakefield Road, Staincross, Barnsley S75 6JZ (01226 382856). *Location:* A61 three miles north of Barnsley, five miles south of Wakefield. Parkland course. 18 holes, 6048 yards, 5529 metres. S.S.S. 69. *Green Fees:* weekdays £7.50; weekends £8.50. *Eating facilities:* meals available. *Visitors:* welcome, no restrictions. *Society Meetings:* course extremely busy and not suitable for Societies. Professional: M. Melling (01226 382954). Secretary: L.E. Lammas (01226 382856).

BARNSLEY. **Silkstone Golf Club,** Field Head, Elmhirst Lane, Silkstone, Barnsley S75 4OD (01226 790328). *Location:* one mile beyond Dodworth village on the A628 and one mile from M1. Parkland. 18 holes, 6045 yards. S.S.S. 70. Practice area. *Green Fees:* weekdays £23.00 per day. *Eating facilities:* available. *Visitors:* welcome weekdays only. *Society Meetings:* by arrangement. Package £34.00. Professional: Kevin Guy (01226 790128). Secretary: L. Depledge (01226 287053).

DONCASTER. **Austerfield Park Golf Club,** Cross Lane, Austerfield, Doncaster DN10 6RF (Tel & Fax: 01302 710841). *Location:* two miles from Bawtry on the A614. Parkland. 18 holes, 6828 yards. S.S.S. 73. 10 bay floodlit golf range, flat bowling green. *Green Fees:* midweek £13.00 per round, £17.00 per day; weekends £17.00 per round, £21.00 per day. *Eating facilities:* bar snacks and full restaurant. *Visitors:* welcome without reservation. *Society Meetings:* welcome, special package rates. Professional: Trevor Parkinson (01302 710850). Secretary: Alan Bradley (01709 540928).

DONCASTER. **Crookhill Park (Municipal) Golf Club,** Crookhill Park, Conisborough, Doncaster (01709 862974). *Location:* leave A1(M) Doncaster by-pass, on to A630 Sheffield, after two miles turn left in Conisborough on to B60694. 18 holes, 5846 yards. S.S.S. 68. Practice area. *Green Fees:* weekdays £8.50; weekends £9.00. *Eating facilities:* buffet lunches at club. *Visitors:* welcome. Professional: Richard Swaine (01709 862979). Hon. Secretary: M. Belk.

DONCASTER. **Doncaster Golf Club,** Bawtry Road, Doncaster DN4 7PD (01302 868316). *Location:* four miles south of Doncaster town centre on the A638. Wooded, heathland course. 18 holes, 6220 yards. S.S.S. 70. Practice area, putting green. *Green Fees:* weekdays £20.00 per round, £24.00 per day; weekends £25.00 per round, £30.00 per day. *Eating facilities:* all day catering Monday to Saturday, up to 7pm Sundays. *Visitors:* welcome weekdays, Wednesday Ladies Day; restricted tee times at weekends and Bank Holidays. *Society Meetings:* by arrangement, contact Secretary. Professional: G. Bailey (01302 868404). Secretary: R. Collingwood (01302 868632; Fax: 01302 865994).

DONCASTER. **Doncaster Town Moor Golf Club,** Bawtry Road, Belle Vue, Doncaster DN4 5HU (01302 535286). *Location:* clubhouse approximately 300 yards from racecourse roundabout travelling south towards Bawtry, same entrance as Doncaster Rovers Football Club. Flat wooded parkland. 18 holes, 6094 yards. S.S.S. 69. *Green Fees:* weekdays £13.00 per round, £7.00 with a member; £15.00 per day, £8.00 with a member; weekends and Public Holidays £15.00 per round, £8.00 with a member; £17.00 per day, £9.00 with a member. *Eating facilities:* restaurant and bar meals. *Visitors:* welcome without reservation, not before 11.30am Sundays. *Society Meetings:* catered for by arrangement with Secretary. Professional: Steve Poole (01302 535286). Secretary: Gerry Sampson (01302 538423). *

DONCASTER. **Hickleton Golf Club,** Hickleton, Near Doncaster (01709 892496). *Location:* six miles from Doncaster on A635 to Barnsley. In Hickleton village turn right to Thurnscoe, 500 yards on right. Undulating parkland. 18 holes, 6403 yards. S.S.S. 71. Practice facilities. *Green Fees:* weekdays £18.00; weekends £20.00, Bank Holidays £25.00. *Eating facilities:* available by arrangement with Steward/ess. *Visitors:* welcome by arrangement, restricted times at weekends. *Society Meetings:* welcome by arrangement. Professional: Paul Shepherd (01709 895170; Fax: 01709 888436). Secretary: R. Jowett (01709 896081 office).

DONCASTER. **Owston Park Golf Course,** Owston, Doncaster DN6 9JF (01302 330821). *Location:* signposted from A19. Flat parkland, surrounded by woods. 9 holes, 3042 yards. S.S.S. 71. *Green Fees:* weekdays £3.75 9 holes, £6.50 18 holes; weekends £3.75 9 holes, £7.50 18 holes. £3.25 for Juniors and Senior Citizens. *Visitors:* welcome, pay as you play; no restrictions. *Society Meetings:* welcome. Professional: M. Parker.

DONCASTER. **Serlby Park Golf Club,** Serlby, Doncaster DN10 6BA (01777 818268). *Location:* 12 miles south of Doncaster, between A614 and A638. Parkland, wooded course. 9 holes, 5370 yards. S.S.S. 66. *Green Fees:* weekdays £8.00 per round; weekends £11.00 per round. *Eating facilities:* catering and bar. *Visitors:* welcome only if playing with member. *Society Meetings:* some visiting parties allowed. Hon. Secretary: R. Wilkinson. *

DONCASTER. **Thorne Golf Club,** Kirkton Lane, Thorne, Near Doncaster (01405 815173). *Location:* A18. Parkland. 18 holes, 5366 yards. S.S.S. 66. Practice ground. *Green Fees:* weekdays £8.00 per round; weekends and Bank Holidays £9.00 per round. *Eating facilities:* snacks or full meals booked in advance. *Visitors:* welcome, no restrictions. *Society Meetings:* welcome, please book in advance. Professional: R.D. Highfield (01405 812084). Secretary: Mrs C. Highfield (01405 812084).

DONCASTER. **Wheatley Golf Club,** Armthorpe Road, Doncaster DN2 5QB (01302 831655). *Location:* follow East Coast route alongside Racecourse boundary to water tower at first crossroads. Flat parkland, water hazards between 10th and 18th holes. 18 holes, 6209 yards, S.S.S. 70 (yellow markers); 6405 yards, S.S.S. 71 (white markers). Practice area and putting green. *Green Fees:* information not provided. *Eating facilities:* restaurant and bars. *Visitors:* welcome if member of another club. Non-members may play in the company of a member. *Society Meetings:* catered for weekdays only on written application. Professional: S. Fox. Secretary: T.A.D. Crumpton.

ROTHERHAM. **Grange Park Golf Club,** Upper Wortley Road, Kimberworth Park, Rotherham (01709 558884). Municipal golf course, private clubhouse. *Location:* A629 from Rotherham, easy access from M1. Parkland. 18 holes, 6353 yards. S.S.S. 71. Practice ground. *Green Fees:* £8.00 weekdays; £9.00 weekends. *Eating facilities:* licensed bar and full catering. *Visitors:* welcome without restriction. *Society Meetings:* contact Professional in first instance. Professional: Eric Clark (01709 559497). Secretary: R. Charity (01709 583400).

ROTHERHAM. **Phoenix Golf Club,** Pavilion Lane, Brinsworth, Rotherham (01709 363864). *Location:* M1 Tinsley roundabout, Bawtry Road, Pavilion Lane one mile on left. 18 holes, 6145 yards. S.S.S. 69. *Green Fees:* weekdays £21.00 per day, £8.00 with a member; weekends £28.00, £12.00 with a member. *Eating facilities:* snacks or full meals. *Visitors:* welcome weekdays. *Society Meetings:* welcome, reduced rates for parties. Professional: A. Limb (01709 382624). Secretary: J. Burrows (01709 370759).

ROTHERHAM. **Rotherham Golf Club Ltd,** Thrybergh Park, Thrybergh, Rotherham S65 4NU (01709 850466). *Location:* three and a half miles east of Rotherham on A630. Wooded parkland. 18 holes, 6234 yards, 5701 metres. S.S.S. 70. Practice ground. *Green Fees:* weekdays £26.50; weekends £31.50. Reductions for societies over 16. *Eating facilities:* full catering, bar and restaurant. *Visitors:* welcome all day with limitations. *Society Meetings:* catered for weekdays only except Wednesdays. Professional: Simon Thornhill (01709 850480). Secretary: G.F. Smalley (01709 850812).

ROTHERHAM. **Roundwood Golf Club,** Green Lane, Rawmarsh, Rotherham (01709 523471). *Location:* half a mile from the A633. Parkland course – easy walking. 9 holes, 5713 yards, S.S.S. 67. *Green Fees:* weekdays £12.00; weekends £15.00. *Eating facilities:* bar open seven days a week, meals available Wednesdays to Saturdays. *Visitors:* welcome midweek. *Society Meetings:* welcome Mondays, Tuesdays and Thursdays. Secretary: D. Abel (01709 826134; Fax: 01709 826691).

ROTHERHAM. **Sitwell Park Golf Club,** Shrogswood Road, Rotherham S60 4BY (01709 700799). *Location:* A631 off M18, Bramley turn off to Rotherham thence to Sheffield, Exit 33 off M1, follow A631 to Bawtry. Undulating parkland. 18 holes, 6203 yards. S.S.S. 70. Practice ground. *Green Fees:* weekdays £22.00 per round, £26.00 per day; weekends and Bank Holidays £26.00 per round, £30.00 per day. Parties of 30 or more players 10% discount. *Eating facilities:* restaurant and bar. *Visitors:* welcome with reservation, Saturdays only with member, Sundays after 11.30am. *Society Meetings:* catered for if pre-arranged with Secretary. Not Saturdays; Sundays after 11.30am only. Professional: N. Taylor (01709 540961). Secretary: G. Simmonite (01709 541046).

ROTHERHAM. **Wath Golf Club,** Abdy, Rawmarsh, Rotherham S62 7SJ (01709 872149). *Location:* A633 from Rotherham, through Rawmarsh, taking B6090 towards Wentworth, right along B6089 taking signed road to Clubhouse 300 yards on right. Flat parkland course with small green, dykes and two ponds. 18 holes, 5857 yards. S.S.S. 68. Limited practice area. *Green Fees:* weekdays £16.00; weekends with a member £16.00. *Eating facilities:* lounge bar and dining area with seating for up to 150 people. *Visitors:* weekdays only. No jeans or collarless shirts allowed. *Society Meetings:* welcome weekdays only by prior arrangement. Golf/meal Package £25.00. Professional: Chris Bassett (01709 878677). Secretary: Mr Anthony Buckler (01709 873153 day, 01709 580112 evening; Fax: 01709 760179).

SHEFFIELD. **Abbeydale Golf Club,** Twentywell Lane, Dore, Sheffield S17 4QA (01742 360763). *Location:* A621 five miles south of Sheffield. Parkland. 18 holes, 6419 yards. S.S.S. 71. Practice ground. *Green Fees:* weekdays £28.00, weekends and Bank Holidays £33.00. *Eating facilities:* restaurant and bar meals. *Visitors:* welcome by arrangement. Starting time restrictions April-October. *Society Meetings:* catered for Tuesdays and Fridays by arrangement. Professional:

N. Perry (01742 365633). Secretary: Mrs K.M. Johnston (01742 360763; Fax: 01742 360762).

SHEFFIELD. **Beauchief Golf Club,** Abbey Lane, Beauchief, Sheffield S8 0DB (01742 620040). *Location:* the entrance to course is on the Sheffield Outer Ring Road, between the A621 Bakewell Road and the A61 Chesterfield Road. Mainly flat parkland with some hilly holes. 18 holes, 5452 yards, 4984 metres. S.S.S. 66. Practice area available (small charge). *Green Fees:* £8.00 per round. Juniors half price. *Eating facilities:* cafe/bar, open from 8am to dusk each day. *Visitors:* welcome anytime but starting times get booked up early and cannot be booked by telephone. *Society Meetings:* Contact Sports Development Section, Tower Lodge, Firth Park Road, Sheffield S5 6WS (01742 431253). Professional: A.P. Highfield (01742 367274). Bookings: (01742 367274). Secretary: J.G. Pearson (01742 306720).

SHEFFIELD. **Birley Wood Golf Club,** Birley Lane, Sheffield S12 3BP (0114 264 7262). *Location:* Junction 30 M1 or Junction 33 M1. Undulating meadowland course with well varied features, open plan and good views. 18 holes, 5452 yards. S.S.S. 67. Practice field near course. *Green Fees:* £7.50 per round. *Eating facilities:* bar and snacks at nearby Fairway Inn. *Visitors:* welcome anytime. *Society Meetings:* Contact Sports Development Section, Tower Lodge, Firth Park Road, Sheffield S5 6WS (01742 431253). Professional: P. Ball (01742 647262).

SHEFFIELD. **Concord Park Municipal Golf Course,** Shiregreen Lane, Sheffield S5 6AE. *Location:* one-and-a-half miles from M1 Junction 34. Hilly wooded parkland. 18 holes, 4321 yards, 3929 metres. S.S.S. 62. *Green Fees:* £5.95 per round. *Eating facilities:* available at adjacent Sports Centre. *Visitors:* welcome any time. *Society Meetings:* contact Sports Development Section, Tower Lodge, Firth Park Road, Sheffield S5 6WS (0114 243 1253). Secretary: B. Shepherd (0114 245 6806). *

SHEFFIELD. **Dore and Totley Golf Club,** The Clubhouse, Bradway Road, Bradway, Sheffield S17 4QR (01742 360492). *Location:* leave M1 at Junction 33. Parkland. 18 holes, 6265 yards. S.S.S. 70. *Green Fees:* weekdays £28.00 per round or day; weekends with a member only. *Eating facilities:* bar available, catering facilities available except Mondays. *Visitors:* unintroduced visitors restricted to the hours of 9.30am to 12 noon and after 2pm. Restrictions also exist on Wednesday (Ladies' Day). Handicap Certificates may be requested. *Society Meetings:* catered for Tuesday, Thursday, Friday by prior arrangement. Special rates for parties; catering by arrangement with Stewardess. Professional: Neil Cheetham (01742 366844). Secretary: Mrs C. Ward (01742 369872).

SHEFFIELD. **Hallamshire Golf Club Ltd,** Sandygate, Sheffield S10 4LA (01742 301007). *Location:* A57 out of Sheffield, four miles out of city then fork left for Lodge Moor. Moorland course. 18 holes, 6359 yards, 5815 metres. S.S.S. 71. *Green Fees:* £27.00 weekdays; £34.00 weekends. *Eating facilities:* full catering except Tuesdays – prior notice required. *Visitors:* welcome weekdays by arrangement, some weekends. Snooker table. *Society Meetings:* catered for by arrangement with Secretary. Professional: Geoffrey Tickell (01742 305222). Secretary: K. Sharrocks (01742 302153).

SHEFFIELD. **Hallowes Golf Club,** Hallowes Lane, Dronfield, Near Sheffield S18 6UA (01246 413734). *Location:* six miles south of Sheffield on old A61 (not by-pass to Chesterfield). Moorland/parkland. 18 holes, 6342 yards. S.S.S. 70. Large practice area. *Green Fees:* weekdays £20.00 per round, £27.00 per day. *Eating facilities:* bars, dining room (no catering Mondays). *Visitors:* weekdays only, no visitors at weekends and Bank Holidays except with members. *Society Meetings:* E.G.U. registered societies welcome. Professional: Philip Dunn (01246 411196). Secretary: L.F. Smith (01246 413734).

SHEFFIELD. **Hillsborough Golf Club Ltd,** Worrall Road, Sheffield S6 4BE (0114 234 9151/0114 234 3608). *Location:* three miles from city centre. Worrall Road via Middlewood Road, Dykes Hall Road. Undulating wooded parkland and heath. 18 holes, 6035 yards. S.S.S. 70. Practice field. *Green Fees:* weekdays £28.00. *Eating facilities:* snacks available; lunches, teas, evening meals by arrangement (not Fridays). *Visitors:* welcome weekdays, weekends with a member only. *Society Meetings:* catered for by arrangement with Secretary. Professional: G. Walker (0114 233 2666). Secretary: K.A. Dungey (0114 234 9151).

SHEFFIELD. **Lees Hall Golf Club Ltd,** Hemsworth Road, Norton, Sheffield S8 8LL (0114 255 4402). *Location:* three miles south of Sheffield, between A61 and A6102 ring road. Undulating parkland with extensive views over Sheffield. 18 holes, 6137 yards. S.S.S. 69. *Green Fees:* information not provided. *Eating facilities:* available daily except Tuesdays. *Visitors:* welcome, except Saturday and Sunday before 10.30am. *Society Meetings:* by arrangement only. Professional: J.R. Wilkinson (0114 255 4402). Secretary: N.E. Westworth (0114 255 2900). *

SHEFFIELD. **Stocksbridge and District Golf Club Ltd,** 30 Royd Lane, Deepcar S30 5RZ (01742 882003). *Location:* 10 miles from Sheffield on A616 heading towards Manchester. Moorland course. 18 holes, 5200 yards. S.S.S. 65. Practice ground. *Green Fees:* weekdays £15.00; weekends £24.00. *Eating facilities:* available. *Visitors:* welcome weekdays, restrictions weekends. *Society Meetings:* catered for by arrangement. Secretary: Stuart Lee (01742 882408).

SHEFFIELD. **Tankersley Park Golf Club,** High Green, Sheffield S30 4LG (01742 468247). *Location:* M1 north to Junction 35a, A616, golf club on right. M1 south Junction 36, A61 Sheffield, left on A616, golf club on left. Parkland. 18 holes, 6212 yards. S.S.S. 70. Practice area. *Green Fees:* £18.00 per round, £23.00 per day weekdays; £23.00 weekends. 10% discount for parties of 30 or more players. *Eating facilities:* sandwiches, bar meals, full evening meals; seven day catering. *Visitors:* welcome on weekdays without reservation but not before 3pm weekends. *Society Meetings:* catered for by prior arrangement. Professional: I. Kirk (01742 455583). Secretary: Mr P.A. Bagshaw (01742 468247).

SHEFFIELD. **Tinsley Park Golf Club (Municipal),** High Hazels Park, Darnall, Sheffield (0114 256 0237). *Location:* three miles from Junction 33 M1, exit – A6102. Wooded course. 18 holes, 6086 yards. S.S.S. 69. Practice facilities. *Green Fees:* £6.95. *Eating facilities:* cafe (closed Tuesday); meals if ordered from Stewardess. Time must be booked on arrival. *Visitors:* welcome without restriction, no booking facilities. *Society Meetings:* book through Sheffield City Council. Professional: Mr A.P. Highfield (0114 256 0237). Secretary: Mr C.E. Benson (0114 287 3110). *

SHEFFIELD. **Wortley Golf Club,** Hermit Hill Lane, Wortley, Near Sheffield S30 7DF (01742 882139). *Location:* leave M1 Junction 36 or 35A – A61 to A629 west of Wortley Village. Parkland. 18 holes, 6037 yards, 5520 metres. S.S.S. 69. *Green Fees:* £21.00 per day or round weekdays; £25.00 weekends and Bank Holidays. *Eating facilities:* order in advance, not Mondays. *Visitors:* welcome by arrangement. *Society Meetings:* parties catered for by arrangement Wednesdays and Fridays. Professional: Jeremy Tilson (01742 886490). Secretary: J. Lewis Dalby (01742 885294).

West Yorkshire

BINGLEY. **Bingley (St. Ives) Golf Club,** The Mansion, St. Ives Estate, Harden, Bingley (Tel & Fax: 01274 562436). Parkland/moorland. 18 holes, 6480 yards. S.S.S. 71. Practice ground. *Green Fees:* weekdays £20.00; weekends and Bank Holidays £25.00. *Eating facilities:* daily. *Visitors:* welcome weekdays, limited availability weekends. *Society Meetings:* welcome, book through Professional. Professional: R.K. Firth (01274 562506). Secretary: Mary Welch (01274 562436).

BRADFORD. **Bradford Moor Golf Club,** Scarr Hill, Pollard Lane, Bradford BD2 4RW (01274 638313). *Location:* A658 two miles from top of M606. Moorland, undulating course. 9 holes, 5854 yards. S.S.S. 68. *Green Fees:* weekdays £12.00 (with a member £6.00); weekends with a member only (£8.00). *Eating facilities:* available except Tuesdays. *Visitors:* welcome weekdays. *Society Meetings:* welcome weekdays. Professional: Mr R.J. Hughes (01274 626107). Secretary: Mr Chris Bedford (01274 870108).

BRADFORD. **Clayton Golf Club,** Thornton View Road, Clayton, Bradford BD14 6JX (01274 880047). *Location:* two miles south west of Bradford, via Thornton Road, then Listerhills Road. Moorland course, testing par 3 at third hole. 9 holes, 5515 yards. S.S.S. 67. *Green Fees:* weekdays £10.00 (£8.00 with a member); weekends £12.00 (£10.00 with a member). *Eating facilities:* diningroom – meals and snacks daily; evening meals by arrangement; two bars. *Visitors:* welcome at all times except before 4.00pm on Sundays. Snooker room. *Society Meetings:* catered for by arrangement. Secretary: F. V. Wood (01274 574203).

BRADFORD. **East Bierley Golf Club,** South View Road, East Bierley, Bradford (01274 681023). *Location:* situated about three miles east of Bradford on the Wakefield/Heckmondwike Road. Turn off at Bierley Bar and down South View Road. Undulating semi-moorland course. 9 holes, 4308 metres. S.S.S. 63. *Green Fees:* £12.00 per round weekdays; Saturdays and Bank Holidays £15.00. *Eating facilities:* lunchtime and evening catering. *Visitors:* welcome, not Sunday or Mondays after 4pm. Secretary: Mr R.J. Welch (01274 683666). Steward: (01274 680450).

BRADFORD. **Headley Golf Club,** Headley Lane, Thornton, Bradford BD13 3LX (01274 833481). *Location:* five miles west of Bradford. Hilly parkland. 9 holes, 4914 yards. S.S.S. 64. *Green Fees:* weekdays £10.00, £5.00 if playing with a member. *Eating facilities:* dining and bar. *Visitors:* weekdays only. *Society Meetings:* restricted facilities. Hon. Secretary: K. Allan (01274 670398).

BRADFORD. **Northcliffe Golf Club,** High Bank Lane, Shipley BD18 4LJ (01274 584085). *Location:* three miles west of Bradford on A650 Bradford-Keighley. Undulating wooded parkland. 18 holes, 6104 yards. S.S.S. 69. *Green Fees:* weekdays £20.00; weekends and Bank Holidays £25.00. *Eating facilities:* bars, dining room (no catering Mondays). *Visitors:* tee restricted to members weekdays 8.30/9.30am, 12.30/1.30pm, 4.30/6pm. *Society Meetings:* welcome Tuesdays to Fridays. Handicap Certificate required. Professional: M. Hillas (01274 587193). Secretary: H.R. Archer (01274 596731).

BRADFORD. **Queensbury Golf Club,** Brighouse Road, Queensbury, Bradford BD13 1QF (01274 882155). *Location:* M62 Junction 25, A644 to Brighouse, Hipperholme and Queensbury. Wooded course. 9 holes, 5024 yards. S.S.S. 65. *Green Fees:* weekdays £13.00; weekends £20.00. *Eating facilities:* lunches, teas except Monday. Bar available. *Visitors:* welcome any day, must have Handicap. No parties at weekends. *Society Meetings:* by arrangement. Professional: Mr Geoff Howard (01274 882956). Secretary: Mr H. Andrew (01422 201565). *

BRADFORD. **Shipley Golf Club,** Beckfoot Lane, Cottingley Bridge, Bingley BD16 1LX (01274 563212). *Location:* off A650 at Cottingley Bridge, Bradford six miles, Bingley one mile (from Bradford left before Cottingley Bridge). Flat parkland. 18 holes, 6218 yards. S.S.S. 70. Practice area and net putting green. *Green*

Fees: weekdays £26.00; weekends and Bank Holidays £35.00. *Eating facilities:* available by arrangement with Steward, except Mondays. *Visitors:* welcome (Tuesdays after 2pm, Saturdays after 4pm). *Society Meetings:* catered for by arrangement with Secretary. Professional: J.R. Parry (01274 563674). Secretary: G. Martin Shaw (01274 568652).

BRADFORD. **South Bradford Golf Club,** Pearson Road, Odsal, Bradford BD6 1BH (01274 679195). *Location:* follow signs for Odsal Stadium, roundabout at Stadium turn left and first left again, road leads down to clubhouse. Parkland type course with some hilly sections. 9 holes, 6004 yards. S.S.S. 69. Practice ground. *Green Fees:* weekdays £14.00 per day (£8.00 with member); weekends £22.00 per day (£10.00 with member). *Eating facilities:* bar meals available except Mondays. *Visitors:* welcome; not before 3.30pm on weekends and Bank Holidays. Must provide Handicap Certificate. *Society Meetings:* welcome – must apply in writing. Professional: Mr Ian Marshall (01274 673346). Secretary: Mr D.W. Clow (01274 690643).

BRADFORD. **The Manor Golf Club,** Bradford Road, Drighlington, Bradford (0113 285 2644). *Location:* between Leeds and Bradford, just off M62 Junction 27. Undulating parkland. 18 holes, 6506 yards, 5947 metres. S.S.S 71, Par 72. 20 bay floodlit driving range, 6 hole Par 3 course. *Green Fees:* on application. *Eating facilities:* clubhouse. *Visitors:* welcome at all times but prior enquiry advised. *Society Meetings:* welcome with reservation. Professional: Jim Crompton. Secretary: Mr B. Cook.

BRADFORD. **West Bowling Golf Club Ltd,** Newall Hall, Rooley Lane, Bradford BD5 8LB (01274 724449). *Location:* junction of M606 (off M62) and Bradford ring road (east). Parkland. 18 holes, 5657 yards. S.S.S. 67. Practice facilities. *Green Fees:* weekdays £24.00 (£20.00 with Handicap Certificate); weekends and Bank Holidays £30.00 (restricted). *Eating facilities:* available daily in summer, closed Mondays in winter. *Visitors:* by arrangement with Professional for individuals, with Secretary for parties. Weekends severely restricted, no parties. *Society Meetings:* by arrangement as above. Professional: A. Swaine (01274 728036). Secretary: M.E. Lynn (01274 393207).

BRADFORD. **West Bradford Golf Club Ltd,** Chellow Grange Road, Haworth Road, Bradford BD9 6NP (01274 542767). *Location:* three miles west of city centre off Haworth Road. Undulating course. 18 holes, 5788 yards. S.S.S. 68. *Green Fees:* £15.00 weekdays; £22.00 weekends, including VAT. *Eating facilities:* available every day except Mondays. *Visitors:* welcome, except Saturdays. *Society Meetings:* welcome Wednesday to Friday. Golf package deals Wednesday to Friday £24.00. Professional: Nigel M. Barber (01274 542102). Secretary: D. Ingham (01274 820417).

BRIGHOUSE. **Castlefields Golf Club,** Rastrick Common, Rastrick, Brighouse HD6 3HL. *Location:* one mile out of Brighouse on A643. Parkland. 7 holes, 2406 yards. S.S.S. 50, Par 54. *Green Fees:* weekdays £5.00; weekends £7.00. Juniors £2.00. *Eating facilities:* Globe Inn 200 yards away. *Visitors:* welcome at all times but must be accompanied by a member. Secretary: B.J. Davies (01422 376687).

CLECKHEATON. **Cleckheaton and District Golf Club Ltd,** Bradford Road, Cleckheaton BD19 6BU (01274 874118). *Location:* four miles south of Bradford on A638, 200 yards from Junction 26 M62. Parkland course. 18 holes, 5860 yards. S.S.S. 68. Practice area. *Green Fees:* £22.00 weekdays (winter £18.00); £28.00 weekends and Bank Holidays (winter £25.00). *Eating facilities:* available except Mondays. *Visitors:* welcome except Saturdays, suggest prior enquiry. *Society Meetings:* catered for by prior arrangement with Secretary except Saturdays. Professional: Mike Ingham (01274 851267). Secretary: Herbert Thornton (01274 851266).

CLIFTON. **Willow Valley Golf and Country Club,** Highmoor Lane, Off Walton Lane, Clifton, Brighouse HD6 4JB (01274 878624). *Location:* 500 yards from Armytage Arms, Clifton. Parkland with plantation areas and feature fountain lake. 9 holes, 1696 yards, 1565 metres. S.S.S. 30. 18-hole course under construction. Covered practice range and free putting area. *Green Fees:* £5.00. *Eating facilities:* snacks and beverages available. *Visitors:* no restrictions – pay and play course. (Membership scheme planned). *Society Meetings:* welcome, particularly Monday to Thursday. Professional: Chris Stock. Manager: Glyn Selway.

DEWSBURY. **Hanging Heaton Golf Club,** White Cross Road, Dewsbury WF12 7DT (01924 461606). *Location:* one mile from town centre on main A653 Dewsbury to Leeds road. 9 holes, 5870 yards (for 18 holes). S.S.S. 67. *Green Fees:* weekdays £12.00 (£8.00 with member); weekends with member £10.00. Green fees not taken weekends or Bank Holidays without member's introduction. *Eating facilities:* available. *Visitors:* welcome without reservation, except weekends. *Society Meetings:* catered for by arrangement with Steward. Professional: (01924 467077). Secretary: S.M. Simpson (01924 430100).

ELLAND. **Elland Golf Club,** Hammerstones, Leach Lane, Elland HX5 0TA (01422 372505). *Location:* M62 Junction 24 exit off roundabout for Blackley. Parkland. 9 holes, 5630 yards. S.S.S. 66. *Green Fees:* weekdays £12.00; weekends £20.00. *Eating facilities:* meals/bar snacks except Mondays. *Visitors:* welcome mid-week. *Society Meetings:* by arrangement. Professional: M. Allison (01422 374886). Secretary: A.D. Blackburn (01422 372014).

GUISELEY. **Bradford Golf Club,** Hawksworth Lane, Guiseley, Leeds LS20 8NP (01943 877239). *Location:* Shipley to Ilkley road, left at top of Hollins Hill, one mile up Hawksworth Lane. Moorland/parkland. 18 holes, 6259 yards. S.S.S. 71. *Green Fees:* weekdays £20.00 per round, £25.00 per day; weekends £32.00 (half price with member). *Eating facilities:* every day, preferably by prior arrangement. *Visitors:* welcome without reservation weekdays, not on weekends without prior arrangement. *Society Meetings:* catered for on weekdays (except Tuesdays) by prior arrangement. Professional: Sydney Weldon (01943 873719). Secretary: P. Atkinson (01943 875570).

HALIFAX. **Bradley Hall Golf Club,** Holywell Green, Halifax HX4 9AN (01422 374108). *Location:* three miles south of Halifax on B6112. Moorland, undulating. 18 holes, 6213 yards. S.S.S. 70. Practice ground. *Green Fees:* weekdays £18.00 per round, £16.00 per round with a Handicap Certificate; weekends £28.00 per round, with a Handicap Certificate £24.00 per round. *Eating facilities:* full catering by arrangement except Tuesdays, seven day bar. *Visitors:* welcome. Snooker. *Societies:* welcome with prior reservation weekdays. Professional: P. Wood (01422 370231). Secretary: John R. Burton (01422 715797 evenings).

HALIFAX. **Lightcliffe Golf Club,** Knowle Top Road, Lightcliffe, Halifax (01422 202459). *Location:* three miles east of Halifax on A58 (Leeds) road. Parkland. 9 holes, 5368 metres. S.S.S. 68. *Green Fees:* weekdays £15.00; weekends £18.00. *Eating facilities:* bar snacks and meals (except Mondays). *Visitors:* welcome without reservation but must confirm with Professional. Not Wednesdays. *Society Meetings:* catered for. Professional: D.W. Lockett (01422 202459). Secretary: T.H. Gooder (01422 201051).

HALIFAX. **Ryburn Golf Club,** The Shaw, Norland, Near Halifax (01422 831355). *Location:* Station Road Halifax to Sowerby Bridge, turn right up hill, right towards Hobbit Inn (signposted), left after cottages. Demanding, hilly, windy course. 9 holes, 4907 yards. S.S.S. 64. *Green Fees:* information not available. *Eating facilities:* good catering facilities and bar. *Visitors:* welcome weekdays, weekends by prior arrangement. *Society Meetings:* welcome by prior arrangement. Secretary: Jack Hoyle (01422 843070 home).

HALIFAX. **The Halifax Golf Club Ltd,** Union Lane, Ogden, Halifax HX2 8XR (01422 244171). *Location:* three miles out of Halifax, A629 towards Keighley. Moorland. 18 holes, 6037 yards. S.S.S. 70. *Green Fees:* weekdays £20.00; weekends £30.00. *Eating facilities:* luncheons and dinners served. Good restaurant facilities. *Visitors:* welcome most days by arrangement. *Society Meetings:* catered for by arrangement – mid-week £32.00; weekends £40.00. Professional: Mr Steve Foster (01422 240047). Secretary: Mr J.P. Clark (01422 244171).

HALIFAX. **West End Golf Club (Halifax) Ltd,** Paddock Lane, Highroad Well, Halifax HX2 0NT (01422 353608). *Location:* two miles west of town centre. Parkland. 18 holes, 5951 yards. S.S.S. 69 (White markers). *Green Fees:* weekdays £17.50 per round, £20.00 per day; weekends and Bank Holidays £20.00 per round, £25.00 per day. *Eating facilities:* full bar and catering except Mondays. *Visitors:* welcome except Saturdays – please check with Professional. No visiting parties on Saturdays. *Society Meetings:* catered for by arrangement with Secretary. Professional: D. Rishworth (01422 363293). Secretary: B.R. Thomas (01422 341878).

HEBDEN BRIDGE. **Hebden Bridge Golf Club,** Wadsworth, Hebden Bridge HX7 8PH (01422 842896). *Location:* one mile upwards past Birchcliffe Centre. Moorland with superb Pennine views. 9 holes, 5202 yards. S.S.S. 65. *Green Fees:* weekdays £10.00; weekends £15.00. 50% reduction for Juniors or if playing with member. *Eating facilities:* bar and dining-room facilities. *Visitors:* welcome, please check first at weekends. *Society Meetings:* welcome midweek only except by special arrangement.

HUDDERSFIELD. **Bradley Park Municipal Golf Course,** Off Bradley Road, Huddersfield HD2 1PZ (01484 539988). *Location:* M62 Junction 25, one mile up A6107. Parkland, rolling hills with panoramic views. 18 holes, 6220 yards. S.S.S. 70. Floodlit driving range, 9 hole Par 3 course. *Green Fees:* weekdays £8.50; weekends £10.00. *Eating facilities:* full catering. *Visitors:* no restrictions except booking at weekends. *Society Meetings:* all welcome. Professional: P.E. Reilly. Secretary: D.W. Miller.

HUDDERSFIELD. **Crosland Heath Golf Club Ltd,** Felk Stile Road, Crosland Hill, Huddersfield HD4 7AF (01484 653216). *Location:* three miles from town centre off A62 Oldham road. Flat heathland with extensive views. 18 holes, 5963 yards. S.S.S. 70. Practice facilities. *Green Fees:* on application. *Eating facilities:* full catering except Mondays. *Visitors:* welcome, suggest prior enquiry. *Society Meetings:* catered for by arrangement. Professional: Christopher Gaunt (01484 653877). Secretary: D. Walker (01484 653262).

HUDDERSFIELD. **Huddersfield Golf Club,** Fixby Hall, Lightridge Road, Fixby, Huddersfield HD2 2EP (01484 426203). *Location:* M62 Junction 24; A643 from Hilton Hotel; turn right first traffic lights by Sun Inn. Parkland course. 18 holes, 6432 yards. S.S.S. 71. Practice ground. *Green Fees:* weekdays £30.00 for 18 holes, £40.00 for 27/36 holes; weekends and Public Holidays £40.00 for 18 holes, £50.00 for 27/36 holes. £10.00 playing with a member. *Eating facilities:* available. *Visitors:* always welcome, reservation advised but not essential. Tuesday is Ladies' day and no visitors Saturdays. Snooker. *Society and Company Days:* catered for except weekends, well appointed private rooms. Catering to suit all occasions. Professional: P. Carman (01484 426463). Secretary: Mrs D. Lockett (01484 426203). General Manager: D.L. Bennett (01484 426203).

HUDDERSFIELD. **Longley Park Golf Club,** Maple Street, Aspley, Huddersfield HD5 9AX (01484 426932). *Location:* one mile town centre, Wakefield side. 9 holes, 5324 yards. S.S.S. 66. *Green Fees:* weekdays £13.50; weekends and Bank Holidays £16.00. *Eating facilities:* available. *Visitors:* welcome Tuesdays and Fridays. *Society Meetings:* welcome only by previous arrangement with Secretary. Professional: Paul Middleton (01484 422304). Secretary: D. Palliser.

HUDDERSFIELD. **Marsden Golf Club,** Hemplow, Marsden, Huddersfield HD7 6JL (01484 844253). *Location:* eight miles south of Huddersfield on A62 to Manchester. Moorland. 9 holes, 5702 yards. S.S.S. 68. *Green Fees:* weekdays £10.00. *Eating facilities:* lunches and snacks available except Tuesdays. *Visitors:* welcome weekdays, with a member only weekends. *Society Meetings:* catered for by arrangement. Professional: A. Bickerdike. Secretary: D. Horncastle (01484 647433).

HUDDERSFIELD. **Woodsome Hall Golf Club,** Woodsome Hall, Fenay Bridge, Huddersfield HD8 0LQ (01484 602971). *Location:* leave Huddersfield A629. Parkland. 18 holes, 6080 yards. S.S.S. 69. Practice ground. *Green Fees:* weekdays £25.00; weekends and Public Holidays £30.00 (subject to review). *Eating facilities:* available. *Visitors:* welcome Wednesday, Thursday and Friday. *Society Meetings:* welcome. Professional: M. Higginbottom (01484 602034). Secretary: W.D.N. Woodhouse (01484 602739; Fax: 01484 608260). Office Administrator: Mrs T.J. Mee.

ILKLEY. **Ben Rhydding Golf Club,** High Wood, Ben Rhydding, Ilkley (01943 608759). *Location:* one mile south-east of Ilkley town centre along Ben Rhydding Road. Parkland course with fine panoramic views over Wharfedale and surrounding moors. 9 holes, 4711 yards (18 holes). S.S.S. 64. *Green Fees:* weekdays £10.00 per round/day; Bank Holiday Mondays £15.00. *Visitors:* welcome weekdays and Bank Holidays; as members' guests only at weekends. Secretary: J.D.B. Watts (01374 246249).

ILKLEY. **Ilkley Golf Club,** Nessfield Road, Ilkley (01943 607277). *Location:* 15 miles north of Bradford. Flat course. 18 holes, 6262 yards. S.S.S. 70. *Green Fees:* weekdays £30.00; weekends £35.00. Subject to review. *Eating facilities:* by arrangement. *Visitors:* welcome by arrangement. *Society Meetings:* catered for by arrangement. Professional: J.L. Hammond (01943 607463). Secretary: Arthur K. Hatfield (01943 600214).

KEIGHLEY. **Branshaw Golf Club,** Branshaw Moor, Oakworth, Keighley BD22 7ES (01535 643235). *Location:* one mile from Haworth. Moorland with extensive views. 18 holes, 5858 yards. S.S.S. 69. *Green Fees:* weekdays £15.00 per day; weekends £20.00. Juniors half price. *Eating facilities:* meals and bar snacks served (except Monday). *Visitors:* welcome anytime by prior arrangement with the Professional. *Society Meetings:* catered for weekdays only, contact Professional. Professional: Stephen Bassil (01535 647441). Secretary: Mr D.A. Town (01535 605003).

KEIGHLEY. **Keighley Golf Club,** Howden Park, Utley, Keighley BD20 6DH (01535 603179). *Location:* one mile west of Keighley on A629. Parkland. 18 holes, 6149 yards. S.S.S. 70. *Green Fees:* weekdays £25.00 per day, £21.00 per round; weekends £23.00 per round, £27.00 per day. *Eating facilities:* full catering available. *Visitors:* welcome by prior arrangement. Ladies' day, Tuesday. *Society Meetings:* catered for by arrangement. Professional: Mike Bradley (01535 665370). Secretary: C.L. Hodge (01535 604778).

KEIGHLEY. **Riddlesden Golf Club,** Howden Rough, Riddlesden, Keighley BD20 5QN (01535 602148). *Location:* A650 Keighley-Bradford road, left into Bar Lane, left on Scott Lane, which leads on to Scott Lane West and Elam Wood Road, approximately two miles. Moorland, with spectacular par 3s. 18 holes, 4247 yards. S.S.S. 61. *Green Fees:* weekdays £10.00 (£6.00 with member); weekends £15.00 (£10.00 with member). *Eating facilities:* catering available during bar hours – weekdays 12 noon to 3pm then 7pm onwards, weekends noon onwards. *Visitors:* welcome except between 10am – 2pm Saturdays and until after 2pm Sundays. *Society Meetings:* catered for by prior arrangement. Secretary: Mrs K.M. Brooksbank (01535 607646).

KEIGHLEY. **Silsden Golf Club,** High Brunthwaite, Silsden, Near Keighley BD20 0NH (01535 652998). *Location:* five miles north of Keighley. Undulating downland. 14 holes, 4870 yards. S.S.S. 64. Practice area and putting green. *Green Fees:* £10.00 weekdays; £16.00 weekends. *Eating facilities:* licensed bar, food available. *Visitors:* restrictions at weekends – details from Secretary. *Society Meetings:* by arrangement with Secretary. Secretary: G. Davey (01535 656128).

KNOTTINGLEY. **Ferrybridge "C" P.S. Golf Club,** PO Box 39, Stranglands Lane, Knottingley WF11 8SQ. *Location:* off the A1 at Ferrybridge and quarter of a mile towards Castleford on the B6136. Undulating land within the boundaries of and surrounding the power station. 9 holes, 5211 yards. S.S.S. 66. Practice ground. *Green Fees:* £5.00 weekdays; £6.00 weekends. *Visitors:* welcome when accompanied by a member only because of security restrictions. *Society Meetings:* by special arrangement in parties of not more than 12. Secretary: Mr T.D. Ellis (01977 709847).

LEEDS. **Alwoodley Golf Club,** Wigton Lane, Alwoodley, Leeds LS17 8SA (0113 268 1680). *Location:* five miles north of Leeds on A61 (Leeds to Harrogate). 18 holes, 6686 yards. S.S.S. 72. *Green Fees:* £35.00 weekdays; £45.00 weekends. *Eating facilities:* available. *Visitors:* welcome by arrangement. *Society Meetings:* catered for by arrangement. Professional: J. Green (0113 268 9603). Secretary: R.C.W. Banks.

LEEDS. **Calverley Golf Club,** Woodhall Lane, Pudsey, Leeds LS28 5QY (0113 256 4362). *Location:* Leeds seven miles, Bradford four miles. Parkland. 27 holes: 18 holes – 5527 yards, 9 holes – 2581 yards. S.S.S. 67. *Green Fees:* weekdays 18 holes £12.00, 9 holes £6.00; weekends 18 holes £17.00, 9 holes £6.00. *Eating facilities:* available. *Visitors:* welcome, must book 18 hole course. *Society Meetings:* welcome. Professional: Derek Johnson (0113 256 9244). Secretary: W. Gardner.

LEEDS. **Cookridge Hall Golf Club,** Cookridge Lane, Leeds LS16 7NL (0113 2300641; Fax: 0113 2300640). 18 holes, 6345 yards, 5800 metres. S.S.S. 72. Course due to open 1995 – details not yet available.

LEEDS. **Garforth Golf Club Ltd,** Long Lane, Garforth, Leeds LS25 2DS (0113 286 2021. *Location:* six miles east of Leeds on A63, then turn left on to A642. Flat parkland. 18 holes, 6306 yards. S.S.S. 70. Practice area. *Green Fees:* information not provided. *Eating facilities:* available. *Visitors:* welcome, but not before 9.30am or between 12 noon and 2.30pm or after 4.30pm. Weekend as members' guest only. *Society Meetings:* catered for. Professional: K. Findlater (0113 286 2063). Secretary/Manager: F.A. Readman (0113 286 3308). *

LEEDS. **Gotts Park Municipal Golf Club,** Gotts House, Gotts Park, Armley Ridge Road, Leeds LS12

2QX (0113 231 0492). *Location:* three miles east of city centre off A647 Stanningley Road. Parkland, hilly, hard walking. 18 holes, 4960 yards. S.S.S. 64. Putting green and practice ground, lessons available. *Green Fees:* as set by Municipal Authority. *Eating facilities:* cafeteria, bar facilities evening only. *Visitors:* welcome, tee reserved weekends for members until 11am. Professional: J.F.K. Simpson (0113 263 6600). Secretary: M. Gill (0113 256 2994).

LEEDS. **Headingley Golf Club,** Back Church Lane, Adel, Leeds LS16 8DW (01532 673052). *Location:* leave Leeds/Otley road (A660) at Church Lane, Adel about five miles from city centre. 18 holes, 6298 yards. S.S.S. 70. *Green Fees:* £25.00 per round, £30.00 per day weekdays; £36.00 per round or day weekends and Bank Holidays. *Eating facilities:* full catering except Fridays. *Visitors:* members of other golf clubs welcome, preferably with prior reservation. *Society Meetings:* catered for by arrangement. Professional: Andrew Dyson (01532 675100). Secretary: R.W. Hellawell (01532 679573).

LEEDS. **Horsforth Golf Club Ltd,** Layton Road, Layton Rise, Horsforth, Leeds LS18 5EX (0113 258 6819). *Location:* north-west of Leeds on A65 to Ilkley. 18 holes, 6243 yards. S.S.S. 70. *Green Fees:* £24.00 weekdays, £30.00 weekends and Bank Holidays. *Eating facilities:* full catering (except Monday), order in advance for dinner. *Visitors:* welcome, must be bona fide member of another club. *Society Meetings:* catered for by arrangement with Secretary. Professional: P. Scott (0113 258 5200). Secretary: B. Brown (0113 258 6819).

LEEDS. **Howley Hall Golf Club,** Scotchman Lane, Morley, Leeds (01924 472432). *Location:* turn off the A650 Bradford/Wakefield road at the Halfway House Public House, take the B6123 towards Batley – the course is on the left. Parkland. 18 holes, 6058 yards, 5540 metres. S.S.S. 69. Practice ground. *Green Fees:* weekdays £19.00 per round, £23.00 per day; weekends £26.00. *Eating facilities:* dining room, meals available up to 7pm. *Visitors:* welcome. *Society Meetings:* catered for by reservation. Professional: S.A. Spinks. Secretary: Mrs A. Pepper.

LEEDS. **Leeds Golf Centre,** Wike Ridge Lane, Shadwell, Leeds LS17 9JW (0113 2886000; Fax: 0113 2738128). *Location:* eight miles north of Leeds, in village of Wike. Rolling heathland – built to USGA Spec. Donald Steel design. 18 holes, 6620 yards, S.S.S. 72. 9 hole Par 3 course. 18 bay driving range and golf academy. Membership currently available. *Green Fees:* £12.50. *Eating facilities:* lounge bar and grill. *Visitors:* welcome. *Society Meetings:* welcome weekdays. Professional (Golf Academy): David Leadbetter. Secretary: C. Brockbank.

LEEDS. **Leeds Golf Club,** Cobble Hall, Elmete Lane, Leeds LS8 2LJ (0113 265 8775). *Location:* Leeds ring road to A58, turn left if from east, right if from west, fork right at next roundabout, turn right after 250 yards. 18 holes, 6097 yards. S.S.S. 69. *Green Fees:* £25.00 per day, £19.00 per round weekdays, weekends with member only. *Eating facilities:* full catering, apply in advance. *Visitors:* welcome. *Society Meetings:* catered for. Professional: J. Longster. Secretary: G.W. Backhouse. *

LEEDS. **Middleton Park (Municipal) Golf Club,** Ring Road, Beeston, Middleton, Leeds LS10 4NX (0113 270 0449). *Location:* ring road to Middleton off A653 (Water Tower). Parkland, wooded course. 18 holes, 5036 yards. S.S.S. 66. Practice ground. *Green Fees:* on request – fixed by Leeds County Council. *Visitors:* weekdays, contact the Professional. *Society Meetings:* contact the Professional. Professional: David Bulmer (0113 270 9506). Secretary: Fred Ramsey (0113 253 3993).

LEEDS. **Moor Allerton Golf Club,** Coal Road, Wike, Leeds LS17 9NH (01532 661154; Fax: 01532 371124). *Location:* accessible from A61 at Alwoodley or from Harvester Scarcroft on A58. Undulating parkland, designed by Robert Trent Jones. 18 holes, 6552 yards. S.S.S. 72. 9 holes, 3541 yards. S.S.S. 37. 6 bay driving range, practice field. *Green Fees:* £37.00 per day weekdays; Saturdays only £50.00 per day. Winter rate November to March. Subject to review. *Eating facilities:* bars, full restaurant and snack facilities. *Visitors:* no visitors Sundays; restricted to small parties Saturdays. Crown green bowling, sauna, private room hire for seminars/conferences and dinner parties. *Society Meetings:* can cater for up to 250 for golf and banqueting. Richard Lane (01532 665209). Secretary: Mr S. Mack (01532 661154). Executive Vice-President: J.J. Harris.

LEEDS. **Moortown Golf Club,** Harrogate Road, Alwoodley, Leeds LS17 7DB (01532 681682). *Location:* five miles north of Leeds centre, A61 Leeds to Harrogate road. 18 holes, 6515 yards. S.S.S. 72. Large practice field. *Green Fees:* weekdays £35.00 per round, £40.00 per day, weekends £40.00 per round, £45.00 per day. *Eating facilities:* lunches every day, evening meals Tuesday to Saturday. *Visitors:* welcome weekdays, some tee-off time restrictions. *Society Meetings:* catered for. Professional: B. Hutchinson (01532 683636). Secretary: T. Hughes (01532 686521).

LEEDS. **Rawdon Golf and Lawn Tennis Club,** Buckstone Drive, Micklefield Lane, Rawdon, Leeds LS19 6BD (0113 250 6040). *Location:* eight miles north of Leeds on A65, left at Rawdon traffic lights on to Micklefield Lane. Undulating parkland, with trees a special feature. 9 holes (18 tees), 5964 yards. S.S.S. 69. *Green Fees:* weekdays £16.00; £11.00 weekends with a member only. *Eating facilities:* meals and bar snacks except Mondays. *Visitors:* welcome, weekends must play with a member. Facilities for tennis, visitors welcome with members. *Society Meetings:* catered for on application to Secretary. Professional: Syd Weldon (of Bradford Golf Club) (0113 250 5017). Secretary: Ray Adams (0113 250 6064).

LEEDS. **Roundhay Golf Club,** Park Lane, Leeds LS8 3QW (01532 662695). *Location:* four miles north of Leeds city centre, leave A58 to Wetherby at Oakwood. Wooded parkland. 9 holes, 5322 yards. S.S.S. 65. Practice ground. *Green Fees:* weekdays £6.80; weekends and Bank Holidays £7.40. *Eating facilities:* bar for members and guests, restaurant in evenings. *Visitors:* welcome without reservation. *Society Meetings:* arrangements to be made with Leeds City Council. Professional: J. Pape (01532 661686). Hon. Secretary: R.H. McLauchlan (01532 492523).

LEEDS. **Sand Moor Golf Club,** Alwoodley Lane, Leeds LS17 7DJ (0113 2681685). *Location:* five miles north of Leeds off A61. Moorland, overlooking picturesque Wharfedale. 18 holes, 6429 yards, 5876 metres. S.S.S. 71. *Green Fees:* weekdays £28.00 per round, £35.00 per day; weekends £35.00 per round. *Eating facilities:* lunches daily, evening meals Tuesday to Friday. *Visitors:* welcome most weekdays by arrangement. *Society Meetings:* catered for. Professional: L.P. Tupling (0113 2683925). Secretary: B.F. Precious (0113 2685180).

LEEDS. **Scarcroft Golf Club,** Syke Lane, Leeds LS14 3BQ (01532 892263). *Location:* A58 Wetherby road; turn left at New Inn, Scarcroft village seven miles north of Leeds. Undulating parkland. 18 holes, 6426 yards. S.S.S. 71. Practice ground and indoor net. *Green Fees:* £25.00 per round, £30.00 per day weekdays; £35.00 per round weekends. *Eating facilities:* bar and restaurant except Mondays. *Visitors:* casuals after 9.30am. *Society Meetings:* accepted Tuesdays to Fridays April to October. Must have official Handicaps. Party rates for groups of 20 or more. Professional: Martin R. Ross (01532 892780). Secretary: R.D. Barwell (01532 892311).

LEEDS. **South Leeds Golf Club,** Parkside Links, Gipsy Lane, Leeds LS11 5TU (0113 270 0479). *Location:* M62 and M1 within five minutes' drive, Leeds City Centre 5 minutes' drive. Parkland course with undulating fairways. 18 holes, 5769 yards. S.S.S. 69. Practice ground and net. *Green Fees:* £18.00 weekdays; £26.00 weekends and Bank Holidays (rates may change). *Eating facilities:* full catering except Mondays; bar. *Visitors:* welcome weekdays. *Society Meetings:* catered for by prior arrangement. Professional: Mr Mike Lewis (0113 270 0598). Secretary: Mr John Neal (0113 277 1676).

LEEDS. **Temple Newsam Golf Club,** Temple Newsam, Leeds 15 (0113 264 5624). *Location:* easily reached by public transport from City (to Temple Newsam or Halton). Two 18 hole courses. No. 1 Course 6448 yards. S.S.S. 71. No. 2 Course 5731 yards. S.S.S. 70. *Green Fees:* as decided by City Council. *Eating facilities:* cafe open Saturdays and Sundays 7.30am till 4.00pm. *Visitors:* welcome without reservation, except that parties must book in advance. *Society Meetings:* catered for. Professional: David Bulmer (0113 264 1464). Secretary: G. Gower.

MELTHAM. **Meltham Golf Club,** Thick Hollins Hall, Meltham, Huddersfield HD7 3DQ (01484 850227). *Location:* half mile east of Meltham, six miles south west of Huddersfield (B6107). Gently sloping course in wooded valley. 18 holes, 6202 yards, 5673 metres. S.S.S. 70. Restricted practice area. *Green Fees:* weekdays £20.00; weekends £25.00. *Eating facilities:* lunches, dinners (with reservation). *Visitors:* welcome weekdays and Sundays without reservation, not Saturdays. *Society Meetings:* catered for by arrangement. Professional: P. Davies (01484 851521). Secretary: J. Holdsworth.

MIRFIELD. **Dewsbury District Golf Club,** The Pinnacle, Sands Lane, Mirfield WF14 8HJ (01924 491928). *Location:* turn off A644 opposite Swan Inn, two miles west of Dewsbury. Undulating moorland/parkland with panoramic views over surrounding countryside. 18 holes, 6267 yards. S.S.S. 71. Practice field, putting green. *Green Fees:* weekdays £16.00 per round, £20.00 per day; weekends £18.00 after 4pm. *Eating facilities:* bar and restaurant (catering every day except Mondays). *Visitors:* welcome without reservation weekdays, weekends with member only before 4pm. *Society Meetings:* welcome by prior arrangement. Parties over 12 – day package £28.00 per person including meals. Professional: N.P. Hirst (01924 496030). Secretary: C.B. Rhodes (01924 492399).

NORMANTON. **Normanton Golf Club,** Snydale Road, Normanton WF6 1PA (01924 892943). *Location:* Junction 30 M62, A655 towards Wakefield, left at lights, half a mile on left. Flat course with internal out of bounds. 9 holes, 5823 yards. S.S.S. 66. Large practice area. *Green Fees:* weekdays £10.00, £6.00 with a member; Saturday and Bank Holidays £17.50, £10.00 with a member. No green fees Sundays. *Eating facilities:* full catering and bar facilities. *Visitors:* welcome, no visitors on Sundays. *Society Meetings:* catered for weekdays only. Professional: Martin Evans (01924 220134). Secretary: Jack McElhinney (01977 702273).

OTLEY. **Otley Golf Club,** West Busk Lane, Otley LS21 3NG (01943 461015). *Location:* off main Bradford to Otley road. Parkland with magnificent views across Wharfedale. 18 holes, 6229 yards. S.S.S. 70. Good practice ground. *Green Fees:* weekdays £23.00; weekends £28.00. *Eating facilities:* large dining rooms. *Visitors:* welcome without reservation except Tuesday mornings and Saturdays. *Society Meetings:* catered for by arrangement. Professional: Simon Poot (01943 463403). Secretary/Manager: Mrs Pat Bates (01943 465329).

OUTLANE. **Outlane Golf Club,** Slack Lane, off New Hey Road, Outlane, Near Huddersfield HD3 3YL (01422 374762). *Location:* from Huddersfield (A640) through Outlane Village, entrance on left just after bus terminus. Semi moorland course, part wooded. Offers panoramic views and is challenge to the amateur. 18 holes, 6003 yards. S.S.S. 69. Practice areas and nets available. *Green Fees:* £18.00 mid week; £30.00 weekends and Bank Holidays. Reduced rates playing with member and after 3pm Sunday. *Eating facilities:* full catering available except Mondays. *Visitors:* welcome except Saturdays; Sundays by arrangement. *Society Meetings:* welcome with reservation. Professional: D. Chapman. Secretary: J.S. Donnelly.

PONTEFRACT. **Pontefract and District Golf Club,** Park Lane, Pontefract WF8 4QS (01977 792241). *Location:* M62 Exit 32, one mile from Pontefract on B6134. Parkland. 18 holes, 6227 yards. S.S.S. 70. Practice ground. *Green Fees:* weekdays £25.00; weekends £32.00. *Eating facilities:* available except Mondays. *Visitors:* welcome, must be members of a golf club. *Society Meetings:* catered for Tuesdays, Thursdays and Fridays by arrangement. Professional: Nick J. Newman (01977 706806). Secretary: W.T. Smith (01977 792115).

PUDSEY. **Fulneck Golf Club Ltd,** Fulneck, Pudsey LS28 8NT (01532 565191). *Location:* between Leeds and Bradford. Undulating wooded parkland course. 9 holes, 5564 yards. S.S.S. 67. *Green Fees:* £12.00 (£6.00 with member) weekdays, weekends with a member only. *Society Meetings:* catered for by arrangement. Secretary: J.A. Brogden (01532 574049).

PUDSEY. **Woodhall Hills Golf Club Ltd,** Woodhall Road, Calverley, Pudsey (01532 564771). *Location:* one mile from Pudsey roundabout on A647 Leeds to Bradford road, signposted Calverley. 18 holes, 6102 yards. S.S.S. 69. *Green Fees:* weekdays £20.50 per round/day, weekends and Bank Holidays £25.50. Juniors £10.50 any day. *Eating facilities:* available daily except Mondays. *Visitors:* welcome without reservation. *Society Meetings:* catered for by previous arrangement. Professional: D. Tear (01532 562857). Secretary: D. Harkness (01532 554594).

SHIPLEY. **Baildon Golf Club,** Moorgate, Baildon, Shipley BD17 6ES (01274 582428). *Location:* five miles north-west of Bradford via Shipley. Hilly, moorland course. 18 holes, 6225 yards. S.S.S. 70. *Green Fees:* weekdays £16.00, weekends and Bank Holidays £20.00. Reduced rates for groups of 12 and over. *Eating facilities:* catering except Mondays. Bar and separate dining room. *Visitors:* welcome, restricted at weekends and Tuesdays. *Society Meetings:* welcome weekdays only, by written application. Professional: R. Masters (01274 595162). Secretary: E. Northard.

TODMORDEN. **Todmorden Golf Club,** Rive Rocks, Cross Stone Road, Todmorden (01706 812986). *Location:* A646 Halifax Road, one mile left Cross Stone Road, one mile, bear left at top. Moorland. 9 holes, 5818 yards. S.S.S. 68. *Green Fees:* weekdays £15.00; weekends and Bank Holidays £20.00. Packages for parties of four or more. *Eating facilities:* available, order in advance. *Visitors:* welcome without reservation. *Society Meetings:* catered for Monday to Friday by prior arrangement. Secretary: P.H. Eastwood.

WAKEFIELD. **City of Wakefield Golf Club,** Lupset Park, Horbury Road, Wakefield WF2 8QS (01924 367442). *Location:* one mile from city centre, two miles from M1 Junctions 39/40. Undulating partially wooded parkland. 18 holes, 6299 yards, 5760 metres. S.S.S. 70/71. *Green Fees:* on application. *Eating facilities:* full or snack catering, bar available, except Thursdays. *Visitors:* weekdays ball chute operates, weekends – booked times only. *Society Meetings:* only by arrangement with Stewardess (01924 367242). Professional: Roger Holland (01924 360282). Secretary: Mrs P. Ambler (01924 367442 club or 01924 375008 home).

WAKEFIELD. **Low Laithes Golf Club Ltd,** Parkmill Lane, Flushdyke, Ossett, Wakefield WF5 9AP (01924 273275). *Location:* one mile from Junction 40 M1, or along A638 Dewsbury to Wakefield road. Parkland, undulating. 18 holes, 6456 yards. S.S.S. 71. Practice area. *Green Fees:* £22.00 weekdays. *Eating facilities:* bar and catering. *Visitors:* welcome weekdays after 9.30am, no visitors weekends and Bank Holidays. *Society Meetings:* by arrangement, not weekends or Bank Holidays. Professional: Paul Browning (01924 274667). Secretary: Donald Wilford (Tel & Fax: 01924 378363).

WAKEFIELD. **Painthorpe House Golf and Country Club,** Painthorpe Lane, Crigglestone, Wakefield WF4 3HE (01924 255083). *Location:* half a mile from Junction 39 M1. Undulating parkland. 9 holes, 4520 yards. S.S.S. 62. *Green Fees:* weekdays £6.00; Saturdays £10.00. *Eating facilities:* extensive catering for private functions. Two ballrooms (one holding 450, the other 60), Saturday dinner dances. *Visitors:* welcome weekdays. Bowling green. *Society Meetings:* by arrangement. Secretary: H. Kershaw (01924 274527).

WAKEFIELD. **Wakefield Golf Club,** Woodthorpe Lane, Sandal, Wakefield WF2 6JH (01924 255380). *Location:* leave M1 at Junction 39, golf club off Barnsley Road. Parkland. 18 holes, 6611 yards. S.S.S. 72. *Green Fees:* weekdays £20.00 per round, £25.00 per day, with a member £12.00; weekends and Bank Holidays £27.00, with a member £13.00. *Eating facilities:* full catering available. *Visitors:* visiting parties by arrangement Wednesdays, Thursdays and Fridays. *Society Meetings:* welcome, catered for by arrangement. Professional: I.M. Wright (01924 255380). Secretary: Mr R.E. Guiver (01924 258778).

WETHERBY. **Wetherby Golf Club,** Linton Lane, Linton, Wetherby LS22 4JF (01937 582527). *Location:* three quarters of a mile west from A1 roundabout. Parkland course adjoining River Wharfe. 18 holes, 6235 yards. S.S.S. 70. Two practice grounds. *Green Fees:* weekdays £23.00 per round, £28.00 per day; weekends £34.00 per round/day. *Eating facilities:* available seven days a week. *Visitors:* welcome, advisable to phone first. *Society Meetings:* catered for weekdays except Tuesdays. Professional: D. Padgett (01937 583375). Secretary/Manager: J.R. Nicholson (01937 580089).

Golf in Scotland

WHERE TO PLAY • WHERE TO STAY

Golf in Scotland is special! Scotland is the home of golf and offers the golfer unrivalled opportunities not least because so many great championship courses are open for play to the average club golfer. A directory of clubs and courses in Scotland therefore includes the oldest golfing societies, clubs and courses in the world as well as new developments which keep the game up-to-date. It also includes such world-famous courses as the Old Course St. Andrews, Turnberry, Carnoustie and Muirfield.

Scotland is, of course, also fortunate in its scenery and much of golf in Scotland is played on scenic courses – whether links or inland. Golfing hotels are well-established and in popular golfing centres such as Fife, the Edinburgh area, Perthshire and Ayrshire, there is a wide choice of accommodation. Indeed throughout Scotland, golfing guests and their families are generally welcome.

Where an asterisk (*) follows an entry, details have not been confirmed by the club for 1995.

Aberdeenshire

ABERDEEN. **Auchmill Golf Course,** City of Aberdeen District Council, Arts and Recreation Division, St. Nicholas House, Broad Street, Aberdeen AB9 1XJ (01224 276276). *Location:* approximately four miles from city centre, turn off A96 into Aberdeen at Howes Road. Open, fairly flat. 18 holes, 5082 metres. *Green Fees:* £6.10 adult per round, £3.05 Junior per round. *Visitors:* welcome. Starter: (01224 714577).

ABERDEEN. **Balnagask Golf Course,** City of Aberdeen District Council, Arts and Recreation Division, St. Nicholas House, Broad Street, Aberdeen AB9 1XJ (01224 276276). *Location:* on coast beside Girdleness Lighthouse between Aberdeen Harbour and Nigg Bay, south east side of city. Seaside links. 18 holes, 5472 metres. *Green Fees:* £6.10 adult, £3.05 Juniors. *Visitors:* welcome. Starter: (01224 876407).

ABERDEEN. **Bon Accord Municipal Golf Club,** 19 Golf Road, Aberdeen (01224 633464). *Location:* next to Pittodrie Stadium at Aberdeen beach. Seaside links. 18 holes, 6433 yards, 5880 metres. S.S.S. 70. *Green Fees:* information not provided. *Eating facilities:* meals on request. *Society Meetings:* bookings in advance. Secretary: J.B. Miller (01224 879204).

ABERDEEN. **Caledonian Golf Club,** Kings Links, Aberdeen (01224 632443). 18 holes, 6396 yards. S.S.S. 71. *Green Fees:* information not provided. *Visitors:* welcome. *

ABERDEEN. **Deeside Golf Club,** Golf Road, Bieldside, Aberdeen (01224 867697). *Location:* A93 from Aberdeen to Braemar. Wooded parkland. 18 holes, 5971 yards. S.S.S. 69. Also 9 hole course. Practice area. *Green Fees:* £20.00 per day weekdays; £25.00 weekends and Public Holidays. Weekly tickets available. *Eating facilities:* full meal service and bar. *Visitors:* welcome all week including Sundays, Saturdays after 4pm. *Society Meetings:* by arrangement, Thursdays only. Professional: F.G. Coutts (01224 861041). Secretary: A.G. MacDonald (01224 869457).

ABERDEEN. **Hazlehead Golf Course,** City of Aberdeen District Council, Arts and Recreation Division, St. Nicholas House, Broad Street, Aberdeen AB9 1XJ (01224 276276). *Location:* situated on west edge of city, four miles from city centre. From A944 into Aberdeen turn off into Groats Road. Two courses – 18 holes, 5673 metres; 18 holes, 5303 metres. 9 hole course, 2531 metres. *Green Fees:* 18 holes £6.10 adult, £3.05 Junior; 9 holes £3.05 adult, £1.55 Junior. *Eating facilities:* restaurant adjoining park. *Visitors:* welcome. Professional: Mr I. Smith (01224 317336). Starter: (01224 321830).

ABERDEEN. **King's Links Golf Course,** City of Aberdeen District Council, Arts and Recreation Division, St. Nicholas House, Broad Street, Aberdeen AB9 1XJ (01224 276276). *Location:* beach front course near Bridge of Don. Open plan, near Pittodrie Stadium. 18 holes, 5731 metres. 6 hole course, 1251 metres; driving range next door. *Green Fees:* 18 holes £6.10 adult, £3.05 Junior; 9 holes £2.00 adult, £1.00 Junior. *Eating facilities:* four pubs all doing bar lunches etc nearby. *Visitors:* some bookings for after 4pm, must be done day before in person except Wednesday, Saturday and Sunday. *Society Meetings:* all welcome by writing to Aberdeen District Council (14 days notice). Professional: Mr R. McDonald (01224 641577). Starter: (01224 632269).

ABERDEEN. **Murcar Golf Club,** Murcar, Bridge of Don, Aberdeen AB23 8BD (01224 704345). *Location:* off A92 approximately five miles from Aberdeen centre. Seaside links. White Markers – 18 holes, 6241 yards. S.S.S. 70; Yellow Markers – 18 holes, 5809 yards. S.S.S 68. *Green Fees:* weekdays £16.00 per round, £20.00 per day; weekends £22.50 after 4pm Saturdays, after 12 noon Sundays. *Eating facilities:*

See our colour advertisement on page 26.

diningroom/bars. *Visitors:* welcome, restrictions Wednesdays and weekends. *Society Meetings:* catered for. Professional: A. White (Tel & Fax: 01224 704370). Secretary: R. Matthews (01224 704354).

ABERDEEN. **Nigg Bay Golf Club,** St. Fitticks Road, Torry, Aberdeen (01224 871286). *Location:* Junction of Victoria Road and St. Fitticks Road. Seaside links. 18 holes, 5986 yards, 5472 metres. S.S.S. 69. 9 hole pitch and putt. *Green Fees:* £6.00. *Eating facilities:* private club. *Visitors:* welcome anytime (Municipal course); golfers welcome in clubhouse after playing. Secretary: Arthur Taylor. *

ABERDEEN. **Northern Golf Club,** 22 Golf Road, Aberdeen AB2 1QB (01224 636440).*Location:* Adjacent to Beach Esplanade near Pittodrie Stadium. Kings Links course, 18 holes, 6347 yards, S.S.S.71. *Green Fees:* £6 per round. *Eating facilities:* not Tuesdays and Thursdays. *Visitors:* welcome Monday to Friday. *Society Meetings:* by prior arrangement only. Secretary: F. Sutherland. Steward: (01224 632443). *

ABERDEEN. **Royal Aberdeen Golf Club,** Links Road, Balgownie, Bridge of Don AB23 8AT (01224 702571; Fax: 01224 826591). *Location:* on A92, north side of Aberdeen, cross Bridge of Don, second right. Seaside links. Two Courses – Championship (Balgownie): 18 holes, 6372 yards, 5828 metres. S.S.S. 71; Silverburn: 18 holes, 4033 yards, 3717 metres. S.S.S. 60. Practice area. *Green Fees:* weekdays £35.00 per round, £45.00 per day; weekends and Public Holidays after 3.30pm only £45.00 per round. (Silverburn course green fees are half those quoted for Balgownie). *Eating facilities:* two bars and full catering. *Visitors:* welcome weekdays 9.30am to 12 noon and 2pm to 4pm, weekends after 3.30pm. Letter of introduction and Handicap Certificate required. *Society Meetings:* welcome. Professional: R.A. MacAskill (01224 702221). Secretary: Mrs Sandra Nicolson (01224 702571; Fax: 01224 826591).

ABERDEEN. **Tarland Golf Club,** Aberdeen Road, Tarland, Aboyne (013398 81413). *Location:* from Aberdeen – A944 then A974. Parkland/wooded, easy walking, difficult upland course. 9 holes, 5816 yards for 18 holes, S.S.S. 68. Small practice area. *Green Fees:* on application. Weekly and fortnightly tickets available. *Eating facilities:* catering available, bar 11am to midnight. *Visitors:* welcome without reservation, phone call advisable due to club competitions. *Society Meetings:* catered for except weekends. Secretary: Mr J.H. Honeyman.

ABOYNE. **Aboyne Golf Club,** Formaston Park, Aboyne (013398 86328). *Location:* A93, 30 miles west of Aberdeen. Part parkland, part hilly with lovely views. 18 holes, 5910 yards. S.S.S. 68. Practice ground. *Green Fees:* weekdays £14.00 per round, £18.00 per day; weekends £21.00 per day. *Eating facilities:* full restaurant and bar facilities. *Visitors:* welcome without reservation. *Society Meetings:* by arrangement with Secretary. Professional: Innes Wright (013398 86328). Secretary: Mrs M. MacLean (013398 87078).

ALFORD. **Alford Golf Club,** Montgarrie Road, Alford AB33 8AE (019755 62178). *Location:* A944, 26 miles west of Aberdeen. Flat, parkland course. 18 holes, 5290 yards. S.S.S. 66, ladies 70. Practice area. *Green Fees:* £8.00 per round, £12.00 per day weekdays; £14.00 per round, £18.00 per day weekends. *Eating facilities:* snacks available, meals to order, bar. *Visitors:* always welcome; call club to book tee, weekends very busy. Changing rooms, showers. *Society Meetings:* catered for by arrangement. Secretary: Mrs M.J. Ball (019755 62843).

BALLATER. **Ballater Golf Club,** Victoria Road, Ballater AB35 5QX (013397 55200). *Location:* Aberdeen 42 miles east, Perth 62 miles south. Flat parkland course. 18 holes, 5638 yards. S.S.S. 69. Practice ground, putting. *Green Fees:* £16.00 per round, £24.00 per day weekdays; £19.20 per round, £28.80 per day weekends. Half rates for players aged under 18. *Eating facilities:* dining room April to October; bar lounge. *Visitors:* welcome, book through Pro's shop. *Society Meetings:* all welcome, book well in advance. Professional: Joe Blair (013397 55658). Secretary: Bert Ingram (Tel & Fax: 013397 55567).

BRAEMAR. **Braemar Golf Club,** Cluniebank Road, Braemar AB35 5XX (013397 41618). *Location:* about one mile from centre of the village, signposted opposite Fife Arms Hotel. Flat parkland, highest 18 hole course on mainland Great Britain, course split in two by River Clunie. 18 holes, 5011 yards. S.S.S. 64. Practice ground. Small practice area. *Green Fees:* weekdays £10.00 per round, £14.00 per day; weekends £13.00 per round, £17.00 per day. Weekly ticket £50.00. *Eating facilities:* meals served until 7pm, bar open 11am to midnight. *Visitors:* no restrictions, best phone day in advance for weekends. *Society Meetings:* welcome by booking through Secretary. Secretary: John Pennet (01224 704471).

ELLON. **McDonald Golf Club,** Hospital Road, Ellon AB41 9AW (01358 20576). *Location:* A92 from Aberdeen to Ellon. One mile down A948, on left. Flat parkland with trees and stream. 18 holes, 5986 yards. S.S.S. 69. Putting green and practice nets. *Green Fees:* on application. *Eating facilities:* full catering and bar facilities all week. *Visitors:* welcome at all times weekdays, after 10am and booking advisable at weekends. *Society Meetings:* must book in advance. Professional: Ronnie Urquhart (0358 22891). Secretary: George Ironside (01358 720576).

ELLON. **Newburgh-on-Ythan Golf Club,** c/o Andrew C. Stevenson, 51 Mavis Bank, Newburgh, Ellon, Aberdeen AB4 0FB (013586 89438). *Location:* 12 miles north of Aberdeen. Seaside links course. 9 holes, 6300 yards, 5758 metres. S.S.S. 70. *Green Fees:* weekdays £10.00; weekends £12.00. Reduction of £2 for Senior Citizens. *Eating facilities:* at local hotels. *Visitors:* welcome, but tee reserved Tuesday evenings (Club competitions), Monday evenings (Juniors have priority) and Wednesday evenings (Ladies have priority). *Society Meetings:* by arrangement. Secretary: Andrew C. Stevenson. *

FRASERBURGH. **Fraserburgh Golf Club,** Corbie Hill, Fraserburgh (01346 518287). *Location:* turn right at roundabout on entry to town from Aberdeen then first right. Seaside links. 18 holes, 6279 yards. S.S.S. 70. Practice area. *Green Fees:* weekdays £12.00; weekends £16.00. Weekly £48; fortnightly £84. *Eating facilities:* full catering provided Tuesday to Sunday, bar open seven days. *Visitors:* welcome, some restrictions weekends. *Society Meetings:* welcome, book in advance. Secretary: A.J. Bolt (01346 518413).

HUNTLY. **Huntly Golf Club,** Cooper Park, Huntly AB54 4SH (01466 792643). *Location:* north side of Huntly, 38 miles from Aberdeen on A96. Open parkland course between Rivers Deveron and Bogie. 18 holes, 5399 yards. S.S.S. 66. Practice area. *Green Fees:* weekdays £12.00 day ticket; weekends £18.00. Weekly ticket £60.00. *Eating facilities:* full catering by arrangement, lounge bar. *Visitors:* welcome, no restriction except Wednesday and Thursday evenings. *Society Meetings:* by arrangement with Secretary, maximum of 40. Secretary: Gordon Alexander (01466 792877).

INSCH. **Insch Golf Club,** Golf Terrace, Insch (01464 20363). *Location:* A96 from Aberdeen. Parkland – trees, water hazards. 9 holes, 5632 yards. S.S.S. 67. *Green Fees:* £8.00 per day weekdays; £10.00 weekends. *Eating facilities:* available. *Visitors:* welcome except Mondays from 4.30pm, Tuesdays from 5pm and Wednesdays from 4.30pm. *Society Meetings:* welcome. Secretary: James G. McCombie (01464 20291).

INVERALLOCHY. **Inverallochy Golf Club,** Inverallochy, Fraserburgh (01346 582000). *Location:* three miles south of Fraserburgh. Seaside links course. 18 holes, 5137 yards. S.S.S. 65. *Green Fees:* weekdays £10.00; weekends £10.00. *Eating facilities:* limited, unlicensed, advance booking required. *Visitors:* welcome. *Society Meetings:* catered for on limited basis. Secretary: R.A. Mutch.

INVERURIE. **Inverurie Golf Club,** Davah Wood, Blackhall Road, Inverurie (01467 620207; Fax: 01467 621051). *Location:* main Aberdeen/Inverness trunk road, 16 miles west of Aberdeen. Parkland, partly wooded course. 18 holes, 5711 yards. S.S.S. 68. Practice area. *Green Fees:* weekdays £12.00; weekends £18.00. *Eating facilities:* bar lounge, catering. *Visitors:* welcome anytime – reserve through Golf Shop (01467 620193). *Society Meetings:* catered for. Secretary: David L. Taylor (01467 624542).

INVERURIE. **Kintore Golf Club,** Balbithan Road, Kintore, Inverurie AB5 0UR (01467 632631). *Location:* off A96 12 miles north of Aberdeen. Undulating moorland course. 18 holes, 5985 yards. S.S.S. 69. *Green Fees:* weekdays £9.00 per round, £12.00 per day; weekends £12.00 per round, £17.00 per day. Weekly tickets available. *Eating facilities:* bar available, catering if booked in advance. *Visitors:* welcome daily except Mondays, Wednesdays and Fridays after 4pm. *Society Meetings:* welcome weekdays. Secretary: Jim Smith.

KEMNAY. **Kemnay Golf Club,** Monymusk Road, Kemnay (01467 642225). *Location:* from A96 main Aberdeen/Inverness road. Take B994 signposted Kemnay and pass through village of Kemnay to find golf course on left hand side on leaving village. Flat wooded parkland. 18 holes, 5903 yards, 5398 metres. S.S.S. 68. *Green Fees:* weekdays £10.00; weekends £12.00; weekends £15.00 per round, £18.00 per day. *Eating facilities:* bar, catering by prior arrangement. *Visitors:* welcome all week, Sundays if starting times available. *Society Meetings:* weekdays and weekends by arrangement, maximum number 25. Secretary: D. Imrie (01467 643047).

NEWMACHAR. **Newmachar Golf Club,** Swailend, Newmachar AB2 0UU (01651 863002). *Location:* two and a half miles north of Dyce on A947. Championship standard wooded parkland course with ponds being main feature. 18 holes, 6623 yards. S.S.S. 74. 12 bay driving range and large practice area. *Green Fees:* weekdays £16.00 per round; weekends £20.00 per round. *Eating facilities:* fully licensed clubhouse, catering available. *Visitors:* welcome by prior arrangement. Handicap Certificate required. *Society Meetings:* welcome by prior arrangement. Professional: Glenn Taylor (01651 862127). Secretary/ Manager: George McIntosh.

OLDMELDRUM. **Oldmeldrum Golf Club,** Kirk Brae, Oldmeldrum, Inverurie AB51 0DJ (01651 872648). *Location:* 17 miles north-west of Aberdeen on A947 to Banff. First on right entering from Aberdeen direction. Undulating parkland with tree-lined fairways and water features. 18 holes, 5988 yards, 5479 metres. S.S.S. 69. Practice area. *Green Fees:* weekdays £10.00 per day, weekends £15.00. *Eating facilities:* fully licensed bar, full catering. *Visitors:* welcome, advisable to phone first. *Society Meetings:* catered for by arrangement. Secretary: Douglas Petrie (01651 872383).

PETERCULTER. **Peterculter Golf Club,** Oldtown, Burnside Road, Peterculter, Aberdeen AB1 0LN (Tel & Fax: 01224 734994). *Location:* from North Deeside Road (A93). Scenic, undulating parkland. 18 holes, Medal 5924 yards, Forward Tees 5601 yards; S.S.S. Medal 69, Forward Tees 68. Small practice/teaching area. *Green Fees:* weekdays £16.00 per day, £11.00 per round (after 2.30pm); weekends £21.00 per day, £15.00 per round (after 4.30pm). *Eating facilities:* dining room. *Visitors:* welcome except weekdays 4pm to 6pm. *Society Meetings:* welcome Tuesdays to Fridays. Not Public/local holidays. Professional: Dean Vannet. Secretary: Robert C. Burnett.

PETERHEAD. **Cruden Bay Golf Club,** Aulton Road, Cruden Bay, Peterhead AB42 7NN (01779 812285; Fax: 01779 812945). *Location:* seven miles south of Peterhead, 23 miles north east of Aberdeen. Traditional seaside links with magnificent views near Bay of Cruden. 18 holes, 6370 yards, 5859 metres. S.S.S. 71; 9 holes, 4710 yards. S.S.S. 62. Practice range. *Green Fees:* weekdays £22.00; weekends £30.00. *Eating facilities:* full bar and catering facilities. *Visitors:* welcome but restricted at weekends, telephone for details. *Society Meetings:* welcome weekdays only. Professional/Administrator: Robbie Stewart (01779 812414).

PETERHEAD. **Peterhead Golf Club,** Craigewan Links, Peterhead AB42 6LT (01779 472149). *Location:* off Golf Road at north end of town at mouth of River Ugie. Seaside links. Old Course – 18 holes, 6189 yards. S.S.S. 70; New Course – 9 holes, 2237 yards. S.S.S. 62. Small practice area. *Green Fees:* £14.00 weekdays; £18.00 weekends. *Eating facilities:* snacks available, meals by arrangement, lounge bar. *Visitors:* welcome anytime, no restrictions, except on a Saturday. *Society Meetings:* catered for anytime except Saturdays, prior booking necessary. Handicap Certificate may be asked for. Secretary: W. Bradford.

PORTLETHEN. **Portlethen Golf Club,** Badentoy Road, Portlethen, Aberdeen AB1 4YA (01224 782575). *Location:* five miles south of Aberdeen on main Stonehaven Road. Rolling parkland. 18 holes, 6707 yards. S.S.S. 72. Large practice area. *Green Fees:* weekdays £10.00 per round, £18 per day; weekends £18 per round. *Eating facilities:* bar and restaurant. *Visitors:* welcome, no visitors Saturdays, Sundays also difficult in summer. *Society Meetings:* welcome weekdays and some Sundays, by arrangement. Professional: Muriel Thomson (01224 782571). Secretary: David Black (01224 781090).

ROSEHEARTY. **Rosehearty Golf Club,** C/o Secretary, 24 Brucklay Street, Rosehearty AB43 4JN. *Location:* south of Rosehearty on Fraserburgh Road. Seaside links. 9 holes, 3368 yards. Par 58 (18 holes). *Green Fees:* weekdays £6.00; weekends £10.00. Annual fees £60 plus £10 joining fee (subject to review). *Eating facilities:* Masons Arms adjacent to course. *Visitors:* always welcome. *Society Meetings:* welcome with prior arrangement. Secretary: T. Keith Bruce (01346 571645).

TORPHINS. **Torphins Golf Club,** Bog Road, Torphins, Banchory AB31 4JU (013398 82115). *Location:* through village towards Lumphanan, club signposted to right. Parkland with lovely views to Highlands. 9 holes, 4684 yards (18 holes). S.S.S. 64. *Green Fees:* £10.00 weekdays; £12.00 weekends. Juniors half price, after 6.30pm £6.00. *Eating facilities:* light refreshments, unlicensed. *Visitors:* no play on medal days (alternate Saturdays or Sundays); members only Tuesday evenings. *Society Meetings:* welcome except weekends. Secretary: Mrs Sue Mortimer (013398 82563).

TURRIFF. **Turriff Golf Club,** Rosehall, Turriff AB53 7HB (01888 62745). *Location:* A947 signposted on south side of Turriff. Wooded parkland course. 18 holes, 5877 yards. S.S.S. 69. Small practice area, small putting green. *Green Fees:* weekdays £13.00 per round, £16.00 per day; weekends £17.00 per round, £22.00 per day. *Eating facilities:* catering by arrangement, licensed 11am to 11pm. *Visitors:* no visitors before 10am weekends, slight restrictions Wednesdays. Tee reservation by contacting Professional – during the week up to four days in advance, weekends on day only. *Society Meetings:* by arrangement with Secretary. Professional: Robin Smith (01888 63025). Secretary: James D. Stott (Tel & Fax: 01888 62982).

WESTHILL. **Westhill Golf Club,** Westhill Heights, Westhill, Skene (01224 743361). *Location:* six miles from Aberdeen on A944. Undulating parkland course (hilly in places). 18 holes, 5921 yards. S.S.S. 69. Practice ground. *Green Fees:* weekdays £12.00 per round, £16.00 per day; Sundays and Public Holidays £15.00 per round, £20.00 per day. Special package Monday-Friday for parties of 20 or more (two rounds and catering) £20.00. Subject to review. *Eating facilities:* lounge bar and dining area. *Visitors:* welcome weekdays except betweem 4pm and 7pm, no visitors on Saturdays. *Society Meetings:* welcome per visitors' times by arrangement. Professional: Ronnie McDonald (01224 740159). Secretary: John L. Webster (01224 740957).

Angus

ARBROATH. **Arbroath Golf Course,** Elliot, By Arbroath (01241 72069). *Location:* one mile south on Dundee to Arbroath Road A92. Seaside links. 18 holes, 6095 yards. S.S.S 69. Practice area, putting green and new sprinkler system. *Green Fees:* weekdays £10.00 per round, £15.00 per day; weekends £16.00 per round, £24.00 per day. *Eating facilities:* full catering and bar facility. *Visitors:* welcome, no visitors before 10am weekends. *Society Meetings:* all welcome (good rates midweek). Professional: L. Ewart (01241 75837). Secretary: Gary Pyott (01241 74946).

ARBROATH near. **Letham Grange Golf Course,** Colliston, By Arbroath DD11 4RL (01241 890373). *Location:* four miles north west of Arbroath on A993. Two courses – Old Course is a blend of tree-lined parkland and open rolling fairways; water plays a major role which makes the course both scenic and dramatic. New Course is slightly shorter and without water hazards, offers golfers a more relaxed and less arduous round; however, it could be deceptive! 36 holes, Old 6968 yards, New 5528 yards. S.S.S. Old 73, New 68. Large practice ground, putting green, chipping green. *Green Fees:* weekdays Old £20.00, New £12.00; weekends £25.00 Old, £15.00 New. Juniors 50% reduction. *Eating facilities:* welcome. Members' times Tuesday both courses 9am-10am, Friday New Course 9am-10am, weekends 8am-9.30am and 12.30pm-2pm. Juniors must be accompanied by an adult on the Old Course. 20 bedroomed Hotel rated 3 star by AA and RAC and 4 Crowns Commended by STB. *Society Meetings:* must book more than 7 days in advance. Professional: Mr David F.C. Scott (Tel & Fax: 01241 890377). Secretary: Miss Pamela A. Ogilvie (01241 890373; Fax: 01241 890414).

BARRY. **Panmure Golf Club,** Burnside Road, Barry, By Carnoustie DD7 7RT (01241 853120). *Location:* two miles west of Carnoustie on A930, signposted from centre of Barry village. Championship links. 18 holes, 6317 yards, 5776 metres. S.S.S. 70. *Green Fees:* £23.00 per round, £35.00 per day. Subject to review. *Eating facilities:* full catering seven days a week. *Visitors:* welcome daily except Saturdays. *Society Meetings:* catered for. Professional: A. Cullen (01241 852460). Secretary: Major (Rtd) Graeme Paton (01241 855120).

Please mention this guide when you write or phone to enquire about accommodation.

BRECHIN. **Brechin Golf and Squash Club,** Trinity, By Brechin DD9 6BJ (01356 622383). *Location:* Trinity Village, one mile north of Brechin on A94. Rolling parkland. 18 holes, 6123 yards. S.S.S. 69. Practice area. *Green Fees:* weekdays £12.00 per round, £17.00 per day; weekends £16.00 per round, £25.00 per day. *Eating facilities:* excellent catering available at all times; large bar. *Visitors:* welcome without reservation. Two squash courts. *Society Meetings:* catered for, but prior booking necessary. Midweek packages for parties of 12 or more. Professional: Steven Rennie (01356 625270). Secretary: A.B. May (01356 622326).

CARNOUSTIE. **Carnoustie Golf Links,** Links Parade, Carnoustie DD7 7JE (01241 853789; Fax: 01241 852720). *Location:* 12 miles east of Dundee. Three 18-hole courses. Championship Course 6936 yards. S.S.S. 74; Burnside Course 6020 yards. S.S.S. 69; Buddon Links 5196 yards. S.S.S. 66. Golf trolleys permitted from May to October only. *Green Fees:* (1994 only) Weekly tickets for play over three courses £144.00. Three-day tickets for play over three courses £108.00. Championship Course: Single round £36.00. Burnside Course: Single round £14.00. Buddon Links Course: Single round £10.00. *Eating facilities:* catering facilities can be arranged with the local golf clubs. *Visitors:* welcome, times must be booked and ballot system in operation. Handicap Certificates required for play on Championship Course. *Society Meetings:* catered for by arrangement. Secretary: Earle J.C. Smith.

DUNDEE. **Caird Park Golf Club,** Mains Loan, Dundee DD4 9BX (01382 453606). *Location:* northern edge of city, off Kingsway. Wooded parkland. 18 holes, 6273 yards, 5740 metres. S.S.S. 70. Practice range on course. *Green Fees:* information not available; telephone Starter 01382 451147. *Eating facilities:* at clubhouse. *Visitors:* welcome, must book in advance to ensure game. *Society Meetings:* see Dundee District Council, Parks Department. Professional: Jackie Black (01382 459438). Secretary: Greg Martin. *

DUNDEE. **Camperdown Golf Club,** Camperdown House, Camperdown Park, Dundee (01382 623398). *Location:* two miles north-west of city, enter at Kingsway/Coupar Angus road junction. Wooded parkland. 18 holes, 6561 yards. S.S.S. 72, Par 71. *Green Fees:* information not provided. *Eating facilities:* (must be ordered beforehand) all year round. *Visitors:* welcome, bookable all week, contact Art and Recreation Division, Leisure Centre, Dundee. *Society Meetings:* by arrangement, catered for once booked by Parks Dept. for date and times. Professional: R. Brown (01382 623398). Secretary: K. McCreery (01382 642925). *

DUNDEE. **Downfield Golf Club,** Turnberry Avenue, Dundee DD2 3QP (01382 825595; Fax: 01382 813111). *Location:* off Coupar Angus road, follow signs "Clatto Country Park". Wooded, parkland course. 18 holes, 6804 yards, 6222 metres. S.S.S. 73. Large practice area. *Green Fees:* weekdays £36.00 per day, £24.00 per round; weekends £24.00 per round (limited). *Eating facilities:* full catering available. *Visitors:* welcome weekdays 9.30am to 11.45am then 2.15pm to 3.30pm. *Society Meetings:* welcome, prebooking essential. Professional: Kenneth Hutton (01382 89246). Secretary: Brian Mole (01382 825595; Fax: 01382 813111).

EDZELL. **Edzell Golf Club,** High Street, Edzell DD9 7TF (01356 648235). *Location:* turn left onto B966 from A94 north of Brechin by-pass on Forfar to Aberdeen road. Undulating heathland course. 18 holes, 6348 yards. S.S.S. 71. Practice area and putting green. *Green Fees:* weekdays £18.00 per round, £27.00 per day; weekends £24.00 per round, £36.00 per day. *Eating facilities:* dining room, lounge and bar. *Visitors:* welcome with some restrictions. *Society Meet-*

ings: welcome with some restrictions, apply to Secretary. Professional: Alistair J. Webster (01356 648462). Secretary: J.M. Hutchison (01356 647283). Caterer: Mr Robert Stubbs.

FORFAR. **Forfar Golf Club,** Cunninghill, Forfar (01307 462120). *Location:* one mile from Forfar on A932 to Arbroath. Undulating wooded heathland course. 18 holes, 6033 metres. S.S.S. 69. *Green Fees:* weekdays £16.00 per round, £20.00 per day; weekends £30.00 per day, £20.00 after 3pm. *Visitors:* welcome. *Society Meetings:* catered for. Professional: Peter McNiven (01307 465683). Secretary: W. Baird (01307 463773).

KIRRIEMUIR. **Kirriemuir Golf Club Ltd,** Northmuir, Kirriemuir DD8 4LN (01575 573317; Fax: 01575 574608). *Location:* on A926 and A928, just on edge of Kirriemuir, north of town centre. Parkland and heathland course, relatively flat. 18 holes, 5591 yards, 5336 metres. S.S.S. 67. Putting green, practice ground. *Green Fees:* weekdays £14.00 per round, £19.00 per day; weekends with member only. *Eating facilities:* restaurant. *Visitors:* welcome weekdays only unless accompanied by a member. *Society Meetings:* weekdays only, numbers restricted to around 40. Professional/Director of Golf: A. Caira (01575 573317; Fax: 01575 574608).

MONIFIETH. **Broughty Golf Club,** 6 Princes Street, Monifieth, Dundee DD5 4AW (01382 532147). Starter (01382 532767). *Location:* eight miles east of Dundee, in village of Monifieth. Seaside links, some fairways fringed with trees. Medal Course: 18 holes, 6657 yards, 6087 metres. S.S.S. 72. Ashludie Course: 18 holes, 5123 yards. S.S.S. 66. Practice area. *Green Fees:* on request. *Eating facilities:* full catering; no catering Tuesdays or Thursdays. *Visitors:* no visitors before 2pm on Saturdays or before 10am Sundays. All tee times must be booked through Starters Box. *Society Meetings:* by arrangement. Professional: Mr I. McLeod. Secretary: Mr S.D.J. French.

MONIFIETH. **Monifieth Golf Links,** Princes Street, Monifieth, Dundee DD5 4AW (01382 532767). *Location:* seven miles east of Dundee, Monifieth High Street. Seaside links. Medal Course 18 holes, 6657 yards. S.S.S. 72; Ashludie Course 18 holes, 5123 yards. S.S.S. 64. *Green Fees:* Medal Course £22.00 per round, £32.00 per day; Ashludie Course £14.00 per round, £20.00 per day – Mondays to Fridays; Medal Course £24.00 per round, £36.00 per day Saturdays/Sundays. Ashludie Course £15.00 per round, £22.00 per day Saturdays/Sundays. Composite ticket available, one round on each course – weekdays £24.00, weekends £28.00. *Eating facilities:* clubs and Hotel. *Visitors:* welcome Monday to Friday at any time except before 9.30am; Saturdays after 2pm; Sundays after 10am. *Society Meetings:* parties over 12, must provide club Handicap Certificates. Professional: Ian McLeod (01382 532945). Secretary: H.R. Nicoll (01382 535553).

MONTROSE. **Montrose Links Trust,** Traill Drive, Montrose DD10 8SW (01674 672932). *Location:* A92 runs from Dundee to Aberdeen, through Montrose. Links Medal Course 6443 yards. Par 71. S.S.S. 71. Broomfield Course 4815 yards. Par 66. S.S.S. 63. *Green Fees:* 1994/1995. Medal: weekdays £24.00 per day, £14.00 per round, Juniors £7.00 per round; weekends £33.00 per day, £21.00 per round, Juniors £10.00 per round; weekly tickets £76.00 adult, £38.00 Juniors. Broomfield: weekdays £13.00 per day, £9.00 per round, Juniors £3.00 per round; weekends £20.00 per day, £13.00 per round, Juniors £5.00 per round; weekly ticket £50.00 adult, £25.00 Junior. "Special Deal" to parties for two rounds plus catering, details on request. *Eating facilities:* catering facilities available by arrangement in golf clubs. *Visitors:* welcome, except on Medal Course Saturdays and before 10am Sundays. *Society Meetings:* welcome by arrangement. Temporary membership available at the following clubs: Caledonia Golf Club (01674 672313); Mercantile Golf Club (01674 672408); Royal Montrose (01674 672376). Professional: Kevin Stables. Secretary: Mrs Margaret Stewart (01674 672932; Fax: 01674 671800).

MONTROSE. **Royal Montrose Golf Club,** Dornard Road, Montrose DD10 8SW (01674 72376). *Location:* A92 north from Dundee. Private club playing over the Montrose courses. 18 holes, 6442 yards. S.S.S. 71. *Green Fees:* information not provided. *Eating facilities:* available. *Visitors:* apply Montrose Links Trust. *Society Meetings:* apply Montrose Links Trust. Hon. Secretary: J D. Sykes (01674 73956). *

Argyll

CAMPBELTOWN. **Machrihanish Golf Club,** Machrihanish, by Campbeltown PA28 6PT (01586 810213). *Location:* five miles west of Campbeltown on B843 road. Championship standard seaside links course. 18 holes, 6228 yards. S.S.S. 70. Also 9 holes, 2395 yards. Practice area. *Green Fees:* weekdays £18.00 per round, £25.00 per day; weekends day ticket only, £25.00. Discounts for parties of 12 and over. Advance booking necessary. Subject to review. *Eating facilities:* full catering and bar facilities. *Visitors:* welcome, some restrictions on competition days. Open competitions in summer. Special Flight/Golf packages available through Loganair, Glasgow Airport, Paisley. *Society Meetings:* as visitors. Professional: Ken Campbell (Tel & Fax: 01586 810277). Secretary: Mrs Anna Anderson.

CARRADALE. **Carradale Golf Club,** Carradale PA28 6QT. *Location:* 15 miles north of Campbeltown on B842. Seaside course, short but very demanding, unbelievable views. 9 holes, 2700 yards. S.S.S. 63 (18 holes). *Green Fees:* £6.00 per day. County Membership £48 per annum (may take part in competitions). *Eating facilities:* hotel at first tee. *Visitors:* all welcome, no restrictions. Secretary: J.A. Duncan (015833 387).

DALMALLY. **Dalmally Golf Club,** Old Saw Mill, Dalmally PA33 1AS. *Location:* alongside the A85, two miles west of Dalmally. Flat course alongside River Orchy. 9 holes, 2217 yards. S.S.S. 62. *Green Fees:* £8.00. *Visitors:* welcome at all times. *Society Meetings:* all welcome. Secretary: A.J. Burke (01838 200370).

DUNOON. **Blairmore and Strone Golf Club,** High Road, Strone, by Dunoon PA23 8TH (01369 84676). *Location:* take A880, five miles north of Dunoon and first left after leaving Kilmun. A Braid designed course set above the Clyde with spectacular views, mixture of hill and flatter parkland. 9 holes, 2112 yards, 1933 metres. S.S.S. 62. *Green Fees:* weekdays £8.00 per day; weekends £10.00 per day. *Eating facilities:* bar facilities Saturdays and lunchtimes in Summer. *Visitors:* welcome but some restrictions on competition days. *Society Meetings:* welcome, apply through Secretary. Secretary: J. Clark (01369 84467).

DUNOON. **Cowal Golf Club,** Ardenslate Road, Kirn, Dunoon PA23 8LT (01369 2216). *Location:* quarter mile off A815 at Kirn (north-east boundary of Dunoon). Rising wooded parkland with superb views over Firth of Clyde. 18 holes, 6251 yards. S.S.S. 70. Practice area. *Green Fees:* weekdays £13.00 per round, £20.00 per day; weekends £20.00 per round, £30.00 per day (prices may be subject to increase). *Eating facilities:* full service available. *Visitors:* welcome weekdays, some restrictions weekends. Local hotels offer golf holidays – apply Secretary for details. *Society Meetings:* welcome, special rates available. Professional: R.D. Weir (01369 2395). Secretary: Brian Chatham (Tel & Fax: 01369 5673).

DUNOON. **Innellan Golf Club,** Innellan, By Dunoon (01369 83242). *Location:* four miles west of Dunoon. In elevated position overlooking Firth of Clyde. 9 holes, 2343 yards. S.S.S. 63. *Green Fees:* weekdays £8.00; weekends £10.00. *Eating facilities:* bar and snacks; new clubhouse. *Visitors:* welcome, except Monday evenings. *Society Meetings:* catered for on application. Secretary: J.G. Arden (01369 3546; Fax: 01369 3016).

INVERARAY. **Inveraray Golf Club,** c/o 2 Dalmally Road, Inveraray. *Location:* on the A83, one mile west of Inveraray, signposted. Wooded with natural trees, oak, birch, etc. Flat, some water hazards. 9 holes, 2799 yards. S.S.S. 67. Practice net. *Green Fees:* weekdays £6.00, half price for Senior Citizens and Juniors; weekends £8.00, half price for Senior Citizens and Juniors. *Eating facilities:* none at course but good choice locally. *Visitors:* very few restrictions except occasionally at weekends. *Society Meetings:* welcome by prior arrangement through Secretary. Secretary: (01499 2267).

LOCHGILPHEAD. **Lochgilphead Golf Club,** Blairbuie Road, Lochgilphead PA31 8LE (01546 602340). *Location:* next to Argyll and Bute Hospital, Lochgilphead. Parkland. 9 holes, 2500 yards. S.S.S. 63. Practice fairway. *Green Fees:* weekdays £7.00; weekends £10.00. *Eating facilities:* limited – weekends and most evenings. *Visitors:* welcome but some restriction on competition days. *Society Meetings:* welcome by arrangement. Secretary: Mr A. Law. *

OBAN. **Glencruitten Golf Club,** Glencruitten Road, Oban (01631 62868). *Location:* one mile from town centre. Hilly parkland. 18 holes, 4452 yards. S.S.S. 63. Practice area. *Green Fees:* weekdays £11.00 per round, £13.00 per day; weekends £12.50 per round, £14.50 per day. *Eating facilities:* full catering and bar facilities. *Visitors:* welcome, restrictions on Saturdays and Thursdays during competition times. *Society Meetings:* welcome. Shop: (01631 64115). Starter: (01631 64115). Secretary: A.G. Brown (01631 64604 after 6pm).

SOUTHEND. **Dunaverty Golf Club,** Southend, By Campbeltown (01586 83677). *Location:* about 10 miles south of Campbeltown on B842. Scenic seaside course. 18 holes, 4799 yards. S.S.S. 64. *Green Fees:* £9.00 per round, £11.00 per day. *Eating facilities:* light snacks, meals, etc. *Visitors:* welcome at all times except during competition ballot times (mainly Saturdays), telephone above number. *Society Meetings:* catered for on limited basis on prior application. Secretary: J. Galbraith (01586 83698).

TARBERT. **Tarbert Golf Club,** Kilberry Road, Tarbert PA29 6XX (01880 820565). *Location:* approximately one mile south of Tarbert on B8024. Hilly wooded parkland. 9 holes, 4460 yards. S.S.S. 64. *Green Fees:* £5.00 9 holes, £8.00 18 holes. *Eating facilities:* licensed clubhouse, open weekends. *Visitors:* welcome at all times. *Society Meetings:* by arrangement. Secretary: Peter Cupples (01880 820536).

TAYNUILT. **Taynuilt Golf Club,** Taynuilt. *Location:* 12 miles east of Oban on A85. Parkland course, gently undulating with unrivalled views. 9 holes, 4018 yards, 3674 metres. S.S.S. 62. *Green Fees:* £4.00 9 holes, £5.00 per day Adults; £1.00 9 holes, £3.00 per day Juniors. Weekly ticket (Mon-Fri) £20.00 Adults, £12.00 Juniors. *Visitors:* welcome, some restrictions Tuesday afternoons, Saturdays and Sundays for competitions. Secretary: Mairead MacLeod (0186 62429). *

TIGHNABRUAICH. **Kyles Of Bute Golf Club,** Ravenswood, Tighnabruaich PA21 2EE. *Location:* access from Dunoon and Strachur. Clubhouse by Kames Farm, turn south off B8000 Kames to Millhouse road. Hillside course with magnificent views. 9 holes, 4778 yards. S.S.S. 64. *Green Fees:* £6.00 per day. *Eating facilities:* no bar, but snacks and soft drinks available. *Visitors:* welcome, except Sunday mornings. *Society Meetings:* by special arrangement only. Secretary: Dr Jeremy Thomson (01700 811603).

Ayrshire

AYR. **Belleisle Golf Course,** Doonfoot Road, Ayr KA7 4DU (01292 441258). *Location:* follow main road south through Ayr. Gently sloping parkland course with fine mature trees. 18 holes, 6477 yards. S.S.S. 71. Practice area. *Green Fees:* £15.00. Day ticket one round Belleisle, one round Seafield £22.00. *Eating facilities:* hotel and bars with catering. *Visitors:* no restrictions but booking in advance advisable. Juniors under 17 must have handicap of 9 or under. *Society Meetings:* catered for, groups up to 40. Professional: David Gemmell (Tel & Fax: 01292 441314). Starter: (01292 441258).

AYR. **Dalmilling (Municipal) Golf Club,** Westwood Avenue, Ayr KA8 0QY (01292 263893; Fax: 01292 610543). *Location:* A77, on north-east boundary, one mile from town centre. Parkland. 18 holes, 5724 yards. S.S.S. 68. Practice area. *Green Fees:* £10.00 per round, £18.00 per day. Subject to review. *Eating facilities:* snacks/lunches/high teas, table licence. *Visitors:* welcome, not before 9.30am weekends, telephone to ensure availability. *Society Meetings:* welcome by arrangement. Professional: Philip Cheyney. Secretary: Stewart Graham.

AYR. **Seafield Golf Course,** Doonfoot Road, Ayr KA7 4DU (01292 441258). *Location:* follow main road south through Ayr. Parkland and links, gently sloping. 18 holes, 5498 yards. S.S.S. 67. *Green Fees:* £10.00. Day ticket one round Seafield, one round Belleisle £22.00. *Eating facilities:* hotel and bars with catering. *Visitors:* welcome, no restrictions but booking in advance advisable. *Society Meetings:* catered for, groups up to 40. Professional: David Gemmell (Tel & Fax: 01292 441314). Starter: (01292 441258).

BEITH. **Beith Golf Club,** Threepwood Road, Beith KA15 5JR (01505 503166). *Location:* off Beith bypass road. Wooded and hilly course. 9 holes, 2559 yards. S.S.S. 68 (for 18 holes). Practice area available. *Green Fees:* weekdays £8.00 per round, £10.00 per day; Sundays £12.00. *Eating facilities:* snack meals available, bar open 11am to 11pm. *Visitors:* welcome weekdays (off course by 5pm), no play on Saturdays, Sundays off course by 1pm. *Society Meetings:* welcome by prior arrangement with Secretary. Secretary: M.E. Armstrong (01505 503166).

DAILLY. **Brunston Castle Golf Club,** Dailly KA26 9RH (01465 81471; Fax: 01465 81545). *Location:* AA signposted from A77. Parkland course with river running through. 18 holes, 6792 yards. S.S.S. 72. Putting green, bunker range. *Green Fees:* weekdays £20.00 per round, £30.00 per day; weekends £25.00 per round, £35.00 per day. *Eating facilities:* bar meals. *Visitors:* welcome. *Society Meetings:* welcome. Professional: Dereck McKenzie. Clubmaster: George Ferguson.

GALSTON. **Loudoun Gowf Club,** Galston KA4 8PA (01563 820551). *Location:* five miles east of Kilmarnock on A71. Flat parkland. 18 holes, 5844 yards. S.S.S. 68. *Green Fees:* £15.00 per round, £25.00 per day weekdays. Subject to review. *Eating facilities:* full catering. *Visitors:* welcome weekdays only. *Society Meetings:* welcome by arrangement. Secretary: T.R. Richmond (01563 821993).

GIRVAN. **Girvan Golf Club,** Golf Course Road, Girvan (01465 4272). *Location:* A77 from Glasgow, through Ayr, on coast road to Stranraer. Links/parkland course with testing Par 3 holes and scenic views of Firth of Clyde. 18 holes, 5132 yards. S.S.S. 65. Practice area. *Green Fees:* information not available. *Eating facilities:* full catering available in clubhouse. *Visitors:* welcome, book through Starter (01465 4346). *Society Meetings:* welcome, book through Starter. Secretary: W.B. Tait (01465 2011). *

IRVINE. **Glasgow Golf Club,** Gailes, Irvine KA11 5AE (01294 311347). *Location:* six miles from Kilmarnock, three miles south of Irvine, four miles north of Troon. Links. 18 holes, 6510 yards. S.S.S. 72. *Green Fees:* weekdays £27.00 per round, £33.00 per day; Saturdays and Sunday afternoons £30.00 per round. *Eating facilities:* full catering and bar facilities. *Visitors:* welcome weekdays, and Saturday and Sunday afternoons if no club competitions. *Society Meetings:* by application to Club Secretary. Professional: Jack Steven (0141-942 8507). Secretary: D.W. Deas (0141-942 2011; Fax: 0141-942 0770).

IRVINE. **Irvine Ravenspark Golf Club,** Municipal Clubhouse, Kidsneuk Lane, Irvine KA12 0SR (01294 71293). *Location:* on A78 between Irvine and Kilwinning at Ravenspark Academy. Flat parkland course. 18 holes, 6453 yards. S.S.S. 71. *Green Fees:* weekdays £6.00 per round, £10.00 per day; weekends £10.00 per round, £15.00 per day. *Eating facilities:* dining-room, bar. *Visitors:* welcome, except on Saturdays March to October. No jeans or training shoes allowed in the clubhouse. *Society Meetings:* welcome, by arrangement weekends. Professional: P. Bond (01294 276467). Secretary: G. Robertson (01294 554617).

IRVINE. **The Irvine Golf Club,** Bogside, Irvine KA12 8SN (01294 275979). *Location:* through Irvine going towards Kilwinning, turn left at Ravenspark Academy. Flat links course. 18 holes, 6408 yards. S.S.S. 73. Practice ground. *Green Fees:* weekdays £25.00 per round, £35.00 per day; weekends £35.00. *Eating facilities:* full catering every day. *Visitors:* welcome, after 3pm weekends. *Society Meetings:* catered for. Professional: Keith Erskine (01294 275626). Secretary: Andrew Morton (01294 275979).

IRVINE. **Western Gailes Golf Club,** Gailes, By Irvine KA11 5AE (01294 311649 Fax: 01294 312312). *Location:* three miles north of Troon. Seaside links. 18 holes, 6639 yards, 6179 metres. S.S.S. 72. *Green Fees:* weekdays £38.00 per round, £50.00 per day. *Eating facilities:* full bar and catering facilities. *Visitors:* welcome Monday, Tuesday, Wednesday and Friday, no ladies on a Tuesday, must contact club in advance. Handicap Certificate required. *Society Meetings:* welcome by arrangement with Secretary. Secretary: Andrew M. McBean C.A.

KILBIRNIE. **Kilbirnie Place Golf Club,** Largs Road, Kilbirnie (Kilbirnie (01505) 683398). *Location:* on main Kilbirnie to Largs Road, left hand side just outside town boundary. Parkland. 18 holes, 5116 yards. S.S.S. 69. *Green Fees:* weekdays £10.00; weekends £17.50. Party bookings on application. *Eating facilities:* catering and bar. *Visitors:* welcome weekdays. No visitors Saturdays, no visiting parties Sundays. Secretary: J.C. Walker (01505 683283). *

KILMARNOCK. **Annanhill Golf Club,** Irvine Road, Kilmarnock KA3 2RT (01563 21644). *Location:* between Kilmarnock and Crosshouse on road to Irvine. Parkland course with excellent views. 18 holes, 6285 yards. S.S.S. 70. *Green Fees:* weekdays £12.00; weekends £16.00. *Eating facilities:* full catering available. *Visitors:* no parties on Saturdays, but welcome Sundays and weekdays by reservation. *Society Meetings:* catered for. Secretary: Mr D. McKie.

KILMARNOCK. **Caprington Golf Club,** Ayr Road, Kilmarnock (01563 23702). Parkland/wooded course. *Green Fees:* information not available. *Eating facilities:* available. *Visitors:* welcome except Saturdays. *Society Meetings:* all welcome. Secretary: F. McCulloch (01563 25848). *

LARGS. **Inverclyde National Golf Training Centre,** Scottish Sports Council, Burnside Road, Largs KA30 8RW (01475 674666). *Location:* Largs-Greenock-Glasgow (M8). Parkland, links, training bunkers. 6 holes, driving range. *Green Fees:* on application. *Eating facilities:* cafeteria, dining room, accommodation and bar. *Visitors:* two and four day courses for groups and individuals, pre booking required. Professionals: Jack Steven, David Scott. Secretary: John Kent (Deputy Director).

LARGS. **Largs Golf Club,** Irvine Road, Largs KA30 8EU (01475 673594). *Location:* on A78 28 miles from Glasgow. Parkland with scenic views. 18 holes, 6220 yards. S.S.S. 70. *Green Fees:* weekdays £24.00 per day, £18.00 per round; weekends £24.00 per round or day. *Eating facilities:* full catering and bar. *Visitors:* welcome, no restrictions except on competition days and weekends. *Society Meetings:* catered for Tuesdays and Thursdays only by prior arrangement. Professional: Bob Collinson (01475 686192). Secretary: Frank Gilmour (01475 672497).

LARGS. **Routenburn Golf Club,** Routenburn, Largs (01475 673230). Hilly moorland course. 18 holes, 5765 yards. S.S.S. 67. *Green Fees:* information not provided. *Eating facilities:* lunches at club except Thursdays, order in advance. *Visitors:* welcome with reservation. *Society Meetings:* catered for on application to club. Professional: Greig McQueen (01475 687240). Secretary: Mr John Thomson.

MAUCHLINE. **Ballochmyle Golf Club,** Mauchline KA5 6LE (01290 550469). *Location:* on B705 off A76, one mile south of Mauchline. Wooded parkland course. 18 holes, 5952 yards. S.S.S. 69. *Green Fees:* £25.00 per day weekdays; £30.00 per day weekends. *Eating facilities:* all day bar opening from 1st April until 30th September, snacks and meals available during bar hours. *Visitors:* welcome every day except Saturdays. Dress regulations both on and off the course must be adhered to. Two full size snooker tables and squash court. *Society Meetings:* all welcome to a total of 30 per party. Secretary: Douglas Munro (01290 550469).

MAYBOLE. **Maybole Golf Club,** Memorial Park, Kirkoswald Road, Maybole (01292 281511). *Location:* A77 from Glasgow. By-pass Ayr to Girvan road, on main Girvan road at Maybole. Hilly parkland. 9 holes, 5270 yards. S.S.S. 65. *Green Fees:* municipal rates. *Visitors:* welcome. *Society Meetings:* welcome.

NEW CUMNOCK. **New Cumnock Golf Club,** Lochhill, Cumnock Road, New Cumnock. *Location:* A76, half a mile north of New Cummock. Parkland. 9 holes, 5176 yards (18). S.S.S. 65. *Green Fees:* £8.00 adults. Senior Citizens residing within Cumnock and Doon Valley £1.00. *Eating facilities:* clubhouse open for tea/coffee, filled rolls. *Visitors:* welcome at all times except Sunday competition days before 4pm. *Society Meetings:* welcome, contact Secretary. Secretary: Jim Bryce (01290 32037). *

PATNA. **Doon Valley Golf Club,** Hillside, Patna KA6 7JT (01292 531607). *Location:* 10 miles from Ayr on the A713 Ayr to Castle Douglas road. Parkland, hillside course. 9 holes, 5654 yards. S.S.S. 68. *Green Fees:* £8.00 per round, £12.00 per day. *Eating facilities:* can be arranged; bar open weekdays 7pm to 11pm, weekends 12 noon to 11pm. *Visitors:* welcome, groups of six or more must apply for tee off times. *Society Meetings:* welcome. Secretary: Hugh Johnstone MBE (01292 550411).

PRESTWICK. **Prestwick Golf Club,** Links Road, Prestwick M25 9XB (01292 77404). *Location:* one mile from Prestwick airport, 40 minutes by car from Turnberry Hotel, 10 minutes from Troon, 15 minutes from Ayr. 18 holes, 6544 yards. (No LGU tees). S.S.S. 72. *Green Fees:* information not provided. *Eating facilities:* dining room (male only: prior booking required) open from 12.30pm. to 2.30pm. Cardinal Room (light lunches) open to ladies and gentlemen from 10.00am. until 4.00pm. *Visitors:* welcome with reservation. *Society Meetings:* catered for. Professional: F. C. Renine. A. Sproston. Secretary: D.E. Donaldson.

PRESTWICK. **Prestwick St. Cuthbert Golf Club,** East Road, Prestwick KA9 2SX (01292 77101). *Location:* south-east area of Prestwick near A77 and Prestwick Airport. Flat, some trees; semi-parkland. 18 holes, 6470 yards, 6063 metres. S.S.S. 71. Limited practice area. *Green Fees:* £24.00 per day weekdays only. *Eating facilities:* full catering and bar service. *Visitors:* welcome except weekends unless introduced by and playing with member. *Society Meetings:* catered for. Secretary: R. Morton (01292 77101).

PRESTWICK. **Prestwick St. Nicholas Golf Club,** Grangemuir Road, Prestwick KA9 1SN (01292 77608). *Location:* proceed down Grangemuir Road from Main Street, Prestwick. 18 holes, 5952 yards, 5441 metres. S.S.S. 69. *Green Fees:* weekdays £30.00 per day, £20.00 per round. *Eating facilities:* full service. *Visitors:* welcome most weekdays with club introduction, reserved for members at weekends. *Society Meetings:* catered for by arrangement. Professional: S. Smith (01292 79755). Secretary: J.R. Leishman (01292 77608).

SKELMORLIE. **Skelmorlie Golf Club,** Beithglass Road, Skelmorlie PA17 5ES (01475 520152). *Location:* two/three miles from Wemyss Bay Pier. Hillside, moorland course. 13 holes, 5056 yards. S.S.S. 65. *Green Fees:* weekdays £11.00 per round, £15.00 per day; Saturdays after 4pm £12.00 per round, Sundays £18.00 per day. Discounts to local hotel residents. *Eating facilities:* bar with snacks available, catering at weekends. *Visitors:* welcome except Saturdays before 4pm. *Society Meetings:* welcome by arrangement. Parties at discounted "all-in" rate. Secretary: Mrs A. Fahey (01475 520774).

STEVENSTON. **Ardeer Golf Club,** Greenhead, Stevenston KA20 4JX (01294 464542). *Location:* north of Ayr, just outwith Irvine New Town. Parkland course lined with trees incorporating water on several holes. 18 holes, 6407 yards. S.S.S. 71. *Green Fees:* weekdays £10.00 per round, £18.00 per day; weekends £14.00 per round, £24.00 per day. *Eating facilities:* restaurant and bars. *Visitors:* welcome except Saturdays. *Society Meetings:* all parties holding Handicap Certificates welcome. Starter: Paul Rodgers (01294 601327). Secretary: Tom Cumming (01294 465316).

STEVENSTON. **Moorpark Golf Club,** Auchenharvie Golf Complex, Stevenston (01294 469127). *Location:* A738 Stevenston/Saltcoats, Auchenharvie Swimming Pool. Flat parkland, large pond at the side of holes two and three. 18 holes, 4912 yards. S.S.S. 64. *Green Fees:* information not provided. *Visitors:* welcome anytime during the week, weekends after 9am and anytime after 1pm. *Society Meetings:* all welcome. The course is situated right next door to Sandylands Caravan Park and there are plenty of other golf courses to play all within easy reach. Professional: Mr Bob Rodgers (01294 603103). Secretary: Mr William S. Durham (01294 462196).

TROON. **Kilmarnock (Barassie) Golf Club,** 29 Hillhouse Road, Barassie, Troon KA10 6SY (01292 311077). *Location:* two miles north of Troon. Links course. 18 holes, Medal 6473 yards, Visitors 6177 yards. S.S.S. 71. Practice ground. *Green Fees:* £30.00 per round, £40.00 per day weekdays. *Eating facilities:* coffee, lunches, snacks, high teas. *Visitors:* welcome Mondays, Tuesdays, Thursdays and Friday afternoons. All visitors must adhere to club dress code – no demin, trainers, etc. *Society Meetings:* catered for Tuesdays and Wednesdays. Professional: W.R. Lockie (Tel & Fax: 01292 311322). Secretary: Robert L. Bryce (01292 313920).

TROON. **Royal Troon Golf Club,** Craigend Road, Troon KA10 6EP (01292 311555). *Location:* three miles from A77 (Glasgow/Ayr trunk road). Old Course 18 holes, 7097 yards. S.S.S. 74. Portland Course 18 holes, 6274 yards, 5738 metres. S.S.S. 71. *Green Fees:* £78.00 (Old); £48.00 (Portland). *Eating facilities:* full restaurant service available, including bar snacks. *Visitors:* Mondays, Tuesdays and Thursdays between 9.30 and 11.00am and 14.30 and 15.00pm. Letter of introduction from own club and Handicap Certificate required (maximum of 20). (No ladies or those under 18 years on Old Course). *Society Meetings:* parties in excess of 24 not accepted. Professional: R. Brian Anderson (01292 313281). Secretary/Manager: J.D. Montgomerie (01292 311555; Fax: 01292 318204).

TROON. **Troon Municipal Golf Course,** Harling Drive, Troon (01292 312464). *Location:* adjacent to railway station, one mile off the Ayr-Glasgow road. Three 18 hole courses. Lochgreen 6687 yards. S.S.S. 72. Darley 6327 yards. S.S.S. 70. Fullerton 4784 yards. S.S.S. 65. *Green Fees:* information not provided. *Eating facilities:* hot snacks, 8am – 6pm. Bar snacks and lunches, evening meals bookings only. *Visitors:* catered for. Broad wheeled trolleys only. *Society Meetings:*

South Beach Hotel

Troon, Ayrshire KA10 6EG. Tel. (01292) 312033 Fax. (01292) 318438

FULLY LICENSED ♛♛♛♛ Commended RAC ★★★

Privately owned Hotel with a high reputation for friendly and efficient service with health and fitness facilities. All rooms ensuite. In the immediate surrounding area there are 5 Championship Courses including the famous Royal Troon. Another 15 courses within a 20 mile radius. Phone for details.

Manor Park Hotel

A warm welcome awaits guests at The Manor Park Hotel where all bedrooms are ensuite and have TV, teasmade and telephones. The Hotel has recently been refurbished and the new 'Reflections' Restaurant offers excellent food and fine wines in elegant surroundings.

Royal Troon, Old Prestwick and many other golf courses are within 10 minutes of the Hotel, as is Prestwick Airport. Contact: Mr Murray, Manor Park Hotel, by Prestwick Airport, Ayrshire. Telephone/Fax: (01292) 79365.

CRAIGLEA HOTEL

Troon KA10 6EG · Tel/Fax: (01292) 311366 AA RAC****

Ideal for a golfing break this 22 bedroom family run hotel overlooks the Firth of Clyde. We are adjacent to all the Troon Courses (including Royal Troon) and minutes away from Prestwick, Barassie and Western Gailes Golf Courses. Special all year round rates for Golf Parties. Cocktail bar – Restaurant – Rooms with ensuite facilities, tea/coffee makers – TV – Radio – Direct dial telephones etc.

Partners: The Misses J. and M. Calderwood and R. L. Calderwood.

· AYRSHIRE ·

Scotland's Famous Golfing Coast

FREE 52-PAGE COLOUR GOLF GUIDE AVAILABLE

ROYAL TROON • LARGS • TURNBERRY • PRESTWICK OLD COURSE

... and many more exciting and challenging courses are waiting to test your skill.

There's lots to do once you leave the 19th hole, or why not just relax in our comfortable accommodation. Whether you choose a luxury ♛♛♛♛♛ hotel or homely bed and breakfast, self-catering or a holiday home you'll be delighted with the choice available. Send now for our free colour brochure to:

DEPT. P.G.A.
Ayrshire Tourist Board, Burns House, Burns Statue Square, Ayr KA7 1UP
Telephone: (01292) 262555 Fax: (01292) 269555

catered for. Caterer: John Darge. Professional: Gordon McKinley. Advance booking should be made in writing to Starter's Office, Troon Municipal Golf Courses, Harling Drive, Troon, Ayrshire. *

TURNBERRY. **Turnberry Hotel Golf Courses,** Turnberry KA26 9LT (01655 31000; Fax: 01655 31706). *Location:* on main A77 between Girvan and Maybole. 2 Championship Links Courses, Ailsa (host to British Open) 18 holes, 6976 yards. S.S.S. 72; Arran 18 holes, 6014 yards. S.S.S. 69. Golf practice area, putting greens. *Green Fees:* on application. *Eating facilities:* new clubhouse, restaurant and bar. *Visitors:* written requests only. Accommodation at Turnberry Hotel. *Society Meetings:* written requests only. Professional: Bob Jamieson (01655 31000 extension 77). Club Manager: E.C. Bowman (01655 31000 extension 300).

WEST KILBRIDE. **West Kilbride Golf Club,** 33-35 Fullerton Drive, Seamill, West Kilbride KA23 9HT (01294 823128). *Location:* on A78 Greenock to Ayr Road, signposted in Seamill. Seaside links course. 18 holes, 6452 yards. S.S.S. 71. Practice area. *Green Fees:* on application. *Eating facilities:* diningroom, lounge and casual bar. *Visitors:* welcome weekdays only. *Society Meetings:* catered for Tuesdays and Thursdays. Handicap Certificates required. Professional: Gregor Howie (Tel & Fax: 01294 823042). Secretary: R.J. Whittingham (01294 823911).

Banffshire

ABERLOUR. **Rothes Golf Club,** Blackhall, Rothes, Aberlour AB38 7AN (01340 831443). *Location:* south west of Rothes, off A941 Elgin to Craigellachie road. A hilly course with fine views over the River Spey. 9 holes (18 tees), 2526 yards (5052 yards), 2310 metres (4620 metres). S.S.S. 64. *Green Fees:* weekdays £8.00, Juniors £4.00; weekends £10.00, Juniors £5.00. *Eating facilities:* bar open evenings and weekends. *Visitors:* always welcome, tee reserved for Ladies 5pm to 7.30pm Tuesdays, and 5pm to 6pm Mondays for Juniors. *Society Meetings:* contact Secretary. Secretary: J.P. Tilley (01340 831277).

BANFF. **Duff House Royal Golf Club,** The Barnyards, Banff AB45 3SX (01261 812062; Fax: 01261 812224). *Location:* two minutes from town centre, A97, A98. Level parkland. 18 holes, 6161 yards. S.S.S. 69. *Green Fees:* weekdays £12.00 per round, £16.00 per day; weekends £18.00 per round, £24.00 per day. *Eating facilities:* lounge bar and full catering service. *Visitors:* welcome weekdays without reservation; restricted weekends. *Society Meetings:* catered for by prior arrangement. Professional: R.S. Strachan (01261 812075). Secretary: H. Liebnitz (01261 812062).

BUCKIE. **Buckpool Golf Club (Buckie),** Barhill Road, Buckie AB56 1DU (01542 832236). *Location:* turn off A98 signposted Buckpool. Links course with superlative view over Moray Firth. 18 holes, 6257 yards. S.S.S. 70. *Green Fees:* weekdays £15.00 per day, £8.00 (single rounds only) after 3.30pm; weekends £20.00 per day, £12.00 (single rounds only) after 3.30pm. Half price for Juniors. *Eating facilities:* full catering daily, normal bar hours. *Visitors:* no restrictions except when there are scheduled competitions. Squash, snooker and indoor bowling. *Society Meetings:* welcome by prior arrangement. Secretary: Miss M. Coull.

BUCKIE. **Strathlene Golf Club,** Strathlene, Buckie AB56 2DJ (01542 31798). *Location:* equidistant between Aberdeen and Inverness. Raised links course which follows the natural contours of the land. 18 holes. Practice facilities. *Green Fees:* weekdays £10.00 per round, £12.00 per day; weekends £12.00 per round, £15.00 per day. *Eating facilities:* full catering facilities available, bar open all day. *Visitors:* prior booking essential; avoid Saturday and Sunday mornings. Locker room. *Society Meetings:* booking required. Secretary: G. Clark (01542 34170). *

CULLEN. **Cullen Golf Club,** The Links, Cullen, Buckie AB56 2UU (01542 840685). *Location:* off A98 midway between Aberdeen and Inverness, on Moray Firth coast. Seaside links with elevated section, natural rock landscaping and sandy beach coming into play at several holes. 18 holes, 4610 yards. S.S.S. 62. Putting green and net area. *Green Fees:* day tickets: weekdays £10.00; weekends £13.00. Subject to review. Weekly and fortnightly tickets available. Member of District Council's Rover Golf Ticket scheme. *Eating facilities:* catering and bar facilities. *Visitors:* welcome, may be restrictions Wednesdays and Saturdays (club competitions). *Society Meetings:* catered for. Secretary: I. Findlay (01542 840174).

DUFFTOWN. **Dufftown Golf Club,** Mether Cluny, Tomintoul Road, Dufftown AB55 4BX (Tel & Fax: 01340 820325). *Location:* one mile from Dufftown on Tomintoul Road. Hilly course, spectacular views. 18 holes, 5308 yards. S.S.S. 67. *Green Fees:* £10.00 per round, £12.00 per day. Weekly (five day) ticket £35.00. Reductions for parties of 12 or more. Juniors half price. *Eating facilities:* bar and snacks daily, meals by arrangement. *Visitors:* welcome at all times. *Society Meetings:* welcome by arrangement, catering available. Secretary: Mr D.M. Smith (01340 820033).

BANFF SPRINGS HOTEL

A very special hotel with superb facilities.
Overlooking the Golden Sands of the Moray Firth.
A vast selection of courses within easy reach,
reasonable green fees, long days and low rainfall
make this the perfect location for the Golfer.

AA ★★★ STB ♛♛♛♛ Commended.

Golf factsheet. Special Breaks.
Telephone now for details.

Banff Springs Hotel, Golden Knowes Road,
Banff, Aberdeenshire AB45 2JE.
Tel. 01261 812881. Fax. 01261 815546.

St Andrew's HOTEL

Drive for Scotland's North East

Golf Package between 1st April and 31st October 1995 –
6 nights DB&B + 5 days' golf on 10 local courses for only £205.
3 Day Package also available. Please telephone for details.

Tel: 01542 831227 Fax: 01542 834513
9 St Andrew's Square, Buckpool, Buckie, Banffshire AB5 1BT

Norwood House

11 Seafield Place, Cullen, Banffshire AB5 2TE Telephone (01542) 840314

Family run Guest House in quiet residential area offering B&B or Half Board in ensuite or standard rooms. Close to Bowling Green. Beaches and Unique Cliff and Links Golf Course within easy reach with a further 10 courses within a 20-mile radius.

('Moray for Golf' tickets available on application).

The Seafield Arms Hotel

RAC ★★★ STB ♛♛♛♛

This fine old coaching hotel, which is family run, offers a warm welcome to all its visitors. 25 en-suite bedrooms tastefully decorated, a 'Taste of Scotland' restaurant and lounge bar with open fire. This is the ideal place for relaxation. There are 18 golf courses within a radius of twenty miles. Lying on the sunny southern shores of the Moray Firth, the uncrowded district of Moray offers an excellent range of golf to challenge the most dedicated golfer. From traditional links to parkland and moorland, all courses welcome visitors and most participate in the inclusive golf ticket. If you feel able to foresake your clubs in favour of sightseeing, the only Malt Whisky Trail in the world is on your doorstep, besides a variety of things to do and see for all the family, while the Castle Trail, Loch Ness and the Cairngorms are all within easy reach for a half day excursion. Bed and Breakfast from £30. For that special holiday or golf break please telephone for a tariff or brochure.

The Seafield Arms Hotel, Cullen AB56 2SG Tel: 01542 840791 Fax: 01542 840736

KEITH. **Keith Golf Club,** Fife Park, Keith AB55 3DF (01542 882469). *Location:* main road – A96 Keith. Parkland, open, panoramic views. 18 holes, 5614 yards. S.S.S. 68. Small practice area and putting green. *Green Fees:* Day ticket: weekdays £10.00, with a member £5.00; weekends £15.00 per day. *Eating facilities:* catering available by arrangement, full bar facilities. *Visitors:* welcome anytime, advisable to telephone in advance during playing season. *Society Meetings:* all welcome, applications to Hon. Secretary. Hon. Secretary: G. Edwards (01542 886286).

MACDUFF. **Royal Tarlair Golf Club,** Buchan Street, Macduff (01261 832897). *Location:* A98 Fraserburgh to Inverness road. Seaside links. 18 holes, 5866 yards, 5373 metres. S.S.S. 68. *Green Fees:* weekdays £10.00 per round, £15.00 per day; weekends £12.50 per round, £19.00 per day. *Eating facilities:* full catering and bar available. *Visitors:* welcome. *Society Meetings:* welcome, bookings through Secretary. Secretary: Mrs T. Watt.

Berwickshire

COLDSTREAM. **Hirsel Golf Club,** Kelso Road, Coldstream TD12 4NJ (01890 882678). *Location:* A697 west end of Coldstream. Parkland. 18 holes, 6092 yards, 5570 metres. S.S.S. 69. *Green Fees:* weekdays £15.00; weekends £20.00. Weekly tickets (Monday to Friday) £60.00. Subject to review. *Eating facilities:* bar and catering facilities March/October. *Visitors:* welcome, no restrictions; groups of over 10 players must book in advance. *Society Meetings:* catered for by arrangement. Secretary: John C. Balfour (01890 883052).

DUNS. **Duns Golf Club,** Hardens Road, Duns. *Location:* about one mile west of Duns just off A6105, signposted Longformacus. Upland, undulating course with view south to Cheviot Hills. A burn runs through the course and is the main hazard. 9 holes, 5826 yards (2913 x 2). S.S.S. 68. Practice ground. *Green Fees:* £10.00. Half-price 1st November to 15th March. *Eating facilities:* lounge/bar open weekday evenings and weekends during season, light snacks available. *Visitors:* welcome without restriction except during club competitions and no visitors to start second 9 holes after 3pm Tuesdays. *Society Meetings:* welcome, booking through Secretary. Secretary: A. Campbell (01361 82717).

EYEMOUTH. **Eyemouth Golf Club,** Gunsgreeen House, Eyemouth (018907 50551). *Location:* six miles north of Berwick-on-Tweed, off the A1 towards the coast. Seaside course on cliff tops with panoramic views, spectacular hole over North Sea inlet. 9 holes, 5000 metres. S.S.S. 65. *Green Fees:* information not provided. *Eating facilities:* no eating facilities, normal bar hours in the evenings. *Visitors:* welcome most weekdays; after 10.30am on Saturdays and after 12 noon Sundays. *Society Meetings:* by prior arrangement with Secretary. Secretary: I. Fairbairn (018907 50074). *

LAUDER. **Lauder Golf Club,** Galashiels Road, Lauder. *Location:* off A68, 28 miles south of Edinburgh. Undulating course, originally designed by W. Park of Musselburgh, on Lauder Hill. 9 holes, 6002 yards. S.S.S. 70. Practice ground. *Green Fees:* weekdays £7.00; weekends £8.00. *Eating facilities:* none – good Hotels in Lauder. *Visitors:* welcome except Wednesdays between 5pm and 7pm and Sundays before 12 noon. Secretary: D. Dickson (01578 722526).

Caithness

LYBSTER. **Lybster Golf Club,** Main Street, Lybster. *Location:* 14 miles south from Wick on A9, half-way down village street. One of smallest courses in Scotland, heathland/parkland. 9 holes, 1896 yards. S.S.S. 62. *Green Fees:* £3.00. *Eating facilities:* at nearby hotels in village. *Visitors:* welcome anytime. *Society Meetings:* welcome anytime. Secretary: N. Fraser (0184 784 215). *

THURSO. **Reay Golf Club,** Clubhouse, Reay, By Thurso KW14 7RE (01847 81288). *Location:* 12 miles west of nearest main town of Thurso. Natural seaside links. 18 holes, 5884 yards. S.S.S. 68. *Green Fees:* £10.00 per day. Rates available for week/fortnight – information from Secretary. *Eating facilities:* restricted: bar open 12-3pm, 8-11pm daily June to September. *Visitors:* welcome anytime, restricted during competitions. *Society Meetings:* welcome, advance bookings via Secretary. Captain: Neil McDonald (01847 81233). Secretary: Miss P. Peebles (01847 81537).

THURSO. **Thurso Golf Club,** Newlands of Geise, By Thurso (01847 63807). *Location:* two miles south west of Railway Station. Flat parkland, wonderful views of Pentland Firth and Orkneys. 18 holes, 5610 yards. S.S.S. 69. Driving range. *Green Fees:* £10.00, with member £5.00 (clubs provided). *Eating facilities:* catering 11am to 2.30pm, some evenings; bar 11am to 11pm Summer. *Visitors:* welcome without reservation. *Society Meetings:* catered for. Shop Manager: J. Newton. Secretary: Wendy Meiklejohn (01847 65024).

WICK. **Wick Golf Club,** Reiss, By Wick KW1 4RW (01955 2726). *Location:* three miles north of Wick on A9. Seaside links course. 18 holes, 5976 yards. S.S.S. 69, Ladies 72. Practice area. *Green Fees:* £15.00 per day. *Eating facilities:* licensed; snacks available. *Visitors:* welcome. *Society Meetings:* catered for. Secretary: Mr J.S. Bain (01955 3278).

Clackmannanshire

ALLOA. **Alloa Golf Club,** Shawpark, Sauchie (01259 722745). *Location:* on A908 between Alloa and Tillicoultry. Parkland. 18 holes, 6240 yards. S.S.S. 70. Two practice grounds. *Green Fees:* weekdays £14.00 per round, £22.00 per day. *Eating facilities:* dining room, bar meals. *Visitors:* welcome. *Society Meetings:* catered for. Professional: Bill Bennett (01259 724476). Secretary: A.M. Frame (01259 750100).

ALLOA. **Braehead Golf Club,** Cambus, By Alloa FK10 2NT (01259 722078). *Location:* one mile west of Alloa on A907. Gently undulating parkland course with scenic views and a variety of challenging holes. 18 holes, 6013 yards. S.S.S. 69. Practice area. *Green Fees:* weekdays £12.00 per round, £18.00 per day; weekends £18.00 per round, £24.00 per day. Discounts available for mid-week visiting parties. *Eating facilities:* bar/full catering available all day during Summer months; slightly restricted during Autumn/Spring. *Visitors:* no restrictions but advisable to telephone in advance. *Society Meetings:* catered for with prior booking. Professional: Paul Brookes. Secretary: Paul MacMichael.

ALVA. **Alva Golf Club,** Beauclerc Street, Alva FK12 5LH (01259 760431). *Location:* seven miles from Stirling on A91 Stirling to St Andrews Road – course lies at foot of Ochil Hills. Inland wooded hillside course with fast greens. 9 holes, 2423 yards, 2213 metres. S.S.S. 64. *Green Fees:* on application. *Eating facilities:* bar snacks only. *Visitors:* welcome at all times. Lounge and changing rooms available. Secretary: (01259 760431).

DOLLAR. **Dollar Golf Club,** Brewlands House, Dollar FK14 7EA (01259 742400). *Location:* off A91 in Dollar, signposted. Hillside course. 18 holes, 5242 yards, 4796 metres. S.S.S. 66. *Green Fees:* weekdays £8.00 per round, £12.00 per day; weekends £16.00. *Eating facilities:* full catering except Tuesdays. *Visitors:* welcome. Snooker table available. *Society Meetings:* welcome (maximum 24). Secretary: J.C. Brown.

DOLLAR. **Muckhart Golf Club,** Muckhart, By Dollar FK14 7JH (01259 781423). *Location:* off A91, three miles east of Dollar. Undulating heathland. 18 holes, 6034 yards. S.S.S. 70. Practice ground. *Green Fees:* weekdays £12.00; weekends £18.00. *Eating facilities:* catering and bar available all day, every day. *Visitors:* welcome except before 10am and from 12 noon to 3pm weekends and Public Holidays. *Society Meetings:* catered for. Professional: Keith Salmoni (01259 781493). Secretary: A.B. Robertson.

STIRLING. **Tillicoultry Golf Club,** Alva Road, Tillicoultry FK13 6EB (01259 50124). *Location:* on A91, nine miles from Stirling. Parkland. 9 holes, 5358 yards. S.S.S. 66. *Green Fees:* weekdays £9.00 per round, £11.00 after 4pm; weekends £15.00 per round. *Eating facilities:* licensed bar, bar lunches, snacks, etc from 12 noon to 2pm daily, bookings taken for evenings. *Visitors:* welcome at all times outwith competitions. No children under 15 weekends until 4pm. *Society Meetings:* catered for on application to the Secretary. Secretary: R. Whitehead (01259 51337/50124).

Dumfriesshire

ANNAN. **Powfoot Golf Club,** 27 Bank Street, Annan DG12 6AU (014617 227). *Location:* off Annan/ Dumfries Road B724, signpost to course three miles from Annan. Semi-links course on Solway shore with outstanding views. 18 holes, 6283 yards, 5745 metres. S.S.S. 70. Practice ground. *Green Fees:* weekdays £24.00 per day, £16.00 per round. Sundays after 2.45pm £16.00. *Eating facilities:* morning coffee, lunches and teas in clubhouse – ordering in advance essential for large parties. *Visitors:* welcome weekdays but restrictions at weekends, no formal introduction required. *Society Meetings:* catered for weekdays by prior arrangement (up to 40 in number). Professional: Gareth Dick (014617 327). Secretary: R.G. Anderson (01461 202866/7).

DALBEATTIE. **Dalbeattie Golf Club,** C/o 7 Galla Drive, Dalbeattie (01556 611421). *Location:* outskirts of Dalbeattie. Slightly hilly parkland. 9 holes, 2100 yards. S.S.S. 60. *Green Fees:* £10.00 per round. Reductions for parties. *Eating facilities:* bar and food available. *Visitors:* welcome every day but restricted on three nights – Monday, Wednesday and Thursday. *Society Meetings:* all welcome. Secretary: T. Moffat (01556 610682).

DUMFRIES. **Crichton Royal Golf Club,** Bankend Road, Dumfries DG1 4TH (01387 55301). *Location:* directly opposite Dumfries and Galloway Royal Infirmary, one mile outside Dumfries on Bankend Road. Wooded parkland. 9 holes, 5952 yards. S.S.S. 69. *Green Fees:* weekdays £12.00; weekends £15.00. *Eating facilities:* restricted. *Visitors:* welcome, restrictions depending on club competitions, Tuesdays gents' competitions. *Society Meetings:* on application. Secretary: Alastair B. McKay (01387 55301 extension 2122).

DUMFRIES. **Dumfries and County Golf Club,** Nunfield, Edinburgh Road, Dumfries DG1 1JX (01387 53585). *Location:* one mile north-east town centre on A701. 18 holes, 5928 yards. S.S.S. 68. Limited practice facilities. *Green Fees:* £21.00 weekdays; £25.00 weekends. *Eating facilities:* restaurant and bar snacks. *Visitors:* welcome except on Saturdays. *Society Meetings:* catered for by arrangement. Professional: G. Gray (01387 68918). Secretary: E.C. Pringle (01387 53585).

DUMFRIES. **Dumfries and Galloway Golf Club,** 2 Laurieston Avenue, Dumfries DG2 7NY (01387 53582). *Location:* one mile from Dumfries on Castle Douglas/Stranraer road, A75. Parkland course. 18 holes, 5803 yards. S.S.S. 68. Practice area. *Green Fees:* weekdays £18.00; weekends £22.00. *Eating facilities:* full catering during bar hours except Mondays. *Visitors:* welcome, except on competition days. *Society Meetings:* catered for weekdays, except Tuesdays. Professional: Joe Fergusson (01387 56902). Secretary: Jack Donnachie (01387 63848).

DUMFRIES. **Southerness Golf Club,** Southerness, Kirkbean, Dumfries DG2 8AZ (01387 88677). *Location:* 16 miles south west of Dumfries on A710 (Solway Coast Road). Natural challenging Championship links, designed by MacKenzie Ross, with panoramic views of Solway Firth and Galloway hills. Hosted British Ladies' Amateur 1989 and British Youths' 1990. 18 holes, 6566 yards. S.S.S. 72. Large practice area. *Green Fees:* weekdays £24.00 per day; weekends £32.00 per day. Weekly (Monday to Friday) ticket £96.00. *Eating facilities:* full bar and catering facilities. *Visitors:* welcome 10am to 12 noon, 2pm to 4.30pm; Thursdays 11am to 1pm, 2.30pm to 4.30pm; weekends 10am to 11.30am, 2.30pm to 4.30pm. Must have Handicap. *Society Meetings:* on application to Secretary. Secretary: W.D. Ramage.

GRETNA. **Gretna Golf Club,** "Kirtle View", Gretna DG16 5HD (01461 338464). *Location:* south side of A75, one mile from A74. Scenic parkland course. 9 holes, 3215 yards. S.S.S. 72. Driving range. (£1 per 60+ balls). *Green Fees:* weekdays £5.00 per round, £8.00 per day; weekends £5.00 per round, £10.00 per day. *Eating facilities:* clubhouse, bar meals and refreshments. *Visitors:* welcome, no restrictions. *Society Meetings:* on application. Secretary: Mrs L. Skinner.

LANGHOLM. **Langholm Golf Club,** Whitaside, Langholm DG13 0JS (013873 80265). *Location:*on A7 Carlisle-Edinburgh road. Turn off at market place in centre of town. Hillside course. 9 holes, 5744 yards. S.S.S. 68. Practice area available. *Green Fees:* £10.00; £5.00 playing with a member. *Eating facilities:* on request. *Visitors:* welcome without reservation; restrictions Saturday 9am to 9.45am, 1pm to 2pm and 3pm-4pm, Sunday 9am to 10am and 1pm (Competition times). *Society Meetings:* apply in writing to Secretary. Secretary: W.J. Brown (013873 80395).

LOCKERBIE. **Hoddom Castle Golf Course,** Hoddom, Lockerbie DG11 1BE (01576 300251). *Location:* three miles from A74 via B725, five miles from A75 via B723 north of Annan. Parkland, partially wooded, bounded on two sides by River Annan. 9 holes, 2274 metres. S.S.S. 33. *Green Fees:* weekdays £5.00 per day; weekends £6.00 per day. *Eating facilities:* bar. *Visitors:* welcome anytime.

LOCKERBIE. **Lochmaben Golf Club,** Castlehillgate, Lochmaben, Lockerbie DG11 1NT (01387 810552). *Location:* Lockerbie four miles, Dumfries eight miles. Parkland with excellent views. 18 holes, 5336 yards, 4863 metres. S.S.S. 67. Practice area. New 9 hole course opening 1995. *Green Fees:* weekdays £12.00; weekends £14.00. *Eating facilities:* catering and bar. *Visitors:* welcome Monday to Saturday except on competition days and not after 5pm. Local hotel 50 yards from course. *Society Meetings:* welcome. Secretary: J.M. Dickie (01387 810713).

LOCKERBIE. **Lockerbie Golf CLub,** Corrie Road, Lockerbie DG11 2ND (01576 203363). *Location:* M74 to Lockerbie, take Corrie Road, 500 yards on right. Parkland featuring pond which is in play on three holes. 18 holes, 5418 yards. S.S.S. 66. Small practice area. *Green Fees:* weekdays £16.00; weekends £20.00 Saturday; £18 Sunday. Juniors £4.00. *Eating facilities:* bar and dining area. *Visitors:* welcome, restricted on Sundays. *Society Meetings:* welcome by arrangement. Secretary: Mr J. Thomson (01576 202462).

MOFFAT. **The Moffat Golf Club,** Coatshill, Moffat DG10 9SB (01683 20020). *Location:* leave A74 at Beattock. Take A701 for Moffat, club notice one mile on left. Scenic moorland course. 18 holes, 5218 yards. S.S.S. 66. Putting green; small practice area. *Green Fees:* weekdays £17.00 per day; weekends £25.00 per day. Special Package £25.50 weekdays, £33.50 weekends for parties of eight and over – package includes coffee, snack, lunch, evening meal and two rounds of golf. *Eating facilities:* bar meals served all day. *Visitors:* welcome without reservation, except Wednesday after 12 noon. *Society Meetings:* welcome, make reservations with clubmaster. Secretary: T.A. Rankin (01683 20020). Clubmaster: Mr Ian Preston.

SANQUHAR. **Sanquhar Golf Club,** Euchan Course, Sanquhar (01659 50577). *Location:* situated quarter-of-a-mile from A76 Dumfries-Kilmarnock trunk road. Undulating parkland. 9 holes, 5144 metres. S.S.S. 68. *Green Fees:* weekdays £10.00 per day; weekends £12.00 per day. *Eating facilities:* bar available if requested in advance. *Visitors:* welcome without reservation. *Society Meetings:* catered for with advance notice. Licensed clubhouse with full-size snooker table. Secretary: Mrs J. Murray (01659 58181).

THORNHILL. **Thornhill Golf Club,** Blacknest, Thornhill DG3 5DW (01848 330546) *Location:* 14 miles north of Dumfries on A76. Parkland/open moorland. 18 holes, 6011 yards. S.S.S. 69. Practice ground (two areas). *Green Fees:* weekdays £16.00; weekends £20.00. Weekly ticket £75.00. *Eating facilities:* catering available, except Mondays, bar facility. *Visitors:* welcome without reservation, but please contact Club Steward re competitions, etc. *Society Meetings:* welcome, contact Club Steward. Secretary: J.F.K. Crichton (01848 331752).

Dunbartonshire

ALEXANDRIA. **Vale of Leven Golf Club,** Northfield Road, Bonhill, Alexandria (01389 52351). *Location:* A82 to Dumbarton, follow signs at roundabout at Dumbarton for Bonhill then club signs. Moorland with splendid views of Loch Lomond. 18 holes, 5165 yards. S.S.S. 66. *Green Fees:* weekdays £10.00 per round, £15.00 per day; weekends £15.00 per round, £20.00 per day. *Eating facilities:* catering and bar available. *Visitors:* welcome except Saturdays between April 1st and September 30th. Full changing and locker facilities. *Society Meetings:* on application to Secretary. Secretary: W. McKinlay (01389 52508).

CARDROSS. **Cardross Golf Club,** Main Street, Cardross G82 5LB (01389 841213). *Location:* on A814 west of Dumbarton. Parkland course. 18 holes, 6469 yards. S.S.S. 71. Practice ground. *Green Fees:* weekdays £18.00 per round, £30.00 day ticket. *Eating facilities:* lunches/bar snacks available during bar hours. *Visitors:* weekdays only (by phoning Professional to book time). *Society Meetings:* catered for weekdays by arrangement. Professional: Robert Farrell (01389 841350). Secretary: P.A. Laing (01389 841754).

CLYDEBANK. **Clydebank and District Golf Club,** Glasgow Road, Hardgate, Clydebank G81 5QY (01389 873289). *Location:* Hardgate village. Off A82 10 miles west of Glasgow (off Great Western Road). 18 holes, 5832 yards, 5325 metres. S.S.S. 68. *Green Fees:* £12.00 per round. *Eating facilities:* catering as required. *Visitors:* welcome weekdays only. Professional: David Pirie (01389 878686). Secretary: W. Manson (01389 872832).

CLYDEBANK. **Clydebank Municipal Golf Course,** Overtoun Road, Clydebank G81 3RE (0141-952 8698). *Location:* one mile west of Clydebank centre off Duntocher Road. Parkland course – one of the best Par 3's in Scotland. 18 holes, 5349 yards. S.S.S. 66. *Green Fees:* on application to Secretary. *Eating facilities:* tearoom. *Visitors:* municipal course, tee closed Saturdays in Summer 11am to 2pm. *Society Meetings:* contact District Council. Secretary: District Council (0141-941 1331).

CUMBERNAULD. **Palacerigg Golf Club,** Palacerigg Country Park, Cumbernauld, Near Glasgow G67 3HU (01236 734969). *Location:* Palacerigg Road, three miles south of Cumbernauld off B8039 Lenziemill Road. Wooded parkland with good views to Campsie Hills. 18 holes, 6444 yards, 5894 metres. S.S.S. 71. Practice area, nearby golf range. *Green Fees:* £7.00 per day weekdays; £8.00 per day weekends. *Eating facilities:* bar seven days, all day opening from March to October; meals available Wednesdays to Sundays or by arrangement. *Visitors:* welcome weekdays only. *Society Meetings:* by letter to Secretary. Secretary: David S.A. Cooper. Starter: (01236 721461).

CUMBERNAULD. **Westerwood Golf Club,** Westerwood, Cumbernauld (01236 457171; Fax: 01236 738478). *Location:* off M80 towards Dullatur. Undulating wooded course designed by Seve Ballesteros and Dave Thomas. 18 holes, 6721 yards. S.S.S. 73. Indoor practice facility. *Green Fees:* information on request from Professional. *Eating facilities:* full catering facilities. *Visitors:* welcome at all times, no restrictions. Advance booking of tee-off times recommended. Hotel golf packages available. *Society Meetings:* welcome by arrangement. Professional: Steven Killens (01236 725281; Fax: 01236 738478). Secretary: Gerry McAteer (01324 634662).

DUMBARTON. **Dumbarton Golf Club,** Broadmeadow, Dumbarton G82 2BQ (01389 32830). *Location:* A814, three-quarters of a mile north west of town. Flat parkland. 18 holes, 6071 yards. S.S.S. 69. Small practice area. *Green Fees:* £16.00 weekdays. *Eating facilities:* bar available, meals by previous arrangement with Caterer. *Visitors:* welcome weekdays only except Bank Holidays. No jeans or shellsuits on course or in clubhouse. *Society Meetings:* all welcome with prior bookings through Secretary. Secretary: R. Turnbull.

HELENSBURGH. **Helensburgh Golf Club,** 25 East Abercromby Street, Helensburgh G84 9JD (01436 674173; Fax: 01436 671170). *Location:* A82 from Dumbarton. Moorland course with panoramic views across Loch Lomond and Gareloch. 18 holes, 6058 yards. S.S.S. 69. Practice area. *Green Fees:* £15.00 per round, £23.00 per day weekdays. *Eating facilities:* full catering and bar. *Visitors:* welcome weekdays only, dress in recognised golfing attire. Professional: Robert Farrell (01436 675505). Secretary: David Loch (01436 674173).

KIRKINTILLOCH. **Kirkintilloch Golf Club,** Campsie Road, Kirkintilloch G66 1RN (0141-776 1256). *Location:* from Glasgow to Bishopbriggs, then straight on to Kirkintilloch. Undulating, parkland course. 18 holes, 5269 yards. S.S.S. 66. Par 70. Putting green and practice areas. *Green Fees:* on application. *Eating facilities:* dining room and bar. *Visitors:* weekdays only, must be introduced by member. *Society Meetings:* catered for Mondays and Tuesdays, information from Secretary including catering. Secretary: I.M. Gray (0141-775 2387).

LENZIE. **Lenzie Golf Club,** 19 Crosshill Road, Lenzie, Glasgow G66 5DA (0141-776 1535). *Location:* two miles from A90 Junction to Kirkintilloch. Parkland. 18 holes, 5982 yards. S.S.S. 69. *Green Fees:* weekdays only, £12.50 per round, £20.00 per day. *Eating facilities:* dining room available. *Visitors:* welcome with introduction or prior reservation. *Society Meetings:* welcome. Professional: Jim McCallum (0141-777 7748). Secretary: J.A. Chisholm (0141-776 6020).

Edinburgh and the Lothians

ABERLADY. **Kilspindie Golf Club,** The Clubhouse, Aberlady EH32 0QD (0187 57 216). *Location:* off A198 North Berwick Road at Aberlady. Seaside course. 18 holes, 5417 yards, 4957 metres. S.S.S. 66. Large practice area. *Green Fees:* weekdays £20.00 per round, £27.00 per day; Saturday and Sunday £25.00 per round, £32.00 per day. *Eating facilities:* diningroom and bar. *Visitors:* welcome after 9.15am and before 4pm weekdays, after 11am weekends on non-competition days. *Society Meetings:* welcome subject to above restrictions (no catering Fridays). Professional: Graham Sked (0187 57 695). Secretary: Hugh F. Brown (0187 57 358). *

ABERLADY. **Luffness New Golf Club,** Aberlady EH32 0QA (01620 843114; Fax: 01620 842933). *Location:* A198 – 17 miles east of Edinburgh. One mile from Gullane. Links course, 18 holes, 6122 yards. S.S.S. 69. *Green Fees:* provided on application. *Eating facilities:* dining room except Mondays. *Visitors:* weekdays only (require introduction). *Society Meetings:* by prior arrangement. Secretary: Lt. Col. J.G. Tedford (01620 843336; Fax: 01620 842933).

BATHGATE **Bathgate Golf Club,** Edinburgh Road, Bathgate EH48 1BA (01506 52232; Fax: 01506 636775). *Location:* three miles from M8, 400 yards east of George Square, the town centre. Flat course. 18 holes, 6328 yards. S.S.S. 70. Practice area. *Green Fees:* weekdays £15.00 per round, £20.00 per day; weekends £25.00 per day. *Eating facilities:* diningroom open all week. *Visitors:* welcome without reservation except on Competition days at weekends. Professional: Sandy Strachan (01506 630553). Secretary: W. Gray (01506 630505).

DALKEITH. **Newbattle Golf Club Ltd,** Abbey Road, Dalkeith (0131-663 2123). *Location:* approximately seven miles south-east of Edinburgh A7 to Eskbank Toll (Newbattle exit). Parkland, wooded course. 18 holes, 6012 yards, 5498 metres. S.S.S. 69. Small practice area. *Green Fees:* £14.00 per round, £20.00 per day. *Eating facilities:* full catering available on request. *Visitors:* weekdays only. No jeans/trainers on course or in clubhouse. *Society Meetings:* restricted. Professional: D. Torrance (0131-660 1631). Secretary: H.G. Stanners (0131 663 1819).

If you are writing, a stamped, addressed envelope is always appreciated.

DUNBAR. **Dunbar Golf Club,** East Links, Dunbar EH42 1LP (01368 862317; Fax: 01368 865202). *Location:* on coast half a mile east of Dunbar. Seaside links, used for final qualifying 1992 Open Championship. 18 holes, 6426 yards. S.S.S. 71. *Green Fees:* weekdays £28.00 per day; weekends £40.00. Subject to review. *Eating facilities:* full catering facilities. *Visitors:* no visitors on Thursdays or before 9.30am and between 12.30pm and 2pm weekdays; or before 10am and between 12 noon and 2pm weekends. *Society Meetings:* welcome. Professional: Derek Small (01368 862317). Secretary: Don Thompson (01368 862186; Fax: 01368 865202).

DUNBAR. **Winterfield Golf Club,** North Road, Dunbar (01368 62280). Seaside course. 18 holes, 4686 metres. S.S.S. 65. *Green Fees:* information not available. *Eating facilities:* available. *Visitors:* welcome without reservation. The Pro Shop: (01368 63562). Professional: Keven Phillips. Secretary: Michael O'Donnell (01368 62280/65119).

EDINBURGH. **Baberton Golf Club,** Baberton Avenue, Juniper Green, Edinburgh EH14 5DU (0131-453 3361). *Location:* five miles west of Edinburgh on the A70. 18 holes, 6098 yards. S.S.S. 69. *Green Fees:* weekdays £17.00 per round, £25.00 per day. *Eating facilities:* by arrangement (phone Peter Wilkie 0131-453 3361). *Visitors:* welcome by arrangement with Secretary. *Society Meetings:* catered for. Professional: K. Kelly (0131-453 3555). Secretary: E.W. Horberry (0131-453 4911).

EDINBURGH. **Braids United Golf Club,** 22 Braid Hills Approach, Morningside, Edinburgh EH10 6JY (0131-452 9408). *Location:* Braid Hills on south side of Edinburgh. Two 18 hole courses. No. 1 – 5880 yards. S.S.S. 68. No. 2 – 4495 yards. S.S.S. 64. *Green Fees:* £6.60. *Visitors:* welcome without reservation. (Accommodation in Braid Hills Hotel – 400 yards). Public courses, clubs on hire. Sunday golf on No. 2 course only. Hon. Secretary: Gerald Hind. Starter: (0131-447 6666).

EDINBURGH. **Broomieknowe Golf Club Ltd,** 36 Golf Course Road, Bonnyrigg (0131-663 9317). *Location:* south of Edinburgh, A6094 from Dalkeith. Flat parkland course. 18 holes, 6150 yards. S.S.S. 69. *Green Fees:* weekdays £15.00 per round, £25.00 per day; £25.00 per round at weekends. *Eating facilities:* lunches, high teas except Mondays. *Visitors:* welcome Monday to Friday, weekends by prior arrangement. *Society Meetings:* catered for Monday to Friday by arrangement. Professional: Mark Patchett (0131-660 2035). Secretary: John Guthrie White.

EDINBURGH. **Bruntsfield Links Golfing Society,** The Clubhouse, 32 Barnton Avenue, Edinburgh EH4 6JH (0131-336 2006). *Location:* off A90 to Davidson's Mains. Parkland course. 18 holes, 6402 yards. S.S.S. 71. *Green Fees:* information not provided. *Eating facilities:* morning coffee, lunches and high tea if ordered in advance. *Visitors:* welcome on weekdays if playing with a member or suitably introduced. Maximum Handicap 18. *Society Meetings:* catered for. Professional: Brian MacKenzie (0131-336 4050). Secretary: Lieut Col M.B. Hext (0131-336 1479).

EDINBURGH. **City of Edinburgh Golf Club,** Silverknowes Pavilion, Silverknowes Parkway, Edinburgh EH4. *Location:* main office (Silverknowes) on north side of Edinburgh. Club plays over the following municipal courses – Carrick Knowe: 18 holes, 6150 yards. S.S.S. 69; Braids No.1: 18 holes, 5692 yards. S.S.S. 67; Braids No.2: 18 holes, 4788 yards. S.S.S. 63; Portobello: 9 holes, 4816 yards. S.S.S. 64; Silverknowes: 18 holes, 6198 yards. S.S.S. 69; Craigentinny: 18 holes, 5413 yards. S.S.S. 66. 30-bay driving range and large Pro shop adjacent to Braids No.1; professional coaching available at all times. *Green Fees:* on application. *Eating facilities:* available at Silverknowes Pavilion and Braids No.1 Pavilion. *Visitors:* welcome all year round. Professional: Gary Nicol (Tel and Fax: 0131-447 8030). Secretary: Mrs Andrea Sharrock (0131-312 7222; Fax: 0131 312 7666).

EDINBURGH. **Craigmillar Park Golf Club,** 1 Observatory Road, Edinburgh EH9 3HG (0131-667 2837). *Location:* A702 from City centre on Mayfield Road, right at King's Buildings. Parkland. 18 holes, 5846 yards. S.S.S. 68. *Green Fees:* £15.00 per round, £23.00 per day. *Eating facilities:* lunches, snacks, high teas and dinners. *Visitors:* welcome with reservation on production of Handicap Certificate. Weekdays only before 3.30pm. *Society Meetings:* catered for by previous arrangement. Professional: B. McGee (0131-667 0047). Secretary: J. Brough (0131-667 0047).

EDINBURGH. **Duddingston Golf Club Ltd,** Duddingston Road West, Edinburgh EH15 3QD (0131-661 1005). *Location:* adjacent to A1 Willowbrae Road, turn right at Duddingston crossroads then one mile on Duddingston Road West. Undulating parkland with stream. 18 holes, 6647 yards. S.S.S. 72. *Green Fees:* weekdays only £21.00 per round, £27.50 per day. *Eating facilities:* full catering and bar facilities. *Visitors:* welcome weekdays only. *Society Meetings:* catered for Tuesdays and Thursdays (rates on request). Professional: Alistair McLean (0131-661 4301). Secretary: John C. Small (0131-661 7688).

EDINBURGH. **Kingsknowe Golf Club,** 326 Lanark Road, Edinburgh EH14 2JD (0131-441 1144). *Location:* on Edinburgh Corporation Bus No. 44 route. Parkland course. 18 holes, 5979 yards, 5466 metres. S.S.S. 69. Practice area. *Green Fees:* weekdays £16.00 per round, £20.00 per day; weekends £25.00 per round. *Eating facilities:* lounge bar, snacks and meals available. *Visitors:* welcome Monday to Friday, also weekends subject to availability. *Society Meetings:* catered for. Professional: Andrew Marshall (0131-441 4030). Secretary: R. Wallace (0131-441 1145)

EDINBURGH. **Liberton Golf Club,** 297 Gilmerton Road, Edinburgh EH16 5UJ (0131-664 8580). *Location:* Corporation transport to Lodge Gate, buses 3 and 8 from Edinburgh. By car on A7 (Visitors' car park). Parkland, rolling. 18 holes, 5299 yards, 4845 metres. S.S.S. 66. *Green Fees:* weekdays £15.00 per round, £25.00 per day; weekends £25.00. *Eating facilities:* full catering and bar service. *Visitors:* not before 1.30pm weekends. *Society Meetings:* catered for by arrangememt except Fridays or weekends. Professional: I. Seath (0131-664 1056). Secretary: A. Poole (0131-664 3009).

EDINBURGH. **Lothianburn Golf Club,** 106a Biggar Road, Edinburgh EH10 7DU (0131-445 2206). *Location:* south on the A702 approximately four miles from city centre or easily reached from Edinburgh bypass road coming off at Lothianburn junction. Hill course close to Pentland Hills. 18 holes, 5750 yards. S.S.S. 69. Two practice grounds. *Green Fees:* weekdays £12.00 per round, £18.00 per day; weekends £18.00 per round, £23.00 per day. Special rates November to February on application. *Eating facilities:* normal bar hours, no hot food on Wednesdays. *Visitors:* welcome mid-week, weekends restricted. *Society Meetings:* catered for by prior arrangement with the Secretary. Professional: Kurt Mungall (0131-445 2288). Secretary: W.F.A. Jardine (0131-445 5067).

EDINBURGH. **Merchants Of Edinburgh Golf Club,** 10 Craighill Gardens, Edinburgh EH10 5PY (0131-447 1219). *Location:* car park Glenlockhart Road, Edinburgh EH10. Hilly parkland. 18 holes, 4889 yards. S.S.S. 64. *Green Fees:* weekdays £12.00. *Eating facilities:* by arrangement with Clubmaster, J. Wilson. *Visitors:* welcome weekdays until 4pm, not weekends. *Society Meetings:* catered for except weekends). Professional: N.E.M. Colquhoun (0131-447 8709). Secretary: A.M. Montgomery.

EDINBURGH. **Mortonhall Golf Club,** 231 Braid Road, Edinburgh EH10 6PB (0131-447 2411). *Location:* take A702 south from City to Morningside traffic lights, up Braid Road one mile, course on left. 18 holes, 6548 yards, 5987 metres. S.S.S. 71. *Green Fees:* information not provided. *Eating facilities:* lunch, tea and snacks every day (no lunches Mondays). *Visitors:* welcome with introduction. *Society Meetings:* catered for (not at weekends). Professional: D. Horn. Secretary: Mrs C.D. Morrison (0131-447 6974).

EDINBURGH. **Murrayfield Golf Club,** 43 Murrayfield Road, Edinburgh EH12 6EU (0131-337 1009). *Location:* two miles west of city centre. Parkland on east side of Corstorphine Hill. 18 holes, 5725 yards.

S.S.S. 68. Practice area, net and putting green. *Green Fees:* weekdays £20.00 per round, £26.00 per day. *Eating facilities:* lunch each day, snacks in casual bar, also full bar facilities. *Visitors:* welcome playing with member or by prior arrangement only. No visitors weekends. *Society Meetings:* catered for by prior arrangement. Professional: J.J. Fisher (0131-337 3479). Secretary: Mrs M.K. Hermiston (0131-337 3478).

EDINBURGH. **Portobello Golf Club,** Stanley Street, Portobello, Edinburgh EH15 1JJ (0131-669 4361). *Location:* on A1 at Milton Road East. Parkland course. 9 holes, 2400 yards, 2167 metres. S.S.S. 32. *Green Fees:* £3.30 per round (9 holes). Reductions for Juniors and Senior Citizens. *Visitors:* welcome, restrictions on competition days. *Society Meetings:* not catered for. Professional: J. Boath. Secretary: A. Cook (0131-669 5271).

EDINBURGH. **Prestonfield Golf Club,** 6 Priestfield Road North, Edinburgh EH16 5HS (0131-667 1273). *Location:* off Dalkeith Road, near Royal Commonwealth Pool on A68. Parkland. 18 holes, 6216 yards. S.S.S. 70. Practice area. *Green Fees:* weekdays £17.00 per round, £25.00 per day; weekends and Bank Holidays £25.00 per round, £35.00 per day. *Eating facilities:* full catering. *Visitors:* welcome weekdays anytime, not between 8am and 10.30am or 12 noon to 1.30pm Saturdays, not before 11.30am Sundays. *Society Meetings:* welcome weekdays. Professional: G. MacDonald (0131-667 8597). Secretary: Michael D.A.G. Dillon (0131-667 9665).

EDINBURGH. **Ravelston Golf Club Ltd,** 24 Ravelston Dykes Road, Blackhall, Edinburgh EH4 5NZ (0131-315 2486). *Location:* A90 Queensferry Road (leading to Forth Road Bridge). Left at traffic lights by Kwik-Fit garage to Strachan Road, cross Craigcrook Road, clubhouse on right. Parkland course. 9 holes, 2600 yards, 2377 metres. S.S.S. 66. *Green Fees:* £12.50 weekdays. Subject to review. *Eating facilities;* tea, coffee, soft drinks and light snacks. *Visitors:* welcome during quiet period. *Society Meetings:* permitted by special application only. Secretary: Frank Philip (0131-312 6850).

EDINBURGH. **Royal Burgess Golfing Society of Edinburgh,** 181 Whitehouse Road, Barnton, Edinburgh EH4 6BY. *Location:* A90 to Forth Road Bridge, behind Barnton Hotel. Parkland. 18 holes, 6494 yards. S.S.S. 71. *Green Fees:* on request. *Eating facilities:* snacks and lunches available. *Visitors:* welcome weekdays, male only. *Society Meetings:* male only, catered for Tuesdays, Thursdays and Fridays. Professional: George Yuille (0131-334 6474). Secretary: John Audis (0131-339 2075).

EDINBURGH: **Silverknowes Golf Club,** Silverknowes, Parkway, Edinburgh EH4 5ET (0131-336 5359). *Location:* nearest main road Queensferry Road; signs Davidson Mains, Silverknowes. Parkland, flat. 18 holes, 6216 yards. S.S.S. 71. *Green Fees:* £7.00 per round. *Eating facilities:* clubhouse – by invitation/ Lauriston Farm restaurant. *Visitors:* only by invitation of club member. *Society Meetings:* by arrangement weekdays only. Secretary: D.W. Scobie.

EDINBURGH. **Swanston Golf Club,** 111 Swanston Road, Edinburgh EH10 7DS (0131-445 2239). *Location:* five miles from centreof Edinburgh, west of Biggar Road (A702) on the lower slopes of the Pentland Hills. Parkland course. 18 holes, 5024 yards. S.S.S. 66. *Green Fees:* weekdays £10.00 per round, £15.00 day ticket; weekends £15.00 per round, £20.00 day ticket. *Eating facilities:* full catering facilities. *Visitors:* welcome without reservation weekdays, weekends restricted. *Society Meetings:* catered for. Professional: J. Scott Maxwell (0131-445 4002). Secretary: John Allan (0131-445 2239).

EDINBURGH. **Torphin Hill Golf Club,** Torphin Road, Edinburgh EH13 0PG (0131-441 1100). *Location:* south west of Colinton Village at terminus of No. 9 and No. 10 bus. Holes 5 to 15 on plateau with outstanding views of Edinburgh. 18 holes, 5087 yards, 4652 metres. S.S.S. 66. Practice area. *Green Fees:* weekdays £7.00 per round, £12.00 per day; weekends £10.00 per round, £18.00 per day. *Eating facilities:* dining room and bar snacks. *Visitors:* welcome without reservation except on Competition Days. *Society Meetings:* catered for weekdays only. Reduced rates for parties over 20. Secretary: E.H. Marchant (0131-441 4061).

EDINBURGH. **Turnhouse Golf Club,** Turnhouse, Edinburgh (0131-339 1014). *Location:* to Glasgow first right at Maybury roundabout. 18 holes, 6171 yards. S.S.S. 69. *Green Fees:* weekdays £14.00 per round, £20.00 per day. *Eating facilities:* full service. *Visitors:* welcome only as a group/society or playing with member. Not at weekends, Bank Holidays or Competition days. Professional: John Murray (0131-339 7701). Secretary: A.B. Hay (0131-539 5937).

FAULDHOUSE. **Greenburn Golf Club,** 6 Greenburn Road, Fauldhouse EH47 9AY (01501 770292). *Location:* four miles south of Junctions 4 and 5 of M8 motorway. Undulating moorland with elevated railway line running through, supported by viaduct. 18 holes, 6055 yards. S.S.S. 69. Practice area. *Green Fees:* £11.50 per round, £17.00 per day weekdays; £14.00 per round, £21.50 per day weekends. *Eating facilities:* catering available except Tuesdays (catering on Tuesdays for visiting parties by prior arrangement only). *Visitors:* welcome by prior arrangement. Normal times 9am to 10am and 2pm to 3pm. *Society Meetings:* welcome with prior arrangement. Professional: Howard Ferguson (01501 771187). Secretary: Alexander Stein (01501 741967).

GULLANE. **Gullane Golf Club,** Gullane EH31 2BB (01620 842255). *Location:* 18 miles east of Edinburgh on A198 Edinburgh to North Berwick Road. Links. Three 18 hole courses. No. 1 – 6466 yards, 5913 metres. S.S.S. 71. No. 2 – 6244 yards, 5676 metres. S.S.S. 70. No. 3 – 5166 yards, 4696 metres. S.S.S. 65. *Green Fees:* (1994)No. 1 course £37.00, No. 2 course £17.00, No. 3 course £10.50 weekdays; No. 1 course £47.00, No. 2 course £21.00, No. 3 course £12.50 weekends. *Eating facilities:* new clubhouse with bar, snacks, etc. *Visitors:* welcome with reservation. *Society Meetings:* catered for. Professional: Jimmy Hume (01620 843111). Secretary: A.J.B. Taylor (01620 842255; Fax: 01620 842327). Starters: (01620 843115).

GULLANE. **The Honourable Company Of Edinburgh Golfers,** Muirfield, Gullane EH31 2EG (01620 842123; Fax: 01620 842977). *Location:* 20 miles from Edinburgh along the coast road to North Berwick. Links course. 18 holes, 6601 yards. S.S.S. 73. *Green Fees:* £50.00 per round; £70 for double round (1994 prices). *Eating facilities:* morning coffee, lunches and afternoon teas if ordered in advance. *Visitors:* welcome Tuesdays and Thursdays, maximum Handicap 18 for men, 24 for ladies. Secretary: Group Captain J.A. Prideaux.

HADDINGTON. **Haddington Golf Club,** Amisfield Park, Haddington, East Lothian EH41 4PT (0162-082 3627). *Location:* on A1 Edinburgh. Wooded parkland, slightly undulating. 18 holes, 6280 yards, 5764 metres. S.S.S. 70. Practice area. *Green Fees:* weekdays £11.00 per round, £15.00 per day; weekends £15.00 per round, £19.00 per day. Fees subject to increase. *Eating facilities:* two bars and dining room. *Visitors:* welcome, midweek no restrictions, weekends permitted 10am-12 noon, 2-4pm. *Society Meetings:* catered for. Professional: J. Sandilands (0162-082 2727). Secretary: Tom Speirs.

HADDINGTON near. **Gifford Golf Club,** Edinburgh Road, Gifford, Near Haddington (0162-081 591). *Location:* quarter of a mile south of village. Undulating parkland with burn crossing the course. 9 holes, 6101 yards. S.S.S. 70. *Green Fees:* weekdays £10.00 per day, weekends £10.00 per 9/18 holes. Juniors (under 16's) £3.00 per day, £10.00 weekends. *Visitors:* closed to visitors from 4pm Tuesdays and Wednesdays and from 12 noon weekends. Closed all day first Sunday in the month April to October. Secretary: Donald A. Fantom (0162-081 267).

KIRKNEWTON. **Dalmahoy Hotel, Golf and Country Club,** Kirknewton, Midlothian EH27 8EB (0131-333 4105; Fax: 0131-335 3203). *Location:* seven miles west of Edinburgh on A71. Two courses: East Course, Championship parkland course, host to many major tournaments. 18 holes, 6677 yards. S.S.S. 72. West Course, parkland course featuring two spectacular crossings of Gogar Burn. 18 holes, 5185 yards. S.S.S. 66. Extensive practice area. *Green Fees:* East Course: weekdays £33.00 per round; West Course: weekdays £22.00 per round. *Eating facilities:* Terrace Restaurant and Club Bar in Country Club, restaurant and bars in Hotel also. *Visitors:* welcome weekdays; weekends members and Hotel residents only. Hotel accommodation. Golf carts, buggies and clubs for hire. *Society Meetings:* welcome weekdays only. Director of Golf: Brian Anderson. Secretary: Jennifer Wilson. *

LINLITHGOW. **Linlithgow Golf Club,** Braehead, Linlithgow EH49 6QF (01506 671044). *Location:* M8, M9, 20 miles west of Edinburgh, west end of Linlithgow – fork left. Parkland and wooded course with panoramic views. 18 holes, 5729 yards. S.S.S. 68. Small practice area and net. *Green Fees:* weekdays £11.00 per round, £17.00 per day; Sunday £17.00 per round, £22.00 per day. Weekly tickets £35. *Eating facilities:*

full facilities available. *Visitors:* welcome except Saturdays. *Society Meetings:* welcome. Professional: Derek Smith (01506 844356). Secretary: Tommy Thomson (01506 842585).

LINLITHGOW. **West Lothian Golf Club,** Airngath Hill, Bo'ness EH49 7RH (01506 826030). *Location:* situated midway between Linlithgow and Bo'ness. Undulating parkland course. 18 holes, 6629 yards. S.S.S. 71. Practice area. *Green Fees:* information not provided. *Eating facilities:* available by arrangement. *Visitors:* welcome, no restrictions before 3.30pm midweek. After 3.30pm and at weekends by arrangement only. *Society Meetings:* by arrangement. Secretary: T.B. Fraser (01506 825476). *

LIVINGSTON. **Deer Park Golf & Country Club,** Golf Course Road, Livingston EH54 8PG (01506 31037; Fax: 01506 35608). *Location:* Junction 3 of M8. Parkland course, first 9 holes flat, back 9 holes hilly. 18 holes, 6688 yards. S.S.S. 72. *Green Fees:* £15.00 per round weekdays; £25.00 per round weekends. *Eating facilities:* four bars, catering seven days. *Visitors:* welcome. Snooker, ten pin bowling, pool, sauna, steam room. *Society Meetings:* catered for. Professional: W.J. Yule (01506 38843). Secretary: Alec Strathearn.

LIVINGSTON. **Pumpherston Golf Club,** Drumshoreland Road, Pumpherston, Livingston EH53 0LF (01506 32869). *Location:* one mile east of Livingston, one and a half miles south of M8. Undulating parkland course, well bunkered. 9 holes, 5434 yards, 4969 metres. S.S.S. 66. Small practice area. *Green Fees:* information not supplied. *Eating facilities:* snack meals, lounge bar. *Visitors:* only when introduced by member. *Society Meetings:* Mondays to Thursdays, maximum number 24. Secretary: A.H. Docharty (01506 854652).

LONGNIDDRY. **Longniddry Golf Club Ltd,** The Clubhouse, Links Road, Longniddry EH32 0NL (01875 852623). *Location:* from Edinburgh by A1, left for Longniddry, A198 at Wallyford roundabout or left off A1 one mile after MacMerry. Parkland course with links features. 18 holes, 6219 yards, 5678 metres. S.S.S. 70. Practice ground, putting green, nets. *Green Fees:* weekdays £25.00 per round, £35.00 per day. *Eating facilities:* restaurant Saturday to Thursday, bar snacks seven days a week. *Visitors:* Monday to Thursday parties booked, otherwise Monday to Friday casual bookings arranged within the previous seven days except on local and Public Holidays and competition days. *Society Meetings:* catered for (except Friday – Sunday). Professional: John Gray (01875 852228). Secretary: Neil Robertson (01875 852141).

MUSSELBURGH. **Musselburgh Golf Club,** Monktonhall, Musselburgh EH21 6SA (0131-665 2005). *Location:* from the A1 end of the Edinburgh City bypass, on the B6415 to Musselburgh. Wooded parkland, rivers. 18 holes, 6614 yards. S.S.S. 72. *Green Fees:* on application. *Eating facilities:* catering available except Tuesdays. *Visitors:* welcome with reservation. *Society Meetings:* catered for. Professional: T. Stangoe (0131-665 7055). Secretary: S.Sullivan (0131-665 2005). Administrator (for bookings): G. Finlay.

NEWBRIDGE. **Ratho Park Golf Club Ltd,** Ratho, Newbridge EH28 8NX (0131-333 1252). *Location:* eight miles west of Edinburgh G.P.O., access from A71 or A8. Flat parkland. 18 holes, 5900 yards, 5398 metres. S.S.S. 68. *Green Fees:* weekdays £20.00 per round, £30.00 per day; weekends £30.00 per day. *Eating facilities:* full catering available. *Visitors:* welcome without reservation. *Society Meetings:* catered for Tuesdays, Wednesdays and Thursdays. Professional: Alan Pate (0131-333 1406). Secretary: J.C. McLafferty (0131-333 1752).

NORTH BERWICK. **Glen Golf Club,** East Links, Tantallon Terrace, North Berwick EH39 4LE (01620 2221). *Location:* off A198 one mile east of Railway Station. Seaside links with impressive panoramic views. 18 holes, 6089 yards. S.S.S. 69. Practice area on course. *Green Fees:* weekdays £11.50 per round, £17.00 per day; weekends £15.00 per round, £21.00 per day. (Composite tickets available from hotels in East Lothian). Half price for Senior Citizens and Juniors weekdays. *Eating facilities:* full facilities available. *Visitors:* welcome anytime, no restrictions. *Society Meetings:* catered for with advance booking. Professional: shop only (01620 4596). Secretary: D.R. Montgomery (01620 2221; Fax: 01620 5288). Starter: (01620 2726).

NORTH BERWICK. **The North Berwick Golf Club,** New Clubhouse, Beach Road, North Berwick EH39 4BB (01620 4766; Fax: 01620 3274). *Location:* 24 miles east of Edinburgh, A1 to Meadowmill roundabout then A198 to North Berwick. Seaside links. 18 holes, 6420 yards. S.S.S. 71. Practice ground. *Green Fees:* weekdays £25.00 per round, £35.00 per day; weekends and Public Holidays £35.00 per round, £40.00 per day. *Eating facilities:* diningroom and bar. *Visitors:* welcome from 10am, book ahead Saturdays – restricted when there are club fixtures. Lounge and changing rooms available. *Society Meetings:* catered for by arrangement. Professional: D. Huish (01620 3233). Secretary: William Gray (01620 5040). Advance Bookings: (01620 2135).

PENICUIK. **Glencorse Golf Club,** Milton Bridge, Penicuik EH26 0RD (01968 677177). *Location:* A701 nine miles south of Edinburgh on Peebles Road. Parkland course with stream affecting 10 holes. 18 holes, 5217 yards. S.S.S. 66. *Green Fees:* weekdays £16.00 per round, £21.00 per day, weekends £21.00 per round. Package deals available. *Eating facilities:* full catering and bar. *Visitors:* welcome at all times subject to Club Competitions. *Society Meetings:* catered for Mondays to Thursdays. Professional: Cliffe Jones (01968 676481). Secretary: W. Oliver (01968 677189; Fax: 01968 674399).

PRESTONPANS. **Royal Musselburgh Golf Club,** Prestongrange House, Prestonpans EH32 9RP (01875 810276). *Location:* A198 North Berwick road near Prestonpans. Parkland. 18 holes, 6237 yards. S.S.S. 70. *Green Fees:* weekdays £18.00 per round, £30.00 per day; weekends £30.00 per round, no day tickets.

Eating facilities: full catering and licence. *Visitors:* welcome weekdays, not before 9.30am, not after 3pm, not Friday afternoons. *Society Meetings:* catered for weekdays only – book in advance. Professional: John Henderson (Tel & Fax: 01875 810139). Secretary: (Tel & Fax: 01875 810276).

SOUTH QUEENSFERRY. **Dundas Parks Golf Club,** Dundas Estate, South Queensferry, West Lothian. *Location:* five miles west of Edinburgh, on South Queensferry to Kirkliston road on right of A8000. Parkland course in open countryside. 9 holes (x 2). Small practice area. *Green Fees:* £8.00. *Eating facilities:* not available. *Visitors:* welcome with member, or by prior arrangement with Secretary. *Society Meetings:* by prior arrangement with Secretary. Secretary: Keith D. Love (0131-331 1416). *

UPHALL. **Uphall Golf Club,** Uphall, West Lothian EH52 6JT (01506 856404). *Location:* eight miles west of Edinburgh Airport on the A89 Edinburgh to Glasgow road. Established parkland course. 18 holes, S.S.S. 67. *Green Fees:* weekdays £14.00 per round, £19.00 per day; weekends £19.00 per round, £29.00 per day. *Eating facilities:* hot and cold snacks, lunches, high teas and bars. *Visitors:* welcome weekdays without reservation. A booking through the Professional is required at weekends. *Society Meetings:* catered for. Professional: Gordon Law (01506 855553). Manager: Tony Flood (01506 856404).

WEST CALDER. **Harburn Golf Club,** Harburn, West Calder EH55 8RS (01506 871256). *Location:* two miles south of West Calder on B7008. Parkland course. 18 holes, 5853 yards, 5436 metres. S.S.S. 68. Practice ground. *Green Fees:* £12.50 per round, £18.50 per day weekdays; £18.50 per round, £25.00 per day weekends. *Eating facilities:* full catering and bar service except Tuesdays. *Visitors:* welcome any time – no restrictions. *Society Meetings:* catered for by advance arrangement. Professional: Tom Stangoe (01506 871582). Secretary: Frank Vinter (01506 871131).

WHITBURN. **Polkemmet Golf Course,** Polkemmet Country Park, Whitburn, West Lothian (01501 743905). *Location:* off B7066, one mile west of Whitburn. Inland course set within old private estate, mature varied woodland with belts of rhododendrons. 9 holes, 2969 metres. Par 37. Driving range. *Green Fees:* Monday to Saturday (Summer) £2.80 adults, Juvenile/Senior Citizens/Concessions £1.30; Sunday (Summer) £3.50 adult, Juvenile/Senior Citizens/ Concessions £1.80. Winter reductions. *Eating facilities:* restaurant and bar complex. *Visitors:* welcome. Public course. Facilities include bowling green, picnic areas, etc. Caddy Cart hire 70p. Secretary: West Lothian District Council, Department of Leisure and Recreation, County Buildings, Linlithgow.

WINCHBURGH. **Niddry Castle Golf Club,** Castle Road, Winchburgh EH52 6RQ (01506 891097). *Location:* 10 miles west of Edinburgh on A803 between Kirkliston and Linlithgow. Wooded, natural parkland. 9 holes, 5450 yards. S.S.S. 67. *Green Fees:* £8.00 weekdays; £11.00 weekends. *Eating facilities:* none – but bar lunches available in village. *Visitors:* welcome anytime but not until 2pm on Saturdays of club competitions. *Society Meetings:* by arrangement. Secretary: A. Brockbank.

Fife

ABERDOUR. **Aberdour Golf Club,** Seaside Place, Aberdour KY3 0TX (01383 860688). *Location:* take Shore Road from centre of village. Parkland course situated along the shoreline of the River Forth. 18 holes, 5460 yards. S.S.S. 67. *Green Fees:* £17.00 per round, £27.00 per day. *Eating facilities:* full catering. *Visitors:* welcome on weekdays. *Society Meetings:* catered for on weekdays and Sundays. On Sundays, maximum size of group 24. Professional: Gordon McCallum (01383 860256). Secretary: John Train (01383 860080).

ANSTRUTHER. **Anstruther Golf Club,** Marsfield, Shore Road, Anstruther KY10 3DZ (01333 310956). *Location:* nine miles south of St. Andrews, west side of Anstruther. Seaside links course. 9 holes, 4144 metres. S.S.S. 63. *Green Fees:* weekdays £11.00; weekends £15.00. *Eating facilities:* lounge bar and dining room. *Visitors:* welcome except during club competitions. *Society Meetings:* outwith May/September and competition days. Secretary: J.F. MacLeod (01333 310956/312283).

BURNTISLAND. **Burntisland Golf House Club,** Dodhead, Burntisland KY3 9EY (01592 873247). *Location:* on B924, approximately half a mile east of town centre. Parkland with some hills. 18 holes, 5908 yards. S.S.S. 69. Practice ground and net. *Green Fees:* weekdays £18.00 per round, £25.00 per day; weekends £25.00 per round, £38.00 per day. *Eating* *facilities:* full catering facilities. *Visitors:* welcome. Parties limited to 24 at weekends apart from club competitions. Changing room. *Society Meetings:* welcome with advance bookings. Professional: J. Montgomery (01592 873247). Manager: Ian McLean (01592 874093).

CARDENDEN. **Auchterderran Golf Club,** Woodend Road, Cardenden (01592 721579). *Location:* six miles north of Kirkcaldy. Flat course. 9 holes, 5252 yards. S.S.S. 66. *Green Fees:* weekdays £7.00; weekends £9.00. Concessionary ticket available. *Visitors:* welcome at all times, check with course for members' tournaments. *Society Meetings:* all bookings accepted. Secretary: Michael Dois (01592 721877). *

CRAIL. **Crail Golfing Society,** Balcomie Clubhouse, Fifeness, Crail KY10 3XN (01333 450278). Instituted 1786. *Location:* eleven miles south-east of St. Andrews on A917. Parkland/seaside links. 18 holes, 5720 yards. S.S.S. 68. Practice ground. *Green Fees:* weekdays £17.00 per round, £25.00 per day; weekends £22.00 per round, £33.00 per day. 3/4/5 day £17.00 per day, Fortnightly £140. (except Sundays). *Eating facilities:* quality catering and bar. *Visitors:* welcome. *Society Meetings:* advance booking available for parties. Professional: Graeme Lennie (01333 450960). Secretary: Mrs C.W. Penhale (01333 450686).

CUPAR. **Cupar Golf Club,** Hilltarvit, Cupar (01334 653549). *Location:* near cemetery on Ceres Road. Hillside/parkland course. 9 holes, 5074 yards. S.S.S.

65. Practice putting green. *Green Fees:* weekdays £10.00; Sundays £12.00. *Eating facilities:* full catering/ bar. *Visitors:* welcome, except Saturdays, weekends after 5pm. *Society Meetings:* by arrangement with Secretary. Secretary: C.J. McCulloch (01334 652176).

DUNFERMLINE. **Canmore Golf Club,** Venture Fair, Dunfermline (01383 724969). *Location:* one mile north of town centre on A823. Parkland, undulating. 18 holes, 5347 yards. S.S.S. 66. *Green Fees:* weekdays £12.00 per round, £18.00 per day; weekends £25.00 per day. *Eating facilities:* full catering and bar. *Visitors:* welcome except on weekends. *Society Meetings:* we welcome visiting societies with prior reservation (not at weekends). Professional: John Hamlin (01383 728416). Secretary: J.C. Duncan (01383 726098).

DUNFERMLINE. **Dunfermline Golf Club,** Pitfirrane, Crossford, By Dunfermline KY12 8QV (01383 723534). *Location:* two miles west of Dunfermline on A994 to Kincardine Bridge. Undulating parkland. 18 holes, 6237 yards, 5739 metres. S.S.S. 70. Short 9 hole course and practice area. *Green Fees:* £20.00 per round, £28.00 per day weekdays. *Eating facilities:* full catering except Sunday evenings and Mondays, bar snacks available. *Visitors:* welcome weekdays 10am to 12 noon and 2pm to 4pm. Must have official club Handicap. *Society Meetings:* accepted weekdays by prior arrangement. Professional: Steve Craig (01383 723534). Secretary: Hamish Matheson (01383 723534).

DUNFERMLINE. **Pitreavie (Dunfermline) Golf Club,** Queensferry Road, Dunfermline KY11 5PR (01383 722591). *Location:* M90 Edinburgh/Perth, leave at Junction 2 for Dunfermline. Undulating parkland with views across Firth of Forth. 18 holes, 6008 yards. S.S.S. 69. Practice ground. *Green Fees:* weekdays £14.00 per round, £19.00 per day; weekends £25.00 per round/day. Subject to review. *Eating facilities:* full catering and bar facilities available. *Visitors:* welcome except Competition Days. Please phone in advance, must have recognised Golf Union Handicap. *Society Meetings:* catered for, must be booked through Secretary. Professional: Jim Forrester (Tel & Fax: 01383 723151). Secretary: Mr D. Carter (01383 722591).

DUNFERMLINE. **Saline Golf Club,** Kinneddar Hill, Saline KY12 9NF (01383 852591). *Location:* turn off M90 at Junction 4 for Dollar, near Dunfermline. Hillside course. 9 holes, 5302 yards. S.S.S. 66. Practice net, putting green. *Green Fees:* weekdays £9.00; weekends £11.00. Reductions for Senior Citizens. *Eating facilities:* bar snacks; meals by prior arrangement. *Visitors:* welcome, except Saturdays and certain Sundays. *Society Meetings:* catered for midweek or Sundays; maximum 24. Secretary: R. Hutchison (01383 852344).

ELIE. **Earlsferry Thistle Golf Club,** Melon Park, Elie (01333 310053). *Location:* A917, golf course signs in Elie. Seaside links. 18 holes, 6250 yards. S.S.S. 70. *Green Fees:* set by Elie Golf House Club, on application. *Visitors:* welcome weekdays. Secretary: (0133 450393). The course belongs to Elie Golf House Club, also played by Earlsferry Thistle.

ELIE. **Golf House Club,** Elie KY9 1AS (01333 330327; Fax: 01333 330895). *Location:* 10 miles south of St Andrews on A917. Links course. 18 holes, 6252 yards. S.S.S. 70. *Green Fees:* (1994) weekdays £24.00 per round, £32.00 per day; weekends £36.00 per round, £48.00 per day. *Eating facilities:* lunches, teas, etc. *Visitors:* welcome with reservation. Elie Sports Centre nearby with leisure facilities and cafeteria. *Society Meetings:* catered for except at weekends. Professional: Robin Wilson (01333 330955). Secretary: A. Sneddon (01333 330301).

FALKLAND. **Falkland Golf Club,** The Myre, Falkland KY7 7AA (01337 57404). *Location:* entrance on A912, 12 miles from Kirkcaldy – approximately 20 minutes from St. Andrews. Lies at the foot of East Lomond Hills. Flat meadowland, beautiful views. 9 holes, 2608 yards, 2384 metres. S.S.S. 66 for 18 holes. *Green Fees:* £8.00 per day weekdays; £12.00 weekends. Weekly ticket £35.00. Contact 01337 57404 after 6pm. *Eating facilities:* meals by arrangement, bar available for golfers. *Visitors:* welcome, no problem during weekdays, phone for availability weekends. *Society Meetings:* must book in advance. Secretary: Mrs H.H. Horsburgh (01337 756075).

GLENROTHES. **Glenrothes Golf Club,** Golf Course Road, Glenrothes KY6 2LA (01592 758686). *Location:* at the western end of town, near airfield. Hilly wooded parkland with burn crossing four fairways. 18 holes, 6444 yards. S.S.S. 71. *Green Fees:* weekdays £9.00 per round, £15.00 per day; weekends £11.00 per round, £17.00 per day. Reductions for Senior Citizens and Juniors. *Eating facilities:* full catering service. Temporary day membership of club available to visitors. *Visitors:* welcome, some restrictions weekends. *Society Meetings:* welcome, minimum number 12, contact Secretary. Hon. Secretary: Mrs P.V. Lanbells (01592 754561).

KINCARDINE. **Tulliallan Golf Club,** Alloa Road, Kincardine, by Alloa (01259 30396). *Location:* on A908 five miles east of Alloa, one mile north of Kincardine Bridge. Parkland, slightly wooded, burn winds through the course. 18 holes, 5892 yards, 5463 metres. S.S.S. 69. *Green Fees:* information not provided. *Eating facilities:* diningroom, bar 11am to 11pm. *Visitors:* no visiting parties on Fridays, Saturdays or on local holidays. *Society Meetings:* catered for with reservation, 24 limit on Sundays. Professional: Steven Kelly (01259 30798). Secretary: J.S. McDowall (01324 485420). *

KINGHORN. **Kinghorn Municipal Golf Club,** MacDuff Crescent, Kinghorn (01592 890345). *Location:* bus stop at course, railway station three minutes away. Semi links course with hills. 18 holes, 5217 yards. S.S.S. 67. *Green Fees:* weekdays £9.00 per round, £15.00 per day; weekends £11.00 per round, £17.00 per day. *Eating facilities:* meals at clubhouse, local hotels. *Visitors:* welcome with prior reservation if large party (up to 30). *Society Meetings:* catered for by arrangement. Secretary: George G. Flinn (01592 890380).

NOTE

All the information in this book is given in good faith in the belief that it is correct. However, the publishers cannot guarantee the facts given in these pages, neither are they responsible for changes in policy, ownership or terms that may take place after the date of going to press. Readers should always satisfy themselves that the facilities they require are available and that the terms, if quoted, still apply.

KIRKCALDY. **Dunnikier Park Golf Club,** Dunnikier Way, Kirkcaldy KY1 3LP (01592 261599). *Location:* one mile off A92 on the A910. Parkland course. 18 holes, 6601 yards, 6036 metres. S.S.S. 72. Practice ground adjacent. *Green Fees:* weekdays £9.00 per round, £15.00 per day; weekends £11.00 per round, £17.00 per day. *Eating facilities:* full catering facilities, licensed bar. *Visitors:* welcome by arrangement with Secretary, no restrictions. Adjacent to private hotel. *Society Meetings:* catered for. Professional: Jacky Montgomery (01592 205916). Secretary: Robert A. Waddell (01592 200627).

KIRKCALDY. **Kirkcaldy Golf Club,** Balwearie Road, Kirkcaldy KY2 5LT (01592 260370). *Location:* west end of town adjacent to Beveridge Park. Wooded parkland with stream. 18 holes, 6004 yards. S.S.S. 70. Small practice area. *Green Fees:* weekdays £15.00 per round, £20.00 per day; weekends £18.00 per round, £25.00 per day. *Eating facilities:* full catering facilities available. *Visitors:* welcome except Saturdays, limited Tuesdays. Professional's shop. *Society Meetings:* catered for. Professional: Scott McKay (01592 203258). Secretary: J.I. Brodley (01592 205240).

LADYBANK. **Ladybank Golf Club,** Annsmuir, Ladybank KY7 7RA (01337 830814). *Location:* on B9129 off A91, 15 miles St. Andrews. Wooded heathland. 18 holes, 6641 yards. S.S.S. 72. Practice ground. *Green Fees:* weekdays £25.00 per round, £34.00 per day; weekends £27.00 per round, £37.00 per day. *Eating facilities:* full catering facilities and bar. *Visitors:* welcome without reservation. Party bookings by arrangement with Secretary. *Society Meetings:* by arrangement. Professional: Martin J. Gray (01337 830725). Secretary: A.M. Dick (01337 830814).

LESLIE. **Leslie Golf Club,** Balsillie Laws, Leslie, Glenrothes KY6 3LR (01592 620040). Parkland with small stream running through some fairways. 9 holes, 4940 yards. S.S.S. 64. *Green Fees:* £6.00 weekdays; £10.00 weekends. *Eating facilities:* bar open each evening 7.30pm to 11pm, weekends 12 noon to 5pm and 7.30pm to 11pm. *Visitors:* always welcome, some restrictions on competition days. Secretary: M.G. Burns (01592 741449). *

LEUCHARS. **St. Michael's Golf Club,** Gallowhill, Leuchars KY16 0DX (01334 839365). *Location:* quarter of a mile outside Leuchars on A919 towards Dundee. Undulating parkland course surrounded by plantations. 9 holes, 5158 yards. S.S.S. 66. *Green Fees:* £12.00 day ticket, Juniors £6.00. Five day ticket Monday to Friday £40.00. *Eating facilities:* bar facilities and meals available. *Visitors:* welcome anytime but not before 1pm Sundays. Changing rooms and showers. *Society Meetings:* by prior arrangement. A booking fee is payable before confirmation of reservation. Secretary: Major L.M. McIntosh (01334 55328 after 6pm).

LEVEN. **Leven Golfing Society,** Links Road, Leven KY8 4HS (01333 426096). *Location:* nine miles east of Kirkcaldy on the A955. Links course, flat. 18 holes, 6434 yards, 5939 metres. S.S.S. 71. *Green Fees:* weekdays £18.00 round, £26.00 day; weekends £24.00 round, £36.00 day. *Eating facilities:* full catering available. *Visitors:* welcome (except Saturdays). *Society Meetings:* by arrangement (01333 428859). Parties of under 12 persons (01333 421390). Professional: George Finlayson. Links Secretary: Mr A. Herd (01333 428859).

LEVEN. **Leven Thistle Golf Club,** Balfour Street, Leven (01333 426333). *Location:* 10 miles south west of St. Andrews. Top championship links used for national and international events including Open qualifying. 18 holes, 6434 yards. S.S.S. 71. *Green Fees:* weekdays £18.00 per round, £26.00 per day; weekends £24.00 per round, £36.00 per day. *Eating facilities:* full catering available, two bars, function hall. *Visitors:* welcome without reservation, except Saturdays. *Society Meetings:* for group bookings contact Leven Links Joint Committee, Promenade, Leven, Fife KY8 4HS (01333 428859). Secretary: J. Scott.

LEVEN. **Lundin Golf Club,** Golf Road, Lundin Links KY8 6BA (01333 320202). *Location:* three miles east of Leven, 14 miles east of Kirkcaldy. Seaside links. 18 holes, 6377 yards. S.S.S. 71. Practice ground. *Green Fees:* £20.00 per round, £30.00 per day weekdays; Saturdays after 2.30pm £30.00 per round. *Eating facilities:* bar and diningroom. *Visitors:* welcome Monday/Thursday 9am to 3.30pm; Friday 9am to 3pm; Saturdays no visitors before 2.30pm; Sundays no visitors. *Society Meetings:* limited numbers. Professional: David K. Webster (01333 320051). Secretary: A.C. McBride (01333 320202).

LEVEN. **Scoonie Golf Club,** North Links, Leven KY8 4SP (01333 427057). *Location:* nearest town Leven on coastal road to St. Andrews. Not a proper links course, rather flat, typical seaside bunkers. 18 holes, 5600 yards, 5000 metres. S.S.S. 66. *Green Fees:* weekdays £9.00 per round, £11.00 per day; weekends £11.00 per round, £17.00 per day. *Eating facilities:* one bar, meals and bar snacks available all day. *Visitors:* welcome anytime (Saturday club competitions). *Society Meetings:* all welcome. Secretary: S. Kuczerepa (01333 427057).

LOCHGELLY. **Lochgelly Golf Club,** Cartmore Road, Lochgelly (01592 780174). *Location:* take M90 to Junction 4 Halbeath Interchange, follow signs. Parkland. 18 holes, 5491 yards, 5063 metres. S.S.S. 67. *Green Fees:* £18.00 weekdays; £23.00 weekends. *Eating facilities:* catering available. *Visitors:* welcome, no restrictions weekdays, weekends parties limited to 24. Secretary: R.F. Stuart (01383 512238).

LUNDIN LINKS. **Lundin Ladies Golf Club,** Woodielea Road, Lundin Links KY8 6AR (01333 320832). *Location:* off Leven Road. Excellent parkland course, picturesque. 9 holes, 2365 yards. S.S.S. 67. Practice net, putting green. *Green Fees:* weekdays £6.00 per day; weekends £7.50 per day. *Eating facilities:* tea making facilities. *Visitors:* welcome. Secretary: Eliz Davidson (01333 320490).

MARKINCH. **Balbirnie Park Golf Club,** The Clubhouse, Balbirnie Park, Markinch, Glenrothes KY7 6DD (01592 752006). *Location:* outside Markinch near the A92. Wooded parkland course. 18 holes, 6210 yards. S.S.S. 71. *Green Fees:* weekdays £19.00 per round, £26.00 per day; weekends £27.00 per round, £34.00 per day. *Eating facilities:* snacks, lunch, High Tea and full meals available during clubhouse hours. *Visitors:* no restrictions at present other than maximum number of 24 at weekends and no visitors before 10am weekends. *Society Meetings:* welcome. Secretary: W.A. Black.

ST. ANDREWS. **Balgove Course,** St. Andrews. *Location:* outskirts of St. Andrews on Dundee Road. 9 hole, beginners' course, 1530 yards. S.S.S. 60 (18 holes). Driving range, practice ground. *Green Fees:* £6.00 High Season (1st May to 30th November), £5.00 Low Season (1st December to 30th April). Subject to review. *Eating facilities:* hotels and restaurants in the vicinity. *Visitors:* welcome without reservation. Golf Manager: John Lindsey, Links Management Committee of St. Andrews (01334 475757).

ST. ANDREWS. **Eden Course,** St. Andrews (Starter 01334 474296). *Location:* follow A91 trunk road to St. Andrews, directions to golf course are clearly marked. Seaside links. 18 holes, 6112 yards. S.S.S. 70. Practice facilities, driving range. *Green Fees:* £18.00 High Season (1st May to 30th November), £15.00 Low Season (1st December to 30th April). Subject to review. *Eating facilities:* hotels and restaurants in the vicinity. *Visitors:* welcome with or without reservation. Trolleys are allowed and can be hired at £2.00 per round. *Society Meetings:* catered for except Saturday. Golf Manager: John Lindsey, Links Management Committee of St. Andrews (01334 475757).

ST. ANDREWS. **Jubilee Course,** West Sands, St. Andrews KY16 9JA (Starter 01334 473938). *Location:* follow A91 trunk road to St. Andrews, directions to golf course are clearly marked. Seaside links. 18 holes, 6805 yards. S.S.S. 72. Driving range, practice facilities available. *Green Fees:* £25.00 High Season (1st May to 30th November), £20.00 Low Season (1st December to 30th April). *Eating facilities:* new clubhouse with full facilities is under construction, due for completion Spring 1995. *Visitors:* welcome with or without reservation. *Society Meetings:* catered for except Saturday. Secretary: John Lindsey, Links Management Committee of St. Andrews (01334 475757).

Sporting Laird Hotel & Apartments

5 PLAYFAIR TERRACE
ST. ANDREWS KY16 9HX
Tel: (01334) 475906 Fax: (01334) 473881
RAC Acclaimed STB ♛♛♛ Commended
Old Course – 200 yards

A 2 day weekend / 2 nights DB&B / 3 days Golf (3 day golf ticket at St. Andrews) – £155
B 3 day weekend / 3 nights DB&B / 3 days Golf – £190
C 3 day midweek / 3 nights DB&B / 3 days Golf – £190
D 4 day midweek / 4 nights DB&B / 3 days Golf plus green fees at Lundin Links/Elie/Ladybank – £255
Further golf packages available for 3, 5 & 7 days – prices from £190.
NB. Green Fees are subject to increase.

AA Listed **RAC Acclaimed**

BELL CRAIG HOUSE

A small comfortable house under the personal supervision of the proprietors. Only a few minutes' walk from the world famous 'Old Course'. Ideal for a break in the home of golf. All bedrooms are ensuite and have colour TV, tea/coffee facilities and shaver/hairdryer points. Close to beach, amusements, shops and other amenities. Enjoy the 'home from home' atmosphere. Contact Sheila Black for more details.

Bell Craig House, 8 Murray Park, St. Andrews, Fife KY16 9AW. Telephone: 01334 472962

ST. ANDREWS GOLF HOTEL

AA ★★★ RAC MERIT AWARDS H C R AA HIGHLY COMMENDED

A Most Comfortable Privately Owned 3-Star Hotel Specialising In Golf

- **Sea front location only 200 yards from the famous "Old Course".**
- **Superb restaurant with gourmet food and fine wines.**
- **Golfing holidays tailored to your particular requirements.**

FOR RESERVATIONS & BROCHURE TELEPHONE: (01334) 472611 FAX: (0334) 472188

The Russell Hotel

Situated on **THE SCORES** overlooking St. Andrews Bay, this small friendly hotel personally run by Gordon and Fiona de Vries offers good food and comfortable accommodation with 10 twin/double rooms, all with private facilities; satellite TV, telephones, tea/coffee making. Just two minutes' walk from 1st tee of the **OLD COURSE** and equally convenient for town centre and beaches. **The RUSSELL** has acquired a fine reputation for excellent cuisine and exceptional service. Golf Parties welcome.

Major Credit Cards Accepted. AA★★. Enquiries to:

THE RUSSELL HOTEL, THE SCORES, ST. ANDREWS, Tel: 01334 473447; Fax: 01334 478279

HEAVEN ON EARTH

Overlooking the R&A Clubhouse and St. Andrews Bay, this famous 3-Star, 30 bedroom hotel is literally only yards from the 1st tee of the Old Course and minutes from the other St. Andrews courses. Adjacent to the hotel is The British Golf Museum and the town centre is only a short stroll away. This is a golfers paradise!

All bedrooms are ensuite and hotel facilities include two bars, a coffee shop and a highly regarded restaurant. Ample free parking adjacent. We can assist with golf arrangements in St. Andrews and at most of Fife's famous courses. Please phone for a brochure and details of Golf Breaks at this exceptional hotel.

SCORES HOTEL
- ST ANDREWS

AA ★★★ RAC ★★★

The Scores Hotel, St. Andrews, Fife KY16 9BB, Scotland (Tel: 01334 472451; Fax: 01334 473947)

Adventures in Golf

Customised tours organised throughout Scotland with great emphasis on attention to detail and professional service blended with friendly, personal contact. Tee-times, accommodation, car rental, etc. arranged. Quotations and itineraries prepared according to budget and personal preference. The entire process from initial enquiry to confirmed itinerary can take as little as 72 hours. Extension tours to Ireland, England, Spain, Portugal and France also available.

For more details contact: Golf Quest (St. Andrews) P.G.A., 7 Crawford Gardens, St. Andrews, Fife KY16 8XG
Telephone/Fax: (01334) 479093

ST. ANDREWS. **New Course,** West Sands, St. Andrews (Starter 01334 473938). 18 holes, 6604 yards, 6038 metres. S.S.S. 72. Driving range, practice ground. *Green Fees:* £25.00 High Season (1st May to 30th November), £20 Low Season (1st December to 30th April). Subject to review. *Eating facilities:* a clubhouse with full facilities is under construction and due for completion Spring 1995. *Visitors:* welcome with or without reservation. Two person buggies may be hired for £15.00 – availability cannot be guaranteed. *Society Meetings:* catered for except Saturday. Golf Manager: John Lindsey, Links Management Committee of St. Andrews (01334 475757).

ST. ANDREWS. **Strathtyrum Course,** St. Andrews Links Management Committee, Pilmour Cottage, St. Andrews KY16 9SF (01334 475757). 18 holes, 5094 yards. S.S.S. 65. 24 bay driving range, practice ground. *Green Fees:* £14.00 High Season (1st May to 30th November), £12.00 Low Season (1st December to 30th April). *Eating facilities:* hot and cold drinks and snacks available at Eden Information Centre. *Visitors:* welcome. Two person buggies may be hired at a charge of £15, trolleys allowed at a hire charge of £2.00 per round. Golf Manager: John Lindsey.

ST. ANDREWS. **The Old Course,** St. Andrews KY16 9JA. *Location:* follow A91 trunk road to St. Andrews – directions to golf course are clearly marked. Seaside links. 18 holes, 6566 yards, 6004 metres. S.S.S. 72. Driving range, practice facilities. *Green Fees:* £50.00 High Season (1st May to 30th November), £40.00 Low Season (1st December to 30 April). Subject to review. *Eating facilities:* clubhouse with full facilities is presently under construction and is due for completion Spring 1995. *Visitors:* Handicap Certificate or letter of introduction required from recognised golf club. Trolleys allowed after 12 noon from May to September. *Society*

Meetings: welcome except Saturdays. Golf Manager: John Lindsey (01334 475757). Starter: (01334 473393).

TAYPORT. **Scotscraig Golf Club,** Tayport (01382 552515). *Location:* ten miles north of St Andrews. Seaside links. 18 holes, 6496 yards. S.S.S. 71. *Green Fees:* on application. *Eating facilities:* lunches and high teas, except Tuesdays. *Visitors:* welcome on weekdays or weekends by prior arrangement. *Society Meetings:* catered for subject to approval. Secretary: K. Gourlay (01382 552515).

THORNTON. **Thornton Golf Club,** Thornton KY1 4DW (01592 771111). *Location:* southeast Fife located off A92, midway between Glenrothes and Kirkcaldy. Undulating, wooded parkland. 18 holes, 6177 yards. S.S.S. 69. *Green Fees:* weekdays £12.00 per round, £18.00 per day; weekends £17.00 per round, £27.00 per day. *Eating facilities:* full catering service and bar. *Visitors:* welcome, restricted weekends before 10am and between 12 noon and 2.30pm. *Society Meetings:* catered for. Secretary: Brian Forrester.

Glasgow & District

BISHOPBRIGGS. **Bishopbriggs Golf Club,** Brackenbrae Road, Bishopbriggs G64 2DX (0141-772 1810). Location: quarter mile from Bishopbriggs Cross off Glasgow-Kirkintilloch road. Fairly flat parkland course. 18 holes, 6041 yards. S.S.S. 69. *Green Fees:* on application. *Eating facilities:* full service always available. *Visitors:* weekends/Public Holidays with member only, other times apply to Secretary. *Society Meetings:* catered for Tuesdays and Thursdays by application to committee at least one month in advance. Secretary: John Magin (0141-772 8938).

GLASGOW. **Alexandra Golf Club,** Alexandra Park, Alexandra Parade, Glasgow G31 3SE (0141-554 3991). *Location:* M8 off ramp to Alexandra Parade. Wooded parkland. 9 holes, 1965 yards. S.S.S. 35. Practice area. *Green Fees:* weekdays adults £2.10, weekends £2.00. Juniors 95p, Senior Citizens and UB40 60p. *Eating facilities:* bar, rooms available for functions. *Visitors:* welcome anytime. Blind Club, Unemployed Club. Bowling greens. Professional: S. Wilson. Secretary: A. Clark.

GLASGOW. **Bearsden Golf Club,** Thorn Road, Bearsden, Glasgow G61 4BP (0141-942 2351). *Location:* seven miles north-west of Glasgow. Parkland. 9 holes, 6014 yards. S.S.S. 69. *Green Fees:* information not provided. *Visitors:* welcome, but must be accompanied by member. Secretary: J.R. Mercer (0141-942 2381).

GLASGOW. **Blairbeth Golf Club,** Fernhill, Rutherglen, Glasgow (0141-634 3355). *Location:* two miles south of Rutherglen off Stonelaw Road. Parkland. 18 holes, 5800 yards. S.S.S. 67. *Green Fees:* on application. *Eating facilities:* available. *Visitors:* welcome weekdays. *Society Meetings:* not catered for. Secretary: F.T. Henderson (0141-632 0604).

GLASGOW. **Bonnyton Golf Club,** Eaglesham, Glasgow G76 0QA (013553 2645; Fax: 013553 3151). *Location:* B764. Moorland course. 18 holes, 6252 yards. S.S.S. 71. *Green Fees:* £25.00 per day. *Eating facilities:* full diningroom and snack facilities. *Visitors:* welcome except weekends. Professional: Kendal McWade (013553 2256). Secretary: (013553 2781).

GLASGOW. **Bothwell Castle Golf Club,** Blantyre Road, Bothwell G71 (01698 853177). *Location:* adjacent to M74, three miles north of Hamilton. Parkland course. 18 holes, 6243 yards, 5606 metres. S.S.S. 70. Golf clubs and caddy cars for hire. Practice fields. *Green Fees:* £18.00 per round, £25.00 per day. (Playing times must be booked with Professional). *Eating facilities:* lunches, bar snacks and dinners available, bar. *Visitors:* welcome weekdays 9.30am to 10.30am and 2pm to 3pm only. *Society Meetings:* catered for, courtesy granted by application on Tuesdays only. Professional: Gordon Niven (01698 852052). Secretary: A.D.C. Watson (01698 852395).

GLASGOW. **Buchanan Castle Golf Club,** Buchanan Estate, Drymen, Glasgow G63 0HY (01360 60369). *Location:* Glasgow/Drymen road, half a mile short of village. Flat parkland course. 18 holes, 6086 yards. S.S.S. 69. 9 hole putting area. *Green Fees:* weekdays £25.00, all day £35.00. *Eating facilities:* full catering available. *Visitors:* welcome, Thursdays – official visiting day, Wednesday maximum 12. *Society Meetings:* welcome, maximum 12. Professional: Keith Baxter (01360 60330). Secretary: Richard Kinsella (01360 60307). *

GLASGOW. **Cambuslang Golf Club,** 30 Westburn Drive, Cambuslang (0141-641 3130). *Location:* half a mile north of Cambuslang main street. 9 holes, 6146 yards. S.S.S. 69. *Green Fees:* weekdays £10.00. *Eating facilities:* bar snacks, lunches, evening meals. *Visitors:* welcome Mondays, Wednesdays, Thursdays and Fridays on written application to the Secretary. *Society Meetings:* by arrangement. Secretary: William Lilly (0141-641 1498).

GLASGOW. **Cathcart Castle Golf Club,** Mearns Road, Clarkston, Glasgow G76 7YL (0141-638 0082). *Location:* one and a half miles from Clarkston Toll. Undulating parkland course. 18 holes, 5832 yards. S.S.S. 68. *Green Fees:* £17.00 per round, £25.00 per day. *Eating facilities:* full catering available, lounge bar. *Visitors:* welcome weekdays by prior arrangement. *Society Meetings:* on Tuesdays and Thursdays by application. Professional: David Naylor (0141-638 3436). Secretary: D.A. Howe (0141-638 9449).

GLASGOW. **Cathkin Braes Golf Club,** Cathkin Road, Rutherglen, Glasgow G73 4SE (0141-634 6605). 18 holes, 6208 yards. S.S.S. 71. Practice ground. *Green Fees:* £20.00 per round, £30.00 per day. *Eating facilities:* available. *Visitors:* welcome Monday to Friday by prior arrangement. *Society Meetings:* catered for. Professional: Stephen Bree (0141-634 0650). Secretary/Treasurer: G.L. Stevenson.

GLASGOW. **Cawder Golf Club,** Cadder Road, Bishopbriggs, Glasgow G64 3QD (0141-772 7101; Fax: 0141-772 4463). *Location:* A803 north of city. Parkland. Cawder: 18 holes, 6305 yards, 5737 metres. S.S.S. 71. Keir: 18 holes, 5891 yards, 5373 metres. S.S.S. 68. Practice area. *Green Fees:* £23.00. *Eating facilities:* lunches, high teas, dinners available. *Visitors:* welcome when playing with member. *Society Meetings:* catered for mid-week. Professional: Ken Stevely (0141-772 7102). Secretary: G.T. Stoddart (0141-772 5167).

GLASGOW. **Clober Golf Club,** Craigton Road, Milngavie G62 7HP (0141-956 1685). *Location:* five minutes from Milngavie centre, seven miles from Glasgow city centre. 18 holes, 5068 yards. S.S.S. 65. *Green Fees:* weekdays £10.00 per round. *Eating facilities:* morning coffee, lunches, high teas. *Visitors:* welcome weekdays before 4.30pm (Fridays 4.00pm), weekends if introduced by a member. *Society Meetings:* catered for. Secretary: J. Anderson (0141-956 2499).

GLASGOW. **Cowglen Golf Club,** 301 Barrhead Road, Glasgow G43 1AA (0141-632 0556). *Location:* south-west Glasgow, near the Burrell Collection. Undulating parkland course. 18 holes, 5976 yards. S.S.S. 69. Practice area. *Green Fees:* weekdays £17.00 per round, £25.00 per day. *Eating facilities:* full catering facilities available. *Visitors:* welcome when introduced by a member. Lockers and showers available. *Society Meetings:* restricted numbers, apply to Secretary. Professional: John McTear (0141-649 9401; Fax: 0141-636 5411). Secretary: R.J.G. Jamieson, C.A. (01292 266600; Fax: 01292 610464).

GLASGOW. **Crow Wood Golf Club,** Garnkirk House, Cumbernauld Road, Muirhead G69 9JF (0141-779 2011). *Location:* on A80 on Stirling Road, six miles north east of Glasgow. Wooded parkland. 18 holes, 6249 yards. S.S.S. 70. Practice area. *Green Fees:* weekdays £16.00 per round, £24.00 per day. *Eating facilities:* fully licensed, snacks or full meals served all day. *Visitors:* welcome weekdays except Bank Holidays and only by arrangement with Secretary. *Society Meetings:* catered for as visitors. Professional: Alan Kershaw (0141-779 1943). Secretary: Ian McInnes (0141-779 4954).

GLASGOW. **Deaconsbank Golf Course,** Rouken Glen Golf Centre, Stewarton Road, Thornliebank, Glasgow G46 7UZ (0141-638 7044 or 0141-620 0826). *Location:* on Stewarton Road at Rouken Glen Park, only 250 yards from the A726. Parkland with wooded features, designed by James Braid. 18 holes, 4800 yards. S.S.S. 63 (Par 64). 15-bay floodlit driving range. *Green Fees:* weekdays £7.00; weekends and Public Holidays £8.00; Day Ticket £12.00. *Eating facilities:* catering and bar facilities available. *Visitors:* welcome all year round. Shop, club hire, etc. *Society Meetings:* catered for all year round. Professional: (0141-638 7044). Secretary: Christine Cosh (0141-620 0826).

GLASGOW. **Dougalston Golf Course,** Strathblane Road, Milngavie, Glasgow G62 (0141-956 5750; Fax: 0141-956 6480). *Location:* A81 half a mile Milngavie. Wooded – water; three ponds. 18 holes, 6683 yards. S.S.S. 72. Practice ground. *Green Fees:* information not provided. *Eating facilities:* diningroom and bar meals. *Visitors:* welcome weekdays. Club Manager: Grace Wilson.

GLASGOW. **Douglas Park Golf Club,** Hillfoot, Bearsden, Glasgow G61 2TJ (0141-942 2220). *Location:* adjacent to railway station, Hillfoot, Bearsden, off Milngavie Road. Undulating parkland course. 18 holes, 5982 yards. S.S.S. 69. *Green Fees:* £17.00 per round, £23.00 per day. *Eating facilities:* full service available, usual licensing hours. *Visitors:* must be introduced and play with member. *Society Meetings:* Wednesdays and Thursdays on application to Secretary. Professional: David B. Scott (0141-942 1482). Secretary: D.N. Nicolson.

GLASGOW. **Dullatur Golf Club,** Dullatur, Glasgow G68 0AR (01236 723230). *Location:* 12 miles east of Glasgow, north of Cumbernauld on Kilsyth road via Dullatur. 18 holes, 6229 yards. S.S.S. 70. *Green Fees:* £25.00 per day, £15.00 per round after 1.30pm. *Visitors:* welcome weekdays except Public Holidays and competition days. *Society Meetings:* welcome as above. Professional: Duncan Sinclair. Secretary: W. Laing.

GLASGOW. **East Kilbride Golf Club,** Chapelside Road, Nerston, East Kilbride G74 4PF (013552 20913). Parkland course with variable topography. 18 holes, 6419 yards. S.S.S. 71. *Green Fees:* weekdays £14.00 per round, £20.00 per day. *Eating facilities:* full catering except Tuesdays and Thursdays (bar snacks). *Visitors:* welcome weekdays on application. Letter of introduction from own Club Secretary required for smaller groups in advance of visits. Weekends no visitors unless accompanied by a member. *Society Meetings:* catered for on application, minimum 12, maximum 30. Professional: A.R. Taylor (013552 22192). Secretary: W.G. Gray (013552 47728).

GLASGOW. **Eastwood Golf Club,** Loganswell, Newton Mearns, Glasgow G77 6RX (0135-55 261). *Location:* on main A77 road to Kilmarnock two miles south of Newton Mearns. Parkland. 18 holes, 5864 yards. S.S.S. 68. Practice area. *Green Fees:* £18.00 per round. *Eating facilities:* snacks or full meals available. *Visitors:* welcome weekdays on application to Secretary. *Visiting parties:* welcomed on prior application. Professional: A. McGinness (0135-55 285). Secretary: V.E. Jones (0135-55 280).

GLASGOW. **Glasgow Golf Club,** Killermont, Bearsden, Glasgow G61 2TW (0141-942 1713). *Location:* taking Maryhill Road out of Glasgow turn right at Killermont Avenue, half a mile before Canniesburn Toll. Tree-lined parkland. 18 holes, 5968 yards. S.S.S. 69. Members only. *Visitors:* only if introduced by member. *Society Meetings:* by application to Club Secretary. Professional: Jack Steven (0141-942 8507). Secretary: D.W. Deas (0141-942 2011; Fax: 0141-942 0770).

GLASGOW. **Haggs Castle Golf Club,** Dumbreck Road, Dumbreck, Glasgow G41 4SN (0141-427 0480). *Location:* straight ahead at roundabout at end of M77 from Glasgow. Flat, tree-lined course. 18 holes, 6464 yards. S.S.S. 71. Practice area and putting green. *Green Fees:* weekdays £24.00 per round, £36.00 per day. Weekends, members only. *Eating facilities:* full catering available. *Visitors:* welcome, must book through Professional. Golf shoes must be worn. *Society Meetings:* by arrangement through Secretary. Professional: J. McAlister (0141-427 3355). Secretary: I. Harvey (Tel & Fax: 0141-427 1157).

GLASGOW. **Hayston Golf Club,** Campsie Road, Kirkintilloch, Glasgow G66 1RN (0141-776 1244). *Location:* 10 miles north-east of Glasgow and one mile north of Kirkintilloch. Parkland course with tree-lined fairways. 18 holes, 6042 yards. S.S.S. 69. Practice area. *Green Fees:* weekdays £15.00 per round, £20.00 per day. *Eating facilities:* lunches, dinners, bar snacks. *Visitors:* welcome weekdays before 4.30pm with letter of introduction from own club. Weekends only if introduced by member. *Society Meetings:* Tuesdays/ Thursdays on application to Secretary. Professional: Steve Barnett (0141-775 0882). Secretary: J.V. Carmichael (0141-775 0723). *

GLASGOW. **Hilton Park Golf Club,** Stockiemuir Road, Milngavie, Glasgow G62 7HB (0141-956 5124). *Location:* on A809. Moorland courses. Allander course: 18 holes, 5374 yards. S.S.S. 67. Hilton course: 18 holes, 6054 yards. S.S.S. 70. Practice area. *Green Fees:* £20.00 per round, £26.00 per day. *Eating facilities:* full catering and bar. *Visitors:* on application to the Secretary (not at weekends). *Society Meetings:* as visitors. Professional: W. McCondichie (0141-956 5125). Secretary: Mrs J.A. Warnock (0141-956 4657).

GLASGOW. **Kirkhill Golf Club,** Cambuslang, Glasgow (0141-641 3083 or 8499). 18 holes, 5862 yards. S.S.S. 69. *Green Fees:* £12.00 per round, £20.00 per day weekdays. *Eating facilities:* dining room and bar snacks. *Visitors:* welcome when introduced by member; only introduced visitors at weekends. *Society Meetings:* welcome on written application to the Secretary. Secretary: H.G. Marshall. *

GLASGOW. **Knightswood Golf Club,** Lincoln Avenue, Glasgow G13 (0141-959 2131). *Location:* west along Great Western Road to Lincoln Avenue. Flat parkland course. 9 holes, 2717 yards. S.S.S. 33 (66). *Green Fees:* £2.10, Juniors 95p, Passport to Recreation holders 60p weekdays. *Visitors:* welcome anytime, Municipal course. Secretary: Mr James Dean (0141-954 6495).

GLASGOW. **Letham Hill Municipal Golf Club,** 1240 Cumbernauld Road, Glasgow G33 1AH (0141-770 6220). *Location:* 100 yards off M8 Junction 28. Parkland, many holes with views of Hogganfield Loch. 18 holes, 6073 yards. S.S.S. 68. Pitch and putt course (18 holes) *Green Fees:* weekdays £3.25 adult, £1.85 Junior; weekends £3.80. Passport to Recreation Concession £1.15. Season tickets available. *Visitors:* welcome at all times – this is a public course. *Society Meetings:* available from Course Marker. Secretary: J. Wilson. *

GLASGOW. **Linn Park Golf Club,** Simshill Road, Glasgow G44 (0141-637 5871). *Location:* five miles south of city centre. Parkland. 18 holes, 4952 yards. S.S.S. 65. *Green Fees:* weekdays £4.10 adults, £2.30 Juniors; weekends £4.00. *Visitors:* welcome without restrictions. *Society Meetings:* not catered for. Secretary: Robert Flanagan.

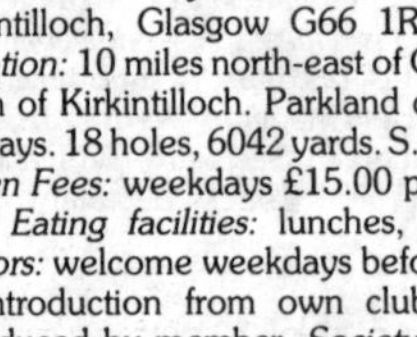

GLASGOW. **Littlehill Golf Club,** Auchinairn Road, Bishopbriggs, Glasgow G64. *Location:* from Glasgow on A803, turn off for Stobhill Hospital. Flat, parkland. 18 holes, 6364 yards. S.S.S. 70. Small practice area. *Green Fees:* £4.00 per round/day. Special rates for Senior Citizens, Juniors and unemployed. *Eating facilities:* canteen open five days in season, three outwith. *Visitors:* welcome without reservation – pay and play. *Society Meetings:* no restrictions. Professional: Kevin Hughes (0141-762 3998). Secretary: W. Burke. *

GLASGOW. **Milngavie Golf Club,** Laigh Park, Milngavie, Glasgow (0141-956 1619). *Location:* situated off Glasgow to Drymen road approximately one mile past Stockiemuir Service Station, turn right at signpost. 18 holes, 5818 yards. S.S.S. 68. *Green Fees:* information not provided. *Eating facilities:* catering available. *Visitors:* welcome when introduced by member only. *Society Meetings:* catered for. Secretary: Mrs A.J.W. Ness.

GLASGOW. **Pollok Golf Club,** 90 Barrhead Road, Glasgow G43 1BG (0141-632 1080). *Location:* A736, four miles south of Glasgow, near end of M77. Wooded parkland. 18 holes, 6257 yards. S.S.S. 70. *Green Fees:* £26.00 per round, £33.00 per day. *Eating facilities:* dining room and bar. *Visitors:* welcome with reservation by letter to Secretary. No visitors Saturday or Sunday. No Ladies. *Society Meetings:* catered for by letter. Secretary: A Mathison Boyd (0141-632 1453).

GLASGOW. **Sandyhills Golf Club,** 223 Sandyhills Road, Glasgow G32 9NA (0141-778 1179). *Location:* three miles east from centre of Glasgow. Parkland. 18 holes, 6253 yards. S.S.S. 70. *Green Fees:* £20.00. *Eating facilities:* lunches at club except Mondays, order in advance. *Visitors:* welcome when introduced by a member. *Society Meetings:* welcome by prior arrangement. Secretary: Paul Ward.

GLASGOW. **The Whitecraigs Golf Club,** 72 Ayr Road, Giffnock, Glasgow G46 6SW (0141-639 4530). *Location:* on A77 south of city. Parkland course, 18 holes, 6230 yards, 5669 metres. S.S.S. 70. *Green Fees:* £23.00 per round, £29.00 per day. *Eating facilities:* diningroom, lounge bar. *Visitors:* letter of introduction required. *Society Meetings:* catered for Wednesday only. Professional: Alastair Forrow (0141-639 2140). Secretary: H.J. Fairley (0141-639 4530).

GLASGOW. **Williamwood Golf Club,** Clarkston Road, Glasgow G44 (0141-637 1783). *Location:* beside Clarkston Toll on Clarkston Road. Attractive parkland course designed by James Braid. 18 holes, 5878 yards. S.S.S. 69. Practice area and putting. *Green Fees:* information not provided. *Eating facilities:* meals must be ordered. *Visitors:* must be introduced by, and play with, a member. *Society Meetings:* weekdays only by arrangement. Professional: J. Gardner (0141-637 2715). Secretary: R.G. Cuthbert CA (0141-226 4311).

GLASGOW. **Windyhill Golf Club,** Baljaffray Road, Bearsden, Glasgow G61 4QQ (0141-942 2349). *Location:* eight miles north-west of Glasgow. Undulating parkland/moorland course. 18 holes, 6254 yards. S.S.S. 70. Practice area. *Green Fees:* £15.00 plus VAT; weekends with member only. *Eating facilities:* full catering and bar. *Visitors:* welcome weekdays, by prior arrangement with Secretary. *Society Meetings:* welcome weekdays by arrangement. Professional: G. Collinson (0141-942 7157). Secretary: A.J. Miller (0141-942 2349).

KILSYTH. **Kilsyth Lennox Golf Club,** Tak-Ma-Doon Road, Kilsyth, Glasgow G65 0RS (01236 824115). *Location:* 12 miles from Glasgow on A80. Parkland/moorland, undulating ground with superb views across central Scotland. 18 holes, 5912 yards. S.S.S. 70. *Green Fees:* weekdays £8.00 per round, £12.00 per day; weekends £12.00 per round, £16.00 per day. *Eating facilities:* new clubhouse. *Visitors:* welcome weekdays up to 5.00pm, Saturdays after 5.00pm, not Sundays. *Society Meetings:* welcome, details on application. Professional: R. Abercrombie. Secretary: A.G. Stevenson (01236 823213).

NEWTON MEARNS. **The East Renfrewshire Golf Club,** Pilmuir, Newton Mearns, Glasgow G77 6RT (0135 55 256). *Location:* on A77, one and a half miles south of Newton Mearns. Moorland course. 18 holes, 6097 yards, 5577 metres. S.S.S. 70. *Green Fees:* weekdays £25.00 per round, £30.00 per day. *Eating facilities:* by prior arrangement with Clubmaster. *Visitors:* welcome except Saturdays but always by prior arrangement with Professional. *Society Meetings:* welcome by prior arrangement with Secretary. Professional: Gordon D. Clark (0135 55 206). Secretary: A. Lindsay Gillespie (0141-226 4311).

Inverness-shire

ARISAIG. **Traigh Golf Course,** Traigh Farm, Arisaig. *Location:* on A830 Fort William to Mallaig Road, between Arisaig and Morar. Seaside links, close to sandy beaches on the beautiful Morar coast. 9 holes, 2400 yards. S.S.S 66. (Course being extended and improved). *Green Fees:* £10.00 per day. *Eating facilities:* unlicensed, soft drinks and confectionery only. *Visitors:* welcome at all times. Clubs may be hired. *Society Meetings:* by arrangement. Manager: Bill Henderson (016875 234).

BEAULY by. **Aigas Golf Course,** By Beauly IV4 7AD (01463 782942 or 782423). *Location:* A831, five miles from Beauly village. Challenging 9 hole course uniquely set in beautiful Strathglass beside the River Beauly. 9 holes, 2439 yards, S.S.S. 64 (2 x 9 holes). *Green Fees:* weekdays £8.00 per day; weekends £10.00 per day. *

BOAT OF GARTEN. **Boat of Garten Golf and Tennis Club,** Boat of Garten PH24 3BQ (01479 831351). *Location:* A9 six miles north of Aviemore. Wooded course, birch tree-lined fairways, very scenic, overlooking Cairngorm Mountains. 18 holes, 5837 yards. S.S.S. 69. Practice net. *Green Fees:* weekdays £16.00; weekends £21.00. Subject to review. *Eating facilities:* catering facilities open 9.30am to 9pm, bar open 11am to 11pm daily. *Visitors:* welcome 9.30am to 5.30pm. *Society Meetings:* catered for. Secretary: J.R. Ingram (01479 831282; Fax: 01479 831523).

CARRBRIDGE. **Carrbridge Golf Club,** Inverness Road, Carrbridge PH23 3AU (01479 841623). *Location:* off A9, 27 miles south of Inverness. Moorland/parkland. 9 holes, 2630 yards. S.S.S. 66 (under review). *Green Fees:* weekdays £9, July, August, September £10; weekends £11.00 per day. *Eating facilities:* snacks, coffee etc. No bar. Clubhouse open April to October only. *Visitors:* welcome, course closed Wednesdays after 5pm for members only, competitions most Sundays. *Society Meetings:* welcome. Secretary: Mrs Anne T. Baird (01479 841506).

FORT AUGUSTUS. **Fort Augustus Golf Club,** Markethill, Fort Augustus (01320 366660). *Location:* one mile from village on Fort William road. Moorland course with tree lined canal to north and heather and birch covered hills to the south. 9 holes (18 tees), 5454 yards. S.S.S. 68. *Green Fees:* on request. *Eating facilities:* soft drinks. *Visitors:* welcome anytime except Tuesdays and Wednesdays after 6pm and Saturday afternoons from 1.30pm to 5pm. *Society Meetings:* catered for. Secretary: I. Aitchison (01320 366460).

INVERNESS. **Inverness Golf Club,** The Clubhouse, Culcabock Road, Inverness IV2 3XQ (01463 233422). *Location:* one mile south of town centre. Parkland course. 18 holes, 6226 yards. S.S.S. 70. Two practice grounds. *Green Fees:* weekdays £18.00 per round, £24.00 per day; weekends and Bank Holidays £21.00 per round, £27.00 per day. *Eating facilities:* sandwiches, lunches, high teas and dinners served at club. *Visitors:* welcome except Saturdays from 25th March to 20th October. *Society Meetings;* catered for, pre-booking preferred. Professional: A.P. Thomson (01463 231989). Secretary: G.B. Thomson (01463 239882).

INVERNESS. **Torvean Golf Club,** Glenurquhart Road, Inverness (01463 236648). *Location:* A82 towards Fort William, approximately one mile from town centre. Parkland course. 18 holes, 5784 yards, 5288 metres. S.S.S. 68. *Green Fees:* weekdays £9.50; weekends £10.50. *Eating facilities:* snacks and bar available; summer season 11am – 11pm. *Visitors:* booking preferred, especially at weekends – telephone 01463 711434. *Society Meetings:* welcome with advance booking through Inverness District Council. Secretary: Mrs K.M. Gray (01463 225651).

KINGUSSIE. **Kingussie Golf Club,** Gynack Road, Kingussie PH21 1LR (01540 661 374). *Location:* turn at Duke of Gordon Hotel, half a mile up road (sign-posted). Hill type course. 18 holes, 5555 yards, 5079 metres. S.S.S. 67. *Green Fees:* weekdays £12.00 per round, £15.00 per day; weekends £14.00 per round, £18.00 per day. Subject to review. *Eating facilities:* bar, catering provided. *Visitors:* welcome, tee reserved for members 8.30am – 9.30am, 12.30pm – 2pm and 5.30pm – 6.30pm at weekends, otherwise no restrictions. Caravan site. *Society Meetings:* welcome. Secretary: Norman MacWilliam (01540 661 600).

NETHYBRIDGE. **Abernethy Golf Club,** Nethybridge PH25 3DE (01479 821305). *Location:* 10 miles from Aviemore lying on the B970 between Boat of Garten and Grantown-on-Spey. Delightful nine hole course close to pine woods and with commanding view of the valley of the River Spey. 9 holes, 4986 yards. S.S.S. 66. *Green Fees:* £9.00 weekdays; £12.00 weekends. *Eating facilities:* clubhouse is unlicensed but there are full catering facilities available. *Visitors:* welcome subject to short restrictions when club competitions being held. *Society Meetings:* by arrangement with the Secretary. Secretary: Mrs E. Knight (01479 873558).

NEWTONMORE. **Newtonmore Golf Club,** Golf Course Road, Newtonmore PH20 1AT (01540 673328). *Location:* turn off A9 at Newtonmore, course in centre of village, 45 miles south of Inverness. Mainly flat course runs along banks of River Spey amidst beautiful scenery. 18 holes, 5880 yards. S.S.S. 68. Practice green. *Green Fees:* weekdays £10.00 per round, £13.00 per day; weekends £13.00 per round, £16.00 per day. *Eating facilities:* full catering and bar facilities. *Visitors:* welcome, restrictions during open competitions and Society days. Locker and shower facilities. *Society Meetings:* welcome by appointment with Secretary. Professional: Robert Henderson. Secretary: R.J. Cheyne (01540 673878). *

SPEAN BRIDGE. **Spean Bridge Golf Club,** Station Road, Spean Bridge PH34 4EU (01397 81340). *Location:* on main A82, eight miles north of Fort William. Wooded course set on the hillside, lovely views. 9 holes, 2203 yards. S.S.S. 64. *Green Fees:* £8.00 per day. *Eating facilities:* Hotel nearby. *Visitors:* welcome, Tuesdays from 5pm reserved for members, competitions some weekends. Full membership and Country membership available: contact Secretary for details. Secretary: John MacLennan (01397 702967).

Kincardineshire

BANCHORY. **Banchory Golf Club,** Kinneskie Road, Banchory AB31 3TA (01330 822365). *Location:* on the A93, 18 miles south west of Aberdeen. Parkland on the banks of the River Dee. 18 holes, 5245 yards, 4795 metres. S.S.S. 66. Practice area. *Green Fees:* weekdays £19.00; weekends £21.00. Weekly and monthly tickets available. *Eating facilities:* full catering service and lounge bar. *Visitors:* welcome, restrictions on Thursdays and weekends. *Society Meetings:* welcome by arrangement. Professional: Mr Charles Dernie (Tel & Fax: 01330 822447). Admin. Secretary: Mrs Anne Smith (01330 822365). Secretary: Mr W.N. Donaldson.

STONEHAVEN. **Stonehaven Golf Club,** Cowie, Stonehaven AB3 2RH (01569 762124). *Location:* A92, one mile north of town. 18 holes, 5128 yards. S.S.S. 65. *Green Fees:* £13.00 weekdays, £18.00 weekends. *Eating facilities:* full catering including bar lunches. *Visitors:* welcome, only a few with reservation. *Society Meetings:* catered for except for Saturday. Secretary: E.A. Ferguson. Club Manager: R.O. Blair.

Kinross-shire

KINROSS. **Green Hotel Golf Course,** Green Hotel, The Muirs, Kinross KY13 7AS (01577 862237). *Location:* turn left in Kinross off M90 Junction 6, course 500 yards on right. Reasonably flat wooded parkland. Two courses: Blue 18 holes, 6456 yards, 5905 metres. S.S.S. 71; Red 18 holes, 6257 yards, 5719 metres. S.S.S. 70. Practice ground. *Green Fees:* weekdays £14.00 per round, £20.00 per day; weekends £20.00 per round, £30.00 per day. *Eating facilities:* in clubhouse and hotel. *Visitors:* welcome, booking recommended. *Society Meetings:* catered for by arrangement. Professional: Stewart Geraghty (01577 865125). Secretary: Mrs M. Smith (01577 863407).

KINNESSWOOD. **Bishopshire Golf Club,** Kinnesswood, By Kinross. *Location:* take road to Glenrothes from M90, three miles. Course has panoramic views overlooking Loch Leven. 10 holes, 4700 yards, 2151 metres. S.S.S. 64. *Green Fees:* weekdays £5.00; weekends £6.00. *Eating facilities:* by arrangement or available at the hotel 400 yards away. *Visitors:* welcome without restriction. *Society Meetings:* by arrangement. Secretary: John Proudfoot (01592 780203).

LAURENCEKIRK. **Auchenblae Golf Club,** Auchenblae, Laurencekirk AB30 1BU. *Location:* five miles north of Laurencekirk, on A94, two miles west of Fordoun. Parkland. 9 holes, 2174 yards. S.S.S. 30. *Green Fees:* Mondays to Fridays £6.00; Saturdays £6.50, Sunday £7.00. Juniors and Senior Citizens half price at all times. *Eating facilities:* two hotels in nearby village. *Visitors:* restrictions Wednesday and Friday evenings (competitions); very busy Sundays. *Society Meetings:* small groups welcome. Secretary: A.I. Robertson (01561 378869). *

MILNATHORT. **Milnathort Golf Club Ltd,** South Street, Milnathort (01577 864069). Parkland course. 9 holes, 5969 yards. S.S.S. 69. *Green Fees:* weekdays £10.00 per day; weekends £15.00 per day. *Eating facilities:* by arrangement. *Visitors:* welcome without reservation. *Society Meetings:* must be booked in advance. All enquiries phone Clubhouse. *

Kirkcudbrightshire

CASTLE DOUGLAS. **Castle Douglas Golf Club,** Abercromby Road, Castle Douglas (01556 502801). *Location:* half a mile from town centre on A713 Castle Douglas to Ayr Road. Parkland. 9 holes, 5408 yards. S.S.S. 66. *Green Fees:* £12.00 per round or day. *Eating facilities:* catering during summer season. *Visitors:* welcome without reservation, except Tuesdays or Thursdays after 4pm and competition days. *Society Meetings:* by arrangement. Secretary: A.D. Millar (01556 502099).

DALBEATTIE. **Colvend Golf Club,** Sandyhills, Colvend, By Dalbeattie (01556 63398). *Location:* six miles from Dalbeattie on the A710, Solway Coast road, between Dalbeattie and Dumfries. Picturesque seaside course on a hill. 9 holes (visitors' tees), 2240 yards. S.S.S. 63. *Green Fees:* £12.00 per day; Juniors £6.00 (full fee Saturdays and Sundays). *Eating facilities:* excellent catering available. *Visitors:* welcome almost anytime. Course must be vacated by 2pm on Tuesdays and 5.30pm on Thursdays, also some Sundays (competitions), from April to September. Secretary: J.B. Henderson (01556 610878).

GATEHOUSE OF FLEET. **Gatehouse of Fleet Golf Club,** Laurieston Road, Gatehouse of Fleet, Castle Douglas. *Location:* quarter of a mile north of Gatehouse on Gatehouse – Laurieston road. Sloping and wooded course with fine views over Fleet Valley and Wigtown Bay. 9 holes, 2500 yards. S.S.S. 63. *Green Fees:* £10.00, Juniors £5.00. *Visitors:* welcome at all times except Sunday mornings to 11.30am. *Society Meetings:* welcome, rates negotiable on application. Secretary: Peter Colville (01557 814734).

KIRKCUDBRIGHT. **Kirkcudbright Golf Club,** Stirling Crescent, Kirkcudbright DG6 4EZ (01557 330314). *Location:* signposted near centre of town. Hilly parkland. 18 holes, 5598 yards. S.S.S. 67. *Green Fees:* £15.00 per round, £20.00 per day. *Eating facilities:* coffee, lunch, evening meal (not Mondays), usual bar hours. *Visitors:* welcome without reservation most days; Tuesday Ladies' Day, Wednesday Men's. Phone and check. *Society Meetings:* welcome, advance bookings. Secretary: John H. Sommerville.

NEW GALLOWAY. **New Galloway Golf Club,** New Galloway, Castle Douglas (016443 455). *Location:* one mile off A731, Ayr to Dumfries road. Scenic with fine turf. 9 holes, 5058 yards. S.S.S. 65. *Green Fees:* £10.00 per round/day. *Eating facilities:* bar. *Visitors:* welcome without reservation. Accommodation and meals available in village. *Society Meetings:* by arrangement. Secretary: Alan R. Brown (016443 455).

Lanarkshire (including the Clyde Valley)

AIRDRIE. **Airdrie Golf Club,** Glenmavis Road, Airdrie (01236 762195). *Location:* one mile north of Airdrie Cross. 18 holes, 6004 yards. S.S.S. 69. *Green Fees:* £12.00 per round, £20.00 per day (both inclusive of VAT). *Eating facilities:* available. *Visitors:* welcome only on application to the Secretary. Professional: A. McCloskey (01236 754360). Secretary: D.M. Hardie. *

AIRDRIE. **Easter Moffat Golf Club,** Plains, Airdrie ML6 8NP (01236 842878). *Location:* three miles east of Airdrie on old Edinburgh Road. 18 holes, 6221 yards. S.S.S. 70. Practice ground. *Green Fees:* £12.00 per round, £18.00 per day (lower rate if visited previous year). *Eating facilities:* bar and dining room. *Visitors:* welcome except weekends. *Society Meetings:* welcome. Professional: Brian Dunbar (01236 843015). Secretary: J.G. Timmons (01236 761440).

BELLSHILL. **Bellshill Golf Club,** Community Road, Orbiston, Bellshill ML4 2RZ (01698 745124). *Location:* Bellshill to Motherwell road, turn right. Parkland course. 18 holes, 6494 yards. S.S.S. 71. *Green Fees:* weekdays £14.00 per day; weekends £20.00. *Eating facilities:* by prior arrangement with Clubmaster. *Visitors:* welcome, parties by prior application (not competition days or Sundays). *Society Meetings:* by prior arrangement with Secretary. Secretary: Jack Sloan.

BIGGAR. **Biggar Golf Club,** Broughton Road, Biggar ML12 6HA (01899 20618). *Location:* from Edinburgh A702, from Glasgow A74 or M8, turn off at Newhouse. Flat, scenic parkland course. 18 holes, 5416 yards. S.S.S. 66. *Green Fees:* weekdays £11.00, weekends £13.00. Reductions for Juniors and Senior Citizens. *Eating facilities:* all day licence, full catering. *Visitors:* unrestricted, casual dress – no jeans. All weather tennis courts and caravan park. 1995 Club centenary, many special events. *Society Meetings:* welcome, early reservation essential. Secretary: W.S. Turnbull (01899 20566). Tee Reservations: (01899 20319).

CARLUKE. **Carluke Golf Club,** Maudslie Road, Hallcraig, Carluke ML8 5HG (01555 771070). *Location:* Carluke Cross, go west along Clyde Street for two miles. Parkland course. 18 holes, 5800 yards. S.S.S. 68. Practice area. *Green Fees:* £15.00 per round, £20.00 per day weekdays. *Eating facilities:* available. *Visitors:* till 4pm weekdays, no visitors weekends or Public Holidays. Tuition. *Society Meetings:* by written application to the Secretary. Professional: A. Brooks (01555 751053). Secretary: J.H. Muir (01555 770620).

COATBRIDGE. **Drumpellier Golf Club,** Drumpellier Avenue, Coatbridge ML5 1RX (01236 428723). *Location:* one mile from town centre. Parkland, wooded. 18 holes, 6227 yards. S.S.S. 70. Practice area. *Green*

Fees: £18.00 per round, £25.00 per day weekdays. *Eating facilities:* catering available except Thursdays. *Visitors:* welcome with reservation. *Society Meetings:* catered for by arrangement. Professional: K. Hutton (01236 432971). Secretary: W. Brownlie (01236 424625).

DOUGLAS WATER. **Douglas Water Golf Club,** Ayr Road, Rigside, Lanark (01555 880361). *Location:* five miles south of Lanark on A70, Junction 11 from M74. Hilly course, small greens, undulating fairways. 9 holes, 2947 yards, 2694 metres. S.S.S. 69. *Green Fees:* weekdays £5.00; weekends £8.00. Subject to review. *Eating facilities:* snacks, etc., rolls weekends. *Visitors:* welcome any time, with reservation on Saturdays because of competitions. *Society Meetings:* contact Secretary. Secretary: Mr R.McMillan (01555 882295).

EAST KILBRIDE. **Torrance House Golf Club,** Calderglen Country Park, Strathaven Road, East Kilbride G75 0QZ (013552 49720). *Location:* East Kilbride boundary on main Strathaven road. Parkland. 18 holes, 6423 yards. S.S.S. 71. Practice area. *Green Fees:* information on request. *Eating facilities:* private clubhouse. *Visitors:* welcome mid-week only. *Society Meetings:* details on request. Secretary: J.B. Asher (013552 49720). Booking Office: (013552 48636).

GARTCOSH. **Mount Ellen Golf Club,** Johnstone Road, Gartcosh (01236 872277). *Location:* approximately six miles north-east of Glasgow, near old Gartcosh steelworks. Flatland. 18 holes, 5525 yards. S.S.S. 68. *Green Fees:* weekdays £10.00 per round. *Eating facilities:* bar and full catering service. *Visitors:* welcome weekdays from 9am to 4pm, no weekend visitors. *Society Meetings:* by arrangement with Secretary. Professional: G. Reilly (01236 872632). Secretary: W.J. Dickson. *

HAMILTON. **Hamilton Golf Club,** Riccarton, Ferniegair, Hamilton ML3 7PZ (01698 282872). *Location:* off M74 Hamilton turn-off, one and a half miles up Larkhall road. Parkland course. 18 holes, 6700 yards. S.S.S. 70. *Green Fees:* information not provided. *Eating facilities:* meals must be ordered. *Visitors:* must be accompanied by a member. *Society Meetings:* by arrangement with Secretary. Professional: M.J. Moir (01698 282324). Secretary: P.E. Soutter (01698 286131).

HAMILTON. **Strathclyde Park Golf Club,** Motehill, Hamilton ML3 6BY (01698 266155 ext. 154). *Location:* M74 north, Hamilton, Motherwell exit, to roundabout second exit, pass ice rink, golf course straight ahead (about one mile from motorway turn off to course). Parkland, wooded course. 9 holes, 3147 yards. S.S.S. 70. Large practice area, putting green and driving range (24 bays). *Green Fees:* adults approximately £2.25 per 9 holes. Reductions for Juniors and Senior Citizens. *Eating facilities:* cafe and separate bar, bar lunches available. *Visitors:* welcome, same day booking system in operation; phone lines open 8.45am. *Society Meetings:* welcome by arrangment with Park's management. Professional: William Walker (01698 285511). Secretary: Kevin Will (01698 825363).

LANARK. **Carnwath Golf Club,** 1 Main Street, Carnwath (01555 840251). *Location:* on main Ayr/ Edinburgh Road. Fairly hilly inland course. 18 holes, 5860 yards. S.S.S. 69. *Green Fees:* £18.00 per day; Sundays and Bank Holidays £22.00. *Eating facilities:* lounge bar and dining room daily. *Visitors:* welcome Mondays, Wednesdays, Fridays and Sundays with prior booking. *Society Meetings:* catered for by prior arrangement. Secretary: W. Bruce (01555 661927).

LANARK. **Lanark Golf Club,** The Moor, Whitelees Road, Lanark ML11 7RX (01555 663219). *Location:* off A73. Tough moorland course. 18 holes, 6423 yards. S.S.S. 71. Also 9-hole course. Two practice grounds. *Green Fees:* £22.00 per round, £34.00 per day weekdays. *Eating facilities:* full catering and bar. *Visitors:* welcome daily until 4pm, no visitors weekends. *Society Meetings:* groups of 24 and over catered for Mondays and Tuesdays. Professional: Ron Wallace (01555 661456). Secretary: G.H. Cuthill.

LANARK. **Mouse Valley Golf Course,** East End, Cleghorn, Lanark ML11 (01555 870015). *Location:* 5 miles from Carluke on A721 Peebles Road. Pay as you play. Links style course, inland undulating terrain. Mouse Water (river) runs through the course. 18 holes, 6600 yards. Par 70. Practice ground. Driving range. *Green Fees:* £8. *Eating facilities:* full bar and catering. *Visitors:* welcome. *Society Meetings:* welcome at all times. Company days. Contact: (01662 366236). *

LARKHALL. **Larkhall Golf Club,** Burnhead Road, Larkhall (01698 881113). *Location:* on A74, close to M74. Parkland. 9 holes, 6684 yards. S.S.S. 72. *Green Fees:* information not provided. *Eating facilities:* meals weekends; bar normal hours. *Visitors:* welcome, but check beforehand; every second Saturday course closed to visitors. Secretary: I. Gilmour (01698 881755). *

LEADHILLS. **Leadhills Golf Club,** Leadhills, Biggar (01659 74222). *Location:* seven miles south of Abington on B797. This short but testing course is the highest in Britain. 9 holes, 2400 yards. S.S.S. 62. *Green Fees:* £4.00. *Eating facilities:* not available. *Visitors:* welcome any time. *Society Meetings:* welcome. Secretary: Graham Shaw. *

LESMAHAGOW. **Hollandbush Golf Club,** Acretophead, Lesmahagow (01555 893484). *Location:* off M74 between Lesmahagow and Coalburn. 18 holes, 6110 yards. S.S.S. 70. Practice area. *Green Fees:* £9.00 weekdays; £11.00 weekends. (Special tourist rates available). *Eating facilities:* meals at club. *Visitors:* welcome without restriction. *Society Meetings:* catered for. Professional: Ian Rae (01555 893646). Secretary: James Hamilton (01555 582 222).

MOTHERWELL. **Colville Park Golf Club,** Jerviston Estate, Merry Street, Motherwell ML1 4UG (01698 263017). *Location:* one mile from station (Merry Street, Motherwell). Parkland, wooded first six holes. 18 holes, 6265 yards. S.S.S. 70. *Green Fees:* £20.00. *Eating facilities:* full facilities. *Visitors:* welcome weekdays only and by prior written arrangement or accompanied by member. *Society Meetings:* by prior written arrangement. Professional: (01698 265779). Secretary: Scott Connacher.

SHOTTS. **Shotts Golf Club,** Blairhead, Benhar Road, Shotts ML7 5BJ (01501 820431). *Location:* off M8 at junction B7057, one and a half miles on Benhar Road. Semi-flat moorland/wooded course. 18 holes, 6204 yards. S.S.S. 70. Practice area, professional tuition. *Green Fees:* weekdays £17.00 per day (off season £10.00); weekends £20.00 per day (off season £12.00). July Monday to Friday weekly ticket £40. *Eating facilities:* full catering, all day licence. *Visitors:* welcome anytime except Saturdays before 4pm, Sundays (prior booking needed) or Public Holidays. *Society Meetings:* weekdays only (not Public Holidays) by arrangement. Professional: Sandy Strachan (01501 822658). Secretary: Jack McDermott (01501 820431, 01698 422584 (evenings)).

STRATHAVEN. **Strathaven Golf Club,** Overton Avenue, Glasgow Road, Strathaven ML10 6NR (01357 20539). *Location:* on A726 on outskirts of town. 18 holes, 6226 yards. S.S.S. 70. *Green Fees:* please contact Secretary for information. *Eating facilities:* full catering and bar. *Visitors:* welcome weekdays, casual visitors before 4pm; party bookings Tuesdays only by prior arrangement. Professional: M.R. McCrorie (01357 21812). Secretary: A.W. Wallace (01357 20421).

UDDINGSTON. **Calderbraes Golf Club,** 57 Roundknowe Road, Uddingston (Uddingston (01698) 813425). *Location:* at end of M74, overlooking Calderpark Zoo. 9 holes, 3425 yards. S.S.S. 67. *Green Fees:* weekdays £12.00. *Eating facilities:* catering available at all times. *Visitors:* welcome weekdays only; must be off course by 5pm. *Society Meetings:* welcome, contact Secretary. Secretary: S. McGuigan.

WISHAW. **Wishaw Golf Club,** 55 Cleland Road, Wishaw (01698 372869). *Location:* 400 yards from Main Street at Wishaw West Cross. Tree-lined parkland course. 18 holes, 6137 yards. S.S.S. 69. Practice area. *Green Fees:* weekdays £12.00 per round, £20.00 per day; weekends £25.00 per day. *Eating facilities:* full catering and two bars. *Visitors:* welcome before 4pm weekdays, after 11am Sundays, no visitors Saturdays. *Society Meetings:* by application to Secretary. Professional: J.G. Campbell (01698 358247). Secretary: J.M. Mitchell (01698 372869).

Morayshire

ELGIN. **Elgin Golf Club,** Hardhillock, Birnie Road, Elgin IV30 3SX (01343 542338; Fax: 01343 542341). *Location:* half a mile south of Elgin on Birnie Road. Undulating parkland on sandy subsoil. 18 holes, 6401 yards, 5853 metres. S.S.S. 71. Practice ground and net. *Green Fees:* weekdays £15.00 per round, £22.00 per day; weekends £22.00 per round, £30.00 per day. *Eating facilities:* bar and catering every day. *Visitors:* no restrictions but parties should book with Secretary. *Society Meetings:* by arrangement with Secretary. Early booking advised. Professional: Ian Rodger (Tel & Fax: 01343 542884). Secretary: Derek J. Chambers.

ELGIN. **Hopeman Golf Club,** Hopeman, Elgin IV30 2YA (01343 830578). *Location:* 7 miles north-east of Elgin on B9012. Seaside links, with spectacular 12th hole. 18 holes, 5474 yards, 5003 metres. S.S.S. 67. *Green Fees:* weekdays £12.00 per day; weekends £17.00 per day. Half price for Senior Citizens and Juniors. *Eating facilities:* bar, catering. *Visitors:* welcome, some restrictions on tee times at weekends. *Society Meetings:* welcome by arrangement. Secretary: W.H. Dunbar (01343 830687).

FOCHABERS. **Garmouth & Kingston Golf Club,** Garmouth, Fochabers (01343 870388). *Location:* west bank of River Spey, 300 yards from North Sea. Flat parkland/part links. 18 holes, 5656 yards. S.S.S. 67. *Green Fees:* weekdays £10.00 per round, £15.00 per day; weekends £15.00 per round, £20.00 per day. Reductions for parties over 10. *Eating facilities:* 11am to 11pm weekends for bar, catering by prior arrangement; snacks available at bar. *Visitors:* welcome, except during local competitions. Local hotel caters for golfing holidays. *Society Meetings:* by arrangement with Secretary, very welcome. Secretary: A. Robertson (01343 870231).

PUBLISHER'S NOTE

While every effort is made to ensure accuracy, we regret that FHG Publications cannot accept responsibility for errors, omissions or misrepresentation in our entries or any consequences thereof. Prices in particular should be checked because we go to press early. We will follow up complaints, but cannot act as arbiters or agents for either party.

FOCHABERS. **Spey Bay Golf Club,** Spey Bay Hotel, Spey Bay, Fochabers IV32 7PJ (01343 820424 Hotel). *Location:* halfway between Inverness and Aberdeen, at the mouth of River Spey. Seaside links, wooded (gorse bushes). 18 holes, 6092 yards. S.S.S. 69. Driving range, practice area and putting green. *Green Fees:* Monday to Friday £10.00 per round, weekends £13.00. Parties of eight or more – two rounds and food £20.00 Monday to Saturday, Sundays £22.00. *Eating facilities:* all meals available at the adjoining hotel. *Visitors:* welcome weekdays without reservation, advise prior phone call on Sundays. *Society Meetings:* catered for by prior arrangement. Special weekend terms including full board and golf available. Any enquiries to the Hotel Manager: Michael Dann. Secretary: Arthur Mitchell (01343 820459).

FORRES. **Forres Golf Club,** Muiryshade, Forres IV36 0RD (01309 672949). *Location:* one mile south from clock tower in town centre. Parkland, part wooded. 18 holes, 6203 yards. S.S.S. 69. Practice ground and putting green. *Green Fees:* weekdays £13.00 per day; weekends £18.00. *Eating facilities:* bar and catering all day every day. *Visitors:* welcome without reservation – can be difficult at weekends due to competitions. *Society Meetings:* welcome. Professional: Sandy Aird (01309 672250). Secretary: D.F. Black (01309 672949).

GRANTOWN-ON-SPEY. **Grantown-on-Spey Golf Club,** The Clubhouse, Golf Course Road, Grantown-on-Spey PH26 3HY (01479 872079). *Location:* situated at north end of town, A9 to A95, then turn right opposite police station. Parkland and woodland. 18 holes, 5745 yards. S.S.S. 68. Practice area and putting green. *Green Fees:* weekdays £13.00 per day; weekends £18.00. *Eating facilities:* bar and full catering available April to December inclusive. *Visitors:* welcome weekdays except between 5.30pm – 6.30pm when members have preference. *Society Meetings:* welcome except before 10am weekends. Professional: Bill Mitchell (01479 872398). Secretary: Dennis W. Elms (01479 872715).

LOSSIEMOUTH. **Moray Golf Club,** Stotfield Road, Lossiemouth IV31 6QS (01343 812018; Fax: 01243 815102). *Location:* six miles north of Elgin. Old Course 18 holes, 6643 yards, 6074 metres. S.S.S. 72. New Course 18 holes, 6005 yards, 5491 metres. S.S.S. 69. *Green Fees:* on request. *Eating facilities:* full catering and bar facilities. *Visitors:* welcome weekdays after 9.30am (except between 1-2pm). Weekends: Saturday (New Course only), Sunday not before 10.30am and not between 1-2pm. *Society Meetings:* all welcome. Handicap Certificate required. Professional: Alastair Thomson (01343 813330). Secretary: James Hamilton (01343 812018).

Nairnshire

CAWDOR CASTLE. **Cawdor Castle Golf Club,** Cawdor Castle, Nairn IV12 5RD (01667 404615; Fax: 01667 404674). *Location:* situated between Inverness and Nairn on the B9090 off A96. Parkland. 9 holes, 1161 yards. S.S.S. 32. *Green Fees:* weekdays £3.00 per round; weekends £4.00 per round. Subject to review. *Eating facilities:* licensed restaurant in Castle, snack bar in grounds. *Visitors:* welcome every day from 11am to 5pm May 1st to first Sunday in October.

NAIRN. **Nairn Dunbar Golf Club,** Lochloy Road, Nairn IV12 5AE (01667 452741; Fax: 01667 456897). *Location:* off A96, one mile east of town. Seaside links. 18 holes, 6431 yards. S.S.S. 71. *Green Fees:* weekdays £17.00 per round, £22.00 per day; weekends £22.00 per round, £27.00 per day. *Eating facilities:* available. *Visitors:* welcome. *Society Meetings:* catered for. Professional: B. Mason (01667 453964). Secretary: Mrs S.J. MacLennan.

NAIRN. **The Nairn Golf Club,** Seabank Road, Nairn IV12 4HB (01667 452103; Fax: 01667 456328). *Location:* Nairn West Shore, on the southern shore of the Moray Firth, 16 miles east of Inverness on A96. Traditional Scottish links championship course. 18 holes, 6722 yards. S.S.S. 72. Also 9 hole course (Newton Course). Practice area. *Green Fees:* weekdays £26.00 per round, £37.00 per day; weekends £32.00 per round, £42.00 per day. Fees subject to review. *Eating facilities:* full catering and bar available. *Visitors:* welcome, no jeans in clubhouse, Handicap Certificate required, restricted times at weekends. Full size snooker table. *Society Meetings:* bookings in advance through Secretary. Professional: Robin Fyfe (01667 452787). Secretary: Mr Jim Somerville (01667 453208; Fax: 01667 456328). Clubmaster: (01667 452103).

Peeblesshire

PEEBLES. **Innerleithen Golf Club,** Leithen Water, Leithen Road, Innerleithen (01896 830951). *Location:* 25 miles south of Edinburgh, just south of Peebles. Situated in valley, easy walking but challenging. 9 holes, 2992 yards (x 2). S.S.S. 69. *Green Fees:* weekdays £10.00 per day; weekends £12.00 per day. *Eating facilities:* by prior arrangement. *Visitors:* welcome without reservation. *Society Meetings:* catered for by arrangement, limit 40. Secretary: S. Wyse (01896 830071).

PEEBLES. **Peebles Golf Club,** Kirkland Street, Peebles EH45 8LF (01721 720197). *Location:* 51 miles from Glasgow, off A72 at west side of town, 23 miles from Edinburgh. Undulating parkland with panoramic views. 18 holes, 6137 yards. S.S.S. 69. *Green Fees:* weekdays £13.00 per round, £20.00 per day; weekends £19.00 per round, £27.00 per day. *Eating facilities:* full catering daily except Tuesdays. *Visitors:* welcome subject to tee availability. Golf buggy hire April to September. *Society Meetings:* catered for subject to prior booking, limited to 24 players in party. Secretary: Hugh Gilmore.

WEST LINTON. **West Linton Golf Club,** West Linton EH46 7HN (01968 660463). *Location:* A702 road 17 miles south west of Edinburgh. Scenic moorland course. 18 holes, 6132 yards, 5607 metres. S.S.S. 69. Two practice areas. *Green Fees:* weekdays £15.00 per round, £21.00 per day; weekends £24.00 per round. Weekly ticket (Mon-Fri) £75.00. Fees subject to review. *Eating facilities:* catering except Tuesdays; lunches, bar snacks, high teas, morning coffee, bar. *Visitors:* welcome at all times except on Medal days and weekends before 1pm. *Society Meetings:* catered for weekdays except Tuesdays. Professional: Ricky Forrest (01968 660256). Secretary: Grahame Scott (01968 660970).

Perthshire

ABERFELDY. **Aberfeldy Golf Club,** Taybridge Road, Aberfeldy PH15 2BH (01887 820535). *Location:* A9 to Ballinluig. Riverside course. 9 holes, 2733 yards, 2655 metres. S.S.S. 67. *Green Fees:* £10.00 per round. *Eating facilities:* snacks and bar. *Visitors:* welcome anytime. *Society Meetings:* catered for. Contact the Secretary at Aberfeldy Golf Club. Secretary: Angus M. Stewart (01887 820117). *

AUCHTERARDER. **Auchterarder Golf Club,** Orchil Road, Auchterarder PH3 1LS (01764 662804). *Location:* off A9 to southwest of town, next to Gleneagles. Flat parkland, part wooded. 18 holes, 5778 yards. S.S.S. 68. Small practice area. *Green Fees:* weekdays £14.00 per round, £20.00 per day; Saturdays £21.00 per round, £28.00 per day; Sundays £30.00. Weekdays weekly ticket (one round per day) £50.00. *Eating facilities:* full catering and bar. *Visitors:* welcome without reservation except major competition days. *Society Meetings:* welcome, must book 3 months in advance. Professional: Gavin Baxter (01764 663711). Secretary: W.M. Campbell (01764 662804).

AUCHTERARDER. **Gleneagles Hotel Golf Courses,** Auchterarder PH3 1NF (01764 62231; Telex 76105; Fax: 01764 62134). *Location:* A9 from Perth, 16 miles south-west: bus meets trains at Gleneagles Station. Gleneagles offers two moorland 18 hole courses. **King's Course: 6125 yards par 69; **Queen's Course: 5660 yards par 67. Also Monarch's Course (18 holes) and a new 9 hole course, The Wee Course: 1481 yards par 27. *Green Fees:* on request. *Eating facilities:* at Dormy House (Bar & Restaurant) and The Gleneagles Hotel. *Visitors:* strictly Hotel residents, and members. Professional: Billy Marchbank. Hotel General Manager: Peter Lederer (01764 62231). Golf Co-ordinator: Suzanne Mailer (01764 663543; Fax: 01764 664440).

Moorfield House Hotel

Coupar Angus, by Blairgowrie PH13 9HS
Telephone (01828) 27303

Deserve a break? We are surrounded by superb golf courses all with something different to offer, be you professional or beginner. Then return to the privacy of our elegant Country House and enjoy the best of Scottish fare accompanied by fine wines and hearty Malts. Luxurious bedrooms all with private facilities, a charming Dining Room and spacious Lounge have all been expertly decorated for your pleasure, and friendly Staff wait to welcome you.

Highly Commended

Nine challenging holes set on a privately owned 6000-acre estate in spectacular and beautiful scenery. The course has been owned and maintained by the Winton family for over 40 years, alongside Dalmunzie House Hotel and Highland Cottages. Why not come to stay, and enjoy carefree golf in spectacular surroundings? Send for details to Simon Winton.

DALMUNZIE GOLF COURSE

SPITTAL OF GLENSHEE, BLAIRGOWRIE, PERTHSHIRE PH10 7QG TEL: 01250 885226

KINLOCH HOUSE HOTEL

By Blairgowrie, Perthshire PH10 6SG

Kinloch House is a fine example of a Scottish country house – set in 20 acres of wooded policies and parkland. An ideal golfing centre, 30 courses within an hour's drive. We should be happy to help plan your golf and book your tee off times. Write or telephone for a brochure.

Tel: (01250) 884237 Fax: (01250) 884333 David & Sarah Shentall

---

The Angus Hotel

BLAIRGOWRIE, PERTHSHIRE PH10 6NQ

Telephone: Blairgowrie (01250) 872838/872455

Carnoustie, St. Andrews, Rosemount, Downfield – need we say more?

All rooms with private facilities. Indoor heated pool, spa bath, sauna, solarium. Ample free parking.

5 days (Half Board) – £35 per day (inc VAT at 17½%).

The Lake Hotel

7 Golf courses within half an hour's drive of our hotel with its Conservatory Restaurant set beside the Lake of Menteith and wonderful views to the hills beyond.

STB **Highly Commended, AA Rosette. Personally run, friendly welcome. Reservations 01877 385258.**

The Lake Hotel, Port of Menteith, Perthshire FK8 3RA

Keppoch House Hotel **Perth Road, Crieff PH7 3EQ Tel: (01764) 654341**

This charming hotel is fully licensed and stands in its own grounds only a short walk from the Crieff Golf Club and Crieff town centre, with a further 20 golf courses within a 20 mile radius. The Keppoch is an ideal base for your holiday or short break. We can arrange all your golfing needs. Relax in the comfort of a family run hotel and enjoy our excellent meals.

For brochure and further details contact: Bob Brown

LOCHEARNHEAD HOTEL

Escape to Perthshire – A family run Hotel with luxury self-catering Chalets overlooking LOCHEARN. Ideal golfing centre, with 7 Golf Courses within 20 miles and many more within an hour's drive. Play 5 local courses in 5 days for approximately £40. Also an ideal centre for touring, water sports (we have our own moorings and slipway), hillwalking, fishing and sailing. Enjoy superb Scottish cooking and stunning views. Families and dogs welcome. Fully licensed. 3 Day and 5 Day midweek breaks available.

Write or phone for brochure to: Lochearnhead Hotel, Lochearnhead, Perthshire
Telephone: 01567 830229 Fax: 01567 830364

BLAIR ATHOLL. **Blair Atholl Golf Club,** Blair Atholl, Pitlochry PH18 5TG (01796 481407). *Location:* off A9, seven miles north of Pitlochry. Flat parkland. 9 holes. S.S.S. 69. Clubs for hire. *Green Fees:* weekdays £10.00 per day; weekends £12.00 per day. *Eating facilities:* bar meals and snacks. *Visitors:* welcome at all times. *Society Meetings:* by arrangement with Secretary, not Sundays. Secretary: Mr J.A. McGregor (01796 481274).

BLAIRGOWRIE. **Alyth Golf Club,** Alyth, Blairgowrie (018283 2268). *Location:* A926 or A927 to Alyth, B954 one mile to Club (five miles from Blairgowrie/Coupar Angus). Heathland course. 18 holes, 6205 yards, 5676 metres. S.S.S. 70. *Green Fees:* weekdays £17.00 per round, £25.00 per day; weekends £22.00 per round, £30.00 per day. *Eating facilities:* full catering and bar facilities. *Visitors:* welcome, tee may be reserved six days in advance. *Society Meetings:* welcome, prior booking essential. Professional: Tom Melville (Tel & Fax: 018283 2411). Secretary: Roy Davidson.

BLAIRGOWRIE. **Blairgowrie Golf Club,** Rosemount, Blairgowrie PH10 6LG (01250 872383; Fax: 01250 875451).*Location:* take A923 out of Perth, turn right at "Rosemount" sign. Flat wooded moorland. Rosemount Course: 18 holes, 6588 yards. S.S.S. 72. Lansdowne Course: 18 holes, 6895 yards. S.S.S. 73. Wee Course: 9 holes, 2307 yards. S.S.S. 65. Three practice grounds. *Green Fees:* on application. No advance booking Wednesdays/Saturdays/Sundays. *Eating facilities:* full catering available. *Visitors:* advance booking Mon/Tues/Thurs/part Fri, 8.30am-4.00pm (through Secretary). Handicap Certificate required. *Society Meetings:* catered for by application to the Secretary. (Maximum 32 without prior permission.) Professional: Gordon Kinnoch (01250 873116). Secretary/Manager: John N. Simpson (01250 872622). *

BLAIRGOWRIE. **Dalmunzie Golf Course,** Spittal O' Glenshee, Blairgowrie PH10 7QG (01250 885226). *Location:* A93 Blairgowrie to Braemar road, left at Spittal O' Glenshee. A small well-kept hill course amid glorious scenery. 9 holes, 2035 yards. Practice area. *Green Fees:* £5.00 per round, £8.50 per day. Under 7 free, 7 – 14 half price (we like young golfers.) *Eating facilities:* restaurant facilities at Dalmunzie Hotel. Bar. *Visitors:* welcome without reservation. Self-catering cottages available. *Society Meetings:* catered for. Secretary: Simon Winton.

CALLANDER. **Callander Golf Club,** Aveland Road, Callander FK17 8EN (01877 330090). *Location:* M9 (Stirling) leave by Crianlarich exit on to A84 to Callander, at east end of town, just off Main Street. Parkland, partly wooded, with panoramic views. 18 holes, 5125 yards. S.S.S. 66. Small practice ground. *Green Fees:* weekdays £14.00 per round, £18.00 per day; weekends £18.00 per round, £22.00 per day. *Eating facilities:* bar snacks, lunches, high teas, dinners by arrangement. *Visitors:* welcome, no restrictions. Handicap Certificate required Wednesdays and Sundays. *Society Meetings:* welcome, book nine months in advance, arrange through Club Office between 10am to 4pm November/March, 9am to 5pm April/October. Professional: W. Kelly (01877 330975). Secretary: Ian A.C. Scott (01877 330090).

CRIEFF. **Comrie Golf Club,** Comrie (01764 670055). *Location:* six miles from Crieff on Crieff/Lochearnhead Road at east end of Comrie village. 9 holes, 5966 yards. S.S.S. 69. *Green Fees:* weekdays £10.00, weekends £12.00. *Eating facilities:* light refreshments during summer months. *Visitors:* welcome without reservation. *Society Meetings:* by arrangement with Secretary. Secretary: D.G. McGlashan (01764 670544).

CRIEFF. **Crieff Golf Club,** Perth Road, Crieff PH7 3LR (01764 652397). *Location:* A85 north-east outskirts of Crieff. Ferntower Course – 18 holes, 6402 yards. S.S.S. 71. Dornock Course – 9 holes, 2386 yards. S.S.S. 63. Two practice areas. *Green Fees:* Ferntower: weekdays £16.00 per round, £27.00 per day; weekends £20.00 per round. Dornock – per 18 holes: weekdays £11.00; weekends £13.00. *Eating facilities:* full restaurant facilities by arrangement (phone 01764 652397) and bar snacks. *Visitors:* welcome with reservation, prior arrangement advisable by phone. *Society Meetings:* book by phone (01764 652909) and confirm in writing. Senior Professional: John Stark (01764 652909). Club Professional: David Murchie. Secretary: L.J. Rundle.

CRIEFF. **St. Fillans Golf Club,** South Loch Earn Road, St. Fillans PH6 2NG (01764 685312). *Location:* thirteen miles west of Crieff on A85 between Crieff and Lochearnhead. M9 nearest motorway. Parkland with one small hill. 9 holes, 5866 yards. S.S.S. 68 (18 holes). Practice net. *Green Fees:* weekdays £8.00 per round, £12.00 per day; weekends £10.00 per round, £14.00

WESTER RIECHIP, Butterstone, Dunkeld

Enjoy the freedom of self catering on your next Golfing Holiday.
This STB ♛♛♛♛ Deluxe Graded house accommodates 8 people in comfort. Centrally situated for access to 30 famous and popular courses in Perthshire and beyond. Cottages and flats also available for smaller groups.

Brochures from: Laighwood Holidays, Butterstone, Dunkeld, Perthshire PH8 0HB. Tel: 01350 724241

THE ROYAL DUNKELD HOTEL

♛♛♛ **STB Commended**

A former Coaching Inn, THE ROYAL DUNKELD HOTEL, some 170 years old is now a comfortable, modern hotel set in the beautiful Cathedral town of Dunkeld. We are members of the Logis of Great Britain group and our restaurant offers excellent value and now boasts membership of the Taste of Scotland scheme. Outstanding bar suppers and a warm, friendly welcome are always assured in our bar. 35 bedrooms, all ensuite. Open all year, we are perfectly situated to tour very many of Scotland's most famous golf courses.

Dunkeld, Perthshire PH8 0AR. Telephone: (01350) 727322 for reservations. Fax: (01350) 728989

Delightful waterside hotel has 38 bedrooms, all ensuite with colour TV. Situated in the beautiful village of Kenmore this hotel offers golfing and fishing breaks. Local produce is heavily relied upon in the Kenmore's kitchen with fresh salmon and seasonal game. Swimming pool and sauna available for residents. There are a variety of golf courses to enjoy nearby. Hotel residents can enjoy a 20% discount on green fees at Taymouth Castle Golf Club.

THE KENMORE HOTEL
Scotland's Oldest Inn
1572

Kenmore Hotel, Kenmore,
Perthshire PH15 2NU
Tel: 01887 830205 Fax: 01887 830262

TAYMOUTH HOLIDAY CENTRE

and KENMORE GOLF COURSE

Taymouth Holiday Centre is situated in the heart of Perthshire amongst the beautiful surroundings of the Tay Valley at the head of the Loch. Holiday accommodation is available in self-catering farm cottages furnished and equipped to the Tourist Board's ♛♛♛♛ Commended standards. There is also a quiet and secluded caravan and camping park (Four Pennants) nearby, with shop and ample children's play areas. The "Byre Bistro" overlooking the first tee offers delicious bar meals, served all day, and there are many other excellent places to dine at in the area. The centre's own KENMORE GOLF COURSE (6030 yards, 9 holes) offers a challenging game on excellent greens. Caddy cars and clubs can be hired and changing rooms are available. As well as golf at this or any of the other 29 courses in Perthshire, visitors can enjoy walking, fishing, cycling and all watersports at the nearby water sports centre.

Brochure available from D. Menzies & Partners, Taymouth Holiday Centre, Kenmore, Aberfeldy, Perthshire PH15 2HN Tel: 01887 830226 Fax: 01887 830211

LOCH TAY HIGHLAND LODGES – *SUPERB SELF CATERING*

Our luxury lodges, on the shore of LochTay in the heart of Scotland, are fully equipped and heated for all-year occupation with spacious comfort for 4 to 6 people.

Golfers can enjoy a local 5-day/5-course ticket at £40, or travel a little further to Kenmore or Rosemount.

Our on-site facilities include riding centre, salmon and trout fishing, pleasure cruising, mini-leisure centre and putting green.

For brochure and details contact:–
Pamela and Clive Booth
Loch Tay Highland Lodges,
Milton Morenish, by Killin, Perthshire FK21 8TY
Tel: 01567 820323 Fax: 01567 820581

per day. *Eating facilities:* light meals, teas, coffees, snacks. No bar. *Visitors:* welcome at all times. *Society Meetings:* welcome with advance booking (not July and August). Maximum 24. Hon. Professional: John Stark. Secretary: J. Allison (01764 670951). *

CRIEFF. **Muthill Golf Club,** Peat Road, Muthill, Crieff PH5 2AD (01764 81523). *Location:* 500 yards off main Crieff/Stirling Road at west end of village. Parkland (noted for panoramic views of Strathearn). 9 holes, 2350 yards. S.S.S. 63 for 18 holes. *Green Fees:* weekdays £8.00 per day; weekends £12.00. Fees subject to review. *Eating facilities:* tea, coffee, soft drinks only. *Visitors:* restricted when competitions and matches are being played, notice displayed at clubhouse. Changing and toilet facilities available. Secretary: W.H. Gordon (01764 653319).

DUNBLANE. **Dunblane New Golf Club,** Perth Road, Dunblane FK15 0LJ (01786 822343). *Location:* one mile off main road A9 at Fourways Roundabout. Parkland/undulating. 18 holes, 5939 yards. S.S.S. 68. *Green Fees:* weekdays £16.00 per round, £23.00 per day. *Eating facilities:* available. *Visitors:* welcome, 9.30am to 12 noon, 2.30pm to 4pm. *Society Meetings:* catered for Mondays and Thursdays only. Professional: R.M. Jamieson (01786 823711; Fax: 01786 825946). Treasurer: Jack Dunsmore.

DUNKELD. **Dunkeld and Birnam Golf Club,** Fungarth, Dunkeld PH8 0AD (01350 727524). *Location:* turn right one mile north of Dunkeld onto A923. Heathland course with panoramic views. 9 holes, 5240 yards. S.S.S. 66. Practice area. *Green Fees:* on application. *Eating facilities:* bar and full catering facilities. *Visitors:* welcome. *Society Meetings:* catered for. Secretary: Mrs W.A. Sinclair (01350 727524).

DUNNING. **Dunning Golf Club,** Rollo Park, Dunning (01764 684747). *Location:* 10 miles south-west of Perth, two miles from A9. Parkland, softly undulating. 9 holes, 4836 yards. S.S.S. 64. Small practice area. *Green Fees:* £8.00 per day adults, £4.00 per day Juniors. £30.00 weekly ticket. *Eating facilities:* tea/coffee, soft drinks, snacks. *Visitors:* welcome weekdays but no visitors after 5pm unless accompanied by member; no visitors before 4pm Saturday, Sundays no visitors before 1pm. *Society Meetings:* welcome weekdays. Secretary: Mr James Slater (01764 684372).

KENMORE. **Kenmore Golf Course,** Mains of Taymouth, Kenmore, Aberfeldy PH15 2HN (01887 830226; Fax: 01887 830211). *Location:* west off A9 at Ballingluig on A827, six and a half miles west of Aberfeldy through village of Kenmore on RHS. Mildly undulating natural terrain, well kept, nestled in Tay Valley. 9 holes, 6052 yards. S.S.S. 69. Practice facilities. *Green Fees:* £12.00 18 holes, £18.00 per day. Junior rates available, rates for parties on application. *Eating facilities:* full bar and catering facilities in pleasant surroundings. *Visitors:* welcome anytime. STB 4 Crown Cottages to let and group accommodation available (self catering included). Pro shop; club and trolley hire; changing and shower facilities. *Society Meetings:* up to 50 welcome. Secretary: Robin Menzies.

KENMORE. **Taymouth Castle Golf Course,** Kenmore, by Aberfeldy PH15 2NT (01887 830228). *Location:* six miles west of Aberfeldy. Flat parkland set in scenic mountain terrain. 18 holes, 6066 yards. S.S.S. 69. Practice area. *Green Fees:* weekdays £15.00 per round, £24.00 per day; weekends and Bank Holidays, £18.00 per round. Half price for Juniors (under 14). Subject to review. *Eating facilities:* restaurant and bar. *Visitors:* welcome except competition days, tee reservations necessary (phone or letter). Tuition available, motorised buggies. *Society Meetings:* catered for by previous arrangement only. Professional: Alex Marshall (01887 820910). Director of Golf: (01887 830228).

KILLIN. **Killin Golf Club,** Killin (01567 820312). *Location:* west end of Loch Tay. Hilly parkland amongst beautiful scenery. 9 holes, 2510 yards. S.S.S. 65. Small practice area includes bunker and net. *Green Fees:* £9.50 per round, £12.50 per day. *Eating facilities:* available all day. *Visitors:* welcome. *Society Meetings:* catered for by arrangement. Secretary: Sandy Chisholm (01838 300235).

PERTH. **Craigie Hill Golf Club (1982) Ltd,** Cherrybank, Perth PH2 0NE (01738 24377). *Location:* at west end of town, easy access from M90 and A9. Hilly course with lovely scenery. 18 holes, 5379 yards. S.S.S. 66. Practice ground and putting green. *Green Fees:* weekdays £10.00 per round, £15.00 per day; Sundays £20.00 per day. Visitors with member £5.00, Juniors (weekdays) £3.00 per round. *Eating facilities:* full catering except Mondays and Tuesdays, bar open every day. *Visitors:* welcome Mondays to Fridays and Sundays by arrangement. *Society Meetings:* catered for by written application in first instance. Professional: Frank L. Smith (01738 22644). Secretary: William A. Miller (01738 20829).

PERTH. **King James VI Golf Club,** Moncrieffe Island, Perth PH2 8NR (01738 625170). Starter (01738 632460). *Location:* situated on Island in River Tay, access by Footbridge alongside railway from Tay Street, Perth. Parkland course. 18 holes, 6038 yards. S.S.S. 69. Practice nets. *Green Fees:* weekdays £12.00 per round, £18.00 per day; Sundays £24.00 per day,

£15.00 per round after 10am. *Eating facilities:* full catering, bar. *Visitors:* welcome, phone for reservation, no visitors on Saturdays. *Society Meetings:* catered for by prior booking. Fully stocked golf shop. Professional: Tony Coles (01738 632460). Secretary: Dorothy Barraclough (01738 632460).

PITLOCHRY. **Pitlochry Golf Course,** Pitlochry (01796 2792). *Location:* half mile from centre of Pitlochry on A9. 18 holes, 5811 yards, S.S.S. 68. *Green Fees:* 1st April to 31st October: weekdays £14.00 per day (£3.00 Juniors); Saturdays £17.00 per day (£5.00 Juniors); Sundays £17.00 per day. Restricted course (1st November to 31st March). Day ticket (any day) Adult £6.00, Junior £1.50. *Eating facilities:* catering and refreshments available in licensed clubhouse, except mid-October to end of March. *Visitors:* welcome. Caddy cars available for hire. *Society Meetings:* catered for. Professional: George Hampton (01796 2792). Secretary: D.C.M. McKenzie (01796 2114 for Group bookings). Fax: 01796 473599. *

SCONE. **Murrayshall Golf Course,** Murrayshall, Scone PH2 7PH (01738 551171; Fax: 01738 552595). *Location:* three miles north of Perth on Coupar Angus Road. Undulating wooded parkland. 18 holes, 6460 yards. S.S.S. 70. Golf range. *Green Fees:* weekdays £20.00 per round, £30.00 per day; weekends £25.00 per round, £40.00 per day. *Eating facilities:* clubhouse open all day. *Visitors:* welcome at all times, no restrictions – advance booking advisable. Hotel; buggies, clubs for hire. *Society Meetings:* welcome – must book. Professional: Neil I.M. MacKintosh (01738 552784).

STRATHTAY. **Strathtay Golf Club,** Strathtay, by Pitlochry PH15. *Location:* on the right, three-quarters of a mile westwards on the minor road to Weem from off the A827 Ballinluig to Grandtully. Wooded, mainly hilly course with beautiful panoramic views. 9 holes, 4082 yards. S.S.S. 63. *Green Fees:* £8.00 weekdays (Juniors £2.00); £10.00 weekends (Juniors £3.00). Five day ticket £30.00. *Eating facilities:* cafe and bar five minutes walk. *Visitors:* pre-teenagers MUST have adult supervision. NO visitors on Sundays 12.30pm to 5pm May to August. Open mixed foursomes every Tuesday evening April/October. New changing room, toilets. *Society Meetings:* must be arranged in advance. Secretary: Thomas D. Lind (01350 727797).

FOR THE MUTUAL GUIDANCE OF GUEST AND HOST

Every year literally thousands of holidays, short-breaks and overnight stops are arranged through our guides, the vast majority without any problems at all. In a handful of cases, however, difficulties do arise about bookings, which often could have been prevented from the outset.

It is important to remember that when accommodation has been booked, both parties — guests and hosts — have entered into a form of contract. We hope that the following points will provide helpful guidance.

GUESTS: When enquiring about accommodation, be as precise as possible. Give exact dates, numbers in your party and the ages of any children. State the number and type of rooms wanted and also what catering you require — bed and breakfast, full board, etc. Make sure that the position about evening meals is clear — and about pets, reductions for children or any other special points.

Read our reviews carefully to ensure that the proprietors you are going to contact can supply what you want. Ask for a letter confirming all arrangements, if possible.

If you have to cancel, do so as soon as possible. Proprietors do have the right to retain deposits and under certain circumstances to charge for cancelled holidays if adequate notice is not given and they cannot re-let the accommodation.

HOSTS: Give details about your facilities and about any special conditions. Explain your deposit system clearly and arrangements for cancellations, charges, etc, and whether or not your terms include VAT.

If for any reason you are unable to fulfil an agreed booking without adequate notice, you may be under an obligation to arrange alternative suitable accommodation or to make some form of compensation.

Renfrewshire

BARRHEAD. **Fereneze Golf Club,** Fereneze Avenue, Barrhead, Glasgow (0141-881 1519). *Location:* nine miles south west of Glasgow. Parkland. 18 holes, 5962 yards. S.S.S. 69. *Green Fees:* on application. *Eating facilities:* lunches served at club except Mondays, order in advance. *Visitors:* welcome by arrangement. *Society Meetings:* welcome, bookings arranged in advance. Professional: Darren Robinson (0141-880 7058). Secretary: A.D. Gourley C.A. (0141-221 6394; Fax: 0141-221 0135).

BISHOPTON. **Erskine Golf Club,** Bishopton PA7 5PH (01505 862302). *Location:* north of M8, leave M8 at Bridge Toll barrier and turn left along B815 for one mile approximately. Parkland course. 18 holes, 6298 yards. S.S.S. 70. Putting green and practice area. *Green Fees:* £20.00 per round, £30.00 per day ticket. *Eating facilities:* restaurant and bar, lunches, teas and dinners served at club. *Visitors:* welcome but must play with a member or be introduced. Professional: Peter Thomson. Secretary: T.A. McKillop.

BRIDGE OF WEIR. **Old Course Ranfurly Golf Club Ltd,** Ranfurly Place, Bridge of Weir PA11 3DE (01505 613612). *Location:* five miles west of Glasgow Airport. Moorland course. 18 holes, 6089 yards. S.S.S. 69. *Green Fees:* weekdays £15.00 per round, £25.00 per day; weekends only if introduced by and playing with a member. *Eating facilities:* restricted catering Mondays and Tuesdays. *Visitors:* welcome weekdays, should contact club beforehand. Must be members of recognised golf clubs with Handicap Certificates. *Society Meetings:* on written application only. Secretary: R. Mitchell (01505 613214).

BRIDGE OF WEIR. **Ranfurly Castle Golf Club Ltd,** Golf Road, Bridge of Weir PA11 3HN (01505 612609). *Location:* M8 from Glasgow exit Junction 29, A240 and A761 to Bridge of Weir. Moorland. 18 holes, 6284 yards. S.S.S. 70. Practice ground. *Green Fees:* weekdays £22.00 per round, £27.00 day ticket. *Eating facilities:* bar snacks all day; lunches, high teas, etc by arrangement. *Visitors:* welcome weekdays, at weekends only if accompanied by member. *Society Meetings:* catered for Tuesdays only. Professional: Tom Eckford (01505 614795). Secretary: Mr J. Walker (01505 612609).

ELDERSLIE. **Elderslie Golf Club,** 63 Main Road, Elderslie PA5 9AZ (01505 322835). *Location:* off M8 at Linwood turn-off, continue to roundabout, follow Elderslie signs A737. Club on main road. Woodland course. 18 holes, 6031 yards. S.S.S. 69. Large practice area. *Green Fees:* £16.10 per round, £22.00 per day weekdays. *Eating facilities:* diningroom, bar and bar snacks. *Visitors:* welcome weekdays, no visitors weekends. *Society Meetings:* welcome weekdays, book through Secretary. Professional: (01505 320032). Secretary: Anne Anderson (01505 323956). *

GOUROCK. **Gourock Golf Club,** Cowal View, Gourock (01475 631001). *Location:* two miles west of Gourock Station above Yacht Club. Heathland/parkland with spectacular views. 18 holes, 6492 yards. S.S.S. 71. *Green Fees:* on application. *Eating facilities:* restaurant, full meals also bar snacks. *Visitors:* welcome with letter of introduction. *Society Meetings:* catered for on application. Professional: A.M. Green (01475 636834). Secretary: M.J. Walker.

GREENOCK. **Greenock Golf Club,** Forsyth Street, Greenock PA16 8RE (01475 720793). *Location:* one mile from town centre. Moorland course. 18 holes, 5835 yards. S.S.S. 68. *Green Fees:* £15.00 weekdays; £20.00 weekends. *Eating facilities:* available. *Visitors:* welcome weekdays, not Saturdays. *Society Meetings:* advance booking required. Professional: Graham Ross (01475 787236). Secretary: Eric J. Black (01475 726819).

GREENOCK. **Greenock Whinhill Golf Club,** Beith Road, Greenock (01475 24694). *Location:* 26 miles from Glasgow. Municipal course. 18 holes, 5454 yards. S.S.S. 68. *Green Fees:* information not provided. Secretary: D. McConnell. *

JOHNSTONE. **Cochrane Castle Golf Club,** Craigston, Johnstone PA5 0HF (01505 322010). *Location:* A737 off Beith Road, Johnstone. Parkland course. 18 holes, 6226 yards. S.S.S. 70. Practice ground. *Green Fees:* weekdays £22.00 per day, £16.00 per round. *Eating facilities:* full catering and bar snacks. *Visitors:* welcome weekdays, maximum 32 players. *Society Meetings:* catered for by arrangement, weekdays only. Professional: Stuart H. Campbell (01505 328465). Secretary: J.C. Cowan (01505 320146).

KILMACOLM. **Kilmacolm Golf Club,** Porterfield Road, Kilmacolm PA13 4PD (01505 872139). *Location:* A761. Moorland course. 18 holes, 5964 yards. S.S.S. 68. Practice area. *Green Fees:* £20.00 per round, £25.00 per day. *Eating facilities:* diningroom and bar. *Visitors:* welcome on weekdays. *Society Meetings:* catered for. Professional: D. Stewart (01505 872695). Secretary: R.F. McDonald.

If you are writing, a stamped, addressed envelope is always appreciated.

LANGBANK. **Gleddoch Golf and Country Club,** Langbank PA14 6YG (0147554 304). *Location:* M8 west of Glasgow, past airport to Langbank; Langbank and Gleddoch House are both signposted. Moorland, woodland and parkland. 18 holes, 6332 yards. S.S.S. 71. Practice area, indoor driving bay and putting green. *Green Fees:* £25.00 day ticket. Hotel residents £12.50. *Eating facilities:* bar, lounge and restaurant open all day. *Visitors:* welcome all week. Gleddoch House Hotel, 39 bedrooms plus self catering lodges. *Society Meetings:* welcome weekdays only. Professional: Keith Campbell (0147554 704). Secretary: David Tierney (0147554 304).

LOCHWINNOCH. **Lochwinnoch Golf Club,** Burnfoot Road, Lochwinnoch PA12 4AN (01505 842153). *Location:* between Johnstone and Beith, off A737 on Largs road A760. Parkland, extremely scenic, set in quiet country village. 18 holes, 6242 yards. S.S.S. 70. Practice area. *Green Fees:* weekdays £15.00 per round, £20.00 per day. *Eating facilities:* licensed bar and catering, except Mondays. *Visitors:* no visitors weekends or Public Holidays. *Society Meetings;* welcome weekdays. Professional: Gerry Reilly (01505 843029). Secretary: Mrs Evelyn McBride.

PAISLEY. **Barshaw Golf Club,** Barshaw Park, Glasgow Road, Paisley (0141-889 2908). *Location:* one mile from Paisley Cross travelling east towards Glasgow (Glasgow Road). Parkland course, flat/hilly. 18 holes, 5703 yards. S.S.S. 68. Putting green. *Green Fees:* (subject to review) £6.00; Senior Citizens and Juniors £3.00. Unemployed £3.00 (proof to be shown). *Eating facilities:* mobile van rear of clubhouse. *Visitors:* welcome anytime, must have a bag of clubs. *Society Meetings:* apply to Superintendent Parks Department (Leisure and Recreation). Secretary: W. Collins (0141-884 2533).

PAISLEY. **Paisley Golf Club,** Braehead, Paisley PA2 8TZ (0141-884 2292). *Location:* up Causeyside Street, Neilston Road, turn right into Glenburn, left at roundabout. Moorland – exposed course. 18 holes, 6220 yards. S.S.S. 71. Practice area. *Green Fees:* weekdays £16.00 per round, £24.00 per day. *Eating facilities:* bar snacks and full meals. *Visitors:* welcome by prior arrangement with Handicap Certificate, midweek before 4pm. Not Public Holidays or weekends. *Society Meetings:* by prior arrangement. Professional: Grant Gilmour (0141-884 4114). Secretary: W.J. Cunningham (0141-884 3903).

PAISLEY. **Ralston Golf Club,** Strathmore Avenue, Ralston, Paisley PA1 3DT (0141-882 1349). *Location:* two miles east of Paisley off Glasgow Road. Parkland course. 18 holes, 6091 yards. S.S.S. 69. *Green Fees:* weekdays £16.00 per round, £24.00 per day. *Eating facilities:* dining room, bar. *Visitors:* welcome subject to course availability. *Society Meetings:* catered for on application subject to course availability. Professional: John Scott (0141-810 4925). Secretary: A. MacFadyen (0141-883 7045).

PORT GLASGOW. **Port Glasgow Golf Club,** Devol Road, Port Glasgow PA14 5XE (01475 704181). *Location:* M8 to Newark Castle to roundabout, follow signs for Industrial Estate. Heathland. 18 holes, 5712 yards, 5224 metres. S.S.S. 68. *Green Fees:* weekdays £12.00 per round, £18.00 per day. *Eating facilities:* meals by arrangement. *Visitors:* welcome weekdays until 4pm, weekends must be introduced. *Society Meetings:* welcome weekdays. Secretary: N.L. Mitchell (01475 706273). *

RENFREW. **Renfrew Golf Club,** Blythswood Estate, Inchinnan Road, Renfrew PA4 9EG (0141-886 6692). *Location:* A8 Renfrew, turn in at Stakis Normandy Hotel. Flat parkland, wooded. 18 holes, 6818 yards, 6231 metres. S.S.S. 72. *Green Fees:* information not provided. *Eating facilities:* daily restaurant facilities and bar. *Visitors:* welcome on introduction by members. Visiting parties by arrangement. *Society Meetings:* catered for on Mondays, Tuesdays and Thursdays only by written application to Secretary. Professional: Mr David Grant (0141-885 1754). Secretary: Alan Brockie. *

UPLAWMOOR. **Caldwell Golf Club,** Uplawmoor, Glasgow G78 4AU (01505 850329). *Location:* five miles south of Barrhead, Glasgow on A736 Irvine Road/A739. Parkland bounded by mature trees and a natural water hazard. 18 holes, 6228 yards, 5526 metres. S.S.S. 70. Practice area. *Green Fees:* £16.00 per round, £24.00 per day weekdays. *Eating facilities:* every day bar menu – filled rolls on Thursdays. *Visitors:* welcome weekdays only before 4.30pm, not weekends and Public Holidays (local and national). *Society Meetings:* weekdays only by prior arrangement. Professional: Stephen Forbes (Tel & Fax: 01505 850616). Secretary: H.I.F. Harper (Tel & Fax: 01505 850366).

Ross-shire

ALNESS. **Alness Golf Club,** Ardross Road, Alness (01349 883877). *Location:* on A9 ten miles north east of Dingwall. 9 holes, 2359 yards (twice round 4718 yards). S.S.S. 63. *Green Fees:* weekdays £6.00 per round (18 holes); weekends £8.00 per round (18 holes). Day ticket £10; weekly ticket £40. Senior Citizens and Juniors half price. *Eating facilities;* licensed bar and snacks served. *Visitors:* welcome without reservation. *Society Meetings:* welcome with advance notice. Secretary: Mrs Betty Taylor (01349 883877).

FEARN. **Tarbat Golf Club,** Tarbatness Road, Portmahomack, Fearn IV20 1YB. *Location:* 10 miles east of Tain. B9165 off A9. Seaside links course. 9 holes, 5054 yards. S.S.S. 65. Practice area. *Green Fees:* weekdays £6.00 per day; weekends £8.00. £25.00 per week. *Eating facilities:* none, local hotels. *Visitors:* welcome, some restrictions Saturdays. *Society Meetings:* welcome, please telephone Secretary. Secretary: D.C. Wilson (0186 287 236; Fax: 01349 852131).

FORTROSE. **Fortrose and Rosemarkie Golf Club,** Ness Road East, Fortrose (01381 620529). *Location:* on the Black Isle. A9 north from Inverness, across Kessock Bridge, through Munlochy, follow signs to Fortrose. Good links course, sea both sides. 18 holes, 5973 yards. S.S.S. 69. Practice area available Summer. *Green Fees:* weekdays £13.00 per round, £18.00 per day; weekends £18.00 per round. Five Day ticket (Mon-Fri) £50.00; 10 Day ticket (Mon-Fri) £80.00. Subject to review. *Eating facilities:* catering available. *Visitors:* welcome without reservation. *Society Meetings:* catered for. Professional: Graham Philp (01381 620733). Secretary: Mrs M. Collier.

GAIRLOCH. **Gairloch Golf Club,** Gairloch IV21 2BE (01445 82407). *Location:* 75 miles west of Inverness on the A832. Seaside links, extensive views. 9 holes, 2093 yards, 1770 metres. S.S.S. 63 over 18 holes. *Green Fees:* daily £10.00, £5.00 per day for Senior Citizens and Juniors; £45.00 weekly. *Eating facilities:* light refreshments available. *Visitors:* welcome without reservation. *Society Meetings:* welcome, no restrictions or reservations. Secretary: A. Shinkins (01445 86346).

INVERGORDON. **Invergordon Golf Club,** King George Street, Invergordon (01349 852715). *Location:* A9 (B817), two miles, west side of town. 9 holes, 3014 yards. S.S.S. 69 over 18 holes. *Green Fees:* weekdays £6.00; weekends £7.50. *Eating facilities:* bar Tuesday/Thursday: evenings: Saturday 12-2pm. *Visitors:* welcome without restrictions except Tuesdays and Thursdays after 5pm (club competitions). Changing rooms and showers. *Society Meetings:* welcome, catering arranged. Secretary: N.R. Paterson (01349 882693).

LOCHCARRON. **Lochcarron Golf Club,** Lochcarron, Wester Ross. *Location:* one mile east of Lochcarron village. Seaside links course – very interesting 2nd hole, a short course but great accuracy required. 9 holes (additional holes being constructed), 1750 yards. S.S.S. 60. *Green Fees:* £5.00. Subject to review. *Eating facilities:* three hotels within two miles of course. *Visitors:* welcome anytime except Saturday afternoons (club matches). Clubs for hire. Secretary: G. Weighill (015202 257).

MUIR OF ORD. **The Muir of Ord Golf Club,** Great North Road, Muir of Ord IV6 7SX (01463 870825). *Location:* 15 miles north of Inverness beside A862, 12 miles north of Inverness on A9/A832. Heathland, moorland course, excellent greens. 18 holes, 5202 yards. S.S.S. 65 Medal. Practice area. *Green Fees:* October to March weekdays £12.00; weekends £15.00. Weekly tickets – six days £30.00. Monthly – seven days £100. *Eating facilities:* snacks, bar lunches; lounge and bar. *Visitors:* visiting parties welcome, weekends times by arrangement. *Society Meetings:* catered for. Professional: Mr G. Vivers (01463 871311). Secretary: Mr H. Brown (01463 870188). Administrator/Manager: Mr D. Noble (01463 870825).

STRATHPEFFER. **Strathpeffer Spa Golf Club,** Strathpeffer IV14 9AS (01997 421219). *Location:* 20 minutes north of Inverness by A9, 5 miles west of Dingwall, quarter of a mile north of Strathpeffer Square (signposted). Upland course, panoramic views of moorland and mountain. No bunkers but plenty of natural hazards. 18 holes, 4792 yards. S.S.S. 64. Small practice area. *Green Fees:* weekdays £10.00 per round, £15.00 per day; weekends £12.00 per round. *Eating facilities:* bar and catering available seven days a week. *Visitors:* welcome without reservation, but check weekends and competition days. *Society Meetings:* catered for by arrangement. Secretary: Norman Roxburgh (01997 421396).

TAIN. **Tain Golf Club,** Chapel Road, Tain IV19 1PA (01862 892314). *Location:* off A9, 33 miles north of Inverness. Travelling north, turn right in middle of High Street – Golf Club one mile. Parkland and seaside links. 18 holes, 6238 yards. S.S.S. 70. Practice putting green. *Green Fees:* weekdays £12.00 per round, £18.00 per two rounds; weekends £18.00 per round, £24.00 per two rounds. Special rates for parties over 10. *Eating facilities:* bar and catering. *Visitors:* welcome, depending on availability. *Society Meetings:* catered for. Professional: (01862 893313). Secretary: Mrs Kathleen Ross.

Roxburghshire

HAWICK. **Hawick Golf Club,** Vertish Hill, Hawick (01450 72293). *Location:* north along A7 from Carlisle for 40 miles or south on A7 from Edinburgh for 50 miles. Wooded parkland. 18 holes, 5929 yards, 5422 metres. S.S.S. 69. Restricted practice area. *Green Fees:* weekdays £15.00 per round, £22.00 per day; weekends £22.00 one round only. Contact Tourist Board re Freedom of Fairways promotions. *Eating facilities:* available all day. *Visitors:* welcome, advisable to book in advance. *Society Meetings:* catered for, advisable to book in advance. Secretary: Jim Reilly (01450 75594).

HAWICK. **Minto Golf Club,** Denholm, Hawick TD9 8SH (01450 87220). *Location:* five miles north-east of Hawick leaving A698 at Denholm village. Parkland, trees, no bunkers. 18 holes, 5460 yards, 4992 metres. S.S.S. 68. Practice area. *Green Fees:* weekdays £12.00 per round, £18.00 per day; weekends £18.00 per round, £25.00 per day. Half price for under 18s. Subject to review. *Eating facilities:* new clubhouse with full facilities, catering. *Visitors:* welcome, with prior booking. *Society Meetings:* accepted with prior booking (weekends difficult). Secretary: Ian Todd.

JEDBURGH. **Jedburgh Golf Club,** Dunion Road, Jedburgh TD8 6LA (01835 63587). *Location:* three quarters of a mile south of Jedburgh on the road to Hawick. Undulating course, with young trees. 9 holes, 5555 yards. S.S.S. 67. *Green Fees:* £10.00. *Eating facilities:* bar from 7.30pm on May to September, meals Friday and weekend evenings. *Visitors:* welcome weekdays, weekends depending on competitions. *Society Meetings:* welcome, if notice given. Secretary: R. Strachan (01835 64175).

KELSO. **Kelso Golf Club,** Berrymoss, Kelso TD5 7SL (01573 223009). *Location:* one mile north-east of town within Kelso Racecourse. Flat parkland within racecourse. 18 holes, 6066 yards. S.S.S. 69. Practice ground. *Green Fees:* weekdays £12.00 per round, £20.00 per day; weekends £16.00 per round, £25.00 per day. *Eating facilities:* catering Wednesday to Sunday. *Visitors:* welcome without reservation. *Society Meetings:* welcome with reservation. Secretary: J.P. Payne (01573 223259).

MELROSE. **Melrose Golf Club,** Dingleton, Melrose (01896 822855). *Location:* A68 south from Edinburgh or north from Darlington. Wooded/sloping scenic course, tree-lined fairways. 9 holes, 5579 yards, 5098 metres. S.S.S. 68. Practice area. *Green Fees:* £14.00 per round/day. Juniors half price. *Eating facilities:* by arrangement. *Visitors:* welcome anytime when no competitions taking place, Ladies' Day Tuesdays. No visitor to tee off after 4pm April to October. Locker room, shower. *Society Meetings:* welcome by arrangement. Secretary: W.G. MacRae (01896 822391; Fax: 01896 822960).

NEWCASTLETON. **Newcastleton Golf Club,** Holm Hill, Newcastleton. *Location:* off A7 Carlisle to Hawick road, Newcastleton is on B6357. Hilly course with splendid views. 9 holes, 5748 yards. S.S.S. 68. *Green Fees:* weekdays £7.00; weekends £8.00. Weekly ticket £35.00. *Eating facilities:* by arrangement. *Visitors:* welcome, no restrictions except competition days. *Society Meetings:* welcome. Secretary: F.J. Ewart (013873 75257).

ST. BOSWELLS. **St. Boswells Golf Club,** St. Boswells, Melrose TD6 0AT (01835 23527). *Location:* quarter of a mile off trunk route A68 at St. Boswells Green. Flat attractive scenery along the banks of the River Tweed. 9 holes, 5250 yards. S.S.S. 65. *Green Fees:* weekdays £10.00, weekends £15.00 (subject to review). *Visitors:* no visitors after 4pm on a weekday and when competitions are being held.

Selkirkshire

ASHKIRK. **The Woll Golf Course,** The Woll Estate, Woll House, Ashkirk (01750 32222). *Location:* half a mile from the village of Ashkirk on the A7. Challenging course (opened in 1993) in natural parkland setting of outstanding beauty incorporating the Woll Burn; flat. 9 holes, 6446 yards. S.S.S. 71. Practice area. *Green Fees:* weekdays £7.00 per day; weekends £10.00. *Eating facilities:* none, but pub and self catering accommodation in village. *Visitors:* welcome. Enquiries to: Ms C.I. Amos. *

GALASHIELS. **Galashiels Golf Club,** Ladhope Recreation Ground, Galashiels TD1 2NJ (01896 753724). *Location:* north end of town, quarter of a mile off A7 on Ladhope Drive. Parkland, hilly – municipal course. 18 holes, 5185 yards. S.S.S. 66. Practice area. *Green Fees:* weekdays £10.00 per round, £14.00 per day; weekends £12.00 per round, £16.00 per day. *Eating facilities:* catering by arrangement with Secretary. *Visitors:* welcome without restriction. *Society Meetings:* catered for. Secretary: R. Gass (01896 755307).

GALASHIELS. **Torwoodlee Golf Club,** Edinburgh Road, Galashiels (01896 2260). *Location:* leave Galashiels on A7 for Edinburgh. Entrance to course one mile on left. Parkland with wooded greens alongside river and splendid par 5. Designed by Braid. 18 holes, 5720 yards. S.S.S. 68. *Green Fees:* weekdays £12.00 per round, £14.00 per day; weekends £15.00 per round, £20.00 per day. Subject to review. *Eating facilities:* bar, dining room. *Visitors:* welcome without reservation. Restriction Saturday and Thursday after 1pm. Showers available. *Society Meetings:* catered for weekdays, booking required. Secretary: A. Wilson (0189-682 2146).

SELKIRK. **Selkirk Golf Club,** The Hill, Selkirk (01750 20621). *Location:* one mile south of Selkirk on A7 road. Undulating moorland with superb views. 9 holes, 5620 yards. S.S.S. 67. *Green Fees:* weekdays £12.00 per round, £16.00 per day; weekends £16.00 per day. *Eating facilities:* bar opens lunchtime and evenings except Mondays, catering available. *Visitors:* ladies only Mondays 2pm onwards, members only weekends and from 5pm Fridays. *Society Meetings:* catered for by arrangement weekdays, meal arranged through Secretary. Secretary: Stuart Wilson (01750 22508).

Stirlingshire

ABERFOYLE. **Aberfoyle Golf Club,** Braeval, Aberfoyle, By Stirling FK8 3UY (01877 382493). *Location:* A81 Glasgow – Stirling. Parkland. 18 holes, 5204 yards. S.S.S. 66. *Green Fees:* weekdays £12.00 per round, £16.00 per day; weekends £16.00 per round, £24.00 per day. *Eating facilities:* catering by arrangement. *Visitors:* welcome anytime but must not tee off before 10.30am at weekends. Secretary: R.D. Steele (01877 382638).

DRYMEN. **Strathendrick Golf Club,** Glasgow Road, Drymen, Glasgow G63 (01360 40582). *Location:* one mile south of Drymen on Glasgow Road. Inland – hilly course. 9 holes, 5116 yards. S.S.S. 65. *Green Fees:* information not provided. *Visitors:* accompanied by a member welcome all week, restrictions on competition days. Secretary: Ronald H. Smith (01360 40582).

FALKIRK. **Bonnybridge Golf Club,** Larbert Road, Bonnybridge FK4 1NV (01324 812645). *Location:* five miles west of Falkirk. Parkland. 9 holes, 6060 yards. S.S.S. 69. Practice area. *Green Fees:* weekdays £10.00 per round. *Eating facilities:* catering by arrangement. *Visitors:* welcome with prior permission, no unaccompanied visitors. Secretary: C. Munn (01324 813694).

FALKIRK. **Falkirk Golf Club,** 136 Stirling Road, Camelon, Falkirk (01324 611061). *Location:* one and a half miles west of town centre on A9. Parkland with streams. 18 holes, 6282 yards. S.S.S. 69. Large practice area. *Green Fees:* weekdays £12.00 per round, £18.00 per day; weekends £25.00 per day. *Eating facilities:* full catering and bar facilities. *Visitors:* welcome Monday to Friday up to 4.00pm unaccompanied, with member only at weekends. *Society Meetings:* weekdays except Wednesdays, Sundays after 10.30am. Make arrangements with Clubmaster. Professional: (01324 612219). Secretary: John Elliott (01324 634118).

FALKIRK. **Polmont Golf Club,** Manvelrigg, Maddiston, Falkirk FK2 0LS (01324 711277). *Location:* first turn to the right past Fire Brigade HQ in Maddiston. Undulating course. 9 holes, 6603 yards. S.S.S. 70. *Green Fees:* weekdays £7.00 per round; Sundays £12.00. *Eating facilities:* lunches and high teas. *Visitors:* welcome without reservation, no visitors after 5pm weekdays or all day Saturday. *Society Meetings:* catered for. Secretary: Peter Lars.

LARBERT. **Falkirk Tryst Golf Club,** 86 Burnhead Road, Stenhousemuir, Larbert FK5 4BD (01324 562415). *Location:* three miles from Falkirk (M9), one mile from Larbert Station. Flat/seaside links style surface. 18 holes, 6053 yards, 5533 metres. S.S.S. 69. Practice area. *Green Fees:* weekdays £13.00 per round, £18.00 per day. *Eating facilities:* full catering – lunches, high teas, bar service. *Visitors:* welcome weekdays only except Bank and local Holidays. *Society Meetings:* catered for weekdays only except Bank and local Holidays. Professional: Mr Steven Dunsmore (01324 562091). Secretary: Mr R.D. Wallace (01324 562054).

LARBERT. **Glenbervie Golf Club Ltd,** Stirling Road, Larbert FK5 4SJ (01324 562983). *Location:* one mile north of Larbert on A9 Falkirk to Stirling road. Parkland course. 18 holes, 6402 yards. S.S.S. 71. Two practice areas. *Green Fees:* £25.00 per round, £35.00 for day ticket. *Eating facilities:* lunches and high teas, bar snacks. *Visitors:* welcome weekdays only with reservation, letter of introduction. Weekends as members' guests only. *Society Meetings:* up to 40 competitors catered for, Tuesdays and Thursdays only. Professional: Mr John Chillas (01324 562725). Secretary: Mrs Mary Purves (01324 562605).

LENNOXTOWN. **Campsie Golf Club,** Crow Road, Lennoxtown, Glasgow G65 7HX (01360 310244). *Location:* on B822 out of Lennoxtown. Hillside course with panoramic views. 18 holes, 5517 yards, 5045 metres. S.S.S. 67. Practice fairway and putting green. *Green Fees:* weekdays £12.00 per round, £20.00 per day; weekends £15.00 per round. Reduced rates for pre-booked parties of over 12. *Eating facilities:* full catering available. *Visitors:* welcome, weekdays unrestricted, weekends by prior arrangement. *Society Meetings:* catered for. Professional: Mark Brennan (01360 310920). Secretary: David Barbour (01360 310407).

POLMONT. **Grangemouth Golf Club,** Polmont Hill, Polmont, Falkirk FK2 0YA (01324 711500). *Location:* quarter of a mile north of Junction 4 M9 motorway. Parkland course. 18 holes, 6314 yards. S.S.S. 70. Practice area. *Green Fees:* £6.30 per round weekdays; £8.40 per round weekends. *Eating facilities:* catering and bar facilities available. *Visitors:* welcome, no restrictions. *Society Meetings:* welcome any day except Saturday. Professional: Stuart Campbell (01324 714355). Secretary: Iain Hutton (01324 712585).

STIRLING. **Bridge of Allan Golf Club,** Sunnylaw, Bridge of Allan (01786 832332). *Location:* from Stirling, three miles, turn right at Bridge, keep taking the high road. Hilly course. 9 holes, 4932 yards, 4508 metres. S.S.S. 65. *Green Fees:* weekdays £8.00, £3.00 with a member; weekends £12.00, £4.00 with a member. *Eating facilities:* by arrangement, licensed bar. *Visitors:* welcome without reservation, Saturdays after 4pm. *Society Meetings:* catered for by arrangement. Secretaries: Sandra Green/Mary Watson (01786 833135/443692).

STIRLING. **Stirling Golf Club,** Queen's Road, Stirling FK8 3AA (01786 473801). *Location:* one mile from town centre, rail and bus stations; two miles from Junction 10 M9. Parkland (undulating) with superb views of mountains and castle. 18 holes, 6400 yards. S.S.S. 71. Practice area. *Green Fees:* £17.00 per round. £23.00 per day. *Eating facilities:* bar and dining facilities. *Visitors:* welcome except at weekends; casual visitors by arrangement with Pro Shop. *Society Meetings:* welcome by arrangement. Professional: Ian Collins (01786 471490). Secretary: W. McArthur (01786 464098).

TORRANCE. **Balmore Golf Club,** Balmore, Torrance (0141-332 0392). *Location:* A803 then A807 from Glasgow. 18 holes, 5641 yards. S.S.S. 67. *Green Fees:* information not provided. *Eating facilities:* full service available. *Visitors:* welcome if introduced by member. *Society Meetings:* catered for. Secretary: G. P. Woolard, 11 Woodside Crescent, Glasgow G3 7UL. *

Sutherland

BONAR BRIDGE. **Bonar Bridge-Ardgay Golf Club,** Market Stance, Migdale Road, Bonar Bridge. *Location:* off the A9, driving north cross Bonar Bridge, straight up hill for half a mile. Wooded heathland. 9 holes, 4626 yards. S.S.S. 63. *Green Fees:* £9.00 per day. Reduced rates for week/fortnight. *Eating facilities:* not available. *Visitors:* always welcome. *Society Meetings:* limited to weekdays. Secretary: A. Turner (0154-982 248).

BRORA. **Brora Golf Club,** Golf Road, Brora KW9 6QS (01408 621417). *Location:* approximately 65 miles north of Inverness on the A9. Seaside links, 18 holes, 6110 yards. S.S.S. 69. Practice ground available. *Green Fees:* £15.00 per day, £65.00 per week. *Eating facilities:* lunches and snacks May to August. *Visitors:* welcome, only restriction on tournament days. Welcome to participate in opens with Certificate of Handicap. *Society Meetings:* catered for by arrangement. Secretary: (01408 621417).

DORNOCH. **Royal Dornoch Golf Club,** Golf Road, Dornoch (01862 810219; Fax: 01862 810792). *Location:* one mile from A9 to Wick. Seaside links. Championship Course and Struie Course. Championship – 18 holes, 6581 yards. S.S.S. 72; Struie – 18 holes, 5221 yards. S.S.S. 68. Practice area. *Green Fees:* on request. *Eating facilities:* available. *Visitors:* welcome, no major restrictions other than competitions – bookings can be heavy. Handicap Certificates – men 24, women 35. *Society Meetings:* must be arranged through the Secretary. Professional: W.E. Skinner (01862 810902). Secretary/Manager: I.C.R. Walker (01862 810219).

DORNOCH. **The Carnegie Golf Club,** Skibo Castle, Dornoch (01862 894600; Fax: 01862 894601). *Location:* A9 between Tain and Dornoch. Seaside links. 18 holes, 6671 yards. S.S.S. 71. Practice ground. *Green Fees:* private club, members only. *Eating facilities:* available. *Visitors:* by invitation only. Professional and Secretary not yet appointed.

DURNESS. **Durness Golf Club,** Balnakiel, Durness. *Location:* 57 miles northwest of Lairg on A838. Links course with final hole played over deep gully. 9 greens, 18 tees, 5555 yards. S.S.S 69. *Green Fees:* £9.00 per day. Weekly ticket £35.00. *Eating facilities:* snacks available 12-5pm June to September. *Visitors:* welcome without reservation, only restriction on Sunday mornings. Course closed during lambing season (April 20th to May 14th approximately). *Society Meetings:* by arrangement. Secretary: Lucy MacKay (01971 511364).

GOLSPIE. **Golspie Golf Club,** Ferry Road, Golspie KW10 6ST (01408 633266). *Location:* off A9 half a mile from Golspie. Fairly flat course, seaside links and wooded. 18 holes, 5836 yards. S.S.S. 68. Practice area available. *Green Fees:* weekdays £14.00; weekends £16.00. *Eating facilities:* bar and catering service, available all day during season. *Visitors:* welcome, no restrictions except on competition days. *Society Meetings:* welcome by prior arrangement. Admin Secretary: Mrs Marie MacLeod.

HELMSDALE. **Helmsdale Golf Club,** Golf Road, Helmsdale KW8 6JA (01431 82240). *Location:* on A9, 28 miles north of Dornoch. Parkland/moorland course. 9 holes, 1860 yards. S.S.S. 60 (2 x 9 holes). *Green Fees:* £5.00 per round, £10.00 per day, £20.00 weekly. Country membership available at reduced rate. *Visitors:* welcome at all times. *Society Meetings:* welcome. Secretary: David Bishop (01431 821339).

FOR THE MUTUAL GUIDANCE OF GUEST AND HOST

Every year literally thousands of holidays, short-breaks and overnight stops are arranged through our guides, the vast majority without any problems at all. In a handful of cases, however, difficulties do arise about bookings, which often could have been prevented from the outset.

It is important to remember that when accommodation has been booked, both parties — guests and hosts — have entered into a form of contract. We hope that the following points will provide helpful guidance.

GUESTS: When enquiring about accommodation, be as precise as possible. Give exact dates, numbers in your party and the ages of any children. State the number and type of rooms wanted and also what catering you require — bed and breakfast, full board, etc. Make sure that the position about evening meals is clear — and about pets, reductions for children or any other special points.

Read our reviews carefully to ensure that the proprietors you are going to contact can supply what you want. Ask for a letter confirming all arrangements, if possible.

If you have to cancel, do so as soon as possible. Proprietors do have the right to retain deposits and under certain circumstances to charge for cancelled holidays if adequate notice is not given and they cannot re-let the accommodation.

HOSTS: Give details about your facilities and about any special conditions. Explain your deposit system clearly and arrangements for cancellations, charges, etc, and whether or not your terms include VAT.

If for any reason you are unable to fulfil an agreed booking without adequate notice, you may be under an obligation to arrange alternative suitable accommodation or to make some form of compensation.

While every effort is made to ensure accuracy, we regret that FHG Publications cannot accept responsibility for errors, omissions or misrepresentation in our entries or any consequences thereof. Prices in particular should be checked because we go to press early. We will follow up complaints but cannot act as arbiters or agents for either party.

Wigtownshire

NEWTON STEWART. **Newton Stewart Golf Club,** Kirroughtree Avenue, Minnigaff, Newton Stewart DG8 6PF (01671 402172). *Location:* from South leave A75 at sign to Minnigaff village. Parkland, mainly flat but has one steep climb. 18 holes, 5588 yards. S.S.S. 68. *Green Fees:* weekdays £14.00 per day; weekends and Bank Holidays £20.00 per day. *Eating facilities:* bar lounge, bar snacks, lunches, high teas, dinners. *Visitors:* welcome 10am to 12 noon, 1.30pm onwards. *Society Meetings:* all welcome, booking required. Secretary: D.C. Matthewson (01671 403236).

NEWTON STEWART. **Wigtownshire County Golf Club,** Mains of Park, Glenluce, Newton Stewart DG8 0NN (01581 300420). *Location:* A75 two miles west Glenluce, eight miles east Stranraer. Seaside links. 18 holes, 5823 yards, 5325 metres. S.S.S. 68. Practice ground. *Green Fees:* weekdays £15.00 per round, £19.00 per day; weekends £17.00 per round, £21.00 per day. *Eating facilities:* available all year round. *Visitors:* unrestricted except Wednesday evenings. *Society Meetings:* catered for. Secretary: R. McKnight (01581 300532).

PORT WILLIAM. **St. Medan Golf Club,** Monreith, Newton Stewart DG8 8NJ (01988 700358). *Location:* on A747, four miles south of Port William. Seaside links course with panoramic views of Mull of Galloway and Isle of Man. 9 holes, 4552 yards. S.S.S. 62. Practice driving net and green. *Green Fees:* 9 holes £6.00, £10.00 per day. £40.00 per week. *Eating facilities:* full catering and bar. *Visitors:* welcome, restrictions only during competitions. *Society Meetings:* welcome, please telephone the Secretary. Reduced green fees for parties. Secretary: D. O'Neill (01988 500555).

PORTPATRICK. **Portpatrick (Dunskey) Golf Club,** Golf Course Road, Portpatrick DG9 8TB (01776 810273). *Location:* A77 to Stranaer, follow signs to Portpatrick; A75 fork right after Glenluce bypass, follow signs to Portpatrick. Enter village, fork right at war memorial, then 300 yards on right. Cliff top links-type course. 18 holes, 5882 yards. S.S.S. 68. Also short 9 hole (Par 3) course, 1504 yards. S.S.S. 27. Practice ground. *Green Fees:* 18 hole course – weekdays £14.00 per round, £21.00 per day; weekends £17.00 per round, £25.00 per day. 9 hole course – £5.00 per round (18 tees), £10.00 per day. *Eating facilities:* full meals all week mid-March to mid-October. *Visitors:* prior booking essential. Handicap Certificate required for 18 hole course. *Society Meetings:* catered for by prior arrangement. Hon. Secretary: J.A. Horberry (01776 810273).

STRANRAER. **Stranraer Golf Club,** Low Creachmore, Leswalt, Stranraer DG9 0LF (01776 870245). *Location:* three miles from Stranraer on the Kirkcolm Road (A718). Parkland, seaside – the last course James Braid designed before he died. 18 holes, 6308 yards. S.S.S. 71. 9 hole putting green. *Green Fees:* weekdays £16.00 per round, £22.00 per day; weekends £21.00 per round, £27.00 per day. Fees subject to review. *Eating facilities:* meals available, order in advance. *Visitors:* welcome, please contact the Starter at golf club or the Steward. *Society Meetings:* catered for. Secretary: W.I. Wilson C.A. (01776 703539).

WIGTOWN. **Wigtown and Bladnoch Golf Club,** Wigtown (01988 403354). *Location:* 200 yards from square in Wigtown. Parkland course. 9 holes, 5400 yards. S.S.S. 67. *Green Fees:* £10.00. Senior Citizens and Juniors half price. *Eating facilities:* light lunches and bar 11.30am to 2.30pm 1st April to 30th September. *Visitors:* welcome most days, tee reserved most evenings and occasional weekends. No prior booking necessary. *Society Meetings:* welcome by arrangement with Secretary. Secretary: J.I. Alexander (01988 403209).

Scottish Islands

ARRAN

BLACKWATERFOOT. **Shiskine Golf and Tennis Club,** Blackwaterfoot, Shiskine. *Location:* off B880 at Blackwaterfoot. Seaside links with only Par 5 on island. 12 holes, 2990 yards. S.S.S. 42. Putting green, nets. *Green Fees:* £8.00 per round, £12.00 per day except July and August. *Eating facilities:* teas, lunches (no bar). *Visitors:* welcome, preferably with Club Handicap. Tennis and bowls. Shop open Easter – October. *Society Meetings:* on application, preferably with Handicap. Match Secretary: Joe Faulkner (01770 860392). Secretary: Fiona Crawford (01770 860293).

BRODICK. **Brodick Golf Club,** Brodick (01770 302349). *Location:* one mile north of pier. Flat seaside course. 18 holes, 4404 yards. S.S.S. 62. Practice area. *Green Fees:* weekdays £8.00 per round, £12.00 per day; weekends £9.00 per round, £14.00 per day. Subject to review. *Eating facilities:* bar snacks available. *Visitors:* welcome without restriction. *Society Meetings:* welcome with reservation by letter. Professional: P.S. McCalla (01770 302513). Secretary: H.M. Macrae (01770 302181).

CORRIE. **Corrie Golf Club,** Sannox, Corrie KA27 8JD (01770 810223). *Location:* seven miles north of Brodick. Hilly course. 9 holes, 1948 yards. S.S.S. 61. *Green Fees:* £6.00 daily. *Eating facilities:* meals available March to October. *Visitors:* very welcome except Saturday afternoon. *Society Meetings:* catered for by arrangement. Secretary: Robert Stevenson (01770 810268).

LAMLASH. **Lamlash Golf Club,** Lamlash KA27 8JU (01770 600296). *Location:* A841 three miles south of Brodick Pier ferry terminal. Undulating heathland course. 18 holes, 4611 yards. S.S.S. 63. *Green Fees:* weekdays £9.00 per day; weekends £11.00. Senior Citizens £6.00. Rates subject to review. *Eating facilities:* tearoom adjacent. *Visitors:* welcome, no restrictions. *Society Meetings:* welcome, book in advance by letter. Secretary: J. Henderson (01770 600272).

LOCHRANZA. **Lochranza Golf,** Isle of Arran KA27 8HL (Tel & Fax: 017701 830273). *Location:* at north end of Island of Arran in Lochranza village. Challenging course in spectacular setting. 18 holes, 5454 yards, 5033 metres. S.S.S. 70. *Green Fees:* £8.00 per day. Weekly ticket £28.00. *Eating facilities:* tearoom, meals and snacks. Home cooking. *Visitors:* welcome daily 8th May to 30th September. Golf packages can be arranged throughout the summer. Caravans to let on adjacent site. *Society Meetings:* catered for by arrangement, at short notice if necessary. Proprietor: I.M. Robertson.

MACHRIE. **Machrie Bay Golf Club,** Machrie, Near Brodick KA27 8HP (0177-085 261). *Location:* on A841, three and a half miles north from Blackwaterfoot. Flat seaside course. 9 holes, 2143 yards, 1957 metres. S.S.S. 32. *Green Fees:* £5.00 per round/day. *Eating facilities:* available Summer season. Tennis court. *Visitors:* welcome, no restriction except on club competition days. *Society Meetings:* can be arranged if pre-booked. Secretary: A.M. Blair (0177-085 261).

WHITING BAY. **Whiting Bay Golf Club,** Golf Course Road, Whiting Bay, Brodick (01770 700487). *Location:* through Whiting village, turn right at signpost. Undulating parkland. 18 holes, 4405 yards. S.S.S. 63. *Green Fees:* £6.00 per round; weekends (Friday to Sunday) £17.50. 10% discount for parties of 10 or over. *Eating facilities:* catering and bar. *Visitors:* welcome anytime. Clubhouse, shower, snooker and pool rooms. *Society Meetings:* by prior booking. Secretary: Irene I'Anson (01770 700307). *

BUTE

ISLE OF BUTE. **Bute Golf Club,** C/o Meadowpark, Kilchattan Bay PA20 9NW. *Location:* 8 miles from Rothesay on the A845, situated on shores of Stravanan Bay. Flat seaside links in beautiful setting. 9 holes, 2497 yards, 2284 metres. S.S.S. 64 (18 holes). *Green Fees:* £6.00 adults, £3.00 Juniors. *Visitors:* welcome any day, Saturdays after 12.30pm. *Society Meetings:* catered for by arrangement. Secretary: J.M. Burnside (01700 83648).

ROTHESAY. **Port Bannatyne Golf Club,** Bannatyne Mains Road, Port Bannatyne. *Location:* two miles north of Rothesay (ferry terminal). Hill course overlooking bays and sea lochs. 13 holes, 4730 yards. S.S.S. 63. *Green Fees:* £8.00 per day, weekly £30.00, 14-day £50.00. *Eating facilities:* snack facilities on course, bar and meal facilities in village, quarter-of-a-mile from course. *Visitors:* welcome – almost unrestricted. *Society Meetings:* very welcome. Secretary: William W. McGeechan (01700 502009).

ROTHESAY. **Rothesay Golf Club,** Canada Hill, Rothesay PA20 9HN (01700 502244). *Location:* island in the Firth of Clyde, ferry terminal Wemyss Bay, 35 miles south west of Glasgow. One of Scotland's most scenic island courses, designed by James Braid and Ben Sayers. 18 holes, 5370 yards. S.S.S. 67. Practice area. *Green Fees:* on application to Professional. *Eating facilities:* full facilities at clubhouse. *Visitors:* very welcome, but at weekends by prior booking through Professional. *Society Meetings:* welcome by arrangement. PGA Professional: James M. Dougal (01700 503554). Secretary: R.D. Strong (01700 502244).

COLONSAY

ISLE OF COLONSAY. **Colonsay Golf Club,** Isle of Colonsay PA61 7YP. *Location:* two miles west of pier. Traditional links course, reputedly 200 years old. 18 holes, 4775 yards. *Green Fees:* information not available. *Eating facilities:* none. *Visitors:* always welcome. Secretary: Kevin Byrne (019512 316). *

CUMBRAE

MILLPORT. **Millport Golf Club,** Golf Road, Millport (01475 530311). *Location:* Caledonian McBrayne car ferry Largs slip to Cumbrae slip (seven minutes). On hill overlooking Firth of Clyde over Bute and Arran to Mull of Kintyre. 18 holes, 5831 yards. S.S.S. 68. Large practice area. *Green Fees:* weekdays £11.00 per round, £15.00 per day; weekends and Bank Holidays £20.00 – unrestricted golf. *Eating facilities:* full catering facilities. *Visitors:* welcome without reservation. Tee reservations available for parties. Well stocked Professional's shop, tuition available. Starter's telephone (01475 530305). *Society Meetings:* catered for. Special open amateur competition, Cumbrae Cup. Secretary: W.D. Patrick C.A. (01475 530308).

GIGHA

ISLE OF GIGHA. **Isle of Gigha Golf Club,** The Croft, Isle of Gigha PA41 7AA. *Location:* by ferry from Tayinloan to Gigha, course half a mile north from Post Office. Seaside course with scenic views looking over the Sound of Gigha and the Kilberry coast. 9 holes, 5026 yards. S.S.S. 66. *Green Fees:* £5.00 per round, £7.00 per day. *Eating facilities:* available at Gigha Hotel. *Visitors:* always welcome. *Society Meetings:* welcome. Secretary: Mr M. Tart (015835 287).

HARRIS

BOROSDALE. **Harris Golf Club,** "Muldoanich", Borosdale. *Location:* 10 miles south of Tarbert, 50 miles south of Stornoway. Machair land, by the sea with sand dunes (outstanding scenery). 9 holes, 2014 yards. S.S.S. 31. *Green Fees:* £5.00. *Visitors:* welcome, but note club is closed in May due to lambing. Match Secretary: Bryce Weir (01859 530262; or Tel & Fax: 01859 520214).

ISLAY

PORT ELLEN. **Islay Golf Club,** Western Cottage, Port Ellen PA42 7AT (01496 302409). *Location:* five miles north of Port Ellen. Championship course. 18 holes, 6226 yards, 5692 metres. S.S.S. 71. *Green Fees:* information not provided. *Eating facilities:* full range at adjoining Hotel. *Visitors:* welcome, apply to the Hotel but usually no restrictions. *Society Meetings:* all welcome. Secretary: Mr T. Dunn.

PORT ELLEN. **Machrie Golf Club,** The Machrie Hotel and Golf Links, Port Ellen PA42 7AN (01496 2310; Golfax: 01496 2404). *Location:* adjacent Airport. Classic links. 18 holes, 6226 yards. S.S.S. 70. *Green Fees:* information not provided. *Eating facilities:* full service in hotel. *Visitors:* welcome any day without reservation. *Society Meetings:* any number catered for. Golf packages available. Secretary: M.R. MacPherson. Proprietor: Murdo MacPherson. *

LEWIS

STORNOWAY. **Stornoway Golf Club,** Lady Lever Park, Stornoway, Isle of Lewis (01851 70 2240). *Location:* close proximity to town of Stornoway, in grounds of Lewis Castle. Inland course, hilly parkland, scenic. 18 holes, 5178 yards. S.S.S. 66. *Green Fees:* £10.00 per day. Weekly tickets £30.00; fortnightly ticket £50.00. Subject to alteration. *Eating facilities:* available. *Visitors:* welcome anytime but no Sunday golf. Car ferry daily (except Sunday) from Ullapool. British Airways service daily (except Sunday) from Glasgow and Inverness. *Society Meetings:* welcome, book through Secretary. Secretary: Gordon Davies.

MULL

ISLE OF MULL. **Craignure Golf Club,** Scallastle, Craignure (016802 370). *Location:* one mile from ferry terminal at Craignure. Seaside links. 9 holes, 2218 metres. S.S.S. 64. *Green Fees:* £8.00. *Eating facilities:* not available. *Visitors:* always welcome, no restrictions except on competition days which are usually Sundays. Hon. Secretary: Sheila M. Weir (016802 370).

TOBERMORY. **Tobermory Golf Club,** Tobermory PA75 6PR. *Location:* situated on the cliffs above the town to the north west. Panoramic views of Sound of Mull; testing terrain, not suitable for powered trolleys. 9 holes, 4921 yards, 4362 metres. S.S.S. 64. *Green Fees:* £10.00 per day, £35.00 per week. *Eating facilities:* none available. *Visitors:* unrestricted except for some competition days. *Society Meetings:* welcome. Secretary: Dr W.H. Clegg (01688 2493 or 2020).

ORKNEYS

KIRKWALL. **Orkney Golf Club Ltd,** Grainbank, Kirkwall (01856 872457). *Location:* half-a-mile west of Kirkwall. Parkland with good views over Kirkwall Bay and North Isles. 18 holes, 5411 yards, 4964 metres. S.S.S. 68. Practice area. *Green Fees:* £10.00 per day. Weekly £35.00, fortnightly £50.00. *Eating facilities:* bar lunches during summer months. *Visitors:* welcome at all times, restrictions only during competitions. *Society Meetings:* welcome, booking advised. Secretary: L. Howard (01856 874165).

STROMNESS. **Stromness Golf Club Ltd,** Ness, Stromness (01856 850772). *Location:* on the outskirts of Stromness. Parkland/seaside links course. 18 holes, 4762 yards. S.S.S 64. *Green Fees:* £10.00 per day. £35.00 weekly ticket. *Eating facilities:* bar in clubhouse; hotels nearby. *Visitors:* welcome, no restrictions. *Society Meetings:* by arrangement through Secretary. Secretary: F.J. Groundwater (01856 850622).

WESTRAY. **Westray Golf Club,** Westray, Orkney Islands (018577 373). *Location:* half a mile from Pierowall Village. Seaside links course. 9 holes, 2316 yards, 2084 metres. S.S.S. 33. *Green Fees:* £3.00 per day, Senior Citizens and Juniors £1.50. £15.00 per week, Senior Citizens and Juniors £7.50. *Visitors:* welcome anytime. Captain: Mr Stephen Hagan (018577 226). Secretary: Mr Michael Harcus (018577 516).

SHETLAND

LERWICK. **Shetland Golf Club,** PO Box 18, Lerwick (01595 84369). *Location:* four miles north of Lerwick on main road. Hilly, undulating course. Excellent greens. 18 holes, 5776 yards. S.S.S 70. *Green Fees:* £8.00. *Eating facilities:* bar snacks. *Visitors:* welcome, no restrictions except on days of open competitions. *Society Meetings:* arrange through Secretary. Secretary: D.C. Gray (01595 2691).

WHALSAY. **Whalsay Golf Club,** Skaw Taing, Symbister, Whalsay. *Location:* five miles from Symbister ferry terminal – ferries run from Laxo to Symbister (018066 259). Seaside course with wonderful scenery and birdlife in abundance – Britain's most northerly 18 holes. 18 holes, 6009 yards. S.S.S. 70. Changing rooms. *Green Fees:* £5.00 per day, £20.00 per week. *Eating facilities:* not available. *Visitors:* welcome anytime. Secretary: H. Sandison.

SKYE

SCONSER. **Isle of Skye Golf Club,** Sconser. *Location:* 20 miles from Kyle/Kyleakin ferry on road to Portree. Seaside course with spectacular views. 9 holes (18 tees), 4798 yards, 4385 metres. S.S.S. 64. *Green Fees:* weekdays £8.00; weekends £10.00. *Visitors:* most welcome; competitions held on Wednesdays after 5pm. Changing and toilet facilities. *Society Meetings:* welcome. Secretary: Alasdair H. MacKenzie (01478 612341 or 01478 613059; Fax: 01478 612543).

SKEABOST BRIDGE. **Skeabost Golf Club,** Skeabost House Hotel, Skeabost Bridge IV51 9NP (01470 532202; Fax: 01470 532454). *Location:* A850 Portree to Dunvegan Road. Wooded course. 9 holes, 3056 yards. S.S.S. 60 (for 18 holes). *Green Fees:* weekdays £6.00. Free play to hotel residents staying three or more days. *Eating facilities:* buffet lunch, evening meals in hotel; bar food in public bar. *Visitors:* welcome, under 13's must be accompanied by an adult. *Society Meetings:* accepted. Club Captain: J.R. Stuart. Secretary: D.J. Matheson (01470 532319).

SOUTH UIST

LOCHBOISDALE. **Askernish Golf Club,** Askernish, Lochboisdale. *Location:* three miles from Lochboisdale ferry terminal. Seaside links, designed by Tom Morris Senior 1891. 9 holes, 5042 yards. S.S.S. 68. *Green Fees:* £3.50. *Eating facilities:* local hotels. *Visitors:* welcome. Secretary: A.L. MacDonald (018784 700541).

TIREE

SCARINISH. **Vaul Golf Club,** Scarinish, Isle of Tiree PA77 6XH. *Location:* two miles from Scarinish and half a mile from Lodge Hotel, ferry from Oban four hours and plane from Glasgow 45 minutes. Links course with crystal white beaches to north and south. 9 holes, 5822 yards (18 holes). S.S.S. 70 (18 holes). *Green Fees:* £5.00 daily. *Eating facilities:* at Lodge Hotel. *Visitors:* welcome, no restrictions, no Sunday golf. *Society Meetings:* catered for, arrangement with Lodge Hotel. Secretary: Mrs D. MacDonald (01879 2737).

Golf in Wales

WHERE TO PLAY • WHERE TO STAY

With a few notable exceptions, golf for the visitor in Wales is most easily available in the North at Harlech and along the north coast, and along the Bristol Channel in the South. Royal St. David's at Harlech, Royal Porthcawl in Mid-Glamorgan and St. Pierre near Chepstow are probably the jewels in the Principality's golfing crown but plenty of lesser gems shine brightly elsewhere and as in Scotland, the scenery is often an added bonus to a satisfying round!

Clwyd

ABERGELE. **Abergele and Pensarn Golf Club,** Tan-y-Gopa Road, Abergele LL22 8DS (01745 824034). *Location:* below Gwrych Castle, Abergele. Parkland in scenic setting. 18 holes, 6520 yards, 5961 metres. S.S.S. 71. Practice area. *Green Fees:* £22.00 weekdays; £27.00 weekends. *Eating facilities:* full catering facilities except Mondays, two bars. *Visitors:* welcome weekdays, Bank Holidays and weekends with official Club Handicap. *Society Meetings:* catered for, by arrangment with Secretary. Professional: I. Runcie (01745 823813). Secretary: Edgar Richards.

CHESTER near. **Northop Country Park Golf Club,** Northop, Near Chester CH7 6WA (01352 840440; Fax: 01352 840445). *Location:* travel west on M56, follow signs for North Wales. A494/A55 for Northop. Parkland course set amongst 300 year old oak trees, designed by John Jacobs. Challenging non-punitive layout. 18 holes, 6735 yards, 6128 metres. S.S.S. 74. Practice range and academy. *Green Fees:* weekdays £25.00; weekends £35.00. 50% reductions when playing with a member, daily packages available. *Eating facilities:* clubroom for snacks, club restaurant for full meals. *Visitors:* welcome. *Society Meetings:* welcome weekdays, weekends depending on availability. Professional: David Llewellyn. Admin Manager: Noel Hynes/Kath Manning.

CHIRK. **Chirk Golf and Country Club,** Chirk, Near Wrexham LL14 5AD (01691 774243). *Location:* just off A5 towards Llangollen. Generally flat course. 18 holes, 6956 yards. S.S.S. 74. 9 hole Par 3 course, 15 bay driving range. *Green Fees:* weekdays Blue Tees £13.00, Yellow Tees £15.00; weekends Blue Tees £17.00, Yellow Tees £19.00. *Visitors:* welcome seven days a week. *Society Meetings:* all welcome. Professional: J.F. Waugh (01691 774407).

COLWYN. **Old Colwyn Golf Club,** The Clubhouse, Woodland Avenue, Old Colwyn LL29 9NL (01492 515581). *Location:* signposted at main Abergele road, Old Colwyn. Parkland. 9 holes (x 2), 5268 yards. S.S.S. 66. Practice area. *Green Fees:* weekdays £12.00; weekends £18.00. *Eating facilities:* bar and meals by arrangement. *Visitors:* welcome except Saturday afternoons or Wednesday evenings. *Society Meetings:* welcome by arrangement with Secretary. Secretary: R.G. Tudor.

DENBIGH. **Denbigh Golf Club,** Henllan Road, Denbigh LL16 5AA (01745 814159). *Location:* one mile from Denbigh town centre on the B5382 road. Parkland with excellent views. 18 holes, 5582 yards. S.S.S. 67. *Green Fees:* weekdays £15.00 per round, £18.00 per day; weekends and Bank Holidays £20.00

per round, £24.00 per day. *Eating facilities:* catering daily, bar. *Visitors:* welcome, no restrictions except Thursdays/Saturdays. *Society Meetings:* by arrangement. Professional: M.D. Jones (01745 814159). Secretary: Mac McCarthy (01745 816669).

DENBIGH near. **Bryn Morfydd Hotel Golf Course,** Llanrhaeadr, Near Denbigh LL16 4NP (01745 78280; Fax: 01745 78556). *Location:* off A525 between Denbigh and Ruthin. Peter Allis designed mature parkland course overlooking the Vale of Clwyd. Two courses. The Duchess Course – 9 holes, 1146 yards. Par 27; The Duke's Course – 18 holes, 5700 yards. S.S.S. 68, Par 71. Practice area, indoor golf range. *Green Fees:* for 18 holes £10.00. *Eating facilities:* courses attached to three star Hotel, two restaurants and two bars. *Visitors:* welcome by arrangement. Home of British School of Golf. Hotel accommodation – 30 rooms en-suite, outdoor swimming pool. *Society Meetings:* welcome by arrangement all year. Secretary/ Director of Golf: Colin Henderson. Proprietor: D. Muirhead.

FLINT. **Flint Golf Club,** Cornist Park, Flint CH6 5HJ (01352 732327). *Location:* A548 coast road, one mile from town centre. Hilly parkland. 9 holes, 5927 yards. S.S.S. 69. Practice area. *Green Fees:* weekdays £12.00 per day; weekends with member. Special rate for golf parties numbering 12 or more. *Eating facilities:* bar; snacks and evening meals by arrangement. *Visitors:* welcome weekdays (no restrictions), weekends with member only. *Society Meetings;* welcome by arrangement. Secretary: E. Owens (01244 812974).

HAWARDEN. **Hawarden Golf Club,** Groomsdale Lane, Hawarden, Deeside CH5 3EH (01244 531447). *Location:* A55, left at Ewloe interchange, follow Hawarden signs. Undulating parkland. 18 holes, 5664 yards, 5089 metres. S.S.S. 67. *Green Fees:* weekdays £20.00. *Eating facilities:* full bar and catering. *Visitors:* welcome, must be playing with a member. *Society Meetings:* catered for by arrangement with Secretary. Professional: Chris Hope. Secretary: Tim Hinks-Edwards.

HOLYWELL. **Holywell Golf Club,** Brynford, Near Holywell CH8 8LQ (01352 713937). *Location:* turn off A55 at Springfield Hotel onto A5206, turn at traffic lights, up hill for one and a half miles, turn right at crossroads. Flat natural terrain, links type course. 18 holes, 6025 yards. S.S.S. 70. *Green Fees:* weekdays £13.00; weekends and Bank Holidays £20.00. *Eating facilities:* full bar facilities and catering on request. *Visitors:* welcome weekdays without reservation; Bank Holidays and weekends by prior arrangement with Secretary. Snooker table. *Society Meetings:* by prior arrangement with Secretary. Professional: Martin Carty (01352 710040). Secretary: E.K. Carney (01352 713937).

LLANGOLLEN. **Vale of Llangollen Golf Club,** The Clubhouse, Llangollen LL20 7PR (01978 860613). *Location:* one mile east of town on the A5. 18 holes, S.S.S. 72. *Green Fees:* on application. *Eating facilities:* full catering service. *Visitors:* welcome. *Society Meetings:* welcome. Professional: D.I. Vaughan (01978 860040). Secretary: T.F. Ellis (01978 860906).

MOLD. **Mold Golf Club,** Cilcian Road, Pantymwyn, Mold CH7 1LW (01352 740318). *Location:* three miles from Mold. Undulating course. 18 holes, 5548 yards. S.S.S. 67. Practice ground. *Green Fees:* weekdays £16.00; weekends and Bank Holidays £21.00. *Eating facilities:* bar and diningroom. *Visitors:* welcome at all times subject to tee availability. *Society Meetings:* written application. Professional: Martin Carty (01352 740318) (Lessons by appointment). Secretary: A. Newall (01352 741513).

MOLD. **Padeswood and Buckley Golf Club,** The Caia, Station Lane, Padeswood, Mold CH7 4JD (01244 543636). *Location:* A5118, one mile west of Castle Cement Works, half a mile off main road. Flat parkland; river, lakes. 18 holes, 5823 yards. S.S.S. 68. *Green Fees:* weekdays £20.00 per round, £25.00 per day; weekends £25.00. *Eating facilities:* daily bar service, catering daily in Caia Restaurant. *Visitors:* welcome except on Sundays. *Society Meetings:* welcome, enquiries through Secretary. If numbers are greater than 20 package deal is available. Professional: David Ashton (01244 543636). Secretary: J.G. Peters (01244 550537).

PADESWOOD. **Old Padeswood Golf Club Ltd,** Station Road, Padeswood, Near Mold CH7 4JL (01244 547401). *Location:* off A5118 Chester to Mold road, eight miles from Chester and three miles from Mold. Situated in the beautiful Alyn Valley – nine holes flat parkland, nine holes slightly undulating. 18 holes, 6668 yards, 6079 metres. S.S.S. 72/Ladies 73. Par 3 9 hole course, 968 yards. Practice ground. *Green Fees:* weekdays £16.00 per round; weekends £20.00 per round. Par 3 weekdays £2.00; weekends £3.00. *Eating facilities:* diningroom, bar meals – two bars. *Visitors:* welcome anytime subject to tee availability. *Society Meetings:* welcome, written applications to Co-Secretary. Professional: Tony Davies (01244 547401). Co-Secretary: B. Jones (01244 550414). Club Secretary: B. Hellen (01352 770506).

PENYCAE. **Penycae Golf Club Ltd,** Ruabon Road, Penycae, Wrexham LL14 1TP (01978 810108). *Location:* from A483 Chester – Oswestry onto A539

Llangollen; half a mile right to Penycae, one mile right to course. Parkland course, suitable for all standards of golfers, with a testing double dogleg hole. 9 holes, 2008 yards. S.S.S. 32. *Green Fees:* weekdays 9 holes £4.00, 18 holes £6.00; weekends 9 holes £5.00, 18 holes £8.00. £1.00 reduction for members' guests. *Eating facilities:* licensed clubhouse, bar snacks and meals to order. *Visitors:* always welcome. *Society Meetings:* always welcome. 48 hours notice preferred but not always necessary. Rates from £12.00 per person (min. 8) for coffee, 9 holes, lunch, 18 holes. Professional: Nick Rothe. Secretary/General Manager: Glyn Williams.

PRESTATYN. **Prestatyn Golf Club,** Marine Road East, Prestatyn LL19 7HS (01745 854320). *Location:* A548, on approaching Prestatyn from Chester direction turn right at sign for Pontins Holiday Village and follow club sign. Seaside links Championship course. 18 holes, 6517 yards, 5959 metres. S.S.S. 72. Practice areas. *Green Fees:* £18.00 weekdays; £25.00 weekends and Bank Holidays. *Eating facilities:* full catering available, bar. *Visitors:* must be members of golf club, with Handicap Certificates. *Society Meetings:* special "all-in" arrangement for 27 holes. Professional: M. Staton (01745 854320). Secretary: Roy Woodruff (01745 888353).

PRESTATYN. **St. Melyd Golf Club,** The Paddock, Meliden Road, Prestatyn LL19 9NB (01745 854405). *Location:* on main Prestatyn to Rhuddlan road, just outside Meliden. Parkland, beautifully set. 18 holes, 5811 yards. S.S.S. 68. *Green Fees:* weekdays £17.00; weekends £19.00. *Eating facilities:* full range of catering facilities except Tuesdays. *Visitors:* welcome. *Society Meetings:* catered for by arrangement with Secretary (various golf packages). Professional: Richard Bradbury (01745 888858). Secretary: Mr Peter M. Storey (01745 853574).

RHUDDLAN. **Rhuddlan Golf Club,** Meliden Road, Rhuddlan LL18 6LB (01745 590217). *Location:* leave A55 at St. Asaph for Rhuddlan, clubhouse 100m from roundabout on Rhyl side of Rhuddlan. Gently undulating, parkland course with natural hazards. 18 holes, 6482 yards. S.S.S. 71. Extensive practice ground. *Green Fees:* £20.00 per day weekdays; £25.00 per round weekends and Bank Holidays. *Eating facilities:* available daily. *Visitors:* welcome at all times when course demand permits. Sundays with member only. No denim. Snooker table. *Society Meetings:* weekdays only, maximum 50. Professional: Ian Worsley (Tel & Fax: 01745 590898). Secretary: David Morris (01745 590217; Fax: 01745 590898).

RHYL. **Rhyl Golf Club,** Coast Road, Rhyl LL18 3RE (01745 353171). *Location:* one mile east of Rhyl on A548. Seaside links. 9 holes, 6153 yards. S.S.S. 69. Practice ground. *Green Fees:* weekdays £12.00 (9 holes £9.00); weekends £15.00. Discounts for parties over 15. *Eating facilities:* bar snacks and meals available, licensed bar. *Visitors:* welcome any time except when competitions in progress. *Society Meetings:* catered for by prior arrangement with Secretary. Professional: Martin Carty, c/o Mold Golf Club. Secretary: Mr F. Bass (01745 338204 home).

RUTHIN. **Ruthin Pwllglas Golf Club,** Pwllglas, Near Ruthin (01824 702296). *Location:* Corwen Road (A494), two miles south of Ruthin. Hilly parkland. 10 holes, 5418 yards. S.S.S. 66. Practice area. *Green Fees:* weekdays £10.00, weekends and Bank Holidays £15.00. *Eating facilities:* none. Secretary can arrange catering for visiting parties. *Visitors:* welcome without reservation, phone call advisable in high season and at weekends. *Society Meetings:* catered for midweek. Hon. Secretary: Ken Roberts (01824 703427).

WREXHAM. **The Plassey Golf Club,** Eyton, Wrexham LL13 0SP (01978 780020). *Location:* Bangor on Dee exit off A483 Chester to Oswestry bypass. Undulating parkland course. 10 holes, 2812 yards. *Green Fees:* weekdays £4.00 per round, £6.00 per two rounds; weekends £5.00 per round, £8.00 per two rounds. £1.00 reduction to visitors to the nearby caravan park. *Eating facilities:* available at Hay Bank Inn. *Visitors:* welcome, no restrictions. Caravan site Leisure Park Complex. *Society Meetings:* welcome any weekday. Professional: Roger Shutt. Secretary: Christine M. Brassey.

WREXHAM. **Wrexham Golf Club,** Holt Road, Wrexham LL13 9SB (01978 261033). *Location:* A543 north east of Wrexham. 18 holes, 6139 yards. S.S.S. 69. Practice facilities. *Green Fees:* weekdays £18.00, weekends £24.00. *Eating facilities:* daily, subject to functions and visiting Societies. *Visitors:* welcome, subject to competitions and Society bookings. Proof of Golf Club membership and/or Handicap Certificate required. *Society Meetings:* catered for, Mondays and Fridays preferred. Professional: D.A. Larvin (01978 351476). Secretary: K.B. Fisher (01978 364268).

Dyfed

ABERYSTWYTH. **Aberystwyth Golf Club,** Brynymor Road, Aberystwyth (01970 615104). *Location:* north end of Promenade, access near to cliff railway. Undulating meadowland. 18 holes, 6150 yards. S.S.S. 71. Practice ground. *Green Fees:* Summer: £15.00 per round, £18.00 per day weekdays; £18.00 per round, £20.00 per day weekends. 50% reduction for Juniors. *Eating facilities:* restaurant and bar. *Visitors:* welcome at all times, pre-booking helpful. *Society Meetings:* welcome, Special Deals available. Professional: Kevin Bayliss (01970 625301). Secretary: Barrie Thomas.

AMMANFORD. **Glynhir Golf Club,** Glynhir Road, Llandybie, Ammanford SA18 2TF (01269 850472). *Location:* seven miles from end of M4, between Ammanford and Llandybie on the A483. Turn right up Glynhir Road and proceed for about two miles. Undulating wooded parkland course. 18 holes, 5952 yards, 5442 metres. S.S.S. 69. *Green Fees:* £15.00 (£10.00 in Winter) weekdays; £20.00 (£12.00 in Winter) weekends and Bank Holidays. *Eating facilities:* full catering available (closed Mondays in Winter). *Visitors:* welcome but preferably on weekdays. Not Sundays. B&B for six/eight persons at clubhouse. *Society Meetings:* welcome weekdays by prior arrangement with Secretary (preferably Mondays, Tuesdays or Fridays). Professional: Ian M. Roberts (01269 851010). Joint Secretaries: E.P. Rees (01269 592345)/D.B. Jones (01269 842583).

BORTH. **Borth and Ynyslas Golf Club Ltd,** Borth SY24 5JS (01970 871796). *Location:* A487 Machynlleth to Aberystwyth, turn off to Borth. Flat links course running by sea and through dunes. 18 holes, 6116 yards. S.S.S. 70. Practice area. *Green Fees:* weekdays £16.00 (August £22.00); weekends £22.00 per day. 20% discount staying at local accommodation or for parties of eight or more. *Eating facilities:* bar and catering, please book. *Visitors:* welcome at all times except during competitions – check with Professional. *Society Meetings:* by prior arrangement with the Secretary. Professional: J.G. Lewis (01970 871557). Secretary: Miss S. Wilson (01970 871202).

CARDIGAN. **Cardigan Golf Club,** Gwbert-on-Sea, Cardigan SA43 1PR (01239 612035). *Location:* three miles north-west of Cardigan. Seaside links course. 18 holes, 6641 yards. S.S.S. 72. *Green Fees:* £15.00 per day weekdays, £20.00 per day weekends and Bank Holidays. *Eating facilities:* catering and bar facilities available. *Visitors:* welcome. Tee reserved for members 1 – 2pm. *Society Meetings:* very welcome. Professional: Colin Parsons. Hon. Secretary: J. Rhapps (01239 612035).

CARMARTHEN. **Carmarthen Golf Club,** Blaenycoed Road, Carmarthen SA33 6EH (01267 281214). *Location:* four miles north-west of town. Undulating parkland – a good test of golf. 18 holes, 6210 yards. S.S.S. 71. Large practice ground. *Green Fees:* weekdays £18.00 Summer, £12.00 Winter; weekends £25.00 Summer, £15 Winter. Half price with a member. *Eating facilities:* catering every day except Wednesday April to November, except Monday and Wednesday November to March. *Visitors:* welcome with proof of Handicap, telephone call advisable at weekends. *Society Meetings:* by arrangement. Professional: Pat Gillis (01267 281493). Secretary: Jonathan Coe (01267 281588).

CARMARTHEN. **Llanstephan Golf Course,** Llanstephan, Carmarthen SA33 5LU. *Location:* on coast two miles south west of Llanstephan village on old Ferry Road. Dylan Thomas "Under Milkwood" Course; spacious coastal downland course between two estuaries with magnificent views of the Gower, North Devon, Caldy Island and Prescelly Mountains. 9 holes, 2200 yards. S.S.S. 30. Practice net and putting green. *Green Fees:* £3.00; Juniors £2.00. *Eating facilities:* "tuck shop" only (further facilities to be added soon). *Visitors:* always welcome. Hire of five clubs in a bag £2; trolley £1. *Society Meetings:* very welcome, please telephone in advance. Director of Golf: Roger Fry (01267 83526).

HAVERFORDWEST. **Haverfordwest Golf Club,** Arnolds Down, Haverfordwest SA61 2XQ (01437 763565). *Location:* one mile east of Haverfordwest on A40. S.S.S. 69. Practice fairway and putting green. *Green Fees:* £16.00 weekdays (£13.00 playing with a member); £23.00 weekends (£16.00 playing with member). *Eating facilities:* bar snacks available, meals by arrangement – 40 seater diningroom (food 8.30am to 9.30pm). *Visitors:* bona fide golfers welcome. *Society Meetings:* catered for by arrangement. Professional: A.J. Pile (01437 768409). Secretary: M.A. Harding (01437 764523).

KIDWELLY. **Pontnewydd Golf Centre,** Trimsaran, Kidwelly SA17 4LB (01554 810056). *Location:* leave Llanelli following signs for Trimsaran, at the Bird in Hand turn right to Carway, course is second on the left. Wooded parkland with 52 bunkers. 18 holes, 6173 yards. *Green Fees:* weekdays £11.25, weekends £13.00. Discounts for groups of over 10 persons. *Eating facilities:* Bryn Fforest Inn adjacent to 17th fairway. *Visitors:* advisable to book weekends. *Society Meetings:* welcome at all times. Professional: (01554 810278; Fax: 01269 861825). Secretary: G. Lowe (01554 810278).

LAMPETER. **Cilgwyn Golf Club,** Llangybi, Lampeter SA48 8NN (01570 45286). *Location:* five miles north-east of Lampeter, off A485 at Llangybi. Flat parkland course. 9 holes, 5309 yards, S.S.S. 67. Practice area. *Green Fees:* weekdays £10.00, £6.00 with a member; weekends £15.00, £9.00 with a member. Weekly £60.00. *Eating facilities:* full bar and catering. *Visitors:* welcome without reservation, please telephone at weekends April to September. Golf shop, pool table, TV. Caravan parking and golf for Caravan Club members. *Society Meetings:* catered for, Thursdays and Fridays by prior arrangement. Special packages offered for parties of six or more – contact Anne James (01570 45286). Secretary: N. Hill.

LLANELLI. **Ashburnham Golf Club,** Cliffe Terrace, Burry Port SA16 0HN (01554 832466). *Location:* south side of A484, four miles west of Llanelli. Seaside links with Championship status. 18 holes, 6627 yards. S.S.S. 72. Practice area. *Green Fees:* weekdays £22.50 per round; weekends and Bank Holidays £30.00 per round. *Eating facilities:* catering except Mondays, two bars. *Visitors:* welcome, starting times available from the Secretary. *Society Meetings:* by arrangement with Secretary. Professional: Robert A. Ryder (01554 833846). Secretary: D.K. Williams (01554 832269). *

LLANRHYSTYD. **Penrhos Golf and Country Club,** Llanrhystyd SY23 5AY (Tel & Fax: 01974 202999). *Location:* nine miles south of Aberystwyth on A487. Parkland and meadowland with lakes and terrific views. 18 holes, 6641 yards. S.S.S. 72. Practice ground. *Green Fees:* weekdays £15.00 per round; weekends £18.00 per round. *Eating facilities:* bar meals and à la carte restaurant. *Visitors:* welcome at all times. Accommodation in Holiday Park, full leisure facilities. *Society Meetings:* welcome. Professional: Paul Diamond. Secretary: R. Rees-Evans.

MILFORD HAVEN. **Milford Haven Golf Club,** Woodbine House, Hubberston, Milford Haven (Milford Haven [01646] 692368). *Location:* one mile from Milford Haven on Dale Road. Parkland overlooking magnificent harbour. 18 holes, 6071 yards. S.S.S. 70. *Green Fees:* weekdays £13.00 per day; weekends and Bank Holidays £18.00. Half price if with a member. *Eating facilities:* lunches, bar snacks; dinners available at clubhouse. *Visitors:* welcome at all times. *Society Meetings:* welcome, special rates depending on numbers. Professional: Stephen Laidler (0646 697762). Secretary: I.S. Harvey (0646 692368, 0646 693234 evenings; Fax: 0646 697018 evenings). *

NEWPORT. **Newport (Pembs) Golf Club,** The Golf Club, Newport SA42 OMR (01239 820244). *Location:* two miles off A487 Cardigan-Fishguard at Newport, Dyfed. Flat seaside links course with mountain views. 9 holes, 5815 yards. S.S.S. 68. *Green Fees:* £14.00 per day. Rates for two, three and four days negotiable. *Eating facilities:* full catering and bar facilities available. *Visitors:* welcome at all times, please telephone at weekends and Bank Holidays. Self-catering accommodation available adjoining clubhouse. *Society Meetings:* catered for at any time by arrangement with the Secretary. Professional: Mr Colin Parsons. Secretary: A.R.T. Dietrich.

PEMBROKE. **South Pembrokeshire Golf Club,** 1 Rose Valley, Pembroke SA71 5NJ. *Location:* on hilltop overlooking Pembroke Dock and The Haven. Parkland. 9 holes, 5804 yards. S.S.S. 69. *Green Fees:* £10.00 per day, £8.00 with a member. *Eating facilities:* none at present, in the process of building a new clubhouse. *Visitors:* welcome except during special competitions. *Society Meetings:* catered for by arrangement. Secretary: W.D. Owen (01646 682650).

ST. DAVID'S. **St. David's City Golf Club,** Whitesands Bay, St. David's SA62 6QY (01437 721751). *Location:* follow signs to Whitesands Bay, on Fishguard

Road out of St. David's, for two miles. Car park is situated on crossroads with club sign at entrance. If you reach the beach you've gone too far! Seaside links course with spectacular panoramic views over Whitesands Bay and St. David's Head. 9 holes, 5961 yards. S.S.S. 70. *Green Fees:* £11.00 per day. *Eating facilities:* available at our 19th hole in Hotel adjacent to course. *Visitors:* welcome at all times but please check at weekends and Bank Holidays; Ladies' Day Friday afternoons. *Society Meetings:* welcome, book with Secretary. Secretary: C.W.J. Snushall (01437 720312). *

TENBY. **Tenby Golf Club,** The Burrows, Tenby SA70 7NP (01834 842787). *Location:* on A478, near Tenby Railway Station. Seaside links, Championship course, oldest in Wales. 18 holes, 6330 yards. S.S.S. 71. Practice ground. *Green Fees:*weekdays £18.00; weekends £22.50. *Eating facilities:* complete dining facilities; licensed bar. *Visitors:* always welcome, subject to club competitions. Handicap Certificate required. Billiards rooms. Sky TV. *Society Meetings:* catered for by advance booking. Professional: Terence Mountford PGA (01834 844447). Secretary: J.A. Pearson (01834 842978).

Mid-Glamorgan

ABERDARE. **Aberdare Golf Club,** Abernant, Aberdare (01685 871188). *Location:* half a mile from town centre. Mountain course with parkland features and view of whole Cynon Valley. 18 holes, 5845 yards. S.S.S. 69. *Green Fees:* weekdays £14.00, (with member £8.00); weekends and Bank Holidays £18.00, (with member £10.00). *Eating facilities:* bar, lounge and diningroom. *Visitors:* welcome without reservation weekdays. Saturdays with member only, Sundays if no competition. Handicap Certificates required. Snooker room, ladies' lounge and changing room. *Society Meetings:* catered for by prior arrangement with Secretary. Professional: A. Palmer (01685 878735). Secretary: L. Adler (01685 872797).

BARGOED. **Bargoed Golf Club,** Heolddu, Bargoed CF8 9GF (01443 830143). *Location:* A469 to Bargoed town centre – Moorland Road. Mountain top course. 18 holes, 6012 yards. S.S.S. 70. *Green Fees:* weekdays £15.00; weekends £10.00 with a member only. *Eating facilities:* lunches, dinners and snacks. *Visitors:* welcome, only with member at weekends, no other restrictions. *Society Meetings:* catered for weekdays only. £3 reduction for parties of 12 or more. Secretary: W.R. Coleman (01443 830143 or 822377).

BRIDGEND. **Southerndown Golf Club,** Ewenny, Bridgend CF32 0QP (01656 880326). *Location:* three miles from Bridgend on the Ogmore Road. Downland overlooking Bristol Channel. 18 holes, 6417 yards, 5868 metres. S.S.S. 72. Practice area. *Green Fees:* £30.00 weekdays; £36.00 weekends. £20.00 after 2pm. *Eating facilities:* full diningroom and bar facilities. *Visitors:* welcome any time except on competition days (check with Secretary). Handicap Certificate required. *Society Meetings:* catered for on Tuesdays and Thursdays or by arrangement with Secretary. Special rates dependent on number. Professional: D. McMonagle (01656 880326). Secretary: K.R. Wilcox (01656 880476).

CAERPHILLY. **Caerphilly Golf Club,** Pencapel, Mountain Road, Caerphilly CF8 1HJ (01222 883481). *Location:* seven miles north of Cardiff on A469, 250 yards south of both railway and bus stations opposite Magistrates' Court. Mountainside course with undulating features and areas of woodland. 13 holes, 6028 yards. S.S.S. 71 (course is in development stage of 18 holes). Limited practice facilities. *Green Fees:* weekdays £22.00, £11.00 with a member; weekends only if playing with a member £14.00. *Eating facilities:* men's bar, mixed lounge, ladies' lounge, dining area (by arrangement). *Visitors:* welcome weekdays only, weekends and Bank Holidays by arrangement if with a member. *Society Meetings:* only a limited number by arrangement. Professional: Richard Barter (01222 869104). Secretary: H.M. Matthews (01222 863441).

CAERPHILLY. **Castell Heights Public Golf Course,** Blaengwynlais CF8 1NG (01222 861128). *Location:* approximately four miles north of Cardiff on A469, two miles south of Caerphilly. 9 holes, 2688 yards. S.S.S. 66 for 18 holes. *Green Fees:* information not provided. *Eating facilities:* snacks, lunches and afternoon tea available. Restaurant meals booking only (01222 886686). *Visitors:* welcome, booked times only. Professional: S. Bebb. Secretary: A.H. Godsall. *

CAERPHILLY. **Mountain Heights Golf Club,** Castell Heights Golf Course, Blaengwynlais CF8 1NG (01222 886686). *Location:* approximately four miles north of Cardiff on A469, two miles south of Caerphilly. Wooded course with lakes. 18 holes, 5981 yards. S.S.S. 72. 9 holes, 2688 yards. S.S.S. 66 for 18 holes. Driving range. *Green Fees:* £15.00 (£10.00 as member's guest), for 18 hole course. *Eating facilities:* two bars and cafeteria. *Visitors:* welcome except competition days. Professional: S. Bebb (01222 886666). Secretary: Mrs J. Bull (01222 861128). *

CAERPHILLY. **Mountain Lakes Golf and Country Club,** Caerphilly CF8 1NG (01222 886686). *Location:* approximately four miles north of Cardiff on A469, two miles south of Caerphilly. M4 Junction 32. Part parkland, part wooded, undulating. 20 water hazards, large penncross greens. 18 holes, 6550 yards. S.S.S. 73. 20 bay driving range. *Green Fees:* weekdays £15.00 (£10.00 with member); weekends £15.00. *Eating facilities:* full restaurant and three bars. *Visitors:* welcome at all times but must have registered Handicap. *Society Meetings:* welcome at all times but players must have registered Handicap. Professional: Sion Bebb (01222 886666). Golf Secretary: D.C. Rooney (01222 627041 or 01443 238374). Company Secretary of Proprietors Club: Jean Bull (01222 861128; Fax: 01222 869030).

CAERPHILLY. **Virginia Park Golf Club,** Virginia Park, Caerphilly CF8 3SW (01222 863919). *Location:* off Pontygwindy Road, Caerphilly, next to Caerphilly Recreation Centre. Totally flat course with two lakes, plenty of trees; six Par 4's and three Par 3's. 9 holes, 2566 yards. S.S.S. 66. 20 bay floodlit driving range. *Green Fees:* £6.00 per 9 holes, £11.00 per 18 holes. *Eating facilities:* bar facilities, bar meals, etc. *Visitors:* welcome anytime. *Society Meetings:* welcome. Professional available on range Monday and Friday evenings.

HENGOED. **Bryn Meadows Golf and Country Hotel,** The Bryn, Near Hengoed CF8 7SM (01495 225590/224103; Fax: 01495 228272). *Location:* A472 between stretch from Ystrad Mynach to Blackwood, turn up lane at Texaco Service Station at Crown roundabout. Parkland course. 18 holes, 6200 yards. S.S.S. 69. *Green Fees:* weekdays £17.50; weekends £22.50. *Eating facilities:* restaurant, 70 covers. Functions up to 120. Conferences catered for from five to 120. Bar snacks served daily. *Visitors:* welcome, but not Sunday mornings. The "Fairways" Leisure Club including – indoor heated swimming pool, jacuzzi, sauna and steam rooms and "state of the art" multigym available. *Society Meetings:* welcome Tuesdays and Thursdays. Professional: B. Hunter (01495 221905). Secretary: B. Mayo.

KENFIG. **Pyle and Kenfig Golf Club,** Waun-y-Mer, Kenfig CF33 4PU (01656 782060). *Location:* one mile off M4 at Junction 37. Seaside links and downland course. 18 holes, 6650 yards, 6081 metres. S.S.S. 73. Five practice holes, practice driving range. *Green Fees:* weekdays £26.00 per round, £31.00 day; weekends only as a member's guest £15.50. *Eating facilities:* full bar and catering facilities. *Visitors:* welcome weekdays by arrangement, proof of membership of a club and Handicap Certificate required. *Society Meetings:* welcome Tuesdays and Fridays. Professional: R. Evans (Tel & Fax: 01656 772446). Secretary: Roger Thomas (01656 783093).

MAESTEG. **Maesteg Golf Club,** Mount Pleasant, Neath Road, Maesteg CF34 9PR (01656 732037). *Location:* half a mile out of Maesteg town centre on the Port Talbot road (B4282). Reasonably flat hilltop course with scenic views over wooded hills and valleys down to Swansea Bay. 18 holes, 5900 yards. S.S.S. 69. *Green Fees:* weekdays £15.00; weekends £20.00. Special rates for Societies. *Eating facilities:* bar and dining facilities available daily. *Visitors:* welcome without reservation, groups of more than 12 by arrangement. *Society Meetings:* catered for weekdays only by arrangement. Professional: Bill Evans (01656 735742). Secretary: W.H. Hanford (01656 734106).

MERTHYR TYDFIL. **Merthyr Tydfil (Cilsanws) Golf Club,** Cloth Hall Lane, Cefn Coed, Merthyr Tydfil (01685 723308). *Location:* off A470 two miles north of Merthyr Tydfil town centre. Mountain course in National Park area with outstanding views. 11 holes, 5957 yards. S.S.S. 69. *Green Fees:* £14.00 weekdays; £18.00 weekends. Half price playing with member. *Eating facilities:* weekends only. *Visitors:* welcome anytime except competition days (usually Sundays). *Society Meetings:* catered for by prior arrangement. Secretary: Vivian Price.

MERTHYR TYDFIL. **Morlais Castle Golf Club,** Pant, Dowlais, Merthyr Tydfil CF48 2UY (01685 722822). *Location:* near "Heads of Valley Road", Dowlais roundabout, follow signs for Brecon Mountain Railway. Very pleasant moorland course with excellent views. 18 holes, 6320 yards, 5744 metres. S.S.S. 71. Practice area. *Green Fees:* weekdays £14.00 per day, £8.00 with member; weekends £16.00, £10.00 with a member. *Eating facilities:* bar meals/restaurant, dining area. *Visitors:* welcome, weekends by prior arrangement with/or by application to the Secretary. *Society Meetings:* weekdays only, please contact Secretary. Secretary: Mr J.N. Powell.

MOUNTAIN ASH. **Mountain Ash Golf Club,** Cefn Pennar, Mountain Ash (01443 472265). *Location:* A470 Pontypridd to Aberdare road, approximately 10 miles from Pontypridd, four miles north of Abercynon. Partly wooded course. 18 holes, 5553 yards. S.S.S. 68. *Green Fees:* weekdays £18.00, £10.00 with member, weekends and Bank Holidays £18.00 only with member. *Eating facilities:* catering at club. *Visitors:* welcome anytime without reservation. *Society Meetings:* catered for. Professional: Ceri Hiscox (01443 488770). Secretary: Geoffrey Matthews (01443 479459).

NELSON. **Whitehall Golf Club,** The Pavilion, Nelson, Treharris CF46 6ST (01443 740245). *Location:* 15 miles north of Cardiff, take A4054 off A470. Hillside course with pleasant views. 9 holes (x2), 5666 yards. S.S.S. 68. *Green Fees:* on application. *Eating facilities:* available, contact Steward for cooked meals. *Visitors:* welcome weekdays, weekends with members. *Society Meetings:* by prior arrangement. Secretary: V.E. Davies.

PONTYCLUN. **Llantrisant and Pontyclun Golf Club,** The Clubhouse, Lanelay Lane, Talbot Green, Pontyclun CF7 8HZ (01443 222148). *Location:* 10 miles north of Cardiff, two miles north of Junction 34 M4. Parkland. 12 holes, 5712 yards. S.S.S. 68. *Green Fees:* weekdays £20.00, £10.00 with member; weekends and Bank Holidays £10.00 with member only. *Eating facilities:* by arrangement with Steward. *Visitors:* welcome with proof of membership and weekends with member only. *Society Meetings:* catered for by arrangement. Professional: Nick Watson (01443 228169). Secretary: John Williams (01443 224601).

PONTYPRIDD. **Pontypridd Golf Club,** Ty Gwyn Road, Pontypridd CF37 4DJ (01443 402359). *Location:* east side of town, off A470, 12 miles from Cardiff. Wooded mountain course. 18 holes, 5721 yards. S.S.S. 68. *Green Fees:* on application. *Eating facilities:* bar, restaurant (restaurant closed Thursdays, snacks available). *Visitors:* welcome weekdays, Ladies' Day Tuesdays; weekends with member only. Must be member of recognised golf club in possession of Handicap Certificate. *Society Meetings:* catered for weekdays with prior reservation. Professional: Wade Walters (01443 491210). Secretary: J.G. Graham (01443 409904; Fax: 01443 491622).

PORTHCAWL. **Royal Porthcawl Golf Club,** Rest Bay, Porthcawl CF36 3UW (01656 782251; Fax: 01656 771687). *Location:* 25 miles west of Cardiff off Junction 37 M4, 14 miles east of Swansea. Seaside links. 18 holes, 6691 yards. S.S.S. 74. 27 acre practice area. *Green Fees:* £35.00 weekdays, £45.00 weekends. *Eating facilities:* full catering and bar facilities. *Visitors:* playing with member only at weekends, reservations required and must have Handicap Certificate. *Society Meetings:* by arrangement with the Secretary. Professional: Mr Peter Evans (01656 773702). Secretary: A.W. Woolcott.

RHONDDA. **Rhondda Golf Club,** Golf House, Penrhys, Ferndale, Rhondda CF43 3PW (01443 433204). *Location:* on the Penrhys road joining Rhondda Fach and Rhondda Fawr. Mountain course. 18 holes, 6206 yards. S.S.S. 70. *Green Fees:* £15.00 weekdays, £10.00 with a member; £20.00 weekends, £15.00 with member. *Eating facilities:* all facilities daily except Mondays. *Visitors:* welcome without reservation weekdays. Handicap Certificate required. Telephone for weekend availability. *Society Meetings:* welcome on written application. Professional: Rhys Davies (01443 441385). Secretary: G. Rees (Tel & Fax: 01443 441384).

South Glamorgan

BARRY. **Brynhill (Barry) Golf Club,** Port Road East, Colcot, Barry CF62 8PN (01446 735061). *Location:* leave M4 at Junction 33 (A4232), follow signs for Barry and Cardiff (Wales) Airport onto the A4050. Club on right of road. Undulating meadowland course. 18 holes, 6077 yards. S.S.S. 69. Par 71. *Green Fees:* weekdays: £20.00 per day, £9.00 with member; Saturdays and Bank Holidays: £25.00, £9.00 with member. Societies £17.00. With County Cards £9.00. Juniors £7.00. *Eating facilities:* the Steward Mr Phil Jones and his wife Susan extend a warm welcome, and will provide morning coffee, lunches between 12 noon and 2pm. Afternoon teas and dinner from 4.30pm. Your order prior to playing is requested. *Visitors:* welcome, except Sundays; must produce membership card and Handicap Certificate. *Society Meetings:* by arrangement with Secretary – no weekends, must be members of a golf club. Professional: Peter Fountain (01446 733660). Secretary: Keith Atkinson (01446 720277).

BARRY. **RAF St. Athan Golf Club,** Flemingstone Road, St. Athan, Barry CF62 4WA (01446 751043). *Location:* eight miles from Barry, turn left through St. Athan Village. Parkland. 9 holes, 6452 yards. S.S.S. 71. Practice area and nets. *Green Fees:* £8.00/£10.00 weekdays; £10.00/£15.00 weekends with or without member. *Eating facilities:* available except Mondays. *Visitors:* welcome except Sunday mornings, telephone for information. Handicap Certificate required. *Society Meetings:* apply through the Secretary. Professional: Neil Gillette (01222 373923). Secretary: P.F. Woodhouse (01446 797186).

BARRY. **St. Andrews Major Golf Club,** Coldbrook Road, Near Cadoxton, Barry (01446 722227). *Loca-*

tion: off Barry Docks new link road, Junction 33 M4. Flat parkland course. 9 holes, 3000 yards. S.S.S. 68. *Green Fees:* 9 holes £8.00, 18 holes £13.00. *Eating facilities:* restaurant and snacks; full bar facilities. *Visitors:* welcome anytime, but advisable to ring for bookings (especially at weekends). *Society Meetings:* special rates available, details on request. Secretary: Tom Gallimore.

CARDIFF. **Cardiff Golf Club,** Sherborne Avenue, Cyncoed, Cardiff (01222 753067). *Location:* two miles north of city centre or M4, A48 or A48M from east to Pentwyn exit on Eastern Avenue, and take Pentwyn Industrial Road to top of hill at Cyncoed Village, turn left at Spar shop into Sherborne Avenue. Undulating parkland, all greens bunkered. 18 holes. S.S.S. 70. *Green Fees:* £28.00. Winter rate 1st October to 31st March £20.00. *Eating facilities:* catering available lunchtime and evening weekdays except Mondays. *Visitors:* welcome; Saturdays must play with a member. Professional: Terry Hanson (01222 754772). Secretary: Keith Lloyd (01222 753320). *

CARDIFF. **Creigiau Golf Club,** Cardiff Road, Creigiau, Cardiff CF4 8NN (01222 890263). *Location:* seven miles north-west of Cardiff, two miles Exit 34 M4. 18 holes, 6015 yards. S.S.S. 69. *Green Fees:* £21.00 per day (£10.00 with member). *Eating facilities:* meals on request. *Visitors:* welcome without reservation except weekends when with members only. *Society Meetings:* catered for by arrangement. Professional: Mark Maddison (01222 891909). Secretary/Manager: D. Bryan Jones (01222 890263).

CARDIFF. **Llanishen Golf Club,** Cwm, Lisvane, Cardiff CF4 5UD (01222 752205). *Location:* five miles north of Cardiff city centre, one mile north of Llanishen village. Wooded mountain course with spectacular views. 18 holes, 5296 yards, 4844 metres. S.S.S. 66. *Green Fees:* £22.00. Special rates for County Cards or visitors playing with member weekdays except Bank Holidays. *Eating facilities:* full bar and catering except Mondays. *Visitors:* welcome weekdays; weekends only with member. Handicap Certificate required. *Society Meetings:* catered for Thursday only on written application. Visitors must be bona fide members of a golf club. Professional: R.A. Jones (01222 755076). Secretary/Manager: Elfed Davies (01222 755078).

CARDIFF. **Radyr Golf Club,** Drysgol Road, Radyr, Cardiff CF4 8BS (01222 842442). *Location:* Junction 32 M4, A470 to Merthyr Tydfil, first exit. Parkland course. 18 holes, 6015 yards. S.S.S. 70. *Green Fees:* £25.00 weekdays. *Eating facilities:* snacks, lunches and evening meals. Please order in advance (01222 842735). *Visitors:* welcome except weekends, Handicap Certificate from recognised club required. *Society Meetings:* catered for Wednesdays, Thursdays and Fridays only. Professional/Manager: Steve Gough (01222 842476/842408). *

CARDIFF. **St. Mellons Golf Club,** St. Mellons, Cardiff CF3 8XS (01633 680401). *Location:* just off M4 at Junction 28 on to A48. Parkland. 18 holes, 6225 yards. S.S.S. 70. *Green Fees:* £20.00 weekdays. *Eating facilities:* available. *Visitors:* welcome with Handicap Certificates weekdays only, weekends with member only. *Society Meetings:* catered for on written application. Professional: Barry Thomas (01633 680101). Secretary: Mrs K. Newling (01633 680408).

CARDIFF. **Wenvoe Castle Golf Club Ltd,** Wenvoe, Cardiff CF5 6BE (01222 591094). *Location:* exit Junction 33 M4, follow signs for Cardiff Airport. Parkland. 18 holes, 6422 yards. S.S.S. 71. *Green Fees:* weekdays £22.00; weekends £15.00 with a member only. *Eating facilities:* bar snacks and restaurant meals. *Visitors:* welcome weekdays only. *Society Meetings:* catered for Monday to Thursday, parties of 16 or more. Professional: R. Day (01222 593649). Secretary: Mr M. Burke (01222 594371).

CARDIFF. **Whitchurch (Cardiff) Golf Club,** Pantmawr Road, Whitchurch, Cardiff CF4 6XD (01222 620125; Fax: 01222 529860). *Location:* Junction 32 M4. 18 holes, 6319 yards. S.S.S. 70. *Green Fees:* £25.00 weekdays, £30.00 weekends and Bank Holidays. *Eating facilities:* restaurant and two bars. *Visitors:* welcome every day, limited over weekends. *Society Meetings:* catered for Thursdays only. Professional: Eddie Clark (01222 614660). Secretary/Manager: Lieutenant Commander R.G. Burley (01222 620985).

DINAS POWIS. **Dinas Powis Golf Club,** Golf House, Old Highwalls, Dinas Powis CF64 4AJ (01222 512157). *Location:* M4 Cardiff, thereafter signposted Dinas Powis, Penarth and Barry. Mostly parkland, three holes quite hilly. 18 holes, 5151 yards. S.S.S. 66. Limited practice area. *Green Fees:* weekdays £20.00; weekends £25.00. Half fee if playing with a member. Reduced rates for Societies depending on numbers. *Eating facilities:* diningroom/bar snacks except Mondays. *Visitors:* welcome weekdays, weekends by arrangement. *Society Meetings:* welcome, no restrictions. Professional: G. Bennett (01222 513682). Secretary: J.D. Hughes (01222 512727).

PENARTH. **Glamorganshire Golf Club,** Lavernock Road, Penarth CF64 5UP (01222 707048). *Location:* five miles west Cardiff, one mile west Penarth Centre. Parkland course overlooking Bristol Channel. 18 holes, 6150 yards. S.S.S. 70. Practice area. *Green Fees:* weekdays £24.00; weekends and Bank Holidays £30.00. *Eating facilities:* full restaurant and bar snacks, Men's bar and mixed lounge bar. *Visitors:* welcome providing no competitions in progress and/or Societies on course. Telephone call recommended. All visitors must possess current Handicap Certificate. *Society Meetings:* applications to Secretary/Manager. Reductions for parties exceeding 20. Professional: Mr A.K. Smith (01222 707401). Secretary/Manager: W.G. Davies (01222 701185).

Where an asterisk (*) follows an entry, details have not been confirmed by the club for 1995.

West Glamorgan

CLYDACH. **Inco Golf Club,** Clydach (01792 844216). *Location:* outskirts of Swansea, easily accessible from M4. Flat, tree-lined course, with river. 12 holes, 6230 yards. S.S.S. 70. *Green Fees:* information not available. *Eating facilities:* none. Bar only. *Visitors:* welcome. *Society Meetings:* catered for by arrangement through Secretary: Mr S. Murdoch (01792 843336). *

GLYNNEATH. **Glynneath Golf Club,** 'Penygraig', Pontneathvaughan, Near Glynneath SA11 5UH (01639 720452). *Location:* A465 trunk road to Glynneath onto B4242 to Pontneathvaughan. Picturesque hillside course overlooking the Vale of Neath, fairly flat, half parkland, half wooded in Brecon Beacons National Park. 18 holes, 5566 yards. S.S.S. 67. *Green Fees:* weekdays £12.00; weekends £18.00 per day. *Eating facilities:* snacks, hot drinks and bar. *Visitors:* welcome weekdays only. *Society Meetings:* welcome by prior arrangement, catering can be provided. Secretary: R.M. Ellis (01639 720679).

NEATH. **Earlswood Golf Club,** Jersey Marine, Neath SA10 6JP. *Location:* half a mile southeast of Jersey Marine village, take B4290 turning off A483 then first right. Scenic, gently undulating course. 18 holes, 5174 yards. S.S.S. 68. *Green Fees:* £8.00, £7.00 for members. *Visitors:* pay as you play course, all visitors welcome. *Society Meetings:* by arrangement. Professional: Mike Day (01792 321578). Secretary: (01792 812198).

NEATH. **Neath Golf Club,** Cadoxton, Neath SA10 8AH (01639 643615). *Location:* two miles from Neath town centre. 18 holes, 6492 yards. S.S.S. 72. *Green Fees:* weekdays £17.00; £12.00 with a member. Weekends with a member only. *Eating facilities:* full catering facilities available. *Visitors:* welcome weekdays only, Tuesday Ladies' Day. Snooker room. *Society Meetings:* Wednesday, Thursday and Friday by arrangement with Secretary. Professional: Mr E.M. Bennett. Secretary: Mr D.M. Hughes (01639 632759).

NEATH. **Swansea Bay Golf Club,** Jersey Marine, Neath SA10 6JP (01792 812198). *Location:* half a mile south east of Jersey Marine village. Take B4290 turning off A483 then first right. Seaside links. 18 holes, 6605 yards. S.S.S. 72. *Green Fees:* weekdays £16.00; weekends and Bank Holidays £22.00. *Eating facilities:* bar/catering available every day from 10.30am; dinners by arrangement. *Visitors:* welcome without reservation. Indoor bowling stadium available for private hire summer months. *Society Meetings:* by arrangement. Professional: M. Day (01792 816159). Secretary: Mrs D. Goatcher (01792 814153).

SWANSEA. **Clyne Golf Club,** 120 Owls Lodge Lane, The Mayals, Swansea SA3 5DP (01792 401989). *Location:* west of Swansea, South Gower road before Mumbles. Moorland course. 18 holes, 6323 yards. S.S.S. 71. Large practice area and 9 hole putting green. *Green Fees:* weekdays £20.00; weekends £25.00. *Eating facilities:* full catering available and fully licensed. *Visitors:* welcome. *Society Meetings:* welcome by application. Professional: Mark Bevan (01792 402094). Secretary: K. Crawford. *

SWANSEA. **Fairwood Park Golf Club Ltd,** Blackhills Lane, Upper Killay, Swansea SA2 7JN (01792 203648). *Location:* A4118 road – follow signs to "Sketty" and "Killay"; road to club opposite Swansea Airport. Parkland, many new trees planted, five lakes. Championship course. 18 holes, 6741 yards. S.S.S. 72. Practice field and net. *Green Fees:* £25.00 per day weekdays; £30.00 per day weekends and Bank Holidays. *Eating facilities:* full range, from bar snacks to three course meals, licensed bar. *Visitors:* welcome, large parties by appointment. If playing with a member £1.00 reduction. *Society Meetings:* welcome all through the year. Apply to Professional. Professional: Mark Evans (01792 299194). Secretary: Mrs C.J. Beer (01792 297849). Administrator: Bryn Morgan (01792 297849). Steward: J. Pettifer (01792 203648).

SWANSEA. **Langland Bay Golf Club,** Langland Road, Langland, Swansea SA3 4QR (01792 366023). *Location:* Swansea main road to Mumbles, followed by Langland Bay. Parkland/seaside course. 18 holes, 5857 yards. S.S.S. 69. *Green Fees:* weekdays £24.00; weekends and Bank Holidays £26.00. *Eating facilities:* bar snacks, lunches and supper. *Visitors:* welcome without reservation. *Society Meetings:* restricted, by arrangement; £20.00 per person for groups of 12 or more. Professional: T. Lynch (01792 366186). Secretary: T.J. Jenkins (01792 361721).

SWANSEA. **Morriston Golf Club,** 160 Clasemont Road, Morriston, Swansea SA6 6AJ (01792 771079). *Location:* off Junction 46 M4, turn first left follow road for one mile, clubhouse on left hand side of road. Parkland course, rather difficult. 18 holes, 5891 yards. S.S.S. 67. *Green Fees:* weekdays £18.00, £12.00 with a member; weekends and Bank Holidays £25.00, £16.00 with member. Special rates for parties of 10 or over with prior notice. *Eating facilities:* catering by arrangement with caterer (01792 700310), three bars. *Visitors:* welcome, restrictions only at weekends and Bank Holidays. *Society Meetings:* welcome. Professional: D.A. Rees (01792 772335). Secretary: W.A. Jefford (01792 796528).

SWANSEA. **Palleg Golf Club,** Lower Cwmtwrch, Swansea SA9 2QQ (01639 842193). *Location:* off A4067 (A4068) north of Swansea 14 miles, 25 miles Brecon. 9 holes, 6510 yards. S.S.S. 72. *Green Fees:* information not provided. *Eating facilities:* evening bar meals Tuesday, Thursday, weekend lunches. *Visitors:* welcome, restrictions Saturday (Summer) and Sunday mornings (Winter). *Society Meetings:* welcome if arranged. Secretary: Mr D.W. Moses (01792 862303). *

SWANSEA. **Pennard Golf Club,** 2 Southgate Road, Southgate, Swansea SA3 2BT (01792 233131). *Location:* eight miles west of Swansea A4067, B4436. Seaside links. 18 holes, 6289 yards. S.S.S. 71. Practice areas. *Green Fees:* weekdays £24.00, with a member £12.00; weekends and Bank holidays £30.00, with a member £15.00. *Eating facilities:* dining room and two bars. *Visitors:* welcome at any time. Squash courts, snooker room. *Society Meetings:* catered for weekdays only. Professional: M.V. Bennett (01792 233451). Secretary: E.M. Howell (01792 233131).

SWANSEA. **Pontardawe Golf Club,** Cefn Llan, Pontardawe, Swansea SA8 4SH (01792 863118). *Location:* four miles north of M4 Junction 45 on A4067 Swansea-Brecon road. Wooded course. 18 holes, 6162 yards. S.S.S. 70. *Green Fees:* £19.00 weekdays; £29.00 weekends. *Eating facilities:* restaurant open daily except Mondays. *Visitors:* welcome, weekends by prior arrangement only. Handicap Certificate required. *Society Meetings:* catered for by application/appointment. Professional: G. Hopkins (01792 830977). Secretary: Lyn Jones (01792 830041).

Gwent

ABERGAVENNY. **Monmouthshire Golf Club,** Llanfoist, Abergavenny NP7 9HE (01873 853171). *Location:* two miles out of Abergavenny on Llanfoist to Llanellen Road (A40). Parkland with scenic mountain views. 18 holes, 6045 yards. S.S.S. 70. Practice ground. *Green Fees:* weekdays £21.00, weekends and Bank Holidays £26.00. *Eating facilities:* full catering except Tuesday when bar snacks available. *Visitors:* welcome. Proof of membership of recognised golf club required. *Society Meetings:* catered for. Booking to be confirmed before Jan. 31st each year. Professional: P. Worthing (Tel & Fax: 01873 852532). Secretary: B. Jackson (Tel & Fax: 01873 852606).

ABERGAVENNY. **Wernddu Golf Centre,** Old Ross Road, Abergavenny NP7 8NG (01873 856223). *Location:* one and a half miles east of Abergavenny on B4521 off A465. Sloping site with three ponds. 9 holes, 2000 yards. S.S.S. 60. 26 bay driving range, 9 hole pitch and putt. *Green Fees:* £6.00 per 9 holes. *Eating facilities:* bar and snacks. *Visitors:* welcome. *Society Meetings:* welcome. Professional: A.A. Ashmead. Secretary: L. Davies (01873 853426).

BLACKWOOD. **Blackwood Golf Club,** Cwmgelli, Blackwood (01495 223152). *Location:* one mile north of Blackwood on Tredegar road A494. 9 holes, 5350 yards. S.S.S. 66. *Green Fees:* weekdays £12.50; weekends and Bank Holidays £15.00. *Visitors:* welcome weekdays only. *Society Meetings:* by arrangement. Secretary: A.M. Reed-Gibbs.

CAERLEON. **Caerleon Public Golf Course,** The Broadway, Caerleon, Newport (01633 420342). *Location:* three miles off M4 at turnoff for Caerleon. Flat parkland. 9 holes, 3000 yards. S.S.S. 68. Driving range. *Green Fees:* weekdays £3.00; weekends £3.80. Senior Citizens and Juniors £2.20. *Eating facilities:* cafe and bar. *Visitors:* welcome. *Society Meetings:* welcome. Professional: Alex Campbell. Secretary: R. Morgan. *

CHEPSTOW. **St. Pierre Hotel Resort Country Club,** St. Pierre Park, Chepstow NP6 6YA (01291 625261; Fax: 01291 629975). *Location:* five minutes from M4/Severn Bridge on A48 to Newport. Two courses set in 400 acre deer park, 11 acre lake. One of the toughest finishing holes in Golf – 18th on Old

Course. Old Course 18 holes, Championship/Medal 6700 yards, S.S.S. 73; standard tees 6285 yards, S.S.S. 71. Mathern Course 18 holes, 5762 yards, S.S.S. 68. *Green Fees:* Old Course – £40.00; Mathern Course £25.00. *Eating facilities:* two restaurants, bar snacks, three bars. *Visitors:* welcome with current membership of a bona fide golf club, book seven days in advance for weekday and 48 hours in advance for weekends. *Society Meetings:* weekdays only, except when resident in hotel which has 150 bedrooms with bathrooms, including 42 executive lodge bedrooms, conference rooms and extensive leisure facilities. Professional: Renton Doig (01291 621400). Secretary: T.J. Cleary.

CWMBRAN. **Greenmeadow Golf and Country Club,** Treherbert Road, Croesyceiliog, Cwmbran NP44 2BZ (01633 869321). *Location:* M4 Junction 26 north on A4042. Turn right off Croesyceiliog by-pass. Next to Gwent Crematorium. Parkland course. 18 holes, 6200 yards. S.S.S. 71. Driving range. *Green Fees:* weekdays £14.00; weekends £17.00. *Eating facilities:* diningroom with 80 covers, patio restaurant 50 covers. *Visitors:* welcome by prior arrangement. No jeans allowed and golf shoes must be worn. *Society Meetings:* always welcome, bookings via our Professional. Package deals with meals available. Professional: Ian Roberts (01633 862626). Secretary: David Williams (Fax: 01633 868430).

CWMBRAN. **Pontnewydd Golf Club,** West Pontnewydd, Cwmbran (01633 482170). *Location:* two miles north of Cwmbran on B4244. 9 holes, 5403 yards. S.S.S. 67. *Green Fees:* weekdays £16.00; weekends £16.00 only with a member. *Visitors:* welcome all week, must play with member at weekends. *Society Meetings:* not catered for. Secretary: H. R. Gabe.

LLANWERN. **Llanwern Golf Club,** Tennyson Avenue, Llanwern NP6 2DY (01633 412380). *Location:* four miles east of Newport, one mile from M4 Junction 24. Parkland. 18 holes, 6202 yards, 5581 metres. S.S.S. 70. 9 holes, 5674 yards, 5186 metres. S.S.S. 69. Large practice area. *Green Fees:* £20.00 weekdays. *Eating facilities:* full catering and bar. *Visitors:* welcome weekdays and Thursdays especially, must have Handicap Certificate. No casual visitors at weekends. *Society Meetings:* catered for by arrangement. Professional: S. Price (01633 413233). Secretary: D.J. Peak (01633 412029).

MONMOUTH. **Monmouth Golf Club,** Leasbrook Lane, Monmouth (01600 712212). *Location:* outskirts of town on Monmouth – Ross-on-Wye dual carriageway, entrance 100 yards past roundabout; signposted. Undulating parkland. 18 holes, 5700 yards. S.S.S. 69. Practice area. *Green Fees:* £15.00 per day. Weekly ticket (Monday/Friday inclusive) £35.00. *Eating facilities:* lunch and evening meals provided each day. *Visitors:* welcome, no restrictions. *Society Meetings:* contact the Secretary in advance. Secretary: P.C. Harris (01600 712212).

MONMOUTH. **The Rolls of Monmouth Golf Club,** The Hendre, Monmouth NP5 4HG (01600 715353; Fax: 01600 713115). *Location:* four miles west of Monmouth on the B4233 Monmouth/Abergavenny road. Wooded, hilly parkland course on private estate. 18 holes, 6723 yards. S.S.S. 72. Practice area, practice net, putting green. *Green Fees:* on request. *Eating facilities:* full catering. *Visitors:* welcome any day. *Society Meetings:* welcome on any day including weekends. Bookings Secretary: Mrs S. Orton.

NANTYGLO. **West Monmouthshire Golf Club,** Pond Road, Nantyglo, Brynmawr NP3 4QT (01495 310233; Fax: 01495 311361). *Location:* Heads of the Valleys Road to Brynmawr, roundabout to Nantyglo, signposted. Mountain and heathland course. 18 holes, 6118 yards. S.S.S. 69. *Green Fees:* Mondays to Saturdays £15.00, £10.00 with a member; Sundays £15.00 as members' guests only. *Eating facilities:* 24 hours notice required. *Visitors:* welcome except Sundays. *Society Meetings:* welcome on application to the Secretary. Special package for parties – details on request. Secretary: Colin Lewis (01495 312746).

NEWPORT. **Dewstow Golf Club,** Caerwent, Newport NP6 4AH (01291 430444; Fax: 01291 425816). *Location:* one mile from Severn Bridge, then A48 to Newport one mile, left at Caerwent (total five miles from Severn Bridge). Undulating parkland courses, special features include totem pole, bridge, views. 26 bay floodlit covered driving range. Two Courses – Valley Course 18 holes, 6123 yards, S.S.S. 72; Park Course 18 holes, 6147 yards, S.S.S. 69. *Green Fees:* weekdays £11.00; weekends £15.00. winter rates available. *Eating facilities:* restaurant, bars. *Visitors:* welcome all day every day. Acceptable standard of dress. *Society Meetings:* welcome. Professional: Mark Kedward. Golf Secretary: Mr Eric Tose. Club Secretary: Mrs Barbara Hill.

NEWPORT. **Newport Golf Club,** Great Oak, Rogerstone, Newport NP1 9FX (01633 892683; Fax: 01633 896676). *Location:* four miles west of Newport, one and a half miles west of Junction 27 of M4 on B4591. Parkland. 18 holes, 6314 yards, 5830 metres. S.S.S. 71. Two practice areas. *Green Fees:* £30.00 weekdays, £40.00 weekends. 50% reduction 1st November to 31st March. *Eating facilities:* full dining facilities at club. *Visitors:* welcome weekdays without reservation. *Society Meetings:* book only through Secretary. Professional: Roy Skuse (01633 893271). Secretary: J.M. Seatter (01633 892643; Fax: 01633 896676).

NEWPORT. **Parc Golf Club,** Church Lane, Coedkernew, Newport NP1 9TU (01633 680933; Fax: 01633 681011). *Location:* Junction 28 M4, A48 three miles from Newport. Flat links course. 18 holes, 5512 yards. S.S.S. 70. Golf range; putting machine and putting green. *Green Fees:* weekdays £10.00, weekends £12.00. *Eating facilities:* bar, conservatory, function room (can cater for 120). *Visitors:* always welcome. *Society Meetings:* all catered for. Professional: B. Edwards PGA (01633 680955). Secretary: M.V. Cleary.

NEWPORT. **Peterstone Golf Club,** Peterstone, Wentloog, Cardiff CF3 8TN (01633 680009; Fax: 01633 680563). *Location:* Leave the M4 at Junction 28, take the A48 towards Castleton. Parkland/links course bordering the Bristol Channel. 18 holes, 6555 yards. S.S.S. 71. Indoor teaching academy. *Green Fees:* weekdays £15.00; weekends £17.50. £12.00 Mondays and Tuesdays. *Eating facilities:* lounge bar, Fairways Restaurant, Crystal Suite. *Visitors:* welcome, strongly recommend telephone enquiry for a tee time. *Society Meetings:* welcome. Professional: Mike Pycroft. Manager: Bob Williams.

NEWPORT. **Tredegar Park Golf Club Ltd,** Bassaleg Road, Newport NP9 3PX (01633 895219). *Location:* Junction 28 M4. Mature parkland course with River Ebbw running across. 18 holes, 6095 yards, 5626 metres. S.S.S. 70. Practice area. *Green Fees:* weekdays £25.00; weekends and Bank Holidays £30.00. *Eating facilities:* restaurant and bar. *Visitors:* welcome, must be member of affiliated club. *Society Meetings:* groups of 16 and over catered for; package at £35 per head. Professional: M.L. Morgan (01633 894517). Secretary: Mr R.T. Howell (01633 894433; Fax: 01633 897152).

PONTYPOOL. **Pontypool Golf Club,** Lasgarn Lane, Trevethin, Pontypool NP4 8TR (Pontypool (01495) 763655). *Location:* Pontypool A4042 to St. Cadoc's Church, Trevethin. Undulating hillside course, with mountain turf and fine views. 18 holes, 6046 yards. S.S.S. 69. Practice area. *Green Fees:* £16.50 weekdays, £22.50 weekends and Bank Holidays. *Eating facilities:* diningroom and bar snacks. *Visitors:* welcome with Handicap Certificates. *Society Meetings:* catered for by arrangement. Professional: Jim Howard (01495 755544). Secretary: Mrs E. Wilce (01495 763655). *

PONTYPOOL. **Woodlake Park Golf and Country Club,** Glascoed, Pontypool NP4 0TE (01291 673933; Fax: 01291 672764). *Location:* Llandedfedd Reservoir approached from Usk. Undulating parkland. 18 holes, 6300 yards. S.S.S. 72. Indoor golf centre with bunkers and chipping bays, 9 hole pitch and putt course. *Green Fees:* weekdays £15.00; weekends £20.00. *Eating facilities:* spikes bar open 8am to 11pm. *Visitors:* welcome, no restrictions. Function room for 130, games room, snooker. *Society Meetings:* welcome, must pre book. Professional: Clive Coombs. Secretary: M.J. Wood.

RHYMNEY. **Tredegar and Rhymney Golf Club,** Cwmtysswg, Rhymney NP2 3BQ (01685 840743). *Location:* junction of A4048 and A465 Heads of the Valley road. Mountain course. 9 holes, 5564 yards. S.S.S. 68. *Green Fees:* weekdays £12.00 (with member £9.00); weekends and Bank Holidays £15.00 (with member £12.00). *Eating facilities:* bar snacks. *Visitors:* welcome without reservation. *Society Meetings:* catered for without reservation. Secretary: V. Davies (01495 726096).

USK. **Alice Springs Golf Club,** Bettws Newydd, Usk NP5 1JY (01873 880708; Fax: 01873 880838). *Location:* three miles north of Usk on B4598. Two undulating parkland courses. King's Course: 18 holes, 6185 yards. S.S.S. 72. Queen's Course: 18 holes, 6041 yards. S.S.S. 69. *Green Fees:* weekdays £12.50 per round; weekends and Bank Holidays £15.00. Discounts for parties of 12 or more. *Eating facilities:* available. *Visitors:* welcome at all times, telephone for tee time. Professional: Jim Howard (01873 880914). Secretary: Keith R. Morgan (01873 880244).

Where an asterisk (*) follows an entry, details have not been confirmed by the club for 1995.

Gwynedd

ABERDOVEY. **Aberdovey Golf Club,** Aberdovey LL35 0RT (01654 767210). *Location:* west end of Aberdovey on A493, adjacent to railway station. Classic Championship links. 18 holes, 6445 yards. S.S.S. 71. Practice ground, limited. *Green Fees:* weekdays £20.00; weekends £25.00. Concessions for guests at local hotels. *Eating facilities:* restaurant and bar. *Visitors:* welcome on production of Handicap Certificate, restrictions at weekends. Snooker. *Society Meetings:* catered for by prior arrangement (not August or Bank Holidays). Professional: J. Davies (01654 767602). Secretary: J.M. Griffiths (01654 767493).

ANGLESEY. **Baron Hill Golf Club,** Beaumaris, Anglesey (01248 810231). *Location:* turn left on approach to Beaumaris from Menai Bridge on A545. Parkland. 9 holes, 5062 metres. S.S.S. 67. *Green Fees:* weekdays £12.00, £5.00 with a member. Weekly £45.00. *Eating facilities:* clubhouse destroyed by fire – hope to resume full facility in near future. *Visitors:* welcome, competitions most Sundays, tee reserved for ladies on Tuesdays 10.30 – 12.30. *Society Meetings:* welcome, prior arrangement with Secretary. Secretary: A. Pleming.

ANGLESEY. **Bull Bay Golf Club Ltd,** Bull Bay, Amlwch, Anglesey LL68 9RY (01407 830213). *Location:* one mile west of Amlwch on A5025 coastal road towards Cemaes Bay and Holyhead. Coastal heathland championship course – Wales' northernmost golf course. 18 holes, 6217 yards. S.S.S. 70. Practice ground and puttinggreen. *Green Fees:* £15.00 per round, £20.00 per day weekdays; £20.00 per round, £25.00 per day weekends and Bank Holidays. Discount for parties of 12 and over of £2 per person. *Eating facilities:* bar snacks, dining room; limited facilities on Tuesdays. *Visitors:* welcome, competitions permitting; advance bookings advised. All visitors should have current Handicap Certificates or satisfy Professional of competence to play. *Society Meetings:* welcome (not usually on Saturdays), booking essential. Professional: Neil Dunroe PGA (01407 831188). Secretary/Manager: David W. Lewis OBE (01407 830960; Fax: 01407 832612).

BALA. **Bala Golf Club,** Penlan, Bala LL23 7YD (01678 520359). *Location:* turn right before coming to Bala Lake on the main Bala-Dolgellau road. Upland course with superb views in the Snowdonia National Park. 10 holes, 4970 yards, 4512 metres. S.S.S. 64. *Green Fees:* weekdays £12.00 per day; weekends and Bank Holidays £15.00 per round. Weekly tickets £30.00. *Eating facilities:* bar with snacks available. *Visitors:* welcome all year, some restrictions on Bank Holidays and weekends. Snooker table and small golf shop. *Society Meetings:* very welcome by prior arrangement. Professional: David Larvin (visiting). Secretary: (01678 520359).

BANGOR. **St. Deiniol Golf Club,** Penybryn, Bangor LL57 1PX (01248 353098). *Location:* at A5/A55 intersection, follow A5122 for one mile to eastern outskirts of Bangor. Parkland course with magnificent views. 18 holes, 5545 yards, 5068 metres. S.S.S. 67. *Green Fees:* weekdays £12.00 per day; weekends and Bank Holidays £16.00 per day. Discount for parties over eight. *Eating facilities:* two bars; full catering Mondays excepted. *Visitors:* welcome without reservation, restrictions at weekends. *Society Meetings:* welcome by prior arrangement. Secretary: E.W. Jones.

BETWS-Y-COED. **Betws-y-Coed Golf Club,** The Clubhouse, Betws-y-Coed LL24 0AL (01690 710556). *Location:* turn north off A5 in village. Parkland, flat scenic course on valley floor of River Conwy. 9 holes, 4996 yards. S.S.S. 64. *Green Fees:* £12.50 weekdays, £17.50 weekends. Rates for parties negotiable. *Eating facilities:* catering, bar 12 – 2pm and from 4.30pm. *Visitors:* no restrictions provided there are no club competitions. *Society Meetings:* catered for. Secretary: F.R. Slater (01690 710556).

CAERNARFON. **Caernarfon Golf Club,** Aberforeshore, Llanfaglan, Caernarfon LL54 5RP (01286 673783). *Location:* two miles from town along the Menai Straits. Parkland course in superb sea and mountain setting. 18 holes, 5891 yards. S.S.S. 69. *Green Fees:* weekdays £18.00; weekends £22.00. Special rates for visiting parties, weekdays only. *Eating facilities:* excellent catering and bar facilities. *Visitors:* welcome Monday to Friday. *Society Meetings:* welcome, subject to pre-arranged bookings. Secretary: G. Jones (01286 678359).

CONWY. **Conwy (Caernarvonshire) Golf Club,** Morfa, Conwy LL32 8ER (01492 593400). *Location:* follow signs for Conwy Marina off A55. Seaside links. 18 holes, 6647 yards. S.S.S. 72. Practice facilities. *Green Fees:* weekdays £22.00; weekends and Bank Holidays £27.00. Weekly ticket £88.00 (Monday to Friday). *Eating facilities:* available except Monday evening and all day Tuesday. *Visitors:* welcome with reservation, restrictions at weekends. *Society Meetings:* catered for on application to Secretary. Professional: Peter Lees (01492 593225). Secretary: E.C. Roberts (01492 592423).

CRICCIETH. **Criccieth Golf Club,** Ednyfed Hill, Criccieth (01766 522154). *Location:* in High Street (A497) turn right past Memorial Hall, keep going up lane to Club. 18 holes, 5755 yards. S.S.S. 68. *Green Fees:* £12.00; £15.00 Sundays. *Eating facilities:* light meals available April to September. *Visitors:* welcome without reservation. *Society Meetings:* catered for with prior reservation. Secretary: M.G. Hamilton (01766 522697).

DOLGELLAU. **Dolgellau Golf Club,** Ffordd Pencefn, Dolgellau (01341 422603). *Location:* half-a-mile from town centre. 9 holes, 4671 yards. S.S.S. 63. *Green Fees:* weekdays £12.00; weekends £15.00. *Eating facilities:* bar and catering facilities available. *Visitors:* welcome without reservation. *Society Meetings:* catered for. Secretary: H.M. Edwards (01341 422603).

FFESTINIOG. **Ffestiniog Golf Club,** Y Cefn, Ffestiniog (01766 762637). *Location:* located on B4391, one mile from Ffestiniog village. Upland course. 9 holes, 5032 yards. S.S.S. 66. *Green Fees:* approximately £8.00. *Eating facilities:* available by prior arrangement. *Visitors:* welcome at any time, some restrictions mainly at weekends during club competitions. *Society Meetings:* by prior arrangement. Secretary: Andrew M. Roberts (01766 831829).

HARLECH. **Royal St. David's Golf Club,** Harlech LL46 2UB (01766 780203; Fax: 01766 781110). *Location:* A496 lower Harlech road. Seaside links. Championship course. 18 holes, 6427 yards. S.S.S. 72. Large practice ground. *Green Fees:* weekdays £24.00 per day; weekends £30.00 per day (subject to review). *Eating facilities:* full catering and bar facilities available. *Visitors:* must be members of bona fide golf clubs with Handicap – booking advisable. *Society Meetings:* catered for by prior arrangement. Professional: John Barnett (01766 780857). Secretary: R.I. Jones (01766 780361).

LLANDUDNO. **Llandudno Golf Club (Maesdu) Ltd,** Hospital Road, Llandudno LL30 1HU (01492 876016; Fax: 01492 871570). *Location:* Llandudno General Hospital. A55 and then A470. Parkland. 18 holes, 6513 yards. S.S.S. 72. *Green Fees:* weekdays £22.00 per day; weekends and Bank Holidays £30.00 per day. *Eating facilities:* full catering, bar (large) available. *Visitors:* welcome everyday, tee reservations for members. *Society Meetings:* must be booked, catered for. Professional: S. Boulden (01492 875195). Secretary: George Dean (01492 876450).

LLANDUDNO. **North Wales Golf Club Ltd,** 72 Bryniau Road, West Shore, Llandudno LL30 2DZ (01492 875325). *Location:* one-and-a-half miles from Llandudno town centre on West Shore. Seaside links. 18 holes, 6132 yards, 5580 metres. S.S.S. 69. *Green Fees:* weekdays £22.00 per day; weekends and Bank Holidays £28.00 per day. Inclusive package available November to March. *Eating facilities:* full bar and catering facilities. *Visitors:* welcome with reservation after 9.45am. Some other time restrictions. Current Handicap Certificate required. *Society Meetings:* catered for by arrangement. Professional: R.A. Bradbury (01492 876878). Secretary: G.D. Harwood (01492 875325).

LLANDUDNO. **Rhos-on-Sea Residential Golf Club,** Penrhyn Bay, Llandudno LL30 3PU (01492 549100). *Location:* A55 to Colwyn Bay follow signs to Rhos-on-Sea, one mile past Rhos-on-Sea on coast road in Penrhyn Bay. Flat seaside parkland course. 18 holes, 6064 yards. S.S.S. 69. *Green Fees:* £15.00 weekdays; £20.00 weekends. *Eating facilities:* available, bar meals 12 -2pm, teas, coffees, snacks available all day. Evening meals by arrangement. Licensed bar open 11am – 3pm lunch, 5.30pm – 11pm evenings; Sundays 12 – 2pm lunch, 7pm – 10.30pm evenings. *Visitors:* all welcome any time, prior booking required particularly weekends. 18 bedrooms, two full size snooker tables, small TV lounge. Two £100 jackpot fruit machines. *Society Meetings:* catered for. Professional: Mr Matthew Jones (01492 548115). Secretary: Mr I.H. Taylor (01492 544551). Stewards: Mr and Mrs J. John.

LLANFAIRFECHAN. **Llanfairfechan Golf Club,** Llannerch Road, Llanfairfechan LL33 0EB (01248 680144). *Location:* signposted off old A55, 300 yards west of traffic lights. Hillside parkland. 9 holes, 3119 yards. S.S.S. 57. *Green Fees:* weekdays £10.00; weekends £15.00. *Eating facilities:* no eating facilities, bar open weekends and weekday evenings. *Visitors:* welcome anytime except Sundays. *Society Meetings:* by arrangement, weekdays only in Summer. Secretary: M.J. Charlesworth (01248 680524).

LLANGEFNI. **Llangefni Public Golf Course,** Llangefni, Isle of Anglesey. Short, parkland course. 9 holes, 1467 yards, 1342 metres. S.S.S. 28. Practice net. *Green Fees:* information not provided. Reduced rates Juniors and Senior Citizens. *Eating facilities:* light refreshments only. *Visitors:* welcome at all times, no booking. Golf equipment available for hire. Professional: Paul Lovell (01248 722193). *

MORFA BYCHAN. **Porthmadog Golf Club,** Morfa Bychan, Porthmadog LL49 9UU (01766 512037). *Location:* turn in Porthmadog High Street at Woolworths towards Black Rock Sands, club on left hand side of road one mile west. Part parkland, part seaside links. 18 holes, 6240 yards. S.S.S. 70. Practice area. *Green Fees:* £15.00 weekdays, £20.00 weekends, £25.00 Bank Holidays. *Eating facilities:* new clubhouse with much enlarged dining facilities; lunches, teas and evening meals; two bars serving bar snacks. *Visitors:* welcome, no restrictions except for competition days. Snooker. *Society Meetings:* catered for by prior arrangement. Bookings via Match Secretary. Professional: Peter Bright (01766 513828). Secretary: Glyn Humphreys (01766 514124). Match Secretary: Dennis Morrow (01766 514286 evenings). *

NEFYN. **Nefyn and District Golf Club,** Golf Road, Morfa Nefyn, Pwllheli LL53 6DA (01758 720218; Fax: 01758 720476). *Location:* north coast of Lleyn Peninsula, two miles west of Nefyn. Seaside course. 27 holes. Main Course – 18 holes, 6548 yards. S.S.S. 71. Practice area. *Green Fees:* weekdays £20.00 per round, £25.00 per day; weekends and Bank Holidays £25.00 per round, £35.00 per day. 10% discount for parties of 12 or more players. *Eating facilities:* full restaurant facilities and two bars. *Visitors:* welcome without reservation, except club competition days. Snooker. *Society Meetings:* catered for by arrangement with Secretary. Professional: John Froom (01758 720102). Secretary: T.G. Owen (01758 720966).

PENMAENMAWR. **Penmaenmawr Golf Club,** Conwy Old Road, Penmaenmawr LL34 6RD (01492 623330). *Location:* A55 expressway three miles west of Conwy. Parkland with panoramic views. 9 holes (18 tees), 5306 yards. S.S.S. 67. Two practice areas. *Green Fees:* £15.00 weekdays, £18.00 weekends. *Eating facilities:* bar and bar snacks, meals by arrangement. *Visitors:* welcome anytime except Saturdays. *Society Meetings:* welcome by arrangement (not Saturdays). Secretary: Mrs J. Dryhurst Jones (01492 623330).

PWLLHELI. **Abersoch Golf Club,** Golf Road, Abersoch, Pwllheli (01758 712622). *Location:* on left beyond village along the shore. Parkland and seaside links course. 18 holes, 5881 yards. S.S.S. 69. *Green Fees:* £15.00. *Eating facilities:* catering, bar. *Visitors:* welcome, booking required. Handicap Certificate required. Shop. *Society Meetings:* catered for. Secretary: Brian Guest.

PWLLHELI. **Pwllheli Golf Club,** Golf Road, Pwllheli LL53 5PS. *Location:* A499 from Caernarvon (20 miles). Parkland/seaside links. 18 holes. 6091 yards. S.S.S. 69. Two practice areas and putting green. *Green Fees:* £20.00 per day weekdays; £25.00 weekends. Reductions for parties. *Eating facilities:* two large lounge bars and diningroom. Steward: (01758 701633). *Visitors:* welcome without reservation. Pro shop. *Society Meetings:* catered for by prior arrangement. Professional: G.D. Verity (01758 612520). Secretary: R. Eric Williams (01758 701644).

RHOSNEIGR. **The Anglesey Golf Club Ltd,** Station Road, Rhosneigr, Anglesey (01407 810219). *Location:* turn south off A5 between Gwalchmai and Bryngwram onto A4080. In about three miles turn right at Llanfaelog church about one mile from course. Links course. 18 holes, 5713 yards. S.S.S. 68. *Green Fees:* information not provided. *Eating facilities:* bar meals and restaurant. *Visitors:* welcome, preferably after 10am and 1.30pm. Handicap Certificate required. *Society Meetings:* catered for, reservation advised. Professional: Paul Lovell (01407 811202). Manager: Mr Arfon Jones (01407 810930/810219). *

TREARDDUR BAY. **Holyhead Golf Club,** Lom Carreg Fawr, Trearddur Bay, Anglesey (01407 762119). *Location:* two miles from Holyhead. Heathland, heavy gorse cover, superb sea views. Course designed by James Braid. 18 holes, 6058 yards. S.S.S. 70. *Green Fees:* weekdays £20.00; weekends £25.00. *Eating facilities:* all catering services available. *Visitors:* welcome, must possess current Handicap and have third party public liability insurance (available from Professional). *Society Meetings:* catered for if members of bona fide golf clubs. Dormy House accommodation available for up to 14. Professional: Steve Elliot (01407 762022). Secretary: D. Entwistle (01407 763279).

Powys

BRECON. **Brecon Golf Club,** Newton Park, Brecon (01874 2004). *Location:* on A40 west of town, half a mile from centre. 9 holes, 5218 yards. S.S.S. 66. *Green Fees:* £10.00 at all times. *Visitors:* welcome without reservation. *Society Meetings:* catered for. Secretary: D.H.E. Roderick.

BUILTH WELLS. **Builth Wells Golf Club,** Golf Club Road, Builth Wells LD2 3NF (01982 552737). *Location:* off A483, on outskirts of town on Llandovery Road. Parkland, reasonably flat. 18 holes, 5386 yards. S.S.S. 67. Practice area. *Green Fees:* £15.00 per day weekdays, £20.00 weekends and Bank Holidays. Five day and seven day tickets available. *Eating facilities:* catering all day, two bars. *Visitors:* welcome, Handicap Certificate required. *Society Meetings:* welcome, Handicap Certificate required. Professional: Roy Truman (01982 553296). Secretary: Ainsleigh Jones (01982 553296).

BUILTH WELLS. **Rhosgoch Golf Club,** Rhosgoch, Builth Wells LD2 3JY (01497 851251). *Location:* near Hay-on-Wye. Parkland course. 9 holes, 4842 yards. S.S.S. 64. *Green Fees:* £7.00 weekdays, £10.00 weekends. *Eating facilities:* bar/restaurant meals, two bars. *Visitors:* welcome anytime. Accommodation available. *Society Meetings:* anytime. Secretary: C. Dance (0154422 286). *

CRADOC. **Cradoc Golf Club,** Penoyre Park, Cradoc, Brecon LD3 9LP (01874 623658). *Location:* about two miles north of the market town of Brecon, off B4520 Upper Chapel Road (signposted) past Brecon Cathedral. Attractive parkland course situated in the Brecon Beacons National Park. 18 holes, 6301 yards. S.S.S. 71. Separate practice ground. *Green Fees:* £18.00 weekdays, £20.00 weekends. *Eating facilities:* full catering facilities daily except Mondays. *Visitors:* welcome daily but restricted on Sundays when must be playing with a member. *Society Meetings:* welcome during weekdays. Professional: Douglas Beattie (01874 625524). Secretary: G.S.W. Davies. Host of 1982 Welsh Stroke Play Championships. Home of the Welsh Brewers Champion of Champions Tournament.

CRICKHOWELL. **Old Rectory Hotel and Golf Club,** Llangattock, Crickhowell NP8 1PH (01873 810373). *Location:* Crickhowell is between Abergavenny and Brecon. Course is on a hill with spectacular views. 9 holes, 2878 yards. S.S.S. 54. *Green Fees:* information not provided. *Eating facilities:* restaurant, bar meals, two bars. *Visitors:* welcome at all times. Accommodation available, outdoor swimming pool. *

KNIGHTON. **Knighton Golf Club,** Little Ffryd Wood, Knighton LD7 1DG (01547 528646). *Location:* on the A488 to Llandrindod Wells, signposted. Undulating hill course with spectacular views. 9 holes, 5500 yards. S.S.S. 66. *Green Fees:* weekdays £8.00; weekends £10.00. *Eating facilities:* bar, meals can be arranged. *Visitors:* welcome, no visitors before 4.30pm on Sundays. *Society Meetings:* catered for by prior arrangement. Secretary: P.J. Isherwood (01547 528917).

LLANDRINDOD WELLS. **Llandrindod Wells Golf Club,** Llandrindod Wells LD1 5NY (01597 822010). *Location:* well signposted from A483 and centre of town. Hill top course with beautiful views, designed by Harry Vardon. 18 holes, 5687 yards. S.S.S. 68. *Green Fees:* £12.00 weekdays, £20.00 weekends and Bank Holidays. Parties of eight or more £1.00 per person reduction. *Eating facilities:* every day (except Tuesday), order in advance. *Visitors:* welcome, advisable to book in advance. *Society Meetings:* welcome, special day packages, must book in advance. Secretary/Manager: Mr F.T. James (01597 823873).

LLANIDLOES. **St. Idloes Golf Club,** Penrallt, Llanidloes (01686 412559). *Location;* take road to Trefeglwys from Llanidloes for one mile, turn left at house on extreme bend near top of hill. Slightly undulating terrain. 9 holes (x2), 5320 yards. S.S.S. 66. *Green Fees:* weekdays £10.00; weekends £12.00. *Eating facilities:* bar, snacks. *Visitors:* welcome Monday to Saturday. *Society Meetings:* welcome weekdays and Saturdays. Secretary: J.C. Green (01686 430479).

MACHYNLLETH. **Machynlleth Golf Club,** Ffordd Drenewydd, Machynlleth SY20 8UH (01654 702000). *Location:* A489 from Newtown, left hand turn before the speed restriction sign on entering Machynlleth. Undulating meadowland course. 9 holes, 5726 yards, 5285 metres. S.S.S. 67. Small practice area. *Green Fees:* weekdays £12.00; weekends £15.00. £7.00 with a member. *Eating facilities:* by arrangement. Bar. *Visitors:* welcome except during competition days. *Society Meetings:* welcome.

NEWTOWN. **St. Giles Golf Club,** Pool Road, Newtown (01686 625844). *Location:* convenient to town centre, quarter-of-a-mile on A483 from Newtown. Pleasant riverside course. 9 holes, 5936 yards. S.S.S. 68. *Green Fees:* weekdays £12.50 per day, weekends and Bank Holidays £15.00 per day. *Eating facilities:* bar and catering facilities, no catering on Mondays except Bank Holidays. *Visitors:* welcome, with reservation Saturday afternoons and Sunday mornings. Handicap Certificate required. Golf shop and Professional. *Society Meetings:* catered for. Professional: Mr D.P. Owen. Secretary: Mr T.A. Hall (01686 622223).

WELSHPOOL. **Welshpool Golf Club,** Y Golfa, Welshpool (01938 83249). *Location:* A458 West from Welshpool four miles, signpost on right at junction with main road. Rather hilly but very beautiful scenery. 18 holes, 5708 yards. S.S.S. 69. *Green Fees:* £10.00 weekdays; £20.00 weekends. *Eating facilities:* open most of the day for food and drink. *Visitors:* welcome weekdays, must contact the Steward for weekend starting times. *Society Meetings:* must contact Mr F. Knight. Secretary: D.B. Pritchard (01938 552215). *

GOLF IN IRELAND

Golf in Northern Ireland

Antrim

ANTRIM. **Massereene Golf Club,** 51 Lough Road, Antrim BT41 4DQ (01849 429293). *Location:* one mile S.W. of town, 3 miles from Aldergrove Airport, situated alongside the shores of Lough Neagh. 18 holes, 6440 yards. S.S.S. 71. *Green Fees:* weekdays £18.00; weekends £23.00. *Eating facilities:* full catering facilities 12 noon till 9pm. *Visitors:* welcome. *Society Meetings:* catered for. Professional: Jim Smyth (01849 464074). Secretary: Mrs Marie Agnew (01849 428096).

BALLYCASTLE. **Ballycastle Golf Club,** Cushendall Road, Ballycastle (012657 62536). *Location:* approximately 50 miles along the coast road west of Larne Harbour. Seaside links/undulating. 18 holes, 5662 yards, 5177 metres. S.S.S. 68. *Green Fees:* (1994) weekdays £13.00 (with member £7.00); weekends and Public Holidays £18.00 (with member £9.00); subject to review. *Eating facilities:* catering by arrangement. *Visitors:* welcome, best days during the week, no particular restrictions. *Society Meetings:* by arrangement. Professional: Mr I. McLaughlin (012657 62506). Hon. Secretary: Mr M.E. Page (012657 62536).

BALLYCLARE. **Ballyclare Golf Club,** 25 Springvale Road, Ballyclare BT39 9JW (01960 342352).*Location:* one and a half miles north of Ballyclare. Parkland, lakes and river. 18 holes, 5840 metres. S.S.S. 71. Practice ground. *Green Fees:* weekdays £14.00; weekends £20.00. *Eating facilities:* catering available. *Visitors:* welcome weekdays except Thursday. *Society Meetings:* catered for. Special rates for 20 plus. Secretary: H. McConnell (01960 322696).

BALLYMENA. **Ballymena Golf Club,** 128 Raceview Road, Ballymena (01266 861207). *Location:* two miles north east of town on A42. Flat/parkland. 18 holes, 5245 metres. S.S.S. 67. *Green Fees:* weekdays £13.00, £8.00 with a member; weekends £16.00, £9.00 with a member. *Eating facilities:* restaurant and bar snacks. *Visitors:* welcome at all times, except Tuesdays and Saturdays. *Society Meetings:* catered for except Tuesdays and Saturdays. Professional: (01266 861652). Secretary: Carl McAuley (01266 861487).

BELFAST. **Cliftonville Golf Club,** 44 Westland Road, Belfast BT14 6NH (Belfast (0232) 744158). Parkland with rivers bisecting three fairways. 9 holes, 6210 yards, 5672 metres. S.S.S. 70. Practice fairway and nets. *Green Fees:* weekdays £12.00, playing with a member £8.00; weekends £15.00, playing with a member £10.00. Special rates – 25% discount for parties of 20 or over. *Eating facilities:* bars, catering on request. *Visitors:* no visitors after 5pm weekdays, until 6pm Saturdays and after 12 noon Sundays. *Society Meetings:* very welcome, especially by arrangement. Hon. Secretary: Martin Henderson (0232 746595).

BELFAST. **Dunmurry Golf Club,** 91 Dunmurry Lane, Dunmurry, Belfast BT17 9JS (01232 621402). *Location:* one mile off M1, between Lisburn Road and Malone Road. Parkland, partially wooded. 18 holes, 5333 metres. S.S.S. 68. Practice area. *Green Fees:* weekdays £14.00; weekends £20.00. Subject to review. *Eating facilities:* restaurant and bar. *Visitors:* welcome except Friday and Saturday. *Society Meetings:* welcome. Professional: Paul Leonard (01232 621314). Secretary/Manager: Allan Taylor (01232 610834).

BELFAST. **Fortwilliam Golf Club,** Downview Avenue, Belfast BT15 4EZ (01232 776798). *Location:* one mile Fortwilliam Junction M2. Parkland. 18 holes, 5973 yards. S.S.S. 70. *Green Fees:* weekdays £16.00; weekends £21.00. *Eating facilities:* excellent catering and bar. *Visitors:* welcome every day except Saturdays. *Society Meetings:* catered for Tuesdays and Thursdays, special rates available. Professional: Peter Hanna (Tel & Fax: 01232 770980). Secretary: M. Purdy (01232 370770).

BELFAST. **Gilnahirk Golf Club,** Manns Corner, Upper Braniel Road, Gilnahirk, Belfast (01232 448351). *Location:* two miles from city centre, east Belfast. Parkland. 9 holes, 2699 metres. S.S.S. 68. Practice area and putting green. *Green Fees:* £3.85 weekdays for 9 holes; £4.80 weekends for 9 holes. *Visitors:* welcome, no restrictions. *Society Meetings:* all welcome. Professional: Mr K. Gray (01232 448477). Secretary: Mr H. Moore (01232 659653).

BELFAST. **Malone Golf Club,** 240 Upper Malone Road, Dunmurry, Belfast BT17 9LB (Belfast (0232) 612695). *Location:* three miles south of Belfast. Parkland, wooded course with large lake. 18 holes, 6476 yards. S.S.S. 71. 9 holes, 2895 yards. S.S.S. 72. Two practice grounds. *Green Fees:* £23.00 weekdays (except Wednesday when fee is £26.00); £26.00 weekends and Bank Holidays. *Visitors:* welcome weekdays except Wednesdays. After 5pm Saturdays and time sheet on Sundays. Dress code observed on course and in clubhouse. *Society Meetings:* Mondays and Thursdays. Professional: Michael McGee (0232 614917). Secretary: Thomas H. Young (0232 612758; Fax: 0232 431394).

CARRICKFERGUS. **Carrickfergus Golf Club,** 35 North Road, Carrickfergus BT38 8LP (01960 362203). *Location:* North Road, one mile from main shore road. Fairly flat parkland course, partially wooded. 18 holes, 5752 yards. S.S.S. 68. *Green Fees:* weekdays £13.00; weekends £18.00. Societies £11.00. *Eating facilities:* full catering and bar facilities. *Visitors:* welcome except on Friday afternoons and weekends. *Society Meetings:* catered for on weekdays but not after 1pm on Fridays. Professional: Ray Stevenson (01960 351803). Secretary/Manager: R.J. Campbell (01960 363713).

CARRICKFERGUS. **Greenisland Golf Club,** 156 Upper Road, Greenisland, Carrickfergus BT38 8RW (Whiteabbey (0232) 862236). 9 holes, 5596 metres. S.S.S. 69. *Green Fees:* weekdays £10.00, Sundays £15.00. *Eating facilities:* lunches at club, order in advance. *Visitors:* welcome except before 5.30pm Saturdays. Secretary: J. Wyness.

CARRICKFERGUS. **Whitehead Golf Club,** McCrae's Brae, Whitehead, Carrickfergus (01960 353792). *Location:* Whitehead, 15 miles from Belfast, 10 miles from Larne. 18 holes, 6362 yards. S.S.S. 71. *Green Fees:* weekdays £11.00; weekends with a member only £7.00. *Eating facilities:* by arrangement with Steward. *Visitors:* welcome Monday to Friday, weekends with a member only. *Society Meetings:* by prior arrangement. Professional: T. Loughran (01960 353118). Secretary/Manager: J.M. Niblock (01960 353631 9am – 1pm).

CUSHENDALL. **Cushendall Golf Club,** Shore Road, Cushendall (012667 71318). *Location:* 25 miles north on Antrim coast road from Larne Harbour. Seaside – wooded. River comes into play in seven out of nine holes. 9 holes, 4678 yards, 4030 metres. S.S.S. 63. *Green Fees:* weekdays £9.00 per day, weekends and Bank Holidays £11.00; £3.00 concession if playing with member. *Eating facilities:* normal bar hours – by arrangement with caterers. *Visitors:* welcome without reservation, time sheet in operation on Sundays. *Society Meetings:* by arrangement. Hon. Secretary: Shaun McLaughlin (01266 758366).

LARNE. **Cairndhu Golf Club Ltd,** 192 Coast Road, Ballygally, Larne BT40 2QG (Tel & Fax: 01574 583248). *Location:* four miles north of Larne. Parkland course. 18 holes, 6122 yards, 5598 metres. S.S.S. 69. Practice area. *Green Fees:* £12.00 weekdays; £20.00 weekends. *Eating facilities:* dining and bar facilities available. *Visitors:* welcome except Saturdays. *Society Meetings:* welcome. Professional: R. Walker (01574 583417). Secretary: Mrs Josephine Robinson (01574 583324).

LARNE. **Larne Golf Club,** 54 Ferris Bay Road, Islandmagee, Larne BT40 3RT (01960 382228). *Location:* six miles north of Whitehead on Browns Bay Road. Part links, part parkland. 9 holes, 6066 yards. S.S.S. 69. Practice ground. *Green Fees:* weekdays £8.00, with a member £4.00; weekends £15.00, with a member £8. *Eating facilities:* bar, restaurant. *Visitors:* welcome Mondays to Thursdays, and Sundays. Snooker table. *Society Meetings:* welcome on application (not Friday or Saturday). 10% reduction for societies of 20 or more. Secretary: J.B. Stewart.

LISBURN. **Lisburn Golf Club,** Blairs Lodge, 68 Eglantine Road, Lisburn BT27 5QR (01846 677216; Fax: 01846 603608). *Location:* three miles south of Lisburn on A1. Parkland. 18 holes, 6647 yards. S.S.S. 72. Practice area. *Green Fees:* £25.00 weekdays; weekends £30.00. *Eating facilities:* bar and restaurant. *Visitors:* welcome weekdays, Tuesdays Ladies have preference. Saturday after 5.30pm only, Sundays with member only. Snooker room. *Society Meetings:* catered for Mondays, Thursdays and Fridays. Professional: B.R. Campbell (01846 677217). Secretary: G. Graham (01846 677216).

NEWTOWNABBEY. **Ballyearl Golf and Leisure Centre,** 585 Doagh Road, Newtownabbey BT36 8RZ (01232 848287). *Location:* eight miles north of Belfast, 15 miles south of Larne. From Belfast follow signs to Larne via M2 (A8), turn right to Mossley approximately one mile from Corrs Corner Pub. Ballyearl is one mile on left. Parkland. 9 holes, 2402 yards, 2196 metres. Par 3. 27 bay covered floodlit driving range, outdoor grass teeing area. *Green Fees:* weekdays adults £3.00, Juniors £2.00, Senior Citizens £1.50; weekends adults £4.00, Juniors £3.00, Senior Citizens £2.00. *Eating facilities:* snacks available in Squash Club bar. *Visitors:* no restrictions – pay and play. Squash courts, hi-tech fitness suite and arts theatre. Golf lessons available by appointment, golf equipment tailored to individual requirements and can be tested on driving range. Professional: Jim Robinson (01232 840899).

PORTBALLINTRAE. **Bushfoot Golf Club,** 50 Bushfoot Road, Portballintrae BT57 8RR (012657 31317). *Location:* off Ballaghmore Road, Portballintrae. Seaside links course. 9 holes, 5054 yards. S.S.S 68. *Green Fees:* weekdays £12.00; weekends £15.00. *Eating facilities:* full diningroom, bars. *Visitors:* welcome, restrictions weekends June to September. *Society Meetings:* all welcome weekdays. Secretary: J. Knox Thompson.

PORTRUSH. **Rathmore Golf Club,** Bushmills Road, Portrush BT56 8JG (01265 822285). *Location:* north east coast – six miles from Coleraine, beside roundabout on road to Bushmills. Royal Portrush Golf Club (valley links). Flat seaside links. 18 holes, 6273 yards. S.S.S. 71. *Green Fees:* £16.00 weekdays; £20.00 weekends. *Eating facilities:* bar but no eating facilities. *Visitors:* Saturday and Sunday 1.30 to 2.30pm, Monday to Friday no restrictions except Tuesday after 11am

Please mention this guide when you write or phone to enquire about accommodation.

September to March and Thursday from 5-6pm May to August. *Society Meetings:* must register at Royal Portrush Golf Club and pay green fees before commencement of play. Professional: Dai Stevenson (R.P.G.C.) (01265 823335). Secretary: Derek Ross Williamson (01265 822996).

PORTRUSH. **Royal Portrush Golf Club,** Dunluce Road, Portrush BT56 8JQ (Portrush (0265) 822311). *Location:* one mile from Portrush on the main Portrush/Bushmills Road. Dunluce Course – natural seaside links. 18 holes, 6794 yards. S.S.S. 73. Valley Course – flat seaside links. 18 holes, 6273 yards. S.S.S. 71. Two practice grounds. *Green Fees:* Dunluce: £35.00 per day weekdays; £40.00 per day weekends. Valley: £15.00 per day weekdays; £20.00 per day weekends. *Eating facilities:* three bars, restaurant with snacks and a la carte. *Visitors:* Dunluce Course: must contact Secretary prior to visit. Restrictions Wednesday and Friday afternoons and Saturday and Sunday mornings. Valley Course: welcome weekdays, plus limited tee times at weekends. *Society Meetings:* accepted with prior booking. Professional: Dai Stevenson (0265 823335). Secretary: Miss W. Erskine (0265 822311; Fax: 0265 823139).

Armagh

ARMAGH. **County Armagh Golf Club,** The Demesne, Newry Road, Armagh BT60 1EN (01861 522501). *Location:* Newry Road out of Armagh. Parkland. 18 holes, 6157 yards, 5649 metres. S.S.S. 70. Practice area available. *Green Fees:* £12.00 weekdays, £18.00 weekends. During the months of November to February (inclusive) reduction of £1.00. *Eating facilities:* diningroom/bar meals Tuesdays to Sundays, bar facilities daily. *Visitors:* welcome by arrangement. Not Saturdays or Thursdays. *Society Meetings:* welcome by arrangement except Saturdays or Thursdays. Professional: Alan Rankin (01861 525864). Secretary: June McParland (01861 525861).

CRAIGAVON. **Craigavon Golf and Ski Club,** Turmoyra Lane, Lurgan, Craigavon (Lurgan (0762) 326606; Fax: 0762 347272). *Location:* half a mile from motorway, one mile from town centre, adjacent to ski slope. Parkland/wooded. 18 holes, 5901 metres. S.S.S. 72. 9 hole Par 3; 12 hole pitch and putt. Driving range. *Green Fees:* weekdays £8.00; weekends £11.00. *Eating facilities:* full restaurant facilities. *Visitors:* always welcome. Modern clubhouse, showers and lockers. *Society Meetings:* welcome – book beforehand. Professional: D. Paul.

CULLYHANNA. **Ashfield Golf Club,** Freeduff, Cullyhanna (01693 868180). *Location:* two miles from Crossmaglen, 15 miles from Newry. Parkland course. 18 holes, 5616 yards. S.S.S. 67. Par 69. Driving range. *Green Fees:* weekdays £8.00; weekends £10.00. *Eating facilities:* fully licensed restaurant. *Visitors:* welcome at all times except before 11am on Sundays. *Society Meetings:* welcome, special rates available. Secretary: Sean McCann.

LURGAN. **Lurgan Golf Club,** The Demesne, Lurgan, Craigavon BT67 9BN (01762 322087; Fax: 01762 325306). *Location:* one mile from motorway, half a mile from town centre. Parkland. 18 holes, 5561 metres. S.S.S. 70. Small practice area, putting green. *Green Fees:* weekdays £15.00; weekends £20.00. Reductions if playing with a member. Students £10.00, under 18's £5.00. *Eating facilities:* restaurant and lounge bar. Caterer: (01762 322337). *Visitors:* welcome Mondays, Thursdays, Friday mornings and Sundays. *Society Meetings:* welcome as per visitors. Professional: D. Paul (01762 321068). Secretary: Mrs G. Turkington (01762 322087).

PORTADOWN. **Portadown Golf Club,** 192 Gilford Road, Portadown, Craigavon BT63 5LF (01762 355356). *Location:* A59 south east of Portadown for two miles, entrance on right. Parkland. 18 holes, 5621 metres. S.S.S. 70 off white tees; 68 off green tees, 67 off yellow tees. Practice net. *Green Fees:* weekdays £15.00 (men), £12.00 (ladies); weekends and Bank Holidays £18.00 (men), £15.00 (ladies). Eating facilities: bar snacks, restaurant, members' bar and lounge. *Visitors:* welcome at all times except Tuesdays and Saturdays. Squash, indoor bowling and snooker. *Society Meetings:* catered for. Professional: Paul Stevenson (01762 334655). Secretary: Mrs Lily Holloway (01762 355356).

TANDRAGEE. **Tandragee Golf Club,** Markethill Road, Tandragee, Craigavon BT62 2ER (01762 840727). *Location:* approximately five miles from Portadown on road to Newry and Dublin. Hilly parkland and wooded. 18 holes, 5519 metres. S.S.S. 69. Practice area and net. *Green Fees:* weekdays £12.00, £10 for Ladies and Juniors; weekends £18.00. *Eating facilities:* full catering and bars. *Visitors:* welcome all days except Thursdays (Ladies Day) and Saturdays (competition day). *Society Meetings:* welcome by arrangement, except Saturdays; £11.00 weekdays, £17.00 weekends. Professional: E. Maney (01762 841651). Secretary: H. McCready (Tel & Fax: 01762 841272).

Down

ARDGLASS. **Ardglass Golf Club,** 4 Castle Place, Ardglass BT30 7TP (01396 841219; Fax: 01396 841841). *Location:* nearest town – Downpatrick. Situated on the coast 30 miles due south of Belfast. Seaside links. 18 holes, 5515 metres. S.S.S. 69. *Green Fees:* weekdays £15.00; weekends £20.00. *Eating facilities:* bar and diningroom. *Visitors:* welcome. *Society Meetings:* catered for. Advance booking necessary. Professional: Kevin Dorrian (01396 841022). Secretary: Alan Cannon (01396 841219).

BALLYNAHINCH. **Spa Golf Club,** 20 Grove Road, Ballynahinch BT24 8PN (01232 562365). *Location:* Ballynahinch half mile, Belfast 11 miles. Parkland, wooded. 18 holes, 5938 yards. S.S.S. 72. Practice area. *Green Fees:* weekdays £12.50, playing with a member £8.50; Sundays and Public Holidays £16.50. *Eating facilities:* bar snacks/restaurant service. *Visitors:* welcome except Saturdays. *Society Meetings:* welcome, discount for large party. Hon. Secretary: John M. Glass (01232 812340).

BANBRIDGE. **Banbridge Golf Club,** Huntly Road, Banbridge (Banbridge (08206) 62342). *Location:* half-a-mile out of Banbridge on Huntly Road. Parkland. 18 holes, 5453 yards, 5003 metres. S.S.S. 67. Practice ground. *Green Fees:* weekdays £7.00, with a member £5.00; weekends £12.00, with a member £6.00. *Eating facilities:* bar facilities. Meals for Societies by arrangement. *Visitors:* welcome. Restrictions on Ladies' Day (Tuesday) and Men's Competition (Saturday). *Society Meetings:* catered for. Arrange with Secretary/Manager. Secretary/Manager: Thomas F. Fee (08206 23831).

BANGOR. **Bangor Golf Club,** Broadway, Bangor BT20 4RH (01247 465133). *Location:* one mile from town centre off Donaghadee Road. Parkland. 18 holes, 6424 yards. S.S.S. 71. Practice facilities. *Green Fees:* weekdays £17.00; weekends £23.00. *Eating facilities:* diningroom (booking essential), lunches and evening meals, bar snacks. *Visitors:* welcome Monday and Wednesday, Tuesday Ladies' Day; not Saturdays. *Society Meetings:* advance booking necessary. Professional: Norman Drew (01247 462164). Secretary: Tom Russell (01247 270922).

BANGOR. **Carnalea Golf Club,** Station Road, Bangor BT19 1EZ (01247 465004). *Location:* one minute walk from Carnalea Railway Station. Seaside parkland. 18 holes, 5574 yards. S.S.S. 67. *Green Fees:* weekdays £11.00; weekends £15.00. *Eating facilities:* full restaurant and two bars. *Visitors:* welcome without reservation. *Society Meetings:* catered for. Parties comprising over 20 persons – £10.00 each. Golf Shop (01247 270122). Secretary: J.H. Crozier (01247 270368; Fax: 01247 273989).

BANGOR. **Helen's Bay Golf Club,** Golf Road, Helen's Bay, Bangor BT19 1TL (01247 852601). *Location:* A2 from Belfast – 9 miles. Parkland. 9 holes, 5176 yards. S.S.S. 67. *Green Fees:* weekdays £12.00; weekends £15.00. *Eating facilities:* available – full restaurant, bar and lounge bar. *Visitors:* welcome Monday, Wednesday and Friday; Tuesday is Ladies' Day. *Society Meetings:* catered for by prior booking confirmed by the Hon. Secretary (maximum 40). Hon. Secretary: (01247 852815).

BELFAST. **Balmoral Golf Club Ltd,** 518 Lisburn Road, Belfast BT9 6GX (01232 668540). *Location:* two miles south of Belfast City Centre, next door to King's Hall. Parkland course. 18 holes, 5702 metres. S.S.S. 70. *Green Fees:* weekdays £20.00, (Wednesdays £24.00); weekends £30.00. 10% off for Societies numbering over 20. *Eating facilities:* mixed lounge, Fred Daly Bar and Restaurant. *Visitors:* welcome except Saturdays. *Society Meetings:* Mondays and Thursdays only. Professional: G. Bleakley (01232 667747; Fax: 01232 669505). Secretary: Robert McConkey (01232 381514).

BELFAST. **Belvoir Park Golf Club,** 73 Church Road, Newtownbreda, Belfast BT8 4AN (01232 491693; Fax: 01232 646113). *Location:* three miles from city centre on road to Newcastle. Parkland – well wooded. 18 holes, 6501 yards, 5943 metres. S.S.S. 71. Practice area. *Green Fees:* weekdays (excluding Wednesday) £27.00; weekends and Wednesdays £32.00. *Eating facilities:* dining and snack meals – bar. *Visitors:* welcome except Saturday. *Society Meetings:* by prior booking only. Professional: M. Kelly (01232 646714). Secretary: Kenneth H. Graham (01232 692817).

BELFAST. **Knock Golf Club,** Summerfield, Dundonald, Belfast BT16 0QX (01232 482249). *Location:* Upper Newtownards Road in east of the city of Belfast. Parkland with huge trees, large bunkers and a stream running through the course. 18 holes, 6435 yards. S.S.S. 71. Limited practice. *Green Fees:* weekdays £20.00, weekends and Bank Holidays £25.00. Fees subject to review. Parties over 25 or more (must book in advance) £16.00 per player. *Eating facilities:* full catering and bar facilities available. *Visitors:* welcome except Saturday but it is advisable to ring Professional first. *Society Meetings:* catered for Mondays and Thursdays. Professional: G. Fairweather (01232 483825). Secretary/Manager: S.G. Managh (01232 483251).

BELFAST. **Mahee Island Golf Club,** Comber, Newtownards, Belfast BT23 6ET (01238 541234). *Location:* Comber/Killyleagh Road. After half a mile turn left signpost Ardmillan. Keep left for six miles to course. Parkland/seaside. 9 holes, 5588 yards, 5108 metres. S.S.S. 67. Par 68 over 18 holes. Practice net, green and chipping area. *Green Fees:* weekdays £11.00; weekends £16.00. *Eating facilities:* eating by prior arrangement with caterer (Dundonald 484038). *Visitors:* welcome, restricted Wednesdays after 4pm and Saturdays until 5pm. *Society Meetings:* welcome, by prior arrangement. 50p reduction when 16 or more. Professional: (Shop) Archie McCracken (01238 541234). Secretary: John McMillen (01247 278219).

BELFAST. **Mount Ober Golf and Country Club,** 20-24 Ballymaconaghy Road, Knockbracken, Belfast BT8 4SB (01232 792100; Fax: 01232 705862). *Location:* south from the centre of Belfast on the Ormeau Road to "Four Winds" public house and restaurant, half a mile out on Ballymaconaghy Road, on left by ski slopes. Parkland on undulating ground. 18 holes, 5391 yards. S.S.S. 68. Practice area, floodlit driving range. *Green Fees:* £10.00 weekdays, £9.00 with member; £12.00 weekends and Public Holidays, £10.00 with member. *Eating facilities:* full meals and snacks served. *Visitors:* welcome anytime, weekends advised to check availability of tee times. *Society Meetings:* weekdays anytime, not on Saturdays/after 10.30am on Sundays. Professional: David Jones (01232 795666). Secretary: M. Grose (01232 401811).

BELFAST. **Ormeau Golf Club,** 50 Park Road, Belfast BT7 2FX (01232 641069). *Location:* Belfast south/east; Ravenhill Road. Flat, parkland wooded course. 9 holes, 2678 yards, 2447 metres. S.S.S. 65. *Green Fees:*

£9.00 weekdays, £11.00 weekends and Holidays. *Eating facilities:* bars and restaurant. *Visitors:* welcome, restrictions on Tuesdays and Saturdays. Snooker. *Society Meetings:* welcome Thursdays or Sundays. Shop Manager: Mr B. Wilson (01232 640999). Secretary/Manager: G.E. McVeigh (01232 640700). Caterer: (01232 641999).

BELFAST. **Shandon Park Golf Club,** 73 Shandon Park, Belfast BT5 6NY (01232 793730). Parkland. 18 holes, 5714 metres. S.S.S. 70. *Green Fees:* weekdays £20.00 per round; weekends £25.00 per round. *Eating facilities:* restaurant facilities, bar snacks. *Visitors:* welcome everyday subject to advance clearance by Professional. *Society Meetings:* Mondays and Fridays only. Professional: Barry Wilson (01232 797859). Secretary: Mr Michael Corsar (01232 401856; Fax: 01232 402773).

DONAGHADEE. **Donaghadee Golf Club,** 84 Warren Road, Donaghadee BT21 0PQ (01247 888697; Fax: 01247 888891). *Location:* five miles south of Bangor on coast road. Part links and inland open, magnificent views over Copeland Islands to Scottish coast. 18 holes, 6100 yards, 5561 metres. S.S.S. 69. Practice ground. *Green Fees:* weekdays £14.00; Sundays £18.00. *Eating facilities:* restaurant, bar and snacks except Mondays. *Visitors:* welcome any day except Saturdays. *Society Meetings:* welcome, reductions for groups numbering over 24. Professional: Gordon Drew (01247 882392). Secretary/Manager: M.E. Dilley (01247 883624).

DOWNPATRICK. **Bright Castle Golf Club,** 14 Coniamstown Road, Bright, Downpatrick BT30 8LU (0396 841319). *Location:* off the main Downpatrick Killough Road approximately two and a half miles off main road. Parkland – excellent fairways and greens, plenty trees. 18 holes, 7143 yards. S.S.S. 74. Putting green. *Green Fees:* information not provided. *Eating facilities:* snacks available. *Visitors:* very welcome, no restrictions. *Society Meetings:* very welcome, tee must be reserved. Secretary: Raymond Reid.

DOWNPATRICK. **Downpatrick Golf Club,** 43 Saul Road, Downpatrick BT30 6PA (01396 612152). *Location:* one and a half miles from town centre, south-east direction. Parkland, challenging upland course. 18 holes, 6400 yards. S.S.S. 69. Putting area. *Green Fees:* weekdays £14.00; weekends £18.00. 20% discount on weekdays for groups of 20 plus. *Eating facilities:* two lounges, diningroom and snack bar. Catering: (01396 615244). *Visitors:* welcome. Snooker room. *Society Meetings:* welcome by prior arrangement. Professional: (01396 615167). Secretary: Daniel McGreevy (01396 615947).

HOLYWOOD. **Holywood Golf Club,** Nuns Walk, Demesne Road, Holywood BT18 9LE (01232 422138). Parkland. 18 holes, 5430 yards. S.S.S. 68. *Green Fees:* weekdays £15.00; weekends £20.00. *Eating facilities:* bars and restaurant. *Visitors:* welcome, Thursday is Ladies' Day. *Society Meetings:* welcome Mondays, Tuesdays, Wednesdays and Fridays and between 8am and 9am Sundays. Discounts for groups of 20 plus weekdays. Professional: Michael Bannon (01232 425503). General Manager: Robin Kirk (01232 423135; Fax: 01232 425040).

HOLYWOOD. **The Royal Belfast Golf Club,** Craigavad, Holywood BT18 0BP (01232 422368). *Location:* two miles past Holywood, off main Belfast to Bangor Road. Mainly parkland, bordering shores of Belfast Lough. 18 holes, 5963 yards. S.S.S. 69. Practice ground. *Green Fees:* weekdays £25.00; Saturday after 4.30pm and Sundays £30.00. *Eating facilities:* full catering and bar facilities. *Visitors:* with letter of introduction and by arrangement only. *Society Meetings:* by arrangement. Professional: D.H. Carson (01232 428586). Secretary: I.M. Piggot (01232 428165).

KILKEEL. **Kilkeel Golf Club,** Mourne Park, Kilkeel (016937 62296). *Location:* 16 miles from Newcastle and three miles from Kilkeel on main road to Newry. Parkland, wooded, undulating. 18 holes, 6650 metres. S.S.S. 72. Practice area available. *Green Fees:* weekdays £16.00 for 18 holes; weekends £18.00 for 18 holes. *Eating facilities:* full catering services on application, bar facilities. *Visitors:* welcome all week except Saturdays. *Society Meetings:* catered for by prior arrangement. Secretary: S.C. McBride (016937 63787).

LISBURN. **Down Royal Park,** Dunygarton Road, Maze, Lisburn BT27 5RT (0846 621339). *Location:* inside Maze Racecourse. Heathland. 18 holes, 6824 yards. *Green Fees:* weekdays £11.00; Saturdays £13.00; Sundays £17.00. *Eating facilities:* licensed restaurant. *Visitors:* welcome at all times. *Society Meetings:* welcome. Secretary: N.F. Ewing (acting).

NEWCASTLE. **Royal County Down Golf Club,** Newcastle BT33 0AN. *Location:* adjacent to north side of Newcastle, approach from town centre. Championship Course: 18 holes, 6968 yards. Course: 18 holes, 4100 yards. S.S.S. 60. *Green Fees:* weekdays Summer £43.00, Winter £32.00; weekends Summer £55.00, Winter £43.00. *Eating facilities:* light lunches and bar, weekdays only. *Visitors:* welcome with prior reservation. *Society Meetings:* catered for. Professional: Kevan J. Whitson (013967 22419). Secretary: P.E. Rolph (013967 23314; Fax: 013967 26281).

NEWTOWNARDS. **Clandeboye Golf Club,** Tower Road, Conlig, Newtownards BT23 3PN (01247 271767). *Location:* Conlig village off A21 between Bangor and Newtownards. Wooded, undulating parkland/heathland. Two courses: (1) 18 holes, 6548 yards, S.S.S. 71. (2) 18 holes, 5755 yards, S.S.S. 68. Practice ground. *Green Fees:* weekdays £21.00 and £17.00; weekends £13.00 and £12.00 with a member only. *Eating facilities:* full catering and bar. *Visitors:* welcome weekdays; Saturdays and Sundays must be accompanied by member. (Thursday ladies' day). *Society Meetings:* welcome weekdays except Thursdays (in winter Mondays and Wednesdays only). Reduced rates for parties over 20. Professional: Peter Gregory (01247 271750). Secretary/Manager: Ian Marks (01247 271767).

NEWTOWNARDS. **Kirkistown Castle Golf Club,** 142 Main Road, Cloughey, Newtownards (012477 71353). *Location:* A20 west of Belfast then B173. Seaside links. 18 holes, 6176 yards. S.S.S. 70. *Green Fees:* £13.00 weekdays; £25.00 weekends and Public Holidays. Weekly ticket £50. Subject to review. Tourists 10% discount in approved hotels. *Eating facilities:* full catering and snacks. *Visitors:* welcome, Friday Ladies' Day, tee reserved 10.30-11.30am, 1.30-2.30pm and 5.30-6pm. Saturday Men's competition day, tee opens approximately 2.30pm, Sunday tee reserved 9-10.30am and 12 noon to 1.30pm. *Society Meetings:* welcome by arrangement. Professional: Jonathan Peden (Tel & Fax; 012477 71004). Secretary: D.J. Ryan (012477 71233; Fax: 012477 71699).

NEWTOWNARDS. **Scrabo Golf Club,** 233 Scrabo Road, Newtownards BT23 4SL (01247 812355). *Location:* approximately 10 miles from Belfast off main Belfast to Newtownards dual carriageway. Upland course. 18 holes, 5699 metres. S.S.S. 71. *Green Fees:* weekdays £15.00; weekends £20.00. Societies weekdays £12.00; weekends £19.00. *Eating facilities:* highly recommended full catering facilities. *Visitors:* welcome except Saturdays. *Society Meetings:* over 20 players, welcome. Professional: G. Fairweather (01247 817848) Secretary/Manager: James Fraser (01247 812355).

WARRENPOINT. **Warrenpoint Golf Club,** Lower Dromore Road, Warrenpoint (Warrenpoint (06937) 52219). *Location:* five miles south of Newry on coast road. Parkland. 18 holes, 5640 metres. S.S.S.70. *Green Fees:* weekdays £15.00, weekends £21.00. *Eating facilities:* full catering and bar facilities. *Visitors:* welcome Sunday, Monday, Thursday, Friday. Squash, snooker facilities available. *Society Meetings:* catered for by prior arrangement. Professional: Nigel Shaw (06937 52371). Secretary: John McMahon (06937 53695; Fax: 06937 52918).

Fermanagh

ENNISKILLEN. **Ashwoods Golf Centre,** Ashwoods, Enniskillen (0365 325321). *Location:* one and a half miles west of Enniskillen on main road to Sligo. Meadowland, wooded and landscaped. 9 holes, 1250 yards. Golf driving range. *Green Fees:* weekdays £3.00; weekends £4.00. *Eating facilities:* available. *Visitors:* welcome, no restrictions. 12 bedroomed guesthouse (licensed). Golf clubs available for hire. *Society Meetings:* welcome, bookings in advance. Professional: Thomas Loughran. Secretary: Mrs Peggy McManus.

ENNISKILLEN. **Castle Hume Golf Club,** Castle Hume, Enniskillen (01365 327077). *Location:* Belleek Road, Enniskillen. Parkland course; 11th fairway, 15th green and 16th tee are situated on the lough shore. 18 holes, 5941 metres. S.S.S. 72. Putting green and practice area. *Green Fees:* weekdays £10.00; weekends £12.00. Excess of 12 players £2.00 reduction per person. *Eating facilities:* available by arrangement. *Visitors:* welcome, no restrictions. *Society Meetings:* all welcome. Secretary: Daphne Gibson.

ENNISKILLEN. **Enniskillen Golf Club,** Castlecoole, Enniskillen BT74 6HZ (01365 325250). *Location:* off Enniskillen to Tempo Road on outskirts of town. Undulating parkland with many mature trees. 18 holes, 5990 yards, 5574 metres. S.S.S. 70. *Green Fees:* weekdays £10.00; weekends £12.00. *Eating facilities:* bar snacks daily – full catering by arrangement. *Visitors:* welcome at all times, Ladies have priority on Tuesdays. *Society Meetings:* welcome. Special rates. Hon. Secretary: W.J. Hamilton (01365 323206).

Londonderry

CASTLEROCK. **Castlerock Golf Club,** 65 Circular Road, Castlerock, Coleraine BT51 4TJ (01265 848215; Fax: 01265 848314 office hours only). *Location:* A2, six miles west of Coleraine. Seaside links, stream in play at four holes. 18 holes, 6687 yards. S.S.S. 72. 9 holes, 2457 metres. S.S.S. 67. Practice area. *Green Fees:* weekdays £18.00 per round; weekends £30.00. Subject to review. *Eating facilities:* full restaurant facilities, two bars. *Visitors:* weekdays no restrictions; casual green fees welcome Sundays. *Society Meetings:* welcome weekdays. Professional: R. Kelly (01265 848314). Secretary: R.G. McBride (01265 848314).

COLERAINE. **Brown Trout Golf and Country Club,** 209 Agivey Road, Aghadowey, Near Coleraine (01265 868209; Fax: 01265 868878). *Location:* on A54 between Kilrea and Coleraine. Parkland course, heavily wooded, crossing water seven times in nine holes. 9 holes, 2755 metres. S.S.S. 68. *Green Fees:* weekdays £8.00; weekends £12.00. *Eating facilities:* à la carte restaurant, bar snacks, barbecues. *Visitors:* always welcome. 15 new luxurious en suite bedrooms available. *Society Meetings:* welcome. Professional: Ken Revie. Secretary/Manager: Bill O'Hara.

LIMAVADY. **Benone Golf Course,** 53 Benone Avenue, Benone, Limavady (015047 50555; Fax: 015047 22010). *Location:* situated on the A2 coast road, 12 miles from Limavady. Parkland course with characteristic stream. 9 holes, 1427 yards, 1305 metres. S.S.S. 27. Practice range, putting green. *Green Fees:* weekdays £3.20 adults, £1.85 Juniors; weekends £3.75 adults, £2.70 Juniors. *Eating facilities:* coffee shop open July/August, restaurants within one mile. *Visitors:* welcome. Secretary: The Warden (015047 50555).

MAGHERAFELT. **Moyola Park Golf Club,** Shanemullagh, Castledawson, Magherafelt BT45 8DG (01648 68468). *Location:* 40 miles north of Belfast on M2. Attractive, spacious mature parkland. 18 holes, 6517 yards. S.S.S. 71. Practice ground, putting green. *Green Fees:* weekdays £12.00, with a member £8.00; weekends £22.00, with a member £12. *Eating facilities:* bars and restaurant. *Visitors:* welcome weekdays except Wednesdays and Sundays (1.30pm to 2.30pm only, must be pre-booked). *Society Meetings:* welcome with prior notice. Professional: Mr V. Teague (01648 68830). Secretary: Mr L.W.P. Hastings (01648 32796/ 31271).

PORTSTEWART. **Portstewart Golf Club,** Strand Head, Portstewart (0126583 2015; Fax: 0126583 4097). *Location:* north from Coleraine. Coastal links. No 1 Strand – 18 holes, 6784 yards, S.S.S. 73. No 2 Riverside – 9 holes, 2622 yards. No 3 Old – 18 holes, 4733 yards, S.S.S. 64. Practice area. *Green Fees:* weekdays Strand £22, Riverside £10, Old £7; weekends Strand £30, Riverside £15, Old £11. *Eating facilities:* meals available – advance orders. *Visitors:* welcome Mondays to Fridays. Prior booking essential on Strand. Enquire about special rates for parties. *Society Meetings:* catered for by arrangement. Professional: Alan Hunter (0126583 2601). Secretary: Michael Moss.

PREHEN. **City of Derry Golf Club,** 49 Victoria Road, Prehen BT47 2PU (01504 46369). *Location:* three miles from city centre on the road to Strabane – follow the River Foyle. Parkland, wooded. 18 holes, 6362 yards. S.S.S. 71. Also 18 hole course, 4708 yards. Par 71. Practice area. *Green Fees:* weekdays £11.00, with a member £9.00; weekends £13.00, £11.00 with a member. *Eating facilities:* catering and bar facilities available. *Visitors:* welcome on weekdays up to 4.30pm, weekends please contact Professional. Convenient for hotels and guest houses. *Society Meetings:* welcome, please contact Secretary. Professional: Mr Michael Doherty (01504 311496). Secretary: Mr Colum Murphy (01504 46369).

Tyrone

COOKSTOWN. **Killymoon Golf Club,** Killymoon Road, Cookstown (016487 62254). *Location:* private road off A29. Signposted at Dungannon end of town opposite Drum Road. Mainly flat parkland. 18 holes, 5513 metres. S.S.S. 69. Practice area. *Green Fees:* weekdays £14.00; weekends and Bank Holidays £18.00. *Eating facilities:* full catering at club (large groups please book). *Visitors:* welcome. No visitors Saturdays until after 5pm; Thursdays Ladies' Day. Booking essential. *Society Meetings:* Sundays limit 32, Saturdays none, weekdays welcome but ladies have priority Thursdays. Societies of 20 or more £11.00 weekdays, £15.00 weekends. Professional: Barry Hamill (016487 63460). Secretary: Les Hodgett (016487 63762).

DUNGANNON. **Dungannon Golf Club,** 34 Springfield Lane, Dungannon BT70 1QX (018687 27338). *Location:* one mile west of Dungannon, to right of Dungannon to Donaghmore Road. Flat first nine holes, hilly last nine holes. 18 holes, 5904 yards. S.S.S. 68. Putting area. *Green Fees:* £10.00 weekdays; £13.00 weekends and Bank Holidays. £2.00 discount if playing with a member. *Eating facilities:* catering by prior arrangement. *Visitors:* welcome, precluded by timesheets weekends/competitions. *Society Meetings:* welcome, especially midweek. Secretary: L.R.P Agnew (018687 27338/22098).

FINTONA. **Fintona Golf Club,** Kiln Street, Ecclesville, Demesne, Fintona (0662 841480). *Location:* eight miles south of Omagh, county town of Tyrone. Parkland with a river running through the course. 9 holes, 5716 metres. S.S.S. 70. *Green Fees:* information not provided. *Eating facilities:* bar food. *Visitors:* welcome daily but check by telephoning at weekends. Snooker tables. *Society Meetings:* catered for by advance booking. Secretary: G. McNulty (0662 841514).

NEWTOWNSTEWART. **Newtownstewart Golf Club,** 38 Golf Course Road, Newtownstewart, Omagh BT78 4HH (016626 61466). *Location:* signposted from Strabane Road (A57) at Newtownstewart, two miles west of Newtownstewart on B84. Parkland and wooded course. 18 holes, 5869 yards, 5341 metres. S.S.S. 69. Practice ground adjacent to clubhouse. *Green Fees:* weekdays £10.00; weekends £15.00. Weekly £60.00. Monthly £90. *Eating facilities:* available. *Visitors:* welcome at all times except during club competitions. Accommodation available in chalets beside clubhouse. *Society Meetings:* all welcome but should be affiliated to G.U. Secretary/Manageress: Mrs D. Marshall (016626 71487).

If you are writing, a stamped, addressed envelope is always appreciated.

OMAGH. **Omagh Golf Club,** 83a Dublin Road, Omagh BT78 1HQ (01662 243160). *Location:* one mile from Omagh town centre on Belfast/Dublin Road. Parkland. 18 holes, 5636 metres. S.S.S. 70. *Green Fees:* weekdays £10.00; weekends and Bank Holidays £15.00. £2.00 reduction if playing with a member, Senior Citizens and students half price. *Eating facilities:* snacks and bar facilities. *Visitors:* welcome any day except Tuesday and Saturday. Special arrangements with Royal Arms Hotel for guests. *Society Meetings:* welcome. Secretary: Florence E.A. Caldwell (01662 241442).

STRABANE. **Strabane Golf Club,** Ballycolman Road, Strabane (0504 382271). *Location:* Omagh – Strabane main road. Parkland. 18 holes, 5552 metres. S.S.S. 69. *Green Fees:* weekdays £10.00, £8.00 with a member; weekends £12.00, £10.00 with a member. *Eating facilities:* two bars, catering by arrangement. *Visitors:* welcome by arrangement. *Society Meetings:* by arrangement with Secretary. Secretary: Terry Doherty (0504 382007).

Republic of Ireland

COUNTY CARLOW

CARLOW. **Carlow Golf Club,** Deer Park, Carlow (0503 31695). *Location:* 52 miles south of Dublin, two miles north of Carlow town on N9. Parkland. 18 holes, 5844 metres. S.S.S. 70. *Green Fees:* weekdays IR£20.00; weekends IR£25.00. Weekly ticket IR£70.00. Groups of 12 or more IR£18.00 weekdays, £22.00 weekends. *Eating facilities:* restaurant open all day, bar open from 9.30am – 12 midnight. *Visitors:* welcome Monday to Friday, avoid Tuesday (Ladies' Day), Saturdays difficult, Sundays impossible, pre-booking advisable. *Society Meetings:* must be pre-booked with Secretary. Professional: Andrew Gilbert (0503 41745). Secretary: Margaret Meaney (0503 31695; Fax: 0503 40065).

COUNTY CAVAN

BLACKLION. **Blacklion Golf Club,** Toam, Blacklion, via Sligo (072 53024; from the UK 010 353 72 53024). *Location:* Blacklion/Belcoo on Enniskillen to Sligo Road. Flat parkland, wooded copses, lake partially in play, scenic. 9 holes, 6175 yards, 5614 metres. S.S.S. 69. *Green Fees:* IR£5.00 weekdays; IR£8.00 weekends. Group rates by prior arrangement. *Eating facilities:* bar with bar snacks. *Visitors:* welcome weekdays, Sundays after 4pm. *Society Meetings:* by arrangement. Hon. Secretary: Robert Thompson.

DRUMELIS. **County Cavan Golf Club,** Aranmore House, Drumelis (049 312 83). *Location:* county town of Cavan. Parkland course. 18 holes, 5519 metres.

NOTE

All the information in this book is given in good faith in the belief that it is correct. However, the publishers cannot guarantee the facts given in these pages, neither are they responsible for changes in policy, ownership or terms that may take place after the date of going to press. Readers should always satisfy themselves that the facilities they require are available and that the terms, if quoted, still apply.

S.S.S 69. *Green Fees:* information not provided. *Eating facilities:* available. *Visitors:* welcome throughout the year. *Society Meetings:* welcome with pre-booking. Secretary: Donal Crotty (049 31643).

COUNTY CLARE

LAHINCH. **Lahinch Golf Club,** Lahinch (065 81003; Fax: 065 81592). *Location:* 30 miles north west of Shannon Airport, 200 yards from Lahinch Village on Lisconner Road. Links course. Old Course – 18 holes, 6699 yards. S.S.S. 67. *Green Fees:* on application. *Visitors:* weekdays only, by arrangement. *Society Meetings:* catered for by arrangement. Professional: R. McCavery (065 81408). Secretary: M. Murphy.

COUNTY CORK

CARRIGROHANE. **Muskerry Golf Club,** Carrigrohane (021 385104). *Location:* seven and a half miles north west of Cork City. Parkland/wooded, two rivers. 18 holes, 5426 metres. S.S.S. 70. *Green Fees:* weekdays £15.00; weekends £17.00. *Eating facilities:* available. *Visitors:* welcome weekdays – Monday and Tuesday all day, Wednesday up to 11.30am, Thursday after 12.30pm and Friday up to 3.30pm; weekends as available. Members' hour weekdays 1pm to 2pm. *Society Meetings:* welcome. Professional: W.M. Lehane (021 381445). Secretary: J.J. Moynihan (Tel & Fax: 021 3852970).

CASTLETOWNBERE. **Berehaven Golf Links,** Filane, Castletownbere, Beara (027 70700). *Location:* by the main Castletownbere – Glengarriff Road. Seaside links. 9 holes, 4748 metres. S.S.S. 64. *Green Fees:* £8.00 weekdays; £10.00 weekends. *Eating facilities:* bar and restaurant. *Visitors:* welcome at all times. Tennis, crazy golf and swimming facilities. Camping site. *Society Meetings:* welcome by appointment. Secretary: A. Harrington.

CHARLEVILLE. **Charleville Golf Club,** Charleville (063 81257; Fax: 063 81274). *Location:* main road from Limerick to Cork, 25 miles from Limerick. Parkland, very wooded. 18 holes, 6430 yards. S.S.S. 70. Practice area. *Green Fees:* weekdays £12.00; weekends £15.00. *Eating facilities:* full eating facilities and bar. *Visitors:* welcome, weekends by appointment. *Society Meetings:* welcome. Special rates apply. Secretary: James A. Murphy (063 81257).

DOUGLAS. **Douglas Golf Club,** Douglas (021 891086; Fax: 021 895297). *Location:* in Douglas Village, three miles to the south of Cork City. Parkland course – very flat. 18 holes, 5664 yards. S.S.S. 69. *Green Fees:* weekdays £17.00 (18 holes); weekends £19.00. *Eating facilities:* full restaurant and bar available. *Visitors:* Monday, Wednesday, Thursday, Friday mornings, preferably mid-morning; Saturday and Sunday after 2pm. Advisable to check in advance. *Society Meetings:* welcome but bookings are made in January each year. Professional: Gary Nicholson (021 362055). Secretary/Manager: Brian Barrett (021 895297).

LITTLE ISLAND. **Cork Golf Club,** Little Island (021 353451; Fax: 021 353410). *Location:* five miles east of Cork City N25, signposted. Parkland, very scenic championship course. 18 holes, 6065 metres. S.S.S. 72, 70. Practice ground. *Green Fees:* weekdays £23.00; weekends £26.00. Special rates for groups of 20 or more: Monday and Tuesday £18.00, Friday, Saturday and Sunday £20.00. Subject to review. *Eating facilities:* full catering facilities, bar. *Visitors:* welcome Mondays, Tuesdays, Wednesdays and Fridays except 12.30 to 2pm; Thursday, weekends ring in advance. *Society Meetings:* catered for, arrange with Secretary/Manager. Professional: Ted Higgins (021 353451). Secretary: Matt Sands (021 353451).

LITTLE ISLAND. **Harbour Point Golf Club,** Clash Road, Little Island (021 353094; Fax: 021 354408). *Location:* enter Little Island by taking a right off the main Cork/Rosslare Road, then take your next left and then right. Parkland course by banks of River Lee. 18 holes, 6630 yards, 6063 metres. S.S.S. 72. 21 bay floodlit driving range. *Green Fees:* £20.00. £10.00 before 11am Monday, Wednesday, Thursday and Friday. *Eating facilities:* full restaurant and bar facilities. *Visitors:* welcome anytime by appointment. *Society Meetings:* welcome every day; £15.00 per person for groups of 20 or more.

TIVOLI. **Silver Springs Golf Club,** Tivoli, Cork (021 507533; Fax: 021 507641). *Location:* five minutes from Cork city centre. Hilly parkland. 9 holes, 1420 metres. S.S.S. 64 for 18 holes. *Green Fees:* weekdays £5.00; weekends £7.00. Special rates for groups of 20 or more. *Eating facilities:* full catering facilities and beverage facilities. *Visitors:* welcome, ring beforehand. Hotel on site, accommodation available. Full sports centre, indoor pool, squash, indoor tennis, sauna & steam bath, gym. *Society Meetings:* all welcome, phone bookings in advance. Manager: Ria Hunt.

YOUGHAL. **Youghal Golf Club,** Knockaverry, Youghal (024 92787; Fax: 024 92641). *Location:* N25 main road from Rosslare to Cork. Parkland, seaside course with panoramic views of Youghal Bay/Blackwater Estuary. 18 holes, 6300 yards. S.S.S. 69. *Green Fees:* £14.00 IR. *Eating facilities:* full bar and restaurant facilities. *Visitors:* welcome mid-week, phone re weekends and Wednesdays (Ladies' Day). *Society Meetings:* welcome, please phone. Special rates available. Professional: Liam Burns (024 92590). Secretary: Margaret O'Sullivan.

COUNTY DONEGAL

BUNDORAN. **Bundoran Golf Club,** Great Northern Hotel, Bundoran (072 41302). *Location:* 25 miles from Sligo on edge of Bundoran Town. Parkland, seaside; not wooded. 18 holes, 6121 yards, 5599 metres. S.S.S. 70. Practice ground. *Green Fees:* weekdays £12.00; weekends £14. *Eating facilities:* snacks in bar. *Visitors:* preferably weekdays but always welcome. Locker rooms. *Society Meetings:* very welcome with due notice. Professional: David Robinson (072 41302). Secretary: Liam M. Devitt.

LAGHEY. **Donegal Golf Club,** Murvagh, Laghey (073 34054; Fax: 073 34377). *Location:* N15 off main Donegal/Ballyshannon Road. Seaside links course. 18 holes, 6867 yards, 6243 metres. S.S.S. 73. Practice ground. *Eating facilities:* restaurant and bar. *Visitors:* welcome, restrictions weekends and Mondays. *Society Meetings:* all welcome. Administrator: John McBride (073 34054).

LETTERKENNY. **Dunfanaghy Golf Club,** Dunfanaghy, Letterkenny (074 36335). *Location:* on main Letterkenny to Dunfanaghy Road – N56. Seaside links. 18 holes, 5066 metres. S.S.S. 66. *Green Fees:* IR£10.00 weekdays; IR£12.00 weekends. *Eating facilities:* bar snacks – soup, tea and sandwiches. *Visitors:* welcome at all times, restriction on weekend mornings. *Society Meetings:* welcome most days by booking. Club Secretary: Mary Quinn.

LETTERKENNY. **Portsalon Golf Club,** Portsalon, Fanad (074 59459). *Location:* 20 miles north of Letterkenny. Seaside links. 18 holes, 5878 yards, 5379 metres. S.S.S. 68. *Green Fees:* £12.00, playing with a full member £7.00. *Eating facilities:* diningroom and bar in clubhouse. *Visitors:* welcome, please telephone for weekends. *Society Meetings:* welcome weekdays and some weekends, must book in advance with Secretary. Secretary: C. Toland.

COUNTY DUBLIN

BALBRIGGAN. **Balbriggan Golf Club,** Blackhall, Balbriggan (018412173). *Location:* quarter of a mile south of Balbriggan on main Belfast/Dublin Road. Parkland course with fine views of Cooley Peninsula and Mourne Mountains. 18 holes, 2968 metres. S.S.S. 71. *Green Fees:* £14.00 weekdays; £18.00 weekends. *Eating facilities:* full restaurant and snacks. *Visitors:* welcome, Tuesday Ladies' Day, Saturdays and Sundays not good as club competitions take place. *Society Meetings:* catered for Mondays, Wednesdays, Thursdays and Fridays. Secretary: Michael O'Halloran (018412229).

CLONSILLA. **Luttrellston Castle Golf and Country Club,** Clonsilla (8208210; Fax: 820427). *Location:* in the west of Co. Dublin beside Phoenix Park (off N4 and M50). Six miles from Dublin City and Airport. Parkland setting with ornamental lakes. 18 holes, 7091 yards, 6447 metres. S.S.S. 73. *Green Fees:* weekdays £30.00, weekends £35.00. Reductions for parties over 40 in number. *Eating facilities:* two restaurants and bars. *Visitors:* some tee times reserved for members – details on request. Accommodation available at Luttrellston Castle. *Society Meetings:* welcome at weekends subject to availability. Acting Secretary: Linda Halpin (8213237; Fax: 8213241).

DONABATE. **Corballis Public Golf Course,** Donabate (8436583). *Location:* main Dublin to Belfast Road. Links course. 18 holes, 4791 yards. S.S.S. 64. *Green Fees:* weekdays £7.00; weekends £8.00. Unemployed, Senior Citizens and Students £3.00. *Eating facilities:* snack food. *Visitors:* welcome anytime. *Society Meetings:* welcome. Secretary: P.J. Boylan.

DUBLIN. **Deer Park,** Howth, Co. Dublin (01 832 2624. Fax: 01 839 2405). *Location:* Deer Park Hotel, 9 miles east of the city centre, 3rd turn after Sutton Cross. Public parkland courses of 18 holes (6770 yards) par 72; two 9-holes (3100 yards and 3370 yards) each par 3 and 12-hole par 3. Pitch and putt. *Green Fees:* 18 holes weekdays £7.60; weekends £9.60. 9 holes from £3.80 weekdays. *Eating facilities:* full facilities and Hotel on site. *Visitors:* welcome at all times, weekends very busy. *Society Meetings:* welcome weekdays and Saturdays.

DUBLIN. **Elm Park Golf and Sports Club,** Nutley House, Donnybrook, Dublin 4 (0001 2693438; Fax: 2694505). *Location:* between R.T.E. and St. Vincent's Hospital. Flat parkland course. 18 holes, 5929 yards, 5422 metres. S.S.S. 68. *Green Fees:* £30.00 weekdays; £35.00 weekends. Subject to review. *Eating facilities:* full bar and dining facilities. *Visitors:* welcome but must telephone to arrange times with Professional. *Society Meetings:* by special arrangement. Professional: S. Green (0001 2692650). Secretary: A. McCormack.

DUBLIN. **The Royal Dublin Golf Club,** North Bull Island, Dollymount, Dublin 3 (0001 337153). *Location:* three and a half miles north east of city centre on coast road to Howith. Seaside links. 18 holes, 6850 yards, 6262 metres. S.S.S. 71. Large practice ground. *Green Fees:* weekdays £35.00 IR; weekends £45.00 IR. *Eating facilities:* grill room, restaurant, two bars. *Visitors:* Monday, Tuesday, Thursday, Friday and Sunday 10.30 to 12.30. *Society Meetings:* catered for, written application must be made. Tournament Professional: Christy O'Connor. Professional: Leonard Owens (0001 336477). Secretary: J.A. Lambe (0001 336346; Fax: 0001 336504).

DUN LAOGHAIRE. **Dun Laoghaire Golf Club,** Eglinton Park, Tivoli Road, Dun Laoghaire (01 2805116). *Location:* half a mile from town centre and ferry port. Parkland. 18 holes, 5495 metres. S.S.S. 68. *Green Fees:* IR£25.00. *Eating facilities:* restaurant, snacks and bar. *Visitors:* welcome except Saturdays. *Society Meetings:* welcome. Professional: Owen Mulhall (01 2801694). Secretary: Terry Stewart (01 2803916; Fax: 01 2804868).

FOXROCK. **Leopardstown Golf Course,** Foxrock Village, Dublin 18 (01 2895341). *Location:* five miles south of Dublin city centre, situated in Leopardstown race course. Flat parkland. 18 holes, 5300 yards. S.S.S. 69. 80 bay floodlit driving range. *Green Fees:* weekdays £IR6.50; weekends £IR9.00. *Eating facilities:* restaurant. *Visitors:* welcome. *Society Meetings:* welcome. Professional: Mr Dominic Reilly (01 2893511). Manager: Michael Hoey.

PORTMARNOCK. **Portmarnock Golf Club,** Portmarnock (0001 8462969; Fax: 0001 8462601). *Location:* 8 miles NE of Dublin along north coast, four miles from Airport. Seaside links – winds. Three courses: 'A' – 27 holes, 7097 yards. S.S.S. 75. 'B' – 7047 yards. S.S.S. 75. 'C' – 6596 yards. S.S.S. 74. Practice area. *Green Fees:* IR£40.00 weekdays (Ladies IR£30.00); IR£50.00 weekends. *Eating facilities:* available. *Visitors:* by arrangement, restriction weekends and Bank Holidays. *Society Meetings:* on application, 12 or more Mondays, Tuesdays and Fridays only. Professional: J. Purcell (0001 8462634). Secretary: W. Bornemann (0001 8462968).

ST. MARGARET'S. **St. Margaret's Golf and Country Club,** St. Margaret's (8640400; Fax: 8640289). *Location:* eight miles north of Dublin city centre, three miles from Dublin Airport. Parkland, ultra-modern design by Craddock and Ruddy. 18 holes, 6900 yards. Putting and practice areas. *Green Fees:* £30.00 weekdays; £35.00 weekends. 10% discount for groups. *Eating facilities:* full bar and restaurant facilities. *Visitors:* welcome at all times. *Society Meetings:* welcome. Director of Golf: Paul Henry. General Manager: Denis Kane.

SUTTON. **Howth Golf Club,** St. Fintan's, Carrickbrack Road, Sutton, Dublin 13 (01 8323055; Fax: 01 8321793). *Location:* one and a half miles from Sutton Cross on city side of Hill of Howth. Moorland course with scenic views of Dublin Bay – very hilly. 18 holes, 5419 metres. S.S.S. 68. *Green Fees:* Mondays to Thursdays £16.00, Fridays £18.00. *Eating facilities:* bar snacks from 11am. *Visitors:* welcome weekdays except Wednesdays. *Society Meetings:* bookings accepted by arrangement with Secretary. Reduced rates for large groups. Professional: John McGuirk (01 322844). Secretary: Mrs Ann MacNeice.

COUNTY GALWAY

CLIFDEN. **Connemara Golf Club,** Aillebrack, Ballyconneely, Near Clifden (095 23502/23602; Fax: 095 23662). *Location:* nine miles south west of Clifden. Seaside links. Championship course: 18 holes, 6790 yards, 6173 metres. S.S.S. 73. Medal course: 18 holes, 6173 metres. S.S.S. 73. Practice fairway. *Green Fees:* £18.00 per round. *Eating facilities:* à la carte restaurant and bar. *Visitors:* Monday to Saturday preferable, booking in advance advised particularly during Summer. *Society Meetings:* groups of 20 or more £12.00 per person (rate does not apply from July to August inclusive). Secretary: John McLaughlin.

LOUGHREA. **Loughrea Golf Club,** Loughrea (091 41049). Location: one and a half miles north east of town, on New Inn Road. Parkland, undulating, with beautiful views of town and Sl. Aughty Mountains in background. 18 holes, 5613 yards. Par 69. Practice area. *Green Fees:* information not provided. *Eating facilities:* light snacks and bar. *Visitors:* welcome weekdays and open days. *Society Meetings:* welcome, please telephone. Secretary: Brendan Blake (091 41339).

COUNTY KERRY

BALLYBUNION. **Ballybunion Golf Club,** Saudhill Road, Ballybunion (068 27146; Fax: 068 27387). *Location:* 20 miles from Tralee, 10 miles from Listowll. Seaside links. Two courses. 36 holes, 6800 yards. S.S.S. 71. *Green Fees:* £30.00 single round; £40.00 to play both courses. *Eating facilities:* full bar and catering facilities. *Visitors:* welcome, subject to availability. *Society Meetings:* catered for. Professional: Brian O'Callaghan (068 27146). Secretary: Jim McKenna (068 27146).

Please mention this guide when you write or phone to enquire about accommodation.

BALLYFERRITER. **Ceann Sibeal (Dingle) Golf Club,** Ballyferriter (066 56255; Fax: 066 56409). *Location:* turn right quarter of a mile after Ballyferriter. Traditional links, most westerly golf course in Europe. 18 holes, 6650 yards. S.S.S. 71. Practice ground. *Green Fees:* weekdays £18.00 per round, £21.00 per day; weekends £18 per round, £23.00 per day. *Eating facilities:* diningroom, bar, full facilities. *Visitors:* welcome at all times, book in advance. Hotel adjacent. *Society Meetings:* all welcome. Professional: Dermot O'Connor. Secretary: Garry Partington.

KENMARE. **Kenmare Golf Club,** Kenmare (064 41291). *Location:* outside Kenmare town on main Cork/Kilgarvan Road. Partly links, partly parkland surrounded by some breathtaking views. 18 holes, 5950 yards. S.S.S. 68. Putting green. *Green Fees:* £12.50. Groups of 18 and over £10.00 each. *Eating facilities:* snacks only in bar. *Visitors:* welcome, please enquire as to availability on weekends. Club hire, pull-cart hire. *Society Meetings:* welcome, must book well in advance and deposit required. Manager: Michael Fitzgerald. Secretary: Siobhan O'Connor.

KILLARNEY. **Killarney Golf and Fishing Club,** Mahony's Point, Killarney (064 31034; Fax: 064 33065). *Location:* Killarney town, two miles west on Ring of Kerry road. Undulating parkland courses – lakeside. Mahony's Point: 18 holes, 6152 metres. S.S.S. 72. Killeen: 18 holes, 6457 yards. S.S.S. 73. Practice area. *Green Fees:* information on request. *Eating facilities:* available all day. *Visitors:* welcome at all times, reservations in advance, Handicap Certificate required. *Society Meetings:* welcome. Professional: T. Coveney (064 31615). Secretary: T. Prendergast.

KILLORGLIN. **Killorglin Golf Club,** Stealrue, Killorglin (066 61979; Fax: 066 61437). *Location:* three km from Killorglin on N70, just off Ring of Kerry road; Killarney 20 km. Parkland course overlooking Dingle Bay. 18 holes, 6464 yards. S.S.S. 72. *Green Fees:* £14.00. Group rates available on request. *Eating facilities:* restaurant facilities all day. *Visitors:* always welcome, booking necessary at weekends. Accommodation can be arranged. *Society Meetings:* all welcome, rates on request. Secretary: Barry Harmon.

SNEEM. **Parknasilla Golf Club,** Parknasilla, Sneem (064 45122). *Location:* on the Ring of Kerry route, two miles east of Sneem Village. Hilly seaside course, wooded. 9 holes, 4894 yards. S.S.S. 65. *Green Fees:* £9.00. *Eating facilities:* available at Great Southern hotel, 10 minutes' walk. *Visitors:* welcome, no restrictions. *Society Meetings:* contact 064 45122. Professional: Charlie McCarthy. Secretary: Maurice Walsh (064 45233).

TRALEE. **Tralee Golf Club,** West Barrow, Ardfert, Tralee (066 36379). *Location:* Tralee to Barrow via the Spa and Churchill. Seaside links. 18 holes, 6252 metres. S.S.S. 72. *Green Fees:* £25.00 weekdays, £30.00 weekends. *Eating facilities:* bar and restaurant. *Visitors:* unrestricted except Wednesdays and weekends. *Society Meetings:* by arrangement. Secretary: Peter Colleran (066 36379; Fax: 066 36008).

WATERVILLE. **Waterville Golf Links,** Waterville (066 74102; Fax: 066 74482). *Location:* 50 miles from Killarney on the Ring of Kerry. Seaside links course. 18 holes, 7184 yards. S.S.S. 74. Practice range and putting green; golf clinics from Professional. *Green Fees:* £35.00 (subject to review). *Eating facilities:* full catering facilities and bar. *Visitors:* welcome; course open all year round. Accommodation available at Waterville House. *Society Meetings:* all welcome. Professional: Liam Higgins (066 74102; Fax: 066 74482). Secretary/Manager: Noel Cronin (066 74545; Fax: 066 74482).

COUNTY KILDARE

CURRAGH. **The Curragh Golf Club,** Curragh, Newbridge (045 41238). *Location:* three miles south of Newbridge. Hilly heathland course. 18 holes, 6003 metres. S.S.S. 71. Practice ground. *Green Fees:* weekdays £14.00; weekends and Bank Holidays £18.00. *Eating facilities:* bar and restaurant. *Visitors:* restricted, please check in advance for course availability. *Society Meetings:* by appointment. Professional: Mr Phil Lawlor (045 41896). Secretary: Ann Culleton (045 41714).

DONADEA. **Knockanally Golf and Country Club,** Donadea, North Kildare (Tel & Fax: 045 69322). *Location:* three miles off N4 between Enfield and Kilcock. Parkland. 18 holes, 6495 yards. S.S.S. 72. *Green Fees:* IR£16.00 weekdays; IR£20.00 weekends. *Eating facilities:* available. *Visitors:* welcome, no restrictions. *Society Meetings:* by arrangement. Professional: Peter Hickey. Secretary: Noel A. Lyons (045 69322/ 6287716).

COUNTY KILKENNY

THOMASTOWN. **Mount Juliet Golf Club,** Thomastown (010 353 56 24455). *Location:* Thomastown – on main Dublin to Waterford Road. Parkland, designed by Jack Nicklaus, home of the 1993 Carrolls Irish Open. 18 holes, 7142 yards, 6493 metres. S.S.S. 74. 3 hole teaching academy and driving range. *Green Fees:* £57.00. Group rate £45.00 weekdays, £46.00 weekends. *Eating facilities:* full catering and bar facilities. *Visitors:* welcome, no restrictions but please book in advance. Handicap Cards essential. 53 bedroom de luxe Hotel. *Society Meetings:* please book in advance.

COUNTY LAOIS

PORTLAOISE. **The Heath Golf Club,** The Heath, Portlaoise, Co Laois (0502 46533). *Location:* three and a half miles northeast of Portlaoise, off main Dublin road. Relatively flat with furze, gorse and three lakes. 18 holes, 5736 metres. S.S.S. 70 white, 69 Green. 10 bay all weather floodlit driving range and practice area. *Green Fees:* weekdays £10.00; weekends £16.00. 50% reduction if with a member. *Eating facilities:* full bar and catering facilities available. *Visitors:* welcome at all times but advance booking required for weekends and Public Holidays. *Society Meetings:* welcome by prior arrangement. Professional: Eddie Doyle (0502 46622). Secretary: Patrick A. Malone (0502 21074).

COUNTY LIMERICK

BALLYNEETY. **Limerick County Golf and Country Club,** Ballyneety (353 61 351881; Fax: 351384). *Location:* five miles from Limerick City, R512 direction of Lough Gur/Kilmallock. Championship standard, parkland course with water hazards bordering 8 holes. 18 holes, 6712 yards, 6137 metres. S.S.S. 74. Driving range, putting greens, 3 hole short game area, golf school with professional tuition. *Green Fees:* weekdays £25.00 approximately; weekends £30.00 approximately. Early bird discounts and for holiday cottage residents. *Eating facilities:* excellent restaurant serving international cuisine, light snacks, lunch and dinner menus, full bar service. *Visitors:* welcome, telephone in advance to assure tee space. 12 four star Holiday Cottages. *Society Meetings:* welcome. Professional: Philip Murphy. Secretary: Liam Meade.

CASTLETROY. **Castletroy Golf Club,** Castletroy, Co. Limerick (061 335261; Fax: 061 335373). *Location:* three miles from Limerick City on N7 (Dublin Road). Parkland with numerous trees. 18 holes, 6330 yards. S.S.S. 71. *Green Fees:* weekdays £20.00; weekends with a member only, £12.00. *Eating facilities:* full catering service, bar. *Visitors:* welcome most weekdays, restrictions weekends and Thursday afternoons, Tuesdays is Ladies' Day – advisable to phone. *Society Meetings:* welcome Mondays, Wednesdays and Fridays, group rates available. Professional: M. Cassidy (061 338283). Secretary: Laurence Hayes (061 335753).

COUNTY LOUTH

DROGHEDA. **County Louth Golf Club,** Baltray, Drogheda (041 22327). *Location:* Drogheda, five miles north east. Championship links course. 18 holes, 6783 yards. S.S.S. 72. *Green Fees:* weekdays £27.00; weekends £35.00. *Eating facilities:* restaurant, coffee shop and bar. *Visitors:* welcome weekdays except Tuesdays on application, weekends restricted. Accommodation available for 20 persons. *Society Meetings:* on application. Professional: Paddy McGuirk (041 22444). Secretary: Michael Delany (041 22329; Fax: 041 22969).

DROGHEDA. **Seapoint Golf Club,** Termonfeckin, Drogheda (041 22333; Fax: 22331). *Location:* on Drogheda to Termonfeckin road. Links course. 18 holes, 6339 yards. S.S.S. 74. Practice range. *Green Fees:* weekdays £17.00, weekends £22.00. *Eating facilities:* restaurant and bar. *Visitors:* welcome at all times; members' tee times 1-2pm daily and up to 10.30am weekends. Professional: David Carroll. Secretary: Amelia Smith.

PALMA. **Son Vida Golf,** Urb. Son Vida, 07013 Palma de Mallorca (0034-(9)71-79.12.10; Fax: 79.11.27). *Location:* five km north-west of Palma. Majorca's first course (1964) winding through trees and estate villas with lakes and gentle slopes. 18 holes, 6276 yards. S.S.S. 71. Driving range, Pro Shops, car, trolley and club rental. *Green Fees:* on application. *Eating facilities:* snacks and lunches in the comfortable clubhouse, excellent restaurant El Pato (The Duck) overlooking 18th hole. *Visitors:* welcome. Nearby hotels (20% discount on green fees) include Arabella Golf Hotel (5 stars), Hotel Son Vida (5 stars) on the course, 10% discount on green fees for guests at Melia Victoria, Son Caliu (4 stars). Manager: Peter Haider.

POLLENSA. **Golf Pollensa,** Ctra. Palma Pollensa, 07460 Pollensa (00-34-71 533216; Fax: 00-34-71 533265). *Location:* in the north of the island, 45 km from Palma Airport and 2 km from Pollensa. On the south side of a hill with smooth and beautiful undulations and sea views. 9 holes, 5304 metres. S.S.S. 70. Driving range. *Green Fees:* 5,300pts. Groups (more than 10 people) 10% discount. *Eating facilities:* snack bar. *Visitors:* welcome, tee reservation recommended. Changing room, swimming pool. *Society Meetings:* welcome. Professional: Carlos Insua. Secretary: Teresa and Sabrina.

SANTA PONSA. **Santa Ponsa Golf Club One,** Santa Ponsa, 07184 Calvia (690211; Fax: 693364). *Location:* 18km on motorway from Palma to Andratix, turn off roundabout Santa Ponsa. Gently sloping fairways with water hazards. 18 holes, 6170 metres. S.S.S. 72 men, 73 ladies. Practice range, two putting greens. *Green Fees:* 6500pts. Subject to review. *Eating facilities:* restaurant and bar in clubhouse, also small bar on golf course. *Visitors:* welcome; maximum Handicaps – 28 men, 36 ladies. Guests at the hotel receive 50% reduction on green fees. Accommodation available, swimming pool, paddling pool, tennis. *Society Meetings:* welcome. Professionals: Diego Lopez/George Oosterlynck. Director: Jose M. Comez. Secretary: Vicky Garcia.

SANTA PONSA. **Santa Ponsa Golf Club Two,** Santa Ponza, Calvia (690211/102732; Fax: 693364/102732). *Location:* as Sant Ponza One. A very interesting and enjoyable course, it has a mixture of holes, some with very tight fairways and others with many water hazards. Designed by Jose Gancedo. White Stakes – 6036 metres, Par 72; Yellow Stakes – 5672 metres, Par 70; Blue Stakes – 5144 metres, Par 72; Red Stakes – 4883 metres, Par 70. S.S.S. 72. Practice range, putting green. *Green Fees:* on request. *Eating facilities:* as Santa Ponza One. *Visitors:* at moment only open for shareholders.

SON SERVERA. **Son Servera Golf Club,** Costa de los Pinos, 07550 Son Servera (56.78.02; Fax: 56.81.46). *Location:* Palma – Manacor – San Llorens – Son Servera. Fairly flat, narrow, seaside course, set among pine trees. 9 holes, 2978 metres. S.S.S. 72. *Green Fees:* 6000pts. Groups of four persons 20% discount. *Eating facilities:* bar and restaurant. *Visitors:* welcome, no restrictions. Handicap Certificate required. Nearby hotels include Eurotel Golf Punta Roja, Flamenco, Royal Mediterranea, Gran Sol. Professional: Santiago Sota Bedia. Secretary: Pedro Canellas Ramis.

Golf in the USA

WHERE TO PLAY • WHERE TO STAY

by Michael Gedye

GOLFING in the States need no longer be a holiday dream. Cheaper flights, shorter travel times, a wealth of choice and a good selection of all-in packages from many specialist tour operators can put you on the tee Stateside at no greater cost than many similar packages to southern Europe. If you fancy the idea of reliable winter sunshine, immaculate courses manicured to perfection, the luxury of travelling around the fairways on four wheels with regular snack stops between holes and an environment where customer service comes as second nature, you need look no further than the USA. For this initial taste of the holiday golf that awaits you, a mere nibble at the literally thousands of resort courses available, we have chosen three of the most popular destinations with British players – Florida and the two Carolinas. Direct flights from the UK to Tampa, Orlando and Miami provide easy access to Florida, while Raleigh/Durham, Charlotte and Atlanta provide convenient gateway links to the resorts of North and South Carolina.

FLORIDA is the ultimate holiday golf destination. With over 1,000 golf courses, superb winter weather and a longstanding resort tradition to maintain, the visitor is spoiled for choice. Our selection covers the western coast along the Gulf of Mexico, central Orlando and the Palm Beach coastline a little north of Miami. We have included the championship venues of Innisbrook and PGA National but also friendly family resorts such as Saddlebrook and Naples Beach. Enough variety to suit all tastes, all with a warm welcome for the British visitor.

The discerning golfer has much to whet his golfing appetite in both Carolinas. Pride of NORTH CAROLINA is the Pinehurst Resort, a sheltered inland jewel of traditional excellence which manages to combine all the charm and elegance of its historic past with playing conditions over its seven courses matched to courteous service.

SOUTH CAROLINA has two resort areas of unparalleled quality. Hilton Head Island, just offshore from its southernmost corner, and the bountiful chain of over 80 golf courses and non-stop nightlife that forms the Grand Strand of Myrtle Beach. The choice is very much one of contrasts – the peace of Hilton Head or the colourful bustle of Myrtle Beach. Careful preservation of the environment and a realisation that its quiet island situation and climate lent itself admirably to resort golf has made Hilton Head a mecca for those seeking the very best. Fairways lined with pine, oak, magnolia and palm skirt lakes and subtle sand traps on a rich selection of well-kept courses. Pride of place goes to Harbour Town, the Pete Dye links that stages the annual Heritage Classic and which US professionals voted as having six of the toughest eighteen holes on the Tour.

Up the coast to Myrtle Beach and life moves up a gear. Here it is not so much a matter of where to play as where to start.

There are more courses in the 60-mile seaside stretch of the Grand Strand than one could reasonably ever visit. Yet the quality, the roster of great designers, the range of golfing tests makes any selection difficult. We have given you a preliminary taste to whet your appetite and encourage you to discover more of the charms that can only be found holiday golfing in the USA.

FLORIDA

BOCA RATON. **The Boca Raton Resort & Club,** 501 East Camino Real, Boca Raton, Fl. 33431 (407) 395 3000; Fax: (407) 391 3183. 22 miles from Palm Beach. Historic golf resort which combines links with the past and contemporary luxury. 36 holes: Country Club Course 6564 yards Par 72; Resort Course 6682 yards Par 71. Full facilities.

FORT MYERS. **Pelican's Nest Golf Club,** 4450 Bay Creek, Bonita Springs, Fl. 33923 (813) 947 4600. 15 miles from Fort Myers. A superb test by Tom Fazio, top rated and demanding in a highly attractive setting. 27 holes: Hurricane 3459 yards; Gator 3491 yards; Seminole 3478 yards, each Par 36. Full facilities.

NAPLES. **Lely Resort,** 8202 Lely Resort Boulevard, Naples, Fl. 33962 (813) 793 2200; Fax: (813) 775 2333. 40 miles from Fort Myers. Great golf in substantial homesite development. Golf design by Jones, Player and Trevino. 54 holes Flamingo Course 7171 yards Par 72. Full facilities.

NAPLES. **Naples Beach Hotel & Golf Club,** 851 Gulf Shore Boulevard North, Naples, Fl. 33940 (813) 261 2222; Fax: (813) 261 7380. 40 miles from Fort Myers. Beachside hotel and golf resort with much tradition. Very popular with British players. 18 holes 6642 yards Par 72. Full facilities.

NORTH MIAMI. **Turnberry Isle Resort & Club,** 19999 West Country Club Drive, Aventura, Fl. 33180 (305) 932 6200; Fax: (305) 933 6560. North Miami Beach. Luxury lifestyle by the sea for sports holiday fanatics with a taste for elegance. 36 holes: North 6323 yards Par 70; South 7003 yards Par 72. Full facilities.

ORLANDO. **Grand Cypress Resort,** 1 North Jacaranda, Orlando, Fl. 32819 (407) 239 4700. At Lake Buena Vista, near Disney World. Superb resort complex including an 18-hole replica of the Old Course, St. Andrews by Jack Nicklaus. 45 holes: New Course 6469 yards Par 71; Saddlebrook 6603 yards Par 70. Full facilities.

ORLANDO. **Grenelefe Golf & Tennis Resort,** 3200 SR 544, Haines City, Fl. 33844 (813) 422 7511. 25 miles south-west of Disney World. A comprehensive golf and tennis resort in a rolling, wooded setting. Popular also for conventions. 54 holes: East 6802 yards Par 72; South 6869 yards Par 71; West 7325 yards Par 72. Full facilities.

PALM BEACH. **PGA National Golf Club,** 400 Avenue of the Champions, Palm Beach Gardens, Fl. 33418 (407) 627 1800. 15 miles from West Palm Beach. Golf for all levels, including beginners, at a superb resort which hosted the 1983 Ryder Cup. 90 holes: Champion Course 7022 yards Par 72. Full facilities including teaching academy.

TAMPA. **Saddlebrook Resort,** 5700 Saddlebrook Way, Wesley Chapel, Fl. 33543 (813) 973 1111; Fax: (813) 973 4504. 20 miles north of Tampa. A complete family sports resort with some fine golf designed by Arnold Palmer. 36 holes: Palmer 6469 yards Par 71; Saddlebrook 6603 yards Par 70. Full facilities.

TARPON SPRINGS. **Innisbrook Hilton Resort,** PO Drawer 1088, Tarpon Springs, Fl. 34688 (813) 942 2000. 20 miles from Tampa. A total golf resort with superb facilities. The Copperhead course ranks in Florida's top five. 63 holes: Copperhead 7087 yards Par 71; Island 6999 yards Par 72. Full facilities.

NORTH CAROLINA

PINEHURST. **Pinehurst Resort & Country Club,** Pinehurst, North Carolina (910) 295 8141. 70 miles from Raleigh. Truly historic with great golf, an old-world atmosphere and service to match. 136 holes: No. 2 Course 7020 yards Par 72; No. 7 Course 7114 yards Par 72. Full facilities including inter-course transportation.

SOUTH CAROLINA

HILTON HEAD. **Harbour Town Golf Links,** Sea Pines Plantation, Hilton Head Island, South Carolina (803) 842 1892. Home of the Heritage Classic and a true thoroughbread regularly ranked in US top 25. 18 holes 6912 yards Par 71. Full facilities.

HILTON HEAD. **Palmetto Dunes Resort,** Hilton Head Island, South Carolina (803) 785 1138. Rolling dunes and fairways make a contrast at this popular, exciting golf complex. 54 holes: Arthur Hills Course 6651 yards Par 72; George Fazio Course 6873 yards Par 70; Robert Trent Jones Course 6710 yards Par 72. Full facilities.

HILTON HEAD. **Port Royal Golf Club,** Hilton Head Island, South Carolina (803) 686 8801. Three fine courses winding past magnolia and oak to a hospitable plantation-style clubhouse. 54 holes: Robber's Row 6711 yards Par 72; Planter's Row 6520 yards Par 72; Barony 6530 yards Par 72. Full facilities.

HILTON HEAD. **Shipyard Golf Club,** Hilton Head Island, South Carolina (803) 785 2402. Plenty of water hazards on these well-established tree-lined holes near the sea. 27 holes: Galleon 3364 yards; Brigantine 3352 yards; Clipper 3466 yards, all Par 36. Full facilities.

MYRTLE BEACH. **Litchfield Country Club,** PO Drawer 320, Pawleys Island, SC 29585 (803) 237 3411. Fine plantation-style golf winding past giant oaks, cypress, marshland and strategic lakes. 18 holes 6752 yards Par 72. Full facilities.

MYRTLE BEACH. **Pine Lakes International Country Club,** Woodside Drive, Central Myrtle Beach, South Carolina (803) 449 6459. Old fashioned service and style colour every aspect of this mature Scottish-designed golf setting. 18 holes 6709 yards Par 71. Full facilities.

MYRTLE BEACH. **The Witch Golf Club,** Highway 544 between Conway and Myrtle Beach, South Carolina (803) 448 1300. 5 miles from Myrtle Beach. A natural spellbinding course winding through dense forest and mangrove swamp. 18 holes 6702 yards Par 71. Full facilities.

MYRTLE BEACH. **Tidewater Golf Club,** Cherry Grove Beach, North Myrtle Beach, South Carolina (803) 249 3829. Full of potential, a tough course which makes good use of coastal water hazards. 18 holes 7020 yards Par 72. Full facilities.

MYRTLE BEACH. **Wild Wing Plantation,** Myrtle Beach, South Carolina (803) 347 9464. A new complex of courses featuring much-acclaimed bent grass greens. 54 holes: Avocet Course 7127 yards Par 72; Hummingbird Course 6853 yards Par 72; Wood Stork Course 7044 yards Par 72. Full facilities.

Driving Ranges

LONDON

CHINGFORD. **Chingford Golf Range,** Waltham Way, Chingford E4 8AQ (0181-529 2409). *Location:* two miles south of Junction 26 M25. 23 bay two tier driving range. *Fees:* information not provided. *Opening hours:* 9.30am to 10pm. Practice putting green, practice bunker; new multi-level practice mat; video, tuition available at all times. Professional: Gordon Goldie PGA and Susan Wood WPGA.

LONDON. **Docklands Golf Range Ltd.,** Brunswick Wharf, Leamouth Road, London E14 0JG (0171-712 9944). *Location:* follow City Airport signs from Tower of London through the Limehouse Link Tunnel and pick up signs to golf range (entrance on Prestons Road). 29 bay covered floodlit range. *Fees:* £2.00 for 50 balls. *Eating facilities:* full bar and cafe facilities. *Opening hours:* 10am to 10pm weekdays, 9am to 9pm weekends. Fully qualified PGA coaching staff, group and individual tuition (including video facilities) available. Fully equipped Pro shop.

LONDON. **Ealing Golf Range,** Rowdell Road, Northolt, Middlesex UB5 6AG (0181-845 4967). *Location:* A40 Target roundabout, Northolt. Golf range with 40 floodlit bays – 36 covered and 4 open. *Fees:* £2.00 for 50 balls. *Eating facilities:* bar and snack bar. *Opening hours:* 10am to 10pm. Three professionals, tuition, large golf shop, repair shop. Squash courts, health club. Head Professional: David Elliott (0181-845 4967).

NORTHOLT. **London Golf Centre,** Ruislip Road, Northolt UB5 6QZ (0181-845 3180). *Location:* 500 yards south of Polish War Memorial roundabout off A40, two miles inside M25. 20 bay covered, floodlit, grassed driving range. *Fees:* on application. *Eating facilities:* full bar and catering facilities (bar open 11am to 11pm). *Opening Hours:* daybreak to sunset. Two PGA Professionals, golf superstore, public golf course. Social club with pool and snooker; functions catered for.

THAMESMEAD. **Riverside Golf Club,** Summerton Way, Thamesmead, London SE28 8PP (0181-310 7975). 31 bay covered, floodlit and grassed driving range. *Fees:* basket of 52 balls £2.00. *Eating facilities:* restaurant and two bars. *Opening Hours:* 8am to 11pm. Fully equipped golf shop, golf tuition available. Many social functions; function rooms to hire.

AVON

BRISTOL. **Hambrook Golf Range,** Common Mead Lane, Filton Road, Bristol BS16 1QQ (Tel & Fax: 0117 970 116). *Location:* behind Crest Hotel on Junction 1 of the M32. 26 bay covered, floodlit range. *Fees:* £2.50 for 55 balls. *Eating facilities:* public bar and restaurant. *Opening hours:* 8am to 11pm. Grass putting green, austroturf green, bunker; indoor video studio; tuition by PGA qualified Professional. Professional: Michael Smedley.

BRISTOL. **Mendip Spring Golf Club,** Honeyhall Lane, Congresbury, Bristol BS19 5JT (01934 852322). *Location:* between A370 and A38. 15 bay covered, floodlit driving range with a grassed area. *Fees:* £2.50 per 100 balls, £1.75 per 50 balls. *Eating facilities:* none at range but available at the clubhouse. Practice bunker and putting green available. There is also an active members' social club.

TICKENHAM. **Tickenham Golf Centre,** Clevedon Road, Tickenham BS21 6SB (01275 856626). *Location:* M5 Junction 20, follow Nailsea signs. Centre on left after Tickenham village. 24 bay covered, floodlit driving range. *Fees:* 75 balls for £3.00. *Eating facilities:* can be arranged locally. *Opening Hours:* open normal hours including evenings. Professional tuition, group lessons etc; practice bunkers, 9-hole course.

BEDFORDSHIRE

DUNSTABLE. **Tilsworth Golf Centre,** Dunstable Road, Tilsworth, Near Leighton Buzzard LU7 9PU (01525 210721/2). *Location:* two miles north of Dunstable, off A5, Tilsworth turn-off. 30 bay covered floodlit driving range. *Fees:* information not provided. *Opening hours:* 10am – 10pm. *Eating facilities:* restaurant and bar (extensive menu), function suite. Large Pro shop, repairs, tuition and group lessons. 18 hole golf course open to public.

LEIGHTON BUZZARD. **Aylesbury Vale Golf Club,** Wing, Leighton Buzzard LU7 0UJ (01525 240196). *Location:* four miles west of Leighton Buzzard on the Wing to Stewkley Road. 10 bay covered, floodlit range. *Fees:* £2.00 for 65 balls, £1.50 for members. *Eating facilities:* downstairs bar and restaurant, first floor bar and balcony. *Opening hours:* 7.30am to 10pm. 18 hole golf course, 6622 yards, Par 72. Professional: Lee Scarbrow (01525 240197). Secretary/Manager: Chris Wright (01525 240196).

BERKSHIRE

BINFIELD. **Blue Mountain Golf Centre,** Wood Lane, Binfield RG12 5EY (01344 300200). *Location:* from M4 Junction 10, 329M Bracknell direction, Wokingham Exit B3408. 33 bay covered, floodlit driving range. *Fees:* £2.00 for 50 balls. *Eating facilities:* public bar, dining for up to 500. *Opening hours:* 8am to 9pm. PGA instructors, Pro shop, 18 hole golf course. Conference and dining facilities.

MAIDENHEAD. **Bird Hills Golf Centre,** Drift Road, Hawthorn Hill, Near Maidenhead SL6 3ST (01628 771030). *Location:* on A330 Ascot to Maidenhead road. 38 covered, floodlit bays. 18 hole 'pay and play' course. Professional's Tuition. *Fees:* approx 55 balls £2. *Opening hours:* 7.30am to 10pm daily. *Eating facilities:* "Racecourse Restaurant" and Golfers bar and terrace.

WARGRAVE. **Hennerton Golf Club,** Crazies Hill Road, Wargrave RG10 8LT (01734 401000). *Location:* between Maidenhead and Reading. 8 bay covered, floodlit driving range. *Fees:* on request. *Eating facilities:* clubhouse with full facilities. Two professionals, tuition available.

WOKINGHAM. **Downshire Driving Range,** Easthampstead Park, Wokingham RG11 3DH (01344 302030). *Location:* between Bracknell and Wokingham, off the Nine Mile Ride. 30 bay covered floodlit driving range. *Fees:* £1.50 bucket. *Eating facilities:* bar and restaurant, bar snacks available. *Opening hours:* 7.30am to 10pm. Tuition, 18 hole course, 9 hole pitch and putt; golf superstore. Societies welcome. *

WOKINGHAM. **Sindlesham Driving Range,** Mole Road, Wokingham RG11 5DJ (01734 788494). *Location:* two minutes from M4 Junction 11. 25 covered, floodlit bays. Professional tuition available. *Fees:* £2.00 per bucket. *Opening hours:* 7am to 10pm. *Eating facilities:* restaurant and bar. *Visitors:* open to the public. Health club and squash club. Professional: Andrew R. Wild (01734 788494). *

BUCKINGHAMSHIRE

AYLESBURY. **Aylesbury Golf Centre,** Hulcott Lane, Bierton, Aylesbury HP22 5GA (01296 393644). *Location:* north of Aylesbury on the A418. 30 bay covered, floodlit driving range. *Fees:* information not provided. *Eating facilities:* available. *Opening hours:* weekdays 7am to 10pm; weekends 8am to 10pm. Professional coaching, 9 hole golf course.

COLNBROOK. **Colnbrook Golf Range,** Galleymead Road, Colnbrook SL3 0EN (01753 682670). *Location:* one mile from Junction 5 M4, one mile Junction 14 M25. 27 bay floodlit, grassed range; 14 covered bays. *Fees:* £1.00 dispensing machine (35 balls). *Eating facilities:* fully licensed bar 11am to 11pm six days a week, catering, anything from snacks to full à la carte – excellent resident chef. *Opening hours:* 9am to 10.30pm. Professional: Graham Hepsworth; Assistant: Alistair McKay. Very well equipped golf shop. Full tuition, video assisted lessons given.

MILTON KEYNES. **Windmill Hill Golf Range,** Tattenhoe Lane, Bletchley, Milton Keynes MK3 7RB (01908 378623). *Location:* off A421 at Bletchley. 23 bay covered floodlit driving range, 5 bays outside. *Fees:* small bucket (46 balls) £1.60; large bucket (92 balls) £3.00. *Eating facilities:* public bar and catering. *Opening hours:* 9am to 9pm weekdays, 8am to 8pm weekends. Professional tuition, public course – 18 holes, Par 73. Club membership available, apply to Secretary.

STOWE. **Silverstone Golf Club,** Silverstone Road, Stowe MK18 5LH (01280 850005). 12 bay covered range. *Fees:* weekdays £8.00; weekends £12.00. Memberships available. *Eating facilities:* licensed bar, good food. *Opening hours:* dawn to 11pm. Tuition available – group or private.

CAMBRIDGESHIRE

HUNTINGDON. **Old Nene Golf and Country Club and Edrich Range (Ramsey) Ltd.,** Muchwood Lane, Bodsey, Ramsey, Huntingdon PE17 1XQ (01487 813519). 60 bay driving range, 24 covered, 36 floodlit, all grassed. *Fees:* £1.00 for 30 balls, £2.60 and £3.90. *Eating facilities:* coffee lounge and golf club house catering. *Opening hours:* dawn to 10pm. Professional tuition, 9 hole course. Free instruction on range Wednesdays 5pm to 7pm; instruction in school holidays Thursdays 10am to 10.30am. Five places for coarse fishing on lake, Ramsey Miniature Car Racing Club meetings.

PETERBOROUGH. **Thorney Golf Centre,** English Drove, Thorney, Peterborough PE6 0TJ (01733 270570). *Location:* A47 Leicester to Wisbech, turn left in Thorney, first right out of village. 13 bay covered, floodlit, grassed range. *Green Fees:* £1.50 for 50 balls. *Eating facilities:* full bar and restaurant open to public. *Opening Hours:* 8am to 8pm seven days. 18 hole course and nine hole Par 3 course.

ROYSTON. **Whaddon Golf Centre,** Whaddon, Royston SG8 5RX (01223 207325). *Location:* four miles north of Royston off A1198, nine miles south of Cambridge off A603. 9 open bays, 14 bays covered, floodlit and grassed. *Fees:* £1.00 for 50 balls. *Eating facilities:* available. *Opening hours:* 8am to 9pm weekdays, 8am to dusk weekends. Three Professionals – coaching by appointment. Putting green and Par 3 approach course.

ST. NEOTS. **Abbotsley Golf and Squash Club,** Eynesbury, Hardwicke, St Neots PE19 4XN (01480 215153/474000). *Location:* A45 St. Neots bypass to Abbotsley, south east of St. Neots Junction 13 M11. 21 bay range and grass. *Fees:* £2.00 per bucket (80 balls). *Opening hours:* 8am to 10pm. *Eating facilities:* bar and food available all day. Two courses (36 holes), residential golf school, shop, tuition; residential schools for golf with Vivien Sanders and John Stirling. 15 bedroom hotel, 6 squash courts, snooker, 2 sun beds, sauna.

CHESHIRE

CHESTER. **Carden Park,** Carden, Chester CH3 9DQ (01829 731000). *Location:* take A41 Chester to Whitchurch road, turn right onto the A543 Wrexham road, Carden Park is one and a half miles on the left. 13 bay covered driving range. *Eating facilities:* full catering facilities. *Opening Hours:* 8am to 11pm. Professional tuition with the latest in split-screen video. Various sporting activities catered for including clay shooting, archery and tennis; conference facilities, hotel, cottage accommodation.

NORTHWICH. **Hartford Golf Range,** Burrows Hill, Hartford, Northwich CW9 8AP. *Location:* off A556 Northwich, near ICI. 30 bay floodlit driving range. Bunker. Golf shop. Professional: (01606 871162; Fax: 01606 851808).

STOCKPORT. **Cranford Golf Centre,** Harwood Road, Heaton Mersey, Stockport SK4 3AW (0161-432 8242). *Location:* five minutes from M63 and M56 motorways. 43 all-weather covered tees, fully floodlit. *Fees:* £2.50 per bucket (50 balls). No booking or membership required. *Eating facilities:* drinks and snacks available. *Opening hours:* seven days a week 10am to 11pm. Two indoor bunkers, 9 hole indoor putting course, changing rooms and golf shop. Group facilities and lessons available. Professional: Anthony Murray.

CLEVELAND

STOCKTON-ON-TEES, **Knotty Hill Golf Centre,** Sedgefield, Stockton-on-Tees TS21 2BB (01740 620320). *Location:* A1M Junction 60, one mile north of Sedgefield on A177. 14 bays covered and floodlit, 14 tees open and grassed. *Fees:* small basket of balls £2.00, large basket £3.00. *Eating facilities:* restaurant and bar. *Opening Hours:* 8am to 9pm. Professional tuition, golf shop; 18-hole course, chipping and putting greens. Secretary: J.A. Reynolds.

CORNWALL

REDRUTH. **Radnor Golf and Ski Centre,** Radnor Road, Redruth TR16 5EL (01209 211059). *Location:* follow signs from Old Redruth by-pass (A3047) or crossroads at north county. 18 bay covered floodlit driving range. *Fees:* £1.50 for 50 balls. Subject to review. *Eating facilities:* bar available. *Opening hours:* weekdays 8.30am to 9pm; weekends and Bank Holidays 8.30am to 6pm. PGA Approved. Teaching, club repairs, shop. Indoor ski machine, snooker. 9 hole Par 3 course.

TRURO. **Killiow Park Golf Club Driving Range,** Killiow Golf Park, Kea, Truro TR3 6AG (01872 70246). *Location:* take A39 from Truro direct to Falmouth, 2.75 miles. Large sign on right into park. All weather floodlit driving range with bunker and putting facilities. *Fees:* £1.60 for 50 balls. *Eating facilities:* bar with bar snacks. *Opening hours:* weekdays 9.30am to 9pm; weekends 9.30am to 6pm. *Visitors:* some restrictions – check with Reception. Tuition available by appointment. Wide range of golf equipment and sundries available in the shop. Secretary: John Crowson (01872 72768).

CUMBRIA

CARLISLE. **The Eden Golf Course,** Crosby-on-Eden, Carlisle CA6 4RA (01228 573003; Fax: 01228 818435). *Location:* M6 Junction 44, A689 to Crosby-on-Eden village. 16 bay floodlit, covered range. *Green Fees:* £1.50 per basket (55 balls). *Eating facilities:* full catering facilities available in clubhouse. *Opening hours:* 8am to 9pm. Professional tuition, 18 hole parkland course also available.

DERBY

CHESTERFIELD. **Grassmoor Golf Centre,** North Wingfield Road, Grassmoor, Chesterfield S42 5EA (01246 856044). *Location:* M1 Junction 29 or A61 near Chesterfield. 26 bay covered, floodlit range. *Fees:* per bucket (approximately 80 balls) £1.50 members, £2.00 non-members. *Eating facilities:* catering available 8am to 11pm weekdays, 7.30am to 11pm weekends; bar open 11am to 11pm weekdays, till 10.30pm weekends. *Opening hours:* seven days a week 9am to 9.30pm. Golf lessons £9.50 with video.

DEVON

IVYBRIDGE. **Dinnaton Golf Club,** Dinnaton Sporting and Country Club, Ivybridge PL21 9HU (01752 892512). *Location:* leave A38 at Ivybridge, follow signs for Dinnaton Golf Club. 6 bay covered, floodlit driving range. *Fees:* £2.00 per basket (approximately 50 balls). *Eating facilities:* coffee lounge, club bar, restaurant. *Opening hours:* dawn till dusk. Professional, 9 hole course, squash, badminton, volleyball, table tennis, gymnasium, snooker room, sauna solarium, steam room, 25 metre heated indoor pool. Accommodation for up to 20 people, conference facilities available.

UPOTTERY. **Otter Valley Golf Centre,** Upottery, Honiton EX14 9QP (01404 86266). *Location:* just off the A303 before Monkton. 4 indoor bays and 8 grassed bays. *Fees:* from £5.00. *Eating facilities:* none available. *Opening Hours:* open daily. Residential and non-residential school; tuition; practice putting, chipping and approach greens; golf shop; lounge (video instruction etc).

DORSET

SHAFTESBURY. **Twyford Golf Range,** Twyford, Shaftesbury SP7 0JN (01747 811356). *Location:* situated one and a half miles west of Fontmell Magna, four and a half miles south of Shaftesbury off A350. 20 bay grassed range, 6 covered. 310 yards long with markers and flags. *Fees:* £1.50 per basket of 50 balls. *Opening hours:* open all day until dusk.

ESSEX

BRAINTREE. **Towerlands Driving Range,** Panfield Road, Braintree CM7 5BJ (01376 326802; Fax: 01376 347951). *Location:* take A120 into Braintree then B1053. 6 grassed bays. *Fees:* £1.25 for 50 balls. *Eating facilities:* full bar and restaurant. *Opening hours:* 8.30am till dark. 9 hole course, professional tuition, indoor bowls, squash, full sports hall and equestrian facilities.

CHADWELL HEATH. **Warren Park Golf Centre,** Whalebone Lane North, Chadwell Heath RM6 6SB (0181-597 1120; Fax: 0181-590 5457). *Location:* on A12 opposite "Moby Dick" public house. 27 bay covered, floodlit driving range. *Fees:* 40 balls £1.40, 80 balls £2.80, 120 balls £3.50. *Eating facilities:* bar and snacks; function suite. *Opening Hours:* 9am to 10pm Sunday to Friday, 9am to 9pm Saturday. Seven PGA Professionals, individual lessons from £10.00 per half hour. Fully stocked golf shop.

COLCHESTER. **Colchester Golf Range,** Old Ipswich Road, Ardleigh, Colchester (01206 230974). *Location:* next to the Crown Inn, Old Ipswich Road. Covered, floodlit range, 12 bays. Professional tuition available. Putting green. *Fees:* £1.75 for 50 balls. request. *Opening Hours:* weekdays 10am to 9pm, weekends 10am to 5pm. *Eating facilities:* The Crown Inn, 50 yards from golf range.

COLCHESTER. **Earls Colne Golf and Country Club,** Earls Colne, Colchester CO6 2NS (01787 224466; Fax: 01787 224410). *Location:* B1024 between A120 and A604 Earls Colne. 20 bay covered floodlit driving range. *Fees:* £1.75 for 50 balls. *Eating facilities:* full restaurant and bar facilities in the main clubhouse which is 200 yards from the driving range. *Opening hours:* weekdays 9am to 10pm, weekends 8am to 9pm. Tuition available. 18 hole and 9 hole courses, 4 hole teaching course. Leisure centre – swimming pool, gym, sun beds, beauty parlour, spa bath. Creche. Trainee Golf Professional: L. Cocker. Golf Director: Owen McKenna.

ILFORD. **Fairlop Waters,** Forest Road, Barkingside, Ilford IG6 3JA (0181-500 9911). *Location:* two miles north of Ilford, half a mile from A12, one and a half miles from southern end of M11. Covered, floodlit range, 36 bays. 18 hole golf course, 9 hole Par 3 course. Individual or group tuition available. *Fees:* information not provided. *Opening hours:* 9am to 10pm. *Eating facilities:* bars and American Diner. Banqueting facilities and conferences. 38 acre sailing lake, 25 acre country park, children's play area. Professional: Tony Bowers (0181-501 1881). Manager: Keith Robson.

GLOUCESTERSHIRE

CHURCHDOWN. **Brickhampton Court Golf Club,** Cheltenham Road, Churchdown GL2 9QF (01452 859444; Fax: 859333). *Location:* midway between Cheltenham and Gloucester on B4063, within Brickhampton Court Golf Club. 26 bays floodlit and covered. *Fees:* 60 balls £2.50 (card available – 10 baskets for £22.50). *Eating facilities:* light refreshments available. *Opening hours:* weekdays 10am to 9pm; weekends 10am to 5.30pm. 18 hole, par 71 and 9, hole par 31 courses. P.G.A. qualified teaching staff available for group and individual lessons.

GLOUCESTER. **Gloucester Hotel and Country Club,** Robinswood Hill, Matson Lane, Gloucester GL4 9EA (01452 525653). 12 bays covered and floodlit. *Fees:* £2.00 per basket of balls for driving range. *Opening hours:* 9am to 9.30pm. *Eating facilities:* available. Five professional instructors, private and group tuition available. Sebastian Coe Health Park, dry ski slope, golf course, indoor swimming pool, sauna, solarium, gymnasium, 6 squash courts, two tennis courts, snooker, pool, skittles etc.

HAMPSHIRE

BORDON near. **Kingsley Golf Club,** Main Road, Kingsley, Near Bordon GU35 9NG (014203 88195). *Location:* B3004 off A325 Farnham to Petersfield road. *Fees:* information not provided. Indoor computerised driving bay, equipment store, golf school for tuition. Professional/Acting Secretary: Richard Adams.

ROMSEY. **Paultons Golf Centre,** Old Salisbury Road, Ower, Near Romsey SO51 6AN (01703 813992). *Location:* off M3 at Junction 2, A36 towards Salisbury, at first roundabout take first exit, then first right at the Vine Public House. 24-bay covered floodlit driving range. *Fees:* £1.00 for 25 balls, £1.75 for 50, £3.00 for 100. *Eating facilities:* full bar and restaurant. *Opening Hours:* 8am until 9pm. Full Professional shop and teaching facilities; 27 holes.

HEREFORD & WORCESTER

BROMSGROVE. **Bromsgrove Golf Centre,** Stratford Road, Bromsgrove B60 1LD (01527 575886/ 570505). *Location:* two miles south on A38 off Junction 4 M5, five miles north on A38 off Junction 5 M5. Golf Centre on junction of A38/A448, two minutes off M42. 41 bay covered, floodlit driving range. *Fees:* £2.40 per 100 balls, £1.60 per 55 balls, £1.20 per 35 balls. *Eating facilities:* snack refreshments available. Professional tuition available, 9 hole course (Hawtree), pay and play and an additional 9 holes under construction. *Opening Hours:* 9am to 10pm weekdays; 9am to 6pm Sat/Sun. Large Golf Shop (John Reay).

LEOMINSTER. **The Grove Golf Centre,** Fordbridge, Leominster HR6 0LE (01568 611804). *Location:* adjacent to Leominster Golf Club, three miles south of Leominster on A49. 18 bay floodlit range (four outdoor). *Fees:* £1.00 per 30 balls. *Opening hours:* 8am to 9pm. Also 9 hole putting green, practice bunker, club hire, tuition available. Professional: Gareth Bebb. *

HERTFORDSHIRE

WARE. **Whitehill Golf Centre,** Dane End, Ware SG12 0JS (01920 438495; Fax: 01920 438891). *Location:* turn at Happy Eater, High Cross on A10 north of Ware. 25 bays covered, floodlit, grassed. *Fees:* £1.50 45 balls, £2.50 90 balls. *Eating facilities:* bar and restaurant. *Opening hours:* Wednesday to Friday 7am to 10pm, Tuesday 10am to 10pm, Monday 7am to 10pm, weekends and Bank Holidays 7am to dusk. Professional tuition, 18 hole golf course, practice bunkers, snooker.

WELWYN GARDEN CITY. **Gosling Golf Range,** Gosling Sports Park, Stanborough Road, Welwyn Garden City AL8 6XE (01707 331056). *Location:* A1(M) Junction 4, follow signs for Welwyn Garden City. 22 bays covered floodlit driving range. *Fees:* £1.90 bucket of 48 balls non members, members £1.65. *Opening hours:* 9am to 10pm weekdays, weekends 9am to 8pm. *Eating facilities:* extensive bar/catering within Sports Park. Resident Professional, tuition and shop. Extensive facilities with ski-ing, tennis, athletics, bowls, cycling, badminton. Health suite, etc. Brochure available. *

HUMBERSIDE

SCUNTHORPE. **Grange Park Golf Range,** Butterwick Road, Messingham, Scunthorpe DN17 3PP (01724 764478). *Location:* five miles south of Scunthorpe between Messingham and East Butterwick, four miles south of Junction 3 of M180. 20 bay covered floodlit driving range. *Fees:* £1.25 for 50 balls. *Opening hours:* 9am to 10pm weekdays, 9am to 9pm weekends. Large Pro shop and exclusive golf ladies' wear shop. Professional available. 9 hole pay and play course on site.

KENT

CHATHAM. **Chatham Golf Centre,** Street End Road, Chatham ME5 0BG. *Location:* five minutes' drive from Rochester Airport. Covered, floodlit range, 30 bays. Tuition available. *Fees:* £2.00 per 65 balls. *Opening hours:* 10am to 10pm. *Eating facilities:* licensed snack bar. Fully stocked Pro Shop. Competitive prices. Professional: Colin Bentley (01634 848925). Secretary: R. Burden (01634 848907).

CHISLEHURST. **Mulligan's Golf Park,** A20 Sidcup By-pass, Chislehurst BR7 6RP (0181-295 0606). *Location:* six minutes from Junction 3 on M25 heading towards London on the A20. 54 bay covered, floodlit driving range. *Fees:* £2.50 for 50 balls, £4.50 for 100 balls. *Eating facilities:* small bar and restaurant. *Opening Hours:* 9am to 9pm daily. 18-hole adventure putting course, 9-hole Par 3 golf course, practice putting green and floodlit practice bunkers. Large golf and tennis store, club and racquet repair shop; tennis courts.

MAIDSTONE. **Langley Park Driving Range,** Sutton Road, Langley, Maidstone ME17 3NQ (01622 863163). *Location:* south of Maidstone on A274, first turning after Park Wood Industrial Estate. 26 covered, floodlit bays. *Fees:* £1.50 for 45 balls. *Eating facilities:* licensed bar, snacks available. *Opening hours:* 10am to 10pm weekdays, 10am to 9pm weekends. PGA tuition, computerised putting machine – £1.00 per 9 holes, putting green. Professional: Nick McNally.

ORPINGTON. **Ruxley Park Golf Centre,** Sandy Lane, St. Pauls Cray, Orpington BR5 3HY (01689 871490; Fax: 01689 891428). *Location:* off old A20 at Ruxley Corner. 24 bays, covered, floodlit, grassed. *Fees:* information not provided. *Opening hours:* 9am to 10.30pm. *Eating facilities:* breakfast, lunch available, bar open all day. 18 hole Par 71 golf course.

SITTINGBOURNE. **The Oast Golf Centre Ltd,** Church Road, Tonge, Sittingbourne ME9 9AR (01795 473527). *Location:* one mile north A2 between Faversham and Sittingbourne, take the turning to Tonge at Bapchild. 17 bay covered floodlit driving range. *Fees:* £1.00 per bucket of 30 balls. *Eating facilities:* fully licensed. Par 3 approach course, 9 holes pay and play basis. Tuition available, golf shop. Two short mat bowls facility £2.00 per hour per mat. *Opening Hours:* 8.30am to 10pm Range; 8am to dusk Par 3 course. Professional: Mr Gordon Nixon.

SWANLEY. **Olympic Golf Range,** Beechenlea Lane, Swanley BR8 8DR (01322 615126). *Location:* Junction 3 M25, take Swanley exit then first on right. 30 floodlit bays (18 covered and 12 grassed). *Fees:* weekdays 10am to 5pm 50 balls for £1.00, at other times £2.00. *Eating facilities:* bar and restaurant. *Opening Hours:* 10am to 11pm Monday to Saturday, 10am to 10.30pm Sunday. PGA tuition, discount golf shop, club repair centre. Snooker centre and bowling green.

TONBRIDGE. **Hilden Golf Centre,** Rings Hill, Hildenborough, Tonbridge TN11 8LX (01732 833607). *Location:* take exit off A21 for Tonbridge North/Hildenborough; take second turning right (Watts Cross Road), follow road past station to bottom of the hill, Golf Centre is on the left. 40 bay covered, floodlit and grassed driving range. *Fees:* basket of 45 balls £2.00. *Eating facilities:* fully licensed cafe bar. *Opening Hours:* Summer: 7am to 10pm, Winter: 8am to 10pm. Two PGA Professionals (tuition available); large golf shop; golf course and putting green.

LANCASHIRE

BLACKBURN. **Blackburn Golf Driving Range,** Queens Park Playing Fields, Haslingden Road, Blackburn BB2 3HQ. *Location:* east side of Blackburn, one mile from town centre. 27 bay covered, floodlit range. *Fees:* £1.65 for 55 balls, £3.00 for 100 balls. *Visitors:* welcome. *Opening hours:* 9am to 9pm. Two bunkers and two greens for outdoor practice. Professional: Jeff Mathews. Owner: Jim Gornall (01254 581996).

BLACKPOOL. **The Village Golf Club Driving Range,** Herons Reach Golf Course, East Park Drive, Blackpool FY3 8LL (01253 838866). *Location:* from Junction 4 off M55 follow signs for Blackpool Zoo, complex is opposite Stanley Park and next to the Zoo. 18 bay covered, floodlit range. *Fees:* £2.00 for multiples of 50 balls. *Eating facilities:* Spikes Bar, leisure bar, grill restaurant. *Opening Hours:* 8am to 10pm, open to the general public. *Visitors:* welcome. Must hold current Handicap Certificate. 166 bedroomed hotel, leisure facilities, conference and banqueting facilities. Hotel Reservations (01253 838866; Fax: 01253 798800). *Society Meetings:* welcome. Golf Packages available. Group and individual tuition, all standards, video aids. Golf trolleys and buggies for hire. Professional: Richard Hudson. Golf Manager: David Hughes.

KEARSLEY. **Kearsley Golf Driving Range,** Moss Lane, Kearsley, Bolton BL4 8SF (01204 75726). *Location:* Manchester to Bolton A666. Floodlit driving range, 10 covered, 12 grassed. *Fees:* £1.25 for multiples of 25 balls. *Opening hours:* weekdays 11am to 9.30pm; weekends 11am to 4.30pm. *Eating facilities:* bar and snack bar. *Visitors:* welcome. Small 3 hole pitch and putt with practice sand bunker, 18 hole pay as you play course immediately adjacent. Open to the public. Professional/Owner: E. Raymond Warburton.

LEICESTER

LEICESTER. **Kingstand Golf Course,** Beggars Lane, Leicester Forest, Leicester LE3 3NQ (0116 238 7908). 16 bay grassed, covered, floodlit range. *Fees:* £1.00 per basket. *Eating facilities:* available. *Opening hours:* 7am to 10pm. Par 33 9 hole course, gymnasium.

GREATER MANCHESTER

ROCHDALE. **Castle Hawk Golf Club,** Chadwick Lane, Castleton, Rochdale OL11 3BY (01706 40841). *Location:* five minutes from Exit 20 on M62. 25 bay covered, floodlit, grassed driving range. *Fees:* £3.00 for large bucket of balls. *Eating facilities:* available at Golf Club. *Opening Hours:* dawn till dusk. Professional tuition available.

MERSEYSIDE

MORETON. **Wirral Golf and Drive Centre,** Tarran Way, Moreton, Wirral L46 4TP (0151-677 6606). *Location:* off Pasture Road, opposite Cadbury's factory. *Fees:* 30 balls £1.00, 65 balls £2.00. *Eating facilities:* not available. *Opening Hours:* 10am to 8.30pm. Golf shop, PGA Professionals, golf lessons.

NORTHAMPTONSHIRE

NORTHAMPTON. **Delapre Golf Complex,** Eagle Drive, Nene Valley Way, Northampton NN4 7DU (01604 764036). *Location:* three miles from Junction 15 M1 towards Wellingborough. 40 covered, floodlit bays plus 30 grassed areas. *Fees:* practice balls dispensed from machines at £2.00 for approximately 60 balls. *Opening hours:* 7.30am to 10.30pm daily. *Eating facilities:* hot and cold meals served all day, bar facilities available during licensing hours. PGA qualified teaching staff available for individual or group tuition. 27 holes of main golf; two Par 3 courses, pitch and putt course, practice putting greens.

NOTTINGHAMSHIRE

CALVERTON. **Ramsdale Park Golf Centre,** Oxton Road, Calverton NG14 6NU (0115 965 5600). *Location:* north east Nottingham city, on B6386 Oxton Road. 25 bay covered floodlit range. *Fees:* small bucket of balls £2.00, medium £3.00, large £3.75. *Eating facilities:* available. *Opening hours:* 7.30am to 10pm. Professional tuition, 18 hole main course and 18 hole Par 3 course.

LONG EATON. **Trent Lock Golf Centre,** Lock Lane, Sawley, Long Eaton, Nottingham NG10 3DD (0115 946 4398/1184). 24 bay covered, floodlit driving range. *Fees:* small basket of balls £1.75, large basket £3.00. *Eating facilities:* restaurant, bar and function room. *Opening Hours:* 8am until midnight. Professional tuition available, five PGA staff. 18-hole golf course.

NOTTINGHAM. **Richard Herrod Leisure Centre,** Foxhill Road, Carlton, Nottingham NG4 1RL (0115 961 2949). *Location:* east side of Nottingham. 28 bay covered, floodlit range. *Fees:* off peak £2.15 per basket, peak £2.35 per basket; approximately 75 balls. Special discount for Juniors, Senior Citizens, UB40's and students. *Eating facilities:* luxury bar and restaurant. *Opening hours:* Monday noon to 10.30pm, Tuesday-Sunday 9.30am to 10.30pm. Professional tuition available. Golf shop, snooker, indoor bowls, dry ski slope, sledging, indoor bowls, snooker, function rooms. Newly formed golf society, new members most welcome, all standards. Professional: Mr John Down. Centre Manager: Mrs B. Neal.

RADCLIFFE-ON-TRENT. **Cotgrave Place Golf and Country Club,** Stragglethorpe, Near Radcliffe-on-Trent NG12 3HB (0115 933 3344). *Location:* A52 from Nottingham, turn right at traffic lights to Cotgrave, first right, then first again. 20 bay covered, floodlit and grassed driving range. *Fees:* basket of balls £2.00. *Eating facilities:* food available all day in the golf clubhouse. *Opening Hours:* 8am to dusk seven days a week. Professional tuition £7.00 for 30 minutes. 27-hole golf course, 6-hole Par 3 Academy course. Limited membership still available. Professional: Greg Towne.

OXFORDSHIRE

DRAYTON. **Drayton Park Golf Course and Driving Range,** Steventon Road, Drayton (01235 550607). *Location:* south of Abingdon, between Drayton and Steventon. 21 bay covered, floodlit driving range. *Fees:* £2.00 for 45 balls, £3.00 for 75 balls. *Eating facilities:* full facilities available. *Opening hours:* 8am to 9pm. PGA qualified Professionals (including Lady Pro), individual and group tuition and Junior classes and Award Scheme.

OXFORD. **Oxford Golf Centre,** Binsey Lane, Botley Road, Oxford OX2 0EX (01865 721592). *Location:* within city boundary, past railway station, fourth turn on right going south. 17 bay covered, floodlit bays with mats. *Fees:* large basket £3.00, small £2.00. *Eating facilities:* light refreshments. *Opening Hours:* 10am to 8.30pm. Two professionals, individual tuition available. Shop and video room.

OXFORD. **Waterstock Golf Club Driving Range,** Thame Road, Waterstock, Oxford OX33 1HT (01844 338093). *Location:* direct access from Junction 8 M40; four miles east of Oxford, three miles west of Thame on A418. 22 bay covered, fully floodlit driving range. *Fees:* £2.20 for 50 balls. *Eating facilities:* full bar and catering facilities. *Opening Hours:* 7.30am to 11pm. Resident Professional offers tuition; Pro shop with many demonstration clubs; 18-hole golf course; clubhouse with full social facilities (societies and functions catered for).

WITNEY. **Witney Golf Centre,** Downs Road, Witney OX8 5SY (01993 779000). *Location:* two miles west of Witney town centre. 24 bay covered, floodlit driving range. *Fees:* £2.00 for 60 balls, £3.50 for 120 balls. *Eating facilities:* available all day. *Opening Hours:* 8am to 10pm weekdays, 9am to 9pm weekends. 4 Professional teaching staff, two fully stocked shops, club repair service. Two large putting greens, 18-hole golf course. Clubhouse with conference/function room.

SHROPSHIRE

OSWESTRY. **Oswestry Golf Driving Range,** Mile End, Oswestry SY11 4JE (01691 670580/671246). *Location:* signposted "Mile End Golf Club" off A45, one mile south-east of Oswestry. 12 bay covered, floodlit driving range. *Fees:* £1.00 for 30 balls. *Eating facilities:* available to members and green fee paying visitors. *Opening Hours:* Summer: 8.30am until dusk daily; Winter: 8.30am to 8pm weekdays, 8.30am to 6pm weekends. Professional tuition available, fully stocked Pro shop. 9-hole Par 35 golf course.

TELFORD. **The Shropshire Golf and Leisure Complex,** Muxton Grange, Muxton, Telford TF2 8PQ (01952 677866). *Location:* M54 from M6 Junction 4, turn right and follow signs. 31 bay covered, floodlit driving range. *Fees:* £2.00 for 75 balls, £1.00 for 35 balls. *Eating facilities:* restaurant, bars and function rooms. *Opening Hours:* 7am to 9pm. Teaching professional, 27 hole golf course, 12 hole short course, 18 hole putting green. Trout fishing and equestrian centre also available.

SOMERSET

CHEDDAR. **Cheddar Valley Golf Driving Range,** Penstown, Lyppiatt Lane, Cheddar BS27 3QT (01934 742531). 10 bay driving range. *Fees:* £2.50 per basket (80 balls). *Opening hours:* 9am to 9pm. Putting green and bunker also available, free.

LANGPORT. **Long Sutton Golf Club,** Langport TA10 9JU (01458 241017). *Location:* three miles north of A303 from Podimore roundabout on A372 to Langport and Taunton. 12 bay covered, floodlit, grassed range. *Fees:* £2.00 for 60 balls. *Eating facilities:* available. *Opening Hours:* 8am till dusk. 18 hole golf course and large practice putting green. Professional tuition.

STAFFORDSHIRE

BURTON-ON-TRENT. **Craythorne Golf Centre,** Craythorne Road, Stretton, Burton-on-Trent DE13 0AZ (01283 64329). *Location:* Stretton, one and a half miles north of Burton – A5121/A38 Junction. 14 bay covered floodlit driving range. *Fees:* £1.50 per bucket. *Opening hours:* weekdays 9am to 9pm; weekends 9am to dusk.

SUFFOLK

HALESWORTH. **St. Helena Golf Club,** Bramfield Road, Halesworth IP19 8NB (01986 875567). *Location:* A12, A144 to and through Bramfield, over crossroads and then first right. 18 bays floodlit (10 covered). *Fees:* small basket £1.50, large basket £2.00. *Eating facilities:* available. *Opening Hours:* 8am until dark. Professional tuition and fully equipped Pro shop; 27-hole golf course, putting and chipping greens. Professional: P.M. Heil.

WOODBRIDGE. **Seckford Golf Club,** Seckford Hall Road, Great Bealings, Near Woodbridge IP13 6NT (01394 388000). *Location:* signposted from A12. 11 bay driving range. *Fees:* £1.75 for small bucket of balls, £2.50 for large bucket. *Eating facilities:* available. *Opening Hours:* 7.30am to 7.30pm daily. Golf school, three Professional staff. Full membership available.

SURREY

CHESSINGTON. **Chessington Golf Centre,** Garrison Lane, Chessington KT9 2LW (0181-391 0948). *Location:* off A243, 500 yards from Chessington World of Adventure. Opposite Chessington South Station, Junction 9 M25. Covered, floodlit range, 18 bays. 9 hole course. Private and group tuition available. *Fees:* £1.00 token per 35 balls. *Opening hours:* 9am to 10pm. *Eating facilities:* bar and catering. Tuition, public course.

COBHAM. **Silvermere Driving Range,** Redhill Road, Cobham KT11 1EF (01932 867275). *Location:* half a mile from Junction 10 on M25, take B366; 30 minutes from central London. Covered, floodlit range, 34 bays. *Fees:* £1.50 and £2.50 per bucket of balls. *Eating facilities:* full service available. *Opening hours:* 8.30am to 9.30pm. Tuition available. Public golf course. Telephone bookings taken.

CROYDON. **Croydon Driving Range,** 175 Long Lane, Addiscombe, Croydon CR0 7TE (0181-656 1690). *Location:* on A222 about two miles east of Croydon. 24 bay covered, floodlit, grassed driving range. *Fees:* £2.00 for 40 balls, £3.75 for 80 balls. *Eating facilities:* snacks/coffee. *Opening hours:* weekdays 9am to 10pm, weekends 9am to 9pm. *Visitors:* very welcome at all times, open to the public. Lessons and club repairs available. Professional: Nick Parfrement (0181-656 1690).

ESHER. **Sandown Golf Centre,** More Lane, Esher KT10 8AN (01372 463340). *Location:* centre of Sandown Park Racecourse. 33 bay covered floodlit range plus grassed area. *Fees:* information not provided. *Eating facilities:* coffee shop and bar. *Opening hours:* 10am to 10pm weekdays; 10am to 9pm weekends. Three PGA Professionals. Snooker club.

GODALMING. **Broadwater Park Golf Club,** Guildford Road, Farncombe, Near Godalming GU7 3DD (01483 429955). 16 bay covered, floodlit driving range. *Fees:* £2.35 for 55 balls. *Eating facilities:* available. *Opening Hours:* 8am to 10pm. Professional, tuition and 9 hole Par 3 course.

LEATHERHEAD. **Pachesham Golf Centre,** Oaklawn Road, Leatherhead KT22 0BT (01372 843453; Fax: 01372 844076). *Location:* half a mile outside Leatherhead, just off A244. Junction 9 M25. 33 bay covered floodlit range. *Fees:* 30 balls £1.00, 60 balls £1.75, 90 balls £2.00. *Eating facilities:* available. *Opening hours:* weekdays 9am to 10pm, weekends 9am to 9pm. PGA teaching professional, 9 hole golf course.

NEWDIGATE. **Rusper Golf Club and Driving Range,** Rusper Road, Newdigate RH5 5BX (01293 871871). *Location:* Dorking-Horsham A24, Beare Green roundabout, left to Newdigate, in village turn right to Rusper, club approximately one mile on right hand side. 12 bay floodlit, grassed driving range. *Fees:* £1.50 for 51 balls. *Eating facilities:* snacks and bar. *Opening Hours:* dawn till dusk. Qualified professional tuition; club hire. Attached to Rusper Club, membership available, monthly payments. Professional: Karl Spurrier.

NEW MALDON. **Beverley Park Golf Range,** Beverley Way, New Maldon KT3 4PH (0181-949 9200). *Location:* Kingston bypass A3. *Eating facilities:* licensed restaurant. *Opening Hours:* 8am to 10pm weekdays, 8am to 9pm weekends and Bank Holidays.

OLD WOKING. **Hoebridge Golf Centre,** Old Woking Road, Old Woking GU22 8JH (01483 722611). Covered, floodlit range. 25 bays. Two 18 hole courses and 9 hole course. *Fees:* £3.75 large basket, £2.75 medium basket, £1.75 small basket. *Opening hours:* dawn to dusk in summer, 8am to 11pm in winter. *Eating facilities:* available.

RICHMOND. **Richmond Golf Range,** The Athletic Ground, Twickenham Road (A316), Richmond TW9 2SS (0181-332 9200). *Location:* next to Richmond swimming pool on the A316 road. 24 bay covered, floodlit driving range, grassed area. *Fees:* information not provided. *Eating facilities:* coffee shop. *Opening hours:* weekdays 9.30am to 10pm, weekends 9am to 9.30pm; September to May closed Saturday afternoons at 1pm. Professional tuition available.

EAST SUSSEX

HELLINGLY. **Wellshurst Golf and Country Club,** North Street, Hellingly BN27 4EE (01435 813456). *Location:* two miles from the A22 London to Eastbourne Road on A267. 16 bay covered, floodlit range. *Fees:* £2.00 per large bucket of quality two piece balls. *Eating facilities:* full bar and catering facilities available at all times. *Opening hours:* 7.30am to 9.30pm. Full professional staff for lessons, well stocked pro shop, 18 hole course, two sand bunker bays.

HORAM. **Horam Park Golf Course and Floodlit Driving Range,** Chiddingly Road, Horam TN21 0JJ (014353 3477, Fax: 014353 3677). *Location:* 13 miles north of Eastbourne, 7 miles east of Uckfield. Covered, floodlit, Astroturf range. 16 bays. 5 PGA golf Professionals, lessons and tuition available. Golf shop. *Fees:* £2.00 per bucket; £1.00 after 8.30pm. *Opening hours:* weekdays 8am to 10.30pm. *Eating facilities:* restaurant bar and spike bar.

SEDLESCOMBE. **Sedlescombe Golf Club,** Kent Street, Sedlescombe TN33 0SD (01424 870898; Fax: 01424 870855). *Location:* five miles north of Hastings on the A21. 24 bay covered, floodlit range; mats. *Fees:* £2.00 per bucket, £1.00 after 8.30pm. *Eating facilities:* bar and catering available. *Opening hours:* 8am to 10.30pm. All professional services available.

WEST SUSSEX

CHICHESTER. **Chichester Golf Centre,** Hunston Village, Chichester PO20 6AX (01243 533833). *Location:* take B2145 off A27 to Selsey, golf centre is on the left after Hunston Village. 26 bay covered, floodlit, grassed driving range. *Fees:* £2.50 per bucket (60 balls). *Eating facilities:* fully licensed clubhouse. *Opening hours:* 9am to 8pm. Tuition available, two 18 hole courses and a 9 hole course also. Society Golf Days available, membership available.

CRAWLEY. **Gatwick Manor Golf Club,** Gatwick Manor Hotel, London Road, Lowfield Heath, Crawley RH10 2ST (01293 526301 (Hotel); 01293 538587 (Club)). *Location:* A23 Crawley to Gatwick Airport on London Road on right. 9 grassed tees. *Fees:* £3 for 9 holes. *Eating facilities:* hotel facilities at Gatwick Manor. *Opening hours:* 9am to 8.00pm seven days a week. *

LITTLEHAMPTON near. **Rustington Golf Centre,** Golfers Lane, Rustington, Near Littlehampton BN16 4NB (01903 850786/850790). *Location:* on A259 between Worthing and Littlehampton. 30 bay covered, floodlit, grassed range. *Fees:* £2.95 per basket of balls, £1 club hire. *Eating facilities:* coffee shop. *Opening hours:* 9am to 9pm seven days. Teaching Professional, well stocked golf shop. 9 hole Par 3 course £4.95 per round.

TYNE AND WEAR

NEWCASTLE-UPON-TYNE. **Gosforth Park Golfing Complex Ltd,** High Gosforth Park, Newcastle-Upon-Tyne NE3 5HQ (0191-236 4480). *Location:* off A1 for Gosforth Park. 45 bay covered, floodlit range. *Fees:* £2.00 per basket of balls. *Opening hours:* 8am to 10.30pm. *Eating facilities:* bar and restaurant. Professional tuition, 18 hole golf course, 9 hole pitch and putt.

WASHINGTON. **Washington Moat House Golf Club,** Stone Cellar Road, High Usworth, District 12, Washington NE37 1PH (0191-417 2626). *Location:* just off A1(M), take A194 then exit A195 Washington. 21 bay floodlit grassed range. 18 hole pitch and putt. *Fees:* information on request. *Eating facilities:* Bunkers Bar 9am to 11pm, serves snacks. Buffets etc by arrangement. *Opening hours:* 9.30am to 10pm. Golf professional, tuition available. Leisure club with sauna, pool, solarium, multi gym, spa and squash.

WARWICKSHIRE

COVENTRY. **John Reay Golf Centres,** Sandpits Lane, Keresley, Coventry CV7 8NJ (01203 333920). *Location:* three miles from Coventry city centre along A51 Tamworth Road. Covered, floodlit driving range. 30 bays. Golf club repair facility. Teaching professionals using latest video techniques. *Fees:* 45 balls £1. *Opening hours:* weekdays 9am to 10pm. *Eating facilities:* Hogan's Bar & Bistro open every day. *Visitors:* open to the public. Large Golf Shop with all the leading brands of golf equipment. Professional: John Reay (01203 333920/333405). *

WARWICK. **Warwick Golf Centre,** The Racecourse, Warwick CV34 6HW (01926 494316). *Location:* A46 off the M40 (middle of Warwick). 26 bay covered, floodlit, grassed range. *Fees:* large basket £2.30, medium basket £2.00 and small basket £1.20. *Opening hours:* weekdays 10am to 9pm, weekends 9am to 6pm. *Eating facilities:* bar only. Professional tuition, 9 hole golf course (Par 34) open to the public.

WEST MIDLANDS

DUDLEY near. **Swindon Ridge Golf Driving Range,** Bridgnorth Road, Swindon, Near Dudley DY3 4PU (01902 896191). *Location:* B4176 Bridgnorth/Dudley Road, three miles from Himley A449 Junction. 27 bay floodlit range (22 covered). *Fees:* £1.40 for small bucket, £2.20 for large bucket, £2.95 for extra-large bucket. Tuition £8.00 per half hour with large bucket free. *Opening hours:* 9am to 9.30pm weekdays, 8.30am to 6pm weekends. *Eating facilities:* licensed bar and restaurant. 18 hole private golf club on site plus 9 hole Par 3. Snooker table in bar.

WOLVERHAMPTON. **Three Hammers Golf Complex,** Old Stafford Road, Coven, Wolverhampton WV10 7PP (01902 790428). *Location:* Junction 2 M54 north on A449, one mile on right. 24 covered floodlit bays. *Fees:* balls from £1.00. *Eating facilities:* bookings taken from 10.30am, details on (01902 791917). *Opening hours:* weekdays £9.30am to 10pm, weekends 9.30am to 9pm. 18 hole Par 3 course, two teaching Professionals.

WILTSHIRE

SWINDON. **Broome Manor Golf Complex,** Pipers Way, Swindon SN3 1RG (01793 532403/495761). *Location:* two miles from Junction 15 on M4, follow signs for Golf Complex. 35 bays, 30 covered, five uncovered, floodlit range. *Fees:* large basket £2.85, standard £2.00. *Eating facilities:* full service available. *Opening hours:* 8am to 9pm. 18 hole course, 9 hole course, short game practice area, pitch and putt. Professional tuition available.

TROWBRIDGE near. **Wingfield Golf Range,** Radstock Road, Wingfield, Near Trowbridge BA14 9LW (01225 776365). *Location:* Radstock Road out of Trowbridge, A366 approximately two miles. 28 bay covered, floodlit driving range. *Fees:* £2.00 for 50 balls, £3.00 for 100 balls. *Eating facilities:* snacks, hot and cold drinks, ice creams, sweets. *Opening Hours:* 9.30am to 9.30pm Monday to Saturday, 9.30am to 6pm Sunday. Resident Professional seven days a week; £9.50 per lesson including balls (25 minutes). Competitions arranged, Winter League Monday nights. Known as one of the best ranges around for atmosphere, views, home cooking.

WESTBURY near. **Thomstone Park Golf Club and Driving Range,** Chapmanslade, Near Westbury BA13 4AQ (01373 832825). *Location:* three miles north-west of Warminster on A36. 20 bay covered floodlit, grassed range. *Fees:* £2.00 per 50 balls, £3.00 per 100 balls. *Eating facilities:* coffee shop and bar in clubhouse. *Opening hours:* weekdays and Saturdays 8am to 9pm, Sundays 8am to 6pm. Professional available for lessons, Pro shop, 18 hole course, sauna, solarium. *

NORTH YORKSHIRE

HARROGATE. **Rudding Park Golf,** Rudding Park, Harrogate HG3 1DJ (01423 872100). *Location:* off Harrogate bypass, brown tourist signs indicate Rudding Park. 16 bay covered range, four bays grassed. *Fees:* telephone for details. *Eating facilities:* available at Rudding Golf Course. *Opening Hours:* 8am to dusk. Golf academy.

WEST YORKSHIRE

BRADFORD. **Shay Grange Golf Centre,** Long Lane, off Bingley Road, Heaton, Bradford BD9 6RX (01274 483955). *Location:* take the A650 Bradford to Bingley road, turn left at Cottingley lights, the Centre will be found on the left after two miles. 32 bay covered, floodlit, grassed range. *Fees:* £2.00 for 60 balls. *Eating facilities:* coffee shop. *Opening hours:* weekdays 9am to 10pm, weekends 9am to 7pm. Golf instruction school, all weather putting green, sand bunker. Discount golf shop. Professional: Steve Dixon. *

LEEDS. **Leeds Golf Centre,** Wike Ridge Lane, Shadwell, Leeds LS17 9JW (0113 288 6186). *Location:* two miles north of Leeds between A61 and A58 at the village of Wike. 20 bay covered, floodlit, grassed range; artificial turf mats. *Fees:* £2.00 per basket. *Eating facilities:* full catering available 8am to 9.30pm. *Opening hours:* 8am to 10pm. David Leadbetter Golf Academy, 18 hole course and short course. Brochure gives full details of facilities available.

SCOTLAND

ABERDEENSHIRE

ABERDEEN. **Kings Links Golf Centre,** Golf Road, Aberdeen AB2 1RZ (01224 641577; Fax: 01224 639410). *Location:* behind Pittodrie Stadium, on the Kings Links, by the beach. 58 covered bays, on two tiers, floodlit range. *Fees:* £2.00 per 48 balls. *Eating facilities:* sandwiches at lunchtime, vended drinks and snacks. *Opening hours:* 9.00am to 10pm weekdays, 9am to 5.30pm weekends. Adjoins Kings Links Golf Course, PGA qualified Professionals for tuition and club repair. Short game area (bunkers and putting) and putting green. Concessions available for Senior Citizens and under 14's.

AYRSHIRE

DAILLY. **Brunston Castle Golf Course,** Dailly KA26 9RH (01465 81471). *Location:* five miles north of Girvan on B471. *Fees:* information not provided. *Eating facilities:* full facilities available. *Opening hours:* 8am to 6pm. 18 hole course available. PGA Professional: D. McKenzie.

EDINBURGH & LOTHIANS

DALKEITH near. **Melville Golf Centre and Driving Range,** South Melville, Lasswade EH18 1AN (0131-663 8038; Fax: 0131-654 0814). *Location:* three minutes from Edinburgh City Bypass (Exit A7 Galashiels); signposted "Golf Range". 22 floodlit, covered bays plus 12 outdoor mats. 300 yards long; target practice. *Fees:* top quality two piece balls from £1.80 for 50, various concessions. *Eating facilities:* hot and cold beverages available. *Opening Hours:* weekdays 9am to 10pm; weekends 9am to 8pm. Club hire and repairs, golf shop; Professional tuition for individuals and groups; practice bunker and putting green. 9-hole pay and play course opening mid-1995.

EDINBURGH. **Braid Hills Golf Centre,** 91 Liberton Drive, Edinburgh EH16 6NS (0131-658 1755; Fax: 0131-658 1653). *Location:* leave Edinburgh bypass at Straiton Junction, head towards city centre, take left turn at second set of traffic lights, proceed half a mile along Liberton Drive. 30 bay covered, floodlit astroturf range. *Fees:* £2.00 for basket of 50 balls. *Opening Hours:* 9am to 9pm weekdays, 9am to 6pm weekends. Scotland's top Professionals available for group and individual tuition, large comprehensive golf shop with stock of all leading brand names.

EDINBURGH. **Port Royal Golf Range,** Eastfield Road, Ingliston, Edinburgh EH28 8TR (0131-333 4377). *Location:* follow signs to Edinburgh Airport, on slip road approximately 100 yards from airport entrance. Five miles from centre of Edinburgh. 36 bays, 24 covered, floodlit and 12 grassed. 1000 square yard putting green and 9 hole Par 3 golf course. Pro shop, Professional and tuition. *Fees:* £1.40 per basket. *Eating facilities;* bar and lounge area, bar meals all day. *Opening hours:* 10am to 10pm. Open all year. *

FIFE

ST. ANDREWS. **St. Andrews Links Trust Golf Practice Centre,** St. Andrews, KY16 9SF *(01334 75757; Fax: 01334 77036). *Location:* situated alongside the Old Course, just 10 minutes' walk from the town centre and only a few minutes by car. 12 indoor bays, 12 outdoor bays. *Fees:* 50 balls £1.75, Senior Citizens/students £1.45, children (under 18) 85p. *Eating facilities:* light refreshments and seated viewing area. *Opening hours:* 8am to 9pm daily (balls dispensed until 8pm). Pitching, putting, bunker area using own balls (£1.00 for 45 minutes). Golf club hire available. Centre Manager: Brendan Duffy (01334 474489).

GLASGOW

UDDINGSTON. **Clydeway Golf Centre,** Blantyre Farm Road, Uddingston G71 7RR (0141-641 8899). *Location:* B758 off Main Street, Uddingston, near Glasgow Zoo. 25 covered floodlit bays. *Fees:* £1.70 for 60 balls. *Opening hours:* 10am to 5.30pm (to 8.30pm April to September). Tuition and repairs, very large modern shop including ladies' department. *

PERTHSHIRE

MIDDLEBANK. **Middlebank Golf Range,** Middlebank, Errol PH2 7SX (01821 670320). 21 bay driving range. *Fees:* £1.50 per 50 balls. *Eating facilities:* no bar but coffee, etc available. *Opening Hours:* 9am to 9pm seven days. Tuition available and well stocked golf shop.

RENFREWSHIRE

RENFREW. **Normandy Golf Range,** Inchinnan Road, Renfrew PA4 9EG (0141-886 7477). *Location:* take M8, then take Glasgow Airport turn-off, then take Renfrew Road one mile away. 25 bays covered, floodlit. *Fees:* £1.50 per token for 48 balls. *Opening hours:* 9.30am to 10.00pm seven days. *Eating facilities:* full hotel facilities. Professional, assistants, tuition anytime. Adjacent to Renfrew Golf Club. Large comprehensive stock of all leading golf equipment.

WALES

CLWYD

CHESTER near. **Bannel Golf Driving Range,** Mold Road, Penymynydd, Near Chester CH4 0EN. *Location:* A5118 Penymynydd to Mold road. *Fees:* £2.00 50 balls, £3.50 100 balls. Happy Hour Monday to Friday – reduced rates. *Eating facilities:* refreshments available. Putting green, sand bunker, golf shop. Happy Hour Monday to Friday – reduced rates. Proprietor: Mrs J. Povey.

ST. ASAPH. **North Wales Golf Driving Range and 9 Hole Course,** Llannerch Park, St. Asaph LL17 0BD (01745 730805). *Location:* on the A525, one and a quarter miles from St. Asaph Cathedral. 14 bay covered, floodlit driving range. *Fees:* £1.00 for 36 balls, pro rata; four bucket sizes. *Eating facilities:* refreshments, hot and cold drinks, sandwiches, burgers, sweets. *Opening Hours:* 10am to 9pm seven days a week during Summer, early closing in Winter 5pm Friday to Monday. Lessons with non-resident Professional by arrangement £7.00 per half hour including balls. 9 hole course also on site – £2.00 pay and play, Non-members welcome.

MID GLAMORGAN

CAERPHILLY. **Virginia Park Golf Club,** Virginia Park, Caerphilly CF8 3SW (01222 863919). *Location:* off Pontygwindy Road, next to recreation centre. 20 bay covered, floodlit driving range. *Fees:* two piece balls £1.50 basket, one piece range balls £1.00 basket. *Eating facilities:* available. *Opening Hours:* 7am to 10pm seven days a week. 9 hole golf course.

SOUTH GLAMORGAN

BARRY. **South Wales Golf Range and Course,** 101 Port Road East, Barry CF6 7PX (01446 742434). *Location:* A4050 road Cardiff to Barry. 16 covered floodlit bays. *Fees:* from £2.00. *Opening Hours:* weekdays 9am to 8pm; weekends 9am to 6pm. Professional tuition available from Simon Cox, former Welsh Champion; 9-hole Par 3 course and 18-hole putting green.

GWENT

ABERGAVENNY. **Wernddu Golf Centre,** Old Ross Road, Abergavenny NP7 8NG (01873 856223). *Location:* one and a half miles east of Abergavenny on B4521. 36 bay driving range - 26 covered and floodlit, 10 grassed. *Fees:* £1.50 for 50 balls. *Eating facilities:* available. *Opening Hours:* 8am to 10.30pm. *Visitors:* welcome. Professional tuition, 9 hole pitch and putt and a 9 hole course.

COEDKERNEW. **Parc Golf Club.** Church Lane, Coedkernew NP1 9TH (01633 680933). *Location:* Junction 28 M4, then A48. 38 bay covered, floodlit driving range. *Fees:* 50 balls for £1.00. *Eating facilities:* available. *Opening Hours:* weekdays 7.30am to 10pm, weekends 7.30am to 8.30pm. Three Professionals, individual and group tuition. Full social calendar.

NORTHERN IRELAND

ANTRIM

NEWTOWNABBEY. **Ballyearl Golf and Leisure Centre,** 585 Doagh Road, Newtownabbey BT36 8RZ (01232 848287). *Location:* six miles north of Belfast on M2 then first right onto Doagh Road from Belfast to Larne Road. 32 bay covered, floodlit range, 20 grassed bays. *Fees:* £2.00 small bucket (70 balls), £2.70 large bucket (110 balls). *Eating facilities:* bar – may be signed in. *Opening hours:* 9am to 10.15pm. Professional: Jim Robinson. Five squash courts, sunbed, theatre, golf, fitness suite and art classes. Various courses available.

ARMAGH

CRAIGAVON. **Craigavon Golf and Ski Centre,** Turmoyra Lane, Silverwood, Lurgan, Craigavon BT66 6NE (01762 326606; Fax: 01762 347272). *Location:* A76 off M1 motorway. Floodlit driving range with 10 covered and 10 grassed bays. *Fees:* £1.60 per bucket. *Eating facilities:* full restuarant. *Opening hours:* 9am to 9pm. Professional, equipment hire, ski slope.

COUNTY DOWN

KNOCKBRACKEN. **Knockbracken Golf Centre,** 24 Ballymaconaghy Road, Knockbracken, Belfast BT8 4SB (01232 792108). *Location:* outskirts of Belfast, approximately three miles from centre along Ormeau Road near "Four Winds" Restaurant and Public House. 36 bays covered, floodlit and grassed. *Fees:* £2.20 for 100 balls, £1.80 for 70 balls, £1.25 for 40 balls. *Opening hours:* 9am to 11pm. *Eating facilities:* bar open seven days a week during normal opening hours, catering available seven days a week 11am to 10pm. Tuition available at Golf Academy by PGA Professionals. Snooker, playing machines, ski slope in season, equipment hire available, bowling (indoors).

WARRENPOINT. **Newry and Mourne Golf Centre,** Milltown Street, Burren, Warrenpoint BT34 3RJ (016937 73247). *Location:* six miles south of Newry, at Warrenpoint roundabout turn left for Burren: approximately one mile. Driving range – 10 covered, 20 grassed bays, all floodlit. *Fees:* £1.50 per 50 balls, £2.00 for 80 balls, £2.50 for 120 balls. *Opening Hours:* weekdays £10am to 10pm; weekends £10am to 8pm. Tuition available at all times for individuals, groups and schools. 9 hole pitch and putt course. Professional: Pat Trainor.

FERMANAGH

ENNISKILLEN. **Ashwoods Golf Centre,** Ashwoods, Sligo Road, Enniskillen (01365 325321 or 322908). *Location:* one and a half miles west of Enniskillen on main Sligo Road. 7 bay covered, floodlit range. *Fees:* £2.00 per bucket of 70 balls. *Eating facilities:* none on site, available 300 yards away. *Opening hours:* 9am to 10pm summer, 9am to 8pm winter. Resident Professional, 9 hole Par 3 course, club hire available.

REPUBLIC OF IRELAND

DUBLIN

FOXROCK. **Leopardstown Driving Range,** Foxrock (01 895341). *Location:* five miles south of Dublin city centre situated in Leopardstown race course. 38 indoor, 38 outdoor floodlit bays. *Fees:* information not provided. *Opening hours:* 9am to 10pm. *Eating facilities:* restaurant. Professional tuition – practice green. 9 hole golf course and 18 hole par 3.

CHANNEL ISLANDS

ST. OUEN'S. **Les Mielles Golf and Country Club,** St. Ouen's Bay, Jersey (01534 482787). *Location:* centre of St. Ouen's Bay. 20 bay covered driving range. *Fees:* information not provided. *Opening hours:* dawn till dusk. *Eating facilities:* restaurant, seasonal barbecue, kiosk. NZPGA Professional Jeremy Phillips. Public golf facility. Putting green; golf shop. Manager: J.A. Le Brun.

PORTUGAL

LISBON

ESTORIL. **Quinta da Marinha Golf Range,** Quinta da Marinha Hotel Village Resort, Casa 36, 2750 Cascais, Portugal (4869881/9). *Location:* highway from Lisbon to Cascais. New driving range opened in April 1994. Pro shop, Professional, all facilities.

Index

DUNDALK. **Dundalk Golf Club,** Blackrock, Dundalk (042 21379; Fax: 042 22022). *Location:* Dundalk coast road to Blackrock, three miles. Parkland. 18 holes, 6776 yards, 6160 metres. S.S.S. 72 (Par 72). Six acre field practice ground. *Green Fees:* weekdays £18.00; weekends £20.00. *Eating facilities:* full restaurant and bar. *Visitors:* welcome Mondays, Wednesdays, Thursdays and Fridays, restrictions Tuesdays and weekends. *Society Meetings:* welcome except Tuesdays and Sundays. Professional: James Cassidy. Secretary: Joe Carroll (042 21731).

COUNTY MAYO

ACHILL. **Achill Golf Club,** Keel, Achill. *Location:* N59 from Westport and R319 from Mulranny to Achill. Seaside links in scenic setting. 9 holes, 2723 yards, 2489 metres. S.S.S. 66. *Green Fees:* on application. *Visitors:* welcome at all times, no restrictions. *Society Meetings:* by prior arrangement. Secretary: Patrick Lavelle.

BALLINROBE. **Ballinrobe Golf Club,** Castleton Road, Ballinrobe (Tel & Fax: 092 41448). *Location:* one mile from town on the Castleton road. Flatland with four holes in the middle of a racecourse. 9 holes, 5540 metres. S.S.S. 68. Practice ground. *Green Fees:* £8.00. *Eating facilities:* snacks and bar facilities. *Visitors:* welcome at all times except Tuesday evenings and Sundays. Excellent shooting and beside two of the best trout fishing lakes in Europe. *Society Meetings:* welcome. Secretary: Pat Holian (092 41659).

BELMULLET. **Carne Golf Course,** Carne, Belmullet (097 82292; Fax: 097 81477). *Location:* three km from centre of Belmullet town. Pure links course – feature holes 9th, 14th and 18th. 18 holes, 6042 metres. Medal S.S.S. 71, Par 72; Championship S.S.S. 72, Par 72. Practice ground. *Green Fees:* £15.00. Groups of more than six persons or staying in local registered approved accommodation get a discount. *Eating facilities:* bar and meals available in clubhouse. *Visitors:* welcome at all times. *Society Meetings:* welcome at all times. Secretary: Liam McAndrew (097 81051; Fax: 097 81477).

COUNTY MONAGHAN

CASTLEBLAYNEY. **Castleblayney Golf Club,** Onomy, Castleblayney (042 46194). *Location:* Hope Castle Estate, 500 yards from town centre. Scenic parkland course with lakes and forest in centre of Leisure Park. 9 holes, 5345 yards. S.S.S. 66. *Green Fees:* £5.00 weekdays; £8.00 weekends. *Eating facilities:* restaurant and bar. *Visitors:* welcome at all times except during major competitions. Accommodation in Hope Castle Complex. *Society Meetings:* welcome. Secretary: Des McGlynn (042 40197).

COUNTY MEATH

NAVAN. **Royal Tara Golf Club,** Bellinter, Navan (046 25244 and 25508). *Location:* 25 miles north of Dublin off National Primary Route N3. Parkland, private course. 18 holes, 5757 yards. S.S.S. 70. 9 hole course, 3184 yards. S.S.S. 35. *Green Fees:* IR£14.00 weekdays; IR£18.00 weekends. *Eating facilities:* bar and full catering facilities. *Visitors:* welcome, Tuesday Ladies' Day, please check with club in advance. *Society Meetings:* welcomed Monday, Thursday, Friday and Saturday. Professional: Mr Adam Whiston (046 26009). Secretary: Mr Paddy O'Brien (046 25508).

COUNTY ROSCOMMON

ROSCOMMON. **Roscommon Golf Club,** Mote Park, Roscommon (0903 26382). *Location:* half a mile south of Roscommon town. Rolling parkland. 9 holes (course will be extended to 18 holes and opened for limited play in August 1995), 5784 metres. S.S.S. 70. Practice ground. *Green Fees:* £10.00 per day. *Eating facilities:* full catering during main golf season. *Visitors:* welcome, restrictions Tuesdays and Saturdays and no visitors Sundays except on open days. *Society Meetings:* welcome with restrictions as for visitors. Secretary: Cathal McConn (0903 26062).

COUNTY SLIGO

ENNISCRONE. **Enniscrone Golf Club,** Enniscrone (096 36657). *Location:* on coast road from Sligo to Ballina, about nine miles from Ballina. Championship links course – host to the Irish Close Championship 1993. 18 holes, 6570 yards. S.S.S. 72. Practice area and putting green. *Green Fees:* weekdays £15.00 to £18.00; weekends £12.00 to £15.00. *Eating facilities:* bar and full catering facilities. *Visitors:* welcome. *Society Meetings:* groups of 12 or more, Green Fee £10.00 to £12.00. Professional: Charlie McGoldrick. Secretary: John Fleming.

COUNTY TIPPERARY

CARRICK-ON-SUIR. **Carrick-on-Suir Golf Club,** Garravoone, Carrick-on-Suir (051 40047). *Location:* one mile from Carrick-on-Suir on Dungarvan Road. Scenic 9 hole course on elevated ground close to town. 9 holes, 5948 yards. S.S.S. 68. *Green Fees:* £10.00. *Eating facilities:* full meals and bar snacks available by prior arrangement. *Visitors:* welcome Monday to Saturday, avoid Tuesday and Wednesday evenings in summer (competitions). Special rates for groups. *Society Meetings:* all welcome by prior arrangement. Secretary: Francis Comerford (051 43328).

CLONMEL. **Clonmel Golf Club,** Lyreanearla, Mountain Road, Clonmel (052 21138). *Location:* three miles up the mountain road from Clonmel town. Parkland set on the scenic slopes of the Comeragh Mountains. 18 holes, 5538 (white), 5297 (green) metres. S.S.S. 69 white, 68 green. Practice area. *Green Fees:* £13.00 per round weekdays; £15.00 per round weekends. Reductions for groups over 25 persons. *Eating facilities:* bar, sit-down meals available on request. *Visitors:* always welcome but contact Secretary/Manager re weekends. Golf range across the road with B&B accommodation. *Society Meetings:* welcome, contact Secretary/ Manager for weekends. Professional: Mr Robert Hayes (052 24050). Secretary/Manager: Ms Aine Myles Keating (052 24050).

COUNTY WATERFORD

BALLINAKILL. **Waterford Castle Golf Club,** The Island, Ballinakill (051 71633; Fax: 051 79316). *Location:* Waterford City. Parkland. 18 holes, 6209 metres. S.S.S. 73. *Green Fees:* weekdays £18.00; weekends £20.00. *Eating facilities:* bar food in clubhouse. *Visitors:* welcome, no restrictions, subject only to availability. Five star Waterford Castle Hotel with all its facilities including tennis and heated swimming pool. *Society Meetings:* enquiries welcomed. Secretary: Dick Brennan.

DUNGARVAN. **West Waterford Golf Club,** Coolcormack, Dungarvan (353 58 43216; Fax: 353 58 44343). *Location:* Aglish Road on roundabout on N25 bypass road, five km west of Dungarvan. Parkland course with natural water hazards, mature trees, abundant wildlife, etc. 18 holes, 6771 yards, 6162 metres. S.S.S. 72, 73, 74. *Green Fees:* weekdays £15.00; weekends £20.00. Discounts for groups and societies. *Eating facilities:* full bar and catering facilities, light snacks all day or avail yourself of our full dining room service. *Visitors:* always welcome, pre-booking in advance if possible. *Society Meetings:* always welcome, book in advance if possible. Secretary: Nora J. Spratt.

LISMORE. **Lismore Golf Club,** Ballyin, Lismore (058 54026). *Location:* one kilometre north of Lismore Heritage Town, just off the N72. Undulating parkland with mature trees, course surrounded by woodlands. 9 holes, 5291 metres. S.S.S. 67. *Green Fees:* £8.00 weekdays; £10.00 weekends and Bank Holidays. Reductions for Societies. *Eating facilities:* tea, coffee, snacks. *Visitors:* welcome weekdays, restriction may apply on Wednesday (Ladies' day). *Society Meetings:* welcome weekdays except Wednesday. Secretary: Shaun Moynihan (058 54016).

WATERFORD. **Faithlegg Golf Club,** Faithlegg House, Co. Waterford (051 382241; Fax: 051 382664). *Location:* from Waterford city turn off main Dunmore East road towards Cheekpoint village. Parkland course with undulating fairways, contoured greens and a number of lakes to put a premium on shot-making. 18 holes, 6662 yards, 6057 metres. S.S.S. 72. Practice ground and putting green. *Green Fees:* £20.00 per round, £16.00 before 9am (except Saturdays); golf and Dinner £27.00; groups of 20 or more £18.00 per round. *Eating facilities:* full bar and restaurant facilities available every day. *Visitors:* always welcome. Ranked in the top ten best new courses in Britain and Ireland by Golf World Magazine in December 1993. *Society Meetings:* always welcome. Professional: Ted Higgins. Secretary: Vari McGreevy (051 382688; Fax: 051 382664).

COUNTY WEXFORD

ROSSLARE. **Rosslare Golf Club,** Rosslare Strand, Wexford (053 32113; Fax: 053 32203). *Location:* Rosslare harbour ferry terminal, six miles. Seaside links course, beside the Irish Sea. Two courses. Old Course – 18 holes, 6554 yards. S.S.S. 71. New Course – 9 holes 3153 yards. S.S.S. 70, Par 35. Practice ground. *Green Fees:* Old Course weekdays £18.00; weekends £23.00. New Course £12.00 per round (18 holes), £8.00 for 9 holes. Reductions for Societies and off season. *Eating facilities:* available all day. *Visitors:* welcome, telephone for booking. *Society Meetings:* welcome, telephone for booking. Professional: Austin Skerritt (053 32238). Secretary/Manager: J.F. Hall (053 32203).

ROSSLARE HARBOUR. **St. Helen's Bay Golf and Country Club,** St. Helens, Kilrone, Rosslare Harbour (053 33669/33234; Fax: 053 33803). *Location:* two miles from Rosslare Harbour. Part links, part parkland. 18 holes, 6091 metres. S.S.S. 72. *Green Fees:* weekdays £15.00 (low season), £17.00 (high season); weekends £18.00 (low season), £22.00 (high season). Special Society and "Early Bird" rates. *Eating facilities:* full bar and restaurant facilities. *Visitors:* always welcome. Cottage accommodation on site. *Society Meetings:* always welcome. Secretary: Larry Byrne.

COUNTY WEST MEATH

ATHLONE. **Glasson Golf and Country Club,** Glasson, Athlone (0902 85120; Fax: 0902 85444). *Location:* take the N55 from Athlone to Glasson village and turn left. Parkland course bordering Lough Ree and the Shannon – spectacular scenery. 18 holes, 7043 yards, 6410 metres. S.S.S. 72. Practice range, 3 hole golf academy. *Green Fees:* weekdays IR£22.00; weekends IR£25.00. Group rates on request. *Eating facilities:* restaurant and bar, spike bar and snack bar, private rooms available. *Visitors:* welcome every day, members' times up to 10.30am and after 4.30pm. Private jetty with mooring facilities. *Society Meetings:* welcome, no restrictions, all facilities available. Director of Golf/Professional: Peter O'Hagan. Operations Manager/Secretary: Fidelma Reid.

COUNTY WICKLOW

BRITTAS BAY. **The European Club,** Brittas Bay, Wicklow (0404 47415). *Location:* one mile south of main Brittas Bay beach on coast road, 40 miles south of Dublin City Centre. Rolling linksland overlooking Arklow Bay, designed and owned by Pat Ruddy. 18 holes, 6900 yards. S.S.S. 72. Extensive practice areas. *Green Fees:* IR£20.00 weekdays; IR£25.00 weekends. Discounts for groups of 20 plus. *Eating facilities:* full services. *Visitors:* welcome to all golfers, advisable to book. *Society Meetings:* welcome. Secretary: Pat Ruddy (0404 47415; Fax: 01 2808457).

Isle of Man

DOUGLAS. **Douglas Golf Club,** Pulrose Golf Course, Pulrose Road, Douglas IM2 1AE (01624 675952). *Location:* one mile from town centre, next to power station. Undulating parkland. 18 holes, 5922 yards. S.S.S. 68. Practice and putting area. *Green Fees:* information not provided. *Eating facilities:* bar meals always available. *Visitors:* welcome, no restriction. *Society Meetings:* catered for by arrangement with Professional. Professional: Mr K. Parry (01624 661558). Secretary: Mr G. Allen.

DOUGLAS. **Pulrose Golf Course,** Douglas. *Location:* one mile from town centre, next to power station. Undulating parkland with memorable 17th hole. 18 holes, 5922 yards. S.S.S. 68. Putting and practice area. *Green Fees:* information not provided. *Eating facilities:* bar; meals available at all times. *Visitors:* welcome, no restrictions. *Society Meetings:* by arrangement with Professional. Professional: K. Parry (01624 75952). Secretary: G. Allen. *

FORT ISLAND. **Castletown Golf Club,** Castletown Golf Links Hotel, Fort Island, Derbyhaven (01624 822201). *Location:* 12 miles from Douglas, three miles from Ronaldsway Airport. Seaside links course. 18 holes, 6731 yards. S.S.S. 73. *Green Fees:* weekdays £19.00 per person per day; weekends £25.00 per person per day. *Eating facilities:* table d'hôte/à la carte restaurant, daytime and evening bistro snacks. *Visitors:* welcome without reservation. Accommodation available, plus sauna, sunbeds, swimming pool, changing rooms. *Society Meetings:* catered for. Professional: Murray S. Crowe (01624 822211). General Manager: Miss J.M. Mitchell (01624 822201). Hon. Secretary: Mr A. Karran. *

ONCHAN. **King Edward Bay Golf Club,** Groudle Road, Howstrake, Onchan (01624 620430). *Location:* north headland of Douglas Bay. Stunning views from Headland links course. Watered greens, excellent fairways. 18 holes, 5450 yards. S.S.S. 67. Practice area. *Green Fees:* weekdays £12.00; weekends £14.00. *Eating facilities:* full catering available, three bars. *Visitors:* welcome without reservation but not before 9.30am Sundays. *Society Meetings:* most welcome by arrangement. Special rates. Professional: Donald Jones (01624 672709). Secretary: Miss C. Nightingale (Tel & Fax: 01624 676794).

PEEL. **Peel Golf Club,** Rheast Lane, Peel (01624 842227). *Location:* outskirts of Peel on main Douglas Road. Combination of links and heathland. 18 holes, 5914 yards. S.S.S. 68. Practice ground. *Green Fees:* weekdays £14.00 per day; weekends £18.00. *Eating facilities:* full bar service and meals. *Visitors:* welcome, but check in advance for weekend availability. *Society Meetings:* catered for, check in advance. Pro Shop. Professional: R. Garrard (01624 844232). Secretary: T.P. Kissack (01624 843456).

PORT ERIN. **Rowany Golf Club,** Rowany Drive, Port Erin IM9 6LN (01624 834108). *Location:* off the Promenade, five minutes from Port Erin. Hilly setting and meadowland. 18 holes, 5480 yards. S.S.S. 69. Practice ground. *Green Fees:* £13.00 per day weekdays; £18.00 weekends. 25% discount for parties of 20 and over. *Eating facilities:* restaurant and bar meals. *Visitors:* welcome by arrangement, little restriction. Accommodation can be arranged. *Society Meetings:* welcome. Secretary: W.H. Vincent (01624 834072).

PORT ST. MARY. **Port St. Mary Golf Club,** Point Road, Port St. Mary (01624 834932). *Location:* clearly signposted after entering Port St. Mary. Seaside links with beautiful panoramic views. 9 holes, 2754 yards. S.S.S. 66. *Green Fees:* weekdays £8.50; weekends £11.50. 10% reductions for Societies. *Eating facilities:* restaurant and bar open all day. *Visitors:* welcome at all times, only restrictions weekends between 8am to 10.30am. Handicap Certificate required. Secretary: T.M. Boyle (01624 832274).

RAMSEY. **Ramsey Golf Club,** Brookfield (01624 813365). *Location:* west boundary of Ramsey. Parkland. 18 holes, 6019 yards. S.S.S. 69. Practice ground. *Green Fees:* weekdays £10.00 winter, £15.00 summer; weekends £12.00 winter, £18.00 summer. *Eating facilities:* bar snacks and lunches available every day, a la carte restaurant available Thursday, Friday and Saturday. *Visitors:* welcome, teeing off between 10am – 12 noon and 2pm – 4pm only. *Society Meetings:* welcome weekdays only. Professional: Calum Wilson (01624 814736). Secretary: Major B.C. Hodgson (01624 812244 or 814736).

SANTON. **Mount Murray Golf Club,** Mount Murray, Santon (01624 661111; Fax: 01624 661116). *Location:* three miles from Douglas on the Castletown road. Wooded parkland set on hills with panoramic views. Seventh hole (612 yards) believed to be the longest in the UK. 18 holes, 6709 yards. S.S.S. 73. 24-bay driving range, two-tier putting green. *Green Fees:* weekdays £18.00, weekends £24.00. Special rates for societies and hotel guests. *Eating facilities:* full hotel catering, bistro, dining room, two bars. *Visitors:* welcome at any time by arrangement with the Secretary. *Society Meetings:* welcome at any time by arrangement with the Secretary. Secretary: Ronald G. Jackson (01624 661111 Ext. 597).

Channel Islands

ALDERNEY. **Alderney Golf Club,** Route des Carrieres, Alderney (01481 822835; Fax: 01481 823609). *Location:* one mile east of St. Annes. Seaside links with sea views from every hole. 9 holes, 2528 yards. S.S.S. 65. Putting and practice area. *Green Fees:* weekdays £10.00, £5.00 with a member; weekends £15.00, £7.50 with a member. Half price for Juniors. *Eating facilities:* friendly lounge bar, extensive lunch menu and bar meals all day. *Visitors:* welcome all year, tees reserved for competitions only. *Society Meetings:* welcome by arrangement. Secretary: Tim Butler.

GUERNSEY. **Royal Guernsey Golf Club,** L'Ancresse, Vale, Guernsey GY3 5BY (01481 47022). *Location:* three miles north of St. Peter Port. Seaside links. 18 holes, 6206 yards. S.S.S. 70. Driving range. *Green Fees:* £25.00, £15.00 playing with a member. *Eating facilities:* restaurant and bar. *Visitors:* welcome except Thursday and Saturday afternoons and Sundays unless playing with a member. Must have Handicap Certificate. Professional: Norman Wood (01481 45070). Secretary: M. De Laune (01481 46523; Fax: 01481 43960).

GUERNSEY. **St. Pierre Park Golf Club,** Rohais, St. Peter Port, Guernsey (01481 728282 ext 564). *Location:* 10 minutes from St. Peter Port. Wooded parkland with numerous lakes. 9 holes, 2511 yards. S.S.S. 27. Driving range, putting green. *Green Fees:* information not provided. *Eating facilities:* two restaurants and two bars in hotel. *Visitors:* welcome subject to rules and regulations on display. Hotel accommodation in 135 luxurious rooms and suites. Pro shop. Shop Manager: R. Corbet. *

JERSEY. **Jersey Recreation Grounds,** Greve d'Azette, St. Clement, Jersey (01534 21938). *Location:* inner coast road near St. Helier. Flat course with some water hazards. 9 holes, 2244 yards. S.S.S. 30. Practice range and putting green. *Green Fees:* information not provided. *Eating facilities:* licensed buffet. *Visitors:* welcome at all times. *Society Meetings:* welcome. Managing Director: P.A.O. Graham. *

JERSEY. **La Moye Golf Club,** St. Brelade, Jersey (01534 42701). *Location:* on road to Corbiere Lighthouse at La Moye, St. Brelade. Turn right at airport crossroads, right again at crossroads traffic lights. Seaside links championship course. 18 holes, 6512 yards. S.S.S. 72. Practice ground. *Green Fees:* on application. *Eating facilities:* full restaurant/snack facilities, three bars. *Visitors:* weekdays 9.30-11am and 2-3.30pm, weekends 2.30pm onwards. Must have Handicap Certificate. *Society Meetings:* by prior appointment only. Professional: Mr Mike Deeley (01534 43130). Secretary: Mr Pat Clash (01534 43401).

Royal Jersey Golf Course and Mont Orgueil.

JERSEY. **Royal Jersey Golf Club,** Grouville, Jersey (01534 854416; Fax: 01534 854684). *Location:* take coast road from St. Helier, head towards Gorey. Seaside links course. 18 holes, 6059 yards. S.S.S. 70. *Green Fees:* weekdays £30.00 per round; weekends and Bank Holidays £35.00 per round (after 2.30pm). *Eating facilities:* bar snacks. *Visitors:* welcome weekdays between 10am and 12 noon or 2pm to 4pm; weekends after 2.30pm. Handicap Certificate required. *Society Meetings:* welcome by prior arrangement. Professional: Tommy A. Horton (01534 852234). Secretary: R.C. Leader.

JERSEY. **Wheatlands Golf Course,** Off Old Beaumont Hill, St Peter, Jersey JE3 7ED (01534 888844; Fax: 01534 69880). *Location:* Le Vieux Beaumont, which is road forking off to right by Cannon, and then first right at top of hill. Jersey's only inland/ parkland course; undulating setting and extensive countryside vistas. 9 holes, 1326 yards, 1226 metres. S.S.S. 27. *Green Fees:* weekdays £10.00 for 9 holes, £15.00 for 18 holes; weekends £12.00 for 9 holes, £18.00 for 18 holes. *Eating facilities:* "Tenth Hole Bar", "Garden Terrace" – snacks and meals. *Visitors:* pay and play course; telephone bookings accepted. *Society Meetings:* welcome.

ST. OUEN'S. **Les Mielles Golf and Country Club,** St. Ouen's Bay, Jersey JE3 2PQ (01534 482787; Fax: 01534 485414). *Location:* centre of St. Ouen's Bay. American design "bent grass" greens, fairways of "dwarf rye". 18 holes, 5700 yards (white tees). S.S.S. 68. Putting green. *Green Fees:* weekdays £15.00; weekends £17.00; subject to review. *Eating facilities:* restaurant, bar facilities; seasonal barbecue. *Visitors:* always welcome, pre-booking necessary. Large Pro shop, hire equipment available, carts and buggies for visitors. Smart golfing attire required, no jeans code. *Society Meetings:* welcome, pre-booking required. Professional: Jeremy Phillips N.Z.P.G.A. Manager: J. A'C Le Brun.

PUBLISHER'S NOTE

While every effort is made to ensure accuracy, we regret that FHG Publications cannot accept responsibility for errors, omissions or misrepresentation in our entries or any consequences thereof. Prices in particular should be checked because we go to press early. We will follow up complaints, but cannot act as arbiters or agents for either party.

Golf in France

WHERE TO PLAY • WHERE TO STAY

by Michael Gedye

PROBABLY no other country in Europe has managed to produce so much memorable golf that is as closely interlinked with its history, heritage and culture as has France. Dramatic, highly playable courses wind through the deer parks and forests of great estates, fairways sweep past ancient vineyards, grand châteaux provide stately clubhouses and even, in some cases, alternative venues for concerts and cultural events. From sandy shorelines sprinkled with pine to holes carved out against spectacular mountain backdrops, the holiday courses of France offer great variety, well-maintained golf of high quality, clubhouse facilities to match and a warm welcome to all visitors, whatever their handicap. Spread across such a large country, the choice covers a variety of landscape and climatic seasons. For convenience, our selection of courses is grouped under seven regions.

The NORTH comprises those areas nearest Britain, that region just across the Channel which formed the holiday golfing playgrounds in the early part of this century. Nord, Pas-de-Calais, Picardy

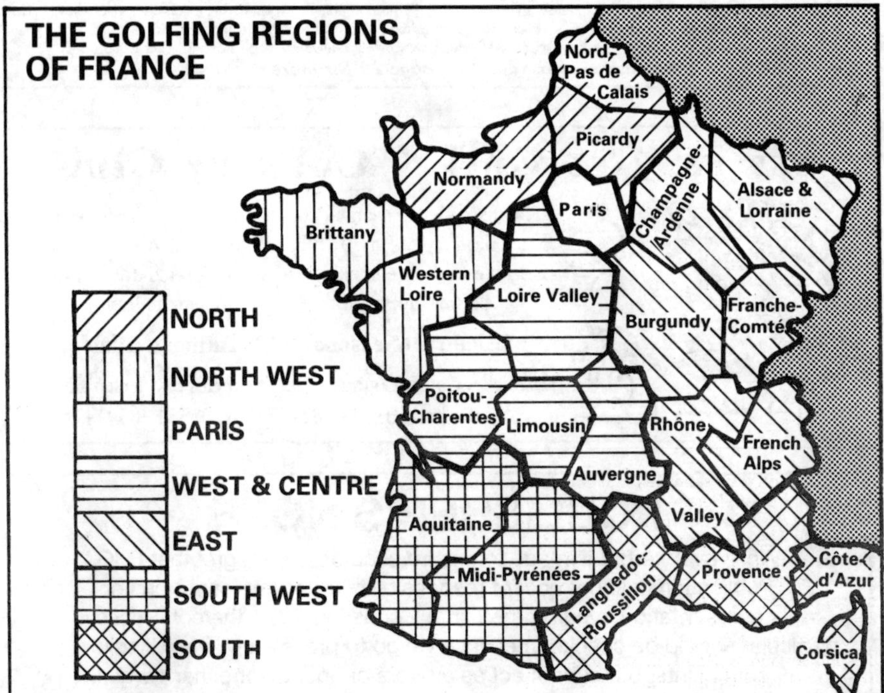

and Normandy offer such historic golfing gems as Wimereux, Granville, Le Touquet, Hardelot and Deauville alongside more recent additions such as Omaha Beach and Champ de Bataille.

The NORTH WEST area of Brittany and the Western Loire has long been a golfing favourite for its ease of access by ferry and car plus the timeless ambience of its southern reaches and unique micro-climate. Golf in Brittany tends to follow the coast, with such treats as St. Malo le Tronchet, Brest Iroise, Val Queven and St. Laurent. Inland, Rennes has three courses, of which La Freslonnière is well worth a detour for its understated charm. The historic château and wine regions of the Western Loire yield further riches, notably La Baule and La Bretesche near the coast in the north, St. Jean de Monts and La Domangere further south plus the pleasures of the Anjou Country Club and Sable Solesmes inland near Angers.

A visit to the capital, PARIS, can well include golf, often of very high quality. Tigers will want to test their skills on the tough fairways of Golf National, home of the French Open. Lesser lights can enjoy the wooded beauty of Yvelines.

The WEST & CENTRE region includes the Loire Valley, Poitou-Charentes, Limousin and Auvergne. For a real test, visit Les Bordes with its many hazards in a sylvan setting or for sheer magnificence, tackle the plunging fairways of Royan near the sea.

Quite the largest area is the EAST, which includes Champagne-Ardennes, Lorraine, Alsace, Burgundy, Franche-Comte, French Alps and the Rhone Valley. Golfers at Chamonix play under picture-postcard views of the eternal snows of Mont Blanc while others can be cossetted at Evian overlooking a vista of Lake Leman.

The richest area for golf, in fact where it all began in France, lies in the SOUTH WEST along the stretch of Atlantic coastline from Bordeaux down to Biarritz. Golf du Medoc and Château des Vigiers manage the happiest of links between golf and wine, Pessac and Gujan offer pure holiday enjoyment while further down the coast the litany of old and new delights includes Moliets, Seignosse, Hossegor, Chiberta, Biarritz du Phare, Arcangues, la Nivelle and Makila – a superb selection to satisfy everyone. Finally, in the SOUTH, find the colourful, sunsplashed courses of Languedoc-Roussillon, Provence and the Cote d'Azur, where natural beauty and elegance go in hand. The rugged, strategic slopes of Golf de Fregate and Les Baux contrast with the manicured excellence of Cannes and St. Raphael while, for a real test of your skill, visit the trio of Massane, La Grande Motte and Nimes, fine championship courses worthy of the best. The last in a fine selection to suit players of every calibre.

NORTH

BAYEUX. **Golf d'Omaha Beach,** Ferme St. Sauveur, 14520 Port-en-Bessin (31.21.32.32; Fax: 31.22.36.77). *Location:* from Paris, autoroute de Normandy A13 towards Caen. Don't go into the city, take the peripheral highway towards Bayeux, follow signs to Port-en-Bessin. Hilly course. 18 holes, 6229 metres, S.S.S. 72. 9 holes, 2875 metres, S.S.S. 35. Driving range, practice, pitch and putt course. *Green Fees:* weekdays 240f; weekends 270f. *Eating facilities:* bar and restaurant (31.21.32.32). *Visitors:* welcome. Tennis. Professional: Marc Eve. Secretary: (31.21.72.94; Fax: 31.51.79.61).

BOULOGNE. **Golf de Wimereux,** Route d'Ambleteuse, 62930 Wimereux (21.32.43.20). *Location:* north of Wimereux on the D940 approximately seven km north of Boulogne. Venerable Scottish-style links course with broad fairways between sea and dunes. 18 holes, 6150 metres, Par 72. Practice ground, putting green. *Eating facilities:* clubhouse, bar and restaurant. Trolley and club hire.

CAEN. **Golf de Caen,** Le Vallon, 14112 Biéville Beuville (31.43.98.93; Fax: 31.47.45.30). *Location:* follow road to Guistreham car ferries, first on your right to Château de Beauregard. A hilly course, wooded. 18 holes, 6155 metres, Par 72; 9 holes, 2950 metres, Par 36. Practice area, putting green. *Green Fees:* weekdays 200f; weekends 250f. *Eating facilities:* available except Tuesdays. Pro shop. Professional: Christian Carle (31.95.17.70). Secretaries: Corinne/Elizabeth (31.94.72.09).

DEAUVILLE. **Golf de St Gatien Deauville,** Le Mont Saint Jean, 14130 Saint-Gatien-des-Bois (31.65.19.99; Fax: 31.65.11.24). *Location:* about eight km inland and eight km east of Deauville. An interesting course with 9 holes, sloping steeply through woodland, plenty of sand and strategic water. 18 holes, 6200 metres, Par 72. 9 holes, 3035 metres, Par 36. Driving range, putting green. *Eating facilities:* bar and restaurant in rustic 18th century clubhouse. *Visitors:* welcome. Pro shop; cart, trolley and club hire. *Society Meetings:* welcome, special rates available. Two professionals.

DEAUVILLE. **New Golf Lucien Barriere Deauville,** 14800 Deauville, Saint-Arnoult (31.88.20.53; Fax: 31.88.06.00). *Location:* on the south-western side of Deauville with the sea to the north. A scenic and varied course, hilly in part with fast greens. 18 holes, 5934 metres, Par 71. 9 holes, 3033 metres, Par 36. Practice ground and putting green. *Green Fees:* weekdays 250f; weekends 350f. *Eating facilities:* bar and restaurant in clubhouse; all facilities at the adjoining Golf Hotel. *Visitors:* welcome, Handicap Certificates required. Pro shop; club, cart and trolley hire.

GRANVILLE. **Association du Golf de Granville,** Route de la Plage, 50290 Breville-sur-Mer (33.50.23.06; Fax: 33.61.91.87). *Location:* near Granville, towards Coutances and Cherbourg. Seaside links. 18 holes, 5854 metres, Par 71. 9 holes, 2323 metres, Par 33. Driving range, putting green. *Green Fees:* weekdays 140f; weekends 200f, Holidays 220f. *Eating facilities:* bar and restaurant in clubhouse. Pro shop; trolley and club hire. *Visitors:* welcome, no restrictions. Special rates for groups over 10.

HARDELOT. **Golf d'Hardelot "Les Dunes",** 3 Avenue du Golf, 62152 Hardelot (010 33 21.83.73.10). *Location:* at Hardelot Plage, 15km south of Boulogne. Undulating dunes with attractive pine trees. 18 holes, 6014 metres, Par 73. Golf academy. *Green Fees:* weekdays Summer 270ff; Winter 200ff; weekends Summer 320ff, Winter 200ff. *Eating facilities:* clubhouse. *Visitors:* welcome. Handicap Certificate required. *Society Meetings:* welcome. Professionals: Louis Maisonnave/David Amat (21.91.89.80/21.91.90.90). Secretary: S. Devilliers (21.83.73.10; Fax: 21.83.24.33). Director of Golf: Peter Dawson.

HARDELOT. **Golf d'Hardelot "Les Pins",** 3 Avenue du Golf, 62152 Hardelot (010 33 21.83.73.10). *Location:* the beach-resort of Hardelot Plage is 15 km south of Boulogne. Attractive course carved through a pine forest. 18 holes, 5870 metres, Par 72. Practice ground, putting green. *Green Fees:* weekdays Summer 270ff, Winter 200ff; weekends Summer 320ff, Winter 200ff. *Eating facilities:* clubhouse with bar and fine restaurant. Handicap Certificate required. Pro shop; club and trolley hire. Professionals: Louis Maisonnave/David Amat (21.91.89.80/21.91.90.90). Secretary: (21.83.73.10; Fax: 21.83.24.33). Director of Golf: Peter Dawson.

LAON. **Golf de l'Ailette,** 02860 Cerny-en-Laonnois (23.24.79.10). *Location:* about 12km south of Laon, autoroute A26 exit Laon. An interesting course laid out on the edge of a forest flanked by large areas of water. 18 holes, 6127 metres, Par 72. 9 holes, 1753 metres, Par 32. Practice ground, pitch and putt, putting green. *Green Fees:* weekdays 185f; weekends 240f. *Eating facilities:* bar and restaurant. *Visitors:* welcome, closed Tuesday mornings. Handicap required (maximum 35). *Society Meetings:* welcome, 20% to 30% discount for groups. Professional: Eric Censier. Secretaries: Miss Sylvie Dolat and Mrs Marie Christine Harant (23.24.83.99; Fax: 23.24.84.66).

LE TOUQUET. **Golf du Touquet,** Avenue du Golf, 62520 Le Touquet (21.05.68.47; Fax: 21.05.40.19). *Location:* 20km from Boulogne, on the coast, 3km from Le Touquet centre. The Forest Course – in the heart of an old pine forest. 18 holes, 6032 metres, Par 72. The Sea Course – a championship links course laid out amongst sand dunes. 18 holes, 6347 metres, Par 74. The Manoir Course – perfect for beginners. 9 holes, 2584 metres, S.S.S. 34. Practice range and putting green. *Green Fees:* The Forest Course and The Sea

Course weekdays 120ff to 250ff, weekends 180ff to 320ff; The Manoir Course weekdays 65ff to 130ff, weekends 90ff to 180ff. *Eating facilities:* bar and restaurant in clubhouse. *Visitors:* welcome. Maximum Handicaps: The Forest Course 35, The Sea Course 24 Gentlemen, 28 Ladies, no handicap for The Manoir Course. *Society Meetings:* welcome. Pro Shop. Professionals: P. Philippon, J.P. Harismendy, C. Dachicourt.

LILLE. **Golf de Bondues,** Château de la Vigne, BP 54, 59587 Bondues Cedex (20.23.20.62). *Location:* about 10km north of Lille, west of the N17. In the grounds of an 18th century château, the courses have well protected greens with deep bunkers and several water hazards. 18 holes, 6261 metres, Par 73. 18 holes, 6000 metres, Par 72. Driving range, putting green. *Green Fees:* weekdays 200f; weekends 300f. Discounts for groups of 20 plus. *Eating facilities:* bar and restaurant in clubhouse. Pro shop, trolley hire. Lessons available. Professional: (20.23.13.87). Secretary: (20.23.20.62; Fax: 20.23.24.11).

NEUBOURG. **Golf Club du Champ de Bataille,** 27110 Le Neubourg (32.35.03.72; Fax: 32.35.83.10). *Location:* south-west of Rouen, about 28km north-west of Evreux. A fine test of golf attractively laid out through the wooded estate of the elegant château. Par 3 holes. 18 holes, 6575 yards, 5983 metres, Par 72. Driving range, putting green. *Green Fees:* weekdays 220f (full season); weekends 330f (full season). Special rates to tour operators under contract with the club. *Eating facilities:* bar and restaurant in château clubhouse. *Visitors:* welcome, no restrictions. Pro shop; cart, trolley and club hire. Guest rooms available in the château. *Society Meetings:* welcome.

ST. OMER. **Aa Saint-Omer Golf Club,** Chemin des Bois, Acquin-Westbecourt, 62380 Lumbres (21.38.59.90; Fax: 21.38.59.90). *Location:* from Calais take A26 auto route, Junction 3 St. Omer, right onto RN42 Expressway, first exit Acquin/Lumbres (30 minutes from Calais). Undulating parkland and mature trees overlooking the valley of the River Aa. 18 holes, 6400 metres, Par 72. 9 holes, 2003 metres, Par 31. Practice ground and putting green. *Green Fees:* weekdays winter 190f, summer 230f; weekends winter 230f, summer 270f. *Eating facilities:* clubhouse bar and restaurant. *Visitors:* welcome all year, no restrictions. Pro shop; trolley and club hire. Secretary: (UK) Philip Bramall.

NORTH WEST

ANGERS. **Anjou Golf and Country Club,** Route de Cheffes, 49330 Champigne (41.42.01.01; Fax: 41.42.04.37). *Location:* about 20km north of Angers, from Paris A11, exit Durtal. Flat course with a few lakes and trees. 18 holes, 6227 metres, Par 72. Short 6 hole course, 750 metres, Par 19. Practice facilities. *Green Fees:* weekdays 200/160f; weekends 160/120f. Discount for hotel residents. *Eating facilities:* bar and restaurant in clubhouse. *Visitors:* welcome. Starting times must be booked in advance. Professional: D. Dalies. Secretary: F. Guel. Pro shop; cart, trolley and club hire.

ANGERS. **Golf de Sablé-Solesmes,** Domaine de l'Outinière, Route de Pincé, 72300 Sablé-sur-Sarthe (43.95.28.78; Fax: 43.92.39.05). *Location:* east of the A11, about 40km north of Angers, south-east of Le Mans. Three totally different 9's – Forest and River: 18 holes, 6207 metres, Par 72; Waterfall: 9 holes, 3069 metres, Par 36, radiate from the large clubhouse. Testing and spectacular with park, woodland and lakeside holes. Driving range, putting green. *Green Fees:* weekdays 260f; weekends 390f. Discounts for groups over 10 persons. *Eating facilities:* bar and restaurant in clubhouse. Pro shop; cart, trolley and club hire. Professional: Olivier Gaudin. Secretary: Angèle Goyer. Director: Moraly Michel.

AURAY. **Golf de Baden,** Kernic, 56870 Baden (97.57.18.96; Fax: 97.57.22.05). *Location:* between the village of Baden and the sea, south of the RN 165 at Auray exit. Undulating course partly through pine woods and around lakes. 18 holes, 6112 metres, Par 72. 3 hole, 535 metres pitch and putt course. Practice area, putting green, approach green. *Green Fees:* on application. *Eating facilities:* bar and snacks in clubhouse. Pro shop; trolley and club hire; club repair. Neighbouring hotels "Le Gavrinis" and "du Loch" offer year-round golfing breaks.

AURAY. **Golf de Saint Laurent,** 56400 Auray, Ploemel (97.56.85.18; Fax: 97.56.89.99). *Location:* about five km west of Auray and not far from Carnac with its ancient standing stones. High quality championship course, undulating through mature trees. 18 holes, 6112 metres, Par 72. 9 hole course, 2705 metres, Par 35. *Green Fees:* 18 holes 150f – 230f; 9 holes 100f – 150f. *Eating facilities:* bar and restaurant in on-course Fairway Hotel St. Laurent; also on-course "Maeve" self catering cottages available. Pro shop; cart, trolley and club hire. Professionals: Paul Braun, Dominique Jouan.

BENODET. **Golf de l'Odet,** Menez Groas, Clohars-Fouesnant, 29950 Bénodet (98.54.87.88; Fax: 98.54.61.40). *Location:* south of Quimper, towards the sea at Be1nodet. An undulating partly wooded course. 18 holes, 6235 metres, Par 72. 9 holes, 1100 metres, Par 27. Driving range, putting green, pitching green. *Eating facilities:* bar, restaurant and on-site Hotel Eurogreen, whose residents have reduced green fees. *Visitors:* welcome, no restrictions but advisable to book tee times. Other accommodation nearby. Pro shop; cart, trolley and club hire. Professional: Yva Bechu. Secretary: J.P. Chaton (98.54.87.88; Fax: 98.52.61.40).

BREST. **Golf de Brest Iroise,** Parc de Loisirs de Lann Rohou, 29800 Landerneau (98.85.16.17; Fax: 98.21.52.08). *Location:* east of Brest, five km south of Landerneau. A tough course, open to the breeze in a beautiful natural setting. 18 holes, 5885 metres, Par 72. 9 holes, 3329 metres, Par 37. Driving range, putting green. *Eating facilities:* bar and restaurant and all facilities at the Golf Hotel d'Iroise. Pro shop; cart, trolley and club hire.

LA BAULE. **Golf de la Baule,** Domaine de St. Denac, 44117 St. André-des-Eaux (40.60.46.18; Fax: 40.60.41.41). *Location:* to the east of La Baule, 3km from St. Andre des Eaux. A parkland course winding through mature trees with hills and a large lake affecting the back nine. 18 holes, 6700 yards, 6157 metres, S.S.S. 73, Par 72. Practice ground and putting greens. *Green Fees:* from 170f – 320f depending in time of year. 20% reduction for groups of 15 or more. *Eating facilities:* bar and restaurant. *Visitors:* welcome by reservation booked the day before. Pro shop; cart, club and trolley hire. *Society Meeting:* welcome by arrangement. Professional: Eric Mauger (40.60.34.04). Secretary: Eric Stoquer.

LA BAULE. **Golf de la Bretesche,** Domaine de la Bretesche, 44780 Missillac (40.88.30.05). *Location:* 20km north-east of La Baule; 50km north-west of Nantes on the N165. In a wooded parkland with narrow fairways. 18 holes, 6080 metres, S.S.S. 72. Practice ground, putting green, training bunker, pitch and putt. *Green Fees:* 140f – 280f. 20% reduction for residents in the hotel. *Eating facilities:* bar and restaurant. *Visitors:* welcome. *Society Meetings:* welcome. Professional: Thierry Mathon (40.88.30.03; Fax: 40.88.36.28). Secretary: Isabelle Moreau (40.88.30.03; Fax: 40.88.36.28).

LA ROCHE-SUR-YON. **Golf Club de la Domangère,** Route de la Rochelle, 85310 Nesmy (51.07.60.15; Fax: 51.07.64.09). *Location:* approximately 10km south of La Roche-sur-Yon west of the D747. A long and majestic course with plenty of strategic water, mature trees and bordered by the River Yon. 18 holes, 6480 metres, Par 72. 4 hole practice course, driving range, putting green. *Green Fees:* on request. *Eating facilities:* bar, grill-room and restaurant in the on-site Hotel de la Domangère. *Visitors:* welcome. Club, cart and trolley hire. *Society Meetings:* welcome, booking required. Professional: Mr Magnou Olivier.

LORIENT. **Golf du Val Quéven,** Kerrousseau RD 6, 56530 Quéven (97.05.17.96: Fax: 97.05.19.18). *Location:* nearest main road RN165, Quéven situated between Lorient and Pont Scorff. A varied course, wooded and with water hazards. 18 holes, 6140 metres, Par 72. Driving range, putting green. *Green Fees:* 150f, 190f, 230f. *Eating facilities:* bar and restaurant. *Visitors:* welcome. Pro shop; club and trolley hire. Professional: Jean-Luc Leroux. Secretaries: Mlle Sylvie Jochmans and M. Frédéric Dellsperger.

LORIENT. **Golf Ploemeur Ocean,** Saint Jude-Kerham, 56270 Ploemeur (97.32.81.82; Fax: 97.32.80.90). *Location:* main route Rennes-Lorient, exit Ploemeur. Seaside course, huge American style greens, water hazards. 18 holes, 5957 metres, S.S.S. 72. Covered driving range. *Green Fees:* from 140f – 230f depending on season. 20% reduction for tour operators. *Eating facilities:* bar and restaurant. *Visitors:* welcome. Hotels in immediate surroundings. *Society Meetings:* managed by the SEM of Ploemeur. Professionals: M. Zimmermann and M. Queffelec. Manager: Bertrand Hellegouarch.

RENNES. **Golf de la Freslonnière,** 35650 Rennes Le Rheu (33.99.14.84.09; Fax: 33.99.14.94.98). *Location:* three km from Rennes towards Lorient. Woodland course with water features and banks of rhododendrons. 18 holes, 5671 metres, Par 71. Practice ground and putting green. *Green Fees:* weekdays 180f/200f; weekends 200f/230f. *Eating facilities:* clubhouse, restaurant and bar. Golf holiday packages from nearby Novotel Rennes. Pro shop; club, cart and trolley hire. Professional: Richard Triaire.

RENNES. **Golf de Rennes,** St. Jacques de la Lande, 35136 Rennes (99.31.52.52). *Location:* eight km south of Rennes, off the D177 to Redon. Set amongst mature woodland with several water hazards; a new course to enjoy. 18 holes, 6150 metres, Par 72. 9 holes, 2068 metres, Par 32. Short 9 hole course. *Green Fees:* weekdays 190f; weekends 230f. *Eating facilities:* bar and restaurant in clubhouse. *Visitors:* welcome, no restrictions. Pro shop; trolley and club hire.

ST. MALO. **Golf de St-Malo-le-Tronchet,** Le Tronchet, 35540 Miniac Morvan (99.58.96.69). *Location:* 23km south of St. Malo, 12km east of Dinan, south of the N176. Rolling parkland designed on a grand scale with vast greens and sand traps, strategic water. 18 holes, 6049 metres. Par 72. 9 holes, 2684 metres, Par 36. Driving range, putting green. *Green Fees:* £220f. Reduced rares for students. *Eating facilities:* bar and restaurant. *Visitors:* welcome. "Hostellerie Abbatiale" close by the course with all hotel facilities and golf holiday packages. Pro shop; trolley and club hire. *Society Meetings:* welcome, bookings required. Professional: M. Cyril Bourakhowitch. Secretary: Mme Raquel Watbot.

ST.-JEAN-DE-MONTS. **Golf Club de St. Jean-de-Monts,** Avenue des Pays de Monts, 85160 St. Jean-de-Monts (51.58.82.73; Fax: 51.59.18.32). *Location:* a partly links-style course along the seaside with pine trees and dunes. On the Atlantic coast some 60/70km south-west of Nantes. 18 holes, 5962 metres, Par 72. Short 5 hole course. Practice ground and putting greens. *Eating facilities:* clubhouse with bar and restaurant. The Hotel de la Plage in nearby Notre Dame de Monts offers golfing breaks. Pro shop; cart, club and trolley hire.

PARIS

PARIS. **Golf de Forges-les-Bains,** Rue de General Leclerc, 91470 Forges-les-Bains (64.91.48.18; Fax: 64.91.40.52). *Location:* A10 Orleans, exit Les Ulis then towards Limours and Forges-les-Bains. Wooded course. 18 holes, 6207 metres, Par 72. Driving range, practice area. *Green Fees:* weekdays 200f; weekends 300f. *Eating facilities:* bar and restaurant in clubhouse. *Visitors:* welcome, no restrictions but reservations preferred. Pro shop; trolley and club hire. Professionals: Sydney Kershaw, Martino Proenca. Secretary: Fabrice Gicquiaud.

PARIS. **Golf de la Vaucouleurs,** 78910 Civry-la-Forêt (34.87.76.04). *Location:* off the A13 at the Mantes interchange, south off the road to Houdan. Two 18 hole courses. "The River" – very varied with trees, water and hills, 6298 metres, Par 73; "The Little Valley" – a links-type course, 5638 metres, Par 70. Practice ground, putting green. *Green Fees:* weekdays 350f, weekends 200f. *Eating facilities:* bar and restaurant in clubhouse; also at nearby Hotel la Dousseine at Anet. Pro shop; club and trolley hire. Professional: Raymond Marro (34.87.62.29; Fax: 34.87.70.09).

PARIS. **Golf de St. Quentin-en-Yvelines,** RD 912, 78190 Trappes (30.50.86.40; Fax: 34.82.88.82). *Location:* about 20km west of Paris off the D912. A very popular public facility of 36 holes. White Course – 18 holes, 6048 metres, Par 72; Red Course – 18 holes, 5969 metres, Par 70. Also 3 hole compact course, driving range, putting green. *Eating facilities:* bar and restaurant in clubhouse. Pro shop; trolley and club hire.

PARIS. **Golf des Yvelines,** Château de la Couharde, 78940 La Queue-les-Yvelines (34.86.48.89; Fax: 34.86.50.31). *Location:* about 45km west of Paris by N12, near Montfort-l'Amaury. Built around the elegant château, with fairways cut through thick woods. 18 holes, 6344 metres, S.S.S. 72. 9 holes, 2065 metres, S.S.S. 31. Practice ground, putting green. *Green Fees:* weekdays 190ff, weekends 330ff. *Eating facilities:* bar and restaurant. *Visitors:* all visitors welcome. Club and trolley hire. Professional: Jean Paul Chardonnet.

PARIS. **Golf National,** 2 Avenue du Golf, 78280 Guyancourt (30.43.36.00; Fax: 34.43.85.58). *Location:* about 25km south-west of Paris off the D91. A public facility of 45 holes laid out in three courses. "The Albatross" (now the venue for the French Open) – 18 holes, 6500 metres championship course with severe water hazards and winding fairways, Par 72; "The Eagle" – 18 holes, 6000 metres, Par 72 for experienced players; "The Birdie" – 9 holes, 2100 metres beginners' course, Par 32 and driving range; "The Par" – a warm-up, practice course. Putting greens. *Eating facilities:* on-site Hotel Novotel. Club and trolley hire.

WEST & CENTRE

CHEVERNY. **Golf du Château de Cheverny,** La Rousselière, 41700 Contres (54.79.24.70; Fax: 54.79.25.52). *Location:* on the south of Cheverny 15km south of Blois. Built over the former hunting grounds of the Château with large well-kept greens. 18 holes, 6272 metres, Par 71. 3 hole practice course, driving range and putting green. *Eating facilities:* bar and restaurant in clubhouse. *Visitors:* welcome. Pro shop; club and trolley hire. *Society Meetings:* 20% reduction on fees.

COGNAC. **Golf du Cognac,** Saint-Brice, 16100 Cognac (45.35.38.50; Fax: 45.35.10.76). *Location:* five km east of Cognac, north of the N141 across the River Charente. Undulating fairways with views of vineyards and the river; some water hazards. 18 holes, 6122 metres, Par 72. 4 hole practice course, putting green and driving range. *Green Fees:* 200f. *Eating facilities:* clubhouse with restaurant and bar. Pro shop; cart, club and trolley hire. Professional: Jean-Marc Lecuona (45.32.37.60). Secretary: Emmanuel Ballongue (45.32.18.17).

LOUDUN. **Golf de Loudun,** Domaine St. Hilaire, 86120 Roiffe (49.98.78.06; Fax: 49.98.72.57). *Location:* 15km north of Loudun towards Saumur on the D147. An attractive woodland course with a few water hazards and well guarded greens. 18 holes, 6280 metres, Par 72. 6 hole practice course, driving range and putting green. *Green Fees:* weekdays low season 170f, high season 190f; weekends low season 210f, high season 230f. *Eating facilities:* restaurant on site catering for up to 140 people, bar. *Visitors:* welcome, no restrictions. Two star hotel with 47 rooms and 13 self catering apartments. Pro shop; trolley and club hire. *Society Meetings:* welcome. Professional: D. Sheen.

ORLÉANS. **"Les Bordes" Golf International,** 41220 St-Laurent Nouan (54.87.72.13; Fax: 54.87.78.61). *Location:* from Paris motorway A10 exit Meung sur Loire. Laid out on a former hunting park. 18 holes, 7041 yards, 6412 metres, Par 75. Driving range, putting green. *Green Fees:* weekdays 400f per person, 600f per couple; weekends and Holidays 700f per person, 1000f per couple. Reductions November to

March inclusive. *Eating facilities:* bar and restaurant in clubhouse. *Visitors:* welcome every day. Pro shop; carts, trolleys and clubs for hire. Professional: M. Kitamura.

POITIERS. **Golf du Haut-Poitou,** Parc de Loisirs de St. Cyr, 86130 Jaunay-Clan (49.62.53.62; Fax: 49.60.28.58). *Location:* 20km north of Poitiers and 15km south of Chatellerault. Undulating course with a lake and water hazards and wooded hills. 18 holes, 6590 metres, S.S.S. 75. 9 holes, 1800 metres, Par 31. Practice ground, driving range, putting and pitching greens. *Green Fees:* Mondays to Saturdays 9 hole course 120ff, 18 hole course 170ff; Sundays 9 hole course 140ff, 18 hole course 200ff. *Eating facilities:* clubhouse with restaurant and bar. *Visitors:* welcome without restriction. Pro shop and equipment hire. *Society Meetings:* welcome. Professional: David Maxwell. Secretaries: Catherine Marchais and B. Guignard (49.62.53.62; Fax: 49.60.28.58).

ROYAN. **Golf de Royan,** Maine-Gaudin, 17420 St-Palais-sur-Mer (46.23.40.80). *Location:* on the D25 coast road, nine km north-west of Royan. An exciting course with narrow fairways undulating through tall pines. 18 holes, 5970 metres, S.S.S. 73. 6 hole pitch and putt, 920 metres, S.S.S. 20. Practice ground with driving range, putting green. *Green Fees:* weekdays 130f – 230f; weekends 170f – 230f. *Eating facilities:* restaurant and bar in clubhouse. *Visitors:* welcome. Course closed Tuesdays from December until end of March. Pro shop with equipment hire. *Society Meetings:* welcome by arrangement with the Secretary. Professionals: Gilles Delavallade and Christine Wenandy (46.23.16.24). Secretary: Nathalie and Christelle (46.23.16.24; Fax: 46.23.23.38).

TOURS. **Golf d'Ardrée,** 37360 St.-Antoine-du-Rocher (47.56.77.38; Fax: 47.56.79.96). *Location:* 10km north of Tours. An attractive parkland course with strategic water and sand. 18 holes, 5507 metres, Par 70. Practice ground and putting green. *Green Fees:* weekdays 190f; weekends 260f. Special rates for groups of 20 or more (20% discount). *Eating facilities:* restaurant and bar in clubhouse. *Visitors:* welcome. Pro shop; club and trolley hire. Visitors may participate in Club's Sunday competitions held in high season.

TOURS. **Golf du Château des Sept Tours,** 37330 Courcelles de Tourraine (47.24.69.75; Fax: 47.24.23.74). *Location:* on the D34 between Château la Vallière and Langeais. A fairly long course but relatively flat with attractive trees and water, excellent greens. 18 holes, 6194 metres, Par 72. Practice ground and putting green. *Green Fees:* weekdays 180f; weekends 240f. *Eating facilities:* bar and restaurant in on-site Hotel Château des Sept Tours. Pro shop; club and trolley hire. Professionals: Brian Sparks/Yannick Saillour.

EAST

AIX-LES-BAINS. **Golf Club d'Aix-les-Bains,** Avenue de Golf, 73100 Aix-les-Bains (79.61.23.35; Fax: 79.34.06.01). *Location:* three km south of Aix by the Lac du Bourget. An attractive parkland course on sloping land surrounded by wooded hills. 18 holes, 5595 metres, Par 71. Driving range, putting green. *Eating facilities:* bar and restaurant in clubhouse. Pro shop; trolley and club hire.

CHAMONIX. **Golf de Chamonix,** 35 Route du Golf, BP 31, 74400 Chamonix (50.53.06.28; Fax: 50.53.38.69). *Location:* on the N506 three km north of Chamonix. A subtle and technical course, enhanced by water obstacles and numerous bunkers. Spectacular mountain views including Mont Blanc. 18 holes, 6076 metres, S.S.S. 72. Driving range, putting green. *Green Fees:* weekdays 200f; weekends 250f. July/August 300f per day. *Eating facilities:* restaurant. *Visitors:* welcome every day with a Handicap Certificate, tee off times must be booked one day in advance. Pro shop; cart, trolley and club hire. *Society Meetings:* welcome, 10% reduction. Professional: Jean Claude Bonnaz. Secretary: Caroline de Chardon (50.53.06.28; Fax: 50.53.38.69).

EVIAN. **Royal Golf Club Evian,** Rive Sud du Lac de Genève, 74500 Evian-les-Bains (50.26.85.00; Fax: 50.75.65.54). *Location:* on high ground above Evian. 8kms from Thonon, 45kms west of Geneva. Hilly fairways overlooking Lake Leman, sloping greens guarded by deep bunkers. 18 holes, 6674 yards, 6006 metres, Par 72. Covered and uncovered practice range, two putting greens, chipping green, pitching green, training bunkers, pitch and putt. *Green Fees:* weekdays 190/310f according to season; weekends 290/380f according to season. Free to hotel guests – guaranteed tee times. *Eating facilities:* restaurant and bar: Le Chalet du Golf. *Visitors:* welcome, Handicap 35 or course authorization. Pro shop – clubs, bags and carts. *Society Meetings:* welcome (up to 180 people). Professionals: Jean-Marc Bochaton (lessons) and Lamberto Capoccia (courses). Secretary: Sylvie Martin. Director: Delphine Bourson.

GRENOBLE. **Golf International de Grenoble,** Route de Montavie, Bresson, 38320 Eybens (76.73.65.00; Fax: 76.73.65.51). *Location:* five km south of Grenoble. A long course with winding fairways, small lakes, trees – architect Robert Trent Jones Jnr. Bresson Course 18 holes, 6343 metres, Par 74; Uriage Course 9 holes, 2005 metres. S.S.S. 62. Practice ground and putting green; driving range. *Green Fees:* Bresson weekdays 220f, weekends 320f; Uriage weekdays 140f, weekends 180f. *Eating facilities:* clubhouse and nearby hotel. *Visitors:* welcome at all times.

LYON. **Golf Club de Lyon,** 38280 Vilette d'Anthon (78.31.11.33; Fax: 72.02.48.27). *Location:* Lyon, motorway A42 exit Balan. Brocards – flat, wooded; Sangliers – hilly, wooded. Brocards 18 holes, 6167 metres. S.S.S. 72; Sangliers 18 holes, 6727 metres. S.S.S 72. Practice ground, putting green, 7 holes pitch and putt. *Green Fees:* weekdays 200f; weekends 300f. *Eating facilities:* bar and restaurant in clubhouse. *Visitors:* welcome anytime. Pro shop; equipment hire.

ST. JULIEN (Geneva). **Golf and Country Club de Bossey,** Château de Crevin, Bossey, 74160 St.-Julien-en-Genevois. *Location:* just near the main road between St. Julien en Genevois and Annemasse about five miles from each of these towns. Just in France on the southern outskirts of Geneva. Challenging mountain golf with fine views. Well wooded with water hazards. 18 holes, 6002 metres, Par 72. Driving range, putting green. *Green Fees:* weekdays only, on application. *Eating facilities:* bar and restaurant in cha3teau clubhouse. *Visitors:* welcome weekdays only, maximum of three times a year. Maximum handicap 35. No jeans allowed on course. Contact General Manager for details. Pro shop; cart, trolley and club hire. *Society Meetings:* catered for, contact General Manager. Professional: Mark Cobley (50.43.65.66). Secretary: (50.43.75.25; Fax: 50.95.32.57).

SOUTH-WEST

ANGLET. **Golf de Chiberta,** 104 Boulevard des Plages, 64600 Anglet (59.63.83.20; Fax: 59.63.30.56). *Location:* three km from Biarritz and from Bayonne. A well-established combination of seashore and wooded parkland. 18 holes, 5650 metres, Par 71. Driving range, putting green. *Green Fees:* weekdays from 200f, weekends from 240f. *Eating facilities:* bar and restaurant in clubhouse. *Visitors:* welcome, Handicap Certificate required. Pro shop; trolley and club hire. Professional: H. Brouson, P du Foure, C. Lecuona.

ARCACHON. **Golf de Gujan Mestras,** B P 74, Route de Sanguinet, 33470 Gujan Mestras (56.66.86.36; Fax: 56.66.10.93). *Location:* a spectacular course with well-located water obstacles. 12 km east of Arcachon, 40km west of Bordeaux, north of the A66. 18 holes, 6225 metres, Par 72. 9 holes, 2630 metres, Par 35. Practice facilities available. *Green Fees:* weekdays 200f 18 holes, 140f 9 holes; weekends 250f 18 holes, 170f 9 holes. *Eating facilities:* restaurant, clubhouse and at nearby hotel. Pro shop; equipment and trolley hire.

BAYONNE. **Golf de la Côte d'Argent,** 40660 Moliets (58.48.54.65; Fax: 58.48.54.88). *Location:* about 30km north of Bayonne on the Atlantic coast at Moliets. Part of a leisure seaside complex with links and wooded inland holes. 18 holes, 6164 metres, Par 72. 9 holes, 1905 metres, Par 31. Practice ground, putting green. *Green Fees:* 220f (280f in July and August). *Eating facilities:* bar and restaurant in clubhouse and in on-site hotels. *Visitors:* welcome. Pro shop; cart, club and trolley hire; tennis, archery. *Society Meetings:* welcome. Professionals: Franck Ducousso, Patrick Talon.

BAYONNE. **Golf de Seignosse,** Carrefour de Bocau, 40510 Seignosse (58.43.17.32; Fax: 58.43.16.67). *Location:* about 25km north of Bayonne on the D79 north of Hossegor. Very hilly, exciting and undulating course, a pleasure to look at as well as play. 18 holes, 6140 metres, Par 72. Practice ground. *Green Fees:* High Season 300f, Low Season 220f. *Eating facilities:* bar and restaurant; Hotel. Pro shop; cart, club and trolley hire. *Visitors:* welcome.

BIARRITZ. **Golf de Biarritz Le Phare,** 2 Avenue Edith Cavell, 64200 Biarritz (59.03.71.33). *Location:* in Biarritz, facing the ocean with cooling breezes. A historic course (1888) with fast greens, level, many bunkers. 18 holes, 5379 metres, S.S.S. 69. Practice ground, putting green. *Green Fees:* off season 220ff, main season 300ff. *Eating facilities:* bar and restaurant in clubhouse, the nearby Hôtel du Palais and other hotels. Pro shop; club and trolley hire. Secretary: (59.03.71.80; Fax: 59.03.26.74).

BIARRITZ. **Golf d'Arcangues,** Argelous, 64200 Arcangues (59.43.10.56; Fax: 59.41.12.60). *Location:* three km south-east of Biarritz. A fine rolling test in modern but natural style. Mounded bunkers and strategic water. 18 holes, 6142 metres, Par 72. *Eating facilities:* bar and restaurant in clubhouse. Pro shop and equipment hire.

BORDEAUX. **Golf de Bordeaux Cameyrac,** 33450 St. Sulpice et Cameyrac (56.72.96.79; Fax: 56.72.86.56). *Location:* 15km from Bordeaux N89 (Exit no. 15) close to the famous vineyards of St. Emilion and Pomerol. Fairways run through forest, alongside ponds and vineyards. 18 holes, 5972 metres, Par 72. 9 holes, 1188 metres, Par 28. Practice ground, putting green. *Green Fees:* weekdays 150f 18 holes, 110f 9 holes; weekends 200f 18 holes, 140f 9 holes. *Eating facilities:* bar and restaurant (56.72.94.51). *Visitors:* welcome every day 8.30am to 7.30pm. Pro shop; equipment hire. *Society Meetings:* welcome. Professional/Manager: Mr Christian Chabrier. Secretary: Mr Alexis Champion.

BORDEAUX. **Golf de Pessac,** Rue de la Princesse, 33600 Pessac (56.36.24.47; Fax: 56.36.52.89). *Location:* on the western outskirts of Bordeaux, four km from the city and close to the airport, St. Jean d'Illiac road. A level course with large bunkers and some water. 27 holes providing alternative 9 hole layouts plus 9 hole practice course. 18 holes, 6300 metres, all Par 72. Driving range, putting green. *Green Fees:* weekdays 200f; weekends 250f. *Eating facilities:* restaurant and bar. *Visitors:* welcome. *Society Meetings:* welcome. Pro shop; cart, club and trolley hire. Professional: Thierry Minaud. Secretary: Christophe Fouquet.

BORDEAUX. **Golf du Médoc,** Chemin de Courmateau, 33290 Le Pian Médoc (56.70.21.10; Fax: 56.70.23.44). *Location:* 20 minutes by car from international Bordeaux Airport. Two courses, the original with widespread fairways, water and banks; 18 holes, 6940 yards, 6316 metres. S.S.S. 74. The newer course "Des Vignes", winding through lakes and pine trees, has each of its 18 holes named after a Médoc wine château: 6835 yards, 6220 metres, Par 73. Practice ground, pitching and putting greens. *Green Fees:* weekdays 200f; weekends 270f. Special rates for groups of over 15 people. *Eating facilities:* clubhouse with bar and quality restaurant. *Visitors:* welcome. *Society Meetings:* please contact Secretary. Professional: Gilles Arnaud. Secretary: Eric Destaras.

CASTELJALOUX. **Golf de Casteljaloux,** Avenue du Lac, 47700 Casteljaloux (53.93.51.60; Fax: 53.93.04.10). *Location:* situated on the D933 facing Lake Clarens on the road to Mont-de-Marsan, 15km from the exit of the motorway, 90km from Bordeaux, 170km from Toulouse. Gentle slopes and some difficult greens. 18 holes, 5916 metres, Par 72. Practice holes, bunkers and tees, driving range and putting green. *Green Fees:* weekdays low season 150f, high season 180f; weekends low season 200f, high season 220f. *Eating facilities:* bar and restaurant in clubhouse with fine views. *Visitors:* welcome. Pro shop; club and trolley hire. *Society Meetings:* by arrangement. Professional: Francois Thollon Pommerol. Secretary: Véronique Huix.

DORDOGNE. **Château des Vigiers Golf and Country Club,** 24240 Monestier (53.61.50.00; Fax: 53.61.50.20). *Location:* about an hour's drive east of Bordeaux on D936, bearing right on D18 at Ste-Foy-la-Grande. New course, rolling past orchards, vineyards, woods, lakes surrounding charming 16th century château clubhouse which is also a luxury hotel. 18 holes, 6003 metres. Par 72. 9 hole practice course, driving range and putting green. *Green Fees:* weekdays 220ff; weekends 280ff. The higher charge at all times during July and August. *Eating facilities:* restaurant and bar. Pro shop, club, cart and trolley rental. Professional: Vincent Trojani.

HOSSEGOR. **Golf d'Hossegor,** Avenue du Golf, 40150 Hossegor (58.43.56.99; Fax: 58.43.98.52). *Location:* about 15km north of Bayonne just west of the A63. Fine classic test of golf over gently undulating, heavily wooded land. 18 holes, 5867 metres, Par 71. Driving range, putting green. *Eating facilities:* bar and restaurant in clubhouse. Pro shop; trolley and club hire.

PAU. **Pau Golf Club,** Rue du Golf, 64140 Billère (59.32.02.33; Fax: 59.62.42.57). *Location:* RN 117 Commune de Billère 5km from Pau towards Bayonne. The first course in continental Europe (1856). Flat, wooded, along the River Gave. 18 holes, 5312 metres, S.S.S. 69. Practice facilities including three practice holes. *Green Fees:* weekdays 200f; weekends 250f. Special rates available on request. *Eating facilities:* bar and restaurant in clubhouse. *Visitors:* welcome. *Society Meetings:* by arrangement. Professional: D. Loustalet (59.32.79.24). Secretary: Mme Nicole Larre (59.32.02.33).

SAINT-JEAN-DE-LUZ. **Golf de la Nivelle,** Place William Sharp, 64500 Ciboure (59.47.18.99; Fax: 59.47.21.16). *Location:* two km south of Saint-Jean, on the banks of the River Nivelle. A "town" course; classic parkland with mature trees and harbour views. 18 holes, 5513 metres, Par 70. Practice ground, putting green. *Green Fees:* weekdays 200ff; weekends 250ff. *Eating facilities:* bar and restaurant in clubhouse. Self catering flats on golf course. Pro shop; equipment hire.

Please mention this guide when you write or phone to enquire about accommodation.

TOULOUSE. **Golf International de Toulouse Seilh,** Route de Grenade, 31840 Seilh (61.42.59.30; Fax: 61.42.34.17). *Location:* about 12km north-west of Toulouse near the A62. "Yellow" Course of moderate difficulty, 18 holes, 4202 metres, Par 64; "Red" Course of competition standard, 18 holes, 6200 metres, Par 72. Extensive practice and training facilities. *Eating facilities:* bar and restaurant in clubhouse. Pro shop; club, cart and trolley hire.

VILLENEUVE-SUR-LOT. **Golf de Castelnaud,** "La Menuisière", 47290 Castelnaud de Gratecambe (53.01.74.64; Fax: 53.01.78.99). *Location:* on the N21 10km north of Villeneuve, between the scenic valleys of the Lot and the Dordogne. Inland course with water and many trees. 18 holes, 6322 metres, Par 72. 9 hole practice course, 1092 metres, Par 27. Practice ground, putting green. *Eating facilities:* the clubhouse is an 18th century manor house with what is reputed to be the best golf course restaurant in France. Pro shop; equipment hire.

SOUTH

AIX-EN-PROVENCE. **Golf International de Château L'Arc,** Domaine de Château L'Arc, 13710 Fuveau (42.53.28.38; Fax: 42.29.08.41). *Location:* about 15km south-east of Aix-en-Provence just south of the A8. A challenging course of varying terrain through trees, sloping fairways and water hazards. 18 holes, 6300 metres, Par 73. Driving range, putting green. *Eating facilities:* bar and restaurant in clubhouse. Pro shop; cart, trolley and club hire.

AVIGNON. **Golf des Baux de Provence,** Domaine de Manville, 13520 Les Baux de Provence (0800 890 033 90.54.40.20; Fax: 90.54.40.93). *Location:* 25km from Avignon, 18km from Arles, 80km from Marseille (Airport), the course is on the D27 between Les Baux and Maussane-les-Alpilles. Designed by the British architect Martin Hawtree, the course is set between pines, olive trees and scented lavender. 9 holes, 2842 metres. Par 36. Practice, putting green, 9 hole pitch and putt course 836 metres, Par 27. *Green Fees:* weekdays 120ff; weekends 150ff. Extra for 18 holes. Special rates for pairs, Juniors and for 9 holes. *Eating facilities:* bar and restaurant in clubhouse. *Visitors:* always welcome. Hire of clubs, trolleys and golf cars. *Society Meetings:* welcome by arrangement. Professional: Frèdéric Monréal. Secretary: Sylvie Martin-Raget.

BANDOL. **Golf de Fregate,** Route de Bandol, RD 559, 83270 St-Cyr-sur-Mer (94.32.50.50; Fax: 94.29.96.94). *Location:* about 7km from St-Cyr-sur-Mer on the road to Bandol on the right hand side. A dramatic new course in a vineyard setting overlooking the Mediterranean. 18 holes, 6500 metres. Par 72. Also 9 holes, 1500 metres. Par 29. Practice ground and putting green. *Green Fees:* information not provided. *Eating facilities:* bar and restaurant. Also on-site hotel by 18th green. Pro shop, club, cart and trolley hire.

See our Colour Advertisement on page 33.

BEZIERS. **Golf du Cap d'Agde,** 4 Avenue des Alizès, 34300 Cap d'Agde (67.26.54.40; Fax: 67.26.97.00). *Location:* autoroute A9 exit Agde. Seaside links. 18 holes, 6301 metres, Par 72. Practice ground; 9 hole pitch and putt, 800 metres, S.S.S. 27. *Green Fees:* weekdays 190f; weekends 230f; Holidays 210f. *Eating facilities:* bar and restaurant in clubhouse. *Visitors:* welcome, no restrictions. Club, trolley and cart hire. *Society Meetings:* welcome by reservation. Professionals: Xavier Bernard, Vincent Denis. Secretary: Marguerite Bouvier.

CANNES. **Golf Club de Cannes-Mandelieu,** Route de Golf, 06210 Mandelieu-la-Napoule (93.49.55.39; Fax: 93.49.92.90). *Location:* across the mouth of the small River Siagne, about seven km west of Cannes, south of the A8. A short, level course, third oldest and most popular in France. 18 holes, 5867 metres, Par 71. 9 holes, 2409 metres, Par 33. Practice ground, putting green. *Green Fees:* weekdays 260f 18 holes, 180f 9 holes; weekends 300f 18 holes, 180f 9 holes (per day). *Eating facilities:* bar and restaurant in attractive clubhouse. *Visitors:* welcome. *Society Meetings:* welcome.

CANNES. **Golf Country Club de Cannes-Mougins,** 175 Route d'Antibes, 06250 Mougins (93.75.56.59; Fax: 93.75.27.60). *Location:* eight km north of Cannes, near the A8. A high-class private course, undulating through wooded hills, part of the annual Volvo Tour. 18 holes, 6263 metres, S.S.S. 72. Driving range, putting green, pitching green. *Green Fees:* weekdays 330f; weekends 370f. *Eating facilities:* restaurant, bar, snacks. *Visitors:* welcome, no restrictions. Sauna. Pro shop; cart, trolley and club hire. Professionals: Michel Damiano, Patrick Lemaire, Richard Sorrell. Secretary: Danielle Menager (93.75.79.13; Fax: 93.75.27.60).

CANNES. **Riviera Golf Club,** Avenue des Amazones, 06210 Mandelieu (92.97.67.67; Fax: 92.97.66.57). *Location:* less than five km west of Cannes, just south of the A8, Fréjus direction. A new 18 hole course by American master Robert Trent Jones; mostly level, some hills and lakes. 18 holes, 5736 metres, Par 72. Driving range, putting green. *Green Fees:* weekdays 220f; weekends 270f. *Eating facilities:* in clubhouse. *Visitors:* welcome, Handicap of 35 and insurance required. Professional/Manager: Mr Stumpler. Secretary: Mme Merna Laetitia.

CORSICA. **Golf de Sperone,** Domaine de Sperone, 20169 Bonifacio (95.73.17.13; Fax: 95.73.17.85). *Location:* near Bonifacio, southern point of Corsica. Another new Trent Jones creation, part on rocky maquis inland, part overlooking the Mediterranean. 18 holes, 6130 metres, Par 73. Practice facilities. *Green Fees:* 300f to 390f. *Eating facilities:* bar and restaurant in the clubhouse. *Visitors:* welcome every day, please make a reservation. Pro shop. *Society Meetings:* welcome except July and August. Professional: Philippe Allain. Secretaries: A. Minier, P. Vichera.

FREJUS. **Golf de Roquebrune,** CD 7, 83520 Roquebrune-sur-Argens (94.82.92.91; Fax: 94.82.94.74). *Location:* inland, midway between Cannes and St. Tropez. A natural and attractive course, hilly and with water traps. 18 holes, 6241 metres, Par 71. Large 3 hole practice area, driving range and putting green. *Eating facilities:* bar and restaurant in clubhouse. Pro shop; club and trolley hire.

GRASSE. **Golf de la Grande Bastide,** Chemin des Picholines, 06740 Châteauneuf de Grasse (93.77.70.08; Fax: 93.77.72.36). *Location:* autoroute A8 exit Cannes towards Mougin-Valbonne-Opio. Gently rolling, of equal challenge to all grades of player. 18 holes, 6105 metres, S.S.S. 72. Driving range, putting green. *Green Fees:* weekdays 240f; weekends 270f. *Eating facilities:* bar and restaurant in clubhouse. *Visitors:* welcome anytime. Trolley and club hire. *Society Meetings:* welcome. Professional: S. Damiano. Secretary: Jean Paul Mugnier.

MARSEILLES. **Golf d'Aix Marseille,** Domaine de Riquetti, 13290 Les Milles (42.24.20.41; Fax: 42.39.91.48). *Location:* between Marseille and Aix-en-Provence, west of the A51. A mature parkland course in a natural setting with a wealth of established trees. 18 holes, 6291 metres, Par 73. Driving range, putting green. *Green Fees:* weekdays 220f; weekends 300f. From 15th July to 31 August 200f. *Eating facilities:* bar and restaurant in clubhouse. *Visitors:* welcome, closed Tuesdays. Pro shop; trolley and club hire.

MONTPELLIER. **Golf de la Grande Motte,** BP16, 34280 La Grande Motte, ph ([33].67.56.05.00; Fax: [33].67.29.18.84). *Location:* by the Mediterranean Sea, 18 km south-east of Montpellier. A Robert Trent

Jones Sr 42-hole course, in the Floridian style with fast greens, water and bunkers. "Les Flamants Roses" – 18 holes international, Par 72, 6200 meters. "Les Goélands" – 18 holes compact, Par 58, 3200 meters. "Les Mouettes" – 6 holes compact, Par 19, 765 metres. Driving range, putting green and pitch. *Green Fees:* weekdays 180/100/70f; weekends 230/130/70f. *Eating facilities:* bar and restaurant in the clubhouse. Accommodation: 2 on-course hotels. Pro shop. Teaching school with courses for all levels of players. Trolley, buggy and club hire. Professionals: V. Etchevers, S. Etchevers, P.-H. Milhau and A. Schneider. Open all year round.

MONTPELLIER. **Golf de Massane,** Domaine de Massane, 34670 Baillargues (67.87.87.89; Fax: 67.87.87.90). *Location:* seven km from airport, 10km from Montpellier and two km from autoroute. Tough championship layout which hosts the annual Volvo Tour qualifying. Elevated greens protected by sand and water. 18 holes, 6375 metres, Par 72. 9 hole compact course. Extensive teaching school with large driving range, pitching and putting greens. *Green Fees:* weekdays 195ff; weekends 270ff. *Eating facilities:* bar and restaurant in clubhouse, hotel on course. Pro shop. *Society Meetings:* yes. Professional: Nicolas Armand (67.87.87.91). Secretary: Chantel Tisserand (67.87.87.89).

MONTPELLIER. **Golf Hotel de Fontcaude,** Route de Loclère, Domaine de Fontcaude 34990 Juvignac (67.03.34.10; Fax: 67.03.34.51). *Location:* at Juvignac, six km west of Montpellier. Undulating over a rolling, scrub-covered landscape, this course provides a fair and interesting challenge. Two courses: International 18 holes, 6292 metres, Par 72. Executive 9 holes, 1290 metres, Par 29. Driving range, putting green, pitching green. *Green Fees:* weekdays 160f 18 holes, 100f 9 holes; weekends 210f 18 holes, 150f 9 holes. *Eating facilities:* bar and restaurant in clubhouse. *Visitors:* welcome, no restrictions. Pro shop; cart, trolley and club hire. *Society Meetings:* welcome. Professional: Bruno Tancogne. Secretaries: Cathy Laniboire, Nathalie Rossi (67.03.34.30). Manager: Jean Claude Lenoire.

MONTPELLIER. **Montpellier-Massane Golf Club,** Domaine de Massane, 34670 Baillargues (67 87 87 87; Fax: 67 87 87 90). *Location:* seven km from airport, 10 km from Montpellier and two km from highway. Championship layout which hosts the annual PGA Qualifying School. Elevated greens protected by sand and water. 18 holes, 6375 metres, Par 72. 9-hole compact course. Large practice range. *Green Fees:* weekdays 195ff, weekends 270ff. *Eating facilities:* bar and restaurant in clubhouse, hotel on course. Golfy Leadbetter Academie offers all year round golf tuition with English-speaking Professionals (67 87 87 97; Fax: 67 87 87 99).

MONTE CARLO. **Monte Carlo Golf Club,** Route du Mont Agel, 06320 La Turbie (93.41.09.11; Fax: 93.41.09.55). *Location:* from Nice, take autoroute A8 Exit for La Turbie. Signpost at end of town, left turn for Mont Agel. Golf course entrance after 5 kms. Picturesque course with exceptional views of the Mediterranean sea and southern Alps. 18 holes, 5700 metres, Par 71. Driving range, practice, putting green. *Green Fees:* weekdays 350f; weekends 450f. *Eating facilities:* bar and restaurant. *Visitors:* welcome, Handicap Certificate required. *Society Meetings:* welcome by prior arrangement. Professionals: F. Ruffier-Meray, J.M. Loustalan. Secretary: C. Houtart.

NIMES. **Golf de Nîmes Vacquerolles,** , Route de Sauve, 30900 Nîmes (66.23.33.33; Fax: 66.23.94.94). *Location:* five minutes from Nîmes. New course (1990) running up a valley and over steeply wooded hills. 18 holes, 6289 metres, Par 73. Practice area, putting green. *Green Fees:* weekdays 160f; weekends 230f. *Eating facilities:* bar and restaurant in clubhouse. *Visitors:* welcome. *Society Meetings:* welcome. Open Golf Club. Professionals: Gye Clerigues and Emmanuel Thomas.

NIMES. **Golf de Nîmes-Campagne,** Route de Saint-Gilles, 30900 Nîmes (66.70.17.37). *Location:* about three km south of Nîmes, by the airport. A classic parkland course of championship calibre built around a hill. 18 holes, 6135 metres, Par 72. Driving range, putting green. *Eating facilities:* bar and excellent restaurant in imposing hilltop clubhouse. Pro shop; cart, trolley and club hire.

PERPIGNAN. **Golf de St-Cyprien,** Mas d'Huston, 66750 Saint-Cyprien Plage, Perpignan (68.21.01.71; Fax: 68.21.11.33.). *Location:* just south of Perpignan, a renowned course between sea and lake with the Pyrenees mountains in the background. Challenging championship course with water hazards. 18 holes, 6480 metres, Par 73. South Course – 9 holes, 2724 metres, Par 35. *Green Fees:* information not provided. *Eating facilities:* bar at clubhouse. Bars, restaurants and accommodation at Le Mas d'Huston, on-course hotel. Open all year. Pro shop, golf clinic.

ST. RAPHAÈL. **Golf de l'Estérel,** Avenue du Golf, 83700 St. Raphaèl (94.82.47.88; Fax: 94.44.64.61). *Location:* inland just a few metres north of St. Raphaèl, close to Golf de Valescure. Not long but rated difficult; many trees, narrow fairways and water hazards protecting beautiful greens. 18 holes, 5941 metres, Par 71. 9 holes, 1400 metres, Par 29. Driving range, 9 hole school. *Green Fees:* weekdays 260f; weekends 290f. *Eating facilities:* bar, clubhouse and restaurant. On-site Hotel Latitudes-Valescure (30% reduction in green fees for residents). Pro shop; club, cart and trolley hire.

ST. RAPHAÈL. **Golf et Tennis Club de Valescure,** BP451, Route de Golf, 83700 St.-Raphaèl (94.82.40.46; Fax: 94.82.41.42). *Location:* about five km east of St.-Raphaèl. An established course (1895), winding attractively through the umbrella pine trees. 18 holes, 5067 metres, Par 68. Driving range, putting green. *Eating facilities:* bar and restaurant in period clubhouse. Also at golf hotel nearby. Pro shop; trolley and club hire.

DUBAI

DUBAI. **Dubai Creek Golf and Yacht Club,** PO Box 6302, Dubai (971-4-821000; Fax: 971-4-822565). *Location:* beside the Al Garhoud Bridge, close to the city centre and airport. Long, rolling course with green dunes and palm trees, man-made lake and large sandy waste. 18 holes, 6900 yards, Par 72. Floodlit 9-Hole Par 3 course. Golf academy, caddy cart and club hire; floodlit driving range, pitching/putting area. *Green Fees:* on application. *Eating facilities:* clubhouse with restaurants and bars. *Visitors:* welcome; overseas pass available. Restrictions on Thursdays and Fridays. Swimming pool, tennis courts, yacht club and marina. Professional: Peter Downie (971-4-822789; Fax: 971-4-823591). Secretary: Sandy Meyer (971-4-825777; Fax: 971-4-821776).

DUBAI. **Dubai Golf and Racing Club,** PO Box 52872, Dubai (971-4-363666; Fax: 971-4-363717). *Location:* on the Al Awir Road, within the race track, a few kilometres from the city centre. A links-type course with undulating fairways, heavily bunkered. 9 holes, 3100 yards, Par 35. 18 holes (2x9), Par 70. Fully floodlit. Golf clinics, floodlit driving range, practice area, chipping and putting. *Green Fees:* on application. *Eating facilities:* well equipped clubhouse with restaurant and Spike Bar. *Visitors:* welcome; overseas pass available. Restrictions on race days, Fridays and Saturdays. Professional: Adrian Flaherty.

DUBAI. **Emirates Golf Club,** PO Box 24040, Dubai (971-4-480222; Fax: 971-4-481888). *Location:* on the Abu Dhabi Highway, leaving Dubai. Long, championship standard 18-hole course with palm-edged fairways, lakes and immaculate greens. Taxing, full-size 9-hole course with water hazards and bunkers. 18 holes, 7100 yards, Par 72. 9 holes, Par 37. Coaching, driving range, pitching/putting greens. *Green Fees:* on application. *Eating facilities:* clubhouse in unique setting with bars, snack bars and restaurant. *Visitors:* welcome; overseas pass available. Restrictions on Thursdays and Fridays. Tennis, squash and gym available. *Society Meetings:* restrictions on Thursdays and Fridays. Professional: James Williams. Secretary: William Richardson.

Golf in Portugal

WHERE TO PLAY • WHERE TO STAY

by Michael Gedye

ALTHOUGH there are golf courses to play in the northern port-wine area of the country as well as the semi-tropical islands of the Azores and Madeira, the prime regions for the holiday player lie along the holiday coasts of the Costa do Estoril and Costa Azul, either side of Lisbon and the southern sunshine beaches of the Algarve.

Golf in the north, the COSTA VERDE, is best known for the Oporto Golf Club (oldest in Portugal – 1890) and one of the newest, Estela at Povoa de Varzim. Rapidly gaining ground as a focal point for golf is the COSTA DE LISBOA, with a choice of four courses to the west of the capital around the holiday resort of Estoril plus three to the south in the Costa Azul. Golf along the western coast towards Cascais always centred around the classic Mackenzie Ross layout at Estoril but now the new course at Penha Longa demands attention. Part of a 27-hole complex with luxury hotel built on a palatial estate near Sintra, it hosted the 1994 Portuguese Open. South of Lisbon's Tagus river lies relatively unsung treasure. Three very different courses, each worthy of interest. The Portuguese Country Club at Aroeira is an unheralded masterpiece by English architect Frank Pennink, carved through a natural pine forest in delightful solitude

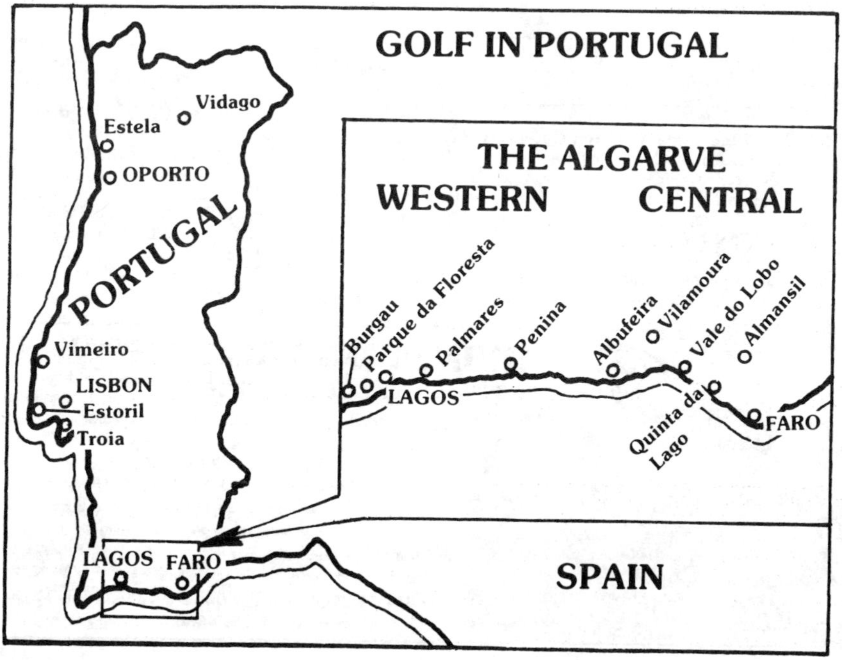

yet only a short drive from the city. Montado, the most recent course, flanks working vineyards near Setubal, providing a link in the golfing chain running south to Troia. The latter, built by Robert Trent Jones on a pine-encrusted seaside sandbar, presents a tough and often breezy test for anyone.

Down south in the sunny ALGARVE, nearly half the courses in Portugal form an elegant green chain along a series of craggy cliffs, stunning white beaches and rolling orchards of orange and olive. To the west, six locations await, from the dramatic challenge of Parque da Floresta, past the popular slopes of Palmares, the classic demands of Penina and the new Alto Club to the two Ronald Fream layouts at Carvoeiro, of which the Vale da Pinta course, carved through ancient olive groves, is a gem. Centrally, the extensive residential, hotel and marina complex of Vilamoura offers three quite varied courses to play while nearby, Vila Sol is a fine Donald Steel layout in good condition and Pine Cliffs has nine holes in keeping with its name. The best concentration of golf is found near Faro in the east. The classic quartet of Vale do Lobo, Quinta do Lago, San Lorenzo and Pinheiros Altos provide a total of 99 holes laid out over a rolling, sandy, pine-sprinkled landscape with sparkling sea views. Manicured fairways lead to immaculate greens, splashes of white sand bordering tempting strategic water – here is the essence of ideal holiday golf.

ALGARVE

ALBUFEIRA. **Pine Cliffs Golf and Country Club,** Pinhal do Concelho, 8200 Albufeira (00 351 89 501090; Fax: 00 351 89501200). *Location:* seven km from Vilamoura, situated outside Olhos d'Agua. Seaside links. 9 holes, 2557 yards, 2324 metres, Par (equivalent) 67. 9 holes Par 3 course. *Green Fees:* 4,000 9 holes. Discounts for hotel guests. *Eating facilities:* bar, restaurant. *Visitors:* welcome, advance booking required. Golf academy, changing facilities. *Society Meetings:* all groups welcome. Professional/Golf Director: David J. Marsh.

ALMANSIL. **Sociedade do Golfe da Quinta do Lago,** Quinta do Lago, 8135 Almansil (089 396002/3; Fax: 089 394013). *Location:* 15 minutes west of Faro Airport, nearest town Almansil. Gently undulating sandy land covered with umbrella pines, wild flowers and lakes. 4 courses – A,B,C,D. A/D 6850 yards, A/C 7040 yards, B/C 7137 yards, B/D 6915 yards. S.S.S. A/D 73, A/C 73, B/D 73, B/C 73. Driving range. *Green Fees:* Visitors: 11,000 esc; Residents: 8,250 esc. *Eating facilities:* pizzeria, clubhouse restaurant and bar.

Visitors: welcome subject to availability. Pro Shop, boutique and golf academy. Professional: Domingos Silva (089 394529). Secretary: José A. Capele (089 394529).

ALMANSIL. **San Lorenzo Golf Club,** Quinta do Lago, 8135 Almansil, Loule 8100 (00 351 89 396522; Fax: 00 351 89 396908). *Location:* 20km from Faro Airport towards west. Parkland with seaside view surrounded by wildlife and umbrella pine trees. 18 holes, 6238 metres. S.S.S. 73. Practice range. *Green Fees:* 2500esc Free to Hotel Dona Filipa guests. *Eating facilities:* bar and restaurant. *Visitors:* welcome, please reserve a day before wishing to play. *Society Meetings:* welcome if staying in Dona Filipa Hotel. Professional: A. Rodrigues. Secretary: Antonio Santos (010 351 89 396534).

ALMANSIL. **Vale do Lobo Golf Club,** Vale do Lobo, Almansil, Loule 8137 (00 351 89 394589; Fax: 394713. Telex: 56842). *Location:* on the cliff edge, overlooking the sea, 15 minutes' drive west from Faro. 27 holes, three loops of 9; average 18-hole length 6600 yards. S.S.S. 72. *Green Fees:* 10,000esc. *Facilities:* clubhouse with restaurant, bar and shop. Nearby the 5 star Dona Filipa Hotel and luxury villa estate with leisure complexes. Professional: Steven Walker. Secretary: J.A. Walker.

ALVOR. **Alto Golf Club,** Quinto do Alto do Poco, Alvor, 8500 Portimao (082 416913; Fax: 082 401046). *Location:* in Alvor, overlooking the Atlantic ocean and the Bay of Lagos. A parkland course designed by Sir Henry Cotton with gently undulating fairways and challenging sloping greens. Stunning views of the Monchique Mountains in the background. 18 holes, 6125 metres, Par 72. Driving range, putting green. *Eating facilities:* bar and restaurant in clubhouse. Pro shop; cart, trolley and club hire.

BUDENS/SALEMA. **Parque da Floresta Golf and Country Club,** Vale do Poco, Budens, 8650 Vila do Bispo (082 65333/4; Fax: 082 65157). *Location:* N125, 16k west of Lagos. Located just past Budens on right. Undulating course with spectacular views. 18 holes, 6477 yards, 5888 metres. S.S.S. 72. Large practice ground, driving range, putting green. *Green Fees:* 6000esc. *Eating facilities:* restaurant and bar. *Visitors:* most welcome with no restrictions. Advisable to book starting times by phone. Enquire about Special Rates. Pro shop. *Society Meetings:* welcome, catered for by arrangement with Golf Manager. Professional/General Manager: Peter Dolan. Golf Director: B.H. Murphy.

LAGOA. **Carvoeiro Golf and Country Club,** Carvoeiro, Apartado 24, 8400 Lagoa (082 52670; Fax: 082 52649). *Location:* 2km south of Lagoa on the Estrada Nacional 125, follow road signs. A superb course undulating through olive groves. Double 9 hole course (course played twice but with alternate tees and greens). 9 holes, 5919 metres. S.S.S. 71, Par 72. Driving range, putting green. *Green Fees:* 8000esc 18 holes, 5000esc 9 holes. *Eating facilities:* restaurant, bar plus magnificent terrace. *Visitors:* welcome anytime after booking starting times. Pro shop, rental of pull trolleys, electric trolleys and clubs. *Society Meetings:* welcome by arrangement. Professional: Roel Gritter.

LAGOA. **Palmares Golf Club,** Meia Praia, Lagoa 8600 (082 762961; Fax: 082 762534). *Location:* five kilometres from centre of Lagoa on main Meia Praia beach. Five link type holes – very scenic. 18 holes, 5961 metres. S.S.S. 72. Driving range, putting green, pitch and putt. *Green Fees:* 7000esc. *Eating facilities:* restaurant and bar. *Visitors:* always welcome. *Society Meetings:* always welcome by prior arrangement. Professional: Luis Espadinha. Secretary: Dennis Garvey (082 762953).

LAGOA. **Vale da Pinta,** Carvoeiro Golfe (2nd course), Apt. 24, 8400 Lagoa (082 52670; Fax: 082 52649). *Location:* 2kms south of Lagoa on the Estrada Nacional 125, follow road signs. Parkland in ancient olive groves with trees 600/700 years old. 18 holes, 5861 metres. S.S.S. 71, Par 71. Driving range, putting green. *Green Fees:* 8000esc. *Eating facilities:* restaurant and bar plus magnificent terrace. *Visitors:* welcome any time, after booking starting times. Handicap Certificate required: men 28, ladies 34. Accommodation available locally (082 357262). Golf School, Pro shop, rental of pull trolleys, electric trolleys, clubs and buggies. *Society Meetings:* welcome anytime by arrangement. Professional: Roel Gritter. Director of Golf: Aart C. Spaans.

PORTIMAO/PENINA. **Penina Golf Club,** Penina Golf Resort Hotel, PO Box 146, Penina, 8502 Portimao (082 415415; Fax: 082 415000). *Location:* five km from Portimao, 12km from Lagos. Long, flat course with lakes, trees and bunkers. 18 holes (plus two 9 hole courses), 7041 yards, 6439 metres. S.S.S. 73. Also Monchique Course 9 holes, 3268 yards, 2987 metres. S.S.S. 35 and Quinta Course 9 holes, 2035 yards, 1851 metres. S.S.S. 31. Golf academy, putting greens. *Green Fees:* Championship course 9.500Esc; Monchique course 6.000Esc; Quinta 5.000Esc. Special tickets June, July, August. *Eating facilities:* clubhouse and Hotel restaurants. *Visitors:* welcome, Handicap Certificate required to play Championship Course. Professional: Jose Lourenco and Robin Liddle. Secretary: Leonel Rio.

QUINTA DO LAGO. **Pinheiros Altos Golf Club,** Quinta do Lago, 8135 Almansil, Algarve (089 394340; Fax: 089 394392). *Location:* south of Almansil just east of the Quinta do Lago and San Lorenzo courses. A combination of elevated holes through pines and low lying marshland with strategic water. 18 holes, 6049 metres. S.S.S. 72. Large practice ground, bunker, chipping green and three putting greens. *Green Fees:* 9000esc. Subject to review. *Eating facilities:* restaurant and bar. *Visitors:* welcome, Handicap Certificate required: Men 28, Ladies 36. Extensive Pro shop; trolley, club hire available, caddies by request. *Society Meetings:* welcome. Professional: Wayne Johnson.

VILAMOURA. **Golf Vila Sol,** Vila Sol, Alto do Semino (089 302144; Fax: 089 302147). *Location:* just east of Vilamoura off the road leading down to Quarteira. An excellent natural course undulating through umbrella pines with good water hazards and superb greens. 18 holes, 6183 metres, Par 72. Driving range, putting green. *Eating facilities:* bar and restaurant in clubhouse. Pro shop; cart, trolley and club hire.

VILAMOURA. **Vilamoura One (The Old Course),** Vilamoura, Quarteira 8125 (089 321652; Fax: 089 380726). *Location:* 20km from Faro Airport, 25km from Faro. Narrow fairways through pine woods, sea views. 18 holes, 6331 metres. S.S.S. 72. Practice and putting greens. *Green Fees:* information on request. *Eating facilities:* restaurant and bar. *Visitors:* course open to all players with Handicap Certificate. Pro shop, hire of trolleys. Professional: Joaquim Catarino (089 321652). Sales Director: Susete Calado (089 380724).

VILAMOURA. **Vilamoura Two (The New Course),** as Vilamoura One (089 321562; Fax: 089 380726). *Location:* as Vilamoura One. Pine wood setting. Sea views. 18 holes, 6256 metres. S.S.S 71. Driving range. *Green Fees:* on request. *Eating facilities:* bar and restaurant. *Visitors:* open to players with Handicap Certificate all year round. *Society Meetings:* welcome at any time. Professional: Manuel Pardal (089 321562). Sales Director: Susete Calado (089 380724).

VILAMOURA. **Vilamoura Three and Four,** Vilamoura – 8125 Quarteira (089 380724; Telex: 56018 VIGOLF; Fax: 089 380726). *Location:* 20 kms from Faro Airport – 25 kms from Faro. 27 challenging holes set up overlooking the sea, although not particularly long for a modern layout; its 10 different lakes being the principal hazards. 3 x 9-holes. Driving range, putting green. *Green Fees:* on request. *Eating facilities:* restaurant and bar. *Visitors:* Vilamoura Three is open to players with Handicap Certificate, Vilamoura Four is open to beginners all year round. *Society Meetings:* welcome at all times. Professional: Abilio Coelho (089 380724). Sales Director: Susete Calado (089 380724).

LISBON

AROEIRA. **Clube de Campo da Ardeira,** Herdade da Aroeira, 2825 Monte de Caparica, Aroeira, Costa Lisboa (01 2971314; Fax: 01 2971358). *Location:* south from Lisbon across the bridge, turn right to Costa Caparica and follow signs. This well-established course remains one of Portugal's best kept secrets. A superb test through a floral pine forest by Frank Pennink; one for purists to savour. 18 holes, 6040 metres, Par 72. Practice ground with shelters for bad/hot weather. *Eating facilities:* restaurant, snack bar, cocktail bar and lounge. *Visitors:* welcome, no restrictions; subject only to having a valid Handicap and availability of tees. Professional: Joaquim Noura. Director: Duarte Leal.

ESTORIL. **Estoril Palacio Golf Course,** Estoril (4680400). *Location:* an undulating links course with views of the Atlantic, north west of Lisbon. Pine trees and natural hazards. 27 holes including 18-hole championship course, 5700 yards. S.S.S. 69. *Facilities:* clubhouse with restaurant, bar and swimming pool. The 5 star Hotel Palacio one mile away with superb amenities. Hotel's guests are entitled to special privileges at the Estoril Palacio Golf Course. Golf Director: E. Pinheira.

ESTORIL. **International Golf Academy,** Estoril Sol Golf Club, Quinta do Outeiro, Linho, Sintra 2710 (351-1-9232461; Telex: 12624). *Location:* take the main Cascais-Sintra road and turn left at the village of Linho towards Lagoa Azul. 9 holes (18 tees), 3341 metres. S.S.S. 62. Purpose-built golf academy – practice facility, chipping greens, putting green. *Green Fees:* 4000esc. 50% discount after 5pm. *Eating facilities:* restaurant and bar. *Visitors:* no restrictions. *Society Meetings:* welcome. 10% discount for groups of eight or more players. Professionals: Geoff Hutchinson/ Roger Marios. Golf Manager: Nuno Teixeira Bastos.

ESTORIL. **Penha Longa Golf Club,** Lagoa Azul, Linho, 2710 Sintra (01 9249022; Fax: 01 9249024). *Location:* half an hour west of Lisbon, just north of Estoril on the main road to Sintra. A new course of quality laid out over craggy hills, wooded slopes and valleys surrounding an ancient royal palace; hosted the Portuguese Open in 1994 and again in 1995. 18 holes, 6910 yards, 6290 metres. S.S.S. 73. Driving range, two putting greens. *Eating facilities:* two bars and three restaurants. *Visitors:* welcome, Handicap Certificate required. Golf Academy, Pro shop, cart, trolley, club and shoe hire. Sauna, jacuzzi. No jeans. Professional: Keath Ashdown. Director: Nelson Ramalho (01 9240014).

ESTORIL. **Quinta da Marinha Golf Club,** Casa 36, Quinta da Marinha, Cascais 2750 (4869881/9). *Location:* highway from Lisbon to Cascais, Cascais to Quin Cho. Championship golf course designed by Robert Trent Jones. Open sandy course with pine trees, lakes and spectacular views over the mountains and ocean. 18 holes, 6684 yards. S.S.S. 71. *Green Fees:* weekdays 6500esc; weekends 7500 esc. 2900esc for guests of resort. *Eating facilities:* bar and restaurant. *Visitors:* welcome. Men's Handicap 28, Ladies' Handicap 36. Club hire, trolley rental; Pro shop. *Society Meetings:* welcome (one person free for every eight). Sports Director: Nuno Teixeira Bastos (4869881/9; Fax: 4869032).

LISBON. **Lisbon Sports Club,** Casal da Carregueira, Belas, Queluz 2745 (01 4310077). *Location:* 25 km from Lisbon. Parkland. 18 holes, 5278 metres. S.S.S. 69. *Green Fees:* 6,000esc weekdays, 8,000esc weekends. 10% discount for groups. *Eating facilities:* clubhouse with restaurant, bar and swimming pool. *Visitors:* welcome weekdays, Handicap Certificate required. Professional: Jose Baltazar (01 4321474). Secretary: Mrs Manuela De Sousa (Tel & Fax: 01 4312482).

PRAIA DE MIRAMAR. **Clube de Golf de Miramar,** Av. Sacadura Cabral, Miramar, Valadares 4405 (02 7622067; Fax: 02 7627859). *Location:* approximately 13 km south of Oporto. Flat coastal course amongst dunes alongside the beach. 9 holes, 5146 metres. S.S.S. 67. *Green Fees:* 9.000esc. *Eating facilities:* clubhouse with restaurant and bar. Hotels, restaurants and casino nearby. Pro Shop. 50% discount on green fees given by some hotels. Professional: Manuel Ribeiro/Joao Couto. Secretary: Manuela Pinto Leite.

TROIA. **Troia Golf Club,** Troia, Setubal 2900 (065 4412; Fax: 065 44162; Telex: 18138). *Location:* on the Troia Peninsula, 42 km south of Lisbon by motorway. Seaside links, small greens, long fairways and sandy roughs. 18 holes. S.S.S. 74. Two putting areas and driving range. *Green Fees:* on application. Special rates

for Hotel Magnoliamar guests. *Eating facilities:* clubhouse with bar/restaurant. *Visitors:* welcome, no restrictions all year round. Golf/Hotel Special Packages available. *Society Meetings:* welcome, special rates. Secretaries: Madalena O'Neil, Pinheiro de Mello (065 44151).

VIMEIRO. **Vimeiro Golf Club,** Praia do Porto Novo, Vimeiro, Torres Vedras 25600 (98157; Telex: 43353). *Location:* approximately 70 km north of Lisbon, overlooking the sea. A level course, divided by a river and sheltered by rocky cliffs. 9 holes with 18 tees, 5228 yards. S.S.S. 67. *Facilities:* the neighbouring Hotel Golf Mar offers all facilities.

MADEIRA

MADEIRA. **Campo de Golfe da Madeira,** Santo Antonio da Serra, 9100 Santa Cruz (091 552345; Fax: 091 552367). *Location:* main highway to Airport (Santa Cruz) Machilo. Wooded, mountainous with view over Atlantic Ocean. 27 holes, 6082 metres. Driving range, putting and chipping green. *Green Fees:* 7000esc 18 holes. *Eating facilities:* restaurant, snack bar, lounge bar. *Visitors:* welcome to play in tournaments except PGA Madeira Island Open (January). Pro shop; cart, trolley and club hire. Professional: Joao Sousa. Secretary: Anthony Barton (acting).

THE AZORES

TERCEIRA. **Terceira Golf Club,** Caixa Postal 15, 9760 Praia da Vitoria, Terceira. (Tel: [00 351 95] 92444/92299. Fax: 92445). *Location:* a few km from Angra do Heroismo and Praia da Vitoria on the island of Terceira in the Azores. Landscaped course through trees and low hills, with small lakes. S.S.S. 70. *Green Fees:* no information supplied. *Hotel accommodation:* Hotel Angra and Hotel Nasce Agua, both nearby.

OPORTO

ESPINHO. **Oporto Golf Club,** Lugar do Sisto, Paramos, Espinho 4500 (02 722008; Fax: 02 726895). *Location:* 18 miles south of Oporto, one mile south of Espinho. Seaside links, few trees, founded in 1890. 18 holes, 6500 yards. S.S.S. 70. Practice ground. *Green Fees:* weekdays 8,000esc; weekends 10,000esc. Half price for guests of Hotels mentioned below. *Eating facilities:* bar with snacks (restaurant – members only). *Visitors:* welcome Tuesdays to Fridays (closed Mondays); weekends and Bank Holidays till 10.30am. Handicap Certificate required. Beach, hotels – Hotel Solverde, Hotel Praia – Golf, casino nearby. Professional: Eduardo Maganinho. Secretary: Antonio Pais.

ESTELA. **Estela Golf Club,** Rio Alto-Estela, 4490 Povoa de Varzim (52 601567/612400; Fax: 52 612701; Telex: 25654). *Location:* 30 km north of Oporto, 24 km from the international airport. Seaside links. 18 holes, 6095 metres. S.S.S. 73. *Green Fees:* 6,000esc. *Eating facilities:* full bar and catering facilities. *Visitors:* welcome anytime when no competitions taking place. Sopete Hotel guests entitled to special privileges. *Society Meetings:* by arrangement. Professionals: Carlos Alberto, Carlos Henrique. Secretary/ Manager: Salete Correia.

VIDAGO. **Vidago Golf Club,** Vidago 5425 (97106; Telex: 238888). *Location:* mountain valley course, in spa/resort area well inland, only 25 km from Spanish border. Short 9-hole course, 1000ft high, 2678 yards. S.S.S. 63 (18 holes). *Facilities:* Vidago Palace Hotel.

Golf in Spain

WHERE TO PLAY • WHERE TO STAY

by Michael Gedye

FOR MANY people, holiday golf is inextricably linked with Spain. For the past thirty years, the development of coastal resorts where golf is allied to hotels and real estate, served by package holiday operators providing relatively inexpensive and convenient 'golf in the sun' has been a Spanish speciality. The game of golf is still a minority sport amongst its resident population; the bulk of its 230-odd courses, mostly fringing the Mediterranean coasts and the Balearic islands, have been built with the foreign visitor in mind, particularly as a winter season opportunity. Our selection is concentrated in the five most popular areas for resort golf – the Costa del Sol and other coastal areas of Andalucia in the south; the central/eastern regions of Murcia and Valencia; the sunshine island of Majorca and golf in Catalonia in the north-east. A total of forty-three courses,

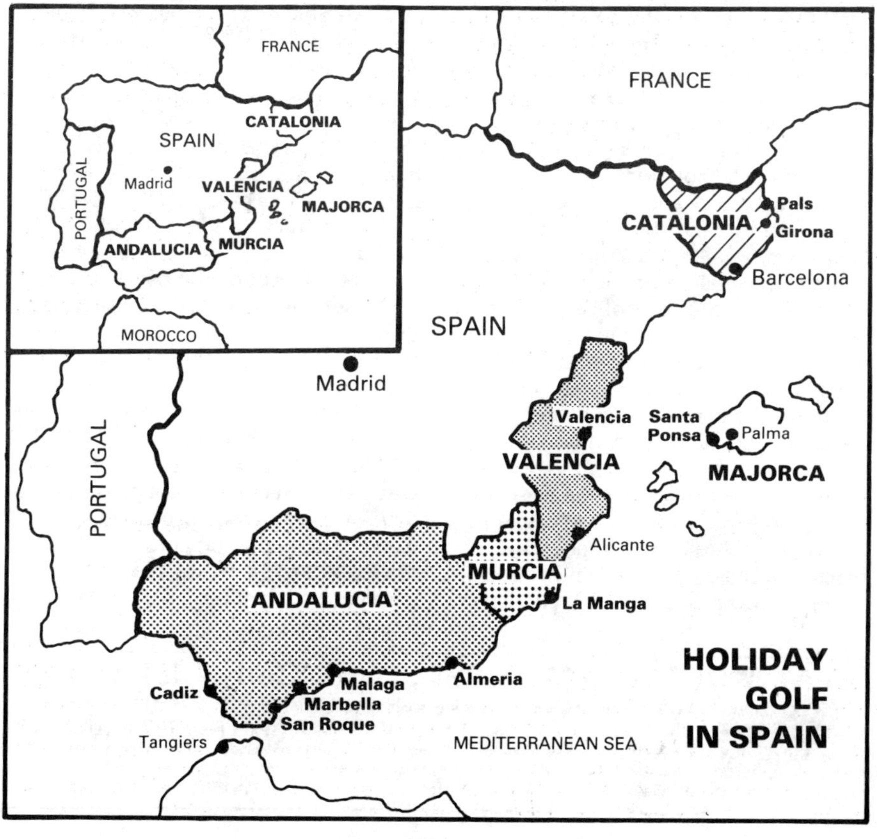

all offering a warm welcome to the visitor and golf of excellent calibre.

Golf in the vast region of ANDALUCIA subdivides into three sections of coastal plain – West, Central and East. To the west, there is a strong contrast between old and new yet all golf of quality. Cadiz now has Montecastillo and Novo Sancti Petri while just to the east of Gibraltar, the complex of San Roque has joined the mature and highly respected layouts of Sotogrande and Valderrama, the latter due for the 1997 Ryder Cup.

The central area clusters around the bright lights of Marbella, spreading east to just beyond Malaga, a rich vein of golf dating back to 1925. Guadalmina, opened in 1959, was the first of the true resort courses, heading a steadily increasing trend of development over the years that followed until the region can now claim a concentration of holiday golf to rival Florida or Myrtle Beach. Here is golf to test the most demanding as well as mere mortals, from the world-famous championship holes of Las Brisas to the dramatic subtlety of Torrequebrada; from the understated class of Rio Real to the spectacular mountainous challenge of Monte Mayor. Many have been carved from the river valleys and low hills which lie inland from the strips of beach hotels, running back up towards the blue shadow of the Sierra Nevada and Ronda mountain ranges, rugged terrain which has tested the course designer and placed a premium on earth-moving for the constructor and accuracy for the player.

There is more golf along the Costa del Sol than you can ever hope to play on a holiday, with a full range of attendant practice facilities, golf academies and even, for insomniacs, a 9-hole floodlit course of 2,700 metres par 36 open 24 hours a day! The number of major championships contested here include the World Cups of 1973 and 1989 and the Spanish Opens of 1970 and 1983 (all over Las Brisas) plus further Spanish Opens in 1966 (Sotogrande) and 1979 (Torrequebrada) plus the end-of-season Volvo Masters held each year at Valderrama. Other courses, of more gentle character, allow players of all abilities to enjoy this golfing feast. East of Malaga lies Almeria and the pleasant resort location of Almerimar right by the sea.

The pride of MURCIA is the La Manga Club. Host to five Spanish Opens between 1973 and 1977, the complex now boasts three fine courses as well as a wide range of leisure and sporting facilities. Shielded by a crescent of low hills, with views down to the Mar Menor and the sea beyond, it offers Europe's first self-contained golf and sports resort.

A little farther north through Alicante to VALENCIA, lies a string of golfing treasure of rare quality. El Saler, twice host to the Spanish Open, is arguably (with St. Andrews and Carnoustie) one of the finest public course tests anywhere. Add in Golf Escorpion (Spanish Open 1980) and the more recent examples of El Bosque, Villamartin and others along the way to form a further 'golfing coast' to reckon with.

In the far north-east of Spain, nudging the border with France, one finds CATALONIA, where in the Girona and Costa Brava regions recent golf development has supplemented some well-established resort golf, and includes the PGA European Tour-supported Catalyuna Club at Caldes de Malavella.

Long a traditional holiday favourite with the British, the Costa Brava and the surrounding province of Girona supports a wide variety of hotel and self-catering accommodation overlooking its attractive bays and beaches and now supported by a good selection of interesting and challenging golf.

Not to be outdone, MAJORCA has a good choice of golf linked to its range of general holiday activity, which also benefits from the mild year-round climate. Best known are the two 18-hole courses at Santa Ponsa which undulate gently past trees and water open to the coastal breeze. The last area from a fine selection of first-class holiday golf with opportunities for all, whatever their ability or interest, in a country blessed with winter sun and a tradition of hospitality.

ANDALUCIA: Central

BENAHAVIS. **La Quinta Golf and Country Club,** Carratera de Ronda, Benahavis, Marbella (95.278.34.62; Fax: 95.278.34.66). *Location:* up Ronda Road, 3km from San Pedro; at top of the Golf Valley. 18 holes, 5517 metres, Par 72, S.S.S. 71; also 9 hole course, 2848 metres, Par 36, S.S.S. 71. Driving range. *Green Fees:* 6800pts. Discounts for groups over 10 people. *Eating facilities:* full catering facilities. *Visitors:* welcome. Professional: Manuel Pinero.

BENAHAVIS. **Monte Mayor Golf Club,** Los Naranjos Country Club, Nueva Andalucia, 29660 Marbella, Malaga (908 75 83 37). *Location:* in the hills between San Pedro de Alcantara and Estepona; inland from Ctra. N-340, km. 165.6. Possibly the Costa del Sol's most spectacular course, a challenging layout over mountainous terrain for the bold and accurate. 18 holes, 5593 metres, Par 71. *Green Fees:* information not provided. *Eating facilities:* bar and restaurant in clubhouse. Cart hire.

BENALMADENA. **Golf Torrequebrada,** Apartado 120, 29630 Benalmadena-Costa, Malaga (952-44 27 42; Fax: 952-56 11 29). *Location:* north of the Malaga-Cadiz coast road at km 220. A dramatic and highly strategic test, not too long but full of interest with elevated sea views. 18 holes, 5806 metres, Par 72. Driving range and putting green. *Green Fees:* information not provided. *Eating facilities:* bar and restaurant. Pro shop; club, cart and trolley hire.

ESTEPONA. **Atalaya Park,** Estepona-Malaga, Crta. Benahavis, 29680 Estepona, Malaga. *Location:* between Marbella and Estepona, off N340 going west, turn inland for Benahavis just past Guadalmina. One of the coast's well-established courses (1966). The fairly open parkland holes are lined with eucalyptus and pine. 18 holes, 6177 metres, Par 72. Large practice ground and putting greens. *Green Fees:* information not provided. *Eating facilities:* bar and restaurant in Swiss chalet style clubhouse. Pro shop; club, cart and trolley hire.

ESTEPONA. **Golf El Paraiso,** Carretera de Cadiz-Malaga, 29680 Estepona, Malaga. *Location:* west on N340, turn right at Benavista then inland 3 km. A fine rolling parkland style course opened in 1974. The holes run over and around a hill surmounted by the El Paraiso Hotel. 18 holes, 6116 metres, Par 71. Practice ground and putting green. *Green Fees:* 5000pts. June/September 4000pts, July/August 3000pts. *Eating facilities:* bar and restaurant. Pro shop; club, cart and trolley hire.

MALAGA. **Guadalhorce Club de Golf,** Ctra de Cartama, Apartado 48, 28950 Campanillas, Malaga (952-24 36 82; Fax: 952-24 16 78). *Location:* east towards Malaga on N340 past airport; turn right at sugar refinery taking underpass towards Bacardi distillery. A combination of classic parkland on level land with sculptured holes with raised greens and strategic water. 18 holes, 6194 metres, Par 72. Practice ground and putting green. Also 9 short holes. *Green Fees:* information not provided. *Eating facilities:* bar and restaurant in classical 19th century Andalucian manor house. Pro shop; club, cart and trolley hire.

MARBELLA. **Aloha Golf,** Nueva Andalucia, 29660 Marbella, Malaga (952-81 37 50; Fax: 952-81 23 89). *Location:* 3 km inland from Puerto Banus, 8 km east of Marbella. A fine course, opened in 1975. Tight fairways with numerous trees running through mountain valleys. 18 holes, 6261 metres, Par 72. Practice ground and putting green. *Green Fees:* information not provided. *Eating facilities:* bar and restaurant. Pro shop; club, cart and trolley hire.

MARBELLA. **Club de Golf Las Brisas,** Apartado 147, Nueva Andalucia, 29660 Marbella, Malaga (952-81 08 75; Fax: 952-81 55 18). *Location:* turn right of N340 at Puerto Banus. Over hill past bullring, then right and follow signs to Hotel Golf Plaza. A fine course which has played host to two World Cups and numerous other major Opens. Tough, with plenty of water and fast, sloping greens. 18 holes, 6163 metres, Par 72. Practice ground and putting green. *Green Fees:* information not provided. *Eating facilities:* bar and restaurant. Pro shop; club, cart and trolley hire.

MARBELLA. **Golf Rio Real,** Apartado 82, 29600 Marbella (952-77 37 76; Fax: 952-77 21 40). *Location:* 5km east from Marbella on N340, take overpass to Incosol and follow signs for 2.5km. A relatively gentle test of golf amongst mature and exotic trees. Well-cared for and closely linked to Hotel Los Monteros and Incosol Clinic. 18 holes, 6057 metres, Par 72. Practice ground and putting green. *Green Fees:* information not provided. *Eating facilities:* bar.

MARBELLA. **Guadalmina Club de Golf,** Guadalmina Alta, San Pedro de Alcantara, 29678 Marbella (952-88 33 75; Fax: 952-2883483). *Location:* turn right off N340 approximately 2km west of San Pedro de Alcantara. A development which now boasts 45 holes – the original South course, the North which is more open despite some strategic water, and a short 9 hole layout. North: 18 holes, 6065 metres, Par 71. South: 18 holes, 5825 metres, Par 71. Driving range and putting greens. *Green Fees:* information not provided. *Eating facilities:* bar and restaurant. Pro shop; club, cart and trolley hire.

MARBELLA. **Los Naranjos Golf Club,** Apartado 64, 29660 Nueva Andalucia, Malaga (952-81 52 06; Fax: 952-81 14 28). *Location:* turn right of N340 (going west) at Puerto Banus. Past bullring and over hill for 2km. The sister course to Las Brisas. The front nine run through fragrant orange groves while later holes are tougher and more undulating. 18 holes, 6437 metres, Par 72. Practice ground and putting green. *Green Fees:* information not provided. *Eating facilities:* bar and restaurant in grand new clubhouse. Pro shop; club, cart and trolley hire.

MIJAS. **Club de Golf de Mijas,** Apartado 145, 29640 Fuengirola (952-47 68 43; Fax: 952-46 79 43). *Location:* from Marbella on N340 take the Fuengirola bypass and turn left at underpass. Then 2 km before turning right. Two excellent courses: Los Lagos - 18 holes, 6348 metres, Par 71; and Los Olivos - 18 holes, 5896 metres, Par 72. The former course is relatively open although the greens are well protected by sand and water; the latter is narrower with smaller greens, favouring finesse over power. Driving range and putting green. *Green Fees:* information not provided. *Eating facilities:* bar and restaurant. Pro shop; club, cart and trolley hire.

MIJAS. **Golf del Chaparral,** Urbanizacion El Chaparral, CN-340, 29648 Mijas-Costa, Malaga (3452 494665; Fax: 3452 2494051). *Location:* on CN 340 driving east, directly off this road, two miles past El Faro lighthouse. A new course in undulating land; tough with elevated tees, winding pine-lined valleys and superb views over the Mediterranean. 18 holes, 5700 metres, Par 70. Practice ground and putting green. *Green Fees:* 4000pts daily; after 4pm 2000pts. *Eating facilities:* bar and restaurant. *Visitors:* welcome, no restrictions. *Society Meetings:* welcome. Professional: Juan Rosa Flores. Secretary: Patrick Murphy (3452 493800; Fax: 3452 2494051).

MIJAS. **La Cala Golf and Country Club,** La Cala de Mijas, 29647 Mijas Costa (95-2589100; Fax: 95-2589105). *Location:* from La Cala del Mijas between Fuengirola and Marbella, turn inland for about 5km on new road. Set in a high inland valley, La Cala offers elevated greens, large bunkers, playable and challenging holes and some magnificent views. 36 holes, 6160 metres, S.S.S. 73 North Course; 5960 metres, S.S.S. 71 South Course; Golf Academy and putting green. *Green Fees:* 4500pts. 25% discount for groups of 15 plus. *Eating facilities:* bar and restaurant. *Visitors:* always welcome. Gym, squash and tennis. *Society Meetings:* welcome. Professional: Ricardo de Miguel. Director: Jan Sonneui.

RINCON DE LA VICTORIA. **Anoreta Golf,** Urbanizacion Anoreta Golf Avda. del Golf s/n, 29730 Rincon de la Victoria, Malaga (952-40 40 00; Fax: 952-40 40 50). *Location:* 12 km east of Malaga at Rincon de la Victoria, only second course to be built east of Malaga. Fairly open parkland at present, with water hazards on 11 holes. 18 holes, 5976 metres, Par 72. Driving range and putting green. *Green Fees:* weekdays before 12 noon 3000pts; weekends 4000pts. Groups of more than 10 people 2000pts. *Eating facilities:* bar and restaurant. *Visitors:* welcome, no restrictions. Pro shop; club, cart and trolley hire.

ANDALUCIA: East

ALMERIA. **Golf Almerimar,** Golf Hotel Almerimar, El Ejido, 04700 Almeria (951-48 02 34; Fax: 951-48 46 19). *Location:* 7 km from El Ejido, which is some 35 km from Almeria on the main Malaga road. This is a well-established course in a relatively level situation, with a wealth of trees and the chance of a breeze from the sea alongside. 18 holes, 6111 metres, Par 72. Practice ground and putting green. *Green Fees:* information not provided. *Eating facilities:* bar and restaurant. Pro shop; club, cart and trolley hire.

ANDALUCIA: West

CADIZ. **Club de Golf Novo Sancti Petri,** Playa de la Barrosa, 11130 Chiclana de la Frontera, Cadiz (956-49 44 50; Fax: 956-49 43 50). *Location:* end of the La Barrosa road at Chiclana. This is a 27 hole layout along a stretch of virgin coastline. Mostly parkland with lakes which affect play on eight holes. Fairly flat with a wealth of young trees. 27 holes – M&C 6466 metres, M&P 6476 metres, P&C 6510 metres, all Par 72. Practice ground and putting green. *Green Fees:* information not provided. *Eating facilities:* bar and restaurant. Pro shop; club, cart and trolley hire; eight tennis courts, two paddle-tennis courts.

CADIZ. **Montecastillo,** Ctra de Arcos, 11406 Jerez de la Frontera (956-151200; Fax: 956-151209). *Location:* half a mile main road, four miles Jerez, 46 miles Sevilla. A relatively level but rolling layout with a distinct links flavour. Plenty of mounds and elevated tees, vast bunkers and water. 18 holes, 6424 metres, Par 72. Driving range and putting green. *Green Fees:* 4500pts; 3000pts hotel guests. Subject to review. *Eating facilities:* restaurant, two coffee shops. *Visitors:* welcome. Special packages available. *Society Meetings:* welcome. Professional: Cristobal Jaime (956-151216). Secretary: Maria Luisa (956-151203).

SAN ROQUE. **Club de Golf Sotogrande,** Paseo del Parque, Apartado 14, 11310 Sotogrande (956-79 50 50; Fax: 956-79 50 29). *Location:* right at Sotogrande entrance off N340 going west; then 2.5 km towards sea. Well established (1964) and a major golfing landmark in Europe. Rolling slopes and strategic water are offset by cork oak, eucalyptus, palm and pine. A demanding golfing feast. 18 holes, 6224 metres, Par 72. Also 9 hole short course. Practice ground and putting green. *Green Fees:* information not provided. *Eating facilities:* bar and restaurant. Pro shop; club, cart and trolley hire. Telephone in advance.

SAN ROQUE. **Club de Golf Valderrama,** Avda Los Cortijos, s/n, 11310 Sotogrande (956-79 57 75; Fax: 956-79 60 28). *Location:* access through the main Sotogrande entrance (right of N340 going west); then 2.5 km inland. Over heavily rolling hills with a commitment to excellence, this is a course to savour and appreciate. 18 holes, 6311 metres, Par 71. Practice ground and putting green. *Green Fees:* information not provided. *Eating facilities:* bar and restaurant. *Visitors:* must book in advance. Pro shop.

SAN ROQUE. **San Roque Club,** Apartado de Correos 127, 11360 San Roque (956-61.30.30; Fax: 956-61.30.12). *Location:* go west on N340 past Sotogrande 3 km and turn right at sign. Telephone first. The good variety of challenging holes of championship calibre are lined with olive trees and strategic water. 18 holes, 6440 metres, Par 72. Practice ground and putting green. *Eating facilities:* bar and restaurant. Pro shop; club, cart and trolley hire.

CATALONIA

GERONA. **Emporda Golf Club,** Ctra Pala Frugell a Torroella, S/N, 17257 Gualta, Gerona (34 72 760450; Fax: 34 72 108206). *Location:* from A7 highway Exit 6 in the direction of La Bisbal/Torroella. Llevant Course is a wooded links course; Gold Course is wooded. Llevant Course: 18 holes, 5595 metres. S.S.S. 70. Gold Course: 9 holes, 3135 metres. S.S.S. 36. Two driving ranges, Pro shop. *Green Fees:* weekdays 4500 pts, weekends 6000 pts. *Eating facilities:* snack bar and restaurant. *Visitors:* all welcome, Handicap Certificate required. *Society Meetings:* welcome; special rates. Professional: Mr Riera. Secretary: Mrs Angels (34 72 760136).

GIRONA. **Costa Brava Golf Club,** 17246 Santa Cristina d'Aro, Costa Brava (Girona) ([972] 83 71 50; Fax: [972] 83 72 72). *Location:* in Santa Cristina d'Aro, 30 km south east of Girona, five/six km from the coast. From a hilly, wooded first 9 holes with fine views, the back 9 holes slope down by the river to flatter ground. 18 holes, 5570 metres. S.S.S. 70. Putting greens and practice areas. *Green Fees:* on application. *Eating facilities:* restaurant, bar and snack bar. Pro shop, changing rooms.

GIRONA. **Girona Golf Club,** Travessia del Carril 2, 17001 Girona ([972] 17.16.41; Fax: [972] 22.14.38). *Location:* four km north of Girona town centre, near the Girona North Exit (6) of the Girona-La Jonquera Motorway (A7). An undulating course around wooded valleys and hills and three man-made lakes. 18 holes, 6100 metres. S.S.S. 72. Practice course, golf school. *Grees Fees:* on application. *Eating facilities:* snack bar. Pro shop, caddie carts for hire.

GIRONA. **Mas Nou Golf Club,** 17250 Platja d'Aro, Costa Brava (Girona) ([972] 82 60 84; Fax: [972] 82 61 17). *Location:* on the Costa Brava, behind Platja d'Aro, 35 km east of Girona. A scenic course with panoramic views of the Costa Brava from its situation on the Les Gavarres mountains. Trees and lakes add to the course's charm. 18 holes, 6200 metres. S.S.S. 72. 9 hole Par 3 course, practice area. *Green Fees:* on application. *Eating facilities:* clubhouse with bar, snack bar and restaurant. Caddies.

PALS. **Emporda Golf Club,** Ctra. Palafrugell-Torroella de Montgri, 17257 Gualta (Girona) ([972] 76 04 50; Fax: [972] 76 00 33). *Location:* almost on the coast, north of Pals and approximately 40 km east of Girona. 27 holes. *Green Fees:* on application. *Eating facilities:* clubhouse with bar and restaurant. Clubs and trolleys for hire.

PALS. **Pals Golf Club,** 17256 Platja de Pals, Costa Brava (Girona) ([972] 63 60 06; Fax: [972] 63 70 09). *Location:* on the coast at Playa de Pals beach, eight km from Begur and 40 km east of Girona. A demanding, flattish course, heavily treed and with bunkers. 18 holes, 6200 metres. S.S.S. 72/74. *Green Fees:* on application. *Eating facilities:* restaurant and bar. Clubs, caddy cars and golf carts can be hired.

See our Colour Advertisement on page 39.

MURCIA

MURCIA. **La Manga Club,** Los Belones, Cartagena, 30385 Murcia (968-56 45 11; Fax: 968-56 47 50). *Location:* 30 km from Cartagena, 75 km from Murcia and 100 km from Alicante airport. Access off road to Murcia Airport. A true sporting resort in all aspects, with 54 holes of palm-lined golf backed by low hills as well as tennis, squash, bowls, health club and watersports at the Mar Menor close by. Five star La Manga Club hotel on site. Three courses: North 18 holes, 5780 metres, Par 71; South 18 holes, 6361 metres, Par 72; La Princesa 18 holes, 5971 metres, Par 72. Driving range and putting green. *Green Fees:* information not provided. *Eating facilities:* bar and restaurant. Pro shop; club, cart and trolley hire.

VALENCIA

BETERA. **Club de Golf Escorpion,** Apartado 1, 46117 Betera, Valencia (96-160 12 11; Fax: 96-169 01 87). *Location:* take the road from Valencia to Liria, turning off at San Antonio de Benageber. Go 4 km to the right, direction Betera. A fine private club offering parkland-style golf with a mountain backdrop. Tree-lined and interesting. 18 holes, 6319 metres, Par 72. Driving range and putting green. *Green Fees:* information not provided. *Eating facilities:* bar and restaurant. Pro shop; club, cart and trolley hire.

CHIVA. **Club de Golf El Bosque,** Carretera Godelleta, 46370 Chiva-Valencia (96-180 41 42; Fax: 96-180 40 09). *Location:* take the Nacional III road (Madrid-Valencia) to km 324, turn off for Godelleta. Modern American design in an attractive location backed by wooded hills. Plenty of strategic sand. A course kept in excellent condition. 18 holes, 6276 metres, Par 72. Driving range and putting green. *Green Fees:* 5000pts. Special rate Monday, Tuesday and Wednesday – breakfast, lunch, golf 5000pts. *Eating facilities:* cafeteria, restaurant. *Visitors:* welcome. Professional: Alfonso Pinto. Secretary: J.L. Mendez.

ORIHUELA. **Campo de Golf Villamartin,** Apartado 35, Torrevieja, 03300 Orihuela, Alicante (96-676 03 50; Fax: 96-676 03 58). *Location:* on the Torrevieja-Cartagena road at km 7.6, near San Javier Airport and El Alted. Two courses laid out on interesting coastal sandy land with some pines. A good test of golf, open to the breeze. 18 holes, 6132 metres, Par 72; 18 holes, 5770 metres, Par 72. Driving range and putting green. *Green Fees:* information not provided. *Eating facilities:* bar, coffee shop and restaurant. Pro shop; club, cart and trolley hire.

VALENCIA. **Campo de Golf El Saler,** Parador Nacional "Luis Vives", El Saler, Valencia (96-161 11 86; Fax: 96-162 70 16). *Location:* at km 18 on the road from Nazaret to Oliva, right by the sea. One of the great Spanish tests of golf, with open links fairways and tight holes lined with umbrella pine; a public facility offering true seaside conditions. 18 holes, 6355 metres, Par 72. Driving range and putting green. *Green Fees:* information not provided. *Eating facilities:* bar, restaurant and coffee shop. Pro shop; club, cart and trolley hire.

MAJORCA

CALA D'OR. **Vall D'Or Golf Club,** Apartado 23, 07660 Cala D'Or (971 837001; Fax: 971 837299). *Location:* approximately 60km east of Palma on the road from Porto Colom to Cala D'Or. Undulating, winding course, with trees. 18 holes, 5881 metres. S.S.S. 71. Driving range, club hire. *Green Fees:* on application. 10% discount if player comes with a card from hotel. *Eating facilities:* clubhouse, bar and restaurant. *Visitors:* welcome with Handicap. Nearby hotels include Cala D'Or, Rocador, Rocador Playa. Professional: Antonio Gonzalez (971 837001). Secretary: Celestino Padial (971 837068).

MAGALLUF. **Poniente Golf Club,** Crta. Cala Figuera S/N, Costa de Calvia (03471 130148). *Location:* 18km west of Palma, one km from Magalluf on the Andraix Road. The course is considered long and difficult, surrounded by trees and water, with large and fast greens. 18 holes, 6430 metres. S.S.S. 72. Driving range, putting green. *Green Fees:* information not provided. *Eating facilities:* clubhouse, restaurant and bar. Nearby hotels include Son Calliv, Club Galatzo.

PALMA. **Real Golf de Bendinat,** Campoamor S/N, 07015 Calvia, Baleares (3471 405200; Fax: 3471 700786). *Location:* five km west from Palma centre. A short, hilly but interesting course. 9 holes, 4988 metres. S.S.S. 68. Driving range, putting green. *Green Fees:* 5000ptas. *Eating facilities:* snack bar and Restaurant "Hoyo 10". *Visitors:* welcome, 20% discount for large groups. Please reserve tee-off times through our Fax No: (3471 700786). Professional: Ricardo Galiano (3471 405450). Secretary: Beatriz Arnau (3471 405200).

Index to Advertisers

ORDER NOW! *See Overleaf*

ONE FOR YOUR FRIEND 1995

FHG Publications have a large range of attractive holiday accommodation guides for all kinds of holiday opportunities throughout Britain. They also make useful gifts at any time of year. Our guides are available in most bookshops and larger newsagents but we will be happy to post you a copy direct if you have any difficulty. We will also post abroad but have to charge separately for post or freight. The inclusive cost of posting and packing the guides to you or your friends in the UK is as follows:

Farm Holiday Guide ENGLAND, WALES and IRELAND
Board, Self-catering, Caravans/Camping, Activity Holidays. Over 400 pages. **£4.80**

Farm Holiday Guide SCOTLAND
All kinds of holiday accommodation. **£3.00**

SELF-CATERING & FURNISHED HOLIDAYS
Over 1000 addresses throughout for Self-catering and caravans in Britain. **£4.20**

BRITAIN'S BEST HOLIDAYS
A quick-reference general guide for all kinds of holidays. **£3.30**

The FHG Guide to CARAVAN & CAMPING HOLIDAYS
Caravans for hire, sites and holiday parks and centres. **£3.30**

BED AND BREAKFAST STOPS
Over 1000 friendly and comfortable overnight stops. Non-smoking, The Disabled and Special Diets Supplements. **£4.40**

CHILDREN WELCOME! FAMILY HOLIDAY GUIDE
Family holidays with details of amenities for children and babies. **£4.40**

Recommended SHORT BREAK HOLIDAYS IN BRITAIN
'Approved' accommodation for quality bargain breaks. Introduced by John Carter. **£4.20**

Recommended COUNTRY HOTELS OF BRITAIN
Including Country Houses, for the discriminating. **£4.20**

Recommended WAYSIDE INNS OF BRITAIN
Pubs, Inns and small hotels. **£4.20**

PGA GOLF GUIDE
Where to play and where to stay
Over 2000 golf courses in Britain with convenient accommodation. Endorsed by the PGA. Holiday Golf in France, Portugal, Spain and USA. **£9.50**

PETS WELCOME!
The unique guide for holidays for pet owners and their pets. **£4.60**

BED AND BREAKFAST IN BRITAIN
Over 1000 choices for touring and holidays throughout Britain. Airports and Ferries Supplement. **£3.30**

THE FRENCH FARM AND VILLAGE HOLIDAY GUIDE
The official guide to self-catering holidays in the 'Gîtes de France'. **£9.50**

Tick your choice and send your order and payment to FHG PUBLICATIONS, ABBEY MILL BUSINESS CENTRE, SEEDHILL, PAISLEY PA1 1TJ (TEL: 0141-887 0428. FAX: 0141-889 7204). **Deduct** 10% for 2/3 titles or copies; 20% for 4 or more.

Send to: NAME ....

ADDRESS ....

....

.... POST CODE ....

I enclose Cheque/Postal Order for £ ....

SIGNATURE .... DATE ....

Please complete the following to help us improve the service we provide. How did you find out about our guides:

☐ Press ☐ Magazines ☐ TV ☐ Radio ☐ Family/Friend ☐ Other.

SHETLAND ISLANDS
YELL
MAINLAND
Lerwick
Sumburgh
ORKNEY
MAINLAND
Kirkwall
Stromness
HOY
0 10 20 30 40 50 Kilometres
0 10 20 30 Miles
Grid interval is 30 miles
A
B
C
D
E
F
G
1
2
3
4
5
6
7
8
9
10
11
John o'Groats
Thurso
Durness
Bettyhill
Tongue
Wick
Scourie
LEWIS
WESTERN ISLES
Lochinver
Helmsdale
Lairg
Golspie
Ullapool
Bonar Bridge
Dornoch
Gairloch
Poolewe
Tain
Dingwall
Rosemarkie
Fortrose
Nairn
Forres
Elgin
Cullen
Banff
Fraserburgh
Fochabers
Keith
Turriff
Peterhead
HIGHLAND
Beauly
Inverness
Daviot
Portree
RAASAY
SKYE
Huntly
Kyle of Lochalsh
Dornie
Kyleakin
Broadford
Grantown-on-Spey
Carrbridge
Tomintoul
GRAMPIAN
Inverurie
Aviemore
Fort Augustus
Kingussie
Aberdeen
HEBRIDES
Mallaig
Braemar
Banchory
Stonehaven
Fort William
Kinlochleven
Glencoe
Ballachulish
Kinloch Rannoch
Pitlochry
Brechin
Montrose
Tobermory
INNER
Aberfeldy
TAYSIDE
Forfar
Dunkeld
Blairgowrie
Arbroath
MULL
Oban
Taynuilt
Killin
Dundee
Carnoustie
Monifieth
Dalmally
Crianlarich
Lochearnhead
Perth
Crieff
Cupar
St Andrews
Inveraray
Auchterarder
FIFE
Arrochar
Tarbet
Callander
Aberfoyle
Kinross
CENTRAL
Stirling
Dunfermline
Kirkcaldy
JURA
Lochgilphead
Luss
Drymen
Ardrishaig
North Berwick
Dunoon
Gourock
Balloch
Dumbarton
EDINBURGH
Dunbar
Tarbert
Greenock
Glasgow
Dalkeith
Haddington
Eyemouth
ISLAY
Rothesay
Paisley
LOTHIAN
Largs
Chirnside
Berwick upon Tweed
STRATHCLYDE
Hamilton
Duns
Lauder
Ardrossan
Kilmarnock
Lanark
Peebles
Coldstream
Cornhill-on-Tweed
KINTYRE
Brodick
Irvine
Troon
Biggar
Galashiels
Bamburgh
Lamlash
Prestwick
Selkirk
Kelso
Wooler
Seahouses
Campbeltown
ARRAN
Ayr
Abington
BORDERS
Jedburgh
New Cumnock
Hawick
Alnwick
Maybole
Moffat
Beattock
Girvan
NORTHUMBERLAND
Langholm
Bellingham
Morpeth
DUMFRIES & GALLOWAY
New Galloway
Dumfries
Whitley Bay
Newton Stewart
Castle Douglas
Gretna
Longtown
Stranraer
Annan
Greenhead
Newcastle-upon-Tyne
Hexham
Corbridge
Wigtown
Gatehouse of Fleet
Carlisle
Portpatrick
Kirkcudbright
Silloth
Port William
CUMBRIA
Alston
Durham
Bassenthwaite
Penrith
5
6
A9
A99
A836
A838
A894
A837
A835
A832
A890
A87
A82
A830
A96
A95
A939
A93
A98
A92
A94
A86
A85
A84
A91
A90
A93
A83
A815
A816
A8
A73
M8
M9
A71
A702
A703
A7
A68
A697
A1
A77
A76
A713
A701
A74
A75
A69
A696
A689
M6

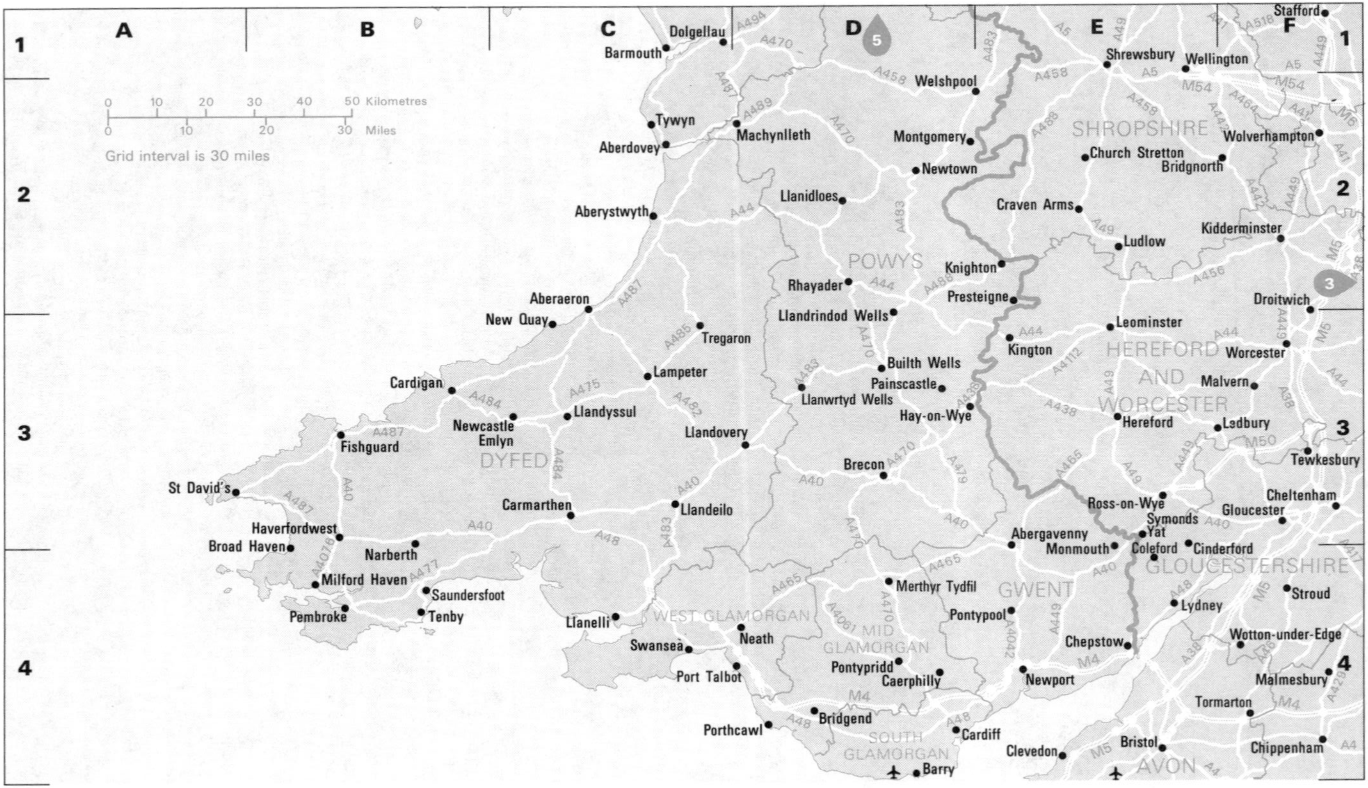

A
B
C
D
E
F
1
2
3
4
0 10 20 30 40 50 Kilometres
0 10 20 30 Miles
Grid interval is 30 miles
SHROPSHIRE
POWYS
HEREFORD AND WORCESTER
DYFED
GLOUCESTERSHIRE
GWENT
WEST GLAMORGAN
MID GLAMORGAN
SOUTH GLAMORGAN
AVON
Stafford
Shrewsbury
Wellington
Wolverhampton
Church Stretton
Bridgnorth
Kidderminster
Droitwich
Worcester
Malvern
Ledbury
Tewkesbury
Cheltenham
Gloucester
Stroud
Wotton-under-Edge
Malmesbury
Tormarton
Chippenham
Bristol
Clevedon
Barry
Cardiff
Newport
Chepstow
Lydney
Cinderford
Coleford
Symonds Yat
Ross-on-Wye
Monmouth
Abergavenny
Hereford
Leominster
Ludlow
Craven Arms
Knighton
Presteigne
Kington
Hay-on-Wye
Painscastle
Builth Wells
Llanwrtyd Wells
Llandrindod Wells
Rhayader
Llanidloes
Newtown
Montgomery
Welshpool
Machynlleth
Dolgellau
Barmouth
Tywyn
Aberdovey
Aberystwyth
Aberaeron
New Quay
Tregaron
Lampeter
Cardigan
Newcastle Emlyn
Llandyssul
Llandovery
Llandeilo
Brecon
Merthyr Tydfil
Pontypool
Pontypridd
Caerphilly
Bridgend
Porthcawl
Port Talbot
Neath
Swansea
Llanelli
Carmarthen
Fishguard
St David's
Haverfordwest
Broad Haven
Narberth
Milford Haven
Saundersfoot
Tenby
Pembroke

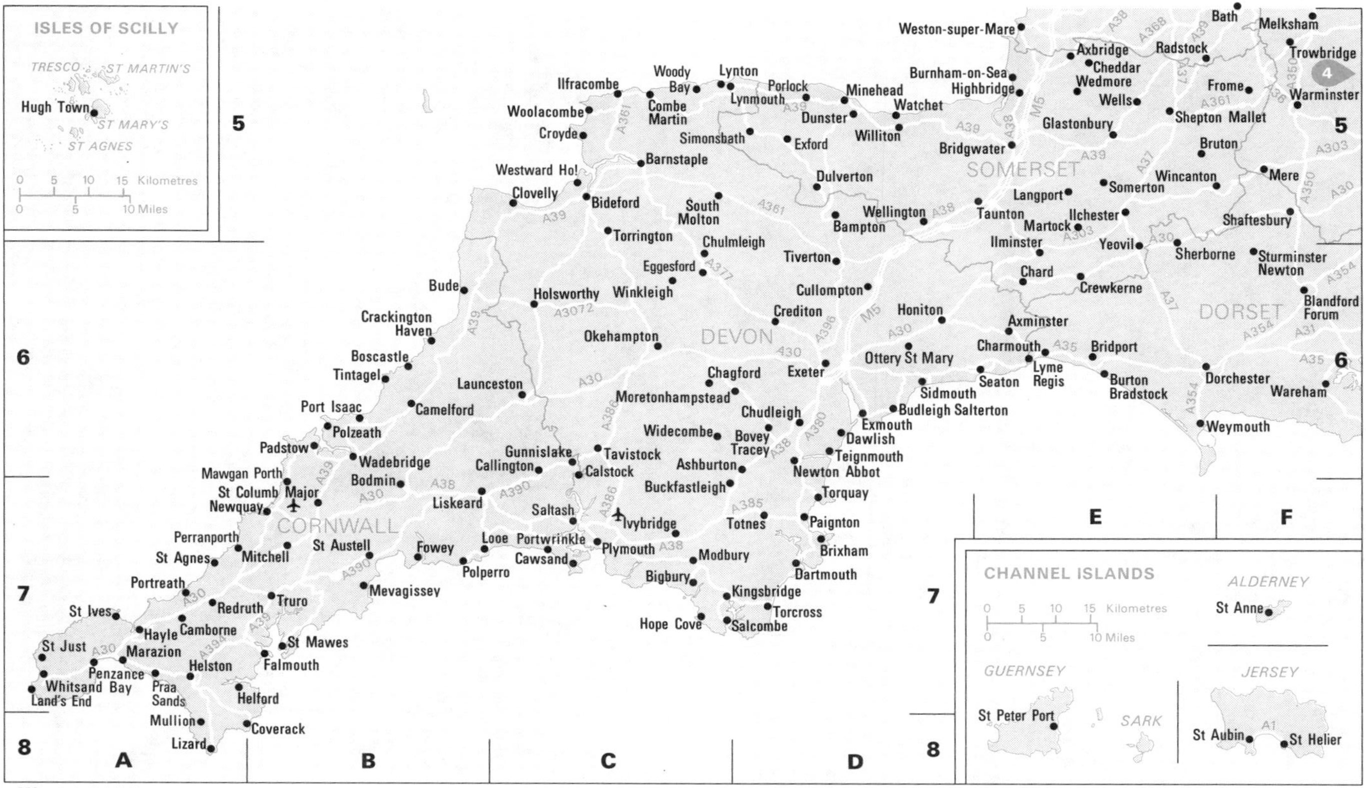
ISLES OF SCILLY
TRESCO
ST MARTIN'S
Hugh Town
ST MARY'S
ST AGNES
0 5 10 15 Kilometres
0 5 10 Miles
CHANNEL ISLANDS
0 5 10 15 Kilometres
0 5 10 Miles
ALDERNEY
St Anne
GUERNSEY
St Peter Port
SARK
JERSEY
St Aubin
St Helier
CORNWALL
DEVON
SOMERSET
DORSET
A B C D E F
5 6 7 8
Bath
Melksham
Trowbridge
Warminster
Weston-super-Mare
Axbridge
Cheddar
Wedmore
Wells
Radstock
Frome
Shepton Mallet
Burnham-on-Sea
Highbridge
Glastonbury
Bruton
Bridgwater
Wincanton
Mere
Somerton
Langport
Taunton
Ilchester
Martock
Shaftesbury
Ilminster
Yeovil
Sherborne
Sturminster Newton
Chard
Crewkerne
Blandford Forum
Axminster
Charmouth
Lyme Regis
Bridport
Dorchester
Wareham
Burton Bradstock
Weymouth
Ilfracombe
Woolacombe
Croyde
Woody Bay
Combe Martin
Lynton
Lynmouth
Porlock
Minehead
Watchet
Dunster
Williton
Simonsbath
Exford
Barnstaple
Dulverton
Westward Ho!
Clovelly
Bideford
South Molton
Wellington
Bampton
Torrington
Chulmleigh
Tiverton
Eggesford
Winkleigh
Holsworthy
Cullompton
Bude
Crediton
Honiton
Crackington Haven
Okehampton
Ottery St Mary
Boscastle
Tintagel
Chagford
Exeter
Seaton
Sidmouth
Launceston
Moretonhampstead
Budleigh Salterton
Port Isaac
Camelford
Chudleigh
Exmouth
Polzeath
Widecombe
Bovey Tracey
Dawlish
Padstow
Wadebridge
Gunnislake
Tavistock
Teignmouth
Callington
Calstock
Ashburton
Newton Abbot
Mawgan Porth
Bodmin
St Columb Major
Newquay
Liskeard
Buckfastleigh
Torquay
Saltash
Ivybridge
Totnes
Paignton
Perranporth
St Austell
Fowey
Looe
Portwrinkle
Plymouth
Brixham
St Agnes
Mitchell
Polperro
Cawsand
Modbury
Dartmouth
Portreath
Mevagissey
Bigbury
Kingsbridge
Truro
Redruth
Torcross
St Ives
Hayle
Camborne
Hope Cove
Salcombe
St Just
Marazion
St Mawes
Penzance
Helston
Falmouth
Whitsand Bay
Land's End
Praa Sands
Helford
Mullion
Coverack
Lizard
A30
A39
A38
A361
A3072
A377
A386
A390
A396
A380
A385
A35
A37
A303
A350
A354
A31
A368
A361
A36
A1
M5
4

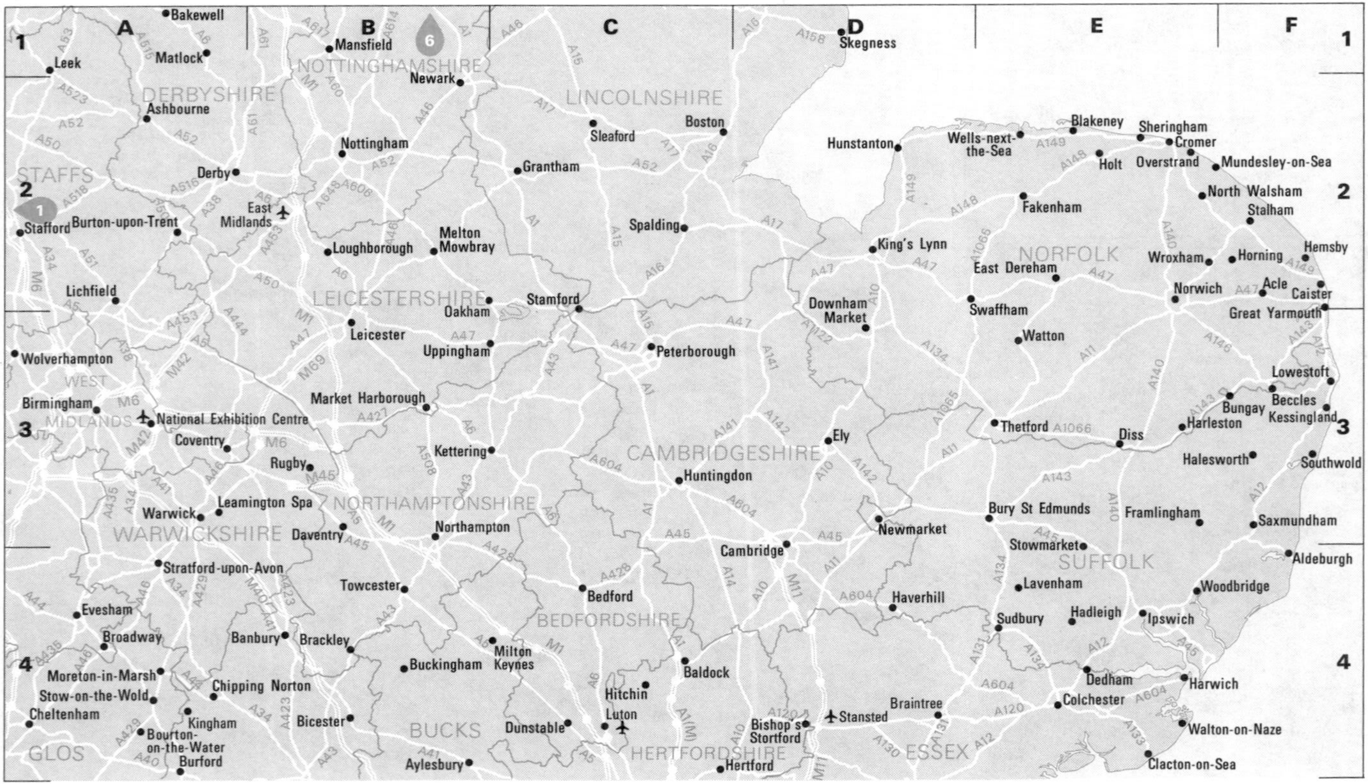
A
B
C
D
E
F
1
2
3
4
NOTTINGHAMSHIRE
DERBYSHIRE
LINCOLNSHIRE
STAFFS
LEICESTERSHIRE
NORFOLK
WEST MIDLANDS
CAMBRIDGESHIRE
NORTHAMPTONSHIRE
WARWICKSHIRE
SUFFOLK
BEDFORDSHIRE
BUCKS
HERTFORDSHIRE
ESSEX
GLOS
Bakewell
Mansfield
Skegness
Leek
Matlock
Newark
Ashbourne
Boston
Sleaford
Nottingham
Hunstanton
Wells-next-the-Sea
Blakeney
Sheringham
Cromer
Holt
Overstrand
Mundesley-on-Sea
Derby
Grantham
East Midlands
Stafford
Burton-upon-Trent
Spalding
Fakenham
North Walsham
Stalham
King's Lynn
Loughborough
Melton Mowbray
Hemsby
Horning
Wroxham
East Dereham
Lichfield
Leicester
Oakham
Stamford
Downham Market
Swaffham
Norwich
Acle
Caister
Great Yarmouth
Uppingham
Peterborough
Watton
Wolverhampton
Lowestoft
Beccles
Bungay
Kessingland
Harleston
Birmingham
Market Harborough
National Exhibition Centre
Thetford
Diss
Coventry
Ely
Halesworth
Southwold
Kettering
Rugby
Huntingdon
Leamington Spa
Warwick
Bury St Edmunds
Framlingham
Saxmundham
Daventry
Northampton
Newmarket
Stowmarket
Cambridge
Aldeburgh
Stratford-upon-Avon
Towcester
Bedford
Lavenham
Haverhill
Woodbridge
Evesham
Sudbury
Hadleigh
Ipswich
Broadway
Banbury
Brackley
Milton Keynes
Buckingham
Baldock
Dedham
Harwich
Moreton-in-Marsh
Chipping Norton
Hitchin
Stow-on-the-Wold
Colchester
Braintree
Cheltenham
Kingham
Luton
Stansted
Bicester
Bishop's Stortford
Walton-on-Naze
Bourton-on-the-Water
Dunstable
Burford
Aylesbury
Hertford
Clacton-on-Sea

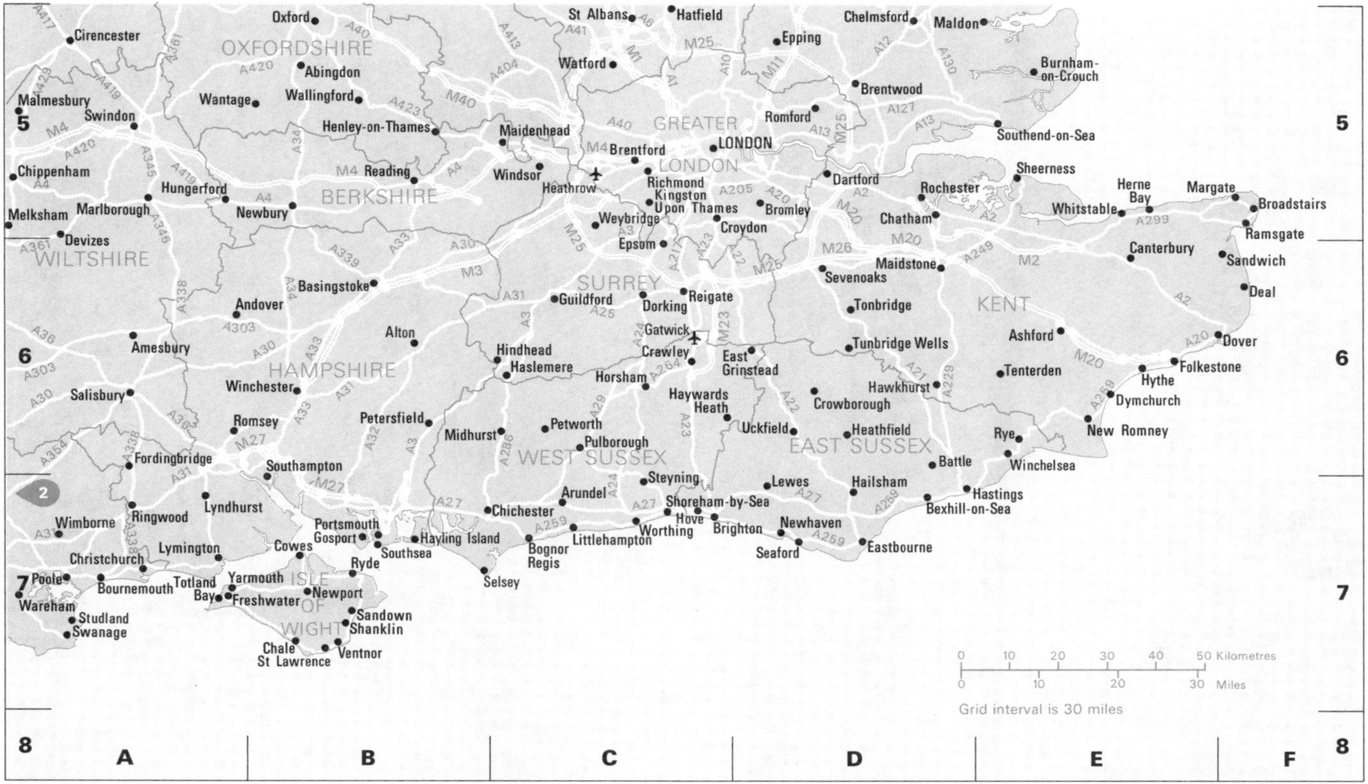
OXFORDSHIRE
BERKSHIRE
WILTSHIRE
HAMPSHIRE
SURREY
GREATER LONDON
KENT
WEST SUSSEX
EAST SUSSEX
ISLE OF WIGHT
Oxford
Cirencester
Malmesbury
Swindon
Abingdon
Wantage
Wallingford
Henley-on-Thames
Maidenhead
Chippenham
Hungerford
Reading
Windsor
Heathrow
Melksham
Marlborough
Newbury
Devizes
Basingstoke
Andover
Amesbury
Alton
Salisbury
Winchester
Romsey
Petersfield
Fordingbridge
Southampton
Ringwood
Lyndhurst
Wimborne
Portsmouth
Gosport
Southsea
Hayling Island
Lymington
Cowes
Christchurch
Ryde
Poole
Bournemouth
Totland Bay
Yarmouth
Freshwater
Newport
Wareham
Studland
Swanage
Sandown
Shanklin
Chale
St Lawrence
Ventnor
St Albans
Hatfield
Watford
Epping
Chelmsford
Maldon
Burnham-on-Crouch
Brentwood
Romford
LONDON
Southend-on-Sea
Brentford
Richmond
Kingston Upon Thames
Bromley
Croydon
Weybridge
Epsom
Dartford
Sheerness
Rochester
Chatham
Herne Bay
Whitstable
Margate
Broadstairs
Ramsgate
Canterbury
Sandwich
Deal
Maidstone
Sevenoaks
Tonbridge
Guildford
Dorking
Reigate
Gatwick
Crawley
East Grinstead
Tunbridge Wells
Ashford
Dover
Folkestone
Hythe
Dymchurch
New Romney
Tenterden
Hindhead
Haslemere
Horsham
Haywards Heath
Crowborough
Hawkhurst
Midhurst
Petworth
Pulborough
Uckfield
Heathfield
Rye
Winchelsea
Battle
Steyning
Lewes
Hailsham
Hastings
Bexhill-on-Sea
Chichester
Arundel
Shoreham-by-Sea
Hove
Brighton
Newhaven
Worthing
Littlehampton
Bognor Regis
Selsey
Seaford
Eastbourne
0 10 20 30 40 50 Kilometres
0 10 20 30 Miles
Grid interval is 30 miles
A B C D E F
5 6 7 8
2

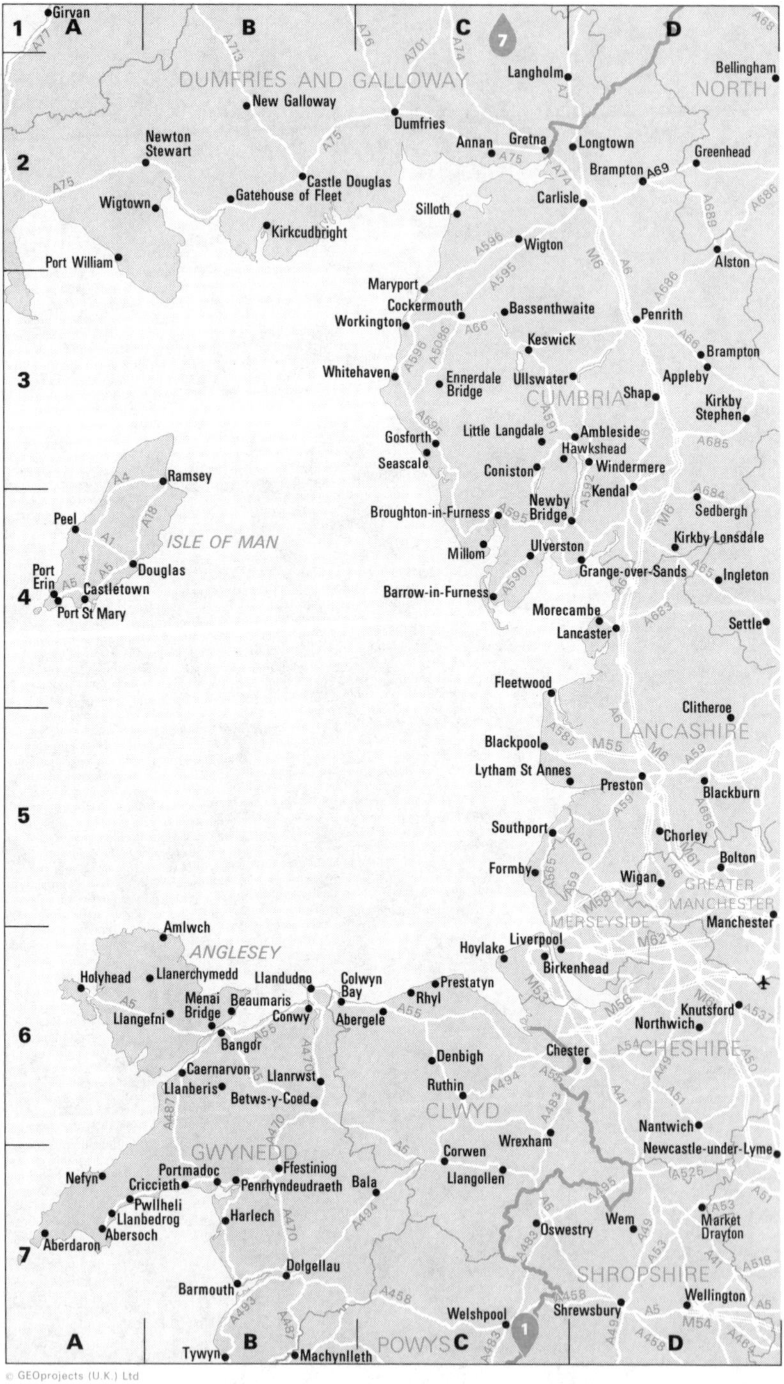
DUMFRIES AND GALLOWAY
NORTH
CUMBRIA
ISLE OF MAN
LANCASHIRE
GREATER MANCHESTER
MERSEYSIDE
ANGLESEY
CHESHIRE
CLWYD
GWYNEDD
SHROPSHIRE
POWYS
Girvan
Langholm
Bellingham
New Galloway
Dumfries
Annan
Gretna
Longtown
Newton Stewart
Castle Douglas
Gatehouse of Fleet
Wigtown
Kirkcudbright
Silloth
Carlisle
Brampton
Greenhead
Port William
Wigton
Alston
Maryport
Cockermouth
Bassenthwaite
Workington
Penrith
Keswick
Brampton
Whitehaven
Ennerdale Bridge
Ullswater
Appleby
Shap
Kirkby Stephen
Gosforth
Seascale
Little Langdale
Ambleside
Hawkshead
Coniston
Windermere
Kendal
Sedbergh
Ramsey
Broughton-in-Furness
Newby Bridge
Kirkby Lonsdale
Peel
Millom
Ulverston
Grange-over-Sands
Ingleton
Port Erin
Douglas
Castletown
Port St Mary
Barrow-in-Furness
Morecambe
Lancaster
Settle
Fleetwood
Clitheroe
Blackpool
Lytham St Annes
Preston
Blackburn
Southport
Chorley
Bolton
Formby
Wigan
Manchester
Amlwch
Liverpool
Hoylake
Birkenhead
Holyhead
Llanerchymedd
Llandudno
Colwyn Bay
Prestatyn
Rhyl
Menai Bridge
Beaumaris
Conwy
Abergele
Knutsford
Llangefni
Northwich
Bangor
Chester
Denbigh
Caernarvon
Llanrwst
Llanberis
Ruthin
Betws-y-Coed
Nantwich
Wrexham
Newcastle-under-Lyme
Corwen
Portmadoc
Ffestiniog
Nefyn
Criccieth
Penrhyndeudraeth
Llangollen
Bala
Pwllheli
Llanbedrog
Abersoch
Harlech
Oswestry
Wem
Market Drayton
Aberdaron
Dolgellau
Barmouth
Welshpool
Shrewsbury
Wellington
Tywyn
Machynlleth

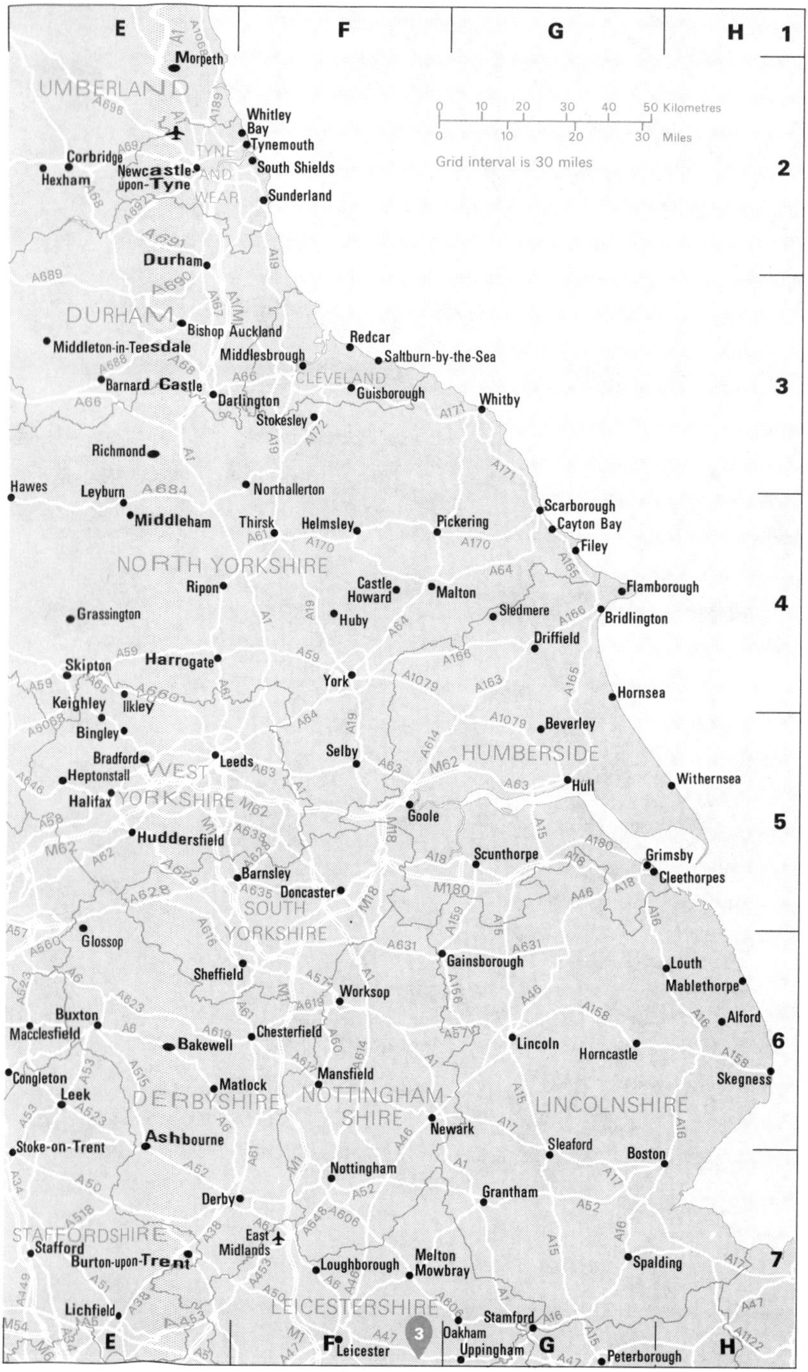

E
F
G
H
1
2
3
4
5
6
7
0 10 20 30 40 50 Kilometres
0 10 20 30 Miles
Grid interval is 30 miles
Morpeth
UMBERLAND
Whitley Bay
Tynemouth
South Shields
Sunderland
Corbridge
Hexham
Newcastle-upon-Tyne
TYNE AND WEAR
Durham
DURHAM
Bishop Auckland
Middleton-in-Teesdale
Middlesbrough
Redcar
Saltburn-by-the-Sea
CLEVELAND
Guisborough
Barnard Castle
Darlington
Stokesley
Whitby
Richmond
Hawes
Leyburn
Northallerton
Middleham
Thirsk
Helmsley
Pickering
Scarborough
Cayton Bay
Filey
NORTH YORKSHIRE
Ripon
Castle Howard
Malton
Flamborough
Sledmere
Bridlington
Grassington
Huby
Driffield
Harrogate
Skipton
York
Hornsea
Keighley
Ilkley
Beverley
Bingley
Bradford
Leeds
Selby
HUMBERSIDE
Heptonstall
WEST YORKSHIRE
Hull
Withernsea
Halifax
Goole
Huddersfield
Scunthorpe
Grimsby
Cleethorpes
Barnsley
Doncaster
SOUTH YORKSHIRE
Glossop
Gainsborough
Sheffield
Louth
Mablethorpe
Worksop
Buxton
Alford
Macclesfield
Chesterfield
Lincoln
Bakewell
Horncastle
Skegness
Congleton
Mansfield
Leek
Matlock
DERBYSHIRE
NOTTINGHAM-SHIRE
LINCOLNSHIRE
Newark
Stoke-on-Trent
Ashbourne
Sleaford
Boston
Nottingham
Derby
Grantham
STAFFORDSHIRE
East Midlands
Stafford
Burton-upon-Trent
Loughborough
Melton Mowbray
Spalding
Lichfield
LEICESTERSHIRE
Stamford
Oakham
Uppingham
Leicester
Peterborough
3

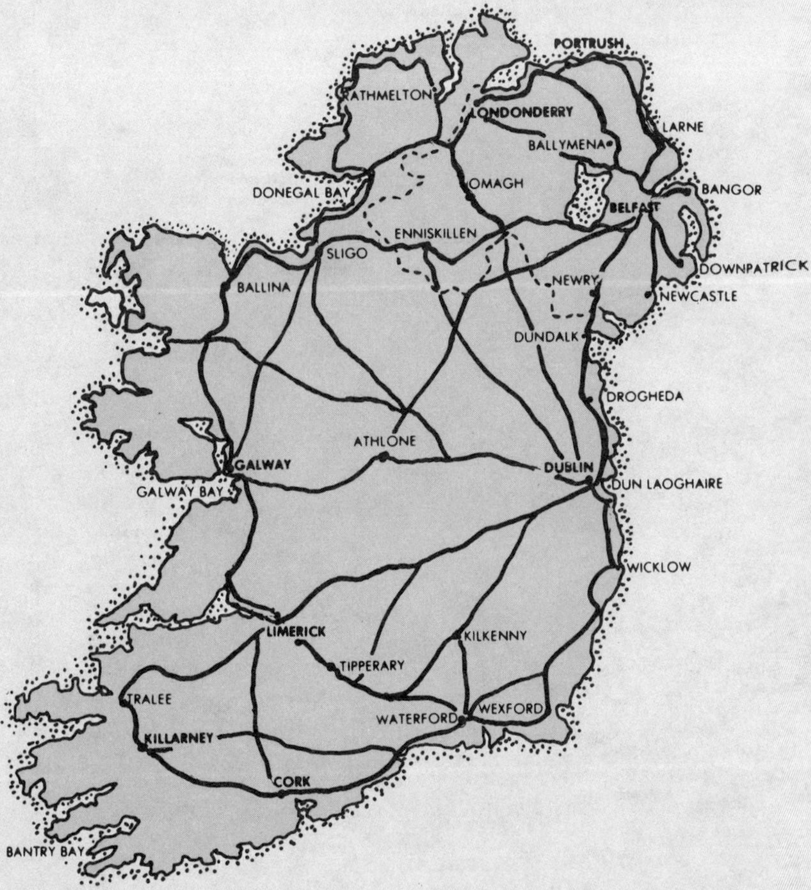

PORTRUSH
RATHMELTON
LONDONDERRY
LARNE
BALLYMENA
DONEGAL BAY
OMAGH
BANGOR
BELFAST
ENNISKILLEN
SLIGO
DOWNPATRICK
BALLINA
NEWRY
NEWCASTLE
DUNDALK
DROGHEDA
ATHLONE
GALWAY
DUBLIN
GALWAY BAY
DUN LAOGHAIRE
WICKLOW
LIMERICK
KILKENNY
TIPPERARY
TRALEE
WATERFORD
WEXFORD
KILLARNEY
CORK
BANTRY BAY